# Wiley CIA

## EXAM REVIEW

### VOLUME 2
### Conducting the Internal Audit Engagement

## THIRD EDITION

# S. RAO VALLABHANENI

**WILEY**

JOHN WILEY & SONS, INC.

# CONTENTS

# PREFACE

The Certified Internal Auditor (CIA) Examination is a program of the Institute of Internal Auditors (IIA), Inc. The CIA examination certifies a person as a professional internal auditor and is intended to measure the knowledge, skills, and competency required in the field of internal auditing. The Certified Internal Auditor designation is the mark of an expert in internal auditing. The new exam, effective from May 2004, tests knowledge at two levels of comprehension—proficiency and awareness—as indicated in the IIA's content specifications outlines (*www.theiia.org*). These levels require allocating more preparation time to proficiency-level topics and less time to awareness-level topics.

A series of four-volume review guides have been prepared for the candidate to utilize for all four parts of the new CIA exam. Each volume covers one part of the exam.

Each volume includes a comprehensive coverage of the subject matter (theory) followed by hundreds of previous CIA exam multiple-choice questions with answers and explanations (practice). The structure and topics of each book matches the content specifications as closely as possible. In volume 2, a total of 1,092 questions have been included from previous CIA exams and other sources. The actual CIA exam for each part consists of 125 multiple-choice questions to be completed in 3½ hours. The breakdown of questions by chapter is

| | |
|---|---|
| Chapter 1 | 216 questions |
| Chapter 2 | 427 questions |
| Chapter 3 | 52 questions |
| Chapter 4 | 101 questions |
| Chapter 5 | 296 questions |
| Total | 1,092 questions |

The objective of this book is to provide single-source, comprehensive review materials to assist the CIA exam candidate in successfully preparing for the exam. Major highlights of these review books include

- Easy to navigate, comprehend, learn, and apply the subject matter since it was written from a student's perspective in a textbook style and format.
- It contains fully developed theories and concepts with complete thoughts as opposed to mere outlines. The candidate needs to know more than outlines to pass the difficult CIA exam.
- The theoretical topic at the beginning of each chapter is shown with a range of percentages to indicate the relative weights given to that topic in the exam. The candidate is expected to plan study time in proportion to the relative weights suggested. A clear linkage is provided between theory and practice presented in the same chapter, in the same book, to provide consistency.
- The multiple-choice questions are organized in the same sequence as the theoretical topics for quick and easy access to the subject matter and for better integration between theory and practice. Each question is labeled with its subject area and is identified with its source (i.e., CIA, CBM, and Author). The author is S. Rao Vallabhaneni.
- Greater use of comparisons and contrasts of subject matter make the key concepts come alive by providing lasting impressions. These comparisons show interrelationships between key concepts.
- The four volumes offer full coverage of all of IIA's *Standards,* all of the Practice Advisories, and the Code of Ethics in their entirety, issued as of February 2003.
- A total of 4,013 multiple-choice questions are provided in all four volumes together.

These books focus on the student: the candidate preparing for the CIA exam. They provide a positive learning experience for candidates by helping them to remember what they read through the use of tree diagrams, line drawings, memory aids (which is what), tables, charts, and graphic text boxes. In other words, an attempt has been made to bring life to static words through visual aids. *The positive learning experience system provided through visual aids and memory recalls will enable candidates to form long-lasting study impressions of the subject matter on their minds.* In short, these books are student-focused and learning-oriented.

In these volumes, the needs of the students have been recognized. Learning is made easier, more convenient, and more enjoyable for our customer, the student. A great deal of planning and thought went into the creation of these books with the single goal of making the study program (whether individual or group) relatively easier, more relevant, and meaningful. We hope that these books meet or exceed expectations in terms of quality, content coverage, and presentation of the subject matter.

We were excited and challenged while writing these books, and we hope that you, too, will be excited to study, remember, and achieve lifelong benefit from them. We believe that the knowledge gained from these books will remain with the candidate even after passing the CIA exam, assisting on-the-job as reference material, as well as a training source.

Our goal is to be responsive to the CIA exam candidate's needs and provide customer (student) satisfaction through continuous quality improvement. This goal can be met only through timely feedback from the candidate. Please help us to serve you better—your input counts.

## How to Use This Book

Volume 2 is entitled *Conducting the Internal Audit Engagement* (Part II). It has five chapters: Chapter 1 deals with conducting engagements, Chapter 2 addresses conducting specific engagements, Chapter 3 covers monitoring engagement outcomes, Chapter 4 discusses fraud knowledge elements, and Chapter 5 explains engagement tools.

We suggest a sequential approach, that is, study the theory first and then answer the multiple-choice questions. Both the theory and the practice are highly integrated, and the theory provides good input and clear framework to the practice. Since some theoretical topics are covered in multiple chapters, students are strongly advised to read all the theory chapters first, followed by the practice questions. Also, practice questions can be grouped into multiple chapters in the same part or even multiple parts due to overlapping coverage of the subject matter.

## Exam-Taking Tips and Techniques

The types of questions a candidate can expect to see in the CIA exam are objective, multiple-choice questions. Answering multiple-choice questions requires a good amount of practice and effort.

These tips and techniques will be helpful in answering the multiple-choice questions.

- Stay with your first impression of the correct choice.
- Know the subject area or topic. Do not read too much into the question.
- Remember that questions are independent of specific country, products, practices, vendors, hardware, software, or industry.
- Read the last sentence of the question first followed by all choices and then the body of the question. Underline or circle the keywords.
- Read the question twice or read the underlined or circled key words twice, and watch for tip-off words such as **not, except, all, every, always, never, least,** or **most**, which denote absolute conditions.
- Do not project the question into your organizational environment, practices, policies, procedures, standards, and guidelines. The examination is focused on the IIA's *Professional Standards* and publications and on the CIA's exam syllabus (i.e., content specifications).
- Try to eliminate wrong choices quickly by striking or drawing a line through the choices, or other ways convenient to you.
- When you get down to two semifinal choices, take a big-picture approach. For example, if choices A and D are the semifinalists, and choice D could be a part of choice A, then select choice A; or if choice D could be a more complete answer, then select choice D.
- Do not spend too much time on one question. If you are not sure of an answer, move on, and go back to it if time permits. The last resort is to guess the answer. There is no penalty for guessing the wrong answer.
- Transfer all questions to the answer sheet either after each question is answered individually or in small groups of ten or fifteen questions. Allocate sufficient time to do this task since it is a very important one. Place the right answer on the correct dot of the answer sheet.

Remember that success in the examination depends on your time management skills, preparation effort levels, education and experience, recall of the subject matter, and decision-making skills.

## Administrative Matters

We encourage the new, prospective candidate to write directly to the Institute of Internal Auditors, 247 Maitland Avenue, Altamonte Springs, FL 32701-4201 U.S.A., to obtain a copy of the CIA program "Information for Candidates" brochure. This brochure contains everything the candidate needs to know about the CIA exam (i.e., application form, exam fees, exam dates, and exam sites). Phone: 407-937-1100, Fax: 407-937-1111. Web site: www.theiia.org.

Your comments are important to us in order to improve quality and presentation of future editions. Please send us your feedback through the Web site www.srvbooks.com. Thank you.

## Acknowledgments

The author is indebted to these individuals and sources for helping to improve the quality of this book: Angela Philips Woodward, Director of Certification at the Institute of Internal Auditors, Altamonte Springs, Florida, for providing great assistance during the writing of these books. Special thanks for providing previous CIA exam questions, answers, and explanations, and IIA *Standards* and other sources of materials. *Certified Business Manager (CBM) Examination Preparation Guides,* Volumes 1 through 6, Thomson Learning (South-Western), Mason, OH, 2003-2004 (www.apbm.org). ITT Audit Manual, ITT Corporation, New York, New York, 1983.

# CIA EXAM CONTENT SPECIFICATIONS

The CIA exam tests a candidate's knowledge of current internal auditing practices and understanding of internal audit issues, risks, and controls. The exam is offered in four parts, each part consisting of 125 multiple-choice questions. The following is a breakdown of topics for Part II (Volume 2).

## Part II: Conducting the Internal Audit Engagement

A.  Conduct Engagements (25–35%)

    1.  Research and apply appropriate standards

        a.  IIA Professional Practices Framework (Code of Ethics, *Standards,* Practice Advisories)
        b.  Other professional, legal, and regulatory standards

    2.  Maintain an awareness of the potential for fraud when conducting an engagement

        a.  Notice indicators or symptoms of fraud
        b.  Design appropriate engagement steps to address significant risk of fraud
        c.  Employ audit tests to detect fraud
        d.  Determine if any suspected fraud merits investigation

    3.  Collect data
    4.  Evaluate the relevance, sufficiency, and competence of evidence
    5.  Analyze and interpret data
    6.  Develop workpapers
    7.  Review workpapers
    8.  Communicate interim progress
    9.  Draw conclusions
    10.  Develop recommendations when appropriate
    11.  Report engagement results

        a.  Conduct exit conference
        b.  Prepare report or other communication
        c.  Approve engagement report
        d.  Determine distribution of report
        e.  Obtain management response to report

    12.  Conduct client satisfaction survey
    13.  Complete performance appraisals of engagement staff

B.  Conduct Specific Engagements (25–35%)

    1.  Conduct assurance engagements

        a.  Fraud investigation

            (1)  Determine appropriate parties to be involved with investigation
            (2)  Establish facts and extent of fraud (e.g., interviews, interrogations and data. analysis)
            (3)  Report outcomes to appropriate parties
            (4)  Complete a process review to improve controls to prevent fraud and recommend changes

        b.  Risk and control self-assessment

            (1)  Facilitated approach

                 (a)  Client-facilitated
                (b)  Audit-facilitated

            (2)  Questionnaire approach
            (3)  Self-certification approach

        c.  Audits of third parties and contract auditing
        d.  Quality audit engagements
        e.  Due diligence audit engagements
        f.  Security audit engagements
        g.  Privacy audit engagements

h. Performance (key performance indicators) audit engagements
i. Operational (efficiency and effectiveness) audit engagements
j. Financial audit engagements
k. Information technology (IT) audit engagements

    (1) Operating systems

        (a) Mainframe
        (b) Workstations
        (c) Server

    (2) Application development

        (a) Application authentication
        (b) Systems development methodology
        (c) Change control
        (d) End-user computing

    (3) Data and network communications/connections (e.g., LAN, VAN, and WAN)
    (4) Voice communications
    (5) System security (e.g., firewalls, access control)
    (6) Contingency planning
    (7) Databases
    (8) Functional areas of IT operations (e.g., data center operations)
    (9) Web infrastructure
    (10) Software licensing
    (11) Electronic funds transfer (EFT) and Electronic data interchange (EDI)
    (12) E-commerce
    (13) Information protection (e.g., viruses, privacy)
    (14) Encryption
    (15) Enterprise-wide resource planning (ERP) software (e.g., SAP R/3)

l. Compliance audit engagements

2. Conduct consulting engagements.

    a. Internal control training
    b. Business process review
    c. Benchmarking
    d. Information technology (IT) and systems development
    e. Design of performance measurement systems

C. Monitor Engagement Outcomes (5–15%)

1. Determine appropriate follow-up activity by the internal audit activity
2. Identify appropriate method to monitor engagement outcomes
3. Conduct follow-up activity
4. Communicate monitoring plan and results

D. Fraud Knowledge Elements (5–15%)

1. Discovery sampling
2. Interrogation techniques
3. Forensic auditing
4. Use of computers in analyzing data
5. Red flag
6. Types of fraud

E. Engagement Tools (15–25%)

1. Sampling

    a. Nonstatistical (judgmental)
    b. Statistical

2. Statistical analyses (process control techniques)

3. Data gathering tools

    a. Interviewing
    b. Questionnaires
    c. Checklists

4. Analytical review techniques

    a. Ratio estimation
    b. Variance analysis (e.g., budget versus actual)
    c. Other reasonableness tests

5. Observation
6. Problem solving
7. Risk and control self-assessment (CSA)
8. Computerized audit tools and techniques

    a. Embedded audit modules
    b. Data extraction techniques
    c. Generalized audit software (e.g., ACL, IDEA)
    d. Spreadsheet analysis
    e. Automated workpapers (e.g., Lotus Notes, Auditor Assistant)

9. Process mapping including flowcharting

# 1 CONDUCT ENGAGEMENTS (25–35%)

## THEORY

### 1.1 Audit Scheduling

An audit schedule is an essential part of planning internal auditing department activities. Since audit resources, in terms of available time and the number of auditors, are limited, the audit manager needs to balance the needs of the audit plan and the availability of resources. It is prudent to hire auditors with different skill and experience levels so that all required skills are available among the audit staff even though each auditor may not have all the required skills.

It is the audit manager's responsibility to match the available audit resources to the audit requirements. If the required resources are not available, the audit manager should try to acquire them from either internal or external sources.

The audit manager will notice that there are constraints on the conduct of the audit that may affect the completion of the audits as planned. Some examples of such constraints are staff unavailability due to illness or termination; auditee not ready for the audit due to some business considerations such as mergers, demergers, and other extraordinary events; and time constraints, such as accounting month closing work, quarter-end work, or year-end work. The audit manager needs to consider all these constraints with alternative plans in place.

When it comes to assigning the audit staff to particular audit responsibilities, the two approaches most often taken are the "team" concept and the "pool" concept. Under the team concept, individuals are given responsibility only for certain segments of the organization.

Under the pool concept, individuals are made available for assignment to any audit. What works best is determined by the needs of individual organizations, but both approaches have their advantages and drawbacks.

The team approach offers the opportunity for the individual staff members to become proficient in given areas quickly. Experienced audit staff members are more likely to work in specialized team-type areas. The pool approach allows the individual staff member to gain experience in a broader sense in many areas of the organization. What usually works in practice is a blending of the two approaches, with new staff auditors being available under the pool concept and more experienced auditors developing supervisory skills as well as expertise in more specialized areas.

During the planning of the audit, the audit manager needs to break down the audit project into small and manageable tasks, which can be assigned to audit staff to facilitate monitoring the audit results and progress. Project management tools and techniques, such as program evaluation and review techniques (PERT), critical path methods (CPM), and periodic progress reports, might help the audit manager to plan and control major and complex audit projects.

## KEY CONCEPTS TO REMEMBER: MANAGING AN AUDIT ASSIGNMENT

- An audit department can use the pool concept to assign all staff and most senior auditors to engagements. Monthly audit work schedules would most likely ensure effective staff utilization.
- The effectiveness of an audit assignment is related to the findings and the action taken on those findings. Conducting an exit interview with auditees would contribute to assignment effectiveness.
- The internal audit department time budgets normally should be prepared in terms of hours or days.
- A primary purpose of an exit conference is to ensure the accuracy of the information used by an internal auditor. A secondary benefit of an exit conference is to improve relations with auditees. One purpose of the exit conference is for the internal auditor to review and verify the appropriateness of the audit report based on auditee input.
- The primary reason that the auditor should document a closing conference is that information may be needed if a dispute arises.
- A purpose of an audit closing conference is to generate commitment for appropriate managerial action.
- A primary purpose of the audit closing conference is to resolve remaining issues.
- The best purpose of an exit conference is to ensure that there have been no misunderstandings or misinterpretation of fact. The auditors are required to discuss conclusions and recommendations at appropriate levels of management before issuing final written reports. The purpose of the exit conference is not whether the objectives of the audit and the scope of the audit work are known by the auditee, the auditee understands the audit program, or the list of persons who are to receive the final report are identified.
- The primary purpose of conducting a closing conference with the manager of an organizational unit audited should be to confirm the soundness of audit results and make such modifications as seem justified.
- During an exit conference, an auditor and an auditee disagreed about a well-documented audit finding. Assuming that the disagreement cannot be resolved prior to issuing the audit report, it should be handled by presenting both the audit finding and the auditee's position on the finding. Reasons for disagreement should be stated.
- Audit objectives of the audit closing or exit conference are to discuss the findings, to resolve conflicts, and to identify management's actions and responses to the findings.
- Recommendations in audit reports may or may not actually be implemented.
- Working papers should include identifying concerns for future audits, but such concerns are not an objective of the audit closing conference.
- Interim reports are issued during an audit to communicate information requiring immediate action.
- An oral report is appropriate when there are significant problems discovered during the audit.
- If an audit is done in a sales department, a copy of the audit report should be sent to the sales director and vice president of marketing.
- Participants who would be appropriate to attend an exit conference include the responsible internal auditor, representatives from management who are knowledgeable of detailed operations, and those who can authorize implementation of corrective action.
- After an audit report with adverse findings has been communicated to appropriate auditee personnel, proper action is to schedule a follow-up review.
- Due professional care calls for consideration of the possibility of material irregularities during every audit assignment.
- Due care in the conduct of an audit implies the conduct of examinations and verifications to a reasonable extent.

- When written performance standards established by management are vague and have to be interpreted by the auditor, the auditor should establish agreement with the auditee as to the standards needed to measure performance.
- An auditor begins an audit with a preliminary evaluation of internal controls, the purpose of which is to decide on the extent of future auditing activities. If the auditor's preliminary evaluation of internal controls results in a finding that controls may be inadequate, the next step would be an expansion of audit work prior to the preparation of an audit report.
- The performance appraisal system for evaluating an auditor should include specific accomplishments directly related to the performance of the audit program (i.e., based on task outcomes).

## 1.2 Audit Supervision

The most effective way to ensure the quality and expedite the progress of an audit assignment is by exercising proper supervision from the start of the planning process to the completion of audit work and reporting. Supervision adds seasoned judgment to the work performed by less experienced staff and provides necessary on-the-job training for them.

Assigning and using staff is important to satisfying audit objectives. Since skills and knowledge vary among auditors, work assignments must be commensurate with skills and abilities.

Supervisors should satisfy themselves that staff members clearly understand their assigned tasks before starting the work. Staff should be informed not only of what work they are to do and how they are to proceed but also why the work is to be conducted and what it is expected to accomplish. With experienced staff, the supervisors' role may be more general. They may outline the scope of the work and leave details to assistants. With a less experienced staff, a supervisor may have to specify not only how to gather data but also techniques for analyzing them.

Effective supervision ensures that audit assignments are properly planned and produce a high- quality and consistent product. A competent supervisor can help in preparing audit plans, developing and controlling budgets and schedules, improving auditor and auditee relationships, ensuring the preparation of consistent and quality working papers, and reviewing audit reports.

Supervision is a continuing process, beginning with audit planning and ending with the conclusion of audit assignments and distribution of the final audit report. Supervisors should attend the initial and final meetings with the auditee, when possible. Supervisors should approve both the initial audit work program and any revisions to the audit work program. Nonconformance to the approved audit work program should be recorded in the working papers, giving adequate reasons. Supervisors should review the working papers and monitor and control audit budgets and schedules through observation and periodic progress and time reports. When supervisors review the audit report, they should refer to the working papers to ensure that all evidence and findings are adequately supported and that the deficiency audit findings are objective, fair, significant, and factual.

---

### KEY CONCEPTS TO REMEMBER: AUDIT SUPERVISION

- "The proficiency of the internal auditors and the difficulty of the audit assignment" best describes what should determine the extent of supervision required for a particular internal audit assignment. The extent of supervision is not determined by whether the audit involves possible fraud on the part of management, whether the audit involves possible violations of laws or government regulations, or the audit organization's prior experience in dealing with the particular auditee.
- Time budgets, weekly status reports, and time reports would be of most assistance in the supervision of a specific audit assignment. An assignment board would be of least assistance.
- Using only daily, close supervision and written memoranda is an acceptable approach for managing a small department, but is not appropriate for use with a large audit department.
- Supervising an audit engagement properly includes ensuring that the approved audit program is carried out.

- Audits should be properly supervised to produce professional audits of consistently high quality. This requires review of all audit programs, working papers, and draft audit reports.
- Best control over the work on which audit opinions are based is a supervisory review of all audit work. An audit opinion is the auditor's professional judgment of the situation, which was reviewed by an audit supervisor.
- When reviewing the audit working papers, the audit supervisor is to determine whether working papers adequately support the audit findings, conclusions, and audit reports.
- "An audit finding recorded in the working papers and report draft that omits the criteria used for evaluation" should be a deficiency found by an audit supervisor when reviewing a set of working papers.
- An audit supervisor should evaluate the evidence collected by the auditor during the review of the audit working papers. Substantive testing supports the "sufficient" evidence; tests of control support "competent" evidence. The relationship of the sample to the audit objectives supports "relevant" evidence. An example of relevant evidence is selecting a stratified sample of billings by an agency specializing in newspaper advertising when the company is requesting an artwork for a magazine advertising. "Insufficient" evidence is when an auditor interviews the firm's advertising manager, products marketing director, and major customers to determine the adequacy of contract and compliance with fair trade regulations. The auditor should have talked to legal counsel also.

## 1.3 Collecting Data and Information

Information is the heart of the problem-solving process. Decisions are made using the information to solve existing problems and to make decisions. For the information to be useful in so many ways, it has to meet certain quality attributes, such as availability, timeliness, accuracy, and relevancy.

Knowledge is power. Knowledge is the result of information. The amount and the right kind of information a person has can make the difference between an informed decision and a guess, between success and failure. Knowledge is a synthesis of information. In this information age, knowing means winning. The more one knows about something, the more control one has over one's own destiny. *The need for relevant information is not only to avoid present failures, but also to maximize future opportunities and minimize potential future problems.*

As changes create a need for more information, the value of information will begin to increase significantly. The successful executives and professionals (e.g., auditors) will be those who have mastered the art of being information conscious. Information consists of facts, figures, rules, news, statistics, data, values, impressions—pieces of intelligence that singly or jointly increase awareness of the subject matter.

Information should be differentiated from assumptions. An assumption is a conclusion based on noninformation, which can be true or false. It has no evidence. Assumptions are made all the time. We make false assumptions, such as certain data are: easy to find when in fact they are difficult to find, difficult to find when in fact they are easy, inexpensive to buy when in fact they are expensive, and expensive to buy when in fact they are inexpensive.

Information is obtained only by asking questions or searching for it. Information is an outcome of a process that involves fact gathering, data collection, measurement, interpretation, analysis, and forecasting.

Information can be said to be the result of data. Data consist of raw numbers and facts. Information consists of meaningful numbers and facts. Information involves the addition of a certain value to data through some level of selection, interpretation, or rearrangement.

Since management makes decisions and auditors use information, they need to know how and where the information is coming from. At least four sources of information are available: primary and secondary information and internal and external sources (see Exhibit 1.1).

**Sources of Information**

- Primary information (original, expensive)
- Secondary information (not original, inexpensive)
- Internal sources (facts about the firm, used in planning)
- External sources (facts about the economy, markets)

**Exhibit 1.1: Sources of information**

**Primary information** is firsthand information from an original source. **Secondary information** is secondhand. Primary information is usually expensive to gather while secondary information is inexpensive.

**Internal sources** involve facts about an organization (sales data, customer data, financial data, and product data). Internal sources are used in planning and performance measurement.

**External sources** are facts about the world outside the organization. This information involves facts about competitors, markets, demographics, the environment, and the economy. Managers often make decisions without external sources. External sources are not usually perceived as being that important; they are more difficult to obtain and often are neglected, resulting in bad consequences. The goal should be to combine external sources with internal sources.

Managers should think of problems and opportunities as information needs, as a series of questions that need to be answered. *Information consciousness means to think information when thinking about problems.*

## 1.4 Evaluate the Audit Evidence

(a) **Types of Audit Evidence.** Audit evidence is information that provides a factual basis for audit opinions. It is the information documented by the auditors and obtained through observing conditions, interviewing people, examining records, and testing documents. Audit evidence may be categorized as physical, documentary, testimonial, and analytical (see Exhibit 1.2).[1]

Types of audit evidence
- Physical (direct inspection and observation)
- Documentary (letters, contracts, records)
- Testimonial (obtained from others)
- Analytical (computations, comparisons)

**Exhibit 1.2: Types of audit evidence**

**Physical evidence** is obtained by direct inspection or observation of people, property, or events. Such evidence may be documented in the form of memoranda summarizing the matters inspected or observed, photographs, charts, maps, or actual samples. An auditor's observation of the functioning of an internal control system produces physical evidence.

Examples of physical evidence include: taking a photograph of the auditees' workplace, such as improperly stored materials or unsafe conditions; observing conditions; test counting a batch of inventory; and testing the existence of an asset.

**Documentary evidence** consists of created information, such as letters, contracts, accounting records, invoices, and management information on performance.

Examples of documentary evidence include: a page of the general ledger containing irregularities placed there by perpetrator of a fraud; and determining whether erroneous billings occurred when the auditor for a construction contractor finds material costs increasing as a percentage of billings and suspects that materials billed to the company are being delivered to another contractor. A contract is the most appropriate evidence for the auditor to obtain and review when evaluating the propriety of a payment to a consultant.

**Testimonial evidence** is obtained from others through statements received in response to inquiries, through interviews, or through responses to questionnaires. Testimonial evidence needs to be evaluated from the standpoint of whether the individual may be biased or have only partial knowledge about the area. Testimonial evidence obtained under conditions where persons may speak freely is more credible than testimonial evidence obtained under compromising conditions (e.g., where persons may be intimidated).

Examples of testimonial evidence include: a written, signed statement from an interviewee in response to a question asked by an auditor during an interview; a written statement by or a letter from an

---

[1] *Comptroller General of the United States, **Government Auditing Standards** (Washington, DC: US General Accounting Office, 1994).*

auditee in response to a specific inquiry made by an auditor; and a letter from the company's attorney in response to inquiries about possible litigation.

**Analytical evidence** includes computations, comparisons, reasoning, and separation of information into components.

Examples of analytical evidence include: to evaluate the reasonableness of the quantity of scrap material resulting from a certain production process compared to industry standards; to evaluate the reasonableness of account balances; and concluding that there was an adequate separation of duties in the counting and recording of cash receipts.

(b) **Standards of Audit Evidence.** All audit evidence should meet the three standards of sufficiency, competence, and relevance. Evidence is sufficient if it is based on facts. Competent evidence is reliable evidence. The term "relevance" refers to the relationship of the information to its use. When audit evidence does not meet these three standards, additional (corroborative) evidence is required before expressing an audit opinion (see Exhibit 1.3).

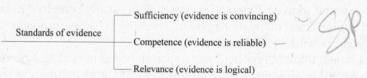

Standards of evidence
- Sufficiency (evidence is convincing)
- Competence (evidence is reliable)
- Relevance (evidence is logical)

**Exhibit 1.3: Standards of evidence**

(c) **Appropriateness of Audit Evidence.** The phrase "appropriateness of audit evidence" refers to persuasiveness (sufficiency), relevance, and competence (reliability). The following discussion helps auditors determine what constitutes sufficient, relevant, and competent evidence to support their findings and conclusions.

Evidence is **sufficient** if there is enough of it to support the auditors' findings. In determining the sufficiency of evidence, it may be helpful to ask: Is there enough evidence to persuade a reasonable person of the validity of the findings? An essential factor in evaluating the "sufficiency" of evidence is that it must be convincing enough for a prudent person to reach the same decision.

Therefore, *sufficiency deals with the persuasiveness of the evidence* (see Exhibit 1.4 for hierarchy of persuasive evidence). When appropriate, statistical methods may be used to establish sufficiency. When sampling methods are used, the concept of sufficiency of evidence means that the samples selected provide reasonable assurance that they are representative of the sampled population. Interviewing the auditee is not enough to provide sufficient evidence.

Some examples of sufficient evidence follow:

- Verifying the quantity of fixed assets on hand by physical observation would provide the most persuasive evidence of quantity on hand.
- Using test data, an auditor has processed both normal and atypical transactions through a computerized payroll system to test calculations of regular and overtime pay amounts. Sufficient competent evidence of controls exists if test data results are compared to predetermined results or expectations.
- The audit procedure that provides the most persuasive evidence about the loan's collectibility is to examine the documentation of a recent, independent appraisal of the real estate that was used a security.
- The most persuasive evidence that the incoming supply counts are made by the receiving department is a periodic observation by the internal auditor over the course of the audit.
- "A positive confirmation received directly from the customer" is the most persuasive evidence concerning the existence and valuation of a receivable.
- If the audit objective is to gain evidence that payment has actually been made for a specific invoice from a vendor, the most persuasive evidence would be obtained by a canceled check, made out to the vendor and referenced to the invoice, included in a cutoff bank statement, which the auditor received directly from the bank.
- If an auditor wants assurance of the existence of inventory stored in a warehouse, the most persuasive evidence is to physically observe the inventory in the warehouse.
- Externally prepared documents (e.g., invoice) would provide the most persuasive evidence regarding an asset value that was acquired.

- A physical examination would provide the most persuasive evidence for testing the existence of an asset.

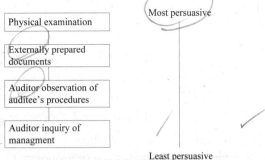

**Exhibit 1.4: Hierarchy of persuasive evidence**

Evidence used to support a finding is **relevant** if it has a logical, sensible relationship to that finding. Relevant evidence is consistent with the audit objectives and supports audit findings and recommendations. Evidence is **competent** to the extent that it is consistent with fact (i.e., evidence is competent if it is valid). "Competent" evidence is satisfied by an original signed document, but copies do not provide competent evidence. *Evidence that is both available and reliable is competent. Competent information is reliable and the best available through the use of appropriate audit functions.*

The next presumptions are useful in judging the competence of evidence. However, these presumptions are not to be considered sufficient in themselves to determine competence.

- Evidence obtained from a credible independent source is more competent than that secured from the audited organization. An external source of evidence should impact audit conclusions most.
- Evidence developed under an effective system of management controls is more competent than that obtained where such control is weak or nonexistent.
- Evidence obtained through the auditors' direct physical examination, observation, computation, and inspection is more competent than evidence obtained indirectly. An example of external and internal evidence is when an auditor reviews the count sheets, inventory printouts, and memos from the last inventory during determination of causes of inventory shortages shown by the physical inventories.

Examples of competent evidence follow:

- An audit objective of an accounts receivable function is to determine if prescribed standard procedures are followed when credit is granted. An audit procedure providing the most competent evidence would be selecting a statistical sample of credit applications and testing them for conformance with prescribed procedures.
- The most "reliable" (competent) evidence of determining a company's legal title to inventories is paid vendor invoices.
- A contract dispute has arisen between a company and a major supplier. To resolve the dispute, the most competent evidence would be the original contract.
- A positive confirmation of an accounts receivable that proves that it actually exists is competent evidence.
- In deciding whether recorded sales are valid, most "competent" evidence would be obtained by looking at the shipping document, the independent bill of lading, and the invoice for the merchandise.

Auditors should, when they deem it useful, obtain from officials of the audited entity written representations concerning the competence of the evidence they obtain. Written representations ordinarily confirm oral representations given to the auditor, indicate and document the continuing appropriateness of such representations, and reduce the possibility of misunderstandings concerning the matters that are the subject of the representations.

An example of relevant evidence is aging of accounts receivables, which provides relevant evidence regarding the validity of receivables and thus the allowance account.

(d) **Information Sources for Audit Evidence.** The auditors' approach to determining the sufficiency, relevance, and competence of evidence depends on the source of the information that constitutes the evidence (see Exhibit 1.5). Information sources include original data gathered by auditors and existing data gathered by either the auditee or a third party. Data from any of these sources may be obtained from computer-based systems.

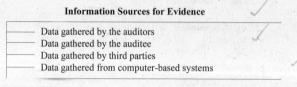

**Information Sources for Evidence**

- Data gathered by the auditors
- Data gathered by the auditee
- Data gathered by third parties
- Data gathered from computer-based systems

**Exhibit 1.5: Information sources for evidence**

(i) **Data gathered by the auditors.** These data include the auditors' own observations and measurements. Among the methods for gathering these types of data are questionnaires, structured interviews, and direct observations. The design of these methods and the skill of the auditors applying them are the keys to ensuring that these data constitute sufficient, competent, and relevant evidence. When these methods are applied to determine cause, auditors are concerned with eliminating rival explanations of cause. Doing so involves considering three types of validity (1) internal validity, (2) construct validity, and (3) external validity.

1. Internal validity means that A (the program as defined for the particular audit) caused B (the effect measured in the audit).
2. Construct validity refers to whether the auditors are measuring or observing what they intend to.
3. External validity refers to the ability to generalize the auditors' findings to a broader universe.

(ii) **Data gathered by the auditee.** Auditors can use data gathered by the auditee as part of their evidence. If those data are significant to the overall body of evidence supporting their findings, auditors should obtain additional evidence of the reliability of those data. Statements by auditee management or personnel about the reliability of operations data should be corroborated with other evidence. Auditors can obtain the necessary evidence by testing the effectiveness of the entity's controls over the reliability of the data, by direct tests of the data, or by a combination of the two.

When the auditors' tests of data disclose errors in that data, the auditors should consider the significance of those errors in relation to the audit objectives. If the auditors conclude that these errors are so significant that the data are not valid or reliable, they should consider whether to

- Seek evidence from other sources
- Redefine the audit's objectives to eliminate the need to use the invalid or unreliable data, or
- Use the data, but clearly indicate in their report the data's limitations and refrain from making unwarranted conclusions or recommendations

Similar considerations apply when the auditors are unable to obtain sufficient, competent, and relevant evidence about the validity and reliability of the auditee's data.

(iii) **Data gathered by third parties.** The auditors' evidence may also include data gathered by third parties. In some cases, these data may already have been audited, or the auditors may be able to audit this evidence themselves. Often, however, it will not be practical to obtain evidence of the data's validity and reliability.

How the use of unaudited third-party data affects the auditors' report depends on the data's significance to the overall body of evidence supporting the auditors' findings. If it is significant, the auditors should clearly indicate in their report the data's limitations and refrain from making unwarranted conclusions or recommendations based on those data.

(iv) **Data gathered from computer-based systems.** Auditors should obtain sufficient evidence that computer-processed data are valid and reliable when those data are significant to the overall body of evidence supporting the auditors' findings, and any conclusions or recommendations. (When the reliability of a computer-based system is the primary objective of the audit, the auditor should conduct a review of the system's general and application controls.) This is necessary regardless of whether the data are provided to auditors or auditors independently extract them. (When the auditor uses computer-processed data or includes them in the report for background or information purposes, and when those data are not significant to the auditor's results, citing the source of the data and stating that they were not verified will satisfy the reporting standards for accuracy and completeness).

Auditors should determine if other auditors have worked to establish the validity and reliability of the data or the effectiveness of the controls over the system that produced it. If they have, auditors may be able to use that work. If not, auditors can obtain evidence about the validity and reliability of computer-processed data from tests of general and application controls, direct tests of the data, or a combination of both.

## 1.5 Develop and Review Audit Working Papers

Working papers document the basis for findings, conclusions, and auditors' recommendations, and should contain sufficient information to enable an experienced auditor previously not connected with the audit to ascertain from them what work the auditors performed to support the findings, conclusions, or recommendations.[2] This is the ultimate objective of the audit working papers. The working papers not only document the auditors' work, but also allow for the review of audit quality.

Working papers are the link between fieldwork and the audit report. The requirements to prepare working papers may be satisfied with documentation maintained on disks, tapes, or film. Working papers serve three purposes: (1) they provide the principal support for the auditors' report, (2) aid the auditors in conducting and supervising the audit, and (3) allow others to review the audit's quality (see Exhibit 1.6).

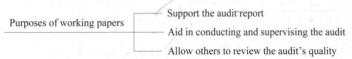

Purposes of working papers
- Support the audit report
- Aid in conducting and supervising the audit
- Allow others to review the audit's quality

**Exhibit 1.6: Purposes of audit working papers**

Audit organizations should establish policies and procedures to ensure the safe custody and retention of working papers for a time sufficient to satisfy legal and administrative requirements. These policies should also cover the need to make the working papers available for others to review audit quality. These quality reviewers need a written explanation of the basis for the auditor's significant judgments. Arrangements need to be made to ensure that the director of internal audit will make working papers available to others after approval.

Working papers should contain

- The objective, scope, and methodology, including any sampling criteria used, and results of the audit
- Evidence of the work performed to support findings, judgments, and conclusions
- Evidence of supervisory reviews of the work conducted

Working papers can be prepared electronically. The contents of the working papers will be the same whether they are paper or electronic. However, the electronic media requires additional considerations due to technological factors. These considerations include generating backup copies of working papers, security and control procedures to access working papers, and data file retention procedures. Exhibit 1.7 presents major advantages and disadvantages for both manually and electronically prepared working papers.

| *Manually prepared working papers* | *Electronically prepared working papers* |
| --- | --- |
| *Advantages* | *Advantages* |
| • Can feel and touch the paper | • Do not take valuable space to file and store |
| • Can make notes and comments easily | • Easy to transport among auditors |
| • Approved by tax authorities | • Cross-referencing is easy to do |
| • Easy to work with due to familiar media | • Changes can be made quickly and easily |
| | • Save time overall |
| | • Quick sharing of information among audit staff when used through a computer network |
| | • Approved by tax authorities |
| *Disadvantages* | *Disadvantages* |
| • Materials are bulky to handle | • Require specific technical training |
| • Take value space for filing and storage | • Cannot put normal signature |
| • Difficult to make changes; take more time | • Require elaborate access controls |
| • Difficult to transport especially when there are multiple volumes | • Cannot feel and touch like the "paper" |
| • Paper can easily be destroyed by fire, flood | • Not easy to work with compared to paper |
| • Cross-referencing is difficult and time-consuming to do | • Require access to a computer |
| | • Cross-referencing is difficult to verify |

**Exhibit 1.7: Advantages and disadvantages of manually and electronically prepared working papers**

---

[2] *Ibid.*

## KEY CONCEPTS TO REMEMBER: AUDIT WORKING PAPERS

- The functions of audit working papers are to: facilitate third-party reviews; aid in the planning, performance, and review of audits; provide the principal evidential support for the auditor's report; explain all audit verification symbols properly; and make cross-references between the working papers and the audit report. However, the working papers are not to aid in the professional development of the operating staff or teach auditing skills to nonauditors.
- The purpose of "summaries" in working papers is to distill the most useful information from several working papers into a more usable form.
- A working paper is complete when it satisfies the audit objectives for which it is developed.
- Working papers document the auditing procedures performed, the information obtained, and the conclusions reached. Each individual working paper should, at a minimum, contain a descriptive heading.
- When determining the retention period for the working papers of a contract audit, it is best to seek the assistance of the legal department to ensure compliance with contract provisions.
- Working papers provide the principal evidential support for the internal auditor's report and are the principal purpose for retaining the working papers.
- Working papers should include documentation of the examination and evaluation of the adequacy and effectiveness of the system of internal control.
- When reviewing the audit working papers, the audit supervisor must determine that working papers adequately support audit findings, conclusions, and audit reports.
- To properly control working papers, the auditor should not make them available to people who have no authority to use them. With working papers, the auditor can share the results of an audit with the auditee, permit access to external auditors, and permit access to government auditors.
- Audit working papers should be reviewed to ensure that no issues are open at the conclusion of the fieldwork.
- The director of internal auditing should establish policies for indexing and the type of working papers files maintained.
- An adequately documented working paper should be concise but complete.
- Working papers are the property of the auditor. Good control of working papers requires that only the auditor who created a working paper can change an electronic working paper.
- When audit conclusions are challenged, the auditor's factual rebuttal is best facilitated by cross-referencing the working papers.
- Working papers should be disposed of when they are of no further use and in accordance with departmental policy. Retention and destruction policies should be approved by legal counsel.
- A primary purpose of an auditor's working papers is to provide evidence of the planning and execution of audit procedures performed.
- Working papers on fraud audits should not be retained indefinitely. Some guidelines are: working papers should be disposed of when they have no further use, working paper retention schedules should be approved by legal counsel, and working paper retention schedules should consider legal and contractual requirements. Working papers should not be retained indefinitely.
- Audit working papers should not be overdocumented by including unnecessary forms, reports, and documents.
- Statistical summaries of working papers are used to consolidate numeric data scattered among several schedules.
- An auditor's working papers should support the findings and recommendations to be reported and should facilitate peer reviews.

- The primary purpose for indexing working papers is to permit cross-referencing and simplify supervisory review.
- The supervisory review of working papers determines that working papers adequately support findings, conclusions, recommendations, and audit reports.
- The primary objective of maintaining security over working papers is to prohibit unauthorized changes or removal of information.
- An internal auditor's working papers should be reviewed by the management of the internal auditing department and should contain certain standard information, such as heading, date work sheet completed, auditor's initials, and index number. Including all forms and directives used by the auditee department in the working papers would constitute inappropriate working paper preparation.

A working paper can include flowcharts, findings cross-referenced to supporting documentation, and tick marks explained in footnotes. The question of whether a working paper is complete or not is determined by whether the audit objective has been met and supported. Working papers should describe objectives, procedures, facts, conclusions, and recommendations. Working paper summaries can be used to promote efficient working paper review by supervisors. Working paper control is best described by a restricting access to only those who have a legitimate need to know.

## 1.6 Audit Reporting

(a) **Audit Report Purpose.** Written audit reports serve multiple purposes. They communicate the results of the audit work to auditees and others, make the results less susceptible to misunderstanding, and facilitate follow-up reviews to determine whether appropriate corrective actions have been taken.[3]

(b) **Audit Report Timeliness.** To be of maximum use, the audit report must be timely. A carefully prepared report may be of little value to decision makers if it arrives too late. Therefore, the audit organization should plan for the prompt issuance of the audit report and conduct the audit with this goal in mind.

The auditors should consider interim reporting, during the audit, of significant matters to appropriate auditees. Such communication, which may be oral or written, is not a substitute for a final written report, but it does alert auditees to matters needing immediate attention and permits them to correct the problems before the final report is completed.

### ADVANTAGES AND DISADVANTAGES OF INTERIM REPORTS

**Advantages**

- Final report-writing time can be minimized.
- Communication of critical information requiring immediate attention is facilitated.
- Informal and verbal communication can take place.

**Disadvantages**

- A formal, written interim report may negate the need for a final report in certain circumstances.
- It puts more demand on auditors to make sure the evidence is solid and complete.

Summary reports highlighting audit results may be appropriate for levels of management above the auditee. They may be issued separately from or in conjunction with the final report.

(c) **Audit Report Contents.** The contents of the audit report should include: objectives, scope, and methodology; audit findings, conclusions, and recommendations; compliance with standards, regulations, and laws; management (auditee's) responses; and noteworthy accomplishments (see Exhibit 1.8).

---

[3] *Ibid.*

Components of Report Contents

| |
| --- |
| Objectives, scope, and methodology |
| Audit findings, conclusions, and recommendations |
| Compliance with standards, regulations, and laws |
| Auditee's (management) responses |
| Auditee's noteworthy accomplishments |

**Exhibit 1.8:  Components of report contents**

(i) **Objectives, scope, and methodology.** Readers need knowledge of the objectives of the audit, as well as the audit scope and methodology for achieving the objectives, to understand the purpose of audit, judge the merits of the audit work and what is reported, and understand any significant limitations.

The statement of objectives being reported on should explain why the audit was made and state what the report is to accomplish. Articulating what the report is to accomplish normally involves identifying the audit subject and the aspect of performance examined. Because what is reported depends on the objectives, the statement should also communicate what finding elements are discussed and whether conclusions and recommendations are given.

## Effective Communication

Effective communication (written and oral) skills are crucial for advancement in today's team-oriented workplace. Such skills are more important than technical skills and greatly needed to solve problems.

The statement of objectives tells the reader the boundaries of the audit. To preclude misunderstanding in cases where the objectives are particularly limited and broader objectives can be inferred, it may be necessary to clearly define the audit boundaries by stating objectives that were **not** pursued.

The statement of scope should describe the depth and coverage of the audit work conducted to accomplish the audit's objectives. As applicable, it should explain the relationship between the universe and what was audited, identify organizations and geographic locations at which audit work was conducted and the period covered, cite the kinds and sources of evidence used and the techniques used to verify it, and explain any quality or other problems with the evidence. Significant constraints imposed on the audit approach by data limitations or scope impairments must be disclosed.

The statement on methodology should clearly explain the evidence-gathering and analysis techniques used to accomplish the audit's objectives. The explanation should identify any assumptions. It should describe any comparative techniques applied and measures and criteria used to assess performance in conducting the audit. If sampling is involved, the statement should describe the sample design and state why it was chosen.

Every effort should be made to avoid any misunderstanding on the part of the reader concerning the work that was and was not done to achieve the audit objectives, particularly when the work was limited because of constraints on time or resources.

## DETERMINING THE SIGNIFICANCE OF AUDIT FINDINGS

Audit findings and recommendations have a direct link in that recommendations should address or correct the findings. The benefit from audit work is not in the recommendations made, but in their effective implementation. Important measures of audit organization's effectiveness are the type of issues it tackles and the changes or improvements it is able to effect.

Audit findings need to be significant to be of any use to the audited organization. This is because correcting a deficient audit finding requires resources. The significance of audit findings can be assessed from two aspects: (1) the nature of the finding itself and (2) the quality of the recommendations.

With respect to the nature of the finding itself, both quantitative and qualitative aspects of a finding should be considered when determining its significance. Examples of quantitative aspects include: revenues increased, costs decreased, and number of defects reduced. Examples of qualitative aspects include: customer satisfaction increased, employee morale improved, and compliance to laws and regulations is achieved.

With respect to quality, recommendations should be action-oriented and effective. To achieve the desired action, action-oriented recommendations must be

- Properly directed
- Hard-hitting
- Specific
- Convincing
- Significant

To be effective, recommendations must identify a course of action that will correct identified problem or cause significant improvements. Effective recommendations

- Deal with underlying causes
- Are feasible
- Are cost-effective
- Consider alternatives

The significance of a recommendation depends on the subject matter and the specific situation. Frequently, significance can be assessed in terms of dollars. For example, assume that implementation of an audit recommendation would correct inadequate internal controls in an area where very significant amounts of money are subject to theft or manipulation. The inadequate controls are readily recognizable as a significant deficiency. A recommendation to strengthen the internal controls in an area of such significance and susceptibility would be key and worthy of special emphasis.

However, dollars are only one measure of significance, not necessarily the most important one. For example, the need to ensure implementation of recommendations to provide safe operations of a manufacturing or nuclear plant can hardly be overemphasized. Implementing such recommendations could prevent the loss of life, substantial bodily injury, or environmental contamination.

There is a vast difference between recommendations dealing with conditions that are imminently life threatening and those that are just significant enough to be reportable.

The significance of a finding and a recommendation should be known to the auditor and communicated to the auditee early during an assignment. The fact that a recommendation is considered to be a key one should not come as a surprise to the auditee being audited. It should have been made apparent during early discussions with the auditee and certainly at the exit conference.

Emphasis on key recommendations should be continued as the findings and recommendations are reported. Key recommendations should be identified and highlighted in reports in a context that makes their significance apparent. Executive summaries and transmittal memorandums can be used to further establish and emphasize the significance of key recommendations.

---

(ii) **Audit findings, conclusions, and recommendations.** The report should include a full discussion of the significant audit findings and, where applicable, auditors' conclusions.

The report should present the significant findings developed in response to each audit objective. Any audit finding not included in the audit report because of insignificance should be separately communicated to management, preferably in writing. The audit report should reference findings communicated in a management letter.

All communications should be documented in the working papers. Sufficient, competent, and relevant information about findings should be included to promote adequate understanding of the matters reported and to provide convincing but fair presentations in proper perspective. Appropriate background information that readers need to understand the findings should also be included.

Audit findings have often been regarded as containing the elements of criteria, condition, and effect, plus causes when problems are found. However, the elements needed for a finding depend entirely on the objectives of the audit. Thus, a finding or set of findings is complete to the extent that the audit objectives are satisfied and the report clearly relates those objectives to the finding's elements.

## DESIRABLE ATTRIBUTES OF A DEFICIENCY AUDIT FINDING

Audit findings have often been regarded as containing the elements of criteria, condition, and effect, plus cause when problems are found.[4] However, the elements needed for a finding depend entirely on the objectives of the audit. This means the elements "cause" and "effect" may be optional for a compliance audit, but they are musts for an operational audit. Thus, a finding or set of findings is complete to the extent that the audit objectives are satisfied and the report clearly relates those objectives to the finding's elements. A deficiency audit finding should have four elements or attributes, with a recommendation as optional (see Exhibit 1.9).

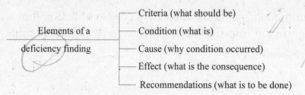

Exhibit 1.9:  Elements of a deficiency audit finding

**Criteria.** Criteria are the standards used to determine whether an operation, function, or program meets or exceeds expectations. Criteria provide a context for understanding the results of the audit. The audit plan, where possible, should state the criteria to be used. In selecting criteria, auditors have a responsibility to use only criteria that are reasonable, attainable, and relevant to the matters being audited. Some examples of different types of criteria are

- Targets or goals set by management or prescribed by law or regulation
- Technically developed standards or norms
- Expert opinions
- Prior years' performance
- Performance of similar entities
- Expected direction of change in outcomes

When the criteria are vague, the auditors should seek interpretation. If interpretation is not available, auditors should strive to agree on the appropriateness of these measures with the interested parties or, if applicable, indicate that they were unable to report on performance because of the lack of definite criteria. It represents "what should be" at the time of the audit.

**Condition.** Condition is a situation that exists. It has been observed and documented during the audit. It represents "what is" at the time of the audit.

**Cause.** Cause has two meanings, which depend on the audit objectives. When the auditors' objective is to explain why the poor (or good) performance observed in the audit happened, the reasons for the observed performance are referred to as "cause." Identifying the cause of problems is necessary before making constructive recommendations for correction. Because problems can result from a number of plausible factors, auditors need to clearly demonstrate and explain with evidence and reasoning the link between the problems and the factor(s) they identified as the cause. When the auditors' objective includes estimating the impact of a program on changes in physical, social, or economic conditions, they seek evidence of the extent to which the program itself is the "cause" of those changes.

**Effect.** Like cause, effect also has two meanings, which depend on the audit objectives. When the auditors' objectives include identifying the actual or potential consequences of a condition that varies (either positively or negatively) from the criteria identified in the audit, "effect" is a measure of those consequences. Auditors often use effect in this sense to demonstrate the need for corrective action in response to identified problems. When the auditors' objectives include estimating the effectiveness of an operation or a program in causing changes in physical, social, or economic conditions, "effect" is a measure of the impact achieved by the operation or program. Here effect is the extent to which positive or negative changes in actual physical, social, or economic conditions can be identified and attributed to program or operations.

**Recommendations.** Recommendations state what an audit organization believes should be done to accomplish beneficial results. They do not direct what must be done but seek to convince others (e.g., the auditee) of what needs to be done.

Recommendations should be action-oriented, convincing, well supported, and effective. When appropriately implemented, they should get the desired beneficial results.

---

The audit report should contain conclusions when called for by the audit objectives. Conclusions are logical inferences about the function or operation based on the auditors' findings. Conclusions should be specified and not left to be inferred by readers. The report should not be written on the basis that a bare recital of facts makes the conclusions inescapable. The strength of the auditors' conclusions depends on the persuasiveness of the evidence supporting the findings.

The audit report should contain recommendations when the potential for significant improvement in operations and performance is substantiated by the reported findings. Recommendations to effect compliance with laws and regulations and improve management controls should also be made when significant instances of noncompliance are noted or significant weaknesses in controls are found. The audit report should also disclose the status of known uncorrected significant findings and recommendations from prior audits that affect the objectives and findings of the current audit.

Reports containing constructive recommendations can encourage improvements in the conduct of audited activities. Recommendations are most constructive when they are directed at resolving the cause of identified problems, are action-oriented and specific, and are addressed to parties that have the authority to act, and are feasible and, to the extent practical, cost-effective.

(iii) **Compliance with standards, regulations, and laws.** The statement of conformity refers to the applicable standards that the auditors should have followed during the audit. The statement need not be qualified when standards that were not applicable were not followed. When applicable standards were not followed, the auditors should modify the statement to disclose in the scope section of their report the required standard that was not followed, why, and the known effect htat not following the standard had on the results of the audit.

The auditors' report should include all instances of noncompliance that auditors determine are significant. All instances of fraud or other illegal acts that could result in the entity, or manager or employee of the entity, being subject to criminal prosecution should also be reported.

In reporting significant instances of noncompliance identified in response to the audit objectives, the auditors should place their findings in proper perspective. To give the reader a basis for judging the prevalence and consequences of noncompliance, the instances of noncompliance should be related to the universe or the number of cases examined and is quantified in terms of dollar value, if appropriate.

(iv) **Management responses.** One of the most effective ways to ensure that a report is fair, complete, and objective is to obtain advance review and comments by responsible auditee (management) and others, as may be appropriate. Including the views of the auditee produces a report that shows not only what was found and what the auditors think about it, but also what the responsible persons think about it and what they plan to do about it.

Auditors should normally request that the responsible auditees' views on significant findings, conclusions, and recommendations adversely affecting the audited entity be submitted in writing. When written comments are not obtained, oral comments should be requested.

Advance comments should be objectively evaluated and recognized, as appropriate, in the report. A promise or plan for corrective action should be noted, but should not be accepted as justification for dropping a significant finding or a related recommendation.

When the comments oppose the report's findings, conclusions, or recommendations, and are not, in the auditors' opinion, valid, the auditors may choose to state their reasons for rejecting them. Conversely, the auditors should modify their report if they find the comments valid.

(v) **Noteworthy accomplishments.** Significant management accomplishments identified during the audit that were within the scope of the audit should be included in the audit report, along with deficiencies. Such information is necessary to fairly present the situation the auditors found and to provide appropriate balance to the report. In addition, inclusion of such accomplishments may lead to improved performance by other department heads or managers that read the report.

(d) **Report Presentation.** The audit report should be complete, accurate, objective, convincing, and as clear and concise as the subject permits (see Exhibit 1.10).

**Characteristics of Report Presentation**

Complete (contains all related information)
Accurate (evidence presented is true)
Objective (balanced in content and tone)
Convincing (findings are persuasive)
Clear (easy to read and understand)
Concise (conveys just the message)

**Exhibit 1.10: Characteristics of report presentation**

(i) **Complete.** Being complete requires that the report contain all information needed to satisfy the audit objectives, promote an adequate and correct understanding of the matters reported, and meet the applicable report content requirements. It also means including appropriate background information.

Giving readers an adequate and correct understanding means providing perspective on the extent and significance of reported findings, such as frequency of occurrence relative to the number of cases or transactions tested and the relationship of the findings to the entity's operations.

Except as necessary to make convincing presentations, detailed supporting data need not be included. In most cases, a single example of a deficiency is not sufficient to support a broad conclusion or a related recommendation. All that it supports is that there was a deviation, an error, or a control weakness.

## HOW TO GET ACTION ON AUDIT RECOMMENDATIONS

Four basic principles to ensure the benefits of the audit work include (1) quality recommendations, (2) commitment, (3) monitoring and follow-up system, and (4) special attention to key recommendations.

1. **Quality Recommendations.** Whether audit results are achieved depends on the quality of the recommendation. A recommendation that is not convincing will not be implemented. A recommendation that does not correct the basic cause of a deficiency may not achieve the intended result.

   Basic to effective audit work are recommendations that, when adequately implemented, accomplish a defined and worthwhile result. They must state a clear, convincing, and workable basis for implementation. Their utility and continued relevance should be reevaluated as follow-up action progress.

2. **Commitment.** When the auditor is committed to the need for action on a recommendation, he or she will do what needs to be done to get it implemented. Without that commitment, a recommendation may not achieve the desired action.

   Auditors and audit organizations must be committed to identifying and bringing about needed change. The auditor's commitment should be personal and professional. The audit organization should be supportive and reinforce the commitment to its staff.

3. **Aggressive Monitoring and Follow-up.** Acceptance of a recommendation does not ensure results; effective implementation does. Continued attention is required until results are achieved.

   The audit organization should have a system that provides the structure and discipline needed to promote action on audit recommendations. It should ensure that recommendations are aggressively pursued until they have been resolved and successfully implemented. Also, auditors should assess whether the audited organizations have a follow-up system internally that adequately meets their basic responsibility for resolving and implementing audit recommendations.

4. **Special Attention to Key Recommendations.** While all recommendations require follow-up, some deal with particularly serious or flagrant matters. They should receive special attention.

   Auditors should ensure that key recommendations are fairly considered when effective use of the first three principles has not done so. They should reassess strategies to get positive action on those recommendations. Outside intervention (e.g., senior management, audit committee) should be considered when it would help to get necessary action on key recommendations of great significance.

*SOURCE: "How to Get Action on Audit Recommendations" (Washington, DC: U.S. General Accounting Office, 1991).*

---

(ii) **Accurate.** Accuracy requires that the evidence presented be true and that findings be correctly portrayed. The need for accuracy is based on the need to assure readers that what it reported is credible and reliable. One inaccuracy in a report can cast doubt on the validity of an entire report and can divert attention from its substance. Also, inaccurate reports can damage the credibility of the issuing audit organization and reduce the effectiveness of reports it issues.

The report should include only information, findings, and conclusions that are supported by competent and relevant evidence in the auditors' working papers. That evidence should demonstrate the correctness and reasonableness of the matters reported. The term "correct portrayal" means describing accurately the audit scope and methodology, and presenting findings and conclusions in a manner consistent with the scope of audit work.

(iii) **Objective.** Objectivity requires that the presentation of the entire report be balanced in content and tone. A report's credibility is significantly enhanced when it presents evidence in an unbiased manner so that readers can be persuaded by the facts.

The audit report should be fair and not be misleading, and should place the audit results in proper perspective. This means presenting the audit results impartially and guarding against the tendency to exaggerate or overemphasize deficient performance. In describing shortcomings in performance, auditors should present the explanation of responsible auditees, including the consideration of any unusual difficulties or circumstances they faced.

The tone of reports should encourage favorable reaction to findings and recommendations. Titles, captions, and the text of reports should be stated constructively. Although findings should be presented clearly and forthrightly, the auditors should keep in mind that one of their objectives is to persuade and that this can best be done by avoiding language that generates defensiveness and opposition. Although criticism of past performance is often necessary, the report should emphasize needed improvements.

(iv) **Convincing.** Being convincing requires that the audit results are responsive to the audit objectives, the findings are presented persuasively, and the conclusions and recommendations follow logically from the facts presented. The information presented should be sufficient to enable the readers of the validity of the findings, the reasonableness of the conclusions, and the desirability of implementing the recommendations. Reports designed in this way can help focus the attention of management on the matters that warrant attention and can help stimulate correction.

(v) **Clear.** Clarity requires that the report be easy to read and understand. Reports should be written in language as clear and simple as the subject permits. Use of straightforward, nontechnical language is essential to simplicity of presentation. If technical terms and unfamiliar abbreviations and acronyms are used, they should be clearly defined. Acronyms should be used sparingly.

Both logical organization of material and accuracy and precision in stating facts and in drawing conclusions are essential to clarity and understanding. Effective use of titles and captions and topic sentences make the report easier to read and understand. Visual aids (i.e., pictures, charts, graphs, and diagrams) should be used when appropriate to clarify and summarize complex material.

(vi) **Concise.** Being concise requires that the report be no longer than necessary to convey the message. Too much detail detracts from a report, may even conceal the real message, and may confuse or discourage readers. Also, needless repetition should be avoided. Although room exists for considerable judgment in determining the content of reports, those that are complete but still concise are likely to receive greater attention.

(e) **Report Distribution.** First, the final report should be distributed to auditees directly interested in the audit work results and those responsible for acting on the findings and recommendations. Higher-level members in the organization may receive only a summary report. Reports may also be distributed to other interested or affected parties, such as external auditors and the board of directors.

Certain information may not be appropriate for disclosure to all report recipients because it is privileged, proprietary, or related to improper or illegal acts. Such information, however, may be disclosed in a separate report. If the conditions being reported involve senior management, report distribution should be to the board of the organization.

(f) **Oral Reports.** In some circumstances, it might be appropriate for auditors to issue oral reports. If they issue an oral report, the auditors should keep a written record of what they communicated and the basis for not issuing a written report. An oral report may be most appropriate when emergency action is needed. Before issuing an oral report, auditors should determine that both of these conditions exist

1. An oral report would effectively meet decision makers' needs for information about the results of the audit.
2. It is unlikely that parties other than those who would receive the oral report would have a significant interest in the results of the audit.

(g) **Summary Reports.** Summary written audit reports are generally intended for high-level management and/or the audit committee. However, a detailed audit report dealing with payroll department with significant control weaknesses should be most useful to the payroll department manager.

---

**KEY CONCEPTS TO REMEMBER: AUDIT REPORTS**

- The first-line supervisor is the lowest organizational level to receive the final report of the operational audit of the production department.
- The scope statement of an audit report should identify the audited activities and describe the nature and extent of the auditing performed.
- Interim reports are issued during an audit to communicate information requiring immediate attention.
- An audit report recommendation should address the "cause" of an audit finding.
- "Significance of deficiencies" is a proper element in an audit results section of a report.
- After an audit report with adverse findings has been communicated to appropriate auditee personnel, proper action is to schedule a follow-up review.
- An oral report to auditee management would be appropriate when an internal auditor observed that assembly-line workers without protective clothing were being exposed to dangerous chemicals.
- An oral report is appropriate when significant problems are discovered during the audit.
- The auditor can use oral reports to give immediate information to management and to exchange thoughts more accurately with a face-to-face discussion.
- The director of internal auditing or designee is responsible for the distribution of an audit report.
- If an audit is done in the sales department, a copy of the audit report should be sent to the sales director and vice president of marketing.
- An audit report should never be viewed as providing an infallible truth about a subject under the "due professional care" standard.
- An auditor found that employees in the plant maintenance department were not signing their time cards. This situation also existed during the last audit. The auditor should include this finding in the current audit report.
- "An evaluation of the impact ("effect") of the findings on the activities reviewed" is not always required in an audit report. The audit report should include a statement that describes the audit objectives and identifies the audited activities, conducted, and presents pertinent statements of facts.
- When there is a disagreement between the auditor and the auditee concerning audit findings and recommendations, the most appropriate method of reporting would be to state both positions and identify the reasons for the disagreement
- An audit report with routine findings in the accounts payable department should be distributed to the accounts payable supervisor, the department manager, division general manager, external auditor, and the corporate controller, not to the board of directors or audit committee

- The reason for requiring auditees to promptly reply and outline the corrective action that has been implemented on reported deficiencies is to effect savings or to institute compliance as early as possible
- A report issued by an internal auditor should contain an expression of opinion when an opinion will improve communications with the reader of the report. An audit opinion is the auditor's professional judgment of the situation, which was reviewed. Due professional care requires that the auditor's opinions be based on sufficient factual evidence that warrants the expression of the opinions. Due care does not require the performance of extensive audit examinations. It requires the conduct of examination and verifications to a reasonable extent, the reasonable assurance that compliance does exist, and the consideration of the possibility of material irregularities.
- Certain information may not be appropriate for disclosure to all report recipients because it is privileged, proprietary, or related to improper or illegal acts. If conditions being reported involve improper acts of a senior manager, the audit report should be distributed to the board of directors.
- Internal audit reports should contain the purpose, scope, and results. The audit results should contain the criteria, condition, effect, and cause of the finding. The cause is the reason for the difference between the expected and actual conditions.
- Internal auditing reports should be distributed to those members of the organization who are able to ensure that audit results are given due consideration. For higher-level members of the organization, that requirement can be satisfied with summary reports.
- The final audit report should be reviewed, approved, and signed by the internal auditing director or designee.
- The chairman of the board of directors would normally not receive an internal auditing report related to a review of the purchasing cycle. Others who would receive such a report include the director of purchasing, the external auditor, and the general auditor.
- When a member of senior management commits illegal acts, such information may be disclosed in a separate audit report and distributed to the company's audit committee of the board of directors.
- The summary audit report for an accounts payable audit should be issued to the audit committee of the board of directors, not to the accounts payable manager, external auditor, and controller.
- Issuing an audit report eight weeks after the audit was concluded is not timely—two or three weeks is timely.
- An audit report containing significant internal control weaknesses in the accounts payable system of a company whose securities are publicly traded should be distributed to the audit committee and the external auditor due to potential for misstated financial statements.
- The findings in the audit report should include pertinent factual statements concerning the control weaknesses that were uncovered during the course of the audit.
- An audit policy should state that final audit reports will not be issued without a management response. An audit report with significant findings is completed except for management response. The best alternative is to issue an interim report regarding the important issues noted.
- Audit findings often emerge by a process of comparing "what should be" with "what is." Findings are based on the attributes of criteria, condition, cause, and effect. The effect of the audit finding is risk or exposure encountered because of the condition.
- An objective audit report is one that is described as factual, unbiased, and free from distortion.
- It is important to develop a distribution list for each audit report, because the list specifies those individuals who have responsibilities with regard to the report.
- The most appropriate use of an oral audit report is to communicate conditions that demand immediate action.

- When an auditor has agreed to keep the marketing department vice president informed of the marketing audit progress on a regular basis, oral or written interim reports should be used for those progress reports.
- To enhance communications with senior management, auditors include a summary report with each written audit report. The summary report should contain highlights of the audit results.
- The primary reason for issuing a written audit report is to achieve precision by pinpointing problems and to achieve permanence. Oral reports do not have these attributes.
- The primary audience for the written report issued by the internal auditing department at the completion of an audit should be those managers inside or outside the audited area who can take corrective action.
- A concise statement of audit findings would be most appropriate for inclusion in the management summary section of a final internal auditing report.
- The final operational audit report regarding supply activities of a division would be circulated to the lowest level of management with sufficient authority to take action on audit recommendations, as it is their responsibility.
- A reason to use interim audit reports is to communicate a change in audit scope.
- The "Purpose" section of the final audit report would include a discussion of audit objectives.
- When illegal acts are being performed by several of the highest-ranking officers of the company, the audit report should be addressed to the audit committee of the board of directors.
- Opinions in the audit reports are the auditor's evaluations of the effects of the findings on the activities reviewed.
- In a review of warranty programs for new products introduced by a company with low and declining profits, an auditor has determined, and management has acknowledged, that the company will be unable to fulfill promised warranty coverage. The auditor should inform the audit committee.
- During an audit of a joint venture, the auditor discovered numerous audit exceptions where some credits would be due to each party. The audit report should contain all material audit exceptions and provide each partner with a net amount due.
- IIA *Standards* require auditors to follow up to see that the corrective action satisfies the audit recommendations.

## 1.7 IIA's *Performance Standards*

### (a) Performing the Engagement

**2300—Performing the Engagement**—Internal auditors should identify, analyze, evaluate, and record sufficient information to achieve the engagement's objectives.

**2310—Identifying Information**—Internal auditors should identify sufficient, reliable, relevant, and useful information to achieve the engagement's objectives.

**2320—Analysis and Evaluation**—Internal auditors should base conclusions and engagement results on appropriate analyses and evaluations.

**2330—Recording Information**—Internal auditors should record relevant information to support the conclusions and engagement results.

**2330.A1**—The chief audit executive should control access to engagement records. The chief audit executive should obtain the approval of senior management and/or legal counsel prior to releasing such records to external parties, as appropriate.

**2330.A2**—The chief audit executive should develop retention requirements for engagement records. These retention requirements should be consistent with the organization's guidelines and any pertinent regulatory or other requirements.

**2330.C1**—The chief audit executive should develop policies governing the custody and retention of engagement records, as well as their release to internal and external parties. These policies should be consistent with the organization's guidelines and any pertinent regulatory or other requirements.

**2340—Engagement Supervision**—Engagements should be properly supervised to ensure objectives are achieved, quality is assured, and staff is developed.

**IIA's Practice Advisory 2300-1: The Internal Auditor's Use of Personal Information in Conducting Audits**

*Nature of This Practice Advisory*

Internal auditors should consider these suggestions when considering the use of personal information in the conduct of an assurance or consulting engagement. This practice advisory is not intended as comprehensive guidance related to the use of personal information, but rather a reminder of the importance of its appropriate use in accordance with the laws and policies of the relevant jurisdiction where the audit is being conducted and where the organization conducts business. *Compliance with Practice Advisories is optional.*

1. Concerns relating to the protection of personal privacy and information are becoming more apparent, focused, and global as advancements in information technology and communications continually introduce new risks and threats to privacy. Privacy controls are legal requirements for doing business in most of the world.
2. "Personal information" generally refers to information that can be associated with a specific individual or that has identifying characteristics that might be combined with other information to do so. It can include any factual or subjective information, recorded or not, in any form or media. Personal information might include, for example

   - Name, address, identification numbers, income, or blood type
   - Evaluations, comments, social status, or disciplinary actions
   - Employee files, credit records, loan records

3. For the most part, laws require organizations to identify the purposes for which personal information is collected at or before the time the information is collected and that organizations do not use or disclose personal information for purposes other than those for which it was collected, except with the consent of the individual or as required by law.
4. It is important that internal auditors understand and comply with all laws regarding the use of personal information in their jurisdiction and those jurisdictions where their organization conducts business.
5. The internal auditor must understand that it may be inappropriate, and in some cases illegal, to access, retrieve, review, manipulate, or use personal information in conducting certain internal audit engagements.
6. The internal auditor should investigate issues before initiating audit effort and seek advice from in-house legal counsel if there are any questions or concerns in this respect.

**IIA's Practice Advisory 2310-1: Identifying Information**

*Nature of This Practice Advisory*

Internal auditors should consider these suggestions when identifying information. This guidance is not intended to represent all the considerations that may be necessary, but simply a recommended set of items that should be addressed. *Compliance with Practice Advisories is optional.*

1. Information should be collected on all matters related to the engagement objectives and scope of work. Internal auditors use analytical auditing procedures when identifying and examining information. Analytical auditing procedures are performed by studying and comparing relationships among both financial and nonfinancial information. The application of analytical auditing procedures for identifying information to be examined is based on the premise that, in the absence of known conditions to the contrary, relationships among information may reasonably be expected to exist and continue. Examples of contrary conditions include unusual or nonrecurring transactions or events; accounting, organizational, operational, environmental, and technological changes; inefficiencies; ineffectiveness; errors; irregularities, or illegal acts.

2.  Information should be sufficient, competent, relevant, and useful to provide a sound basis for engagement observations and recommendations. Sufficient information is factual, adequate, and convincing so that a prudent, informed person would reach the same conclusions as the auditor. Competent information is reliable and the best attainable through the use of appropriate engagement techniques. Relevant information supports engagement observations and recommendations and is consistent with the objectives for the engagement. Useful information helps the organization meet its goals.

## IIA's Practice Advisory 2320-1: Analysis and Evaluation

### *Nature of This Practice Advisory*

Internal auditors should consider these suggestions when using analysis and evaluation to reach conclusions. This guidance is not intended to represent all the considerations that may be necessary during such an evaluation, but simply a recommended set of items that should be addressed. *Compliance with Practice Advisories is optional. This guidance is repeated in Part 1 and Part 2 for proper coverage of the subject matter.*

1.  Analytical audit procedures provide internal auditors with an efficient and effective means of assessing and evaluating information collected in an engagement. The assessment results from comparing information with expectations identified or developed by the internal auditor. Analytical audit procedures are useful in identifying, among other things

    *   Differences that are not expected
    *   The absence of differences when they are expected
    *   Potential errors
    *   Potential irregularities or illegal acts
    *   Other unusual or nonrecurring transactions or events

2.  Analytical audit procedures may include

    *   Comparison of current period information with similar information for prior periods
    *   Comparison of current period information with budgets or forecasts
    *   Study of relationships of financial information with the appropriate nonfinancial information (e.g., recorded payroll expense compared to changes in average number of employees)
    *   Study of relationships among elements of information (e.g., fluctuation in recorded interest expense compared to changes in related debt balances)
    *   Comparison of information with similar information for other organizational units
    *   Comparison of information with similar information for the industry in which the organization operates

3.  Analytical audit procedures may be performed using monetary amounts, physical quantities, ratios, or percentages. Specific analytical audit procedures include, but are not limited to, ratio, trend, and regression analysis; reasonableness tests; period-to-period comparisons; comparisons with budgets, forecasts, and external economic information. Analytical audit procedures assist internal auditors in identifying conditions that may require subsequent engagement procedures. Internal auditors should use analytical audit procedures in planning the engagement in accordance with the guidelines contained in Section 2200 of the *International Standards for the Professional Practice of Internal Auditing (Standards)* (Practice Advisory 2210-1).

4.  Analytical audit procedures should also be used during the engagement to examine and evaluate information to support engagement results. Internal auditors should consider the factors listed next in determining the extent to which analytical audit procedures should be used. After evaluating these factors, internal auditors should consider and use additional audit procedures, as necessary, to achieve the engagement objective.

    *   The significance of the area being examined
    *   The assessment of risk and effectiveness of risk management in the area being examined
    *   The adequacy of the system of internal control
    *   The availability and reliability of financial and nonfinancial information
    *   The precision with which the results of analytical audit procedures can be predicted

- The availability and comparability of information regarding the industry in which the organization operates
- The extent to which other engagement procedures provide support for engagement results

5. When analytical audit procedures identify unexpected results or relationships, internal auditors should examine and evaluate such results or relationships. This examination and evaluation should include making inquiries of management and application of other engagement procedures until internal auditors are satisfied that the results or relationships are sufficiently explained. Unexplained results or relationships from applying analytical audit procedures may be indicative of a significant condition, such as a potential error, irregularity, or illegal act. Results or relationships that are not sufficiently explained should be communicated to the appropriate levels of management. Internal auditors may recommend appropriate courses of action, depending on the circumstances.

## IIA's Practice Advisory 2330-1: Recording Information

### *Nature of This Practice Advisory*

Internal auditors should consider these suggestions when recording information. This guidance is not intended to represent all the considerations that may be necessary, but simply a recommended set of items that should be addressed. *Compliance with Practice Advisories is optional.*

1. Working papers that document the engagement should be prepared by the internal auditor and reviewed by management of the internal audit activity. The working papers should record the information obtained and the analyses made and should support the bases for the observations and recommendations to be reported. Engagement working papers generally

   - Provide the principal support for the engagement communications
   - Aid in the planning, performance, and review of engagements
   - Document whether the engagement objectives were achieved
   - Facilitate third-party reviews
   - Provide a basis for evaluating the internal audit activity's quality program
   - Provide support in circumstances such as insurance claims, fraud cases, and lawsuits
   - Aid in the professional development of the internal audit staff
   - Demonstrate the internal audit activity's compliance with the *International Standards for the Professional Practice of Internal Auditing (Standards)*

2. The organization, design, and content of engagement working papers will depend on the nature of the engagement. Engagement working papers should document these aspects of the engagement process.

   - Planning
   - Risk assessment
   - The examination and evaluation of the adequacy and effectiveness of the system of internal control
   - The engagement procedures performed, the information obtained, and the conclusions reached
   - Review
   - Communication
   - Follow-up

3. Engagement working papers should be complete and include support for engagement conclusions reached. Among other things, engagement working papers may include

   - Planning documents and engagement programs
   - Control questionnaires, flowcharts, checklists, and narratives
   - Notes and memoranda resulting from interviews
   - Organizational data, such as organization charts and job descriptions
   - Copies of important contracts and agreements
   - Information about operating and financial policies
   - Results of control evaluations
   - Letters of confirmation and representation

- Analysis and tests of transactions, processes, and account balances
- Results of analytical auditing procedures
- The engagement's final communications and management's responses
- Engagement correspondence if it documents engagement conclusions reached

4. Engagement working papers may be in the form of paper, tapes, disks, diskettes, films, or other media. If engagement working papers are in the form of media other than paper, consideration should be given to generating backup copies.

5. If internal auditors are reporting on financial information, the engagement working papers should document whether the accounting records agree or reconcile with such financial information.

6. The chief audit executive should establish working paper policies for the various types of engagements performed. Standardized engagement working papers such as questionnaires and audit programs may improve the efficiency of an engagement and facilitate the delegation of engagement work. Some engagement working papers may be categorized as permanent or carry-forward engagement files. These files generally contain information of continuing importance.

7. These are typical engagement working paper preparation techniques.

- Each engagement working paper should identify the engagement and describe the contents or purpose of the working paper.
- Each engagement working paper should be signed (or initialed) and dated by the internal auditor performing the work.
- Each engagement working paper should contain an index or reference number.
- Audit verification symbols (tick marks) should be explained.
- Sources of data should be clearly identified.

## IIA's Practice Advisory 2330.A1-1: Control of Engagement Records

### *Nature of This Practice Advisory*

Internal auditors should consider these suggestions involving control of engagement records. This guidance is not intended to represent all the considerations that may be necessary, but simply a recommended set of items that should be addressed. *Compliance with Practice Advisories is optional.*

1. Engagement working papers are the property of the organization. Engagement working paper files should generally remain under the control of the internal audit activity and should be accessible only to authorized personnel.

2. Management and other members of the organization may request access to engagement working papers. Such access may be necessary to substantiate or explain engagement observations and recommendations or to utilize engagement documentation for other business purposes. These requests for access should be subject to the approval of the chief audit executive (CAE).

3. It is common practice for internal and external auditors to grant access to each other's audit working papers. Access to audit working papers by external auditors should be subject to the approval of the CAE.

4. In some circumstances, parties outside the organization other than external auditors request access to audit working papers and reports. Prior to releasing such documentation, the CAE should obtain the approval of senior management and/or legal counsel, as appropriate.

## IIA's Practice Advisory 2330.A1-2: Legal Considerations in Granting Access to Engagement Records

### *Nature of This Practice Advisory*

Internal auditors should consider these suggestions when considering granting access to engagement records to those outside the internal audit activity. This guidance is not intended to represent all the considerations that may be necessary. *Compliance with Practice Advisories is optional.*

***CAUTION: Internal auditors are encouraged to consult legal counsel in all matters involving legal issues as requirements may vary significantly in different jurisdictions. The guidance contained in this Practice Advisory is based primarily on the legal system in the United States of America.***

1. Internal audit engagement records include reports, supporting documentation, review notes, and correspondence, regardless of storage media. Internal auditors, with the support of management and governing boards to whom they provide audit services, develop the engagement records. En-

gagement records are generally produced under the presumption that their contents are confidential and may contain a mix of both facts and opinions. However, those who are not immediately familiar with the organization or its internal audit process may misunderstand these facts and opinions. Access to engagement records by outside parties has been sought in several different types of proceedings, including criminal prosecutions, civil litigation, tax audits, regulatory reviews, government contract reviews, and reviews by self-regulatory organizations. Virtually all of an organization's records that are not protected by the attorney-client privilege are accessible in criminal proceedings. In noncriminal proceedings, the issue of access is less clear and may vary according to the legal jurisdiction of the organization.

2. Explicit practices in the documents of the internal audit activity may increase the control of access to engagement records. These suggestions are discussed in the paragraphs below.

   - Charter
   - Job descriptions
   - Internal department policies
   - Procedures for handling investigations with legal counsel

3. The internal audit charter should address access to and control of organizational records and information, regardless of media used to store the records.

4. Written job descriptions should be created for the internal audit activity and should include the complex and varied duties auditors perform. Such descriptions may help internal auditors when addressing requests for engagement records. They will also help internal auditors understand the scope of their work and external parties to comprehend the duties of internal auditors.

5. Internal department policies should be developed with regard to the operation of the internal audit activity. These written practices should cover, among other matters, what should be included in engagement records, how long departmental records should be retained, how outside requests for access to department records should be handled, and what special practices should be followed in handling an investigation with legal counsel. These are discussed below.

6. A policy relating to the various types of engagements should specify the content and format of the engagement records and how internal auditors should handle their review notes (i.e., retained as a record of issues raised and subsequently resolved or destroyed so third parties cannot gain access to them). Also, a policy should specify the length of retention for engagement records. These time limits will be determined by the needs of the organization as well as legal requirements. (It is important to check with legal counsel on this issue.)

7. Departmental policies should explain who in the organization is responsible for ensuring the control and security of departmental records, who can be granted access to engagement records, and how requests for access to those records are to be handled. These policies may depend on the practices followed in the industry or legal jurisdiction of the organization. The CAE and others in internal auditing should be alert to changing practices in the industry and changing legal precedents. They should anticipate those who might someday seek access to their work products.

8. The policy granting access to engagement records should also address these issues.

   - Process for resolving access issues
   - Time period for retention of each type of work product
   - Process for educating and reeducating the internal audit staff concerning the risks and issues regarding access to their work products
   - Requirement for periodically surveying the industry to determine who may want access to the work product in the future

9. A policy should provide guidance to the internal auditor in determining when an audit warrants an investigation, that is, when an audit becomes an investigation to be handled with an attorney and what special procedures should be followed in communicating with the legal counsel. The policy should also cover the matter of executing a proper retention letter to have any information given to the attorney be privileged.

10. Internal auditors should also educate the board and management about the risks of access to engagement records. The policies relating to who can be granted access to engagement records, how those requests are to be handled, and what procedures are to be followed when an audit warrants an investigation should be reviewed by the audit committee of the board of directors (or

equivalent governing body). The specific policies will vary depending on the nature of the organization and the access privileges that have been established by law.

11. Careful preparation of engagement records is important when disclosure is required. These steps should be considered.

    • Disclose only the specific documents requested. Engagement records with opinions and recommendations are generally not released. Documents that reveal attorneys' thought processes or strategies will usually be privileged and not subject to forced disclosure.
    • Release copies only, keeping the originals, especially if the documents were prepared in pencil. If the court requests originals, the internal audit activity should keep a copy.
    • Label each document as confidential and place a notation on each document that secondary distribution is not permitted without permission.

## IIA's Practice Advisory 2330.A2-1: Retention of Records

### Nature of This Practice Advisory

Internal auditors should consider these suggestions when developing record retention requirements. This guidance is not intended to represent all the considerations that may be necessary, but simply a recommended set of items that should be addressed. *Compliance with Practice Advisories is optional.*

1. Record retention requirements should be designed to include all engagement records, regardless of the format in which the records are stored.

## IIA's Practice Advisory 2340-1: Engagement Supervision

### Nature of This Practice Advisory

Internal auditors should consider these suggestions when supervising engagements. This guidance is not intended to represent all the considerations that may be necessary, but simply a recommended set of items that should be addressed. *Compliance with Practice Advisories is optional.*

1. The chief audit executive (CAE) is responsible for assuring that appropriate engagement supervision is provided. Supervision is a process that begins with planning and continues throughout the examination, evaluation, communication, and follow-up phases of the engagement. Supervision includes

    • Ensuring that the auditors assigned possess the requisite knowledge, skills, and other competencies to perform the engagement.
    • Providing appropriate instructions during the planning of the engagement and approving the engagement program.
    • Seeing that the approved engagement program is carried out unless changes are both justified and authorized.
    • Determining that engagement working papers adequately support the engagement observations, conclusions, and recommendations.
    • Ensuring that engagement communications are accurate, objective, clear, concise, constructive, and timely.
    • Ensuring that engagement objectives are met.
    • Providing opportunities for developing internal auditors' knowledge, skills, and other competencies.

2. Appropriate evidence of supervision should be documented and retained. The extent of supervision required will depend on the proficiency and experience of internal auditors and the complexity of the engagement. The CAE has overall responsibility for review but may designate appropriately experienced members of the internal audit activity to perform the review. Appropriately experienced internal auditors may be utilized to review the work of other less experienced internal auditors.

3. All internal audit assignments, whether performed by or for the internal audit activity, remain the responsibility of the CAE. The CAE is responsible for all significant professional judgments made in the planning, examination, evaluation, report, and follow-up phases of the engagement. The

CAE should adopt suitable means to ensure that this responsibility is met. Suitable means include policies and procedures designed to

- Minimize the risk that professional judgments may be made by internal auditors or others performing work for the internal audit activity that are inconsistent with the professional judgment of the CAE such that a significant adverse effect on the engagement could result.
- Resolve differences in professional judgment between the CAE and internal audit staff members over significant issues relating to the engagement. Such means may include (a) discussion of pertinent facts; (b) further inquiry and/or research; and (c) documentation and disposition of the differing viewpoints in the engagement working papers. In instances of a difference in professional judgment over an ethical issue, suitable means may include referral of the issue to those individuals in the organization having responsibility over ethical matters.

4. Supervision extends to staff training and development, employee performance evaluation, time and expense control, and similar administrative areas.
5. All engagement working papers should be reviewed to ensure that they properly support the engagement communications and that all necessary audit procedures have been performed. Evidence of supervisory review should consist of the reviewer initialing and dating each working paper after it is reviewed. Other techniques that provide evidence of supervisory review include completing an engagement working paper review checklist; preparing a memorandum specifying the nature, extent, and results of the review, and/or evaluation; and acceptance within electronic working paper software.
6. Reviewers may make a written record (review notes) of questions arising from the review process. When clearing review notes, care should be taken to ensure that the working papers provide adequate evidence that questions raised during the review have been resolved. Acceptable alternatives with respect to disposition of review notes are

- Retain the review notes as a record of the questions raised by the reviewer and the steps taken in their resolution.
- Discard the review notes after the questions raised have been resolved and the appropriate engagement working papers have been amended to provide the additional information requested.

## (b) Communicating Results

**2400—Communicating Results**—Internal auditors should communicate the engagement results.
**2410—Criteria for Communicating**—Communications should include the engagement's objectives and scope as well as applicable conclusions, recommendations, and action plans.

**2410.A1**—Final communication of engagement results should, where appropriate, contain the internal auditor's overall opinion and or conclusions.
**2410.A2**—Internal auditors are encouraged to acknowledge satisfactory performance in engagement communications.
**2410.A3**—When releasing engagement results to parties outside the organization, the communication should include limitations on distribution and use of the results.
**2410.C1**—Communication of the progress and results of consulting engagements will vary in form and content depending on the nature of the engagement and the needs of the client.

**2420—Quality of Communications**—Communications should be accurate, objective, clear, concise, constructive, complete, and timely.
**2421—Errors and Omissions**—If a final communication contains a significant error or omission, the chief audit executive should communicate corrected information to all *parties* who received the original communication.
**2430—Engagement Disclosure of Noncompliance with the *Standards***—When noncompliance with the *Standards* impacts a specific engagement, communication of the results should disclose the

- *Standard(s)* with which full compliance was not achieved
- Reason(s) for noncompliance
- Impact of noncompliance on the engagement

**2440—Disseminating Results**—The chief audit executive should communicate results to the appropriate *parties.*

**2440.A1**—The chief audit executive is responsible for communicating the final results to *parties* who can ensure that the results are given due consideration.

**2440.A2**—If not otherwise mandated by legal, statutory, or regulatory requirements, prior to releasing results to parties outside the organization, the chief audit executive should

- Assess the potential risk to the organization
- Consult with senior management and/or legal counsel as appropriate
- Control dissemination by restricting the use of the results

**2440.C1**—The chief audit executive is responsible for communicating the final results of consulting engagements to clients.

**2440.C2**—During consulting engagements, risk management, control, and governance issues may be identified. Whenever these issues are significant to the organization, they should be communicated to senior management and the board.

### IIA's Practice Advisory 2400-1: Legal Considerations in Communicating Results

*Nature of This Practice Advisory*

Internal auditors should consider these suggestions when communicating the results of audit engagements. This guidance is not intended to represent all the considerations that may be necessary when communicating results. *Compliance with Practice Advisories is optional.*

***CAUTION: Internal auditors are encouraged to consult legal counsel in all matters involving legal issues as requirements may vary significantly in different jurisdictions. The guidance contained in this Practice Advisory is based primarily on the legal system in the United States of America.***

1. Internal auditors should exercise caution when including results and issuing opinions in audit communications and working papers regarding law and regulatory violations and other legal issues. Established policies and procedures regarding the handling of these matters and a close working relationship with other appropriate areas (legal counsel, compliance, etc.) is strongly encouraged.
2. Internal auditors are required to gather evidence, make analytical judgments, report their results, and ensure corrective action is taken. Internal auditors' requirement for documenting engagement records may conflict with legal counsel's desire not to leave discoverable evidence that could harm a defense. For example, even if an internal auditor conducts an investigation properly, the facts disclosed may harm the organization counsel's case. Proper planning and policy making is essential so that a sudden revelation does not place the corporate counsel and internal auditor at odds with one another. These policies should include role definition and methods of communication. The internal auditor and corporate counsel should also foster an ethical and preventive perspective throughout the organization by sensitizing and educating management about the established policies. Internal auditors should consider the following guidelines, especially in connection with engagements that may give rise to disclosing or communicating results to parties outside the organization.
3. There are four elements necessary to protect the attorney-client privilege. There must be

- A communication
- Made between "privileged persons"
- In confidence
- For the purpose of seeking, obtaining, or providing legal assistance for the client

This privilege, which is used primarily to protect communications with attorneys, can also apply to communications with third parties working with the attorney.

4. Some courts have recognized a privilege of critical self-analysis that shields from discovery self-critical materials such as audit work product. In general, the recognition of this privilege is premised on the belief that the confidentiality of the reviews in the instances involved outweighs the valued public interests. As one court explained

> *The self-critical analysis privilege has been recognized as a qualified privilege that protects from discovery certain critical self-appraisals. It allows individuals or businesses to candidly assess their compliance with regulatory and legal requirements without creating evidence that may be*

*used against them by their opponents in future litigation. The rationale for the doctrine is that such critical self-evaluation fosters the compelling public interest in observance of the law.*

5. In general, three requirements must usually be met for the privilege to apply.

   - The information subject to the privilege must result from a self-critical analysis undertaken by the party asserting the privilege.
   - The public must have a strong interest in preserving the free flow of the information contained in the critical analysis.
   - The information must be of the type whose flow would be curtailed if discovery were allowed.

   In some instances, courts also have considered whether the critical analysis preceded or caused the plaintiff's injury, where the analysis comes after the events giving rise to the claim, the justification for the privilege is said to be at its strongest.

6. The courts have generally been more reluctant to recognize self-evaluative privileges when the documents are sought by a government agency rather than a private litigant; presumably this reluctance results from recognition of the government's relatively stronger interest in enforcing the law. The self-evaluative privilege is particularly relevant to functions and activities that have established self-regulatory procedures. Hospitals, security brokers, and public accounting firms are among those that have established such procedures. Most of these procedures are associated with quality assurance procedures that have been added to an operating activity such as financial auditing.

7. Three elements must be satisfied to protect documents from disclosure under the work-product doctrine. Documents must be

   - Some type of work product (i.e., memo, computer program).
   - Prepared in anticipation of litigation.
   - The party preparing must be an agent of the attorney.

8. Documents prepared before the attorney-client relationship comes into existence are not protected by the work-product doctrine. Delivering documents, prepared before the attorney-client relationship is formed, to the attorney will not protect those documents under the work-product doctrine. In addition, the doctrine is qualified. The documents will not be protected under the doctrine if a substantial need for the information exists and the information is not otherwise available without undue hardship. Thus in *R: Grand Jury,* the audit committee of the corporation conducted interviews to determine if any questionable foreign payments were made. Their report was protected from discovery under the work-product doctrine except for those portions that contained the results of the interviews with deceased persons (599 F.2d 1224 [1979]).

## IIA's Practice Advisory 2410-1: Communication Criteria

### *Nature of This Practice Advisory*

Internal auditors should consider these suggestions when communicating the results of engagements. This guidance is not intended to represent all the considerations that may be necessary, but simply a recommended set of items that should be addressed. *Compliance with Practice Advisories is optional.*

1. Although the format and content of the engagement final communications may vary by organization or type of engagement, they should contain, at a minimum, the purpose, scope, and results of the engagement.
2. Engagement final communications may include background information and summaries. Background information may identify the organizational units and activities reviewed and provide relevant explanatory information. It may also include the status of observations, conclusions, and recommendations from prior reports and an indication of whether the report covers a scheduled engagement or is responding to a request. Summaries, if included, should be balanced representations of the engagement communication's content.
3. Purpose statements should describe the engagement objectives and may, where necessary, inform the reader why the engagement was conducted and what it was expected to achieve.
4. Scope statements should identify the audited activities and include, where appropriate, supportive information such as time period reviewed. Related activities not reviewed should be identified if

necessary to delineate the boundaries of the engagement. The nature and extent of engagement work performed also should be described.

5. Results should include observations, conclusions, opinions, recommendations, and action plans.
6. Observations are pertinent statements of fact. Those observations necessary to support or prevent misunderstanding of the internal auditor's conclusions and recommendations should be included in the final engagement communications. Less significant observations or recommendations may be communicated informally.
7. Engagement observations and recommendations emerge by a process of comparing what should be with what is. Whether there is a difference or not, the internal auditor has a foundation on which to build the report. When conditions meet the criteria, acknowledgment in the engagement communications of satisfactory performance may be appropriate. Observations and recommendations should be based on these attributes.

   - *Criteria:* The standards, measures, or expectations used in making an evaluation and/or verification (what should exist).
   - *Condition:* The factual evidence that the internal auditor found in the course of the examination (what does exist).
   - *Cause:* The reason for the difference between the expected and actual conditions (why the difference exists).
   - *Effect:* The risk or exposure the organization and/or others encounter because the condition is not consistent with the criteria (the impact of the difference). In determining the degree of risk or exposure, internal auditors should consider the effect their engagement observations and recommendations may have on the organization's operations and financial statements.
   - *Observations and recommendations* may also include engagement client accomplishments, related issues, and supportive information if not included elsewhere.

8. Conclusions and opinions are the internal auditor's evaluations of the effects of the observations and recommendations on the activities reviewed. They usually put the observations and recommendations in perspective based on their overall implications. Engagement conclusions, if included in the engagement report, should be clearly identified as such. Conclusions may encompass the entire scope of an engagement or specific aspects. They may cover, but are not limited to, whether operating or program objectives and goals conform with those of the organization, whether the organization's objectives and goals are being met, and whether the activity under review is functioning as intended. An opinion may include an overall assessment of controls or area under review or may be limited to specific controls or aspects of the engagement.
9. Engagement communications should include recommendations for potential improvements, acknowledgments of satisfactory performance, and corrective actions. Recommendations are based on the internal auditor's observations and conclusions. They call for action to correct existing conditions or improve operations. Recommendations may suggest approaches to correcting or enhancing performance as a guide for management in achieving desired results. Recommendations may be general or specific. For example, under some circumstances, it may be desirable to recommend a general course of action and specific suggestions for implementation. In other circumstances, it may be appropriate only to suggest further investigation or study.
10. Engagement client accomplishments, in terms of improvements since the last engagement or the establishment of a well-controlled operation, may be included in the engagement final communications. This information may be necessary to fairly present the existing conditions and to provide a proper perspective and appropriate balance to the engagement final communications.
11. The engagement client's views about engagement conclusions, opinions, or recommendations may be included in the engagement communications.
12. As part of the internal auditor's discussions with the engagement client, the internal auditor should try to obtain agreement on the results of the engagement and on a plan of action to improve operations, as needed. If the internal auditor and engagement client disagree about the engagement results, the engagement communications may state both positions and the reasons for the disagreement. The engagement client's written comments may be included as an appendix to the engagement report. Alternatively, the engagement client's views may be presented in the body of the report or in a cover letter.

13. Certain information may not be appropriate for disclosure to all report recipients because it is privileged, proprietary, or related to improper or illegal acts. Such information, however, may be disclosed in a separate report. If the conditions being reported involve senior management, report distribution should be to the board of the organization.

14. Interim reports may be written or oral and may be transmitted formally or informally. Interim reports may be used to communicate information that requires immediate attention, to communicate a change in engagement scope for the activity under review, or to keep management informed of engagement progress when engagements extend over a long period. The use of interim reports does not diminish or eliminate the need for a final report.

15. A signed report should be issued after the engagement is completed. Summary reports highlighting engagement results may be appropriate for levels of management above the engagement client. They may be issued separately from or in conjunction with the final report. The term "signed" means that the authorized internal auditor's name should be manually signed in the report. Alternatively, the signature may appear on a cover letter. The internal auditor authorized to sign the report should be designated by the chief audit executive. If engagement reports are distributed by electronic means, a signed version of the report should be kept on file by the internal audit activity.

## IIA's Practice Advisory 2420-1: Quality of Communications

### Nature of This Practice Advisory

Internal auditors should consider these suggestions when preparing communications. This guidance is not intended to represent all the considerations that may be necessary, but simply a recommended set of items that should be addressed. *Compliance with Practice Advisories is optional.*

1. Accurate communications are free from errors and distortions and are faithful to the underlying facts. The manner in which the data and evidence are gathered, evaluated, and summarized for presentation should be done with care and precision.

2. Objective communications are fair, impartial, and unbiased and are the result of a fair-minded and balanced assessment of all relevant facts and circumstances. Observations, conclusions, and recommendations should be derived and expressed without prejudice, partisanship, personal interests, and the undue influence of others.

3. Clear communications are easily understood and logical. Clarity can be improved by avoiding unnecessary technical language and providing all significant and relevant information.

4. Concise communications are to the point and avoid unnecessary elaboration, superfluous detail, redundancy, and wordiness. They are created by a persistent practice of revising and editing a presentation. The goal is that each thought will be meaningful but succinct.

5. Constructive communications are helpful to the engagement client and the organization and lead to improvements where needed. The contents and tone of the presentation should be useful, positive, and well meaning and contribute to the objectives of the organization.

6. Complete communications are lacking nothing that is essential to the target audience and include all significant and relevant information and observations to support recommendations and conclusions.

7. Timely communications are well timed, opportune, and expedient for careful consideration by those who may act on the recommendations. The timing of the presentation of engagement results should be set without undue delay and with a degree of urgency so as to enable prompt, effective action.

## IIA's Practice Advisory 2440-1: Recipients of Engagement Results

### Nature of This Practice Advisory

Internal auditors should consider these suggestions when reporting results. This guidance is not intended to represent all the considerations that may be necessary, but simply a recommended set of items that should be addressed. *Compliance with this Practice Advisory is optional.*

1. Internal auditors should discuss conclusions and recommendations with appropriate levels of management before issuing final engagement communications.

2. Discussion of conclusions and recommendations is usually accomplished during the course of the engagement and/or at postengagement meetings (exit interviews). Another technique is the review of draft engagement issues, observations, and recommendations by management of the audited activity. These discussions and reviews help ensure that there have been no misunderstandings or misinterpretations of fact by providing the opportunity for the engagement client to clarify specific items and to express views of the observations, conclusions, and recommendations.

3. Although the level of participants in the discussions and reviews may vary by organization and by the nature of the report, they will generally include those individuals who are knowledgeable regarding detailed operations and those who can authorize the implementation of corrective action.

4. The chief audit executive (CAE) or designee should review and approve the final engagement communication before issuance and should decide to whom the report will be distributed. The CAE or a designee should approve and may sign all final reports. If specific circumstances warrant, consideration should be given to having the auditor-in-charge, supervisor, or lead auditor sign the report as a representative of the CAE.

5. Final engagement communication should be distributed to those members of the organization who are able to ensure that engagement results are given due consideration. This means that the report should go to those who are in a position to take corrective action or ensure that corrective action is taken. The final engagement communication should be distributed to management of the activity under review. Higher-level members in the organization may receive only a summary communication. Communications may also be distributed to other interested or affected parties, such as external auditors and the board.

### IIA's Practice Advisory 2440-2: Communications outside the Organization

*Nature of This Practice Advisory*

Internal auditors should consider these guidance if called on to disseminate information outside the organization. Such situations can arise when internal auditors are requested to provide a report or other information to someone outside the organization for which the internal audit services were provided. This guidance is a recommended set of items to be addressed and is not intended to represent all the considerations that may be necessary. *Compliance with Practice Advisories is optional.*

1. Internal auditors should review guidance contained in the engagement agreement or organizational policies and procedures related to reporting information outside the organization. The audit activity charter and the audit committee charter may also contain guidance related to reporting information outside the organization. If such guidance does not exist, the internal auditor should facilitate adoption of appropriate policies by the organization. Examples of information that could be included in the policies are

   - Authorization required to report information outside the organization
   - Process for seeking approval to report information outside the organization
   - Guidelines for permissible and nonpermissible types of information that can be reported
   - Outside persons authorized to receive information and the types of information they can receive
   - Related privacy regulations, regulatory requirements, and legal considerations for reporting information outside the organization
   - Nature of assurances, advice, recommendations, opinions, guidance, and other information that can be included in communications resulting in dissemination of information outside the organization

2. Requests can relate to information that already exists; for example, a previously issued internal audit report. Requests can also be received for information that must be created or determined, resulting in a new internal audit engagement. If the request relates to information or a report that already exists, the internal auditor should review the information to determine whether it is suitable for dissemination outside the organization.

3. In certain situations it may be possible to revise an existing report or information to make it suitable for dissemination outside the organization. In other situations it may be possible to generate a new report based on work previously conducted. Appropriate due professional care should be exercised when revising, customizing, or creating a new report based on work previously conducted.

4. When reporting information outside the organization, these matters should be considered.
    - Need for a written agreement concerning the information to be reported
    - Identification of information providers, sources, report signers, information recipients, and related persons to the report or information disseminated
    - Identification of objectives, scope, and procedures to be performed in generating applicable information
    - Nature of report or other communication, including opinions, inclusion or exclusion of recommendations, disclaimers, limitations, and type of assurance or assertions to be provided
    - Copyright issues and limitations on further distribution or sharing of the information

5. Engagements performed to generate internal audit reports or communications to be reported outside the organization should be conducted in accordance with applicable *International Standards for the Professional Practice of Internal Auditing (Standards)* and include reference to such *Standards* in the report or other communication.

6. If during the conduct of engagements to disseminate information outside the organization the internal auditor discovers information deemed to be reportable to management or the audit committee, the internal auditor should provide suitable communication to appropriate individuals.

**IIA's Practice Advisory 2440-3: Communicating Sensitive Information within and outside the Chain of Command**

*Related Standard*

**2600—Resolution of Management's Acceptance of Risks**—When the chief audit executive believes that senior management has accepted a level of residual risk that may be unacceptable to the organization, the chief audit executive should discuss the matter with senior management. If the decision regarding residual risk is not resolved, the chief audit executive and senior management should report the matter to the board for resolution.

*Related Rules of Conduct of the Code of Ethics—Integrity*

Internal auditors

1.1 Shall perform their work with honesty, diligence, and responsibility.
1.2 Shall observe the law and make disclosures expected by the law and the profession.
1.3 Shall not knowingly be a party to any illegal activity, or engage in acts that are discreditable to the profession of internal auditing or to the organization.
1.4 Shall respect and contribute to the legitimate and ethical objectives of the organization.

*Related Rules of Conduct of the Code of Ethics—Confidentiality*

Internal auditors

3.1 Shall be prudent in the use and protection of information acquired in the course of their duties.
3.2 Shall not use information for personal gain or in any manner that would be contrary to the law or detrimental to the legitimate and ethical objectives of the organization.

*Nature of This Practice Advisory*

An internal auditor may discover information about exposures, threats, uncertainties, fraud, waste and mismanagement, illegal activities, abuse of power, misconduct that endangers public health or safety, or other wrongdoings. In some cases, the new information will have significant consequences, and the supporting evidence will be substantial and credible. The dilemma posed to internal auditors in these types of situations is complex, often involving cultural and business practice differences, legal structures, local and national laws, as well as professional standards, ethical codes, and personal values. The manner in which the internal auditor seeks to resolve the situation may create reprisals and potential liability. Because of those risks and ramifications, the internal auditor should proceed with care to evaluate the evidence and the reasonableness of his or her conclusions and to examine the various potential actions that could be taken to communicate the sensitive information to persons who have the authority to resolve the matter and to stop the improper activity. In some countries, certain actions may be prescribed by local laws or regulations.

This Practice Advisory is offered to stimulate thinking about the many issues and challenges that the internal auditor may face in these situations. While providing information and suggesting factors that may be considered by an internal auditor, the Practice Advisory is not a comprehensive examination of the topic, and it does not offer legal or expert advice for the auditor. Internal auditors should seek legal counsel when the situation is sensitive and has significant consequences. This Practice Advisory was developed with the utmost care and after lengthy deliberation. However, the IIA does not assume responsibility for the use of the information contained in this Practice Advisory or for its applicability to specific situations in practice, and it does not give assurance that the suggested actions will be successful. *Compliance with Practice Advisories is optional.*

1.  Internal auditors often come into the possession of information that is critically sensitive and substantial to the organization and has significant potential consequences. That information may relate to exposures, threats, uncertainties, fraud, waste and mismanagement, illegal activities, abuse of power, misconduct that endangers public health or safety, or other wrongdoings. Those types of matters may adversely impact the organization's reputation, image, competitiveness, success, viability, market values, investments and intangible assets, or earnings. They are likely to increase an organization's risk exposures.

### Communicating Sensitive Information to Those in the Chain of Command

2.  Once the internal auditor has decided that the new information is substantial and credible, the auditor would normally communicate the information, on a timely basis, to those in management who can act on it. In most instances, those communications will resolve the matter from an internal audit perspective, so long as management takes the appropriate action to manage the associated risks. If the communications result in a conclusion that management, by inadequate actions or lack of actions, is exposing the organization to an unacceptable level of risk, the chief audit executive (CAE) should consider other options to achieve a satisfactory resolution.

3.  Among those possible actions, the CAE could discuss concerns about the risk exposure with senior management within his or her normal chain of command. Since the audit or other committee of the governing board would also be expected to be in the CAE's chain of command, the members of the board committee would normally be apprised of the CAE's concerns. If, after those discussions with senior management, the CAE is still unsatisfied and concludes that senior management is exposing the organization to an unacceptable risk and is not taking appropriate action to halt or correct the situation, senior management and the CAE would present the essential information and their differences of opinion to the members or a committee of the governing board.

4.  That simple chain-of-command communication scenario may be accelerated for certain types of sensitive occurrences because of national laws, regulations, or commonly followed practices. For instance, in the case of evidence of fraudulent financial reporting by a company with publicly traded securities in the United States of America, regulations prescribe that the audit committee of the board be immediately informed of the circumstances surrounding the possibility of misleading financial reports, even though senior management and the CAE may be in substantial agreement on what actions need to be taken. Laws and regulations in several countries specify that members or a committee of the governing board should be informed of discoveries of violations of criminal, securities, food, drugs, or pollution laws and other illegal acts, such as bribery or other improper payments to government officials or to agents of suppliers or customers.

### Communicating outside the Chain of Command

5.  In some situations, an internal auditor may face the dilemma of considering whether to communicate the discovered information to persons outside the normal chain of command or even outside the organization. The act of disclosing adverse information to someone in the organization who is outside the individual's normal chain of command, or to a governmental agency or other authority that is wholly outside the organization, is commonly referred to as "whistle-blowing."

6.  In studies about whistle-blowing, it has been reported that most whistle-blowers disclose the sensitive information internally, even if outside the normal chain of command, particularly if they trust the policies and mechanisms of the organization to investigate an allegation of an illegal or other improper activity and to take appropriate action. However, some persons possessing sensitive information may decide to take the information outside the organization, particularly if they fear retribution by their employers or fellow employees, doubt that the issue will be properly investigated,

believe that it will be concealed, or possess evidence about an illegal or improper activity that jeopardizes the health, safety, or well-being of people in the organization or community. The primary motive of most whistle-blowers who are acting on good faith is to halt the illegal, harmful, or improper behavior.

7. An internal auditor who is facing a similar dilemma and needs to consider all possible options must evaluate alternative ways to communicate the risk to some person or group outside his or her normal chain of command. Because of risks and ramifications associated with these approaches, the internal auditor should proceed with care to evaluate the evidence and the reasonableness of his or her conclusions and to examine the merits and disadvantages of each potential action. It may be appropriate for an internal auditor to take this type of action if doing so will result in responsible action by persons in senior management or in governance positions, such as members of the governing board or one of its committees. An internal auditor would likely consider communicating outside the organization's governance structure to be a last option. An internal auditor would reserve this type of action for those rare occasions when he or she is convinced that the risk and its possible consequences are serious and there is high probability that the organization's existing management and governance mechanisms cannot or will not effectively address the risk.

8. Many member countries in the Organization for Economic Cooperation and Development (OECD) have laws or administrative regulations requiring public servants with knowledge of illegal or unethical acts to inform an inspector general, other public official, or ombudsman. Some national laws pertaining to whistle-blowing–type actions protect citizens if they come forward to disclose specific types of improper activities. Among the activities listed in the laws and regulations of those countries are

- Criminal offenses and other failures to comply with legal obligations
- Acts that are considered miscarriages of justice
- Acts that endanger the health, safety, or well-being of individuals
- Acts that damage the environment
- Activities that conceal or cover up any of the above

Other countries offer no guidance or protection. The internal auditor should be aware of the laws and regulations of the various localities in which the organization operates and should take actions that are consistent with those legal requirements. The internal auditor should consider obtaining legal advice if he or she is uncertain of the applicable legal requirements.

9. Many professional associations hold their members to a duty to disclose illegal or unethical activities. The distinguishing mark of a "profession" is its acceptance of broad responsibilities to the public and its protection of the general welfare. In addition to examining the legal requirements, IIA members and all Certified Internal Auditors should follow the requirements outlined in the IIA's Code of Ethics concerning illegal or unethical acts.

### Internal Auditor's Decision

10. An internal auditor has a professional duty and an ethical responsibility to evaluate carefully all the evidence and the reasonableness of his or her conclusions and decide whether further actions may be needed to protect the interests of the organization, its stakeholders, the outside community, or the institutions of society. Also, the auditor will need to consider the duty of confidentiality imposed by the IIA's Code of Ethics to respect the value and ownership of information and avoid disclosing it without appropriate authority, unless there is a legal or professional obligation to do so. In this evaluation process, the auditor should seek the advice of legal counsel and, if appropriate, other experts. Those discussions may be helpful in providing a different perspective on the circumstances as well as offering opinions about the potential impact and consequences of various possible actions. The manner in which the internal auditor seeks to resolve this type of complex and sensitive situation may create reprisals and potential liability.

11. Ultimately, the internal auditor must make a personal decision. The decision to communicate outside the normal chain of command should be based on a well-informed opinion that the wrongdoing is supported by substantial, credible evidence and that a legal or regulatory imperative or a professional or ethical obligation requires further action. The auditor's motive for acting should be the desire to stop the wrongful, harmful, or improper activity.

**MULTIPLE-CHOICE QUESTIONS (1-216)**

## Collect Data and Evaluate Audit Evidence

**1.** An operational audit is being performed to evaluate the productivity of telephone sales representatives relative to last year. The organization sells two similar products, one of which is priced 20% higher than the other. Prices did not change during the two years subject to the audit, and the gross profit percentage is the same for both products. The sales representatives are paid a base salary plus a commission. Which one of the following items represents the **best** evidence that the organization's sales representatives are more productive this year than last year?

    a.    The revenue per representative is higher this year than last year.

    b.    The number of sales calls is higher this year than last year.

    c.    The ratio of the number of new customers to the number of prospects contacted is higher this year than last year.

    d.    Unit sales increased at a higher rate this year than last year.

**2.** Data gathered in support of an audit conclusion can be rated on a continuum of reliability. The most reliable form of evidence would be an

    a.    Internal document obtained from the auditee.

    b.    External document obtained directly from an outside source.

    c.    Internal document subject to rigorous internal review procedures.

    d.    Internal document that has been circulated through an outside party.

**3.** The purchasing manager of a manufacturing company was concerned with the rising prices of some direct materials provided by a supplier. The purchasing manager told the supplier to either maintain the current prices or withdraw as a supplier for the company's direct materials. The supplier devised a plan to circumvent the purchasing manager's intent without actually violating the purchasing manager's mandate. Which one of the following is the probable action taken by the supplier?

    a.    The supplier maintained prices in the short run but later returned to a pattern of increasing prices.

    b.    The supplier decided to stop providing the direct materials to the manufacturing company, since holding the line on prices would have a negative impact.

    c.    The supplier maintained prices but substituted a lower grade of direct materials.

    d.    The supplier worked through the president of the manufacturing company to force the purchasing manager to cancel the mandate.

**Items 4 through 9** are based on the following:

The internal auditing department has just completed an audit of loan processing and commercial loan account balances for a financial institution. Following are a few excerpts from their working papers indicating potential audit findings:

    A.    We took a statistical sample of 100 loan applications and determined that only 85 loans were granted.

    B.    Of the 85 loans granted, we noted that four loans should have been reviewed and approved by the

loan committee but were not. Company policy states that the committee, prior to funding, must approve all loans. The vice president, however, approved each of the four loans. The matter was discussed with the vice president, who indicated it was a competitive loan situation to a new customer and in the best interests of the financial institution to expedite the loan and establish a firm relationship with a growing customer. The loan committee formally approved all of the other loans.

    C.    Of the 81 loans approved by the loan committee, we found 7 where the actual amount loaned exceeded the approved amount.

    D.    We noted 3 instances in which loans were made to related groups of companies without an analysis of the total amount of loans made to the controlling entity. There may be statutory limitations on the amount of loans that can be made to any individual controlling organization.

    E.    Of the 81 loans approved by the loan committee, we found that 14 contained either insufficient documentation or were not received by the committee in a timely fashion in advance of their meeting.

The statistical sample was taken with a 95% confidence level using attribute sampling with a tolerable error limit of 4%. You may assume that the sampling plan was implemented correctly.

**4.** Regarding item A only, which of the following audit conclusions is justified?

    a.    There is a 15% deviation rate in total loans processed.

    b.    There is a problem in processing that should be followed up by the auditor to determine why 15 of the loans may have been lost.

    c.    The loans that have been made comply with company procedures while the loans that were not made do not.

    d.    None of the above.

**5.** Regarding item B, which of the following would be correct?

  I.    The sample deviation rate exceeds 4%.

  II.    The auditor should examine the nature of the loans approved by the vice president to see if there is a pattern.

  III.    The audit finding should be included in the auditor's report with a suggestion that the loan committee review the loans.

    a.    II only.

    b.    II and III only.

    c.    III only.

    d.    I, II, and III.

**6.** Assume that, with regard to item B, the vice president asks the loan committee to review the loans on an after-the-fact basis. Assume further that, upon this subsequent review, the loan committee approves the loans on the after-the-fact basis. Which of the following conclusions would be correct regarding the reporting of the audit finding in the auditor's report?

  I.    The sample deviation rate would drop to 0%.

  II.    The item should still be reported in the audit report because it was not approved in a timely manner in accordance with company policies.

III. The item should be reported as a nondeviation because subsequent action validated the vice president's approach.

    a.   I only.
    b.   II only.
    c.   III only.
    d.   I, II, and III.

**7.** Regarding item C, which of the following actions would be **inappropriate** on the part of the auditor?

    a.   Examine the loans to determine if there is a pattern of the loans to companies. Summarize amounts and include in the audit report.
    b.   Report the amounts to the loan committee and leave it up to them to correct. Take no further follow-up action at this time and do not include the items in the audit report.
    c.   Follow up with the vice president and include the vice president's acknowledgment of the situation in the audit report.
    d.   Determine amount of differences and make an assessment as to whether the dollar differences are material. If the amounts are not material, not in violation of government regulations, and can be rationally explained, omit the finding from the audit report.

**8.** Regarding item D, which of the following would be correct?

   I. The deviation rate is under 4%; therefore, the finding need not be reported to management and the audit committee.
  II. The auditor should review appropriate regulations and possibly get legal counsel opinion on the finding prior to including the finding in the final audit report.
 III. The auditor should report the finding to the vice president who approved the loans and ask for a follow-up report during the audit scheduled next year. No further action need be taken at this time.
 IV. Review a plan by the loan committee to prevent such occurrences in the future and include a summary and analysis of the plan in the final audit report.

    a.   I only.
    b.   III only.
    c.   II and IV.
    d.   II only.

**9.** Regarding item E, which of the following conclusions/ audit actions is appropriate?

    a.   There is no audit finding since the loan committee approved all of the loans.
    b.   Before issuing a final audit report, the auditor should investigate to determine the reasons for the lack of documentation and timely submittal to the loan committee and include that analysis in the report.
    c.   The auditor should include the audit findings in the report only if the auditor is able to determine the cause of the findings.
    d.   Both choice (b) and (c) are correct.

**10.** Which of the following documents would provide the best evidence that a purchase transaction has actually occurred?

    a.   Canceled check issued in payment of the procured goods.
    b.   Ordering department's original requisition for the goods.
    c.   Receiving memorandum documenting the receipt of the goods.
    d.   Supplier's invoice for the procured goods.

**Items 11 through 15** are based on the following:

The internal auditor of a financial institution is performing an audit of the real estate loans portfolio. The auditor wants to test the basic assertions on the existence and valuation of the loans and to determine that the loans do not exceed the bank's policy that loans to any single entity do not exceed 8% of the total loan portfolio. The auditor wants to be 95% confident in the test results. Consequently, the auditor took a judgment sample of 100, which included the 20 largest account balances and selected others. The auditor was aware that some of the account balances were controlled by common holding corporations, but did not feel the need to combine the accounts since they were all listed as separate accounts in the bank's computer files and represented different real estate developments with separate legal entities. The auditor sent confirmations to the 100 entities and received the following results:

- 82 of the 100 returned the positive confirmations and reported no exceptions, 53 did so in response to a first inquiry, 25 responded to a second request, and the remaining four responded after management called the customer and asked them to respond.
- Of the remaining 18 accounts, the auditor found the following:

    A.   For seven accounts, customers returned confirmations showing differences in either the terms of the loan or a disagreement on the amount outstanding. Most were minor, but one customer reported that the account had a zero balance. Upon subsequent investigation, it was found the cash payment had been recorded to a commercial account with the same company. The bank agreed to adjust the loan balances to the amounts confirmed; therefore, the auditor concluded there were no differences on the account balances.
    B.   For five accounts, the auditor traced the loan balance to a signed loan contract, a check disbursing the funds, and examined a payment subsequent to year-end.
    C.   For two accounts, the auditor examined payments made on the account in the subsequent period and verified it was for the correct balance.
    D.   For the remaining four accounts, there were no payments, but the auditor examined the bank's internal file, which showed a signed contract and a loan application signed by the customer.

The auditor was satisfied that all 100 account balances had been accounted for and, with the possible exception of the last four, was confident in the correct balances. The auditor reasoned that there was positive assurance that 96 out of 100 were correct and some assurance that the other 4 were correct because of a valid loan application and contract. The auditor concluded that the 95% confidence level had been achieved. The auditor also noted that none of the 100 account balances exceeded 8% of the real estate loan portfolio.

**11.** Which of the following would constitute an **error** on the part of the auditor in interpreting the data and drawing a conclusion?

I. Concluding that the 95% confidence level had been achieved.

II. Concluding there were no significant differences in the account balances because most of the differences on the returned items were minor and the bank agreed to change them.

III. Concluding that the five account balances described in item B represented valid account balances and were appropriately recorded.

   a.   I and II.
   b.   I only.
   c.   II and III.
   d.   I, II, and III.

**12.** The auditor often has to evaluate the reliability of data to reach audit conclusions. Consider the following four sources of audit evidence gathered by the auditor and rank from the most persuasive to least persuasive:

I. The twenty-five positive responses received in connection with the second request.

II. The four positive responses received in response to a call by management.

III. The five accounts tested by alternative means in item B.

IV. The seven responses in item A that showed account balance differences.

   a.   III, II, IV, I.
   b.   I, II, III, IV.
   c.   II, IV, I, III.
   d.   I, IV, III, II.

**13.** Assuming the responses obtained from the customers are accurate, which of the following auditor conclusions is/are justified by the data?

I. There is no violation of the bank's policy on the total loan balance for a single entity.

II. The portfolio account balance as recorded exists.

III. The portfolio account balance as recorded is properly valued.

   a.   I only.
   b.   I and II.
   c.   II only.
   d.   I, II, and III.

**14.** If the auditor had decided to utilize an integrated test facility instead of using confirmations to test the account balance, the auditor would have gathered evidence to test which of the following assertions?

I. Existence.

II. Valuation.

III. The computer program properly accrues interest income.

IV. Payments entered into the system are properly matched to account balances by the computer program.

   a.   III and IV only.
   b.   I and II only.
   c.   I and III only.
   d.   I, II, III, and IV.

**15.** The auditor decides to expand the audit tests to gather more information about the collectibility and cash realization of the account balances. As a first step, the auditor wants to understand more about the procedures used by the organization to deal with collectibility and the ultimate cash realization of the account balances. Which of the following techniques would be the **least** effective in gathering the information?

   a.   Develop a questionnaire and administer to appropriate personnel.

   b.   Obtain a systems flowchart describing the processing of normal loan transactions.

   c.   Make inquiries of the credit department on criteria used and evidence gathered to support loan write-offs. Document in a narrative.

   d.   Interview the credit department and develop a flowchart of the key decisions made regarding collectibility of account balances.

**16.** The auditor wants to understand the actual flow of data regarding cash processing. The most convincing evidence would be obtained by

   a.   Reviewing the systems flowchart.

   b.   Performing a "walk-through" of the processing and obtaining copies of all documents used.

   c.   Reviewing the programming flowchart for evidence of control procedures placed into the computer programs.

   d.   Interviewing the treasurer.

**17.** The following are potential sources of evidence regarding the effectiveness of the division's total quality management program. Assume that all comparisons are for similar time periods and duration and current items are compared with similar items before the implementation of the total quality management program. The **least persuasive** evidence would be a comparison of

   a.   Employee morale over the two time periods.

   b.   Scrap and rework costs over the two time periods.

   c.   Customer returns over the two time periods.

   d.   Manufacturing and distribution costs per unit over the two time periods.

**18.** The auditor is concerned with the overall valuation of inventory. Rank the following sources of audit evidence from most persuasive to least persuasive in addressing the assertion as to the valuation of inventory.

I. Calculate inventory turnover by individual product.

II. Assess the net realizability of all inventory items with a turnover ratio of 2.0 or less by interviewing the marketing manager as to the marketability of the product.

III. Calculate the net realizable value (NRV) of all inventory products (using audit software to calculate NRV based on the last selling price) and compare NRV with cost.

IV. Take a statistical sample of inventory and examine the latest purchase documents (invoices and receiving slips) to calculate inventory cost.

   a.   I, II, III, IV.
   b.   I, IV, II, III.
   c.   IV, I, III, II.
   d.   II, III, IV, I.

**19.** The auditor wishes to test the assertion that all claims paid by a medical insurance company contain proper authorization and documentation, including but not limited to the validity of the claim from an approved physician and an indi-

cation that the claim complies with the claimant's policy. The most appropriate audit procedure would be to
   a. Select a random statistical sample of all policyholders and examine all claims for the sampled items during the year to determine if they were handled properly.
   b. Select a sample of claims filed and trace to documentary evidence of authorization and other supporting documentation.
   c. Select a sample of claims denied and determine that all claims denied were appropriate. The claims denied file is much smaller, and the auditor can obtain greater coverage with the sample size.
   d. Select a sample of paid claims from the claims (cash) disbursement file and trace to documentary evidence of authorization and other supporting documentation.

**Items 20 through 22** are based on the following:

An auditor of a public company has the following information available to write a memorandum on the progress of developing new audit software for accounts receivable:

> The programmers, who were to start on the sampling software last week, will not be able to start until next week. The programmers want to spend $5,000 for a commercially available software package. The $5,000 for the software is not in the budget. By using the software, the programmers expect to complete their work on schedule. Programming costs will be reduced by $12,500 if the programmers can use the purchased software. The programming of the sampling techniques is expected to be completed one week early. The overall project is expected to be completed on time. Except for the software package and the programming costs, the project is on budget.

**20.** The most important message for the auditor to convey to senior management is
   a. The development of the new audit software is behind schedule.
   b. The programmers want to buy new software that costs $5,000.
   c. The project is expected to be completed on time and within budget.
   d. The programming of the sampling techniques will be completed one week early.

**21.** To emphasize information in a memorandum, it is best to place the information
   a. In the middle of the memorandum and use passive voice.
   b. In the middle of the memorandum and use active voice.
   c. At the beginning of the memorandum and use passive voice.
   d. At the beginning of the memorandum and use active voice.

**22.** Regarding the unbudgeted $5,000 for the purchase of a software package, the auditor should
   a. Disclose it with the $12,500 reduction in programming costs to show the complete picture.
   b. Leave it out of the report because it is irrelevant.
   c. Emphasize it because it is outside the budget.
   d. Leave it out of the report to avoid criticism.

**23.** In evaluating the validity of different types of audit evidence, which one of the following conclusions is **incorrect**?
   a. Recomputation, although highly valid, is limited in usefulness due to its limited scope.
   b. The validity of documentary evidence is independent of the effectiveness of the control system in which it was created.
   c. Internally created documentary evidence is considered less valid than externally created documentary evidence.
   d. The validity of confirmations varies directly with the independence of the party receiving the confirmation.

**24.** Which of the following is generally **not** true when evaluating the persuasiveness of evidence?
The evidence is considered more persuasive if
   a. Verified by internally maintained documents rather than by written inquiry of third party.
   b. Obtained under conditions of strong controls rather than weak controls.
   c. Known by an auditor's personal knowledge rather than from a third-party confirmation.
   d. Obtained from an external source rather than from an internal source.

**Items 25 through 27** are based on the following:

Listed below are four examples of common types of audit evidence. Use the evidence types to answer the three questions.

   I. Inquiry of management.
   II. Observation of auditee's procedures.
   III. Physical examination.
   IV. Documentation prepared externally.

**25.** The **most** persuasive evidence to test the existence of newly acquired computers for the sales department would be
   a. Inquiry of management
   b. Observation of auditee's procedures
   c. Physical examinations
   d. Documentation prepared externally

**26.** The **most** persuasive evidence regarding the asset value of the acquired computers would be
   a. Inquiry of management
   b. Observation of auditee's procedures
   c. Physical examinations
   d. Documentation prepared externally

**27.** Which of the following represents the general order of persuasiveness, from **most** to **least,** for the evidence types listed above?
   a. (III, IV, II, I).
   b. (IV, I, II, III).
   c. (II, IV, I, III).
   d. (IV, III, I, II).

**28.** Which of the following procedures would provide the **most** relevant evidence to determine the adequacy of the allowance for doubtful accounts receivable?
   a. Confirmation of the receivables.
   b. Analysis of the following month's payments on the accounts receivable balances outstanding.
   c. Test the controls over the write-off of accounts receivable to ensure that management approves all write-offs.
   d. Analyze the allowance through an aging of receivables and an analysis of current economic data.

**29.** Which of the following audit procedures would provide the **least** relevant evidence that the company had included all of its outstanding debt on a recent disclosure statement that was made public?

    a. Send bank confirmations to all banks that have done business with the company, asking for information on outstanding notes.

    b. Prepare a schedule of outstanding notes using the company's list of notes payable, and trace them to the general ledger and disclosure statement.

    c. Compare the notes listed in last year's audited disclosure statement with the notes listed this year and reconcile the differences.

    d. Analyze the interest expense and notes payable accounts to determine if interest has been recorded for notes that are not on the disclosure statement.

**30.** Which of the following audit procedures would provide the **least** relevant evidence in determining that payroll payments were made to bona fide employees?

    a. Reconcile time cards in use to employees on the job.

    b. Examine canceled checks for proper endorsement and compare to personnel records.

    c. Test for segregation of the authorization for payment from the hire/fire authorization.

    d. Test the payroll account bank reconciliation by tracing outstanding checks to the payroll register.

**Items 31 and 32** are based on the following:

The two statements below are the result of an audit of an organization's cash controls. Specifically, the statements were part of the evidence gathered to satisfy the audit objective of "determining whether all cash receipts are deposited intact daily."

  I. During an interview, the controller assured an internal auditor that all cash receipts are deposited as soon, as is reasonably possible.

  II. A comparison of a sample of cash receipts lists with the total of daily cash receipts journal entries and daily bank deposit slip amounts revealed that (1) each cash receipts list equaled cash journal entry amounts but not daily bank deposit amounts and (2) each cash receipts list totals equaled bank deposit totals in the long run.

**31.** As evidence that can be used to satisfy the audit objective stated above, Statement I taken alone is

    a. Sufficient but not competent or relevant.

    b. Sufficient, competent, and relevant.

    c. Not sufficient, competent, or relevant.

    d. Relevant but not sufficient or competent.

**32.** As evidence to support a finding that "Cash deposits are not deposited intact daily," Statement II is

    a. Sufficient but not competent or relevant.

    b. Sufficient, competent, and relevant.

    c. Not sufficient, competent, or relevant.

    d. Relevant but not sufficient or competent.

**33.** The most persuasive means of assessing production quality control is to

    a. Evaluate the number and reasons for sales adjustments.

    b. Analyze labor efficiency variances.

    c. Analyze materials efficiency variances.

    d. Evaluate the production/inventory/sales mix.

**34.** Which of the following forms of evidence represents the most competent evidence that a receivable actually exists?

    a. A positive confirmation.

    b. A sales invoice.

    c. A receiving report.

    d. A bill of lading.

**35.** In testing the write-off of a deteriorated piece of equipment, the best evidence of the condition of the equipment would be

    a. The equipment manager's statement regarding condition.

    b. Accounting records showing maintenance and repair costs.

    c. A physical inspection of the actual piece of equipment.

    d. The production department's equipment downtime report.

**36.** Which of the following audit procedures provides the best evidence about the collectibility of notes receivable?

    a. Confirmation of note receivable balances with the debtors.

    b. Examination of notes for appropriate debtors' signatures.

    c. Reconciliation of the detail of notes receivable and the provision for uncollectible amounts to the general ledger control.

    d. Examination of cash receipts records to determine promptness of interest and principal payments.

**37.** Assuming all of the procedures below are satisfactorily performed, to test the valuation of receivables, the auditor should rely most on

    a. Mailing positive confirmation requests.

    b. Completing an aging schedule of accounts receivable.

    c. Comparing the accounts receivable total with totals from prior periods.

    d. Recalculating the value of selected individual accounts receivable.

**38.** What standard of evidence is satisfied by an original signed document?

    a. Sufficiency.

    b. Competence.

    c. Relevance.

    d. Usefulness.

**39.** The director of internal auditing is reviewing the working papers that were produced by an auditor during a fraud investigation. Among the items contained in the working papers is a description of an item of "physical evidence." Which of the following is the most probable source of this item of evidence?

    a. Observing conditions.

    b. Interviewing people.

    c. Examining records.

    d. Computing variances.

**40.** Evidence that is both the best available and reliable is

    a. Sufficient.

    b. Competent.

    c. Relevant.

    d. Documentary.

**41.** When sampling methods are used, the concept of sufficiency of evidence means that the samples selected provide

    a.  Reasonable assurance that they are representative of the sampled population.

    b.  The best evidence that is reasonably obtainable.

    c.  Reasonable assurance that the evidence has a logical relationship to the audit objective.

    d.  Absolute assurance that a sample is representative of the population.

**42.** An internal auditor takes a photograph of the auditee's workplace. The photograph is a form of what kind of evidence?

    a.  Physical.

    b.  Testimonial.

    c.  Documentary.

    d.  Analytical.

**43.** Which of the following is an example of "documentary'" evidence?

    a.  A photograph of an auditee's workplace.

    b.  A letter from a former employee alleges a fraud.

    c.  A page of the general ledger containing irregularities placed there by the perpetrator of a fraud.

    d.  A page of the auditor's working papers containing the computations that demonstrate the existence of an error or irregularity.

**44.** Which of the following techniques would best result in sufficient evidence with regard to an audit of the quantity of fixed assets on hand in a particular department?

    a.  Physical observation.

    b.  Analytical review of purchase requests and subsequent invoices.

    c.  Interviews with department management.

    d.  Examination of the account balances contained in general and subsidiary ledgers.

**45.** Which technique is most appropriate for testing the quality of the preaudit of payment vouchers described in an internal control questionnaire (ICQ)?

    a.  Analysis.

    b.  Evaluation.

    c.  Verification.

    d.  Observation.

**46.** Which of the following is an essential factor in evaluating the sufficiency of evidence? The evidence must

    a.  Be well documented and cross-referenced in the working papers.

    b.  Be based on references that are considered reliable.

    c.  Bear a direct relationship to the finding and include all of the elements of a finding.

    d.  Be convincing enough for a prudent person to reach the same decision.

**47.** Accounts payable schedule verification may include the use of analytical evidence. Which of the following is most appropriately described as analytical evidence?

    a.  Comparing the items on the schedule with the accounts payable ledger or unpaid voucher file.

    b.  Comparing the balance on the schedule with the balances of prior years.

    c.  Comparing confirmations received from selected creditors with the accounts payable ledger.

    d.  Examining vendors' invoices in support of selected items on the schedule.

**48.** Of the following, audit evidence is **best** described as:

    a.  The records of preliminary planning and surveys, the audit program, and the results of fieldwork.

    b.  The information documented by the auditors and obtained through observing conditions, interviewing people, and examining records.

    c.  An intermediate fact, or group of facts, from which the auditor can infer the fairness of an assertion being audited.

    d.  Detailed documentation for systems that do not achieve desired objectives, actions that were taken improperly, and actions that should have been taken but were not.

**49.** Which of the following documents would provide the **most** persuasive evidence concerning the existence and valuation of a receivable?

    a.  A credit approval document supported by the customer's audited financial statements.

    b.  A copy of a sales invoice to the customer in the auditee's records.

    c.  A positive confirmation received directly from the customer.

    d.  A customer's purchase order in the auditee's records related to the credit sale.

**50.** Which of the substantive fieldwork procedures presented below provides the **best** evidence about the completeness of recorded revenues?

    a.  Reconciling the sales journal to the general ledger control account.

    b.  Vouching charges made to the accounts receivable subsidiary ledger to supporting shipping records.

    c.  Vouching shipping records to the customer order file.

    d.  Reconciling shipping records to recorded sales.

**51.** Which of the following types of tests would be the **most** persuasive if an internal auditor wanted assurance of the existence of inventory stored in a warehouse?

    a.  Examination of the shipping documents supporting recorded transfers to and from the warehouse.

    b.  Obtaining written confirmation from management.

    c.  Physically observing the inventory in the warehouse.

    d.  Examination of warehouse receipts contained in the auditee's records.

**52.** Documents provide evidence that is of differing degrees of persuasiveness. If the audit objective is to gain evidence that payment has actually been made for a specific invoice from a vendor, which of the following documents would generally provide the **most** persuasive evidence?

    a.  An entry in the auditee's cash disbursements journal supported by a voucher package containing the vendor's invoice.

    b.  A canceled check, made out to the vendor and referenced to the invoice, included in a cutoff bank statement that the auditor received directly from the bank.

    c.  An accounts payable subsidiary ledger that shows payment of the invoice.

    d.  A vendor's original invoice stamped "PAID" and referenced to a check number.

**53.** One objective of an internal audit of the receiving function is to determine whether receiving clerks independently count incoming supplies before completing the "quantity received" section of the receiving report. Which of the following is the **most** persuasive evidence that the counts are made?

    a.   The receiving section supervisor's assurance based on personal observation that the counts are made.

    b.   A receiving clerk's initials on all receiving reports attesting to the fact that the count was made.

    c.   Assurance from the warehouse supervisor that the accuracy of the perpetual inventory is the result of the reliability of the entries in the quantity received section.

    d.   Periodic observations by the internal auditor over the course of the audit.

**54.**  An internal auditor is auditing the corporate advertising function. The company has engaged a medium-size local advertising agency to place advertising in magazine publications. As part of the review of the audit working papers, the internal auditing supervisor is evaluating the evidence collected.

The auditor reviewed the language in the advertising for its legality and compliance with fair trade regulations by interviewing the firm's advertising manager, the products marketing director (who may not have been objective), and five of the firm's largest customers (who may not have been knowledgeable). The supervisor can justifiably conclude that the evidence is

    a.   Competent.

    b.   Irrelevant.

    c.   Conclusive.

    d.   Insufficient.

**55.**  During an audit of cash controls, an auditor compared a sample of cash receipts lists with (1) the total of daily cash receipts journal entries and (2) daily bank deposit slip amounts. The comparison revealed that (1) each cash receipts list equaled cash journal entry totals but not daily bank deposit amounts and (2) totals for cash receipts lists equaled bank deposit totals in the long run.

To support a finding that "Cash receipts are not deposited intact daily," the above evidence is

    a.   Sufficient, but not competent or relevant.

    b.   Sufficient, competent, and relevant.

    c.   Not sufficient, competent, or relevant.

    d.   Relevant, but not sufficient or competent.

**56.**  Which of the following procedures would provide the **best** evidence of the effectiveness of a credit-granting function?

    a.   Observe the process.

    b.   Review the trend in receivables write-offs.

    c.   Ask the credit manager about the effectiveness of the function.

    d.   Check for evidence of credit approval on a sample of customer orders.

**57.**  An auditor performs an analytical review of division operations and notes the following:

- Current ratio is increasing
- Quick ratio is decreasing
- Number of days sales in inventory is increasing
- Sales are constant
- Current liabilities are constant

From this, the auditor can conclude that

    I.   The company has produced fewer products this year than last year.

   II.   Cash or accounts receivable have decreased.

  III.   The gross margin has decreased.

    a.   I only.

    b.   II only.

    c.   I and III.

    d.   II and III.

**Items 58 and 59** are based on the following:

During a review of a division's operations, an auditor notes that

- Sales revenue has remained the same.
- Customer base is unchanged.
- Inventory has increased significantly.
- Gross margin has increased significantly.

**58.**  Which of the following statements, if true, could explain the change noted in gross margin?

    I.   The company has developed a new manufacturing process that is much more efficient.

   II.   Sales price per unit has increased.

  III.   Inventory is overstated.

    a.   I only.

    b.   I and II only.

    c.   III only.

    d.   I, II, and III.

**59.**  Assume that divisional management stated that the gross margin increase is due to increased efficiency in manufacturing operations. The auditor wishes to investigate this assertion. Which of the following audit procedures would be most relevant to the assertion?

    a.   Obtain a physical count of inventory.

    b.   For a sample of products, compare costs per unit this year to those of last year, test cost buildups, and analyze standard cost variances.

    c.   Take a physical inventory of equipment to determine if there were significant changes.

    d.   Take a sample of finished goods inventory and trace raw materials cost back to purchase prices in order to determine the accuracy of the recorded raw materials price.

**60.**  Audit findings must be based on sufficient, competent, relevant, and useful evidence. Which of the following statements is true about evidence?

    a.   Physical observation provides the most reliable evidence of the existence of accounts receivable.

    b.   Purchase orders are relevant evidence that goods paid for have been received.

    c.   An appropriate conclusion about a population based on a sample requires that the sample be representative of the population.

    d.   A copy of an original document is as reliable as the original document.

**61.**  An auditor must weigh the cost of an audit procedure against the persuasiveness of the evidence to be gathered. Observation is one audit procedure that involves cost-benefit trade-offs. Which of the following statements regarding observation as an audit technique is(are) correct?

I. Observation is limited because individuals may react differently when being observed.

II. When testing financial statement balances, observation is more persuasive for the completeness assertion than it is for the existence assertion.

III. Observation is effective in providing evidence on how the company's processes differ from that specified by written policies.

    a.   I only.
    b.   II only.
    c.   I and III only.
    d.   I, II, and III.

**62.** Which of the following is the **best** source for an audit team to use to identify common risks faced by a company?
    a.   Checklists or reminder lists.
    b.   Flowcharts.
    c.   Questionnaires.
    d.   Research reported in professional journals and textbooks.

**63.** The audit effort most likely to yield relevant evidence in determining the adequacy of an organization's "disaster recovery plan" should focus on
    a.   The completeness of the plan as to facilities, operations, communications, security, and data processing.
    b.   The sufficiency of the list of replacement equipment needed in event of a disaster.
    c.   Whether the plan is in the planning or developmental stage.
    d.   The role of the internal auditing department in developing and testing the plan.

**64.** Which of the substantive fieldwork procedures presented below provides the **best** evidence about the completeness of recorded revenues?
    a.   Reconciling the sales journal to the general ledger control account.
    b.   Vouching charges made to the accounts receivable subsidiary ledger to supporting shipping records.
    c.   Vouching shipping records to the customer order file.
    d.   Reconciling shipping records to recorded sales.

**65.** The IIA *Standards* define competent evidence as
    a.   Factual, adequate, and convincing.
    b.   Reliable and the best attainable through the use of appropriate audit techniques.
    c.   Consistent with the audit objectives, findings and recommendations.
    d.   Information that helps the organization meets its goals.

**66.** You are an internal auditor whose company is in the process of acquiring another company. You have been requested to verify that cash for the company being acquired is properly stated. The audit technique that will yield the most persuasive evidence is
    a.   Examination of the company's escheatment account.
    b.   Interview with the company's treasurer and cash manager.
    c.   Preparation and review of standard bank confirmation inquiries.
    d.   Analytical computations comparing current cash in the bank with previous accounting periods.

**67.** An auditor would primarily rely on which type of evidential matter when evaluating the collectibility of accounts receivable?
    a.   Positive confirmation.
    b.   Negative confirmation.
    c.   Aged accounts receivable listing.
    d.   Management's representations.

**68.** What evidence is appropriate to determine that recorded purchase transactions were valid and at the best price?
    a.   Purchase requisitions, journal voucher entries, and bid quotes.
    b.   Purchase requisitions, purchase orders, and bid quotes.
    c.   Receiving reports, purchase orders, and purchase requisitions.
    d.   Purchase orders, receiving reports, and bid quotes.

**69.** Audit information is generally considered relevant when it is
    a.   Derived through valid statistical sampling.
    b.   Objective and unbiased.
    c.   Factual, adequate, and convincing.
    d.   Consistent with the audit objectives.

**Items 70 through 72** are based on the following:

An internal auditor is auditing the corporate advertising function. The company has engaged a medium-size local advertising agency to place advertising in magazine publications. As part of the review of the audit working papers, the internal auditing supervisor is evaluating the evidence collected.

**70.** The auditor examined the company's advertising agency's internal controls and, based on the preliminary survey, has determined that there are no problems. The supervisor believes there should be substantive testing and has decided that the evidence gathered to date is **not**
    a.   Competent.
    b.   Relevant.
    c.   Sufficient.
    d.   Useful.

**71.** The auditor examined a statistical sample of the agency's billings to clients for newspaper advertising space. The agency specializes in newspaper advertising that is predominantly typeset plates or mats; however, the agency's work for the company is essentially artwork for magazine advertising. The supervisor, concerned with the relationship of the sample to the work performed for the company, has decided that the evidence is **not**
    a.   Competent.
    b.   Relevant.
    c.   Sufficient.
    d.   Reliable.

**72.** The auditor reviewed the language in the advertising for its legality and compliance with fair trade regulations by interviewing the firm's advertising manager, the products marketing director (who may not have been objective), and five of the firm's largest customers (who may not have been knowledgeable). The supervisor has decided that the evidence is
    a.   Competent.
    b.   Relevant.
    c.   Conclusive.
    d.   Insufficient.

**73.** One criticism of the banking industry is that loan committees were not properly carrying out their function of examining proposed loans, determining that proper collateral exists, and assessing the associated risk before approving the loan. In gathering evidence to determine if the loan committee is operating effectively, the auditor should

    a. Interview loan officers to see if their individual loan recommendations were followed.

    b. Reconcile the total amount of loans made plus those rejected with the total amount of loans submitted to the committee for approval.

    c. Examine individual loans for signatures of the committee members and determine the amount of loans made during each meeting and an approximation of time spent in approving the loans.

    d. All of the above.

**74.** Which of the following procedures would provide the **most** relevant evidence to determine the adequacy of the allowance for doubtful accounts receivable?

    a. Confirm the receivables.

    b. Analyze the following month's payments on the accounts receivable balances outstanding.

    c. Test the controls over the write-off of accounts receivable to ensure that management approves all write-offs.

    d. Analyze the allowance through an aging of receivables and an analysis of current economic data.

**75.** Observation is considered a reliable audit procedure, but one that is limited in usefulness. However, it is used in a number of different audit situations. Which of the following statements is true regarding observation as an audit technique?

    a. It is the most effective audit methodology to utilize in filling out internal control questionnaires.

    b. It is the most persuasive methodology to learn how transactions are really processed during the period under audit.

    c. It is rarely sufficient to satisfy any audit assertion other than existence.

    d. It is the most persuasive audit technique for determining if fraud has occurred.

**76.** An internal auditor at a savings and loan concludes that a secured real estate loan is collectible. Which of the following audit procedures provides the **most** persuasive evidence about the loan's collectibility?

    a. Confirming the loan balance with the borrower.

    b. Reviewing the loan file for proper authorization by the credit committee.

    c. Examining documentation of a recent, independent appraisal of the real estate.

    d. Examining the loan application for appropriate borrowers' signatures.

**77.** The internal auditor for a construction contractor finds material costs increasing as a percentage of billings and suspects that materials billed to the company are being delivered to another contractor. What type of evidence would **best** enable the auditor to determine whether erroneous billings occurred?

    a. Documentary.

    b. Physical examination.

    c. Confirmation.

    d. Analytical review.

**78.** One of the audit objectives of an audit of the organization's accounts receivable function is to determine if prescribed standard procedures are followed when credit is granted. Which of the following audit procedures would produce the **most** competent evidence?

    a. Ask management of the credit department if specific policies and procedures are followed when granting credit.

    b. Select a statistical sample of credit applications and test them for conformance with prescribed procedures.

    c. Analytically review the relationships between trends in credit sales and bad debts.

    d. Review procedures for periodically aging accounts receivable.

**79.** Which of the following tests can help the auditor evaluate the adequacy of the company's allowance for doubtful accounts?

    a. Reconciling the accounts receivable subsidiary ledgers with the control account.

    b. Preparing an aging analysis.

    c. Reviewing authorization of credit terms.

    d. Tracing a sample of credit memos to the accounts receivable subsidiary ledger.

**80.** To identify shortages of specific items in an inventory of expensive goods held for retail sale, the most appropriate audit work step is to

    a. Apply the retail method of inventory valuation.

    b. Compare physical inventory counts to perpetual records.

    c. Develop inventory estimates based on the gross profit percentage method.

    d. Analyze current and previous inventory turnover rates.

**Items 81 and 82** are based on the following:

An internal auditor is examining the purchasing function. Competitive bids are required on purchases exceeding $2,000 unless the executive vice president signs a waiver from the bid requirement. During the most recent year the firm issued 3,000 purchase orders, of which 180 were for amounts exceeding $2,000.

**81.** Which of the following audit procedures will result in the **most competent** evidence of compliance with the bid procedure?

    a. Select a representative sample of requests for bids and trace them back to the related purchase orders, ascertaining that the amount of the purchase exceeds $2,000.

    b. Select a representative sample of purchase orders exceeding $2,000 and examine underlying documentation, ascertaining that requests for bids or properly signed waiver forms are on file.

    c. Interview the head of the purchasing department and inquire as to whether there have been any departures from the bid procedure.

    d. Interview the executive vice president and inquire as to the frequency and circumstances of occasions where waivers from the bid requirement have been signed.

**82.** Before purchase invoices are approved for payment, an accounting clerk is supposed to compare invoice prices with purchase order prices and indicate their agreement by signing in a designated space on the payment voucher form. Which of the following audit procedures would result in **sufficient** evidence that this requirement is being followed?

- a. Select the 20 largest payment vouchers and examines them for the signature of the accounting clerk.
- b. Select the 20 largest payment vouchers, examine them for signature, and compare the prices on the invoices and related purchase orders.
- c. Select a representative sample of payment vouchers and examine them for the signature of the accounting clerk.
- d. Select a representative sample of vouchers, examine them for the signature of the accounting clerk, and compare the prices on the invoices and related purchase orders.

**Items 83 through 85** are based on the following:

A company provides valves, pipe and specialty items to chemical plants in a large metropolitan area. Stock reorder decisions are based on quarterly sales reports and must be approved by the vice president of sales. The company has a highly motivated and well-paid sales force.

Often a good salesperson can earn more in commissions than from base salary. Salespeople use portable computers to enter orders while in the field. As sales orders are entered, all out-of-stock conditions are noted. Restocking orders are created whenever inventory levels fall below reorder points. The products handled by the company are subject to rapid obsolescence and have little scrap value once obsolescence is reached. The annual inventory is performed by an inventory service using professional counters. All count information is given to the company for entry and balancing. Over the past several years, the company has experienced unusually large write-offs as a result of its annual physical inventory.

**83.** An auditor's objective is to determine the cause of inventory shortages shown by the physical inventories. The auditor addresses this objective by reviewing the count sheets, inventory printouts, and memos from the last inventory. The source of information and the sufficiency of this evidence are

- a. Internal and not sufficient.
- b. External and sufficient.
- c. Both external and internal and sufficient.
- d. Both external and internal and not sufficient.

**84.** In order to identify the amount of obsolete inventory that may exist in an organization, the internal auditor probably would collect evidence using all of the following procedures except:

- a. Confirmation.
- b. Scanning.
- c. Recomputation.
- d. Analytical review.

**85.** During interviews with the inventory management personnel, the auditor learned that salespeople often order inventory for stock without receiving the approval of the vice president of sales. Also, detail testing showed that there are no written approvals on purchase orders for replacement parts. The detail testing is a good example of

- a. Indirect evidence.
- b. Circumstantial evidence.
- c. Corroborative evidence.
- d. Subjective evidence.

**86.** In an audit of the procurement system, which of the following procedures would an auditor perform to determine whether competitive bidding procedures were adequate?

- I. Bids are solicited based on properly approved requests.
- II. A sufficient number of vendors were selected to ensure competition.
- III. Incoming bids are first returned to the buyer for control purposes.

- a. I and III.
- b. II and III.
- c. I, II, and III.
- d. I and II.

**87.** Which of the following audit procedures would be **most** effective in determining whether vendor invoices are being processed on a timely basis while maximizing the company's use of cash?

- a. Determine the length of processing time between the receipt of the vendor's invoice to the payment date for the related disbursement.
- b. Interview the accounts payable manager to determine the procedures and standards for processing vendor invoices.
- c. Compare the vendor's invoice due date with the payment date as indicated on the canceled check.
- d. Compare the date stamped on the invoice for receipt with the corresponding payment date for the disbursement.

**88.** Behavioral scientists have identified human tendencies that can erode the quality of decision making. Which of the following **best** describes a behavioral decision error referred to as "framing error"?

- a. Evaluating positive information favorably and negative information unfavorably.
- b. Getting locked into losing courses of action because of personal commitment.
- c. Evaluating the probabilities of outcomes as point estimates instead of ranges.
- d. Becoming overconfident because of past successes.

**89.** When an internal auditor encounters active opposition, as when auditees remain unconvinced of the auditor's reasonably presented point of view, the **most** effective way to gain consensus is to

- a. Refer the matter to the auditees' superior.
- b. Wait to reason with auditees late in the day when they may be more reasonable.
- c. Rely on logic and explain the auditor's point again.
- d. Find a point of agreement by letting auditees explain their position again.

**Items 90 and 91** are based on the following:

An audit of environmental controls, including regulatory compliance, has been concluded. Possible corrective actions are being discussed at a closing conference.

**90.** The environmental manager states that funds are not available in this year's budget to make necessary changes and repairs to the hazardous-waste storage yard. The deficiencies prevent management from complying with controls established to manage waste safely and to comply with regulations. The auditor should

- a. Insist that the changes and repairs be made, regardless of any apparent budget constraints.

b. Agree that corrective action may be postponed until funds can be provided in the following year's budget.

c. Accept temporary, but clearly incomplete, corrective action in order to improve the situation.

d. Involve senior management in the decision.

**91.** The environmental manager proposes a minimal approach that will safely manage waste as well as keep the company in compliance with applicable regulations. The auditor prefers an approach that would correct the deficiencies but also enhance operations, believing that the company has an obligation to go beyond compliance. How should the auditor resolve this difference?

a. Accept the proposed corrective action.

b. Elevate this issue to senior management, citing benchmarking studies in support of the auditor's position.

c. Report management's inadequate action to the audit committee.

d. Accept the corrective action as satisfactory in the short term, but insist that the environmental manager agree to adopt the auditor's approach as soon as it is feasible.

**92.** During fieldwork to test controls over access into restricted work areas, two employees approached the auditor and stated that they experience headaches and other symptoms as a result of some of the chemicals used in certain processes. The auditor should

a. Take detailed statements from each of the employees and pursue the allegations.

b. Tell the employees that the internal audit department is not interested in such information.

c. Advise the employees that such information be better communicated through management channels, and inform audit management.

d. Refer the employees to the company's legal department.

**93.** Because of the nature of work at a company's plants, radiation safety is important. An audit to test the system of controls over the purchase, distribution, and use of radioactive material is being conducted. The process is well documented, and employees in the safety department are very familiar with the department's procedures. Since the purchasing and facilities departments are involved in the process, the auditor is considering reviewing their radioactive material handling procedures as well. The auditor should

a. Have confidence in the rigorous and detailed safety department procedures, since that department has the main responsibility for radiation safety, and do not use audit time to review other departments.

b. Adjust the audit schedule and budget, if needed, and interview the appropriate individuals in purchasing and facilities to ascertain whether additional controls exist that complement those identified within the safety department.

c. Test the controls identified within the safety department; if results are unfavorable, consider whether to involve the other departments.

d. Defer questions regarding purchasing, facilities, and other departments until audit projects can be scheduled for those departments.

**94.** During an interview with a data input clerk to discuss a computerized system used to track employee training requirements and compliance, an auditor identifies a potentially significant weakness in the system. The auditor should

a. Not mention the weakness, directly or indirectly, to avoid making the clerk uncomfortable.

b. Ask indirect questions that will help get more factual information relating to the potential weakness.

c. Ask the clerk about the weakness and determine immediately if the finding should be reported.

d. Conduct a second interview after determining whether the weakness actually exists.

**95.** As part of an audit of safety management programs, an auditor interviews the individual responsible for writing, issuing, and maintaining safety procedures. While the auditor's primary interest is to identify the controls that ensure that procedures are kept current, the individual has a tremendous amount of information and seems intent on telling the auditor most of it. What might the auditor do to guard against missing what is important?

a. Write down everything the individual says. If the auditor gets behind, ask for a pause and catch up. After the interview, the auditor can sift through the notes and be confident of finding the key information.

b. Tape record the interview and later extract the relevant information.

c. Do not sort through extraneous information. Revisit the topic with the individual's supervisor and get any needed information at that time.

d. During the conversation, make an effort to anticipate the approach of a point of critical interest.

**96.** In evaluating the validity of different types of audit evidence, which of the following conclusions is **incorrect**?

a. Recomputation, although highly valid, is limited in usefulness due to its limited scope.

b. The validity of documentary evidence is independent of the effectiveness of the control system in which it was created.

c. Internally created documentary evidence is considered less valid than externally created documentary evidence.

d. The validity of confirmations varies directly with the independence of the party receiving the confirmation.

**97.** An internal auditor is discussing an audit problem with an auditee. While listening to the auditee, the internal auditor should

a. Prepare a response to the auditee.

b. Take mental notes on the speaker's nonverbal communication, as it is more important than what is being said.

c. Make sure all details, as well as the main ideas of the auditee, are remembered.

d. Integrate the incoming information from the auditee with information that is already known.

**98.** An internal auditor would trace copies of sales invoices to shipping documents in order to determine that

a. Customer shipments were billed.

b. Sales that are billed were also shipped.

c. Shipments to customers were also recorded as receivables.

d. The subsidiary accounts receivable ledger was updated.

**99.** To test whether debits to accounts receivable represent valid transactions, the auditor should trace entries from the

a. Sales journal to the accounts receivable ledger.

b. Accounts receivable ledger to the cash receipts journal.

c. Accounts receivable ledger to sales documentation.

d. Cash receipts documentation to the accounts receivable ledger.

**100.** An auditor traces individual time tickets to the payroll cost distribution and also traces totals from the payroll cost distribution to the various work-in-process accounts. If no exceptions are found, this constitutes evidence that

a. The work-in-process accounts have not been "padded" by the inclusion of unsupported payroll costs.

b. Individual time tickets have been properly authorized.

c. Payroll costs have been accurately distributed to work in process accounts.

d. Employees have been paid only for time actually worked.

**101.** Shipping documents should be traced to and compared with sales records or invoices to

a. Determine whether payments are properly applied to customer accounts.

b. Ensure that shipments are billed to customers.

c. Determine whether unit prices billed are in accordance with sales contracts.

d. Ascertain whether all sales are supported by shipping documents.

**102.** A manufacturer of earth-moving equipment is occasionally unable to ship replacement parts on time. The late shipments keep the manufacturer from meeting delivery commitments to its customers. The **best** approach for determining the cause of the late shipments is to

a. Trace replacement parts that were shipped late through production and handling records.

b. Track the production and handling processes to find average turnaround times.

c. Compute the production and handling capacities for replacement parts.

d. Examine the terms and conditions of the delivery commitments to customers.

**103.** In deciding whether recorded sales are valid, which of the following items of evidence would be considered **most** competent?

a. A copy of the customer's purchase order.

b. A memorandum from the director of the shipping department stating that another employee verified the personal delivery of the merchandise to the customer.

c. Accounts receivable records showing cash collections from the customer.

d. The shipping document, independent bill of lading, and the invoice for the merchandise.

**104.** The **most** reliable evidence an auditor can assess when determining a company's legal title to inventories is

a. Monthly gross profit and inventory levels.

b. Purchase orders.

c. Paid vendor invoices.

d. Records of inventories stored at off-site locations.

**105.** During an investigation of unexplained inventory shrinkage, an internal auditor is testing inventory additions as recorded in the perpetual inventory records. Because of internal control weaknesses, the information recorded on receiving reports may not be reliable. Under these circumstances, which of the following documents would provide the best evidence of additions to inventory?

a. Purchase orders.

b. Purchase requisitions.

c. Vendors' invoices.

d. Vendors' statements.

**Develop and Review Workpapers**

**106.** Each individual workpaper should, at a minimum, contain

a. An expression of an audit opinion.

b. A tick mark legend.

c. A complete flowchart of the system of internal controls for the area being reviewed.

d. A descriptive heading.

**107.** Working papers serve the following purpose for the internal auditor:

a. Provide the auditee a place to make responses to audit recommendations.

b. Make the audit report more readable by providing a place to append exhibits.

c. Provide the principal evidential support for the internal auditor's report.

d. Provide a place to summarize overall audit recommendations.

**108.** Working papers should include

a. Documentation of the examination and evaluation of the adequacy and effectiveness of the system of internal control.

b. Copies of all source documents examined in the course of the audit.

c. Copies of all procedures which were reviewed during the audit.

d. All workpapers prepared during a previous audit of the same area.

**109.** When reviewing audit working papers, the primary responsibility of an audit supervisor is to determine that

a. Each worksheet is properly identified with a descriptive heading.

b. Working papers are properly referenced and kept in logical groupings.

c. Standard departmental procedures are adhered to with regard to workpaper preparation and technique.

d. Working papers adequately support the audit findings, conclusions, and reports.

**110.** To properly control working papers, the auditor should **not**

a. Share the results of an audit with the auditee.

b. Permit access to external auditors.

c. Permit access to government auditors.

d. Make them available to people who have no authority to use them.

**111.** An audit working paper is complete when

a. The audit objective has been met.
b. Operational activity describing the essential basis of the audit has been included.
c. Condensation and careful summarization of detail is present.
d. Working papers are properly indexed and cross-indexed.

**112.** When determining the retention period for the workpapers of a contract audit, it is best to
a. Review the corporate policy manual developed by the records management area for the section regarding business records.
b. Seek the assistance of the legal department to ensure compliance with contract provisions.
c. Check with the corporate accounting department since accounting records are involved.
d. Follow the contractor's own record retention policies.

**Items 113 through 115** are based on the following:

You are an audit supervisor, reviewing the working papers of a staff auditor's overall examination of the firm's sales function. The pages are not numbered or cross-referenced. Further, the working papers were dropped and reassembled at random before they were brought to you.

You decide to put the working papers in the proper order according to the IIA *Standards*. The first stage of this activity is to identify each page as a part of (1) the preliminary survey, (2) the review of the adequacy of the system of internal control, (3) the review for effectiveness of the system of internal control, or (4) the review for quality of performance.

**113.** The first page you select documents a compliance test performed during the course of the audit. This page belongs with the following activity:
a. Preliminary survey.
b. Review for adequacy of the system.
c. Review for effectiveness of the system.
d. Review for quality of performance.

**114.** The second page you select documents an interview with a salesperson discussing the overall sales cycle. This page belongs with the following activity:
a. Preliminary survey.
b. Review for adequacy of the system.
c. Review for effectiveness of the system.
d. Review for quality of performance.

**115.** The third page you select is a blank copy of the sales contract form now in use by the firm. Annotated on the form in several places are the words "key control" followed by a brief explanation. You recognize the writing as that of the staff auditor who performed the audit. This document belongs with the following activity:
a. Preliminary survey.
b. Review for adequacy of the system.
c. Review for effectiveness of the system.
d. Review for quality of performance.

**116.** Productivity statistics are provided quarterly to the board of directors. An auditor checked the ratios and other statistics in the four most recent reports. The auditor used scratch paper and copies of the board reports to verify the accuracy of computations and compared the data used in the computations with supporting documents. The auditor wrote a note describing his work for the working papers and then discarded the scratch paper and report copies. The auditor's note stated

> The ratios and other statistics in the quarterly board reports were checked for the last four quarters and appropriate supporting documents were examined. All amounts appear to be appropriate.

In this situation
a. Four quarters is not a large enough sample on which to base a conclusion.
b. The auditor's working papers are not sufficient to facilitate an efficient review of the auditor's work.
c. The auditor should have included the scratch paper in the working papers.
d. The auditor did not consider whether the information in the board report was compiled efficiently.

**117.** Auditors use a variety of indexing and cross-referencing methods in their audit workpapers. An internal auditing manager might devise a workpaper indexing method tailored to a specific organization's needs. A government audit agency would devise one method for all organizations under the agency's jurisdiction. Which of the following **best** explains the reason for this difference between the two workpaper indexing methods?
a. The internal auditing manager devises a method that simplifies the review process within a particular organization, but the government audit agency devises one uniform method to simplify the review process of the vastly different organizations to be audited.
b. The method of the internal auditing manager is prescribed by the Standards, but the method of the government audit agency is required by agency policy.
c. The method of the internal auditing manager is prescribed by the *Standards*, but law requires the method of the government audit agency.
d. The internal auditing manager devises a method specified by the organization's audit committee, but the government audit agency devises one uniform method that is required by law.

**118.** Working papers provide the documentary support for the internal auditor's report. Which of the following is **not** a good practice for working papers?
a. Working papers should be sufficient to support the internal auditors' report without additional verbal elaboration by the internal auditor.
b. Working papers should be kept secure at all times to prevent accidental loss or unauthorized access.
c. Working papers should be organized chronologically, that is, with the papers prepared earliest at the front of the file.
d. Internal auditors within a given organization should develop standardized methods for organization and documentation.

**119.** A good working paper for a bank reconciliation should include (either directly or through cross-reference) all of the following **except:**
a. A legend explaining all tick marks employed.
b. A list of outstanding checks.
c. A list of all deposits made during the period in question.
d. The cash balance per the general ledger as of the reconciliation date.

**120.** Which of the following microcomputer applications would be **least** helpful in preparing audit working papers?
- a. Spreadsheet software.
- b. Word processing software.
- c. Utilities software.
- d. Database software.

**121.** When hiring entry-level internal audit staff, which of the following will **most** likely predict the applicant's success as an auditor?
- a. Grade point average on college accounting courses.
- b. Ability to fit well socially into a group.
- c. Ability to organize and express thoughts well.
- d. Level of detailed knowledge of the company.

**122.** An internal auditing supervisor, when reviewing a staff member's working papers, identified an unsupported statement that the auditee's unit was operating inefficiently. What action should the supervisor direct the auditor to take?
- a. Remove the comment from the working paper file.
- b. Obtain the auditee's concurrence with the statement.
- c. Research and identify criteria to measure operating efficiency.
- d. Explain that it is the opinion of the staff member.

**123.** Internal auditors often include summaries within their working papers. Which of the following **best** describes the purpose of such summaries?
- a. Summaries are prepared to conform to the IIIA Standards.
- b. Summaries are usually required for the completion of each section of an audit program.
- c. Summaries distill the most useful information from several working papers into a more usable form.
- d. Summaries are used to document the fact that the auditor has considered all relevant evidence.

**124.** A working paper is complete when it
- a. Complies with the auditing department's format requirements.
- b. Contains all of the elements of a finding.
- c. Is clear, concise, and accurate.
- d. Satisfies the audit objective for which it is developed.

**125.** Working papers should be disposed of when they are of no further use. Retention policies
- a. Should specify a minimum retention period of three years.
- b. Should be prepared by the audit committee.
- c. Should be approved by legal counsel.
- d. Should be approved by the external auditor.

**126.** An adequately documented working paper should
- a. Be concise but complete.
- b. Follow a unique form and arrangement.
- c. Contain examples of all forms and procedures used by the auditee.
- d. Not contain copies of auditee records.

**127.** Working papers are the property of the auditor. Good control of working papers
- a. Precludes showing working papers to auditees.
- b. Requires retention of working papers for at least three years.
- c. Requires that only the auditor who created the working paper change electronic working papers.

- d. Prevents surrender to a summons issued by a governmental agency.

**Items 128 and 129 are based on the following:**

An internal auditing department has a project under way to determine whether it can go to electronic working papers. Decision criteria will be based primarily on the requirements of internal auditing standards and on the experience of other audit departments.

**128.** The feasibility study should recognize that internal auditing standards specify that for the design and content of working papers in the form of media other than paper
- a. Conversion to paper should occur no later than the time of final review.
- b. Consideration should be given to generating backup copies of working papers.
- c. The media selected should determine working paper design and content.
- d. Working paper retention should be solely a function of the media used.

**129.** Which of the following long-term effects associated with electronic working papers is most likely to occur after conversion from manual working papers?
- a. Significant training needs for auditors.
- b. Reductions in the average time to complete audits.
- c. More comprehensive working papers.
- d. Working papers must be printed.

**130.** Working papers have the following characteristic:
- a. They are the property of the organization and are available to all company employees.
- b. They document the auditing procedures performed, the information obtained, and the conclusions reached.
- c. They become the property of the independent outside auditors when completed.
- d. They should be retained permanently in the organization's records.

**131.** An internal auditing department has been piloting the use of electronic working paper files. Full implementation is expected in the near future. Select a **disadvantage** of electronic working papers.
- a. Each staff auditor must have a personal computer.
- b. Critical working papers must still be printed off.
- c. Cross-referencing is more tedious.
- d. They require specific technical training.

**132.** The primary purpose of an auditor's working papers is to
- a. Provide evidence of the planning and execution of audit procedures performed.
- b. Serve as a means with which to prepare the financial statements.
- c. Document deficiencies in internal control structure with recommendations to management for improvement.
- d. Comply with the auditing standards of the profession.

**133.** Which of the following statements relating to the retention of audit working papers is an inappropriate policy?
- a. Working papers should be disposed of when they have no further use.

b.   Working papers on fraud audits should be retained indefinitely.

c.   Legal counsel should approve working paper retention schedules.

d.   Working paper retention schedules should consider legal and contractual requirements.

**134.** Auditors use a variety of indexing and cross-referencing methods in their audit working papers. An internal auditing manager might devise a working paper indexing method tailored to a specific organization's needs. A government audit agency would devise a method for all organizations under the agency's jurisdiction. Which of the following **best** explains the reason for this difference in working paper index methods between the two?

a.   The internal auditing manager devises a method that simplifies the review process within a particular organization, but the government audit agency devises one uniform method to simplify the review process of the vastly different organizations to be audited.

b.   The method of the internal auditing manager is prescribed by the IIA Standards, but the method of the government audit agency is required by the regulatory agency.

c.   The method of the internal auditing manager is prescribed by the IIA Standards, but law requires the method of the government audit agency.

d.   The internal auditing manager devises that method specified by the organization's audit committee, but the government audit agency devises one uniform method that is required by law.

**135.** Which of the following should be identified as a **deficiency** by an audit supervisor when reviewing a set of working papers?

a.   A memorandum explaining why the time budget for a part of the audit was exceeded.

b.   An audit finding recorded in the working papers and report draft that omits the criteria used for evaluation.

c.   A memorandum explaining why an audit program step was omitted.

d.   A letter to the auditee outlining the scope of the audit.

**136.** In general, internal auditing working papers should be

a.   Retained according to the guidelines published by the federal government.

b.   Retained for three years as specified in the IIA Standards.

c.   Disposed of in accordance with departmental policy.

d.   Disposed of after the performance of two subsequent audits.

**137.** A recent fire in a company's warehouse has destroyed a large portion of its inventory. Management is in the process of filing an insurance claim and needs to use the internal auditors' inventory working papers in preparing the claim. According to the IIA *Standards*, which of the following is correct?

a.   Management may not use any of the internal auditors' working papers in preparing the insurance claim.

b.   Management may use the internal auditors' inventory working papers in preparing the insurance

claim, but the director of internal auditing should approve such use.

c.   Management should be precluded from preparing the insurance claim and such function should be given to the internal auditing department.

d.   Management may use the internal auditors' inventory working papers in preparing the insurance claim, but both the company's external independent auditors and the director of internal auditing should approve such use.

**138.** An internal audit manager is reviewing the audit working papers prepared by the staff. Which of the following review comments is true?

a.   Each working paper should include the actual and the budgeted time related to such audit work.

b.   Including copies of all the forms and directives of the auditee department constitutes "unnecessary" overdocumentation.

c.   Conclusions need not be documented in the working papers when the audit objectives are achieved.

d.   Each working papers should include a statement regarding the auditees' cooperation during the conduct of the audit.

**139.** Which of the following concepts distinguishes the retention of computerized audit working papers from the traditional hard-copy form?

a.   Analyses, conclusions, and recommendations are filed on electronic media and are therefore subject to computer system controls and security procedures.

b.   Evidential support for all findings is copied and provided to local management during the closing conference and to each person receiving the final report.

c.   Computerized data files can be used in information technology audit procedures.

d.   Audit programs can be standardized to eliminate the need for a preliminary survey at each location.

**140.** When audit conclusions are challenged, the auditor's factual rebuttal is best facilitated by

a.   Summaries in the audit program.

b.   Pro forma working papers.

c.   Cross-referencing of the working papers.

d.   Explicit procedures in the audit program.

**Report Engagement Results**

**141.** Which of the following techniques is **best** for emphasizing a point in a written communication?

a.   Place the point in the middle rather than at the beginning or end of the paragraph.

b.   Use passive rather than active voice.

c.   Highlight the point through the use of nonparallel structure.

d.   Use a short sentence with one idea rather than a longer sentence with several ideas.

**142.** Which of the following statements conveys negative information in such a way that a favorable response from the auditee may still be achieved?

a.   Your bookkeeper has failed to reconcile the bank statement each month.

b.   The bank statements have not been reconciled each month.

c.   Unfortunately, your bookkeeper has not taken the time to reconcile the bank statement each month.

d. You have apparently failed to inform your bookkeeper that the bank statements should be reconciled on a timely basis.

**Items 143 and 144** are based on the following:

A company recently experienced a substantially reduced net profit from sales of product-line A. Line A is produced in a dedicated machine shop. The internal auditors have been assigned the task of determining the cause of the reduced net profit.

**143.** The in-charge auditor should, as a first step
   a. Test material vouchers for validity.
   b. Evaluate the elements of cost and compare to prior periods.
   c. Compare production records with cost standards.
   d. Analyze scrap and surplus records.

**144.** Which of the following would most likely identify the problem?
   a. A review of prior audit results.
   b. A walk-through of the machine shop.
   c. Interviews with the staff engaged in the production of line A.
   d. An analysis of the financial and operational reports.

**145.** An internal audit director has noticed that staff auditors are presenting more oral reports to supplement written reports. The best reason for the increased use of oral reports by the auditors is that such reports
   a. Reduce the amount of testing required to support audit findings.
   b. Can be delivered in an informal manner without preparation.
   c. Can be prepared using a flexible format, thereby increasing overall audit efficiency.
   d. Permit auditors to counter arguments and provide additional information that the audience may require.

**Items 146 through 150** are based on the following:

The following information is to be included in a finding of an inventory control audit of a tent and awning manufacturer. The issue relates to overstocked rope.

I. The quantity on hand at the time of the audit represented a 10-year supply based on normal usage.
II. The company had held an open house of its new factory two months prior to the audit and had used the rope to provide safety corridors through the plant for visitors. This was not considered when placing the last purchase order.
III. Rope is reordered when the inventory level reaches a one-month supply and is based on usage during the previous twelve months.
IV. The quantity to be ordered should be adequate to cover expected usage for the next six months.
V. The purchasing department should review inventory usage and inquire about any unusual fluctuations before placing an order.
VI. A public warehouse, costing $500 per month, was required to store the rope.
VII. The purchasing agent receives an annual salary of $59,000.

**146.** Which of these statements should be in the criteria section of the finding?
   a. II only.
   b. III only.
   c. III and IV only.
   d. V only.

**147.** Which of these statements should be in the condition section of the finding?
   a. I only.
   b. IV only.
   c. VI only.
   d. VII only.

**148.** Which of these statements should be in the cause section of the finding?
   a. I only.
   b. II only.
   c. VI only.
   d. VII only.

**149.** Which of these statements should be in the effect section of the finding?
   a. II only.
   b. III only.
   c. V only.
   d. VI only.

**150.** Which of these statements should be in the recommendation section of the finding?
   a. III only.
   b. III and IV only.
   c. V only.
   d. VI only.

**Items 151 and 152** are based on the following:

The internal audit department of a major financial institution completed an audit of the company's derivatives trading operations in its foreign branch. The audit report was critical of the lack of controls in the trading process and the lack of effective monitoring of successful traders by the home office. The auditor suspected, but did not state, that the reason that the home office tolerated the behavior of the foreign branch trading unit was that the branch, and in particular one individual trader, had been very successful. The success created enormous profits and thereby influenced the bonuses of all members of senior management. After receiving the audit report, senior management indicated that corrective action was under way. Based on the imminent corrective action, the auditor did not report the finding to the audit committee.

**151.** Which of the following statements is/are correct regarding the company's compensation system and related bonuses?

I. The bonus system should be considered part of the control environment of the organization and should be considered in formulating a report on internal control.
II. Compensation systems are not part of an organization's control system and should not be reported as part of an organization's control system.
III. An audit of the compensation system should be performed independently of an audit of the control system over the company's derivatives trading activities and should not be considered an integral part of the derivatives audit.

   a. I only.

b. II only.
c. III only.
d. II and III.

**152.** Which of the following statements, if true, could have justified the auditor's decision not to report the control concerns to the audit committee?
  a. Management plans to initiate corrective action.
  b. The board of directors has a separate committee to make recommendations on compensation.
  c. The amounts of trading and the potential risks associated with the foreign branch are not material to the overall organization.
  d. Derivatives are complex, and the auditor should rely on management's analysis of the extent of the problem.

**153.** An internal auditor has completed an audit of an organization's activities and is ready to issue a report. However, the auditee disagrees with the internal auditor's conclusions. The auditor should
  a. Withhold the issuance of the audit report until agreement on the issues is obtained.
  b. Perform more work, with the auditee's concurrence, to resolve areas of disagreement. Delay the issuance of the report until agreement is reached.
  c. Issue the audit report and indicate that the auditee has provided a scope limitation that has led to a difference as to the conclusions.
  d. Issue the audit report and state both the auditor and auditee positions and the reasons for the disagreement.

**154.** According to the IIA *Standards*, reported audit findings emerge by a process of comparing "what should be" with "what is." In determining "what should be" during an audit of a company's treasury function, which of the following would be the **least** desirable criteria against which to judge current operations?
  a. The operations of the treasury function as documented during the last audit.
  b. Company policies and procedures delegating authority and assigning responsibilities.
  c. Finance textbook illustrations of generally accepted good treasury function practices.
  d. Codification of best practices of the treasury function in relevant industries.

**155.** Which of the following is **not** a major purpose of an audit report?
  a. Inform.
  b. Get results.
  c. Assign responsibility.
  d. Persuade.

**156.** Which of the following would **not** be included in the statement of scope in an audit report?
  a. Period covered by the audit.
  b. Audit objectives.
  c. Activities not audited.
  d. Nature and extent of the auditing performed.

**157.** Providing useful and timely information and promoting improvements in operations are goals of internal auditors. To accomplish this in their reports, auditors should

  a. Provide top management with reports that emphasize the operational details of defective conditions.
  b. Provide operating management with reports that emphasize general concerns and risks.
  c. Provide information in written form before it is discussed with the auditee.
  d. Provide reports that meet the expectations and perceptions of both operational and top management.

**Items 158 and 159** are based on the following:

An auditor has submitted a first draft of an audit report to an auditee in preparation for an exit interview. The following is an excerpt from that report:

The audit was performed to accomplish several objectives.

• Verify the existence of unused machinery being stored in the warehouse.
• Determine whether machinery had been damaged during storage.
• Review the handling procedures being performed by personnel at the warehouse.
• Determine whether proper accounting procedures are being followed for machinery kept in the warehouse.
• Calculate the current fair market value of warehouse inventories.
• Compare the total value of the machinery to company accounting records.

It was confirmed that, of the thirty machines selected from purchasing records for the sample, thirteen were present on the warehouse floor and another five were on the loading dock ready for conveyance to the production facility. Twelve others had already been sent to the production facility at a previous time. An examination of the accounting procedures used at the warehouse revealed the failure by the warehouse accounting clerk to reconcile inventory records monthly, as required by policy. A sample of twenty-five machines was examined for possible damage, and all but one was in good condition. It was confirmed by the auditors that handling procedures outlined in the warehouse policy manual appear to be adequate, and warehouse personnel apparently were following those procedures, except for the examination of items being received for inventory.

When communicating with auditees, there exist both situational factors and message characteristics that can damage the communication process. An auditor has only limited control over situational factors but has substantial control over message characteristics.

**158.** Which of the following would seem to be a message characteristic that the auditor who prepared the above report overlooked?
  a. Sequence of message.
  b. Nature of the audience.
  c. Noise.
  d. Prior encounters with the auditee.

**159.** The following elements are usually included in final audit reports: purpose, scope, results, conclusions, and recommendations. Which of the following describes all of the elements missing from the above report?
  a. Scope, conclusion, recommendation.
  b. Purpose, result, recommendation.

c. Result, conclusion, recommendation.
d. Purpose, scope, recommendation.

**160.** Successful communication between the auditor and the auditee partially depends on achieving appropriate emphasis so both parties are aware of the most important points in their discussion. Which of the following approaches would provide the most emphasis in an audit report?
a. Graphics, repetition, and itemization.
b. Solid paragraphs and detailed appendices.
c. Calm discussion in a conversational tone.
d. Key points embedded in discussion.

**Items 161 through 164 are based on the following:**

An internal auditor in a retail company reports to the corporate director of internal audit. The auditor is assigned to audit a regional division. The audit reports are to be sent both to the corporate office and the division controller in the region. The auditor has been on location for six months and has submitted monthly reports, each month auditing a part of the operation as assigned by corporate internal auditing. This month, for the first time, the auditor has audited the inventory controls, following procedures established by the corporate internal auditing staff.

After seeing the audit report on inventory control, the divisional controller called and requested a meeting with the auditor. At the meeting, the divisional controller loudly and abusively criticized the accuracy of the auditor's work, the soundness of the auditor's methods, and the results presented in the reports. In the past, while not always agreeing with the auditor's conclusions, the divisional controller always had rational discussions and developed appropriate follow-up steps to correct the problems the auditor found.

**161.** Despite never having said so, the divisional controller had always thought the auditor's work was substandard. The divisional controller could have handled the situation better by
a. Providing training on auditing of inventory controls so the auditor would do a better job the next time.
b. Documenting shortcomings regularly and reporting them to the director of internal auditing.
c. Discussing the auditor's work with other internal auditors to compare the auditor's methods with others used in the company.
d. Calling the corporate director of internal audit and insist that the auditor be replaced.

**162.** The divisional controller could have handled the situation better by
a. Accepting the report because the auditor has consistently done good work, and this one report is not that important.
b. Accepting the report but informing the director of internal auditing that the report was unsatisfactory.
c. Changing the methods used by corporate audit.
d. Discussing the objections to the inventory report with the auditor to get agreement on changes and appropriate additional work.

**163.** If the internal auditor believes the criticism is completely unjustified, the auditor should
a. Ask the divisional controller to identify specific areas of disagreement and document them in the management response section of the audit report.

b. Confront the divisional controller just as loudly to communicate that the auditor can be just as aggressive and can survive in the corporate environment.
c. Offer to personally rewrite the report and develop the follow-up steps to correct the inventory problems to show the accuracy of the work.
d. Ignore the divisional controller's response.

**164.** This particular audit was not the auditor's best work, and the auditor realizes this. The auditor should
a. Defend the work now and try to improve it in the future.
b. Ask the divisional controller to identify specific areas in which the report is deficient, and, if the objections are justified, revise the report.
c. Explain the personal problems that kept the auditor from working as hard on this report as could be expected.
d. Ask for time off for training in the weak areas.

**Items 165 through 169 are based on the following:**

The following information is extracted from a draft of an audit report prepared on the completion of an audit of the inventory warehousing procedures for a division.

*Findings*

[#5]
We performed extensive tests of inventory recordkeeping and quantities on hand. Based on our tests, we have concluded that the division carries a large quantity of excess inventory, particularly in the area of component parts. We expect this be due to the conservatism of local management that does not want to risk shutting down production if the goods are not on hand. However, as noted earlier in this report, the excess inventory has led to a higher than average level of obsolete inventory write-downs at this division. We recommend that production forecasts be established, along with lead times for various products, and used in conjunction with economic order quantity concepts to order and maintain appropriate inventory levels.

[#6]
We observed that receiving reports were not filled out when the receiving department became busy. Instead, the receiving manager would fill out the reports after work and forward them to accounts payable. There is a risk that all items received might not be recorded, or that failing to initially record might result in some items being diverted to other places. During our tests, we noted many instances in which accounts payable had to call to receiving to obtain a receiving report. We recommend that receiving reports be prepared.

[#7]
Inventory is messy. We recommend that management communicate the importance of orderly inventory management techniques to warehouse personnel to avoid the problems noted earlier about (1) locating inventory when needed for production and (2) incurring unusually large amounts of inventory write-offs because of obsolescence.

[#8]
We appreciate the cooperation of divisional management. We intend to discuss our findings with them and follow up by communicating your reaction to those recommendations included within this report. Given additional time for analysis, we feel there are substantial opportunities available for sig-

nificant cost savings and we are proud to be a part of the process.

**165.** A major deficiency in paragraph [#5] related to the completeness of the audit report is
   a. There is no indication of the potential cause of the problem.
   b. The report does not contain criteria by which the concept of "excessive inventory" is judged.
   c. The report does not adequately describe the potential effect of the conditions noted.
   d. The recommendations are not required and are not appropriate given the nature of the problem identified.

**166.** A major writing problem in paragraph [#5] is
   a. The use of potentially emotional words such as "conservatism" of local management.
   b. The presentation of findings before recommendations. The report would have more impact if recommendations were made before the findings are discussed.
   c. The specific identification of "component parts" may be offensive to the personnel responsible for those parts and may reflect negatively on them.
   d. The reference to other parts of the audit report citing excessive inventory write-downs for obsolescence is not appropriate. If there is a problem, it should all be discussed within the context of the specific audit finding.

**167.** A major deficiency in paragraph [#6] related to the completeness of the audit report is
   a. The factual evidence for the audit finding is not given.
   b. The cause of the problem is not defined.
   c. The risk is presented in an "overdramatic" fashion.
   d. The recommendation is incomplete.

**168.** A major deficiency in paragraph [#7] related to the completeness of the audit report is
   a. There is not a separate section adequately discussing the risks associated with the audit finding.
   b. The recommendation does not follow from the findings. The recommendation could have been reached without any audit findings.
   c. The condition for the audit finding is not clearly explained.
   d. The reference to other parts of the audit report citing excessive inventory write-downs for obsolescence is not appropriate. If there is a problem, it should all be discussed within the context of the specific audit finding.

**169.** A major deficiency in paragraph [#8] is
   a. The nature of the follow-up action is inappropriate.
   b. The findings have not been discussed with division management before they are presented to upper management.
   c. The cost savings mentioned are not supported in the report.
   d. All of the above.

**170.** The auditor completed work on a segment of the audit program. It was clear that a problem existed that would require a modification of the organization's distribution procedures. The auditee agreed and has implemented revised procedures. The internal auditor should
   a. Research the problem and recommend in the audit report measures that should be taken.
   b. Jointly develop and report an appropriate recommendation.
   c. Report the problem and assume that management will take appropriate action.
   d. Indicate in the audit report that the auditee determined and implemented corrective action.

**171.** An audit report relating to an audit of a bank categorizes findings into "deficiency findings" for major problems and "other areas for improvement" for less serious problems. Which of the following excerpts would properly be included under "other areas for improvement"?
   a. Many secured loans did not contain hazard insurance coverage for tangible property collateral.
   b. Loan officers also prepare the cashier's checks for disbursement of the loan proceeds.
   c. The bank is incurring unnecessary postage cost by not combining certain special mailings to checking account customers with the monthly mailing of their statements.
   d. At one branch a large amount of cash was placed on a portable table behind the teller lines.

**172.** The following is the complete text of a deficiency finding included in the internal audit report for a bank: The late charges were waived on an excessive number of delinquent installment loan payments at the Spring Street Branch. We were informed that an officer does not approve late charge waivers. Approximately $5,000 per year in revenues is being lost. In order to provide a better control over late charges waived and loss of income, we recommend that a lending officer be responsible for waiving late charges and that this approval be in writing.
   Which of the following elements of a deficiency finding is **not** properly addressed?
   a. Criteria or standards.
   b. Condition.
   c. Cause.
   d. Effect.

**173.** An auditor for a bank noted a significant deficiency relating to access to cash in the bank's vault at one of the branch banks. Which of the following is the **most** satisfactory means of addressing this deficiency? The auditor should
   a. Discuss the deficiency with the branch manager before drafting the written audit report. If the auditor and branch manager agree on corrective action and the action is initiated before the report is published, the deficiency need not be included in the report.
   b. Discuss the deficiency with the branch manager before drafting the written audit report. If the auditor and branch manager agree on corrective action, include both the deficiency and corrective action in the audit report.
   c. Discuss the deficiency with the branch manager only after the audit report is published.
   d. Not discuss the deficiency with the branch manager before or after the audit report is published; discussion may dilute the impact of the written report.

**174.** Several levels of management are interested in the results of the marketing department audit. What is the **best** method of communicating the results of the audit?
   a. Write detailed reports for each level of management.
   b. Write a report to the marketing management and give summary reports to other management levels.
   c. Discuss results with marketing management and issue a summary report to top management.
   d. Discuss results with all levels of management.

**Items 175 through 178** are based on the following:

An auditor has submitted a first draft of an audit report to an auditee in preparation for an exit interview. The following is an excerpt from that report:

> The audit was performed to accomplish several objectives: verify the existence of unused machinery being stored in the warehouse, determine whether machinery had been damaged during storage, review the handling procedures being performed by personnel at the warehouse, determine whether proper accounting procedures are being followed for machinery kept in the warehouse, calculate the current fair market value of warehouse inventories, and compare the total value of the machinery to company accounting records. It was confirmed that of the thirty machines selected from purchasing records for the sample, ten were present on the warehouse floor and another five were on the loading dock ready for conveyance to the production facility. Twelve others had already been sent to the production facility at a previous time. An examination of the accounting procedures used at the warehouse revealed the failure by the warehouse accounting clerk to reconcile inventory records monthly, as required by policy. A sample of twenty-five machines was examined for possible damage, and all but one was in good condition. It was confirmed by the auditors that handling procedures outlined in the warehouse policy manual appear to be adequate, and warehouse personnel apparently were following those procedures, except for the examination of items being received for inventory.

When communicating with auditees, both situational factors and message characteristics can damage the communication process. An auditor has only limited control over situational factors but has substantial control over message characteristics.

**175.** Which of the following would seem to be a message characteristic that the auditor who prepared the above report overlooked?
   a. Sequence of message.
   b. Nature of the audience.
   c. Noise.
   d. History of prior events leading to the current encounter.

**176.** The objectives of an audit report are to inform and to influence. Whether these objectives are met depends on the clarity of the writing. Which of the following principles of report clarity was violated in the above audit report?
   a. Appropriately organize the report.
   b. Keep most sentences short and simple.
   c. Use active voice verbs.
   d. All of the above.

**177.** The following elements are usually included in final audit reports: purpose, scope, results, conclusions, and recommendations. Which of the following describes all of the elements missing from the above report?
   a. Scope, conclusion, recommendation.
   b. Purpose, result, recommendation.
   c. Result, conclusion, recommendation.
   d. Purpose, scope, recommendation.

**178.** The behavioral science literature identifies diffusion as an effective approach to resolving conflict. An auditor effectively using diffusion in working with a confrontational auditee would
   a. Set aside critical issues temporarily and try to reach agreement on less controversial issues first.
   b. Emphasize differences between the parties.
   c. Avoid the conflict situation.
   d. Identify the sources of conflict and address them directly.

**179.** An internal audit director has noticed that staff auditors are presenting more oral reports to supplement written reports. The best reason for the increased use of oral reports by the auditors is that they
   a. Reduce the amount of testing required to support audit findings.
   b. Can be delivered in an informal manner without preparation.
   c. Can be prepared using a flexible format thereby increasing overall audit efficiency.
   d. Permit auditors to counter arguments and provide additional information that the audience may require.

**180.** When making a presentation to management, the auditor wants to report findings and to stimulate action. These objectives are best accomplished by
   a. Delivering a lecture on the findings.
   b. Showing a series of slides or overheads that graphically depict the findings; limit verbal commentary.
   c. Using slides/overheads to support a discussion of major points.
   d. Handing out copies of the report, asking the participants to read the report, and asking for questions.

**181.** In which section of the final report should the internal auditor describe the audit objectives?
   a. Purpose.
   b. Scope.
   c. Criteria.
   d. Condition.

**182.** An internal auditor can use oral reports to
   a. Give immediate information to management and more accurately exchange thoughts with a face-to-face discussion.
   b. Report interim findings more efficiently by eliminating the preparation time for a written report.
   c. Eliminate the need for a lengthy final report by reaching verbal agreement on the handling of significant findings with the auditee.
   d. Impress the auditee with a polished presentation using graphics to enhance the credibility of audit findings.

**183.** Summary written audit reports are generally intended for
   a. Local operating management.
   b. Review by other auditors only.
   c. High-level management and/or the audit committee.
   d. Midlevel staff management.

**184.** An oral audit report may be most appropriate when
   a. A permanent record of the report is needed.
   b. Emergency action is needed.

c.   Higher-level management needs a summary of individual audits.
d.   It is used only for internal reporting within the internal auditing department.

**185.** An audit report recommendation should address what attribute of an audit finding?
a.   Cause.
b.   Statement of condition.
c.   Criteria.
d.   Effect.

**186.** Which of the following is a proper element in an audit results section of a report?
a.   Status of findings from prior reports.
b.   Personnel used.
c.   Significance of deficiencies.
d.   Engagement plan.

**187.** After an audit report with adverse findings has been communicated to appropriate auditee personnel, proper action is to
a.   Schedule a follow-up review.
b.   Implement corrective action indicated by the findings.
c.   Examine further the data supporting the findings.
d.   Assemble new data to support the findings.

**188.** The scope statement of an audit report should
a.   Describe the audit objectives and tell the reader why the audit was conducted.
b.   Identify the audited activities and describe the nature and extent of auditing performed.
c.   Define the standards, measures, or expectations used in evaluating audit findings.
d.   Communicate the internal auditor's evaluation of the effect of the findings on the activities reviewed.

**189.** In beginning an audit, an internal auditor reviews written procedures that detail segregation of duties adopted by management to strengthen internal controls. These written procedures should be viewed as the following attribute of a finding:
a.   Criteria.
b.   Condition.
c.   Cause.
d.   Effect.

**190.** Interim reports are issued during an audit to
a.   Explain the purpose of the audit.
b.   Eliminate the need for a final report.
c.   Communicate information requiring immediate attention.
d.   Define the scope of the audit so the final report can be brief.

**191.** A senior member of management who is several organizational levels above the head of the operational area being audited has asked for a report of the findings of the audit. The most appropriate means of communicating audit findings to this senior member of management is by
a.   Sending a copy of the final audit report.
b.   Orally communicating the findings.
c.   Sending copies of interim reports.
d.   Sending the summary section of the report.

**192.** Recommendations in audit reports may or may not actually be implemented. Which of the following **best** describes

internal auditing's role in follow-up on audit recommendations? Internal auditing
a.   Has no role; follow-up is management's responsibility.
b.   Should be charged with the responsibility for implementing audit recommendations.
c.   Should follow up to ascertain that appropriate action is taken on audit recommendations.
d.   Should request that independent auditors follow up on audit recommendations.

**193.** An internal auditor found that employees in the maintenance department were not signing their time cards. This situation also existed during the last audit. The auditor should
a.   Include this finding in the current audit report.
b.   Ask the manager of the maintenance department to assume the resulting risk.
c.   Withhold conclusions about payroll internal control in the maintenance department.
d.   Instruct the employees to sign their time cards.

**194.** Which one of the following elements of an audit report is not always required?
a.   A statement that describes the audit objectives.
b.   A statement that identifies the audited activities.
c.   Pertinent statements of fact.
d.   An evaluation of the impact of the findings on the activities reviewed.

**195.** An internal auditing department is conducting an audit of the payroll and accounts receivable departments. Significant problems related to the approval of overtime have been noted. While the audit is still in process, which of the following audit reports is appropriate?
a.   A summary report.
b.   A written report.
c.   A questionnaire-type report.
d.   An oral report.

**196.** During an audit of sales representatives' travel expenses, it was discovered that 152 of 200 travel advances issued to sales representatives in the past year exceeded the prescribed maximum amount allowed. Which of the following statements is a justifiable audit opinion?
a.   The majority of travel advances in the organization exceed the prescribed maximum.
b.   Travel advances are not controlled in accordance with existing policy.
c.   The prescribed maximum travel advance is too low.
d.   76% of all travel advances exceed the management-prescribed maximum.

**Items 197 through 200** are based on the following:

The following data was gathered during an internal auditor's investigation of the reason for a material increase in bad debts expenses. In preparing a report of the finding, each of the items might be classified as criteria, cause, condition, effect, or background information.

1.   Very large orders require management's approval of credit.
2.   Audit tests showed that sales personnel regularly disregard credit guidelines when dealing with established customers.
3.   A monthly report of write-offs is prepared but distributed only to the accounting department.

4. Credit reports are used only on new accounts.
5. Accounting department records suggest that uncollectible accounts could increase by 5% for the current year.
6. The bad debts loss increased by $100,000 during the last fiscal year.
7. Even though procedures and criteria were changed to reduce the amount of bad-debt write-offs, the loss of commissions due to written-off accounts has increased for some sales personnel.
8. Credit department policy requires the review of credit references for all new accounts.
9. Current payment records are to be reviewed before extending additional credit to open accounts.
10. To reduce costs, the use of outside credit reports was suspended on several occasions.
11. Since several staff positions in the credit department were eliminated to reduce costs, some new accounts have received only cursory review.
12. According to the new credit manager, strict adherence to established credit policy is not necessary.

**197.** Criteria are best illustrated by items numbered
   a. 1, 8, and 9.
   b. 2, 10, and 11.
   c. 3, 4, and 12.
   d. 5, 6, and 7.

**198.** Cause is best illustrated by items numbered
   a. 2, 10, and 11.
   b. 3, 4, and 12.
   c. 5, 6, and 7.
   d. 1, 8, and 9.

**199.** Condition is best illustrated by items numbered
   a. 5, 6, and 7.
   b. 1, 8, and 9.
   c. 2, 10, and 11.
   d. 3, 4, and 12.

**200.** Effect is best illustrated by items numbered
   a. 3, 4, and 12.
   b. 5, 6, and 7.
   c. 1, 8, and 9.
   d. 2, 10, and 11.

**201.** Audit fieldwork has identified a number of significant findings. Additional audit tests from the original audit program still have to be performed; however, data are not readily available. Evaluate the following and select the **best** alternative.
   a. Do not issue the audit report until all testing has been completed.
   b. Issue an interim report to management regarding the negative findings noted.
   c. Identify other alternative tests to complete prior to reporting the audit findings.
   d. Perform audit tests when the final data is available.

**202.** Upon reviewing the results of the audit report with the audit committee, executive management agreed to accept the risk of not implementing corrective action on certain audit findings. Evaluate the following and select the **best** alternative for the internal auditing director.
   a. Notify regulatory authorities of management's decision.

   b. Perform additional audit steps to further identify the policy violations.
   c. Conduct a follow-up audit to determine whether corrective action was taken.
   d. Internal audit responsibility has been discharged, and no further audit action is required.

**203.** The internal auditing department for a chain of retail stores recently concluded an audit of sales adjustments in all stores in the southeast region. The audit revealed that several stores are costing the company an estimated $85,000 per quarter in duplicate credits to customers' charge accounts.

The audit report, published eight weeks after the audit was concluded, included the internal auditors' recommendations to store management that should prevent duplicate credits to customers' accounts. Which of the following standards for reporting has been disregarded in the above case?
   a. The follow-up actions were not adequate.
   b. The auditors should have implemented appropriate corrective action as soon as the duplicate credits were discovered.
   c. Auditor recommendations should not be included in the report.
   d. The report was not timely.

**204.** An audit finding is worded as follows:

The capital budget includes funds to purchase 11 new vehicles. Review of usage records showed that 10 vehicles in the fleet of 70 had been driven less than 2,500 miles during the past year. Vehicles have been assigned to different groups whose usage rates have varied greatly. There was no policy requiring rotation of vehicles between high- and low-usage groups. Lack of criteria for assigning vehicles and a system for monitoring their usage could lead to purchasing unneeded vehicles.

Based on the facts presented in this finding, it would be **appropriate** to recommend that management
   a. Establish a minimum of 2,500 miles per quarter as criteria for assigning vehicles to user groups.
   b. Establish a system to rotate vehicles among users periodically.
   c. Delay the proposed vehicle purchases until the apparent excess capacity is adequately explained or absorbed.
   d. Withhold approval of the capital budget until other projects can be reviewed by internal auditing.

**205.** An audit of a company's payroll department has revealed various control weaknesses. These weaknesses along with recommendations for corrective actions were addressed in the internal audit report. This report should be most useful to the company's
   a. Treasurer.
   b. Audit committee of the board of directors.
   c. Payroll manager.
   d. President.

**206.** The IIA *Standards* require that the director of internal auditing or designee decide to whom the final audit report will be distributed. Findings concerning significant internal control weakness are included in an audit report on the accounts payable system of a company whose securities are publicly traded. The director of internal auditing has chosen to send copies of this audit report to the audit committee and the external auditor. Which of the following is the **most likely** reason for distributing copies to the audit committee and the external auditor?

- a. The audit committee and external auditor are normally sent copies of all internal audit reports as a courtesy.
- b. The audit committee and external auditor will need to take corrective action on the deficiency findings.
- c. The activities of the audit committee and external auditor may be affected because of the potential for misstated financial statements.
- d. A regulatory agency's guidelines require such distribution.

**207.** An operational audit report that deals with the scrap disposal function in a manufacturing company should address

- a. The efficiency and effectiveness of the scrap disposal function and include any findings requiring corrective action.
- b. Whether the scrap material inventory is reported as a current asset.
- c. Whether the physical inventory count of the scrap material agrees with the recorded amount.
- d. Whether the scrap material inventory is valued at the lower of cost or market.

**208.** The internal auditing unit has recently completed an operational audit of its company's accounts payable function. The audit director decided to issue a summary report in conjunction with the final report. Who would be the most likely recipient(s) of just the summary audit report?

- a. Accounts payable manager.
- b. External auditor.
- c. Controller.
- d. Audit committee of the board of directors.

**209.** Which of the following is **not** an advantage of issuing an interim report?

- a. Final report-writing time can be minimized.
- b. An interim report allows information requiring immediate attention to be communicated.
- c. An interim report can be conducted on an informal basis and may be communicated only verbally.
- d. A formal, written interim report may negate the need for a final report in certain circumstances.

**210.** During the course of an audit of cash handling, the auditor notices that considerable cash is stored overnight in a work area that has ready access from a busy street. Furthermore, there is no security system or any armed guard in the vicinity. When discussed with the appropriate manager, the auditor is informed, "We have never experienced a robbery or loss of cash from this fund; why should we spend unnecessary amounts to improve security?" The auditor should

- a. Make a verbal interim report. In the final report, concentrate on the corrective measures to be taken.
- b. Explain all the facts but allow management the opportunity to tell their story so that corrective action is more likely to be adopted.
- c. Since the company has never suffered any losses from the cash-handling procedures, there is no need to report the finding.
- d. Widely distribute the report; this is a big problem that everyone in the company needs to know about.

**211.** Certain information may not be appropriate for disclosure to all report recipients because it is privileged, proprietary, or related to improper or illegal acts. If conditions being reported involve improper acts of a senior manager, the report should be distributed to

- a. The external auditor.
- b. The board of directors.
- c. The stockholders.
- d. Senior management.

**212.** Which of the following individuals would normally **not** receive an internal auditing report related to a review of the purchasing cycle?

- a. The director of purchasing.
- b. The independent external auditor.
- c. The general auditor.
- d. The chairman of the board of directors.

**Items 213 and 214** are based on the following:

An excerpt from an audit finding indicates that travel advances exceeded prescribed maximum amounts. Company policy provides travel funds to authorized employees for travel. Advances are not to exceed forty-five days of anticipated expenses. Company procedures do not require justification for large travel advances. Employees can and do accumulate large, unneeded advances.

**213.** The cause of the above audit finding is

- a. Company advance procedures do not require specific justification.
- b. Company policy provides travel funds to authorized employees.
- c. Employees accumulate large travel advances.
- d. Travel advances have not been cleared in timely manner.

**214.** In the above audit finding, the element of an audit finding known as "condition" is

- a. Advances are not to exceed estimated expenses for forty-five days.
- b. Employees accumulate large unneeded advances.
- c. Procedures do not require justification for large advances.
- d. Travel advances exceeded prescribed maximum amounts.

**215.** An internal auditor observed that assembly line personnel without protective clothing were being exposed to dangerous chemicals. The auditor should immediately notify management through the use of a(n)

- a. Summary written report.
- b. Formal written report.
- c. Follow-up report.
- d. Oral report.

**216.** An audit report with routine findings in the accounts payable department is being issued. Distribution should include the accounts payable supervisor, manager, and unit general manager. It may also be sent to the

- a. External auditors and the corporate controller.
- b. Unit purchasing manager and the operations director.
- c. Unit receiving manager, the purchasing manager and the operations director.
- d. External auditors, the corporate controller, and the chairman of the board of directors.

## MULTIPLE-CHOICE ANSWERS AND EXPLANATIONS

| | | | | |
|---|---|---|---|---|
| 1. a __ __ | 45. c __ __ | 89. d __ __ | 133. b __ __ | 177. a __ __ |
| 2. b __ __ | 46. d __ __ | 90. d __ __ | 134. a __ __ | 178. a __ __ |
| 3. c __ __ | 47. b __ __ | 91. a __ __ | 135. b __ __ | 179. d __ __ |
| 4. d __ __ | 48. b __ __ | 92. c __ __ | 136. c __ __ | 180. c __ __ |
| 5. d __ __ | 49. c __ __ | 93. b __ __ | 137. b __ __ | 181. a __ __ |
| 6. b __ __ | 50. d __ __ | 94. b __ __ | 138. b __ __ | 182. a __ __ |
| 7. b __ __ | 51. c __ __ | 95. d __ __ | 139. a __ __ | 183. c __ __ |
| 8. c __ __ | 52. b __ __ | 96. b __ __ | 140. c __ __ | 184. b __ __ |
| 9. b __ __ | 53. d __ __ | 97. d __ __ | 141. d __ __ | 185. a __ __ |
| 10. c __ __ | 54. d __ __ | 98. b __ __ | 142. b __ __ | 186. c __ __ |
| 11. a __ __ | 55. b __ __ | 99. c __ __ | 143. b __ __ | 187. a __ __ |
| 12. d __ __ | 56. b __ __ | 100. c __ __ | 144. d __ __ | 188. b __ __ |
| 13. c __ __ | 57. b __ __ | 101. b __ __ | 145. d __ __ | 189. a __ __ |
| 14. a __ __ | 58. d __ __ | 102. a __ __ | 146. c __ __ | 190. c __ __ |
| 15. b __ __ | 59. b __ __ | 103. d __ __ | 147. a __ __ | 191. d __ __ |
| 16. b __ __ | 60. c __ __ | 104. c __ __ | 148. b __ __ | 192. c __ __ |
| 17. a __ __ | 61. c __ __ | 105. c __ __ | 149. d __ __ | 193. a __ __ |
| 18. c __ __ | 62. d __ __ | 106. d __ __ | 150. c __ __ | 194. d __ __ |
| 19. d __ __ | 63. a __ __ | 107. c __ __ | 151. a __ __ | 195. d __ __ |
| 20. c __ __ | 64. d __ __ | 108. a __ __ | 152. c __ __ | 196. b __ __ |
| 21. d __ __ | 65. b __ __ | 109. d __ __ | 153. d __ __ | 197. a __ __ |
| 22. a __ __ | 66. c __ __ | 110. d __ __ | 154. a __ __ | 198. b __ __ |
| 23. b __ __ | 67. c __ __ | 111. a __ __ | 155. c __ __ | 199. c __ __ |
| 24. a __ __ | 68. d __ __ | 112. b __ __ | 156. b __ __ | 200. b __ __ |
| 25. c __ __ | 69. d __ __ | 113. c __ __ | 157. d __ __ | 201. b __ __ |
| 26. d __ __ | 70. c __ __ | 114. a __ __ | 158. a __ __ | 202. d __ __ |
| 27. a __ __ | 71. b __ __ | 115. b __ __ | 159. a __ __ | 203. d __ __ |
| 28. d __ __ | 72. d __ __ | 116. b __ __ | 160. a __ __ | 204. c __ __ |
| 29. b __ __ | 73. c __ __ | 117. a __ __ | 161. b __ __ | 205. c __ __ |
| 30. d __ __ | 74. d __ __ | 118. c __ __ | 162. d __ __ | 206. c __ __ |
| 31. d __ __ | 75. c __ __ | 119. c __ __ | 163. a __ __ | 207. a __ __ |
| 32. b __ __ | 76. c __ __ | 120. c __ __ | 164. b __ __ | 208. d __ __ |
| 33. a __ __ | 77. a __ __ | 121. c __ __ | 165. b __ __ | 209. d __ __ |
| 34. a __ __ | 78. b __ __ | 122. c __ __ | 166. a __ __ | 210. a __ __ |
| 35. c __ __ | 79. b __ __ | 123. c __ __ | 167. d __ __ | 211. b __ __ |
| 36. d __ __ | 80. b __ __ | 124. d __ __ | 168. c __ __ | 212. d __ __ |
| 37. b __ __ | 81. b __ __ | 125. c __ __ | 169. d __ __ | 213. a __ __ |
| 38. b __ __ | 82. d __ __ | 126. a __ __ | 170. d __ __ | 214. d __ __ |
| 39. a __ __ | 83. d __ __ | 127. c __ __ | 171. c __ __ | 215. d __ __ |
| 40. b __ __ | 84. a __ __ | 128. b __ __ | 172. a __ __ | 216. a __ __ |
| 41. a __ __ | 85. c __ __ | 129. b __ __ | 173. b __ __ | |
| 42. a __ __ | 86. d __ __ | 130. b __ __ | 174. b __ __ | |
| 43. c __ __ | 87. c __ __ | 131. d __ __ | 175. a __ __ | 1st: __/216 = __% |
| 44. a __ __ | 88. a __ __ | 132. a __ __ | 176. d __ __ | 2nd: __/216 = __% |

### Collect Data and Evaluate Audit Evidence

**1.** **(a)** Revenue per representative measures productivity because it relates an output to input. It is better than the other responses as explained below. Choice (b) is incorrect. Choice (a) is better than choice (b) because number of sales calls does not measure output. Choice (c) is incorrect. Choice (a) is better than choice (c) because the higher ratio could be achieved even if unit sales, revenue, and gross profit declined and the number of sales representatives increased. Choice (d) is incorrect. Choice (a) is better than choice (d) because the unit sales increase could be achieved by an uneconomic addition of sales representatives and would not necessarily result in higher revenue.

Subject Area: Conduct audit engagements—audit evidence. Source: CIA 1195, II-5.

**2.** **(b)** The auditee cannot alter an external document obtained directly from its source. Choice (a) is incorrect. The auditee may alter internal documents. Choice (c) is incorrect. The auditee may alter internal documents, even if internal control procedures are followed. Choice (d) is incorrect. Circulation through an outside party does not mean the document is correct, unless it is received directly by the auditor.

Subject Area: Conduct audit engagements—audit evidence. Source: CIA 596, II-4.

**3.** **(c)** This would permit the supplier to "increase" his profit without actually raising the price. Choice (a) is incorrect. This is a violation of the purchasing manager's mandate. Choice (b) is incorrect. This is not a way to circumvent the purchasing manager's mandate. It follows the choices enumerated by the purchasing manager. Choice (d) is incorrect. This action does not provide enough information to determine if the supplier violated the purchasing manager's mandate.

Subject Area: Conduct audit engagements—audit evidence. Source: CIA 596, II-5.

**4.** **(d)** From the information given, none of the conclusions above is correct. Choice (a) is incorrect. The deviation rate applies to errors that were noted in the sample. The 15 items on which loans were not made are not necessarily errors. Choice (b) is incorrect. There is no evidence that there is a problem with the processing. Choice (c) is incorrect. There is no evidence that the loans made (or not made) comply with company procedures.

Subject Area: Conduct audit engagements—audit evidence. Source: CIA 1195, I-1.

**5.** **(d)** This is the most comprehensive answer. All of the actions are appropriate. Choice (a) is incorrect. The deviation rate is greater than 4% (4/85), but choice (d) is more comprehensive. Choice (b) is incorrect. The auditor should examine the nature of the loans, but choice (d) is more comprehensive. Choice (c) is incorrect. The item should be reported in the auditor's report, but choice (d) is more comprehensive.

Subject Area: Conduct audit engagements—audit evidence. Source: CIA 1195, I-2.

**6.** **(b)** The loans were not approved in a timely fashion prior to funding according to company policies and procedures. Therefore, it should be reported as a deviation, and the auditor should note that the loan committee subsequently reviewed the loans. Choice (a) is incorrect. The loan was not approved in accordance with company policies; therefore, the four items are still deviations and the rate would not drop to zero. Choice (c) is incorrect. The loans were not processed in accordance with company policy and therefore represent deviations. Choice (d) is incorrect. Items I and III are not correct actions.

Subject Area: Conduct audit engagements—audit evidence. Source: CIA 1195, I-3.

**7.** **(b)** This is the least appropriate response per the IIA *Standards*. Choice (a) is incorrect. This is an appropriate follow-up action. The auditor should attempt to determine the causes of audit findings and, where appropriate, include them in the audit report. Choice (c) is incorrect. This is an appropriate follow-up step to determine the cause of the audit finding. Choice (d) is incorrect. The action is appropriate as long as the auditor has concluded that the amounts are clearly not material and not in violation of governmental regulations and that a rationale for the deviations exist.

Subject Area: Conduct audit engagements—audit evidence. Source: CIA 1195, I-4.

**8.** **(c)** Both II and IV are appropriate. The auditor should independently determine the significance of the finding and should consult outside legal services if deemed appropriate. It would also be appropriate to review plans taken by the loan committee and include that analysis in the audit report. Choice (a) is incorrect. Item D represents a violation of good business practice and, statistics not withstanding, should therefore is reported. The need to include an item in an audit report is based on the significance of the finding, not just the tolerable error rate. Further, the upper error rate (although not computed here) would be higher

than the tolerable error rate. Choice (b) is incorrect. This would not be appropriate because it may represent significant violations of both federal regulations and company policy. Waiting a full year for follow-up action without reaching a conclusion on the seriousness of the problem would not be appropriate. Choice (d) is incorrect. Item IV is also an appropriate response.

Subject Area: Conduct audit engagements—audit evidence. Source: CIA 1195, I-5

**9.** **(b)** The auditor should attempt to determine the cause of the deficiencies and include constructive suggestions in the audit report. See Section 430 of the IIA *Standards*. Choice (a) is incorrect. Even though the loan committee approved the loans, the procedure was not conducted in accordance with company policies. Choice (c) is incorrect. The findings should be included in an audit report with a recommendation that management perform follow-up to determine the causes of the deviations and take corrective action. Choice (d) is incorrect. Response (c) is not correct.

Subject Area: Conduct audit engagements—audit evidence. Source: CIA 1195, I-6.

**10.** **(c)** The receiving memorandum indicates that the goods were received; therefore, a purchase transaction has occurred. Choice (a) is incorrect. The canceled check indicates that the goods have been paid for, not received. Choice (b) is incorrect. The supervisor's signature indicates the ordering of the goods was authorized, not that the goods were received. Choice (d) is incorrect. The invoice indicates the goods have been billed but provides no evidence as to their receipt.

Subject Area: Conduct audit engagements—audit evidence. Source: CIA 596, II-14.

**11.** **(a)** The conclusion about 95% confidence level is unjustified because the statistical parameters of the account balance are not known. Further, it is incorrect to assume no material differences exist in the account balance just because the bank agreed to adjust the account balances to the errors found. Choice (b) is incorrect. Response II is incorrect. Choice (c) is incorrect. The conclusion reached in Response III is valid. The auditor has examined both internal and external documentation to reach this conclusion. Choice (d) is incorrect. Response III is a valid conclusion.

Subject Area: Conduct audit engagements—audit evidence. Source: CIA 595, II-14.

**12.** **(d)** Items I and IV represent external evidence received directly by the auditor, and both have a high degree of reliability. Item IV merits further investigation because customers sometimes make mistakes. Item III is ranked third because it contains a combination of internal evidence (loan contract, payments, etc.) and external evidence (a current payment for the correct amount on the account balance). Item II is the least reliable because, although it comes from an outside party, it was derived in direct response to pressure from management. Choice (a), (b), and (c) are incorrect. See the rationale in choice (d).

Subject Area: Conduct audit engagements—audit evidence. Source: CIA 595, II-15.

**13.** **(c)** Only Item II is a justifiable conclusion. The auditor can conclude that the recorded account balance does exist per the IIA Standard. Choice (a) is incorrect. Item I is not justified because the auditor is aware that a number of loans are made to holding companies, all controlled by one entity. Until the auditor examines the nature of the holding companies, no conclusion can be made regarding this assertion. Choice (b) is incorrect. Item I is not justified because the auditor is aware that a number of loans are made to holding companies, all controlled by one entity. Until the auditor examines the nature of the holding companies, no conclusion can be made regarding this assertion. Choice (d) is incorrect. Items I and III are not justified. The loans should be valued at net realizable value. The auditor has only gathered information on the gross amount of the loans receivable.

Subject Area: Conduct audit engagements—audit evidence. Source: CIA 595, II-16.

**14. (a)** An integrated test facility (ITF) only provides assurance about the correctness of processing of the computer portion of the application. It does not provide evidence on existence and valuation. To do so, there must be complementary audit procedures to see that all loans are initially entered into the computer application. Choice (b) is incorrect. The ITF does not provide evidence on existence and valuation. To do so, there must be complementary audit procedures to see that all loans are initially entered into the computer application. Choice (c) is incorrect. Item IV is addressed, but not item I. Choice (d) is incorrect. Items I and II are not addressed. See choice (a) or (b).

Subject Area: Conduct audit engagements—audit evidence. Source: CIA 595, II-17.

**15. (b)** This would be the least effective audit procedure. There are two problems with it: (1) It deals with normal processing of account transactions, not with potential write-off or extra collection efforts on the accounts; and (2) there is always the danger that the flowcharts may be out of date per the IIA *Standards*. Choice (a) is incorrect. The auditor can custom design a questionnaire to gather key information on the processes used in evaluating collectibility and the individuals responsible for actions. Choice (c) is incorrect. Inquiries would be an effective procedure and could easily be documented in a narrative. Choice (d) is incorrect. A flowchart of key decisions and flow of information regarding collectibilty might be useful. Flowcharts need not be limited to the ordinary processing of transactions.

Subject Area: Conduct audit engagements—audit evidence. Source: CIA 595, II-18.

**16. (b)** This is the most persuasive evidence because the auditor reviews actual documents and finds out what personnel actually do with the documents. Choice (a) is incorrect. This is less persuasive because the systems flowchart might not indicate how processing may have evolved over time. Choice (c) is incorrect. The program flowchart shows only the computer program portion of the application. Choice (d) is incorrect. The manager may not know how the specific clerical processing may have changed. Further, the manager may be biased in presenting a picture of processing that might not reflect actual processing.

Subject Area: Conduct audit engagements—audit evidence. Source: CIA 595, I-6.

**17. (a)** Employee morale is important and often is a side-benefit of total quality management programs. However, employee morale is not a sufficient reason to implement TQM; there should be some evidence of greater customer satisfaction or reduced costs. Choice (b) is incorrect.

Reduction in scrap should be one of the outcomes as TQM is implemented. Choice (c) is incorrect. TQM should lead to product quality improvements resulting in a lower level of customer returns. Choice (d) is incorrect. TQM is supposed to reduce costs.

Subject Area: Conduct audit engagements—audit evidence. Source: CIA 595, I-9.

**18. (c)** Item IV. This is the most persuasive because it uses an external source. Inventory should be valued at the lower of cost or market. Thus, it is important to first begin with the establishment of cost. Item I Changes in inventory turnover or a very low level of inventory turnover indicates potential obsolescence of inventory and that the auditor should do more investigation, for example, looking at subsequent sales to determine whether inventory should be written down. Item iii. Calculation of net realizable value is a good indication of a lower of cost or market problem. The only difficulty with this procedure is that the auditor needs to make sure that the sales prices used in the calculation are for sufficient amounts to support the conclusion about existing inventory quantities. This evidence is useful, but it is a form of testimonial evidence from an individual who may have a biased, or vested, interest in persuading the auditor that the goods will be sold at their normal prices in the normal course of business. Item II. In addition, the arbitrary cutoff value of 2.0 may not be justified. The cutoff should be based on the nature of the client's inventory.

Subject Area: Conduct audit engagements—audit evidence. Source: CIA 595, I-10.

**19. (d)** The auditor is interested in whether the actual claims paid are properly supported. The most appropriate population from which to sample is the claims-paid file. Choice (a) is incorrect. Sampling from a population of policyholders would be very inefficient for the audit assertion, as many policyholders may not have any activity during the year. Choice (b) is incorrect. A sample of claims filed does provide evidence on the overall processing of claims and thus provides some evidence related to the assertion. However, given the assertion, choice (a) is more efficient because it deals with paid claims. Choice (c) is incorrect. The claims denied filed provides evidence on the claims denied, but the auditor cannot conclude that all claims that were not denied should have been paid.

Subject Area: Conduct audit engagements—audit evidence. Source: CIA 595, I-11.

**20. (c)** The reader, given this information, may not need to know any of the other details. Choice (a) is incorrect. Although the reader needs to know this negative information, emphasizing it will make the reader unduly concerned about the progress of the project. Choice (b) is incorrect. This news, which may require approval of the reader, is otherwise relatively unimportant. Choice (d) is incorrect. The information is relatively unimportant.

Subject Area: Conduct audit engagements—audit evidence. Source: CIA 1196, II-4.

**21. (d)** Both initial placement and active voice are strong ways to emphasize information. Choice (a) is incorrect. Both middle placement and passive voice subordinate information. Choice (b) is incorrect. Middle placement subordinates information. Choice (c) is incorrect. Passive voice subordinates information.

Subject Area: Conduct audit engagements—audit evidence. Source: CIA 1196, II-5.

**22. (a)** Choice (a) is the correct answer. This gives the reader a context in which to understand both the magnitude of the request and the reason for it. Choice (b) is incorrect. An unbudgeted expenditure is relevant. Choice (c) is incorrect. The expenditure is not important enough, by itself, to emphasize. Choice (d) is incorrect. Omitting negative information from a report will not avoid criticism when the reader finds out that the writer is hiding things.

Subject Area: Conduct audit engagements—audit evidence. Source: CIA 1196, II-6.

**23. (b)** The validity of documentary evidence depends on the internal control system. Choices (a), (c), and (d) are incorrect because each choice is a true statement.

Subject Area: Conduct audit engagements—audit evidence. Source: CIA 594, II-47.

**24. (a)** Written inquiry/confirmation obtained from outside third parties is more persuasive than internal company documents. Choice (b) is incorrect. Evidence obtained under conditions of strong control is always more persuasive than if controls had been weak. Choice (c) is incorrect. Personal knowledge is generally more persuasive than knowledge obtained from other parties. Choice (d) is incorrect. Generally evidence from outside the organization is more persuasive than evidence obtained from organizational sources. The above justifications are based on the general theory of audit evidence.

Subject Area: Conduct audit engagements—audit evidence. Source: CIA 594, I-1.

**25. (c)** Examination of the asset is generally considered one of the most persuasive types of evidence for the "existence" assertion, if not the most persuasive type. Choice (a) is incorrect. Unsubstantiated inquiry of management is generally considered the least persuasive evidence. Choice (b) is incorrect. Observation of procedures for acquisition would not be as persuasive as examination of the asset. Choice (d) is incorrect. Documentation is less relevant for existence than is physical examination of the asset.

Subject Area: Conduct audit engagements—audit evidence. Source: CIA 594, I-21.

**26. (d)** Documentation of the purchase provides very persuasive evidence regarding the cost of the asset. Choice (a) is incorrect. Unsubstantiated inquiry of management is generally considered the least persuasive evidence. Choice (b) is incorrect. Observation of procedures for acquisition would not be as persuasive as documents showing the cost of the asset. Choice (c) is incorrect. Physical examination of the asset reveals only limited information as to the asset's value.

Subject Area: Conduct audit engagements—audit evidence. Source: CIA 594, I-22.

**27. (a)** Evidence is arranged in general order of persuasiveness. Choices (b), (c), and (d) are incorrect because inquiry of management is considered one of the least persuasive evidence types, particularly in regard to physical examination.

Subject Area: Conduct audit engagements—audit evidence. Source: CIA 594, I-23.

**28. (d)** Aging of receivables lends direct, relevant evidence regarding the valuation of receivables and thus the allowance account. Choice (a) is incorrect. Although some valuation information is implied from the confirmation, aging is more relevant and persuasive. Choice (b) is incorrect. One month's receipts is too little information on which to base the collectibility of accounts. Choice (c) is incorrect. Controls over write-offs is not relevant to the account's valuation, but to the authorization of the write-off.

Subject Area: Conduct audit engagements—audit evidence. Source: CIA 594, I-24.

**29. (b)** A list prepared from the company's notes would not include unrecorded notes. Choice (a) is incorrect. Bank confirmations are relevant and a common audit procedure for unrecorded liability tests. Choice (c) is incorrect. Comparison to previous year's outstanding debt and verifying payment or inclusion on this year's disclosure is a relevant and common procedure. Choice (d) is incorrect. Analytical tests of interest expense to debt is relevant and a common audit procedure.

Subject Area: Conduct audit engagements—audit evidence. Source: CIA 594, I-25.

**30. (d)** A payroll account proof would test for completeness but not for validity of cash flow. Choice (a) is incorrect. Verification that an employee is actually working is a common procedure to test for nonexistent employees. Choice (b) is incorrect. Examining for proper endorsements and comparing to records would possibly detect improper payments. Choice (c) is incorrect. Segregation of payroll authorization from hire/fire would help to eliminate fictitious employees.

Subject Area: Conduct audit engagements—audit evidence. Source: CIA 594, I-26.

**31. (d)** Statement I is relevant. Choice (a) is incorrect. Although relevant, it is neither sufficient nor competent. Choice (b) is incorrect. Statement I is not sufficient or competent. Choice (c) is incorrect. Statement I is not sufficient.

Subject Area: Conduct audit engagements—audit evidence. Source: CIA 1193, I-15.

**32. (b)** Statement II is sufficient (factual, adequate, and convincing), competent (reliable and the best attainable through appropriate audit techniques), and relevant (consistent with audit objectives). Choice (a) is incorrect. Statement II is competent and relevant. Choice (c) is incorrect. Statement II is all three. Choice (d) is incorrect. Statement II is sufficient and competent.

Subject Area: Conduct audit engagements—audit evidence. Source: CIA 1193, I-16.

**33. (a)** The fewer the adjustments, the higher the production quality. Choice (b) is incorrect. Labor efficiency variances relate to inputs of labor and do not relate directly to quality of production. Choice (c) is incorrect. Materials efficiency variances relate to inputs of materials and do not relate directly to quality of production. Choice (d) is incorrect. Production/inventory/sales mix is meaningless.

Subject Area: Conduct audit engagements—audit evidence. Source: CIA 591, II-22.

**34. (a)** A confirmation from a customer is the most reliable evidence that a receivable exists. Choice (b) is incorrect. An invoice is not particularly reliable because it is not developed external to the company. Choice (c) is incorrect.

This is not evidence of a receivable. Choice (d) is incorrect. This is not as reliable as a confirmation.

Subject Area: Conduct audit engagements—audit evidence. Source: CIA 591, II-16.

**35.** **(c)** A physical inspection provides the best evidence of current condition. Choice (a) is incorrect. Testimonial evidence, standing alone, is not conclusive. Choice (b) is incorrect. The record of repair and maintenance costs is an internal record providing little evidence of current condition. Choice (d) is incorrect. As an internal document, the production department's downtime report provides little persuasive evidence of current condition.

Subject Area: Conduct audit engagements—audit evidence. Source: CIA 591, II-27.

**36.** **(d)** The procedure providing the best evidence of the collectibility of notes receivable. Choice (a) is incorrect. Confirmation establishes existence, not collectibility. Choice (b) is incorrect. Inspection helps verify the validity (not collectibility) of the notes. Choice (c) is incorrect. This merely tests bookkeeping procedures.

Subject Area: Conduct audit engagements—audit evidence. Source: CIA 1191, II-25.

**37.** **(b)** An aging schedule is a primary means of assessing valuation. Choice (a) is incorrect. Positive confirmations primarily indicate existence of the receivable, but not valuation. Choice (c) is incorrect. Analytical procedures provide little direct evidence of valuation. Choice (d) is incorrect. Valuation of the total accounts receivable is determined by probability of collection rather than mathematical correctness of extensions.

Subject Area: Conduct audit engagements—audit evidence. Source: CIA 1191, II-15.

**38.** **(b)** Competent evidence is reliable. It is the best available. An original document is the prime example of such evidence, per the IIA *Standards*. Choice (a) is incorrect. Sufficiency has to do with factual, adequate and convincing evidence. The information contained on the document may be none of those things. Choice (c) is incorrect. Relevancy has to do with the relationship of the evidence to some objective of the audit. Since no audit objective is disclosed in the stem of the question, the observer has no way to tell whether the information on the document is or is not relevant to the investigation. Choice (d) is incorrect. Usefulness is achieved if the item of evidence helps the organization (the auditor, in this case) to accomplish predetermined goals. Since no such goals are specified, there is no way to determine whether the information on the document will help the auditor accomplish some goal established for the audit.

Subject Area: Conduct audit engagements—audit evidence. Source: CIA 1191, II-18.

**39.** **(a)** The observation of people, property and events, which takes graphic form, is "physical evidence." Choice (b) is incorrect. Interviewing people produces "testimonial evidence." Choice (c) is incorrect. The examination of records requires "documentary evidence" and produces "analytical evidence." Choice (d) is incorrect. Computations and verifications lead to "analytical evidence."

Subject Area: Conduct audit engagements—audit evidence. Source: CIA 1191, II-19.

**40.** **(b)** Competent evidence is the best, which is available to the internal auditor. It is also reliable for audit judgments. Choice (a) is incorrect. Sufficient evidence is factual, convincing, and adequate. It would enable a reasonably prudent person to reach the internal auditor's conclusion. Choice (c) is incorrect. Relevant evidence has a logical connection to its intended use. Choice (d) is incorrect. Documentary evidence is available in written form, such as accounting records and receipts.

Subject Area: Conduct audit engagements—audit evidence. Source: CIA 1191, II-20.

**41.** **(a)** A sample need only provide reasonable assurance. Because of cost-benefit considerations, absolute assurance is not necessary. Choice (b) is incorrect. The best reasonably obtainable is a test of competence. Choice (c) is incorrect. The logical relationship is a test of relevance. Choice (d) is incorrect. Because of cost-benefit considerations, absolute assurance is not necessary.

Subject Area: Conduct audit engagements—audit evidence. Source: CIA 1191, II-21.

**42.** **(a)** All graphic evidence is classified as "physical." This includes such other forms as graphs, charts, and maps. Choice (b) is incorrect. "Testimonial" evidence is restricted to the written response to inquiry or interview. Choice (c) is incorrect. "Documentary" evidence is nongraphical. It takes the form of records, memoranda, correspondence, and related written material. Choice (d) is incorrect. "Analytical" evidence is the result of the division of a complex entity into its constituent parts, with the subsequent review of each subset of the original whole.

Subject Area: Conduct audit engagements—audit evidence. Source: CIA 1191, I-19.

**43.** **(c)** "Documentary" evidence is any nongraphical item that is already in existence at the time the evidence is sought. Choice (a) is incorrect. All graphical evidence is "physical." Choice (b) is incorrect. All statements received in response to inquiries or interviews are "testimonial." Choice (d) is incorrect. All evidence of the process leading to a conclusion is "analytical."

Subject Area: Conduct audit engagements—audit evidence. Source: CIA 1191, I-20.

**44.** **(a)** Physical observation provides evidence that can be given full reliance. Choice (b) is incorrect. Items purchased may no longer reside in the department being audited, even though they were originally purchased for that department. Choice (c) is incorrect. Interviews are useful in gaining insight into operations and understanding exceptions, but are not sufficient by themselves. Choice (d) is incorrect. Ledger balances may not indicate if assets have been moved or stolen.

Subject Area: Conduct audit engagements—audit evidence. Source: CIA 1191, I-22.

**45.** **(c)** Verification is the process of determining the validity of previously provided information. Choice (a) is incorrect. Analysis is pointed toward the "why" objective. Choice (b) is incorrect. Evaluation involves weighing what has been gathered. It would not be appropriate for the yes and no responses of an ICQ. Choice (d) is incorrect. Observation is a physical exploration process.

Subject Area: Conduct audit engagements—audit evidence. Source: CIA 592, II-14.

**46. (d)** This is one of the quoted qualities of sufficiency. Choice (a) is incorrect. This is a mechanical aspect of evidence; it has no specific relationship to any of the characteristics of evidence. Choice (b) is incorrect. This is a quality of competence of evidence. Choice (c) is incorrect. This is a quality of relevance of evidence.

Subject Area: Conduct audit engagements—audit evidence. Source: CIA 592, II-21.

**47. (b)** Analytical evidence includes comparisons with budgeted amounts, past operations, and similar operations. Choices (a), (c), and (d) are incorrect because these are detailed tests, not a study of relationships.

Subject Area: Conduct audit engagements—audit evidence. Source: CIA 592, II-10.

**48. (b)** This definition properly implies the inclusion of physical, testimonial, documentary, and analytical evidence per the IIA *Standards*. Choice (a) is incorrect. This is the definition of working papers, not of evidence. The records of preliminary planning, for example, do not constitute audit evidence. Choice (c) is incorrect. This is a modified definition of circumstantial evidence. It does not leave room for direct evidence, such as counting cash on hand. Choice (d) is incorrect. This is the definition of deficiency findings, not of evidence. Evidence underlies positive, as well as negative, findings.

Subject Area: Conduct audit engagements—audit evidence. Source: CIA 1192, II-25.

**49. (c)** This is the most persuasive form of documentary evidence because it is received directly from a knowledgeable third party. Choice (a) is incorrect. Documentary evidence in the hands of the auditee does not relate directly to the receivable. Choice (b) is incorrect. Documentary evidence which is not original and which is completely controlled by the auditee is not the most persuasive evidence. Choice (d) is incorrect. While such documents are originated by third parties, the auditee has an opportunity to alter them, hence this is not the most persuasive evidence.

Subject Area: Conduct audit engagements—audit evidence. Source: CIA 1192, II-26.

**50. (d)** This is the procedure giving the best evidence of completeness of recorded revenues. Choice (a) and (b) are incorrect because they would fail to detect unrecorded sales, which would result in no entries to the sales journal or accounts receivable. Choice (c) is incorrect because it merely establishes that goods shipped were ordered, not that they were recorded as sales.

Subject Area: Conduct audit engagements—audit evidence. Source: CIA 1192, II-13.

**51. (c)** This would provide personal knowledge of existence of the inventory. This is direct and conclusive evidence, which is the highest form of evidence per the IIA *Standards*. Choice (a) is incorrect. This would provide a fairly low form of documentary evidence, which is not as good as personal knowledge. Choice (b) is incorrect. This would provide a high form of documentary evidence, but it is not as good as personal knowledge. Choice (d) is incorrect. This would provide a fairly high form of documentary evidence, but it is not as good as personal knowledge.

Subject Area: Conduct audit engagements—audit evidence. Source: CIA 1192, I-27.

**52. (b)** This includes both internal and external evidence. The evidence was generated internally, but it passed through outsiders who did something to confirm it before it went directly to the auditor. This is high-quality evidence, which is very persuasive. Choice (a) is incorrect. The auditee has either initiated or had an opportunity to alter all of this evidence, and this adversely affects its persuasiveness. Choice (c) is incorrect. This is internal evidence. Choice (d) is incorrect. This includes external evidence of debt but not of payment. The evidence concerning payment is internal and not strong at all, that is, it is reference to a check and not the check itself. This is a not very persuasive form of documentary evidence.

Subject Area: Conduct audit engagements—audit evidence. Source: CIA 1192, I-28.

**53. (d)** This evidence can be considered the most persuasive. Choices (a) and (b) are incorrect. This evidence would require corroboration since it is internal. Choice (c) is incorrect. This evidence may attest to the accuracy of vendor shipments but it does not verify that the clerks actually make an independent count.

Subject Area: Conduct audit engagements—audit evidence. Source: CIA 1193, II-14.

**54. (d)** Evidence is not convincing. Choice (a) is incorrect because the firm's advertising director and the firm's product marketing director are not objective (competent). Choice (b) is incorrect because the information is relevant, but it is not sufficient. Choice (c) is incorrect because it cannot be conclusive because the information is not competent and relevant.

Subject Area: Conduct audit engagements—audit evidence. Source: CIA 1193, II-17.

**55. (b)** The evidence is sufficient (factual, adequate, and convincing), competent (reliable and the best attainable through appropriate audit techniques), and relevant (consistent with audit objectives). Choice (a) is incorrect. The evidence is competent and relevant. Choice (c) is incorrect. The evidence is sufficient, competent, and relevant. Choice (d) is incorrect. The evidence is sufficient and competent.

Subject Area: Conduct audit engagements—audit evidence. Source: CIA 597, I-6.

**56. (b)** The purpose of the credit-granting function is to minimize write-offs while at the same time accepting sales likely to result in collection. Reviewing the trend in write-offs will provide some insight concerning the minimization of write-offs. Choice (a) is incorrect. Observation will provide evidence on whether the credit personnel are following the procedures while being observed. However, since they know they are being watched, they will probably do what they believe they should do, not what they normally do. Choice (c) is incorrect. Responses from the credit manager will lack objectivity, a key attribute of competent evidence. Choice (d) is incorrect. The credit limits may be set too high or not properly revised every six months. The existence of approval will not detect these problems.

Subject Area: Conduct audit engagements—audit evidence. Source: CIA 597, I-23.

**57. (b)** The only way the quick ratio could be decreasing while the current ratio is increasing is if cash or accounts receivable has decreased (item II). Choice (a) (item I) is incorrect. Sales are constant, but number of days sales in inventory has increased. Therefore, production or raw materials would have increased. Choice (c) and choice (d)(Item III) are incorrect because there is no information given regarding the gross margin.

Subject Area: Conduct audit engagements—audit evidence. Source: CIA 597, II-8.

**58. (d)** Each of the three items is a potential explanation for the increase in gross margin.

Subject Area: Conduct audit engagements—audit evidence. Source: CIA 597, II-10.

**59. (b)** An analysis of operations would be relevant in determining the efficiency of operations. Choice (a) is incorrect. This procedure would be useful to determine if the cause was due to overstated inventory. Choice (c) is incorrect. Changes in equipment may signal an improvement in efficiency, but would not be as relevant as choice (b). Choice (d) is incorrect. This procedure would be relevant in determining the correctness of raw material purchases, but would not provide any evidence regarding the efficiency of operations.

Subject Area: Conduct audit engagements—audit evidence. Source: CIA 597, II-11.

**60. (c)** A representative sample is more likely to lead to a proper conclusion about a population than a sample that is not representative of the population. Choice (a) is incorrect. Accounts receivable cannot be observed. Choice (b) is incorrect. Purchase orders are evidence of authorization of a purchase, not of the actual receipt of the items ordered. Choice (d) is incorrect. Copies of original documents can be doctored to change information contained on the original document. Therefore, original documents are more reliable.

Subject Area: Conduct audit engagements—audit evidence. Source: CIA 597, II-14.

**61. (c)** Both statements I and III are correct. Observation provides a good oversight on the nature of processing. Choice (a) is incorrect. This statement is true, but so is statement III. One of the limitations of observation is that individuals may act differently when observed than they otherwise do normally. Choice (b) is incorrect. Observation is more persuasive for the existence assertion than for the completeness assertion. Choice (d) is incorrect because statement II is not correct.

Subject Area: Conduct audit engagements—audit evidence. Source: CIA 1196, II-3.

**62. (d)** Magazines and textbooks are two of many sources of information available to the auditor for the assessment of risks. Choice (a) is incorrect. A reminder list is used in planning an audit, not for data gathering. Reminder lists help organize working papers more methodically and make subsequent audit steps easier (source: Sawyer's Internal Auditing, IIA). Choice (b) is incorrect. A flowchart is a portrait of a process. Flowcharts can also bring key controls into sharper focus. The flowchart however is not suitable for identifying measures of audit risk (source: Sawyer's Internal Auditing IIA). Choice (c) is incorrect. Questions (questionnaires) are developed from permanent files, prior audit reports, and management's charter. A questionnaire might be used to determine if risk is present, but is not suitable for determining a measure of audit risk (source: Sawyer's Internal Auditing IIA).

Subject Area: Conduct audit engagements—audit evidence. Source: CIA 596, II-7.

**63. (a)** Ascertaining the completeness of the plan as to all key functions, the needed facilities, and the supporting elements in the organization best meet the audit objective of "adequacy." Choice (b) is incorrect. Scope is too limited to provide a good indication of adequacy of the plan. Choice (c) is incorrect. Determining the stage of development of the plan is important but is of little help in determining adequacy of the total plan. Choice (d) is incorrect. The role of internal auditing can be helpful in assuring the quality of the plan, but does not assure adequacy. If the role has been fulfilled, then this aspect is potentially of great value in assuring adequacy.

Subject Area: Conduct audit engagements—audit evidence. Source: CIA 590, II-13.

**64. (d)** Shipping records form a link to recorded sales. Choices (a), (b), and (c) are incorrect because they are not connected with recording of revenues.

Subject Area: Conduct audit engagements—audit evidence. Source: CIA 590, II-14.

**65. (b)** This defines competent information. Choice (a) is incorrect. This defines sufficient information. Choice (c) is incorrect. This defines relevant information. Choice (d) is incorrect. This defines useful information.

Subject Area: Conduct audit engagements—audit evidence. Source: CIA 590, II-16.

**66. (c)** Standard bank confirmation inquiries prepared independently of company records is not only compelling in that it was prepared by a party independent of the company but also would lead to the detection of any restrictions on cash. Choice (a) is incorrect. This analytical evidence would be one item reviewed, but it is less compelling than evidence from an external source. Choice (b) is incorrect. Testimonial evidence drawn from company officials is not as strong as external evidence. Choice (d) is incorrect. Analytical computations would be less likely to identify major misstatements in cash than would an independent source such as bank confirmation.

Subject Area: Conduct audit engagements—audit evidence. Source: CIA 1190, I-19.

**67. (c)** This is the best evidential matter for an auditor to utilize. It reflects how long the accounts receivable are outstanding and puts overdue accounts in perspective. This is the primary document to work from in utilizing other audit procedures, such as discussions with management and review of confirmation replies. Choice (a) is incorrect. It is a valid audit procedure regarding the validity, not necessarily the collectibility, of accounts receivable. Choice (b) is incorrect. It is a valid audit procedure regarding the validity, not necessarily the collectibility, of accounts receivable. Choice (d) is incorrect. Although discussion with management about the collectibility of accounts receivable is part of the overall process, it cannot be considered as a primary procedure since management's responses could be self-serving.

Subject Area: Conduct audit engagements—audit evidence. Source: CIA 1190, I-20.

**68. (d)** Evidence that the material was ordered (purchase order), valid (receiving reports), and best priced (bid quotes) is cited. Choice (a) is incorrect. Evidence of receipt (receiving report) is necessary to confirm validity. Choice (b) is incorrect. Evidence of recording (journal voucher entry) is needed as a starting point. Choice (c) is incorrect. Evidence of best price (bid quotes) is needed.

Subject Area: Conduct audit engagements—audit evidence. Source: CIA 590, II-15.

**69. (d)** Relevant information supports the audit findings and is consistent with the audit objectives. Choice (a) is incorrect. Although an accepted audit procedure, this does not address the basis for information requirements. Choice (b) is incorrect. Being objective and unbiased does not assure that information will be consistent with the audit objectives. Choice (c) is incorrect. Such information is "sufficient" so that a prudent, informed person would reach the same conclusion as the auditor.

Subject Area: Conduct audit engagements—audit evidence. Source: CIA 1190, II-20.

**70. (c)** It is not complete—there is no substantive testing. Choice (a) is incorrect. It is just not complete. Choice (b) is incorrect. The work is relevant, just not complete. Choice (d) is incorrect. It is useful, but not sufficient.

Subject Area: Conduct audit engagements—audit evidence. Source: CIA 1190, II-21.

**71. (b)** The firm uses magazine advertising and artwork; the agency specialized in newspaper advertising hence it is not relevant. The sampling should relate only to that type of advertising purchased. Choices (a), (c), and (d) are incorrect. They maybe competent, sufficient and reliable for what is being measured, newspaper advertising, and typeset plates.

Subject Area: Conduct audit engagements—audit evidence. Source: CIA 1190, II-22.

**72. (d)** Choices (a), (b), and (c) are not true. Choice (a) is incorrect. The firm's advertising director and the firm's product marketing director are not objective (competent). Choice (b) is incorrect. The customers are not knowledgeable—the information they provide is not relevant. Choice (c) is incorrect because the evidence cannot be conclusive.

Subject Area: Conduct audit engagements—audit evidence. Source: CIA 1190, II-23.

**73. (c)** This is the most comprehensive procedure since it provides evidence on approval as well as additional evidence on how conscientiously the process was carried out (i.e., it provides evidence as to whether any meaningful discussion took place during the committee meetings). Choice (a) is incorrect. The audit emphasis is on the effectiveness of the loan committee. The loan committee acts as a constraint on the lending officers. Thus, while this procedure would provide some evidence, it is not sufficient evidence. Choice (b) is incorrect. Reconciliation controls are important in the banking industry. This reconciliation, however, only provides evidence that all proposed loans are accounted for; it does not present any evidence on the effectiveness of the loan committee review process. Choice (d) is incorrect because choices (a) and (b) do not directly address the audit question.

Subject Area: Conduct audit engagements—audit evidence. Source: CIA 1195, I-69.

**74. (d)** Aging of receivables provides direct, relevant evidence regarding the valuation of receivables and thus the allowance account. Choice (a) is incorrect. Although some valuation information is implied from the confirmation, aging is more relevant and persuasive. Choice (b) is incorrect. One month's receipts is too little information on which to base the collectibility of accounts. Choice (c) is incorrect. Controls over write-offs are not relevant to the account's valuation, but to the authorization of the write-off.

Subject Area: Conduct audit engagements—audit evidence. Source: CIA 1196, II-20.

**75. (c)** Observation is good in verifying existence, but has limited value in addressing other assertions. Choice (a) is incorrect. Interviews are the most effective method to fill out the questionnaire. The interview results should be supplemented with observations of practice. Choice (b) is incorrect. Observation provides information on how transactions are handled at one particular point in time, not how they are processed throughout the period under audit investigation. Choice (d) is incorrect. The auditor will very seldom be able to observe a fraud; thus, observation is of limited value in documenting a fraud.

Subject Area: Conduct audit engagements—audit evidence. Source: CIA 595, I-41.

**76. (c)** Real estate appraisals are based on estimated resale value and/or future cash flows. A recent, independent appraisal would provide evidence about the borrower's ability to repay the loan. Choice (a) is incorrect. A confirmation provides evidence about a loan's existence, not its collectibility. Choice (b) is incorrect. This procedure would provide evidence about the loan's authorization, not its collectibility. Choice (d) is incorrect. This procedure would not provide evidence about the borrower's ability to repay the loan.

Subject Area: Conduct audit engagements—audit evidence. Source: CIA 1193, I-17.

**77. (a)** By matching invoices received from vendors with receiving documents prepared by company personnel, the nonreceipt of items billed to the company can be detected. Also, the invoices received may well note the delivery made to an address other than the company's storage area or a construction site. Choice (b) is incorrect. It is not usually possible because the materials will not be available on any company premises now or ever. Choice (c) is incorrect. Testimonial through confirmation is unlikely to be helpful because the supplier will confirm shipment of goods and the amount of the invoice but will not report the delivery address on the confirmation returned. Choice (d) is incorrect. It is not likely to be effective unless budgets were very carefully drawn up, all conditions remained virtually constant, and the amounts were relatively large.

Subject Area: Conduct audit engagements—audit evidence. Source: CIA 593, II-18.

**78. (b)** Detailed testing of actual credit applications produces direct evidence of the application (or lack of the application) of specific procedures. Choice (a) is incorrect. Such interviews produce testimonial evidence, which is more useful in gaining an understanding of operations or providing insight into the reasons for exceptions. Choice (c) is incorrect. Analytical procedures can be used to isolate unusual or unexplained fluctuations but do not locate the cause. Choice (d) is incorrect. An aged accounts receivable schedule would provide evidence of whether a particular account might be collected, not the application of credit procedures.

Subject Area: Conduct audit engagements—audit evidence. Source: CIA 593, II-19.

**79. (b)** The aging analysis yields an estimate of the total bad debts, based on the age of the unpaid account balances. This helps the auditor evaluate the adequacy of the company's credit policies and collection efforts. Choice (a) is incorrect. This would test whether the total balance of all individual accounts equals the balance of the control account. Choice (c) is incorrect. This would test only whether the terms for individual accounts were properly authorized. It does not evaluate the adequacy of the company's credit policies and collection efforts. Choice (d) is incorrect. This would test whether the credit memos were properly recorded.

Subject Area: Conduct audit engagements—audit evidence. Source: CIA 1192, I-17.

**80. (b)** A comparison of physical inventory counts to perpetual records is required. Choice (a) is incorrect. Applying the retail method of inventory valuation will not identify specific item shortages. Choice (c) is incorrect. Use of the gross profit percentage will not identify specific shortages. Choice (d) is incorrect. Analysis of inventory turnover rates will not identify specific shortages.

Subject Area: Conduct audit engagements—audit evidence. Source: CIA 1192, I-23.

**81. (b)** The documentation underlying purchase orders provides the most reliable evidence that bids are being obtained in situations where required per the IIA *Standards*. Choice (a) is incorrect. The auditor is searching for possible deviations from the bid procedure. Starting with requests for bids will not turn up instances where the purchasing department should have, but failed to, request bids. Choice (c) is incorrect. Uncorroborated oral statements by a person who is apt to be biased are not a reliable form of evidence. Choice (d) is incorrect. While the executive vice president might be able to estimate the frequency with which waivers are requested, he would not be in a position to identify situations where waivers should have been obtained but were not.

Subject Area: Conduct audit engagements—audit evidence. Source: CIA 1192, II-27.

**82. (d)** When samples are used, they are more apt to provide sufficient evidence when there is reasonable assurance that they are representative of the population from which they were selected. Comparison of the prices by the auditor is a more direct, and therefore more convincing, form of evidence than merely looking for the signature of the accounting clerk who is supposedly performing this function. Choice (a) is incorrect for three reasons. (1) The 20 vouchers do not constitute a representative sample because of the way they were selected.(2) Twenty appears to be too small of a sample from this large of a population. (3) As explained in choice (c) below, the accounting clerk's signature is not as convincing as directly comparing the invoice and purchase order prices. Choice (b) is incorrect. See reasons 1 and 2 listed in choice (a). Choice (c) is incorrect. It is possible that due to time pressures, temporary distractions, and so on, the accounting clerk signed the voucher without effectively comparing the purchase order and invoice prices.

Subject Area: Conduct audit engagements—audit evidence. Source: CIA 1192, II-28.

**83. (d)** The information is not sufficient because it does not explain why the shortages exist. Choices (a) and (b) are incorrect. The company employs an external inventory service and internal personnel for data entry and balancing. Choice (c) is incorrect. Although the company utilizes both external (the counting service) and internal sources (data entry and balancing) for gathering and validating inventory information, the information is not sufficient to determine the **cause**.

Subject Area: Conduct audit engagements—audit evidence. Source: CIA 592, II-23.

**84. (a)** Confirmation is used to verify the physical existence of an item. Obsolete inventory represents a question of value, not physical existence. Choice (b) is incorrect. Scanning is an excellent means of noting unusual relationships, such as very old items with no activity. Choice (c) is incorrect. Recomputation of the value of identified obsolete items is necessary in order to establish current inventory carrying value. Choice (d) is incorrect. Analytical review offers a means to identify part numbers that have a high likelihood of being obsolete.

Subject Area: Conduct audit engagements—audit evidence. Source: CIA 592, II-24.

**85. (c)** Corroboration occurs whenever evidence collected from two separate sources confirms each other. Choice (a) is incorrect. While this is direct evidence here, the situation is really more than that. Choice (b) is incorrect. Circumstantial evidence is received from secondary sources such as the interviews noted above, but this situation is really more than that. Choice (d) is incorrect. Subjective evidence is generally opinion oriented and is not dependable for reaching audit conclusions. No subjective evidence is present in this situation.

Subject Area: Conduct audit engagements—audit evidence. Source: CIA 592, II-25.

**86. (d)** Bids should be solicited based on properly approved requests and a sufficient number of vendors should be selected to ensure competition. Choice (a) is incorrect. Although bids should be solicited based on properly approved requests, the incoming bids should first be returned to an independent third party, such as a bid registrar, for recording and control purposes. Choice (b) is incorrect. A sufficient number of vendors should be selected to ensure competition. However, the incoming bids should first be returned to an independent third party, such as a bid registrar, for recording and control purposes. Choice (c) is incorrect. Bids should be solicited based on properly approved requests. Also, a sufficient number of vendors should be selected to ensure competition. However, the incoming bids should first be returned to an independent third party, such as a bid registrar, for recording and control purposes.

Subject Area: Conduct audit engagements—audit evidence. Source: Transition Question No.1, IIA 1994.

**87. (c)** By comparing the vendor invoice due date with the payment date indicated on the canceled check, the auditor would be able to assess whether invoices were being processed timely. Also, the auditor could determine that cash use was being maximized, that is, payments were not being made before their due dates. Choice (a) is incorrect. This interval would represent the number of days required to process an invoice and indicate whether invoices were being processed timely. However, it would not allow the auditor to determine whether disbursements were being made to maximize the use of company cash. Choice (b) is incorrect. Discussions with the manager would not provide any documentary evidence regarding the timeliness of process while maximizing the company's use of cash. Choice (d) is incorrect. The comparison of these dates would provide an indication of whether invoices were being processed timely. However, it would not allow the auditor to assess whether cash use was being maximized.

Subject Area: Conduct audit engagements—audit evidence. Source: Transition Question No.2, IIA 1994.

**88.** **(a)** This is the definition of framing error. Choice (b) is incorrect. This is the definition of escalation of commitment. Choice (c) is incorrect because it deals with statistical terms, not behavioral terms. Choice (d) is incorrect. Past successes can lead to overconfidence that adversely affects decision making, but overconfidence does not relate to framing error as it has been defined.

Subject Area: Conduct audit engagements—audit evidence. Source: CIA 1194, II-5.

**89.** **(d)** Agreeing on some point can be an opening wedge to more productive discussions. Choice (a) is incorrect. This will only alienate the individual. Choice (b) is incorrect. A tired or distracted person is not a good audience for the auditor's discussion. Choice (c) is incorrect. A closed mind does not accept logic, an open mind does.

Subject Area: Conduct audit engagements—audit evidence. Source: CIA 1196, II-23.

**90.** **(d)** Complete and timely corrective action is needed, but funds appear not to be available. This situation poses a significant risk to the company, and senior management must participate in the decision. It is unlikely that senior management will choose to accept the risk of noncompliance for an extended period of time; funds may be available from another source not accessible to the environmental manager. Choice (a) is incorrect. Disregarding real constraints does not show consideration for the environmental manager's situation and will not achieve the goal of improving hazardous-waste management. Choice (b) is incorrect. If the waste is not being stored properly, the company is probably not in compliance with environmental and safety regulations; postponing action is not acceptable. Choice (c) is incorrect. Inadequate corrective action will not make the facility in compliance and may perpetuate an unsafe condition.

Subject Area: Conduct audit engagements—audit evidence. Source: CIA 597, II-16.

**91.** **(a)** It is management's responsibility to determine policy and set performance goals; the auditor is not necessarily in a position to insist on actions that may be perceived as extraordinary by operations management. Choice (b) is incorrect. Unless senior management is committed to a policy of "environmental excellence" and the auditor is auditing performance toward such a goal, it is inappropriate to raise this issue. Choice (c) is incorrect. This should not be included as part of the audit or audit report. Choice (d) is incorrect because this is inappropriate.

Subject Area: Conduct audit engagements—audit evidence. Source: CIA 597, II-17.

**92.** **(c)** Most companies have a program to receive and address employee concerns. Employees who fortuitously encounter auditors may see an opportunity to bypass the

normal process. Until the process has had a chance to work, internal auditors should encourage its use. It is important that audit management be aware of such contact between auditors and other employees. Choice (a) is incorrect. Potential legal issues are presented whenever an employee complains about working conditions. Unless the internal auditing department is specifically under the guidance of counsel, the auditor should not pursue this information. Choice (b) is incorrect. Although it may not be appropriate for the internal auditing department to investigate such informal allegations or complaints, it is not appropriate simply to disregard employee concerns. Choice (d) is incorrect. Although the legal department may eventually interview the employees, at this stage it is more appropriate to encourage them to use the program in place to address employee concerns.

Subject Area: Conduct audit engagements—audit evidence. Source: CIA 597, II-18.

**93.** **(b)** The risk of having radioactive materials on site that are not accounted for in the facility's inventory is sufficiently serious that all key controls should be identified and evaluated. The auditor is obliged to note that the risk extends beyond the safety department, and should request resources to finish this important planning. Choice (a) is incorrect. Although a procedure may be comprehensive, controls do not exist if people do not take appropriate action. In this situation, the safe handling of radioactive materials requires actions by outsiders not under the control of the safety department. Choice (c) is incorrect. Planning is the most important part of an audit. If an activity crosses organizational lines, the auditor should endeavor to understand the entire system and identify all key controls before making decisions about which controls are appropriate to test. Choice (d) is incorrect. Although another audit project dealing with one of these other departments might touch on controls over radioactive materials, it is not likely to be comprehensive. A review of purchasing, for example, might not result in testing of controls designed specifically to track radioactive materials. Also, the auditors at that time may not have the same technical expertise.

Subject Area: Conduct audit engagements—audit evidence. Source: CIA 597, II-19.

**94.** **(b)** Indirect questions may allow the auditor to obtain some information without making the clerk feel accused. Choice (a) is incorrect. The auditor has an obligation to obtain information. Unless the weakness is something that compromises the security of the company, the auditor should not simply avoid the issue. Choice (c) is incorrect. Since the auditor believes there is a system weakness, the clerk is not likely to have sufficient knowledge to determine if the finding should be reported immediately. Choice (d) is incorrect. This is probably an inefficient approach. The auditor should learn as much as possible from this interview, speak to others who may have additional information, and return to this clerk only if needed to clarify something specific about this employee's duties.

Subject Area: Conduct audit engagements—audit evidence. Source: CIA 597, II-20.

**95.** **(d)** This is one approach the auditor can use to maintain focus during a far-ranging discussion. It assumes that the auditor has done some homework and is prepared to listen intelligently. Choice (a) is incorrect. This is a sign of a poor listener, as the auditor will likely miss important things in the effort to record everything. The auditor should write down key points or issues and then listen to the support or argument offered. Choice (b) is incorrect. This would waste the auditor's time. Choice (c) is incorrect. This would be a waste of everyone's time, and the auditor still may not get the information sought.

Subject Area: Conduct audit engagements—audit evidence. Source: CIA 597, II-22.

**96. (b)** The validity of documentary evidence depends on the internal control system. Choices (a), (c), and (d) are incorrect because each one is a true statement.

Subject Area: Conduct audit engagements—audit evidence. Source: CIA 597, II-24.

**97. (d)** Since the mind can process information three times as fast as most people speak, you should use the extra brain time to sort out the speaker's important points and integrate the new information with what you already know. After having done this to absorb the information, you are in a better position to respond to the speaker later. Choice (a) is incorrect. If you are planning a reply before you have heard the speaker out, you are likely to miss an important point or assume information the speaker does not say. When you are thinking about a reply, you are *not* listening. Choice (b) is incorrect. If you are thinking your own thoughts while someone speaks, you are *not* listening. This is not a productive use of listening time. Choice (c) is incorrect. To listen effectively, you need to sift the main ideas from the details and try to remember the important points. You cannot let yourself be distracted by interesting details, as oral communication is hard to remember.

Subject Area: Conduct audit engagements—audit evidence. Source: CIA 596, II-6.

**98. (b)** If all the invoices in the sample can be correctly matched with shipping documents, then there is some assurance that all or most items billed are also shipped. Choice (a) is incorrect. The tracing procedure originated with a sample of billed sales; thus, all the items in the sample were billed. However, this does not determine if all shipped items were billed. Choice (c) is incorrect. Receivables are not examined at all. Choice (d) is incorrect. Again, receivables are not examined.

Subject Area: Conduct audit engagements—audit evidence. Source: CIA 592, I-23.

**99. (c)** Tracing accounts receivable debit entries to the sales documentation tests whether those debits represent actual sales. Choice (a) is incorrect. This would test whether credit sales were properly recorded in the accounts receivable ledger. It would not ensure that all debit entries to accounts receivable represent valid sales. Choice (b) is incorrect. The auditor would trace accounts receivable credit entries to the cash receipts journal to test whether those entries represent actual payments. Choice (d) is incorrect. Tracing entries from the cash receipts documentation to the accounts receivable ledger tests whether customer payments were credited to accounts receivable.

Subject Area: Conduct audit engagements—audit evidence. Source: CIA 1192, I-16.

**100. (c)** An item distributed to an improper work-in-process account (i.e., one different from that listed on the time ticket) could be discovered by this test. Choice (a) is incorrect. The direction of tracing to establish this is from the work in process account to the individual time tickets. Choice (b) is incorrect. To establish this, the auditor would have to verify proper authorization of the time tickets. Choice (d) is incorrect. To establish this, the auditor would also have to reconcile total payroll costs to the payroll cost distribution.

Subject Area: Conduct audit engagements—audit evidence. Source: CIA 1192, I-29.

**101. (b)** For each shipment, there should be a valid sales record or invoice. Choice (a) is incorrect. These records would not include payment information. Choice (c) is incorrect. This would be done by comparing invoices with sales contracts or price lists, noting the propriety of any discounts. Choice (d) is incorrect. All sales might not require shipping.

Subject Area: Conduct audit engagements—audit evidence. Source: CIA 1192, II-12.

**102. (a)** Tracing the production and handling of replacement parts that were shipped late and comparing the process times to parts that were shipped on time should detect the cause of the late shipments. Choice (b) is incorrect. Tracking the production and handling processes to find average turnaround times will give an overall measure of capacity, but will not determine the cause of late shipments. Choice (c) is incorrect. Computing the production and handling capacities for replacement parts will give an overall measure of capacity, but will not determine the cause of late shipments. Choice (d) is incorrect. Examining the terms and conditions of the delivery commitments to customers will verify the actual delivery terms and conditions, but will not determine the cause of late shipments.

Subject Area: Conduct audit engagements—audit evidence. Source: CIA 1193, II-28.

**103. (d)** The shipping document and invoice provide direct evidence that the sale was made. Choice (a) is incorrect. The customer's purchase order only proves that the item was requested, not sold. Choice (b) is incorrect. This is hearsay evidence, and it is uncorroborated. Choice (c) is incorrect. This evidence is less direct than the shipping document and invoice and provides only circumstantial evidence regarding the validity of the sale.

Subject Area: Conduct audit engagements—audit evidence. Source: CIA 1191, I-21.

**104. (c)** Payment on vendor invoices represents the culmination of the buying process. The paid invoice would evidence the purchaser's ownership of inventory. Choice (a) is incorrect. Although informative, this procedure has no bearing on legal ownership. Choice (b) is incorrect. Purchase orders represent a commitment only to purchase, not legal ownership. Choice (d) is incorrect. This type of confirmation would verify the existence of the inventory, not the legal ownership.

Subject Area: Conduct audit engagements—audit evidence. Source: CIA 1191, I-23.

**105. (c)** Vendors' invoices provide an external source of information regarding quantities shipped, which should be equal to quantities added to inventory (after possible adjustment for items returned to the vendor due to damage, etc.). Choice (a) is incorrect. The quantity ordered may not be equal to the quantity shipped by the vendor due to stockouts. Choice (b) is incorrect. The quantity requested per purchase requisition may not be equal to the quantity shipped by the vendor due to (1) modification by the purchasing department, or (2) vendor stock-outs. Choice (d) is incorrect. Vendors' statements normally list only the invoice number, date, and total. They do not list invoice detail such as quantities shipped.

Subject Area: Conduct audit engagements—audit evidence. Source: CIA 1193, I-18.

## Develop and Review Workpapers

**106. (d)** Every workpaper should contain a descriptive heading. Choice (a) is incorrect. Findings of tests may be documented, but expression of an audit opinion in the working papers is premature and an indication of bias. Choice (b) is incorrect. A tick mark legend is a minor point, although it is helpful to the auditor, Choice (c) is incorrect. A flowchart of internal controls will likely be a working paper at the beginning of a significant audit segment, but each workpaper will not contain a flowchart.

Subject Area: Conduct audit engagements—workpapers. Source: CIA 1190, I-27.

**107. (c)** Working papers provide the primary support for the internal auditor's report. Choice (a) is incorrect. Although a copy of the auditee's responses to audit findings will likely be filed with the working papers, the auditee will normally prepare a formal response to the final audit report or to interim reports. Choice (b) is incorrect. The working papers are not an exhibit appended to the audit report. Choice (d) is incorrect. Overall audit recommendations are properly summarized in the audit report. Individual test conclusions may be documented in the working papers.

Subject Area: Conduct audit engagements—workpapers. Source: CIA 1190, II-25.

**108. (a)** Documentation concerning the adequacy of internal controls will always be a part of the working papers. Choice (b) is incorrect. Many documents may be examined that prove to be irrelevant to the audit objectives. These documents need not be included in the working papers. Choice (c) is incorrect. In many circumstances the exact wording of a procedure is not needed to support a finding. A reference to the procedure in the working papers is adequate in this situation. Choice (d) is incorrect. Some previous workpapers may be so outdated as to be useless. Parts of previous audit working papers may be included in current working papers subject to updating.

Subject Area: Conduct audit engagements—workpapers. Source: CIA 1190, II-26.

**109. (d)** The IIA *Standards* require that appropriate audit supervision include the determination that workpapers adequately support findings, conclusions, and reports. This is of primary importance because nothing reduces the credibility of an internal audit department as much as ineptly developed findings that can collapse under attack. Choice (a) is incorrect. While it is true that a descriptive heading generally should be on each worksheet, it is not of primary importance. Choice (b) is incorrect. Again, while it is desirable that working papers be properly referenced, it is not of primary importance. Choice (c) is incorrect. Although a supervisor would be concerned as to whether departmental procedures are followed, it is not of primary importance.

Subject Area: Conduct audit engagements—workpapers. Source: CIA 1190, II-27.

**110. (d)** The auditor should know exactly where workpapers are during an audit and who has access to them. Choice (a) is incorrect. Audit workpapers may be shown to the auditee so that the auditors are helped to evaluate significance, perspective, accuracy, and relevance. Choice (b) is incorrect. If company policy permits, external auditors may be permitted access to workpapers to avoid duplicate work. Choice (c) is incorrect. If company policy permits, government auditors may be permitted access to workpapers to avoid duplicate work.

Subject Area: Conduct audit engagements—workpapers. Source: CIA 1190, II-28.

**111. (a)** The general test in all cases is whether audit working papers reasonably achieve the purposes of the internal auditor. Choice (b) is incorrect. Description of operational procedures is frequently desirable, but is secondary to the need to document completion of audit objectives. Choice (c) is incorrect. Condensation of detail is desirable, but is secondary to meeting the audit objective. Choice (d) is incorrect. Indexing is a matter of form as opposed to substance.

Subject Area: Conduct audit engagements—workpapers. Source: CIA 590, II-18.

**112. (b)** This is the primary reason why the legal department needs to be involved. Choice (a) is incorrect. This is adequate for internal company records but does not address the legal provisions of the contract, particularly if it is a one-time audit. Choice (c) is incorrect. Again this area is more concerned with in-house routine accounting records which have nothing to do with contractor audits. Choice (d) is incorrect. It is best to have one's own legal department involved in order to make sure the company is adhering to the contract provisions, Contractor's policies are irrelevant regarding company's own audit workpapers.

Subject Area: Conduct audit engagements—workpapers. Source: CIA 1190, I-29.

**113. (c)** Compliance tests are used in reviews for effectiveness of the system. Choice (a) is incorrect. An old compliance test from a former audit might be found in the preliminary survey as background material. A current compliance test would not yet be performed. Choice (b) is incorrect. Compliance tests are not used in reviews for adequacy of the system. Choice (d) is incorrect. Compliance tests are not used in reviews for quality of performance.

Subject Area: Conduct audit engagements—workpapers. Source: CIA 1190, I-21.

**114. (a)** A checklist that outlines the types of errors and irregularities that can occur in the sales cycle identifies the risks faced in the sales cycle. This is properly a function served by the preliminary survey. Choice (b) is incorrect. The review for adequacy of the system determines whether there are controls that will prevent or detect the errors and irregularities suggested in the preliminary survey. Choice (c) is incorrect. The review for effectiveness of the system determines whether the key controls are applied as designed. Choice (d) is incorrect. The review for quality of performance is designed to determine whether the organization's objectives and goals are being achieved.

Subject Area: Conduct audit engagements—workpapers. Source: CIA 1190, I-22.

**115. (b)** This document indicates: (1) that a control system has been contemplated and (2) the portion covered by the standard sales contract can work. Choice (a) is incorrect. The standard sales contract form might be picked up during the on-site survey portion of the preliminary survey. Its analysis, indicating the existence and adequacy of key controls, could also be performed as part of the preliminary survey. In spite of this, there are three reasons why the audit supervisor should not place this document among those from the preliminary survey: (1) The checklist of possible errors and irregularities fits the preliminary survey criteria only. (2) The stub demands that there be no duplications. (3) The activity outlined is a review for adequacy of the system procedure, regardless when it is accomplished. Choice (c) is incorrect. The form is blank. A completed form would be required to indicate that the system is effective. Choice (d) is incorrect. The form is blank. No data are available for substantive testing.

Subject Area: Conduct audit engagements—workpapers. Source: CIA 1190, I-23.

**116. (b)** It is not possible for a reviewer to check any of the auditor's work without obtaining additional copies of the quarterly reports and independently checking the computations. The review would be much more efficient if the auditor included the board reports in the working papers and had used tick marks with explanations to show which computations were checked and to describe what the auditor did to verify the amounts used in the computations. Choice (a) is incorrect. The problem did not state or imply that sampling was used. Four quarters was the population, and it was apparently tested 100%. Choice (c) is incorrect. Scratch papers are generally not suitable for working papers. Unorganized working papers are difficult to review and difficult to understand in the future if it is ever necessary to refer to them. Choice (d) is incorrect. The problem did not state or imply that an objective of the audit was to evaluate efficiency.

Subject Area: Conduct audit engagements—workpapers. Source: CIA 1195, II-6.

**117. (a)** Since there are many differences between organizations (e.g., type, size, location, etc.), the internal auditing manager devises the workpaper indexing method that best suits the organization. A government audit agency, however, audits many different organizations that come under the agency. Therefore, the government audit agency devises one uniform indexing method that is compatible with all of the organizations that it audits so that the review process can be simplified. Choices (b) and (c) are incorrect. The *Standards* require only that the audit workpapers contain an index number, but they do not discuss or require a particular indexing method. Furthermore, there are no laws that require a particular indexing method to be used by government auditors. Choice (d) is incorrect. The audit committee does not specify any workpaper indexing method.

Subject Area: Conduct audit engagements—workpapers. Source: CIA 597, I-8.

**118. (c)** Chronological organization would be ineffective. Choices (a), (b), and (d) are incorrect because these are examples of good practices.

Subject Area: Conduct audit engagements—workpapers. Source: CIA 594, II-41.

**119. (c)** Bank statement reconciliations do not show a list of all deposits, only deposits in transit. Choices (a), (b), and (d) are incorrect because each one of them should be present in a bank's statement reconciliation.

Subject Area: Conduct audit engagements—workpapers. Source: CIA 594, II-42.

**120. (c)** Computer utilities software would be useful during the audit in manipulating and selecting data. However, spreadsheet, word processing, and database software provide flexible options in preparing and editing working papers in a variety of formats, allowing for a combination of narratives, data matrices, graphic presentations, and so on. Choices (a), (b), and (d) are incorrect because each choice would be of great help in preparing audit working papers. In fact, some vendors have developed integrated software that includes spreadsheet, word processing, and database applications.

Subject Area: Conduct audit engagements—workpapers. Source: CIA 594, III-9.

**121. (c)** No characteristic gets to the heart of an internal auditor's job more than the ability to gather, analyze, and draw conclusions from facts. The internal auditor's success in implementing well-founded recommendations is most closely tied to his or her ability to communicate. Choice (a) is incorrect. Accounting educational performance is undoubtedly one criterion that must be examined. Reviewing the performance in only one subject area is much too limited a criterion when the broad scope of internal auditing work is considered. Choice (b) is incorrect. The ability to get along well socially is a benefit to any internal auditor but cannot be considered the most important characteristic of a good candidate. Choice (d) is incorrect. Entry-level internal auditors would typically have relatively little detail knowledge of the company. It is desirable for applicants to demonstrate a general knowledge of the company, but this is not the most reliable predictor of successful performance as an internal auditor.

Subject Area: Conduct audit engagements—workpapers. Source: CIA 591, I-8.

**122. (c)** As a minimum, this would be needed to comply with IIA *Standards* as to having the working papers complete. A standard or norm for efficient operation has to be used to measure how inefficient an operation is before such an opinion can be rendered. Choice (a) is incorrect. While this might become necessary, if the staff auditor has reason to believe inefficiency, an attempt to support that belief is the first priority. Choices (b) and (d) are incorrect. Without support, these statements do not have credibility. They are conjecture and violations of *Standard 420*.

Subject Area: Conduct audit engagements—workpapers. Source: CIA 1191, II-24.

**123. (c)** This is the primary reason for such summaries. Choice (a) is incorrect because it is not required by the IIA *Standards*. Choice (b) is incorrect because audit programs do not usually require it. Choice (d) is incorrect because it is too comprehensive.

Subject Area: Conduct audit engagements—workpapers. Source: CIA 1191, I-24.

**124. (d)** This is the objective of each working paper: to support the particular purpose for which the working paper was generated. Choice (a) is incorrect. Format requirements are superficial and indicate only that mechanical requirements have been met. They do not relate to content.

Choice (b) is incorrect. A working paper may relate to only a part of the finding—one element or several. Choice (c) is incorrect. These items are characteristics of the working paper content. The qualities may be present without the working paper being complete.

Subject Area: Conduct audit engagements—workpapers. Source: CIA 1191, I-25.

**125. (c)** Legal counsel should approve retention policies. Choice (a) is incorrect because minimum retention is for the period of further use, not simply three years. Choice (b) is incorrect because the audit committee should not prepare retention policies. Choice (d) is incorrect because the external auditor need not approve retention policies.

Subject Area: Conduct audit engagements—workpapers. Source: CIA 592, II-27.

**126. (a)** Working papers should include only what is essential. Choice (b) is incorrect. Working papers should be uniform and consistent. Choice (c) is incorrect. Working papers should contain only information related to an audit objective. Choice (d) is incorrect. Copies of auditee records should be used whenever possible.

Subject Area: Conduct audit engagements—workpapers. Source: CIA 592, I-25.

**127. (c)** Because electronic working papers do not bear the initials or signature of the auditor who created them, special rules are needed to protect their integrity. Choice (a) is incorrect. Working papers may be shown to the auditee. Choice (b) is incorrect. Working papers should be retained only until no longer needed. Choice (d) is incorrect. If working papers are only potentially relevant, the courts have held that they must be surrendered.

Subject Area: Conduct audit engagements—workpapers. Source: CIA 592, I-27.

**128. (b)** The IIA *Standards* specify that for working papers in media other than paper, consideration should be given to generating backup copies. Choice (a) is incorrect. Conversion to a paper media is not specified nor is it necessarily desired. Choice (c) is incorrect. The nature of the audit, and not the media, determines working paper design and content. Choice (d) is incorrect. Retention policies are a function of several factors, including legal guidelines.

Subject Area: Conduct audit engagements—workpapers. Source: CIA 1193, I-19.

**129. (b)** Reductions in the average time to complete an audit have been shown. Choice (a) is incorrect. Auditors can learn to use the personal computer with a minimum of training. Choice (c) is incorrect. The IIA *Standards* require comprehensive working papers, and the use of computers should not affect their completeness. Choice (d) is incorrect. Working papers need not be and, in fact, rarely are printed.

Subject Area: Conduct audit engagements—workpapers. Source: CIA 1193, I-20.

**130. (b)** Working papers do document auditing procedures, information obtained, and the conclusions reached. Choice (a) is incorrect. While working papers are the property of the organization, they should be made available only to authorized personnel. Choice (c) is incorrect. Although it is common practice for internal auditors to grant access to working papers to the independent outside auditors, the internal audit working papers are the property of the organization. Choice (d) is incorrect. Working paper retention should

be consistent with the guidelines of the organization and should satisfy pertinent legal or regulatory requirements.

Subject Area: Conduct audit engagements—workpapers. Source: CIA 1190, I-26.

**131. (d)** Training would be required to effectively use any software package. Choice (a) is incorrect. Only access to a personal computer would be a must. Full allocation to each auditor may not be necessary or economically feasible. Choice (b) is incorrect. If adequate measures are taken to safeguard the working paper disks, paper documentation is redundant. Choice (c) is incorrect. Search capabilities actually ease cross-referencing.

Subject Area: Conduct audit engagements—workpapers. Source: CIA 593, I-7.

**132. (a)** Working papers serve the primary purpose of showing that audit procedures were properly planned and executed. Choice (b) is incorrect. Working papers do not provide the means for preparation of the financial statements. Choice (c) is incorrect. Documentation of control deficiencies is only one example of working paper contents, not their primary purpose. Choice (d) is incorrect. The preparation of adequate working papers is a requirement of the IIA *Standards* but not the primary purpose of their existence.

Subject Area: Conduct audit engagements—workpapers. Source: CIA 1192, II-29.

**133. (b)** Although working papers pertaining to a fraud audit might be kept apart from other working papers, no working paper will have to be kept indefinitely. Choices (a), (c), and (d) are true statements regarding working paper retention.

Subject Area: Conduct audit engagements—workpapers. Source: CIA 1192, II-30.

**134. (a)** Since there are many differences between organizations (e.g., type, size, location, etc.), the internal auditing manager devises the working paper index method that best suits the organization. A government audit agency, however, audits many different organizations that come under the agency. Therefore, the government audit agency devises one uniform indexing method that is compatible with all of the organizations that it audits so that the review process can be simplified. Choices (b) and (c) are incorrect. The *Standards* only require that the audit working papers contain an index number, but they do not discuss or require a particular index method. Furthermore, government audit agencies do not require their auditors to follow a specific index method. Furthermore, there are no laws that require government auditors to use a particular index method. Choice (d) is incorrect. The audit committee does not specify any working paper indexing method.

Subject Area: Conduct audit engagements—workpapers. Source: CIA 1193, I-21.

**135. (b)** This would indeed be a deficiency because the basis for comparing what was, with what should have been would be missing. Choices (a), (c), and (d) are incorrect because each is appropriate to include in working papers.

Subject Area: Conduct audit engagements—workpapers. Source: CIA 1193, I-22.

**136. (c)** Each set of working papers should be individually considered for disposal. Choice (a) is incorrect. Internal audit working papers are the property of the organization.

Only those dealing with government contracts could be affected by such guidelines. Choice (b) is incorrect. The *Standards* do not specify a retention period. Choice (d) is incorrect. See choice (c). Some might be destroyed after the next audit.

Subject Area: Conduct audit engagements—workpapers. Source: CIA 1193, I-23.

**137. (b)** Management may use the internal auditors' working papers in preparing the insurance claim, as long as the director of internal auditing approves such use. Choice (a) is incorrect because the IIA *Standards* state: "management and other members of the organization may request access to audit working papers. Such access may be necessary to substantiate or explain audit findings or to utilize audit documentation for other business purposes. The director of internal auditing should approve these requests." Accordingly, the insurance claim should be considered under "other business purposes," and management may use the internal auditors' working papers in preparing the claim. Choice (c) is incorrect. There is nothing in the IIA *Standards* that precludes management from preparing insurance claims. In fact, management typically has such responsibility. Choice (d) is incorrect. The use of the internal auditor's working papers requires the approval by the director of internal auditing only.

Subject Area: Conduct audit engagements—workpapers. Source: CIA 1193, II-19.

**138. (b)** Only those forms and directives that are relevant to the auditor or to the audit findings should be included in the audit working papers. Choice (a) is incorrect. Actual and budgeted audit time is documented in the budget section of the working papers and not on each working paper. Choice (c) is incorrect. Audit conclusions should be documented in the working papers, whether the audit objectives are achieved or not. Choice (d) is incorrect. The cooperation of the auditees during the conduct of an audit is not documented on each working paper. It is typically documented on one working paper, and usually this is done when the auditees were not cooperative.

Subject Area: Conduct audit engagements—workpapers. Source: CIA 1193, II-20.

**139. (a)** This concept invokes the use of computer-based procedures to ensure the retention and availability of audit records and documentation. Choice (b) is incorrect. Evidential support would be retained and provided on the basis of the nature of the finding and not the media used for working papers. Choice (c) is incorrect. This capability is not an exclusive function of computerized working papers. Choice (d) is incorrect. Although the nature of the preliminary survey may change in some cases, the requirement for this phase of the audit is not eliminated by computerized working papers.

Subject Area: Conduct audit engagements—workpapers. Source: CIA 1193, II-23.

**140. (c)** Cross-referencing aids the factual rebuttal of challenges by clearly identifying source and location of facts. Choice (a) is incorrect. Audit programs are not generally summarized; such summaries are applicable to the working papers. Choice (b) is incorrect. Pro forma working papers save time in the evidence collection process by guiding the auditor to ensure that all significant points are covered. Choice (d) is incorrect. Explicit procedures in the audit program guide the collection of evidence, but appropriately cross-referenced facts in the working papers assist in the factual rebuttal to challenges.

Subject Area: Conduct audit engagements—workpapers. Source: CIA 592, II-26.

**Report Engagement Results**

**141. (d)** Long sentences with several ideas will create information overload and disguise the important point. Choice (a) is incorrect. Placing it at the beginning or end of the paragraph best emphasizes the point. Choice (b) is incorrect. Use of the active voice best emphasizes the point. Choice (c) is incorrect. Parallel structure will emphasize the point better. Nonparallel structure will usually detract from the point.

Subject Area: Conduct audit engagements—audit reporting. Source: CIA 597, II-1.

**142. (b)** Using the passive version without placing blame or making the statement personal is more likely to make the reader react positively. Choice (a) is incorrect. Placing the blame and using words such as "failed" will make the individual react negatively. Choice (c) is incorrect. Placing the blame in a manner that seems mean-spirited and using words such as "unfortunately" will make the reader react negatively. Choice (d) is incorrect. Placing the blame on the reader and using words such as "failed" will make the reader react negatively.

Subject Area: Conduct audit engagements—audit reporting. Source: CIA 597, II-2.

**143. (b)** Analysis of elements of cost can point out problem areas. Choice (a) is incorrect. Material is only one element of cost. Choice (c) is incorrect. There is no assurance that the standards are valid. Choice (d) is incorrect. This would only point to one element, production.

Subject Area: Conduct audit engagements—audit reporting. Source: CIA 597, II-3.

**144. (d)** The analysis of these reports should identify where the problem lies. Choice (a) is incorrect. The problem is recent; it was not identified in prior audits. Choice (b) is incorrect. Physical layout and condition of equipment or materials are not likely candidates. Choice (c) is incorrect. It is unlikely that staff would know about the problem.

Subject Area: Conduct audit engagements—audit reporting. Source: CIA 597, II-4.

**145. (d)** Oral reports permit auditors to counter arguments and provide additional information that the audience may require. Since oral reports evoke face-to-face responses, the auditors can provide an immediate response to any auditee objections or provide additional information as appropriate. Choice (a) is incorrect. The amount of testing required to support audit findings is unrelated to the use of oral reports. Whether findings are reported through oral or written reports, they still must be adequately supported. Choice (b) is incorrect. Even though audit reports are delivered orally, they still should be prepared carefully. Poorly planned and delivered oral reports will be difficult for the audience to follow and may create unnecessary misunderstandings. Choice (c) is incorrect. The format of the report will depend on the audience. Factors to consider in delivering reports may include the background and expectations of the audience as well as the time available. This applies to both written and oral reports. Since oral reports do not eliminate the need for a final report, overall audit efficiency is not affected.

Subject Area: Conduct audit engagements—audit reporting. Source: CIA 597, II-7.

**146. (c)** Both statements should be in the criteria section. Choice (a) is incorrect. This should be reported in the cause section of the report. Choice (b) is incorrect. This is only one of the two statements that should be reported in the criteria section. Choice (d) is incorrect. This should be in the recommendation section of the report.

Subject Area: Conduct audit engagements—audit reporting. Source: CIA 1196, II-66.

**147. (a)** This belongs in the condition section. Choice (b) is incorrect. This should be in the criteria section. Choice (c) is incorrect. This should be in the effect section. Choice (d) is incorrect. This should not be included in the report.

Subject Area: Conduct audit engagements—audit reporting. Source: CIA 1196, II-67.

**148. (b)** This belongs in the cause section. Choice (a) is incorrect. This belongs in the condition section. Choice (c) is incorrect. This belongs in the effect section. Choice (d) is incorrect. This should not be included in the report.

Subject Area: Conduct audit engagements—audit reporting. Source: CIA 1196, II-68.

**149. (d)** This belongs in the effect section. Choice (a) is incorrect. This belongs in the cause section. Choice (b) is incorrect. This belongs in the criteria section. Choice (c) is incorrect. This belongs in the recommendations section.

Subject Area: Conduct audit engagements—audit reporting. Source: CIA 1196, II-69.

**150. (c)** This belongs in the recommendation section. Choice (a) is incorrect. This belongs in the criteria section. Choice (b) is incorrect. These belong in the criteria section. Choice (d) is incorrect. This belongs in the effect section.

Subject Area: Conduct audit engagements—audit reporting. Source: CIA 1196, II-70.

**151. (a)** Compensation systems influence behavior and should be considered an integral part of an organization's control structure. Thus, they should be considered as an important part of the control structure over derivatives trading. Choices (b) and (c) are incorrect. Although compensation or payroll audits are often conducted independently of the control structure over related activities, the compensation system should be considered whenever the control structure is evaluated. Choice (d) is incorrect. Both statements II and III are incorrect.

Subject Area: Conduct audit engagements—audit reporting. Source: CIA 1196, II-7.

**152. (c)** The only justification for not reporting the items to the audit committee is the auditor's judgment that the deficiency and the risks associated with it cannot be considered to be material. Choice (a) is incorrect. Significant deficiencies in control should be reported to the audit committee even if corrective action is planned. Choice (b) is incorrect. The compensation system influences employee behavior and is part of the control environment. The auditor's reservations about its effect on the organization's control structure should be communicated to the audit committee. Choice (d) is incorrect. Auditors should ensure they have adequate expertise

to conduct an audit. Thus, the complexity of the audit should have no bearing on the auditor's responsibilities.

Subject Area: Conduct audit engagements—audit reporting. Source: CIA 1196, II-8.

**153. (d)** This would be consistent with the IIA *Standards*. Choice (a) is incorrect. As long as the auditor is satisfied that the audit is completed, it would be inappropriate to delay the issuance of the audit report. Further, agreement may never be obtained. Choice (b) is incorrect. The auditor is satisfied with the audit conclusions. There would be little justification for expanding the audit work. Choice (c) is incorrect. The disagreement is not caused by a scope limitation.

Subject Area: Conduct audit engagements—audit reporting. Source: CIA 1196, II-10.

**154. (a)** Past practices may or may not have been at the level of "best practices" or may not have been in compliance with company procedures. This would not be an appropriate criterion. Choice (b) is incorrect. Company policies and procedures specify what should be a part of the treasury function's operations. Choice (c) is incorrect. Generally accepted good practices can usually be found in leading textbooks describing the field. The auditor should look to the finance discipline for a description of good practices. Choice (d) is incorrect. Industry identification of "best practices" can serve as relevant criteria for both the auditor and the organization.

Subject Area: Conduct audit engagements—audit reporting. Source: CIA 1196, II-11.

**155. (c)** Assigning responsibility is a function of management. Choices (a), (b), and (d) are incorrect because each one is a major purpose.

Subject Area: Conduct audit engagements—audit reporting. Source: CIA 1196, II-14.

**156. (b)** This should be included in the purpose section. Choices (a), (c), and (d) are incorrect because each one should be included in the scope section.

Subject Area: Conduct audit engagements—audit reporting. Source: CIA 1196, II-15.

**157. (d)** The audit report needs to address the expectations and perceptions both of the top management and the operating management. As a result, it needs general concepts as well as details of operations. Choice (a) is incorrect. Top management can best perceive general concepts. Choice (b) is incorrect. Operating management can best perceive details of operations. Choice (c) is incorrect. Do not surprise auditees; discuss the matters with them before they are reported.

Subject Area: Conduct audit engagements—audit reporting. Source: CIA 1196, II-25.

**158. (a)** Complex messages are more understandable if they follow a logical sequence. Thus, the sequence or organization of the message is a characteristic that is within the control of the sender. Choice (b) is incorrect. The nature of an audience is a situational factor that is outside the control of the auditor. Choice (c) is incorrect. Noise is a situational factor that interferes with the effective communication of intended messages. Choice (d) is incorrect. The history of previous encounters is a situational factor that is outside the control of the auditor.

Subject Area: Conduct audit engagements—audit reporting. Source: CIA 1196, II-16.

**159. (a)** While a portion of the scope is discussed (30 machines selected), the reader cannot recognize the significance or insignificance of this amount without knowing the total amount of machines that could have been selected. The value of the machinery is not given. Also, the conclusion or auditor's opinion of the operation is not given, and the report does not make any recommendations. Choices (b), (c), and (d) are incorrect. The purpose or objective of the audit was clearly stated. Results of the audit were also given.

Subject Area: Conduct audit engagements—audit reporting. Source: CIA 1196, II-18.

**160. (a)** Graphic illustrations, oral and written repetition such as summaries, and itemized lists (bulleted or numbered) are good ways of emphasizing information in a report. Choice (b) is incorrect. Long paragraphs may bury important information, and appendexes hide it because readers may not use them. Choice (c) is incorrect. Vocal emphasis comes from raising or lowering the projection of the voice to attract attention to the idea being stated, not from keeping the voice even. Choice (d) is incorrect. Embedding ideas subordinates them rather than emphasizes them.

Subject Area: Conduct audit engagements—audit reporting. Source: CIA 1196, II-21.

**161. (b)** Since the auditor does not report to the divisional controller, the divisional controller can help alleviate the problem by making the director of internal audit aware of the perceived shortcomings. Choice (a) is incorrect. Training on only one part of the job will not improve the rest of the internal audit reports. Choice (c) is incorrect. Good management involves dealing directly with problems, not gossiping about employees within the company. Choice (d) is incorrect. Without awareness of previous problems, the director of internal audit will not fire the auditor and may consider the controller's demand an unreasonable encroachment on corporate audit's responsibilities.

Subject Area: Conduct audit engagements—audit reporting. Source: CIA 1195, II-20.

**162. (d)** The controller should not let anger create more problems. The controller should identify and solve the actual work problems and retain good relations with the auditor. Choice (a) is incorrect. If the auditor's work is not acceptable in this case, the auditor needs to know about it and help to find the solution in order to learn from the process. Choice (b) is incorrect. The divisional controller should not go behind the auditor's back by bringing in someone else. The auditor has done good work so far; the controller should deal directly with the problem. Choice (c) is incorrect. This is a usurpation of authority, and the divisional controller cannot implement such a change.

Subject Area: Conduct audit engagements—audit reporting. Source: CIA 1195, II-21.

**163. (a)** Specific comments will both help revise the report and defuse the potentially explosive interpersonal situation. Choice (b) is incorrect. Confrontation will not solve the internal audit problem. The auditor's personality is not an issue here, but the auditor's work apparently is; the auditor, therefore, should focus on finding out specifically what is wrong. Choice (c) is incorrect. This response will weaken the auditor's ability to continue doing audits, because the auditee has intimidated the auditor. Choice (d) is incorrect. Unless the auditor finds out what specifically the divisional controller thinks is wrong, the auditor will not be

able to decide whether the controller's objections are justified.

Subject Area: Conduct audit engagements—audit reporting. Source: CIA 1195, II-22.

**164. (b)** Asking for specific objections will improve both the auditor's work and the working relationship with the divisional controller by defusing this situation. Choice (a) is incorrect. If the auditor really needs to make changes to the report, they will have to be made eventually, and the divisional controller may ask someone else to make them if the auditor refuses to admit any mistakes. Choice (c) is incorrect. The issue here is work, not personal problems. Choice (d) is incorrect. Again, the issue here is work and getting it done. The auditor should find out what specific areas need work, revise the report, and apply for related training when it is next available.

Subject Area: Conduct audit engagements—audit reporting. Source: CIA 1195, II-23.

**165. (b)** An audit report dealing with findings should discuss the criteria, the conditions found, the cause, and the effect of the findings. Recommendations may also be included, where appropriate. Paragraph [#5] is silent on the criteria the auditor used in determining that the division had excessive levels of inventory. Choice (a) is incorrect. There is a brief discussion of the "cause" of the problem as being due to divisional management's conservative nature in avoiding risks of shutdowns. Choice (c) is incorrect. The report discusses the effect as one leading to unusually large levels of inventory write-downs because of obsolescence. Choice (d) is incorrect. The recommendations are logically derived from the findings and represent an approach that should be considered by management. Recommendations may be included, where appropriate, in audit reports.

Subject Area: Conduct audit engagements—audit reporting. Source: CIA 595, II-1.

**166. (a)** The auditor should avoid using emotionally charged words since doing so might create an unexpected, and negative, reaction from the auditee. The types of actions and attitudes of divisional management could have been adequately described as a cause without the use of the emotionally charged word. Choice (b) is incorrect. The excerpt is from the findings part of the audit report, not the management executive summary. Thus, it is appropriate to present the findings, and the basis for the findings, before presenting the auditor's recommendations. Choice (c) is incorrect. Given that the auditor has a basis for making the observation about component parts, it is appropriately to do so since it presents specifics on which both management and divisional management can focus action. Choice (d) is incorrect. The problem of excessive inventory has been noted in relationship to this finding. As long as the dollar amounts of excessive write-downs have been noted earlier in the report, it is appropriate to refer to that section for more detail.

Subject Area: Conduct audit engagements—audit reporting. Source: CIA 595, II-2.

**167. (d)** The recommendation given is not complete. Receiving reports are being prepared, but they are not being prepared on a timely basis, or concurrently with the receipt of the goods. The recommendation needs to be more detailed. Choice (a) is incorrect. The factual evidence comes from observation. Choice (b) is incorrect. The cause of the problem (or at least the excuse given by the receiving department) is noted. The receiving department does not prepare concurrent receiving reports when it is busy. Choice (c) is incorrect. This is a well-known risk, and the auditor is not "overdramatic" in factually detailing the result that might occur if the control deficiency is not adequately addressed.

Subject Area: Conduct audit engagements—audit reporting. Source: CIA 595, II-3.

**168. (c)**    The description used is that inventory is "messy," but "messy" is a word that does not clearly convey the condition. Choice (a) is incorrect. The risks are pointed out, in some detail, to management. Choice (b) is incorrect. The recommendation is logically presented. The problem is that the author has mixed a finding and a cause. Choice (d) is incorrect. The problem of excessive inventory has been noted in relationship to this finding. As long as the dollar amounts of excessive write-downs have been noted earlier in the report, it is appropriate to refer to that section for more detail.

Subject Area: Conduct audit engagements—audit reporting. Source: CIA 595, II-4.

**169. (d)**    All of the choices items are problems with the paragraph as it is currently written.

Subject Area: Conduct audit engagements—audit reporting. Source: CIA 595, II-5.

**170. (d)**    Choices (a), (b), and (c) are possible actions. However, choice (d) will appeal to the auditee's esteem needs by crediting the auditee in the audit report with the determination and implementation of the corrective action. Choice (b) is part of this solution, but the crediting in the report of the auditee's action responds to the auditee's needs.

Subject Area: Conduct audit engagements—audit reporting. Source: CIA 1194, II-13.

**171. (c)**    This appears to be more a matter of operating efficiency than an internal control weakness or violation of bank policy. Choice (a) is incorrect. This appears to be a serious violation of a standard bank policy. Destruction of uninsured collateral by fire or other catastrophe could easily result in significant uncollectible loan losses. Choice (b) is incorrect. This is a violation of the fundamental internal control concept of separation of duties and could result in major employee defalcations. Choice (d) is incorrect. This is a violation of the fundamental internal control concepts relating to access to assets and accountability, and could result in cash shortages that would be impossible to pin down.

Subject Area: Conduct audit engagements—audit reporting. Source: CIA 1194, II-14.

**172. (a)**    "Excessive" is a subjective term. The finding would be more complete if it indicated the percentage of late payments on which late charges were waived at the Spring Street Branch compared to a standard percentage, or the average percentage at other locations. Choice (b) is incorrect. The condition is the fact that an excessive number of late charges are being waived. Choice (c) is incorrect. The cause is the fact that approval by an officer is not required. Choice (d) is incorrect. The effect is the annual loss of $5,000 of revenues.

Subject Area: Conduct audit engagements—audit reporting. Source: CIA 1194, II-15.

**173. (b)**    This approach takes nothing away from the auditor, and it builds a problem-solving partnership between the auditor and branch manager. Choice (a) is incorrect. Top

management should be made aware of significant deficiencies that have existed, even though they may have been corrected by the time the audit report is issued. Choices (c) and (d) are incorrect. Discussion prior to issuing the report helps ensure that there have been no misunderstandings or misinterpretations of fact and provides the branch manager the opportunity to clarify specific items.

Subject Area: Conduct audit engagements—audit reporting. Source: CIA 1194, II-16.

**174. (b)**    A written report should be issued after completion of an audit. The report should be addressed to the level of management capable of agreeing to and correcting deficiencies noted in the report. Top management should be aware of internal audit's activities and any major deficiencies noted. This could be accomplished in a discussion or in a summary report. Choice (a) is incorrect. A written report should be issued after completion of an audit. However, writing detailed reports for each level of management is not an efficient use of an auditor's time. A summary report for top management could be issued along with a detailed report for the appropriate operational level of management. Choice (c) is incorrect. See choice (b). Choice (d) is incorrect. Conclusions and recommendations should be discussed with the appropriate levels of management, but an audit report should still be issued.

Subject Area: Conduct audit engagements—audit reporting. Source: CIA 1194, II-17.

**175. (a)**    Complex messages are more understandable if they follow a logical sequence. Thus, the sequence or organization of the message is a characteristic that is within the control of the sender. Choice (b) is incorrect. The nature of an audience is a situational factor that is outside the control of the auditor. Choice (c) is incorrect. Noise is a situational factor that interferes with the effective communication of intended messages. Choice (d) is incorrect. The history of previous encounters is a situational factor that is outside the control of the auditor.

Subject Area: Conduct audit engagements—audit reporting. Source: CIA 1194, II-18.

**176. (d)**    All of the listed principles of report clarity were violated in the audit report. Choice (a) is incorrect. The report is not organized in a clear and concise manner. Choice (b) is incorrect. The opening sentence is 73 words, while the next sentence is 37 words. Choice (c) is incorrect. There are at least two passive sentences.

Subject Area: Conduct audit engagements—audit reporting. Source: CIA 1194, II-19.

**177. (a)**    While a portion of the scope is discussed (30 machines selected), the reader cannot recognize the significance or insignificance of this amount without knowing the total amount of machines that could have been selected. The value of the machinery is not given. Also, the conclusion or auditor's opinion of the operation is not given and the report does not make any recommendations. Choice (b), (c), and (d) are incorrect because the purpose or objective of the audit was clearly stated. Results of the audit were also given.

Subject Area: Conduct audit engagements—audit reporting. Source: CIA 1194, II-20.

**178. (a)**    Diffusion involves setting aside the conflict situation and concentrating on less controversial issues. Choice (b) is incorrect. Under diffusion, differences are downplayed. Choice (c) is incorrect. Avoiding the conflict situation would be an example of an avoidance approach, not a diffusion approach. Choice (d) is incorrect. Directly addressing the sources of conflict would be an example of a confrontation approach, not a diffusion approach.

Subject Area: Conduct audit engagements—audit reporting. Source: CIA 1194, II-21.

**179. (d)** Oral reports permit auditors to counter arguments and provide additional information that the audience may require. Since oral reports evoke face-to-face responses, the auditors can provide an immediate response to any auditee objections or provide additional information as appropriate. Choice (a) is incorrect. The amount of testing required to support audit findings is unrelated to the use of oral reports. Whether findings are reported through oral or written reports, they still must be adequately supported. Choice (b) is incorrect. Even though audit reports are delivered orally, they still should be prepared carefully. Poorly planned and delivered oral reports will be difficult for the audience to follow and may create unnecessary misunderstandings. Choice (c) is incorrect. The format of the report will depend on the audience. Factors to consider in delivering reports may include the background and expectations of the audience as well as the time available. This applies to both written and oral reports. Since oral reports do not eliminate the need for a final report, overall audit efficiency is not affected.

Subject Area: Conduct audit engagements—audit reporting. Source: CIA 1194, II-23.

**180. (c)** This method of "show and tell" results in the most retention of information: 85% of the information is remembered after 3 hours and 65% is remembered after 3 days. Choice (a) is incorrect. According to research, observers will remember only 70% of the information after 3 hours and 10% after 3 days. Choice (b) is incorrect. Research indicates that observers will remember 72% of information after 3 hours and 20% after 3 days. Choice (d) is incorrect. This is the equivalent of choice (c) above— a "show" without the "tell." Observers can be expected to remember 72% of the information after 3 hours and 20% after 3 days.

Subject Area: Conduct audit engagements—audit reporting. Source: CIA 1194, II-24.

**181. (a)** "Purpose statements should describe the audit objectives" per the IIA *Standards.* Choice (b) is incorrect. "Scope statements should identify the audited activities and include, where appropriate, supportive information such as time period audited. Related activities not audited should be identified if necessary to delineate the boundaries of the audit. The nature and extent of auditing performed also should be described." This requirement does not include a statement of audit objectives. Choice (c) is incorrect. "Criteria: The standards, measures or expectations used in making an evaluation and/or verification (what should exist)." This requirement does not include a statement of audit objectives. Choice (d) is incorrect. "Condition: The factual evidence, which the internal auditor found in the course of the examination (what does exist)." This requirement does not include a statement of audit objectives.

Subject Area: Conduct audit engagements—audit reporting. Source: CIA 590, I-33.

**182. (a)** Oral reports give immediate response to management and are a more accurate form of communication since they provide visual feedback of the auditee's responses and questions and make immediate two-way communication possible. Choice (b) is incorrect. Oral reports must be presented with the same preparation and care as a written report if the auditor is to have credibility with the auditee. Choice (c) is incorrect. Agreements on significant audit findings should be formalized in the final report. Choice (d) is incorrect. The auditor should focus on oral report on the ideas being presented, not on a flashy presentation, which is excessive for the audience or the subject matter.

Subject Area: Conduct audit engagements—audit reporting. Source: CIA 590, I-38.

**183. (c)** Summary written reports are generally intended for audit committees of boards of directors and/or higher-level management. Choice (a) is incorrect. Summary written reports contain insufficient detail for local operating management. Choice (b) is incorrect. No document classified as an "audit report" is restricted to auditors only. Choice (d) is incorrect. Summary written reports contains insufficient detail for mid-level staff management.

Subject Area: Conduct audit engagements—audit reporting. Source: CIA 1190, I-42.

**184. (b)** Oral reports allow a response to emergency action needs. Choice (a) is incorrect. Oral reports do not provide a permanent record of the report. Choice (c) is incorrect. A summary of individual audits is best presented in a summary written report. Choice (d) is incorrect. Questionnaire-type reports are normally used for internal reporting within the internal auditing department.

Subject Area: Conduct audit engagements—audit reporting. Source: CIA 1190, I-43.

**185. (a)** Cause provides the answer to the question "Why?" and should be the basis for corrective action. Choice (b) is incorrect. Statement of condition simply describes "what is" to serve as a basis for comparison with a given criteria. Choice (c) is incorrect. Criteria describe "what should be" and are compared to the statement of condition. Choice (d) is incorrect. Effect addresses the importance of a finding.

Subject Area: Conduct audit engagements—audit reporting. Source: CIA 1190, II-42.

**186. (c)** The significance of deficiencies from prescribed procedures is an audit finding and belongs in the audit findings section of the report. Choice (a) is incorrect. This is not part of audit findings, but instead comes later in the report. Choice (b) is incorrect. This is not an audit finding. Choice (d) is incorrect. The engagement plan precedes the audit findings report.

Subject Area: Conduct audit engagements—audit reporting. Source: CIA 1190, II-43.

**187. (a)** This is appropriate action, so that lack of follow-up action, if any, can be noted on the next audit report. Choice (b) is incorrect. It is not ordinarily the responsibility of the auditor to implement corrective action. Choice (c) is incorrect. Data have already been examined. Choice (d) is incorrect. Data have already been assembled.

Subject Area: Conduct audit engagements—audit reporting. Source: CIA 1190, II-44.

**188. (b)** Audited activities, time period audited, related activities not audited, and the nature and extent of auditing performed may all be appropriately included in the scope statement. Choice (a) is incorrect. Audit objectives and the reason for conducting the audit are described in the purpose statement. Choice (c) is incorrect. The standards, measures, or expectations used in evaluating audit findings are attributes of findings that emerge during the review of the activities identified in the scope statement. Choice (d) is incorrect. The internal auditor's evaluation of the effect of the findings on the activities reviewed is properly presented in the conclusion or results section of the audit report.

Subject Area: Conduct audit engagements—audit reporting. Source: CIA 590, II-33.

**189. (a)** The written procedures represent the standard against which audit finding concerning segregation of responsibility would be measured. This standard is the condition that should exist. Choice (b) is incorrect. Condition is the factual evidence that the internal audit gathers in the course of the audit work. It represents what does exist. Choice (c) is incorrect. Cause is the reason why the condition observed is different from the criteria established. Choice (d) is incorrect. Effect measures the impact on the organization of the condition being different from the criteria.

Subject Area: Conduct audit engagements—audit reporting. Source: CIA 590, II-34.

**190. (c)** Interim reports can be used to report significant findings that require immediate attention to management. Choice (a) is incorrect. The purpose of the audit is formally defined in the final report and is discussed with the auditee's management prior to beginning the audit. Choice (b) is incorrect. The issuance of interim reports does not diminish or eliminate the need for a final report. Choice (d) is incorrect. The scope of the audit cannot be formally defined until the final report since interim findings may alter the scope during the audit.

Subject Area: Conduct audit engagements—audit reporting. Source: CIA 590, II-35.

**191. (d)** The summary report will serve as a useful tool for the senior management member. This tool will allow him or her to review quickly the major findings of the audit and to delve into more detail on those parts that are of interest. Choice (a) is incorrect. Senior members of management have enormous demands on their time. The final report will almost certainly have more detailed information than a senior management member will want to review. Choice (b) is incorrect. Oral communications will not give a senior manager a written record to use as a basis for further action. Choice (c) is incorrect. Interim reports will typically address specific segments of the audit and will not present the overview needed by a senior manager.

Subject Area: Conduct audit engagements—audit reporting. Source: CIA 590, II-36.

**192. (c)** This is what the IIA *Standards* require. Choice (a) is incorrect. Internal auditing has some follow-up responsibility. Choice (b) is incorrect. This would make internal auditing part of management and cause loss of independence. Choice (d) is incorrect. This responsibility cannot be passed to the independent auditor.

Subject Area: Conduct audit engagements—audit reporting. Source: CIA 590, II-39.

**193. (a)** This situation needs corrective action, and management should be made aware that it still exists. Choice (b) is incorrect. This is not within the internal auditor's authority, and it would not remedy the situation. The auditor would ascertain whether higher-level management has decided to assume the resulting risk, however. Choice (c) is incorrect. The audit report must contain conclusions regarding payroll internal control in the maintenance department. Choice (d) is incorrect. This would place the internal auditor in the position of supervising maintenance department employees.

Subject Area: Conduct audit engagements—audit reporting. Source: CIA 591, II-19.

**194. (d)** The evaluation of the impact of audit findings on audited activities is the statement of conclusions (opinions). A statement of conclusions (opinions) is required only where appropriate. Choice (a) is incorrect. The description of the audit objectives is the statement of purpose. A statement of purpose is always required. Choice (b) is incorrect. The identification of audited activities is the statement of scope. A statement of scope is always required. Choice (c) is incorrect. The listing of pertinent facts is the statement of findings. A statement of findings is always required.

Subject Area: Conduct audit engagements—audit reporting. Source: CIA 591, II-41.

**195. (d)** An oral report is appropriate as an interim audit report when significant problems are discovered. Choice (a) is incorrect. A summary report is an abbreviated explanation of major audit findings. It is generally submitted to top management and the audit committee of the board of directors. Choice (b) is incorrect. A written report is required for each audit. However, when a significant problem is discovered, an oral report should be used to get immediate action. Choice (c) is incorrect. A questionnaire-type report is normally used within the internal auditing department. It has a limited range of value.

Subject Area: Conduct audit engagements—audit reporting. Source: CIA 1191, II-41.

**196. (b)** This statement puts the findings in perspective based on the overall implications. It provides a capsule comment on the conditions found. Choice (a) is incorrect. The statement is not consistent with an overall opinion. It is a statement of condition. Choice (c) is incorrect. This is a possible cause or explanation for the problem and not legitimately part of the auditor's opinion. Choice (d) is incorrect. This is information used to prove a point or finding. It is a statement of condition and is not appropriate for an audit opinion.

Subject Area: Conduct audit engagements—audit reporting. Source: CIA 1191, II-42.

**197. (a)** These items are the standards, what the credit department is supposed to do. Choice (b),(c) and (d) are incorrect because they are not the standards.

Subject Area: Conduct audit engagements—audit reporting. Source: CIA 592, II-44.

**198. (b)** These items best explain why the deviation from the standards occurred.
Choice (a),(c) and (d) are incorrect because they are not the standards.

Subject Area: Conduct audit engagements—audit reporting. Source: CIA 592, II-45.

**199. (c)** These items show what is occurring and result from the observations, analysis, or verification of the internal auditor. Choice (a),(b) and (d) are incorrect because they do not show what is occurring.

Subject Area: Conduct audit engagements—audit reporting. Source: CIA 592, II-46.

**200. (b)** These items describe the real or potential impact (effect) according to the standards. Choice (a),(c), and (d) are incorrect because they don't comply with the standards.

Subject Area: Conduct audit engagements—audit reporting. Source: CIA 592, II-47.

**201. (b)** An interim report should be submitted to management. Choice (a) is incorrect. Significant audit findings should be communicated to management. Choice (c) is incorrect. Significant audit findings should be communicated to management with mention of other tests to be performed. Choice (d) is incorrect. Significant audit findings should be reported without delay for final audit testing.

Subject Area: Conduct audit engagements—audit reporting. Source: CIA 1193, II-41.

**202. (d)** Audit responsibility has been fulfilled. Choice (a) is incorrect. Regulatory authorities do not need to be notified since management has agreed to accept responsibility and no regulatory violations were mentioned. Choices (b) and (c) are incorrect. No further audit action is required.

Subject Area: Conduct audit engagements—audit reporting. Source: CIA 1193, II-42.

**203. (d)** The report, which was not published until eight weeks after the audit was concluded, was not issued in a timely fashion, given the significance of the findings and the need for prompt, effective action. Choice (a) is incorrect. There is not enough information to evaluate the effectiveness of follow-up. Choice (b) is incorrect. Auditors may properly make recommendations for potential improvements but should not implement corrective action. Choice (c) is incorrect. Auditor recommendations are one of the recommended elements of an audit finding.

Subject Area: Conduct audit engagements—audit reporting. Source: CIA 1191, I-41.

**204. (c)** This would be an appropriate recommendation. Choice (a) is incorrect. Specific criteria would not be an appropriate recommendation. Choice (b) is incorrect. This would not be an appropriate recommendation; it would require further analysis. Choice (d) is incorrect. This would be excessive given the results of the audit just completed.

Subject Area: Conduct audit engagements—audit reporting. Source: CIA 593, I-8.

**205. (c)** Control weaknesses over the payroll function should be most useful to the payroll manager because this is the individual who is directly responsible for this department. Choice (a) is incorrect. Control weaknesses in a company's payroll department would not be most useful to the treasurer because he or she is not responsible for taking corrective action for weaknesses in that department. Choice (b) is incorrect. The audit committee of the board of directors would not have a direct interest in a report dealing with weaknesses over the payroll function, and thus, such a report would not be most useful to such individuals. Choice (d) is incorrect. A company's president is responsible for the overall operations of the company. Accordingly, control weak-

nesses over payroll would not be most useful to such individual.

Subject Area: Conduct audit engagements—audit reporting. Source: CIA 593, I-36.

**206. (c)** This is in accordance with the IIA *Standards,* which state: "Reports may also be distributed to other interested or affected parties such as external auditors or the audit committee." The potential for misstated financial statements created by the internal control deficiencies should be of interest to the audit committee and the external auditors. Choice (a) is incorrect. Normal distribution is to department heads of units audited and others in a position to take corrective action or ensure that corrective action is taken. Choice (b) is incorrect. Operating management takes corrective action. Choice (d) is incorrect. There is no such requirement.

Subject Area: Conduct audit engagements—audit reporting. Source: CIA 593, I-41.

**207. (a)** An operational audit report should inform management about the efficiency and effectiveness of the given operations and should discuss findings requiring corrective action. Choice (b) is incorrect. An operational audit report should address the propriety of the function being audited rather than with valuation of item being audited. Choice (c) is incorrect. An operational audit report should address the propriety of the function being audited rather than with the agreement between the records and the items being audited. Choice (d) is incorrect. An operational audit report of the scrap disposal function would not address the valuation of the scrap material inventory at the lower of its cost or market.

Subject Area: Conduct audit engagements—audit reporting. Source: CIA 593, I-37.

**208. (d)** Choice (d) is the correct answer. According to the IIA *Standards*, "Summary reports highlighting audit results may be appropriate for levels of management above the head of the audited unit." Choice (a) is incorrect. The accounts payable manager would be best served by receiving a copy of the full final audit report. Choice (b) is incorrect. External auditor would receive copy of full report. Choice (c) is incorrect. The controller, like the accounts payable manager, would need a copy of the full final report so that details of deficiencies are known and so audit recommendations may be implemented.

Subject Area: Conduct audit engagements—audit reporting. Source: CIA 593, I-39.

**209. (d)** According to the IIA *Standards,* the use of interim reports does not diminish or eliminate the need for a final report. Choice (a) is incorrect. The interim report can minimize report writing time. Choice (b) is incorrect. Improved communications is an advantage. Choice (c) is incorrect. Per the IIA *Standards,* interim reports may be written or oral and may be transmitted formally or informally.

Subject Area: Conduct audit engagements—audit reporting. Source: CIA 593, II-38.

**210. (a)** Since this is very confidential information that could be detrimental to the welfare of the employer, it is not advisable to include these details in the formal audit report. The final report should concentrate on corrective actions needed and avoid unnecessary details that could expose employees to a robbery. A verbal interim report could effectively sell the danger and importance of immediate action in this matter. Choice (b) is incorrect. While this is a good approach on most findings, it is not satisfactory here because of the high exposure to theft and danger to employees. Therefore, immediate corrective action and a low profile are dictated. Choice (c) is incorrect. It shows a lack of good judgment bordering on incompetence. The lack of loss is the product of pure luck and not any internal control system. Choice (d) is incorrect. This is unacceptable because it does not react quickly enough to a dangerous situation, and a full disclosure of this weakness could represent real danger to company employees and heighten the chances that a theft would occur.

Subject Area: Conduct audit engagements—audit reporting. Source: CIA 593, II-43.

**211. (b)** The board of directors should receive the report. Choice (a) is incorrect. The report should not go to the external auditor and bypass chain of command. Choice (c) is incorrect. The report should not go to stockholders. Choice (d) is incorrect. The report should not go to senior management since they may be involved.

Subject Area: Conduct audit engagements—audit reporting. Source: CIA 1192, I-40.

**212. (d)** The board chairman would not normally receive a copy. Choice (a) is incorrect. The director of purchasing should receive a copy. Choice (b) is incorrect. The external auditors should receive a copy. Choice (c) is incorrect. The general auditor should receive a copy.

Subject Area: Conduct audit engagements—audit reporting. Source: CIA 1192, II-45.

**213. (a)** The cause of the finding is that advance procedures do not require specific justification. Choice (b) is incorrect. Policy provides for advances only to authorized employees. Choice (c) is incorrect. Accumulating large travel advances is the effect of the audit finding. Choice (d) is incorrect. Not clearing travel advances in a timely manner is the effect of the audit finding.

Subject Area: Conduct audit engagements—audit reporting. Source: CIA 1192, II-41.

**214. (d)** "Travel advances exceeded prescribed maximum amounts" is the condition. Choice (a) is incorrect. "Advances are not to exceed estimated expenses for 45 days" represents criteria. Choice (b) is incorrect. "Employees accumulate large advances" is the effect. Choice (c) is incorrect. The cause of the finding is procedures do not require specific justification.

Subject Area: Conduct audit engagements—audit reporting. Source: CIA 1192, II-42.

**215. (d)** An oral report is appropriate for a situation that requires emergency action. Of course, a written report should follow. Choice (a) is incorrect. A summary written report summarizes various written reports filed in a specific period. Choice (b) is incorrect. A formal written report is issued at the completion of the audit. This hazardous situation requires immediate action, however. Choice (c) is incorrect. The auditor should file a follow-up report on this situation later. However, management must be alerted about the situation now.

Subject Area: Conduct audit engagements—audit reporting. Source: CIA 591, I-19.

**216. (a)** The report may be distributed to other interested or affected parties. Choices (b) and (c) are incorrect. The purchasing manager and operations director would not be interested or affected by a report with only routine findings in another department. Choice (d) is incorrect. A report with routine findings does not warrant being sent to the chairman of the board of directors.

Subject Area: Conduct audit engagements—audit reporting. Source: CIA 591, II-43.

# 2 CONDUCT SPECIFIC ENGAGEMENTS (25%–35%)

## THEORY

### 2.1 Conduct Assurance Engagements

Assurance auditing provides an assessment of the reliability and/or relevance of data and operations in specific areas of business functions. The scope of assurance engagements includes fraud investigation, risk and control self-assessment, third-party and contract audit, quality audit, due diligence audit, security audit, privacy audit, performance audit, operational audit, financial audit, information technology audit, and compliance audit. With these engagements, internal auditors provide reasonable assurance whether organizational goals are being accomplished.

(a) **Fraud Investigation.** The objectives of fraud investigation are to determine whom, why, and how. Possible approaches include testimonial evidence, documentary evidence, physical evidence (forensic analysis), and personal observation; theft act investigative methods, such as surveillance and covert operations, invigilation (close supervision of suspects); concealment investigative methods, such as document examination, audits, computer searches, and physical asset counts; conversion investigative methods, such as public record searches and net worth analysis; and inquiry investigative methods, such as interviewing and interrogation.[1] The latter approach is presented in detail.

(i) **Interviewing and interrogating in fraud investigations.** Auditors will encounter situations where they would be interviewing employees who were suspected of fraudulent activities. Handling a fraud situation is a very delicate matter with associated financial and legal risks. Knowing what questions to ask and how to ask them of suspects and knowing the difference between interviewing and inter-

---

[1] W. Steve Albrecht, Gerald W. Wernz, and Timothy L. Williams, *Fraud: Bringing Light to the Dark Side of Business* (Burr Ridge, IL: Irwin Professional Publishing, 1995).

rogating would help auditors immensely from being exposed to legal and financial risks. These risks arise simply because of the auditors' lack of technical knowledge in the subject area.

Auditors would meet many parties during the interviewing and interrogating process, including security staff, prosecutors, and other law enforcement officials. Auditors should clearly understand their own role and the role of others in this process.

(ii) **Interpretation of behavior.** Interviewers/interrogators should remember that extremes in a suspect's behavior often indicate deception.[2] At least, they should recognize that the stress of not telling the truth often causes changes in attitudes and verbal and nonverbal behavior. These changes should be compared with what is normal for the individual and the population in general. A profile of the truthful and untruthful suspect follows.

(iii) **Verbal behavior.** Truthful individuals are generally calm, relaxed, and cooperative while being interviewed. As suspects become more comfortable with the situation, they become more relaxed. Overall, truthful individuals are cordial, friendly, and relatively easy to handle.

The attitude displayed by untruthful suspects is usually impatience, both in word and action. They are tense and defensive while questioning, look at their watch, and suggest that they need to be somewhere else.

Truthful individuals generally respond to questions and make timely responses. Untruthful suspects are usually vague and stammering in their responses. There may be long pauses when speaking or answers that are too quick, too short, too long, or too elaborate. The guilty talk softly, mumble, and in many cases talk through their hand.

Guilty suspects often attempt to take an overly friendly, polite, or cooperative attitude toward the interviewers/interrogators. Guilty suspects use this tactic in an attempt to keep the interviewer as a friend rather than as an enemy. Guilty people hope this cooperative attitude will get them a break or even that they will be overlooked as a suspect. Excessive friendliness and politeness by a suspect should immediately alert the interviewer to the suspect's probable deception. This politeness often seems quite out of place.

### Verbal Behavior

The ultimate goal is to elicit the truth from the reluctant suspect. The difficulty in assessing verbal behavior is that the words spoken to the interviewer may be exactly the same for both the truthful and the untruthful suspect. Only the differences in the nonverbal behavior, tone of voice, loudness, and speed of delivery may differentiate truth from deception.

A delay in response to an interviewer's question is a good indicator of a suspect's guilt. Innocent individuals rarely need to think about a response. They simply answer the question posed directly and promptly. The guilty, however, often pause or delay a response while they think. Inappropriate laughter by a suspect is an attempt to make the interviewer's question seem petty. The laughter can be used to cover the deceptive suspect's delay.

Truthful suspects respond directly and deny the allegation, saying, for example, "I did not steal any money." The guilty respond by denying specifically "I did not steal that $300." The qualified response is an indication of a deceptive individual.

Some guilty suspects will attempt to take the offensive by portraying a surly, nasty, aggressive attitude toward interviewers. This surly attitude is designed to put interviewers on the defense and cause them to back off from the confrontation with suspects.

(iv) **Nonverbal behavior.** Interviewers should remember that the entire body must be considered when observing nonverbal behavior. Also, both verbal and nonverbal behavior must be considered together.

- The guilty may perspire excessively, particularly on the trunk of the body. However, the perspiration may not be a relevant clue if the suspect has engaged in strenuous activity or come from an extremely hot environment just prior to the meeting.

---

[2]  *David E. Zulawski and Douglas E. Wicklander, Practical Aspects of Interview and Interrogation (Boca Raton, FL: by CRC Press, 1993).*

- The hands and the arms may provide the guilty with a barrier to protect the abdominal cavity and relieve the stress of sitting across from an interviewer/interrogator. The hands and the arms are used to perform created jobs or grooming gestures.

## Nonverbal Behavior

The interviewer should attempt to establish a behavioral norm for the suspect. Consideration should be given to the suspect's voice pattern, word choice, eye movement, attitude, and physical behavior.

- Scratching the nose, rubbing the brow, or adjusting the glasses could also be used as a ruse to cover the actual purpose of the hand movement.
- The drumming of fingers indicates a suspect's impatience. Clenched fists may show a suspect's frustration or a negative attitude toward the discussion or interviewer.
- Many guilty individuals begin to itch and scratch immediately after the introduction of a stressful topic.
- Suspects may use the thumbs to indicate a defensive or superior attitude. They will lean back in the chair, arms crossed and fingers tucked underneath the armpits with the thumbs extended upward.
- Crossed arms often indicate negative thoughts or displeasure with the conversation. They may also be used in situations where an individual feels uncertain or insecure. Individuals also cross their arms when they feel cold.
- Crossing the ankles or legs typically provides a defensive barrier against the interviewer. As a general rule, the more defensive an individual becomes, the higher the knee rise to protect the abdominal region.
- Truthful individuals will generally have good eye contact with the interviewer. Often the deceptive individual's eyes will be cold and hostile. They have a flat look to them that does not allow the interviewer to look beneath the surface of the eyes.
- In order to reduce the suspect's level of defensiveness, chairs should be positioned directly across from each other or slightly off to one side, which will lessen the confrontational feel of the meeting.

(v) **Role of interviewer/interrogator.** Interviewers blame denials only on the suspect's fear of consequences. Interviewers can also cause denials because of strategies or tactics employed during the interrogation. The suspect's perception of the interviewer and/or the interviewer's strategy often dictates whether the suspect will deny.

Interrogators who are overbearing, aggressive, or nonempathic toward a suspect often increase the suspect's defensiveness, resulting in denial. When a suspect dislikes an interviewer, the dislike often turns into distrust and denial. Interrogators' attitudes should be that of mediators seeking the truth rather than that of dominant, authoritative figures. They should display professionalism.

When interviewers attempt to rush the suspect into a confession due to lack of time or other, the suspect may elect to deny simply because he or she believes the interviewers' hurried demeanor is a weakness to be exploited. By making denials and waiting interviewers out, the suspect believes that he or she can win the encounter.

The verbal and physical behavior displayed by interviewers/interrogators during the interrogation can also directly affect a suspect's decision to deny. If interviewers are perceived as unsure, inconsistent, or weak, the suspect will make a denial to test the interviewer's assertions.

If interviewers are uncertain of the case facts, misquote commonly known facts, or seem unprepared, suspects are encouraged to deny. The suspect's decision to deny is based on a belief that he or she has not been clearly identified with the case. The suspect is taking a chance that the interviewer's bumbling of the facts is directly related to the competency of the investigation. *Most suspects recognize that an incompetent investigation will be unlikely to result in their being proved guilty of the offense.*

Interrogators' word choices may cause denials, as might long pauses or silence. The use of silence by interviewers rarely enhances the likelihood of a confession. To the contrary, it allows the suspect an opportunity to think and assess other possibilities that might convince the interrogator of his or her innocence. In an interrogation, silence invites the suspect to join the conversation. Long pauses by the interrogator invite a denial from the suspect.

## ROLE OF SILENCE IN INTERVIEWS AND INTERROGATIONS

- Silence in an interview is an effective strategy since it can be filled with more conversation. Remember that in an interview, the interviewee (suspect) does all the talking.
- Silence in an interrogation is not an effective strategy since the suspect can deny. Remember that in interrogation, the interviewer (auditor or investigator) does all the talking.

(vi) **Interviewing versus interrogation.** An interview is a fact-gathering process that attempts to answer the six journalistic (investigative) questions: who, what, when, where, how, and why. The suspect who responds to questions posed by the interviewer dominates talking during the interview. During the interview, the suspect may be asked behavior-provoking questions by the interviewer to determine the suspect's truthfulness. The setting of an interview also tends to be much less formal than that of interrogation. In an interview, the interviewer may often pick a time and location convenient for the person being interviewed. In the earliest stages of investigation, the interview is broad-based, with the interviewer attempting to give direction to the investigation.

*An interview can turn into an investigation at any time.* The change in the process from nonaccusatory to accusatory can be very direct or very subtle. In either case, the amount of talking done by the interviewee and suspect changes dramatically. During the interview process, the investigator has made the majority of questions broad and open-ended to elicit a narrative response from the suspect. To clarify specific points, the interviewer may have used closed-end questions. However, once the interviewer has elected to confront the suspect, the interviewer begins to do all the talking and offers face-saving rationalizations that minimize the seriousness of the suspect's involvement.

By contrast, an interrogation is designed to obtain information that might be incriminatory from a suspect who may be reluctant to give the information. The purpose of interrogation is to overcome the suspect's initial resistance and open a dialogue that will encourage the suspect to give information against his or her interests. An interrogator is still attempting to answer the six investigative questions (who, what, when, where, how, and why), but there are two basic differences between an interview and interrogation.

1. In interrogation, the suspect talks only when he or she is confessing.
2. The suspect resists telling the truth until he or she is convinced of the need to do otherwise.

Victims and witnesses typically are interviewed at a time and place convenient to them. If the interviewer/interrogator believes that the individual might ultimately be the suspect, an interrogation could follow. In such a case, the interviewer/interrogator should ask the suspect come to his or her office or at a location where a more formalized setting can be arranged. Regardless of whether the interviewer plans a nonaccusatory interview or an interrogation of a suspect, the interviewer's behavior should seem reasonable and fair.

There is never room for mistreatment of a witness or suspect by an interviewer. Yelling, screaming, or pounding fists on the table to obtain information from a reluctant witness have no place in either an interview or an interrogation.

### Interview versus Investigation

An interview is a noncustody and nonaccusatory situation. An investigation is quite the opposite.

In the interview, the interviewer should open the lines of communication so that the victim, witness, or suspect will begin to talk about the incident under investigation. It may be worthwhile to prepare specific written questions to assure the accuracy of the way that they were asked. The key questions need to be camouflaged during the interview so that the interviewer does not highlight their importance. For example, when conducting a kickback investigation, an investigator may look at a buyer's phone records for investigative leads, but the interviewer does not request the buyer's phone number alone. To conceal the target of the investigation, the entire buying department's phone records may be requested. Although investigators may not be able to conceal the fact that they are looking at telephone records, at least they can conceal who they are looking at.

**Rapport** is needed both in normal interviewing and investigative situations. Rapport is more than just smiling. Even the most cooperative, agreeable witness can be turned off by an interviewer who fails to establish rapport. Interviewers who are too blunt and to the point, who attempt to obtain information without establishing rapport, are often faced with witness who are cold and uncooperative.

How is rapport established? The interviewer should attempt to establish rapport by finding some common ground or interest about which to speak to the individual. People tend to like people who have similar interests and personalities. The interrogator should avoid using words like "steal," "embezzle," or "fraud" when talking to the suspect. People who have a genuine smile are judged to be more honest and trustworthy than those who have cold, expressionless faces. *The kind of words used and the facial expressions displayed lead to good rapport.*

Words alone are not enough to build good rapport between the interviewer and the suspect. Interviewers should practice other techniques, such as mirroring. People who have a high level of rapport tend to mirror each other's behavior. **Mirroring** includes modeling the speech patterns, speed of delivery, breathing, posture, and gestures of the individual to whom the interviewer is speaking. This mirroring shows up as similar body positioning, physiology, tone of voice, and even choice of words used between the two parties. When interviewers mirror an individual's posture, gestures, and physiology, they can create within themselves the same emotions that the suspect is feeling.

## TRUTH VERSUS UNTRUTH IN INTERVIEWS AND INTERROGATIONS

- Individuals who are telling the truth about the issue under investigation are more likely to give direct answers during the interview. In addition, they are often helpful and cooperative in their responses.
- Individuals who are not telling the truth are not as specific, direct, or helpful. In many cases, their responses are vague, too elaborate, short, or evasive.

## AWARENESS OF COMMON-LAW CAUSES OF ACTION

Employers or interviewers must be aware of these common law causes of action before conducting any interviews. Even though the employee has common law rights, the public or private employer has the right to investigate and to expect loyalty from the employee.

**False imprisonment.** This cause of action generally requires that an employee be detained without his or her consent or a legal justification to restrain the employee. A false imprisonment is a detention where no arrest warrant has been issued, or if one has been issued, it is void. For an employee to prove a case of false imprisonment, he or she must prove that: an arrest or forcible detention took place; the arrest or imprisonment was caused by the company; the detention was unlawful or made without a warrant; and there was malice on the part of the company. An employer is entitled to interview an employee on company premises about violations of company policy without liability for false imprisonment. In a number of cases where false imprisonment was found to have occurred, the employee was physically restrained from leaving.

**Defamation.** Defamation of character is the most often occurring allegation made by a suspect regarding an incident of misconduct. The defamation of character may occur in the form of a slander or libelous statement. *Slander* is a false statement that was not written down but was spoken to one or more individuals. *Libel* is an untrue statement that was written down and was communicated to others.

In order for employees to establish that they have suffered a defamation of character, they must prove four things.

1. They must prove that particular words were actually spoken, including proving both the time and place that the activity took place.

2. They must also prove that these words were spoken or published to third persons.
3. They must show that the words written or spoken were actually false.
4. They must also show other facts that prove that the words are libelous or slanderous. This would include that there was malice on the part of the company or investigator and that the libel or slander was not privileged in any way.

An employer has a qualified privilege to communicate allegations during an investigation. However, this qualified privilege is lost if false communication were made out of spite or malice with knowledge that the statements were, in fact, false. In addition, these knowingly false statements must have been communicated to an excessive number of people. During the course of investigative interviews, interviewers should avoid repeating any information or allegations of which they are uncertain to third parties. *As a practical matter, the interview process is one of gathering information rather than giving information to the interviewee.*

An investigator should limit communicating allegations to those who have a need to know as part of the investigation or decision-making process relating to the consequences of the suspect's actions. An investigator can establish the qualified privilege by noting on investigative reports that the document is privileged for counsel. This establishes an attorney-client privilege and protects many documents during an investigation.

The interviewer/interrogator should understand that a qualified privilege exists to express oral charges to superiors, police, prosecutors, or other persons having a need to know within the company. Care should be taken that the report of what happened during the investigation, interview, or interrogation is fair and that statements made are fair and done without malice to the suspect.

**Malicious prosecution.** Companies investigating employee theft, illegal drug use, or other illegal activities within a company must decide whether it is in their best interest to contact a law enforcement agency. Certain businesses, such as financial institutions, are required to report thefts to the Federal Bureau of Investigation. Illegal activities, such as the theft of firearms or controlled substances, are also closely monitored by federal and state agencies. Since most companies do not have a requirement to notify public law enforcement of problems within their company, they generally do not do so because of the cost of prosecution and the difficulty of proving circumstantial cases. A corporation's bonding company may also need to be made aware of loss to keep the insurance contract in force.

Once the company has decided to prosecute an employee, the company can be opening the door to potential liability for an allegation of malicious prosecution and false arrest. For an employee to establish a malicious prosecution claim against the company, the employee must prove that (1) the employer instituted or continued a criminal proceeding, (2) the proceeding was terminated in the employee's favor, (3) no probable cause existed for initiating a proceeding, and (4) the employer's motive in initiating the proceeding was malice or some purpose other than bringing the employee to justice.

Private-sector investigators can limit their and the company's potential liability for a malicious prosecution allegation by allowing the prosecution or police officer to make the decision to prosecute. Malice on the part of the company or an employer may be shown through personal animosity between the person making the accusation and the accused employee. It can also be inferred from the lack of a complete investigation on the part of the company. Furthermore, the company may show the element of malice if it conveys facts that are untrue or withholds facts that might mitigate the conclusion reached by police investigators.

**Assault and battery.** Although assault and battery are related, they are fundamentally different. Battery is bodily contact that either causes harm or is offensive to a reasonable person's sense of dignity; assault is words or actions that place the employee in fear of receiving a battery. Actual physical contact is not an element of assault, but violence, either threatened or offered, is required. An assault can occur when the person uses threatening words or gestures and has the ability to commit the battery.

*SOURCE: David E. Zulawski and Douglas E. Wicklander, **Practical Aspects of Interview and Interrogation** (Boca Raton, FL: CRC Press, 1993).*

(b) **Controls to Prevent or Detect Fraud.** Fraud prevention results in big savings because when fraud is prevented, there are no detection or investigation costs. This means a dollar spent in preventing fraud saves many more dollars later on. Therefore, greater attention should be paid to preventive controls.

(i) **Preventive controls in general.** Some examples of preventive controls include: sharing the company vision with all employees; distributing fraud policies and programs; conducting proactive audits using discovery sampling techniques; database query facilities and data mining tools; providing a hotline for fraud reporting by employees and others; monitoring employee performance; enforcing employee vacation privileges; discouraging collusion between employees, customers, or vendors with policies clearly explained to them; establishing a sound system of internal controls (both formal and informal); providing fraud awareness training programs; providing employee assistance programs to deal with personal and work-related pressures; establishing physical security and information systems security controls; enforcing existing internal controls and fraud policies with the understanding that dishonesty will be punished; establishing separation of duties, dual custody, and dual controls; establishing total quality management programs; creating a positive work environment with open-door policy to facilitate open communications; creating teamwork with self-directed teams or quality circles; assigning responsibility for fraud prevention programs; hiring honest employees; publishing a code of ethics; establishing a system of authorizations and independent checks and balances; and encouraging employee empowerment.

(ii) **Detective controls in general.** Some examples of detective controls include: building audit trails in business transactions (whether automated or not); testing controls; conducting regular internal audits; conducting surprise internal audits; conducting employee performance evaluations; watching employee lifestyle changes; observing employee behavior toward work, the organization, and other employees; and periodically taking physical inventory of assets, financial securities, and other valuable items.

(iii) **Computer fraud–related controls.** Management (directive) controls, such as performing pre-employment screening procedures, requiring employees to sign a code of conduct, and conducting periodic training programs in computer security and privacy policies and procedures are good business practices. System-based preventive, detective, and recovery controls are also needed to effectively combat computer crime and fraud in the electronic age.

---

**Auditing for Fraud Guidelines**

- Good fraud auditors must be nosy.
- To catch a thief, auditors must learn to think like one.
- Detection of fraud takes a long time and hard work.
- Question the validity of any unusual transactions.

---

**Preventive controls** can help in restricting the access of potential perpetrators to the computer facility, computer terminals, data files, programs, and system libraries. Separation of duties, rotation of duties, backup personnel, and a good system of internal controls are some examples of preventive controls.

**Detective controls** can help in discovering fraud in the event perpetrator slips past established prevention mechanisms. Some tips and procedures for fraud detection include: take a fresh approach to looking at the data (middle-of-the-month review instead of month-end), break the normal pattern of reporting (obtain early or late reports, ad hoc reports instead of scheduled), change review timing to throw things off their track (random times, not month-end, quarter-end, or year-end), and run normal reports at unusual times. Audit hooks can help in monitoring the computer fraud. Audit hooks are embedded in the application program and are flagged when incoming and processed transactions meet prescribed criterion. If the auditors requested and designed the audit hooks, they should provide the test data and assist in testing the computer system.

**Recovery controls** can help in limiting losses (financial or other) resulting from a well-planned and well-executed computer fraud and crime.

Prior to auditing for fraud, the organization must answer these questions.

- What does the organization have that someone would want to steal?

- How would someone go about stealing from the organization?
- How vulnerable is the organization?
- How can the organization detect fraud and crime?

(c) **Audit Steps to Detect Fraud.**  It has been said that most frauds are detected by accident, not by planned effort. This should not stop auditors from planning to detect of fraud. Some known approaches to detect fraud include testing, statistical sampling, computer-assisted audit techniques, data query, and data mining tools.

Some examples of tests include analytical techniques, charting techniques, recalculations, confirmations, observations, physical examinations, inquiries, and document reviews.

Examples of statistical techniques include discovery sampling, a type of sampling procedure that has a specified probability of including at least one item that occurs very rarely in the population. Multiple regression analysis can be used to find relationships between two or more variables of interest.

Examples of computer-assisted audit techniques include finding exceptions in data through analysis of computer files. These files are searched for duplication of invoices or payments, or other anomalies.

Data query tools are used to search the database for known conditions of data sequencing and data dependencies. Auditors can query many points within a database. Data mining tools can be used to detect abnormal patterns in data.

(d) **Steps to Take When Fraud Is Suspected.**  Handling suspected fraud is a difficult thing to do. It must be handled properly and with care. Amateurs in the personnel or audit department playing at the investigative business can cause many unforeseen problems and unpleasant surprises. If cases of suspected fraud are not handled properly, employee morale and trust can easily be shattered. Unsubstantiated charges can bring on lawsuits for defamation, illegal firing, false arrest, invasion of privacy, and stress. Confrontations with the suspected employee can be staged before the allegations are even documented or verified. Evidence that may support the charges can often go uncollected or be mishandled.

Jack Bologna provides these tips that could help in investigating internal corruption charges.

- Qualify the source of the allegation (i.e., check on the source's identity, credibility, knowledgeability, and reliability).
- Determine whether the source knows the information firsthand (personal knowledge) or whether it has been passed on by another (hearsay).
- Determine the motives of the source (revenge, spite, jealousy, pique, and money).
- If the source demands money before disclosing details, beware. Do not "front" money until verifiable information has been given and has been confirmed through independent means (other credible witnesses or documents).
- Qualify all further information about the alleged corruption; that is, verify and corroborate the charges through other independent sources and documents.
- Never take disciplinary action without a complete record of the corruption allegation, including the identity of the source of the allegations and his or her written account of the allegations (an oral account is not enough).
- Confirm the allegations through documents and the testimony (written and subscribed to) of other knowledgeable witnesses.
- Approach the vendors, suppliers, or others alleged to be involved; elicit their response and enlist their cooperation.
- Interview the suspected employee to seek his or her version of the situation. (e.g., did the vendor make the offer or did the employee solicit the vendor?)[3]

Another related question that should be asked is: Should the investigation and audit proceed with inside resources (i.e., security department staff, legal department staff, or audit department staff, or a combination)? If the insiders are trained properly, work can proceed in-house. If they are not properly trained, it is advisable to go outside to a reputable and experienced private detective, legal firm, consultant, public accounting firm, or other.

(i) **Document examination.**  Document examination is a part of gathering evidence for fraud. Document examination is a technique that uncovers perpetrators' efforts to conceal fraud by cover-up schemes involving documents. Documents can be altered, forged, created, changed, duplicated, or

---

[3]  *Jack Bologna, **Handbook on Corporate Fraud** (Stoneham, MA: Butterworth-Heinemann, 1993).*

misplaced. According to Joseph Wells, most internal frauds are concealed by manipulating source documents, such as purchase orders, sales invoices, credit memorandums, and warehouse removal slips.[4] Investigators should be aware that missing documents, destroyed records, modified records, errors, or omissions can be attributed to human error, carelessness, or accident as well as deliberate action on the part of a suspect.

## GUIDELINES FOR DOCUMENT EXAMINATION

- Always search for the strongest possible evidence.
- Investigate without delay.
- Do not ignore small clues or leads.
- Look for facts you can confirm or refute.
- Be persistent and creative.
- Concentrate on the weakest link in the fraud chain.

*SOURCE: Joseph Wells, Association of Certified Fraud Examiners (ACFE), Austin, Texas, 1992.*

(ii) **Examining accounting records.** According to Wells, one of the easiest ways to detect fraud in the accounting records is by looking for weaknesses in the various steps of the accounting transaction cycle. Legitimate transactions leave a trail that can be followed. Most transactions start with a source document, such as an invoice, a check, or a receiving report.

These source documents become the basis for journal entries, which are chronological listings of transactions with their debit and credit amounts. Journal entries are made in various accounting journals. The entries in the journals are then posted or entered into the accounts. The amounts in the accounts are summarized to become the financial statements for a period.

When fictitious entries are made to the accounting records, source documents are normally absent, fabricated, or altered. These documents, together with the journal entries, accounts, and financial statements, leave a trail that can reveal many frauds. These guidelines help in searching for overstatement or understatement of amounts in financial statements.

- When searching for an understatement in the financial statements, one usually begins with the source documents and works forward to the financial statements. If the financial statements are understated, sometimes the information from the invoice will be deleted or altered.
- When searching for an overstatement in the financial statements, one starts with the financial statement and works backward to the source documents. Normally true overstatements will not have legitimate support documentation.

Analyzing past records can reveal some insights that can be used to establish the operating standards. These records should include

- The normal rate of loss per a specific time period
- The number and nature of transactions processed per day
- The number and nature of exceptional transactions handled
- The number and nature of people movement in and out per day

(iii) **Documenting fraud.** Documenting fraud is as important, if not more, as conducting the fraud investigation. Documenting fraud is a continuous effort from inception to completion of the fraud investigation. During the documentation period, a great deal of evidence is in the form of documents. Wells states that many examiners (auditors) pay too much attention to documents. It is easy to get bogged down in details when examining records and lose sight of a simple fact: Documents do not make cases; witnesses do. The documents make or break the witness. So-called paper cases often confuse and bore juries. Only relevant documents should be collected. In order to guarantee document acceptance by the courts, one should provide

- Proof that the evidence is relevant and material
- Proper identification of the item
- Proof of the chain of custody of the document

---

[4] *Joseph T. Wells, **Fraud Examination: Investigative and Audit Procedures** (New York: Quorum Books, 1992).*

Early in the case, the relevance of documents cannot be easily determined. For that reason, it is recommended that all documents possible be obtained; if they are not needed, they can always be returned or destroyed. General rules regarding the collection of documents include

- Obtain original documents where feasible. Make working copies for review, and keep the original segregated.
- Do not touch originals any more than necessary; they may later be needed for forensic analysis.
- Maintain a good filing system for the documents. This is especially critical where large volumes of documents are obtained. Voluminous documents can be sequentially stamped for easy reference.[5]

(iv) **Obtaining documentary evidence.** Three principal methods exist for obtaining documentary evidence: subpoenas, search warrants, and voluntary consent[6] (see Exhibit 2.1).

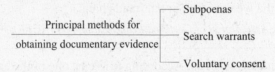

**Exhibit 2.1:  Principle method for obtaining documentary evidence**

**Subpoenas** are ordinarily issued by the court or grand jury and can take three forms. A subpoena *duces tectum* calls for the production of documents and records, whereas a regular subpoena is used for witnesses. If the examiner is not an agent of the grand jury or the court, obtaining documents by subpoena is not possible. Subpoenas can call for the production of documents at a grand jury or deposition at a specified time. A forthwith subpoena is usually served by surprise, and reserved for those instances where it is thought the records will be secreted, altered, or destroyed.

**Search warrants** are issued by a judge upon presentation of probable cause to believe the records are being used or have been used in the commission of a crime. An affidavit is usually used to support the request for the search warrant. The affidavit must describe the reason(s) the warrant is requested, along with the place the evidence is thought to be kept.

Courts do not issue search warrants lightly, as the Constitution protects individuals against unreasonable searches and seizures. Search warrants are almost never used in civil cases. Although there are provisions in the law for warrantless search, examiners should avoid such searches at all costs. Searches can be conducted by voluntary consent.

Documents can be obtained by **voluntary consent,** and this is the preferred method. The consent can be oral or written. In the case of obtaining information from possible adverse witnesses or from the target of the examination, it is recommended that the consent be in writing.

(v) **Types of evidence.** The examiner or auditor needs to be familiar with the types of evidence in order to obtain the right kind of evidence. Basically, evidence falls into one of two categories, either direct or circumstantial (see Exhibit 2.2).

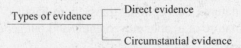

**Exhibit 2.2:  Types of evidence**

**Direct evidence** is that which shows *prima facie* the facts at issue. What constitutes direct evidence depends on the factors involved. For example, in the case of kickbacks, direct evidence might be a check from the person making the kickback directly to the target.

**Circumstantial evidence** is that which would indirectly show culpability. For example, in the case of a kickback allegation, cash deposits of unknown origin deposited to the account of the target around the time of the suspect transaction could be circumstantial evidence.

---

[5] *Ibid.*
[6] *Ibid.*

(vi) **Organization of evidence.** One of the biggest problems in fraud cases is keeping track of the amount of paper generated. Good organization of documents in complex cases usually includes these guidelines.

- Segregate documents by either witness or transaction. Chronological organization is the least preferable method. The idea is to have the witness introduce the document, not the examiner or auditor.
- Make a "key document" file for easy access to the most relevant documents. Purge this file periodically of less important documents.
- Establish a database early on in the case of volumes of information, preferably a computerized database. The database should include, at a minimum, date of the document, individual from whom the document was obtained, date the document was obtained, brief description of the document, and subject to whom the document pertains.

## LEGAL RULES OF EVIDENCE

There are strict legal rules regarding the handling of evidence and the chain of custody thereof. If the examiner is operating under a lawful order of the courts that compels a custodian of records to furnish original documents, they should be copied, preferably in the presence of the custodian, before being removed from the premises. If not operating under a court directive and the records are being provided voluntarily by the custodian, the examiner may retain copies instead of originals.

- Maintain a control log of events and documents in the case of voluminous evidence and complex cases. The purpose of maintaining a brief chronology of events is to establish the chain of events leading to the proof. The chronology may or may not be made a part of the formal report. At a minimum, it can be used for analysis of the case and kept in a working paper binder.

(vii) **Charting techniques.** Three types of charting techniques for documenting fraud are link network diagrams, time flow diagrams, and matrices (see Exhibit 2.3).[7]

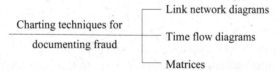

**Exhibit 2.3: Charting techniques for documentary fraud**

**Link network diagrams** show the relationships between persons, organizations, and events. Different symbols can be used consistently to represent different entities (e.g., a square for an organization, a circle for a person, and a triangle for an event). A solid line can represent connection between entities and broken lines can show presumed relationships. The diagram should be clear and simple to understand.

**Time flow diagrams** show the relationships of significant events, in the order they occurred. A **matrix** is a grid that shows the relationship or points of contact between a number of entities. Known contact can be differentiated from presumed contact by use of different marks, such as a solid dot or an open dot. In complex cases a matrix is a useful preliminary step to identify the relative status of the parties by showing the number of contacts of each. Later the matrix can be converted into a table or a chart. For example, a matrix can be used to identify the direction and frequency of telephone traffic between suspect parties.

(viii) **Business and individual records.** Original documents are preferred and should be obtained wherever possible. If necessary, the examiner should furnish the record custodian a receipt for the property. If the originals cannot be obtained, the examiner can settle for copies. The exact records obtained will vary from case to case, but where applicable, basic business records often include

- Organization of the business such as article of incorporation

---

[7] *Ibid.*

- Financial statements and tax returns
- Customer lists
- Business diaries, address, and telephone and facsimile records
- Personnel records, including employment application
- Bank account records, deposit slips, and canceled checks
- Relevant contracts or agreements
- Computer programs and data file diskettes

Originals of individual records are usually easier to obtain than originals of business records. Some of the more relevant individual records include

- Bank account records, deposit slips, and canceled checks
- Financial statements and tax returns
- Credit card statements and payment records
- Telephone and facsimile toll records

(ix) **Memorandum of interview.** It is a good practice to write a memorandum addressed to the case file any time evidence comes into or leaves the hands of the fraud examiner or auditor. Whether it is included in the final report or working papers or not, each official contact during the course of a fraud examination should be recorded on a "memorandum of interview" on a timely basis. Some guidelines for properly handling the memorandum of interview follow.

- Include all facts of possible evidence on the memorandum of interview.
- Reconfirm dates and supporting information with the interviewee to ensure their accuracy. Reconfirmation acts as a precautionary measure to make certain all facts are accurate before the report is written, not after.
- Include the quotations of the interviewee in the memorandum of interview.
- Transcribe all interviews in writing as soon as practicable following the interview. The main reason timeliness is so important is to ensure the accuracy of witness testimony. The longer the examiner waits to record the interview, the more will be forgotten.
- Record each witness interviewed on a separate memorandum of interview. Recordings of witnesses should not be mixed, since a request by the courts or others for a particular witness's statement can then be fulfilled without providing the entire report.

The contents of a memorandum of interview for a witness should contain these details.

- The nature of the inquiry
- The nature of the interviewer (e.g., voluntary or not)
- The date the interview was conducted
- The method of conducting the interview (i.e., in person or on the telephone)
- The identity of the interviewer (i.e., fraud examiner, auditor, detective)
- Each source or informant contact should be documented on a memorandum of interview, but always referring to the source or informant by a symbol number (S-2, I-2). State the reliability of the individual source (e.g., job title, expertise). When a source or informant is paid money for information, ensure that the payment is noted in the body of the memorandum of interview. Do not pay an informant or source without obtaining a receipt of payment.
- The identities of informants or sources should be fully documented and retained in a secure file, available only on a need-to-know basis. The symbol number used in the memorandum of interview should be cross-referenced to the secure file.

(x) **Writing fraud reports.** Writing reports of fraud investigation is one of the most demanding and important tasks of a fraud examiner or an auditor. Some reasons why a written report is so important include

- The report is an evidence of the work performed.
- The report conveys to the litigator all the evidence needed to evaluate the legal status of the case.
- The written report adds credibility to the examination and to the examiner.
- The report forces the fraud examiner to consider his or her actions before and during the interview, so that the objectives of the investigation can be best accomplished.

- The report omits immaterial information so that the facts of the case can be clearly and completely understood.

(xi) **Characteristics of fraud reports.** Important characteristics of good report writing include accuracy, clarity, impartiality, relevance, and timeliness (see Exhibit 2.4).

**Characteristics of Fraud Reports**

———— Accuracy (deals with reporting factual information)
———— Clarity (conveys the proper message)
———— Impartiality (means reporting facts without bias)
———— Relevance (dictates including only appropriate matters)
———— Timeliness (dictates issuing the report in a timely fashion)

**Exhibit 2.4: Characteristics of fraud reports**

**Accuracy** deals with reporting factual information that is correct and that can be verified. There is no room for error. **Clarity** means conveying the proper message in the clearest possible language. If necessary, the interviewed person can be quoted, provided the quotation does not distort the context of the memorandum of interview. Complex terms should be explained since persons who are not familiar with technical terminology might read the report. **Impartiality** means reporting facts without bias. **Relevance** dictates including only matters appropriate to the examination. Irrelevant information confuses and complicates the written report and leaves the examiner open to criticism of his or her methodology. **Timeliness** dictates issuing the draft and the final reports in a timely manner so that they will accomplish their objective(s).

(xii) **Written report.** In the absence of an established system of report writing, Wells recommends including five major sections: *cover page, witness statements, cover letter, working papers, and index.*[8] **The cover page** of a report typically includes all pertinent data gathered during the course of an examination. It includes file number, case description, perpetrator (employee) name, the lead investigator name, date of report, case status (pending, inactive, closed), report number, type of inquiry (civil, criminal, administrative), referrals, synopsis, financial data (all costs incurred, projected losses), final disposition, and predication (basis under which the investigation commenced to establish a reason for investigation).

## Due Professional Care

The IIA *Standard* (Due Professional Care) requires that a written report be issued at the conclusion of the investigation phase. It should include all findings, conclusions, recommendations, and corrective action taken.

The final report should include all relevant **witness statements**. Typically a **cover letter** to the requester of the investigation is included with the report. The purpose of the cover letter is to

- Accompany the report
- Set forth a succinct summary of witness testimony
- Provide details on the location of potential witnesses
- Set forth the apparent violation of law, if any, that the report addresses

Summarized **working papers,** when necessary, should be enclosed as attachments to the report. If working papers are enclosed with the report, they should be so described in the cover letter of the report.

If there are a limited number of memorandums of interviews, the **index** may be omitted; otherwise it is a good idea to provide an index. The index should be in chronological order rather than alphabetical, so the reader of the report may easily follow the development of the case.

(xiii) **Privileged reports.** According to Wells, there is no privilege, per se, for investigative reports and notes, or for any fraud examination, forensic audit, or similar services. However, there are two exceptions.

---

[8] *Ibid.*

1. If the examiner is conducting an investigation at the request of an attorney in anticipation of litigation, the report is considered in most courts as an attorney/client work product, that is, privileged.
2. If a public authority, such as the police, federal agents, the courts or grand jury, or the like, is conducting the investigation, the report can be considered privileged.[9]

If the examination is being conducted under the authority of the lawyer-client-court privilege, each page of the report should be marked "Privileged and Confidential."

(xiv) **Mistakes to avoid in writing fraud reports.** Mistakes are costly, especially in fraud reports. Careless errors should be avoided and are inexcusable. Mistakes and errors can make a report useless. A brief description of areas to be careful about in writing fraud reports, based on Wells, follows.

- **Conclusions.** One of the most significant mistakes made by fraud examiners and auditors is the statement of conclusions in the written report. Under no circumstances should conclusions be made, as they may come back to haunt the examiner in litigation. The opposing counsel's main tactic is usually to try to impeach whatever testimony is given and to show that the examiner is biased. The conclusions of the investigations should be self-evident and able to stand alone. If not, the report has not been properly prepared.
- **Opinions.** Like conclusions, opinions have no place in the report. Under no circumstances should an opinion be written concerning the guilt or innocence of any person or party, as this is purview of the courts; it is up to the jury to decide guilt or innocence.
- **Informant and source information.** Under no circumstances whatsoever should the name of a confidential source or informant be disclosed in the report, nor anywhere else in writing. It is recommended that the source or informant be referred to by symbol number (e.g., S-1, I-1).[10]

(e) **IIA's *Attribute Standards***

**IIA's Practice Advisory 1210.A2-1: "Identification of Fraud"**

*Nature of This Practice Advisory*

Internal auditors should consider these suggestions in connection with the identification of fraud. This guidance is not intended to represent all the considerations that may be necessary, but simply a recommended set of items that should be addressed. *Compliance with Practice Advisories is optional. This guidance is repeated in Part 1 and Part 2 for proper coverage of the subject matter.*

1. Fraud encompasses an array of irregularities and illegal acts characterized by intentional deception. It can be perpetrated for the benefit of or to the detriment of the organization and by persons outside as well as inside the organization.
2. Fraud designed to benefit the organization generally produces such benefit by exploiting an unfair or dishonest advantage that also may deceive an outside party. Perpetrators of such frauds usually accrue an indirect personal benefit. Examples of frauds designed to benefit the organization include

- Sale or assignment of fictitious or misrepresented assets.
- Improper payments such as illegal political contributions, bribes, kickbacks, and payoffs to government officials, intermediaries of government officials, customers, or suppliers.
- Intentional, improper representation or valuation of transactions, assets, liabilities, or income.
- Intentional, improper transfer pricing (e.g., valuation of goods exchanged between related organizations). By purposely structuring pricing techniques improperly, management can improve the operating results of an organization involved in the transaction to the detriment of the other organization.
- Intentional, improper related-party transactions in which one party receives some benefit not obtainable in an arm's-length transaction.
- Intentional failure to record or disclose significant information to improve the financial picture of the organization to outside parties.

[9] *Ibid.*
[10] *Ibid.*

- Prohibited business activities, such as those that violate government statutes, rules, regulations, or contracts.
- Tax fraud.

3. Fraud perpetrated to the detriment of the organization generally is for the direct or indirect benefit of an employee, outside individual, or another organization. Some examples are

- Acceptance of bribes or kickbacks.
- Diversion to an employee or outsider of a potentially profitable transaction that would normally generate profits for the organization.
- Embezzlement, as typified by the misappropriation of money or property, and falsification of financial records to cover up the act, thus making detection difficult.
- Intentional concealment or misrepresentation of events or data.
- Claims submitted for services or goods not actually provided to the organization.

4. Deterrence of fraud consists of those actions taken to discourage the perpetration of fraud and limit the exposure if fraud does occur. The principal mechanism for deterring fraud is control. Primary responsibility for establishing and maintaining control rests with management.

5. Internal auditors are responsible for assisting in the deterrence of fraud by examining and evaluating the adequacy and the effectiveness of the system of internal control, commensurate with the extent of the potential exposure/risk in the various segments of the organization's operations. In carrying out this responsibility, internal auditors should, for example, determine whether

- The organizational environment fosters control consciousness.
- Realistic organizational goals and objectives are set.
- Written policies (e.g., code of conduct) exist that describe prohibited activities and the action required whenever violations are discovered.
- Appropriate authorization policies for transactions are established and maintained.
- Policies, practices, procedures, reports, and other mechanisms are developed to monitor activities and safeguard assets, particularly in high-risk areas.
- Communication channels provide management with adequate and reliable information.
- Recommendations need to be made for the establishment or enhancement of cost-effective controls to help deter fraud.

6. When an internal auditor suspects wrongdoing, the appropriate authorities within the organization should be informed. The internal auditor may recommend whatever investigation is considered necessary in the circumstances. Thereafter, the auditor should follow up to see that the internal audit activity's responsibilities have been met.

7. Investigation of fraud consists of performing extended procedures necessary to determine whether fraud, as suggested by the indicators, has occurred. It includes gathering sufficient information about the specific details of a discovered fraud. Internal auditors, lawyers, investigators, security personnel, and other specialists from inside or outside the organization are the parties that usually conduct or participate in fraud investigations.

8. When conducting fraud investigations, internal auditors should

- Assess the probable level and the extent of complicity in the fraud within the organization. This can be critical to ensuring that the internal auditor avoids providing information to or obtaining misleading information from persons who may be involved.
- Determine the knowledge, skills, and other competencies needed to carry out the investigation effectively. An assessment of the qualifications and the skills of internal auditors and of the specialists available to participate in the investigation should be performed to ensure that engagements are conducted by individuals having appropriate types and levels of technical expertise. This should include assurances on such matters as professional certifications, licenses, reputation, and the fact that there is no relationship to those being investigated or to any of the employees or management of the organization.
- Design procedures to follow in attempting to identify the perpetrators, extent of the fraud, techniques used, and cause of the fraud.

- Coordinate activities with management personnel, legal counsel, and other specialists as appropriate throughout the course of the investigation.
- Be cognizant of the rights of alleged perpetrators and personnel within the scope of the investigation and the reputation of the organization itself.

9. Once a fraud investigation is concluded, internal auditors should assess the facts known in order to

- Determine if controls need to be implemented or strengthened to reduce future vulnerability.
- Design engagement tests to help disclose the existence of similar frauds in the future.
- Help meet the internal auditor's responsibility to maintain sufficient knowledge of fraud and thereby be able to identify future indicators of fraud.

10. Reporting of fraud consists of the various oral or written interim or final communications to management regarding the status and results of fraud investigations. The chief audit executive has the responsibility to report immediately any incident of significant fraud to senior management and the board. Sufficient investigation should take place to establish reasonable certainty that a fraud has occurred before any fraud reporting is made. A preliminary or final report may be desirable at the conclusion of the detection phase. The report should include the internal auditor's conclusion as to whether sufficient information exists to conduct a full investigation. It should also summarize observations and recommendations that serve as the basis for such decision. A written report may follow any oral briefing made to management and the board to document the findings.

11. Section 2400 of the *International Standards for the Professional Practice of Internal Auditing (Standards)* provides interpretations applicable to engagement communications issued as a result of fraud investigations. Additional interpretive guidance on reporting of fraud is

- When the incidence of significant fraud has been established to a reasonable certainty, senior management and the board should be notified immediately.
- The results of a fraud investigation may indicate that fraud has had a previously undiscovered significant adverse effect on the financial position and results of operations of an organization for one or more years on which financial statements have already been issued. Internal auditors should inform senior management and the board of such a discovery.
- A written report or other formal communication should be issued at the conclusion of the investigation phase. It should include all observations, conclusions, recommendations, and corrective action taken.
- A draft of the proposed final communications on fraud should be submitted to legal counsel for review. In those cases in which the internal auditor wants to invoke client privilege, consideration should be given to addressing the report to legal counsel.

12. Detection of fraud consists of identifying indicators of fraud sufficient to warrant recommending an investigation. These indicators may arise as a result of controls established by management, tests conducted by auditors, and other sources both within and outside the organization.

13. In conducting engagements, the internal auditor's responsibilities for detecting fraud are to

- Have sufficient knowledge of fraud to be able to identify indicators that fraud may have been committed. This knowledge includes the characteristics of fraud, the techniques used to commit fraud, and the types of fraud associated with the activities reviewed.
- Be alert to opportunities, such as control weaknesses, that could allow fraud. If significant control weaknesses are detected, additional tests conducted by internal auditors should include tests directed toward identification of other indicators of fraud. Some examples of indicators are unauthorized transactions, override of controls, unexplained pricing exceptions, and unusually large product losses. Internal auditors should recognize that the presence of more than one indicator at any one time increases the probability that fraud may have occurred.
- Evaluate the indicators that fraud may have been committed and decide whether any further action is necessary or whether an investigation should be recommended.

- Notify the appropriate authorities within the organization if a determination is made that there are sufficient indicators of the commission of a fraud to recommend an investigation.

14. Internal auditors are not expected to have knowledge equivalent to that of a person whose primary responsibility is detecting and investigating fraud. Also, audit procedures alone, even when carried out with due professional care, do not guarantee that fraud will be detected.

## IIA's Practice Advisory 1210.A2-2: "Responsibility for Fraud Detection"

### *Nature of This Practice Advisory*

Internal auditors should consider these suggestions in relation to the responsibility for fraud detection. This guidance is not intended to represent all the considerations that may be necessary, but simply a recommended set of items that should be addressed. *Compliance with this Practice Advisory is optional. This guidance is repeated in Part 1 and Part 2 for proper coverage of the subject matter.*

1. Management and the internal audit activity have differing roles with respect to fraud detection. The normal course of work for the internal audit activity is to provide an independent appraisal, examination, and evaluation of an organization's activities as a service to the organization. The objective of internal auditing in fraud detection is to assist members of the organization in the effective discharge of their responsibilities by furnishing them with analyses, appraisals, recommendations, counsel, and information concerning the activities reviewed. The engagement objective includes promoting effective control at a reasonable cost.
2. Management has a responsibility to establish and maintain an effective control system at a reasonable cost. To the degree that fraud may be present in activities covered in the normal course of work as defined above, internal auditors have a responsibility to exercise "due professional care" as specifically defined in *Standard* 1220 with respect to fraud detection. Internal auditors should have sufficient knowledge of fraud to identify the indicators that fraud may have been committed, be alert to opportunities that could allow fraud, evaluate the need for additional investigation, and notify the appropriate authorities.
3. A well-designed internal control system should not be conducive to fraud. Tests conducted by auditors, along with reasonable controls established by management, improve the likelihood that any existing fraud indicators will be detected and considered for further investigation.

(f) **Risk and Control Self-Assessment.** Control self-assessment (CSA) deals with evaluating the system of internal control in any organization. CSA is a shared responsibility among all employees in the organization, not just of internal auditing or senior management. The examination of the internal control environment is conducted within a structured, documented, and repetitive process. The formal assessment approach takes place in workshop sessions with business users as participants (process owners) and internal auditors as facilitators (subject matter experts) and nonfacilitators (note takers). The purpose of the sessions is conversation and mutual discovery and information sharing.

   (i) **Elements of CSA.** CSA has five elements: (1) up-front planning and preliminary audit work, (2) the gathering of process owners with a meeting facilitator, (3) a structured agenda to examine the process's risks and controls, (4) a note taker and electronic voting technology to input comments and opinions, and (5) reporting the results and the development of corrective action plans.

   (ii) **Scope of CSA.** CSA can be done either as a stand-alone project or as a supplement to traditional audit work. The CSA is not suitable to situations such as finding fraud, compliance reviews (e.g., regulatory audits), or when participants have conflicting objectives, as in third-party contracts. CSA can be applied to numerous situations, business issues, and industries, regardless of their size. It is a management tool that has equal application to horizontal (organization-wide), vertical (a single department), or diagonal (process inquiries) issues.

   (iii) **Effect of CSA on internal auditors.** CSA can be used to assess business and financial statement risks, control activities, ethical values, and control effectiveness; the controls that mitigate those risks; and overall compliance with policies and procedures.

   During the assessment process, there is a constant interactive dialogue between the auditor and the auditee and between the auditees. This interaction increases communications and builds trust and confidence of each party in the other. At the same time, it is educational to both parties since a knowledge transfer takes place between the auditor and the auditee. The auditors will have a greater knowledge of business functions while the auditees will have a better understanding of and appreciation for controls and the business process in which they are a part.

The increased communication and the knowledge transfer add value to the organization in these ways.

- Auditors accomplish control assessment.
- Auditees understand the purpose of controls.
- Management takes responsibility for the development and maintenance of the control environment.
- Process improvement issues are identified and resolved (i.e., implemented or deferred).

(iv) **Interrelationships among CSA, CoCo, and COSO.** CSA can be an effective tool for accomplishing the Criteria of Control (CoCo) sponsored by the Canadian Institute of Chartered Accountants and the Committee of Sponsoring Organizations (COSO) sponsored by the Treadway Commission. CSA acts as a link to the CoCo and COSO.

The CSA audit can address the four elements of CoCo framework (i.e., purpose, commitment, capability, and monitoring and learning). Both commitment and capability are examples of soft controls (e.g., risk assessment, the achievement of business objectives and goals, and the attitude of people toward controls).

The CSA audit can address the five elements of COSO framework (control environment, risk assessment, control activities, information and communication, and monitoring). The COSO addresses both soft controls and hard controls.

## TRADITIONAL AUDITING VERSUS CONTROL SELF-ASSESSMENT

- Traditional auditing techniques address hard controls (e.g., authorization, accurate and timely recording of transactions, limit controls, segregation of duties). They do not address the soft controls.
- CSA techniques address the soft controls as well as the hard controls.
- Traditional auditing techniques create an atmosphere of hostility and mistrust and an attitude of "us against them."
- CSA techniques create an atmosphere of partnership and an attitude of "us against us."

(v) **Implications of CSA for internal auditors.** Auditor judgment is still needed in the CSA process. Additional testing may be needed for issues that arise during the discussion that cannot be addressed during the CSA session. The level of reliance on CSA is a function of organization's culture and auditor judgment.

The auditor should still perform follow-up work to monitor the progress of the implementation of action items related to control issues. The business unit and its management should have the primary responsibility of executing the action plan. Since the business unit managers and employees are part of the resolution process, implementation of action items becomes somewhat easier.

(vi) **CSA approaches and workshop formats.**

(A) *CSA approaches.* The IIA's "Perspective on Control Self-Assessment" identifies three primary approaches to CSA: (1) facilitated team meetings (also known as workshops), (2) questionnaires (also known as surveys), and (3) management-produced analysis. Two types of facilitated approach exist: (1) client facilitated and (2) audit facilitated. Most organizations prefer a CSA approach using facilitated workshops with the internal auditors as facilitators. Note that organizations can use more than one approach in their self-assessment process. Workshops (70%) and surveys (30%) are the more popular formats of CSA.

There are five types of CSA workshops: (1) objective-based (deals with controls and residual risks), (2) risk-based (deals with risks and controls), (3) control-based (follows the traditional audit), (4) process-based (deals with business process reengineering and total quality management), and (5) the departmental or situational approach (identifies enablers and hindrances). The objective-based and the risk-based types are recommended by COSO; CoCo recommends the departmental or situational approach.

The questionnaire (survey) approach to CSA uses a survey form that offers opportunity for simple "Yes/No" or "Have/Have Not" responses. Process owners can use the survey results to assess their control structure. Surveys or questionnaires are used in about 30% of CSA efforts and are almost always followed by workshops or interviews of the results.

Self-certification approach is based on management-produced analysis, which includes opinions about internal controls required by a law or regulation, investigations into the reasons why a particular control breakdown or fraud occurred, implications of a new computer system being developed, or effect of combination of business units.

(B) *CSA workshop formats.* Depending on the approach taken, the workshop formats have different characteristics.

- The workshop flow for the objective-based format: Objectives → Controls → Residual Risks → Assessment.
- The workshop flow for the risk-based format: Objectives → Risks → Controls → Residual Risks → Assessment.
- The workshop flow for the control-based format: Objectives → Agreement (risks and controls) → Assessment.
- The workshop flow for the process-based format: Objectives → Activity Levels → Assessment.
- The workshop flow for the departmental or situational format: Enablers → Hindrances → Solutions.

(vii) **Conclusions for CSA.** CSA is a dynamic business process improvement and control-enhancing technique. The CSA to internal auditing is like total quality management and continuous process improvement techniques to other parts of the organization. The only difference is how the CSA program is implemented in each organization. The benefits are real and long lasting.

(g) **IIA's** *Performance Standards*

**IIA's Practice Advisory 2120.A1-2: "Using Control Self-Assessment for Assessing the Adequacy of Control Processes"**

*Nature of This Practice Advisory*

Control self-assessment (CSA) methodology can be used by managers and internal auditors to assess the adequacy of the organization's risk management and control processes. Internal auditors can utilize CSA programs to gather relevant information about risks and controls; to focus the audit plan on high-risk, unusual areas; and to forge greater collaboration with operating managers and work teams. *Compliance with Practice Advisories is optional. This guidance is repeated in Part 1 and Part 2 for proper coverage of the subject matter.*

1.  Senior management is charged with overseeing the establishment, administration, and evaluation of the processes of risk management and control. Operating managers' responsibilities include assessment of the risks and controls in their units. Internal and external auditors provide varying degrees of assurance about the state of effectiveness of the risk management and control processes of the organization. Both managers and auditors have an interest in using techniques and tools that sharpen the focus and expand the efforts to assess risk management and control processes that are in place and to identify ways to improve their effectiveness.

2.  A methodology encompassing self-assessment surveys and facilitated workshops called control self-assessment (CSA) is a useful and efficient approach for managers and internal auditors to collaborate in assessing and evaluating control procedures. In its purest form, CSA integrates business objectives and risks with control processes. Control self-assessment is also referred to as control/risk self-assessment (CRSA). Although CSA practitioners use a number of different techniques and formats, most implemented programs share some key features and goals. An organization that uses self-assessment will have a formal, documented process that allows management and work teams that are directly involved in a business unit, function, or process to participate in a structured manner for the purpose of

- Identifying risks and exposures

- Assessing the control processes that mitigate or manage those risks
- Developing action plans to reduce risks to acceptable levels
- Determining the likelihood of achieving the business objectives

3. The outcomes that may be derived from self-assessment methodologies are

- People in business units become trained and experienced in assessing risks and associating control processes with managing those risks and improving the chances of achieving business objectives.
- Informal, "soft" controls are more easily identified and evaluated.
- People are motivated to take ownership of the control processes in their units and corrective actions taken by the work teams are often more effective and timely.
- The entire objectives-risks-controls infrastructure of an organization is subject to greater monitoring and continuous improvement.
- Internal auditors become involved in and knowledgeable about the self-assessment process by serving as facilitators, scribes, and reporters for the work teams and as trainers of risk and control concepts supporting the CSA program.
- Internal audit activity acquires more information about the control processes within the organization and can leverage that additional information in allocating their scarce resources so as to spend a greater effort in investigating and performing tests of business units or functions that have significant control weaknesses or high residual risks.
- Management's responsibility for the risk management and control processes of the organization is reinforced, and managers will be less tempted to abdicate those activities to specialists, such as auditors.
- The primary role of the internal audit activity will continue to include the validation of the evaluation process by performing tests and the expression of its professional judgment on the adequacy and effectiveness of the whole risk management and control systems.

4. The wide variety of approaches used for CSA processes in organizations reflects the differences in industry, geography, structure, organizational culture, and degree of employee empowerment, dominant management style, and the manner of formulating strategies and policies. That observation suggests that the success of a particular type of CSA program in one enterprise may not be replicated in another organization. The CSA process should be customized to fit the unique characteristics of each organization. Also, it suggests that a CSA approach needs to be dynamic and change with the continual development of the organization.
5. The three primary forms of CSA programs are facilitated team workshops, surveys, and management-produced analysis. Organizations often combine more than one approach.
6. Facilitated team workshops gather information from work teams representing different levels in the business unit or function. The format of the workshop may be based on objectives, risks, controls, or processes.

- The objective-based format focuses on the best way to accomplish a business objective. The workshop begins by identifying the controls currently in place to support the objective and then determining the residual risks remaining. The aim of the workshop is to decide whether the control procedures are working effectively and are resulting in residual risks within an acceptable level.
- The risk-based format focuses on listing the risks to achieving an objective. The workshop begins by listing all possible barriers, obstacles, threats, and exposures that might prevent achieving an objective and then examines the control procedures to determine if they are sufficient to manage the key risks. The aim of the workshop is to determine significant residual risks. This format takes the work team through the entire objective-risks-controls formula.
- The control-based format focuses on how well the controls in place are working. This format is different from the two above because the facilitator identifies the key risks and controls before the beginning of the workshop. During the workshop, the work team assesses how well the controls mitigate risks and promote the achievement of objectives. The aim of

the workshop is to produce an analysis of the gap between how controls are working and how well management expects those controls to work.

- The process-based format focuses on selected activities that are elements of a chain of processes. The processes are usually a series of related activities that go from some beginning point to an end, such as the various steps in purchasing, product development, or revenue generation. This type of workshop usually covers the identification of the objectives of the whole process and the various intermediate steps. The aim of the workshop is to evaluate, update, validate, improve, and streamline the whole process and its component activities. This workshop format may have a greater breadth of analysis than a control-based approach by covering multiple objectives within the process and supporting concurrent management efforts, such as reengineering, quality improvement, and continuous improvement initiatives.

7. The survey form of CSA utilizes a questionnaire that tends to ask mostly simple "Yes/No" or "Have/Have Not" questions that are carefully written to be understood by the target recipients. Surveys are often used if the desired respondents are too numerous or widely dispersed to participate in a workshop. They are also preferred if the culture in the organization may hinder open, candid discussions in workshop settings or if management desires to minimize the time spent and costs incurred in gathering the information.

8. The form of self-assessment called management-produced analyses covers most other approaches by management groups to produce information about selected business processes, risk management activities, and control procedures. The analysis is often intended to reach an informed and timely judgment about specific characteristics of control procedures and is commonly prepared by a team in staff or support role. The internal auditor may synthesize this analysis with other information to enhance the understanding of controls and to share the knowledge with managers in business or functional units as part of the organization's CSA program.

9. All self-assessment programs are based on managers and members of the work teams possessing an understanding of risks and controls concepts and using those concepts in communications. For training sessions, to facilitate the orderly flow of workshop discussions and as a check on the completeness of the overall process, organizations often use a control framework such as the COSO and CoCo models.

10. In the typical CSA facilitated workshop, a report will be largely created during the deliberations. A group consensus will be recorded for the various segments of the discussions, and the group will review the proposed final report before the end of the final session. Some programs will use anonymous voting techniques to ensure the free flow of information and viewpoints during the workshops and to aid in negotiating differences between viewpoints and interest groups.

11. Internal audit's investment in some CSA programs is fairly significant. It may sponsor, design, implement, and, in effect, own the process, conducting the training; supplying the facilitators, scribes, and reporters; and orchestrating the participation of management and work teams. In other CSA programs, internal audit's involvement is minimal, serving as interested party and consultant of the whole process and as ultimate verifier of the evaluations produced by the teams. In most programs, internal audit's investment in the organization's CSA efforts is somewhere between the two extremes described above. As the level of internal audit's involvement in the CSA program and individual workshop deliberations increases, the chief audit executive should monitor the objectivity of the internal audit staff, take steps to manage that objectivity (if necessary), and augment internal audit testing to ensure that bias or partiality do not affect the final judgments of the staff. *Standard* 1120 states: "Internal auditors should have an impartial, unbiased attitude and avoid conflicts of interest."

12. A CSA program augments the traditional role of internal audit activity by assisting management in fulfilling its responsibilities to establish and maintain risk management and control processes and to evaluate the adequacy of that system. Through a CSA program, the internal audit activity and the business units and functions collaborate to produce better information about how well the control processes are working and how significant the residual risks are.

13. Although it provides staff support for the CSA program as facilitators and specialists, the internal audit activity often may reduce the effort spent in gathering information about control procedures and eliminate some testing. A CSA program should increase the coverage of assessing control processes across the organization, improve the quality of corrective actions made by the process owners, and focus internal audit's work on reviewing high-risk processes and unusual situations. It can focus on validating the evaluation conclusions produced by the CSA process, synthesizing the information gathered from the components of the organization, and expressing its overall judgment about the effectiveness of controls to senior management and the audit committee.

(h) **Audits of Third Parties and Contract Auditing**

(i) **Audits of third parties.** There will be at least three parties to several business transactions such as electronic procurement, electronic payment, computer-based applications service providers (ASPs), computer system outsourcing services, and computer service bureaus. Key parties include the purchaser, the third-party provider, and the supplier. The purpose of third-party auditing is to ensure that controls are adequate and that proper evidence is collected in the event of a dispute between the parties.

Individual trading partners (i.e., purchasers and suppliers) will have specific controls, such as data entry and application system controls over the business transactions, while the third-party provider will have common controls. These common controls include general, translation, transaction, access authorization, balancing, data integrity, confidentiality, and privacy controls.

The internal auditor should review general controls and transaction controls at the third-party provider's computer center. Examples of general controls include system development and program change controls; security and access control methods; backup, recovery, and business continuity controls; operating system controls; and audit trails. Examples of transaction controls include transaction authorization, accuracy, completeness, compensating, and user controls.

## OVERVIEW OF THIRD PARTIES

Four types of third parties that often work with information technology (IT) and users of the client organization include system integrators, vendors, consultants/contractors, and service providers.

### System Integrators

System integrators are independent organizations hired to

- Manage the software acquisition process
- Manage the system development process
- Manage the network development and services
- Integrate hardware and software from different platforms

In this role, system integrators focus on how best to integrate the client's hardware and network configurations, applications software, and systems software acquired from different vendors operating at various locations.

### Vendors

Both hardware and software vendors work with their clients (customers) from planning to installation of hardware devices and software products. Here software includes applications software and systems software. Often vendors

- Help in software product integration and implementation
- Help in hardware installation
- Provide technical assistance in problem troubleshooting
- Conduct training programs for the client
- Provide educational materials
- Provide maintenance and service agreements
- Conduct hardware and software diagnosis in response to client's problems
- Coordinate new software releases and updates

## Consultants and Contractors

Consultants or contractors are usually hired for a short time period to perform specific tasks, such as

- Conduct special studies in computer operations, operating systems, databases, capacity planning, network services, and other areas of information systems (IS) and making recommendations to management to improve operating efficiency and system effectiveness
- Develop computer-based application systems from planning to implementation stages
- Maintain or enhance existing application systems from inception to completion stages

## Service Providers

Use of service providers is growing and should be based on cost-benefit analysis. Organizations outside the user/customer organization provide several types of third-party IS services, including

- **Service bureau.** A private organization provides IS services to its clients for a fee, basically to process certain applications. Controls required by a service bureau systems and operations are no different from in-house systems and operations.
- **Timesharing facilities.** A private organization provides IS services to process certain applications for a fee (based on time used).
- **Outsourcing or facilities management.** A private organization takes over operating the user organization's IS computer center operations and network services based on a contract.

  Outsourcing means an IS organization goes "outside" for the knowledge and experience required to do a specific job. In simpler terms, it means subcontracting or farming out for systems and services. The scope of outsourcing includes telecommunications and network support, facilities (computer center) management, disaster recovery services, education and training, ongoing hardware maintenance, data center design and construction, equipment relocation services, systems integration, application development and maintenance, and other services. The scope is broad and could include partial and full-line services.

  Organizations turn to outsourcing to improve performance (system and people) and to reduce operating costs. From a positive side, outsourcing offers solutions when there is a shortage of in-house skills, when a high-risk and high-overhead project needs to be managed, and when there is an unacceptable lead time to complete a project using company personnel.

  The benefits from outsourcing usually focus on performance improvements and/or cost reduction. Another benefit is that it allows internal management's time and resources to be devoted more to the core business and the company's future. Outsourcing prevents hiring additional employees to meet temporary needs. However, outsourcing does not mean surrendering control and internal management responsibility of subcontracted functions and projects to outside vendors.

  Some of the organization's IS employees could work for the outsourcing vendor. The key point here is to monitor the performance of the outsourced vendor during the contract period. Selection of an outsourcing vendor is no different from selecting other types of vendors. Selection factors such as proximity of the vendor, attitude of the vendor's personnel, vendor's reputation and knowledge, and the vendor's financial condition and management's integrity are important to consider.

  The fixed-price-type contract is best for the user organization, although this may not be feasible in all situations. The contract should spell out vendor performance-level guarantees and the remedies for nonperformance. Usually contract periods range from five to six years.

  From the economics point of view, the outsourcing approach provides an option to buy IS services from outsiders rather than from the organization's IS department. Users can perform "make-or-buy" analysis.

- **Third-party network services.** A private organization provides telecommunication network and data interchange services between two user organizations, or trading partners. An example is an electronic data interchange (EDI) service being provided between a buying organization (e.g., retailer) and a selling organization (e.g., manufacturer of merchandise) of goods and services.

- **Financial services.** A financial organization providing charge or credit services to its customers will arrange for the processing of charge card transaction validation and updating of its customer data files from a user organization such as a retailer, a financial institution, or a business entity.

(ii) **Contract auditing.** Many opportunities exist in contract auditing in terms of cost recovery in such areas as fraud, kickbacks, overcharges, and conflict of interest. Similar to IT system development audits, internal auditors should participate early in contract audits such as construction audits. Early participation is required in bidding procedures, cost estimates, contractual terms, contractors' accounting (billing) systems, cost control, and project control procedures. A provision should be provided in the contract for overall project reviews, billing reviews, progress reviews, and cost recovery audits.

Construction audits generally fall into one of the three categories: (1) fixed price (lump sum), (2) cost plus, and (3) unit price. Under the fixed price contract, contractors agree to work for a fixed amount. The auditor should review escalation clauses, progress payments, incentive provisions, adjustments for excess labor and materials costs, and change orders. Risks in fixed-price contract include: inadequate insurance and bond coverage; charges for equipment and materials that are not received; overhead cost items included as additional charges; inadequate inspection relative to specifications; and extra costs, changes, and revisions that are already part of the original contract.

Under the cost-plus contract, the contractor is reimbursed for costs plus a fixed fee (which is encouraged) or costs plus a fee based on percentage of costs (which is discouraged). Some cost-plus contracts provide for maximum costs and sharing of any savings generated. Risks in cost-plus contract include: overhead cost items are also billed directly; duplication of costs between head-quarters and field offices; poor-quality work practices; poor physical protection of materials and equipment; excessive costs incurred due to idle rented equipment; excessive manning of project; and uncontrolled overtime costs.

The unit-price contracts are useful when large amounts of similar work is required from the contractor (e.g., clearing land by the acre and surveillance of a building). A price is agreed on for each unit of work. Risks in the unit-price include: excessive progress payment; improper or inaccurate reporting of units completed; unauthorized escalation adjustments; and inaccurate field records. Exhibit 2.5 shows a comparison of the three categories of contracts.

| Contract category | Fixed price | Cost-plus | Unit-price |
|---|---|---|---|
| Requires built-in hedges for unknowns | Yes | No | Not applicable |
| Contractor self-policing | Yes | No | Not applicable |
| Recordkeeping is crucial | Not applicable | Yes | Yes |

**Exhibit 2.5: Comparison of contracts**

(i) **Quality Audit Engagements.** Quality audit engagements can take place in two areas: quality audit of a company's products and services and quality audit of internal audit function. Each area is briefly discussed next.

(i) **Quality audit of a company's products or services.** Most organizations view quality of a product or service as a competitive weapon. Quality can increase revenues and sales, decrease costs, and increase profits. Auditing the quality department is very important for the internal audit department since it is one of the assurance functions in the organization. Both audit and quality departments provide assurance to management that organizational resources are used efficiently and effectively.

The internal audit scope of quality function includes review of the charter, organization chart, quality policies and procedures, quality control tools, quality costs (cost of quality), quality management tools, quality standards, applicable laws and regulations, and six-sigma metrics.

The internal auditor needs to understand how quality management tools (affinity diagrams, tree diagrams, process decision program charts, matrix diagrams, interrelationship digraphs, prioritization matrices, and activity network diagrams) are used, including their frequency and applicability, how six-sigma metrics are implemented or planned to be implemented, how quality control tools (check sheets, histograms, scatter diagrams, Pareto diagrams, flowcharts, cause-and-effect diagrams, and control charts) are used, including their frequency and applicability, how quality costs (preventive, appraisal, internal failures, and external failures) are accumulated and reported to management and their reasonableness with the industry norms and company targets, and how service quality characteristics (intangibility, inseparability, heterogeneity, and perishability) are measured and reported.

(ii) **Quality audit of internal audit function.** Many audit departments installed total quality management (TQM) approaches to improve audit operations. One such approach is recommended by the US General Accounting Office, which outlined eight steps to TQM in audit operations.

1. **Initial quality assessment.** This step includes: identifying the audit department's customers; establishing the needs of the customers; setting priorities so as to best meet the customers' needs; assessing the quality of the audit products (audit reports) as perceived by the audit customers as to timeliness, usefulness, responsiveness, and cost; and interviewing customers so as to reveal pertinent information about the audits, audit staff performance, and the audit department as a whole.

2. **Chief audit executive awareness.** Awareness training should stress the importance of TQM as a philosophy or an approach, not a program.

3. **Formation of a quality council.** Audit managers, audit supervisors, and audit staff members should be part of the quality council, and they should acquire the knowledge of TQM principles, practices, and tools. This council should report to the chief audit executive. It should coordinate training and participate in prototypes.

4. **Fostering teamwork in audits.** The audit department should establish a participative environment that fosters teamwork and quality work. Audit plans, audit work programs, fieldwork, working papers, and audit reports all require quality orientation and thinking.

5. **Development of prototypes.** To convince some auditors who are doubtful about the TQM philosophy, the quality council should demonstrate the practical value of new ways of organizing the audit work with highly visible prototype and productivity initiatives. When tested and proven successful, these prototypes can convince the cautious of the audit staff.

6. **Celebration of success.** The audit department should publicize the achievements of the prototype to encourage the cautious and hesitant audit staff.

7. **Organizational implementation.** All units and all locations of the audit department should successfully implement audit quality methods, and appropriate recognition should be given for those units that are most successful. This provides motivation and promotes healthy competition.

8. **Annual audit quality review.** There should be an annual audit quality review for audit departments that are spread throughout the organization. The annual review, together with a rating system, will demonstrate the success of the implementation of quality in the audit department.

## INTERNAL AUDIT AND TQM

An audit assignment can go wrong at any stage. It can be ill conceived, improperly directed, poorly planned, or badly implemented, and its results can be ineffectively communicated. For a variety of reasons, it can fail to meet its customers' needs.

An appropriate quality control system identifies or flags those factors that could jeopardize the quality of an audit and establishes processes or procedures that promptly identify and correct problems before they occur. For example, it will be more effective to correct a planning-related problem in the planning phase than in a later phase (e.g., reporting phase).

An effective quality control system needs to do more than ensure the quality with which work was performed. It also needs to determine what the work accomplished and how customers and stakeholders viewed the result. This can be done by system approaches, such as surveys of customers and stakeholders, recommendation tracking and reporting systems, and auditor performance measurements and award/reward systems.

(j) **Due Diligence Audit Engagements.** Due diligence audits provide a safety valve to management that is planning to acquire, manage, or consolidate with other businesses. Joint ventures and environmental audits are also subject to due diligence audits. These audits are the minimum managerial requirements to ensure that all applicable laws and regulations are met and that risks and exposures are minimized. For example, due diligence audits are a risk management tool for banks, land buyers, and lending agencies when a buyer is purchasing land or accepting it as a gift. Here the buyer wants to minimize the potential legal liability resulting from the land acquisition.

Due diligence audits are team-based effort with internal auditors, external auditors, lawyers, engineers, IT staff, and other specialists. Three phases in this audit include information gathering (phase 1), information analysis (phase 2), and information reporting (phase 3). Information gathering involves collecting information through document reviews, interviews, and meetings. Information analysis may include analytical reviews, including ratio analysis, regression analysis, and other quantitative techniques. Information reporting includes writing a balanced report based on facts with an executive summary. In addition to writing reports, oral reports can be used for immediate response and clarification of issues and findings.

(k) **Security Audit Engagements.** The scope of security audits, which can be unannounced audits, includes logical security, physical security, computer storage medium, and safety. Logical security focuses on determining whether a person attempting access should be allowed into a computer system and what the user can do once on the system. Specific controls in logical review include authentication controls such as composition and change of passwords and user identification codes (IDs), encryption methods and routines, and restricting transactions to particular terminals and employees. Terminal-related controls include time-out limits and displaying the last time and date a user ID was used.

The scope of physical security audits can include a review of physical access to storerooms, cash vaults, research laboratories, plants and factories, computer centers, preventive maintenance procedures, and environmental controls. Physical access controls include limiting unauthorized access using electronic cards and biometrics access devices (voice recognition, electronic signature verification), fire prevention techniques, and electric power supply and conditioning.

The scope of computer storage media audits includes review of rotation of computer files to and from off-site storage, electronic vaulting at remote locations, environmental controls off-site as well as on-site, and adequacy of storage media capacity for future computing needs.

The scope of safety audit includes review of safety policies and procedures and accident statistics and investigations. The internal auditor needs to make sure that corrective actions to safety problems are proper and timely and that all applicable labor laws are complied with.

The internal auditor would need to coordinate safety audit activities with other internal assurance functions, such as quality, health, security, and industrial engineering. Possible areas of coordination include sharing work plans and schedules, conducting periodic meetings, exchanging reports, developing work statistics, providing control training, and participating in investigations and corrective actions.

(l) **Privacy Audit Engagements.** Privacy is the right of an individual to limit access to information regarding that individual. The term "privacy" refers to the social balance between an individual's right to keep information confidential and the societal benefit derived from sharing information, and how this balance is codified to give individuals the means to control personal information. The term "confidentiality" refers to disclosure of information only to authorized individuals and entities.

Privacy means that the rights of the accused (suspect) cannot be violated during the investigation. The accused can use protective orders if his or her privacy rights are ignored or handled improperly. If accused persons can prove that evidence brought against them would do more harm to them than good, the courts will favor the accused in suppressing such evidence from being presented.

The organization can protect itself from privacy and confidentiality problems by developing a policy statement and by showing the amount of damage done by the accused. A policy statement

- Is a prerequisite to handling privacy issues properly and legally. An incomplete or unclear policy could result in legal action against the organization by employees (suspects) when they find out that their privacy rights are violated.
- The organization must show that the perpetrator actually broke into a computer system, violated its proprietary rights to the system, and show the extent of damage caused. Organizations should have

controls such as passwords, encryption, access controls, hidden files, and warning banners to establish proprietary rights to a computer system. A policy statement should define this area.

In general, internal auditors are concerned about accidental or intentional disclosure of confidential data. They are also concerned about collection and use of such data. Legal requirements dictate the collection, disclosure, and use of data, both in public and private sectors. Internal auditors must understand that there is a trade-off between the level of protection (security) and the cost of that protection and that there is no absolute (perfect) security.

Threats to security come from individuals already having authorized access to a computer system as well as from those unauthorized to have access to a computer system. The internal auditor needs to make sure that known threats, exposures, and risks are addressed during system design, that proper controls are established, and that the established controls are working effectively on a continued basis.

Privacy laws affecting the public sector include the US Privacy Act of 1974, the Freedom of Information Act, and the Health Insurance Portability and Accountability Act of 1996 (HIPAA). Privacy laws affecting the private sector include Securities and Exchange Commission (SEC) requirements, the Foreign Corrupt Practices Act (FCPA), and others.

Most, if not all, of these privacy laws require establishing appropriate safeguards (controls) to ensure the confidentiality and integrity of personal or corporate records and protecting against anticipated threats that could result in substantial harm to individuals or corporations.

The internal auditor should be concerned not only with actual compliance with privacy laws but also with how such compliance can be proved to authorities should the question arise. Documentation, in the form of manuals, should provide such proof, as documentation contains work rules, standard operating procedures, controls, and references to laws and regulations.

(m) **Performance Audit Engagements.** Any operation or function, whether it is production or service, needs to be measured in terms of its performance. To measure performance, performance standards, which are tied to the primary objectives of the operation or function, must be developed and monitored. In addition, each performance standard must be expressed in terms of efficiency and effectiveness criteria. If too many performance standards or indicators exist, employees may not be able to handle them properly, which can lead to waste of resources. Therefore, both management and employees should focus on a few meaningful, key performance indicators (KPIs).

For example, the KPIs in a production plant safety operation might include

- Number of safety inspections conducted in a month, quarter, and year
- Number of factory equipment tested and calibrated in a month, quarter, and year
- Number of factory operations observed for safety conditions in a month, quarter, and year
- Number of safety accidents investigated and reported in a month, quarter, and year
- Number of accidents reduced from month to month, quarter to quarter, and year to year
- Amount of machine downtime reduced resulting from reduced accidents in a month, quarter, and year
- Amount of worker's compensation insurance premiums reduced resulting from reduced accidents

The internal auditor needs to be aware that some employees may deceive the KPIs to survive and that performance results may be distorted to receive larger bonuses and promotions. Therefore, the auditor should compare the KPIs with the industry norms as well as with the same company data from period to period. Also, the auditor should be careful in analyzing KPIs that look too good as well as those KPIs that do not meet standards.

(n) **Operational Audit Engagements.**

(i) **Overview of operational audits.** The economic events and business transactions of an entity are usually classified into several cycles for convenience of grouping similar and related activities and in order to manage the audit effectively and efficiently. For example, typical cycles for a manufacturing organization are (see Exhibit 2.6)

- Revenue
- Expenditure
- Production/conversion
- Treasury (financing/investing)

- Financial reporting (external)

The production/conversion cycle is the only one that will be different between manufacturing and nonmanufacturing organizations. Regardless of the nature of the organization, an internal control structure must meet several detailed internal control objectives to prevent, detect, and correct errors, omissions, fraud, and irregularities during handling of the business transaction cycles. These objectives, which are applicable to all transaction cycles, include

- Transactions are properly authorized
- Existing transactions are recorded
- Recorded transactions are valid
- Transactions are properly classified
- Transactions are properly valued
- Transactions are recorded at the proper time and that they are reasonable
- Transactions are properly posted to journals, ledgers, books, and subsidiary records
- Transactions are properly and promptly reconciled, properly summarized and reported

**Overview Diagram for Operational Audits**

**Revenue Cycle**
- Credit management
- Billing
- Accounts receivable
- Cash receipts
- Warranty accounting
- Commissions
- Advertising and sales promotion
- Marketing administration
- Product distribution
- Intercompany transfers

**Expenditure Cycle**
- Purchasing
- Receiving
- Quality assurance of materials
- Accounts payable
- Personnel administration
- Payroll

**Production\Conversion Cycle**
- Inventory control
- Production control
- Shipping
- Traffic
- Quality control
- Fixed assets
- Plant maintenance
- Cost accounting

**Treasury Cycle**
- Debt management
- Cash management
- Equity management
- Investment management
- Dividends management
- Risk and insurance management
- Foreign currency exchange management
- Write-off accounting

**Financial Reporting Cycle**
- Journal entry preparation
- Consolidation and general ledger posting
- Financial report preparation and issuance
- Tax accounting and reporting

**Exhibit 2.6:  Overview diagram for operational audits**

For each transaction cycle and for each auditable area within a transaction cycle, we present "what can go wrong," that is, potential or actual risks and exposures along with controls or control procedures needed to reduce or eliminate those risks and exposures. An audit program that includes audit objectives and audit procedures follows. Audit objectives are broad statements developed by auditors and define intended audit accomplishments. Audit procedures are the means to attain audit objectives.

Four types of controls apply to all five transactions cycles: (1) directive, (2) preventive, (3) detective, and (4) corrective. Since directive controls are broad in nature and apply to all situations, they are described here only once. Examples include organization structure and chart, policies, procedures, management directives, guidance statements, circulars, and job\position descriptions. However, as preventive, directive, and corrective controls are specific to each function, they are described for each auditable area, and labeled PC (preventive control,) DC (detective control), and CC (corrective control).

At the end of audit programs, sample audit findings are presented to describe what went wrong during a review of the auditable area. These are the auditor's actual findings and recommendations. These sample audit findings should help the candidate to crystallize the key concepts from a real-world point of view, which will increase comprehension of the subject matter.

(ii) **Introduction to revenue cycle.** Major activities in a revenue cycle would include: granting of credit to the customer; receiving, accepting, and processing of customer orders; shipping of goods or delivery of service; billing of customers and adjustments; updating inventory records and the customers' accounts; recording of sales and adjustments; costing of sales and services; receiving, processing, and recording of cash receipts; accounting for product warranties; providing allowances for, and writing off, bad debts; recording of sales and billing, and cash receipts and adjustments, by journalizing and posting to appropriate accounts; protecting cash and accounts receivable records; and maintaining the accuracy and completeness of cash records and accounts receivable record balances and warranty records.

(A) *Audit cycle/area: Revenue—Credit management.*

*Risks and exposures*
- Improper (e.g., loose or tight) credit may be granted.

- Loans made to fictitious borrowers.

- Unauthorized shipping of goods.

*Controls or control procedures*
- Customer background verification, financial statement analysis, and segregation of duties between credit and sales functions (PC).
- Approval of secured collateral (PC).
- Test sample for properly completed loan documents (DC).
- Segregation of duties between credit, billing, and shipping functions (PC).

*Audit objectives for credit management*
- To determine whether the credit management function is administered properly.

- To determine if credit controls are inconsistently applied, preventing valid sales to creditworthy customers.

*Audit procedures for credit management*
- Ensure that a thorough investigation is made of all new customers before a credit limit is established. Verify that a credit file is established for each customer with all available financial and operating background information. Verify that credit limits are reviewed, updated, and used for all customers on a continuing basis.
- Ensure that the customer's orders are subject to review and approval by the credit department before acceptance of the sales order. Individual customer requests for credit in excess of established limits are reviewed by authorized higher-level management. An example of attribute sampling would be to determine whether the credit department requires a credit check for credit sales when needed.
  A possible scenario is: Individual salespeople were allowed to approve credit and determine product availability and delivery increased sales. Later, write-offs of accounts receivables increased. An appropriate corrective action is an independent review and approval of credit.
- Select a representative number of sales orders and the corresponding invoices, and verify that: (1) the terms and amounts for credit extended are within those authorized limits, and (2) proper approval had been obtained prior to acceptance of the order when the credit limits and/or terms have been exceeded.
- Compare credit histories for those receiving credit and for those denied credit. Evaluate the adequacy of controls.

### EXAMPLES OF APPLICATION OF COMPUTER-ASSISTED AUDIT TECHNIQUES: CREDIT MANAGEMENT

- List all shipments exceeding the customer credit limits in order to understand reasons of noncompliance.
- Compare the percentage of credit applications that were rejected with standards to determine whether the credit approval process is strict or lax.

---

(B) ***Audit cycle/area: Revenue—Billing.***

| Risks and exposures | Controls or control procedures |
|---|---|
| • Unauthorized persons may be accessing the order entry system via a dial-up using personal computers. | • A frequent access revalidation with logical access controls such as callback and passwords (PC). |
| • Shipments may not be billed. | • Shipping documents, packing slips, sales order forms, credit memoranda, customer invoices should be prenumbered and their use is controlled (PC).<br>• Reconciliation between shipping and billing (DC). |
| • Improper services or goods may be billed. | • Reconcile a sample of invoices to service pickup receipts or goods receiving reports (DC). |
| • Potential for fraud or irregularities. | • Segregation of duties between billing, credit, shipping, and marketing functions (PC). |

| Audit objectives for billing | Audit procedures for billing |
|---|---|
| • To determine whether controls over order entry and order processing is adequate. | • Ensure that the order system does not process any customer orders when the customer order exceeds his credit limits. Identify exceptions and overrides.<br>• Identify all preventive, detective, and corrective controls present in the system, and evaluate their adequacy.<br>• Examine the order entry system manual for completeness, clarity, and currency.<br>• Review system availability and computer terminal response times, and compare them with service level objectives to ensure the system performance meets its operating goals. |
| • To ascertain whether customer invoices are based only on shipments made and those invoices are mailed within the established time limits. | • In order to evaluate compliance with controls designed to ensure that all shipments are billed, select "prenumbered shipping documents" as the population from which to draw a sample.<br>• Select a sample of customer invoices and compare date of invoice with the date on the relevant shipping documents. Verify that the quantity shipped and billed is the same. |
| • To ensure that the price charged on the invoice is the approved price. | • Compare that the price charged on the invoice is the same as the one found in the approved price list. Identify exceptions and reasons for it.<br>• Select a number of missing numbers from shipping documents, sales order forms, and credit memoranda, and customer sales invoices and check as to the follow-up action taken. Analyze the reasons given for missing documents. |
| • To determine whether sales order backlog is properly controlled. | • To ensure prompt delivery of out-of-stock items, match the back-order file to goods received daily.<br>• Analyze open sales orders for backlog and compute the number of active orders that were recently shipped but not closed, the number of orders for future delivery, the number of orders on which delivery is past due, the number of orders which appear to be closed, and the number of inactive orders for other reasons. Ensure that additional billings are forthcoming for the orders that appeared to be closed. |
| • To determine whether invoices and credit memoranda are handled properly and in a timely manner by the billing department. | • Review a sample of invoices to ensure that they contain invoice number, date, customer number, product identification code, price, payment terms, amount due, tax information, freight terms, and so forth.<br>• Select a sample of credit memoranda, trace and analyze supporting documentation. Verify the reasons for issuing the credit memoranda to customers.<br>• Trace the customer invoices to the detailed accounts receivable records. Trace totals of one month's sales summary to the sales and receivables general ledger account. |

## EXAMPLES OF APPLICATION OF COMPUTER-ASSISTED AUDIT TECHNIQUES: SALES/BILLING/INVOICING

- Compare shipping records with sales invoices by line item for testing to determine whether all inventory shipments were billed to customers.
- Identify discrepancies between quantities shipped and quantities billed for understanding reasons.
- Use "controlled reprocessing" techniques to identify lost or incomplete sales accounting record updates.

## CREDIT MEMOS VERSUS DEBIT MEMOS

- Credit memos are used to adjust accounts receivable balances.
- Debit memos are used to adjust accounts payable balances.

### (C) *Audit cycle/area: Revenue—Accounts receivable.*

#### *Risks and exposures*
- A division may be intentionally shipping unordered merchandise to customers near the end of each quarter to meet its sales goals.
- Allowance for bad debts may be misstated.
- Potential for fraud or irregularities.

#### *Controls and control procedures*
- Send accounts receivable confirmations to selected customers as of the end of the quarter (DC).
- Perform an aging analysis of accounts receivable accounts (DC).
- Segregation of duties between accounts receivable, credit and collection, shipping, billing, and marketing functions (PC).
- Receivable clerk should not have physical access to and control of cash receipts (PC).

#### *Audit objectives for accounts receivable*
- To determine whether accounts receivable represent valid sales.
- To ascertain whether the total billed sales and cash receipts are accurately classified, summarized, and reported on a timely basis.
- To ensure that all cash sales are recorded.
- To determine whether refunds granted to customers were properly approved.
- To determine if the allowance for doubtful accounts is accurately stated and that trade accounts receivable are carried at net collectible amounts.
- To determine whether statement of accounts are mailed to customers on a regular basis.
- To evaluate the collectibility of past due accounts.
- To ensure those receivables adjustments are properly approved and controlled.

#### *Audit procedures for accounts receivable*
- Trace a sample of accounts receivable debit entries to customer invoices and related shipping documents.
- Check the timeliness of receivable postings to individual accounts receivable records. Verify that postings are made directly from customer invoices and/or credit memoranda.
- Establish that postings for daily cash receipts are made from remittance advices rather than from check receipts.
- Observe cash sales to determine if customers are given written receipts.
- Trace accounts receivable entries to credit memos. Credit memos are used to grant refunds to customers.
- Prepare and analyze the aging schedule of trade accounts receivable, and discuss all potentially doubtful accounts which are material in amount with management.
- Test whether statements of accounts are mailed on a designated schedule, and make sure that an employee who has no access to cash remittance or the detailed accounts receivable records does these mailings and reconciliations.
- Review the collectibility of past due accounts with the credit manager and ascertain that the reserve for doubtful accounts is adequate. "Aged accounts receivable listing" is the primary document to rely on when evaluating the collectibility of receivables and their valuation.
- Evaluate the reasons given for accounts written off during the period under review by examining bankruptcy, discharge notices, and other sources to make sure that accounts written off actually had not been collected (i.e., bad and doubtful).
- Examine whether write-off of bad debts, discounts in excess of normal credit lines, refunds, and authorized management approves allowances.

| *Audit objectives for accounts receivable* | *Audit procedures for accounts receivable* |
|---|---|
| • To determine whether controls over notes receivable are adequate and are being followed. | • Verify that a note register is kept, which includes identification of the customer, amount, maturity date, and collateral. Determine that the note register is reconciled periodically to the control account. Ascertain that a record is kept of the discount notes to reflect the contingent liability.<br>• The audit procedure providing the best evidence about the collectibility of notes receivable would be an examination of cash receipts records to determine promptness of interest and principal payments. |
| • To ensure that the aged trial balance report is prepared and confirmations are mailed on a timely basis. | • Inquire whether an aged trial balance report is prepared and that positive confirmations are sent for all accounts over a certain amount and negative confirmations are sent to the remaining accounts. Test the accuracy of the aged trial balance by tracing a number of accounts to the detail records. Add the open items for a number of accounts in the ledger and trace the totals to the aging schedules and invoices. |
| • To determine whether the receivable sub-ledger is reconciled regularly to the general ledger. | • Analyze the receivables general ledger control account for each category of receivables and trace the postings to supporting documentation such as sales journal summaries, sales adjustment records, and other correspondence. |

## Accounts Receivable Turnover

When the accounts receivable turnover rate falls from 6.2 to 4.2 over the last two years, a more liberal credit policy would be the most likely cause of the decrease in the turnover rate. When the other variables are constant, a decrease in the turnover rate indicates liberal while an increase indicates a tight (conservative) credit policy.

## EXAMPLES OF APPLICATION OF COMPUTER-ASSISTED AUDIT TECHNIQUES: ACCOUNTS RECEIVABLE

- Develop a control total to verify that the dollar amounts for all debits and credits for incoming transactions are posted properly and completely to an accounts receivable master file.
- Recompute provisions for doubtful accounts and compare with management's estimates.
- List all credit balances for further analysis and interpretation because debit balances are normal.
- List all outstanding receivables balances in excess of customer credit limits for understanding reasons of noncompliance.
- Recompute customer receivables account-aging categories, and compare them with management's computations.

### (D) *Audit cycle/area: Revenue—Cash receipts.*

| *Risks and exposures* | *Controls or control procedures* |
|---|---|
| • Inadequate physical access controls over cash. | • Restricted areas, money safes, controls over night collections (PC). |
| • Alteration of petty cash balances by petty cash custodian. | • Separate responsibility for imprest fund checking account reconciliation from the petty cash custodian's duties (PC). |
| • Misappropriation of cash receipts. | • Separate the cash receipt function from the related record-keeping function (PC). |
| • Improper handling of cash receipt transactions. | • One employee issues a prenumbered cash receipt form for all cash collections; another employee reconciles daily total of prenumbered receipts to bank deposits (PC, DC). |
| • Potential for fraud or irregularities. | • Segregation of duties between cash receipts and bank reconciliation; vouching for payment; credit; opening incoming mail; and posting cash receipts to the general ledger functions (PC).<br>• Use of fidelity bonds and employee background checks (PC). |

*Audit objectives for cash receipts*

- To determine whether access to cash receipts is permitted only in accordance with management's authorization.

*Audit procedures for cash receipts*

- Verify that all bank account openings and closings have been approved by the treasurer of the organization.
- Ensure that incoming cash is handled by the least possible number of employees while maintaining segregation of duties. Check that cash receipts are promptly deposited intact and not commingled with other cash items or petty cash funds.
- Determine that employees handling cash funds are properly bonded. Based on the volume of cash receipts, analyze the need for the use of a lockbox. Ensure that when branch offices collect cash receipts, only the head/home office–authorized personnel deposit those collections in a bank account subject to withdrawal.
- Select a representative sample of checks returned by the bank as uncollectible. Ascertain that an individual not responsible for preparing the cash deposit has investigated and taken appropriate action.

- To determine whether controls over checks arriving in the mail are adequate.

- Ensure that all cash receipts are deposited in the bank daily. To ensure compliance, compare cash receipt journal entries with the monthly bank statements.

- To determine whether controls over petty cash are adequate.

- Compare monthly balances and use change and trend analysis to detect fraud. In one situation, a remote unit's petty cash custodian had responsibility for the imprest fund checking account reconciliation. The cashier concealed a diversion of funds by altering the beginning balance on the monthly reconciliations sent to the headquarters.

- To ascertain whether cash receipts are accurately summarized and reported in a timely manner.

- Ensure that cash receipts are prelisted at the initial point of receipt by preprinted cash receipt forms. Verify that cash receipts are posted to detail accounts receivable records from collection advice, not the checks. Find out if an independent person promptly compares the totals with entries in the cash receipts records. *Requiring preparation of a prelist of incoming cash receipts, with copies of the prelist going to the cashier and to the accounting department, is an example of a preventive control.*
- Trace the amount received to the daily bank deposit. Note any differences.
- Ensure that no payroll or personal checks are cashed from cash receipts.
- Examine the account distribution of the cash receipt total, and compare to the detail receivables posting and the invoice as to amount and date entered. Ensure discount and allowances taken are proper. Ensure that cash receipts regarding taxes are accurately classified and reported to the tax authorities in a timely manner. *In order to determine whether customers took undeserved cash discounts, compare cash receipt journal entries with related remittance advices and sales invoices.*
- Obtain bank statements and verify that deposits are being made on a daily basis. Investigate any unusual amounts.

## EXAMPLES OF APPLICATION OF COMPUTER-ASSISTED AUDIT TECHNIQUES: CASH RECEIPTS

- List outstanding customer payment checks that were not applied to their account receivables records.
- Compare the accuracy of posting of cash receipts journal entries to general ledger cash accounts.

### (E) *Audit cycle/area: Revenue—Warranty accounting.*

*Risks and exposures*

- Manipulation of warranty reserves.
- Underestimation of warranty liabilities.

*Controls or control procedures*

- Conduct trend analysis and ratio analysis (DC).
- Recompute and compare actual experience with accruals (DC).

Warranty costs are defined as costs incurred after passage of title to a customer in connection with defective products shipped to customers.

*Audit objectives for warranty accounting*
- To determine whether provisions to the reserve account for warranty are made, classified, and recorded on a consistent basis.

- To ascertain whether the warranty reserve account is reviewed periodically for adequacy.

*Audit procedures for warranty accounting*
- Obtain the supporting detail or analyses of an individual warranty reserve account, and reconcile the detail to the general ledger account, compare the balance at the audit date with those of the previous year, and investigate all significant changes. Check the warranty reserve calculation for consistency with the established rates, review the propriety of the contra accounts by examining entries to the reserve accounts, and verify that all significant charges are costs of the nature for which the warranty reserve was set up originally.
- Inquire whether a detailed analysis and evaluation are made at the end of each accounting year to verify the adequacy of the reserve balance. This is to cover known and probable exposures and to ensure the compliance to local tax laws and regulations.
- Assess the basis for calculating the warranty reserves. Ensure that these items were taken into consideration for determining the base: prior experience ratings, specific sales and major contracts identified as major exposure, known past warranty claims, and known or expected quality problems uncovered in production.
- With the help of legal and marketing management, ensure that accrued warranty liabilities are properly estimated, provided for, and reported.
- Examine the justification of deductibility of warranty expenses for income tax purposes.

## (F) *Audit cycle/area: Revenue—Commissions.*

*Risks and exposures*
- Sales commissions for the year were too large.

- Impropriety of sales commissions paid.

*Controls or control procedures*
- Compute a selected sales commissions to ensure the accuracy of recorded commissions (DC).
- Perform a detailed commission account analysis to detect exceptions (DC).

*Audit objectives for commissions*
- To determine whether all commission payments to dealers, brokers, distributors, and agents are based on written agreements.

- To ascertain whether commission payments are only made for valid business reasons and payments are properly computed and accounted for.

*Audit procedures for commissions*
- Inspect all written agreements with the agents and ensure that a master file of agreements is maintained with control numbers assigned to the agreements for tracking and controlling purposes. Inquire whether all agreements have been reviewed and approved by legal counsel. Look for any noncash considerations agreed to in the agreements, that is, sales of merchandise at "distressed" prices, which should be discouraged and brought to senior management's attention.
- Ensure that approved requests for the payment of commissions are independently verified by the accounting department before processing. This includes not only the accuracy of calculations but also the proper application of the base and rates, and limits.
- Obtain canceled checks and review for proper endorsement. Also, compare payee's name per check with agent named in the agreement.
- Ensure those journal entries for commissions earned are prepared for each accounting period. Ensure that all commissions are accurately classified, summarized, and reported in the proper period.
- Perform an analytical review of commissions paid in relation to performance goals. Some measures include sales by product; sales by location; collections received; and individual agent's performance. Assess the reasonableness of commission expenses as a percent of sales for several periods and investigate any unusual variations.

## EXAMPLES OF APPLICATION OF COMPUTER-ASSISTED AUDIT TECHNIQUES: COMMISSIONS

- Recompute sales commissions to salespersons and distributors, and compare them with management calculations and contracts.
- Verify that sales commissions were adjusted to reflect customer returns and other credits not resulting in a sale.

---

### (G) *Audit cycle/area: Revenue—Advertising and sales promotion.*

*Risks and exposures*

- Unreasonable advertising expense.

- Disputes over charges and expenses billed by an independent advertising agency.
- Informal function for advertising and sales promotion.

- Potential for fraud or irregularities.

*Controls or control procedures*

- Analytical evidence developed by comparing the ratio of advertising expense to sales with historical data for the company and industry (DC).
- A written agreement containing provisions as to charges and expenses billable (PC).
- Plans, goals, budgets, and comparison of the actual with budgets (PC).
- Segregation of duties among advertising, purchasing, receiving, and accounts payable functions (PC).

*Audit objectives for advertising and sales promotion*

- To determine whether approved budgets exist for advertising and sales promotion activities and that those advertising expenditures are properly classified for performance measurement.

- To ascertain whether a detailed budget is prepared for each advertising project and closed properly after the work is completed and that costs are documented and are reasonable.

*Audit procedures for advertising and sales promotion*

- Examine and evaluate the method of determination of approved budget amounts. Determine that the budget elements (e.g., production costs, media, and materials) are classified in a form that can be coordinated with accounting.
- Perform an analytical review by comparing this year's budget with prior years' budgeted levels. Inquire as to reasons for any significant variations. Examine actual expenditures by month to determine whether large expenditures are being made at year-end to use up budget balances. Conversely, determine that advertising budgets do not phase out prior to the year-end. Neither situation is desirable.
- Inquire whether analyses were conducted with regard to outsourcing the advertising work to an outside agency. Evaluate the advantages and disadvantages for outsourcing.
- Obtain the breakdown of the advertising and sales promotion budget by project, and study the actual expenditures against the budget, and investigate any variances.
- Select several projects and: examine contracts with advertising agencies and determine that they include duration, cancellation, and proper approval; basis of allocating direct and indirect agency costs; check estimation sheets showing media, estimated cost, description of advertising, date of appearance, and agency fee, review billings, and supporting vouchers from the agency, and determine that all items are billed in accordance with the agreements and purchase orders, find out if independent verification of exhibition and date of advertising is obtained from the agency or an independent service, and verify that claims have been made for unsatisfactory items, such as wrong position in publication, poor printing, radio and television station interruptions, torn billboard, or lack of illumination at night on billboards.
- Verify that media billings are accompanied by evidence of appearance in such forms as tearsheets from magazines, newspapers, and classified directories; performance affidavits from radio and television stations; and location lists for outdoor advertising. Check the calculation of the agency's commissions. Verify, by examination of published price lists, that the proper rates were used for media billings. Examine the advertising department's time sheets and vouchers for purchased materials and determine that these production charges have been properly allocated to the project.

*Audit objectives for advertising and sales promotion*

*Audit procedures for advertising and sales promotion*

- Where agency contracts give the right to audit, visit the advertising agency and examine appropriate vouchers, time reports, overtime records, and inventory records for accuracy and completeness of work and charges. Inquire whether the agency has given due consideration to discounts and special rates and that the savings are passed to the company. Find out if the agency and the company use competitive bidding where appropriate, and understand the criteria used for agency selection. Evaluate whether existing controls are sufficient to eliminate the risk of duplicate payment of invoices to the agency.

- To determine whether the quality and quantity of advertising and sales promotion materials are adequately controlled.

- Review the physical controls as well as financial controls maintained over advertising and sales promotion materials, and note any significant variations with budgeted costs, levels of expenditures compared to prior years, and any write-offs. These materials include artwork, display items, tearsheets, sales brochures, and catalogs.
- Examine the charges for materials distributed to the proper budget and expense accounts, and understand the reasons for significant deviations from budget and confirm that appropriate management approvals were obtained for overexpenditures.
- Examine payment arrangements with various supply sources and determine that payments are made accordingly. Select a representative number of invoices for materials and compare the finished advertising with the specifics of the contract as to layout, composition, and artwork to verify the work performed and that materials supplied to studios were used as intended.
- Where suppliers maintain material in their warehouses awaiting shipping instructions, examine the propriety of custody, control over access, and the accountability for this inventory. Verify that proper shipping evidence is received prior to payment of charges.

## (H) *Audit cycle/area: Revenue—Marketing administration.*

*Risks and exposures*
- Excessive sales adjustments.


- Individual sales staff approving credit for customers.

*Controls or control procedures*
- Assess production quality control by evaluating the number of adjustments and ascertaining the reasons for sales adjustments (DC).
- Implement independent review and approval of credit by credit department staff (PC).

*Audit objectives for marketing administration*
- To determine whether the marketing function is organized properly and that adequate documentation exists in support of the objectives, goals, and funding for each program proposal.



- To ascertain whether the marketing function develops long- and short-range sales forecasts and to assess their reasonableness.

*Audit procedures for marketing administration*
- Review the marketing organization structure to determine the degree to which it is established along functional lines, product lines, regional and customer lines, and so forth, and evaluate whether the structure is logically suited to the needs of the company. Analyze the turnover of personnel to determine whether it appears excessive, and if so, ascertain the reasons.
- Obtain copies of latest market surveys, market share analyses, new product development plans, and long-range and short-range sales forecasts.
- Evaluate the nature and reasonableness of the basis used in developing sales forecasts and the amount and degree of detail supporting the forecast development. Verify whether the sales forecast prepared by marketing is used in the development of the manufacturing forecast.
- Verify whether the marketing management periodically reviews sales forecasts and revises them in accordance with changing conditions. Ascertain whether a formal program exists for the recurring analysis of variances between actual sales to budgets and forecasts. Determine that notices of revisions to sales forecasts are distributed to the same parties who received the original forecast.
- Establish whether the marketing department coordinates with engineering and research and development departments to develop markets for new products.

| *Audit objectives for marketing administration* | *Audit procedures for marketing administration* |
|---|---|
| | • Perform sales trend analysis by product lines and review product lines where sales are declining. Investigate the reasons for any downward trend and recommend corrective action to reverse the trend. |
| • To determine whether product line profitability analyses are prepared for increasing profits and decreasing losses. | • Confirm whether periodic reports are prepared reflecting the profitability of the various product lines and/or territories. |
| | • Investigate which lines are contributing less than budgeted profit margin and why. Review the corrective actions planned or already taken. Verify whether marketing management allocates sales and whether customer service effort is in accordance with the related product line profitability. |
| | • Determine marketing management prepares a lost-business report to reflect the extent and reasons for unsuccessful bidding. |
| • To ascertain whether all hired sales personnel are carefully screened and provided adequate training and supervision. | • Review and evaluate policies and procedures for the selection and hiring of sales personnel. Determine whether the selection process provides for formal testing techniques to verify professional qualifications and experience levels. |
| | • Inquire whether a formal training program is available on a continuing basis. Verify whether the training program is adequate and complete in course content and sales staff attendance. Evaluate the information provided to determine its ability to enhance sales staff knowledge of product familiarization. |
| | • Verify whether the sales manager accompanies new sales personnel in the initial selling stages. Inquire whether salespeople are periodically and formally advised of changes in product features, selling techniques, prices, and payment terms and credit policy. |
| • To determine whether the sales force is geographically allocated and adequately controlled. | • Review geographical allocation of field sales force for reasonableness, taking into consideration of the size of the area and actual/potential sales volume. Review how long vacancies remain open and any corrective action taken by management. |
| | • Review sales statistics of sales person and by territory to determine whether sales staff is logically assigned to each area on the basis of sales potential. |
| | • Review for timeliness, adequacy, and completeness sales call reports used by the field sales force and the use made by sales management. Verify whether an evaluation is made of calls planned versus calls accomplished. Review salespeople's expense reports for adequacy and reasonableness. |
| • To ascertain whether sales personnel are employed on an incentive pay plan, preferably based on a written agreement. | • Obtain the employment contract for a typical salesperson who is not on a straight pay basis. Confirm that signed formal agreements covering commission rates and terms of employment are on file. |
| | • Obtain a summary of total sales personnel indicating whether they are paid on a straight salary basis, an incentive basis, or on a combined salary and incentive basis. Verify the type of incentive programs in effect, and review and evaluate the basis on which the incentive factor is developed. Evaluate whether the incentive factor is correlated with the gross margin contributed by the product. |
| | • Determine that existing incentive compensation plans provide for penalties to be assessed for cancellations and returns by customers. Review reasons for cancellations and returns. |

## (I)  *Audit cycle/area:  Revenue—Product distribution.*

| *Risks and exposures* | *Controls or control procedures* |
|---|---|
| • Inefficient practices. | • Product distribution policies and procedures (PC). |
| • Nonperformance and poor-quality work. | • Written agreements and contracts with agents and distributors (PC). |

*Audit objectives for product distribution*
- To determine whether the company products are distributed in an efficient and economical manner and at the same time meet customer needs and market requirements.



- To ascertain whether controls over product distributors and agents are proper to facilitate timely information exchange between parties.

*Audit procedures for product distribution*
- Document the various methods used to distribute the company's products, such as direct shipment from the manufacturing plant, outlying company warehouses, consignments, and commission merchants. Ask marketing management whether the distribution channels meet the current and future marketing requirements.
- Inquire whether studies are conducted periodically to determine the profitability of warehouse operations and distribution methods.
- Obtain a list of all agents and distributors along with their written agreements. Examine a number of files containing data used for qualifying selected agents and distributors. Evaluate the adequacy of data for qualifying purposes.
- Test whether payments to agents and distributors comply with the written agreements, are properly authorized, and are correctly recorded.
- Verify and test the means by which marketing management continually updates outside agents regarding product changes. Inquire whether formal programs have been established to increase the sales competence of outside distributors.

### (J)  *Audit cycle/area:  Revenue—Intercompany transfers.*

*Risks and exposures*
- Improper intercompany prices to show excessive profits or to avoid taxes.
- Untimely reconciliations between intercompany accounts.

*Controls or control procedures*
- Establish a transfer pricing methodology (PC).

- Competent staff supported by clear written policies and procedures (PC).

*Audit objectives for intercompany transfers*
- To determine whether all intercompany transactions are accurately classified and promptly recorded in the proper category of accounts.






- To ascertain whether all intercompany accounts are reconciled on a monthly basis.

*Audit procedures for intercompany transfers*
- Ensure that all financial transactions arising between company units and the originating unit through issuance of debit/credit advices reports.
- Select a representative number of intercompany transactions and check whether they have been promptly and accurately recorded in the proper accounts.
- Select a representative number of intercompany sales invoices received during the month under review and check for evidence of having matched against the related purchase orders and receiving reports.
- Check the reconciliation as of the month-end under review of statements received to the division's own records for evidence of having been reviewed by management.
- Obtain a trial balance of the detailed intercompany accounts and reconcile to the general ledger control account.
- Find out what measures have been taken or will be taken to clear the imbalances.
- Scan intercompany account balances for aging or unsettled accounts or disputed items and obtain explanations for overdue accounts.
- Review suspended intercompany items and obtain and evaluate explanations for their nonclearance.

(iii) **Introduction to expenditure cycle.** Major activities in an expenditure cycle would include: selecting reliable, trustworthy, and competent vendors; initiating and requisitioning assets, goods, services, and labor; issuing purchase orders and ordering the goods requested; receiving the goods or services and storing the goods received for inventory; accounting for accrued expenses; processing the vendor invoices and receiving reports and comparing them with the purchase order; hiring employees and authorizing pay rates, deductions, and terminations; preparing daily attendance and timekeeping records; preparing and paying payroll; paying liabilities by disbursing cash; filing and paying payroll taxes; recording goods and services purchased, cash, and payroll disbursements by journalizing and posting to appropriate accounts; updating inventory records and employee earning records; costing and reporting labor time and variances; protecting physical inventory of goods and records and payroll funds, and records; and maintaining the accuracy and completeness of inventory records, payroll bank accounts, and accounts payable records.

## (A) *Audit cycle/area: Expenditure—Purchasing.*

### *Risks and exposures*

- Buyers receiving expensive gifts from a vendor in return for directing a significant amount of business to that vendor.
- Buyers purchasing from a vendor-relative.
- Inability to cancel a purchase order resulting in unneeded materials and legal liabilities.

- Excessive or unwanted open purchase commitments.

- Buyers favoring certain suppliers in placing orders for personal gain.
- Goods may not be purchased at the best price, and buyers may use their positions for personal gain.
- High inventory holding costs.
- Buyers routinely initiate, authorize, and execute both the purchase requisition and purchase order forms for materials ordered for all departments.
- Employees not understanding the purchasing procedures.
- Quantities in excess of needs may be ordered.

- Buyers ordering materials which at that time were being disposed of as surplus.
- Buyer irregularities or obtaining kickbacks.

### *Controls or control procedures*

- A policy stating competitive bids should be solicited on purchases to the maximum extent that is practicable (PC).
- Maintain an approved-vendor file for purchases (PC).
- Purchase order review by legal counsel; description of conditions for cancellation; formal agreements with suppliers specifying the terms, conditions, and time intervals required (PC).
- Rules on commitments and contracts, policies and procedures; clear responsibilities between local purchase and central purchases, authorization levels; delegation of authority for approving purchases (PC)
- Periodic rotation of buyer assignments (PC).
- Implement a team approach to vendor selection (PC, DC).
- Obtain competitive bids from approved vendors (PC).

- Reduce purchasing lead time for materials ordered (CC)
- Segregation of duties between initiating and authorizing the purchase requisitions and executing the purchase orders (PC).

- Develop a procedure manual for purchasing (PC).
- Have a department supervisor receive each purchase requisition prior to its being forwarded to the purchasing department (PC).
- Develop and distribute periodic reports of surplus stock (PC).

- Conduct analytical techniques such as change analysis and trend analysis of buyer or vendor activity (DC).

### *Audit objectives for purchasing*

- To determine whether product demand forecasting techniques produce reliable data for purchasing decisions to be made.

- To ascertain whether product demand forecasts are updated throughout the year to reflect actual demand patterns and changing market conditions.

- To determine whether purchase transactions are authorized and are for needed materials only, and that the inventory is obtained at the best price.

### *Audit procedures for purchasing*

- Analyze the method of forecasting product demand: salesperson's projections, market surveys, economic indicators, management's input.
- Evaluate the method of exploding forecast demand down to component parts and that forecast is time phased throughout the year.
- Test to see if purchase order firm commitments are made much earlier than established lead times.
- Inquire about the method of updating forecasts, that is, regeneration, net change, and exponential smoothing. Regeneration involves discarding the old forecast and substituting a new one. This technique is generally appropriate where there are widely varying forecasts and relatively few inventory levels. Net change involves updating only those items for which a forecast change is indicated, either in quantities or timing. This technique is appropriate where there are few changes and many levels in the bills of materials. Exponential smoothing technique uses the formula of New forecast = Old forecast + (Sales – Old forecast).
- Review techniques for tracking actual demand to the forecast, and comment on significant deviations from forecast and adequacy of tracking techniques.
- Review a sample of purchase orders and their related purchase requisitions for proper approval signatures. "Predetermined stocking levels" help ensure that unnecessary purchases of inventory are not made. Ascertain that production budgets and economic order quantities are integrated and have been used in determining quantities purchased.
- Purchase orders, receiving reports, and bid quotations provide evidence appropriate to determine that recorded purchase transactions were valid and at the best price.

*Audit objectives for purchasing*

- To determine whether the company has established a formal process of appraisal for selecting vendors.

- To ascertain whether procedures for sourcing vendors are adequate.

*Audit procedures for purchasing*

- Determine whether the company has published comprehensive vendor appraisal criteria. Understand the procedures, including form layout, document flow, and authorization requirements for the appraisal process.
- Confirm, for each of the A-class items in the sample, that at least two alternative suppliers have been identified. Examine the procedures to test financial and technical reliability, including obtaining credit reports, financial statements, and bank references.
- Inquire if the purchasing department has a formal procedure for periodic review of appraisals. Verify that the purchasing department has a mechanism for monitoring the performance of vendors and that it uses this information to update vendor appraisals. Review quality records and collect a sample of goods rejected on quality grounds. Review goods delivery records and collect a sample of significantly late deliveries. Trace these problem samples to the vendor appraisal files and confirm they have been updated.
- Verify that each production item is classified into one of these categories: make inside only, make and buy, make or buy, buy outside only. Confirm that the head of the purchasing department is one of the members of the make-or-buy committee and is active in that role.
- Ascertain whether the purchasing department has a reliable indication of total amount of usage for each part.
- Confirm that the purchasing department receives quality specifications for the goods or services to be purchased. Test for a sample of such specifications and confirm that they exist and are up-to-date.
- Take a sample of orders and compare actual delivery dates with those originally requested. Find out how lead times are monitored. Ensure that regular contacts are maintained with the vendor so that purchasing is aware of problems as they develop and that they are resolved promptly.
- Review the mechanisms used to ensure that the purchasing department is aware of current prices quoted by suppliers. Confirm that for each part on the A-class item list, there are at least two suppliers with price quotations received.
- Confirm that the purchasing department documents the vendor selection process. Review the process for getting quotations and ensure that they are considered confidential and in no case divulged to a vendor's competition. Confirm that low bids from reputable suppliers are not to be used to reduce prices from existing suppliers.
- Determine whether there is a policy about single sourcing and multiple sourcing. Prepare a schedule of the significant one-vendor purchases indicating the items, vendors, and amount purchased. Determine the dollar impact of one-vendor purchases in relation to total purchases. Investigate the reasons for significant one-vendor purchases and evaluate the risks for using only one source of supply.
- Review the policy about acceptance of gifts from vendors. Interview purchasing department staff about their views on receiving gifts. Obtain a list of visits and meetings with suppliers on the part of purchasing staff, review the expense reports for the associated periods, and confirm whether the expenses were shared each time or alternatively with the vendor.
- Inquire whether there is a program to qualify minority-owned suppliers who are capable of providing quality materials, supplies, and services. Determine whether the company is able to identify which of its suppliers are minority-owned business enterprises.
- Inquire whether the company has a program of cost reduction and cost increase avoidance integrated into its vendor relations policy. Obtain the most recent calculation of money saved through cost reduction or cost increase avoidance. Evaluate the rationale of the calculation and prove the validity of the figures.

*Audit objectives for purchasing*

*Audit procedures for purchasing*

- Confirm that all employees in the purchasing department are aware of the US antitrust laws. Review all of the correspondence files for any indication of an illicit attempt, by either the buyer or a supplier, to introduce reciprocity as a criterion for doing business (i.e., placing orders). Identify all businesses that are both suppliers and customers. From that list of suppliers or customers, select a sample of those where the volume of business is significant and is of the same magnitude in each direction. Understand the reasons for this activity and inform management about the possible reciprocity.

- To determine whether placement of the order for purchase of goods is proper and timely.

- Confirm that the purchase order cannot be processed unless there is a corresponding requisition, which can be verified by the requisition number on the order. Verify that requisitioners have been given lists of delivery lead times for major commodities and groups of commodities and that the lists are updated as significant changes occur. The listed lead times should include an adequate allowance for administrative and clerical time. Inquire whether traveling requisitions are used on repetitive items purchased—some constant information is not printed each time a request is made, and all subsequent requests will be cross-referenced to the original requisition number for convenience.

- Confirm that purchasing staff is following the rules prescribed for open purchase commitments. This is described as the maximum allowable limit of dollars that can be spent for each type of materials, such as production materials, interplant materials, subcontracted material, and installation materials. Confirm that the maximum allowable limit for total purchase commitments placed during a time period does not exceed the management-approved limits. Ask about the frequency of updating these open purchase commitments.

- Verify that all purchase orders are printed with a sequential numbering system. Identify and investigate missing numbers. Confirm that there is regular review of missing numbers by the purchasing department.

- Verify that all individual purchase orders for A-class items are written on a single-item basis only for each required production item for better tracking. Take a sample of an A-class item purchase orders and test for the presence of this information: purchase order number and date; vendor name and address; part number and description; quantity, including correct unit or measure; unit cost; purchase and payment discounts; freight terms, including method of shipment.

- Perform analytical reviews in the form of calculating time lags or elapsed times among identifying a need to purchase, initiating the purchasing order, and issuing the purchase order. The purpose is to make sure that the time taken to issue orders is not adding significantly to the need to forecast demand for material requirements planning items or to hold safety stocks for order point items.

- Test to see if buying practices reflect rush or emergency conditions, and determine if these practices have had any impact on price or possible quality of material accepted.

- To ascertain whether the procedures for canceling the purchase order are adequate.

- Verify that each major type of material has a time classification by the freedom to cancel the purchase order (e.g., not at all, up to one week before delivery, up to two weeks, etc.) and confirm that these time frames were approved by the legal department and are continually updated by the purchasing department.

- Compute the proportion of cancellations rejected by the vendor by classifying the rejections by reason, and obtain explanations for these rejections. Perform trend analysis for the number of cancellations over a certain time period.

- Identify a sample of canceled orders on which a deposit had been paid and the deposit had been repaid by the vendor.

*Audit objectives for purchasing*

*Audit procedures for purchasing*

- Confirm that the documentation canceling a purchase order is distributed to the same parties as the original order and that the cancellation notice is issued in a timely manner. Identify the communication media used: regular mail, electronic mail, or special carrier. Compute the time lags between the rising of the cancellation and issuing the cancellation, and find out how the purchasing department is planning to speed up communication for unacceptable delays.

---

### KEY CONCEPTS TO REMEMBER: ABC METHOD OF INVENTORY

- Inventory items are classified according to their value and frequency of usage expressed in dollars. "Number of items" would be least likely be used as criteria to classify inventory items. Inventory with high value and greater frequency of usage is labeled as A-class, followed by B-class and C-class. This labeling is referred to as the ABC inventory classification method. From a cycle counting perspective, A-class items could be counted monthly, B-class items quarterly, and C-class items annually. A-class items are likely to have the fewest days' supply in inventory, and C-class items will have many days' of supply. The ABC method suggests that expensive, frequently used, high stock-out cost items with long lead times should be reviewed more frequently than others.
- The ABC method of inventory control would be appropriate to use to reduce the safety stock investment without materially increasing the probability of stock-outs in a company in which a few products account for most of its costs and a large number of products have low total cost. The ABC method can understate the potential stock-out cost of C-class parts in manufacturing companies. To compensate, some companies invest in safety stock. Note that shortage costs are excluded from classic order point formulas.

---

### Computer Simulation in Purchasing

Computer simulation technique can be used to evaluate a company's purchasing function with respect to the effect of alternative purchasing policies on investment in inventory and stock-out costs.

---

### KEY CONCEPTS TO REMEMBER: EVIDENCE IN PURCHASING AND ACCOUNTS PAYABLE

- Competitive bids are required on purchases exceeding $3,000 unless a waiver from the executive management is obtained. The audit procedure that will result in the most "competent" evidence of compliance with the bid procedure would be to select a representative sample of purchase orders exceeding $3,000 and examine underlying documentation, ascertaining that requests for bids or properly signed waiver forms are on file.
- Before purchase invoices are approved for payment, an accounting clerk is supposed to compare invoice prices with purchase order prices and indicate their agreement by signing in a designated space on the payment voucher form. The audit procedure that would result in sufficient evidence that this requirement is being followed is to select a representative sample of vouchers, examine them for the signature of the accounting clerk, and compare the prices on the invoices and related purchase orders.

**Risks in Purchasing Systems**

When a manual purchasing process is converted to an online computer system, traditional duties will be less segregated than before.

## EXAMPLES OF APPLICATION OF COMPUTER-ASSISTED AUDIT TECHNIQUES: PUIRCHASING

- Produce a list of all purchase transactions processed after the cut-off date in order to determine whether all material liabilities for trade accounts payable have been recorded.
- List all new suppliers/vendors to determine whether they were properly approved with competitive bids obtained, where applicable.
- List all suppliers or vendors who exceeded certain dollar threshold limits (e.g., budgets) for further analysis and justification of doing business with them.
- List the top 10 suppliers or vendors for further analysis and identification of improprieties or irregularities, if any.

## TOTAL QUALITY MANAGEMENT AND PURCHASING

The application of total quality management (TQM) concepts and principles to the purchasing function has many control implications that an internal auditor should be concerned about.

The approach to TQM purchasing changes the traditional role of purchasing, material acquisition strategies, buyer/supplier working relationships, and buyer/vendor performance measurements to a partnership concept. Some policy and control implications include

- **Identify customers.** For example, suppliers are external customers and purchase requisitioners are internal customers.
- **Implement just-in-time (JIT) purchasing principles.** The scope includes supplier selection and evaluation, bidding practices, incoming inspection procedures, inbound freight responsibilities, paperwork reduction, value analysis practices, and packaging needs. JIT purchasing eliminates parts stock-out situations. A formal requisition form is no longer required as the requirements are driven by materials requirements planning (MRP) system.
- **Establish policies that encourage prime contractors to establish long-term partnerships with their supplier base.** Devote more time and effort to getting suppliers involved in the design of the product. Developing a partnership with a supplier does not eliminate the need for good negotiations.
- **View the supplier as the customer.** The buyer is required to provide the supplier with the right tools and right information, such as part drawings, specifications, and delivery dates, that will allow the supplier to provide products or services as needed. The objective is to have the supplier and the buyer share common goals and benefits. It promotes a win-win situation. Competitive bidding is still required prior to selecting the needed suppliers.
- **Require vendor certification.** Qualify the supplier base to reduce rework and to improve quality.
- **Develop single-source strategies.** Use multiple sources only when a unique technology is required or when one source cannot provide all the parts. This strategy could be a professional challenge to the internal auditor for control evaluation. The risk here is too much dependence on one supplier without a fallback.
- **Develop both quantitative and qualitative performance measurements for suppliers.** They should be rated on delivery, quality, cost, and service. Specific examples of quantitative performance measurement techniques include: on-time deliveries, quality of prod-

ucts, number of problems solved, and control of production processes. Some examples of qualitative performance measurements include: the degree of cooperation, technical assistance provided, responsiveness to inquiries and problems, and compliance with instructions provided.

- **Develop performance measurements for buyers.** Examples include requisition cycle time, meeting required dates, quality of products, and responsiveness to requisitioner.

---

### (B) *Audit cycle/area:  Expenditure—Receiving*.

#### *Risks and exposures*

- Inadequate control over receipts.

- Not ensuring that ordered quantities are actually received, that is, receiving department employees signing receiving documents without inspecting or counting the goods received.

- Failure to detect substandard materials received.
- Unauthorized shipments are accepted.

- Inefficient receiving operations.

#### *Controls or control procedures*

- Maintain purchase order with the units described, but both prices and quantities omitted (PC).
- For a sample of receipt: (1) compare quantities per receiving reports to quantities per supporting purchase orders, and (2) look for authorized signatures on the receiving reports indicating that quantities had been verified (DC).
- Perform unobtrusive or hidden measures when goods are received (DC).
- Establish inspection procedures for incoming materials (DC).
- Maintain a file of purchase orders in the receiving department for merchandise ordered but not yet received (PC).
- Maintain a written receiving manual describing how to handle damaged materials, overshipments and undershipments, valuable items, after-hours deliveries, and materials sent directly to storage or productive facilities (PC).

#### *Audit objectives for receiving*

- To determine whether procedures and practices of receiving materials are proper and reasonably controlled.

#### *Audit procedures for receiving*

- Establish whether receiving department employees prepare and sign a formal receiving report for all items received at each receiving point showing vendor's name, purchase order number, description of material, date received, count and weight of the materials received.
- Determine whether the receiving report is based on facts in that it: shows weights of materials only if they have been actually weighed, shows numbers only if they have been counted, and describes the materials only if they have been checked. Ensure that the receiving department personnel simply do not take information from documents such as company's purchase order or vendor's bill of lading, packing slip, or shipping document. Determine whether guidelines have been issued on what is to be 100% counted or weighed, what is to be sampled, and when reliance will be placed on supplier information.
- In order to make sure whether the receiving department verifies the materials and quantities are correct, these audit tests are suggested: determine the extent to which receipts from suppliers are independently counted, weighed, or otherwise measured and identified without reference to the packing slips or purchase orders; ascertain the extent to which primary verification by the receiving department is limited because of mutual confidence between the company and its vendors; establish the degree of acceptance of container markings and packing slips as evidence of quantity and material identification; verify the extent to which test checks are used in counting or measuring materials received; and determine that quantities received are later verified by store staff or operations staff.
- Confirm that discrepancies in the quality and quantity of materials received are promptly recorded and reported to purchasing, accounts payable, and traffic departments. Determine that goods damaged or lost in transit are properly noted on carrier's receipts and covered by loss or damage reports and that copies of these reports are forwarded to accounting and traffic departments for filing claims.
- Select a sample of material waiting to be returned to vendors. Confirm that this is not the material that should have been rejected by the receiving department in the first place.

| *Audit objectives for receiving* | *Audit procedures for receiving* |
|---|---|
| | • Select a sample of damaged materials and analyze whether the goods are (1) identifiably damaged before arrival, (2) found to be damaged when unpacked, or (3) damaged while in the company's possession. Ensure that the damage report clearly reflects the actual condition. Determine whether the material is (1) to be returned to the vendor, (2) to be reworked, (3) to be scrapped, or (4) awaiting a decision. |
| | • Select a sample of receiving reports and look for quantities received more than preestablished guidelines (say 5% greater than the quantity ordered on the purchase order). Classify them into those where the overshipped quantity was retained or returned. For each excess quantity retained: (1) calculate the holding cost, (2) establish who authorized retention, and (3) determine advantages from retaining and that it offsets the additional holding costs. |
| | • Inquire whether the receiving department follows up with the purchasing department about open items in the receiving file by matching with the past due receiving report. Take a sample of open purchase orders and classify them into: no purchase order number given, invalid purchase order number given, and purchase order number is valid but a copy of the purchase order not received. Ensure that a copy of the purchase order is used to receive only authorized purchases. |
| • To ascertain whether goods received are physically secured from theft, loss, or damage until transferred to other areas. | • Examine the labeling of all materials, whether they are stored for testing, sent in error, defective, surplus, or other. Take a sample from the receiving reports and confirm that each item is: clearly labeled; physically secured and stored in the correct predesignated location; or passed to store or user. |
| | • Match selected fields of the purchase invoice to goods received to ensure that goods received are the same as those shown on the purchase invoice. |
| | • Identify goods received, not billed, for establishing proper liabilities. |
| | • List discrepancies between quantities received and quantities billed for further analysis and examination. |
| • To determine whether the receiving department dispatches the goods received to users in a timely manner. | • Determine whether targets are available for the maximum and average time lags between delivery and receipt by store or user. Select a sample from receiving reports and prepare a schedule showing the dates of delivery and the dates received by stores or users. Investigate and obtain reasons for any time lags in excess of established standards. |
| | • Determine the time lags between the date on which materials are received and the dates the receiving reports are received in the accounts payable department by comparing dates on receiving reports with dates received in accounts payable. |
| • To ascertain whether materials flow through the receiving area effectively and efficiently and that physical arrangement of the receiving area is conducive to effective operation. | • Observe the physical location(s) of the receiving area(s) and the layout. Evaluate the effectiveness of material flow through the receiving area to incoming quality control and storerooms. |
| | • Review the volume and nature of materials received at the various points and determine whether receiving areas could be consolidated for more efficient operation. Analyze the plant layout. Determine whether the receiving areas are near the points of incoming quality control, the storerooms, and the start of the production lines, rather than having to transport received material to the other end of the facility. |
| | • Observe whether work areas are adequate. Verify that scales and other mechanical or electrical measurement equipment are regularly calibrated. Review the adequacy of uncrating and counting areas. Check the receiving department storage area. Ensure material is stored in an orderly manner and is properly identified while awaiting transfer to stores or production lines. |
| | • Review the effectiveness of protection against fire with the use of sprinklers and/or fire extinguishers. Review the effectiveness of protection against intrusion or unauthorized removal of goods with the presence of locked doors, restriction of access to essential employees, employment of security guards, use of security alarms, and so on. |

*Audit objectives for receiving*

*Audit procedures for receiving*

- Determine if the receiving department was subject to a work measurement system for analyzing work flow and to enhance productivity and performance. Evaluate whether the receiving department is keeping up with its workload. Prepare a list of items of backlog and determine loss of purchase discounts resulting from delays in the receiving department.
- Select a number of cases where payment was made for demurrage and trace them to determine reasons for demurrage payment and demurrage cost versus overtime pay for unloading the trucks. Analyze demurrage expenditures month-by-month for the last twelve months and comment on the effectiveness of operation.

---

**KEY CONCEPTS TO REMEMBER: RECEIVING**

- When the number of units shipped in the shipping document does not agree with the quantity shown on the receiving report, the error might be that the amounts ordered on the receiving department's copy of the purchase order or actual count was different from quantity on shipping document.
- One operating department of a company does not have adequate procedures for inspecting and verifying the quantities of goods received. To evaluate the materiality of this control deficiency, the auditor should review the department's annual inventory purchases.
- Upon receipt of purchased goods in a retail company, receiving department employees match the quantity received to the packing slip quantity and mark the retail price on the goods based on a master price list. The annotated packing slip is then forwarded to inventory control and goods are automatically moved to the retail sales area.

---

**TQM and JIT Receiving**

Total quality management principles and just-in-time receiving practices can eliminate the need for inspection of incoming materials received due to trust and reliance placed on the supplier. This practice can have a control implication and be a professional challenge to the internal auditor.

## Examples of Application of Computer-Assisted Audit Techniques:  Goods Receiving

(C) *Audit cycle/area: Expenditure—Quality assurance of materials.*

*Risks and exposures*
- Poor-quality material supplied.
- Poor inspection procedures resulting in accepting inferior-quality materials.

*Controls or control procedures*
- Supplying engineering specifications and drawings to the vendors (PC).
- A written manual describing inspection and test procedures, continuous training of inspectors (PC).

*Audit objectives for quality assurance of materials*
- To determine whether quality control function is adequately prepared for the job of preventing the escape of defective goods into the production operations.

*Audit procedures for quality assurance of materials*
- Confirm whether the quality assurance manual covers topics such as receiving inspection, sampling inspection, nonconforming supplies, quality control records, and corrective action. Confirm that the detailed test procedures include: sampling techniques and risk levels, specific test procedures, acceptable tolerances, and accept or reject decisions including tagging and documentation flow to purchasing, inventory control, and accounts payable departments.
- Review the statistical sampling techniques being used. Determine that they are: the least complex possible without compromising the sample results, at least simple enough to be workable at the plant location, and being carried out according to instructions provided.
- Determine the extent to which vendors are required to submit actual test results with each delivery of material and whether the tests were conducted by the vendor or a reliable private testing agency.

<u>*Audit objectives for quality assurance of materials*</u>

- To ascertain whether quality control staff members are carrying out inspection properly and that they are adequately trained and equipped to accomplish this objective.

- To determine whether cost of quality reports are prepared accurately and promptly.

<u>*Audit procedures for quality assurance of materials*</u>

- Evaluate the adequacy of training given to quality control inspectors and vendors for the purpose of preventing defects and errors.
- Ascertain that quality control management prepares a monthly quality status report, describing significant problems and actions planned, major actions accomplished, and the general situation of the quality program. Determine if the quality control staff has the authority to cause production to cease immediately due to nonconforming materials or operations, instead of waiting for a written report recommending such action.
- Evaluate whether defective material reports for all nonconforming material are prepared and that they include, at a minimum: part name and number, purchase order number, date of inspection, quantity received, quantity defective, nature of discrepancy with inspector's name, further action required, and disposition suggestions.
- Check whether the quality team has implemented a zero-defects program where applicable at the plant. Examine a sample of inspection reports covering high-usage and high-dollar items to see that instructions are properly followed.
- Conduct a plant tour and determine whether incoming quality inspection has adequate facilities, tools, and staff to perform its duties. Establish whether adequate and satisfactory equipment is provided and that the plant has its own calibrating measuring equipment. Review calibration records maintained and comment on their content and adequacy in comparison to guidelines provided.
- Determine whether targets were established for the average and maximum time lags between receipt of an item by the quality control department and its dispatch to the final destination (e.g., store, user, vendor, and scrap). Evaluate the frequency of time lag measurements and monitoring of actual against targets. Age materials on hand awaiting inspection by comparing the date on receiving reports with the audit date, and label them time lag of five working days or more, time lag between two and five days, time lag of less than two days, and so on. Note and investigate with quality control management unusual time lags and obtain reasons for delay.
- Ascertain whether the purchasing management initiates effective and timely actions on inspection deficiencies requiring follow up with vendors. Calculate the average time taken by the purchasing agent in disposing of defective material, and compare actual with targets.
- Evaluate the technical qualifications of the quality control staff to determine the degree to which the individuals are qualified to substitute for one another.
- Analyze the latest month's cost of quality reports, tracing amounts on reports to general ledger accounts. Summarize the costs of rework expense, scrap expense, and warranty expense in each work center by responsibility for a given accounting period. In order to locate the source of a quality problem, prepare a schedule for each class of expense in detail, reflecting part name and number, date inspected, reason for defect, quantity defective, total cost, and vendor supplying the basic material. Identify those costs that relate to failure of purchased parts or material.
- Determine that a work order procedure has been established to accumulate costs of reworking vendor defective material. Ascertain that formal procedures have been established for charging rework costs back to vendors for nonconforming material resulting from vendor cause. Review the procedures and evaluate for adequacy. Take a sample of rework orders completed and determine whether the costs were billed back to the vendor or absorbed by the company. Obtain reasons for deviations from established procedures.

## (D) *Audit cycle/area:  Expenditure—Accounts payable.*

*Risks and exposures*

- Merchandise billed by the vendor was not received by the company.
- Payment had been made for items without a purchase order and receiving report.
- Duplicate requests for checks to pay vendors for specific invoices.
- Unauthorized withdrawal of items from the goods received and unauthorized payment for goods received.
- Overpaying a vendor.
- Payment for goods not received.
- Alteration of employee expense report.

*Controls or control procedures*

- Compare the vendor's invoice with a copy of the receiving department's receiving report (DC).
- Have accounts payable department match the purchase order with the receiving report (PC). Purchasing department should not be performing this match due to possibility of fraud.
- Cancel the paid invoices (PC).
- Periodic spot checks of payments by accounts payable staff (DC).
- Separate the incompatible functions of access to goods received and authorization of payment of vouchers (PC).
- Review and cancel supporting documents when a check is issued (PC).
- Have a departmental supervisor other than the employee ordering the goods approve vendor invoices (PC).
- Verify copies of receipts from vendors to the amount submitted by the employee (DC).

*Audit objectives for accounts payable*

- To determine whether all known liabilities arising from the receipt of goods or services have been recorded in proper accounts and in a timely and accurate manner.

*Audit procedures for accounts payable*

- Examine that all purchase requisitions, purchase orders, receiving reports, and vendor invoices are filed under numerical control by the accounts payable department. Select a number of missing numbers and voided numbers, and query as to the follow-up action taken. Analyze the reasons given and trace to appropriate source documents.
- Review open files of receiving reports and vendor invoices in accounts payable department and conduct these audit tests: obtain an aging schedule of these documents; review for correspondence with vendor on billing differences; check for duplicate posting by verifying with vendor's statement; inquire about actions taken to resolve "unmatched" items. Verify those unmatched receiving reports, unpaid invoices, and open purchase orders are followed up on a current basis.
- In order to determine if any substantial liabilities existed or should have been accrued as of the audit date but had not been booked, perform these audit tests: examine vouchers recorded and payments made after the audit date; examine receiving reports for the last few days of the audit date; examine monthly statements received from creditors having large balances; examine large construction contracts; examine correspondence regarding disputed items; and consider confirming a randomly selected number of creditors, including regular suppliers with zero balances.
- In order to test the year-end cutoff for unrecorded liabilities, examine shipment date and terms of shipment on vendor invoices received prior and subsequent to year-end. A possibility of understated payable exists.
- In order to ensure that all debit or credit memoranda have been properly approved and recorded in accounts, conduct these audit tests: Inspect if debit/credit memos are prenumbered, and verify that all adjustments are approved by management outside the accounts payable department that issued the debit or credit.
- In order to test the accuracy and completeness of invoices entered into an accounts payable system, conduct these audit tests: batch totals processed equal the charges to general ledger accounts and the credits reflected in the accrued accounts payable; and batch totals plus opening balance in accrued accounts payable minus payments made equal closing balance in accrued accounts payable.

| *Audit objectives for accounts payable* | *Audit procedures for accounts payable* |
|---|---|
| | • In order to verify the propriety of account distribution, compare account distributions on selected vouchers with voucher register and/or account distribution sheets. Investigate any charges to accounts that appear to be unusual. Make sure that standard journal entries are used to record items charged to prepaid and deferred accounts, and inquire if a single journal entry is prepared for write-offs and amortization and that management approved them. |
| | • In order to test whether the general ledger balance agrees with the detailed accounts payable subledger, conduct these audit tests: reconcile the total to the general ledger control account; confirm that detailed records are maintained supporting the general ledger control accounts for prepaid expenses and deferred charges; test if the general ledger control totals can be derived independently of the detailed vouchering function; inquire if monthly reconciliations are made of unpaid vouchers with the general ledger accounts; and find out the reasons for delays in payment of past due items and make sure that they are actual liabilities. Scan the trial balance of open accounts payable for significant debit balances and determine the reason for their existence. |
| | • Verify that proper control is exercised over purchase orders and sales invoices in cases where merchandise is purchased for direct shipment to customers. These are called "drop shipments." |
| • To ascertain whether vendor statements have been reconciled properly and promptly. | • Inquire who is responsible for reconciling vendor statements with the vendor's accounts in the accounts payable department, and determine the extent to which vendor's statements are checked. |
| | • Review files of selected vendors and trace their vendor statements to appropriate documents such as purchase orders, receiving reports, vendor invoices, and debit/credit memos, to determine whether transactions and liabilities appear to be normal and that they are accurately recorded. Investigate unusual items. |
| • To determine whether controls over payments are proper, including taking trade discounts and refunds. | • Inquire if there is an approved list of authorized signatures prescribing the scope of authority and expenditure limitation of each individual who can sign and approve the payment. Make sure this list is current. |
| | • Review the policy document explaining when to make payment to vendors and the procedures to ensure those payments can be made promptly. Select a sample of paid invoices and compute elapsed times between actual date and due date of payment. |
| | • In order to ensure whether trade discounts are being taken, conduct these audit tests: review procedures about when to take discounts and under what conditions; review invoices paid for several major vendors who regularly allow trade discounts and investigate the reasons for lost discounts noted; and establish the extent to which discounts are taken after the payment date authorized for the taking of the discount. To determine the cost of late payment of invoices containing trade discounts, the file of paid vendor invoices is the appropriate population from which a sample would be drawn. |
| | • Verify whether invoices and supporting documents have been canceled to prevent their reuse, preferably showing the date of cancellation. |
| | • For refund payment processing, make sure refund checks are issued only after proper authorization is obtained. |
| • To ascertain whether controls over approved vendors are appropriate. | • Examine whether the accounts payable department has a list of approved vendors and that this list is current and used as a control tool prior to processing payments to vendors. |
| | • Inquire as to who is responsible for maintaining the vendor information, including controls over vendor additions, changes, and deletions to the master vendor file. Make sure that system access privileges given to this person are in accord with his or her job duties. |

*Audit objectives for accounts payable*

*Audit procedures for accounts payable*

- To determine whether controls over advance payments to vendors and employees are proper.

- Inquire whether historical files are maintained for vendors, including price history, purchase orders, part numbers, job number, and quantity ordered. Ensure that these historical files are summarized and archived for future reference.
- Evaluate the reasons for advance payments to vendors. Verify that trade discounts are taken before making payments for materials not received at the time of payments. Identify the system in place to ensure that materials are subsequently received. Select a sample to test that materials are subsequently received by tracing receiving reports to vendor invoices.
- Evaluate the reasons for advance payment to employees, whether officers or not. Identify the system in place to ensure that advance monies are recovered through offsets to business expense payments or payments received directly from employees. Select a sample to test that those tracing business expense reports or checks to the employee advance payment register subsequently receive monies.

## Risks in Sampling

An internal auditor suspects that the invoices from a small number of vendors contain serious errors and therefore limits the sample to only those vendors. A major disadvantage of selecting such a directed sample of items to examine is the inability to quantify the sampling error related to the total population of vendor invoices.

## KEY CONCEPTS TO REMEMBER: CREDIT MEMOS VERSUS DEBIT MEMOS

- The vendor for returns and adjustments of goods or services issue credit invoices (memos) to vendor accounts. The vendor owes or gives credit to the purchaser (customer), which results in a debit balance with a supplier. Debit balances with vendors can be a result of the normal delays in recovering monies due from them under the "request for credit" procedure.
- Debit invoices (memos) are issued by the purchaser for vendor errors, rebates, overcharges, corrections, allowances due the company, and recovery of overpayment. The purchaser charges the vendor. Debit memos are charge backed to the vendor and applied to vendor accounts.

## EXAMPLES OF APPLICATION OF COMPUTER-ASSISTED AUDIT TECHNIQUES: ACCOUNTS PAYABLE

- Identify unauthorized vendors in a vendor database for testing to determine existence of valid recorded liabilities. The presence of unauthorized vendors is an indication of fraud and overstates liabilities.
- Identify debit balances for further analysis and interpretation since credit balances are normal.
- Use the test data method to test the accuracy of application program controls over the purchase transactions.
- List payable balances with no scheduled payment date, which is an indication of a lapse in procedures.
- Recompute the file balance to reconcile the accounts payable balance listed in the company's month-end trial balance report to the master accounts payable file.
- Use generalized audit software to verify that all purchases were authorized, that all goods paid for were received, and that there were no duplicate payments.

### (E) *Audit cycle/area: Expenditure—Personnel administration.*

<u>Risks and exposures</u>

- Hiring a highly qualified person with questionable background.

- High employee turnover.

- Employment discrimination suits.

- Errors in payroll rates for new employees.

- No career guidance to management trainees.

- Listing of bogus agencies as referring the candidate for recruiting.

<u>Controls or control procedures</u>

- Perform an adequate check on prior employment background for all new employees (PC).
- Compensation package, including salary, benefits, and bonuses, that is competitive; ongoing training; employee development programs (PC).
- At least two levels of functional management conduct interviews of candidates after initially screened by personnel staff; standard interview and evaluation procedures; use of a checklist to ensure that all points are covered regarding job requirements, qualifications, work conditions, fringe benefits; use of standard and competency measurement tests (PC).
- Have personnel department verify the payroll changes processed in the form of an edit listing (DC)
- Develop a plan for recruiting, selecting, training, and development (PC).
- Verify new agency names and addresses through the telephone book or call the other agencies to see if they have heard about the new agencies (PC, DC).

<u>Audit objectives for personnel administration</u>

- To determine whether controls over employee hiring, indoctrination, and termination procedures are proper and in accordance with policies.

<u>Audit procedures for personnel administration</u>

- *Hiring procedures.* Examine the job/position descriptions of randomly selected positions. Establish that these are consistent with official job grade, job category, and other job classifications by analyzing the job duties and responsibilities. Establish that all approved position descriptions are represented in the organization charts and that no positions in the organization charts lack a position description. Ensure that the job description indicates requirements such as education, training, experience, and special skills. Match these job descriptions to personnel requisition forms, interview forms, and performance evaluation forms. Investigate any discrepancies.
- Make sure that the actual count of employees classified as permanent, temporary, and seasonal is within the limits of budgets or plans. If actual numbers exceed budgets or plans, find out the causes for the excess and the effectiveness of measures taken and planned toward reducing the excess.
- Where applicable, ensure that all new employees are hired subject to their passing physical, psychological, mental, or other specific-capability examinations. Confirm that education, work experience, reference, credit, security, and background checks have been conducted prior to making a job offer.
- Ascertain that the hiring function is adequately organized and staffed and that its employees are suitably trained and are knowledgeable concerning the company personnel policies and procedures.
- Review the company's policy regarding hiring internal candidates versus external candidates. Establish that the employee search methods (i.e., newspaper advertisement, use of professional recruiting firm, advertisement in professional/business journal, use of employment agency) utilized are responsive to the needs of the company and that they are effective and economical.
- Select a random sample of completed application forms in the personnel files and establish the degree to which they are clearly and completely filled out. This is to ensure that all legal requirements (i.e., privacy laws, antidiscrimination laws) have been satisfied or not violated.
- Verify that decisions on offers or rejections of job applicants and candidates are supported by properly filled-out application and interview forms and signed evaluations by the personnel and requisitioning functional department management.

*Audit objectives for personnel administration*

- To ascertain whether policies and practices over employee promotions and transfers are fair and effective.

- To determine whether policies and practices over employee salary/wages and bonuses are fair, equitable, and competitive.

*Audit procedures for personnel administration*

- *Employee indoctrination procedures.* Establish that the personnel department has formal procedures for the indoctrination of new employees. The indoctrination should cover topics such as pension plans, group insurance, medical service, employee loans, travel arrangements, vacation, holidays, sick pay allowances, education reimbursement programs. Select a sample of new employees who have gone through the indoctrination process, and check their files to see if these documents are available in their personal folders: employment agreement; fidelity bond application; covenant against disclosure agreements; conflict-of-interest statements; patent agreement; payroll authorization and deduction forms; employee acknowledgment to return company assets such as keys, manuals, badges, tools, and computers at the time of termination.

- *Termination procedures.* Take a random sample of terminated employees, obtain their personnel folders, and ensure the presence of these documents: exit interview form completely filled out first by the functional department management and then by the personnel department management, use of a checklist by personnel department to make sure that company property has been turned in by the terminated employee. (The checklist should include items for manuals, automobiles, instruments, tools, computers, credit cards, uniforms, identification badges, protective clothing, loans, advances, etc.)

- Verify that the payroll department does not release the final paycheck or separation allowances without approved release forms signed by personnel management, functional department management, and general management.

- Inquire whether information collected from an exit conference is communicated to concerned management and whether it is combined with other exit interview data to yield statistical information on the stated reason for voluntary and involuntary separation.

- Review the policy document regarding employee promotions and transfers. Ensure that it is based on objective criteria and in the best interests of the company, while being fair to employees concerned.

- Establish that employee transfers and promotions are effected as a consequence of formal requests by the management of the initiating department. From personnel records, randomly select a representative number of employees transferred or promoted and examine the pertinent requests, memoranda, and supporting documentation. Ensure that: (1) policies and good business practices have been followed by interviewing the concerned management and employees as required, and (2) approvals were based on documented review of concerned employees' performance evaluations and qualifications against the position requirements.

- Establish that there is a separate group within the personnel department responsible for administering formal compensation (salary) and benefit policies and programs. Make sure that salary, wages, and benefits are related to grade levels or salary ranges that are, in turn, formally related to each position as indicated in the position description and organization chart. Ensure that the benefits provided are cost-effective for the organization. "A system of compensation based on a current job analysis" is a good control to ensure a fair and equitable compensation program administration.

- Examine employee records for completeness and accuracy of wage and salary rates and check records are easily retrievable. Compare the actual grade or salary against the published grade or salary levels. Obtain explanations for apparent deviations from policy or for any evidence of inequitable treatment. Inquire about the frequency of updating the salary and benefits after taking into account changing labor markets (demand and supply forces), inflation factors, budget impact, turnover of specific key positions, and labor union requests.

| *Audit objectives for personnel administration* | *Audit procedures for personnel administration* |
|---|---|
| | • Establish the actual bases utilized in selecting employees entitled to annual bonuses and for determining the amount of bonus to be paid. Ascertain, through a review of policy and interview of the employees concerned and their management, that the bonuses paid were not arbitrarily established through an inadequately supported decision by the employee's management, but rather were the result of a properly documented and executed performance evaluation. Inquire if the personnel management was fully involved in the bonus establishment and execution. |

## EXAMPLES OF APPLICATION OF COMPUTER-ASSISTED AUDIT TECHNIQUES: PERSONNEL ADMINISTRATION

- List employees who have not taken vacations, which is an indication of a fraud.
- List employees who have taken excessive sick leave, which is an indication of an abuse.
- Compare employee pay rates used in calculating payroll to official pay rates to find out discrepancies.

---

(F) *Audit cycle/area: Expenditure—Payroll.*

Major activities and responsibilities of a payroll department include: maintenance of employee records showing authorized pay rates and payroll deductions for each employee; maintenance of control totals for each class of fixed payroll deductions, such as group insurance and savings bonds, or investment plans; determination of total hours on which gross amounts payable for hourly wages will be calculated; maintenance of record showing eligibility and payments for time not worked (i.e., vacation, holidays, sick leave, excused absences, jury duty); processing employee travel advance and business expense reports; and maintaining timekeeping records.

| *Risks and exposures* | *Controls or control procedures* |
|---|---|
| • Unauthorized changes to the payroll. | • Have the personnel department authorize the hiring of all employees, setting pay levels and pay rate changes; ensure that there exist management approvals; dual controls; system access controls; supervisory reviews (PC, DC). |
| • Misappropriation of unclaimed payroll checks. | • Unclaimed payroll checks should be controlled by accounting employees who have no payroll or cash functions; unclaimed pay envelopes should be returned promptly to the treasury department for interim hold and subsequent redeposit; unclaimed paychecks should be voided by the treasury department after a specified period (PC, DC) |
| • Fraudulent practices in payroll preparation. | • Ensure the existence of: segregation of duties; periodic audits by internal and/or external auditors; good recordkeeping; periodic and surprise reviews by supervisors for unusual entries, big adjustments, unusually high payments, and checks to nonemployees (PC, DC). |
| • Employees might be paid for hours not worked or submitting excessive hours for payment. | • Have the time cards approve by the department supervisor and submit them to timekeeping department (PC). |
| • Unauthorized alteration of computer payroll programs for fraudulent purposes. | • Implement authorization, testing, and software quality assurance procedures for payroll program changes (PC, DC). |
| • Terminated employees had not been removed from the payroll. | • Reconcile payroll and timekeeping records (DC). |
| • Payroll checks are drawn for improper amounts. | • Obtain supervisory approval of employee time cards (PC). |
| • Unauthorized alteration of hourly pay rates by payroll clerks. | • Limit access to master payroll records to payroll supervisors only (PC). |
| • Payroll clerk adding fictitious employees to the payroll. | • Allow changes to the payroll to be authorized only by the personnel department (PC). |
| | • Perform periodic floor checks of employees on the payroll (DC). |
| | • Ensure that all hiring and terminating is performed by the personnel department (PC). |
| • Payments to unauthorized recipients. | • Examine procedures for proper distribution of paychecks (DC). |
| • Payroll fraud. | • Authorize payroll master-file additions and deletions by personnel department (PC). |

<u>*Audit objectives for payroll*</u>

- To determine whether payroll preparation procedures are effective in preventing the processing of unauthorized transactions.

<u>*Audit procedures for payroll*</u>

- Establish that: there is adequate segregation of duties regarding time reporting, payroll preparation, payroll approval, check deposit/bank transfer preparation, journal entry preparation, input (data entry) to computer, and reconciliation of system output; only designated, appropriate persons are authorized to input payroll information to the computer and that system access privileges are based on employee job duties; and there are built-in automated program edit checks to prevent improper, erroneous, or unusual inputs to the computer.
- For selected payroll periods, verify that: batch control totals of entered data and pay period totals of output data were maintained and compared by the payroll department and that these totals were either agreed or reconciled and exceptions were resolved in a timely manner. Some examples of control totals that can be made of include total number of hours, number of employees, number of documents, number of transactions.
- In order to ensure the accuracy and completeness of the payroll calculations, conduct these audit tests: foot and cross-foot the payroll register; trace payroll totals to the general ledger; trace the total net pay to the reimbursement of the imprest payroll account. Verify that any unusual entries, adjustments, checks to nonemployees have been noted and investigated by the payroll department; and compare the payroll by department with that of the previous month for reasonableness.
- Select a representative number of employees from one or two departments and perform these audit tests: check the name, job classification, clock card number, employee number to the employment authorization and personnel data records; check the propriety of job classification with the job description; check the rates of pay to the wage authorization, incentive plan, and union contract; check the computation of gross and net pay and check the calculations and propriety of each deduction; check the recorded shift time and premium to ensure correctness of the shift differentials applied; trace gross pay, net pay, and deduction amounts to employee earnings records; verify that deductions are formally authorized by the employee; if the payroll is paid by check, examine paid, endorsed payroll checks for agreement with the payee name, payment amount, check number, date of payment as indicated in the payroll register, and if the payroll is paid by direct deposit in the employee bank, check bank payment report for agreement with the payee name, payment amount, bank deposit number, date of payment as indicated in the payroll register.
- Verify that when an employee's pay rate or deduction has just been changed or when the initial pay of a new employee is being prepared, the pay rates, deductions, and computations are verified and signed by an uninterested second employee or by the supervisor of the payroll department.

- To determine whether payroll disbursement procedures are effective to prevent the receipt of unauthorized payroll.

- From an examination of the payroll run, verify that amounts actually paid for wages and salaries are readily traceable to the totals for all employees and to the pay period.
- Ensure that payroll checks are prenumbered and the numerical sequence is accounted for by the payroll department. Ensure that canceled, voided, and missing check numbers are accounted for.
- Establish that for each pay period, the computer-based payroll system lists all employee names and amounts paid even when the amount is zero. This is to ensure that all employees are accounted for, which can be easily and readily compared to other records of employee count.
- Evaluate procedures, interview employees concerned, and inspect storage facilities to verify that blank payroll checks are stored in a locked area accessible only to authorized employees and issued only in blocks, with the check number sequence monitored.

| *Audit objectives for payroll* | *Audit procedures for payroll* |
|---|---|
| | • Verify that payroll checks are distributed to employees by non-payroll department employees, by a nonsupervisory employee of the functional department with no payroll authorization or preparation duties, or by internal auditors. Employees should wear the company identification badge during the payoff of wages. |
| | • To determine if salaried employees are taking more paid vacation time than they have earned, observe which employees on the audit day were absent because of vacations and trace those absences through the payroll records to subtractions from accumulated vacation time. |
| | • To ascertain that no payments to fictitious employees were made, perform a payroll payoff test. |
| | • Payoff of cash wages should be discouraged, where possible. If cash wages are used, verify that dated payroll receipts exist or that the proper employee signs listings immediately on being paid. Verify that these receipts are subsequently compared with payroll records, that signatures are spot-checked, and that the receipts are canceled to prevent reuse. Employees should wear the company identification badge during the payoff of wages. |
| | • In order to ensure that controls over unclaimed paychecks are proper, these audit tests should be conducted: obtain all unclaimed pay envelopes and checks; trace these back to the payroll registers and signed receipts; and verify that the receipts for these unclaimed paychecks have not been signed. Verify that the liability had been correctly and promptly set up for these unclaimed wages. |
| | • To determine whether persons on the payroll of a particular department actually work there, observe for the physical presence of properly identified employees during a surprise department floor check. This test provides the best source of evidence. |
| • To ascertain whether accounting for payroll is adequate and proper, including bank account reconciliations. | • Through an examination of bank account authorizations, deposit and transfer documents, and recent bank statements, verify that all payroll funding is controlled through separate imprest bank account(s). |
| | • Trace the amounts deposited and/or transferred into and out of the payroll bank account(s) to respective payroll registers and other related internal memoranda. Investigate any discrepancies. Ensure that there is no mixed application of funds between payroll-related expenditures and nonpayroll types of expenditures. |
| | • Establish that payroll bank accounts are reconciled promptly by an employee independent of all payroll functions, preferably by treasury department employees. Select a sample of bank accounts and conduct these audit tests: verify that: each reconciliation has been dated and signed by the preparer; the reconciliations are correct as to format and content (i.e., descriptions, amounts, totals); and reconciling items have been promptly followed up and resolved. |
| | • In order to ensure that good accounting practices are followed, conduct these audit tests: the gross payroll is reconciled to the respective accrual and the accrual is reconciled to the respective labor distribution; all employee compensation payments are promptly recorded in the accrued payroll account. Where detailed labor distributions are not prepared, ensure that: each payroll is regularly reconciled with the previous one; vacation pay is accrued properly; bonus payments and other performance awards are accrued each month rather than recorded when paid; and general ledger control accounts for each payroll deduction are supported by subsidiary records detailed by employee. |
| | • In order to ensure the accuracy of the distribution of payroll, labor charges, and payroll adjustments, these audit tests are suggested: confirm that labor distributions and adjustments are reviewed by a responsible person other than the preparer, inquire if adjustments are signed by an authorized person; and confirm that labor distributions and adjustments are made in accordance with generally accepted accounting principles. |

| _Audit objectives for payroll_ | _Audit procedures for payroll_ |
|---|---|
| | • Review the payroll accounting procedure manual to ensure that it describes how to compute, record, classify, summarize, and report these transactions: amounts due the employee, employer's contributions, employees' contributions, income tax and social security deductions, payroll taxes, and payroll adjustments. Verify that general ledger subaccounts are maintained in sufficient detail for all categories of taxes withheld to facilitate management analysis, investigation of erroneous entries, and the timely development of tax information for reporting to the tax authorities. |
| • To determine whether payroll records are retained long enough to meet statutory requirements. | • In order to ensure that all salary data and personnel and payroll records are stored securely and protected against damage, loss by fire or flood, or unauthorized access, these tests or inquiries should be conducted: verify that all sensitive records are stored in a locked, fireproof area accessible only to authorized employees; and examine whether stored documents are not exposed to excessive heat, humidity, chemical vapors, steam, water leaks, rain, and so on. |
| | • Ensure that sensitive records are retained in accordance with statutory period requirements and approved by the legal counsel and the taxing authorities. Establish that the controls and procedures followed in destroying or disposing of expired records are adequate. |
| • To ascertain whether controls over employee travel advance and business expense reports and accounting procedures are accurate and timely. | • Ensure that these activities are separated and performed by different employees: review of travel authorizations, vouchers, requests for advances, and approval of these documents; preparation of journal entries and approval of these entries; preparation of check requisitions for travel advances or for employee expense reimbursement and approval or check signing; and maintenance of employee advance records and the preparation of related journal entries. |
| | • _Employee travel advances._ Verify that the company shall not provide any employee with an advance for business travel without a properly approved cash requisition on which the travel is stipulated. Ascertain how emergency conditions are handled. Verify that the related vouchers had been submitted with a copy of a properly completed and approved travel authorization form. |
| | • Ascertain whether the person requesting an advance is refused if the person: has a significant outstanding balance due the company, and is soon to be terminated and has an unsettled balance due the company. Confirm that the personnel department is responsible for notifying, with sufficient lead time, the payroll department of any impending transfer or termination of an employee. |
| | • Confirm that the payroll department is responsible for ascertaining the status of an employee's advance account before computing the final net pay of any employee it has been notified shall be shortly transferred or terminated. |
| | • Determine if there have been any instances of any employee having been denied an advance because of unsettled, excessive balances. Ensure that this procedure is consistently followed in all departments and at all grade levels. |
| | • Ascertain if balances due the company were either reimbursed by the employee prior to separation or deducted from the employee's final paycheck. |
| | • _Business expense reports._ Ensure that expenses incurred by employees are for business travel or other specified business-related expenses. Verify that these expense reports are prepared using a standard form and submitted within a few days after returning from the business trip. Examine whether all expense reports are reviewed by the functional department management for accuracy and propriety and by the accounting department in that sequence. _Fraudulent use of corporate credit cards would be minimized by subjecting credit card charges to the same expense controls as those used on regular company expense forms._ |

*Audit objectives for payroll*

*Audit procedures for payroll*

- Make sure that travel and related costs that are incurred but not recorded by the close of an accounting period are properly accrued and that these accruals are reversed in the following accounting month.

- Examine copies of the three most recent reconciliations of individual account balances or advances with the general ledger control accounts. Examine a sample of employee expense account statements and verify that periodic confirmation of significant balances is actually solicited and followed up by accounting department.

- To determine whether controls over timekeeping and labor utilization practices and reporting are proper.

- Ensure that written policies and procedures are available describing how to account for time and attendance for all categories of positions. Establish that labor utilization objectives and performance monitoring and reporting requirements are formally defined in production control, the personnel department, and the cost accounting department policies and procedures. Determine that these policies and procedures contain guidelines: performance reporting, controls over direct and indirect labor, controls over overtime pay and shift premium rates, application of labor standards, and reporting of idle time and cost variances.

- *Timekeeping practices and reporting.* Select a sample of employees from different departments who were paid for authorized absences, such as vacation, holiday, illness, military service, approved leave of absence, and so on. Trace the hours or days of authorized absence back to supporting departmental or timekeeping records and ascertain that proper departmental approvals have been documented and are reasonable. Investigate major instances or patterns of deviations from policy.

- Examine the departmental or timekeeping records documenting lateness or early departures. For hourly employees, trace the time not worked forward to the payroll wage computation sheets and backward to the time sheets or cards. For salaried employees, trace the lateness and early departures recorded by the employees' departments or by the timekeeping function. Ensure that follow-up and corrective actions have been adequate and effective for any cases of chronic lateness or early departure.

- Ascertain that any manual adjustments or changes made to the hours originally entered are adequately explained, appear reasonable, and are signed by authorized persons in accordance with the company policy.

- Conduct spot observations of time clock punching by employees on an entirely surprise basis in an unobtrusive manner from a position not readily visible to those approaching the time clock. Observe that: no one has punched in or out for anyone but him- or herself or punched using someone else's time card, and that all persons, once punching in or out, remain in or out and do not subsequently leave or enter the facility without again punching the time clock.

- Obtain payroll records for selected departments and verify that all the employees listed on the payroll are physically present at their place of work or otherwise accounted for (e.g., business travel, training, illness, and authorized absence).

- Verify, through interview of accounting and production managers, that the time actually worked on each job is being charged to the job and that the system for distributing direct and indirect labor costs to jobs is reliable. Select a random sample of completed time sheets or clock cards. Trace summary time and cost figures to jobs charged through the use of journal entries. Ensure that supervisors approve any modifications to these time cards.

<u>*Audit objectives for payroll*</u>

<u>*Audit procedures for payroll*</u>

- *Labor utilization practices and reporting.* To ensure that overtime and premium pay are effectively controlled, conduct these audit tests: verify that overtime hours and premium pay are regularly accumulated on a departmental basis; review the procedures for deriving actual overtime hours worked and overtime pay; check for prior solicitation in writing by designated supervisors; compare the overtime hours paid to the actual basic time cards and verify that they are the same, and investigate any differences; and compare approval signatures on the time cards and on overtime requests with those approved to sign.

- To ensure that production statistics facilitate realistic evaluation of performance and the derivation of specific corrective measures, perform these audit tests: review whether proper records are maintained showing the actual and targeted production by major cost center and product line; review whether proper records are maintained showing direct labor hours actually worked and indirect labor costs distributed; compare standard direct labor hours against with actual hours; analyze production performance indices (e.g., productivity ratios and nonproductive time by department or product line); and ensure that labor efficiency variances from budget are regularly developed on a departmental basis. Ensure that performance records are maintained in sufficient detail to provide a basis for evaluating the utilization of labor by function, cost center, or department.

- To ensure that standard times are derived independent of production operations, preferably by industrial engineering time studies, conduct these audit tests: ascertain that standards are developed based on either time studies or historical data, or a combination of both; review the policies and procedures for deriving standard times and for updating them to cover engineering changes, time studies of estimated standards, and the correction of errors; examine the supporting documentation for time studies or historical data; verify the accuracy of calculations on a sample basis and that these standards are periodically updated as needed; obtain copies of standard time process sheets covering a representative number of production operation steps, and compare them to the standards used in computing labor efficiency variances.

- To test the adequacy and effectiveness of worker incentive plans, these audit tests are suggested: understand the policies and procedures describing how to calculate incentive pay; select a random sample of employees receiving incentive pay and verify that each payment is supported by approved production counts and authorized rate schedules, correctly computed, complies with the established policies and procedures; interview a representative sample of workers and supervisors and ascertain whether incentive plans motivate them or not and whether incentive plans are administered fairly or not; and ensure that the function administering the incentive plans is separate from the function who granted incentives for maximum reliability and effectiveness. Conduct a trend analysis of incentive payments relating them to productivity and labor efficiency.

## Compatible and Incompatible Functions in Payroll

Preparing attendance data and preparing the payroll activities are incompatible. Examples of compatible activities include: hiring employees and authorizing changes to pay rates, preparing the payroll and filing payroll tax forms, and signing and distributing payroll checks. It is a control weakness when a payroll clerk has custody of the check signature stamp machine.

**Audit Procedures for Payroll**

### Sampling in Payroll

In testing payroll transactions, an auditor discovers that in 4 out of 100 (statistical sample) the appropriate supervisor did not sign selected time cards. To evaluate the materiality or significance of this control deficiency, the auditor should compute an upper precision limit and compare with the tolerable error.

## EXAMPLES OF APPLICATION OF COMPUTER-ASSISTED AUDIT TECHNIQUES: PAYROLL

### Use of Mainframe Computer Audit Software

Use the test data method to test the accuracy of computations of employee withholding for tax and benefit deductions, and compare the actual results with predetermined results. Identify unusually small tax deductions.

Use the parallel simulation technique to ensure that the payroll program is reliable and to test the accuracy of the payroll calculation.

Use the test data method to test calculation of regular and overtime pay amounts and compare the results with predetermined or expected results.

Produce a cross-reference list after matching individual employee payroll time card information to personnel department records and files to conclude that individuals are bona fide employees.

### Use of Microcomputer Audit Software

Compare current period amounts with previous period amounts for employee gross and net payroll wages. Identify employees with unusual pay amounts after performing reasonableness tests.

Select all transactions in specified activity codes and in excess of predetermined amounts. Trace them to proper authorization in personnel files in order to determine if payroll changes are authorized.

---

(iv) **Introduction to production/conversion cycle.** Major activities in a production/conversion cycle would include: initiating production or manufacturing orders; requesting withdrawal of raw materials from stores; scheduling of production orders; processing of raw materials according to process sheets or other specifications; performing quality control inspection work; accounting for costs of production and processing; preparing production and cost accounting reports; storing of processed goods; shipping of processed goods; recording of production activities by journalizing and posting of manufacturing transactions; analyzing production or manufacturing variances for corrective actions; updating of production and work-in-process records; protecting physical inventory of raw materials, work-in-process, and finished goods; and maintaining the accuracy and completeness of inventory records and of property, plant, and equipment records.

(A) *Audit cycle/area: Production/conversion—Inventory control.*

| Risks and exposures | Controls or control procedures |
|---|---|
| • Defects in finished goods due to poor-quality raw materials. | • Implement specifications for purchase of raw materials and parts (PC, DC). |
| • Excessive investment in raw materials inventory. | • Implement total quality management and just-in-time principles in purchasing and receiving functions (PC). |
| • Unsatisfactory customer service levels. | • Establish service-level goals (PC) and obtain customer feedback periodically (DC). |

<u>*Audit objectives for inventory control*</u>

- To determine whether inventory levels are sufficient to achieve satisfactory customer service levels and to maintain balanced production throughput without requiring excessive investment in inventory.

<u>*Audit procedures for inventory control*</u>

- Ascertain that the inventory control function is organizationally separate from the manufacturing function to ensure that inventory decisions are not overridden by production considerations.
- Review the overdue backlog of customer orders to determine the extent to which original promised delivery dates are not being achieved. Prepare a schedule showing total customer orders: total orders meeting on-time delivery and total orders with overdue delivery expressed as a range of delivery slippage in weeks. Determine the percentage of orders that have been delayed due to inventory problems.
- Determine the extent of production line disruptions, downtime, rescheduling due to material shortages. Review production department reports of production line downtime due to material shortages and/or out-of-specification material. Determine the frequency and the effect of multiple line setups due to material shortages.
- Ensure that inventory turnover goals are achieved and that the inventory mix is in proper balance. Select a representative sample of items in each A-B-C inventory and calculate the turnover rates as follows: Annualized usage for the period in units / Average inventory for the period in units. Compare the actual turnover rates with the established goals. Discuss exceptions with management.
- Compare the actual turnover rates with the established goals for each category of inventory. Discuss exceptions with management.

- To ascertain whether the inventory control techniques used are appropriate considering the composition of the products and the demand patterns.

- By discussion with inventory control and marketing management, determine the demand patterns for finished goods. Also, determine the demand patterns for inventory items (both manufactured items and purchased parts) by discussion with purchasing and production control management. Determine the degree of common parts between the manufactured items and purchased parts. Based on these discussions, determine whether order point (OP) or materials requirements planning (MRP) techniques are appropriate.
- These guidelines would help in this matter: An order point system is useful where the life of the product is long, demand patterns are stable, and many parts have a high degree of commonality of usage. A material requirement planning system is useful where product life is uncertain and demand patterns are subject to significant fluctuations. For order point systems, determine that the reorder point is calculated properly using the formula

  Reorder point = Lead time × Demand during the lead time + Safety stock

- Select representative samples of manufactured and purchased parts and calculates the reorder points. For purchased items, determine that the lead time includes processing time for requisitions, purchase orders, receiving, inspection, stocking, and vendor lead time. For manufactured items, determine that the lead time includes production scheduling time, sequencing time, move time, queue time, setup time, run time, inspection time, and stocking time. Compare actual lead times to stated lead times and comment on discrepancies. For the sample selected, verify that new orders are placed when the reorder point is reached, not before.
- Check the actual historical on-hand balances when the new orders are received. If the safety stock level is not being reached, the reorder point is probably too high. If there is never a stock-out, the reorder point and/or safety stock levels are probably too high.

| *Audit objectives for inventory control* | *Audit procedures for inventory control* |
|---|---|
| | • For order point systems, select a representative sample of manufactured and purchased items and calculate the economic order quantity (EOQ). Compare the calculated EOQs against the order quantities actually used. In the event of significant discrepancies, determine the management overrides that allow other than an EOQ to be ordered and comment on the appropriateness after calculating the overall effect on inventory levels. *For MRP systems*, analyze the method of forecasting demand and determine whether forecasts represent reliable data on which accurate materials decisions can be based. Review marketing's forecasting techniques for adequacy and appropriateness, be they salesperson's projections, market surveys, economic indicators, or a variable combination of all. Evaluate the method of exploding forecasts down to component parts. Ensure the forecast is time phased throughout the year. |
| | • Review techniques for tracking actual demand to the forecast and comment on significant deviations from the forecast and adequacy of tracking techniques. Determine the method of updating the forecast: exponential smoothing, regeneration, and net change. |
| | • Determine whether or not a new components parts explosion is generated when revised finished goods or subassembly requirements are identified. |
| | • Determine whether scrap and shrinkage are given adequate consideration in requisitioning parts. Determine basis for scrap and shrinkage factors. Test scrap factors against recent experience. |
| • To determine whether controls over perpetual inventory records are proper. | • Ensure that: only inventory control staff can update perpetual inventory records and that they do not have access to the physical inventory; all perpetual inventory records maintenance flows through a centralized, controlled function; all changes to inventory records are properly authorized and approved; and individuals charged with the custodianship of physical inventories do not have access to the perpetual records. |
| | • Determine that inventory control staff is notified of all receipts of materials and all material that fails incoming quality inspection. Determine whether satisfactory actions are taken to obtain substitute material, rework failed material. |
| | • Verify the adequacy of paperwork controls to ensure that inventory control is assured of receiving all documentation relative to material movement. This includes relief of preprocess inventory to work in progress (WIP), bookings to finished goods from WIP, and relief of finished goods based on sales. |
| | • Ensure that perpetual inventory quantity balances are periodically verified by cycle counts. Ensure those significant differences between the cycle counts and the perpetual records are verified independently prior to updating the perpetual records. Investigate reasons for negative balances in inventory. This procedure identifies inventory shortages. |
| | • Ensure that there are general ledger control accounts for raw materials, purchased parts, manufactured parts, WIP inventory, finished goods inventory, goods at suppliers, consigned goods, shop supplies, and small tools. Ensure that individuals who maintain the perpetual records do not have access to the general ledger inventory accounts. |
| | • In order to ensure that all inventory transactions are promptly and accurately posted to the general ledger, perform these audit tests: review accounts payable controls for properly coding the preprocess inventory; review procedures that relieve preprocess inventory and charge WIP; review controls that charge direct labor and overhead to WIP; review controls that relieve WIP and charge finished goods; and review controls that relieve finished goods inventory. |

<u>Audit objectives for inventory control</u>

<u>Audit procedures for inventory control</u>

- Review controls over material sent to suppliers for processing (e.g., plating, anodizing). Ensure that controls cover: authorized shipping documentation, physical counts of parts shipped; notification sent to accounting; segregation of the inventory in a goods-at-supplier inventory account in the general ledger at standard cost; verification of counts of inventory received back from the suppliers and any discrepancies are accounted for by the supplier; and preparation by accounting of appropriate general ledger inventory records relieving the goods at supplier account and charging the appropriate inventory account at the new standard.

- Verify that accounting records for material stored or consigned away from the plant include: proper approvals prior to shipment; warehouse, consignment, or other agreements in effect to protect the company in the event of fire, theft, negligence; periodic confirmation from consignee of quantities on hand; reconciliation of consignee's confirmation with company records; and taking of physical inventories at least once a year of quantities on consignment and reconciliation with the company records.

- Verify that the accounting department maintains separate records of material owned by others but in the hands of the company (goods consigned in, materials being processed for others). Ensure that: received quantities are verified; the goods are physically safeguarded; periodic confirmations are made with the owner; quantities shipped are accurate and are reconciled to consigned quantities; and the company is adequately covered against loss in the event of fire, theft, deterioration.

- Ensure small tools and shop supplies are accurately accounted for and are controlled. Ensure that: accounting controls are appropriate to account for all receipts and issues of small tools and shop supplies; and physical controls over small tools and shop supplies are sufficient to preclude unauthorized removal.

- To ascertain whether controls over excess and obsolete inventory and reserve provisions are adequate.

- Obtain copies of the perpetual inventory records and identify excess and obsolete inventory items. Verify that the items identified are included in the company's excess and obsolete inventory stock listing. Understand the methods used to identify slow-moving stock: annually at physical inventory time, at the time of cycle counts, periodic reviews, and judgment. Evaluate the adequacy of method(s) used to identify slow-moving stock.

- Compare the calculated excess and obsolete reserve requirement to that actually provided in the general ledger and comment on discrepancies. Obsolete inventory may be defined as inventory that has had no movement in the last year. Excess inventory may be defined as the quantity in excess of one year's supply on hand. Scanning, recomputation, and analytical review are procedures that can be used to identify the amount of obsolete inventory and to collect audit evidence.

- Ensure that excess and obsolete inventory to be disposed of is physically segregated and securely stored, is accounted for separately, and that an aggressive disposal program is in effect. Review the dollar value of inventory disposed of in light of total excess and obsolete inventory and comment on the effectiveness of disposal activities.

- Determine that surplus stock disposal efforts are sequenced in order to minimize loss: returning to vendors, selling to other companies or other divisions of the same company, reworking or modifying, selling to customers at a reduced price, and selling for scrap. Determine that once stock has been identified for disposal, it is physically segregated and maintained in a secured area. Ascertain that the proper management level authorizes inventory disposal. Ensure that authorized write-offs and write-downs are promptly and accurately charged against the appropriate inventory and reserve accounts.

## FORMULAS IN INVENTORY

Calculate the turnover rates for raw material, work in process (WIP), and finished goods using the following formulas:

Raw materials = Relief of preprocess inventory (raw material) to WIP in dollars / Average preprocess inventory in dollars

Work in process = Relief of finished goods inventory in dollars / Average WIP inventory in dollars

Finished goods = Cost of goods sold in dollars / Average finished goods inventory in dollars

## GUIDELINES FOR FORECASTING TECHNIQUES

**Exponential smoothing.** New forecast = Old forecast + (Sales – Old forecast)

**Regeneration.** This technique involves discarding the old forecast and substituting a new one. This technique is generally appropriate where there are widely varying forecasts and relatively few inventory levels.

**Net change.** This technique involves updating only those items for which a forecast change is indicated (either in quantities or timing). This technique is generally appropriate where there are few changes and many levels in the bills of materials.

---

### KEY CONCEPTS TO REMEMBER: INVENTORY CONTROL

- If controls over the perpetual inventory system are weak, a good recommendation is to schedule a physical inventory count.
- Statistical sampling would be appropriate to estimate the value of a firm's inventory because statistical sampling is reliable and objective.
- During an investigation of unexplained inventory shrinkage, the auditor is testing inventory additions as recorded in the perpetual inventory records. Because of internal control weaknesses, the information recorded on receiving reports may not be reliable. Under these conditions, the vendors' invoices would provide the best evidence of additions to inventory.
- During the year-end physical inventory process, the auditor observed items staged in the shipping area and marked "Sold—Do Not Inventory." The customer had been on credit hold for three months because of bankruptcy proceedings, but the sales manager had ordered the shipping supervisor to treat the inventory as sold for physical inventory purposes. The auditor noted the terms of sale were "FOB warehouse." The auditor should recommend that the inventory staged in the shipping area be counted and included along with the rest of the physical inventory results. Conclusions: The inventory belongs to the company and was not sold to the customer due to FOB warehouse and the title to the goods remains with the company. Risk was not passed to the customer.

## EXAMPLES OF APPLICATION OF COMPUTER-ASSISTED AUDIT TECHNIQUES: INVENTORY CONTROL

- Use "tagging and tracing" techniques to provide a computer trail of all relevant processing steps applied to a specific inventory transaction in an online perpetual inventory system. To accomplish this, certain file-updating transactions need to be selected for detailed testing. Inquiry-type transactions will not be useful since they are merely data lookups, with no file updating. File updating is a critical, risky activity since the file contents can be changed.

- List old or slow-moving inventory items for possible write-offs.
- List large differences between the last physical inventory and the perpetual book inventory for further analysis and review of adjustments.
- Test the numerical sequence of physical inventory count sheet numbers to account for all numbers, whether used or not.
- List inventory items with negative balances for further analysis and follow-up.
- Test the accuracy of reduction of inventory relief for cost of sales.
- Calculate inventory turnovers by product (including finished goods, raw materials, and WIP components), and compare them to targets.
- Use the control flowcharting technique to review the overall business control context of the work-in-process computer processing application system. This technique is similar to a normal flowchart except that it will focus more on controls and control points in a work-in-process flow in a manufacturing environment.

---

### (B) *Audit cycle/area: Production/conversion—Production control.*

*Risks and exposures*

- Production delays as a consequence of equipment breakdowns and repairs.
- Building of unnecessary finished goods inventory.

*Controls or control procedures*

- Establish a preventive maintenance program for all production equipment (PC).
- Comparison of actual inventory against production schedules by time period (DC).

*Audit objectives for production control*

- To determine whether inputs to the annual production plan are proper.

- To ascertain whether short-term production schedules support the overall annual production plan.

*Audit procedures for production control*

- Ascertain that the production control function is organizationally independent of manufacturing to ensure that production control decisions are not overridden by manufacturing considerations.
- Determine the inputs or basis of the annual planned production, that is, a finished goods replenishment plan based on reorder point techniques, a plan based on forecasted demand using materials requirement planning techniques, or a combination of techniques.
- Ascertain the degree of participation and involvement by the marketing, manufacturing, and inventory control staff and management in developing the production plan. This is very critical since subsequent decisions, such as acquisition of capital equipment, manpower, inventory, and facility expansion, are made based on the production plan.
- Analyze the production schedules and detail significant deviations from the production plan. Where significant deviations exist, ensure the deviations are caused by changes in demand patterns, not due to bad production schedules.
- Evaluate the effect of deviations from the production plan on: preprocess inventory levels; production floor balancing to ensure that machines are neither overutilized nor underutilized; and finished goods inventory levels where production is focused on few items at the expense of many other items (i.e., giving unequal weight).
- Verify that production control staff considers existing WIP and current machine loading capacity prior to generating new production schedules.
- Determine whether similar products are scheduled together to minimize setups. This is because the more frequent the setups are, the more interruption to the production schedule and the more cost.
- Ensure that production runs are neither excessively long nor short. Lengthening production runs excessively can result in delivery slippage or bottlenecks in other products. The ultimate goal should be a balanced production throughput that maximizes utilization of the production facilities and yet meets the demand for the products.

<u>*Audit objectives for production control*</u>

- To determine whether product-related documentation exists and that it is complete and current.

- To ascertain whether engineering changes are controlled properly.

- To determine whether manufacturing operations adhere to specifications.

- To ascertain whether production reporting is accurate and timely.

<u>*Audit procedures for production control*</u>

- Verify that appropriate documentation exists for each product so that only approved parts and manufacturing processes are utilized. Select a sample of parts and ensure that drawings, specifications, and manufacturing process sheets are available and that they are current. This includes routing sheets, production process sheets, material travelers, and so on. Ensure that the documentation contains, at a minimum: description of sequence of operations, description of operator motion sequence, indication of standard time allowed for each operation, description of accepted tolerances for scrap and breakages, and description of accepted tolerance for downtime during operation.

- In order to ensure that engineering change notices (ECN) are properly approved and controlled and are processed promptly, identify the conditions leading to ECN (e.g., quality control failures, customer complaints, product returns, and initiating product improvements).

- Determine whether the company has an engineering change review board composed of the managers of production control, inventory control, industrial engineering, design engineering, marketing, and production operations. Inquire if approval levels have been established for each type of change. Determine that full consideration is given to on-hand and on-order material that will be scrapped or become obsolete due to change.

- Review procedures in effect to dispose of material obsolete by engineering changes. Confirm whether consideration is given to using the old parts prior to introducing the new parts into production, reworking the old parts, returning the old parts to the vendor, sales to other companies, and scrap sales.

- Ascertain whether obsolete parts are segregated into a controlled area to prevent accidental use in the production line.

- Select a sample of production orders and ensure that the packet includes an approved production order, a list of component parts that must be withdrawn from stores, routing or process sheets that list the sequence of operations from cost center to cost center, and the manufacturing steps. The production order should also include time standards by labor class and by department, special machines or tools required, and setup instructions.

- Ensure that approved manufacturing orders are delivered to the shop floor and travel with the order detailing customer name, part number, quantity required, start date, and completion date. Ensure that manufacturing operations adhere strictly to the route sheets, which include sequence of operations, drawings of all dimensions, tolerances, and material usage standards including offal and production scrap.

- Determine the extent to which substitute material is used. Indicate and evaluate the approval of substitute material. Calculate the additional cost of substitute material. Determine the reasons why the substitute material was necessary.

- Obtain copies of production reports and ensure that these items are presented: material usage; production direct and indirect labor used; machine utilization; scrap, spoilage, and rework costs; downtime and idle time; good production quantities; percent of compliance with production schedules.

- Ensure that there are adequate controls over preprinted forms for material issuance to the production line, preprinted forms for returns to stock and production floor transfers to finished goods inventory, and method of charging labor and overhead to work-in-progress at pay points.

- Evaluate the method of recording factory direct and indirect labor to specific shop orders. Evaluate machine utilization reporting. Verify actual setup times to standards, actual run times, and machine downtime. Determine incidence of production line downtime and comment on amount of downtime. Evaluate the causes of idle time (e.g., bottlenecks, stock-outs, incorrect scheduling) and comment on shop floor throughput.

| *Audit objectives for production control* | *Audit procedures for production control* |
|---|---|
| | • Evaluate the reporting procedures and controls over scrap, spoilage, and rework costs. Test the accuracy of production quantity reporting. Sample test-count quantities run against reported. |
| | • Determine whether control procedures are adequate to prevent subsequent operations reporting more pieces completed than previous operations. |
| | • Perform production-aging schedules. Select a sample of closed production orders and determine: number of orders completed on schedule, number of orders completed early; and number of orders completed less than a week late, less than a month late, or more than a month late. Evaluate the reasons for production orders that are completed late or early. Where customer orders are to be delivered late, determine whether production control informs the sales department so that the customers can be contacted regarding the delay. Quantify the financial impact of late deliveries resulting in fines, premium freight charges, and changes in shipping schedules of other products. Assess the level of loss of goodwill. |

## EXAMPLES OF APPLICATION OF COMPUTER-ASSISTED AUDIT TECHNIQUES: PRODUCTION CONTROL

- List production orders with no due date of production scheduling and no delivery (shipping) date.
- Compare production counts between production system records and cost accounting system records to ensure that costs are allocated based on correct production count.
- Test the accuracy of accumulation of production costs.

(C)  *Audit cycle/area: Production/conversion—Shipping.*

| *Risks and exposures* | *Controls or control procedures* |
|---|---|
| • Unable to ship replacement parts on time. | • Establish shipping time standards by part category (PC). |
| • Unauthorized shipments. | • Implement strict procedures to ship approved sales orders only (PC). |

| *Audit objectives for shipping* | *Audit procedures for shipping* |
|---|---|
| • To determine whether all material movements into and out of the shipping department are completely and accurately documented and all shipments are promptly reported to billing function. | • Determine that copies of sales orders are forwarded to the shipping department on a timely basis by comparing the dates the sales orders were prepared to the dates received in shipping. Ensure that sales orders are prenumbered and that shipping maintains a numerical control log. Investigate gaps in the numerical sequence. |
| | • Determine whether shipping is responsible for reviewing sales orders and the documents authorizing the transfer of material to shipping for proper approval and for verifying that the proper material has been forwarded for shipment. If it is not, determine why not. |
| | • When many "rush shipments" are found, determine the need for rush shipment services. |
| | • Perform a substantive audit test by selecting bills of lading from the warehouse and tracing the shipments to the related invoices. Relevant facts include: shipments are made from the warehouse based on customer purchase orders, the matched shipping documents and purchase orders are then forwarded to the billing department for sales invoice preparation, and the shipping documents are neither accounted for nor prenumbered. |
| | • Evaluate the method used to notify the billing department of shipment. Sales order form should be used as a shipping advice in both shipping and billing departments. |

*Audit objectives for shipping*

- To ascertain whether the material is physically safeguarded while in the shipping department and that the physical layout facilitates free flow of material.

*Audit procedures for shipping*

- Ascertain that prenumbered bills of lading are properly approved and accounted for. Ensure that copies of bills of lading are sent to the billing function and as support documentation for prepaid freight billings.
- Observe the physical location(s) of the shipping area(s) and the layout. Comment on the material flow to the shipping area(s) and the efficiency of operations within the shipping department. Ensure that shipping is functionally and physically separated from receiving and inventory stores.
- Analyze the plant layout. Observe whether shipping areas are near the point of finished goods storage or the end of the production lines so that materials need not be transported to the other end of the factory for shipment.
- Determine whether the physical locations and layouts of shipping areas are conducive to constant surveillance by security guards. Ensure that the loading dock doors are kept closed and locked when trucks are not actually being loaded and the shipping department is physically secured when unattended. Ensure that all material movement documents and shipping papers are protected to minimize the risk of their loss or destruction.

## EXAMPLES OF APPLICATION OF COMPUTER-ASSISTED AUDIT TECHNIQUES: SHIPPING

- List customer orders that were shipped late by comparing order due date on production records with shipped date on shipping records.
- Identify items shipped but not billed, which is an indication of lapse in procedures.

(D) *Audit cycle/area: Production/conversion—Traffic.*

Major activities and responsibilities of the traffic department include procurement of public carrier services; analysis and study of routes, rates, and carriers; checking of bills submitted by carriers; handling of claims for loss or damage; administration of the day-to-day operations of receipt and shipment of goods.

*Risks and exposures*

- Vehicle theft or loss.

- Movement of trailers not controlled properly.

*Controls or control procedures*

- Maintain vehicles in a secured location with release and return subject to approval by a custodian (PC).
- Have security guards log the time-in and time-out of trailers and compare the actual elapsed time with standards (PC, DC).

*Audit objectives for traffic*

- To determine whether a written procedure manual is available to guide the traffic department.

*Audit procedures for traffic*

- Determine that a current and complete transportation procedure manual exists outlining the activities relative to inbound and outbound traffic procedures and assigning responsibility limits of authority.
- At a minimum, the manual should contain these topics for inbound traffic: scheduling carriers; signing delivery receipt; verifying freight charges; tracing and expediting shipments; filing loss, short, damage, and overcharge claims.
- At a minimum, the manual should contain these topics for outbound traffic: scheduling carriers; preparing packing lists; tracing and expediting shipments; arranging for in-transit insurance; packing to meet tariff requirements.

- To ascertain whether interdepartmental coordination is in effect to minimize inbound and outbound freight expenditure.

- Determine whether close coordination exists between purchasing and traffic for inbound freight; that traffic receives notice of incoming volumes of purchases from purchasing for planning purposes; and traffic furnishes routing instructions to purchasing for inclusion on the purchase orders.

| _Audit objectives for traffic_ | _Audit procedures for traffic_ |
|---|---|
| | • Ascertain the effectiveness of procedures followed in specifying and controlling routings on inbound shipments. Select a representative sample of purchase orders, freight bills, and routing and rate guides. Perform these audit tests to determine: that the procedures followed ensure that adequate shipping information is given to vendors; that the routing was specified by traffic and adhered to; the basis on which the rates were based was verified; the cost of items delivered by premium cost carriers such as express mail, or airmail; the extent to which items normally received in large quantities are delivered on a less than carload or less than truckload basis; whether freight allowances from vendors were verified and the controls existing to ensure that freight bills are not paid on freight-allowed deliveries. Where terms of the purchase orders were based on carload or truckload shipments and delivery was made on a partial basis, determine whether the vendor made an allowance for increased transportation cost. |
| | • Select a representative sample of shipping department records or billings by carriers and perform tests to determine that: the routing was specified by traffic and followed in shipment; proper action was taken when prescribed routing was not followed; routing and rate guides used are current; the controls to ensure that additional costs resulting from using customer routing are collected or there exist approvals for waiver of such costs; and the extent to which shipments were made at premium rates resulting from "rush" shipments to customers or shipping less than a carload or less than a truckload interim shipments to normal carload locations. |
| • To determine whether the selection of carriers and routes is based on economical factors. | • Evaluate the allocation of the overall freight workloads among various carriers and owned or leased vehicles. Obtain reasons for various modes of transportation and the support for the selection of individual carriers. |
| | • Ascertain whether procedures exist for determining whether services of contract truckers should be used in lieu of owned or leased vehicles, railroad facilities, or a combination of transportation modes. Evaluate whether unusual preference appears to have been given to a particular carrier or mode of transportation. Review several major carriers and determine the basis on which their selection was made. Determine the extent to which commercial carriers are selected on the basis of competitive bids and the frequency with which bids are solicited. |
| | • Where numerous carriers are employed, discuss with management whether benefits could be obtained from consolidating shipments using fewer carriers. Ascertain whether action has been taken to determine cost savings that might be obtained by such action. |
| | • Determine whether all contracts with trucking firms are approved by traffic and legal departments and that they are for specific periods and contain provisions for periodic review and adjustment of rates. |
| | • In order to minimize freight charges, determine whether procedures provide for and adequate measures are taken to pool shipments to obtain rate benefits on incoming and outgoing shipments. Select a representative sample of carriers and determine the cost differential incurred by not pooling shipments. |
| | • Review and evaluate procedures relative to shipments to customers from outlying warehouses, basis for selection of warehouse locations, and assignment of responsibility for control of warehouse stock. Consideration should be given to factors such as determination of routing of shipments, minimization of warehouse charges through direct shipments to large-volume customers, or regional warehouse concept. |

<u>*Audit objectives for traffic*</u>

- To ascertain whether procedures and controls are appropriate and adequate to minimize demurrage charges.

- To determine whether procedures and controls are appropriate to collect on shipments that have been completely or partially lost or damaged during shipment.

- To ascertain whether freight invoices are accurately processed for payment.

<u>*Audit procedures for traffic*</u>

- Review records covering payments for demurrage during the past few months, noting the number of occurrences and amounts involved. Determine whether they are separately identified in the accounting records.
- Determine whether truckers assess a penalty for excess waiting time pending loading or unloading of trucks. Relate the penalties to total demurrage.
- In selected cases where demurrage is paid, calculate the differential between cost versus the overtime pay that might have been incurred for unloading. Determine the operating department that is primarily responsible for demurrage charges and establish the action taken by traffic to correct operating inefficiencies to prevent future recurrences.
- Prepare a schedule of all unpaid claims. Establish that goods lost, short, or damaged in transit are properly noted on carrier's receipts and are covered by loss or damage reports. Ascertain whether copies of these reports are forwarded to traffic and accounting departments. Establish whether claims were filed for all items covered by these reports.
- Evaluate the adequacy of the traffic department follow-up action taken with respect to outstanding or unpaid claims. Evaluate the procedures for receiving, handling, and accounting for cash received in the settlement of claims. Determine whether a floor has been established for convenience and speed below which a claim will not be submitted.

    Evaluate the procedures to validate, process for payment, and audit freight invoices. Conduct these audit tests.

- Measure the elapsed times between when the freight bill was received in the mailroom and when it was received in the traffic department, when the freight bill was received in the traffic department and when it was approved by the traffic department, and when the freight bill was received in the accounts payable department and the date the payment was actually made.
- In order to evaluate the procedures established for the in-house audit of freight bills, perform these audit procedures on a sample of paid freight bills: determine that the carrier's charges are valid and that the services billed have been rendered; ascertain whether freight bills were paid prior to the audit by traffic; if so, evaluate the controls that exist to ensure that a postaudit is made; ascertain that rates and weights charged on transportation bills are in accordance with published tariffs, classifications, and agreements with private carriers; determine the basis used for substantiating and approving the weights used for billing purposes; and evaluate the controls in effect to prevent duplication of payment of freight bills.
- Ascertain whether the feasibility of retaining an outside agency to process and/or audit freight bills has been considered. If so, determine the advantages and disadvantages of in-house audit and outside audit of freight bills.

## Audit Approach in a Transportation Department

A transportation department maintains its vehicle inventory and maintenance records in a database on a stand-alone microcomputer in the fleet supervisor's office. The audit approach that is appropriate for evaluating the accuracy of this information is to verify a sample of the records extracted from the database against the supporting documentation.

(E) *Audit cycle/area: Production/conversion—Quality control.*
Major activities and responsibilities of the quality control department include: measuring and test equipment calibration; inspection of incoming materials, production process, and completed assemblies; sampling inspection; identification of nonconforming materials; field inspection; maintaining quality control records and costs; planning and implementing corrective ac-

tions to improve quality. These activities are a continuation of those described for quality assurance of materials in the expenditure cycle.

### Risks and exposures

- Quality control not involving vendor selection.

- Cost-of-quality reports not prepared.
- No charge-back of rework costs to vendors for poor-quality work.

### Controls and control procedures

- Implement quality team concept among purchasing, quality control, inventory control, and production control staff (PC).
- Establish procedures for tracking quality costs (PC).
- Implement a work order cost accounting system to accumulate costs of reworking defective vendor material (CC).

### Audit objectives for quality control

- To ascertain whether quality control staff participates in qualifying new vendors and in assessing vendor quality performance.

- To determine whether procedures for incoming quality inspection of purchased parts and raw materials are timely and adequate.

### Audit procedures for quality control

- Verify that records are maintained, by vendor, of deviations from purchase orders or receipt of out-of-specification material. Determine the disposition of such material: returned to vendor, scrapped, reworked, and used as is. Determine the manufacturing or customer service problems caused by such materials: production delays, multiple line setups, shipping delays, product failures, additional field service expenses. Determine the extent to which the additional costs were billed back to the vendor.
- Determine the adequacy of procedures in effect to evaluate prospective vendors for inclusion on the approved vendor list. Ascertain whether formal checklists outlining the elements required for an acceptable quality control function at the supplier's facility are utilized in this evaluation. Review the criteria used in selecting vendors and that the available data in the vendor file supports the qualification of the vendor.
- Verify that complete engineering specifications and drawings are supplied to the vendors so that there is no misunderstanding of material requirements. Verify that the quality control department has adequate facilities, tools, and human resources to perform its duties and that inspectors measure vendor conformance to the specifications on a timely basis.
- Determine that the quality control department receives copies of all purchase orders with complete sets of specifications and drawings attached. Compare a sample of the drawings and specifications to those maintained in the product engineering department to ensure they are current.
- Establish that written test procedures exist for all products purchased, including: sampling techniques and risk levels, specific test procedures, acceptable tolerances, and "pass" and "reject" material procedures. Age materials on-hand awaiting inspection by comparing the date on receiving reports with the audit date, with details such as time lag five working days or more, time lag more than two working days but less than five, time lag two working days or less. Find out the reasons for the delay.
- Verify the extent to which vendors are required to submit actual test results with each delivery, whether the tests were conducted by the vendor or a reliable private testing agency, and the degree of reliance that the company places on these test results.
- In the case of nonconforming purchased materials, ascertain the time required to notify purchasing department of the defective material by comparing the date of issue of a number of defective material reports to the date received in the purchasing department. Find out the reasons for the delay. Ascertain whether the purchasing agent initiates effective and timely action on inspection deficiencies requiring follow-up with vendors. Calculate the average time utilized by purchasing in disposing of defective material reports by comparing the date on which the defective material report was received in the purchasing department to the date the files reflect final disposition.

*Audit objectives for quality control*

- To determine whether procedures for in-process and finished goods are timely and adequate.

- To ascertain whether quality control management prepares defective material reports and distributes them to interested parties in a timely manner for corrective action and helps accounting or other department in developing cost-of-quality reports.

*Audit procedures for quality control*

- Determine if a vendor evaluation report is prepared by either the purchasing agent or the quality control inspector for defective parts. Determine that a work order procedure has been established to accumulate costs of reworking defective vendor material and that formal procedures are in place to charge rework costs back to vendors. When a work order system is not employed for accumulating rework costs of vendor nonconforming material, understand how such work is accounted for.
- Establish that quality control staff members have the following documents to carry out in-process and finished goods inspection: inspection checklists, applicable drawings and specifications, production work orders, records of nonconformance, operating time logs, accept or reject criteria for statistical sampling.
- Age materials on hand awaiting inspection by comparing the date on selected move tickets transferring the materials to the inspection station with the audit date with details such as time lag five working days or more, time lag more than two working days but less than five, time lag two working days or less. Find out the reasons for the delay.
- Review statistical sampling techniques, establishing that they are simple, workable, and effectively used. Ensure that test results from these sampling techniques are sent to appropriate members of the engineering, production, purchasing, and inventory control departments.
- Take a sample of defective material reports prepared by the quality control department for all nonconforming materials. Ensure that each report contains this information: part number and name, purchase order number, vendor identification number, date of inspection, quantity received and checked, quantity defective, inspector's identification number, nature of discrepancy, further action required, disposition rules. Comment on the timeliness of reporting. Ensure that the defect reports are distributed to the individuals responsible for correcting the problem. Review various control charts available to determine the quality trend at the facility and comment on unfavorable trends.
- Determine if quality control has the authority to cause production to cease due to nonconforming materials or operations, rather than wait for a written report recommending such action. It is too late by that time.
- Ascertain that cost-of-quality reports are prepared regularly and that report amounts are reconciled to general ledger accounts. Ensure that the report elements contain preventive costs, appraisal costs, and failure costs (internal and external). Understand the focus of the quality control program: defect prevention or defect detection. Prevention is better than detection.
- Inquire whether programs such as zero defect committee, quality councils, or quality teams are in place to improve quality continuously. Ensure that formal training programs for error prevention are available to all employees, including supervisors, and that quality awareness is created through the use of periodic meetings between employees and management, display of posters, articles in the company's newsletter, special recognition events, and quality awards.

### (F) *Audit cycle/area: Production/conversion: Fixed assets.*

| *Risks and exposures* | *Controls or control procedures* |
|---|---|
| • Potential for financial losses due to theft of fixed assets. | • Establish physical access controls (PC). |
| | • Obtain insurance coverage in an amount supported by periodic appraisals (PC). |
| • Misclassification of capital acquisitions as expenditures. | • Scan repair and maintenance records and investigate large dollar-value entries (DC). |
| • Overcharge of fees on contractor billings. | • Review of invoices before funds are disbursed (PC). |
| • Contractor could be charging for the use of equipment not utilized in the construction project in a cost-plus contract. | • Comparison of invoice items with the contract terms (DC). |
| • Potential for inflated costs in the cost-plus contract. | • A provision for maximum costs and sharing any savings (PC). |

| _Audit objectives for fixed assets_ | _Audit procedures for fixed assets_ |
|---|---|
| • To determine whether requests for capital budgets and project appropriation for all capital projects are properly controlled. | • Review the capital budget prepared for the current year and determine that adequate data supporting proposed projects have been prepared. Review rejected proposals and ascertain the reason for their rejection in light of accepted proposals.<br><br>• Review project appropriation requests and verify that complete documentation of the project exists, including analysis of available optional course of actions, and that all required approvals were obtained prior to the commitment of funds to the project. Ensure that alternatives to purchasing, such as leasing, in-house manufacture, or transfer from other divisions, have been thoroughly explored prior to commitment of funds. Ensure that adequate coordination exists with all long-term financing needs of the company.<br><br>• Verify that the specific project was included in the approved capital budget. Determine that the project appropriation request and the attached work sheets and schedules provide the necessary detail, including description and purpose of the project, anticipated benefits, estimated costs, and time schedules for starting and completion of the project. Ensure that the estimated cost figure includes cost of material, labor, overhead, and other costs as necessary. Establish that all approvals were obtained prior to commitment of funds. |
| • To ascertain whether postcompletion audits are performed to compare the actual results with the expected. | • Ensure that postcompletion audits are performed by individuals other than the original preparers of the project appropriation request. Select a representative sample of postcompletion audit reports and perform these reviews: compare cost estimates to actual costs and investigate significant differences; trace actual expenditures to construction-in-progress (CIP) detail records; and compare actual benefits with expected benefits. Evaluate the accuracy of explanations for unfavorable variances and assess their implication on overall project planning. Where actual expenditures exceed budget due to changes in specifications, establish the justification of the changes, and verify that proper approvals were obtained prior to the issuance of change orders.<br><br>• During a postcompletion audit of a warehouse expansion, the auditor noted several invoices for redecorating services from a local merchant that were account-coded and signed for payment only by the cost engineer. The auditor should compare the cost and description of the services to the account code used in the construction project and to relate estimates in the construction-project budget. |
| • To determine whether controls over construction-in-progress expenditures are proper and adequate. | • In order to ensure proper accumulation of costs and accounting for capital projects, review the fixed asset accounts for both open and closed projects. Perform these audit tests: compare total expenditures to date plus estimate to complete the approved project appropriation request, including supplemental requests; evaluate estimates to complete by comparison of actual costs to date with original estimate, considering percent of completion, review of open purchase commitments, and discussion with engineers; verify direct purchases by reference to construction contracts, examination of properly approved vendor invoices, and receiving reports; examine material requisitions in support of materials issued from stockrooms; trace labor charges to payroll distribution summary; trace the burden rate used to the master standard listing; for purchase of land and buildings, verify evidence of ownership by examinations of deeds, title abstracts and policies, tax bill descriptions, and real estate contracts; determine the propriety of useful life and salvage value by discussion with engineers; and ensure that material being used on one project is not being charged against the budgets of other projects. |

*Audit objectives for fixed assets*

*Audit procedures for fixed assets*

- Review the open work orders supporting the CIP account to ensure that they are either current items related to property that will be capitalized when the property is put into service or current expense items that will be charged against operations in the current period. Utilizing the work orders closed during the period under audit, review amounts transferred from the CIP account to determine that transfers to property accounts are proper and comply with laws and regulations and that they exclude expense items and that amounts written off to expense accounts do not include capital items.

- To ascertain whether controls are adequate over outside contractors working on capital projects.

- Determine that competitive bids are obtained for all outside construction-related purchases and that the same controls are exercised over these purchases as over routine purchases.

- In order to ensure that appropriate controls are maintained over outside contractors with **cost-plus contracts,** these audit tests are suggested for a sample of projects: review the contracts for inclusion of specifications, estimated costs, and technical and time constraints; where the right of audit is included, review the contractors' time records, vendor invoices, fee calculations (be particularly alert for materials included in fee calculations that should have been excluded, transfer of contractors' materials from their own inventory, discounts and rebates not passed on to the company); where the right of audit is not included, ascertain that appropriate supporting documents (e.g., vendor invoice, payroll summaries) accompany the billing from the contractor. Test vouch a representative number of such billings.

- Inquire as to why the right of audit is not included in the contract and, if feasible, suggest that an attempt be made to insert this right when contracts are negotiated in the future. Ensure that all contractors have provided certificates of insurance.

- Cost-plus construction contracts require early and constant on-site monitoring due to the inherent risk that overcharging or other irregularities can occur.

- In order to ensure that appropriate controls are maintained over outside contractors with **fixed-price contracts,** these audit tests are suggested for a sample of projects: review the bid file to ensure that the lowest bidder was selected (if not, why not); ascertain that the finished work was inspected by company management before final payment was made; where a contractor submits a claim for renegotiation or incentives due under a contract, relate the details of the claim to the contract and analyze for appropriateness; and ensure that all contractors have provided certificates of insurance.

- To determine whether physical controls over fixed assets are proper.

- Ensure that a permanently fixed physical asset identification tag is assigned to each capital asset, that it is uniquely numbered, and that the number is included in the detailed property records.

- Review the procedures for the taking of physical inventories of fixed assets. Ensure that a count is taken periodically and reconciled to the general ledger accounts, and that all adjustments are approved. Observe physical count where possible, and ensure that proper cutoff was observed between before and after the inventory date for assets received and disposed.

- To ascertain whether procedures and controls over disposition of fixed assets (i.e., sales, retirements, and transfers) are proper.

- Select a sample of land, buildings, and other capital assets that had been disposed of during the current fiscal year. Verify that a written procedure is available to be followed in disposing of fixed assets and review it for adequacy. Verify that competitive bids are obtained to ensure that the best price is obtained.

- To ensure that costs and related depreciation reserves applicable to asset retirements have been properly removed from the accounts, review the fixed asset accounts for the period under review and, on a sample basis, perform these audit tests: verify sales proceeds and trace them to the cash receipts book; verify the computation of depreciation against date of sale; trace to the general ledger accounts and the detailed property records the relief of the asset cost and the related accumulated depreciation reserve.

**Audit objectives for fixed assets**

- To determine whether accounting controls over fixed assets are accurate and adequate.

**Audit procedures for fixed assets**

- To ascertain if there have been any unrecorded sales or retirements of fixed assets, perform these audit tests: review work orders for indication of retirements related to additions of property; discuss the existence of any major asset retirements or sales with production operations staff and management; tour the plant facilities to determine if any major assets have been removed; review changes in manufacturing processes that would necessitate replacement or retirement of existing fixed assets; and review credits in nonoperating income and maintenance expense accounts to determine if they are generated by sales of assets.
- Ensure that the accounting department receives copies of project appropriation requests, purchase orders, vendor invoices, work orders, and receiving reports pertaining to capital assets. Reporting should include all actual expenditures and commitments.
- In order to determine whether fixed assets employed in the business are properly reflected in the accounting records, inspect the fixed assets used and trace them to the asset subsidiary ledger.
- Review the property, plant, and equipment (PPE) records and ensure that: separate general ledger control accounts are established and maintained for each major category of PPE; the costs of all items of PPE are recorded in the appropriate account; the cost of labor directly related to overhead employed in the construction and installation of PPE is capitalized as part of the cost of the assets and that its source is the labor distribution summary; and the cost of freight is capitalized as part of the cost of capital assets.
- Ensure that a written policy exists governing the distinction between expenditures to be capitalized and those to be charged to repairs, maintenance, supplies, and small tools accounts and that costs of individual items below a certain amount are expensed when purchased.
- Verify that appropriate amounts of improvement or betterment expenditures are capitalized when such expenditures increase the rate of output, lower operating costs, or extend the useful life of fixed assets. To verify that the proper value of costs are charged to real property records for improvements to the property, the best source of evidence is the original invoices and supporting entries in the accounting records.
- Ascertain that a work order system is maintained for all capital expenditures and major repair jobs whereby all charges applicable to each project are identified and accumulated and that a separate series of work orders is assigned to accumulate costs relative to additions to PPE.
- Ensure that open work orders are balanced to the CIP account each month and that all additions to PPE accounts are cleared through the CIP account and that the CIP account is cleared each month of all charges of a noncapital nature.
- Review the repair and maintenance accounts for the period under the audit to ensure no capital additions have been expensed. Compare the repair and maintenance accounts for significant monthly variations and for variations from budget and from the same period in the prior year.
- Ensure that the detailed asset accounting record contains, at a minimum, this information: date of acquisition; total cost; asset description; asset identification number; estimated salvage value; asset life; depreciation method; and asset location. Ensure that year-end accruals are based on invoices covering work completed or goods received.
- Ensure that leased equipment is properly identified and that company maintenance staff does not attempt to repair broken leased equipment without the specific written permission of the lessor.

| *Audit objectives for fixed assets* | *Audit procedures for fixed assets* |
|---|---|
| | • Review the method(s) of depreciation utilized to ensure there is consistent application for similar categories of property. Verify the adequacy of the detail supporting the general ledger account for accumulated depreciation. Conduct these audit tests: trace the supporting detail for the separate reserve amounts relative to the various depreciation computations to the general ledger control account; ensure that fully depreciated assets are excluded from the computation of depreciation; verify that the cost of fully depreciated equipment is continued in the accounts and shown as gross amount (not net of depreciation) on the balance sheet until retired from service; ascertain that the engineering department has furnished estimates of salvage value to be used in calculating depreciation charges, and review these estimates for reasonableness. |
| | • To test the accuracy of recorded depreciation, compare depreciation schedules with the maintenance and repair logs for the same equipment. |
| | • Make an overall test of depreciation for the period under audit and compare to the same period for the prior year. Explain any major variations between comparable periods as a means of ascertaining changes in depreciation methods or major computation errors. Select a category of fixed assets for a detailed test of depreciation. Verify the computation of the provision to date as to adequacy and consistency with prior periods, and trace the distribution to the general ledger accounts. Where applicable, determine that depreciation rates approved by government regulatory agencies are in use. |

## EXAMPLES OF APPLICATION OF COMPUTER-ASSISTED AUDIT TECHNIQUES: FIXED ASSETS

- List high-dollar-value assets for physical inspection.
- List asset additions and disposal for vouching to supporting documentation.
- List high-dollar-value maintenance expenses for possible capitalization.
- List fully depreciated assets.
- Compare depreciation periods with guidelines provided by management and tax authorities for compliance, and list unusually long or short depreciation periods.
- List assets without any depreciation charges, which would increase income.
- Use the parallel simulation audit technique to calculate depreciation charges using the declining balance method.

---

(G) *Audit cycle/area: Production/conversion—Plant maintenance.*

Major activities and responsibilities of a plant maintenance department would include: maintenance of physical plant, power, light, and water systems; the service, repair, and maintenance of plant equipment and production machinery; a standard preventive maintenance program; keeping maintenance cost records; acquiring, storing, and controlling maintenance supplies and parts; preparation of the maintenance budget; preparation of formal maintenance requests and orders; control of labor and material costs.

| *Risks and exposures* | *Controls or control procedures* |
|---|---|
| • Inadequate documentation over property. | • Issue guidelines for documentation, including the use of checklists (PC). |
| • Excessive machine downtime. | • Establish a preventive maintenance program (PC). |
| • Incorrect and/or improper accounting of costs. | • Implement a work order system for tracking maintenance costs (PC, DC). |

*Audit objectives for plant maintenance*

- To determine whether the plant maintenance department maintains complete records of all property, plant, equipment, and machinery, including drawings, specifications, and maintenance history, and that it performs a preventive maintenance program.

- To ascertain whether the maintenance department utilizes a maintenance work order system to control costs more effectively and to schedule jobs.

- To determine whether effective controls exist over the procurement of maintenance equipment, materials, parts, and outside contract services and that the associated recordkeeping procedures are adequate.

*Audit procedures for plant maintenance*

- Ensure that the maintenance department obtains factory repair manuals and the manufacturer's maintenance schedules for all machinery and equipment at the time of acquisition or later and that the manuals are up-to-date and are utilized by maintenance department staff.

- By discussion with maintenance management and review of maintenance records, ascertain that the preventive maintenance program is operating properly and covers key production equipment and building items. Test a sample of machinery preventive maintenance records to the manufacturer's recommended maintenance routines and intervals. Ascertain whether checklists are used during periodic inspections of plant and equipment.

- Ensure that a complete maintenance history file is maintained for all property items and that this file is reviewed on a regular basis by maintenance department management to revise preventive maintenance schedules and to make replacement recommendations to plant production management.

- Review production time lost due to unplanned machine downtime and preventive maintenance routines that were not completed on schedule during the past year. Calculate the cost of time lost by unplanned downtime, and evaluate the effectiveness of the preventive maintenance program. Compute downtime for selected, critical machines and, where significant, determine what action has been taken to either replace the machine or schedule a major overhaul. Evaluate whether maintenance work can be outsourced.

- Review the maintenance work order system and ensure that all jobs are properly authorized and estimated; that actual costs are accumulated and compared; and that appropriate schedule control is maintained. Determine that the system for the accumulation of actual maintenance costs provides the following information: a formal work order system accumulates costs by job and account number that will be charged to the department initiating the request for service; a comparison of estimated cost to actual cost is done regularly; blanket work orders are issued to cover routine and repetitive-type tasks; allocations of costs to benefiting departments is reasonable and proper; and compliance with established procedures regarding capitalization and expense is followed.

- Evaluate the control over closeout of completed work orders. When possible, physically inspect completed maintenance jobs to determine that work has been completed and is in agreement with the job order. Also, ascertain that the equipment records have been updated to reflect this work. Determine if completed jobs are inspected by maintenance department management under a quality control program.

- Analyze maintenance costs for the year and compare them to the last two years. Obtain explanations for significant increases, if any. Determine whether the preventive maintenance program is effective in reducing costs. Determine whether management has included the maintenance department in the cost reduction programs similar to other service centers.

- Ascertain that appropriate approvals have been obtained prior to initiating the procurement activity for maintenance material, machinery, and equipment. Determine that written bids and quotations are received for maintenance materials, spare parts, equipment, and outside contract services. Determine that purchased maintenance materials are formally received through the receiving department of the company, not straight to the maintenance department.

*Audit objectives for plant maintenance*

*Audit procedures for plant maintenance*

- In order to assure that control procedures are working properly over the maintenance equipment, material, and parts inventory, conduct these audit tests: determine whether there is a significant storage area for small tools, repair parts, and supplies, and that it is well protected; determine whether physical access to the storage area is restricted to authorized personnel; verify that issuance of supplies and parts is supported by approved withdrawal tickets and is in accordance with authorized and approved job orders; and test count selected items and compare them to the perpetual inventory records.
- Review inventory cards to determine economics of purchases. Also determine whether there are any excess, slow-moving, or obsolete parts on hand. Evaluate the adequacy of the records.

## (H) *Audit cycle/area: Production/conversion—Cost accounting.*

*Risks and exposures*

- Unattainable standards affect employee performance negatively.
- Standards may not reflect all cost elements.
- Improper use of cost classification, thus distorting cost picture.

*Controls or control procedures*

- Request employee involvement in developing and updating standards (PC).
- Develop quality control procedures and use checklists (PC).
- Study cost behavior patterns (PC).
- Conduct data validation routines (DC).

*Audit objectives for cost accounting*

- To determine whether standard costs have been developed for each significant cost element and class of inventory, for significant operations and cost centers, and for significant products.

*Audit procedures for cost accounting*

- For a sample of the more significant products, compare standards per the frozen standard cost file to current bills of material and process sheets. Ensure that the structure of the standards is consistent with the bills of material and process sheets and that they are used to control shop operations.
- Determine the extent of materials and operations "not on standard": evaluate the impact on proper inventory valuation and effective cost control due to items not on the standard cost system. If effects appear significant, investigate underlying causes of the problem and evaluate the adequacy of management's corrective action.
- Determine the extent of use of temporary standards: evaluate the method used in developing the temporary standards and whether it is consistently applied; ensure temporary standards are approved at an appropriate level before being implemented; ensure temporary standards and related costs generated are clearly identified; and ensure temporary standards are replaced with engineered standards on a timely basis.

- To ascertain whether direct material specifications and material usage standards are attainable and that efficient performance is achievable.

- Perform a walk-through review of the process to establish material usage standards. Select a small sample of representative items and note the basis for the standards; examine supporting documents; check approval levels; and trace to the current standards file.
- Ensure those unavoidable loss (shrinkage) allowances and scrap recovery allowances have been included in the standards where applicable: analyze shop operations to identify processes that tend to generate significant shrinkage losses and scrap, and relate to the basis of the standards; and ensure loss factors have been developed with reasonable precision, that is, engineered, not estimated.
- Trace a sample of items from the frozen standard cost file to supporting documents to ensure that the material usage standards in the standards file accurately reflect the detailed material usage buildup in the supporting documents.

- To ascertain whether purchase price standards represent average prices expected to prevail in the marketplace.

- Select a small sample of representative purchased items and determine the basis for the standards. Examine supporting documents, check approval levels, and trace to the current standards file. Ensure that standards reflect proper treatment of all cost elements, that is, they include freight and customs charges and exclude discounts.

| *Audit objectives for cost accounting* | *Audit procedures for cost accounting* |
|---|---|
| | • Evaluate the adequacy of documentation supporting the standards: where numerous items and significant time is involved in setting standards, determine whether an ABC inventory classification approach was followed, and ensure documentation is current in relation to the effective date of the standards. Review the basis for any overall assumptions reflected in the standards (e.g., inflation or vendor cost allocation factors). |
| | • Trace a sample of items from the frozen standard cost file to supporting documents to ensure that the purchase price standards in the standards file accurately reflect the detailed prices in the supporting documents. |
| • To determine whether direct labor time and work class standards represent attainable and efficient performance standards. | • Perform a walk-through review of the process to establish labor time and labor grade requirements and standards. Select a small sample of representative labor time standards and labor grades, and determine the basis for the standards. Examine supporting documents, check approval levels, and trace to current standards file. |
| | • Ascertain that standard hours are based on accepted time study and work measurement techniques. Determine whether a work standardization study was performed in developing the standard hours. Evaluate the assumptions made by the engineering staff with regard to operating conditions, and ensure such factors as routing of work, waiting time, and plant layout reflect actual current conditions and are properly considered in setting the standards. |
| | • Trace a sample of labor time standards from the frozen standard cost file to supporting documents to ensure that the time standards accurately reflect the detailed time buildup in the supporting documents. |
| • To determine whether direct labor rate standards represent average labor rates expected to be paid under efficient production levels. | • Perform a walk-through review of the process to establish labor rate standards. Select a small sample of representative labor rates, and determine the basis for the standards. Examine supporting documents, check approval levels, and trace to the current standards file. |
| | • Evaluate the adequacy of the documentation supporting the standards: ensure that the labor rate standards are related to the planned requirements for the various labor grades per the production budget; ensure that shift premiums and other associated labor benefits are treated as indirect costs and are excluded from the standards; and trace labor rates and labor classes used in developing the standards to source data (e.g., current and anticipated union contracts, personnel records, manning tables, employment contracts). |
| | • Trace a sample of labor rate schedules from the frozen standard cost file to the supporting documents to ensure that the rate standards accurately reflect the detailed rate buildup in the supporting documents. |
| • To ascertain whether material burden standards are utilized to absorb the indirect costs of acquiring goods and services and that they are applied in a reasonable and consistent basis. | • Perform a walk-through review of the process to establish material burden standards. Select a small sample of representative departments involved in material acquisition, and review the basis for projected departmental costs. Examine supporting documents, check approval levels, and trace to the current standards file. |
| | • Ensure that the material burden standard is used to recover all anticipated manufacturing burden related to these operations: purchasing, ordering, and expediting; receiving; incoming inspection by quality control. Check the material-burden rate calculation, and trace the cost elements to the departmental budgets or other supporting data. |
| | • Ensure that the standard material burden is applied to purchases of these items: raw materials, packing materials, items for resale, items shipped directly to customers by vendors. Determine whether a single material burden rate is applied or whether multiple, varying rates are used for the different types of purchases. Evaluate the appropriateness and effectiveness of the method utilized. |

*Audit objectives for cost accounting*

- To determine whether standard manufacturing burden rates, excluding the direct material burden rate, are based on detailed departmental flexed budgets representing indirect manufacturing costs expected to be incurred.

- To determine whether standard manufacturing burden rates, excluding direct material burden rate, are based on normal operating capacity and take into account all elements of indirect manufacturing costs.

- To ascertain whether standard burden rates are applied on a consistent basis to ensure accurate and timely absorption of all indirect manufacturing costs.

- To determine whether standard costs are sufficiently detailed and are classified in a manner that permits a timely and meaningful comparison with actual performance and that variance accounting and reporting is proper.

*Audit procedures for cost accounting*

- Ensure that the material burden rate is reflected in the item standards per the standard cost file for all applicable classes of material.
- Perform a walk-through review of the standards-setting process. Using a small sample of burden applicable rates for a selected production department or cost center, note the basis for the standards. Include the basis for individual departmental fixed and variable costs and basis for costs allocated to the selected production department. Examine supporting documents, check approval levels, and trace to the current standards file.
- Review the basis for classifying indirect costs as fixed versus variable and semivariable. Perform these tests: determine whether the cost classification is based on a reasonably current study of cost behavior since cost behavior changes over time and volume; review and assess the adequacy of documentation supporting the determination of fixed versus variable costs; ensure the range of activity (relevant range of production level) used on the fixed versus variable cost study is consistent with current operating plans; and investigate the causes of any major changes in allocation methods between years.
- Ensure that variable indirect costs included in flexed budgets are based on normal plant capacity as reflected in the production budget.
- Evaluate the measurement techniques used in developing standard indirect material and labor costs. Determine whether indirect material physical standards (both quantity and specifications) for significant cost categories are based on engineering measurement techniques.
- Evaluate the reasonableness and consistent application of the method of allocating service department costs to production departments.
- Determine that standard manufacturing burden rates are calculated for each operating department, rather than for the factory as a whole. Determine that the standard manufacturing burden rates are established using direct labor hours, machine hours, direct labor cost, or other as a burden absorption basis. Verify that anticipated production levels are derived from the master production schedule.
- For a sample of items, verify that the application of standard burden rates is appropriate to the particular manufacturing process being reviewed and that there is full absorption of manufacturing overhead.
- Select a sample of indirect manufacturing charges from each manufacturing department and ensure that the correct standard manufacturing burden rates were applied to the direct charges.
- Review the burden variances. Ensure that the total of the standard burden rates plus the total of the burden variances equal the total of all indirect manufacturing costs. That is, ensure there is full burden absorption on a current basis. Ensure that extraordinary burden costs, such as equipment relocation or facility rearrangement costs, special product obsolescence costs, and catastrophe costs, are charged to income.
- Review the process for accumulating actual direct labor and direct material charges. Ensure that all direct labor charges are accumulated and are charged to the proper cost center or operation.
- Ensure that material price variances are accurately calculated and charged to income as period costs at the time the invoice is charged to the inventory account, as opposed to when the material is used.
- Ensure that material usage variances are accurately calculated. Ensure that appropriate controls, such as use of prenumbered material requisition forms, are in place to identify materials usage variances.

| *Audit objectives for cost accounting* | *Audit procedures for cost accounting* |
|---|---|
| | • Ensure the process for accumulating actual burden charges. Ensure that all manufacturing indirect charges are accurately accumulated, including an allocation of utility costs that are chargeable to the factory. Verify that no other charges that would normally be considered general and administrative expense are included in the manufacturing burden costs. |
| | • Ensure that the cost accounting system requires the identification and analysis of causal variances by analysis of the primary variances, by cause, or by establishing specific account codes for the specific causal variances, segregating the costs at the time of original entry on the books, and reporting these variances separately. Examples of causal variances include lot size variance, rework variance, spoilage variance, scrap variance, and the standard revision variance. Examples of primary variances are direct labor, direct materials, and burden variances. Causal variances may contain elements of one or more of the primary variances (e.g., the rework variance is comprised of direct labor, direct materials, and burden variances). |
| • To ascertain whether all inventories are physically counted, priced, and reconciled to the general ledger and that appropriate adjustments are made. | • Ensure that detailed instructions are issued to each of the various groups involved in the physical inventory (i.e., count teams, ticket pullers, ticket checkers). Review the instructions for adequacy. Review the inventory checklist and ensure all items were completed. Note the impact of quantity and price adjustments. Ensure that complete reconciliations are performed and analyses are prepared detailing the causes of all significant inventory adjustments. Ensure that all inventory adjustments are passed through the "Reserve for Inventory Adjustments" account. |
| | • Where **cycle counts** are utilized, review for these items: the method of selecting items for cycle counts; the thoroughness in locating all items; the use of recounts; the reconciliation procedure; booking inventory adjustments; and procedure to fine-tune inventory control techniques where recurring problems are uncovered. |
| | • Check the inventory valuation calculations. Ensure that the period between the physical inventory date and year-end is not excessive, considering the adequacy of the system of internal controls over the inventory and past experience relative to the accuracy of the inventory balances. |
| • To determine whether appropriate controls and documents are in place to ensure that all material is promptly and accurately accounted for and that all material movement is properly authorized and controlled. | • Perform a walk-through of material movement from receipt into the stockroom, to material issues, to the production line, to finished goods. Include material sent to outside vendors for processing, returns to stores from production, returns to inventory from customers, and scrap controls. |
| | • Ensure that material move documentation is generated at the time of issue or return of material and is recorded for inventory control purposes for each of these events: issues to production from raw materials stores, subassembly stores, or directly from third parties, such as vendors or contractors; returns to raw materials stores of excess or unsuitable material; transfers within work in process from one pay point to another; transfers to and returns from outside processors and contractors; scrap or spoiled material; transfers from production to finished goods or subassembly stores; finished goods inventory relief to cost of sales; and material returned from vendors. |
| • To ascertain whether direct labor and overhead charges are promptly and accurately accumulated and reported and whether inventory valuations include all added labor and overhead input. | • Ensure that direct labor and overhead costs are accumulated at definitive stages of production (i.e., pay points) and that these stages are logical break points in the production process. Pay points should not be so large as to preclude meaningful analyses of the production process (i.e., one pay point at the end of all production operations) or so fragmented as to require overly burdensome administrative effort (i.e., multiple pay points at one operation). |

*Audit objectives for cost accounting*

*Audit procedures for cost accounting*

- Ensure that work tickets are prepared by all direct labor employees and include, at a minimum: employee number, date, job number, department, operation, account (work in process, rework), start time, stop time, hourly rate, pieces worked, pieces rejected, good pieces completed. Ensure that the production foreperson or supervisor approves the work tickets. Where incentive pay is involved, review the methods of verifying production counts and hours worked.
- Ensure that the work tickets are summarized by cost accounting, the inventory records are updated for the standard direct labor and associated standard overhead expended, the variances are calculated and charged to income, and variance analysis work is conducted.
- Ensure that the correct overhead rate is being applied in those cases where there are variable overhead rates based on production and where overhead rates vary between departments. Ensure that all overhead is being fully absorbed regardless of actual production levels.

## Actual Costs and Standard Costs

A comparison of actual costs to standard costs will assist management in its evaluation of effectiveness and efficiency of business operations.

## EXAMPLES OF APPLICATION OF COMPUTER-ASSITED AUDIT TECHNIQUES: COST ACCOUNTING

- Use the test data method to determine whether all overhead is completely allocated to cost centers by the computer program.
- List large cost variances (between standard and actual) for further analysis and interpretations.
- Recompute inventory valuation and compare it with actual.
- Compare cost of sales data between summary totals and aggregation of individual item totals to ensure that they are the same.
- Test the accuracy of the accumulation of production costs by cross-referencing to the production system.

## VARIANCE CALCULATIONS

Ensure that the **burden expenditure variance** is calculated as

Actual indirect manufacturing expense incurred – Allowed burden at actual activity level (fixed plus variable) = Burden expenditure variance

Ensure that the **burden efficiency variance** is calculated as

Actual direct labor hours at the fixed portions of the burden rate – Standard direct labor hours earned at the fixed portion of the burden rate = Burden efficiency variance

Ensure that the **burden volume variance** is calculated as

Actual direct labor hours at the fixed portions of the burden rate – Budgeted direct labor hours at the fixed portion of the burden rate = Burden volume variance

## BASIC DEFINITIONS OF VARIANCES

**Lot size variance.** It is the difference between the standard number of units in a standard lot size and the actual number of units in actual lot size times the standard unit setup cost.

**Rework variance.** It is calculated as the cost of actual labor hours at the standard rate plus the standard labor burden plus any material required at the standard cost to correct defective production to meet engineering specifications.

**Scrap variance.** It is calculated as the difference between the actual weight of recovered residual material and the standard allowed weight times the standard scrap price.

**Spoilage variance.** It is calculated as the full standard cost through the last completed operation of spoiled production that does not meet specifications and cannot be reworked to meet specifications less the standard cost of any salvaged parts or components.

**Standard revision variance.** It is calculated as the difference between the old standard and a new standard cost in those cases when standards are revised in the period between general revisions for operating measurements, but the standard cost documents and inventory pricing are left unchanged until the next general revision.

---

(v) **Introduction to treasury cycle.** Major activities in a treasury cycle would include: issuing of capital stock and debt securities; paying dividends and interest; paying debt at maturity; repaying debt and repurchase of securities issued; purchasing of capital stock and bonds; receiving of periodic dividends and interest on investments; selling of capital stock and bonds; conducting cash flow analysis; recording of financing and investing activities by journalizing and posting such transactions; filing of proper tax forms; protecting physical records and inventory of capital stocks, bonds, and other securities; maintaining the accuracy and completeness of securities and shareholder records and financing and investment account balances.

(A) *Audit cycle/area:  Treasury:  Debt management.*

| *Risks and exposures* | *Controls or control procedures* |
|---|---|
| • Improper authorization of company transactions dealing with debt instruments. | • Written company policy requiring review of major repayment of debt proposals by the board of directors (PC). |
| • Loss or theft of debt instruments. | • Install physical security controls (PC). |
| | • Prenumbered debt instruments (PC). |
| | • Reconciliation of physical inventory to perpetual inventory of debt instruments (DC). |
| • Potential for fraud or irregularities. | • Segregation of duties between treasury function and accounting function (PC). |

| *Audit objectives for debt management* | *Audit procedures for debt management* |
|---|---|
| • To determine whether long-term and short-term debt is authorized and issued in accordance with the board of directors' resolutions. | • Review debt instruments on file for approval signatures to ensure that all debt has been authorized by individuals designated to do so by the chief financial officer (CFO). If variances exist, investigate the circumstances and confirm with the CFO. |
| | • Determine that debt placement is only through approved banks or brokers and then only up to amounts authorized by the board of directors' resolutions. Reconcile banks and brokers used and amounts involved to the board of directors' resolutions and credit lines authorized. Review if variance exists and that they have been specifically authorized. If not, investigate the circumstances and confirm with the CFO. |
| | • Ascertain that new debts are incurred only after calculation of total costs of different banks. Ascertain that new debt incurred is reviewed against restrictions in place regarding debt to equity ratio, current ratio, and other relevant financial ratios. Review all debt agreements and determine if there have been any violations of debt restrictions. |
| | • Review debt issuance to cash forecasts and debt planning objectives. Ensure that the issuance of debt is consistent with the cash forecasts and the objectives. If not, comment on the variances that exist and on the exposures, if any. |

| *Audit objectives for debt management* | *Audit procedures for debt management* |
|---|---|
| | • Ascertain that procedures are in place that result in separation of duties in regard to authorization of debt, receipt of funds, and recording of funds and debt (i.e., separation between the treasury function and the accounting function). |
| | • Review transaction registers and monthly reconciliations to ensure that all activity is reflected by a relevant category in both treasury and accounting records. Ensure that all bank debt instruments are prenumbered and kept in locked storage under a perpetual inventory system. Ensure that the system's data are reconciled daily to use record and monthly to a physical inventory. Verify that the custodian of bank debt instruments has no other responsibility in the debt issuance process. Evaluate the adequacy of the storage facilities to prevent theft and casualty loss. Check if the documents are prenumbered. Review record of daily use. Review reconciliations at month-end to physical inventory. |
| • To ascertain whether principal payment of long- and short-term debt is repaid promptly and accurately in accordance with the contractual document. | • Reconcile the debt schedule to the files of banks and brokers involved in debt issuance and the amount of debt to the board of directors' resolutions to ensure all debt is correctly included. Review the debt schedule to a sample of debt agreements and test due dates and other key items. |
| | • Review debt payment procedures. Identify variances and analyze as to causes and if they indicate administrative problem or system control weaknesses. Verify that all required payments are included in the cash forecast. Identify variances and discuss with management. |
| | • Review requests for voucher check or debt payment instrument. For payment of debt, test the authorization by both treasury and accounting management. Test that the payment is accurate and timely and consistent with the terms of the agreement. |
| | • Review control reports and daily transaction registers, and test daily reconciliations to ensure all activity is recorded by relevant category. Reconcile the updated debt balance to payments in total and by specific debt paid. Review paid note documents for endorsements and cancellations. Reconcile debt payments to general ledger debt and cash accounts. Review payment confirmations received from trustees or creditor representatives. |
| • To determine whether interest payments on short- and long-term debt are made in accordance with the requirements of the debt instrument and that they are recorded correctly. | • Review schedules of interest payments due: test that cash flow and budgeting projections have been updated to reflect payments due. If variances exist, explain them, review the reconciliation of interest calculations to the schedules and in total to general ledger records for relevant categories of debt, and verify that interest payment schedules have been reconciled to a trustee or creditor record and that, if variances exist, they have been reconciled. |
| | • Verify interest calculations for payments made for each type of debt reviewed. Review for adequate separation of duties between authorization and recording of payments. If interest payments are confirmed, verify confirmations to payments requested and made. Trace payments made to cash accounts in the general ledger. |
| • To ascertain whether interest is accrued for short- and long-term debt accurately and promptly. | • Verify that interest accrual schedules are reviewed and reconciled to total debt outstanding as of statement date. Review and reconcile interest accrual schedules to total debt outstanding, and ensure that the total accrual appears reasonable. Compare current year's accrual to prior year's accrual and comment on the variance. |
| | • Analyze and reconcile changes to interest accruals to interest payments made, debt payoffs, and new debt incurred. Comment on general reasonableness of the accrual. Ascertain that treasury and accounting records of interest accruals are maintained independently of one another and are reconciled. |
| | • In order to test whether commitment fees are accrued and paid promptly and accurately, the following audit tests are suggested: test calculations of fees paid, verify that all fees have been paid as required, and review accrual balances and reconcile to the appropriate agreements. |

*Audit objectives for debt management*

*Audit procedures for debt management*

- In order to determine that banks confirm commitment fees, the following audit tests are suggested: ascertain that commitment fees recorded are compared with bank's billings, test accrual dates to agreement dates, and analyze variances between accruals and actual.

## EXAMPLES OF APPLICATION OF COMPUTER-ASSISTED TECHNIQUES: DEBT MANAGMENT

- List securities for physical inspection or confirmation.
- List interest payments for vouching to supporting documentation.
- List unusual interest rates on loans after comparing them with management guidelines; unusual rates could indicate a fraudulent situation.
- Conduct reasonableness test between interest amount paid and principal amount for each category of debt and for aggregate.

(B) *Audit cycle/area: Treasury:  Cash management.*

*Risks and exposures*

- Making and concealing unauthorized payments.

- Fraud in electronic cash transfer system.

- Loss or theft of blank checks.

*Controls or control procedures*

- Separation of duties between check preparation and bank reconciliation functions (PC, DC).
- Dual controls, system access controls, system callbacks, and confirmation of transfer requests (PC, DC).
- Establish physical security controls over blank check stock (PC).

*Audit objectives for cash management*

- To determine whether cash receipts are properly secured and promptly deposited to authorized bank accounts.

- To ascertain whether physical security controls, administrative controls, and system controls over cash receipts are adequate and proper.

*Audit procedures for cash management*

- Ensure that receivables due the company or divisions are mailed to lockboxes and are deposited in the company's bank accounts. Review that all cash receipts are clearly labeled as to source (e.g., lockbox and debt). Ensure that all bank accounts used have been authorized and established by the company's treasurer's department.
- Ensure that all banks involved have received instructions as to the correct procedures to be followed in authorizing and confirming cash receipts activity, including the names and signatures of authorized individuals. Review system logs to determine if attempts to record cash deposits to other than approved banks have occurred. Determine responses taken by management. Review data file access controls and verify that computer access is limited based on primary job duties. Verify that all access to the data files is recorded on a system log by access code or other forms of identification of the individual who accessed the system. Ensure that the cash management system generates a daily transaction register that reflects all activity processed.
- Review separation of duties with regard to persons responsible for the application of cash. Test to ensure that they are prohibited from performing the following activities: reconciling bank accounts; opening incoming mail; preparing, recording, or approving vouchers for payment; preparing, signing, mailing, or delivering checks for payroll and other; and performing work on notes payable or any other evidence of indebtedness.
- For mail receipts, test to ensure that they are: opened by someone other than the cashier, accounts receivable, or billing person; listed in detail at the time the mail is opened, and that the listing is reconciled to book entries and deposit slips by an independent person.
- For other than mail receipts, ensure that they are prelisted and accounted for by one of these procedures: tape is prepared by validating machine for receipt forms issued, cash register used, prenumbered receipt forms used, and test that all receipts and prelisting forms are accounted for serially as being recorded in the cash receipts journal.

*Audit objectives for cash management*

*Audit procedures for cash management*

- In order to ensure that all checks received are restrictively endorsed and cash is applied and deposited on a timely basis, these audit tests are suggested: review cash application and deposit procedures for adequacy and completeness; ensure that cash receipts are promptly recorded and deposited; ensure that access to cash receipts is restricted to those parties who have custodial responsibility at each step in the procedure; ensure that cash receipts are deposited in accounts receivable accounts and are not commingled with other funds; ensure that a deposit memo is prepared describing the nature of the receipt and is furnished to the accounting department for each batch of checks received; ensure that payroll or personal checks are not cashed from cash receipts; ensure that undeposited receipts are restrictively endorsed and are under effective physical security control (e.g., lock and key, vault) to prevent theft or loss; ensure that cash receipts are posted to the detailed accounts receivable records from collection advices rather than from cash items; ensure that custody of all other cash funds or securities is separated from the function responsible for applying cash; ensure that there is an adequate safeguard against misappropriation of cash through the recording of fictitious discounts or allowances by persons handling cash; ensure that checks returned unpaid for insufficient funds are delivered directly to a responsible employee (other than cashier) for investigation; ensure that branch offices or divisions making collections deposit these funds in a bank account subject to withdrawal only by the home or head office, ensure that proper physical safeguards and facilities (e.g., safes, restricted areas) are employed to protect cash; and ensure that persons receiving or handling cash funds are properly bonded and take annual vacation time.

- To determine whether cash disbursements are made only to authorized recipients in accordance with management-specific instructions.

- Review the electronic cash transfer systems; observe sign-on procedures, instructions entered, and register(s) generated. Test to documented procedures to determine if variance exists between actual processing and documented procedures. Evaluate the administrative cash transfer procedures in place. Test to ensure that all transfers have been approved in writing by both cash section management and general accounting management and confirmed by the bank to the authorizing parties.

- Review instructions sent to the disbursement banks for adequacy and consistency. Verify that the list of banks to which money can be transferred has been reconciled to treasury letters authorizing establishment of the bank accounts. If variances exist, research and reconcile them. Review to determine if transfers have been attempted to other than an approved bank. Discuss controls that would highlight such an attempt and comment on their adequacy. Determine that all amounts transferred are confirmed by the bank, review confirmations received, and reconcile them to accounting and cash management records. Specifically, review daily cash transfer activity registers to ensure they have been reconciled to source documentation and confirmations and that the reconciliations have been reviewed and approved by management.

- To ascertain whether bank reconciliations are performed promptly and correctly.

- Ensure that bank statements are received by the bank reconciliation section directly from the various authorized banks. Select a sample of bank reconciliations and conduct these audit procedures: observe that the information is supported by bank statements and the general ledger; determine that the reconciliation format used is consistent with the prescribed format; verify that differences are resolved; and test that reconciliations are signed by the person performing the reconciliations and that they are timely.

| *Audit objectives for cash management* | *Audit procedures for cash management* |
|---|---|
| | • In order to test how the differences in reconciliation have been resolved, these audit procedures are suggested: ascertain that all adjustments are adequately supported by acceptable documentation; ensure that documentation is cross-referenced to adjustments; review transmittals of correction entries to the accounting department; and verify that out-of-balance conditions are promptly followed up for correction. Review bank reconciliations for management approval evidenced by signature and date. |
| | • In order to ensure that the canceled checks have authorized signatures, examine a representative sample of signed checks and determine that the signatures are authorized in the corporate signature book. |
| • To determine whether controls are adequate over petty cash disbursement and reimbursement activities. | • In order to ensure that cash disbursed and received by the person handling petty cash is based on approved documentation and that it is timely and accurately recorded, perform these audit tests: review established procedures regarding processing the disbursement of funds and comment on their adequacy; ensure that advances made to employees are approved as required; ensure that a maximum amount for individual payments from the fund has been established; and ensure that petty cash vouchers are: prepared for each disbursement, adequately supported, in ink or typewritten, dated, fully descriptive of the item paid for, clearly marked to show the amount paid, and signed by the person receiving the cash. Ensure that all documents supporting the cash disbursement are canceled to prevent reuse. |
| | • Review reimbursement requests and the attached documentation for compliance to established procedures. Specifically, confirm that: all supporting documents contain authorized approvals, the sums of the individual voucher totals are accurate, and all vouchers and supporting documents are canceled at the time of reimbursement to prevent reuse. |
| | • Ascertain that supervisors perform periodic audits of the petty cash funds and reconcile to the general ledger accounts. Understand how reconciliation problems are resolved. Ascertain that the size of the petty cash imprest funds is based on good business judgment consistent with usage. |

## Audit Concern of a Multinational Corporation

A primary audit concern of a multinational corporation's foreign branch money transfer operations located at international headquarters is ensuring compliance with foreign government money transfer regulations. Good internal control requires that the person making wire transfers should not reconcile the bank statement.

### (C) *Audit cycle/area: Treasury: Equity management.*

| *Risks and exposures* | *Controls or control procedures* |
|---|---|
| • Improper authorization of company transactions dealing with equity instruments. | • A written company policy requiring review of major funding proposals by the board of directors (PC). |
| • Loss or theft of issued stock certificates. | • Physical security controls, sequentially numbered receipts, maintain receipt logs, taking physical inventory, and periodic reconciliations (PC, DC). |
| • Improper or incorrect conversion of instruments. | • Written procedures, management reporting, and recomputations (PC, DC). |

<u>*Audit objectives for equity management*</u>

- To determine whether all stock certificates received are acknowledged properly and documented as to source, number of shares, and certificate numbers to aid in ensuring that all stock certificates are transferred and accounted for.

- To ascertain whether blank stock certificates are adequately protected against theft and loss.

- To determine whether stock transfer requests are processed promptly and accurately.

- To ascertain whether the registrar reviews all stock cancellations and reissues daily, and updates records accordingly.

<u>*Audit procedures for equity management*</u>

- Review stock receiving area for physical security and protection afforded the stock certificates delivered for transfer processing. Evaluate the adequacy of the protection. Observe stock certificate receipt procedures for a selected sample of activity: validate that the stock certificates received are reconciled to accompanying shipping documentation as to total number of shares, certificate numbers, and other information provided; validate that receipts are assigned for stock certificates received by source (e.g., mail, stock exchange, bank, broker, personal delivery, depository trust company) with total number of shares noted; and review receipt log to ensure that all sequentially numbered receipts are accounted for.

- Review a sample of securities in the area for endorsements, guarantees, transfer instructions, and general appearance. Review procedures for handling incomplete stock certificates. Evaluate their adequacy and appropriateness.

- Review blank-certificate storage facilities and access controls: determine that storage facilities adequately protect blank certificates against theft and other casualty damage. All stock certificates released should be accurately recorded and signed for by the individual physically transporting the items. Ascertain that access is restricted to individuals who are independent of the transfer function.

- Review monthly physical inventory and reconciliations to daily use records and the perpetual inventory system: determine if variances have existed, and, if so, verify that they have been researched and resolved on a prompt basis; ascertain that a record of void certificates on hand and certificates destroyed exists. For those destroyed, ensure that destruction has been witnessed; and determine if the physical inventory reconciliation is reviewed and approved by management.

- Review stock certificate preparation for a sample of activity: ascertain that certificates have been prepared consistent with transfer instructions; ensure that unused blank stock certificates are returned to the vault as required; determine that erroneously filled out stock certificates have been voided; and verify that an audit trail exists between old and new certificates.

- Verify that discrepancies between file information and information on the stock certificate being presented for transfer are researched and reconciled on a timely basis. Analyze errors to determine if patterns exist that indicate repetitive processing problems. Determine whether outstanding discrepancies as of the dividend payment date that are effective on the record date are properly recorded to ensure the accuracy of the dividend payment.

- Ensure that transaction registers are reviewed and reconciled daily. Verify that management reviews the reconciliations. Determine that all variances are resolved on a timely basis. Determine that the ability to modify and maintain the stockholder files is assigned to an individual who is independent of the transfer process.

- In order to ensure that the registrar reviews the number of shares canceled and reissued to the number of shares authorized and outstanding, these audit procedures are suggested: review the shipment of canceled stock and newly issued stock certificates to the registrar; observe the controls that ensure all certificates are sent to the registrar; verify that the transaction register is sent with the certificates and that controls are in place to ensure it accurately reflects transfer activity; ensure that packaging and shipment of certificates is performed independently of the treasury department; and determine that the shipping packages are securely bound and sealed prior to shipment.

- Review the daily file reconciliation supplied by the registrar. If variances exist, ascertain that they have been reviewed and resolved on a timely basis and approved by management. Repeat this for month-end, quarter-end, and year-end reconciliations.

| *Audit objectives for equity management* | *Audit procedures for equity management* |
|---|---|
|  | • Observe or ensure that shipments of securities returned by the registrar are sealed, and ascertain that they are properly receipted with the receiving individual(s) clearly identified. |
| • To determine whether newly issued stock certificates returned by the registrar are distributed to the new owner per the original instructions and that canceled stock certificates are securely stored. | • Observe physical security and general safeguards. Ascertain that newly issued certificates are adequately safeguarded to ensure that only people for whom they are intended will receive them. |
|  | • Observe techniques and procedures utilized by the stock distribution area: verify that securities are distributed per original transfer instructions; ascertain that the receipt log for securities distributed is cross-referenced to sources of original securities; and verify that the distribution log is reconciled to the receipt log. |
|  | • For a sample of activity, review to ensure that all canceled stock certificates are physically canceled and stored securely and in a manner consistent with the record retention guidelines. |
| • To ascertain whether preferred stock and debentures are converted into common stock consistent with the terms of the various agreements and are accurately and promptly recorded. | • Review documentation supporting the conversion of preferred stock and debentures into common stock and comment on its adequacy in regard to key operating items. |
|  | • Determine that the conversion calculation (amount of common shares to be issued) is performed and verified independently. Review the conversion calculation procedure and operation: observe that the calculation is performed twice independently to ensure accuracy; verify that controls are in place to ensure that the correct conversion rate is used and that a history file is maintained regarding rate information; for checks issued in lieu of fractional shares, verify that the amount is accurate. |
|  | • Review inventory controls over treasury stock and authorized but not issued shares: test that inventory records are updated daily and are reviewed and approved independently of the area responsible for maintenance; verify that all activity including the issuance of treasury stock and authorized but unissued shares is transmitted to the accounting department daily; ensure that issuance is confirmed independently to both the treasury and accounting departments; and review month-end reconciliations and comment on the discrepancies noted. |
|  | • Review actual issuance of stock certificates: verify that the number of shares issued is consistent with the rate and the amount of preferred stock and debentures presented for conversion; check that the number of shares issued has been transmitted to the accounting department; and ensure that appropriate journal entries have been made to reflect the activity. |
| • To determine whether controls are adequate over the issuance of additional shares. | • Review the board of directors' resolutions. Ensure that the actual issuance of new shares is consistent with the board's authorization. Review to ensure that the issuance of additional shares has been subjected to legal review. |
|  | • Review notifications to regulatory and governmental agencies (e.g., Securities and Exchange Commission) per instructions issued by legal counsel and determine that the notifications are consistent with the instructions. |
|  | • Review procedures followed in regard to actual issuance of new shares and test to ensure consistency with the board of directors' resolutions and specific treasury department instructions. Review entries made by the accounting department to ensure that they are consistent with the board of directors' resolutions and stock transfer activity. Test that the various accounting records affected has been reconciled. |
| • To ascertain whether common stock issued as a result of the exercise of stock options is promptly and accurately recorded consistent with all terms of the option granted. | • Review approvals and documentation supporting procedures regarding the exercise of stock options and comment on their adequacy. Review the stock option plan and ensure that the plan has been approved. |
|  | • Review the list of eligible employees and the specifics of their eligibility. Test the stock option plan for a sample of individuals to ensure that options granted are consistent with the established criteria. Review the procedure followed in notifying individuals of their eligibility: check that all properly approved individuals were notified, and establish that notification was consistent with the specifics of eligibility that were determined. |

| *Audit objectives for equity management* | *Audit procedures for equity management* |
|---|---|
| | • Verify that, when options are exercised, designated individuals in the personnel department have approved the specific request and that all conditions are validated. |
| | • Review requests to exercise the options that have been granted: ensure that they are consistent with the authorization and check that they contain the correct approvals. Verify that a check for the required amount of money accompanied the request and that it has been deposited on a timely basis. |
| | • Review the stock option account file that is compiled as stock certificates are issued for options granted and determine that it is reconciled to source documentation supporting the issuance of shares. Review accounting entries made as the result of the exercise of the options. Verify that they correctly reflect the activity that has taken place. |
| | • Review reporting to governmental and regulatory agencies. Ascertain that it is consistent with the requirements, accurate, and reflective of actual activity. Determine that stock certificates for exercised stock options are issued, registered, and delivered consistent with normal stock transfer processing procedures. |
| • To determine whether conversion of preferred debentures into common stock is performed properly and accurately. | • Verify that documented processing procedures, controls, and management reporting requirements are in place to provide department guidance in regard to conversion activity. Verify that once it has been determined that the preferred debenture submitted is a valid document, it is converted into common stock and the shares are issued, registered, and distributed via the processing procedures in place regarding all other types of transfer activity. |
| | • Review the conversion calculation verification procedure followed. Indicate if they are adequate to ensure that calculations are made correctly. Test a sample of calculations made and comment on their accuracy. |
| • To ascertain whether controls over redemption of securities are proper. | • Verify that the redemption of securities is in accordance with the board of directors' resolutions as to the type of securities to be redeemed, the number of shares or dollar value of securities, monies to be paid, the time period the offer is open, the restrictions as to source, and total or minimum amount from one person. |
| | • Review the selection of the redemption agent; establish that the agent is licensed and that business and character references have been obtained; verify that a contract has been signed, that it details the responsibility of respective parties and specifies payment terms. Test that the contract has been complied with; and ascertain that the payment document has been approved at the appropriate management level. Review the accounting entries made as a result of the board of directors' resolutions. Check that the expenses involved have been correctly accrued. |
| | • Review the register of securities redeemed and payments made. Ensure that amounts paid are consistent with the securities surrendered and authorizing resolutions. Review accounting entries. Test that they correctly reflect the redemption activity that occurred. |
| • To determine whether securities acquired as a result of an acquisition of a company are stored under conditions that are adequate to protect them from theft and loss. | • Review practices and procedures regarding the receipt of security documents: verify that receipt is documented and that it includes time and date, certificate number, and number of shares involved. Test that the record is maintained in duplicate and that it contains a signature or a confirmation from the individual or company delivering the security; determine that the security is subject to adequate safeguarding to protect it from theft or casualty loss; ensure that persons involved in the receipt and transfer of securities are at appropriate job levels and are bonded. |
| | • Review monthly reconciliations between the treasury and accounting departments and, if differences exist, analyze as to causes and determine if they have been resolved. Ascertain that the reconciliations have been reviewed and approved by management. |

*Audit objectives for equity management*

*Audit procedures for equity management*

- Review physical storage of securities and general inventory control procedures: observe and test that storage facilities are adequate to prevent theft and casualty loss except under the most extreme conditions; ascertain that access restrictions are in conformity with requirements. Vaults should be opened for a limited time period each day with **dual persons** attending; check that all employees involved are bonded; verify that securities carry adequate and reasonable insurance coverage; and verify that inventory listings of the securities stored are transmitted to the insurer as required by insurance policies. Perform a count of the securities and trace the results to the treasury's physical inventory records.

- To ascertain whether the divestiture of securities is accurately and timely recorded.

- Confirm divestiture to the board of directors' resolutions. Review inventory records to determine they are adjusted correctly and that, if variances exist, they have been documented. Review confirmation of the receipt and transmittal of securities to the acquirer including signed receipts. Determine that all required parties have been notified.

- Review receipt of cash or other payment (e.g., notes receivable, alternative securities). Determine that they are accurate and consistent with the amount called for in the agreement. Review to ensure they have been correctly receipted and deposited. If variances exist, discuss with the responsible management. Determine that appropriate entries are made in the accounting department to reflect the divestiture and release of the securities.

- To determine whether additional capital contributions are recorded promptly and accurately.

- Review the approved request and verify that it is consistent with the board of directors' resolutions regarding approvals for additional capital contributions. Review journal entries made to record the additional contributions and ensure that they are accurate and consistent with prior entries and with accounting rules and regulations. Review the monthly settlement statement indicating receipt of the funds.

## EXAMPLES OF APPLICATION OF COMPUTER-ASSISTED AUDIT TECHNIQUES:  EQUITY MANAGEMENT

- List capital stock purchases, sales, and redemptions for vouching with supporting documentation.
- Recompute profits and losses on redemption of stock for accuracy and completeness.

---

### (D) *Audit cycle/area: Treasury:  Investment management.*

*Risks and exposures*
- Improper accounting of dividends.

- Improper accounting of notes receivable.
- Improper use of debit/credit advices.

*Controls or control procedures*
- Establish procedures for dividend declaration and payment (PC).
- Perform positive confirmation of notes receivable (DC).
- Issue written guidelines (PC).
Conduct periodic checks to ensure proper use (DC).

*Audit objectives for investment management*
- To determine whether all investment acquisitions are approved by the board of directors and properly recorded.

*Audit procedures for investment management*
- Review initial acquisition proposals. Verify that the terms, conditions, costs, and benefits to the company are clearly stated. Examine that the proposal has been signed and approved by senior management.
- Review approved acquisition proposals. Verify against minutes of the board of directors' meetings. Review external auditors' involvement and check that their comments are consistent with that of the department submitting the proposal. If inconsistencies exist, determine if they have been brought to the attention of senior management.

| *Audit objectives for investment management* | *Audit procedures for investment management* |
|---|---|
| | • Review preliminary agreements. Determine that they are consistent with the board of directors' instructions. Determine if negative confirmations are required from the requesting division and, if so, what subsequent actions occur. Test that the acquisition agreement has been reviewed and approved by the board of directors. If differences exist, evaluate their resolution and management levels involved. Review the letters of intent to ensure that they are consistent with preliminary agreements. |
| | • Review the purchase agreement and closing: test if there are differences from the letter of intent and the approved preliminary agreement. If so, review to determine if the exceptions have been noted and resolved; determine that the closing process has been documented; and inquire whether all affected parties are notified. |
| | • Determine that the acquisition is established in the general ledger and that appropriate documentation is maintained in a permanent file to record the acquisition. |
| | • When the internal auditor is conducting a **due diligence review,** the following audit program is suggested: review articles and bylaws for the company and subsidiaries to be acquired, including major employment contracts, bonus or stock purchase plans, management contracts, insurance polices including the board of directors' liability limits; review federal and state tax returns and audited financial statements, material guaranties, contingent liabilities: class action suits, product liability claims, insider trading issues; review all business activities including material litigation pending and status of tax audits, environmental problems, or any special investigations; review industry regulatory requirements, if any; review compliance with Securities and Exchange Commission (SEC) requirements regarding issuance of financial securities; perform tests in accounts receivables and long-term payables; mail confirmations of significant receivables and payables; ensure that there were no pledged or otherwise encumbered assets; review lease or purchase agreements. Look for generous arrangements, such as an option to purchase equipment for a fraction of its cost, indicating a related-party transaction; review for irrevocable lease arrangements that increase the risk to the acquiring company; conduct a physical count of inventory, and bring in an independent expert if necessary to value the inventory items; ensure that cash is properly stated by preparing and reviewing the standard bank confirmation inquiries; and review fixed asset capitalization procedures for adequacy and compliance with tax guidelines and management directives. |
| • To determine whether all investment divestitures are approved by the board of directors and properly recorded. | • Review the initial divestiture proposal: ensure that it contains signatures of the preparer and management; establish that it clearly presents the proposed divestiture; and verify that it has been approved by senior management and the board of directors. |
| | • Review distribution to prospective buyers for confidentiality of process, quality of buyers, and agents used. Review the preliminary sales agreement and ensure that it has been distributed to all relevant parties. |
| | • Reconcile the final sales agreement to the minutes of the board of directors. Review board of directors' minutes to ensure that all modifications have been made. Research and obtain explanations for any differences that may exist. |
| | • Ascertain that the final sales agreement is distributed to all affected parties. Review distribution controls in place and comment on their adequacy. |
| | • Review accounting entries made as a result of divestiture: verify that accounting entries are consistent with the agreement and ensure that no entries have been omitted; and ensure that accounting entries are consistent with generally accepted accounting principles and company policies and procedures. |

*Audit objectives for investment management*

- To ascertain whether investment escrow cash and/or securities are properly safeguarded and released to the seller in accordance with the purchase agreement.

- To determine whether dividends from subsidiaries are declared and paid properly and promptly.

- To ascertain whether notes received as part of the payment for divestitures are timely and accurately recorded both as to principal and interest accruals and are presented for payment when due.

*Audit procedures for investment management*

- Review the purchase agreement: verify that escrow is deposited consistent with the amount and type called for in the purchase agreement; ensure that the escrow agent is a bank or other financial institution of unquestionable integrity with the technical competence to handle the responsibility and is preselected by the treasury department for this purpose; check that the escrow agent has adequate insurance coverage; and determine that receipt of the escrow payment has been acknowledged or confirmed by the agent and that the treasury has copies of the confirmation.

- Ensure that the funds, if any, involved in an escrow arrangement have been used to purchase interest-bearing instruments consistent with the terms of the agreement. Determine to whom the agreement states the interest accrues and verify that it was paid consistent with the agreement.

- Review escrow payment activity: validate that the trustee has released the escrow to the seller as authorized on a timely and accurate basis. Ensure that confirmations are reviewed promptly and that problems are expeditiously resolved; ascertain that interest earnings, if due, have been paid per the agreement. If paid to the company, determine that they have been recorded as interest income.

- Reconcile dividend declaration and payment to the company by its subsidiaries. Verify that the dividend amounts to be paid are consistent with the percentages of consolidated net income. Ensure that public notice of the intention to declare a dividend has been made as required. Test that the corporate treasury has been notified promptly when a dividend has been declared.

- Ensure that subsidiaries prepare a monthly cash flow forecast, copies of which are sent to both the treasury and accounting departments. Evaluate the adequacy of analysis and follow-up. Review dividends received for a period of time. Verify that dividends have been received in the amounts specified and on the dates due. If the amount received differs from the planned receipt, verify that the difference has been researched, documented, and approved.

- Review debit/credit advices supplied by subsidiaries to ensure that dividends have been correctly reported and the advice forms are utilized correctly. If the dividend was netted or offset against balances owed by corporate, test to determine if treasury management approval was obtained prior to the reduced payment.

- Review final sales agreements for terms of notes receivable. Review notes receivable accounts in the general ledger to determine if they are established consistent with the agreements and if they are subject to control. Specifically, ensure that segregation of duties is maintained between employees who post the detail notes receivable from employees who post general ledger control accounts, have cash functions, and have voucher functions.

- Review the notes receivable schedule system for controls over payment dates. Evaluate the collectibility of questionable items and adequacy of collateral where appropriate, and review the adequacy of the allowance for uncollectible accounts. Review the cash flow forecast system to determine if notes receivable is entered correctly.

- Ensure that the duties of the custodian of notes receivable and related collateral are segregated from general ledger functions, maintaining detailed records of notes receivable and collateral, and cash functions.

- Request positive confirmation of at least a representative sample of notes held by custodians and with makers; specifically confirm the unpaid balances, interest, maturity dates, and collateral pledged with the makers of the notes, and follow up on those for which a reply was not received. Investigate differences reported as a result of the above confirmation requests by examining the underlying data (e.g., sales contracts, billing documents, shipping documents).

## EXAMPLES OF APPLICATION OF COMPUTER-ASSISTED AUDIT TECHNIQUES: INVESTMENT MANAGEMENT

- Recalculate amortization of discounts and premiums on investment accounts, and compare them with management calculations.
- Compare interest and dividend records with investment registers for determining relationships between accounts. Conduct reasonableness tests between the interest amount and the principal amounts of the investment.
- Recompute profits and losses on disposal of investments for accuracy and completeness.

---

**(E)** *Audit cycle/area: Treasury: Dividends management.*

### Risks and exposures
- Inadequate controls over blank dividend checks.

- Misappropriation of funds.
- Violation of state escheat laws.

### Controls or control procedures
- Establish dual-person control (PC).
- Use prenumbered checks (DC).
- Establish controls over returned dividend checks (PC).
- Implement procedures to handle undeliverable dividend checks (PC).
- Conduct periodic reviews for compliance (DC).

### Audit objectives for dividends management
- To determine whether dividends to shareholders are paid promptly and accurately consistent with the board of directors' resolutions and in accordance with governmental and regulatory rules and regulations.

### Audit procedures for dividends management
- Review record date closing procedures: determine that all record date activity up to and including the record date has been updated to the database used to run dividend files by sampling transfers occurring after the record date; ascertain that the record date database is subject to adequate access security controls to prevent accidental destruction and unauthorized modifications; and verify that all stockholder address changes have been updated to record date database between record date and payment date.
- Review preparations for printing of dividend checks: review procedures used in updating the dividend program for proper criteria (e.g., date, rate), and comment on their adequacy and the control procedures followed to ensure the update is accurate and properly authorized; and review preliminary testing regarding calculation accuracy and evaluate procedures followed.
- Review the printing of dividend checks: test that blank dividend check stock is controlled: cartons are sealed; checks are prenumbered and under dual-person control; test that checks are used in sequence; verify that misprints and damaged checks are voided and retained; ascertain that the required calculations have been made prior to signing; determine that checks are signed by facsimile signature under **dual-person control;** and ascertain that the signature plate is adequately secured and is maintained by someone independent of check storage and printing.
- Verify that printed checks are placed in prenumbered cartons in run sequence and sealed prior to shipment to the bank for mailing. Establish that the shipment is subject to adequate physical security. Ensure that the bank confirms the number of checks mailed and that this figure is balanced to the number of checks printed.
- Review the accounting journal entries as a result of dividend checks presented for payment. Test and reconcile to the supporting documents provided. Review the month-end accrual for outstanding dividend payments and verify its accuracy.
- Review monthly bank reconciliations: verify that the bank is being funded as checks are presented consistent with a zero-balance policy; if reconciling items exist, ensure that they have been resolved, documented, and approved by management; and establish that the reconciliations have been formally approved by management.

*Audit objectives for dividends management*

- To ascertain whether controls over undeliverable dividends are adequate to prevent misappropriation of funds or to support eventual transfer to state government as required by the escheat laws.

*Audit procedures for dividends management*

- Verify that all dividend checks that have been returned are reviewed and tested prior to a final determination that they are not deliverable: the addresses as printed are reviewed for obvious printing mistakes; the stock ownership file is checked and the addresses on the envelopes are verified to addresses in the computer database; the prior dividend payment is reviewed to determine if the checks were cashed and, if so, they are reviewed to determine if information on them indicates new addresses or bank account numbers; if a recent stock purchase, transfer tickets are reviewed and the organizations originating the transaction are contacted to determine if they have additional information; and formal letters are sent to the addresses asking for information about the persons involved.
- Ascertain that, once a determination has been made that a check is undeliverable, these activities occur: convert the check to cash and establish the liability in a special account maintained for dividends that have been returned and determined to be undeliverable. Include all relevant information regarding dividend number, number of shares, certificate numbers, and so on; code the stock transfer database so that checks are not printed during future dividend runs; ensure that all nondeliverable coding entered into the database is reviewed and approved by management; verify that undeliverable dividends are grouped by state and date of check; and verify that undeliverable dividends are escheated to the various state governments based on their respective abandoned property laws, where applicable.
- Test the following for compliance with procedures: ascertain that the checks have been canceled and the amounts involved were set up as a liability; review dividend accumulation by state; ensure the record is complete and included holder name, address, dividend date, amount, number of shares of stock, dividend number; review the most recent escheat payment to several states and confirm that a listing by individual and amount is included as a backup to the check; determine that the age of the items included is consistent with state law; and determine that appropriate accounting entries have been made to reflect the payments to the various states.

## EXAMPLES OF APPLICATION OF COMPUTER-ASSISTED AUDIT TECHNIQUES: DIVIDENDS MANAGEMENT

- List dividend payments for vouching with supporting documentation.
- List unusual dividend rates applied to capital stock.
- List missing check numbers for making dividend payments for further analysis.
- Compare dividend records with stock registers to prove that dividends are for the valid stocks.
- Conduct reasonableness test between total dividend amounts paid and the average number of shares and dollar aggregate.

---

### (F) *Audit cycle/area: Treasury: Risk and insurance management.*

*Risks and exposures*

- No insurance due to not reporting property to an insurance company.
- Possibility of excessive insurance coverage.


- Improper handling of loss claims.

*Controls or control procedures*

- Written procedures to notify additions or deletions of property to the insurance carrier (PC).
- A report listing of all properties covered (PC).
- A periodic review for double, overlapping, or no insurance coverage (DC).
- Written procedures describing the required reporting for losses experienced (PC).
- Computation of elapsed time between claim submission date and settlement date (DC).

*Audit objectives for risk and insurance management*

- To determine whether all insurance needs are defined accurately and on a timely basis to reduce or eliminate the exposure of an uninsured loss.

- To ascertain whether the company obtains insurance coverage to satisfy defined needs at the lowest cost and that the coverage is reviewed periodically for adequacy.

- To determine whether claims are filed for losses and that a loss control program is in effect to minimize the potential for theft and casualty loss.

*Audit procedures for risk and insurance management*

- Review the list of assets and exposures whose coverage is requested. Ensure that all coverage provided by a third party (e.g., by lessors in case of leased equipment, forwarding agents for goods shipped, insurance provided by governmental institutions in the export business, legal obligations for producers of purchased goods) is properly reported to the insurance department to prevent double insurance.

- Ensure that all upgrading of security programs and improvements to buildings and equipment that could result in a better insurance rating is properly reported to the insurance department.

- Determine if the company has exposures in the following areas that would appear to require specialized local coverage: new product development, large sales contracts over a predetermined dollar amount, unusual controversies surrounding a product or market, and changing foreign or political conditions relevant to the company.

- Determine that the procedures ensure that all property (e.g., company, vendors, and employees' property) is reported to the insurance department and that the department has controls to ensure it is reported to the insurance carrier where required. Ensure that the insurance carrier is notified of additions or deletions of property.

- Review the insurance coverage in effect. Evaluate types of coverage selected as to optimization of premium expense relative to the coverage provided. Ensure that the file indicates dollar limits and specifics of the coverage. Ascertain that the listing is reconciled to the general ledger and that variances have been analyzed. Review procedures followed in selecting insurance carriers, and ensure that the selection process was documented and indicates single sources, bidding, or negotiations.

- Determine if there are any overlaps in coverage provided. Ensure that certificates of insurance are provided by third parties performing work for the company.

- Review insurance carrier inspection reports. List the exposures pointed out, and determine if they have been corrected. Check that the insurance carriers have made all required inspections or, if they have not been made, that the carrier has been contacted.

- Review the published procedure that describes the required reporting for losses experienced. Ensure that the procedure includes such items as: identifying physical losses or damages; valuing the losses; routines to be followed in reporting the losses; methodology to determine if losses were the result of accidental circumstances, willful acts of sabotage, and frauds or theft; and appropriate documentation to be completed and reporting responsibilities for each of the various types of loss.

- Review the file of loss reports to ascertain that reports have been filed promptly, are consistent with the requirements, and clearly identify and explain the incidents. Ensure that loss notification includes the following information: location of loss, date of loss, cause of loss, description of property damaged, estimated amount of loss, person to be contacted by the insurance adjuster, and if a manufacturer's output–type coverage, the transportation company inspector's report of damage-in-transit claims.

- Review emergency procedures to protect assets from further damage once loss has occurred. Review their implementation in regard to several incidents. Determine if they have protected the property from further loss or damage.

| *Audit objectives for risk and insurance management* | *Audit procedures for risk and insurance management* |
|---|---|

*Audit objectives for risk and insurance management*

*Audit procedures for risk and insurance management*

- Review the receivable that has been established to reflect the claim and perform the following audit tests: check if it is based on the loss estimate; if not, review the support of the entry, determine if aged items are researched to determine their current status, and ensure that management is informed of claims collections problems. In the event of disputed claims, determine: if full documentation of both parties' correspondence is maintained in a secured file, that all contractual avenues of resolution are being explored, and that the advice of legal counsel has been solicited.
- Review access controls to facilities and buildings. Observe that unrestricted access to the facility is limited to employees. Test the means to accomplish this. Observe that all others are directed to a reception area where the purpose of their visit is validated and recorded. Ensure that the employee being visited escorts visitors. Observe that locked facilities are used for the storage of materials with access and inventory controls. Review access and material sign-out procedures.
- Review procedures to identify areas with a high degree of potential for fire and explosion. Ensure access to these areas is restricted to authorized employees by means of locked gates, security guards. Determine whether protective clothing is required for individuals entering dangerous areas. Review emergency procedures and responsibilities (e.g., fire drills, fire-fighting containments, and evacuation) in the event of a disaster. Be alert for conditions such as faulty storage of hazardous material or blocked or locked emergency exits, which could contribute toward the negative effects of an emergency.
- Review reports of facilities inspection conducted. Determine if recommendations to reduce hazards to people, equipment, and property have been implemented, and, if not, that the reasons have been documented and approved by senior management.
- Verify that firefighting equipment is inspected on a regular basis, that safety showers are operative, that first-aid kits are maintained, and that all of these items are readily accessible for use.

## Effectiveness of Insurance Function

One way to assess the effectiveness of the insurance function is to know when final settlements are negotiated after claims are developed and submitted.

### (G) *Audit cycle/area: Treasury: Foreign currency exchange management.*

| *Risks and exposures* | *Controls or control procedures* |
|---|---|

*Risks and exposures*

- Incompatible duties.
- Employees favoring certain banks or customers to do business for personal reasons.
- Incorrect use of exchange rates.

*Controls or control procedures*

- Segregation of duties between foreign exchange function and other functions (PC).
- Require all employees to take annual vacation (DC).
- Test the procedures and verify a sample of exchange transactions (DC).

*Audit objectives for foreign currency exchange management*

- To determine whether foreign currency exchange transactions are consistent with specific policies established by treasury management and the board of directors' resolutions.

*Audit procedures for foreign currency exchange management*

- Review a sample of foreign currency exchange transactions and determine if they are consistent with stated policy. If variances exist, review documentation on file supporting the variances. If documentation is not on file, research the situation and discuss with the appropriate levels of management.
- Review activity that has taken place when procedures indicated a currency should be followed closely for revaluation or devaluation. Verify that it was complied with.

_Audit objectives for foreign currency exchange management_

- To ascertain whether the need to exchange currencies is clearly identified so that exchanges can take place in a manner benefiting the company.

_Audit procedures for foreign currency exchange management_

- Review reporting requirements and ascertain that they specify the receipts and disbursements to be included so that the reports are accurate and comprehensive. Ensure that the coverage includes trade payables and receivables, royalties, service arrangement fees, management fees, dividends, capital funds, and loans.
- Verify that actual receipts and disbursements are compared to forecasts and that the variances are analyzed. Validate that transactions that were to be netted did occur and have been confirmed and recorded correctly in the accounting records.
- To ensure proper segregation of duties, determine that individuals responsible for foreign exchange transactions are excluded from the following functions: preparing, validating, and mailing foreign exchange contracts; recording foreign exchange transactions, maintaining position ledgers and maturity files, and preparing daily activity and position reports; periodically evaluating foreign exchange positions and determining gains and losses; settling transactions and other paying or receiving functions, such as issuing, receiving, and processing cable and mail instructions and foreign drafts; operating and reconciling the due-to and due-from accounts in foreign currencies; and preparing, approving, and posting other accounting entries.
- Ascertain that the function of evaluation, approval, and periodic review of creditworthiness of banks in foreign exchange transactions and establishment of general policy and guidelines for foreign exchange activity are performed by persons outside the foreign exchange department.
- Check that all employees are required to take an annual vacation and that their duties are assigned to others during their absence.
- Review the documentation utilized by the department and determine that it is prenumbered and numerically accounted for by both the foreign exchange and accounting departments.
- In order to ensure that controls are in place to prevent or detect material errors, excessive risks, adverse trends, unreported losses, or transactions engaged in beyond authorized limits, the following audit tests are suggested: ascertain if significant limit excesses are approved in advance and on an individual transaction basis; and review exposure and devaluation or revaluation reports and evaluate their adequacy in regard to: an independent review to ensure that all appropriate foreign currency assets, liabilities, and futures positions are included in these reports; the exchange rates used for revaluation are obtained by someone other than the employee in the area and checked to independent sources; computations are independently checked and reviewed by appropriate management outside the area, evidenced in writing.
- In order to ensure that proper procedures were in place to review the foreign exchange settlements that were made, the following audit tests are suggested: ascertain that settlements are carried out consistent with written instructions; ascertain that settlements are made on a timely and accurate basis; determine that daily activity or transaction registers reflect all settlement activity; and test that all settlement activity is confirmed by the bank involved and the depository or disbursement bank.

- To determine whether accounting controls over foreign currency exchange transactions are proper.

- Compare monthly reconciliations between transaction activity as reported by the foreign exchange department to the activity listing provided by the settlement bank and records maintained in accounting department.

*Audit objectives for foreign currency exchange management*

*Audit procedures for foreign currency exchange management*

- Review to ensure that the rates used in converting foreign currencies to dollars are at prevailing rates and are accurately and consistently applied. Review to ensure that gains and losses on transaction activity have been correctly calculated and recorded and that they comply with generally accepted accounting principles. Review to ensure that forecasted fees are compared to actual fees charged by banks and other financial institutions involved, and that differences are investigated.

### (H) *Audit cycle/area: Treasury: Write-off accounting.*

*Risks and exposures*

- Unauthorized write-offs of investments.
- Improper write-off of goodwill.
- Improper classification of write-off.

*Controls or control procedures*

- Establish write-off and recovery procedures (PC).
- Require management approvals (PC).
- Interview the chief financial officer and review the board of directors' meeting minutes (DC).

*Audit objectives for write-off accounting*

- To determine whether procedures to write off and remove any investment that is deemed worthless from the company's books is based on appropriate management approvals.

*Audit procedures for write-off accounting*

- Review write-off requests. Test that they are properly supported and justified. Examples of justification include judicial decisions, appraisers' reports, financial newspapers, and trade journals. Evaluate the information in relationship to the write-off request.
- Review actual write-offs: establish that they contain the required approvals; establish that the write-offs have been performed consistent with approvals. Review journal entries and test that they are supported by authorization letters; verify that investments written off as worthless have been transferred to a separate memorandum account and are periodically reviewed for possible recovery; review the type of investment written off to verify whether a change in financial statement reporting of the investment is required; and review the reasons for the investment having become worthless and possibly classifying the write-offs as extraordinary items in the financial statements.

- To ascertain whether a goodwill write-off is approved by management.

- Verify that goodwill write-off procedures are in conformity to approved proposals. Review the accounting entries made and ensure that they are correct and conform to the approved proposals. Research and report any differences to management.

- To determine whether write-offs resulting from governmental or political actions are properly recorded.

- Review write-off requests resulting from governmental or political actions such as nationalization of certain industries and economies. Ensure that they are adequately supported and contain independent information to support the write-off. Ensure that the write-off has been approved by the board of directors.
- Review the type of investment written off to verify whether a change in financial statement reporting of the investment is required. (The partial write-off of an investment due to expropriation may decrease the ability to exert significant influence [control] over the investee to the point where a change in financial statement reporting status is required.) Review the reason for the investment having become worthless and whether the write-off can be classified as an extraordinary item in the financial statement.

(vi) **Introduction to financial reporting cycle.** Major activities in a financial reporting cycle would include ensuring that: the financial statements are prepared and presented in conformity with generally accepted accounting principles (GAAP); the GAAP have been observed consistently; the related financial or other informative disclosures are stated adequately; the audit report contains an expression of opinion regarding the financial statements; there exist controls over financial statement valuation processes; accounting principles have been selected properly; and unusual or nonrecurring activities and events are handled properly.

## (A) *Audit cycle/area: Financial reporting: Journal entry preparation.*

| *Risks and exposures* | *Controls or control procedures* |
|---|---|
| • Unauthorized preparation of journal entries. | • Develop a list of employees authorized to prepare journal entries (PC). |
| • Use of incorrect account codes. | • Conduct a periodic comparison of journal entry codes to the chart of accounts (DC). |
| • Possibility of management fraud or irregularities. | • Segregation of duties between journal preparation and approval (PC). |
| | • Conduct periodic audits (DC). |

| *Audit objectives for journal entry preparation* | *Audit procedures for journal entry preparation* |
|---|---|
| • To determine whether journal entries are prepared, reviewed, and authorized in accordance with established procedures. | • Obtain a log of individuals authorized to prepare, review, and approve specific journal entries and compare signatures of prepared journal vouchers to the log. Ensure that all journal entries are assigned to specific individuals. Ascertain that there is an adequate segregation of duties relative to the individuals authorized to prepare or approve specific journal entries (e.g., accounts receivable may be recorded independently from sales). Also, ensure that review and approval of journal entries is by supervisors who did not actively participate in their preparation. Ensure that individuals preparing or approving journal entries have a sufficient understanding of the entry's subject matter to ensure that their preparation or approval is meaningful. |
| | • Review journal entries to ensure they are in compliance with generally accepted accounting principles, regulatory body requirements, and company policies and procedures. Review journal entries to ensure that where alternate accounting methods are acceptable, those used are applied on a consistent basis. |
| | • Review accrual journal entries for vacation pay, dividend rates, inventory obsolescence, and depreciation methods to ensure they are in accordance with underlying union agreements or company policies. |
| • To ascertain whether journal entries include proper documentation and that they are accurately recorded prior to the close of each fiscal period. | • Review journal entries processed for proper documentation. If referenced to documentation that is available elsewhere, trace the journal entry to that documentation. Where documentation includes calculations or assumptions, test the calculation or ascertain the validity of the assumptions made. |
| | • Review the chart of accounts to ensure that all changes to it have been properly approved. Review journal entries to ensure that account coding is accurate and conforms to the proper accounts listed in the chart of accounts. |
| | • Review the current closing schedule to ensure that it is complete and that the journal entry due dates appear reasonable to allow for completion of the financial closing work on schedule. Review the journal entry computer processing system to ensure that it provides for adequate controls in the form of data editing and validation, limited access to data files, batch balancing routines, and transaction logging techniques to give reasonable assurance that all journal entries have been posted to master files or otherwise accounted for. |

## (B) **Audit cycle/area:** *Financial reporting: Consolidation and general ledger posting.*

| *Risks and exposures* | *Controls or control procedures* |
|---|---|
| • Erroneous data entering the financial systems. | • Establish data editing and validation routines in all financially related computer programs (PC, DC, CC). |
| • Delays in processing journal entries. | • Issue a monthly accounting closing schedule (PC). |
| • Lack of audit trails in computer systems. | • Implement "account proofing" routines into financially related computerized application systems (DC). |

*Audit objectives for consolidation and general ledger posting*

- To determine whether all consolidation journal entries have been properly prepared and approved and are accurate reflections of the consolidation worksheets and statements.

- To ascertain whether consolidated reports are prepared accurately and on a consistent basis.

- To determine whether general ledger processing is performed accurately and promptly to ensure that financial statements and reports will be issued at the established due date.

*Audit procedures for consolidation and general ledger posting*

- Verify that a journal entry control log is maintained: ensure that the log includes the assignment of each consolidating journal entry to a particular individual; ensure that the journal entry control log provides for prenumbered, standard, consolidated journal entries and that each consolidating journal entry processed has been logged; and verify posting of the consolidating journal entries to the consolidation working papers.

- Review the written procedures for completeness and ensure that they are consistently followed. Ensure that there are established procedures for checking consolidation working papers and consolidated statements. These procedures should be performed by individuals who did not actively participate in the consolidation and statement preparation process and should include these trace consolidating statements to underlying trial balance; review adjusting, elimination, and reclassification entries, ensuring that: intercompany account balances were in agreement and have been eliminated by entries and intercompany sales, cost of sales, and profits in inventory have been eliminated. Trace foreign exchange rates to documented sources.

- Ensure that there is adequate segregation of duties between the initiation of transactions and their summarization and recording; between custody of company property; and between the maintenance of subsidiary ledgers and control accounts. In particular, cash receipts and disbursements duties should be segregated from general ledger recording duties.

- Ensure that a monthly closing schedule is issued each fiscal period that indicates the due dates for: the completion of journal entries by the department responsible for their entry into the general ledger system, the issuance of preliminary trial balances and submission of corrections thereto, the issuance and review of the final trial balance and subsidiary ledgers, and the issuance of financial statements and reports.

- Verify that a control point and log have been established, and review current and past logs to ensure that journal entries are being received and processed in a timely manner. Obtain explanations of significant delays in processing journal entries, and test validity of the schedule due dates. Review processed journal entries to ensure that documentation has been canceled to prevent reuse. Ensure that control totals are determined and batches are submitted to computer processing. Verify that data editing and validation is performed and that debit and credit amounts and hash totals are in agreement with predetermined totals. Ensure that errors are corrected by preparing offsetting entries using the journal entry forms in order to leave an audit trail of corrections (i.e., debit entry is used to fix the incorrect credit entry).

- Ensure that preliminary general ledger trial balances are reviewed for accuracy and reasonableness by authorized individuals and that any noted discrepancies or unusual items are investigated and corrected prior to issuance of a final trial balance and general ledger. This should include a review for out-of-balance conditions, erroneous account codes, reasonableness of balances, large fluctuations, and absence of balances.

*Audit objectives for consolidation and general ledger posting*

*Audit procedures for consolidation and general ledger posting*

- Ensure that general ledger accounts are reviewed, analyzed, and approved in accordance with a formal monthly closing schedule by authorized employees. The analyses should include these steps: (1) verify the current month's opening balance to the prior month's closing balance; (2) review the current month's transactions, including reversal of the prior month's accruals; (3) review accounts without the current month's activity for possible omission of data; (4) verify the legitimacy of accounts with credit balances that normally carry debit balances and debit balances in accounts that normally carry credit balances; (5) verify balances of an intercompany account with comparable offsetting balances on the other company's general ledger; (6) analyze ending balances and activity in accounts to establish propriety of balances, and investigate large fluctuations in balances from month to month, (7) verify subsidiary ledger balances against the controlling general ledger account balances; (8) verify account balances by cash counts, securities inventory, or property inspection; (9) compare recorded amounts of securities held with market values; and (10) compare account balances with budgeted amounts.
- Ensure that, for accrued liabilities and reserve accounts in particular, the stated account balances appear reasonable and reflect company policies. Review explanations and supporting documentation where account balances change significantly during the year. Examine payment of accrued amounts in subsequent periods to determine adequacy of the accrual balance, and verify that related expense or income accounts are charged to offset accrual and reserve accounts credits (i.e., salary expense should be charged to accrued payroll, tax expense is charged to accrued taxes, etc.).

**(C) *Audit cycle/area: Financial reporting: Financial report preparation and issuance, including records retention.***

*Risks and exposures*

- Data errors between general ledger and financial reports.
- Errors or omissions in financial statement disclosures.

- Inadequate or excessive records retention.

*Controls or control procedures*

- Trace data through the system for accuracy (DC).
- Perform quality assurance reviews by independent third parties (DC).
- Issue written procedures describing record retention and disposition schedules (PC).
- Conduct periodic review to determine its compliance (DC).

*Audit objectives for financial report
preparation and issuance, including record retention*

- To determine whether financial reports are prepared in accordance with various requirements.

*Audit procedures for financial report
preparation and issuance, including record retention*

- Ensure that a monthly closing schedule is issued each fiscal period and that the due dates appear reasonable. Ensure that the responsible individuals are aware of due dates to be met. Test the actual completion dates to the corresponding due dates and obtain explanations for those that have not been met; assess the impact of not meeting critical due dates.
- In order to ensure that financial reports are based on information shown in the final general ledger or consolidating working papers, perform these audit reviews: reconcile key data from selected financial reports to the final general ledger or consolidating working papers, and ascertain that a standard approved format is used to show which general ledger accounts comprise which lines or data elements on financial reports.
- Compare the accounting methods used in the compilation and presentation of financial reports with those of prior periods to ensure that they are consistently applied. Ensure that financial reports are reviewed for reasonableness and that they are compared against forecast data.
- Verify that financial reports are issued by the required due dates, by reference to prescribed monthly closing schedules, dates included on instruction forms.

*Audit objectives for financial report*
*preparation and issuance, including record retention*

*Audit procedures for financial report*
*preparation and issuance, including record retention*

- In order to ensure that all supplementary disclosures of information affecting the financial status of the company is properly presented in the form of notes or other, the following audit tests are suggested: ascertain that all relative disclosures in the financial, legal, and operation areas have been made or have been considered; ensure that prospective disclosure data have been considered in the areas of lease information, tax provisions, earnings per share data, replacement cost data, stock options and purchase plan information, special debt agreements, pending legal settlements, open purchase commitments, loss contingencies, and blocked funds; and ensure that the selection of disclosure data for inclusion in financial reporting has been made by senior management in legal, financial, and operating departments.

- To ascertain whether financial documents and records are retained in accordance with management's and regulatory requirements.

- In order to ensure that documents and records are retained for such periods of time as business needs dictate and considering legal and regulatory requirements, these audit tests are suggested: ensure that records retention and disposition schedules have been established that list, by title, each type of record maintained, retention period, and ultimate disposal date; ensure that such schedules indicate approval by responsible department management; ensure that the records retention facility and procedures permit the withdrawal of stored documents when necessary, under controlled conditions, and ensure their timely return; observe that storage areas are fireproof, contain a sprinkler system, and are locked or alarmed to prevent unauthorized access and use; ensure that tax records for a period are destroyed only after tax audits for that period are completed; and ensure that the final disposition of outdated material is by incineration, shredding, pulping, secured waste basket, or other method, depending on its sensitivity.

## (D) *Audit cycle/area: Financial reporting: Tax accounting and reporting.*

*Risks and exposures*
- Incorrect preparation of payroll-related taxes.

- Incorrect application of sales tax and use tax rules.

*Controls or control procedures*
- Written procedures and training of employees in the tax and payroll departments (PC).
- Periodic review for quality assurance (DC)
- Written procedures and training of employees in the tax and purchasing departments (PC).
- Periodic review for quality assurance (DC).

*Audit objectives for tax accounting and reporting*
- To determine whether tax policies are adequate, that tax effects are considered in all major decisions, and that tax adjustments are properly made.

*Audit procedures for tax accounting and reporting*
- Assess whether tax procedures provide information about how to accumulate: sales and use tax, payroll taxes, state and local income taxes, real estate property taxes, and foreign taxes. Outline tax aspects of key business transactions for tax planning purposes.
- Ensure that tax calendars are prepared to provide reminders to file tax returns and tax payments. Examine whether the tax calendar contains the following information: name and type of tax, taxing authority, due date for filing the tax report, payment dates, lead time to complete the report, and source of data.
- Review the effects of operating loss carryforwards and offsets of other companies in a consolidated return; evaluate whether the tax policy goals will maximize tax benefits. Review opportunities for acceleration or deferral of income. Review situations that will result in minimizing taxes: moving facilities, such as sales office, warehouses, branch offices, plant, from high-tax jurisdiction area to a low-tax jurisdiction area; and verify that calculating depreciation of fixed assets for tax purposes is on a basis that will achieve the most advantageous deductions.

*Audit objectives for tax accounting and reporting*

*Audit procedures for tax accounting and reporting*

- In order to ensure that all required tax adjustments and required analyses are promptly prepared, conduct these audit tests: establish that only accrued income legally enforceable is included for tax purposes; review questionable or controversial items of income with management; ascertain that adjustments recommended by tax agents are corrected; review the ratio of the bad debt reserve to sales for the last fiscal year. If the ratio is materially higher than the previous five years' ratios, determine that appropriate explanations were furnished; review depreciation methods to ensure compliance with tax authorities; review disposition of fixed assets and ascertain that no gain or loss is recognized on a trade-in; ascertain that mixed expenditures (repairs and improvements) made under a general plan for rehabilitating or improving property are capitalized in total; attempt to segregate ordinary gains or losses (treated as ordinary income or loss) and capital gains or losses (subject to capital gains treatment); review inventories and ascertain that obsolete items are written down to realizable values and that there is detailed support for the write-down; review leasehold amortization and ascertain that improvements are amortized over the lease period, including optional extensions, but not exceeding the useful life; and investigate if property taxes and franchise taxes are being expensed for the taxable year in which they accrue, as permitted, regardless of payment date (unless in dispute).

- In order to verify that all required adjustments to income tax accounts are recorded promptly and accurately, conduct these audit tests: ensure that all adjustments to tax accounts, except tax payments, are made by journal entry; obtain tax accounting journal entries and verify the basis of calculations for accuracy; trace the tax accounting journal entries to ensure that they are posted to the proper general ledger accounts prior to the close of the fiscal period; ensure that subledgers are maintained by the taxing authority and reconciled to the relevant general ledger accounts; and ascertain that tax payments are first charged to a balance sheet control account to facilitate control and audit.

- Ensure that there is an account analysis for every income tax account and the analyses indicate that they have been reviewed and approved by financial accounting management. Obtain copies of correspondence with taxing authorities and ensure that all prior year tax adjustments are reflected in the appropriate accounts or in a permanent adjustment schedule.

- Review analyses of all prepaid and accrued tax account balances and ensure that there are no accruals for tax years that have been closed or exorbitant excess accruals for prior tax years. Physically verify the existence of tax working papers and reports in a locked, fireproof file cabinet until the tax audit for the relevant years has been completed.

- To ascertain whether sales taxes are promptly and accurately calculated and recorded on sales invoices.

- In order to ensure that sales taxes are charged and collected as appropriate, these audit tests are suggested: verify that the company is registered in all states where sales taxes are collected and that tax returns are filed in all such states; test sales invoices to ensure that the proper tax is calculated and charged on sales to end-use customers; determine that exemption certificates are on file for every customer claiming exemption from sales and use taxes; verify the recording of sales taxes billed to customers from invoices to a copy of the sales register; and test the accumulation of total sales taxes on the sales register.

| _Audit objectives for tax accounting and reporting_ | _Audit procedures for tax accounting and reporting_ |
|---|---|

**Audit objectives for tax accounting and reporting**

- To determine whether use taxes are promptly and accurately calculated and recorded on vendor invoices.

- To ascertain whether payroll taxes are prepared accurately and filed on a timely basis.

- To determine whether real estate and personal property taxes have been paid on a timely basis.

**Audit procedures for tax accounting and reporting**

- In order to ensure that the company does not pay sales taxes on purchases for resale or use in finished goods, these audit tests are suggested: review vendors' invoices for items purchased for resale and ensure that sales tax is not charged. If charged, follow up to see if an exemption certificate has been filed with the vendor. Also, ensure that the sales tax charged is deducted from the current or a subsequent payment or that a refund has been applied for; and ensure that the purchasing department has an established practice to furnish all suppliers with sales tax exemption certificates where the materials being purchased are exempt from sales taxes.

- In order to ensure that practices have been established to provide for the accurate calculation and recording of use tax, these audit tests should be conducted: ensure that controls have been established to identify vendor invoices subject to use tax and to provide for their calculation and accumulation by assigning account codes for use tax; verify vendors' invoices to ensure that use taxes have been calculated; and ensure that use taxes have been properly recorded to the appropriate general ledger expense and payables accounts. *Coding and accumulating use tax from vendors' invoices is better than making a separate journal entry for the total use tax.*

- Trace the detail of the journal entry to total sales tax from the sales register or subsidiary ledger. Trace the tax accounting journal entries to ensure that they are posted to the proper general ledger accounts prior to the close of the fiscal period. Ensure that sales and use tax returns are prepared and reviewed by authorized individuals and are paid and filed by the scheduled due date.

- Ensure that payroll tax data are promptly and accurately submitted to and processed by the tax department to ensure timely filing of returns. Processing should include verification of data to payroll summaries, verification of rates and calculations, and supervisory review of tax working papers, tax payments, and tax returns.

- Conduct these audit tests: ensure that payroll summaries are the basis for taxes paid; verify data on payroll summaries to payroll registers; trace data from payroll summaries through tax work sheets to the returns and/or depository receipts; verify calculations of the employer's share of payroll taxes, including verification of rates through the worksheets to quarterly and annual tax returns; and determine that sick pay is treated as exempt wages for unemployment and social security tax purposes.

- Ensure that quarterly tax returns are reconciled to payroll tax account balances before they are filed. Obtain journal entries for recording payroll taxes and verify data to payroll summaries and work sheets. Check calculations of employer payroll taxes. Verify tax calculations relative to accrued (unpaid) payrolls, and verify that general ledger account codings are proper. Verify the accuracy of taxes calculated on the accrued (earned but unpaid) payrolls by references to the actual tax calculated in the subsequent period when the payroll is actually paid.

- Review real estate and personal property tax accruals. Ascertain that the monthly amount is based on the most current information and calculated correctly. Research the last payment to ascertain that it was charged against the accrual, and verify that the annual accrual approximates the annual payments.

- Ensure that the property tax statement contains correct values of property for all pertinent assets and is properly approved before submission to the taxing authority. Obtain a copy of the most current property tax statement. Trace the statement total to general ledger property accounts.

<u>*Audit objectives for tax accounting and reporting*</u>

- To ascertain whether foreign taxes are paid in a timely and accurate manner.

<u>*Audit procedures for tax accounting and reporting*</u>

- Ensure that: a schedule for foreign taxes is maintained for all tax returns and reporting dates to ensure timely submission of returns and reports; tax data are promptly and accurately accumulated to facilitate the preparation of tax returns and related accounting entries; adequate working papers and/or records are maintained to support tax data; tax returns and reports are properly prepared, reviewed, and authorized prior to issuance and are filed along with the required payments by the scheduled due date; all tax accounts are accurately summarized, classified, and reported promptly at the close of each fiscal period; and all tax working papers, returns, reports, and tax data are adequately protected from unauthorized access and are secured in fireproof storage containers.

### EXAMPLES OF APPLICATION OF COMPUTER-ASSISTED AUDIT TECHNIQUES: TAX

- In order to detect whether sales taxes are applied properly and computed correctly, sort sales orders by geographic area, compute taxes in aggregate, and compare the aggregate amount with the sum of individual taxes charged for each geographic area.
- Perform reasonableness tests between taxes actually collected and the taxes that should have been collected. Identify discrepancies.

### (o) Financial Audit Engagements

Financial auditing is defined as determining whether financial statements present fairly the financial position and results of operations. More specifically, financial auditing provides reasonable assurance about whether the financial statements of an audited entity present fairly the financial position, results of operations, and cash flows in accordance with generally accepted accounting principles (GAAP). Balance sheet and income statements are the focus; balance sheets provide the financial status of an entity at the end of an accounting period, while income statements report income earned during an accounting period.

During financial auditing, auditors obtain a sufficient understanding of the entity's internal control structure to plan the nature, timing, and extent of tests to be performed; assess the control risk associated with the control environment; and assess the control risk associated with control procedures for safeguarding assets that the auditors conclude are vulnerable to loss or misappropriation.

The **purpose and scope of a financial audit** are to determine whether the overall financial statements of an entity are prepared and reported in accordance with specified criteria (standards). The audit scope is usually limited to accounting-related data. Financial audits are conducted by independent auditors who are "external" to the organization being audited. External auditors express an opinion on the overall fairness of the financial statements. The audit report contains the auditor's opinion. Four types of audit opinions can be included in an audit report. However, only one type of opinion can be included in any one report.

The four types of audit opinions are

**Unqualified opinion.** This is a "clean opinion." It is the standard and most commonly used. This condition applies when all professional standards have been followed on the audit engagement, sufficient evidence has been accumulated, financial statements are presented in accordance with GAAP, or other, and no additional explanatory paragraphs are included in the audit report.

**Qualified opinion.** This is rarely used. The auditor uses the term "except for" in the opinion paragraph. This implies that the auditor is satisfied that the overall financial statements are correctly stated "except for" a particular aspect. A qualified opinion can be issued from an audit scope limitation or failure to conform to GAAP and only when the auditor believes that the overall financial statements are fairly stated. An adverse opinion or a disclaimer must be used when the financial conditions are highly material; the qualified opinion is given for less severe types of conditions. However, a qualified report is still a departure from an unqualified report.

**Adverse opinion.** This is also rarely used and is suitable only when the financial condition is highly material. The auditor will issue such an opinion only when he or she believes that the overall financial statements are so materially misstated or misleading that they do not present fairly the financial position in conformity with GAAP. As a result, the auditor has determined nonconformity to GAAP.

**Disclaimer of opinion.** This is rarely used and is appropriate only when the condition is highly material. Auditors will issue such an opinion only when they have been unable to satisfy themselves that the overall financial statements are fairly presented. This condition arises when the audit scope is severely limited and/or when auditors are not independent from the client. The disclaimer varies from an adverse opinion in that the former can arise only from a lack of knowledge of nonconformity to GAAP by the auditor.

A suggested framework for describing the general audit and control procedures performed by external auditors for conducting **financial audits** is

- Obtain background information about the client.
- Assess preliminary risks and exposures.
- Obtain an understanding of the client's internal control structure.
- Develop an audit plan and audit program.
- Perform compliance tests of controls.
- Perform substantive tests of transactions and account balances.
- Evaluate test results.
- Form an audit opinion.
- Issue the audit report.

External audit reports require strict compliance to professional audit standards in terms of report content, specific wording, and format. In addition to issuing financial statements, external auditors issue "management letters" to their clients to improve internal controls.

General audit objectives for a **financial review** are

- To evaluate whether the account balances appear reasonable in the financial statements
- To determine whether the amounts included in the financial statements are valid
- To determine whether all amounts that should be included have actually been included in the financial statements
- To ensure that assets included in the financial statements are owned by the entity and liabilities belong to the entity
- To determine whether the amounts included in the financial statements are properly valued
- To determine whether correct amounts are included in the correct accounts and those accounts are properly classified in financial statements
- To determine whether transactions near the balance sheet date are recorded in the proper accounting period
- To determine whether details in the account balance agree with related subsidiary ledger amounts, foot to the total in the account balance, and agree with the total in the general ledger
- To ensure that all balance sheet and income statements accounts and related information are correctly disclosed in the financial statements and properly described in the body and footnotes of the statements

---

**KEY CONCEPTS TO REMEMBER: FINANCIAL AUDITING**

- The external auditor would most likely detect an unreported disposal of a fixed asset due to the audit objective.
- Internal auditors are often requested to coordinate their work with that of the external auditors. For example, external auditors would keep the work of attesting to the fairness of presentation of cash position in the balance sheet. Shared audit work between these auditors would be: evaluating the system of controls over cash collections and similar transactions, evaluating the adequacy of the organization's overall system of internal controls, and reviewing the system established to ensure compliance with policies and procedures that could have a significant impact on operations.

**(p) Information Technology Audit Engagements**

Significant progress has taken place in auditing computer-based information systems and operations. This includes new audit methodologies and new techniques such as participating in systems development projects, getting involved in the implementation of new information technologies, and more auditing through the computer instead of auditing around the computer. More research needs to be done to improve audit methodologies.

**(i) Information systems audit scope.** The information technology or systems (IT/IS) audit function is not a stand-alone activity. Rather it is an integral part of the external or internal auditing function (see Exhibit 2.7). Information system audits deal with the review of computer operations and application systems where computer equipment is located and computer-based systems are used. **The purpose and scope of information systems audits** are to determine whether controls over computer systems and information technology assets are adequate. These particular types of audits are conducted by IS auditors, who may be external or internal to the organization being audited.

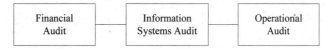

Financial Audit — Information Systems Audit — Operational Audit

**Exhibit 2.7: Integrated information systems audits**

Materiality, as it relates to IS audits, considers the issues for both financial and operational audit situations. Specifically, it deals with issues such as the impact of computer operations control weaknesses on the organization's financial and operating records; impact of system integrity and security control weaknesses on the application system's data and system usefulness to users; and impact of system errors and irregularities (e.g., computer fraud and theft, embezzlement, and abuse) on the financial statements. For example, major computer security breaches can be treated as material weaknesses of the internal control system.

**(ii) Information systems control objectives.** An internal control structure must meet several detailed information systems control objectives to prevent, detect, and correct errors, omissions, irregularities, and computer intrusions, (such as viruses and worms), and to recover from such activities to ensure continuity of business operations. Here the term "system" includes hardware, data, software, people, documentation, and the associated procedures, (whether manual or automated).

Information systems control objectives are

- **System assets are safeguarded.** An organization's technology assets and resources, such as computer facilities, computer equipment, people, programs, and data, are to be safeguarded at all times to minimize waste and loss.
- **System reliability is ensured.** The objective is to ensure that the hardware, software, and data are stable and that people are trustworthy to carry out the organization's mission.
- **Data integrity is maintained. Data integrity** deals with controls over how data are entered, communicated, processed, stored, and reported. The objective is to ensure that the data are authorized, complete, accurate, consistent, and timely.
- **System security is ensured.** An organization's assets and information resources are to be protected from unauthorized access and use.
- **System availability is ensured.** The objective is to ensure that the system (hardware, software, and data) and its components are available when they are needed, where they are needed, and for whom they are needed.
- **System controllability is maintained.** Adequate manual and automated controls and procedures should be available over hardware, software, data, and people.
- **System maintainability is ensured.** The system, which includes hardware and software, should be maintained with existing resources at minimum cost and time.
- **System usability is ensured.** For example, the application system is appropriately user-friendly, or the system design invites the authorized user to use as opposed to inhibiting.
- **System effectiveness is ensured.** For example, system effectiveness is measured by determining that the system performs the intended functions and that users get the information they need, in the right form, and in a timely fashion.

- **System economy and efficiency are maintained.** An economical and efficient system uses the minimum number of information resources to achieve the output level the system's users require. Economy and efficiency must always be considered in the context of system effectiveness.
- **System quality is maintained.** This is an overall goal. In addition to the above, the computer system should have built-in quality-related features such as testability, portability, convertability, modifiability, readability, reliability, reusability, structuredeness, consistency, understandability, and, above all, adequate documentation.

(iii) **Information systems audit objectives.** The objectives of an **information systems** audit are to

- Ensure that adequate audit coverage of major risks and exposures in an IS environment is available
- Ensure that IS resources are allocated to computer hardware, peripheral equipment, software, services, and personnel in an efficient and effective manner to achieve the IS department's and the organization's goals and objectives
- Provide reasonable assurance that computer-related assets (e.g., data, programs, facilities, equipment, and supplies) are safeguarded
- Ensure that information is timely, accurate, available, and reliable
- Provide reasonable assurance that all errors, omissions, and irregularities are prevented, detected, corrected, and reported
- Obtain the most efficient usage of audit resources (staff time and money)

(iv) **Information systems audit and control procedures.** The following is a suggested framework for describing the information systems audit and control procedures performed by auditors for conducting **information systems audits**:

- Obtain background information about the IS operations and the systems.
- Conduct a preliminary evaluation of internal controls.
- Develop an audit plan and audit program.
- Perform compliance tests of controls.
- Perform substantive tests of transactions and account balances.
- Evaluate the test results and issue an audit report.

After an audit work program is developed and approved by audit management, the auditor is ready to perform compliance and substantive reviews and/or tests.

Essentially, compliance reviews and tests in an IS environment include whether policies and documentation are available and that they are followed, and whether management approvals are obtained prior to acquiring technology assets and services.

Basically, substantive tests and reviews in an IS environment include analysis of information or data related to system/program/job/operations activities, service-level exception reporting, system logs, and system/data integrity. These are in addition to: reconciliation of financial accounts; confirmation of amounts and account balances with external sources; and comparison of physical counts with recorded amounts. Scope includes both manual and automated systems as well as manually or system-generated logs and reports (see Exhibit 2.8).

| *Compliance review/test description* | *Substantive review/test description* |
|---|---|
| Whether written IT policies, procedures, and standards are available? | System outage analysis |
| Whether written IT policies, procedures, and standards are followed? | System storage media analysis |
| Whether errors are present? | System aging analysis |
| Whether documentation is available? | System interruption impact analysis |
| Is the required documentation up-to-date? | System resource utilization statistical analysis |
| Whether security and other system-based logs are reviewed? | Transaction activity analysis |
| Whether passwords are changed periodically? | Program activity analysis |
| Whether transactions are approved? | Job activity analysis |
| Whether disaster recovery plan is documented? | Operations activity analysis |
| Whether disaster recovery plan is tested? | System activity analysis |
| Whether disaster recovery plan is updated? | IT financial analysis |
| Whether disaster recovery plan is complete? | IT turnover statistics |
| Whether disaster recovery plan is accurate? | Development of account balance or interest confirmations |
| Whether the disaster recovery plan meets stated objectives? | System response-time analysis |
| Whether system development methodology is available? | Comparison of book computer inventory to actual count |

| *Compliance review/test description* | *Substantive review/test description* |
|---|---|
| Whether the system development methodology is followed? | Service-level exception reporting analysis |
| Whether program changes are approved? | System trend analysis |
| Whether program changes are tested? | System exception analysis |
| Whether program changes are documented? | System availability analysis |
| Are manual overrides approved? | System log analysis |
| Are system overrides approved? | System performance analysis |
| Is hardware acquisition approved? | System/manual reconciliation of accounts and transactions |
| Is software acquisition approved? | System/data integrity analysis |

**Exhibit 2.8: Examples of information technology compliance and substantive reviews and/or tests**

Examples of the first five substantive reviews or tests include

1. **System outage analysis.** Outages can occur due to

    (a) Power failures (brownouts, blackouts)
    (b) Magnetic/optical disk failures
    (c) Operating system-related problems and failures

2. **System storage media analysis.**

    (a) Amount of allocated space by data set
    (b) Amount of allocated space not used by data set

3. **System aging analysis.**

    (a) Inactive data sets with six months, twelve months, or twenty-four months old run dates
    (b) Number of computer jobs run one hour or two hours late

4. **System interruption impact analysis.**

    (a) Estimate revenue loss associated with a one-hour system interruption
    (b) Estimated degree of external customer services lost due to a one-hour system interruption

5. **System resource utilization statistical analysis.**

(v) **Information systems control types.** According to the Committee of Sponsoring Organizations (COSO) of the Treadway Commission study, with widespread reliance on information systems, controls are needed over all information systems, whether financial, operational, large, or small. Two broad groupings of information systems controls can be used. The first is **general or information technology controls,** which ensure the continued, proper operation of computer information systems. General controls are designed to focus on information systems or information technology as a whole.

## Application Controls versus General Controls

The relationship between the application controls and the general controls is such that general controls are needed to support the functioning of application controls, and both are needed to ensure complete and accurate information processing.

The second category is **application controls,** which include computerized steps within the application software and related manual procedures to control the processing of various types of transactions. Together these controls serve to ensure completeness, accuracy, and validity of the financial and other information in the system. General controls and application controls are presented below along with their relationships.

(A) *General controls.* General controls commonly include controls over data (computer) center operations, system software (not applications software) acquisition and maintenance, access security (both physical and logical), application system development and maintenance, and overall IS department administration. These controls apply to all systems—mainframe, minicomputer, and end user computing environments.

**Data center operations controls.** These include job setup and scheduling, operator actions, backup and recovery procedures, and contingency or disaster recovery planning. In a sophisticated environment, these controls also address capacity planning and resource allocation and use.

In a high-technology environment today, the job scheduler is automatic and job control language is online. Storage management tools automatically load data files onto high-speed devices in anticipation of the next job. The shift supervisor no longer needs to initial the console log manually, because it is not printed out; the log is maintained on the system. Hundreds of messages flash by each second on a consolidated console that supports multiple mainframes. Minicomputers run all night, unattended.

**System software controls.** These include controls over the effective acquisition, implementation, and maintenance of system software—the operating system, database management systems, telecommunications software, security software, and utility programs (service aids)—that run the system and allow applications to function. The master director of system activities, system software also provides the system logging, tracking, and monitoring functions. System software can report on uses of utility programs, so that if someone accesses these powerful data-altering functions, at the least the use is recorded and reported for review.

**Access security controls.** These controls have assumed greater importance as telecommunications networks have grown. System users may be halfway around the world or down the hall. Effective access security controls can protect the system, preventing inappropriate access and unauthorized use of the system. If well designed, they can intercept hackers and other trespassers.

Adequate access control activities, such as changing dial-up numbers frequently or implementing dial-back—where the system calls a potential user back at an authorized phone number, rather than allowing direct access into the system—can be effective methods to prevent unauthorized access.

Access security controls restrict authorized users to only the applications or application functions that they need to do their jobs, supporting an appropriate division of duties.

There should be frequent and timely review of the user profiles that permit or restrict access. Former or disgruntled employees can be more of a threat to a system than hackers; terminated employee passwords and user IDs should be revoked immediately. By preventing unauthorized use of and changes to the system, data and program integrity are protected.

**Application system development and maintenance controls.** Development and maintenance of application systems have traditionally been high-cost areas for most organizations. Total costs for IS resources, the time needed, the skills of people to perform these tasks, and hardware and software required are all considerable. To control those costs, most entities have some form of system development methodology. It provides structure for system design and implementation, outlining specific phases, documentation requirements, approvals and checkpoints to control the development or maintenance project. The methodology should provide appropriate control over changes to the system, which may involve required authorization of change requests, review of the changes, approvals, testing results, and implementation protocols, to ensure that changes are made properly.

An alternative to in-house development is the use of packaged software, which has grown in popularity. Vendors provide flexible, integrated systems allowing customization through the use of built-in options. Many system development methodologies address the acquisition of vendor packages as a development alternative and include the necessary steps to provide control over the selection and implementation process.

(B) *Application controls.* As the name indicates, application controls are designed to control application processing, helping to ensure the completeness and accuracy of transaction processing, authorization, and validity.

The scope includes controls over inputs, processing, and output phases of a system. Particular attention should be paid to an application's interfaces, since they are often linked to other systems that in turn need control, to ensure that all inputs are received for processing and all outputs are distributed appropriately.

One of the most significant contributions computers make to control is their ability to prevent errors from entering the system, as well as detecting and correcting them once they are present. To do this, many application controls depend on computerized edit checks. These consist of format, existence, reasonableness, and other checks on the data that are built into each application during its development. When these checks are designed properly, they can help provide control over the data being entered into the system.

(C) *Relationship between general and application controls.* The COSO study went on to say that these two categories of control over computer systems are intertwined. There must be an appropriate balance of both in order for either to function. General controls are needed to ensure the function of application controls that depend on computer processes. For example, application controls such as computer matching and edit checks examine data as they are entered online. They provide immediate feedback when something does not match or is in the wrong format, so that corrections can be made. They display error messages that indicate what is wrong with the data or produce exception reports for subsequent follow-up.

If there are inadequate general controls, it may not be possible to depend on application controls, which assume the system itself will function properly, matching with the right file, or providing an error message that accurately reflects a problem, or including all exceptions in an exception report.

Another example of the required balance between application and general controls is a completeness control often used over certain types of transactions involving prenumbered documents. These are usually documents generated internally, such as purchase orders, where prenumbered forms are employed. Duplicates are flagged or rejected. To effect this as a control, depending on its design, the system will reject an inappropriate item or hold it in suspense, while users get a report that lists all missing, duplicate, and out-of-range items. Or does it? How do those who need to rely on the report content for follow-up know that all items that should be on the report are, in fact, listed?

The answer is the general controls. Controls over system development requiring thorough reviews and testing of applications ensure that the logic of the report program is sound and that it has been tested to ascertain that all exceptions are reported. To provide control after implementation of the application, controls over access and maintenance ensure that applications are not accessed or changed without authorization and that required, authorized changes are made. The data center operations controls and systems software controls ensure that the right files are used and updated appropriately.

The relationship between the application controls and the general controls is such that general controls are needed to support the functioning of application controls and both are needed to ensure complete and accurate information processing.

(vi) **Classification of computer controls.** Computer controls can be classified in different ways. Two basic categories are (1) general controls and (2) application controls, which are described above. Another way to classify controls is by their nature, such as management controls (e.g., policies, procedures, standards, separation of duties), physical controls (e.g., access to computer facilities and equipment), and technical controls (e.g., logical access controls to programs and data files, use of options and parameters). Another way is to classify controls by functional areas, such as application controls, network controls, development controls, operations controls, security controls, and user controls. Still another way is to classify controls on the basis of action or objective, such as directive, preventive, detective, corrective, and recovery (see Exhibit 2.9). The latter category is discussed in detail.

**Two Basic Control Categories**
- General controls
- Application controls

**Controls by Nature**
- Management controls
- Physical controls
- Technical controls

**Controls by Functional Area**
- Application controls
- Network controls
- Development controls
- Operations controls
- Security controls
- User controls

**Controls by Action or Objective**
- Directive controls
- Preventive controls
- Detective controls
- Corrective controls
- Recovery controls

**Exhibit 2.9: Controls by action or objective**

**Directive controls** are management actions, policies, procedures, directives, or guidelines that cause or encourage a desirable event to occur. By their nature, directive controls affect the entire system or operation. Directive controls address system usability, maintainability, auditability, controllability, and securability attributes of software as well as the integrity of data and reliability and availability of system resources.

**Preventive controls** include all standards, methods, practices, or tools and techniques (manual or automated) that will result in quality, reliable systems. Preventive controls also deter or minimize the occurrence of undesirable events, such as computer-related fraud, theft, or embezzlement, as well as possible errors, omissions, and irregularities. Preventive controls address the maintainability, securability, usability, and controllability features of the system. Directive controls can be grouped with preventive controls for convenience, if desired.

**Detective controls** give feedback as to whether the system's directive and/or preventive controls have achieved their objectives and whether standards or guidelines have been met. They detect errors, omissions, and irregularities, and identify aspects of system quality, control, and security features that need management's attention. Detective controls include both manual and automated tools and techniques. Detective controls provide some information about the adequacy and completeness of audit trails, thereby addressing the auditability of the system, as well as its securability and controllability.

## Control Assessment Challenge

The key issues are to know how much control is needed, how to measure it, how to evaluate whether a control is deficient or sufficient, and how to balance it.

**Corrective controls** provide information, procedures, and instructions for correcting the errors, omissions, and irregularities that have been detected. They may simply identify the areas where corrective action is required or may actually facilitate the corrective action. Corrective controls include both manual and automated tools and techniques. These controls address the usability and auditability of the system.

**Recovery controls** facilitate backup, restoration, recovery, and restart of an application system after any interruption in information processing. They promote an orderly environment in which all the required resources would be readily available to ensure a reasonably smooth recovery from disaster. This permits continuation of a specific activity or of the entire operation of the organization. Recovery controls include timely backup and rotation of data and program files, checkpoints, restart/rerun procedures, record and file retention, journaling, recovery logging, and contingency plans. Recovery controls address issues of system usability, auditability, controllability, and securability. Recovery controls can be grouped with corrective controls for convenience, if desired.

During an assessment of control strengths and weaknesses, the auditor might run into situations where a business function, system, or manual/automated procedure is overcontrolled or undercontrolled. This means that there may be too many controls in one area and not enough controls in other areas. Also, there may be a duplication or overlapping of controls between two or more areas. Under these conditions, the auditor should recommend eliminating some user controls, some IT controls, some manual controls, some automated controls, or a combination of them. The same may be true of situations where a system or operation is oversecured or undersecured and where an application system is overdesigned or underdesigned.

This assessment requires differentiating between relevant and irrelevant information, considering compensating controls (which are discussed later in this section), considering interrelationships of controls (which are discussed later in this section), and judging materiality and significance of audit findings taken separately and as a whole.

Rarely will a single finding lead to the conclusion of an unacceptable audit or uncontrolled area. Usually a combination of control weaknesses is required to call an area unacceptable. For example, a finding such as "housekeeping is poor in the data center" alone or in combination with "there are no no-smoking or no-eating signs in the data center" will not qualify for giving an unacceptable or uncontrolled audit rating. The audit findings must be significant. The nature of the operation (e.g., automated or manual and sensitive or routine), criticality of the system (high risk versus low risk), costs to develop and maintain controls, and the materiality (significance) of the finding are more important criteria to consider than simple observation of control weaknesses.

## Attributes of a Control

A control should be appropriate, practical, reliable, simple, complete, operational, usable, cost-effective, timely, meaningful, reasonable, and consistent.

Note that materiality is relative, not absolute. What is material to one organization may not be material to another. Audit judgment plays an important role in deciding what is material, what is a significant control weakness, what is an efficient operation, what is an effective system, and which should be considered separately and as a whole. In other words, the auditor needs to focus on the entire environment of the audited operation or system and take a "big picture" approach instead of taking a finding-by-finding approach. A cost-benefit analysis might help the auditor in the process of evaluating controls.

(vii) **Cost-benefit analysis of controls.** A cost-benefit analysis is advised during the process of designing each type of control into an application system during its development and maintenance as well during its operation. Ideally, costs should never exceed benefits to be derived from installing controls. However, costs should not always be the sole determining factor because it may be difficult or impractical to quantify benefits such as timeliness, improved quality and relevance of data and information, or improved customer service and system response time. When controls are properly planned, designed, developed, tested, implemented, and followed, they should meet one or more of these 12 attributes: appropriate, practical, reliable, simple, complete, operational, usable, cost-effective, timely, meaningful, reasonable, and consistent.

(viii) **Costs versus controls versus convenience.** Costs of controls vary with their implementation time and the complexity of the system or operation. Control implementation time is important to realize benefits from installing appropriate controls. For example, it costs significantly more to correct a design problem in the implementation phase of an application system under development than it does to address in the early planning and design phases.

There are **trade-offs** among costs, controls, and convenience factors. The same is true among system usability, maintainability, auditability, controllability, and securability attributes of systems. For example

• High-risk systems and complex systems and operations require more controls.

- Excessive use of tight security features and control functions can be costly and may complicate procedures, degrade system performance, and impair system functionality, which could ultimately inhibit the system's usability.
- System users prefer as few integrity and security controls as possible, only those needed to make the system really usable.
- The greater the maintainability of the system, the easier it is for a programmer to modify it. Similarly, the greater the maintainability of the system, the less expensive it is to operate in the long run.

(ix) **Compensating controls.** Normally, auditors will find more control-related problems in first-time audits of an area. Generally, the more frequently an area is audited, the less probability of many control weaknesses. Therefore, determining the nature of efficient and effective operations needs both audit instinct and business judgment. During the control evaluation process, the auditor should consider the availability of compensating controls as a way to mitigate or minimize the impact of inadequate or incomplete controls. In essence, the concept of compensating controls deals with balancing of weak internal controls in one area with strong internal controls in other areas of the organization. Here the word "area" can include a section within a user or IT department.

An example of a weak control is a situation where data control employees in the IT department are not reconciling data input control totals to data output control totals in an application system. This control weakness in the IT department can be compensated for by strong controls in the user department where end users reconcile their own control totals with those produced by the application system. Sometimes automated compensating controls and procedures are needed to shorten the lengthy manual controls and procedures (e.g., replacing a manual report balancing system with an automated report balancing system).

Compensating controls are needed whenever

- Manual controls are weak.
  **Solution:** Look for strong computer or other controls.

- Computer controls are weak.
  **Solution:** Look for strong manual or other controls.

- Interface controls between manual and automated systems are weak.
  **Solution:** Look for strong controls in either the receiving or the sending system.

- Functional (system) user controls are weak.
  **Solution:** Look for strong IT or other controls.

- IT controls are weak.
  **Solution:** Look for strong controls in system user or other departments.

- Third-party manual controls are weak.
  **Solution:** Look for strong controls in the in-house system in either the manual or the automated part.

- Third-party computer controls are weak.
  **Solution:** Look for strong controls in the in-house system in either the manual or the automated part.

- Physical access security controls are weak.
  **Solution:** Look for strong logical access security controls.

- Logical access security controls are weak.
  **Solution:** Look for strong physical access security controls, supervisory reviews, or more substantive testing.

- A specific general control is weak.
  **Solution:** Look for a strong and related application control.

- An application system control is weak.
  **Solution:** Look for a strong and related general control.

- Employee performance is weak.

**Solution:** Look for strong supervisory reviews and more substantive testing.

(x) **Review of compensating controls.** One way to strengthen internal controls and reduce the possibility of errors, omissions, and irregularities is to build compensating controls into operations and systems and to review their adequacy. Control-related information should be produced for review by supervisors or managers so that any irregularities are noticed for further action. Some tools and techniques that facilitate a review of compensating controls are

- **Audit trails.** The audit trail is also called processing trail, management trail, information trail, or transaction trail. The audit trail provides the ability to trace a transaction from its initiation to final disposition, including all intermediate points. Similarly, it offers the ability to trace quantitative information, such as financial totals or quantity totals, to its supporting details, including source documents and vice versa. A clear and understandable audit trail is needed for business users, management, auditors, and government agents such as tax collectors. Audit trails offer accountability, reduce fraud, show what actions were taken by people and the system, and provide the ability to reconstruct events or transactions.

  According to Davis and Olson, an audit trail should always be present. Its form may change in response to computer technology, but three requirements should be met.

  1. Any transaction can be traced from the source document through processing to outputs and to totals in which the transaction is aggregated. For example, each purchase of goods for inventory can be traced to inclusion in the inventory totals.
  2. Any output or summary data can be traced back to the transaction or computation used to arrive at the output or summary figures. For example, the total amount owed by a customer can be traced to the sales and payments that were disbursed to arrive at the balance due.
  3. Any triggered transaction (a transaction automatically triggered by an event or a condition) can be traced to the event or condition. An example is a purchase order triggered by a sale that reduced inventory below an order point.[11]

In general, audit trail references begin at the transaction level with one or more of these numbers.

- Preassigned document number
- Number assigned by document preparer at preparation
- Batch number assigned to a batch of documents
- Transaction number assigned by computer

These references are used as processing references in updating master data files records and displaying on control reports and audit trail lists.

- **Control total verifications.** Control totals, such as record counts, document counts, line item counts, financial totals, quantity totals, and hash totals of account numbers and employee numbers, can be used to verify the accuracy of data entry and data processing activities. The control total is entered with transaction data and verified by the computer system as part of its data editing and validation activity. The control totals appear on batch reports, error reports, exception reports, and other reports.

  The rejected totals and accepted totals should be equal to the total input or output. These control totals can be used by both the data control section of the IT department and the functional user department to ensure that all transactions are processed properly. In online application systems, control totals can be provided by terminal, data entry operator, transaction type, or by location.

- **Transaction logs.** In addition to acting as compensating controls, transaction logs help in recovering from a disaster, such as lost or damaged data files and hardware/software failures. These logs are: application transaction log, database log, operating system (console)

---

[11] *Davis and Olson, **Management Information Systems**, 2nd ed. (New York: McGraw-Hill Book Company, 1985).*

log, telecommunication log, access control security log, job accounting log, problem management log, change management log, hardware preventive maintenance log, and system management log. Usually these logs capture pertinent system activity data that can be used for tracing, audit analysis, and substantive reviews/tests. These logs, in turn, can be used to determine whether controls have been circumvented or followed.

- **Error logs.** Manual or automated error logs can be maintained to show errors detected and corrected by the application system. The log can indicate the type of error occurred, who corrected it, and when. Error summary reports by error type, by person, by department, by division, or by application system can be produced according to the volume of data the system collects. The error log can be maintained in either the IT department or the system user department, or in both places.

- **Control grids/matrices.** Two-dimensional control grids/matrices can be developed to show security threats or business and audit risks and exposures on one axis and the controls or control techniques that minimize or eliminate such threats, risks, and exposures on the other axis. Control grids help the auditor in understanding the relation between risks and controls and in evaluating and recommending appropriate controls.

  A single control may reduce more than one type of threat. One control may well compensate or complement the other. An exposure may require several controls to provide reasonable assurance of preventing or detecting failures. Controls could be manual or automated. Control grids/matrices are best to use in a dynamic or constantly changing environment. However, control grids take longer to use since the auditor needs to set the matrix and analyze it. Also, a more complete and clear understanding of the computer center environment must be obtained to effectively use the control grids/matrices approach.

- **Internal control questionnaires.** Many auditors use the internal control questionnaire (ICQ) as a mechanism to obtain an initial understanding of the computer center operations or a computer system. ICQ contains many closed-ended questions requiring a "yes," "no," or "not applicable" answer. One drawback of the ICQ is that the questions are preestablished and not unique to any specific environment. Because of this, ICQ is less flexible than open-ended questions. ICQ is best when used by a new, inexperienced auditor in evaluating controls. ICQ should be supplemented by other information-gathering and control evaluation techniques, such as flowcharting and documentation review.

- **Bank reconciliations.** Monthly reconciliation of the general bank account on a timely basis by someone independent of the handling or recording of cash receipts and disbursements is an essential internal control over the cash balance. The reconciliation is important to make sure the books reflect the same cash balance as the actual amount of cash in the bank after consideration of reconciling items. It also provides the verification of cash receipt and disbursement transactions.

  Since computer-based application systems are used to record and process cash receipt and cash disbursement transactions, an independent reconciliation of bank accounts performed by someone outside the IT department provides a strong compensating control for a possible exposure: perpetration of fraud using the computer system.

- **Independent reviews.** Management can conduct unannounced independent reviews when it has a suspicion about an employee, operation, or activity. Management can delegate this work to auditors or consultants to assess and evaluate the adequacy of controls over certain systems or operations. Such reviews may include the identification of preparer (i.e., verification by signature, initials, date, and system sign-on code) and evidence of approval (i.e., signature, initials, date, and approval codes).

- **Logical access security controls.** If manual controls and physical access controls are weak in certain areas, logical access controls can act as a compensating control device. This includes restricting unauthorized persons accessing computer data and program files. Access rules can be defined in terms of who can do what functions (e.g., add, change, delete, inquire), when, using what devices (visual display unit/cathode ray tube [VDU/CRT] terminal), and from where. Usually both a user identification and password code are required to access computer program and data files, which can be combined with biometric techniques (i.e., fingerprint, signature).

- **Exception and statistical reports.** These reports produce deviations from standards or threshold levels established. This information can then be used to analyze situations leading to such deviations. Patterns, trends, and clues may be obtained about the nature of transactions or operations.
- **Manual/automated reconciliations.** In the absence of manual logging of control totals between input and output operations of an application system and reconciliation of such totals for accuracy and completeness of operations, an automated reconciliation process should take place. This may include run-to-run control totals of computer records or data fields of significance, where totals from one passing or sending application program are verified by the receiving program. In this case automated reconciliations are compensating controls for missing manual control reconciliations. This reconciliation also serves as a check against unauthorized insertions of extra records or program logic into an application system.
- **Report balancing.** Balancing rules for application system-generated reports would help in ensuring data integrity and program processing logic accuracy. The balancing rules can be based on physical quantities, such as the number of units sold, or on financial quantities, such as dollars received or paid. The report balancing task can be done manually or automatically by a computer program.

(xi) **Interrelationships between controls.** Controls are interrelated. Lack of controls in one area may affect other interrelated areas. Similarly, what is an accepted control in one area may not be applicable to another area. This is because life cycles of a system or data are different. For example, a life cycle of an application system can take the phases shown in Exhibit 2.10.

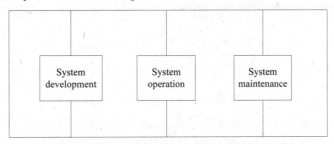

**Exhibit 2.10: Life cycle of an application system**

System development requires different controls from operation and maintenance. For example, the system development process requires more project management controls, system operation requires more operational controls, and system maintenance requires strict program change and configuration controls. However, documentation is common to all these phases, and it acts as a preventive, detective, and corrective control as well. Weak controls during system development impact both operations and maintenance activities.

For example, the life cycle of a data item (or element) can take the phases shown in Exhibit 2.11.

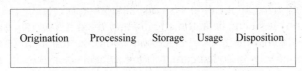

**Exhibit 2.11: Life cycle of a data item**

Different controls are required in each of the phases shown in the exhibit. For example, processing of data requires more data editing and validation controls, and data disposition requires more physical security controls, such as shredding or burning the reports and degaussing the magnetic media.

(xii) **Use of controls.** Implementation of controls requires money and other resources. Hence, judicious use of controls is needed. Proper use of controls depends on many factors, situations, and environments. Some major common considerations are

- The size of the IT department

- The size of the organization in which the IT department is a part
- The availability of financial and other resources
- The value of the assets and resources to be protected
- The level and complexity of computer technology in use
- The type of industry to which the organization belongs
- The risk levels of the system or operation
- Management's tolerance to risk levels
- Management's commitment to and support of controls
- Competitive position of the organization in the industry in which it operates
- Government, tax, accounting, legal, and regulatory requirements placed on the organization

(xiii) **Information systems audit evidence**

(A) *Audit evidence types.* The evidence produced by automated information systems, whether financial or operational, may be different from that produced by manual systems.[12] It is important for the auditor to understand these new forms of evidence because the methods used for auditing will change as the forms of evidence change. A list of **14 traditional forms of evidence** that exist when manual processing is used follows (see Exhibit 2.12). The description provides an example of how the computer can change the forms of that evidence.

**Information Systems Audit Evidence Types**

——— Transaction initiation
——— Hard-copy input
——— Transaction authorization
——— Movement of documents
——— Hard-copy processing
——— Simplified processing
——— Location of information
——— Hard-copy output
——— File of documents
——— Hard-copy audit trail
——— Procedure manual
——— Activity monitoring
——— Segregation of duties
——— Bulk processing techniques

**Exhibit 2.12:  Information systems audit evidence types**

1. **Transaction initiation.** Transactions are originated by people and entered into a system for processing. In computerized applications, transactions can be automatically generated. For example, the application system can automatically issue a replacement order when inventory falls below a reorder point.

2. **Hard-copy input.** The manual recording of information is needed to originate a transaction. In computerized application systems, information can be entered through a terminal that does not leave hard documents. For example, a pay rate change can be entered on a computerized payroll master file through a computer terminal.

3. **Transaction authorization.** Supervisors review transactions and then affix their signatures, initials, or stamps to the document, indicating authorization for processing. In computerized application systems, authorization can be predetermined. For example, sales on credit can be automatically approved if a predetermined credit limit is not exceeded. Other methods of electronic authorization include entering a password, inserting a magnetically encoded card, turning a supervisory key in a terminal, or entering an authorization code into the application function program.

   With electronic data interchange (EDI) systems, for example, employees affixing signatures, initials, and dates on purchase orders, on vendor invoices, or on vendor payments are not present because of electronic transfers of data. Authorization codes and date and time stamps can be captured and made available in a computerized environment.

4. **Movement of documents.** People carry documents from one workstation to another or move the documents by mail or equivalent service from one place of business to an-

---

[12] *National Bureau of Standards (NBS) Special Publication 500-153.*

other. By these methods, a physical document is moved. In computerized application systems, the data can be sent electronically. The data are transcribed, coded, often condensed, and then moved electronically over telecommunication lines. Examples of electronic movement of documents and data are EDI, electronic mail, and electronic fund transfer systems (EFTS).

5. **Hard-copy processing.** Processing is manually performed using the transaction documents. For example, a form might show the steps performed by a procurement officer in selecting a vendor. Normally the documents contain workspace to perform the necessary processing. In computerized application systems, processing is done electronically within computer storage by computer programs following predetermined rules.

6. **Simplified processing.** The processing performed must be simplified so that people can perform the steps repetitively without a high probability of error. In computerized application systems, processing can be extremely complex due to the speed and accuracy of the computer. For example, production scheduling can be calculated hundreds of different ways in order to select the most effective schedule.

7. **Location of information.** The permanent-type information needed for processing, such as pay rates and product prices, is maintained in manuals. In computerized application systems, this information is stored on computer media, such as tapes, cartridges, mass storage, optical disk, and magnetic disk.

8. **Hard-copy output.** The results of processing are listed on hard-copy documents, such as checks and reports. Frequently these documents contain the intermediate processing results. In computerized application systems, processing may not result in the production of hard-copy documents. For example, funds (EFTS) or purchase orders (EDI) can be transferred electronically, with output reports displayed on video screens and CRT terminals. In some systems, routine information is withheld so that the recipient receives only exception items, which require action.

9. **File of documents.** Input, processing, and output documents are stored in file cabinets or similar containers. When the data are needed, they can be manually located and retrieved from the physical storage area. In a procurement system, purchase orders might be stored in a file cabinet. In computerized application systems (e.g., EDI), most files exist on computer media, such as tapes, cartridges, and disks. Retrieving data from these media requires the use of data extract programs, computer-based record retrieval programs, or computer audit software.

10. **Hard-copy audit trail.** The information needed to reconstruct processing is contained in hard-copy documents. These documents contain source data, the authorization signature, methods of processing, and output results. This is normally sufficient information to reconstruct the transaction and to trace the transaction to control totals or from control totals back to the source document. For example, a payroll paper audit trail would permit the reconstruction of each employee's salary.

    In computerized application systems, the audit trail may be fragmented, such as often occurs in a database environment. Also, much of the audit trail information may be stored on computer media. Computerized audit trails frequently require the auditor to understand the rules of processing because it may not be obvious which processing path was taken, especially when computer processing is complex.

11. **Procedure manual.** All of the steps needed to process transactions through a system are contained in one or more procedure manuals. These are guides for people in moving and processing transactions. For example, procedures might be developed to define the steps to follow when a transaction is outside normal processing, such as a claim for a nonreimbursed health care expense. In a computerized environment, procedures are included in help screens and online documentation facilities.

12. **Activity monitoring.** Supervisors oversee and review processing to determine its reasonableness, accuracy, completeness, and authorization. For example, a supervisor would review department purchase orders for correctness and need prior to sending them to procurement. In computerized application systems, much of this monitoring is performed automatically using predetermined program logic, such as data editing and

validation routines. It is difficult to have people monitor processing as computer systems become more integrated and complex and the processing cycle is shortened.

13. **Segregation of duties.** Segregation of duties occurs by dividing tasks among people. In computerized application systems, segregation of duties not only involves the division of tasks among people, but the division of tasks among automated processing steps. For example, one computer program may process one part of a transaction, while another computer program processes a different part. Another example involves one person entering a transaction into the computer system and another person(s) changing or deleting the same transaction based on security clearances established by management and controlled by an access control security system. When the same person enters, changes, and deletes the same transaction, compensating controls such as supervisory review are needed to ensure that the person is discharging his responsibilities properly.

14. **Bulk processing techniques.** The processing of large amounts of data may involve resequencing or matching diverse data elements. This is often difficult and costly in a manual system, so it is done only when necessary. In computerized application systems, large amounts of data can be stored in a single database. The speed and processing capability of the computer makes these data available in any format desired. In a computerized environment, more complex analyses and secondary uses of data can be made. For example, large amounts of data can be sorted, matched, and reported in much less time using the computer.

(B) *Audit evidence-gathering sources.* The information systems auditor uses one or more sources or techniques to gather audit evidence during an audit (whether it is financial or operational in nature). These techniques include

- Reviewing IS organizational structure
- Reviewing IS documentation standards and practices
- Reviewing systems documentation, such as flowcharts, manuals, system/program specifications
- Interviewing appropriate personnel in both IS and functional departments
- Observing operations and employee performance of duties in both IS and functional user departments
- Using audit documentation techniques, such as flowcharts, questionnaires, system narratives, decision trees and tables, control grid charts, security clearance matrices
- Selecting and testing key controls in either the IS or the functional user department
- Applying sampling techniques, where applicable, to select sample accounts (say for confirming accounts receivable balances with customers)
- Using computer-assisted audit techniques (CAATs) to sort, extract, compare, analyze, compute, reperform, and report the required data residing on computer data files. This can be done with the use of generalized data-extraction program report writers, third-generation programming languages (e.g., COBOL), fourth-generation programming language-based software products, Fifth Generation, or computer audit software products.

(xiv) **Operating systems**

(A) *Audit objectives.*

The audit objectives to review operating systems include

- To ensure that the systems software function is administered and managed properly
- To ensure that appropriate control options, parameters, and system commands are selected in the system software products
- To ensure that systems software is installed and used properly and that only authorized personnel have access to the systems software
- To ensure that appropriate control features are included in the systems software being used
- To ensure that changes to systems software are made in a controlled environment to provide an audit or management trail

- To ensure that security over mainframe computers, workstations, and servers is adequate and effective

(B) *Audit procedures.* The audit work programs or procedures for an operating systems software review includes: security over mainframes, workstations, and servers.

### Systems Software Administration

- Ensure that separation of duties exists among systems programming, data security, database, computer operations, and applications programming functions. Inquire whether cross controls are established among these functions.
- Determine whether the systems programming management issues periodic status reports to management describing progress and current and potential problems with planned action.
- The auditor reviewing the systems programmer(s) activities and associated controls should conduct these audit procedures.

  - Inquire whether systems programmers get dedicated test machine time for testing the installation of new releases of operating systems, databases, data communications, utility programs, and other systems software; and for testing the changes to such software. Ascertain whether test members are created using systems programmer's initials embedded in them for easy identification of their source of origination.
  - Ensure that all changes to systems software are documented using online documentation tools and techniques, such as text editors and word processors.
  - Review the functions and uses of supervisor calls (SVCs), whether written in-house or supplied by vendor, and determine their appropriateness. Ascertain whether program code walk-throughs are performed on the SVCs before installing them into production status, and ensure that source code for all SVCs is physically protected (i.e., locked up in a cabinet).
  - Compare the production version of SVCs with its source code to ensure that the object code is derived from its corresponding source code.
  - Inquire whether systems programmer's access to security systems software, data sets, utility programs, and macros is limited to individuals on a need-to-know basis.
  - Determine whether sensitive programs are protected by security systems software by placing them in a protected library. Inquire whether the volume table of contents (VTOC) is protected as a separate data set.
  - Change memory utility programs, which can display and alter computer memory, are powerful and should be used cautiously. Determine whether security features in these utilities are bypassed. Inquire who has "OPER" authority to access these utilities, and confirm that computer operations management properly approves them. Inquire whether automated logs are produced by the use of these utilities, and if so, who is reviewing them.
  - Ensure that systems programmers are restricted from access to production application programs and data files and that only certain commands and parameters are allowed to access from remote areas.
  - Verify whether systems programmers participate in developing contingency plans and that they monitor operating system performance considering seasonal, unexpected demand, volume mix, and other factors.

## CONTROL RISK IN SYSTEMS SOFTWARE ADMINISTRATION

Systems programmers may have direct access to powerful utility programs and sensitive routines that may bypass security controls and logging facilities. They may have the ability to move operating systems software changes between test and production libraries without going through the designated program change control coordinator.

*Operating Systems Software*

1. **Access security features.** Interview technical services manager, systems programming manager, or the person in charge of operating system activities. Assess the following items, and note any exceptions needing improvement:

   - Systems programmer actions should be restricted with the use of passwords and they should be allowed to access the system resources on a need-to-know basis.
   - Inquire whether modifications to the object code (resulting from source code of an application program) and operating system can be controlled through the use of a program library management system similar to the source code of an application program.
   - Determine whether there is a need to use program comparator tools to detect unauthorized modifications to operating systems software in its object code form. Some ways it can be approached are to compare the total bit count at two different points in time.
   
     Any differences to this count indicate modifications to the operating system software. Similarly, security over and integrity of internal tables can be measured by reading hash totals of records or bit counts.
   - Confirm that hardware/software vendor maintenance staff is positively verified with vendor ID card, a phone call from the vendor, and/or other means.
   - The operating system should have a feature to erase all scratch space assigned to a sensitive and critical job after the normal or abnormal termination of the job. This is to prevent unauthorized browsing or scavenging of data files on the system.
   - Certain commands that turn off the operating system-logging feature should be closely controlled and their invocation should be recorded in the log, which should be protected from unauthorized modifications.

2. **Performance measurement and accounting.** Determine whether the operating system performance measurement and accounting software offers these features.

   - Analyzes disk input/output (I/O) activity within a volume and shows where to place data sets to minimize seek contention.
   - Analyzes disk I/O activity across volumes and shows where to place data sets across volumes to balance strings, which reduces path contention and queue time.
   - Simulates the effect of recommended reorganizations and calculates the percentage improvement that would be gained if the reorganizations were implemented.
   - Analyzes and simulates cache control units to evaluate how effectively the cache resource is being used. Determines the model and size of cache storage that should be acquired and identifies which volumes or datasets should be placed under cache.
   - Recommends data set reorganizations based on data set member and directory access analysis.
   - Generates history files that can be used to perform trend analysis.
   - Generates reports showing I/O volume by job name, data set name, and unit name.
   - Produces reports showing I/O volume by job for each data set.
   - Generates reports showing I/O volume by data set from each job.
   - Provides exception reports when user-defined thresholds are exceeded. This means indicating different job names contending for resources on the same volume.
   - Generates response time degradation analysis to examine online application program performance and to identify contention areas. This information helps fine-tune the system to meet its requirements.
   - Monitors individual online system tasks and overall teleprocessing system utilization.
   - Measures activity for CPU, I/O, paging, swapping, real storage, virtual storage, auxiliary storage, and workload.

3. **Buffer management.** For batch and online systems, performance is a major concern. Ascertain the need to install a buffer management system to optimize the performance of storage access methods in order to

- Reduce the number of physical I/O operations
- Reduce the CPU usage
- Increase system throughput
- Reduce run times of heavily I/O intensive batch jobs

However, be aware that there are trade-offs between the above benefits and possible increase in paging rates and storage requirements.

4. **Integrity analysis.** Determine whether operating system software integrity analysis can be provided in the following areas:

- Library analysis detecting inactive system libraries, duplicate modules, superzap activity, and authorized program facility problems
- Hardware display showing operator's consoles, and tape and disk error rates
- Detecting invalid modules, zapped-off bits
- Program freezer detecting program and data file changes
- Providing online comparison of data files, source and load program modules
- Detecting modifications to the operating system by trapdoors, logic bombs, Trojan horses, and computer viruses
- Detecting abnormal conditions and flagging entries needs additional follow-up

### Control Options, Parameters, and System Commands

Interview systems programmers to understand the control options, operating parameters, and system commands selected in the various operating systems software products. Review the product installation document and through online viewing and determine whether

- Parameters used are appropriate to the needs
- Options used are correct to the circumstances
- System commands selected are proper to the tasks
- Incompatible options and parameters are used
- Circumvention of control procedures is possible
- Duplicate system files names and procedures are used

Assess the reasonableness and applicability of options and parameter selections. Note any exceptions.

### Systems Software Changes

1. **Systems software changes.** To ensure effective controls over systems software program changes, the following audit procedures are suggested:

- Select a sample of several systems software library changes.
- Ensure that the change request form is complete in all respects.
- Ensure that the change request form is approved by the appropriate individuals within the technical support or services group.
- Verify the existence of and compliance with all deliverables as defined in the data processing program turnover checklist.
- Document and evaluate the procedures followed by quality control coordinators when assessing individual changes before migration to the production environment.

2. **Emergency database systems software changes.** To ensure effective controls over database program changes, the following audit procedures are suggested:

- Select a sample of several emergency database program changes.
- Determine if the emergency ID and password were obtained according to IT standards.
- Ensure that the emergency change request was completed according to standard and appropriate approvals were obtained.
- Determine if a migration request was submitted to the database administration group to move the change from the emergency dictionary to production.

- Determine if the same modifications were performed to the dialog or table residing in the test area.
- Determine if all changes in this category fit the definition of an emergency change as defined by the IT standard.
- Determine if the production job schedulers were contacted regarding dependent moves associated with the database change migrations.
- Review all items currently residing in the emergency library and determine their status.
- Document and evaluate the procedures followed by quality control coordinators when assessing individual changes before migration to the production environment.

3. **Master catalog changes.** To ensure effective controls over catalog changes, the following audit procedures are suggested:

- Assess the internal procedures in place to control changes to the master catalog for high-level qualifiers. Test a small sample to determine if these procedures are adequate to provide proper control over such changes. Pay particular attention to communication existing between the data security manager or officer and the technical support/service group.
- Review several changes applied to cataloged procedures. Determine if change requests were completed for those changes. In addition, review the method by which the quality control coordinator communicates the successful approval of the proposed change to the technical support group. Determine if any changes are applied before appropriate approvals are obtained.

### *Security over Mainframes, Workstations, and Servers*

- Determine whether all system activities, such as log-on and log-off, are recorded.
- Determine whether system starts and stops of sensitive processes or applications are logged and reviewed by system administrators.
- Ensure that access violations to mainframes, workstations, and servers are recorded and reviewed, including improper time of day, unauthorized directory and terminal, and communications entry mode, or failed access attempts.

(xv) **Application development.** Timely participation of auditors in the application system development process is based on the belief that early detection and correction of inadequate and incomplete controls planned during the system design phase will save time and money in the long run. This is because of the expensive nature of "bringing up" inadequate controls to an acceptable level at a later stage when the same system is put into operational status. Ideally, controls should be built in rather than built on.

The auditor's participation in the system development and maintenance project may take the form of continuous or intermittent reviews and tests. It is important to note that the application systems development and maintenance process should be reviewed against IT/IS standards or methodology.

### Role of Internal Auditor in Systems Development

Internal auditors should refrain from designing and installing any computer systems for their organizations. However, they can review and evaluate any computer system.

The degree of auditor participation really depends on the audit staff's time availability and required skills and on the riskiness of the phase and the application system. Some phases are considered to be more critical from the standpoint of the auditor's contribution to the system development process. The auditor should participate in the early phases where critical decisions are made regarding system requirements, control/security requirements, design approaches, and software testing plans and approaches. The auditor should also participate during file/system conversion and postimplementation reviews.

(A) *How much auditor participation is enough?*

The internal auditor can participate in the review of the systems development process at varying intervals in four ways, as shown in Exhibit 2.13.

**Auditor Participation in the System Development Process**

— Continuous involvement (indication of a proactive management)
— Only at the end of discrete stages (indication of a reactive management)
— After implementation of the entire system (indication of a reactive management)
— During certain stages of the development process (indication of a proactive management)

Exhibit 2.13:  **Auditor participation in the system development process**

1.  **Continuous involvement** requires the auditor to participate in all phases of the system development process and all the time. The advantages would include: improved design and specification of controls, the opportunity to provide significant suggestions to the system design team, reduced need for subsequent rework of controls, and reflection of a proactive management thinking. The disadvantage is cost in terms of time and effort by the auditor and audit management. Auditor's time has an opportunity cost.

2.  The auditor participates **only at the end of discrete stages,** such as system requirement definition, testing, or conversion. The advantages are: reassignment of audit staff to other audits and reduction in audit costs. The disadvantages include: missed opportunity in contributing to strengthening of controls, greater need for subsequent rework of controls, and reflection of reactive management thinking.

3.  The auditor can participate **after implementation of the entire system**. The advantages are: reassignment of audit staff to other audits and reduction in audit costs. Disadvantages are: expensive to add controls later, missed opportunity to strengthen controls, greater need for subsequent rework of controls, and reflection of a reactive management thinking.

4.  Participation **during certain stages of the development process,** such as requirements, design, testing, and conversion. The advantages include: improved design and specification of controls, the opportunity to provide significant suggestions to the system design team, reduced need for subsequent rework of controls in the phases participated, and reflection of a proactive management thinking. The disadvantages are: missed opportunities for not participating in other important phases, greater need for subsequent rework of controls in the phases not participated, and cost in terms of time and effort by the auditor and audit management.

(B) *Audit approaches.* The auditing of software development, acquisition, and maintenance process may require a two-pronged approach. In the first, the auditor reviews the standard systems development, acquisition, and maintenance methodology itself. Based on the review, the auditor suggests improvements when needed. In the second, the auditor reviews an actual application system as it is being developed, acquired, or maintained.

*Approach 1:  Auditing the Software Development, Acquisition, and Maintenance*

**Methodology.** A standard software development, acquisition, and maintenance methodology should contain management's philosophy, guidelines, and direction in developing, acquiring, and maintaining an application system. The directives and guidelines included in the methodology become standards and procedures for IT/IS staff and system users to follow on a day-to-day basis. The methodology should

- Describe the phases or stages and tasks or activities required, including project management techniques for successfully completing a software development, acquisition, and maintenance project
- Identify each task as being either required (mandated) or optional (advisable)
- Define the responsibilities of functional department users and IT staffs
- Describe the expected deliverables (end products) from each phase of the project

- Define guidelines for using software development, conversion, maintenance tools and techniques
- Describe the criteria for automated and manual controls, security, and audit trails
- Define guidelines for software quality, usability, and maintainability

The rationale for having auditors review the methodology itself is that proper guidelines should help systems development and maintenance staff and system users carry out their duties in the system development and maintenance process, even when the auditors themselves cannot participate because of lack of adequate time and staff. Periodically, auditors should review the system development and maintenance methodology to make sure it reflects changes in

- Software development and maintenance tools and techniques
- Control, security, and audit requirements
- Management's overall direction
- Technical improvements in hardware and software
- Business and system strategies

The auditor's review of the methodology will ensure that it is clear, complete, understandable, consistent, practical, and achievable. Here, the term "consistency" refers to compliance with the organization's policies, procedures, and management's philosophy; with generally accepted industry standards and IT/IS standards; with official directives, circulars, and pronouncements; with legal, accounting, tax, government, and regulatory requirements; and with good business and management practices. Auditors need to ascertain whether deviations from the standard system methodology are allowed, whether reasons for deviations and approvals at various levels are required, and whether these requirements are followed.

*Approach 2: Auditing the Software Development, Acquisition, and Maintenance Project.*

The auditors' review of the standard system development, acquisition, and maintenance methodology should not replace their review of the actual system development and maintenance project. There is no other way to be sure that the issued standards and guidelines will be followed uniformly and completely for all of the application systems being developed or maintained.

Therefore, auditors have a professional responsibility and an obligation to their organization to plan and schedule audits of the actual application systems development, acquisition, and maintenance projects. They can conduct risk analysis to determine which of several application systems under development should be audited.

Risk evaluations are used to rank projects as high, medium, and low risk. High-risk systems should be the first to be audited unless the risk is outweighed by other factors, such as management's judgment. Some **risk factors** to be considered for risk assessment and evaluation are

- The scope and the nature of the system
- Assets controlled by the system
- Will system results be used to make management decisions?
- Programming language used
- Total system development cost
- Total system development hours
- System impact on financial statements
- Regulatory agency requirements for the system
- Computer processing mode
- Who is participating in the system development process?
- Systems development methodology used
- Total number of programs/modules including update programs and excluding utility programs

Auditors can use the standard system development, acquisition, and maintenance methodology standards and guidelines in developing audit work programs for use during their participation in the project. The guidelines and standards give them meaningful criteria by measuring the efforts and project activities of the software development staff and system user staff in an objective manner. Without such standards, auditors' evaluations and recommendations are open to question from auditees, and there may be no basis for recommendations.

Auditors and IT quality assurance analysts have the responsibility for reviewing and testing for adherence to standards and for reporting any deficiency findings to management for corrective actions. Senior management has the ultimate responsibility for ensuring adherence to standards by both system users and IT staffs. It is up to management, not the auditor, to take corrective action in response to deficiency reports or to assume the risk resulting from inaction.

(xvi) **Auditor's role in software development, acquisition, and maintenance: Audit objectives and procedures**

(A) *Auditor's role.* The role of the auditor in the auditing of purchased software is similar to in-house application system development efforts, except for participation in the acquisition process of vendor-developed software. The objectives of the auditor in reviewing, testing, and evaluating the vendor-developed applications software packages are to

- Participate in the software evaluation or acquisition, modification or adaptation, installation or implementation processes as a member of the project team consisting of functional users, IT staff, and others
- Review security, audit, control, maintenance requirements, and evaluate software packages against these defined requirements
- Express an opinion on whether the software meets these requirements
- Review software features, functions, and capabilities to determine that they meet user needs, such as ease of use, and IT staff requirements, such as software portability, convertibility, maintainability, and testability
- Assess vendor-supplied documentation for its adequacy and completeness
- Participate in the testing of software to determine whether it performs according to its features as defined in the vendor-supplied documentation

Note that the auditor does **not** make decisions with respect to project's resource allocation and use.

The auditor's role in the software acquisition process is consultative and preventive in nature. This is keeping with traditional, moderate, and participatory concepts. In this independent role, auditors may act as controls specialists and systems consultants to the software project team in determining the adequacy and completeness of software usability, maintainability, auditability, and controllability, and in assessing security features, functions, and capabilities. Auditors may recommend that management should not select an unusable, unsecurable, unauditable, unmaintainable, or uncontrollable system, but they do not make the final decision to acquire a software package. Clearly, the final decision of selecting a software package is the responsibility of the functional user operating management and others.

As user organizations acquire off-the-shelf applications software packages from vendors and others as a viable alternative to in-house software development, the auditor's control review responsibility is shifted from in-house–developed systems to vendor-developed software. The auditor's role has changed because of increased computerization of information systems with software packages.

A major difference between vendor-developed applications software and in-house–developed software is that the auditor's review of vendor software is postdevelopmental in nature. Where validating the system functions and controls (i.e., system features and capabilities, maintainability, securability, testability, usability, auditability, controllability), and assessing the quality and adequacy of documentation are concerned, the auditor's review responsibilities are the same.

(B) **Audit scope.** The auditor needs to focus on five software attributes during software development, acquisition, and maintenance activities. These attributes are in addition to project management controls, such as milestones, planning tools, progress reports, and project structure.

1. Usability
2. Maintainability
3. Auditability

4. Controllability
5. Securability

For each of these five audit attributes, the auditor needs to ask the questions in the following sections prior to or during the software development process.

**Usability.** Is the software easy to use? Is the documentation easy to understand? Are automated and manual procedures flexible enough to handle unexpected business events? Are video display unit (VDU/CRT) screen menu procedures too long? What is the system response time for data inquiry and data editing purposes? In other words, how user-friendly is the software? A simple question might be: What is the purpose of developing a system that cannot be used easily?

Many application systems are developed in both in the public and the private sector that later are discarded because they cannot be used at all or, at most, used only in a limited way. This occurs because system designers did not fully consider software usability criteria. As a result, millions or even billions of dollars are wasted by public and private organizations.

Auditors should review the system design features not so much for the technical accuracy of design specifications but to ensure that the software is usable by the functional users of the system. It is possible that IT staff members might have taken for granted the usability features or not considered them at all when they were concentrating on the technical complexity of the system and its associated design features and functions.

**Maintainability.** Is the software easy to modify? Are the software maintainability criteria addressed during the software development process? Are structured techniques being used during the software development process? Are programs modular in nature? Is the system flexible or expandable as needed? The real question is: What is the use of developing a system that cannot be easily maintained (now or later)?

Typically, IT departments spend more than 50 percent of their operating budget and computer programmers and systems analysts spend 50 to 75 percent of their time and efforts on maintaining the existing software in an operational mode. Simply stated, maintaining the business software consumes more resources than developing new software. Of course, some part of the resource consumption is due to legitimate need for new or changing requirements, which cannot be avoided. However, it has been estimated that a major portion of this resource consumption is due to the fact that the original software was developed without considering its future maintenance. Hence, more time and effort is required when the software needs to be changed, because the system is not easy to modify.

Auditors should ask the designers of the system whether software maintainability criteria (e.g., structured techniques) are addressed and built into the software during its development process (i.e., during software requirements definition, analysis, design, programming, and testing activities). Conventional programs written using nonstructured techniques are like a bowl of "spaghetti code"; they are difficult to handle, control, understand, trace, review, modify, and maintain. When properly planned, structured techniques provide many benefits: Structured analysis produces usable, controllable, securable, and auditable systems; structured design produces flexible and maintainable systems; structured programs produce readable and understandable program code; and structured testing produces reliable and quality results and outputs.

**Auditability.** Is the system auditable? How can a user or an auditor trace transactions from initiation to completion? What kind of audit trails (paper or electronic) are planned and designed into the system? Can the system be audited in accordance with generally accepted auditing standards (GAAS) or generally accepted government auditing standards (GAGAS) or other standards? The important question is: Does the system provide enough data to the auditor to rely on the integrity of the data and the reliability of operations (computer and manual) in order to form an opinion on the financial health of the organization?

Applications software may not have adequate audit trails. Auditors should identify what audit trails are planned and designed into the system and, if necessary, recommend additional audit trails to trace transactions (on paper or electronically) from one point to another.

**Controllability.** How accurate is the input data? How reliable is the output data? Is the input data subject to data editing and validation rules to ensure the integrity of data? How do we correct errors? The question is: How do we control the system inputs, processes, and outputs to ensure data integrity?

Applications software may not have adequate internal program processing (automated) controls planned and designed into the system. Manual controls may not have been well thought out to supplement or complement the automated controls. Controls could be bypassed or circumvented. Compensating controls (access controls and supervisory/management reviews) may not be available to balance the controls between functional user departments and the data processing department. Controls may be overlapped between departments, thus wasting organizational resources. Auditors should identify and assess what controls are available in the software and recommend additional controls necessary to assure data integrity and reliability.

**Securability.** How are computer resources (programs, data, and equipment) protected from undesirable events or actions, such as computer-related fraud, crime, theft, and embezzlement? The basic question is: How secure or vulnerable is the total system including hardware, software, and data?

Applications software may not have adequate built-in security features to protect computer programs, data files, job control procedures, and VDU/CRT terminals from unauthorized access and use. Auditors should identify and assess what security features are planned and designed into the software and, if necessary, recommend additional security measures to prevent, detect, or correct unauthorized access to computer data files, programs, and VDU/CRT terminals and other hardware devices.

## AUDIT/CONTROL RISKS: RESPONSIBILITIES

- Auditors may not participate in the system development, acquisition, and maintenance activities, which would limit their contribution to the organization.
- There may not be a fallback system in place when the new system does not work properly.
- One party (e.g., system users) may over rely on the other party (e.g., data processors) at the expense of self-responsibility.

(C) *Software development.*

**Audit objectives.** The audit objectives are to review an organization's systems development life cycle procedures to determine adherence to generally accepted system development standards. The goal is to develop a usable, securable, auditable, maintainable, and controllable application system that produces consistent results to satisfy user requirements.

**Audit procedures.** The audit work program for an application system development review consists of 14 steps.

1. Review the **user service request** report in detail to determine the reason(s) for the request, user description of new system requirements, anticipated benefits to be derived, and their reasonability and attainability.
2. Review the **feasibility study** report to analyze alternative system solutions for organization problems and determine their relevancy and applicability to the organization problems and final choice. Review all cost-benefit analyses with respect to the alternative solutions to make sure that the appropriate approach has been selected. Review project scope, objectives, tasks, deliverables, work plans, and schedules to determine their reasonability and attainability.

## BUSINESS/CONTROL RISKS IN FEASIBILITY STUDY PHASE

- The feasibility study results may not be available or be incomplete.
- The assumptions made in the feasibility study may not be practical or relevant.
- Cost-capabilities-benefit analysis may not be reasonable and thorough.

3. Review **detail requirements definition** reports or documents

    (a) Determine that during the study of the current system, its weaknesses have been identified and addressed in the new system requirements or specifications.

    (b) Examine the software requirements document for completeness.

    (c) Ensure that the programming language to be used is fairly common and that programming resources will be available during development and maintenance activities.

    (d) Determine the extent of user participation required in developing and understanding the new system specifications.

    (e) Evaluate input, processing, and output control specifications, and determine their adequacy and completeness. Identify preventive, detective, and corrective controls. Recommend additional controls, if necessary. Review and evaluate the planned audit trails, security features, and software maintenance requirements. Identify the need to build audit modules or routines into the system.

    (f) Review and evaluate project organization, scope, and objectives.

    (g) Determine the degree of adherence to the project work plan, budget, and work schedule.

    (h) Verify that project management status reporting is available, accurate, and timely and that all due dates for tasks and deliverables are on schedule. If the project is behind schedule, determine the reasons. Identify applicable problems.

## BUSINESS RISKS IN DETAIL REQUIREMENTS PHASE

- Software requirements may be documented incompletely or not at all.
- Undetected errors and omissions in the software requirements specifications may cast doubt on the quality of the system.
- System user involvement may be low or only superficial.
- Project management control techniques may not be adequate or appropriate.

---

4. Review **general systems design** reports or documents for

    (a) Application systems flowchart.

    (b) Application system input, processing, and output descriptions.

    (c) Database schemas and subschemas.

    (d) Data file characteristics.

    (e) Security features, automated processing controls, and audit trails that include editing, error detection and correction procedures, batch controls, run-to-run controls, and so forth.

    (f) System test and acceptance test criteria and approach.

    (g) Data file conversion criteria and approach.

    (h) Project management written status reports.

    (i) User sign-off letters.

    (j) Evaluate the need for building into the new system audit programs or modules for collecting data during production processing, to be analyzed at a later stage by the auditors and/or data processing staff. Some examples are: integrated test facility (ITF), embedded data collection, extended record, and snapshot techniques. These audit techniques would allow timely evidence collection and evaluation of required data during production processing.

5. Review the **detail systems design** reports or documents to determine the administrative procedures for controlling revisions to design and program specifications, including the recording, evaluation, implementation cost and time, and management and user approval levels.

## BUSINESS/CONTROL RISKS IN SYSTEM DESIGN PHASE

- Software design may be documented incompletely or not at all.
- Software design may be skipped or skimped on as a consequence of time and budget pressures.
- There may be a temptation to do programming (code) first and design later.
- System design may fail to incorporate all criteria from the feasibility study, resulting in only a partial solution.
- Time pressures and resource constraints may lead to taking shortcuts in design, testing, documentation, and quality control review activities.

6. Review **program(s) development** process by observing or participating in program code review walk-through. This may include reviewing computer programs to ensure conformance with the program specifications to prevent logic errors and misinterpretation of user specifications.

## CONTROL RISKS IN PROGRAM DEVELOPMENT PHASE

- Computer programs may have been developed without program or design specifications.
- Walk-throughs, independent inspections, peer reviews, and desk reviews may not have been performed or may not have been thorough, leaving many bugs or errors in the program.
- Programmers may not have made liberal use of comments in the computer application program, making it difficult to understand the purpose of the program.
- Programmers may be accepting user requested changes over the phone, thus leading to incorrect implementation.
- Programmers may produce unmaintainable program code.

7. Review **program/unit test** plan, test data, expected results, and actual results for adequacy.
8. Review **systems test** plan, test data, expected results, actual results, overall systems testing approach, and user sign-off letters. Ensure that the systems testing scope includes all functions, programs, and interface systems. Ensure that all systems test discrepancies were adequately documented, reconciled, and corrected. The test data used in the system test could be actual or created data.
9. Review **manual(s) development** process to ensure those user manuals, terminal operator guides, and computer operations instruction manuals are adequately developed.
10. Review **training** plan and approach to ensure that training objectives were accomplished. Determine whether timely feedback was received from the initially trained users and that it was timely reflected in the training program for later users.
11. Review **user acceptance** of the system by verifying user sign-off letters. This is very important in determining whether users participated in testing and accepting the new system as their own. Review the acceptance test plan, test data, expected results, and actual results.

     Determine whether the acceptance test plan includes system's tolerance to errors and the ability to respond to exceptional circumstances, such as a high volume of input transactions, illogical test conditions, and out-of-sequence transactions processing. Here the objective is to attempt to make the system fail. In other words, users need to identify the errors in the system. Ensure that all acceptance test discrepancies were documented, reconciled, and corrected. This is the last line of defense for the users before accepting the new system.

     Determine how well the users understand their system. The difference between system testing and acceptance testing is that users may or may not participate in the system testing, whereas it is a requirement in acceptance testing. The data processing staff will be participating in unit and systems testing, and may participate in acceptance testing activities. In some organizations, acceptance testing will be conducted by an independent testing team.

## CONTROL RISKS IN USER ACCEPTANCE PHASE

- Criteria for accepting the new system may not have been defined and agreed on by the system users and the data processors.
- Software test data and test conditions may not be sufficiently comprehensive (including both valid and invalid conditions) to provide reasonable assurance that errors and problems (bugs) in the software are detected.
- Expected test results in the form of computer terminal screens, reports, and listings may not be prepared, making it difficult and time-consuming to verify and approve test results.
- Software training processes and materials may be incomplete or ineffective. Some key system users and computer operations and production control staff may not have been trained properly.

12. Review file **conversion** plan and approach to ensure that file control totals are maintained and that problems are identified, documented, reconciled, and corrected quickly and properly. Where applicable, ensure that purchased hardware/software is installed and tested properly. Verify that the results of parallel operation of old and new system are the same, where applicable.

13. Review the **production** trouble reports. Identify the type of production problems encountered, and verify whether sufficient investigation and analysis was made to classify the problems as requiring immediate corrective action or later modification or enhancement.

## CONTROL RISKS IN CONVERSION AND PRODUCTION SUPPORT PHASES

- All data, program, and job files and procedures that need to be converted may not be inventoried or known to the data processing staff and system users.
- Data editing and validation routines in conversion programs may be less complete than in normal programs.
- Operations (production) acceptance testing may not be performed by computer operations and data/production control staff and management.

14. Review the **postimplementation** report to determine the accuracy, timeliness, and completeness of anticipated and actual costs, benefits, and savings. Verify whether the user's original system objectives have been met. Ensure that any lessons learned from the current review are highlighted in the report to improve the quality of future systems development processes.

## BUSINESS/CONTROL RISKS IN POSTIMPLEMENTATION PHASE

- Postimplementation reviews may not be performed at all.
- Production and operational problems may not be logged and monitored adequately.
- System development methodology procedures may not have been updated to reflect the results of postimplementation review or to learn from past mistakes.

(D) *Software acquisition.*

**Audit objectives.** The audit objectives for the software acquisition process are the same as for in-house software development except for determining whether the software vendor selection process is thorough, that the software contractual arrangements are complete, and that the contract document is approved by legal staff to reduce business, technical, and legal risks and exposures.

**Audit procedures.** This list provides audit procedures for reviewing the software acquisition process.

- Review cost-benefit analysis documents and assess its completeness and relevancy.
- Assess whether software selection criteria are fair and reasonable.
- Determine whether vendor selection process is clear and complete.
- Review license/maintenance agreement and contract for completeness and applicability.
- Review the adequacy of system controls, audit trails, and security features within the application system.

## CONTROL RISKS IN SOFTWARE ACQUISITION

- Software contracts may not have been reviewed by qualified legal counsel and auditors, thus exposing the organization to business, technical, and legal risks.
- Software vendors may not have tested the software thoroughly, leaving obvious errors (bugs). Although the software vendor may have been in business for many years with a heavy user base, the software version that an organization gets may not have been tested completely due to constant changes, enhancements, and customization taking place. The original bad design and poor programming practices may not have been corrected due to time pressures to introduce new releases of software.

(E) *Software maintenance or program change control: audit objectives and procedures.*

**Audit objectives.** The audit objectives of a maintenance review or program change control are to ensure that authorized modifications, revisions, or changes to operational application systems are made in a controlled and secured environment.

**Audit procedures.** The audit work programs for a maintenance review consist of these steps.

- Ascertain that a standard maintenance policy is established regarding application program modifications. If a policy is not available, assess risks and exposures relevant to the situation.
- Verify whether users actively participate in program change or modification activities. Review the need for and extent of the auditor and/or data processing quality assurance staff participation.
- Where the auditor could not participate in the software maintenance activities because of time and staff constraints, the auditor may wish to stratify program changes according to the number of hours required or spent (i.e., 10, 20, 40, 80, or 120) by the data processing staff (maintenance analyst, maintenance programmer, etc.) and take samples using judgmental or statistical sampling methods. Then the auditor performs three steps

  **Step 1.** Manually selects load/executable (object) programs whose length (indicated by the number of characters or bits) or address had changed between 1 and $1 + N$ time periods (where $N$ = days or hours).

  **Step 2.** Using generalized audit software or other report writing software, lists any program library activity that had occurred against the correspondingly named source programs during the same time period as in Step 1.

  **Step 3.** Determines whether the changes in source programs as indicated in Step 2 correspond to the authorized user's software change request form.

The purpose of Steps 1 through 3 is to ensure that the object code in the production library is generated from the corresponding source code which is a major problem in the data processing environment and a major concern to the auditor.

- Determine whether each system/program revision or change is supported by a "request for change" form with proper management and user approvals.
- Determine whether each system/program revision or change is supported by adequate systems analysis and detailed design and/or written program specifications.
- Verify whether each system/program revision or change is supported by adequate testing and updating or the systems, program, user, help desk, network control, and computer operations documentation.
- Test to see whether system/program revisions or changes are made in the test library rather than in the production library. This is to prevent the destruction of production programs and data files during program changes and testing processes.

## CONTROL RISK IN SOFTWARE MAINTENANCE

The applications programmer may have direct update access to the production application program and data files although such access is logged and reviewed. The programmer may have the ability to move application program changes between test and production libraries without going through the designated program change control coordinator.

- Evaluate whether descriptions of system/program revisions or changes together with their effective dates are documented so that an accurate chronological record of the system is preserved.
- Determine whether a clearly identifiable and traceable audit trail is available for each program change or modification.
- Determine whether backup computer programs and files and documentation at off-site storage are kept current.
- Ascertain the need for the use of automated software tools to compare source code programs and/or object code programs at different points in time to detect possible unauthorized program changes or modifications.
- For critical and sensitive application systems, review computer programs manually to determine whether program changes or modifications are performed accurately and properly.
- Determine the need for the use of an automated program library system software tool to keep track of all activities (add, change, delete) to a computer program. This can facilitate detection of unauthorized program changes.
- Inquire whether a separate control group in the data center is responsible for planning and coordinating the manual procedures with the automated program library procedures in the areas of
  - Developing and enforcing standard naming conventions to establish relationships between similar programs in different program libraries
  - Developing formal procedures and forms explaining the authorization and approval levels required to transfer programs from test to production status and vice versa
  - Requiring formal recording of program version numbers, effective dates, password protection levels, and name of the person making changes to provide an effective audit trail of program modifications
  - Requiring a program turnover checklist to ensure that important steps or tasks are not omitted or forgotten
- Verify whether user sign-off or other written approvals have been obtained before moving program changes into production status.
- Evaluate whether all system/program revisions or changes are adequately handled in terms of user request, project planning, change analysis, programming, testing, documentation, and user final approvals.
- Ascertain whether it is advisable to completely redesign the application system instead of applying repeated small maintenance changes.
- Recommend developing and monitoring software metrics to increase the software development team's productivity and software quality.

(F) *Software prototyping.*
**Audit objectives.**

- To ensure that potential risks and exposures resulting from incomplete or incorrect prototype goals, analysis, design, development, and testing are minimized, if not eliminated.
- To determine whether software usability, auditability, controllability, security, and maintainability requirements are properly addressed, either prior to or during prototype work, but prior to developing the final software product.
- To ensure that the final software product is not overcontrolled (oversecured) or undercontrolled (undersecured). A balance of controls and security is required.
- To ensure that functional users or data processors do not abuse the prototype approach to bypass certain activities (e.g., system development methodology, project management controls, documentation) that are still required, even in a prototype project environment. However, the degree of detail may vary.

**Audit procedures.** The following audit work program is effective for the auditor. It should be used as a starting point and adjusted as needed. Some of the significant audit procedures are

- Ascertain how a fourth-/fifth-generation programming language (4GL/5GL) is used and for what purpose. Do not include this system in the audit scope if: the 4GL or 5GL is used for developing a new and small application system for the benefit of a single user and/or single department or section for onetime use only, the system is not a critical or sensitive one, or the system is just an automation of a previously manual system. However, use professional skepticism because onetime use systems often stay a long time and continue to run in a production/operational mode. If these symptoms manifest themselves, then this system should be reviewed now or later by the auditor.
- Verify whether the programmer/analyst developing the prototype with the end user(s) is more people-oriented than machine-oriented and has good verbal communication skills, as opposed to writing skills. Effective verbal skills are important in a prototype environment because of frequent interaction with the user. Confirm that the functional (end) user representative(s) has a comprehensive knowledge of the functions and capabilities of the department or section and can assess his department and system needs. These are important for a successful prototype.

## CONTROL/AUDIT RISKS IN SOFTWARE PROTOTYPING

- User attitudes and prototype developer attitudes may not be conducive to a good prototype development environment.
- Online system response time for the prototyped application system in the production environment may be degrading or excessive.
- Overall production system resource requirements may increase due to prototyped application system developed in programming languages that require excessive resources (e.g., CPU memory, disk space).
- Both end users and prototype developers may have mistaken or misguided preconceptions about the prototyping approach and its benefits, which could frustrate or disappoint all participants in the project.

---

- If end users develop prototypes and finally move them to production status without the involvement and participation of IT staff, report this to management and explain the consequences of such practices in terms of missing or inadequate audit trails, controls, and security features that the users may not have been aware of. Inquire whether computer operations or information center consultants reviewed the documentation of such systems and tested the software prior to moving them into production mode. Implementation controls and program version control are still needed for prototyping systems.

- Determine whether high-level systems analysis is conducted for prototyping systems prior to programming. Systems analysis is still needed even for prototyping systems, but the degree of detail may vary.
- Review the end user documentation manual or user's guide for the prototyped system that is being developed before it is moved into production status. Ascertain that it describes how to use the system, not what it does; that complex algorithms, calculations, tables, and codes are explained; and that the documentation is understandable and complete.
- Ascertain whether the prototype project team is considering controls (manual and/or automated), audit trails, and security features as a part of the prototype design.
- Suggest the saving of prototype programs, with their data files that were used to develop a model of the system. Future maintenance work can be performed more effectively using the same prototype to implement program changes and enhancements.
- Inquire whether backup and recovery procedures are included in the prototype system, regardless of who developed them (i.e., user or IT staff). This is to minimize the accidental or intentional destruction of data and program files. Inquire whether periodic backups are done and that floppy disks that contain sensitive data and information are locked up at all times when not in use. This assumes that a personal computer (PC) is used for data entry, updating, and printing purposes. Inquire whether the PC has a security package to control users through a password and log all activities.

## AUDIT/CONTROL RISKS IN SOFTWARE PROTOTYPING

- Software controls and security criteria may not have been addressed properly or were handled incompletely in the prototyped system and/or in the final system.
- System, computer operations, and user documentation may be inadequate, incorrect, incomplete, or unavailable for the prototyped system.
- Backup and recovery procedures may not have been addressed or may not be effective in the prototyped system.
- Walk-throughs, desk reviews, peer reviews, and independent inspections may have not been practiced.
- Data storage and file retention, backup, purging, archiving, and rotating procedures may not have been specified or adequate.
- System/data ownership and system usage responsibilities and accountabilities may not have been established and agreed on among multiple end users sharing the system and its results.

---

- Expand the audit scope when the prototype is planned to be developed exclusively by end users to fully or partly replace a production system that is a heavy-duty transaction processing application system (e.g., accounts payable, general ledger), and/or the system is sensitive from a financial and regulatory agency reporting requirements point of view. Notify management that the system is being developed by end users when it rightfully requires data processing staff expertise.
- A production application system can be developed using a 4GL/5GL, with parts in a 3GL (COBOL), or even a 2GL (BAL). If the 4GL/5GL portion of the system consumes a considerable amount of processing time and computer resources (e.g., main memory, disk and tape space) during its production runs, suggest ways to: redesign the most heavily used sections of the system; recode such sections as subroutines using COBOL or assembler programming languages; recode the entire system when the prototype does not represent all functions in the final system; or use modules of reusable code and change as needed.

(G) *End user computing.*
**Audit objectives.**

- To ensure that end users develop application systems in a controlled and secured manner.

- To ensure those end users extract data files or download from host computer to micro-, mini-, or personal computer for further processing on a need-to-know basis.
- To ensure that end user computing and processing work is performed according to the organization's end user computing and processing guidelines.

**Audit procedures.**

- Inquire whether data processing and senior management have issued guidelines in end user computing in the areas of system request, analysis, design, programming, testing, training, file conversion, documentation, backup and recovery, and program maintenance. Review these guidelines for relevancy and currency.
- Inquire whether end user computing guidelines are issued regarding quality assurance standards and their enforcement. The standards should be verified by the information center (IC) staff and others to certify and validate the system that is being developed. These standards include documentation guidelines: file descriptions, comments in the program code, screen formats, terminal operating procedures, error messages, error correction procedures, complex formula explanations, and use of a data dictionary.

## AUDIT CHALLENGES IN END USER COMPUTING: IIA STUDY RESULTS

The IIA study on end user computing (EUC) identified seven challenges to organizations and auditors: (1) understand the present use or impact of EUC; (2) need to link EUC activities with business objectives; (3) coordinate potentially synergistic EUC activities; (4) ensure connectivity and interoperability; (5) assist end user department managers and staff to identify business risks, control points, and benefits for adopting controls; (6) implement the application selection and development methodology; and (7) expand audit programs to include EUC when significant financial or operational issues exist.

*SOURCE: Larry Rittenberg, Ann Senn, and Martin Bariff,* **Audit and Control of End User Computing** *(Altamonte Springs, FL: Institute of Internal Auditors Research Foundation, 1990).*

- Inquire as to what types of application systems are developed by end users and understand their functions and purposes. Ascertain whether these systems can be better developed on mainframe or minicomputers as opposed to personal computers. If these systems are financial or otherwise sensitive systems, review them to determine the adequacy of controls, security, audit trails, backup and recovery, and documentation.
- Verify whether the functional user initiates a project request form describing the problem with the current system, whether it is manual and/or automated; the scope and objectives of the new system; the known requirements of the proposed system; and the projected costs and benefits of the proposed system. Confirm whether the project request is approved by the user and IT management. If there is no project request document available, assess the potential risks and exposures resulting from an uncontrolled situation, where every user develops his or her own systems without management approval and without following standards.
- Determine whether end user–developed systems use a data dictionary for standard data definitions and that the system includes controls in the form of data editing and validation routines, audit trails, and security features. Inquire whether all probable users were trained by user department staff, that the documentation developed by the users is complete, and that the system (prototype or not) is thoroughly tested by users and Information Center (IC) staff. This approach must be followed whether it is a production system or not.
- Inquire whether user-developed systems handle ad hoc query or data extracting from an existing database. If the systems do not, ascertain whether the IC staff reviews and certifies user-developed systems for adherence to quality assurance standards when the systems

    - Involve the creation of a new database
    - Are to become an integral part of one's job

- Are to be used by others
- Supply data and information to others for decision-making purposes

- Understand the organization's standards regarding data security, integrity, and privacy. Inquire what types of security and access control functions are available in a multiuser microcomputer environment, using multiple systems, to minimize deliberate or accidental errors, irregularities, and omissions. Review the security policies and procedures manual to determine whether it addresses penalties for security violations.

    Ascertain whether uploading of data to a host computer is allowed. If so, ensure that passwords are used for accessing the host data and program files. If the user-developed system feeds data to a central database, review the data control procedures in terms of data preparation, data input, data editing, and validation routines to ensure that the data are accurate, consistent, authorized, current, and complete.

- Take a sample of completed systems. Review the documentation (systems and user) developed by end users for the application that they created. Assess its clarity, understandability, and completeness. The systems documentation, at a minimum, should include: system flowchart; system narrative of its functions; input forms; input and output screen layouts; output reports; and explanation of complex calculations and formulas. The user documentation, at a minimum, should include computer terminal operating procedures including backup and recovery procedures; job submission procedures; data downloading and uploading procedures; data inquiry, updating, and printing procedures.

- Understand the security and access control mechanism in place. Determine whether passwords, lockwords, or other means are used to control access to data and program files residing in a PC as well as when accessing them through a PC when they are stored on a mainframe or minicomputer. Inquire whether the data and program files are uploaded or downloaded from the PC. Where the data are uploaded to a host computer, determine whether data editing and validation routines are in place prior to accepting the data from the PC. This is to prevent or minimize "data contamination" or "data corruption" in the host computer data files. Inquire whether a dial-up and callback procedure is practiced to detect unauthorized people trying to access the host computer from their mini- or microcomputer. Confirm whether the reports and screens generated by end users indicate the program number, name of the user who developed it, and his or her department for tracing and identification purposes.

## CONTROL/AUDIT RISKS IN END USER–DEVELOPED SYSTEMS

- Information (audit) trails, controls, and security features may not be available in the end user–developed application system.
- Data storage and file retention, backup, purging, archiving, and rotating procedures may not be available or adequate.
- Documentation may be inadequate or incorrect.
- Backup and recovery procedures may not be available or effective in the application systems developed by end users.
- Program change controls may not be available or effective.

---

- Understand how "user views" or "user profiles" are established to access corporate or division data files from employee PCs. These profiles should define the data that the user is authorized to access and/or extract for downloading to a PC from the host computer. Understand how downloading of data is performed in terms of

    - Accepting a user's data request entered via a PC
    - Verifying the user's right to access the requested data
    - Receiving the desired data
    - Formatting, converting, and transmitting the data to the PC

- Most mainframe computers use EBCDIC code for data transmission; most microcomputers use ASCII code. Most data communications software packages for mainframe computers use synchronous transmission; microcomputers use asynchronous transmission. Because of lack of standards in this area, error detection and correction is a problem during data transmission. Inquire whether the micro-to-mainframe link software package has error detection, automatic correction, or automatic retransmission features when text files are transferred from mainframe to microcomputers.
- Ascertain who owns and maintains the application system. Understand whether the software maintainer is the same person as the developer. If it is not clear, determine appropriate risks and exposures. For small systems it is preferable that the software maintainer and the developer be the same or have a backup user knowledgeable in the system. Review program change control procedures to determine whether someone other than the maintainer (preferably another end user) reviews program code and other documents to ensure the accuracy of program change.
- Inquire whether there is a policy stating that an application program or system developed by an employee using a PC or minicomputer on company time belongs to the organization and not to the employee. Ensure that all such programs/systems are residing in a central software library so that a backup is available, any changes made by one person will be known to others, and the same software can be used or shared by others to eliminate reinventing of the wheel.
- Ascertain whether the organization's policy forbids its employees from copying the organization's software for personal use at home. Where employees take the organization's software to their homes, ascertain whether management has approved it.
- If the application system is a purchased package from vendors, determine whether the vendor license agreement restricts the use of that software to a specific machine (hardware) or location. If so, inquire whether the vendor software is copied for use on other machines at other locations. (This is illegal.) Usually vendors exempt a software copy for backup from this restriction.

  Assess potential risks and exposures to the organization in terms of legal suits brought by vendors as a result of illegal copying of copyrighted software. Ascertain whether the organization's policy and applicable laws state any punishments or penalties for doing such illegal acts.
- Confirm whether multiple vendor hardware devices and software products are available. If so, determine whether they are compatible. If not, assess the potential risks and exposures. Some exposures are: lack of coordination between users; reinventing of wheels; increased learning curves; no common body of knowledge retained among users; problems with vendor support and training; data communication problems between micros and host computer and operating systems; and loss of price discounts for volume purchases and maintenance contracts.

## SAMPLE AUDIT FINDINGS: WHAT WENT WRONG IN SYSTEMS DEVELOPMENT

**Audit Finding No. 1.** Internal audit was asked to help implement a new customer information system by ensuring that conversion programs were functioning properly. The auditors wrote and ran programs that matched the old and new files and printed exceptions. Several conversion program errors were discovered and corrected. As a result of the audit work, greater reliance was placed on the conversion programs, and implementation time was reduced by four man-weeks.

**Audit Finding No. 2.** During a review of the customer information system file maintenance area, auditors noted that the only documentation for the control programs consisted of the programs themselves. And these were quite complicated.

It was suggested to the information system department that a statement describing these control programs would not only be excellent documentation, but would provide a training tool for computer programmers. In addition, a copy of the test file, developed by the IT audit staff, was turned over to information systems department for its use in conducting independent tests of the system.

**Audit Finding No. 3.** During an audit of a vendor-supplied and remote online computer system, the auditor noted the contract specified that user access to the computer system was guaranteed for a total number of hours per day. The auditor pointed out that this would be meaningless because the contract failed to include any performance standards, such as maximum acceptable terminal response times or the number of file accesses necessary to ensure that the required volume of work could be processed in the designated number of hours. As a result of the auditor's recommendations, tough performance standards for the vendor to meet were included in the new contract. Failure to meet the standards will result in heavy monetary penalties for the vendor, creating a great incentive to provide acceptable service.

**Audit Finding No. 4.** A company's sales incentive plan is complicated by the many incentive earnings determinants based on product type, product profitability, and sales volume. Incentive penalties are also provided. Using a computer program greatly facilitates the calculation of each salesperson's incentive earnings.

The IT auditors employed an audit retrieval program to test the accuracy of computer calculations under various conditions. As a consequence, the auditors found that in the process of amending the program, the company's programmers had inadvertently changed the program so that incentive penalties were no longer calculated and charged to the salespeople.

Overpayments to the salespeople totaling significant amounts were recovered, and procedures were strengthened to guard against unauthorized and/or improper changes in financially sensitive computer programs.

---

(xvii) **Data and network communications and connections: Audit objectives and procedures.** Reviewing controls and procedures in a data and network communication environment is technical in nature and is challenging for the auditor. The auditor should take a business approach instead of a technical approach. Technical assistance should be requested where necessary to supplement the auditor's knowledge and experience in this area. The trend in telecommunications is growing as the demand for network interoperability is increasing.

(A) *Data communications*.
### Audit objectives.

- To evaluate controls over data communication messages.
- To evaluate controls over data communications software.

### Audit procedures.

- Determine whether input and output messages contain sequence numbers. If not, ascertain how messages are controlled.
- Verify whether each message destination is a valid and authorized point in the network.
- Verify that the system acknowledges the successful or unsuccessful transmission and/or receipt of all messages.
- When the data communication network allows incoming dial-up connection, determine whether telephone numbers are changed regularly, kept confidential, and not posted in the computer room.
- For data entry involving network communications, determine that messages are transmitted and logged properly to reduce the risk of loss and that each message is identified as to terminal with a message sequence number and user or operator password number.
- Verify that the number of messages transmitted equals the number of messages received.
- Data communications software supporting online application systems (e.g., CICS for IBM mainframe environment) contains control program modules. These control program modules provide the interfaces between the online application systems and the operating system. Each control program module performs a specific function, such as sending and receiving of terminal messages, obtaining working storage, and loading the application program(s) needed to process each transaction.

Some reviews and tests that can be performed for data communications systems software follow.

- Determine whether accurate and current system initialization tables are used in the production processing.
- Ascertain whether adequate and effective written procedures exist to backup vendor-supplied libraries and source libraries, and verify whether these libraries are protected by appropriate security codes using multiple-level passwords.
- Review user-created tables, such as sign-on tables, to determine whether user- or operator-entered security codes are authorized and matched with the codes established in the security tables.
- Review terminal control tables to determine whether transaction coding restricts terminals to specific transaction types, time of the day, and day of the week.
- Verify whether each user is assigned a unique sign-on system of identification code and password.
- Ascertain that an adequate audit trail in the form of a transaction history file is maintained and available for printing to review for authorized accesses and unauthorized attempts.
- Review authorization levels for table updating for tables, such as terminal control, program control, file control, sign-on, and system initialization. Assess their appropriateness.

## CONTROL/AUDIT RISKS IN DATA COMMUNICATIONS

- System options and parameters (e.g., maximum sessions, maximum users, terminal time-out, terminal inactivity period, error recovery) may not be set up properly, which could affect system performance.
- Not all terminals may be defined to the session manager software, thus risking unauthorized use.
- System default values (undefined users, number of attempts to unlock a locked session, maximum concurrent applications per user) may not be set up properly in order to minimize system overhead and performance degradation problems.
- Who can override default values and parameters, who can update system option tables, and who can access system commands may not be defined clearly, or too many individuals may be defined.

(B) *Network management systems.*
### Audit objectives.

- To review the adequacy of administrative procedures.
- To assess the effectiveness of the configuration management function.
- To assess the effectiveness of the network security function.
- To assess the adequacy of the terminal expansion system and performance management software.

### Audit procedures.

1. **Administration.** The auditor concerned about the adequacy of controls over telecommunications and network facilities should conduct these reviews and tests.

   - Obtain a copy of organization chart for the telecommunications and network function. Determine whether job descriptions are current and that they reflect actual practices.
   - Inquire whether segregation of duties is available among computer operations, data security, systems programming, application programming, and network control group.
   - Understand the type of network services being used. Basically, there are three types: (1) dial-up, which is used to connect terminals from all points; (2) leased line, which is used to connect terminals from one point to another; and (3) micro-

wave, in which data is transmitted by satellite. Leased lines are better from a security standpoint than a dial-up approach.

- Take an inventory of data circuits, both incoming and outgoing, and communications equipment and software. Confirm that the organization is paying only for the items that are being used.
- Identify physical security and controls over data circuits and communications equipment and facilities. Recommend improvements if needed.
- Take an inventory of terminals. Determine whether a log is maintained showing: the location of terminals and hours of use; types of transactions entered, updated, and inquired; terminal model number; whether owned or leased; and the last time the terminal was serviced. Inquire whether transactions can be limited to certain terminals and certain times of the day. Recommend improvements if needed.
- Inquire whether the network control group monitors terminal and network usage in terms of hours of use and unusual low- and high-usage patterns. Ascertain whether security violations are reported for corrective action.
- Review network traffic volumes for identifying trends. Determine whether there is a need for alternative forms of transmission (e.g., half duplex versus full duplex).
- Inquire whether network-balancing procedures are being practiced periodically to reduce the excessive load or stress on the system. This could be done by reviewing the circuit usage and by rerouting the traffic volumes during peak usage.
- Ascertain whether terminal response time is reasonable. Identify causes for low response, and suggest improvements.
- Determine whether backup and recovery procedures for the network are included in the organization's contingency planning document and that these procedures are tested periodically.
- Inquire whether a telecommunications analyst participates in the application system development and maintenance processes for online and distributed processing systems. The role of the telecommunications analyst would be to: review network and load requirements in terms of current and future transaction volumes, and their impact on terminal response time and network throughput rate; recommend network balancing procedures and improvements; and develop a telecommunications manual for users, computer operations, and others.

## CONTROL RISK IN NETWORK ADMINISTRATION

The telecommunications analyst may have the ability to change telecommunications software and hardware without going through the designated program change control coordinator and without using the problem/change management system.

- With the use of audit software or other means and by accessing automated system log records (e.g., telecommunications logs, job accounting logs), determine: connect time, type and volume of transactions transmitted; and inactive and low- and high-volume users. Confirm findings and recommend improvements if needed.

2. **Network configuration management.** Determine the adequacy of network configuration management procedures for these situations.

- When network components malfunction
- When network components are withdrawn from service for replacement, repair, or periodic maintenance
- When nodes are added to or removed from networks either temporarily or permanently

## CONTROL/AUDIT RISKS IN NETWORK CONFIGURATION

- Node numbers may be duplicated, which makes problem determination and isolation difficult.
- Double cables may not be used, although they provide greater protection of critical links and nodes.
- Network testing and network management procedures may vary from department to department.
- Network testing facilities from remote sites may not be available.

Confirm that network management has adequate procedures to address these conditions.

- To diagnose and remedy performance degradation problems in order to provide quality and reliable service to system users
- To assist value-added network service providers in terms of accounting capabilities to support billing for services

## CONTROL/AUDIT RISKS IN NETWORK MANAGEMENT

- Network management may adopt a reactive approach, waiting for something to break down before taking any action. A proactive method of testing network equipment on a regular basis would be better.
- Network equipment may not have been tested end-to-end before it becomes operational. End-to-end testing means both the user organization and the vendor organization test the network from their respective sides.
- Monitoring of the entire network configuration would be more efficient from one console instead of several.

It is difficult to control and maintain large and varied computer networks and to diagnose network-related outages, either with traditional software or using manual methods. Determine whether expert system–based network problem management systems software is available to diagnose and report network-related outages across multiple and dissimilar networks. Knowledge-based modules correlate, format, prioritize, and present network problems and recommend corrective action in a standard method. Specifically, ascertain whether the knowledge-based system

- Produces alerts
- Indicates troubles
- Tracks problems
- Displays alarms
- Notifies failures
- Produces reports

3. **Network security.** Determine whether access can be restricted to a specific time of the day with automatic time zone adjustment.

- Confirm that access can be restricted to a specific day of the week.
- Ensure that terminal locking is provided for users who must leave their terminals.
- Ensure that terminal timeout is available to protect abandoned terminals.
- Ensure that a user ID and password are required to reconnect a session.

## CONTROL RISKS IN NETWORK SECURITY

The network operator may be given access to sensitive and powerful network commands and parameters. Unauthorized connection to business application systems could occur. Access control security could be circumvented.

4. **Network terminal expansion system.** Determine whether the terminal expansion system has the ability to

  - Produce an audible alarm when changes occur in a hidden session
  - Provide duplex support, which allows concurrent access to a single session from two physical terminals
  - Add, drop, or redefine logical terminals to the system
  - Lock dedicated terminals into specific session profiles
  - Initiate the first logical session automatically

Determine whether network performance management software

  - Measures network component response time down to the terminal level
  - Builds log files continuously as events occur
  - Provides threshold-driven, selective, online, and real-time network monitoring information
  - Supports network message and transaction tracing, display, and replay features
  - Provides through network news facility the latest status for each application system
  - Includes network trend and capacity planning reports

## CONTROL/AUDIT RISKS IN NETWORK PERFORMANCE MANAGEMENT

  - The network performance management system standards may not be established to define the ability to: select the events, resources, or measures to be monitored; specify measures or resources to be polled and recorded; and specify the threshold level used to trigger the notification of a performance abnormality.
  - Simulation models may not be used to help determine the effect of network management on efficiency issues.

(C) *System utility programs.*
    **Audit objective.**

  - To evaluate controls over system utility programs.

   **Audit procedures.** Interview systems programmers and application programmers to understand the controls in place to access and use powerful and critical system utility programs. A combination of control procedures is suggested prior to the use of powerful utility programs. Conduct these audit procedures to ensure that utility programs are properly controlled.

  - Determine whether powerful utility programs are removed from disk magnetic media and copied onto a tape or cartridge for later use.
  - Inquire whether powerful utility programs are renamed so only a few authorized people know their existence.
  - Ascertain whether a separate password is required to access and use these powerful utility programs.
  - Examine whether formal approvals with documented procedures and forms are required prior to use.

(D) *Local area networks.*
    **Audit objectives.**

  - To determine the adequacy of security controls over local area networks (LANs).
  - To determine the adequacy of integrity controls over LANs.

   **Audit procedures.**

  - Determine who is responsible for the day-to-day operation of the LAN system.
  - Verify that written procedures are available to use and operate the LAN-based application system.

- Identify who is responsible for updating the LAN system user procedures, and confirm the responsibility with that person.
- Verify that each user has his or her own log-on ID and password and that no group passwords are being used.
- Due to the added risk of shared data, determine if proper levels of security exist for that installation. Conduct these reviews or tests.

  - Consult with management and determine if there is additional need to protect individual files and databases and also data records, data fields, and even byte level in a data field.
  - Ascertain whether there is a need for data encryption to protect sensitive and critical data and program files.

- Determine whether the network operating system provides the security features to

  - Create security groups and classes.
  - Set account expiration dates and time restrictions.
  - Lock account after multiple failed passwords.
  - Designate intruder detect threshold.
  - Set log-in count retention time,
  - Impose mandatory password changes.
  - Limit concurrent connections.
  - Provide an option to allow or forbid a user to set password.
  - Set minimum password length.
  - Disable/lock accounts.
  - Require unique passwords.
  - Restrict to specified workstations.
  - Automatically disconnect after specified inactive period.

- Confirm that the LAN administrator is the only person who can add or delete server names.
- Confirm that the LAN administrator is the only person who can approve the addition or removal of a node on the network.
- Confirm that end user management approves the addition or deletion of organizations, departments, work groups, or sections, authorized to use the LAN system.
- Confirm that the "write verify" switch is not turned off to make the operating system run faster. Be aware that turning off the switch could compromise the integrity of data.

## BUSINESS/CONTROL RISKS IN LOCAL AREA NETWORKS

- There may not be a backup person for the LAN administrator.
- The backup person, even though designated, may not have been trained adequately to take over the LAN administrator's job duties when needed.
- Changes made to the LAN network may not be transparent to end users.

---

  - Confirm that the LAN administrator is the only person who can set up and change server parameters such as

    - Maximum number of simultaneous users per server (e.g., 100, 1000, or unlimited)
    - Maximum server volume size (e.g., expressed in megabytes [MG], gigabytes [GB], terabytes [TB], or unlimited)
    - Maximum number of volumes (e.g., 10 or 32)
    - Maximum number of shared printers per server (e.g., 5 or 10)
    - Maximum number of open files on one server (e.g., 1,000 or 100,000)

  - Inquire whether passwords are required to be changed periodically, forced to be unique, required to be of a minimum length, and have a limited number of **grace log-ins** allowed after expiration. Grace log-ins are extra sign-ons allowed beyond password expiration time.

- Ensure that passwords are sent down the wire in an encrypted form and that encryption is not turned off at the file server console.
- Ascertain whether the vendor-provided documentation is complete, well organized, and consistent. At a minimum, it should contain system administration, network supplements with protocol information, utility program references, system concepts, external bridge supplements, and system messages with help screens.
- Determine whether the LAN network operating system provides this information.

  - Full logs on important file server activities
  - Long-term file server up-time, when it was shut down, and by whom
  - Bad blocks that had been found on the magnetic media, their locations, and where data was redirected to on the media
  - Protocol anomalies like router errors
  - Transaction tracking service
  - Warnings on low disk space, excessive bad password attempts, and notices such as printer out of paper

- Verify the existence of an effective, clear audit trail and that system user staff and management regularly review it.
- Determine whether the LAN administrator measures and tracks network problems and failures. Specifically, inquire whether these items are addressed.

  - The total number of network disabilities per month and year
  - The number of disabilities by single protocol (i.e., AppleTalk or NetWare)
  - The number of disabilities by multiple protocols (i.e., SNA, DECnet, AppleTalk)
  - The number of disabilities by network segment (i.e., ethernet, token ring)
  - The average number of hours lost per each disability
  - The amount of damage suffered when the network is inoperable due to downtime, expressed as the number of dollars lost per hour; the loss can be expressed in lost productivity, lost revenue, or expenses for year

- Determine whether the LAN administrator monitors network performance with the use of network monitoring software or protocol analyzers. Specifically, inquire whether these traffic counts and other items are addressed

  - Number of error packets, including cyclic redundancy check (CRC), alignment, short and long packets
  - Number of workstations: total, active
  - Protocol usage: average, current
  - Packet size distribution
  - Test results for cable breaks on a network
  - Line echo tests
  - Number of frames and bytes: total, current
  - Frames or bytes per second
  - Average frame size
  - Summary statistics on network use over a period of time (filtered and unfiltered network load), displaying average, peak, and error activity

- Confirm that the LAN network file management utility programs are used to provide users and supervisors with the ability to restrict files as well as directories. Examples of file attributes include archive needed, copy and delete inhibit, execute only, hidden, indexed, purge, read and write, read only/read write, shareable. Ensure that supervisors can set up work group managers over disk volumes instead of the whole system.
- Determine whether error-checking routines are available in the wireless LANs and whether security controls can be exercised. Encryption may be necessary as well as implementing transmission in different channels.

(E) *Value-added network.*
### Audit objective.

- To ensure that value-added network (VAN) services are meeting the business needs.

### Audit procedures.

- Review VAN services such as access to the Internet, electronic data interchange (EDI) applications, and dial-in services for proper security and use.
- Review protocols used in the VAN network and determine whether they are properly configured.

(F) *Wide-area network.*
### Audit objective.

- To ensure that wide-area network (WAN) services are meeting the business needs.

### Audit procedures.

- Determine whether WAN devices, such as bridges, repeaters, routers, and switches, are properly protected from logical and physical security viewpoints.
- Review protocols used in the WAN network and determine whether they are properly configured.

(G) *Network changes.*
### Audit objectives.

- To evaluate the network change procedures.
- To assess the adequacy of network change controls.

### Audit procedures.

- Take a sample of changes implemented in the operating system, database system, network operating system, and network management system, and determine the impact of such changes on the access control security systems software. Confirm all such changes are documented, tested, and approved.

  Similarly, take a sample of all changes made to security systems software, and ensure they are recorded in a manual or automated log with request forms approved.

## CONTROL/AUDIT RISKS IN NETWORK CHANGES

- Unauthorized individuals can add or delete a network node.
- Unauthorized individuals can change a node from active to inactive status and vice versa.
- Passwords may not be required to access communications control facility.

---

- Take a sample of network change requests. Determine the elapsed time between the change request date and the completion date. Compare the elapsed time with the stated goal. Understand the reasons for excessive delays and suggest alternatives for improvement.

## SAMPLE AUDIT FINDINGS: WHAT WENT WRONG IN TELECOMMUNICATIONS AND NETWORKS?

**Audit Finding No. 1.** The internal audit department was reviewing expenses for transmitting data across a nationwide network to terminals at remote office. A comparison of all in-service terminals against the supplier's invoices disclosed that many of the terminals charged for having been in service had, in fact, been disconnected. After obtaining copies of requests for disconnection to substantiate the dates, the internal auditor and senior management of the company visited the supplier to discuss this discrepancy. The discussion resulted in the supplier reimbursing the company a significant amount in retroactive billing adjustments.

**Audit Finding No. 2.** During the audit of telephone usage, the auditors found that employees will call direct instead of WATS lines because of convenience. The auditors also found that employees who required a lot of long-distance calls for their work did not have direct access to the WATS lines and had to make long-distance calls through the office switchboard operator. Other employees had direct access, but many of them did not know how to use WATS, and they also placed long-distance calls through the switchboard operator.

The auditor recommended that more WATS-access lines are installed and a WATS-training program is developed. The adoption of these recommendations resulted in a 25% decrease in long-distance telephone costs and a 29% increase in the use of the WATS lines.

*SOURCE: E. Theodore Keys, Jr., ed.,* **The Round Table, How to Save Millions** *(Altamonte Springs, FL: IIA, 1988).*

---

(xviii) **Voice communications: Audit objectives and procedures**
**Audit objectives.**

- To ensure that all risks and opportunities in using voice communications are fully understood before implementation.
- To ensure that quality of service issues, such as latency, jitters, packet losses, and bandwidth congestion, are understood.
- To ensue that proper controls are in place over voice mail to prevent toll fraud.

**Audit procedures.**

- Determine whether all risks and opportunities in using voice communications are documented and distributed.
- Determine small packets, as opposed to large packets, are transmitted through the voice network to reduce latency and bandwidth congestion.
- Determine whether forward error correction and packet loss concealment schemes are implemented to reduce loss of packets.
- Determine whether header compression techniques are implemented to reduce jitters.
- Determine whether controls such as personal identification numbers (PINs) to voice mailboxes are periodically changed, that all unused or unassigned mailboxes are removed, that collect calls are restricted, and that telephone bills are reviewed.

(xix) **System security.** System **security** or logical security is divided into two categories: (1) software security and (2) data security. Within software security, implementation of logical access control (external) security software is discussed first. Then general audit procedures for security controls over systems software, applications software, data communications software, and computer terminals are presented. Firewalls work well with logical security. Physical access security and environmental controls are also discussed as part of the systems security.

(A) *Software security controls review: Access control security software review—Audit objectives and procedures.*
**Audit objectives.**

- To determine whether options and parameters selected in the access control security software are relevant and useful.
- To ensure user profiles established for the information technology staff and functional users for accessing program files are relevant and current.
- To ensure system libraries and user exits are controlled properly.
- To determine whether security software is adequately protected, including related tables.
- To ensure configuration management is properly handled with respect to security.

**Audit procedures**

A. **Implementation of logical access control security software**

1. **Control options and parameters.** In order to evaluate the options and parameters selected in the access control security systems software, these audit procedures are suggested.

   - Obtain a printout of currently used system options and parameters. Some options control the various logging functions, access class protection functions, security modeling functions, and password functions.
   - Review the option settings to be sure no integrity exposures exist.
   - Determine if the password rules and options are adequate to ensure integrity and confidentiality of passwords.
   - Verify access to tape data sets is controlled by security software. Ensure tape bypass label processing (BLP) option is under the control of security software.
   - Verify control over passwords is properly exercised.
   - Verify all disk data sets are protected through the security software.
   - Verify all other required options are properly selected.

2. **Interface validations.** In order to determine if security software performs appropriate validations for interface systems (e.g., CICS, IMS, IDMS, TSO, and CMS), these audit procedures are suggested.

   - Review the table to verify no unnecessary access is given to sensitive or critical data sets.
   - Verify that the online teleprocessing monitor (e.g., CICS) is properly controlled through security software in terms of access to sign-on tables, key parameters, files, transactions, records, and programs.
   - Verify that the database management system (e.g., IMS, IDMS) is properly controlled through security software in terms of tasks, programs, subschemas, and control areas.
   - Verify whether security software controls online programming and development facilities (e.g., TSO, CMS) to limit access to critical and sensitive commands and options.
   - Verify that the interfaces between security software and other systems software products are properly controlled by examining the interface and determining if security software is called for validations of every sign-on attempt.
   - Determine whether online programming facility (e.g., TSO) users defined in the system library are also defined to the security systems software. Evaluate the reasons for any user not defined to the security system.

## AUDIT/CONTROL RISKS IN EXTERNAL SECURITY SOFTWARE

The computer operator may have the option of making the external security software inactive at the time of initial program load.

---

3. **Data ownership and separation of storage resources.** In order to determine who owns the data and to evaluate the separation of storage resources, these audit procedures are suggested.

   - Enter the critical commands from the master console and review the listings for appropriate information.

     - Determine who owns all system disk volumes. Assess whether the ownership is authorized.
     - Determine ownership of all disk/tape data sets by data set name prefix. Assess whether the ownership is authorized.

   - Review the list of all volume profiles and determine that adequate separation of data volumes exist among the various storage media.

4. **Access security rules.** In order to ensure the design and structure of access security rules and user profiles are proper, these audit procedures are suggested.

   - Verify that the log-on IDs used for production jobs are properly defined.
   - Verify that the security database is efficiently and effectively organized from most general to most specific levels of hierarchy.

5. **System and user exits.** To ensure that all operating system and user exits in the security software are properly documented and controlled, these audit procedures are suggested.

   - Identify all active operating system and user exits.
   - Determine what security software exits are used. These exits can control dataset naming corrections, password duplication.
   - Request and examine source code for each active exit for the presence of comments.
   - Evaluate whether these exits are properly controlled.
   - Determine that exit usage is well documented as to its purpose and its effect on the system.

6. **Sensitive privileges.** To ensure that security rules appropriately restrict sensitive privileges, data sets, and utility programs, these audit procedures are suggested.

   - Verify that sensitive privileges are given only to those who need them.
   - Verify that only security administrators at both central and local computer centers have these privileges.
   - Obtain the data set names for the two or three critical application system master files, and verify that these sensitive datasets are adequately protected.
   - Verify that sensitive utility programs are appropriately restricted. These programs can bypass security validations. Determine whether these utility programs are specified as usable only out of a controlled library by a specific log-on ID.

## CONTROL/AUDIT RISKS IN ACCESS PRIVILEGES

- Access control mechanisms cannot be relied on in most cases to protect against an outsider penetration or an insider attack.
- Even the most secure systems are vulnerable to abuse by insiders who misuse their access privileges.
- Detecting legitimate users who abuse their access privileges is difficult, if not impossible.
- Insiders could subvert the security mechanisms so as to masquerade as other users or to evade the security controls altogether.

7. **Protection over programs and libraries.** These audit procedures are suggested to ensure important programs and libraries are secured.

   - Determine who has bypass privileges.
   - Determine if all sensitive programs and libraries are properly protected.
   - Determine if there are any unprotected data sets.

## CONTROL RISK IN SYSTEM LIBRARIES

Too many individuals may have an update access to installation-defined authorized libraries, system parameter libraries, and system data sets.

8. **Access controls over production libraries.** In order to determine whether adequate protection exists for system and production libraries, these audit procedures are suggested.

- Obtain a copy of the data set report. Determine if adequate protection exists for the critical application system production data sets.
- Run data set profile listings on all critical application system data set high-level qualifiers. Determine if a generic code exists for the high-level qualifier to accommodate all data set names not otherwise covered under discretes or qualified generic profiles.
- Determine which disk data sets are defined to the security software. This is a critical audit procedures in the review of either an application or a data center.
- Determine which rights users are granted to data sets. For example, update or alter access to the production job control. Ensure that program libraries are limited to a few individuals.
- Determine what statistics are being kept for analyzing access practices.
- Determine what audit records are being logged to the system logging facility. Determine whether records are maintained for successes and failure access attempts, which can later be reported by either write or read accesses.
- Verify when the passwords were last changed and what the password change interval is for each user.

9. **System logging of events.** In order to ensure all required system records are being logged, these audit procedures are suggested.

- Examine the system logging facility parameters to determine if a computer operator can turn off recording.
- Verify that the system logs these records.

  - Unauthorized attempts to enter the system
  - Authorized and unauthorized attempts to access system-protected resources
  - Authorized and unauthorized attempts to modify profiles on data sets or users
  - Names of each security data set and the data set volume ID

## CONTROL RISKS IN ACTIVITY LOGGING

- Security control procedures could be lax in terms of who can add or delete authorized libraries or who can add, delete, or modify programs in an authorized library.
- External security software may not protect the operating system–based started tasks, system activity logging data sets, system volumes, generation data group records, deletion of user catalogs, and modification and deletion of master catalogs.
- The system logging journal contents may be partially or totally lost in a disk/system crash caused accidentally (e.g., by a power failure to a volatile storage device) or deliberately (e.g., by someone trying to avoid detection).
- Logging of important security violation records produced by the external security software may have been suppressed, allowing security breaches to go unnoticed.

- Ensure that changes to the security database file are captured in the recovery and logging file.
- Determine which reports are being generated from the security software. Inquire how many of these reports are reviewed by the security administrator.

10. **Operational procedures.** In order to ensure proper operational procedures are in place, working, and documented, the following audit procedures are suggested:

- Obtain a copy of security software recovery procedures and review them for adequacy. Inquire whether these recovery procedures were tested to make sure they would work if needed.
- Obtain a copy of procedures used to define security software "exit" specifications. "Exit" specifications should be developed by the data security function

and actual program code developed by the technical services/support function. If no procedures exist, obtain a copy of exit specifications for the current exits and the test plan and sign-off by the data security function.

11. **Controls over security administration.** To ensure the security administration function is properly controlled, these audit procedures are suggested.

- Determine whether documented procedures are available.
- Ensure all terminated employees are no longer active in the security system.
- Obtain a listing from security software showing who has the ability to update the security database. Verify proper request forms are in place to request addition, deletion, and change of users in the security system.
- Ensure the user verification process uniquely identifies each user to the system and the resources he can access.

12. **Administrative procedures.** In order to ensure proper administrative procedures are in place, working, and documented, these audit procedures are suggested.

- Determine the adequacy of procedures for accessing the security database and application systems in production status during normal and emergency situations.
- Obtain a copy of procedures used to review security violation of protected production data sets. Verify these procedures include a daily review of production dataset violations.
- Obtain a copy of security violation follow-up procedures to ensure violations are properly handled once identified. This should include determination of type of violation, severity, and written response requirements based on type and security of violation.
- Test the security system's decentralization of administrative function for adequacy. Determine if the scope of authority for the decentralized administrative function includes only their data.
- Determine whether the security/console log is being printed, reviewed, and initialed on a daily basis.
- Evaluate whether an access control security package is implemented and operated properly to control access to data files, whether database or nondatabase.

13. **Audit trails and reports.** To ensure that all critical audit trail reports, utility programs, and security reports are defined and utilized, these audit procedures are suggested.

- Prepare a workpaper schedule listing all critical reports and utility programs.
- Compare the schedule to actual reports and utility programs used, noting any problems and exceptions.
- Inquire whether data security staff and management review all major security violations and audit trail reports and that they follow up on major problems.

B. **General audit procedures for security over systems software**
   Conduct these reviews and/or tests for security over systems software.

- Determine whether management policies and procedures regarding the access to and use of computer programs have been disseminated.
- Determine whether one or more of the following identification and authentication techniques (a type of combination controls) are used prior to accessing system resources and facilities:

  - Hand-held password-generating devices
  - Multiple-level passwords
  - Identification cards and badges (electronic or mechanical: smart cards or magnetic stripe cards)
  - Reading of eyes

- Reading signature, thumb print, or palm print
- Voice recognition
- Other personal information not easily known to others, such as maiden name, mother-in-law's or father-in-law's name
- Data encryption and scrambling techniques

- Determine whether adequate and clear "electronic separation of duties" is maintained in the application system by establishing password—person—program—terminal—transaction activity matrix relationships. Some examples of transaction activity in computer programs are read only, add, delete, and modify.
- For installations using program library management systems software, ascertain whether data processing management has selected proper default options and indeed is making use of all appropriate control features included in the vendor software. Ascertain the reasons for nonselection of any control features. Ensure that the library management systems software updates and controls both source and object code program libraries; reports all changes, additions, and deletions; and saves prior versions.
- Determine the existence of (or need for) a separate control group to develop, maintain, and control manual procedures and standards required to integrate with library management system procedures. Ascertain whether all program changes are approved and monitored by this control group. Verify whether a program turnover checklist is prepared and followed effectively.
- Ascertain whether only authorized IT staff and IT audit staff are using sensitive utility programs only as required for approved/authorized functions. This is to eliminate the potential misuse of powerful utility programs (e.g., DITTO, SUPER ZAP in the IBM mainframe environment) to bypass or override controls in the application or operating system.

## AUDIT/CONTROL RISK IN UTILITY PROGRAMS

External security software may not protect powerful utility programs, such as the tape initialization program that can destroy tape labels and tape contents and the utility program that can modify the contents of an operating system or application program.

---

- Verify whether a manual log is maintained and reviewed by management describing the reasons for and use of utility programs with control override features.
- For installations using program library management systems software with multiple program libraries, obtain a printout of the volume table of contents (VTOC) for all volumes existing in the system.

    Ascertain whether library and program names and cataloging procedures conform to the established standards. This is to ensure there are no duplicate program names between and within the libraries. Review program change procedures in effect for each type of library, and evaluate the controls practiced to prevent incorrect program versions from being placed into production status. Review the library problem and incident log and evaluate the corrective actions taken.
- For installations having no automated program library systems software, determine if there is a need for it to control updating of both source and object code program libraries, to report all program changes and program version numbers, and to archive prior versions.

## AUDIT/CONTROL RISKS IN PROGRAMMING

- Application programmers may be given the ability to transfer programs between test and production libraries once the development or maintenance work has been completed when, in fact, the operations staff or quality assurance staff should be performing such transfers.

- Unauthorized libraries could be present.
- Unauthorized personnel may purge security rule tables or change security options and parameters for their own benefit.
- Systems programmer's actions may not be auditable at all or may be difficult to audit.

---

- Enter a few innocent or null unauthorized processing jobs and determine whether they are purged from the system. Select a few authorized production jobs and determine whether job priority classes can be changed. Assess the appropriate risks and exposures.
- Review the adequacy of security features, such as backup, restart, rerun, and recovery procedures, for a few critical application systems.

C. **General audit procedures for security over applications software**

1. **General access controls.** Interview the data security officer or person in charge of the security administration function, assess the following issues, and note any exceptions for improvement:

   - Access to all application programs in the production operations environment should be limited to only the programmers responsible for maintaining them, and access privilege rules should be defined in terms of who can read, write, copy, rename, allocate, execute, catalog, delete, and change.
   - Sensitive and critical application programs have restricted rules, such as execute only. Read and copy commands should not be permitted by anyone except the authorized maintenance programmer. Access to such programs should be allowed only at certain times of day and certain days of the week.
   - All versions of programs, whether new or renamed, should receive the same kind of access control protection at all times.

## AUDIT/CONTROL RISKS IN INSIDERS AND OUTSIDERS

- A skilled penetrator could disable or bypass the audit and security mechanisms in order to work undetected.
- Insiders are the most risky of all from a security point of view. They are often shielded by the informal trust system.
- Data input and update areas are the most common places for conducting illegal activities such as fraud and theft.

---

- System and program documentation manuals should be reasonably protected from unauthorized use.
- For both database and nondatabase application systems, a log file should be maintained to post each transaction or, alternately, an image of the transaction record both before and after it is updated in the master file. The log file can be used to back-out transactions, backup transactions, and facilitate recovery and restart processing.
- For application systems involving input data collection or data entry activities through point-of-sale, automatic teller machines, or touch-tone telephone media, incoming data is recorded on mirrored disks (data stored simultaneously in at least two places and on two separate magnetic media).

2. **Access controls over production program changes.** Conduct these audit procedures for assessing security controls over changes to production programs.

   - Assess whether program change control procedures are in place. Inquire whether production operations or application system maintenance staff periodically calculate hash totals of characters or bit counts in production application programs to ensure that there are no unauthorized modifications that might represent computer-related fraud or some other types of abuse.

- Ask whether automated program library management software is in place or being contemplated. Verify whether password-type controls are used to access the library management software through which changes to applications software are made and logged. Determine the possibility of printing program changes (e.g., statement or code additions, deletions, or changes) as an output from the library management software for programmer verification to ensure the accuracy of program changes.

3. **Audit testing of security controls.** Take a sample of application systems in production status. Interview the appropriate functional users and assess the following areas. Note any exceptions for improvements.

  - An electronic separation of duties should be available using the access control security system and application system features. This includes restricting employees to functions such as add, change, delete, read, write, copy, rename, print, inquire, browse, and override errors. When such restrictions cannot be implemented, the transaction logging facility should be turned on.
  - The access privileges granted to employees should be in line with their job descriptions, and all employees listed in the user profiles for an application system should be actively working for the organization.
  - All sensitive blank input forms, such as purchase orders, invoices, blank checks, securities, and other negotiable documents, should be kept in a locked cabinet or similar storage to prevent unauthorized use.
  - Employees should be encouraged to view reports via VDU/CRT terminals rather than automatically receiving hard copy output. Not only does this approach save time and money involved in printing the report, but it also provides additional security because a password is required to print a computer report or to run a job.
  - Sensitive computer and noncomputer reports should be marked or stamped as such and should receive appropriate protection when they are received from other departments or travel from one person to another within the company.
  - All unused and expired reports, computer-generated and otherwise, should be destroyed by shredding, burning, or other means to protect data confidentiality and sensitivity.
  - All required source documents, input forms, tax records, property records, contracts, and government-related documents should be retained according to the established guidelines. These should be cross-referenced to the department of origination, transaction activity period, and retention date. These records should be easily and rapidly retrievable. When a sample is taken from paper media, electronic media, or mechanical media, it should be possible to retrieve the required records by using an inventory list.

D. **General audit procedures for security over data communications software**

Conduct these reviews and/or tests for security over data communications software.

- To ensure the cryptographic device has not been corrupted or replaced with a bogus service, determine whether the host computer is required to authenticate itself to the cryptographic device (and vice versa). Similarly, determine whether a cryptographic device is required to authenticate itself to the user (and vice versa). This would amount to four separate authentication procedures that would have to be performed in order to implicitly authenticate the user to the host and vice versa.
- When the data communication network allows incoming dial-up connection, determine whether telephone numbers are changed regularly, kept confidential, and not posted in the computer room.
- Take an inventory of data communications network nodes, lines, and equipment and compare to inventory records. Note any exceptions.

## AUDIT/CONTROL RISKS IN DATA COMMUNICATIONS

- In a dial-up environment, the length of the access code may be too short (e.g., two or three characters), or one that is easily guessed.
- A special prefix telephone number may not be used for dial-up lines. Sequential numbers help individuals guess other network access phone numbers.
- The "help" function on a sign-on screen could be helping both authorized (legitimate) and unauthorized individuals.
- The modem might have been set to activate after one or two rings so that hackers trying to guess at the phone number would succeed. Try five or six rings so that hackers will go to other target locations.
- Each node may not be carefully protected to prevent access to another network node.
- Network users may not be informed of the status of network resources.
- Components including application-related problems.
- Unauthorized users and operators may have access to network software distribution and updating, and network resources.

---

- Ascertain whether the network hardware and software were changed to take advantage of price reductions and technical improvements.
- Identify any physical security controls, such as locks and keys over the data communications hardware and related equipment.

E. **General audit procedures for security over computer terminals**
   Conduct these reviews and/or tests for security over computer terminals.

- Determine whether management policies and procedures regarding the access to and use of VDU/CRT terminals have been disseminated.
- Ascertain whether written procedures are available for data entry, update, print, and inquiry activities performed through the use of terminals. Test their adequacy and currency.
- Verify whether there is a dedicated printer or terminal assigned to receive all terminal security and access control violation messages. Review these messages for a selected time period and determine whether appropriate corrective actions were taken.
- Ascertain the frequency of password changes. Review the procedures and methods for assigning, scheduling, recording, and communicating password changes. Ensure that the password algorithm is sufficiently complex that it would not be too obvious.
- Ascertain whether terminals have a nonprinting (display) feature when entering user or operator passwords to prevent observation of passwords by others.
- Conduct tests to determine whether terminals become inactive or inoperative after some (three) unsuccessful attempts to sign-on or some time (three minutes), whichever comes first.
- Verify whether each terminal user's identity and authorization levels are established in accordance with the data available from the terminal. Take an inventory of terminals with number of users with access levels. Identify the sensitivity and volume of data being handled and importance to the organization. Inquire whether these terminals are limited to certain hours per day, by the type of transaction entered, or by the location of the terminal.
- Ascertain whether terminals or other devices are authenticated to the computer system through some kind of identification code.
- Evaluate the overall procedures followed in controlling the physical access to computer terminals. Determine whether they are adequate.

(B) *Data security controls review: Audit objectives and procedures.*

### Audit objectives.

- To ensure user profiles established for the IT staff and functional users for accessing data files are relevant and current.
- To determine the adequacy of audit trails and reports, access controls over production libraries, system logging procedures, and granting of sensitive privileges, and to ensure data integrity.

### Audit procedures.

1. **General procedures.** Conduct these audit steps for obtaining a general understanding of controls and procedures that would affect data security.

   - Determine whether management policies and procedures regarding the access to and use of computer data files have been disseminated.
   - Inquire whether the owner of data is identified; who in turn decides who, when, and for what purposes access is permitted to the owner's production data sets or files and programs. Inquire whether data are classified as highly critical, critical, noncritical, or by some other method.
   - Take an inventory of critical data files. For each, identify

     - Owner of the file, and criticality of the file
     - The name of the application system that accepts this file as input or output
     - Reasons for creating and maintaining the data file
     - Security and backup requirements for this file
     - Who can use and modify the file and any limits placed on the total space that can be dynamically allocated to a user so an equitable space allocation service can be provided to all users

   - Ascertain whether a tape librarian function monitors: issuances, returns, and storage of computer data files (tapes, disks, optical disks, diskettes); computer programs (applications and systems software); and documentation (system, program, computer operations, and user) manuals. Reconcile actual computer data files, computer program files, and documentation manuals to the inventory records or logs maintained by the tape librarian. Determine their accuracy, completeness, and currency.
   - Verify whether maintenance procedures call for a regular cleaning and certification of magnetic tape files. Similarly, disk files should be tested periodically. Ascertain whether tape files are scratched or erased before cleaning and recertification. Magnetic tape files can be degaussed before disposition or cleaned by overwriting one time with any one character. Similarly, magnetic disk files can be cleaned by overwriting three times with numbers 1, 0, and any special character in that order.
   - Where applicable, select a random sample of tape files to verify they contain **external labels**. Conduct tests to determine whether label contents are accurate.

### Contents of an External Label

External labels for tape file contain information such as job identification, file names as used by the program, tape density, creating program identification number, creation date, scratch date, or just a reel number.

   - Ascertain that internal file header and trailer records are verified by either operating system or application system.
   - Verify whether computer data file retention periods agree with the requirements of government laws and regulations, other regulatory agencies, and established management policies and procedures. Ascertain that job accounting data or sys-

tem logging data are retained at least six months at a detailed level and in a summary form after that time.

- Verify whether multiple users are sharing the database. Identify the primary and secondary users. Ascertain whether user conflicts exist regarding the use of data. Verify whether user conflicts are resolved properly and in a timely manner by the database administrator.
- For database systems, evaluate the adequacy of edit and validation rules applied to critical and sensitive data elements in the data dictionary.
- For critical and sensitive data elements in database systems, trace key data elements through the application system by reviewing programs, data files, and reports. Determine their accuracy and consistency.
- Review issue and change practices for password and other system identification codes. Verify that passwords are issued on an individual employee basis, that their length is between 6 and 10 characters randomly generated in an alpha/numeric combination, that they would be difficult to guess, and that they do not contain obvious words, such as nicknames, pet names, or date of birth. Determine whether there is a combination of identification codes available (e.g., user ID and password, password and access card) instead of a single type of identification. Review password tables and determine whether they contain passwords for terminated employees.

    Determine whether adequate and clear electronic separation of duties are maintained in the application system by establishing password—person—data—terminal—transaction activity matrix relationships. A typical transaction activity could be to add, change, delete, update, inquire, and retrieve data from computer files. Verify with users whether these matrix relationships are actually followed. Identify any inadequacies and inconsistencies to ensure no single person has complete control and access over entire transaction processing activities. Determine the need for additional or compensating controls if existing controls are not adequate and effective.

- For installations having no automated file management systems software, determine if there is a need for access to computer data files to be controlled and to provide management, audit, processing, transaction, or information trails.
- Ensure that live data is not used for the testing of application systems.
- Determine whether production data is identified and either physically or logically segregated from designated test data by placing them in separate data libraries.
- Verify whether the backup procedures manual contains

    - Data set name, its owner, and the device name
    - Frequency of backup (daily, weekly, monthly), person responsible for backup, rotation scheme (grandfather—father—son or generation levels), and retention periods (six months, year)
    - Backup media issue, return, and scratch procedures
    - Tape certification and cleaning procedures

- Evaluate the overall procedures followed in controlling access to computer data files. Determine whether they are adequate.

2. **Data classification.** Conduct these audit steps to evaluate the data classification system in place.

    - Verify that policy and the procedures manual call for identification of sensitivity and criticality levels of data and protection of sensitive data from beginning to end.
    - Determine whether users have classified data according to sensitivity and criticality levels (e.g., sensitive, confidential) and protect data according to classification scheme at various phases of the data life cycle. Identify whether document/file security protection levels match with the sensitivity and criticality levels.

- Where necessary, ensure data are classified as confidential, secret, top secret, sensitive, and so on. Those data files are internally or externally marked as such, and access restrictions to those files are closely controlled and monitored.

3. **Database user profiles.** If there is a database function, interview the database administrator (DBA) to assess security-related controls over the use of database files.

- Ascertain whether user profiles or user views (subschemas of the database) are created for each user according to his or her job description.
- Determine whether an individual is given access privileges to data, such as the ability to add, change, delete, inquire, or browse, in a file according to his or her specific job functions.
- When a data dictionary or directory is used, access to it is restricted with passwords or by some other means.
- Determine whether before-and-after image reporting is available when functional users perform maintenance on database files.

4. **Data file maintenance reports.** Perform these audit procedures for assessing the control procedures over data file maintenance activity.

- Take a sample of application systems that are subject to heavy file maintenance activity.
- Ask application system functional users whether, for changed data, they receive reports from the IT department showing old data values ("from") and new data values ("to") for each change to a data fields or data element, so they can verify the accuracy and completeness of manual and automated file maintenance procedures. Inquire whether users follow up on discrepancies.
- Look for the evidence of supervisory or employee review of file maintenance reports.

5. **Handling confidential data.** Conduct these audit procedures to determine whether confidential data is handled properly.

- During nonworking hours, sensitive information should be locked in drawers, file cabinets, or vaults. Confidential information should be hand-delivered by messengers to addressees or to their designates. If the receiver is not present, it should be taken back to the sender or secured by the messenger. Color-coded envelopes can be used to signify the confidentiality of information. Confidential information should be controlled by encryption during transmission over telecommunication lines. Assess the adequacy of practices in these areas.
- Inquire how hard copy computer reports, sensitive and confidential documents, and negotiable documents are protected during use and whether they are disposed of by shredding or other means so data cannot be retrieved by unauthorized persons. Ensure that paper is not simply put in trash cans, which would allow for possible misuse. Evaluate security controls over disposition of magnetic media (e.g., tape, cartridge, and disk) by making sure that old media are degaussed prior to being discarded.

6. **Statistical and exception reports.** Conduct these audit procedures to analyze statistical data.

- Take a sample of audit tests using the system logging facility records to search for several occurrences of a record type, in a short period of time, with each occurrence using a different password or pattern of passwords. This could indicate attempted unauthorized access by a person trying to guess a password or a person trying to generate a string of passwords.
- With the help of report writing facilities offered in the security systems software or other report writer, these **statistical reports** can be listed.
  - Frequency of invalid password attempts by user-ID

- Number and the type of warning indicators
- Activities of selected and high-risk users
- Persistent unauthorized use of system commands
- Number of times a password changed in a given time period
- Data files not protected by security access rules

Take a sample and ascertain whether these security violations are properly investigated and resolved in a timely manner.
- Ascertain whether resource access analysis reports are available to data security administration showing who is accessing what resources (e.g., data, programs, and printers). Some categories of **security violations** are

- Violations this period
- Violations by resource type
- Violations by event type
- Violations by event type for specific resources
- Violations for top 10 or 15 users

- Determine whether data set access analysis reports are available to data security administration showing who is accessing which data sets. Some categories of **security violations** are

- Data set logging by reason
- Data set violation and logging for top 10 or 15 users based on number of violations
- Data set logging analysis showing logging patterns
- Data set event type analysis showing different accesses

- Develop **exception reports** indicating

- The number of individuals having update access to production programs and data files
- When security alarm messages are sent to terminals that have been enabled as security officer or operators
- When security/audit journal logging took place due to occurrence of predefined audit events

## CONTROL/AUDIT RISKS IN DATA SECURITY

- Appropriate action may not be pursued when a security variance is reported to the system officer or to the perpetrating individual's supervisor. In fact, procedures addressing such occurrences may not exist.
- Management may simply rely on variance detection as the only safeguard. The objective of variance detection is to allow management to detect and react to departures from established rules and procedures it has determined may constitute hazards. Nevertheless, variance detection can be a very useful technique to encourage a general awareness of security and to discourage dishonest employee behavior. A combination of controls, such as variance detection combined with effective policies and procedures, could be useful.

(C) *Firewalls review.*
**Audit objective.**  To determine whether firewalls are properly configured and placed in the organization at strategic locations.
**Audit procedures.**

- Review firewall configuration reports and make sure that firewalls are properly placed in the organization.
- Understand the types of firewalls used and ensure that they meet the business purpose.

- Understand the advantage and disadvantages of each firewall that is installed. Ensure that advantages outweigh the disadvantages. Assess any potential risks and exposures resulting from the review.

(D) ***Physical access security and environmental controls review.*** Similar to logical access controls, physical access security and environmental controls are important to ensure overall security in the data center.

**Audit objectives.**

- To determine the adequacy of physical access controls, housekeeping controls, and fire prevention, detection, and suppression procedures.
- To ensure that adequate physical security over the data processing installation, facilities, and computer center exists.
- To assess the protective procedures covering water damage, electricity, air-conditioning, natural disasters, and other emergency situations.

**Audit procedures.**

1. **Physical access controls.** Tour the computer center, observe the area, and make notes and drawings (sketches) of the physical layout of the area under consideration. Conduct these audit procedures to evaluate the adequacy of physical access security controls.

    - Verify whether entrance points are adequately controlled to prevent unauthorized access.
    - Identify whether a receptionist controls entrance to the computer center and if a positive identification, such as a photo badge, is required prior to being allowed inside.
    - If no receptionist is available, find out whether keys, cipher locks, combination locks, badge readers, or other mechanical or electronic security devices are used to control access to computer center.
    - If access to the computer center is electrically controlled, ascertain whether a standby battery or electrical generator is available during power failure. Make sure electronic access codes are changed periodically and that one or two people maintain them in confidence.
    - Look for security guards stationed at all major entrances to the computer center. Find out whether security guard services extend to 24 hours.
    - Understand the procedures required for allowing visitors into the computer center, and determine whether a log is maintained with vital information, such as name of the visitor, the organization the visitor is representing, purpose of the visit, the person to see, date and time of the arrival and departure, and whether the visitor is a citizen or not.
    - Inquire whether receptionists or security guards are trained to challenge improperly identified visitors.
    - Find out whether the location of the computer center is obvious through the building lobby entrance index board or signs that enable vandals to target it.
    - Inquire whether doors, locks, bolts, hinges, frames, and other building materials are constructed in such a way as to reduce the probability of unauthorized entry.
    - Determine whether VDU/CRT terminal controllers in the computer room are adequately protected to prevent use of all terminals in the event of a disaster of any nature. A concentration of all terminal controllers in one area is **not** advised because of the adverse effect a disaster would have on all terminals connected to these controllers. Usually terminal controllers are placed in areas where they serve a group of terminals.

2. **Housekeeping controls.** Tour inside the computer center, observe the area, and make notes of impressions about housekeeping practices. These audit procedures are suggested to assess housekeeping controls.

- Look for signs stating "no smoking," "no eating," and "no drinking," and find out whether they are conspicuously displayed so anybody would notice them.
- Observe whether tile floors are clean and are washed regularly to prevent accumulation of dust and dirt.
- Inquire whether carpeting cleaners and floor waxes are of antistatic nature to prevent static electricity from being generated.
- Ascertain whether trash and debris are accumulated in low-fire-hazard waste containers and these containers are emptied outside the computer center to reduce dust discharge.
- Look for plastic sheets to cover the computer equipment in case of water discharge from the ceiling either due to normal water leakage or water sprinkler activation.
- Touch and feel the equipment and work surfaces to determine their degree of cleanliness. Small particles of dust can go into the equipment, which could damage electrical circuits and other internal parts. Similarly, examine reel tapes and unsealed disks.
- Inquire how often the surfaces beneath the raised floors are cleaned.
- Assess whether tile pullers are visible and available to computer operations, cleaning people, and others as needed.
- Inquire whether computer waste (forms, carbons, reports) are disposed of properly by burning, shredding, or other means to make them unreadable and unusable.
- Verify that all magnetic media storage (tapes, cassettes, diskettes) cabinets in the tape library are kept at a distance of 20 to 30 inches from an exterior wall to protect against the potential effects of magnetic fields or radiation.

3. **Fire prevention, detection, and suppression procedures.** Interview the computer center manager, building maintenance engineer, and others as required to understand fire prevention, detection, and suppression techniques available. Conduct these audit procedures to evaluate fire prevention, detection, and suppression procedures and controls.

- Inquire whether the computer room is separated from adjacent areas by noncombustible or fire-resistant partitions, walls, floors, and doors.
- Ascertain that raised floors, suspended ceilings, carpets, furniture, and window coverings are made of noncombustible materials.
- Look for paper stock and combustible supplies, such as toners, cleaners, and other chemicals, and observe whether they are stored outside the computer room area.
- Determine whether computer operations staff is trained in firefighting techniques and assigned individual responsibilities in case of fire.
- Determine the type of **fire, smoke detection, and extinguishing devices** used, and procedures in place to protect the data center from accidental or deliberate damage due to physical or natural hazards. Verify that carbon dioxide or halon fire extinguishers of proper capacity are available for use on electrical fires and that water-type fire extinguishers are available for use on nonelectrical fires. Inquire whether the data center is protected by automatic fire extinguishing systems. If so, conduct these audit steps.

  - If water sprinklers are used, find out whether their activation will sound an alarm and if there is a delay in the release of water in order to prepare for the emergency incident.
  - If a halon sprinkler is used, inquire how long it takes to evacuate the area.
  - If a carbon dioxide sprinkler is used, inquire whether required people were given proper safety precautions to address carbon dioxide discharge.

- Assess whether portable fire extinguishers are placed strategically around the data center with location markers visible, that they are tested periodically, and that people are trained in using them.

- Inquire whether a **shutdown checklist** is available. Find out how easy it is to access emergency power shutdown control switches. Verify shutdown control switches shut off heating, ventilation, and air conditioning as well as computer and support equipment. Assess whether smoke/ionization detection equipment automatically activates the emergency power shutoff.
- Inquire whether smoke and ionization detection devices are installed in ceilings, raised floors, return air ducts, and other important zones. Find out how often these detectors are tested.
- Inquire how often **fire drills** are conducted and that an adequate supply of fire-fighting water and other chemicals are available to combat fire.
- Verify whether periodic fire or evacuation drills are conducted in the computer center and in the entire building where the computer center is located to handle the emergency situations.
- Assess whether fire exit doors are protected by exit alarms.
- Determine the adequacy of the number of fire alarm boxes throughout the data center and that these alarms sound in the local area, such as building maintenance and computer center area, security guard location, help desk, central fire alarm station, and local fire department.
- Ascertain the frequency of fire system testing and certification by the local fire department. Inquire about the rating given to the local fire fighting force by the American Insurance Association's Standards Fire Defense Rating Schedule or other.

4. **Water damage.** Damage due to water leakage is excessive and a common occurrence. These audit procedures are suggested to assess management preparedness and controls to protect equipment from water damage.

- Inquire of the building maintenance engineer whether overhead water and steam pipes, except water sprinklers, are excluded from the computer room. A dry pipe system helps prevent water leaks.
- Ascertain whether adequate drainage is provided under raised floors, on the floor above, and other adjacent areas of the data center.
- Inquire whether electrical junction boxes under raised floors are kept away from the slab to prevent water damage.
- Assess whether exterior doors and windows are watertight to prevent water passage.
- Determine whether there is adequate protection provided against accumulated rainwater or leaks in the roof and rooftop cooling systems.
- For computer rooms not meeting the defined water damage standards, inquire whether floor drains use a sump pump connected to the uninterruptible power supply (UPS) system.

5. **Electricity.** Damage due to power failures is excessive and a common occurrence. Conduct these audit procedures to assess management preparedness and controls to prevent power-related problems such as spikes and outages.

- Inquire how reliable the local power supply is and how many times there have been power failures or power spikes, surges, outages, brownouts. Understand whether alternative measures have been investigated.
- Determine the need to use a UPS system to provide smooth flow of electricity from power spikes, surges, outages, brownouts, and blackouts. There should be enough auxiliary power generators to generate electricity as needed for the computer and support equipment. There should be enough quantity of fuel (gas or propane) for alternate power generators for at least one week.

## BUSINESS RISKS IN ELECTRICAL POWER

- A voltage spike is a sharp but brief increase in voltage, commonly caused by the turning off of heavy loads, such as air conditioners, copiers.
- A voltage surge is similar to a spike, but it is an increase in voltage of longer duration, commonly caused by the removal of heavy loads or equipment shutdown. It is an over-voltage condition.
- A voltage sag is an undervoltage condition, commonly caused by the addition of large loads to a power line within a building, such as turning on a copier, starting an elevator.
- A brownout condition is longer-term sag. It is a deliberate reduction of voltage output at a power generating station to respond to high demand and thus avoid an outage. Computers cannot work during a brownout.
- A blackout is a total loss of power, lasting several hours, commonly caused by weather conditions or damage to power lines and equipment.

---

- Make sure the power supply to the air conditioning, heating, and other source of electricity is leading from a separate power supply. This source should not share with other power sources within the building.
- Make sure that the wiring in the computer room conforms to accepted local and state government electrical codes.

6. **Air conditioning.** Both computer equipment and magnetic storage media (e.g., data and program files on tapes and disks) are susceptible to changes in temperature and humidity levels. In order to minimize the impact from possible adverse effects, these audit procedures are suggested.

- Inquire whether the air conditioning system is exclusively used for the data center and is not being shared with other parts of the building.
- Ascertain whether air duct linings and filters are made of noncombustible materials.
- Observe whether the air compressor is located outside the data center.
- Inspect the cooling system for adequate protection against adverse weather conditions.
- Assess the need for a backup air conditioning system.
- Inquire whether fire dampers are provided in the air-conditioning system. The air-conditioning unit must be shut down automatically when the halon unit is activated.
- Verify that air intakes are

  - Covered with protective screening
  - Located above street level
  - Located to prevent intake of pollutants or other debris

- Verify the existence of separate air-conditioning equipment and electrical power fluctuation control devices to ensure a constant power supply to the computer room.

7. **Natural disaster preparedness.** Natural disasters, such as tornados, earthquakes, hurricanes, and floods, are unpredictable. However, organizations exposed to such disasters should prepare themselves for the inevitable. In order to help minimize the impact from possible adverse effects, these audit procedures are suggested.

- Interview the building architect or maintenance engineer to find out whether the computer center is structurally sound and protected against

  - Hurricanes, tornados, and winds
  - Flood damage
  - Earthquakes

- Winter storms and freezing
- Ascertain whether the building and computer equipment are properly grounded for lightning protection.

8. **Documented emergency procedures.** Written emergency procedures are very important for referencing, testing, and training purposes. In order to minimize the impact from possible adverse effects, these audit procedures are suggested.

- Ascertain whether an emergency lighting system is in place to provide the required illumination automatically in case of interruption of normal lighting for any reason.
- Verify that there is a written emergency procedures manual covering the following items of concern:

  - CPU and air conditioning power cutoff
  - Bomb threats, vandalism, and employee strikes
  - Fire evacuation, fighting, and testing instructions
  - The security of data and program files
  - Restart and recovery procedures due to equipment failures
  - Natural disasters

- Inquire when fire drills, first aid training, and cardiopulmonary resuscitation (CPR) classes were last performed.
- Review the test plans and documents for adequacy and relevancy.

9. **Environmental controls.** Large computers need a clean and controlled environment to operate properly. Conduct these audit procedures to ensure that environmental controls exist in the computer room and tape library rooms.

- Ensure that fire extinguishers, heat and humidity control devices, alarm panels, pressure on halon tanks, and water detectors are tested periodically.
- Ensure those high-speed printers and other equipment that produces paper dust, such as report decollators and bursters, are placed outside of the computer room. This is to prevent dust coming in contact with the computer hardware.
- Determine how often the fire and water detection system is tested.
- Determine the need for an uninterruptible power supply (UPS) machine and standby power generator to accommodate power surges and power losses respectively.
- Test temperature and humidity recordings on a surprise audit basis. Ensure that such measurements are recorded in a timely manner and that proper actions are taken when such measurements go out of the prescribed limits.
- Determine whether monitoring of physical security, environmental controls, and housekeeping activities is adequate.

(xx) **Contingency planning.** Auditing the contingency plan or disaster recovery plan is an important audit function since auditors have the professional and ethical responsibility to the organization for which they work, or to the clients they serve, to ensure continuity of business functions and operations. To discharge this responsibility, auditors must be actively involved in the disaster recovery plan development, testing, and maintenance processes as observers, reviewers, and reporters of actions or lack of actions of IT and end user staff and management. Another responsibility of auditors is to monitor the continual maintenance and periodic testing of the plan to reflect changes in the organization. Auditors should inform senior management if the plan is not updated and tested when needed.

Another major area for auditors to review is to determine the adequacy of insurance coverage on IT resources, such as property, software, and data, and to determine the protection against human errors and omissions, fraud, theft, and embezzlement.

Auditors are interested in both vital records retention and records disposition practices as they affect both the security and confidentiality of records and the ability to resume business operations when interrupted due to a disaster (e.g., fire, flood), either in the computer center or in the functional user area.

(A) *Auditor's role.* The auditor's important role in developing and testing the disaster recovery plan may need clarification for other team participants. Many people participate in the planning and testing efforts, and misunderstandings and misinterpretations can easily develop among team members if they are not properly informed. The auditor should inform all team members of his or her role in the development and testing of the disaster recovery or contingency plan. Although the auditor does not actually prepare the planning document, he or she should advise the team members about its contents. The auditor, as a member of the testing team, reviews test results along with functional users to make sure those critical application system results are correct. The auditor does not make decisions or supervise the team members, which is the management's responsibility.

The auditor's role in the disaster recovery/contingency plan development and testing is clearly a consulting and participative role, where the auditor is a member of the disaster recovery/contingency planning team. The auditor is more of an observer, reviewer, and reporter of disaster planning, testing, and recovery-related actions. Some specific role-related activities in which the auditor participates are

- Attends meetings where issues are raised, problems are discussed, and solutions are suggested in areas related to computer contingency plans
- Reviews planning documents and backup and recovery site vendor's proposals for rendering such services for adequacy and suggests improvements as needed
- Participates in testing of the plan at the backup and recovery vendor's site along with functional users and IT staff, observes the testing process, and suggests cost-effective improvements to the plan based on feedback from the testing experience
- Ensures that functional users review the application test results by comparing them with known values or other means to ensure that the data files are up-to-date and application programs and operating system are the correct version at the primary and backup computer centers
- Where needed, simulates a disaster with the help of senior management to test the recovery and resumption procedures

(B) *Audit objectives and procedures.*

**General audit objectives.**

- To determine the adequacy of risk analysis.
- To evaluate the adequacy and effectiveness of off-site storage facilities.
- To determine whether the disaster recovery-planning document is complete, clear, and understandable.
- To determine the adequacy of management's preparedness to address emergency situations.
- To ensure that disaster recovery plans are tested periodically and that those functional users review such test results for accuracy and completeness.
- To determine the adequacy of plan maintenance procedures.
- To identify concerns, problems, and issues and make cost-effective recommendations for improvements to be included in the disaster recovery plan.
- To ensure that disaster recovery planning, testing, and recovery activities in the computer center and user area are carried out according to the established data processing policies, procedures, standards, and guidelines; good business and management practices; industry standards; and tax, accounting, government, legal, and regulatory requirements.
- To identify overcontrolled (oversecured) and undercontrolled (undersecured) activities in the disaster recovery planning and testing areas. To ensure that weak controls in the disaster recovery planning and testing areas are balanced by strong controls in the end user and other computer center areas.

**Audit procedures.**
The audit procedures for reviewing the continuity of operations include

1. **Information gathering.** Obtain relevant information by interviewing personnel and reading documents such as

   - Risk analysis document indicating possible threats and vulnerabilities and suggested controls to reduce such threats and vulnerabilities
   - Disaster recovery planning committee members, including their commitment, objectives, and responsibilities
   - Critical application systems with their priority levels
   - Disaster recovery requirements document indicating what is needed and where and when it is needed
   - Disaster recovery training document indicating who will be trained, when, and how
   - Disaster recovery plan testing document describing test scenarios and schedules
   - Disaster recovery plan maintenance procedures describing how the planning document will be updated and under what conditions
   - Preaudit survey notes taken during preliminary information-gathering process
   - Audit notification letter with audit scope and specific objectives
   - Copies of relevant IT management, backup computer facility vendor, and end user correspondence
   - Third-party audit report issued as a result of the review of operations at the backup computer facility
   - Alternative processing contracts with backup facilities

2. **Risk analysis.** Only critical application systems need to be processed during a disaster. To support this objective, only critical programs and data/records should be stored at an off-site storage location. These audit procedures are suggested to determine the adequacy of risk analysis.

   - Identify critical application systems with inputs (source paper documents, machine-readable documents, data files) and outputs (reports, data files).
   - Identify minimum hardware configuration needed during a major disaster including CPU, terminals, network controllers, concentrators, printers, and data transmission lines, modems, and so on.
   - Classify critical data according to whether they reside on magnetic/ electronic, paper, or microfiche/microfilm media.
   - Review existing file backup procedures.
   - Formalize data/record retention and rotation schedules between on-site and off-site storage locations.

3. **Off-site storage facilities.** Inquire whether commercial or private off-site storage facilities are used to store magnetic/electronic records, paper records, and microfiche/ microfilm records. If a commercial off-site storage facility (e.g., banks, nonbanks) is used, understand whether the vendor's financial background and reputation have been investigated. Visit the storage facilities, and contact other organizations that are using similar services.

   Also, assess the vendor's compliance with storage standards established by the National Institute of Standards and Technology (NIST), Underwriters Laboratory (UL), American National Standards Institute (ANSI), National Fire Protection Association (NFPA), and state and local governments. In addition, these audit procedures are suggested to evaluate the adequacy and effectiveness of off-site storage vendors.

   - Ask about hours of operation and access privileges during evenings, weekends, and holidays.
   - Inquire how one client's media is separated from other clients' media.
   - Inquire how the media is transported (i.e., using plastic containers, cardboard boxes, or metal boxes with or without the use of seals transported in unmarked

vehicles), security in vehicles, or employee monitoring with antitheft devices controlled by two-way radios for transmission of messages.

- Review media rotation cycles to monitor the flow of media in and out of the facility (whether it is daily, weekly, monthly, or permanent storage).
- Observe how visitors' access is restricted: whether they are required to sign in and out and are escorted at all times.
- Inquire how the confidentiality of data stored on the media is maintained to prevent disclosure or unauthorized use of valuable data either internally or externally.
- Inquire whether the vendor has taken media replacement insurance. This is to protect clients from loss, misplacement, or damage of the media due to the vendor's negligence.
- Understand whether a contract is required to do business with the commercial off-site storage vendor and know its terms and conditions, including media pickup and delivery fee, tape handling and storage fee, and emergency delivery fee.
- Assess whether the traffic at the storage facility is videotaped with concealed cameras or other monitoring devices.
- Understand the procedures to handle emergency or normal requests for media removal and delivery, including authorizations required and contact names and phone numbers.
- Understand employee hiring and termination procedures, and inquire whether employees are bonded.
- Ascertain whether a periodic inventory of media is performed and whether the results are compared to the official list of media.
- Inquire what capabilities are installed to prevent, detect, and correct sonar, vibration, heat, smoke, fire, water, and burglar activities, including alarm systems tied to fire and police departments. Look for automatic halon fire extinguishers.
- Inquire how temperature, heat, humidity, power supply, and contamination are controlled, including backup systems and central-station monitoring twenty-four hours a day.
- Understand the overall vendor's liabilities for media in its possession and penalties for loss or damage of media including deductibles, if any.
- Examine what precautions have been taken in terms of electrical interferences, static electricity, and magnetism.
- Check the facility for extraneous chemical or other pungent odors.
- Ensure that physical security controls are constantly and consistently applied.

Verify that the off-site storage location maintains not only blank checks and other negotiable instruments but also the registers and logs that are used to keep track of the usage of such checks. Ensure that a large enough supply of checks is available from off-site storage or from vendors in case of a disaster. Read letters of understanding negotiated with the vendors.

Determine whether on-site or off-site storage rooms used for magnetic or paper records have adequate environmental controls, such as physical security, fire protection, humidity controls, temperature control, static grounding, and water detection devices.

Ascertain that an inventory list of computer hardware and peripheral equipment is available with manufacturer name, model, and serial number of each unit. Verify the physical existence of each unit.

Ensure that there is only one authorized main entrance to and exit from the data center. Where possible, this main entrance is to be manned by a receptionist or a security guard, preferably with closed-circuit television monitors. Review the training received, performance levels expected, and responsibilities assumed by security guards to handle security violations and emergencies.

Verify whether the off-site storage place has fire-resistant floor-to-ceiling doors or fire-resistant vaults that separate the contents from their surroundings. Ensure that doors have a dead-bolt lock to prevent break-ins.

Obtain a copy of the log maintained to record the movement of media between on-site and off-site. Ensure that a copy of the log is maintained off-site at all times. Examine the log for arrival and departure time of the vendor couriers, and check that the log indicates clearly what was picked up or delivered. Ensure that the logged information is detailed enough to track down media or records that are misplaced at the off-site storage facility or needed on an emergency basis. Take a month of logs and compare them to the vendor invoice to determine the accuracy of volume and the rate used, and compare that to the contract. Note any exceptions.

4. **Planning document.** Obtain a copy of the disaster recovery planning document. Examine it for details. To ensure that the disaster recovery planning document is complete, clear, and understandable, determine whether the document addresses these items.

- There is a balance between the number of subscribers to a backup hot site and the capacity of the computer.
- The vendor's willingness to offer presubscription testing in its facilities prior to signing a contract for backup processing services.
- A clear definition and indication of different types of fee charged by the backup vendor. Some examples of types of fee are: subscription fee, annual test times and corresponding fee, disaster notification fee, daily facility usage fee during a disaster, and extra equipment fee for tape and disk drives used over the base number.
- Whether the backup processing and recovery site vendor also provides off-site storage facilities for storing magnetic media backup, paper records, and supplies.
- Backup and recovery site vendor's liabilities for any loss or damage to media and data during storage and processing at its facilities, including maintaining client confidentiality.
- A temporary and emergency location for employees to work during a disaster, whether it is a warehouse, conference center, hotel/motel, or other prearranged office space.
- Names, phone numbers, and addresses of recovery team members, including their managers, to notify in case of a disaster and to inform where to report for work during a disaster.
- Transportation arrangements, including ground transportation such as special bus or private air transportation (i.e., a charter plane).
- Redirection of telecommunications traffic so business users are connected to remote hot-site processing and recovery facilities.
- Computer-related equipment and supplies, including personal computers, printers, facsimile machines, diskettes, computer paper, and ribbons with two or more suppliers identified with their phone numbers and addresses.
- Names, phone numbers, and addresses of hotels or motels nearby the backup processing and recovery site for stay during recovery from a disaster.
- Consolidation of midrange/minicomputer-based critical application systems on a compatible mainframe computer to be used during a disaster at the midrange/minicomputer work area.
- Network configuration diagram and documentation describing network operations, network topologies and protocol architectures, traffic loads and patterns, and transmission rates and speeds.
- Availability of UPS, proper climate control, suitable fire prevention, detection, or suppression capabilities for both primary and secondary private branch exchange (PBX) installations.
- Migration of LAN-based critical application systems and data to central mainframe or midrange/minicomputer so that users can use these systems through dial-up mode from a backup and recovery site.
- Rerouting of incoming long-distance telephone traffic to the backup processing and recovery site so that user-mainframe connection is made.
- Location of alternate telephone traffic switching equipment offices locally, in case the primary local telephone company fails. The alternate telephone office can be

used as a gateway to long-distance networks. Another alternative could be installation of company-owned microwave satellite link. Still another alternative could be use of independent cable, radio, or microwave links to private-access networks, including privately operated network gateways.

- Emergency team instructions for evacuation and recovery during a disaster. This may include procedures for reporting a fire, detecting a water leakage, powering down the electrical equipment, conducting fire drills, retrieving critical data and program files from off-site storage, testing systems software and application systems at the recovery site, operating from the recovery site, reestablishing the network, transporting users to recovery site, reconstructing the databases, transition procedures from emergency to normal service levels, salvaging of records (paper and microfiche) destroyed.
- Primary and emergency telephone numbers of peripheral equipment, hardware, and software vendors, supply vendors, backup facility vendors.
- Trouble reporting and response escalation procedures to local telephone company during an outage.
- Documentation of contact persons at local, state, and federal governments and for understanding of emergency plan and protection procedures in the event of floods, earthquakes, hurricanes, or other nature-made disasters.
- Procedures to handle bomb threats or arson investigations prepared in conjunction with local police and fire department officials.
- Plan testing procedures at backup vendor site as well as at primary computer site.

5. **Functional user procedures.** Conduct these audit steps to ensure that functional users are prepared themselves to address a disaster.

- Inquire whether fallback plans or alternate manual procedures and forms are developed by functional users to continue critical business operations, such as preparing payroll and invoices. These fallback procedures need to be tested and ready to function in the event of prolonged and delayed attempts to recover from a major disaster in the computer center. A reasonable approach would be to address two major situations separately: data center malfunction and natural disaster.
- In the case of a data center malfunction, functional user management needs to identify plans and procedures to continue critical business operations during the time until the backup computer takes over the critical application system operations and to continue noncritical business operations that are dependent on computer for a period of, say, 10 days until the entire data center's normal operations are restored.
- In the case of natural disasters (e.g., fire, flood, water damage), functional user management needs to identify alternate plans, procedures, equipment, facilities, and people required to operate critical job functions until the original facilities are restored or alternate facilities are located.

  For example, if important application software is not working properly, the contingencies may include reverting to manual processing for some operations, routing information to alternate systems or locations, correcting the software, or doing nothing until the problem is corrected.

6. **Emergency preparedness.** To ensure that management is doing all it can to prepare for unexpected disasters, conduct these audit procedures.

- Determine whether instructions are available for emergency shutdown of the computer system.
- Ascertain whether the location of emergency exits, fire extinguishers, plastic coverings for equipment, power switches, and light switches are visible, and ensure that instructions are clear about operating them during an emergency.
- Examine the building evacuation procedures for reasonableness and applicability and inquire the last time they were tested.

- Inquire about the availability of emergency telephone numbers for local police, ambulance, and fire departments, help desk, or building maintenance desk, and primary and backup recovery people.
- Inquire whether computer floor tile maintenance work, such as adding or changing tiles, is done outside of the computer room instead of inside. This is to prevent fiber and aluminum contaminants getting into the air. The preferred method is to perform all tile maintenance work outside the raised-floor room.
- Ascertain whether filters used in equipment such as humidifiers, air conditioning, and air purifiers are vendor recommended, not generic ones. This is to prevent larger particulate from getting into tape and disk drives and electrical switches. Determine the frequency of maintenance of such equipment and compare that to the manufacturer recommended schedule.
- Verify that the data center manager has conducted proper background investigation about the computer room–cleaning contractor prior to contracting out the services. Some of the areas of investigation include experience in cleaning business, user references, insurance coverage, fidelity bond coverage, and the type of cleaning equipment used.
- Inquire whether the computer room–cleaning contractor uses Occupational Safety and Health Agency (OSHA)–approved nonionic solution and lint-free towels to clean computer room tiles. Similarly, ensure that all equipment exteriors are cleaned with silicon-treated cloths.
- Inquire whether the UPS are online or off-line to the power company source. Online UPS is better than off-line UPS because online UPS remains in the line between the critical load and the power company at all times. Usually it takes longer for off-line UPS to activate and replace failed commercial power than an online model. Also, off-line models may not protect line voltage drops.
- Since the life of UPS is short (15 to 30 minutes), inquire whether private power generators are supplemented to meet prolonged power supply problems. The power generator supplies alternate current to the UPS before the UPS power is exhausted. During this time, the UPS batteries get recharged. Ascertain whether there is adequate supply of backup fuel for the power generator. Confirm that power company representatives and building maintenance engineers were consulted prior to acquiring the UPS model and the private power generator.

7. **Testing and recovery procedures.** The real test of the plan is during the recovery from a disaster. The closest thing to a real recovery is the simulated disaster. These audit procedures are suggested for determining the adequacy of testing and recovery procedures.

   - Participate in the periodic test plans and programs.
   - Observe the project team in action during testing and make notes of concerns.
   - Prepare or obtain a checklist of time-driven actions and plans.
   - Ensure that functional users have reviewed the test results for critical application systems when they are processed at backup computer facility.
   - Ensure that someone in the recovery team is taking notes on the basis of time and action. These notes should include both positive and negative results, which later become part of the test report.
   - Inquire who has access to information about master keys, combination numbers, special codes, or other physical security devices. Ensure that the security administrator has access to this information to facilitate efforts during recovery from a local disaster.

8. **Plan maintenance procedures.** Disaster recovery plan maintenance procedures are more important than plan development. A plan that is out-of-date can be of no use when needed. Conduct these audit procedures to determine the adequacy of plan maintenance procedures.

   - Understand how the plan should be updated, and under what conditions and criteria.

- Determine the adequacy of plan update frequency. Ideally, the plan should be updated prior to the next testing.
- Inquire how plan changes should be communicated, to whom and where.
- Ensure that there is one central location or person assigned the responsibility to update the planning document. In many cases, fragmented responsibility does not work.
- Determine the frequency of updating the hardware and software inventory list with input from all end users and computer centers. A periodic questionnaire should be sent to survey the additions and changes to original inventory list.

9. **Vital records retention program.** Conduct these audit procedures to assess controls over a records retention program.

- Read the organization's published vital records retention guidelines for understanding of specific requirements. Obtain a copy of government and regulatory agency records retention requirements and guidelines in order to understand specific requirements.
- Ensure that hard copy reports are not saved when the same records are microfilmed or microfiched. This is to minimize duplication of records in handling, storing, and retrieving.
- Inquire whether the legal staff has reviewed and updated the record retention schedule to ensure compliance with government and nongovernment records retention requirements.
- Ensure that a manual log for paper-based and magnetic media is maintained that shows the retention label number, the name of the section/department and contact person name, a description of the records, form or record number, the date sent to storage, and the date to be destroyed. Take a sample of record entries from the log, trace them to the storage place indicated, and confirm their existence.
- Ensure that an automated log for electronic (magnetic) media is maintained that shows file name and number, file owner name and department, a business description of the records, transaction types and codes, transaction beginning and ending dates, and expiration date. Ensure that an external label on the tape contains the same information. Take a sample of record entries from the log, trace them to the storage place indicated, and confirm their existence.
- Take a sample of expired records for three types of records (paper, mechanical, and electronic media) from the log. Confirm that after the expiration date, all paper materials were destroyed or recycled and sensitive magnetic materials (e.g., tapes) were degaussed. Where applicable, it is preferable to receive a new copy or replacement copy of the backup material before the old copy is destroyed.
- Observe/inquire whether these methods were used to dispose of sensitive documents.

  - Paper-based reports, documents, letters, and memoranda are fed into a paper shredder by cutting them down the page instead of across to avoid reading the data or letters in the lines. Alternately, paper media can be burned or recycled.
  - When turning in floppy diskettes for reuse or replacement, format them first to prevent people from reading the file contents since the ERASE command does not really erase file contents and material can be recovered with utility programs.
  - Floppy diskettes are cut into two or more pieces before putting them in the trash can so that they will be useless to anybody.

10. **Insurance.** Perform these audit procedures to evaluate the adequacy of insurance coverage to minimize potential business, legal, or financial losses.

- Obtain a copy of risk management reports or industry-specific studies or research reports for better understanding of potential risks and exposures, actual losses, insurance coverage allowed, deductible amounts allowed for each type of coverage, and the type of exclusions practiced. This understanding is required to properly assess the adequacy of insurance programs that are in effect.

- Where needed, coordinate with the risk management analyst to minimize duplication of efforts, to share the analyst's work results, and to exchange ideas, approaches, and audit work programs. However, the auditor's conclusions are his or her own and not those of the analyst. In other words, the auditor can share and use the work results of the analyst, but the auditor has to reach his or her own conclusions based on the auditor's own reviews and test results.

- Verify whether risk management has identified and quantified the possible risks and exposures and associated costs and benefits. Obtain a copy of the inventory of all property and insurable items available in the organization from the risk manager.

- Inquire whether the organization risk management department and legal department's management participated in establishing the dollar limits on insurance policies and policy exclusions, including the amount for coinsurance provisions and liabilities.

- Review the insurance policy for adequate coverage in the areas of business interruption due to computer (hardware and software) failures, physical property (computer and its related equipment) damage, magnetic media (e.g., tapes, disks, cassettes, diskettes) and file reconstruction costs, valuable records retention and damage, errors and omissions, computer crime and fraud insurance, computer viruses, and personal computers.

- Inquire whether fidelity insurance coverage is available to protect against dishonest employees involving computers. Usually fidelity insurance covers the risk of loss due to a dishonest employee committing a fraud, theft, or embezzlement.

- Ascertain whether third-party fraud insurance coverage has been obtained to protect against computer fraud perpetrated by a third party. For example, fraud insurance in a banking environment covers electronic funds transfer (EFT), automated teller machine systems (ATMs), and the computer system, among other things. Some exclusions are extortion; loss of potential income; forged documents; war and nuclear risks; losses where the probable causes are errors, omissions, or mechanical failure; and others.

- Ascertain whether the insurance policy covers liability for bodily injury and property damage resulting from software/hardware vendor representatives and other outsiders (e.g., consultants/contractors). Inquire whether insurance is adequate to cover losses that may occur during the process of transporting computer tapes between on-site and off-site storage areas either done by own truck or by outside truck delivery services, and during on-site storage of program and data files by service bureau operations.

- When an organization opts for self-insurance, understand the rationality for assuming such risk. Determine whether the reserves or contingency funds to cover possible losses are adequate by finding the industry's actual loss experience rate and the past actual losses.

- Verify whether risk management is sending copies of internal and external audit reports to the insurance carrier dealing with security control issues and problems in the coverage items with recommendations and corrective actions for those recommendations. Ascertain whether loss reports are sent to the insurance carrier explaining the circumstances leading to computer-related losses during the past five years. The insurance carrier is interested in knowing the control environment in the client organization and wishes to monitor that environment to minimize potential losses.

### (xxi) Databases

#### (A) *Database management systems software: Audit objectives and procedures.*

**Audit objectives.**

- To determine the adequacy of organizational structure and the reporting relationships.
- To determine whether the database management system (DBMS) software was installed properly.
- To evaluate the security and integrity controls and procedures over the DBMS software for reasonableness and cost effectiveness.
- To assess the operational performance of the DBMS software.

**Audit procedures.**

- Ensure that Data Administrator (DA) reports directly to the data processing manager or executive to provide independence, authority, and responsibility.
- Ensure that the DA is responsible for data requirements, data description, and data standards, as well as procedures regarding data storage, data retrieval, data and program file security, access controls, recovery, and backup.

### CONTROL RISKS IN DATABASE SYSTEMS

- Production databases may not be separated from test databases, thus allowing unauthorized access to production databases.
- The data administration function may not be separated from application system development.
- The database administration group may move database changes between test and production libraries themselves without going through the designated program change control coordinator.

---

- Determine that the Database Administrator (DBA) is not allowed to operate the computer, write application programs, or perform systems programming functions.
- Determine that the DBA has established written procedures for the recovery of the database in the event of total or partial destruction of database files. Verify that the recovery procedures have been tested.
- Ensure that the DBA consults with users and systems analysts regarding data origination, data organization, and data storage and retrieval methods.
- Ensure that the DBA periodically reviews the DBMS software libraries to detect unauthorized libraries.
- Ensure that the DBA approves all modifications to the DBMS software. This includes both custom-developed and vendor-developed software. Determine whether the DBA approves changes to the data dictionary.
- The auditor conducting a review of database structure, audit trails, controls, security, integrity, recovery and restart, and performance should be concerned with

  - Reviewing the schema to understand the physical design of records and segment layouts. Assess whether data are grouped efficiently by analyzing usage maps, query paths, entry points, and primary and secondary keys. The objective here is to have a shorter path.
  - Reviewing the subschema to understand the user's view of the database. These "user views" present a logical database (schema) that is a subset of the physical database structure. Determine whether user views are defined for each transaction in terms of read-only, read and update, add, and delete, and that they are in agreement with employee or department function.
  - Determining whether the DBA has established and documented the audit trail along with its retention periods. Ensure that all transactions are time and date stamped so that they can be recorded in a proper accounting period.

- Identifying what resources need to be protected by passwords or other means. Determine whether violation criteria have been established.
- Determining the frequency of database backup. In general, the larger the database, the more frequent should be the backup. Inquire how database logs are stored and retained.
- Ascertaining who is responsible for database recovery. Ensure that written procedures for system recovery and restart are available for both online and batch portions of the system.
- Inquiring who is monitoring the performance and service levels of the database. Some common ways to improve the performance are by acquiring additional memory and data storage devices, by balancing the work load between peak and normal periods, and by reorganizing the database structure.
- Reviewing database management system deadlock detection and resolution procedures for adequacy.
- Confirming whether user-defined tables (e.g., tax, department, account numbers, interest) are reviewed by functional users for completeness and accuracy.

- After the database is reorganized, ascertain whether the DBA reconciles the control totals before the reorganization with the control totals after the reorganization to ensure the integrity of the data file reorganization.

## CONTROL/BUSINESS RISKS IN DATABASE SYSTEMS

- The database could be overstructured. That is, too many files are defined to a logical model.
- The database may be reorganized too frequently, thus making it unavailable to users.
- The database may be reorganized infrequently, thus creating performance problems.
- There may be too many physical input/output operations performed on the database, which degrades system performance due to its overhead.
- Physical databases are often created by rote, resulting in database performance problems. Physical database design should just be a normal extension of the logical database design in terms of conforming to the design rules.

---

- Confirm that logging and recovery provide transaction back-out initiated either by the application system or automatically for abended (abnormally ended) transactions, with automatic recovery at start-up. Dual logging facility provides continued operation, even in the event of a catastrophic error on the primary log file. Inquire whether a logical close processing facility is available for programs issuing multiple OPENs and CLOSEs while updating records. When a program abend occurs and transaction back-out is requested, this facility ensures that all updates accomplished since the beginning of the task are backed out. Without this facility, transaction back-out is applied only to updates made since the last close.
- Inquire that the DBMS maximizes transaction concurrency by supporting row-level locking so that multiple updates to the same block can be processed without delay. Users can also specify an automatic time-out limit to prevent unnecessary waiting.
- Ensure that the accounting facility is available to collect and report on a variety of access and resource utilization statistics and information.
- The security feature provides add, read, update, and delete protection for each table in the relational database. Review the access rules maintained in the database for accuracy and to ensure that only authorized users are defined to the system.
- Determine whether the database performance management software provides important statistics that can be used to fine-tune the database to achieve the desired performance goals. This, in turn, increases system throughput. Windowing facilities allow multiple logical screens to be viewed on one physical screen. Some of database performance statistics include

  - The number of transactions using the database

- The number of database calls by transaction type
- The number of physical I/Os
- The average time per request
- The number of system and transaction abends

- **Data compression software** is available to compress large volumes of database records. Compression saves disk space requirements, which, in turn, decreases cost and reduced backup/archival processing times
  Determine whether major features include

  - Compression specified at the schema level
  - Compression statistics produced at the end of each compression run
  - Reports showing summary information, such as

    - Percentage of each record type sampled that is compressible
    - Expected compression percentage
    - Expected percentage of compression due solely to the elimination of repeating strings

- For distributed database management software, determine whether multiple copies or replicas of a database can be created. Confirm that updates to a replicated database are automatically posted to all copies of the database, whether local or remote.

(B) *Data dictionary systems software: Audit objectives and procedures*.
**Audit objectives.**

- To determine whether the data dictionary is properly defined, controlled, and secured.
- To evaluate the integrity of data dictionary systems.

**Audit procedures.** The auditor concerned about the adequacy of controls over a data dictionary (DD) system implementation and operation should conduct these reviews and tests.

- Inquire whether the data dictionary is active and interfaces with the database management system. Ensure that the data dictionary includes a data source for each data element, data validation, and data element location and its relationship to other data elements.
- Take a sample of critical and significant data items or elements and review them for adherence to established data standards.
- Ascertain whether passwords or some other security and access controls are defined and followed.
- Test the edit and validation criteria by entering valid and invalid data for critical data items or elements.
- Ensure that backup and recovery procedures are available and that they are followed.
- Determine whether DD system error rates are monitored by data processing staff and that timely corrective actions are taken.
- Interview functional users and others to assess if DD system's reports are clear, correct, and received in time to be useful. Inquire whether users have any problems or concerns in data entry and error correction procedures. In other words, determine whether the DD system is easy to use. Confirm that users have received adequate training in using a DD system.
- Inquire if the data dictionary uses interactive fill-in-the-blank screens that eliminate the need to learn a complex "data definition" language.
- Understand whether users can perform multiple functions simultaneously.
- Determine whether a version management feature is available. This means version numbers are automatically assigned and maintained in "test," "quality assurance," "training," "history," or "production" status.
- Confirm that "history" versions can be deleted selectively.

## CONTROL/AUDIT RISKS IN DATA DICTIONARY SYSTEMS

- Passwords and other access codes may not be required to access, use, and update the data dictionary.
- Nondatabase applications may be loaded to the same data dictionary as the database applications resulting in data corruption. The best procedure would be to use a separate DD for loading nondatabase applications and merge them after data clean up.
- The program record in the DD may not be used to document user-defined comments. If done regularly, program documentation would be current.
- Multiple secondary dictionaries used for multiple system development/maintenance projects may not be in synchronization with the primary and production dictionary.

---

- Examine whether various security levels are provided. Some procedures might include
  - Online user authorization
  - Record/row/file level locking
  - Passwords at the occurrence level
- Inquire whether "user exits" can be coded for specific attribute validation routines that provide for additional security and/or conform with standards.
- Confirm that relational tables can be dynamically defined and put into production status.
- Test and production entity occurrences can be renamed dynamically, permitting naming conventions to be applied incrementally.

(C) *Data warehouse, data mart, and data mining: Audit objectives and procedures.*
**Audit objective.**

- To ensure that organization is using data warehouse, data mart, and data mining techniques to achieve better quality of information and decision making.

**Audit procedures.**

- Review the current plans to implement data warehouse, data mart, and data mining techniques. Understand their business purpose, including cost-benefit analysis.
- If these techniques have already been implemented, determine whether they are achieving the business purpose, that is, timely and quality of information and better decision making in the areas of marketing, fraud detection, and operations. Suggest ways to improve these techniques if they are not achieving their maximum potential.

(xxii) **Functional areas of information technology operations: Audit objectives and procedures.** Major concerns of auditors in reviewing functional areas of IT operations (i.e., data center operations) include how production jobs are scheduled, how storage media are used, how problems and changes are handled, how system backups are scheduled, and how the help desk is functioning.

The audit objectives of a data center operations management review are to ensure the proper implementation and verification of computer operational controls in the data center. This control assurance is needed to determine whether application systems are processed in a controlled and secured environment.

(A) *General operating practices review.*
**Audit objective.** To ascertain whether job descriptions are complete and reflect actual job functions.
**Audit procedures.**

- Review organization charts and job descriptions. Ensure that segregation of duties among data entry, input/output control, systems development, systems maintenance, systems programming, computer operations, and user departments exists, where possible. Determine the need for compensating controls.
- Determine that job descriptions are current and distributed to employees and that they reflect actual conditions and practices.

(B) *Data entry function review.*

**Audit objectives.**

- To determine the adequacy of batch data conversion and data entry activities.
- To determine the adequacy of online data conversion and data entry activities.
- To determine the adequacy of data editing and validation routines and procedures.
- To ensure that all data input errors are handled in a proper and timely manner.

**Audit procedures.**

1. **Batch data conversion and data entry procedures.** Conduct these audit procedures to ensure that controls and procedures over batch data conversion and data entry activities are adequate.

   - Determine if documented procedures exist that explain the manner in which data is converted and entered.
   - Identify the persons performing work in the data input area. Ensure that no person performs more than one of these operations: origination of data, entering of data, processing of data, and distribution of data.
   - Determine if there is a control group either in the functional user department or the IT department that independently controls the data to be entered. Identify control mechanisms used, such as: turnaround transmittal document, batching techniques, record counts, logging techniques, and predetermined control totals.
   - Determine whether source documents used in data conversion or data entry are marked to prevent duplication or reentry into the system.
   - Take a sample of critical business application systems. Ensure that a detailed data entry instruction manual is available, explaining how to enter and key verify the data fields. Assess whether the manual is complete and clear.

2. **Online data conversion and data entry procedures.** In order to ensure that controls and procedures over online data conversion and data entry activities are adequate, these audit procedures are suggested.

   - Confirm that data entry is performed at the point of source or close to the source to prevent delays and errors.
   - Determine whether VDU/CRT terminals used for data entry work are protected from theft or preferably placed in a physically secured room.
   - Determine if data entry can be made only from terminal devices with certain pre-assigned authority levels and that certain terminals are designated for specific application systems, at certain times of the day or certain days of the week.
   - Ascertain if passwords are used to prevent unauthorized use of terminal devices.
   - Determine if the user, through passwords or authorization codes, is allowed to enter only one or a limited number of transaction types.

3. **Online data editing and validation.** Conduct these audit procedures to evaluate the adequacy of data editing and validation control routines and procedures.

   - Determine if preprogrammed keying formats are used to ensure that data are entered in the proper field and format.
   - Ascertain if a prompting technique is used to reduce the number of data entry errors.
   - Determine the point at which input data are validated and edited. Confirm that incorrect data are rejected and not allowed to enter the system.
   - Ascertain that data editing and validation procedures are performed on all data fields of an input record, even though an error may have been detected in an earlier data field of the same input record.
   - Determine if data editing and validation procedures perform these checks: field sizes, date formats, check digit operations, limit/reasonableness tests, footing and cross-footing, sign tests, transaction code validations.

- Ensure that no one is allowed to override or bypass data editing and validation errors. If an override function is needed, limit use of this function to supervisory personnel only.
- Ascertain that the data input/output control group uses batch control totals to validate the completeness and accuracy of batches received as input data. Ensure that a reconciliation process is performed to ensure the completeness and accuracy of data input with system generated reports and manual totals.

## CONTROL RISKS IN DATA ENTRY AND CONVERSION

- The data entry operator may be given access to production data master files and may perform maintenance to production data entry programs.
- Data conversion procedures may not have been documented or documented procedures may not be current.
- Keying errors during data conversion may not be detected or corrected.
- Incomplete or poorly formatted data records may be accepted and treated as if they were complete records.
- A data entry employee may fraudulently add, delete, or modify data records for self or interested parties.

---

4. **Data input error handling.** In order to ensure that all data input errors are handled properly and in a timely manner, these audit procedures are suggested.

- Determine that procedures related to the identification, correction, and resubmission of rejected data have been established and documented.
- Determine whether errors are displayed or printed immediately upon detection to facilitate prompt correction.
- Ascertain that all rejected data are automatically written on to suspense files classified by the application system.
- Review entries in the suspense files to establish whether they include information such as

  - Codes to indicate error types
  - Date and time at which an entry is written to the suspense files
  - Identification of user who originated the input

- Inquire who is authorized to make corrections.
- Ascertain if the suspense files produce follow-up messages and report the status of uncorrected transactions or errors on a regular basis.
- Determine the need for aging the suspense file transactions and errors.
- Determine that, before reentry, all corrections are reviewed and approved by supervisors.
- Ascertain if user department management reviews reports from suspense files to analyze the level of transaction errors and status of uncorrected transactions.

(C) *Report balancing and reconciliation procedures.*
### Audit objectives.

- To ensure that clear responsibilities are assigned for report balancing and reconciliation activities.
- To examine the accuracy of report balancing procedures.

### Audit procedures.

1. **Responsibility for balancing and reconciliation.** Conduct these audit procedures to assess the adequacy of report balancing and reconciliation procedures

- Determine whether the data input/output control group in the data processing department is responsible for reconciling the transactions processed with input batch totals to ensure that no data were added or lost during processing.
- Determine if a log is kept, by application, to provide an audit trail of transactions processed.
- Ascertain if the user department has a control group responsible for reviewing all reports.
- Determine if the user department's control group reconciles report control totals with input batch totals before reports are released.

2. **Report balancing procedures.** In order to ensure that report balancing procedures are performed accurately and according to the application system/user documentation, conduct these audit procedures.

   - Select five major and critical application systems that require report balancing by data control staff.
   - Obtain written balancing procedures and the last system run reports. Conduct the following to determine whether

     - Balancing was done correctly.
     - All the key report fields are balanced.
     - All control totals developed by user's and data control staff are cross-compared.
     - Procedures are up-to-date and accurately reflect the balancing process.
     - All rejected items together with accepted items are balanced.

   - Interview end users to determine whether they

     - Find the data presented on reports accurate, reliable, and useful
     - Should be removed from or added to any report distribution lists
     - Have suggestions concerning the format, content, frequency, and timeliness of reports they receive

(D) *Report handling and distribution procedures.*

**Audit objectives.**

- To evaluate the adequacy of security access controls.
- To assess controls over online viewing of reports.
- To determine the adequacy of report distribution procedures.

**Audit procedures.**

1. **Security access controls.** If an automated report distribution system is being used, conduct these audit procedures to evaluate the adequacy of security access controls in place.

   - Review the security access control software rules to determine if all report distribution system data sets, program libraries, and utility programs are adequately defined and restricted.
   - Review the report distribution system security capabilities and determine if they are adequate, and/or have been utilized effectively.

2. **Online viewing controls.** If an automated report distribution system is being used, conduct these audit procedures to determine if controls over online viewing are adequate.

   - Review use of the distribution control database and surrounding procedures.
   - Review security capabilities of the system and ensure that users who were defined to the system have a business need to view the reports.
   - Determine if the online archival feature is effectively utilized.

3. **Report distribution controls.** If a manual report distribution system is being used, conduct these audit procedures to determine if the report distribution list is up-to-date and that reports are distributed or available to end users in a timely manner.

- Review report distribution instructions for completeness and accuracy. Examine them for name of the recipient, department, location, phone number, number of copies, and so forth.
- Determine if there is a report distribution list for each application system.
- Verify that reports for all applications are included on the relevant report distribution list(s).
- Find out if report distribution lists are updated whenever any change is made in distribution requirements.
- Determine if report distribution lists include

  - Report frequency
  - Disposition of all copies of each report
  - Time schedules for the distribution of each report
  - Special instructions on any given report

- Observe the actual distribution of reports to determine the flow of documents.
- Inspect the report delivery area or boxes and check dates of reports to determine any time lag between report production and delivery. Compare this any time lag against standards.
- Determine that reports are reviewed by data control staff for quality, such as incomplete report contents or missing pages, prior to distribution to end users.
- Understand the procedures used to deliver the reports. Ensure that a systematic and orderly distribution or pickup of reports exists. Assess the method of correcting report distribution errors.
- Determine the need for a report distribution log to indicate the person responsible for report distribution.
- Discuss with report distribution staff and end users their opinions of the current system and their suggestions to improve the system.

(E) *Output error handling review.*
   **Audit objectives.**

- To ensure that clear responsibilities are assigned for correcting output report errors.
- To determine whether all errors are handled properly and in a timely manner.

**Audit procedures.** In order to ensure that all data output errors are handled properly and in a timely manner, these audit procedures are suggested.

- Determine if output error reporting and control procedures have been established and documented.
- Ascertain if the end user is immediately notified of problems in output reports.
- Determine if the user department control group keeps a log of all reports containing errors.
- Establish that reports from rerun jobs are subjected to the same quality control review as the erroneous original reports.

(F) *Report retention and security measures.*
   **Audit objectives.**

- To determine whether retention periods for paper, electronic, and magnetic records have been established.
- To ensure that record retention periods are complied with.

**Audit procedures.**

- Determine if retention periods for paper/electronic/magnetic records have been established.
- Assess whether the retention period is reasonable for system backup and recovery, legal, tax, regulatory, management, and audit purposes.
- Determine if appropriate security methods (e.g., degaussing tapes or cartridges, shredding paper documents) have been used to dispose of unneeded records.

- Determine whether written procedures provide listings of reports classified as critical.
- Evaluate risks associated with critical reports and test procedures used to protect these reports.
- Understand the procedures in place for protecting confidential and critical reports from unauthorized pickup and viewing.
- Assess whether security provisions concerning the protection of critical reports awaiting distribution are adequate and are being followed.
- Assess whether end users receiving critical reports are aware of the criticality status and are taking proper actions to protect their confidentiality.

(G) *Controls over microfiche and microfilm records.*
    **Audit objectives.**

- To determine the adequacy of microfiche/microfilm processing procedures.
- To ensure that retention periods are adequate.
- To determine the adequacy of storage, distribution, and retrieval procedures.

**Audit procedures.**

1. **Accuracy of microfiche/microfilm processing.** Understand how microfiche or microfilm records are generated. Identify the associated end users for each type of microfiche and microfilm record. Conduct the following audit procedures to determine the accuracy of microfiche/microfilm records:

- Inquire whether the microfiche records are generated through off-line or online to the host computer.
- If off-line, understand how data control management and user management ensures that all records that were supposed to be microfiched were indeed microfiched. Understand the relation between microfiche frames (number of records a frame can hold) and computer records.
- If online, inquire whether automated record counts are available to ensure that there is a match between computer-generated records and microfiche-generated records.

2. **Microfiche/microfilm record retention periods.** Select ten critical microfiche or microfilm records judgmentally. In order to determine the adequacy of record retention practices, conduct these audit procedures.

- Ask end users about microfiche and microfilm record retention periods.
- Verify that the retention periods documented in the data control are in agreement with the end user guidelines. Note any exceptions.
- Confirm that the retention periods are in agreement with the organization's records retention policies. Note any exceptions.

3. **Storage, distribution, and retrieval procedures.** Conduct these audit procedures to ensure that controls and procedures over microfiche output distribution, storage, and retrieval are adequate.

- Obtain the microfiche distribution list and determine if it is current and complete and that it is utilized.
- Identify and inspect microfiche storage areas for adequacy and security.
- Request the data control staff to retrieve certain critical and old microfiche and microfilm records. Assess whether the retrieval process is timely and readily available. Suggest any improvements on manual procedures or need for automated record retrieval system.

(H) *Job scheduling review.*
    **Audit objectives.**

- To evaluate the adequacy of job setup procedures.
- To evaluate the adequacy of security access controls.

- To assess the adequacy of operating controls.
- To determine the adequacy of job schedules.
- To evaluate the handling of special processing of jobs.

**Audit procedures.**

1. **Job setup procedures.** These following audit procedures are suggested to assess the accuracy and completeness of job setups:

    - Review operating procedures to obtain familiarity with production job setups, job run sheets, and application program documentation.
    - Judgmentally select five major and important application systems and obtain job run sheets for each.
    - Using the job run sheet, make sure that each job and step procedures were set up in the job control library according to instructions.
    - Using the job run sheet, make sure that the sequence of jobs was set up correctly considering job dependencies (e.g., predecessors and successors; accounts receivable job is a predecessor to a general ledger job while financial statement job is a successor to the general ledger job).

## CONTROL RISK IN JOB DOCUMENTATION

The job documentation specialist may be given access to production job documentation, job control, and report distribution files and libraries, thus causing unnecessary exposure to unauthorized acts.

2. **Security access controls.** These audit procedures are suggested to assess the adequacy of logical security and access controls.

    - For terminal/operator security level, ensure that the terminals defined to the system are in the authorized work area and that all operators defined to the system are using only the terminals they were authorized to use.
    - For the operator/application security level, ensure that operators defined to the application have a business need to access the system.
    - For application/commands security level, ensure that operators defined to the application have access to system commands based on their job needs.
    - For command/function security level, ensure that people defined to the system need a second level of security in addition to application/command security level in order to use certain online screens, commands, functions, and terminals.
    - For user ID/ownership security level, ensure that users defined to the system have access to certain data sets based on business need.

## CONTROL RISK IN JOB DOCUMENTATION

The job control analyst may be given access to production data files and may perform maintenance to production application programs and job control files.

3. **Operational controls.** In order to assess operational controls over the job scheduling activities, these audit procedures are suggested.

    - Review all written procedures and forms for completeness, applicability, and adequacy.
    - Verify whether all jobs are defined to the job scheduling system. If not, find out the reasons for omitting such jobs. Assess the applicability of reasons given.
    - Determine if schedules are defined for each operating shift and that schedules are established at least a week in advance.

- Select the job schedule for a shift, analyze the job priorities and dependencies; assure that all job predecessors and successors were properly taken into account when finalizing the job schedule.
- Draw a sample of application system jobs. Discuss with end users and confirm that they agree with the job priorities and job predecessors and successors.
- Make sure that all job scheduling data sets are backed up regularly both on-site and off-site for disaster recovery purpose. Ensure that backups are retained for at least one week.
- Determine if procedures exist to ensure that scheduled jobs were actually executed. Inquire whether job schedules are reconciled with actual execution.
- Interview computer operations staff and management to find out the adequacy of job mix, availability of job initiators and hardware devices (e.g., tape/disk drives), job timings, and quality of job documentation. Solicit their comments and concerns for possible improvement.

4. **Special jobs.** This section applies to manual handling and scheduling of special jobs. In order to determine whether requests for special jobs are handled properly and in a timely manner, and that the scheduling of special jobs does not conflict with regular production jobs, the following audit procedures are suggested:

- Examine several special job request forms and determine whether the form is complete with job name, date of request, originating department, job due date, location, telephone extension, return to, charge to, and special instructions.
- For each of the special request jobs received, determine whether data control completed the job ID, account number, due date, priority code, and date and initial prior to submission to computer operations.
- Confirm that these special jobs were run by noting dates and initials of computer operations staff.
- Calculate the time lag between date submitted by an end user to date completed by data processing. Assess whether the actual time lag is reasonable and falls within the standards established.

## CONTROL RISK IN PRODUCTION SCHEDULE

The production scheduler may be given access to production data files and may perform maintenance to production application programs and job control files.

(I) *Production job turnover.*

**Audit objective.** To determine the adequacy and appropriateness of software configuration management and production job turnover procedures.

**Audit procedures.**

- Understand the software configuration management and production turnover procedures available to move application system development and maintenance jobs into production. Inquire whether job turnover procedures are manual or automated. Manual procedures are difficult to control and error-prone and may not be suitable for a complex software environment.
- Sometimes the software may be migrated within one CPU, across several CPUs as in a distributed environment, or across a network with increasing order of difficulty. Conduct these audit procedures.
- Ascertain whether computer operations and production control staff conduct production acceptance testing of new or modified software prior to production turnover. If this practice is informal and uses manual procedures, there is a likelihood of greater frequency of production failures and an increase in the number of production-related problems. These problems, in turn, can cause downtime, shut down the system, reduce service levels, corrupt data, increase rerun time, cause overrun of scheduled batch jobs,

disrupt business operations, and cause loss of data processing credibility in the end user community.

- Inquire whether the application system approval process is paper-based or online. Paper processes can cause problems because required information may be omitted or by-passed. If properly implemented, online approvals by managers are relatively more reliable.
- If the problems are excessive, determine the need to automate the production turnover process. Identify its associated benefits.
- Ensure that system implementation checklists or production job turnover procedures include items such as database, production control, technical services/support, network control, security, operations, application, change management, quality assurance, and end user areas.

## CONTROL RISKS IN PRODUCTION OPERATIONS

The operations analyst may be given access to production data files and may perform maintenance to production application programs. Programmers may be given access to production data files.

---

(J) *Computer operations.*
**Audit objectives.**

- To evaluate the controls and procedures over execution of production jobs and programs.
- To determine whether run instructions for critical jobs are complete. Ensure that job setup procedures are clearly documented and that job rerun/restart procedures are clear.
- To determine whether monitoring of system resources is adequate.
- To ensure that computer operations management reviews console/system logs for operator interventions during program/job execution, label overrides, and equipment checks, and to ensure that the log is complete by capturing all activities.
- To ensure that file backup schedules and procedures are adequate.
- To determine whether the options and parameters selected in the system logging facility are relevant and useful.
- To ascertain whether production and operations problems are logged and followed up for corrective action.
- To ensure that good housekeeping practices are followed.
- To ensure that basic emergency procedures are followed and tested.
- To evaluate the adequacy of hardware preventive maintenance practices.

**Audit procedures.**

1.  **Production job processing.** Conduct these audit procedures to ensure that all scheduled production jobs are processed in a timely manner.

    - Obtain a list of all regularly scheduled application program and system backup jobs for a few days of audit time.
    - Ensure that all production jobs are completed per schedule. If not, ascertain the reasons for noncompliance. Determine the job backlog.

2.  **Production job abends.** In order to determine the causes of production job abends and to see how they were disposed, these audit procedures are suggested.

    - Using system logging facility records, extract a list of production job abends for a selected month.
    - Trace these abends to the logs for documentary evidence to determine that

      - Abends are properly reported.
      - Causes for abends are determined.
      - Abends are disposed of.

- The abend logs are reviewed by the computer operations supervisor(s) to prevent their recurrence.

3. **Production job reruns.** In order to determine the causes of production job reruns and to see how they were disposed, these audit procedures are suggested.

- Using system logging facility records, extract a list of production job reruns for a selected month.
- Trace these reruns to the logs for documentary evidence to determine that

  - Reruns are properly reported.
  - Causes for reruns are determined.
  - Correct job control information was entered for the next time.
  - The rerun logs are reviewed by the computer operations supervisor(s) to prevent their recurrence.

4. **System console logs.** Some key commands and information captured by operating system console logs are

- Operator commands and operator responses to system commands
- Equipment problems and failures (tape or disk failures)
- Equipment status
- Frequency of operator commands by command type or code
- Tape bypass label processing overrides
- Abnormal job terminations
- How long a job was executed with start and stop times
- Terminal communication problems such as messages held
- Operating system abends (abnormal ends)
- Database dumps start and completion times
- Database recovery and startup messages
- Print files in queue
- Transactions up (available) or down (not available) requests from users
- Communication management system starts and finish times which are needed to back up databases
- Job reruns and their times

In order to verify that computer operations management does a review of the system console logs to detect operator interventions during program/job execution, label override, and equipment checks, these audit procedures are suggested.

- Inquire how long console logs are retained. If the retention period is too short, say one week, suggest saving them as microfiche records for longer periods, if desired.
- Manually scan console logs for powerful commands and codes for selected operating days or shifts.
- Using automated audit software tool, create reports showing the use of powerful commands and codes.
- Inquire how often the operations supervisors review the console logs.

## CONTROL RISKS IN COMPUTER OPERATIONS

- Computer operators may turn off logging of system activity records, thus losing audit trails.
- The system activity records could be lost due to lack of space on the storage media (overflow).
- Computer console logs may not be retained long enough to facilitate follow-up work.

5. **Backup schedules.** Conduct these audit procedures to evaluate the adequacy and completeness of backup schedules.

- Obtain documentation that describes system backups. This should indicate what programs and data files should be backed up and their frequency. For example, a database may be backed up several times a day.
- Interview computer operators and obtain their assessment of the system backup situation. Determine whether there is enough time in an operating shift to make system backups.
- Determine the need to do incremental system backups instead of full system backups. Only changes since the last backup are backed up in the incremental system backup, which saves time, whereas the entire system is backed up each time a backup is done in the full backup system approach. Full system backups take more time than incremental system backups.

6. **Backup procedures.** In order to ensure that operators follow prescribed backup procedures, these audit procedures are suggested.

- Select a sample of operating days or shifts.
- Compare actual system backups against schedules.
- Note any deviations.

7. **Housekeeping activities.** In order to assess the housekeeping activities in a computer room, these audit procedures are suggested.

- Tour the computer room. Assess whether the place is free from dust and waste materials and that it is neatly organized.
- Ensure that flammable materials are not placed around the computer room to prevent a potential fire hazard.
- Inquire how often the area under the raised floor is cleaned.

8. **Computer operator practices.** Interview the shift supervisor for understanding of security control practices in the computer room, ask the following questions, and note any exceptions for improvement:

- Do computer operators who are required to initiate production jobs have a unique password, not a group password, in order to validate their identify and to exact accountability?

---

**Controls over Computer Operators**

- Separation of duties
- Mandatory vacations
- Activity logging
- Limited access to system documentation

---

- Are computer operators prohibited from initiating, entering, updating, and correcting a record in the transaction or master file of an application system, and are they prohibited from making any significant decisions involved in the running of an application system and its logic?
- Is computer operator decision making kept to a minimum and confined to activities/ areas such as system and job start-up, file backups, system shutdown, equipment reconfiguration, emergency message broadcasting, job rerun, tape mounting and demounting, and file recovery/restart?
- Are all actions taken by computer operators through console terminal commands recorded in a log, and is an exception report available for review by operations supervisors in order to detect any abnormal acts that could lead to computer-related fraudulent activities? Are console logs backed up on a magnetic tape for future retrieval?
- Do computer operators take mandatory vacations with a minimum block of one week at one time, and where practical are operators given a chance to enlarge/enrich their

jobs by rotating between operating shifts or other duties within the computer operations department? It is generally agreed that mandatory and long periods of vacation will help in detecting or surfacing any fraudulent activities.

- Are computer operators aware of the importance of monitoring that temperature and humidity levels are within the manufacturer's suggested tolerance limits? Are they monitoring those levels?
- When was the last time sprinklers or halon was tested by building maintenance and/or other professionals? Was it a successful exercise? Are the locations for the shut-off valves easily accessible and clearly labeled?
- Are there training programs and career development plans for the entire computer operations staff? If so, assess their relevancy and reasonableness. Verify whether employees are allowed to attend professional seminars and conferences and to become members of professional organizations in order to increase their knowledge and to strengthen their career advancement.
- Are computer reports decollated, bursted, and distributed according to the established guidelines, and are carbon papers disposed of securely by burning or shredding to prevent them from being used by unauthorized people?
- Are computer operators given only the operations documentation needed to do their job? Is system/program and user documentation restricted from their use?
- Is the read-after-write option being practiced when online? Are real-time database updates made to magnetic disks?
- How often are the computer room and the area under the raised floors vacuum cleaned to remove paper dust and other debris that could support a fire in the computer room?
- Are excessive computer paper and supplies stored in the computer print room? Excessive storage could support a fire.

## CONTROL RISK IN COMPUTER OPERATIONS

The computer operator may be given access to production data files and may perform maintenance to production application programs and job control files.

9. **Preventive maintenance.** Scheduled preventive maintenance is a good practice to keep hardware in good working condition. Conduct these audit procedures to evaluate the adequacy and timeliness of preventive maintenance activities.

- Understand the frequency of scheduled preventive maintenance work performed on hardware by vendors and/or in-house personnel.
- Compare this frequency to hardware maintenance contracts. Note any exceptions.
- Determine compliance with maintenance contractual agreements by examining maintenance log. Note any deviations.
- Ascertain whether scheduled maintenance has had any adverse effect on normal production schedule or critical business season.
- Determine whether preventive maintenance logs are retained. Identify abnormal hardware and software problems.
- Ensure that the hardware and peripheral equipment maintenance period commences on the same day that the warranty or guarantee period expires. This is to prevent paying additional maintenance charges for services that should be received under warranty or to eliminate the time gap between the maintenance and warranty periods. Here the objective is to obtain a continuity of maintenance service and protection of the hardware and peripheral equipment.
- Verify whether the hardware and peripheral equipment maintenance agreement includes a standard for maintenance call response time (8 to 12 hours is common or within 24 hours) that is defined as the maximum time allowed to elapse between the data processing staff notification of a problem to the vendor and the vendor's maintenance staff arrival on the vendee's premises.

**(K)** *Tape and disk management systems.*
### Audit objectives.

- To determine whether tape/cartridge and disk management system functions are used to their fullest extent.
- To evaluate the adequacy of review and use of system-generated reports for day-to-day management of operations.

**Audit procedures for tape management system.**  The auditor performing a review of magnetic tape files to assure proper usage and control of tapes should

- Inquire whether data in the tapes were classified as highly critical, critical, noncritical, or other.
- Confirm that the number of tape files maintained in the data center agrees with the physical inventory of tapes.
- Take a sample of tapes and confirm that external label descriptions match official descriptions to prevent possible use of incorrect file. External labels can be read by the operator. Computer programs read internal labels only. Internal file labels are better in minimizing the possibility of data or program file destruction than external file labels. Another way of looking at this issue is to treat external file labels as a first layer of protection and internal file labels as a secondary layer of protection, as shown in Exhibit 2.14.

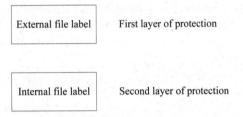

**Exhibit 2.14:  External and internal file labels**

The **Header (first) record** in an internal label usually contains this information.

- File name, reel number
- File ID number
- Volume serial number
- Sequence number
- File creation date
- File expiration date
- Blocking factor
- Record length in bytes
- Record type (i.e., fixed, variable)

The **Trailer (last) record** in an internal label usually contains this information

- End of file indicator
- Number of records
- Control totals such as batch totals

- Inquire whether tapes are degaussed before being sent out for cleaning, certification, or for other purposes.
- Review tape retention tables and confirm that tape retention periods in the tables are in agreement with management policies and regulatory agency guidelines.
- Test whether environmental controls (e.g., heat, humidity) in the tape library area are in compliance with the manufacturer's (vendor) recommended guidelines.

For organizations using an automated tape library management system, these audit procedures are recommended.

- Review the job control language used to describe tape label parameters to ensure that they conform to vendor suggested codes with proper meaning.

- Review data set names, volume serial numbers, and their dispositions for correctness.
- Inquire whether tape management system data sets are protected with password or other means.
- With the use of a batch utility program, print the audit records from the audit backup file (disk or tape) to identify audit exception records and input/output activity records.
- Inquire whether computer operations management is using a tape management system copy utility to back up the tape management catalog data sets and audit datasets and to restore the cataloged data sets if they are destroyed.
- Review security table for proper options such as tape inquiry and update capabilities on the cataloged datasets.

## CONTROL RISK IN TAPE LIBRARY

The tape librarian may be given access to production data files and may perform maintenance to production application programs and job control files.

- Confirm that passwords to tape management system data sets are changed periodically and that passwords for terminated employees are not included.
- Ascertain that the tape management data set used to activate or deactivate the entire tape management systems is password protected, especially for the deactivation task.
- Ascertain whether the tape bypass label processing option in the tape management system is controlled by restricting its use to limited individuals in the computer operations area.

**Audit procedures for disk management system.**  The auditor performing a review of magnetic disk files to ensure proper usage and control of disk resources should

- Verify that access to disk media management systems is restricted through the use of passwords and based on the need-to-know philosophy.
- Determine whether disk media are most frequently used for day-to-day processing and storage and that tape/cartridge media are used for backup purpose only.
- Confirm that computer operations management receives periodic reports on disk media performance.

## AUDIT/CONTROL RISKS IN COMPUTER STORAGE MEDIA

- Data sets may be erased by mistake.
- Data sets may be allowed to expire before their useful life has ended.
- Reel tapes, cartridges, and diskettes could be lost or misplaced.
- Disk drives or tape drives could malfunction, thereby not completing the system backups.
- Software, processing, or operator errors could compromise the integrity of original as well as backup data sets.

(L) *System logs*.
### Audit objectives.

- To determine whether appropriate system logs are produced.
- To ascertain whether system logs are secured.

### Audit procedures.

1. **System logging facility event recording.** To ensure that the system logging facility routines select all system events for recording, these audit procedures are suggested.

   - Identify any selection criteria in effect that will exclude system logging facility records from being logged.

- Ensure that all selected events are written to permanent files to facilitate historical reviews of system activity by identifying the means used to write logging records to permanent files.
- Assess the steps taken by operators to prevent the system logging facility from stopping writing records when the operator forgets to dump records from disk to tape. Ensure that a file dump is taken at the beginning and at the end of every operating shift. Review the storage security and retention controls over system logging facility tape files. Determine their adequacy; usually data are saved for 30 to 40 days.

2. **System logging facility access controls.** To ensure that users or their programs can make no modifications to the system logging facility event records at any time, these audit procedures are suggested.

   - Ensure that parameter library dataset is write-protected.
   - Determine the access authority given to the log files.
   - Determine that no unauthorized supervisor routines exist.
   - Determine that the number of users with special access authority is limited.
   - Determine the adequacy of audit trails.
   - Review the jobs that dump system logging facility data sets. Determine that their execution is in a controlled environment through tests of PROC library execution and access controls.

3. **System logging facility reporting.** With the use of audit software or other report writing program, produce the following information from system logging facilities for further analysis:

   - Number of occurrences of an initial program load
   - Number of jobs or steps that were terminated abnormally
   - Number of times critical data sets opened, deleted, or renamed
   - Number of records lost in any interruption in system logging facility recording
   - Names of data sets scratched, lost, or renamed
   - Number of occurrences of password invalidity

(M) *Help desk function review.*
   **Audit objectives.**

   - To determine whether documentation describing problem isolation and determination is clear and complete.
   - To evaluate the procedures for problem logging, tracking, resolution, and escalation.
   - To ensure that help desk staff is properly trained in their job.

   **Audit procedures.** In order to assure the adequacy and reasonability of the help desk function and hot-line services, conduct the following audit procedures:

   - Determine whether predefined problem isolation and determination procedures are available and that they are documented.
   - Ascertain whether problem logging, tracking, and resolution procedures are available and that they are clearly documented. Inquire whether standard time guidelines are defined for problem resolution.
   - Assess whether procedures are clearly established and reported as to the location of problem sources (i.e., problems resulting from a terminal, host computer, operating system, terminal controller, telecommunications circuits, third-party system, in-house application program, remote/local printer).
   - Verify that contact names and phone numbers in the data processing department are available for problem reporting and routing.
   - Find out if procedures are clear and complete in terms of handling a user problem, such as a user forgot a password, a password has expired, the system denies access although the password is correct, or a user cannot get through an application system because the system requires a multiple-level password.

- Assess whether a call list is available showing whom and how to contact people within the organization, such as data security, technical support, application support, end users, and third-party system support outside the organization.
- Determine the availability of problem escalation procedures for end users and help desk function for reporting to second-level people when problems are not resolved timely and/or first-level people are not available.
- If a voice response system is used either to supplement or substitute for a human-based help desk function, test it by placing some problem calls through the system to ensure that the call routing is properly done and that the response on the receiving end is timely, competent, and adequate.

## AUDIT RISKS IN HELP DESK OPERATION

The auditor may fail to recognize

- Users like to know before the system goes down.
- Help desk staff may not answer the phone quickly or keep the user on hold for long time.
- The help received through the help desk staff is no help at all.
- Weekend, evening, or night shift problems are not resolved properly due to inadequate help desk staff.
- Help desk operators are not courteous and friendly.
- Help desk staff may not return user calls.
- Help desk staff is not knowledgeable in solving problems related to business application systems.

---

(xxiii) **Web infrastructure: Audit objectives and procedures**
**Audit objective.** To ensure that Web management issues are properly addressed and controlled to reduce potential risks and exposures to the organization.
**Audit procedures.**

- Determine how performance issues, such as response time and service bottlenecks, are handled. Suggest using bigger-capacity routers, installing faster modems, and upgrading backbone links to speed Internet access.
- Determine how "cookies" are used or blocked.
- Determine whether Internet firewalls, encryption, and digital signatures are implemented to protect Web resources from unauthorized access and use.

(xxiiv) **Software licensing: Audit objectives and procedures**
**Audit objectives.**

- To ensure that risks and exposures are minimized or eliminated with software licensing practices
- To determine whether software piracy polices are distributed and implemented throughout the organization.
- To ensure that information systems contracts are properly administered and complied with.

**Audit procedures.**

- **Software licensing practices.** Review software licensing agreements in terms of site license, per-server license, or floating license. Understand how they are used in practice.
- **Software piracy policies.** Review the software piracy policies to protect the organization from legal suits by software owners. Test a sample of users for adhering to the software piracy policies.
- **Information systems contracts.** Review the contracts for terms and condition, penalties for nonperformance by vendors or consultants, and software development and maintenance work.

### (xxv) Electronic funds transfer/electronic data interchange

(A) *Electronic funds transfer systems.* A full scope review of an electronic funds transfer (EFT) system should include automated teller machine (ATM) systems, automated clearinghouse (ACH) systems, and wire transfer systems.[13] This review is more applicable to bank auditors.

#### ATM systems

An ATM should have controls similar to a human teller, including frequent reconcilement to the general ledger. Handling of deposits made through ATMs should be under joint custody until the amounts and items have been verified. Remaining procedures for ATM systems deal with controls over plastic cards and personal identification numbers (PINs). The use of PINs to ensure customer account protection is a critical control. Bank employees should not have access to customer PINs. Some banks have been known to retain reports that contain customer PINs. This practice greatly reduces the strength of the control over direct access to customer funds through an ATM. Computer programs used to generate the PINs and the encryption key (base algorithm for generating PINs) should be generally restricted from most employees. Procedures to monitor the use of these programs should be in place.

Strict controls over access to unused plastic cards and to the facilities to emboss and encode information is required. This requirement closely relates to the procedure for controlling cards that have been retained at the ATM. Additionally, a common control practice is to ensure that cards and PIN mailers are not mailed simultaneously to the customer. Returned mail due to wrong address or other invalid information needs to be controlled so a bank employee cannot obtain a customer card and PIN for unauthorized access.

Some ATM systems allow online account maintenance that can associate any account with a specific ATM card. The card could then be used to withdraw funds from an account not owned by that customer or employee. Activity reports should be printed and reviewed to ensure proper use of these transactions. The auditor should test card and account relationships to ensure the integrity of the ATM process.

**Audit objective.** To determine the adequacy of controls over ATM systems.

**Audit procedures.**

- Review procedures related to ATM servicing and balancing functions, including

  - ATM service team members are not employees with incompatible duties.
  - Separation of duties between balancing and servicing is maintained.
  - Control of cash and deposit envelopes to ensure proper posting and handling.
  - Control of "hot cards" retained at ATM to ensure proper distribution and/or destruction.
  - Control of off-line machine transaction cassettes or floppy diskettes to ensure proper posting.

- Observe the servicing and balancing of selected ATM sites to ensure procedures are being followed.
- Determine that there are adequate controls over issuance, maintenance, and customer usage of PINs.
- Ensure that adequate controls exist over any encryption keys and PIN calculation programs.
- Determine that dual control procedures are in effect for accessing, processing, issuing, delivering, and destroying plastic cards.

#### ACH systems

Several problems with processing automated clearing house (ACH) items have been observed over the past few years. Some banks have problems with processing the same ACH items more than once because of poor balancing controls. ACH items may be sent to the bank several days in advance. In these cases, the bank should not give available credit to the customer until

---

[13] *Understanding and Auditing EDI and Open Network Controls* (*Chicago: Bank Administration Institute, 1991*).

the proper date because the bank does not have the funds. Memo postings of ACH items to the online systems for same day withdrawal is another concern for customer satisfaction.

More banks are beginning to originate ACH items for their corporate customers. Many of these systems are PC-based and use dial-up facilities between the customer and the bank. The auditor should carefully review controls over this process to ensure proper accountability for all transactions. Agreements between the bank and the customer should clarify requirements for both parties.

An area where ACH systems most likely will play a major role is in eliminating the paper documents involved in various transactions such as purchasing using electronic data interchange systems and just-in-time inventories. Banks are becoming involved as the third party in the payment side of many of these transactions.

**Audit objective.** To determine the adequacy of controls over ACH systems.

**Audit procedure.** Review procedures for processing ACH transactions to ensure reconcilement to Federal Reserve Bank (Fed) totals and the proper handling of rejected items.

### Wire transfer systems

Wire transfer systems, including manual-based systems, are a very high-risk area for banks of all sizes. Transactions for wire transfer can involve significant cost. Fraud is a major concern. These fraud problems tend to involve insiders, simple schemes, poor security, and inadequate control procedures. If one employee has complete control over executing wire transfers and reconciling due-to, due-from, and Fed accounts, exposures to fraud potential is very high.

**Audit objective.** To ascertain whether controls over wire transfer systems are adequate.

**Audit procedures.**

- Determine that appropriate wire transfer controls are in place, including

  - Callback procedures or use of authorization codes
  - Authentication for nonrepeating wires
  - Documentation of all wire transfers
  - Approvals for unusual wires (e.g., over a certain amount)
  - Recording phone calls relating to wires
  - Access control over authorization codes
  - Separation of duties between reconciling due-to, due-from, and Fed accounts and executing wire transfers
- For PC-based wire transfer systems, ensure that proper physical and data security controls are in place.

(B) *Electronic data interchange systems.*

Documenting the electronic data interchange (EDI) system provides the foundation and scope of the audit program.[14] This helps the auditor understand the EDI environment prior to performing the audit fieldwork, setting the budget, determining the technical resources required, and assessing the overall control evaluation.

**Audit objective.** To review, evaluate, and test the EDI information system in order to determine that controls exist and perform as expected according to standards and policies concerning the management and administration of EDI.

**Audit procedures.** These audit procedures are suggested to ensure that properly authorized transactions are processed.

- Test EDI report distribution. Ensure that it is adequately controlled.
- Verify reject transaction processing. Ensure that all rejected transactions are flagged and reported as rejects and further processing of such transactions ceases.
- Confirm advice notification process. Ensure that input transactions generate advices that are returned to the transaction originator. Find out if transactions initiated by EDI trading partners are advised by the receivers and that these advices are properly reviewed.

---

[14] *EDP Auditing Guide* (Chicago: Bank Administration Institute, 1991).

- Determine that maintenance forms exist; note date of approval. Maintenance forms must be properly approved prior to input.
- Verify that dollar or specific transaction edits perform as expected. Confirm that EDI applications will prevent transactions other than a trading partner, above specified dollar limit from processing or beyond a specific type of transaction. Ensure that the computer program will edit mandatory fields on all incoming transactions.

To determine whether EDI controls ensure that all received transactions are entered into the system, these audit procedures are recommended.

- Examine EDI sequence control process. Ensure that there is computer sequence checking of the control numbers with out-of-sequence numbers getting flagged on the reports.
- Test batch total processing. Ensure that the system uses batch totals and performs reconciliations.
- Sample error processing and advice reconciliation. Ensure that errors and/or rejects are logged in a queue file and an appropriate advice is returned to the sender. Ensure that all transactions received are acknowledged by the system.
- Design and test for duplicate transaction entries. Ensure that duplication transactions are controlled and reviewed. Confirm that the EDI network edits and holds duplicate records.

These audit procedures are advised to ensure that the EDI application controls the accuracy of information that is entered into the system.

- Confirm that there is adequate segregation of duties between the EDI users and the EDI security administrator.
- Identify and test any management overrides. Ensure that the EDI system will prevent the overriding or bypassing of data editing. Inquire if EDI has an automatic interface with the payment system to ensure that customers have the necessary funds to perform the required transaction. The error message clearly indicates corrective action. There is a means of preventing duplicate or reentry of transactions.
- Evaluate exception report use, items reported, and actual use. Understand whether the exception report provides relevant, reliable, and useful information.
- Identify supervisor approval of transactions and test controls. Ensure that supervisors will review sensitive transactions after they are initiated. Ensure that there are controls over job scheduling to prevent unauthorized jobs getting processed.

## AUDIT/CONTROL RISKS IN EDI APPLICATIONS

- For applications involving EDI, proper controls, such as dial-up and dial-back for connecting computers and networks, access security controls, such as positive identification of all users, and audit/information trails may not be established.
- EDI transactions and networks may not be backed up and files/records may not be stored both on site and off site.

To ensure that EDI file update processing occurs in a complete manner, these audit procedures are suggested.

- Verify control over total processing. Confirm that there is an automated check of control totals generated by EDI to final file output.
- Determine the incoming file check to final outbound file. Confirm that there is an automated check of inbound file detail to final outbound file output.
- Validate that rejected and partially processed entries are identified and resolved. Ensure that the EDI application will flag and store rejected and partially processed entries.
- Determine the process to sequence and control outbound transactions. Confirm that the EDI application will assign record sequence control numbers for all outbound transmissions. Ensure that there are standardized default options assigned by users and that there is an error recovery mechanism that includes identification and correction procedures. Find

out if reports are delivered to appropriate areas for reconciliation purposes. Confirm that invalid transactions are rejected before corrupting files.

These audit procedures are suggested to ensure that the EDI application design provides auditable information.

- Verify cross-references that track source to output to provide an auditable link.
- Determine that input process places time and date stamps on all inbound transactions.
- Review report identification controls. Ensure that the reports include title, processing date, program name and an identifying number.
- Review error prevention and detection procedures for adequacy.
- Test EDI audit trail procedures for logging, updating, and monitoring activities. Determine whether the EDI application produces an audit trail of before and after images for all updated files and a transaction log showing time, date, and operator. Ensure that there is logging and reporting of EDI application–generated activities, including the origination of the inbound transaction and destination of the outbound transaction.

To ensure that EDI application's data files, messages, programs, translators, utility programs, databases, and program libraries are secure, these audit procedures are recommended.

- Confirm that passwords are stored in encrypted format and that users can dynamically change their passwords.
- Examine value-added network (VAN) security procedures and controls for adequacy. Make sure that if a security violation occurs, the VAN will log the violation and cease processing.
- Ensure that EDI system activity is logged to allow end-to-end tracing of transmissions.
- Ensure that EDI database resources are adequately protected and access authority is assigned strictly on a need-to-know basis. Verify if access to the database is protected by security software.
- Ensure that utility programs are protected from unauthorized access and that audit trails show the changes made when utility programs are run.
- Ensure that EDI translator programs perform message acknowledgment and that these programs verify messages and identify the trading partner. Note that unacknowledged messages require special handling.
- Review to determine if development (test) libraries, production libraries, system software libraries, and data file libraries are separate from each other and that they are adequately protected with access appropriately assigned to specific individuals.
- Ensure that source program versions are adequately secured and controlled to facilitate concurrent development of multiple versions.
- Find out if there is an effective mechanism to escalate, report, and follow up on access violation.

These audit procedures are suggested to ensure that EDI backup and recovery procedures are tested for disaster recovery.

- Review EDI contingency backup plan. Verify that all data and program libraries are systematically backed up.
- Verify that functional users are familiar with the contingency plan procedures and that they participate in the contingency testing process.
- Ensure that all test events and problems are logged and distributed to all affected parties so that corrective action is taken.

(xxvi) *Electronic commerce: Audit objectives and procedures.*
   **Audit objectives.**

- To ensure that e-commerce software is used for its intended purposes.
- To ensure that e-commerce infrastructure is stable and secure to meet the business needs

   **Audit procedures.**

- Review whether the e-commerce software is facilitating product or service sales, shopping cart facilities are adequate, transaction processing is timely, and Web site traffic data analysis are performed periodically to meet the business needs.
- Review the e-commerce infrastructure for stability and security in terms of hardware, server operating system, server software, virtual private network, and value-added network. Determine whether the Web site is attractive to potential customers and suppliers.

### (xxvii) Information protection: Audit objectives and procedures

#### (A) *Computer viruses.*

**Audit objective.** To ensure that the organization is not severely exposed to computer viruses and that adequate controls are in place to prevent, detect, and correct the effect of viruses.

**Audit procedures.** Review the controls in place to prevent, detect, and correct the computer viruses. Suggested controls to prevent or detect computer viruses follow.

- Computer security education should be a prerequisite to any computer use.
- All system users should be made aware of how to prevent and detect computer viruses.
- All executable program files should be compared daily by system users. Any unexplained change indicates a possible risk of a virus.
- All unlicensed programs should be deleted from PCs and network files by users or data security/LAN administrator. These programs could be a possible source for viruses.
- All inactive user accounts should be purged from the network files and directories by LAN/data security administrator.
- Policies should address whether public domain and shareware software can be used or downloaded.
- An "isolated system" or test system concept should be implemented to test internally developed software and vendor-developed software, and updates to vendor software, prior to use. This is to test the software for a possible virus. The test system should not be used by other users, should not connect to networks, and should not contain any valuable data.
- Technical controls should be implemented to minimize the risk of virus. These include user authentication mechanisms (e.g., passwords), providing selective levels of access to files and directories (read-only, no access, access to certain users), and include write-protection mechanisms on tapes and diskettes.
- Antiviral software should be acquired and used to indicate "typical" malicious software. However, do not download or use pirated copies of antiviral software because they could be infected too.
- System-sweep programs should be acquired and used to automatically check files for changes in size, date, and content.
- When vendor software is purchased, the vendor should be asked what dependencies the product has: what other programs it was developed with or that it depends on to function. This information can be used to gauge the riskiness of using a product in terms of spreading the virus. In general, the fewer software dependencies a network has, the lower the virus risk.
- The number of software products of the same kind should be limited to prevent the spreading of virus. This means it is good to have only one version or copy of spreadsheet, word processing, or desktop publishing software on the network.
- Contingency procedures should be developed for restoring backups after a virus attack.
- Passwords should be sent over the wire in an encrypted manner to prevent tapping into the wire for disclosure of the password.
- Dial-back modems should be established for dial-in access through telephones.
- PC-based software diskettes should be screened for the presence of a virus prior to their use.
- Centralized purchase of PC-based software and hardware should be established.
- PC-based software and hardware should be acquired from reliable and reputable vendors only.

(B) *Electronic mail.*

      **Audit objective.** To evaluate the adequacy of policies, procedures, and controls over electronic-mail system.

      **Audit procedures.** Electronic mail (e-mail) is a substitute for sending critical, time-bound, and time-sensitive short documents and messages in person, by phone, or by postal mail. E-mail arose from the needs of employees at all levels to receive and send documents and messages sooner and faster. These audit procedures are suggested.

- Understand who is authorized to receive and send documents and messages through the use of the e-mail system. Determine whether the use of e-mail is required to do the job.
- Ascertain whether a policy is established defining e-mail usage so only employees at certain job levels, grades, and titles can use the e-mail system.

## BUSINESS/CONTROL RISKS IN ELECTRONIC MAIL

- The privacy policy governing the use of e-mail may not be available to protect the company from legal suits when an employee reads other employee messages.
- A seamless (boundaryless), full-function e-mail system may not be available to key locations throughout the organization regardless of hardware and software vendor platforms.

---

- Inquire whether the e-mail system allocates default passwords to new users based on their initials. This practice should be discouraged. Alternately, the e-mail system should allow default password to new users on their first session, which should be followed by requesting the user to select a new password for second time and for subsequent use.
- Ascertain that the same terminal sign-on procedures used for accessing business systems (e.g., TSO, CICS, and applications) are used to access the e-mail system.
- Find out whether the e-mail system requires both user ID and password to access and use it.
- Determine whether the users of the e-mail system periodically change passwords (e.g., monthly).
- Inquire whether e-mail documents and messages can be printed at authorized and limited printers only.
- Verify if messages can be risk ranked and that high-risk messages cannot be printed at all or printed at authorized and limited printers only.
- Determine how long e-mail documents and messages stay on the system and understand the purging criteria. See that it is not too long. Two weeks is a common practice.
- Ensure that the security system prevents an employee from getting into others' e-mail message boxes.
- By taking a sample of receiving and sending messages, verify that employees are not using the e-mail machines for personal use.
- Verify that employees are not using the e-mail system to transmit bulky and big documents (i.e., more than three pages) when in fact they should be sent through regular postal mail.
- Inquire whether critical messages and documents can be encrypted.
- Test that employees who are authorized to sign-on to e-mail system cannot automatically get into business applications and database systems. This means access to e-mail should be separate from access to other systems.
- Evaluate whether networks used for e-mail are vulnerable to computer viruses, worms, or other kind of security threats.

(xxviii) **Encryption: Audit objectives and procedures**

      **Audit objective.** To determine whether the organization is using encryption methods to protect the confidentiality and privacy of corporate or personal data and information.

      **Audit procedures.**

- Review the encryption methods for their strength, the length of the key (the longer the key, the stronger the protection), and the appropriateness of the encryption key system selected (symmetric or asymmetric key system).
- Ensure that digital signatures and digital certificates are properly issued, controlled, and distributed throughout the organization.

**(xxvix) Enterprise-wide resource planning software: Audit objectives and procedures**

**Audit objective.** To ensure that acquisition and implementation of enterprise-wide resource planning (ERP) system meets the strategic and operational objectives.

**Audit procedures.**

- Review management justification analysis document for acquiring and implementing the ERP system throughout the organization.
- Determine whether implementation of ERP system has improved the value chain.
- Determine whether implementation of ERP system has improved internal work flow. processes, decreased costs, increased revenues, and integrated well with other application systems. Identify problems in relying solely on one vendor for the ERP system.

**(xxx) Operational applications systems: Audit objectives and procedures**

**(A) *Data origination and preparation controls review*.**

**Audit objective.** To evaluate controls and procedures over data origination and preparation activities.

**Audit procedures.**

- Review written procedures for originating, authorizing, collecting, preparing, and approving input transactions. Ascertain whether users understand and follow these procedures.
- Review source documents or other input forms to determine whether they are prenumbered. Also, review transaction identification codes and other frequently used constant data fields to determine whether they are precoded to minimize errors in data preparation, data entry, and data conversion.
- Where applicable, verify that all input for a batch system is sent through a data control section for scanning, reviewing, and logging prior to data entry.
- Determine whether users prepare input-control totals for batch systems and for online systems using a terminal entry and batch-updating method of processing. Verify whether users reconcile input-control totals to output-control totals.
- Ascertain whether the data control section has a cut-off schedule indicating when input data is due from user departments and when reports are due from the data control section.
- Ascertain whether the data control section reconciles input-control totals received from users to totals generated by computer.
- Determine whether filing and retention of source documents and other input forms are logical, documents are easily retrievable, and the retention practices meet the legal, tax, government, and regulatory agency requirements, and the established management policies and procedures.
- Review the adequacy and currency of error correction and resubmission procedures, including whether users perform periodic review of the cumulative error listings. Evaluate the error logging and tracking methods used to ensure that errors are corrected and reentered properly and in a timely manner.

**(B) *Data input controls review*.**

**Audit objective.** To evaluate controls and procedures over data input activities.

**Audit procedures.**

- For batch systems, ascertain whether data conversion or the keypunch instruction manual includes samples of source documents and identification of data fields to be entered and verified.
- For online systems, verify the use of methods to prevent data entry errors, such as self-help features, preselected formats or menu selection, and operator prompting. Evaluate

video display units or computer-terminal user procedures for data-entry and inquiry activities.

- For transactions entered through online terminals, determine whether all input transactions are automatically logged with date and time of transmission, and determine whether user department, terminal, and user identification are included as part of the input transaction record.
- Review transaction logs for online input terminals to detect any unauthorized access and entry of data. Review the computer programs to learn whether they include automated internal program processing controls in the form of data-input edit and validation routines (i.e., check digits, reasonableness tests, batch totals, and record counts). Evaluate their accuracy and relevancy.

## Data Field Validation Controls

- Check digit calculations
- Consistency checks
- Range checks
- Reasonableness checks
- Limit checks
- Completeness checks

- Compare, validate, foot, and recompute selected critical data fields or elements with the use of manual and/or automated testing tools. Evaluate the accuracy and relevancy of test results.
- For online terminals, determine whether input data are validated and errors are corrected as data are entered into the computer system.
- Ascertain whether users review internal tables periodically to ensure the accuracy of their values.
- Review and evaluate the significance of default options or forced value coding features in critical application programs.

## Input Controls

- Batch/hash control totals
- Data editing and validation routines such as transaction limit tests, cross-checks between data fields, sequence checks, completeness tests, logic tests, check-digit tests, anticipation controls, cross-footing or related data fields, test for invalid numeric and sign, date checks, test for valid codes, reasonableness test

- Review and evaluate the rounding and truncating features in mathematical and financial calculations to determine the potential impact of rounding errors.
- Determine whether adequate audit trails are included in the data dictionary. Check to see whether data-input edit and validation routines are described in the data dictionary, and verify whether these data-input edit and validation tests are performed on data before a database master record is updated. Identify program and data interrelationships. This should allow for tracing a data path through the program and the system as a whole.
- Ascertain whether the computer programs have a procedure to use look-up tables for verification of codes (i.e., state, transaction, and account numbers) rather than being hard-coded in the program. (Hard-coded information is difficult to maintain and requires more programmer time and effort than do table-updating methods.)
- Review input error correction and resubmission procedures. When a correction is reentered into the system, ascertain whether it is subject to the same program edit and validation controls as the original transaction. Determine whether users perform periodic reviews of the entire error suspense file contents. Evaluate the error logging and tracking methods.

- Identify, with users, any critical error codes or messages that should have been active but have never appeared on error reports. Determine whether error message routines have been deactivated by reviewing computer program source listings. Evaluate the reasons for any deactivation noted and ascertain whether users are aware of such error code deactivation. (This is to determine whether error codes were deactivated with the knowledge of and/or at the written request of users or whether error codes were simply no longer required because of changes that occurred after the original system design.) Note that the last three audit procedures are also applicable to the area of data processing and update controls.

(C) *Data processing controls review.*
    **Audit objective.** To evaluate controls and procedures over data processing activities.
    **Audit procedures.**

- Review input control totals that facilitate the balancing of processing controls to determine whether all authorized transactions are processed accurately and properly.
- Ascertain whether there are automated run-to-run control totals so that data will not be lost between processing jobs, cycles, or programs.

**Processing Controls**

- Data editing and validation routines (explained in input controls)
- Restart/recovery procedures
- Run-to-run control totals

- Check to see whether the data control section reconciles manual batch control totals with automated batch-control totals; verify run-to-run control totals from one processing job to another before distribution of reports to users.
- Review the movement and control of data from one computer-processing job to another and between or within user departments. Determine whether existing controls are adequate and effective.
- Ascertain whether job-accounting reports are reviewed by computer operations supervisors for detection of unauthorized accesses and acts by users, computer operator, and others.
- Review the computer programs to determine whether they include automated program controls in the form of data-processing edit and validation routines (i.e., record counts, line counts, and reasonableness and relational tests). Evaluate their accuracy and relevancy.
- When data are moved or passed from one processing job or step to another, check to see that control totals are generated by the program and verified, and that data are not merely moved or transferred from one job or step to another without such control.
- Review the default options and forced value coding features included either in vendor-supplied or in-house–developed applications software. Determine whether they work properly and assess the possible consequences of their failure.
- Determine whether control totals are printed at the end of reports to provide adequate management, audit, transaction, information, or processing trails.
- Ascertain whether users' review internal tables (used in master-file updating) periodically to ensure the accuracy of their values.
- Ascertain whether before/after image reporting is available for all transaction, reference, or master-file updating activities.
- Compare, validate, foot, and recompute selected critical data fields or elements with the use of manual and/or automated testing and audit software tools. Evaluate the accuracy and relevancy of test results.

(D) *System-related file maintenance controls review.*
    **Audit objective.** To evaluate controls over system-related data and program files and libraries.

**Audit procedures.**

- For each application system in production status, ascertain whether backup and recovery procedures for data and program files are documented and tested prior to having moved the system from test to production status. Determine their adequacy and currency.
- Review written procedures for movement of backup materials and documents between mainframe computer facility to off-site storage facility. Determine whether these procedures are being followed actively and effectively.
- Verify whether critical computer program files, computer data files, data dictionary, documentation, source documents and input forms, and supplies are stored both at on-site and off-site facilities. Compare actual existence of these materials to a log or book maintained by a tape librarian or similar function. Reconcile any differences and suggest corrective actions, if appropriate.

---
**Controls over Data Files**

---
- Batch totals
- Hash totals
- File label checking
- File cross-footing checks
- Checksums
- File locking controls
- File compression and archiving procedures
- File backup and recovery procedures
- Designating file owners, sponsors, custodians, and users

---

- Verify the existence of a contingency plan and that critical application systems and data files are properly identified in the contingency plan.
- Review the contingency plan and backup arrangement contracts to determine whether they are complete and current. Identify and document any potential risks or exposures that would render the contract inoperative.
- Ascertain whether critical application systems have been tested on the backup computer using only program files, data dictionary, data files, documentation, source documents and input forms, supplies, and contingency plan procedures taken from the off-site storage facility. This is to ensure the accuracy and currency of the contingency plan. Verify whether users have reviewed and reconciled the processing results produced by the backup computer with those produced by the primary computer.

(E) *Data output controls review.*

　　**Audit objective.** To evaluate controls and procedures over system-output activities.
　　**Audit procedures.**

- Determine whether users reconcile input control totals to output control totals via processing control totals. This is to ensure the accuracy of computer program-processing. System-generated reports can be used to perform this reconciliation.
- Determine whether data control personnel scan output reports to detect obvious errors, such as missing data fields, unreasonable values, and incorrect report format, before distributing to users.
- Verify that adequate identification is made of all reports and items on the reports, such as report name and number, date produced, accounting month-end or other effective date, company and department name and number, page number, program number (if necessary), end-of-report messages, subtotals, and report totals.

## Output Controls

- Output distribution procedures
- Security access controls for data viewing, file copying
- Output storage procedures
- Output disposal techniques
- Input/output reconciliation procedures
- Limiting access to spooled data sets
- "End-of-report" markings

- Compare output report distribution lists with users actually receiving the reports and to find out whether unauthorized users are receiving the reports or authorized users are not receiving the reports.
- Determine whether outdated and unneeded output reports are destroyed by shredding instead of placing them in a waste container.
- Determine whether there is a continuing need for generated output report.
- Review output report retention periods. Determine their adequacy.
- Determine whether header and trailer record counts printed out at the end of each output report. If not, ascertain how data file integrity is maintained.
- Review output error correction and resubmission procedures. Determine their adequacy and relevancy. Evaluate the error logging and tracking methods.
- Ascertain whether users review the report balancing rules and reconciliation procedures periodically for accuracy and appropriateness.

(F) *Application system documentation controls review.*

**Audit objective.** To determine the adequacy of application system documentation.

**Audit procedures.**

- Ascertain whether documentation of system, program, computer operations, help desk, network control, and system user functions and procedures are produced as part of system development and maintenance activities.
- Find out whether someone is held responsible and accountable for making various types of documentation available and keeping them current.
- Verify whether documentation problems such as lack of adequate documentation or difficulty in understanding are reported to information systems management for timely and proper corrective action.
- Ascertain whether users and computer operations staff accept new application systems without proper documentation.
- Ascertain whether appropriate documentation is updated to reflect program changes and modifications.
- Determine the need for the use of automated software documentation aids.
- Verify whether documentation librarian maintains a log of people who received various types of documentation.
- Verify whether system, program, computer operations, help desk, network control, and system user documentation manuals are available for each application system in production status (see Exhibit 2.15). Evaluate the contents for consistency and relevancy of documentation. Determine whether the documentation is adequate, complete, and current.

| Documentation type | Documentation contents |
|---|---|
| Systems manual | System flowchart; system requirements; system functions; design specifications; screen layouts; sample reports |
| Program manual | Program flowcharts; program functions; file layouts; program specifications |
| Computer operations manual | Job setup procedures; job narratives; job rerun and restart procedures; file backup procedures; report distribution procedures |
| User manual | System functions; sample screen and report layouts; report balancing procedures; file maintenance procedures; error correction |
| Help-desk manual | Contact names and phone numbers of users and IS staff; problem diagnostic and reporting procedures; problem escalation procedures; problem logging, tracking, and closing procedures |
| Network control manual | Information about circuits, nodes, lines, modems; problem diagnostic procedures; problem reporting and resolution procedures; network backup and contingency procedures |

**Exhibit 2.15: Application system documentation types and contents**

(G) *Data integrity controls review.*

**Audit objective.** To evaluate the adequacy of data integrity controls.

**Audit procedures.**

- Identify and select critical data files for audit review and testing purposes. Obtain and review record layouts and program narratives to understand how certain data fields are updated and the processing logic associated with it.

    Using generalized or customized audit software or utility programs, accumulate total records in a file and/or total dollar value of critical data fields or other control totals. Then compare them to independently available control totals maintained by users. Develop a test plan, test cases, test data, and expected test results for comparison with actual test results. Evaluate the accuracy and relevancy of the test results.

- Evaluate the adequacy of data input and processing edit and validation rules applicable to critical and sensitive data elements contained in the data dictionary. Trace the data elements' paths through the application system by reviewing programs, data files, and reports. Assess their accuracy and consistency.

- Evaluate whether automated program controls, such as data input and data processing edit and validation routines, are logical and appropriate to the application system.

- Verify that computer programs compare transaction dates on input transactions to parameter controlled month-end cutoff dates to ensure consistency and that transactions entering after the cutoff date are included in the following month.

- Evaluate the adequacy of management, transaction, audit, information, or processing trails. Is an audit trail of changes to the database, in the form of a log, produced? If it is not, find out how the database is controlled.

- For online systems, test to see whether data fields are being updated when inquiry requests are being processed.

- For online systems using destructive (buried, in place) updating of random (direct) access files, ensure that there is a log of the status of a master-file record prior to and after the updating. Verify whether the log indicates the source of data.

(H) *User satisfaction review.*

Assessment of system user satisfaction is a very important part of the audit of an application system. This is because it is the system user who paid for, owns, and uses the system. In fact, the system is not successful and useful if the system user is not satisfied with system functions and results. One way to assess user satisfaction is to conduct user surveys periodically. System usability should be a major concern for the user and the auditor.

**Audit objective.** To assess user satisfaction with the results of the system.

**Audit procedures.**

- Determine whether management policies and procedures are available regarding access to and use of information. Assess their adequacy and relevancy.

- Ascertain whether the application system produces accurate, complete, timely, and reliable results.

## Controls to Ensure User Satisfaction

- User involvement in system development and maintenance projects
- User surveys
- Service-level agreements
- Performance standards
- Total quality management programs
- Threshold limits
- Problem management techniques

- Evaluate whether users are able to use the information produced by the application system in their decision-making process.
- Ascertain whether users are able to understand the reports and information produced by the application system.
- Verify whether users are satisfied with the information produced by the application system.
- Review user controls practiced in receiving, storing, securing, and retrieving information available on computer output reports, microfilm, microfiche, optical disk, and other output media. Determine their adequacy and relevancy.
- Ascertain whether users actively participate in developing user requirements, design and program specifications, and review system test and acceptance test results for new or revised application systems.
- Review user controls practiced in transferring information through the exchange of memos, letters, and computer reports to and from the employees/departments. Determine their adequacy and relevancy.
- Where control weaknesses are identified in the data processing department, ascertain whether users have established compensating controls in their department. Determine whether the compensating controls are duplicated between and within user or data processing departments.
- Find out whether users work well with data processing employees in resolving problems, issues, concerns, errors, irregularities, and omissions resulting from various data processing activities.
- Ascertain whether user management periodically reviews and identifies the work areas requiring improvement either by automation or by improved manual procedures and methods. This is to increase employee and management efficiency, effectiveness, productivity, and performance.

(xxxi) **IIA's Performance Standards**

(A) *IIA's Practice Advisory 2110-2: "Internal Auditor's Role in the Business Continuity Process."*

***Nature of This Practice Advisory***

Internal auditors should consider these suggestions when evaluating an organization's activities related to business continuity. Many processes are required to ensure the continuity of an organization after a disaster occurs. The development of a comprehensive plan begins with assessing the potential impact and consequences of a disaster and understanding the risks. (The entire process of ensuring business continuity will incorporate, among other things, business continuity and disaster recovery plans.) Those plans should be constructed, maintained, tested, and audited to ensure that they remain appropriate for the needs of the organization. *Compliance with Practice Advisories is optional. This guidance is repeated in Part 1 and Part 2 for proper coverage of the subject matter.*

1. Business interruption can result from natural occurrences and accidental or deliberate criminal acts. Those interruptions can have significant financial and operational ramifications. Auditors should evaluate the organization's readiness to deal with business

interruptions. A comprehensive plan would provide for emergency response procedures, alternative communication systems and site facilities, information systems
backup, disaster recovery, business impact assessments and resumption plans, procedures for restoring utility services, and maintenance procedures for ensuring the
readiness of the organization in the event of an emergency or disaster.

2. Internal auditing activity should assess the organization's business continuity planning
process on a regular basis to ensure that senior management is aware of the state of
disaster preparedness.

3. Many organizations do not expect to experience an interruption or lengthy delay of
normal business processes and operations due to a disaster or other unforeseen event.
Many business experts say that it is not *if* a disaster will occur, but *when* it will occur.
Over time, an organization will experience an event that will result in the loss of information, access to properties (tangible or intangible), or the services of personnel.
Exposure to those types of risks and the planning for business continuity is an integral
part of an organization's risk management process. Advance planning is necessary to
minimize the loss and ensure continuity of an organization's critical business functions. It may enable the organization to maintain an acceptable level of service to its
stakeholders.

4. A crucial element of business recovery is the existence of a comprehensive and current disaster recovery plan. Internal auditors can play a role in the organization's
planning for disaster recovery. Internal audit activity can (a) assist with the risk analysis, (b) evaluate the design and comprehensiveness of the plan after it has been drawn
up, and (c) perform periodic assurance engagements to verify that the plan is kept up-
to-date.

## Planning

5. Organizations rely on internal auditors for analysis of operations and assessment of
risk management and control processes. Internal auditors acquire an understanding of
the overall business operations and the individual functions and how they interrelate
with one another. This positions the internal audit activity as a valuable resource in
evaluating the disaster recovery plan during its formulation process.

6. Internal audit activity can help with an assessment of an organization's internal and
external environment. Internal factors that may be considered include the turnover of
management and changes in information systems, controls, and major projects and
programs. External factors may include changes in outside regulatory and business
environment and changes in markets and competitive conditions, international financial and economic conditions, and technologies. Internal auditors can help identify
risks involving critical business activities and prioritize functions for recovery purposes.

## Evaluation

7. Internal auditors can make a contribution as objective participants when they review
the proposed business continuity and disaster recovery plans for design, completeness,
and overall adequacy. The auditor can examine the plan to determine that it reflects
the operations that have been included and evaluated in the risk assessment process
and contains sufficient internal control concerns and prescriptions. The internal auditor's comprehensive knowledge of the organization's business operations and applications enables him or her to assist during the development phase of the business continuity plan by evaluating its organization, comprehensiveness, and recommended actions to manage risks and maintain effective controls during a recovery period.

## Periodic Assurance Engagements

8. Internal auditors should periodically audit the organization's business continuity and
disaster recovery plans. The audit objective is to verify that the plans are adequate to
ensure the timely resumption of operations and processes after adverse circumstances,
and that it reflects the current business operating environment.

9. Business continuity and disaster recovery plans can become outdated very quickly. Coping with and responding to changes is an inevitable part of the task of management. Turnover of managers and executives and changes in system configurations, interfaces, and software can have a major impact on these plans. Internal audit activity should examine the recovery plan to determine whether (a) it is structured to incorporate important changes that could take place over time and (b) the revised plan will be communicated to the appropriate people, inside and outside the organization.

10. During the audit, internal auditors should consider

- Are all plans up to date? Do procedures exist for updating the plans?
- Are all critical business functions and systems covered by the plans? If not, are the reasons for omissions documented?
- Are the plans based on the risks and potential consequences of business interruptions?
- Are the plans fully documented and in accordance with organizational policies and procedures? Have functional responsibilities been assigned?
- Is the organization capable of and prepared to implement the plans?
- Are the plans tested and revised based on the results?
- Are the plans stored properly and safely? Is the location of and access to the plans known to management?
- Are the locations of alternate facilities (backup sites) known to employees?
- Do the plans call for coordination with local emergency services?

### Internal Audit's Role after a Disaster

11. There is an important role for the internal auditors to play immediately after a disaster occurs. An organization is more vulnerable after a disaster has occurred and it is trying to recover. During that recovery period, internal auditors should monitor the effectiveness of the recovery and control of operations. Internal audit activity should identify areas where internal controls and mitigating actions should be improved, and recommend improvements to the entity's business continuity plan. Internal audit can also provide support during the recovery activities.

12. After the disaster, usually within several months, internal auditors can assist in identifying the lessons learned from the disaster and the recovery operations. Those observations and recommendations may enhance activities to recover resources and update the next version of the business continuity plan.

13. In the final analysis, it is senior management who will determine the degree of the internal auditor's involvement in the business continuity and disaster recovery processes, considering auditors knowledge, skills, independence, and objectivity.

### (B) *IIA's Practice Advisory 2100-8: "Internal Auditor's Role in Evaluating an Organization's Privacy Framework."*

### Nature of This Practice Advisory

Internal auditors should consider these suggestions when evaluating an organization's activities related to its privacy framework. This guidance is not intended to represent all the procedures necessary for a comprehensive assurance or consulting engagement related to the privacy framework, but rather a recommended core set of high-level auditor responsibilities to complement related board and management responsibilities. *Compliance with Practice Advisories is optional. This guidance is repeated in Part 1 and Part 2 for proper coverage of the subject matter.*

1. Concerns relating to the protection of personal privacy are becoming more apparent, focused, and global as advancements in information technology and communications continually introduce new risks and threats to privacy. Privacy controls are legal requirements for doing business in most of the world.

2. Privacy definitions vary widely depending on country, culture, political environment, and legal framework. Privacy can encompass personal privacy (physical and psycho-

logical); privacy of space (freedom from surveillance); privacy of communication (freedom from monitoring); and privacy of information (collection, use, and disclosure of personal information by others). Personal information generally refers to information that can be associated with a specific individual, or that has identifying characteristics that might be combined with other information to do so.  It can include any factual or subjective information, recorded or not, in any form or media. Personal information might include, for example

- Name, address, identification numbers, income, or blood type
- Evaluations, comments, social status, or disciplinary actions
- Employee files, credit records, loan records

3.  Privacy is a risk management issue. Failure to protect privacy and personal information with the appropriate controls can have significant consequences for an organization. For example, it can damage the reputation of individuals and the organization, lead to legal liability issues, and contribute to consumer and employee mistrust.

4.  There are a variety of laws and regulations developing worldwide relating to the protection of personal information. As well, there are generally accepted policies and practices that can be applied to the privacy issue.

5.  It is clear that good privacy practices contribute to good governance and accountability. The governing body (e.g., the board of directors, head of an agency, or legislative body) is ultimately accountable for ensuring that the principal risks of the organization have been identified and the appropriate systems have been implemented to mitigate those risks. This includes establishing the necessary privacy framework for the organization and monitoring its implementation.

6.  The internal auditor can contribute to ensuring good governance and accountability by playing a role in helping an organization meet its privacy objectives. The internal auditor is uniquely positioned to evaluate the privacy framework in the organization and identify the significant risks along with the appropriate recommendations for their mitigation.

7.  In conducting such an evaluation of the privacy framework, the internal auditor should consider

- The various laws, regulations, and policies relating to privacy in the jurisdictions (including any jurisdiction where the organization conducts business)
- Liaison with in-house legal counsel to determine the exact nature of such laws, regulations, and other standards and practices applicable to the organization and the country/countries in which it does business
- Liaison with information technology specialists to ensure information security and data protection controls are in place and regularly reviewed and assessed for appropriateness
- The level or maturity of the organization's privacy practices. Depending on the level, the internal auditor may have differing roles. The auditor may facilitate the development and implementation of the privacy program, conduct a privacy risk assessment to determine the needs and risk exposures of the organization, or may review and provide assurance on the effectiveness of the privacy policies, practices, and controls across the organization. If the internal auditor assumes a portion of the responsibility for developing and implementing a privacy program, the auditor's independence may be impaired.

8.  Typically, the internal auditor could be expected to identify the types and appropriateness of information gathered by the organization that is deemed personal or private, the collection methodology used, and whether the organization's use of the information so collected is in accordance with its intended use and the laws in the areas that the information is gathered, held, and used.

9.  Given the highly technical and legal nature of the topic, the internal auditor should ensure that the appropriate in-depth knowledge and capacity to conduct any such

evaluation of the privacy framework is available, using third-party experts, if necessary.

(C) *IIA's Practice Advisory 2100-2: "Information Security."*

### Nature of This Practice Advisory

Internal auditors should consider these suggestions when evaluating an organization's governance activities related to information security. This guidance is not intended to represent all the procedures necessary for a comprehensive assurance or consulting engagement related to information security, but simply a recommended core set of high-level auditor responsibilities to complement related board and management responsibilities. *Compliance with Practice Advisories is optional. This guidance is repeated in Part 1 and Part 2 for proper coverage of the subject matter.*

1. Internal auditors should determine that management and the board have a clear understanding that information security is a management responsibility. This responsibility includes all critical information of the organization, regardless of media in which the information is stored.
2. The chief audit executive should determine that the internal audit activity possesses, or has access to, competent auditing resources to evaluate information security and associated risk exposures. This includes both internal and external risk exposures, including exposures relating to the organization's relationships with outside entities.
3. Internal auditors should determine that the board has sought assurance from management that information security breaches and conditions that might represent a threat to the organization will promptly be made known to those performing the internal audit activity.
4. Internal auditors should assess the effectiveness of preventive, detective, and mitigation measures against past attacks, as deemed appropriate, and future attempts or incidents deemed likely to occur. Internal auditors should confirm that the board has been appropriately informed of threats, incidents, vulnerabilities exploited, and corrective measures.
5. Internal auditors should periodically assess the organization's information security practices and recommend, as appropriate, enhancements to, or implementation of, new controls and safeguards. Following an assessment, an assurance report should be provided to the board. Such assessments can either be conducted as separate stand-alone engagements or as multiple engagements integrated into other audits or engagements conducted as part of the approved audit plan.

(D) *IIA's Practice Advisory 2100-6: "Control and Audit Implications of E-commerce Activities."*

### Nature of This Practice Advisory

Growth of e-commerce continues at a fast pace, both for business-to-business or business-to-consumer applications. Effective controls and processes are critical for successful development and implementation of an e-commerce strategy. Thus, an effective e-commerce assessment effort may be a key part of the annual audit plan for many companies. This PA provides an overview of the control and audit implications. Additional resources for practitioners are: IIA's Systems Assurance and Control (SAC) product and other technology reports and publications of the Information Systems Audit and Control Association (ISACA). Both have developed guidelines and criteria for evaluation of electronic systems and models. *Compliance with Practice Advisories is optional. This guidance is repeated in Part 1 and Part 2 for proper coverage of the subject matter.*

1. Electronic commerce (e-commerce) is generally defined as "conducting commercial activities over the Internet." These commercial activities can be business-to-business (B2B), business-to-consumer (B2C), and business-to-employee (B2E). The growth of e-commerce has been dramatic and is anticipated to grow even more rapidly in the years ahead. The recent publication by the IIA Research Foundation, Systems Assur-

ance and Control (SAC), and the success of the Web-based *www.ITAudit.org* and various e-mail IIA newsletters confirms that technology not only supports e-commerce strategies, but also is an integral part. Web-based and other technology changes have a dramatic impact on society, governance, economics, competition, markets, organizational structure, and national defense. Clearly, these changes and the dramatic growth of e-commerce create significant control and management challenges that should be considered by internal auditors in developing and implementing their audit plans.

### Understanding and Planning an E-commerce Engagement

2.  Continuous changes in technology offer the internal auditing profession both great opportunity and risk. Before attempting to provide assurance on the systems and processes, an internal auditor should understand the changes in business and information systems, the related risks, and the alignment of strategies with the enterprise's design and market requirements. The internal auditor should review management's strategic planning and risk assessment processes and its decisions about

    * Which risks are serious?
    * Which risks can be insured?
    * What current controls will mitigate the risks?
    * Which additional compensating controls are necessary?
    * What type of monitoring is required?

3.  The major components of auditing e-commerce activities are to

    * Assess the internal control structure, including the tone set by senior management.
    * Provide reasonable assurance that goals and objectives can be achieved.
    * Determine if the risks are acceptable.
    * Understand the information flow.
    * Review the interface issues (i.e., hardware to hardware, software to software, and hardware to software).
    * Evaluate the business continuity and disaster recovery plans.

4.  The chief audit executive's (CAE's) concerns in performing an e-commerce engagement relate to the competency and capacity of the internal audit activity. Among the possible factors that may constrain the internal audit activity are

    * Does the internal audit activity have sufficient skills? If not, can the skills be acquired?
    * Are training or other resources necessary?
    * Is the staffing level sufficient for the near term and long term?
    * Can the expected audit plan be delivered?

5.  **Internal auditor's questions during risk assessment.** The IIA's SAC publication can assist the internal auditor in audit planning and risk assessment. It includes a list of e-commerce areas that should be of interest to an internal auditor who is undertaking an engagement and assessing risks. The questions for internal auditors to consider are

    * Is there a business plan for the e-commerce project or program?
    * Does the plan cover the integration of the planning, design, and implementation of the e-commerce system with the strategies of the organization?
    * What will be the impact on the performance, security, reliability, and availability of the system?
    * Will the functionality meet the end user's needs (e.g., employees, customers, business partners) as well as management's objectives?
    * Have governmental and regulatory requirements been analyzed and considered?
    * How secure is the hardware and software, and will they prevent or detect unauthorized access, inappropriate use, and other harmful effects and losses?

- Will transaction processing be current, accurate, complete, and indisputable?
- Does the control environment allow the organization to achieve its e-commerce objectives as it moves from concepts to results?
- Does the risk assessment include internal and external forces?
- Have the inherent risks associated with the Internet and Internet provider (i.e., reliability of basic communications, authentication of users, and who has access) been addressed?
- Have other issues been addressed (e.g., disclosures of confidential business information, misuse of intellectual property, violations of copyrights, trademark infringement, libelous statements on Web sites, fraud, misuse of electronic signatures, privacy violations, and reputation damage)?
- If outside vendors are used, has a "going concern" evaluation been conducted by a trusted third party that is qualified to certify the vendor?
- If vendors provide hosting services, do they have a tested business contingency plan? Have they provided a recent Statement on Auditing Standards (SAS 70) report? (SAS 70 reports can offer valuable information about internal controls to user organizations.) Also, have privacy issues been resolved?
- Does the contract include audit rights?

**E-commerce Risks and Control Issues**

6. The e-commerce risk and control environment is complex and evolving. Risk can be defined as the uncertainty of an event occurring that could have a negative impact on the achievement of objectives. Risk is inherent to every business or government entity. Opportunity risks assumed by management are often drivers of organizational activities. Beyond these opportunities may be threats and other dangers that are not clearly understood and fully evaluated and too easily accepted as part of doing business. In striving to manage risk, it is essential to have an understanding of risk elements. It is also important to be aware of new threats and changes in technology that open new vulnerabilities in information security. For management purposes, the seven key questions below can serve to identify organizational risk and target potential ways to control or mitigate the exposures. (Risk practitioners use a variety of different risk management approaches; these questions illustrate one approach.) Risk elements associated with the questions are displayed in brackets.

   (a) **Risk identification and quantification**

   - What could happen that would adversely affect the organization's ability to achieve its objectives and execute its strategies? [threat events]
   - If it happens, what is the potential financial impact? [single-loss exposure value]
   - How often might it happen? [frequency]
   - How probable are the answers to the first three questions? [uncertainty]

   (b) **Risk management and mitigation**

   - What can be done to prevent and avoid, mitigate, and detect risks and provide notification? [safeguards and controls]
   - How much will it cost? [safeguard and control costs]
   - How efficient would that be? [cost-benefit or return on investment analysis]

7. Some of the more critical risk and control issues to be addressed by the internal auditor are

   - General project management risks
   - Specific security threats, such as denial of service, physical attacks, viruses, identity theft, and unauthorized access or disclosure of data
   - Maintenance of transaction integrity under a complex network of links to legacy systems and data warehouses

- Web site content review and approval when there are frequent changes and sophisticated customer features and capabilities that offer around-the-clock service
- Rapid technology changes
- Legal issues, such as increasing regulations throughout the world to protect individual privacy; enforceability of contracts outside the organization's country, and tax and accounting issues
- Changes to surrounding business processes and organizational structures

**Auditing E-commerce Activities**

8. The overall audit objective should be to ensure that all e-commerce processes have effective internal controls. Management of e-commerce initiatives should be documented in a strategic plan that is well developed and approved. If there is a decision not to participate in e-commerce, that decision should be carefully analyzed, documented, and approved by the governing board.

9. Audit objectives for an e-commerce engagement may include

- Evidence of e-commerce transactions
- Availability and reliability of security system
- Effective interface between e-commerce and financial systems
- Security of monetary transactions
- Effectiveness of customer authentication process
- Adequacy of business continuity processes, including the resumption of operations
- Compliance with common security standards
- Effective use and control of digital signatures
- Adequacy of systems, policies, and procedures to control public key certificates (using public key cryptographic techniques)
- Adequacy and timeliness of operating data and information
- Documented evidence of an effective system of internal control

10. The details of the audit program used to audit e-commerce activities in specific organizations will vary depending on industry, country, and legal and business models. An outline of a possible e-commerce audit protocol for key areas follows.

   (a) **E-commerce organization.** The internal auditor should

   - Determine the value of transactions.
   - Identify the stakeholders (external and internal).
   - Review the change management process.
   - Examine the approval process.
   - Review the business plan for e-commerce activities.
   - Evaluate the policies over public key certificates.
   - Review the digital signature procedures.
   - Examine service-level agreements among buyer, supplier, and certification authority.
   - Ascertain the quality assurance policy.
   - Assess the privacy policy and compliance in e-commerce activities.
   - Assess the incident response capability.

   (b) **Fraud.** The internal auditor should be alert for

   - Unauthorized movement of money (e.g., transfers to jurisdictions where the recovery of funds would be difficult).
   - Duplication of payments.
   - Denial of orders placed or received, goods received, or payments made.
   - Exception reports and procedures, and effectiveness of the follow-up.
   - Digital signatures: Are they used for all transactions? Who authorizes them? Who has access to them?

- Protections against viruses and hacking activities (history file, use of tools).
- Access rights: Are they reviewed regularly? Are they promptly revised when staff members are changed?
- History of interception of transactions by unauthorized persons.

(c) **Authentication.** The internal auditor should review the policies for authenticating transactions and evaluating controls.

- Evidence of regular reviews
- Control self-assessment (CSA) tools used by management
- Regular independent checks
- Segregation of duties
- Tools that management should have in place: firewalls (multilevel to partition e-commerce and other activities), password management, independent reconciliation, and audit trails

(d) **Corruption of data.** The internal auditor should evaluate controls over data integrity.

- Who can amend catalogs and prices or rates? What is the approval mechanism?
- Can someone destroy audit trails?
- Who can approve bulletin board amendments?
- What are the procedures for ordering and recording?
- Is the process of online tendering providing adequate documentation?
- Tools that should be in place include intrusion management (monitoring software, automatic time-out, and trend analysis), physical security for e-commerce servers, change controls, and reconciliation.

(e) **Business interruptions.** The internal auditor should review the business continuity plan and determine if it has been tested. Management should have devised an alternative means to process the transactions in the event of an interruption. Management should have a process in place to address these potential conditions.

- Volume attacks
- Denial of service attacks
- Inadequacies in interfacing between e-commerce and financial management systems
- Backup facilities
- Strategies to counter hacking, intrusion, cracking, viruses, worms, Trojan horses, and back doors

(f) **Management issues.** The internal auditor should evaluate how well business units are managing the e-commerce process. Some relevant topics include

- Project management reviews of individual initiatives and development projects
- System development life cycle reviews
- Vendor selection, vendor capabilities, employee confidentiality, and bonding
- Postimplementation economic reviews: Are anticipated benefits being achieved? What metrics are being used to measure success?
- Postimplementation process reviews: Are new processes in place and working effectively?

(xxxii) **Compliance audit engagements.** The section on compliance auditing first provides a general audit direction to conduct a compliance audit. This includes planning, risk assessment, and testing internal controls. Next, guidelines for conducting **specific** audits of compliance are provided. These include environmental auditing and human resource (personnel) policy auditing.

## (A) *General Audits of Compliance.*

*Planning.* In planning the audit, auditors should obtain an understanding of laws and regulations that are relevant to the audit. When laws and regulations are significant to audit objectives, auditors should design the audit to provide reasonable assurance about compliance with them. In all audits, auditors should be alert to situations or transactions that could be indicative of illegal acts or abuse. Auditors should exercise due professional care and caution in pursuing indications of possible fraud or other illegal acts that could result in criminal prosecution so as not to interfere with potential future investigations and/or legal proceedings.[15]

## DEFINITIONS OF KEY TERMS:  GENERAL COMPLIANCE

**Noncompliance** is a failure to follow requirements, or a violation of prohibitions, contained in laws, regulations, contracts, governmental grants, or organization's policies and procedures.

**Illegal acts** are a type of noncompliance; specifically, they are violations of laws or regulations. They are failures to follow requirements of laws or implementing regulations, including intentional and unintentional noncompliance and criminal acts.

**Criminal acts** are illegal acts for which incarceration, as well as other penalties, is available if the organization obtains a guilty verdict.

**Civil acts** are illegal acts for which penalties that do not include incarceration are available for a statutory violation. Penalties may include monetary payments and corrective actions.

**Fraud** is the obtaining of something of value, illegally, through willful misrepresentation. Thus, fraud is a type of illegal act.

**Abuse** occurs when the conduct of an activity or function falls short of expectations for prudent behavior. Abuse is distinguished from noncompliance in that abusive conditions may not directly violate laws or regulations. Abusive activities may be within the letter of the laws and regulations but violate either their spirit or the more general standards of impartial and ethical behavior.

**Errors** are unintentional noncompliance with applicable laws and regulations and/or misstatements or omissions of amounts or disclosures in financial statements.

**Irregularities** are intentional noncompliance with applicable laws and regulations and/or misstatements or omissions of amounts or disclosures in financial statements.

### Understanding Relevant Laws and Regulations

Auditors may obtain an understanding of laws and regulations through review of relevant documents and inquiry of attorneys. Generally more audits of compliance with laws and regulations take place in the public sector than in the private sector. For example, understanding relevant laws and regulations can be important to planning a performance audit because government programs are usually created by law and are subject to more specific rules and regulations than the private sector. What is to be done, who is to do it, the goals and objectives to be achieved, the population to be served, and how much can be spent on what, are usually set forth in laws and regulations. Thus, understanding the laws establishing a program can be essential to understanding the program itself. Obtaining that understanding may also be a necessary step in identifying laws and regulations that are significant to audit objectives.

### Testing Compliance with Laws and Regulations

Auditors should design the audit to provide reasonable assurance about compliance with laws and regulations that are significant to audit objectives. This requires determining if laws and regulations are significant to the audit objectives and, if they are, assessing the risk that significant illegal acts could occur. Based on that risk assessment, the auditors design and perform procedures to provide reasonable assurance of detecting significant illegal acts.

---

[15] *Assessing Compliance with Applicable Laws and Regulations* (Washington, DC: US General Accounting Office, 1989).

*Risk Assessment.*

**Vulnerability assessment.** The probability of risk that noncompliance may occur and be material is the key factor in deciding how much compliance testing is required. A vulnerability assessment is the preferred technique of assessing the probability that applicable laws and regulations may not have been followed, and the internal controls assessment shows the likelihood of such noncompliance being detected or prevented.

> A *vulnerability assessment determines the probability that noncompliance and abuse, which is individually or in the aggregate material, could occur and not be prevented or detected in a timely manner by internal controls.*

The vulnerability assessment evaluates the inherent risk of a law or regulation to noncompliance and abuse before considering internal controls and whether internal controls will prevent or detect noncompliance and abuse.

Inherent risk × Internal controls = Vulnerability or testing extent

The extent of compliance testing is directly related to an activity's degree of vulnerability. The higher the vulnerability, the more extensive the compliance testing needs to be and vice versa. Thus, even though an activity may be generally risky to noncompliance and abuse, strong internal controls can reduce vulnerability to a relatively low level, thereby reducing necessary compliance testing to a relatively low level.

The rationale for performing a vulnerability assessment is that auditors can limit testing and focus on those areas most vulnerable to noncompliance and abuse if internal controls are found to be reliable. This produces a more cost-effective and timely audit.

**Inherent risk.** Inherent risk is the probability that a law or regulation related to audit objectives will not be complied with or that the area being reviewed is highly susceptible to noncompliance (e.g., pilferage of cash). Inherent risk is assessed before considering whether the internal controls would prevent or detect such noncompliance or abuse. Assessing inherent risk involves

- Considering the requirements of applicable laws and regulations
- Establishing susceptibility to noncompliance
- Assessing management's commitment to reduce and control noncompliance
- Determining whether previously identified noncompliance problems have been corrected
- Testing transactions

Auditors should consider the requirements of applicable laws and regulations. Some questions related to identifying the laws and regulations applicable to an audit include

- Are the laws and regulations readily identifiable, vague, complex, or contradictory? Laws and regulations that are clear, understandable, and consistent with other laws and regulations are easier to adhere to and to check for compliance than laws and regulations lacking these characteristics.
- Do the laws and regulations relate to a new program, or have they undergone recent or frequent major changes? Laws and regulations that have recently been implemented or changed may be more likely to be violated because people are less familiar with them.

Auditors should identify the characteristics that increase the susceptibility to noncompliance. Some questions that should be considered include

- Do incentives of noncompliance outweigh the potential penalties? If the law or regulation provides a benefit based on need, individuals will have an incentive to overstate their need in order to qualify or to get a larger benefit.
- Is it practicable or reasonable to expect compliance, or are the laws and regulations so burdensome or onerous that noncompliance could reasonably be expected?
- Does the activity have numerous transactions? The more transactions there are, the greater the chances that noncompliance could occur due to errors, irregularities, and abuse. Also, a large number of transactions increases the difficulty of detecting noncompliance.

---

**KEY CONCEPTS TO REMEMBER: INDICATORS OF SUSCEPTIBILITY TO NONCOMPLIANCE (RED FLAGS)**

- Poor records or documentation
- Complex transactions
- Activities that are dominated and controlled by a single person or small group
- Unreasonable explanations to inquiries by auditors
- Auditee annoyance at reasonable questions by auditors
- Employees' refusal to give others custody of records
- Employees' refusal to take vacations and/or accept promotions
- Extravagant lifestyle of employees
- A pattern of certain contractors' bidding against each other or, conversely, certain contractors' not bidding against each other
- Use of materials on commercial contracts that were intended for use on government contracts
- A high default rate on government-backed loans

---

- Have important activities or programs been contracted out or delegated to those outside the organization without ensuring that adequate internal control systems and active monitoring oversight are in place?
- Does the activity have a significant amount of assets that are readily marketable (i.e., cash, securities) or that could be used for personal purposes (i.e., tools, cars, auto repair parts, or computers)? Such assets are very susceptible to improper use or theft.

Auditors should consider management's commitment to reduce and control noncompliance. A strong commitment by management to comply is a positive factor in reducing the risk of noncompliance. Some questions that should be considered include

- Have problems been repeatedly disclosed in prior audits?
- Does management promptly respond when problems are first identified?
- Are recurring complaints received through "hot line" allegations?
- Is management willing to discuss its approach toward compliance?
- Is management knowledgeable of the subject area and potential problems?
- Does management have a constructive attitude, including a willingness to consider innovative approaches?
- Is there a stable management team with continuity and a good reputation, or is there high turnover and/or a poor management reputation?

The final step of assessing inherent risk involves testing a limited number of transactions. This testing usually occurs during the survey phase of an audit and is not intended to be a representative sample of transactions. The purpose of this testing is to gain a better understanding of the processes an organization follows and to confirm other observations made about the inherent risk of noncompliance.

**Internal controls.** Internal controls consist of policies and procedures used to provide reasonable assurance that goals and objectives are met; resources are adequately safeguarded, efficiently utilized, and reliably accounted for; and laws and regulations are complied with. Evaluating internal controls involves

- Identifying internal control objectives (policies) that management has designed to ensure that laws and regulations are complied with and the control environment
- Identifying key internal control techniques (procedures) that management has established to achieve objectives
- Testing control procedures
- Identifying needed follow-up actions

Auditors should determine what control objectives related to audit objective management have been established. The control objective is a positive thing that management tries to attain or an adverse condition or negative effect that management is seeking to avoid.

The control environment reflects the overall attitude toward and awareness of management regarding the importance of controls. A good control environment is a positive factor in establishing and enhancing the effectiveness of specific policies and procedures, while a poor control environment has the opposite effect. Factors affecting the control environment include

- Management's philosophy and operating style (tone at the top)
- The entity's organizational structure
- Methods of delegating authority and responsibility
- Management's methods for monitoring and following up on performance, including corrective action taken on audit recommendations
- Personnel policies and practices

Control objectives and control environment represent those goals and actions management wished to achieve, while control procedures are the specific steps designed and prescribed by management to provide reasonable assurance that its control objectives will be achieved.

## Examples of Inherent Limitations in Internal Control Systems

- Costs and benefits
- Employee collusion
- Management override
- Incorrect application of control procedures by employees

The auditor can obtain information on the control environment, objectives, and procedures by reading policy and procedure manuals, reviewing past audit reports, interviewing management and employees, and making observations.

Because of inherent limitations in the design and the operation of any internal control system, auditors should **not** expect internal controls to prevent or detect all instances of noncompliance or abuse. The most pervasive limitation is that the cost of internal controls should not exceed their benefits. In deciding how extensive the system of internal controls should be, management compares the costs of more controls with the benefits to be gained.

Other limitations include the possibility that management may override the internal control system; employees may secretly be working together (collusion) to avoid or circumvent the controls; and employees may not be correctly applying the control techniques due to fatigue, boredom, inattention, lack of knowledge, or misunderstanding. As a result, auditors should always test actual transactions to have a reasonable basis for evaluating internal controls.

The auditors' understanding of the internal control system should be documented in the working papers. This can be done through flowcharts; narratives; questionnaire responses; records of interviews; and copies of policies and procedures, documents, and records.

For internal control procedures to be effective, they must be designed to achieve the intended objective(s) and must be correctly and consistently applied by the authorized employee(s). The best-designed internal controls are of little value if the procedures are not correctly followed. For example, if the entity has a procedure requiring the manager's approval for all purchases over $25,000 but the manager does not review the purchase orders, this procedure will not be very effective in preventing or detecting unnecessary purchases.

*Testing internal controls.* Testing internal controls consists of five steps.

1. Defining what constitutes effective internal controls
2. Selecting a small sample of transactions, either randomly or nonrandomly
3. Evaluating whether the sample transactions were executed in accordance with the laws and regulations and internal controls
4. Documenting the evaluation results

5.  Determining the probability that noncompliance will not be detected or prevented by the internal controls

If testing reveals material noncompliance or abuse, the auditor should determine what internal controls were intended to prevent or detect the noncompliance or abuse and ascertain the reasons they did not. If internal controls are weak or nonexistent, many more transactions may be in noncompliance. Auditors should consider expanding tests to determine the impact of weaknesses on audit objectives and of doing follow-up work later.

(B) *Specific Audits of Compliance.* Two areas will be addressed in this section: environmental auditing and human resource policy auditing.

*Environmental auditing.* The 1993 IIA study on environmental auditing defined seven categories under the title of environmental audits.[16] Internal environmental auditing is considered to be the self-evaluation process whereby an organization determines whether or not it is meeting its legal and internal environmental objectives.

## DEFINITION OF KEY TERMS: ENVIRONMENTAL AUDITING

- An **environmental management system** is an organization's structure of responsibilities and policies, practices, procedures, processes, and resources for protecting the environment and managing environmental issues.
- **Environmental auditing** is an integral part of the environmental management system whereby management determines whether the organization's environmental control systems are adequate to ensure compliance with regulatory requirements and internal policies.

---

The seven environmental audit categories include: (1) compliance audits, (2) environmental management system audits, (3) transactional audits, (4) treatment, storage, and disposal facility audits, (5) pollution prevention audits, (6) environmental liability accrual audits, and (7) product audits (see Exhibit 2.16).

1.  Compliance audits
2.  Environmental management system audits
3.  Transactional audits (acquisition and divestiture)
4.  Treatment, storage, and disposal facility audits
5.  Pollution prevention audits
6.  Environmental liability accrual audits
7.  Product audits (appraisal of production processes)

**Exhibit 2.16: Seven categories of environmental audits**

1.  **Compliance audits** are detailed, site-specific assessments of current, past, and planned operations. They assess whether activities and operations are within the legal constraints imposed by regulations. Compliance audits, which are the most common type of environmental audit, may be categorized according to the level of detail and effort they require.

    Preliminary assessment, sometimes called a "document review" or "desktop audit," is used to provide insight into potential problem areas, especially those where projections regarding future conditions may warrant more intensive review.

    An environmental audit is a more detailed audit focusing on operations. This audit includes verification of compliance with permits and consent orders. The auditor typically traces the compliance process through to the reporting requirements to ensure regulatory compliance.

    Environmental investigations or site assessment is a time- and labor-intensive assessment, conducted when the preceding phases indicate the potential risk of contamination or other noncompliance. The audit report includes interpretation of technical analyses, such as laboratory reports.

---

[16] *Rebecca Thomson, Thomas Simpson, and Charles Le Grand, "Environmental Auditing,"* **The Internal Auditor** *(April 1993): 19–21.*

2. **Environmental management system audits** focus on the systems in place to ensure that they are operating properly to manage future environmental risks. These audits are conducted internally when the environmental auditing process matures and organizations become confident in their compliance with regulations.

3. **Transactional audits,** also called acquisition and divestiture audits, property transfer site assessments, property transfer evaluations, and due diligence audits, are an environmental risk management tool for banks, land buyers, lending agencies, charitable organizations, investors, and any organization purchasing land for a facility site. Buyers, lenders, and others need to understand the environmental risks associated with the property they are purchasing, lending on, or accepting as a gift, because the environmental liability can easily exceed the market value of the asset.

4. **Treatment, storage, and disposal facility audits** involve the tracking of hazardous substances throughout their existence. Under US environmental regulations, all hazardous materials are tracked from creation to destruction (cradle to grave), and all "owners" of these materials have liability for them as long as the owners exist.

5. **Pollution prevention audits** are operational appraisals that serve to identify opportunities where waste can be minimized and pollution can be eliminated at the source, rather than controlled at the "end of the pipe." Pollution prevention primarily involves manufacturing facilities. Manufacturing is likely to create pollution within multiple media (air, water, and solid waste) at several operational stages, including raw materials handling and storage, process chemical use, maintenance, finished materials handling, and disposal.

6. **Environmental liability accrual audits** are technical accounting and legal reviews involved with recognizing, quantifying, and reporting liability accruals for known environmental issues. The responsibility for assessing the reasonableness of cost estimates for environmental remediation falls to the internal audit function.

7. **Product audits** are appraisals within the production processes of a facility. Their objective is to provide assurance that the product is in compliance with chemical restrictions and with environmentally sensitive interests. Product auditing is resulting in the development of fully recyclable products.

(C) *An Approach to Conducting an Environmental Audit.* Gerald Vinten recommended the following audit steps in conducting an environmental audit. The audit will address the operating environment, health and safety management, product safety and quality, loss prevention, minimizing resource use, and adverse effects on the environment.[17] The scope of the audit can be comprehensive or limited to a single topic, which can include organization strategy, functional areas of business, operational factors, and reporting and follow-up.

1. **Organization strategy**

   A. **Overall environmental policy**

   These questions should be addressed: Is there an overall environmental policy? Has it the support of the board of directors, top management, and workforce? Is it communicated with shareholders, employees, customers, suppliers, local politicians, neighbors, and control authorities (e.g., the Environmental Protection Agency)? Is there a consistent ecological strategy for the organization? Are the organization's objectives set with due regard for ecological factors?

   B. **Staff training and participation**

   These questions should be addressed: Is there a system for informing staff about ways to improve environmental performance? Are there training programs, suggestion schemes, quality circles, performance targets, and operational and maintenance schedules? What motivation and training methods should be employed, and how are they evaluated? Are environmental matters raised as part of a social occasion to show what the organization is doing? Is there a recognition system for staff? Are staff encouraged

---

[17] *Gerald Vinten, "The Greening of Audit," **The Internal Auditor** (October 1991): 34–35.*

to become involved in environmental projects? *It has been found that "firms that were relatively more prosperous tended more often to pollute illegally."*

With reference to accident and emergency procedures: Are there adequate contingency plans for dealing with accidents and emergencies? Is the public relations department ready to communicate with employees, neighbors, the press, and others? Are there controls to ensure that only public relations statements that will stand up to independent scrutiny are permitted to be issued?

2. **Functional areas of business**

   A. **Marketing function**

   These questions should be addressed: Do marketing initiatives create or reinforce the organization's image and reputation for its concern with environmental issues? Are products marked to draw attention to their environmentally positive features? Is the packaging made from environmentally acceptable materials? Are marketing channels set up by agreement between manufacturers and distributors to make recycling systems possible? If higher prices are attributable to ecological factors, are the price differentials due to the ecological factors highlighted?

   B. **Finance function**

   These questions should be addressed: Is environmental impact taken into account in all investment decisions? Are ethical and green investments chosen wherever feasible? If an investment is likely to increase pollution, has a lower-pollution alternative been investigated, and have the likely costs been included in the project costing? Is a short-term outlook avoided where a longer-term perspective will lead to higher environmental dividends?

   C. **Production function**

   These questions should be addressed: Has the earlier replacement of an existing production plant, and the acquisition of new, nonpolluting machinery, been considered? Are ecological materials and processes in use? Are clean technologies, with better input-output ratios, in use? Are useful materials and heat recovered? Are emissions minimized by postproduction environmental protection measures? Can raw materials specifications be altered without unduly affecting product quality and to improve environmental aspects?

   D. **Insurance function**

   These questions should be addressed: Has a check been made regarding intrinsic damage that could ensue from environmental risks? Have checks been made of the possible risks to third parties caused by damage to the environment?

   Has the risk management strategy been checked to ensure that there is a suitable mix of assumption of risk, transfer of risk, and insurance cover?

   E. **International business divisions**

   These questions should be addressed: Are exports, imports, and foreign production environment-oriented? Is pressure being brought to achieve change?

   F. **Legal department**

   These questions should be addressed: Are all steps taken to comply with official regulations? Are environmental damage and liability risks kept to a minimum?

3. **Operational factors**

   A. **Discharges**

   This question should be addressed: Are process controls and management systems adequate to ensure compliance with legislation and future objectives, as well as to avoid complaints? The scope of discharge includes air, water, and noise.

   B. **Site tidiness**

   These questions should be addressed: Are measures taken to eliminate litter and sources of untidiness inside buildings, outside and in the immediate surroundings? Has suitable landscaping been considered to improve the appearance of the site?

C. **Transport**

These questions should be addressed: Are staff encouraged to use public transport, and could the availability of public transport be increased by providing additional company-funded services? Is the organization using the most efficient and environmentally sound systems for transporting goods, people, and materials? Are only low-pollution vehicles purchased? Are existing vehicles reequipped and serviced with environmental considerations in mind?

D. **Water use**

These questions should be addressed: Is water used efficiently? Can consumption be reduced by using another cooling method or controlling leakages more effectively?

E. **Recycling**

These questions should be addressed: Are all opportunities considered for recycling? Could redundant, used products be recycled?

F. **Wastes**

These questions should be addressed: Are steps taken to minimize, eliminate, or recycle waste? Are recycling opportunities being lost by failure to segregate different types of waste? Is waste disposed of responsibly?

G. **Energy use**

These questions should be addressed: Are electricity, steam, water, and gas meters at the major points of use, and are targets set to reduce their usage? Is full use made of alternative energy sources, such as landfill gas, waste-derived fuel, solar and wind energy, and combined heat and power? Are energy-conservative schemes in existence and adequate? Are buildings and plants properly insulated? Can savings be made in heating and lighting costs?

H. **Canteen food**

These questions should be addressed: Is healthy eating encouraged and health education provided? Is nutritional information provided? Is an improved range of healthy dishes and drinks provided? Are there safeguards to ensure food hygiene?

I. **Occupational heath and safety**

These questions should be addressed: Is there an occupational health department? Does it provide advice on practical accident and injury prevention? Does it look after employees' psychological needs? Does it advise on health education in home and family? Does it advise on stress reduction and time management?

J. **Data processing**

These issues should be addressed: The data collected needs to be analyzed, and then presented in a form that is easily understood and from which clear conclusions may be drawn. Wherever possible, conclusions should be discussed with the staff directly involved.

4. **Reporting and follow-up**

As soon as they are identified, significant defects need to be reported immediately to the chief executive officer for quick action. More routine findings should be presented to the board of directors as an "executive summary" and with clear recommendations for action. These should include an estimate of cost, resource needs, optimum time for introduction, and when the next review should take place. The board should be invited to approve the recommendations and authorized implementation. The implementation plan should include deadlines for action.

A periodic check will be made that the board decisions have been fully implemented, with any noncompliance reported back to the board. A quality assurance review of the audit process itself is also recommended.

(D) ***An Approach to Audit Hazardous Waste Management Program.*** Authors Jerry Kreuze, Gale Newell, and Stephen Newell recommended an audit program entitled "Internal Auditors' Guide to a Comprehensive Hazardous Waste Management Program"[18]

A. **When acquiring new properties**

1. Investigate previous owners and uses of properties.
2. Perform an "environmental audit," to provide assurance that contaminants are not present on the properties.

B. **Be familiar with hazardous waste creation, hauling, and disposal to**

1. Identify the products and by-products that are considered hazardous.
2. Investigate ways to minimize the amount of hazardous waste being created.
3. Confirm that existing hauling and disposal procedures are in conformity with applicable federal, state, and local ordinances, acts, and standards.
4. Verify company compliance with the numerous federal and state acts dealing with clean air and water, solid waste disposal, and toxic substance abuse.
5. Respond to new research findings on toxicity, new regulations, or newly imposed environmental standards.
6. Continuously monitor hazardous waste disposal sites to determine that the disposal methods are adequate and cost-effective.
7. Ensure the availability of insurance, promote favorable rates, and alleviate potential liabilities in excess of insurance limits.

C. **Perform an overall environmental risk assessment to**

1. Identify all environmental concerns faced by the company.
2. Categorize these concerns into three groups: high, moderate, or low risk.
3. Direct financial resources to those concerns that pose the greatest potential threat to the company's long-term existence.
4. Audit the above expenditures to determine if they are effectively reducing the company's overall environmental risk.

(E) ***Another Approach to Environmental Auditing.*** Another approach to environmental auditing is presented by Wayne Socha and Sally Harvey.[19] The authors offered a list of areas for investigation that includes

- Test toxic emissions compliance at all facilities. Smokestacks are not the only sign of potential pollution. For example, the largest polluting company in the western half of Los Angeles County, California, is a one-square-block facility that makes adhesive labels with no "visible" pollution.
- Test pollution levels within the office environment. Recent tests by US universities have shown that standard office equipment, such as laser printers and copiers, can violate federal ozone standards if air filters become clogged with dust.
- Review health and welfare protection for video display terminal workers. Regulations protecting computer users are fairly routine for workers in Europe and South America. In North America, recent landmark legislation by the City of San Francisco signals that American workers may soon be protected. Look for these clues in spotting a concerned employer: polarized lighting, antiglare monitor screens, low-frequency electrical emission blockage on personal computers, adjustable desks and chairs, and wrist rest pads, software that forces personal computer users to take rest breaks, and physical training to relieve stress.
- Review corporate transportation solutions. Is the employer taking an active role in reducing air, traffic, and noise pollution? Subsidized parking increases pollution from cars. Subsidized bus passes and car pools reduce pollution. For an even greater effect, pay people to car pool rather than trying to discourage driving by imposing higher parking

---

[18] Jerry Kreuze, Gale Newell, and Stephen Newell, "Liability for Hazardous Waste and the Internal Auditor," **The Internal Auditor** (June 1990): 53.

[19] Wayne Socha and Sally Harvey, "Mini-Green Audits," **The Internal Auditor** (October 1991): 42–43.

rates. If car-pooling is already encouraged, do corollary policies support the practice? For example, if the driver in a car pool becomes sick in the middle of the day, do the policies allow everyone to go home early? Does the policy provide some other way for the rider employees to get home?

- Perform environmental audits on new products. Does the proposed product increase the depletion of resources? Is this a throwaway product?

---

### Audit Concerns during Environmental Auditing

During an audit of environmental protection devices at a hazardous materials research center, the auditor has reviewed the architect's alarm device specifications, examined invoices for the devices, and interviewed the plant safety officer responsible for installation. The main concern of these procedures is assurance that the specified alarm system was purchased and installed and that it is working properly.

- Review packaging for saving potential. The packaging industry is being generally indicted for increasing the pollution load. While image-enhancing publicity is now being used to reverse the perception, could the company package more responsibly, thereby responding to the concern and saving money? One computer software manufacturer recently looked at the problem and found that 100% of the product could be produced using recycled products, except for the diskette, with large savings in packaging production costs.
- Consider the impact of product content decisions. Environmental organizations may target anything containing tropical or temperate rain forest products.
- Conduct energy audits and encourage efficient building designs.
- Compare corporate mission statements to reality. Most mission statements contain a generic clause professing concern with the community. Is this concern evidenced by action? Are resources allocated to building more responsible products or to fighting regulations designed to correct wasteful industries?
- Investigate the potential for recycling in the company. Recycling is another form of source reduction; in this case, do not buy products that cannot be recycled unless no other substitute exists. The company could use 50% recycled paper for internal reports rather than the same expensive paper used for customer correspondence. Internal publications made from expensive four-color, high-gloss production techniques are not easily recycled and sometimes are printed with inks containing heavy metals. Instead, use low-tech newsprint or even high-tech digital transmission or recyclable videotapes.
- Review hazardous waste exposure on property the firm controls or finances. US banks and insurance firms have been sued for cleanup costs on property they neither controlled nor used. Some courts have held that financing a company that creates hazardous waste, such as gasoline service stations, passes the cleanup liability along to the capital provider.

(xxxiii) **IIA's Performance Standards**

(A) *IIA's Practice Advisory 2100-7: "Internal Auditor's Role in Identifying and Reporting Environmental Risks."*

**Nature of This Practice Advisory**

The purpose of this Practice Advisory is to provide guidance to internal audit organizations on risk and independence issues related to environmental auditing activities. Internal auditors should be alert to the potential risks that may result from the organizational placement and reporting relationships of environmental auditors. This Practice Advisory suggests the minimum safeguards to ensure that important environmental issues are reported on a timely basis and to the appropriate level. The risks related to environmental noncompliance, fines and penalties, and other mismanagement may result in significant losses for the organization. *Compliance with Practice Advisories is optional. This guidance is repeated in Part 1 and Part 2 for proper coverage of the subject matter.*

*Potential Risks*

1.  The chief audit executive (CAE) should include the environmental, health, and safety (EH&S) risks in any entity-wide risk management assessment and assess the activities in a balanced manner relative to other types of risk associated with an entity's operations. Among the risk exposures that should be evaluated are: organizational reporting structures; likelihood of causing environmental harm, fines, and penalties; expenditures mandated by Environmental Protection Agency or other governmental agencies; history of injuries and deaths; record of losses of customers, and episodes of negative publicity and loss of public image and reputation.

2.  If the CAE finds that the management of the EH&S risks largely depends on an environmental audit function, the CAE needs to consider the implications of that organizational structure and its effects on operations and the reporting mechanisms. If the CAE finds that the exposures are not adequately managed and residual risks exist, that conclusion would normally result in changes to the internal audit activity's plan of engagements and further investigations.

3.  The majority of environmental audit functions report to their organization's environmental component or general counsel, not to the CAE. The typical organizational models for environmental auditing fall into one of these scenarios.

    -   The CAE and environmental audit chief are in separate functional units with little contact with each other.
    -   The CAE and environmental audit chief are in separate functional units and coordinate their activities.
    -   The CAE has responsibility for auditing environmental issues.

4.  According to an IIA flash report on environmental auditing issues

    -   About one-half of the environmental auditors seldom meet with a committee of the governing board and only 40% have some contact with the CAE.
    -   Seventy percent of the organizations reported that environmental issues are not regularly included on the agenda of the governing board.
    -   About 40% of the organizations reported that they had paid fines or penalties for environmental violations in the past three years. Two-thirds of the respondents described their environmental risks as material.

5.  The Environmental, Health, and Safety Auditing Roundtable (new name is The Auditing Roundtable) commissioned Richard L. Ratliff of Utah State University and a group of researchers to perform a study of environmental, health, and safety auditing. The researchers' findings related to the risk and independence issues follow.

    -   The EH&S audit function is somewhat isolated from other organizational auditing activities. It is organized separately from internal auditing, only tangentially related to external audits of financial statements, and reports to an EH&S executive, rather than to the governing board or to senior management. This structure suggests that management believes EH&S auditing to be a technical field that is best placed within the EH&S function of the organization.
    -   With that organizational placement, EH&S auditors could be unable to maintain their independence, which is considered one of the principal requirements of an effective audit function. EH&S audit managers typically report administratively to the executives who are responsible for the physical facilities being audited. Thus, poor EH&S performance would reflect badly on the facilities management team, who would therefore try to exercise their authority and influence over what is reported in audit findings, how audits are conducted, and what is included in the audit plan. This potential subordination of the auditors' professional judgment, even when only apparent, violates auditor independence and objectivity.
    -   It is also common for written audit reports to be distributed no higher in the organization than to senior environmental executives. Those executives may have

a potential conflict of interest, and they may curtail further distribution of EH&S audit findings to senior management and the governing board.
- Audit information is often classified as (a) attorney-client privilege or attorney work product, (b) secret and confidential, or (c) if not confidential, then closely held. This results in severely restricted access to EH&S audit information.

### Suggestions for the Chief Audit Executive

6. The CAE should foster a close working relationship with the chief environmental officer and coordinate activities with the plan for environmental auditing. In those instances where the environmental audit function reports to someone other than the CAE, the CAE should offer to review the audit plan and the performance of engagements. Periodically, the CAE should schedule a quality assurance review of the environmental audit function if it is organizationally independent of the internal audit activity. That review should determine if the environmental risks are being adequately addressed. An EH&S audit program could be (a) compliance-focused (i.e., verifying compliance with laws, regulations, and the entity's own EH&S policies, procedures, and performance objectives), (b) management systems–focused (i.e., providing assessments of management systems intended to ensure compliance with legal and internal requirements and the mitigation of risks), or (c) a combination of both approaches.

7. The CAE should evaluate whether the environmental auditors who are not part of the CAE's organization are in compliance with recognized professional auditing standards and a recognized code of ethics. The Board of Environmental, Health, & Safety Auditor Certifications (BEAC) and the IIA publish practice standards and ethical codes.

8. The CAE should evaluate the organizational placement and independence of the environmental audit function to ensure that significant matters resulting from serious risks to the enterprise are reported up the chain of command to the audit or other committee of the governing board. The CAE should also facilitate the reporting of significant EH&S risk and control issues to the audit (or other board) committee.

(B) **Human resource policy auditing.** This section discusses compliance with safety, hazard communication, security, benefits continuation, bulletin boards, exit interview, I-9 employment eligibility, independent contractors, telephone usage, smoking policy, drug testing, substance abuse policy, accommodating disabilities, and sexual harassment.[20]

*Safety.* Firms that have successful safety programs typically share three common characteristics: (1) a management commitment to safety, (2) active employee participation in safety activities, and (3) thorough investigation of accidents. Successful safety programs reduce accidents. Fewer accidents mean less work interruptions, fewer worker's compensation claims, and lower insurance costs.

The US Occupational Safety and Health Administration (OSHA) is the federal government agency responsible for defining and enforcing job standards. The OSHA law covers all employers engaged in a business affecting commerce, but excludes self-employed individuals, family firms, and workplaces covered by other federal safety laws. Employers covered by OSHA have a general duty to maintain a safe and healthful workplace. The general duty requirements mean that the employer must become familiar with safety standards that affect the workplace, educate employees on safety, and promote safe practices in the daily operation of the business.

### Audit Concerns in Employee Safety Review

In a manufacturing operations audit, the audit objective was to determine whether all legal and regulatory requirements concerning employee safety are being properly implemented. The audit procedure would be to examine documentation concerning the design and operation of the relevant systems and to observe operations for compliance.

---

[20] William Hubbartt, **Personnel Policy Handbook** (New York: McGraw-Hill, 1993), pp. 427–500.

**Safety responsibility.** A safety responsibility policy serves as the framework for additional policy guidelines that direct safety activities. Typical safety activities include safety orientation, safety training, safety committee, workplace inspections, and accident investigations. Also effective in promoting safe work practices are safe operating procedures, job safety analysis, and publishing of safety rules. In order to implement this policy, a safety manager should be designated to coordinate day-to-day safety activities and should be supported by higher-level management for having ultimate responsibility for directing workplace safety.

Safety policy guidelines provide a basis for promoting employee participation in safety activities. Active participation in safety is one important way to keep safety in everyone's mind. A safety mindset helps to prevent accidents.

Some risks that could result from noncompliance, or pitfalls to avoid, include not holding supervisors and managers accountable for safety in their respective work areas and not including safety results on a supervisor's performance evaluation and the tendency to publish a few safety rules and then let things slide. Under the law, an employer will be held liable for failing to enforce safety rules. If a company publishes a safety rule but neglects to require employees to comply with the rule, the firm may be subject to a citation.

**Accident investigation.** The purpose of accident investigation is to identify the accident's cause so that future accidents can be avoided. In addition to prevention of accidents, accident investigations serve several other important functions, such as: eliminating unsafe conditions, identifying training needs, redesigning jobs, preventing or combating fraud related to unethical worker's compensation claims, analyzing accident data, and reporting to government.

*Hazard communication.* Millions of workers are exposed to one or more chemical hazards on the job. Improper use of chemicals on the job can cause fire, explosion, contamination of water or sewer systems, and other serious accidents. Further, employees who fail to follow proper chemical-handling procedures may be subject to serious health elements such as heart conditions, kidney and lung damage, sterility, cancer, burns, and rashes.

OSHA has issued Hazard Communication Standards to help prevent employee illness or injury from chemical products. The standards require chemical manufacturers and distributors to identify chemical hazards and communicate this information to employers using the products. Employers, in turn, are responsible for educating employees about workplace hazards.

The Hazard Communication Standards have six main requirements.

1. Determine what chemical hazards are in the workplace.
2. Establish a written Hazard Communication Program.
3. Develop and/or use warning labels on containers of hazardous chemicals.
4. Maintain a file of Material Safety Data Sheets (MSDS) that describe properties and precautions of each chemical used in the workplace.
5. Train employees to recognize chemical hazards and follow safety precautions.
6. Provide disclosure of limited trade secret information when requested by health care professionals dealing with employee chemical exposures.

Some risks that could result from noncompliance, or pitfalls to avoid, include: (1) failing to handle MSDS forms properly, resulting in lost forms, incomplete files, and inadequate information for responding to an emergency; (2) failure to develop a Hazard Communication Plan could result in an OSHA citation; and (3) not discussing chemical hazard issues with employees for fear of generating employee concerns about job safety, when in fact employees will be pleased to see that management is willing to deal with job safety issues. After hazard communication training, employees tend to be cautious and more likely to use personal protective equipment. An employer's failure to address chemical safety issues on their job, however, is more likely to prompt employee concerns and fears.

*Security.* Management in every organization is concerned about protecting company assets from loss and protecting employees from harm. Security issues can range from protecting the premises from unauthorized entry, guarding against unauthorized release of business records, protecting the safety of employees or customers, and preventing theft.

A security policy assigns responsibilities and defines plans to help the firm prevent and control losses. Firms that fail to define certain security guidelines generally incur greater losses than organizations with comprehensive security practices.

Security issues are a matter of great concern in certain industries. Banks define stringent procedures for the handling and storage of cash. Health care facilities and drugstores follow rigid procedures in the handling of drugs. Certain government defense contractors are required to establish sophisticated systems and controls to protect confidentiality of classified defense projects.

*Some major areas that require security focus include:* security services, such as guard services, installation of alarms, and video monitoring systems. These services should be connected to off-site monitoring of alarm and video systems for a timely response, locks and key control, locked files and administrative controls, documented asset and inventory control, visitor control, computer security requiring codes to access confidential data, personnel safety for employees entering or leaving the premises or parking areas. An employee identification system (a badge with picture) may be part of this process. Background checks, reference checks, and surety bonds may be part of this process. Employers are no longer permitted to use polygraph or "lie detector machines" in the employee selection process. The Employee Polygraph Protection Act of 1988 prohibits the use of lie detectors to test an employee or prospective employee. The law also prohibits discipline, discharge, or other discrimination against an employee based on polygraph tests or refusal to take a test. Private security firms, drug companies, and government units are exempted from the law.

A major risk that could result from noncompliance, or pitfalls to avoid, is that workplace security measures have the potential for conflict with individual privacy concerns or rights.

*Benefits continuation.* Employers with 20 or more employees are subject to the Consolidated Omnibus Budget Reconciliation Act (COBRA) of 1986. COBRA defines requirements for employers to offer continued health insurance coverage for employees or covered dependents who become ineligible for benefits.

When certain qualifying events occur under COBRA, the individual must be offered the opportunity to continue group health insurance. Qualifying events include termination of employment, reduction of hours, layoff, divorce, death, or losing dependent status due to age. The law specifies time limits for the period of continued coverage. Also, there are notification responsibilities and limits. Upon expiration of the benefit continuation period, the employee may exercise conversion rights. This means that the employee's coverage is converted to an individual policy with a higher premium rate.

*Bulletin boards.* Many organizations have a bulletin board to communicate information to employees. In addition, various states and federal labor laws require an employer to post notices about certain employee rights under the law. A bulletin board is company property, so the employer has full authority to regulate what items are posted. Bulletin boards may be used to post information on holidays, benefits, company policies, advancement opportunities, company rules, or other company news. Federal labor law posters that must be displayed in the workplace include: equal employment, minimum wage, overtime, child labor, federally financed construction, federal government contracts, occupational safety and health act poster "job safety and health protection," polygraph, and family and medical leave.

*Exit interview.* An exit interview is an important human resource tool for controlling unwanted turnover. An exit interview also promotes compliance with COBRA insurance continuation requirements. In an exit interview, the human resource specialist interviews a separating employee to discuss reasons for separation, explain benefits entitlement, and secure return of company property.

When an unusually large number of employees quit, the exit interview can help identify causes, such as poor supervisory relations, poor employee selection decisions, pay concerns, working conditions, or other problems. The first policy concern is to assign responsibility for exit interviews preferably to an independent third party, such as a human resource specialist. The second policy concern is to act on the information received from the exit interview.

*I-9 Employment eligibility.* The I-9 Employment Verification Form must be completed by all employees after November 6, 1986, per the Immigration Reform and Control Act of 1986. The purpose of the law is to eliminate employment opportunities that attract illegal aliens to the United States. The law makes it the employer's responsibility to verify that the employee is a US citizen or an alien authorized to work in the United States.

An employer may refuse to hire an individual who fails to provide appropriate documents. However, it is illegal to discriminate against an individual because of national origin or citizenship status.

*Independent contractors.* Independent contractors are self-employed individuals who contract with firms to provide a particular service. Some employers treat certain employees as independent contractors. A number of states and federal laws define and regulate the employment relationship.

The US Internal Revenue Service defines employee status and requires income tax withholding from employees. State and federal unemployment insurance laws require employer contributions for employees. Workers' compensation laws require insurance coverage for employees. Wage hour laws stipulate minimum wage and overtime pay requirements for covered employees. Clearly, the determination of whether an individual is an employee or independent contractor has a significant effect on business costs and legal liability.

Unfortunately, there is no single definition for independent contractor. Each government agency that enforces laws relating to the employer-employee relationship has its own definitions and tests to determine whether a covered employment relationship exists. There are some common trends to aid in defining employment relationships.

These factors are typical of independent contractor status.

- Individual operates a separate business on a profit and loss basis.
- Individual performs services for other businesses.
- Individual exercises initiative and judgment in how work is performed.
- Individual maintains own tools, equipment, and separate office or facility.
- Individual is paid on a per-job basis.

These factors are typical of an employer-employee relationship

- Employer exercises direction and control over employee, work methods, and hours of work.
- Employee generally performs tasks at employer's facility.
- Employee works only for employer.
- Employee is compensated on an hourly or weekly salary basis.

*Telephone usage.* Three common policy concerns about employee telephone use include: (1) pleasant telephone manner, (2) use of proper telephone procedures, and (3) controlling abuse of telephones. With regard to abuse of telephones, the major concern is unauthorized use of company telephones for local and long-distance personal calls.

Several telephone use guidelines include

- Limit outgoing personal calls to nonworking time, such as lunch and breaks.
- Limit incoming personal calls to employees, particularly those in public contact jobs.
- Route incoming personal calls to voice mail, message center, or supervisor.
- Not allowing employees in production, service, or public contact jobs to be interrupted from work tasks by personal phone calls.
- Limit outgoing calls to a pay telephone in the plant or work area or use of cellphones during work.

*Smoking policy.* Employee attitudes about smoking have changed significantly over the past 20 years. Along with the changes of public attitudes about smoking, growing numbers of governmental units have defined laws or regulations restricting smoking. A number of these actions are

- OSHA regulations prohibit use of smoking materials when working near flammable substances.
- The federal government and the military adopted policies limiting use of smoking materials in governmental buildings.
- The Federal Aeronautics Administration now prohibits use of smoking materials on all domestic commercial airplane flights.
- Many cities have passed ordinances restricting smoking in public areas.

Advance notice to employees about the new smoking policy is essential. The scope of the smoking policy is a major issue to consider. The policy can range from a total ban on smoking in the workplace to limited restrictions. Incentives to promote employee interest in stopping smoking should be considered. This includes offering smoking clinics, either on-site or off site.

Some common risks resulting from noncompliance or pitfalls to avoid include: smokers' rights versus nonsmokers' rights, impact of smoking or nonsmoking on work tasks not getting done, and impact of new privacy laws. These laws make it illegal for an employer to discipline or otherwise discriminate against an employee for legal off-duty activities. The intent of these laws is to prevent an employer from taking action against an employee for smoking off the job and may serve to bar broad policy criteria, such as hiring only nonsmokers or banning employees from smoking on and off the job.

*Drug testing.* A number of legal issues should be considered when implementing a drug-testing program. Constitutional issues, federal laws, state laws, and various regulations must be considered when defining drug-testing programs. The US Constitution restricts governmental interference with individual rights. This means that public sector employees have been accorded privacy rights from the unreasonable search and seizures of drug tests. Private sector employees, however, have not been accorded the same protection from their employers. Some state constitutions contain privacy protection applicable to both private and public sector's conduct.

Drug testing has grown as a means to combat drug abuse on the job. There are a variety of ways in which firms have used drug testing, such as

- **New hire testing.** A positive test result showing presence of drugs in the body is considered grounds to deny or withdraw a job offer.
- **Reasonable cause testing.** Nuclear plant workers, truck drivers, and railway engineers are subject to drug testing requirements.
- **Random testing.** The unscheduled or surprise testing of an employee or group of employees for the presence of drugs is intended to catch drug-using individuals who may be able to remain drug-free in anticipation of a scheduled drug test in order to pass the test.
- **Universal testing.** Universal testing involves the scheduled or unscheduled drug testing of all employees.

A major risk resulting from noncompliance with policies, or pitfalls to avoid, is sensitivity to an individual's right to privacy. An employer's insensitivity to employee privacy concerns or failure to adequately implement a testing program can cause serious morale problems and costly litigation.

*Substance abuse policy.* Substance abuse can be defined as inappropriate or excessive use of alcoholic beverages, over-the-counter drugs, prescription drugs, or any use of illegal drugs. Substance abuse by employees is a contributing factor to workplace accidents, poor productivity, increased errors, and absenteeism.

A substance abuse policy typically defines specific prohibitions against possession or use of drugs or alcoholic beverages on company time or premises. A substance abuse policy identifies specific action steps that a supervisor can take rather than covering for the employee and enabling the substance abuser to continue.

Several state and federal labor laws may impact on a substance abuse policy. Government contractors are subject to the Drug-Free Workplace Act of 1988. This law requires employers receiving a government contract of $25,000 or more to certify that they maintain a drug-free workplace with a written plan to comply with the law. The employer's drug-free workplace program should include

- A written policy distributed to employees regarding illegal drugs
- A drug awareness program that includes information about hazards of drug use on the job, penalties for violating the policy, and education about available counseling or rehabilitation programs
- Employee compliance with the policy, including the reporting of an employee conviction of a drug offense in the workplace

- Corrective action that the employer will take against an employee for policy violation or drug conviction
- The employer's good-faith effort to comply with the law

The Drug-Free Workplace Act does not require drug testing. Also, the law does not require sanctions for job use or possession of alcoholic beverages. Both of these issues, however, may be included in a substance abuse policy if elected by the employer. The Americans with Disabilities Act (discussed in the next section) specifically defines recovered alcoholics and recovered former drug users as individuals with a disability subject to the law's protection.

Other potential liabilities could result from a substance abuse policy if the employer discharged an employee in a manner contrary to procedures published in a policy manual or employee handbook. Also, careless release of confidential facts or release of false information about an employee in the course of employment or reference check could result in litigation.

*Accommodating disabilities.* The Americans with Disabilities Act (ADA) of 1990 prohibits discrimination against individuals with disabilities. This far-reaching law deals with discrimination issues in employment, among other things. A policy providing guidance to supervisors on accommodating disabilities will help an organization to comply with the law. The policy can focus on those employment practices that involve supervisor decisions affecting disabled persons. The most likely areas for supervisor guidance are hiring processes, reemployment following medical leave or job accident, and other job changes, such as promotions or transfers. Important policy points include

- The firm's employment application should be revised to eliminate inquiries about prior illnesses, physical limitations, or prior workers' compensation claims. These inquiries are now improper inquiries under ADA.
- The ADA specifically recognizes job descriptions prepared before advertising and interviewing candidates as evidence of essential job functions. Old job descriptions need updating to reflect actual job tasks performed on the job. New job descriptions should be prepared where no descriptions currently exist.
- All interview questions, hiring criteria, exams, and tests must be based on job-related standards consistent with business necessity in order to comply with ADA.
- Preemployment medical exams to determine the nature or severity of a disability are prohibited by ADA. A medical examination evaluating the individual's ability to perform job-related functions may be conducted after making an offer of employment but before the applicant begins performing job duties. Any medical exam should be administered to all entering employees in the same job category. An individual's employment may be conditioned on the results of the medical examination.

Enforcement of the employment sections of the ADA rests with the Equal Employment Opportunity Commission (EEOC). Enforcement can include an informal investigation questionnaire, fact-finding conference, conciliation, settlement, dismissal, or federal court enforcement action. Remedies can include reinstatement, back pay, or other actions.

To minimize claims and avoid discrimination findings, here are some pitfalls to avoid.

- Carefully define a disability. ADA defines a disability as a physical or mental impairment that substantially limits one or more of the major life activities of such individual having a record of such impairment and being regarded as having such impairment.
- Make sure that job descriptions are accurate and current.
- Document reasonable accommodation efforts. When a qualified individual with a disability has requested a reasonable accommodation to assist in the performance of a job, the employer should try to accommodate the request.
- Build a file of resource information, where trained specialists can assist in identifying effective accommodations for disabled individuals.

*Sexual harassment.* With the enactment of the Civil Rights Act of 1991, companies may now be held liable for the acts of their employees and supervisors who engage in on-the-job sexual harassment, even if management is not aware of the problem. The US Supreme Court ruled that workers who have suffered harassment do not have to prove psychological damage or the inability to do their jobs to recover significant damages. This ruling makes it easier for claimants to win lawsuits in this area.

Some examples of sexual harassment in nontraditional areas include: if a person is passed over for a promotion or denied benefits in favor of an individual who submitted to sexual advance, the passed-over person is considered to be a victim of sexual harassment under federal and state guidelines; if a worker initially participates in social or sexual contact but then rejects continued unwelcome advances, that constitutes sexual harassment; and if the harassment involved unwanted touching, it could result in wrongful discharge, fraud, intentional infliction of emotional distress for outrageous conduct, invasion of privacy, assault, and civil battery.

The EEOC guidelines specify preventive affirmative steps that may create immunity from liability for employers. In determining whether an employer is liable, some courts look to see if a comprehensive policy against sexual harassment was in place at the time the incident(s) occurred and whether the employer acted promptly and properly.

Penalties include as much as $300,000 in punitive and compensatory damages (i.e., pain and suffering) in a jury trial for charges of sexual harassment. Previously, monetary damages under federal law were limited to back pay and other forms of equitable relief.

## 2.2 Conduct Consulting Engagements

Consulting engagements solve problems and make recommendations to improve a client's operations and processes by making changes. The engagement steps consist of defining problems, developing alternatives, selecting the best alternative, and implementing the best alternative.

(a) **Internal Control Training.** Internal auditors, other employees of the organization, and management at all levels need an understanding of internal control concepts. This is because internal control affects every employee of the organization in terms of policies, work rules, and procedures.

Internal control training should integrate individual and organizational goals because internal control focuses on people, processes, and objectives. Internal auditors can play both student and teacher roles in that they become students to satisfy the continuing education requirement and they become teachers in educating and training other employees in the internal control concepts.

The internal control training syllabus should include: reviewing recommendations of the Treadway Commission regarding internal control framework, understanding control objectives and control procedures in various functional areas of business, explaining employee's duties and responsibilities in promoting internal control in the organization, and discussing limitations of internal controls (what internal control can do and what it cannot do).

(b) **Business Process Review**

(i) **Business process reengineering.** In an effort to increase revenues and market growth, organizations are conducting business process reviews. The idea behind business process reviews, whether for a production process or a service process, is to streamline operations and to eliminate waste. The result is increased efficiencies, which can lead to greater effectiveness. A proven technique is business process reengineering (BPR), which requires big thinking and making major, radical changes in the business processes. Work flow analysis is a part of BPR.

BPR is one approach for redesigning the way work is done to support the organization's mission and reduce costs. BPR starts with a high-level assessment of the organization's mission, strategic goals, and customer needs. Basic questions are asked, such as: Does our mission need to be redefined? Are our strategic goals aligned with our mission? Who are our customers? An organization may find that it is operating on questionable assumptions, particularly in terms of the wants and needs of its customers. Only after the organization rethinks **what** it should be doing does it go on to decide **how** best to do it.

Within the framework of this basic assessment of mission and goals, reengineering focuses on the organization's business processes: the steps and procedures that govern how resources are used to create products and services that meet the needs of particular customers or markets. As a structured ordering of work steps across time and place, a business process can be decomposed into specific activities, measured, modeled, and improved. It can also be completely redesigned or eliminated altogether. Reengineering identifies, analyzes, and redesigns an organization's core business processes with the aim of achieving dramatic improvements in critical performance measures, such as cost, quality, service, and speed.

Reengineering recognizes that an organization's business processes are usually fragmented into subprocesses and tasks that are carried out by several specialized functional areas within the organization. Often no one is responsible for the overall performance of the entire process. Reengineering maintains that optimizing the performance of subprocesses can result in some benefits, but cannot yield dramatic improvements if the process itself is fundamentally inefficient and outmoded. For that reason, reengineering focuses on redesigning the process as a whole in order to achieve the greatest possible benefits to the organization and their customers. This drive for realizing dramatic improvements by fundamentally rethinking how the organization's work should be done distinguishes reengineering from business process improvement efforts that focus on functional or incremental improvement.

Reengineering is not a panacea. There are occasions when functional or incremental improvements are the method of choice, as when a process is basically sound or when the organization is not prepared to undergo dramatic change. When there is a need to achieve order-of-magnitude improvements, reengineering is the method of choice.

(ii) **Business process improvement.** Business process improvement (BPI) should be continuous, not discrete, and it tends to be more of an incremental change that may affect only a single task or segment of the organization. The concept of fundamental or radical change is the basis of the major difference between BPR and BPI. Quite often BPI initiatives limit their focus to a single existing organizational unit. This in itself breaks one of the tenets of BPR, which is that BPR must focus on redesigning a fundamental business process, not on existing departments or organizational units. While BPR seeks to define what the processes should be, BPI focuses more on how to improve an existing process or service.

Through BPI, organizations can achieve significant incremental improvements in service delivery and other business factors (e.g., increase in employee's productivity). The expected outcomes of BPI are not as dramatic as those associated with BPR initiatives, but the process is also not as traumatic as in achieving the radical changes seen with BPR. In many cases, incremental changes may be achieved in situations lacking the support necessary for more radical changes. Exhibit 2.17 shows the key differences between BPR and BPI.

| Element | BPR | BPI |
|---|---|---|
| Degree of change | Radical (e.g., 80%) | Incremental (e.g., 10–30%) |
| Scope | Entire process | Single area, function/unit |
| Time | Years | Months |
| Driver | Business | Technology |
| Focus | Redefine process | Automate/eliminate the function |
| Work structure | Unified | Fragmented |
| Orientation | Outcome | Function |

**Exhibit 2.17:  BPR versus BPI**

**Business Process Reengineering versus Business Process Improvement**

- Business process reengineering focuses on achieving dramatic improvements.
- Business process improvement focuses on achieving incremental improvements.

(c) **Benchmarking**

(i) **Benchmarking defined.** Benchmarking is the selection of best practices implemented by other organizations. Best practices are the best ways to perform a business process. Organizational change and improvement are the major elements of benchmarking. Benchmarks are the result of a study of organizational processes. Arthur Andersen's Best Practices report identified these first-level, basic processes that define a company's operations.

- Understanding markets and customers
- Designing products and services
- Marketing and selling those products and services
- Producing what customers need and want
- Delivering products and services
- Providing service to customers

Supporting these basic operations, management and support processes maximize the value with the use of human resources, information technology, and financial/physical resources.

The best way to practice benchmarking is to

- Analyze business processes (inventory major business processes, conduct documentary research, and attend conferences to understand new developments).
- Plan the benchmark study (define scope, request site visits, and develop a methodology for capturing the new data).
- Conduct the benchmark study (analyze best practices and identify performance gaps).
- Implement the benchmark results (incorporate best practices into business processes and reevaluate the business processes).

(ii) **Types of benchmarking.** Two types of benchmarking exist: business process benchmarking and computer system benchmarking. Business process benchmarking deals with business process improvement and business process reengineering to reduce costs and to improve quality and customer service. Computer system benchmarking focuses on computer hardware/software acquisition, computer system design, computer capacity planning, and system performance. Each has its own place and time.

Business benchmarking is an external focus on internal activities, functions, or operations in order to achieve continuous improvement.[21] The objective is to understand existing processes and activities and then to identify an external point of reference, or standards, by which that activity can be measured or judged. A benchmark can be established at any level of the organization in any functional area, whether manufacturing or service industries. The ultimate goal is to attain a competitive edge by being better than the best.

Value creation is the heart of organizational activity, whether in a profit or a nonprofit entity. Benchmarking provides the metrics by which to understand and judge the value provided by the organization and its resources. Benchmarking focuses on continuous improvements and value creation for stakeholders (i.e., owners, customers, employees, and suppliers), utilizing the best practices to focus improvement efforts.

Benchmarking targets the critical success factors for a specific organization. It considers the mission of an organization, its resources, products, markets, management skills, and others. It requires an identification of customer(s), whether internal or external to the organization. Benchmarking is an early warning system of impending problems and is not a onetime measurement. Benchmarking can focus on improving organization structures, analyzing managerial roles, improving production processes, and developing strategic issues.

What are the sources of information for benchmarking? Benchmarking can be done by using published materials, insights gained at trade association meetings, and conversations with industry experts, customers, suppliers, academics, and others.

(iii) **When is the right time for business process benchmarking?** Benchmarking should be undertaken when "triggers" are present. These triggers can arise internally or externally in response to information needs from some other major project or issue or problem in the company. *Examples of these triggers include* quality programs, cost reduction programs, new management, new ventures, and competitive moves. Benchmarking should be done as needed, without any preconceived notions.

(iv) **Reasons for business process benchmarking.** A company should benchmark for three reasons: (1) it wants to attain world-class competitive capability, (2) it wants to prosper in a global economy, and (3) it simply wishes to survive (desperation). A company can benchmark in six distinct ways: (1) internal benchmarking, (2) competitive benchmarking, (3) industry benchmarking, (4) best-in-class benchmarking, (5) process benchmarking, and (6) strategic benchmarking (see Exhibit 2.18).

---

[21] *C. J. McNair and Kathleen Leibfried,* **Benchmarking** *(New York: Harper Business, 1992).*

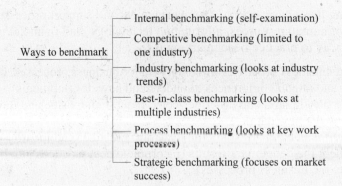

**Exhibit 2.18 Ways to benchmark**

**Internal benchmarking** is the analysis of existing practices within various departments or divisions of the organization, looking for best performance as well as identifying baseline activities and drivers. Drivers are the causes of work: the trigger that sets in motion a series of actions, or activities that will respond to the requests or demands by the stockholders.

In doing internal benchmarking, management is looking downward, examining itself first before looking for outside information. Significant improvements are often made during the internal analysis stage of the benchmarking process. Value-added activities are identified and non-value-adding steps are removed from the process. Internal benchmarking is the first step because it provides the framework for comparing existing internal practices to external benchmark data. *Internal benchmarking focuses on specific value chains or sequences of driver-activity combinations.*

## BPR and BPI

Techniques such as business process reengineering (BPR) and business process improvement (BPI) are used to improve efficiency, reduce costs, and improve customer service. Information technology is an enabler of BPR and BPI, not a substitute for them.

**Competitive benchmarking** looks outward to identify how other direct competitors are performing. Knowing the strengths and weaknesses of the competitors provides good input for strategic and corrective actions.

**Industry benchmarking** extends beyond the one-to-one comparison of competitive benchmarking to look for trends. It is still limited in the number of innovations and new ideas it can uncover because every company is following every other company in the industry. At best, it can help establish the performance baseline or can give an incremental gain. It gives a short-run solution and a quick fix to an existing problem. However, it does not support quantum leaps or breakthroughs in performance since the comparison is limited to one industry.

**Best-in-class benchmarking** looks across multiple industries in search of new, innovative practices, no matter what their source. The best-in-class benchmarking is the ultimate goal of the benchmarking process. It supports quantum leaps in performance and gives a long-run competitive advantage.

**Process benchmarking** centers on key work processes, such as distribution, order entry, or employee training. This type of benchmarking identifies the most effective practices in companies that perform similar functions, no matter in what industry.

**Strategic benchmarking** examines how companies compete and seeks the winning strategies that have led to competitive advantage and market success.

## WHICH BENCHMARKING DOES WHAT?

- Internal benchmarking looks downward and inward.
- Competitive benchmarking looks outward.

- Industry benchmarking looks for trends. It provides a short-run solution and a quick fix to a problem.
- Best-in-class benchmarking looks for the best all around. It provides a quantum jump in improvement.
- Process benchmarking is specific.
- Strategic benchmarking is broad with big impact.

---

### (d) Information Technology and System Development

Information technology (IT) consulting engagements can vary from organization to organization and may include IT strategic planning, computer capacity planning, business and IT continuity planning, customer service, and system development.

Regarding system development, the internal auditor should find out first whether a system development methodology is in place. A methodology can improve the quality of systems, decrease system development and maintenance costs, and increase user service levels and satisfaction. Once a methodology is in place, the internal auditor must ensure the proper application of such methodology. Another area of focus for the auditor is project control to reduce time delays and cost overruns.

During a system development consulting engagement, the internal auditor should

- Determine whether the IT steering committee approves major system development and maintenance projects as part of its charter.
- Review the user's system service request to determine the need for a new system development or maintenance project. Understand the business need for the project.
- Review the feasibility study report for understanding of technical, functional, and economic requirements. Determine whether time and budget estimates are achievable.
- Review general system design to ensure complete coverage of user business needs. Determine whether design of controls is adequate.
- Review detailed system design for inputs (transactions with volumes, input screen formats), process (logic and flow), and outputs (report layouts, output screen formats, and file contents).
- Review system conversion and test plans to determine their adequacy and timing.
- Review system training plans to determine whether appropriate user parties will be trained to do their job properly with the new system.
- Review system implementation plans to determine whether the new system will be implemented all at once or with a phased approach.

### (e) Design of Performance Measurement Systems

Performance measures should be accurately defined, analyzed, and documented so that all interested parties are informed about them. Performance standards should bring meaning to measurements. Employees who are being measured should feel that standards and specific performance measures are fair and achievable. Self-measurement may create confidence and trust, and permit fast feedback and correction from employees. But it can also lead to distortions, concealment, and delays in reporting.

One of the design objectives should be that the performance standards must be simple, meaningful, comparable, reproducible, and traceable given similar business conditions. Care should be taken to compare items that are alike in terms of units of measurements (pounds, grams, liters, or gallons), time frames (hours or days), quantity (volume in units or tons), and quality (meeting the requirements).

During the design of performance measurements, the design team should take both human factors and technical factors into account. From a human factor viewpoint, ensure that the performance measures are not so loose that they present no challenge or so tight that they cannot be attainable. Ideally, both subordinates and superiors must participate in identifying and developing the performance metrics. From a technical factor viewpoint, employees should be given proper tools, training, and equipment to do their job. Otherwise frustration will result. Above all, the performance measures should be based on objective measurement instead of subjective measurement to minimize human bias and suspicion of the reported measurements.

Periodically, the performance measurements should be reviewed and updated to ensure their continued applicability to the situations at hand. Evaluations of performance measures should concentrate on the significant exceptions or deviations from the standards. Therefore, exception reporting is preferred. Significant variances (deviations) require analysis and correction of standards or procedures.

The standards should match the objectives of the operation or function being reviewed. In developing standards, it is better for the auditor to work with the client than alone, with standards later validated by subject matter experts or industry experts for authentication. Usually the standards can be found in standard operating procedures, job descriptions, organizational policies and directives, product design specifications, operating budgets, trade sources, organization's contracts, applicable laws and regulations, generally accepted business practices, generally accepted accounting principles, and generally accepted auditing standards.

(f) **IIA's Attribute Standards**

### IIA's Practice Advisory 1000.C1-1: "Principles Guiding the Performance of Consulting Activities of Internal Auditors"

#### Nature of This Practice Advisory

The definition of internal auditing states: "Internal auditing is an independent, objective assurance and consulting activity designed to add value and improve an organization's operations. It helps an organization accomplish its objectives by bringing a systematic, disciplined approach to evaluate and improve the effectiveness of risk management, control, and governance processes." Internal auditors are reminded that the *Attribute* and *Performance Standards* relate to internal auditors performing both assurance and consulting engagements.

This advisory focuses on broad parameters to be considered in all consulting engagements. Consulting may range from formal engagements, defined by written agreements, to advisory activities, such as participating in standing or temporary management committees or project teams. Internal auditors are expected to use professional judgment to determine the extent to which the guidance provided in this advisory should be applied in each given situation. Special consulting engagements, such as participation in a merger or acquisition project or in emergency engagements, such as disaster recovery activities, may require departure from normal or established procedures for conducting consulting engagements.

Internal auditors should consider these guiding principles when performing consulting engagements. This guidance is not intended to represent all the considerations that may be necessary in performing a consulting engagement, and internal auditors should take extra precautions to determine that management and the board understand and agree with the concept, operating guidelines, and communications required for performing consulting services. *Compliance with Practice Advisories is optional. This guidance is repeated in Part 1 and Part 2 for proper coverage of the subject matter.*

1. **Value proposition.** The value proposition of the internal audit activity is realized within every organization that employs internal auditors in a manner that suits the culture and resources of that organization. That value proposition is captured in the definition of internal auditing and includes assurance and consulting activities designed to add value to the organization by bringing a systematic, disciplined approach to the areas of governance, risk, and control.

2. **Consistency with internal audit definition.** A disciplined, systematic evaluation methodology is incorporated in each internal audit activity. The list of services can generally be incorporated into the broad categories of assurance and consulting. However, the services may also include evolving forms of value-adding services that are consistent with the broad definition of internal auditing.

3. **Audit activities beyond assurance and consulting.** There are multiple internal auditing services. Assurance and consulting are not mutually exclusive and do not preclude other auditing services, such as investigations and nonauditing roles. Many audit services will have both an assurance and consultative (advising) role.

4. **Interrelationship between assurance and consulting.** Internal audit consulting enriches value-adding internal auditing. While consulting is often the direct result of assurance services, it should be recognized that assurance could also be generated from consulting engagements.

5. **Empower consulting through the internal audit charter.** Internal auditors have traditionally performed many types of consulting services, ranging from the analysis of controls built into developing systems, analysis of security products, serving on task forces to analyze operations and make recommendations, and so forth. The board (or audit committee) should em-

power the internal audit activity to perform additional services where they do not represent a conflict of interest or detract from internal audit's obligations to the committee. That empowerment should be reflected in the internal audit charter.

6. **Objectivity.** Consulting services may enhance the auditor's understanding of business processes or issues related to an assurance engagement and do not necessarily impair the auditor's or the internal audit activity's objectivity. Internal auditing is not a management decision-making function. Management should make decisions to adopt or implement recommendations made as a result of an internal audit advisory service. Therefore, internal audit objectivity should not be impaired by the decisions made by management.

7. **Internal audit foundation for consulting services.** Much of consulting is a natural extension of assurance and investigative services and may represent informal or formal advice, analysis, or assessments. The internal audit activity is uniquely positioned to perform this type of consulting work based on (a) its adherence to the highest standards of objectivity, and (b) its breadth of knowledge about organizational processes, risks, and strategies.

8. **Communication of fundamental information.** A primary internal audit value is to provide assurance to senior management and audit committee directors. Consulting engagements cannot be rendered in a manner that masks information that in the CAE's judgment should be presented to senior executives and board members. All consulting is to be understood in that context.

9. **Principles of consulting understood by the organization.** Organizations must have ground rules for the performance of consulting services that are understood by all members of an organization. These rules should be codified in the audit charter approved by the audit committee and promulgated in the organization.

10. **Formal consulting engagements.** Management often engages outside consultants for formal consulting engagements that last a significant period of time. However, an organization may find that the internal audit activity is uniquely qualified for some formal consulting tasks. If an internal audit activity undertakes to perform a formal consulting engagement, the internal audit group should bring a systematic, disciplined approach to the conduct of the engagement.

11. **CAE responsibilities.** Consulting services permit the CAE to enter into dialog with management to address specific managerial issues. In this dialog, the breadth of the engagement and time frames is made responsive to management needs. However, the CAE retains the prerogative of setting the audit techniques and the right of reporting to senior executives and audit committee members when the nature and materiality of results pose significant risks to the organization.

12. **Criteria for resolving conflicts or evolving issues.** An internal auditor is first and foremost an internal auditor. Thus, in the performance of all services the internal auditor is guided by The IIA's Code of Ethics and the *Attribute* and *Performance Standards* of the *International Standards for the Professional Practice of Internal Auditing (Standards)*. Any unforeseen conflicts or activities should be resolved consistent with the Code of Ethics and *Standards*.

**IIA's Practice Advisory 1000.C1-2: "Additional Considerations for Formal Consulting Engagements"**

*Nature of This Practice Advisory*

This Practice Advisory is similar in subject matter to Practice Advisory 1000.C1-1, which discusses the "Principles Guiding the Performance of Consulting Services," and both advisories are useful to internal auditors in performing consulting activities. The definition of internal auditing states: "Internal auditing is an independent, objective assurance and **consulting** activity designed to add value and improve an organization's operations. It helps an organization accomplish its objectives by bringing a systematic, disciplined approach to evaluate and improve the effectiveness of risk management, control, and governance processes." Internal auditors are reminded that the *Attribute* and *Performance Standards* relate to internal auditors performing both assurance and consulting engagements.

This Practice Advisory focuses on broad parameters to be considered in formal consulting engagements. Consulting may range from formal engagements, defined by written agreements, to advisory activities, such as participating in standing or temporary management committees or project teams. Internal auditors are expected to use professional judgment to determine the extent to which the guidance provided in this advisory should be applied in each given situation. Special consulting engagements, such as participation in a merger or acquisition project and in an emergency engagement (e.g., a review of disaster recovery activities), may require departure from normal or established procedures for conducting consulting engagements.

Internal auditors should consider these suggestions when performing formal consulting engagements. This guidance is not intended to represent all the considerations that may be necessary in performing a consulting engagement, and internal auditors should take extra precautions to determine that management and the board understand and agree with the concept, operating guidelines, and communications required for performing formal consulting services. *Compliance with Practice Advisories is optional. This guidance is repeated in Part 1 and Part 2 for proper coverage of the subject matter.*

## Definition of Consulting Services

1. The glossary in the *International Standards for the Professional Practice of Internal Auditing (Standards)* defines "consulting services" as: "Advisory and related client service activities, the nature and scope of which are agreed with the client and which are intended to add value and improve an organization's governance, risk management, and control processes without the internal auditor assuming management responsibility. Examples include counsel, advice, facilitation, and training."

2. The CAE should determine the methodology to use for classifying engagements within the organization. In some circumstances, it may be appropriate to conduct a "blended" engagement that incorporates elements of both consulting and assurance activities into one consolidated approach. In other cases, it may be appropriate to distinguish between the assurance and consulting components of the engagement.

3. Internal auditors may conduct consulting services as part of their normal or routine activities as well as in response to requests by management. Each organization should consider the type of consulting activities to be offered and determine if specific policies or procedures should be developed for each type of activity. Possible categories could include

   • Formal consulting engagements: planned and subject to written agreement.
   • Informal consulting engagements: routine activities, such as participation on standing committees, limited-life projects, ad hoc meetings, and routine information exchange.
   • Special consulting engagements: participation on a merger and acquisition team or system conversion team.
   • Emergency consulting engagements: participation on a team established for recovery or maintenance of operations after a disaster or other extraordinary business event or a team assembled to supply temporary help to meet a special request or unusual deadline.

4. Auditors generally should not agree to conduct a consulting engagement simply to circumvent, or to allow others to circumvent, requirements that would normally apply to an assurance engagement if the service in question is more appropriately conducted as an assurance engagement. This does not preclude where services once conducted as assurance engagements are deemed more suitable to being performed as a consulting engagement.

## "Independence and Objectivity in Consulting Engagements" (*Standard* 1130.C1)

5. Internal auditors are sometimes requested to provide consulting services relating to operations for which they had previous responsibilities or had conducted assurance services. Prior to offering consulting services, the CAE should confirm that the board understands and approves the concept of providing consulting services. Once approved, the internal audit charter should be amended to include authority and responsibilities for consulting activities, and the internal audit activity should develop appropriate policies and procedures for conducting such engagements.

6. Internal auditors should maintain their objectivity when drawing conclusions and offering advice to management. If impairments to independence or objectivity exist prior to commencement of the consulting engagement, or develop subsequently during the engagement, disclosure should be made immediately to management.

7. Independence and objectivity may be impaired if assurance services are provided within one year after a formal consulting engagement. Steps can be taken to minimize the effects of im-

pairment by assigning different auditors to perform each of the services, establishing independent management and supervision, defining separate accountability for the results of the projects, and disclosing the presumed impairment. Management should be responsible for accepting and implementing recommendations.

8. Care should be taken particularly involving consulting engagements that are ongoing or continuous in nature, so that internal auditors do not inappropriately or unintentionally assume management responsibilities that were not intended in the original objectives and scope of the engagement.

**"Due Professional Care in Consulting Engagements"** (*Standards* **1210.C1, 1220.C1, 2130.C1, and 2201.C1)**

9. The internal auditor should exercise due professional care in conducting a formal consulting engagement by understanding the

   - Needs of management officials, including the nature, timing, and communication of engagement results
   - Possible motivations and reasons of those requesting the service
   - Extent of work needed to achieve the engagement's objectives
   - Skills and resources needed to conduct the engagement
   - Effect on the scope of the audit plan previously approved by the audit committee
   - Potential impact on future audit assignments and engagements
   - Potential organizational benefits to be derived from the engagement

10. In addition to the independence and objectivity evaluation and due professional care considerations described above, the internal auditor should

   - Conduct appropriate meetings and gather necessary information to assess the nature and extent of the service to be provided.
   - Confirm that those receiving the service understand and agree with the relevant guidance contained in the internal audit charter, internal audit activity's policies and procedures, and other related guidance governing the conduct of consulting engagements. The internal auditor should decline to perform consulting engagements that are prohibited by the terms of the internal audit charter, conflict with the policies and procedures of the internal audit activity, or do not add value and promote the best interests of the organization.
   - Evaluate the consulting engagement for compatibility with the internal audit activity's overall plan of engagements. The internal audit activity's risk-based plan of engagements may incorporate and rely on consulting engagements, to the extent deemed appropriate, to provide necessary audit coverage to the organization.
   - Document general terms, understandings, deliverables, and other key factors of the formal consulting engagement in a written agreement or plan. It is essential that both the internal auditor and those receiving the consulting engagement understand and agree with the reporting and communication requirements.

**"Scope of Work in Consulting Engagements"** (*Standards* **2010.C1, 2110.C1 and C2, 2120.C1 and C2, 2201.C1, 2210.C1, 2220.C1, 2240.C1, and 2440.C2)**

11. As observed above, internal auditors should reach an understanding about the objectives and scope of the consulting engagement with those receiving the service. Any reservations about the value, benefit, or possible negative implications of the consulting engagement should be communicated to those receiving the service. Internal auditors should design the scope of work to ensure that professionalism, integrity, credibility, and reputation of the internal audit activity will be maintained.

12. In planning formal consulting engagements, internal auditors should design objectives to meet the appropriate needs of management officials receiving these services. In the case of special requests by management, internal auditors may consider these actions if they believe that the objectives that should be pursued go beyond those requested by management.

- Persuade management to include the additional objectives in the consulting engagement; or
- Document the fact that the objectives were not pursued and disclose that observation in the final communication of consulting engagement results; and
- Include the objectives in a separate and subsequent assurance engagement.

13. Work programs for formal consulting engagements should document the objectives and scope of the engagement as well as the methodology to be used in satisfying the objectives. The form and content of the program may vary depending on the nature of the engagement. In establishing the scope of the engagement, internal auditors may expand or limit the scope to satisfy management's request. However, the internal auditor should be satisfied that the projected scope of work will be adequate to meet the objectives of the engagement. The objectives, scope, and terms of the engagement should be periodically reassessed and adjusted during the course of the work.

14. Internal auditors should be observant of the effectiveness of risk management and control processes during formal consulting engagements. Substantial risk exposures or material control weaknesses should be brought to the attention of management. In some situations the auditor's concerns should also be communicated to executive management, the audit committee, and/or the board of directors. Auditors should use professional judgment to (a) determine the significance of exposures or weaknesses and the actions taken or contemplated to mitigate or correct these exposures or weaknesses and (b) ascertain the expectations of executive management, the audit committee, and board in having these matters reported.

**"Communicating the Results of Consulting Engagements"** (*Standards* **2410.C1 and 2440.C1**)

15. Communication of the progress and results of consulting engagements will vary in form and content depending on the nature of the engagement and the needs of the client. Reporting requirements are generally determined by those requesting the consulting service and should meet the objectives as determined and agreed to with management. However, the format for communicating the results of the consulting engagement should clearly describe the nature of the engagement and any limitations, restrictions, or other factors about which users of the information should be made aware.

16. In some circumstances, the internal auditor may conclude that the results should be communicated beyond those who received or requested the service. In such cases, the internal auditor should expand the reporting so that results are communicated to the appropriate parties. When expanding the reporting to other parties, the auditor should conduct the following steps until satisfied with the resolution of the matter:

- Determine what direction is provided in the agreement concerning the consulting engagement and related communications.
- Attempt to convince those receiving or requesting the service to expand voluntarily the communication to the appropriate parties.
- Determine what guidance is provided in the internal audit charter or audit activity's policies and procedures concerning consulting communications.
- Determine what guidance is provided in the organization's code of conduct, code of ethics, and other relative policies, administrative directives, or procedures.
- Determine what guidance is provided by the IIA's Standards and Code of Ethics, other standards or codes applicable to the auditor, and any legal or regulatory requirements that relate to the matter under consideration.

17. Internal auditors should disclose to management, the audit committee, board, or other governing body of the organization the nature, extent, and overall results of formal consulting engagements along with other reports of internal auditing activities. Internal auditors should keep executive management and the audit committee informed about how audit resources are being deployed. Neither detail reports of these consulting engagements nor the specific results and recommendations are required to be communicated. But an appropriate description of these types of engagements and their significant recommendations should be communicated

and is essential in satisfying the internal auditor's responsibility in complying with *Standard* 2060, "Reporting to the Board and Senior Management."

## "Documentation Requirements for Consulting Engagements" (*Standard* 2330.C1)

18. Internal auditors should document the work performed to achieve the objectives of a formal consulting engagement and support its results. However, documentation requirements applicable to assurance engagements do not necessarily apply to consulting engagements.

19. Auditors are encouraged to adopt appropriate record retention policies and address related issues, such as ownership of consulting engagement records, in order to protect the organization adequately and to avoid potential misunderstandings involving requests for these records. Situations involving legal proceedings, regulatory requirements, tax issues, and accounting matters may call for special handling of certain consulting engagement records.

## "Monitoring of Consulting Engagements" (*Standard* 2500.C1)

20. The internal audit activity should monitor the results of consulting engagements to the extent agreed on with the client. Varying types of monitoring may be appropriate for differing types of consulting engagements. The monitoring effort may depend on factors such as management's explicit interest in the engagement or the internal auditor's assessment of the project's risks or value to the organization.

MULTIPLE-CHOICE QUESTIONS (1-427)

## Conduct Assurance Engagements

**1.** Purchases from two new vendors increased dramatically after a new buyer was hired. The buyer was obtaining kickbacks from the two vendors based on sales volume. A possible means of detection is
- a. Periodic vendor surveys regarding potential buyer conflict-of-interest or ethics violations.
- b. The receipt of an invoice to put new vendors on the master file.
- c. The use of purchase orders for all purchases.
- d. The use of change analysis and trend analysis of buyer or vendor activity.

**2.** Due to the small staff, one remote unit's petty cash custodian also had responsibility for the imprest fund checking account reconciliation. The cashier concealed a diversion of funds by altering the beginning balance on the monthly reconciliations sent to the group office. A possible audit test to detect this would be to
- a. Compare monthly balances and use change and trend analysis.
- b. Require additional monitoring by headquarters whenever improper segregation of duties exists at remote units.
- c. Determine if any employees have high personal debt.
- d. Determine if any employees are leading expensive lifestyles.

**3.** In an organization that has a separate division that is primarily responsible for fraud deterrence, the internal auditing department is responsible for
- a. Examining and evaluating the adequacy and effectiveness of that division's actions taken to deter fraud.
- b. Establishing and maintaining that division's system of internal controls.
- c. Planning that division's fraud deterrence activities.
- d. Controlling that division's fraud deterrence activities.

**Items 4 and 5** are based on the following:

During an audit, the internal auditor found a scheme in which the warehouse director and the purchasing agent for a retail organization diverted approximately $500,000 of goods to their own warehouse, then sold the goods to third parties. The fraud was not noted earlier since the warehouse director forwarded receiving reports (after updating the perpetual inventory records) to the accounts payable department for processing.

**4.** Which of the following procedures would have most likely led to the discovery of the missing materials and the fraud?
- a. Take a random sample of receiving reports and trace to the recording in the perpetual inventory record. Note differences and investigate by type of product.
- b. Take a random sample of purchase orders and trace them to receiving documents and to the records in the accounts payable department.

- c. Take an annual physical inventory, reconciling amounts with the perpetual inventory, noting the pattern of differences and investigating.
- d. Take a random sample of sales invoices and trace to the perpetual records to see if inventory was on hand. Investigate any differences.

**5.** Assume the perpetrators confessed to the auditors. What is the appropriate auditor action?
- a. Request the perpetrators sign the auditor's summary of the confession and include it in the working papers. Report the details to senior management for further action.
- b. Omit the documentation from the working papers because it is subjective, sensitive, and may become legal evidence. Report the details to management and have them request legal counsel to document the confession.
- c. Orally report the confession to management and suggest they report it to legal authorities because a crime was involved. Do not document.
- d. Inform the perpetrators of their rights, document their confession on tape, and inform the local legal authorities of the crime.

**6.** An internal auditor who suspects fraud should
- a. Determine that a loss has been incurred.
- b. Interview those who have been involved in the control of assets.
- c. Identify the employees who could be implicated in the case.
- d. Recommend whatever investigation is considered necessary under the circumstances.

**7.** During the audit of payments under a construction contract with a local firm, the auditor finds a $900 recurring monthly reimbursement for rent at a local apartment complex. Each reimbursement is authorized by the same project engineer. The auditor finds no provision for payment of temporary living expenses in the construction contract. Discussion with the project engineer could not resolve the matter. The auditor should
- a. Inform the audit director.
- b. Call the engineer into a private meeting to confront the situation.
- c. Complete the audit as scheduled, noting the $900 recurring reimbursement in the workpapers.
- d. Wait until the engineer is surrounded by plenty of witnesses and then inquire about the payments.

**8.** In the course of performing an audit, an internal auditor becomes aware of illegal acts being performed by several of the highest-ranking officers of the company. To whom should the findings of the audit report be addressed?
- a. Line-level supervision.
- b. Members of the news media.
- c. The officers involved in the illegal acts.
- d. The audit committee of the board of directors.

**9.** An internal auditor has detected probable employee fraud and is preparing a preliminary report for management. This report should include
- a. A statement that an internal audit conducted with due professional care cannot provide absolute assurance that irregularities have not occurred.

b. The auditor's conclusion as to whether sufficient information exists to conduct an investigation.

c. The results of a polygraph test administered to the suspected perpetrator(s) of the fraud.

d. A list of proposed audit tests to help disclose the existence of similar frauds in the future.

**10.** During the course of a bank audit, the auditors discover that one loan officer had approved loans to a number of related but separate organizations, in violation of regulatory policies. The loan officer indicated that it was an oversight and it would not happen again. However, the auditors believe it may have been intentional because the loan officer is related to one of the primary owners of the corporate group that controls the related organizations. The auditors should

a. Inform management of the conflict of interest and the violation of the regulatory requirements and suggest further investigation.

b. Report the violation to the regulatory agency because it constitutes a significant breakdown of the bank's control structure.

c. Not report the violation if the loan officer agrees to take corrective action.

d. Expand the audit work to determine if there may be fraudulent activity on the part of the loan officer and report the findings to management when the follow-up investigation is complete.

**Items 11 through 13** are based on the following:

An auditor is performing an operational audit of a division and observes that an unusually large quantity of goods is on hand in the shipping and materials rework areas. The items are labeled as reship items. Upon inquiry, the auditor is told that they are goods that have been returned by customers and have either been repaired or shipped back to the original customer or repaired and shipped out as new products because they are fully warranted.

**11.** The auditor has not yet performed any detailed audit work. Based on the information given, the **most** appropriate action for the auditor to take would be to

a. Report the items to divisional management and ask for their explanation before determining whether to include the findings in an audit report.

b. Take a sample of the items on hand and trace to underlying documents, such as receiving reports and sales orders, to determine how the goods were handled.

c. Write the finding up, but do not perform any additional work without the approval of the director of internal auditing because it is clearly a scope expansion.

d. Take an inventory of the goods on hand so the dollar amount could be included in the audit report along with the explanation of the problem.

**12.** Assume the auditor found that most of the goods were repaired and sold as new items. Such sales are both against company policy and against governmental regulations. The auditor does not know whether fraud was involved or the extent that divisional management had been involved in the scheme. The auditor should report the finding to

a. Divisional management only, since they are responsible for correcting the problem.

b. Divisional management and relevant regulatory bodies, since it is a clear violation.

c. Divisional management, the audit committee, and senior management.

d. The audit committee and top management only.

**13.** Assume that subsequent investigation shows that previously issued financial statements were materially misstated due to the improper recognition of sales. The auditor's next step should be to

a. Immediately inform the external auditor and the divisional manager.

b. Inform divisional management as a preliminary finding, but wait until a formal audit report is issued to inform the audit committee.

c. Inform the external auditor, senior management, the board, and the audit committee.

d. Inform senior management, the board, and the audit committee.

**14.** Insurance companies are beginning to receive hospitalization claims directly from hospitals by computer media; no paper is transmitted from the hospital to the insurance company. Which of the following control procedures would be **most** effective in detecting fraud in such an environment?

a. Use integrated test facilities to test the correctness of processing in a manner that is transparent to data processing.

b. Develop monitoring programs to identify unusual types of claims or an unusual number of claims by demographic classes for investigation by the claims department.

c. Use generalized audit software to match the claimant identification number with a master list of valid policyholders.

d. Develop batch controls over all items received from a particular hospital and process those claims in batches.

**15.** The auditor suspects a disbursements fraud whereby an unknown employee(s) is submitting and approving invoices for payment. Before discussing the potential fraud with management, the auditor decides to gather additional evidence. Which of the following procedures would be most helpful in providing the additional evidence?

a. Use audit software to develop a list of vendors with post office box numbers or other unusual features. Select a sample of those items and trace to supporting documents such as receiving reports.

b. Select a sample of payments made during the year and investigate each one for approval.

c. Select a sample of receiving reports representative of the period under investigation and trace to approved payment. Note any items not properly processed.

d. Take a sample of invoices received during the past month; examine to determine if properly authorized for payment; and trace to underlying documents such as receiving reports.

**16.** A small city managed its own pension fund. According to the city charter, the funds could be invested in bonds, money market funds, or high-quality stocks only. The auditor has already verified the existence of the pension fund assets. The fund balance was not very large and was managed by the city treasurer. The auditor decided to estimate income from investments for the fund by multiplying the average fund balance by a weighted-average return based on the current portfolio mix. Upon doing so, the auditor found that recorded income was substantially less than was expected. The auditor's next audit step should be to

    a.   Ask the treasurer why that income appears to be less than expected.

    b.   Prepare a more detailed estimate of income by consulting a dividend and reporting service, which lists the interest or dividends paid on specific stocks and bonds.

    c.   Inform management and the audit committee that fraud is suspected and suggest that legal counsel be called in to complete the investigation.

    d.   Select a sample of entries to the pension fund income account and trace to the cash journal to determine if cash was received.

**17.** A disgruntled former employee calls the director of internal auditing to report misappropriations of funds by the supervisor of cash operations. Audit tests subsequently verify the allegations. The director of internal auditing should proceed with which of the following actions based on the above information?

    a.   Notify local law enforcement authorities.

    b.   Confront the supervisor of cash operations with the allegations.

    c.   Inform the treasurer and chief financial officer of the suspected fraud.

    d.   Notify the bonding agency.

**18.** A director of internal auditing uncovers a significant fraudulent activity that clearly involves the executive vice president to whom the director reports. Which of the following **best** describes how the director should proceed?

    a.   Carry out an examination for the purpose of determining the extent of the fraud.

    b.   Interview the executive vice president to obtain essential evidence.

    c.   Notify regulatory authorities and police.

    d.   Report the facts to the chief executive officer and the audit committee of the board of directors.

**19.** The IIA *Standards* require that when an internal auditor identifies multiple factors that have been linked with possible fraudulent conditions and suspects that fraud has taken place, the auditor should

    a.   Immediately notify senior management and the board.

    b.   Immediately inform the audit committee.

    c.   Notify the appropriate authorities within the company and recommend an investigation.

    d.   Extend audit tests to determine the extent of the fraud.

**20.** According to the IIA Standards, internal auditors should be involved in fraud investigations as

    a.   Sole investigators.

    b.   Part of an investigation team.

    c.   Independent observers.

    d.   Nonparticipants.

**21.** A significant employee fraud took place shortly after an internal audit. The internal auditor may **not** have properly fulfilled the responsibility for the deterrence of fraud by failing to note and report that

    a.   Policies, practices, and procedures to monitor activities and safeguard assets were less extensive in low-risk areas than in high-risk areas.

    b.   A system of control that depended on separation of duties could be circumvented by collusion among three employees.

    c.   There were no written policies describing prohibited activities and the action required whenever violations are discovered.

    d.   Divisional employees had not been properly trained to distinguish between bona fide signatures and cleverly forged ones on authorization forms.

**22.** According to the IIA *Standards,* a fraud report is required

    a.   At the conclusion of the detection phase.

    b.   At the conclusion of the investigation phase.

    c.   At the conclusion of both the detection and the investigation phases.

    d.   Neither at the conclusion of the detection phase nor at the conclusion of the investigation phase.

**23.** When conducting fraud investigations, internal auditing should

    a.   Clearly indicate the extent of internal auditing's knowledge of the fraud when questioning suspects.

    b.   Assign personnel to the investigation in accordance with the audit schedule established at the beginning of the fiscal year.

    c.   Perform its investigation independent of lawyers, security personnel, and specialists from outside the organization who are involved in the investigation.

    d.   Assess the probable level and the extent of complicity of fraud within the organization.

**24.** An internal auditor is preparing a report that discusses the possibility of employee fraud by a specific named employee. The auditor should be careful that distribution of the report be limited on a need-to-know basis. Failure to follow this caveat may result in the auditor and/or his employer being found liable for

    a.   Libel.

    b.   Slander.

    c.   Compounding a felony.

    d.   Malicious prosecution.

**25.** Even when there is overwhelming evidence of fraud by a particular employee, internal auditing will usually not initiate a criminal complaint, but rather will leave this action for the law enforcement authorities. By so doing, internal auditing avoids the possibility of being accused of

    a.   False imprisonment.

    b.   Libel.

    c.   Slander.

    d.   Malicious prosecution.

**26.** After completing an investigation, internal auditing has concluded that an employee has stolen a significant amount of cash receipts. A draft of the proposed report on this finding should be submitted for review to

    a.   Legal counsel.

    b.   The audit committee of the board of directors.

    c.   The president of the organization.

    d.   The organization's outside auditors.

**27.** Which of the following is true about interviewing an individual during the investigation of suspected fraud?

a. The internal auditor's role involves collecting facts.

b. Internal auditors should be empowered to confine fraud suspects to the office but only for the purpose of interviewing them.

c. The internal auditor's role involves attempting to obtain confessions of guilt.

d. Internal auditors are authorized to waive punishment of the employee if the employee restores the item(s) stolen.

**28.** An internal auditor is interviewing three individuals, one of whom is suspected of committing a fraud. Which of the following is the **least** effective interviewing approach?

a. Ask each individual to prepare a written statement explaining his or her actions.

b. Take the role of one seeking the truth.

c. Listen carefully to what the interviewee has to say.

d. Attempt to get the suspect to confess.

**29.** An internal auditor is conducting interviews of three employees who had access to a valuable asset that has disappeared. In conducting the interviews the internal auditor should

a. Respond to noncooperation by threatening adverse consequences of such behavior.

b. Conduct the interviews in a group.

c. Not indicate that management will forgo prosecution if restitution is made.

d. Allow a suspect to return to work after the interview so as not to arouse suspicions.

**30.** An internal auditor fails to discover an employee fraud during an audit. The nondiscovery is most likely to suggest a violation of the IIA *Standards* if it was the result of a

a. Failure to perform a detailed audit of all transactions in the area.

b. Determination that any possible fraud in the area would not involve a material amount.

c. Determination that the cost of extending audit procedures in the area would exceed the potential benefits.

d. Presumption that the internal controls in the area were adequate and effective.

**31.** The director of internal auditing is concerned that a recently disclosed fraud was not uncovered during the last audit of cash operations. A review of the work papers indicated that the fraudulent transaction was not included in a properly designed statistical sample of transactions tested. Which of the following applies to this situation?

a. Because cash operation is a high-risk area, 100% testing of transactions should have been performed.

b. The internal auditor acted with due professional care since an appropriate statistical sample of material transactions was tested.

c. Fraud should not have gone undetected in a recently audited area.

d. Extraordinary care is necessary in the performance of a cash operations audit, and the auditor should be held responsible for the oversight.

**32.** In the course of their work, internal auditors must be alert for fraud and other forms of white-collar crime. The important characteristic that distinguishes fraud from other varieties of white-collar crime is that

a. Fraud encompasses an array of irregularities and illegal acts that involve intentional deception.

b. Unlike other white-collar crimes, fraud is always perpetrated against an outside party.

c. White-collar crime is usually perpetrated for the benefit of an organization, whereas fraud benefits an individual.

d. Outsiders usually perpetrate white-collar crime to the detriment of an organization, whereas insiders perpetrate fraud to benefit the organization.

**33.** Internal auditing is responsible for assisting in the prevention of fraud by

a. Informing the appropriate authorities within the organization and recommending whatever investigation is considered necessary in the circumstances when wrongdoing is suspected.

b. Establishing the systems designed to ensure compliance with the organization's policies, plans, and procedures, as well as applicable laws and regulations.

c. Examining and evaluating the adequacy and the effectiveness of control, commensurate with the extent of the potential exposure/risk in the various segments of the organization's operations.

d. Determining whether operating standards have been established for measuring economy and efficiency and whether these standards are understood and are being met.

**34.** The internal auditing department has concluded a fraud investigation that revealed a previously undiscovered materially adverse impact on the financial position and results of operations for two years on which financial statements have already been issued. The director of internal auditing should immediately inform

a. The external audit firm responsible for the financial statements affected by the discovery.

b. The appropriate governmental or regulatory agency.

c. Appropriate management and the audit committee of the board of directors.

d. The internal accounting function ultimately responsible for making corrective journal entries.

**35.** According to the IIA *Standards*, internal auditing has a responsibility for helping to deter fraud. Which of the following **best** describes how this responsibility is generally met?

a. By coordinating with security personnel and law enforcement agencies in the investigation of possible frauds.

b. By testing for fraud in every audit and following up as appropriate.

c. By assisting in the design of control systems to prevent fraud.

d. By evaluating the adequacy and effectiveness of controls in light of the potential exposure or risk.

**36.** According to the IIA *Standards*, which of the following is the correct listing of information that must be included in a fraud report?

a. Purpose, scope, results, and, where appropriate, an expression of the auditor's opinion.

b. Criteria, condition, cause and effect.

c. Background, findings and recommendations.

d.  Findings, conclusions, recommendations, and corrective action.

**37.** An internal auditor reported a suspected fraud to the director of internal auditing. The director turned the entire case over to the security department. Security failed to investigate or report the case to management. The perpetrator continued to defraud the organization until being accidentally discovered by a line manager two years later. Select the most appropriate action for the audit director.

a.  The director's actions were correct.
b.  The director should have periodically checked the status of the case with security.
c.  The director should have conducted the investigation.
d.  The director should have discharged the perpetrator.

**38.** Internal auditing is responsible for reporting fraud to senior management or the board when

a.  The incidence of fraud of a material amount has been established to a reasonable certainty.
b.  Suspicious activities have been reported to internal auditing.
c.  Irregular transactions have been identified and are under investigation.
d.  The review of all suspected fraud-related transactions is complete.

**39.** According to the IIA *Standards*, the role of internal auditing in the investigation of fraud includes all of the following **except:**

a.  Assessing the probable level and extent of complicity in the fraud within the organization.
b.  Designing the procedures to follow in attempting to identify the perpetrators, extent of the fraud, techniques used, and cause of the fraud.
c.  Coordinating activities with management personnel, legal counsel, and other appropriate specialists throughout the investigation.
d.  Interrogating suspected perpetrators of the fraud.

**40.** During the course of an audit, an auditor discovers that a clerk is embezzling company funds. Although this is the first embezzlement ever encountered and the organization has a security department, the auditor decides to personally interrogate the suspect. If the auditor is violating the IIA's Code of Ethics, the rule violated is most likely

a.  Failing to show due diligence.
b.  Lack of loyalty to the organization.
c.  Lack of competence in this area.
d.  Failing to comply with the law.

**Third Parties and Contract Auditing**

**41.** An organization uses a service bureau to process its hourly payroll transactions. The internal auditor is concerned that the hourly payroll for the year has been processed correctly and, in particular, the computation of employee withholding for pension contributions is in accordance with the union contract, which specifies charges each quarter. Which of the following audit procedures would **best** accomplish the audit objective?

a.  Select a random sample of all hourly payroll transactions for the reporting period, recompute pay and withholding items, and compare the result with that obtained from the service bureau.

b.  Select a stratified sample of all hourly and salaried payroll transactions for an entire reporting period, perform the necessary activities, and then compare the result with that obtained from the service bureau.
c.  Select a discovery sampling of all payroll transactions for an entire reporting period and then follow up on any findings.
d.  Submit a set of test data to the service bureau during an annual audit and compare the service bureau's processing with the auditor's predetermined computations on the same test data.

**42.** One concern of a user of a computer service center is that one firm's transactions may accidentally be used in the process of updating a second firm's master files. The control procedure that would **best** provide assurance of the integrity of the master files during updating processes is a check for

a.  Completeness of input, such as a computer sequence check.
b.  Correct master files, such as a header label.
c.  Input accuracy, such as a check of detail reports.
d.  Accuracy of file maintenance, such as review of exception reports.

**43.** An internal auditing department has scheduled an audit of a construction contract. One portion of this audit will include comparing materials purchased to those specified in the engineering drawings. The auditing department does not have anyone on staff with sufficient expertise to complete this audit step. Select the **best** alternative for the director of internal auditing.

a.  Delete the audit from the schedule.
b.  Perform the entire audit using current staff.
c.  Engage an engineering consultant to perform the comparison.
d.  Accept the contractors' written representations.

**Items 44 through 47** are based on the following:

During an audit of a defense contract, the auditor becomes concerned with the possibility of inappropriate charges to overhead. However, when examining the underlying documentation of expenses, the auditor finds that all expenditures are properly supported. All billings show total cost and the application of a percentage overhead rate that appears consistent with previous years.

**44.** Which of the following audit procedures would be **least** effective in addressing the auditor's concern?

a.  Retest the computation of the overhead by multiplying actual costs by the overhead rate.
b.  Take a probability-proportional-to-size sample of expenditures included in the company's overhead expense and examine to determine if they are consistent with the contract.
c.  Recompute the overhead rate to determine if it is properly computed on the appropriate base.
d.  Take a sample of contractor payments to determine if the underlying expense was appropriately classified as contract expense or overhead.

**45.** The auditor calculates a statistical estimate of expenditures by the contractor to determine whether they are in compliance with the contract. The audit working papers document the following evidence, which the auditor is considering for the audit report:

- Total expenditures per the contractor books: $12.3 million
- Total number of items in population: 1,500
- Sample size: 100
- Number of items not in compliance: 5
- Dollar value of items sampled: $700,000
- Dollar amount of items not in compliance: $53,000

Which of the following communications would be correct?

    a.  The best estimate is that 5% of the 1,500 items in the population are not in compliance with the contract.

    b.  The best estimate is that the incorrect charges to the account equal about $795,000.

    c.  The average dollar value of items not in compliance is greater than the average dollar value of items in the population.

    d.  All of the above.

**46.** Assume the contract with the defense contractor states that the government will not pay for costs associated with waste or inefficiency on the part of the contractor. Which of the following sources of evidence would be **least** persuasive regarding potential waste and inefficiency on the part of the contractor?

    a.  Management certification that it has not incurred waste or inefficiencies that are not allowed in the contract.

    b.  A walk-through of the contractor's manufacturing and development facilities.

    c.  An examination of the nature of expenses incurred to determine their intent and relationship to the contract.

    d.  A comparison of contract expense with that of similar projects in the past or similar projects with other companies.

**47.** Assume that the contract also states that the contractor must comply with all applicable environmental regulations because the government is responsible for fines for such regulations. The governmental auditor finds that the environmental protection agency has recently performed an environmental audit of the contractor and found numerous, but minor, deviations from current environmental law. However, there was one major item: the company was not meeting the standard for emissions into the atmosphere. The auditor contacts the environmental regulators and finds the company has acted responsibly. It has fixed all the minor findings and has approved a large capital expenditure to reduce the emission of toxic wastes into the air. Which of the following statements regarding these findings is(are) correct?

    I.  Materiality of the findings should be based on the potential amount of fines that could be imposed, not on the fact that most of the deviations were minor in nature.

    II.  The auditor should report the problem with toxic emissions but should not report the other items because they were of a minor nature.

    III.  Because the report will have a significant effect on the government, the auditor should report the toxic waste emissions only if the nature and type can be substantiated.

    a.  I only.

    b.  II only.

    c.  I, II, and III.

    d.  I and III only.

**48.** A company recently entered into a cost-plus contract to build a new and larger manufacturing plant. Which of the following auditing procedures would be of **most** importance to the auditor reviewing this contract?

    a.  Review the contract to ascertain that it contains a provision for the right of system review and cost audits of the contractor.

    b.  Review the contract for a specific date of completion.

    c.  Review the contract and all of the related bids received to ascertain that the company selected the contractor with the lowest bid.

    d.  Review the business integrity of the contractor through direct inquiry.

**49.** During the audit of a contract for construction that was managed by a general contractor, the internal auditor noted that billings included a fee of 10% for pension benefits for the contractor's personnel. The contractor had no pension plan in effect, and the fee for contract pension was not included in the contract. The internal control most likely to prevent payment of such an overcharge is

    a.  Review of invoices before funds are disbursed thereon.

    b.  Maintenance of adequate records for all construction contracts.

    c.  Segregation of disbursing functions from receiving and inspection functions.

    d.  Employment of well-qualified personnel for the treasury function.

**50.** In auditing a cost-plus construction contract for a new catalog showroom, the internal auditor should be cognizant of the risk that

    a.  The contractor could be charging for the use of equipment not utilized in the construction.

    b.  Income taxes related to construction equipment depreciation may have been calculated erroneously.

    c.  Contractor cash budgets could have been inappropriately compiled.

    d.  Payroll taxes may have been inappropriately omitted from billings.

**51.** Several members of senior management have questioned whether the internal audit department should report to the newly established, quality audit function as part of the total quality management process within the company. The director of internal auditing has reviewed the quality standards and the programs that the quality audit manager has proposed. The director's response to senior management should include

    a.  Changing the applicable standards for internal auditing within the company to provide compliance with quality audit standards.

    b.  Changing the qualification requirements for new staff members to include quality audit experience.

    c.  Estimating departmental cost savings from eliminating the internal auditing function.

    d.  Identifying appropriate liaison activities with the quality audit function to ensure coordination of audit schedules and overall audit responsibilities.

**52.** Internal auditors are often called on either to perform, or assist the external auditor in performing, a due diligence review. A due diligence review is

    a.  A review of interim financial statements as directed by an underwriting firm.

    b.  An operational audit of a division of a company to determine if divisional management is complying with laws and regulations.

    c.  A review of operations as requested by the audit committee to determine whether the operations comply with audit committee and organizational policies.

    d.  A review of financial statements and related disclosures in conjunction with a potential acquisition.

**53.** The IIA *Standards* require an internal auditor to exercise due professional care in performing internal audits. This includes

    a.  Establishing direct communication between the director of internal auditing and the board of directors.

    b.  Evaluating established operating standards and determining whether those standards are acceptable and are being met.

    c.  Accumulating sufficient evidence so that the auditor can give absolute assurance that irregularities do not exist.

    d.  Establishing suitable criteria of education and experience for filling internal audit positions.

**54.** An auditor finds a situation where there is some suspicion, but no evidence, of potential misstatement. The standard of due professional care would be violated if the auditor

    a.  Identified potential ways in which an error could occur and ranked the items for audit investigation.

    b.  Informed the audit manager of the suspicions and asked for advice on how to proceed.

    c.  Did not test for possible misstatement because the audit program had already been approved by audit management.

    d.  Expanded the audit program, without the auditee's approval, to address the highest ranked ways in which a misstatement may have occurred.

**55.** Management asserted that the performance standards the auditors used to evaluate operating performance were inappropriate. Written performance standards that had been established by management were vague and had to be interpreted by the auditor. In such cases auditors may meet their due care responsibility by

    a.  Assuring themselves that their interpretations are reasonable.

    b.  Assuring themselves that their interpretations are in line with industry practices.

    c.  Establishing agreement with auditees as to the standards needed to measure performance.

    d.  Incorporating management's objections in the audit report.

**56.** According to the IIA *Standards* concerning due professional care, an internal auditor should

    a.  Consider the relative materiality or significance of matters to which audit procedures are applied.

    b.  Emphasize the potential benefits of an audit without regard to the cost.

    c.  Consider whether established operating standards are being met and not whether those standards are acceptable.

    d.  Select procedures that are likely to provide absolute assurance those irregularities do not exist.

**57.** "Due care implies reasonable care and competence, not infallibility or extraordinary performance." This statement makes which of the following unnecessary?

    a.  The conduct of examinations and verifications to a reasonable extent.

    b.  The conduct of extensive examinations.

    c.  The reasonable assurance that compliance does exist.

    d.  The consideration of the possibility of material irregularities.

**58.** Internal auditors sometimes express opinions in audit reports in addition to stating facts. Due professional care requires that the auditor's opinions be

    a.  Based on sufficient factual evidence that warrants the expression of the opinions.

    b.  Based on experience and not biased in any manner.

    c.  Expressed only when requested by the auditee or executive management.

    d.  Limited to the effectiveness of controls and the appropriateness of accounting treatments.

## Program and Performance Audit Engagements

**59.** The objective of a program results audit requires the auditor to

    a.  Place an emphasis on outputs rather than inputs.

    b.  Look for cost savings or waste.

    c.  Include only historical data in the audit.

    d.  Render an opinion on the fairness of financial presentation.

**60.** The primary concern in a program results audit is a determination that

    a.  Financial statements are presented in accordance with generally accepted accounting principles.

    b.  Desired benefits are being achieved.

    c.  The entity has complied with laws and regulations.

    d.  Resources are managed economically and efficiently.

**61.** Performance auditing has been described as "evaluating management's performance against a set of accepted objectives and goals." Performance audits generally focus on efficiency and effectiveness, with emphasis on effectiveness. The **best** example of a performance audit would be an evaluation of

    a.  The cost of implementing a major change intended to make the cost accounting system more responsive to user needs.

    b.  The success of a government agency's objective of improving elevator safety.

    c.  The staffing level of a committee established to monitor production planning.

    d.  How well workers conform to established operating procedures on an assembly line.

## Operational Audit Engagements

**62.** A determination of cost savings is most likely to be an objective of

    a.  Program results auditing.

b. Financial auditing.

c. Compliance auditing.

d. Operational auditing.

**63.** An operational audit of the production function includes an audit procedure to compare actual costs to standard costs. The purpose of this operational audit procedure is to

a. Determine the accuracy of the system used to record actual costs.

b. Measure the effectiveness of the standard cost system.

c. Assess the reasonableness of standard costs.

d. Assist management in its evaluation of effectiveness and efficiency.

**64.** During an operational audit, the auditor compares the current staffing of a department with established industry standards in order to

a. Identify bogus employees on the department's payroll.

b. Assess the current performance of the department and make appropriate recommendations for improvement.

c. Evaluate the adequacy of the established internal controls for the department.

d. Determine whether the department has complied with all laws and regulations governing its personnel.

**65.** One objective of a planned audit is to assess the effectiveness of internal controls that safeguard inventories. What type of auditing would **best** achieve that objective?

a. Financial.

b. Compliance.

c. Operational.

d. Program results.

**66.** A manufacturing firm uses large quantities of small inexpensive items, such as nuts, bolts, washers, and gloves, in the production process. As these goods are purchased, they are recorded in inventory in bulk amounts. Bins are located on the shop floor to provide timely access to these items. When necessary, the bins are refilled from inventory, and the cost of the items is charged to a consumable supplies account, which is part of shop overhead. Which of the following would be an appropriate improvement to controls in this environment?

a. Relocate bins to the inventory warehouse.

b. Require management review of reports on the cost of consumable items used in relation to budget.

c. Lock the bins during normal working hours.

d. None of the above controls is needed for items of minor cost and size.

**67.** Which of the following control procedures would be the **least** effective in preventing a fraud conducted by sending purchase orders to bogus vendors?

a. Require that all purchases be made from an authorized vendor list maintained independently of the individual placing the purchase order.

b. Require that only approved vendors be paid for purchases, based on actual production.

c. Require contracts with all major vendors from whom production components are purchased.

d. Require that total purchases for a month not exceed the total budgeted purchases for that month.

**68.** A company controller is concerned that parts may be stolen because there is no formal receiving function (i.e., receiving slips are not filled out). Production raw materials are moved from rail cars directly to the production line, and vendors are paid based on actual production. Which of the following comments correctly portrays the current process?

a. Goods can be paid for only if they have been used in production. Stolen goods or goods not shipped will not be paid for.

b. There is less handling of goods received, thereby decreasing the cost associated with processing goods received as well as decreasing the opportunities for errors to enter the system.

c. Shortages of materials in the system will be brought to a supervisor's attention because of production shutdowns.

d. All of the above.

**Items 69 and 70** are based on the following:

The internal auditors for a large manufacturing company have been requested to conduct a review of the company's production planning system. Production data, collected on personal computers (PCs) connected by a local area network (LAN), are used for generating automatic purchases via electronic data interchange. Purchases are made from authorized vendors based on production plans for the next month and on an authorized materials requirement plan (MRP) that identifies the parts needed per unit of production.

**69.** The production line has experienced shutdowns because needed production parts were not on hand. Management wants to know the cause of this problem. Which of the following audit procedures **best** addresses this objective?

a. Determine if access controls are sufficient to restrict the input of incorrect data into the production database.

b. Use generalized audit software to develop a complete list of the parts shortages that caused each of the production shutdowns, and analyze this data.

c. Take a random sample of parts on hand per the PC databases and compare with actual parts on hand.

d. Take a random sample of production information for selected days and trace input into the production database maintained on the LAN.

**70.** The auditor wants to determine if purchasing requirements have been updated for changes in production techniques. Which of the following audit procedures would be **most** effective in addressing the auditor's objective?

a. Recalculate parts needed based on current production estimates and on the MRP for the revised production techniques. Compare these needs with purchase orders generated from the system for the same period.

b. Develop test data to input into the LAN and compare purchase orders generated from test data with purchase orders generated from production data.

c. Use generalized audit software to develop a report of excess inventory. Compare the inventory with current production volume.

d. Take a sample of production estimates and MRPs for several periods and trace them into the system to determine that input is accurate.

**71.** A potential problem in a manufacturing company is that purchasing agents may take kickbacks or receive gifts from vendors in exchange for favorable contracts. Which of the following would be the **least** effective in preventing this problem?

  a.  A specific corporate policy prohibits the acceptance of anything of value from a vendor.
  b.  A corporate code of ethics that would prohibit such activity.
  c.  A requirement for the purchasing agent to develop a company profile of all vendors before the vendors is added to the authorized vendor list.
  d.  The establishment of long-term contracts with major vendors, with the contract terms approved by top management.

**72.** The transportation department for a large manufacturing company maintains its vehicle inventory and maintenance records in a database on a stand-alone microcomputer in the fleet supervisor's office. Which audit approach is **most** appropriate for evaluating the accuracy of the database information?

  a.  Verify a sample of the records extracted from the database with supporting documentation.
  b.  Submit batches of test transactions through the current system and verify with expected results.
  c.  Simulate normal processing by using test programs.
  d.  Use program tracing to show how, and in what sequence, program instructions are processed in the system.

**73.** An organization uses electronic data interchange (EDI) and online systems. Paper-based documents are not generated for purchase orders, receiving reports, or invoices. An auditor wishes to determine if invoices are paid only for goods received and at approved prices. Which of the following audit procedures would be **most** appropriate?

  a.  Using a statistical sample of major vendors, trace the amounts paid to specific invoices.
  b.  Use generalized audit software to select a sample of payments and match purchase order, invoice, and receiving reports stored on the computer using a common reference.
  c.  Take a monetary-unit sample of accounts payable and confirm the amounts directly with the vendors.
  d.  Use generalized audit software to identify all receipts for a particular day and trace the receiving reports to checks issued.

**74.** Which of the following is **not** likely to be included as an audit step when assessing vendor performance policies?

  a.  Determine whether vendors sent agreed-on lot sizes.
  b.  Determine whether only authorized items were received from vendors.
  c.  Determine whether the balances owed to vendors are correct.
  d.  Determine whether the quality of the goods purchased from the vendors has been satisfactory.

**75.** A production manager for a moderate-sized manufacturing company began ordering excessive raw materials and had them delivered to a wholesale company that the manager was running as a side business. The manager falsified receiving documents and approved the invoices for payment.

Which of the following audit procedures would **most** likely detect this fraud?

  a.  Take a sample of cash disbursements; compare purchase orders, receiving reports, invoices, and check copies.
  b.  Take a sample of cash disbursements and confirm the amount purchased, purchase price, and date of shipment with the vendors.
  c.  Observe the receiving dock and count materials received; compare the counts to receiving reports completed by receiving personnel.
  d.  Perform analytical tests, comparing production, materials purchased, and raw materials inventory levels; investigate differences.

**76.** During a review of purchasing operations, an auditor finds that current procedures differ markedly from stated company procedures. However, the auditor concludes that the procedures currently used represent an increase in efficiency and a decrease in processing time, without a discernible decrease in control. The auditor should

  a.  Report the lack of adherence to documented procedures as an operational deficiency.
  b.  Develop a flowchart of the new procedures and include it in the report to management.
  c.  Report the change and suggest that the change in procedures be documented.
  d.  Suspend the completion of the audit until the auditee documents the new procedures.

**77.** Which of the following describes a control weakness?

  a.  Purchasing procedures are well designed and are followed unless otherwise directed by the purchasing supervisor.
  b.  Prenumbered blank purchase orders are secured within the purchasing department.
  c.  Normal operational purchases fall in the range from $500 to $1,000 with two signatures required for purchases over $1,000.
  d.  The purchasing agent invests in a publicly traded mutual fund that lists the stock of one of the company's suppliers in its portfolio.

**78.** Spreadsheet software would be **most** appropriate for which of the following audit activities?

  a.  Preparing overhead projector slides for an audit presentation.
  b.  Preparing a narrative report summarizing the results of an audit.
  c.  Preparing depreciation schedules for fixed assets.
  d.  Uploading data from a microcomputer to a mainframe computer.

**79.** When an office supply company is unable to fill an order completely, it marks the out-of-stock items as back-ordered on the customer's order and enters these items in a back order file that management can view or print. Customers are becoming disgruntled with the company because it seems unable to keep track of and ship out-of-stock items as soon as they are available. The **best** approach for ensuring prompt delivery of out-of-stock items is to

  a.  Match the back order file to goods received daily.
  b.  Increase inventory levels to minimize the number of times that out-of-stock conditions occur.

c. Implement electronic data interchange with supply vendors to decrease the time to replenish inventory.

d. Reconcile the sum of filled and back orders with the total of all orders placed daily.

**80.** The requirement that purchases be made from suppliers on an approved vendor list is an example of a

a. Preventive control.

b. Detective control.

c. Corrective control.

d. Monitoring control.

**81.** Which of the following audit procedures would be **least** effective in determining whether a division recorded subsequent-year sales in the current year?

a. Perform analytical review procedures that compare like-month sales for the past two years, including the months before and after the year-end.

b. Confirm the amount of year-end accounts receivable with major customers.

c. Use an integrated test facility to run data through the computer during the last month of the year and the first month of the subsequent year to determine if sales were recorded correctly.

d. Perform an analytical review comparing the unit volume of major products shipped during the last month of the year and the first month of the subsequent year.

**82.** A receiving department receives copies of purchase orders for use in identifying and recording inventory receipts. The purchase orders list the name of the vendor and the quantities of the materials ordered. A possible error that this system could allow is

a. Payment to unauthorized vendors.

b. Payment for unauthorized purchases.

c. Overpayment for partial deliveries.

d. Delay in recording purchases.

**83.** The auditor finds a situation where one person has the ability to collect receivables, make deposits, issue credit memos, and record receipt of payments. The auditor suspects the individual may be stealing from cash receipts. Which of the following audit procedures would be **most** effective in discovering fraud in this scenario?

a. Send positive confirmations to a random selection of customers.

b. Send negative confirmations to all outstanding accounts receivable customers.

c. Perform a detailed review of debits to customer discounts, sales returns, or other debit accounts, excluding cash posted to the cash receipts journal.

d. Take a sample of bank deposits and trace the detail in each of the bank deposit back to the corresponding entry in the cash receipts journal.

**84.** An internal auditor is auditing a division's accounts and is concerned that the division's management may have shipped poor-quality merchandise in order to boost sales and profitability for the year and thereby boost the division manager's bonus. Furthermore, the auditor suspects that returned goods are being shipped to other customers as new products without defects being fully corrected. Which of the following audit procedures would be the **least** effective in determining whether such shipments took place?

a. Examine credit memos issued after year-end for goods shipped before year-end.

b. Physically observe the shipping and receiving area for evidence of returned goods.

c. Interview customer service representatives regarding unusual amounts of customer complaints.

d. Require the division to take a complete physical inventory at year-end, and observe the taking of the inventory.

**85.** An auditor notes that production is often stopped or hampered by raw materials inventory not being present when needed. Which of the following statements is(are) correct based on this information alone?

I. The auditor should investigate the quality of communication between production planners and purchasing agents.

II. The auditor should recommend that management implement an economic order quantity (EOQ) model to better manage inventory and meet production needs.

III. The auditor should attempt to quantify the costs to the company related to this problem.

a. I only.

b. I and II.

c. I and III.

d. II and III.

**86.** New credit policies have been implemented in the automated entry order system to control collectability. These policies prevent entering any new sales order that would cause customers' accounts receivable balance to exceed average sales for any two-month period in the prior twelve-month period. Divisional sales management has compiled over a dozen examples that show decreased sales and delayed order entry. Division management contends these examples are a direct result of the new credit policy constraints. Sales management's data and information provide

a. Feedback control data on the new corporate credit policy.

b. Irrelevant argumentative information.

c. Evidence that the new credit policy is not meeting the stated corporate objective to control the collectability of new sales volume.

d. A statistically valid conclusion about the impact on customer goodwill concerning the credit policy.

**Items 87 through 89** are based on the following:

An organization sells products via catalog and takes orders over the phone. All orders are entered online and the organization's objective is to ship all orders within twenty-four hours. The audit trail is kept in machine-readable form. The only papers generated are the packing slip and the invoice sent to the customer. Revenue is recorded upon shipment of the goods. The organization maintains a detailed customer database that allows the customer to return goods for credit at any time.

**87.** Which of the following control procedures would be **least** effective in ensuring that the correct product is shipped and billed at the appropriate price?

a. Self-checking digits are used on all product numbers, and customers must order from a catalog with product numbers.

b. The customer service representative verbally verifies both the product description and price with the customer before the order is closed for processing.

c. The customer service representative prepares batch totals of the number of items ordered and the total dollar amount of the orders.

d. The product database is tightly restricted, and only the director of marketing (and limited personnel in the marketing department) can approve changes to the price file.

**88.** The auditor wants to determine that only the marketing manager and other designated personnel in the department have approved changes to the price of products in the product database. Which of the following audit procedures would provide the **most** persuasive evidence on the effectiveness of the control over price changes?

a. Use an integrated test facility (ITF) and submit product orders to the ITF. Compare the prices invoiced to the prices in the most recent catalog.

b. Use the system control audit review file (SCARF) audit technique to create a listing of all customer orders exceeding a specified dollar limit, and print out the results for subsequent investigation.

c. Obtain a copy of all authorized price changes, and manually trace to the current edition of the organization's catalog.

d. Obtain a computerized log of all changes made to the price database. Take a random sample of changes, and trace to a signed document by the person authorizing the change.

**89.** The auditor wants to gain assurance that all telephone orders received were shipped and billed in a timely fashion. Which of the following audit procedures would be **most** effective in meeting the auditor's objective?

a. Use an integrated test facility (ITF) and submit product orders to the ITF. Compare the prices invoiced to the prices in the most recent catalog. Determine that all submitted items were shipped.

b. Take the computer log of incoming orders, and use generalized audit software to compare order date to invoice and shipping date in the sales invoice file.

c. Use test data to generate batch control totals. Trace the batch control totals from the items submitted to the sales invoice file generated for the test data.

d. Use generalized audit software to randomly select a sample of sales invoices, and have the software match the items selected to the log of transactions maintained for all incoming orders.

**Items 90 through 92** are based on the following:

The internal auditor of a company has been assigned to perform an audit of the company's investment activities with particular emphasis on the company's use of new financial instruments referred to as derivatives.

**90.** The auditor is reviewing the company's policy regarding investing in financial derivatives. The auditor would normally expect to find all of the following in the policy **except:**

a. A statement indicating whether derivatives are to be used for hedging or speculative purposes.

b. A specific authorization limit for the amount and types of derivatives that can be used by the organization.

c. A specific limit on the amount authorized for any single trader.

d. A statement requiring board review of each transaction because of the risk involved in such transactions.

**91.** An investment portfolio manager has the authority to use financial derivatives to hedge transactions but is not supposed to take speculative positions. However, the manager launches a scheme that includes (1) taking a position larger than required by the hedge; (2) putting the speculative gains in a suspense account; and (3) transferring the funds to a nonexistent broker and from there to a personal account. Which of the following audit procedures would be **least** effective in detecting this fraud?

a. Examine individual trades to determine whether the trades violate the authorization limit for the manager.

b. Sample individual trades and determine the exact matching of a hedge. Schedule and investigate all differences.

c. Sample all debits to the suspense account and examine their disposition.

d. Sample fund transfers to brokers and determine if the brokers are on the authorized list for company transactions.

**92.** Assume that the director of internal auditing determines that the department does not have the requisite skills to conduct an audit of the financial derivatives area. Which of the following actions would be the **least** acceptable?

a. Notify the audit committee of the problem, and consult with them regarding outsourcing the audit to a qualified external auditing firm.

b. Determine the requisite knowledge needed, and obtain the proper training for auditors if such training is available within the appropriate time framework outlined by the audit committee.

c. Notify the audit committee of the problem, and assign the most competent auditors to the job.

d. Employ the skills of a financial derivatives expert to consult on the project, and supplement the consulting with a local seminar on financial derivatives.

**93.** Which of the following audit procedures would provide the **least** relevant evidence in determining that payroll payments were made to bona fide employees?

a. Reconcile time cards in use to employees on the job.

b. Examine canceled checks for proper endorsement and compare to personnel records.

c. Test for segregation of the authorization for payment from the hire/fire authorization.

d. Test the payroll account bank reconciliation by tracing outstanding checks to the payroll register.

**94.** An internal auditor was reviewing the operation of the motor pool. The auditor was using the technique of analytical auditing and was observing the trend of expenses for major overhauls of heavy-wheeled vehicles. This trend showed a substantial increase in the last year of the ratios of dollars spent in relation to: (1) the number of vehicles being used; (2) the mileage of the vehicles; (3) the age of the equipment; and (4) environmental conditions. The auditor's investigation indicated that two new maintenance firms were being used. The expenditure packages from the maintenance work were complete; however, there was an unusual regularity in the billings for the work. The identification of the vehicles being serviced did not correspond to the vehicle maintenance reports.

Possible approaches that the auditor could take include

1. Discuss the matter with the superintendent of maintenance and ask for an explanation.
2. Prepare a schedule of the types of maintenance being performed and compare with manufacturers' maintenance guides.
3. Analyze vehicles' trip tickets to determine if they contain indications of problems needing attention.
4. Review deadline reports to determine that vehicles were not in service on the dates of maintenance work.
5. Review dispatch schedules to determine if vehicles were being dispatched for usage on days the maintenance work was reported as performed.
6. Discuss the matter with plant security.

What priority should the above actions have?
- a. 1, 6, and 4.
- b. 4, 5, and 6.
- c. 6, 5, and 1.
- d. 2, 3, and 4.

**95.** A perpetual inventory system uses a minimum quantity on hand to initiate purchase-ordering procedures for restocking. In reviewing the appropriateness of the minimum quantity level established by the stores department, the auditor would be **least** likely to consider
- a. Stock-out costs, including lost customers.
- b. Seasonal variations in forecasting inventory demand.
- c. Optimal order sizes determined by the economic order quantity model.
- d. Available storage space and potential obsolescence.

**96.** To better monitor the performance of operating management, executive management has requested that the internal auditors examine interim financial statements, which are prepared for internal use only. Although interim financial statements have been prepared for several years, this will be the first time that the internal auditors have been involved. The primary reason for this request was that executive management was surprised at the lower-than-anticipated net income eventually reflected in last year's audited financial statements. Earnings had been artificially manipulated on quarterly financial statements. In their work on this year's interim financial statements, internal auditors are likely to focus on which of the following?
- a. Whether payables have been accrued properly at the end of the interim period.
- b. The timing of revenue recognition and the valuation of inventories.
- c. Whether accounting estimates are reasonable given past actual results.
- d. Whether there have been changes in accounting principles that materially affect the financial statements.

Items 97 through 99 are based on the following:

An electric utility company records capital and maintenance expenditures through the use of a computerized project tracking system. Labor, material, and overhead are charged to the applicable project number. Monthly reports are produced that detail individual charges to each project, and expenditure totals are provided for the current month, fiscal year, and project life to date.

**97.** In order to prevent maintenance materials from being charged incorrectly to capital projects, the accounting information system should
- a. Verify that the project number being entered contains the required number of characters.
- b. Authenticate the user identification and verify the input location.
- c. Use tables of project numbers and material requirements.
- d. Require internal file labels for inventory transactions.

**98.** An auditor is reviewing monthly reports distributed by management information system (MIS) output personnel to determine if access to confidential information is limited to project supervisors. Which of the following steps should the auditor perform?

I. Review a sample of report end-of-job indicators.
II. Determine if reports are signed for upon delivery.
III. Review the operating system job control language (JCL) code for abnormal end (ABEND) conditions.
IV. Verify that the correct transaction file was used.
- a. I and III.
- b. II, III, and IV.
- c. II only.
- d. I and II.

**99.** Monthly project reports compare actual costs to original budget estimates and compute variances. Project variations greater than 10% of budget require subsequent explanation and approval by the supervisor. Which of the following audit test(s) would the internal auditor use to determine whether the required procedure is being followed?

I. Select a sample of overbudget explanations and test for subsequent approvals.
II. Trace overbudget explanations to supporting monthly project reports.
III. Use audit software to recompute monthly project report variances and totals.
IV. Compare a sample of project variances to documented approvals and explanations.
- a. IV only.
- b. III and IV.
- c. I, II, and III.
- d. I and II only.

**100.** A manufacturing firm uses large quantities of small inexpensive items, such as nuts, bolts, washers, and gloves in the production process. As these goods are purchased, they are recorded in inventory in bulk amounts. Bins are located on the shop floor to provide timely access to these items. When necessary the bins are refilled from inventory, and the cost of the items is charged to a consumable supplies account, which is part of shop overhead. Which one of the following would be an appropriate improvement to controls in this environment?

   a. Relocate bins to the inventory warehouse.
   b. Require management review of reports on the cost of consumable items used in relation to budget.
   c. Lock the bins during normal working hours.
   d. None of the above controls is needed for items of minor cost and size.

**101.** A manufacturing firm's inventory includes a significant investment in precious metals. The auditors' review of management's system of internal controls over these items most likely would include

  I. Reviewing procedures to ensure that the value of the materials is properly stated on the balance sheet.
  II. Reviewing material acquisition forms for approvals, and tracing release forms to perpetual inventory records to verify that inventory is issued upon proper authorization.
  III. Observing inventory transactions to ascertain if material thefts are occurring.
  IV. Reviewing the manufacturing department's system for comparing the usage of these metals to standards.

   a. III and IV.
   b. I and IV.
   c. I only.
   d. II and III.

**102.** Inventory levels for a packing facility are controlled by the use of just-in-time techniques. If the auditor's objective is to evaluate ordering and stocking standards, which of the following procedures would be relevant?

  I. Using audit software to compute the number of shipping crates used per day.
  II. Reviewing shipping records for product quantity and dates.
  III. Comparing actual stocking levels to industry averages.
  IV. Reviewing sales records for defective returns.

   a. III only.
   b. I and IV.
   c. II and III.
   d. I and II.

**103.** During an audit of the accounts receivable function, the auditor found that the accounts receivable turnover rate had fallen from 7.3 to 4.3 over the last three years. What is the most likely cause of the decrease in the turnover rate?

   a. An increase in the discount offered for early payment.
   b. A more liberal credit policy.
   c. A change from net thirty to net twenty-five.
   d. Greater cash sales.

**104.** You are auditing the payroll system of a company. To satisfy an audit objective of ascertaining that no payments are for fictitious employees, you would

   a. Perform a payroll payoff test.
   b. Examine time cards for supervisory approval.
   c. Make inquiries of payroll personnel concerning internal controls over payroll preparation.
   d. Perform analytical analysis of payroll costs in comparison with industry standards.

**Items 105 and 106** are based on the following:

An internal auditor is examining a production facility shortly after the close of the fiscal year. Each question consists of a specific audit procedure and a choice of four different audit findings. Which of the errors or questionable practices is most likely to be detected by the audit procedure specified?

**105.** The internal auditor tours the production facility.
   a. Insurance coverage on the facility has lapsed.
   b. Overhead has been overapplied.
   c. Necessary facility maintenance has not been performed.
   d. Depreciation expense on fully depreciated machinery has been recognized.

**106.** On randomly selected dates during the month after fiscal year-end, all unrecorded expenditure invoices are examined.
   a. Sales are overstated for the current month.
   b. Expenses are overstated for the fiscal year just ended.
   c. Accounts payable are understated at fiscal year-end (one month previous).
   d. Accounts payable are overstated at fiscal year-end (one month previous).

**107.** A multinational corporation has an office in a foreign branch with a monetary transfer facility. Good internal control requires that
   a. The person making wire transfers not reconcile the bank statement.
   b. The branch manager not deliver payroll checks to employees.
   c. Foreign currency translation rates be computed separately by two branch employees in the same department.
   d. The hiring of individual branch employees be approved by the headquarters office.

**Items 108 and 109** are based on the following:

A rental car company's fleet maintenance division uses a different code for each type of inventory transaction. A daily summary report lists activity by part number and transaction code. The report is reconciled by the parts room supervisor to the day's material request forms and is then forwarded to the fleet manager for approval.

**108..** The reconciliation of the summary report to the day's material request forms by the parts room supervisor
   a. Verifies that all material request forms were approved.
   b. Provides documentation as to what material was available for a specific transaction.
   c. Confirms that all material request forms are entered for all parts issued.
   d. Ensures the accuracy and completeness of data input.

**109.** The use of transaction codes provides the fleet manager with information concerning the types of inventory activity. The auditor is considering an analytical review of transaction codes and materials used. The objective of this review is to
   a. Provide evidence of inventory items that are overstocked.

b. Reveal shortages in perpetual inventory records.
c. Determine whether inventory items are properly valued.
d. Identify possible material lost due to employee theft.

**110.** If a manufacturing firm has established a limit on the number of defects that are tolerable in the final assembly of its product, which of the following quality control procedures should be employed?

  I. Inspect completed goods for compliance with established tolerances.
  II. Review sales returns for defects not detected during the final inspection process.
  III. Compare materials and machinery specifications to original product designs.
  IV. Establish a quality circle that includes management and subordinates to discuss labor efficiency.

    a. I, III, and IV.
    b. II and III only.
    c. I, II, and III.
    d. III and IV only.

**111.** Which of the following is **not** likely to be included as an audit step when assessing vendor performance policies?
    a. Determine whether vendors sent agreed-on lot sizes.
    b. Determine whether only authorized items were received from vendors.
    c. Determine whether the balances owed to vendors are correct.
    d. Determine whether the quality of the goods purchased from the vendors has been satisfactory.

**112.** One of two office clerks in a small company prepares a sales invoice for $4,300; however, the invoice is incorrectly entered by the bookkeeper in the general ledger and the accounts receivable subsidiary ledger as $3,400. The customer subsequently remits $3,400, the amount on the monthly statement. Assuming there are only three employees in the department, the most effective control to prevent this type of error is
    a. Assigning the second office clerk to independently check the sales invoice prices, discounts, extensions, footings, and account for the invoice serial number.
    b. Requiring that monthly statements be prepared by the bookkeeper and verified by one of the other office clerks prior to mailing.
    c. Utilizing predetermined totals to control posting routines.
    d. Requiring the bookkeeper to perform periodic reconciliations of the accounts receivable subsidiary ledger and the general ledger.

**113.** Which of the following activities represents both an appropriate personnel department function and a deterrent to payroll fraud?
    a. Distribution of paychecks.
    b. Authorization of overtime.
    c. Authorization of additions and deletions from the payroll.
    d. Collection and retention of unclaimed paychecks.

**Items 114 through 118** are based on the following:

A retail organization has just implemented electronic data interchange (EDI) to issue purchase orders to major vendors. The client has developed a database of approved vendors. New vendors can be added only after a thorough review by the purchasing manager and marketing director. Only purchasing agents can issue purchase orders, and the amount of purchase orders for a particular product line cannot exceed a budgeted amount specified by the marketing manager.

All purchases go to the distribution center, where they are electronically scanned into the computer system. All incoming items must reference a company purchase order, and any items that do not contain such a reference will not be accepted. Prenumbered receiving slips are not used, but all receipts are referenced to the purchase order. Price tags are generated per the purchase order and for the quantities indicated by the electronically scanned-in receiving report. The number of price tags generated is reconciled with the number of products received.

The vendor sends an invoice to the retailer. The invoices are keypunched and entered into the system. The computer software is programmed to match the vendor invoice, the purchase order, and the receiving report. If the three items are matched within a tolerance of 0.5%, the computer program schedules the items for payment at a time to take advantage of purchase discounts. A check is generated by the cash disbursements program and is electronically signed and mailed. If there is a discrepancy among the three documents, a report is printed and sent to the accounts payable department for investigation.

**114.** The **best** procedure to determine whether the control procedure to limit the amount of purchases for a particular product line was working properly during the past year would be to
    a. Use generalized audit software to prepare a list of purchases by product line. Compare the amounts with the amounts authorized by the marketing manager.
    b. Submit test data to the program controlling purchases. (The amount of data entered should exceed the authorized purchases.) Examine the computer output.
    c. Use parallel simulation techniques to compute the amount of purchases authorized, and compare it with the amount actually purchased.
    d. Implement a snapshot audit approach, which will tag selected transactions and print them out with a listing of items arranged by purchasing agent.

**115.** It is often recognized that one control procedure by itself is not sufficient to achieve a particular control objective. One control objective is to ensure that purchase orders are made only by authorized purchasing agents, to authorized vendors, for authorized goods. Which of the following combination of control procedures would be necessary to accomplish this objective?

  I. Require passwords for each agent, and change the passwords periodically to make them difficult to guess.
  II. Require that someone independent of the purchasing function enter authorized products into the product database.

III. Require that purchase agent functions be periodically rotated among purchasing agents.

IV. Require that someone independent of the purchasing function maintain the authorized vendor database.

     a.    I, II, and III.
     b.    I, II, and IV.
     c.    I only.
     d.    I, II, III, and IV.

**116.** Which of the following items would be considered a control deficiency in the receiving function?
     a.    The number of price tags generated is determined by the receiving reports electronically scanned in during the receiving function.
     b.    Prenumbered receiving documents are not used.
     c.    There is no inspection of goods for quality.
     d.    All of the above.

**117.** The auditor wishes to determine that the program is correctly approving items for payment only when the purchase order, receiving report, and vendor invoice match within the tolerable 0.5%. Assume all the following suggested audit procedures would have been implemented to function over the proper time period. Which of the following computerized audit procedures would provide the **most** persuasive evidence as to the correct operation of the program?
     a.    Using generalized audit software to take a random sample of purchase orders and tracing the selected items to the vendor invoice and receiving document.
     b.    Using a test data approach at year-end by submitting mock purchase orders, vendor invoices, and receiving quantities.
     c.    Implementing a systems control and audit review file (SCARF) audit technique that will automatically select all transactions when the purchase order exceeds a specific dollar limit.
     d.    Implementing an integrated test facility with auditor-submitted test items throughout the period under analysis.

**118.** Which of the following statements, if true, would contribute to the control effectiveness of the computerized environment described above?
     a.    The company uses an automated access control program that identifies all users, data, and actions that can be taken by the users.
     b.    Only the programmer responsible for coding the changes implements all program changes.
     c.    The purchasing agent responsible for purchasing the product lines furnished by the vendor should initiate all changes to the vendor database.
     d.    The receiving department should not have access to the purchase order information.

**Items 119 through 122** are based on the following:

A manufacturer of hospital equipment uses three vendors to supply about half of the materials used in its operations. Invoices from these vendors are transmitted directly to the company through electronic data interchange (EDI) with custom-developed software. In a systems development and postimplementation review, the internal auditor was involved with assessing and testing the EDI system and found no significant problems. Other manufacturing materials are obtained through routine purchase orders prepared by buyers

in the purchasing department. Materials from EDI vendors are delivered to the receiving dock where personnel verify that the goods are authorized purchases, look for shipping damage, and record receipt into the system using barcode technology. Materials purchased from non-EDI vendors are delivered to the receiving dock and recorded manually on receiving reports. Copies of these reports are given to the purchasing and accounts payable departments. The internal audit department is scheduled to complete a full audit of the purchasing and accounts payable cycle before the end of the year. However, there are severe time pressures because other matters delayed the start of the audit.

**119.** Which of the following controls is **least** likely to provide an auditor with assurance that online purchase requisitions are properly authorized?
     a.    Terminal access restrictions.
     b.    Password requirements.
     c.    Hash totals.
     d.    Validity tests.

**120.** The auditor plans to select a sample of transactions to assess the extent that purchase discounts may have been lost by the company. After assessing the risks associated with lost purchase discounts, the auditor was **most** likely to select a sample from which one of the following populations?
     a.    Open purchase orders.
     b.    Paid EDI invoices.
     c.    Paid non-EDI invoices.
     d.    Paid EDI and non-EDI invoices.

**121.** Before authorizing payment of an EDI invoice, the computer automatically compares the invoice with the purchase order and receiving report data. When the system was being developed, the auditor reviewed the payment authorization program and made recommendations. Which one of the following was **most** likely recommended by the auditor for the situation in which the quantity invoiced is greater than the quantity received?
     a.    Prepare an exception report.
     b.    Pay the amount billed and adjust the inventory for the difference.
     c.    Return the invoice to the vendor.
     d.    Authorize payment of the full invoice, but maintain an open purchase order record for the missing goods.

**122.** The auditor determined that the risks associated with the EDI purchases were less than the risks associated with the purchases made through the traditional system. Which one of the following factors **best** supports this prioritization of risks?
     a.    There are three vendors connected through EDI.
     b.    About half of the materials are purchased through EDI.
     c.    The internal auditors were involved with systems development and testing of the EDI software.
     d.    The external auditor did not examine EDI purchase controls during the annual financial audit.

**Items 123 through 126** are based on the following:

Management of a manufacturing company has requested the internal auditing department perform an audit of the cash management system to evaluate the adequacy of existing internal controls over cash management and identify opportunities to increase management control and operating efficiency. The company has four manufacturing divisions located in diverse geographic areas. The company has delegated day-to-day cash management to each local operating division. Excess cash is invested in short-term cash management programs of local financial institutions. These short-term investments are the only source of interest income for the operating divisions. Each division has a line of credit with a local financial institution, but must arrange long-term financing needs through corporate headquarters.

In performing a review of cash management procedures in the divisions during the preliminary audit planning, the internal auditor has noted that management is concerned that

- Some divisions have excess cash balances and might not be investing short-term balances in a manner to maximize returns to the company.
- One division has automated the processing of cash receipts, but has not implemented proper control procedures to ensure that all cash will be recorded.
- The divisions' cash management procedures may not be consistent with overall corporate objectives, that is, there may not be proper coordination between corporate headquarters and divisions regarding cash management.

**123.** Division A has a large number of small customers and has automated cash collection. Customers are requested to return a copy of their invoice (turnaround document) with their payment. The returned document contains the customer's account number, name, and other pertinent information. A cash listing is developed immediately by the cash receipts/mail clerk who then segregates checks and turnaround documents. Checks are given to the treasurer for deposit. Turnaround documents are given to the accounts receivable department for posting. Customer inquiries are referred to the customer service section of the accounts receivable department.

If a customer fails to return the turnaround document, the best control would be to have a substitute document prepared by the

- a. Cash receipts/mail clerk.
- b. Treasurer.
- c. Accounts receivable clerk.
- d. Customer service section.

**124.** If the treasurer took a customer's cash remittance and omitted it from the cash deposit and recorded a debit to cash for the remaining receipts, the omission would best be detected by

- a. Monthly analytical review comparing accounts receivable balances with sales volume and cash receipts.
- b. Customer inquiries to the customer services department.
- c. Periodic confirmation of randomly selected accounts by the internal auditing department and follow-up of all differences.
- d. Batching all receipts and turnaround documents and reconciling the posting of the batches to the receivables and cash account.

**125.** To address management's concern that a division might not be adequately investing short-term funds, management has developed a model that estimates minimum daily cash balances for each division. To determine whether a specific division is failing to maximize its invested cash,

management should implement a control procedure that compares

- a. Interest income per division with industry averages for similar companies.
- b. Interest income for each division with the other three divisions.
- c. Daily cash receipts and interest income across divisions to identify any division with a variance of 5% or more.
- d. Total daily cash balances at each division and interest income for a period with projected interest income based on its model of minimum cash balances.

**126.** Upon investigation, the auditor finds that one division consistently has large amounts of excess cash at a time when the organization is borrowing heavily and using the proceeds to support other divisions. The best control procedure to address this concern, without a major change in procedures, would be to

- a. Centralize all cash processing.
- b. Require each division to handle its own long-term financing, thereby forcing them all to better match their cash needs and sources.
- c. Require each division to prepare detailed cash forecasts and budgets for future periods to be used for centralized cash management.
- d. Implement electronic data interchange with major customers to facilitate the timing of cash receipts.

**127.** Management can **best** strengthen internal control over the custody of inventory stored in an off-site warehouse by implementing

- a. Reconciliations of transfer slips to/from the warehouse with inventory records.
- b. Increases in insurance coverage.
- c. Regular reconciliation of physical inventories to accounting records.
- d. Regular confirmation of the amount on hand with the custodian of the warehouse.

**128.** Which of the following describes a control weakness?

- a. Purchasing procedures are well designed and followed unless otherwise directed by the purchasing supervisor.
- b. Prenumbered blank purchase orders are secured within the purchasing department.
- c. Normal operational purchases fall in the range from $500 to $1,000 with two check signers required for purchases over $1,000.
- d. The purchasing agent invests in a publicly traded mutual fund that lists the stock of one of the company's suppliers in its portfolio.

**129.** Which of the following ensures that all inventory shipments are billed to customers?

- a. Shipping documents are prenumbered and are independently accounted for and matched to sales invoices.
- b. Sales invoices are prenumbered and are independently accounted for and traced to the sales journal.
- c. Duties for recording sales transactions and maintaining customer account balances are separated.
- d. Customer billing complaints are investigated by the controller's office.

**130.** An auditor for a large service company is performing an audit of the company's cash balance. The auditor is considering the most appropriate audit procedure to use to ensure that the amount of cash is accurately recorded on the company's financial statements. The most appropriate audit procedures for the objective are

- a. Review collection procedures and perform an analytical review of accounts receivable; confirm balances of accounts receivable; and verify the existence of appropriate procedures and facilities.
- b. Compare cash receipt lists to the receipts journal and bank deposit slips; review the segregation of duties; observe and test cash receipts.
- c. Review the organizational structure and functional responsibilities; verify the existence and describe protection procedures for unused checks, including security measures.
- d. Examine bank statement reconciliations, confirm bank balances, and verify cutoff of receipts and disbursements; foot totals of reconciliations and compare to cash account balances.

**131.** A manager prepared and signed checks payable to a fictitious supplier and deposited the checks into a personal bank account. Which of the following internal controls would **most** likely have prevented, or at least detected, the embezzlement?

- a. Use of competitive bids for all purchases.
- b. Payments to suppliers must be made by certified check.
- c. A check signer other than the manager must sign checks only when approved invoices are presented with the completed, unsigned check.
- d. A responsible employee must account for the numerical sequence of checks on a regular basis.

**132.** An audit had been scheduled to address unusual inventory shortages revealed in the annual physical inventory process at a large consumer goods warehouse operation. A cycle count program had been installed in the storeroom at the beginning of the year in place of the disruptive process of counting one entire product line at the end of each month. The cycle count program appeared effective based on the fact that only nine minor adjustments had been made for the entire year on the several thousand different products located in the storeroom. The storeroom supervisor explained that each of the fifteen stockroom personnel selected one item each day for cycle count based on how efficiently the item could be counted. The opportunity for control-related problems including fraud has been increased in the stockroom because

- a. Stockroom personnel select items for cycle count.
- b. A cycle count program has been installed in place of a less efficient program.
- c. Only nine minor adjustments have been recorded as a result of the cycle count process.
- d. Stockroom personnel record cycle count information.

**133.** The auditor was reviewing documentation that showed that a customer had recently returned three expensive products to the regional service center for warranty replacement. The documentation showed that the warranty clerk had rejected the claim and sent it to the customer's local distributor. The claim was rejected because the serial numbers listed in the warranty claim were not found in the computer's sales

history file. Subsequently, the distributor supplied three different serial numbers, all of which were validated by the computer system, and the clerk completed the warranty claim for replacements. Which would be the best course of action for the auditor under the circumstances?

- a. Determine if the original serial numbers provided by the customer can be traced to other records, such as production and inventory records.
- b. Notify the appropriate authorities within the organization that there are sufficient indicators that a fraud has been committed.
- c. Verify with the appropriate supervisor that the warranty clerk had followed relevant procedures in the processing and disposition of this claim.
- d. Summarize this item along with other valid transactions in the auditor's test of warranty transactions.

**134.** In the examination of materials receiving operations for a manufacturer of small appliances, the auditor will usually be **most** concerned with the risk of

- a. Failing to detect substandard materials received.
- b. Receiving goods in excess of current needs.
- c. Acquiring goods from related parties at inflated prices.
- d. Receiving unordered goods.

**135.** The cross-reference of individual payroll time cards to personnel department records and reports allows an auditor to conclude that

- a. Individuals were paid only for time worked.
- b. Individuals are bona fide employees.
- c. Individuals were paid at the proper rate.
- d. Personnel department records agree with payroll accounting records.

**136.** A firm's inventory consisted of 1,000 different items, 20 of which accounted for 70% of the dollar value. The most recent regular quarterly manual count revealed that there was an unnecessary two years' supply of several of the more expensive items. The control that would best help to correct this oversupply problem is

- a. Use of a control total over the number of unique inventory items.
- b. Limit check on the total dollar value of the inventory.
- c. Use of authorizing signatures on requisitions for inventory requested by production.
- d. Maintain perpetual inventory of the larger dollar value items in the inventory.

**137.** To determine whether refunds granted to customers were properly approved, an internal auditor should trace accounts receivable entries to

- a. Sales invoices.
- b. Remittance advices.
- c. Shipping documents.
- d. Credit memos.

**138.** Which of the following would help ensure that unnecessary purchases of inventory are not made?

- a. Competitive bidding.
- b. Approved price lists.
- c. Predetermined stocking levels.
- d. Negotiated vendor contracts.

**139.** Which of the following controls would be the **most** appropriate means to ensure that terminated employees had been removed from the payroll?
- a. Mailing checks to employees' residences.
- b. Establishing direct-deposit procedures with employees' banks.
- c. Reconciling payroll and timekeeping records.
- d. Establishing computerized limit checks on payroll rates.

**140.** Management is concerned with the potential for unauthorized changes to the payroll. Which of the following is the proper organizational structure to prevent such unauthorized changes?
- a. The payroll department maintaining and authorizing all changes to the personnel records.
- b. The payroll department being supervised by the management of the human resources division.
- c. Limiting the payroll department's functions to maintaining the payroll records, distributing paychecks, and posting the payroll entries to the general ledger.
- d. The personnel department authorizing the hiring and pay levels of all employees.

**141.** A life insurance company refunds overpayments received from policyholders on their policy loans. The risk of material losses from errors and irregularities related to such refunds are greatest with respect to
- a. Allowing refund checks to be issued before authorization is obtained.
- b. Retaining employees in the same position over long periods of time.
- c. Employing individuals of questionable integrity in the disbursing function.
- d. Posting disbursements of refunds to the wrong policyholder borrower.

**142.** Which of the following would be the **best** procedure to determine whether purchases were properly authorized?
- a. Discuss authorization procedures with personnel in the controller's and purchasing functions.
- b. Review and evaluate a flowchart of purchasing procedures.
- c. Determine whether a sample of entries in the purchase journal is supported by properly executed purchase orders.
- d. Vouch payments for selected purchases to supporting receiving reports.

**143.** The primary objective in the operational audit of an organization's employee benefits program is to
- a. Ascertain that the benefits provided are cost-effective for the organization.
- b. Determine that company policies on providing employee benefits are followed.
- c. Check the adequacy and accuracy of accruals of employee benefit costs in books and records.
- d. Be sure that the program is competitive with programs of other area organizations.

**144.** To determine if credit controls are inconsistently applied, preventing valid sales to creditworthy customers, the auditor should
- a. Confirm current accounts receivable.
- b. Trace postings on the accounts receivable ledger.
- c. Analyze collection rates and credit histories.
- d. Compare credit histories for those receiving credit and for those denied credit.

**145.** Which of the following procedures would be **most** valuable in an audit of traffic department operations in a large manufacturing company?
- a. Obtain written confirmation from the regulatory agencies that all carriers used are properly licensed and bonded.
- b. Review procedures for selection of routes and carriers.
- c. Trace selected items from the weekly demurrage (car detention charge) report to supporting documentation.
- d. Verify that all bills of lading are prenumbered.

**146.** A primary audit concern of a multinational corporation's foreign branch money transfer operations located at international headquarters is
- a. Monitoring the security of foreign property, plant, and equipment.
- b. Ensuring compliance with foreign government money transfer regulations.
- c. Reconciling the foreign branch's petty cash accounts.
- d. Evaluating the exchange rate in effect when foreign fixed assets were purchased.

**147.** Which of the following audit techniques would be **most** persuasive in determining that significant inventory values on the books of a company being acquired are correctly stated?
- a. Obtain a management representation letter stating that inventory values are correctly stated.
- b. Flowchart the inventory and warehousing cycle and form an opinion based on the quality of internal controls.
- c. Conduct a physical inventory and bring in an independent expert if necessary to value inventory items.
- d. Interview purchasing and materials control personnel to ascertain the quality of internal controls over inventory.

**148.** You are an internal auditor who has been assigned to an audit of the material acquisition cycle of a company. To satisfy an audit objective of verifying that purchase transactions are authorized and are for needed materials, you should
- a. Review signatures on a sample of receiving reports.
- b. Discuss a sample of transactions with the purchasing agent.
- c. Review a sample of purchase orders and their related purchase requisition for proper approval signatures.
- d. Examine a sample of vendor invoices.

**149.** An internal auditor found that the supervisor does not properly approve employee time cards in one department. Which of the following could result?
- a. Duplicate paychecks might be issued.
- b. The wrong hourly rate could be used to calculate gross pay.
- c. Employees might be paid for hours they did not work.

d. Payroll checks might not be distributed to the appropriate payees.

**150.** Which of the following controls would **most** likely minimize defects in finished goods due to poor-quality raw materials?
  a. Proper handling of work-in-process inventory to prevent damage.
  b. Implementation of specifications for purchases.
  c. Timely follow-up on unfavorable usage variances.
  d. Determination of spoilage at the end of the manufacturing process.

**151.** Which of the following is an appropriate audit procedure when testing payroll in a company with a satisfactory internal control environment?
  a. Selectively interviewing a sample of employees.
  b. Examining time cards or time sheets for proper approval.
  c. Sending confirmation letters to government authorities.
  d. Verifying all payroll calculations for one pay cycle.

**152.** Which of the following means would be the **most** appropriate to minimize the risk of a company's buyer purchasing from a vendor who is a relative?
  a. Establish a purchasing economic order quantity.
  b. Establish a predetermined reorder point for purchases.
  c. Maintain an approved-vendor file for purchases.
  d. Perform a risk analysis for the purchasing function.

**153.** The president wants to know whether the purchasing function is properly meeting its charge to "purchase the right material at the right time in the right quantities." Which of the following types of audits addresses the president's request?
  a. A financial audit of the purchasing department.
  b. An operational audit of the purchasing function.
  c. A compliance audit of the purchasing function.
  d. A full-scope audit of the manufacturing operation.

**154.** Which account balance is **most** likely to be misstated if an aging of accounts receivable is not performed?
  a. Sales revenue.
  b. Sales returns and allowances.
  c. Accounts receivable.
  d. Allowance for bad debts.

**155.** An internal audit of payroll would **least** likely include
  a. Tests of computations for gross and net wages.
  b. Comparison of payroll costs to budget.
  c. Tracing a sample of employee names to employment records in the personnel department.
  d. Observing the physical distribution of paychecks.

**156.** In response to a confirmation of the June 30 accounts receivable balances, a customer reported that the balance confirmed had been paid by a check dated and mailed June 20. The auditor reviewed the postings of cash receipts in July and found the payment had been recorded on July 13. Given this information, the next audit action should be to
  a. Require an adjusting entry to the payment to June.
  b. Compare deposit slips to posting records.

  c. Trace the billing invoice to the related shipping documents and inventory records, comparing dates "shipped" to "billed" to determine proper period.
  d. Request a bank cutoff statement for July and reconcile the June deposits-in-transit and outstanding checks by examining supporting documentation.

**157.** Cash receipts should be deposited on the day of receipt or the following business day. Select the **most** appropriate audit procedure to determine that cash is promptly deposited.
  a. Review cash register tapes prepared for each sale.
  b. Review the functions of cash handling and maintaining accounting records for proper separation of duties.
  c. Compare the daily cash receipts totals to the bank deposits.
  d. Review the functions of cash receiving and disbursing for proper separation of duties.

**158.** Select the appropriate population from which to draw a sample when the audit objective is to evaluate compliance with controls designed to ensure that all shipments are billed.
  a. Prenumbered customer invoices.
  b. Customer accounts receivable.
  c. Prenumbered shipping documents.
  d. Cash receipts records.

**159.** An audit of the receiving function at the company's distribution center revealed inadequate control over receipts. Which of the following controls would be appropriate for the receiving function?
  a. To ensure adequate separation of duties, the warehouse-receiving clerk should work independently from the warehouse manager.
  b. Ensure that the warehouse-receiving department has a purchase order copy with the units described, but both prices and quantities omitted.
  c. Require that all receipts receive the approval of the warehouse manager.
  d. Ensure that the warehouse-receiving department has a true copy of the original purchase order.

**160.** Due to concern over a worsening economic environment and a belief that most departments were overstaffed, management asked the internal auditing department to perform an audit of the effectiveness of the personnel department. Would such an audit be likely to address the overstaffing problem?
  a. Yes, because recruiting is generally coordinated between personnel and the other departments.
  b. Yes, because a formal job analysis for all key jobs is performed by the personnel department, including all major classes of employees.
  c. No, because the personnel function is generally centralized while other departments might be geographically dispersed.
  d. No, because staffing individual departments is within the individual department's budgetary constraints, which generally sets the staffing levels.

**161.** During a postcompletion audit of a warehouse expansion, the auditor noted several invoices for redecorating services from a local merchant that were account-coded and signed for payment only by the cost engineer. The auditor should

   a. Compare the cost and description of the services to the account code used in the construction project and to related estimates in the construction-project budget.

   b. Consult with the cost engineer for assurance that these purchases were authorized for this construction project.

   c. Obtain a facsimile of the cost engineer's signature from the accounts payable group and compare it to the signature on the invoices.

   d. Recommend reclassifying the expenditure to the appropriate account code for redecorating services.

**162.** An audit assistant found a purchase order form for a regular supplier in the amount of $5,500. The purchase order was dated after receipt of the goods. The purchasing agent explained that he had forgotten to issue the purchase order. Also, a disbursement of $450 for materials did not have a receiving report. The assistant wanted to select additional purchase orders for investigation but was unconcerned about the lack of a receiving report. The audit director should

   a. Agree with the assistant since the amount of the purchase order exception was considerably larger than the receiving report exception.

   b. Agree with the assistant since the receiving clerk had assured the cash disbursement clerk that the failure to fill out a report did not happen very often.

   c. Disagree with the assistant since all problems directly related to cost have an equal risk of loss associated with them.

   d. Disagree with the assistant since the lack of a receiving report has a greater risk of loss associated with it.

**163.** An auditor notes year-to-year increases of over $200,000 for small tool expense at a manufacturing facility that has produced the same amount of identical product for the last three years. Production inventory is kept in a controlled staging area adjacent to the receiving dock, but the supply of small tools is kept in an unsupervised area near the exit to the plant employees' parking lot. After determining that all of the following alternatives are equal in cost and are also feasible for local management, the auditor would **best** address the security issue by recommending that plant management

   a. Move the small tools inventory to the custody of the production inventory-staging superintendent, and implement the use of a special requisition to issue small tools.

   b. Initiate a full physical inventory of small tools on a monthly basis.

   c. Place supply of small tools in a secured area, install a key-access card system for all employees, and record each key-access transaction on a report for the production superintendent.

   d. Close the exit to the employee parking lot, and require all plant employees to use a doorway by the receiving dock that also provides access to the plant employees' parking area.

**164.** The auditor found that the purchasing department has a policy of setting all purchasing lead times to the highest number of days experienced within each product subassembly, even though some subassemblies required three or more months to complete. To address the objective of reducing inventory holding costs related to this policy, the auditor would focus on

   a. Reviewing production requirements for a sample of products to determine at what point in the production process materials and subassemblies are needed.

   b. Evaluating whether product-line assignments were rotated among the members of the purchasing department.

   c. Identifying signature approval authority among members of the purchasing department in relation to any computer system controls.

   d. Testing those products having the highest sales to determine the average number of days that the completed products were held in inventory.

**Items 165 and 166** are based on the following:

An internal auditor is auditing the cash receipts function. The firm is a wholesaler that makes all shipments by private trucking firms. Its billing policy is to require payment of individual invoices. All cash receipts arrive by mail in the form of customer checks.

**165.** The firm's policy is to deposit all cash receipts in its bank intact daily. In order to determine whether this policy is being followed, the auditor should compare

   a. Cash receipts journal entries with the monthly bank statements.

   b. Cash receipts journal entries with entries in the accounts receivable subsidiary ledger.

   c. Duplicate deposit tickets with the monthly bank statements.

   d. Remittance advices with cash receipts journal entries.

**166.** The firm grants a 2% cash discount to customers who pay their bills within fifteen days. When customers improperly deduct a discount from a remittance made after the fifteen-day period, the check is deposited as usual, but the customer's account is credited for only the net (rather than the gross) amount. In order to determine whether undeserved cash discounts are being allowed, the auditor should

   a. Verify account balances by mailing confirmations to a sample of the firm's customers.

   b. Reconcile monthly bank statements with particular emphasis on "deposits in transit" included as reconciling items.

   c. Compare duplicate deposit tickets with related monthly bank statements and remittance advices.

   d. Compare cash receipts journal entries with related remittance advices and sales invoices.

**167.** When an office supply company is unable to fill an order completely, it marks the out-of-stock items as back-ordered on the customer's order and enters these items in a back-order file that management can view or print. Customers are becoming disgruntled with the company because it seems unable to keep track of and ship out-of-stock items as soon as they are available. The **best** approach for ensuring prompt delivery of out-of-stock items is to

   a. Match the back order file to goods shipped daily.

   b. Increase inventory levels to minimize the number of times that out-of-stock conditions occur.

c.  Implement electronic data interchange with supply vendors to decrease the time to replenish inventory.
d.  Reconcile the sum of filled and back orders with the total of all orders placed daily.

**168.**  One operating department of a company does not have adequate procedures for inspecting and verifying the quantities of goods received. To evaluate the materiality of this control deficiency, the auditor should review the department's

a.  Year-end inventory balance.
b.  Annual inventory purchases.
c.  Year-end total assets.
d.  Annual operating expenses.

**169.**  Shipments are made from the warehouse based on customer purchase orders. The matched shipping documents and purchase orders are then forwarded to the billing department for sales invoice preparation. The shipping documents are neither accounted for nor prenumbered. Which of the following substantive tests should be extended as a result of this control weakness?

a.  Select sales invoices from the sales register and examine the related shipping documents.
b.  Select bills of lading from the warehouse and trace the shipments to the related sales invoices.
c.  Foot the sales register and trace the total to the general ledger.
d.  Trace quantities and prices on the sales invoice to the customer purchase order and test extensions and footings.

**170.**  The payroll computer system automatically initiates scheduled pay raises for some employees for whom functional management had intended to withhold the raises. To prevent this situation in the future

a.  The payroll register should be compared to the employee master file.
b.  The payroll master file should be compared to the employee master file.
c.  The payroll department should initiate scheduled pay raises.
d.  Scheduled pay raises should be delayed pending explicit approval by the functional departments.

**171.**  There is generally no incentive for efficiency or economy in a cost-plus construction contract for small, unique projects. There is a potential for inflated costs. An appropriate control to encourage efficiency and economy in these contracts is

a.  Elimination of change orders to the contract.
b.  Provision for maximum costs and sharing any savings.
c.  Use of an agreed-on price for each unit of work.
d.  A checklist approach to the audit of contract costs.

**172.**  During the preliminary survey phase of an audit of the organization's production cycle, management stated that the sale of scrap was well controlled. Evidence to verify that assertion can **best** be gained by

a.  Comparing current revenue from scrap sales with that of prior periods.
b.  Interviewing persons responsible for collecting and storing the scrap.

c.  Comparing the quantities of scrap expected from the production process with the quantities sold.
d.  Comparing the results of a physical inventory of scrap on hand with perpetual inventory records.

**173.**  In order to control daily operating costs, an organization decreased the number of times a messenger service was used each day. In spite of those measures, the monthly bill continued to increase. What procedure should the internal auditor use to detect whether improper services were being billed?

a.  Reconcile a sample of messenger invoices to pickup receipts.
b.  Test the mathematical accuracy of a sample of messenger invoices.
c.  Scan ledger accounts and pickup receipts.
d.  Observe daily use of the messenger service.

**174.**  Identify the audit objective that could be accomplished through the application of the following auditing procedures on a firm's trade accounts receivable: (1) preparing and analyzing an aging schedule of trade accounts receivable; (2) discussing all potentially doubtful accounts which are material in amount with management. The objective is to determine if

a.  Trade accounts receivable represent amounts due to the company on the balance sheet date.
b.  Trade accounts receivable pledged as collateral are properly identified and disclosed.
c.  All material amounts due to the company at the balance sheet date have been recorded.
d.  The allowance for doubtful accounts is accurately stated and trade accounts receivable is carried at net collectible amounts.

**175.**  The results of an audit of cash indicate the bookkeeper signs expense checks and reconciles the checking account. The cash account was properly reconciled and no cash shortages were detected. Select the appropriate overall audit opinion.

a.  In our opinion the system of internal control over cash is adequate.
b.  Based on the audit results, it is our opinion that the system of internal control over cash is inadequate.
c.  The results of the audit indicate bank statement reconciliations have been properly completed.
d.  In our opinion, the physical cash-handling procedures are adequate.

**176.**  To maximize its cash position and increase earnings on invested cash, management has increased the frequency of billings to customers and eliminated all noninterest-bearing accounts. To maintain an undisturbed maximum cash balance for investment purposes, portions of cash received are used to cover current expenditures. By estimating the float on checks received and deposited, the company has reduced excess cash balances otherwise needed to meet normal transaction needs. Interbank transfers have also been employed to consolidate funds available for investment.

A major control weakness in the case described above is the

a.  Elimination of noninterest-bearing accounts.
b.  Use of interbank transfers.
c.  Increased frequency of billings.
d.  Use of cash received to cover cash expenditures.

**177.** A university finds it impractical to have a centralized receiving function for department purchases of books, supplies, and equipment. Which of the following controls would most effectively prevent payment for goods not received, if performed prior to invoice payment?
   a. Vendor invoices should be matched with department purchase orders.
   b. Names and addresses on vendor invoices should be compared to a list of department-authorized vendors.
   c. A departmental supervisor other than the employee ordering the goods should approve vendor invoices.
   d. The vice president of finance should approve invoices over a specified amount.

**178.** The purchase price of a newly acquired subsidiary depends on the subsidiary's profitability during the first year following its acquisition. The former owners of the subsidiary will continue to manage the company. In conducting an audit of the subsidiary, auditors should pay special attention to the
   a. Fixed asset capitalization procedures.
   b. Payroll disbursement procedures.
   c. Bank account reconciliation procedures.
   d. Vendor invoice approval procedures.

**179.** Upon receipt of purchased goods, receiving department personnel match the quantity received to the packing slip quantity and mark the retail price on the goods based on a master price list. The annotated packing slip is then forwarded to inventory control and goods are automatically moved to the retail sales area. The most significant control strength of this activity is
   a. Immediately pricing goods for retail sale.
   b. Matching quantity received to the packing slip.
   c. Using a master price list for marking the sale price.
   d. Automatically moving goods to the retail sales area.

**180.** To minimize potential financial losses associated with property, plant, and equipment, physical assets should be covered by appropriate insurance in an amount that is
   a. Supported by periodic appraisals.
   b. Determined by the board of directors.
   c. Automatically adjusted by the consumer price index.
   d. In agreement with the basis for property tax assessments.

**181.** Which of the following aspects of the administration of a compensation program would be the **most** important control in the long run?
   a. An informal wage and salary policy to be competitive with the industry average.
   b. A plan of job classifications based on predefined evaluation criteria.
   c. A wage and salary review plan for individual employee compensation.
   d. A level of general compensation that is reasonably competitive.

**182.** One risk associated with the purchasing cycle is the possibility that quantities in excess of organizational needs may be ordered. Which of the following controls would address this exposure?

   a. A using department supervisor reviewing each purchase requisition prior to its being forwarded to the purchasing department.
   b. The purchasing department placing all orders when the computer indicates a low inventory level.
   c. The receiving department delaying the unloading of each shipment presented for receipt until an originating purchase order is available.
   d. The warehouse delaying the storage of all goods until the inspection department provides a receiving report that is consistent with the packing slip provided by the vendor.

**183.** Maintaining a file of purchase orders in the receiving department for merchandise ordered but not yet received helps ensure that
   a. Goods are delivered to the appropriate department in a timely manner.
   b. Only authorized shipments are accepted.
   c. Goods are properly counted when they arrive.
   d. Goods received are not misappropriated.

**184.** In an effort to remain competitive, the sales department was authorized to reduce prices and streamline operations. By allowing individual sales personnel to approve credit and determine product availability and delivery, sales were increased. After these changes, write-offs of receivables increased. An appropriate corrective action is
   a. An independent review and approval of credit.
   b. An independent determination of product availability.
   c. The centralization of management control.
   d. An increase in profit margins.

**185.** The cash receipts function should be separated from the related recordkeeping function in an organization in order to
   a. Physically safeguard the cash receipts.
   b. Establish accountability when the cash is first received.
   c. Prevent paying cash disbursements from cash receipts.
   d. Minimize undetected misappropriations of cash receipts.

**186.** An auditor is observing cash sales to determine if customers are given written receipts. The objective of this test is to ensure that
   a. Cash received equals the total of the receipts.
   b. Customers are charged authorized prices.
   c. Cash balances are correct.
   d. All cash sales are recorded.

**187.** Which of the following statements is an audit objective?
   a. Observe the deposit of the day's cash receipts.
   b. Analyze the pattern of any cash shortages.
   c. Evaluate whether cash receipts are adequately safeguarded.
   d. Recompute each month's bank reconciliation.

**188.** To minimize the risk that agents in the purchasing department will use their positions for personal gain, the organization should
   a. Rotate purchasing agent assignments periodically.
   b. Request internal auditors to confirm selected purchase and account payable.

c.   Specify that all items purchased must pass value-per-unit-of-cost reviews.

d.   Direct the purchasing department to maintain records on purchase prices paid, with review of such being required each six months.

**189.** Which of the following controls would help prevent overpaying a vendor?

a.   Reviewing and canceling supporting documents when a check is issued.

b.   Requiring the check signer to mail the check directly to the vendor.

c.   Reviewing the accounting distribution for the expenditure.

d.   Approving the purchase before ordering from the vendor.

**190.** An audit of the payroll function revealed several instances where a payroll clerk had added fictitious employees to the payroll and deposited the checks in accounts of close relatives. What control should have prevented such actions?

a.   Using time cards and attendance records in the computation of employee gross earnings.

b.   Establishing a policy to deal with close relatives working in the same department.

c.   Having the treasurer's office sign payroll checks.

d.   Allowing changes to the payroll to be authorized only by the personnel department.

**191.** One objective of an audit of the purchasing function is to determine the cost of late payment of invoices containing trade discounts. The appropriate population from which a sample would be drawn is the file of

a.   Receiving reports.

b.   Purchase orders.

c.   Canceled checks.

d.   Paid vendor invoices.

**192.** The internal auditing department of a large independent department store chain is auditing the purchasing system. One auditor has been assigned the task of determining if major office equipment is being acquired at the best price. The auditor should determine whether

a.   Purchase order forms are prenumbered and controlled.

b.   Purchase requisitions from user departments are prerequisites to the purchase of equipment.

c.   Competitive bids are obtained from approved vendors.

d.   Acquisitions of the most recent year were approved in the fixed asset budget for the same period.

**193.** Which of the following situations would cause an internal auditor to question the adequacy of internal controls in a purchasing function?

a.   The original and one copy of the purchase order are mailed to the vendor. The copy on which the vendor acknowledges acceptance is returned to the purchasing department.

b.   Receiving reports are forwarded to purchasing where they are matched to purchase orders and sent to accounts payable.

c.   The accounts payable section prepares documentation for payments.

d.   Unpaid voucher files and perpetual inventory records are independently maintained.

**194.** An audit of the purchasing function disclosed that orders were placed for materials that at that time were being disposed of as surplus. What corrective action should be recommended?

a.   Have all purchase requisitions approved by the responsible purchasing agent.

b.   Confirm all orders for replacement material with the user department.

c.   Employ a historical reorder point system.

d.   Develop and distribute periodic reports of surplus stocks.

**195.** A clerk's duties included comparing goods received with vendor shipping documents, authorizing payment for goods received, and updating online inventory totals. From time to time, the clerk removed small valuable items from the goods received, authorized payment for all items shipped, and manipulated inventory totals to match the goods actually added to inventory. The best preventive control over the clerk's unauthorized actions is

a.   Separating the incompatible functions of access to goods received and authorization of payment of vouchers.

b.   Periodically reconciling quantities received with inventory transactions.

c.   Authorizing payment based on vendors' shipping documents.

d.   Requiring passwords for access to the online inventory system.

**196.** A purchasing agent received expensive gifts from a vendor in return for directing a significant amount of business to that vendor. Which of the following company policies would most effectively prevent such an occurrence?

a.   An official who determines compliance with budgetary requirements should approve all purchases exceeding specified dollar amounts.

b.   Important high-volume materials should be purchased regularly from at least two different sources in order to afford supply protection.

c.   The purchasing function should be decentralized so each department manager or foreman does his or her own purchasing.

d.   Competitive bids should be solicited on purchases to the maximum extent that is practicable.

**197.** A new computer operator erroneously submitted duplicate sets of requests for checks to pay vendors for specific invoices. As a result, two copies of all the checks were produced. The best control to prevent this error is

a.   Computer agreement of batch totals of check requests and checks produced.

b.   Manual agreement of a batch check register with computed check totals.

c.   Batch sequence check of invoices.

d.   Cancellation of paid invoices.

**198.** Which of the following documents should the auditor examine to determine if only authorized purchases are being accepted by the receiving department?

a.   A bill of lading.

b.   A copy of the purchase order.

c.   An invoice.

d.   Policies and procedures for the receiving function.

**199.** The treasurer makes disbursements by check and reconciles the monthly bank statements to accounting records. Which of the following **best** describes the control impact of this arrangement?
   a. Internal control will be enhanced since these are duties that the treasurer should perform.
   b. The treasurer will be in a position to make and conceal unauthorized payments.
   c. The treasurer will be able to make unauthorized adjustments to the cash account.
   d. Controls will be enhanced because the treasurer will have two opportunities to discover inappropriate disbursements.

**200.** When testing the year-end balance for trade accounts payable, the use of an audit software package to identify unauthorized vendors in a vendor database is most useful in developing tests to determine
   a. Existence of valid recorded liabilities.
   b. Accuracy of the receiving cutoff used.
   c. Ownership of the recorded payables.
   d. Valuation of recorded transactions.

**201.** Management believes that some specific sales commissions for the year were too large. The accuracy of the recorded commission expense for specific salespersons is best determined by
   a. Computation of selected sales commissions.
   b. Calculating commission ratios.
   c. Use of analytical procedures.
   d. Tests of overall reasonableness.

**202.** A payroll clerk working through a computerized payroll system increased the hourly pay rate for two employees and shared the resulting overpayments with the employees. Which of the following would have **best** served to prevent this illegal act?
   a. Requiring that all changes to pay records be recorded on a standard form.
   b. Limiting access to master payroll records to supervisory personnel in the payroll department.
   c. Reconciling pay rates per personnel records with those of the payroll system annually.
   d. Monitoring of payroll costs by department heads on a monthly basis.

**203.** For an upcoming audit, an auditor's objective is to determine whether costs are both documented and reasonable. This is most likely an audit of
   a. Advertising agency billings.
   b. Allowance for doubtful accounts.
   c. Asset disposals.
   d. Accounts payable.

**204.** A control that prevents purchasing agents from favoring certain suppliers in placing orders is
   a. A monthly report of total dollars committed by each buyer.
   b. Requiring buyers to adhere to detailed product specifications.
   c. Periodic rotation of buyer assignments.
   d. Monitoring the number of orders placed by each buyer.

**205.** A means of ensuring that payroll checks are drawn for properly authorized amounts is to

   a. Conduct periodic floor verification of employees on the payroll.
   b. Require that undelivered checks be returned to the cashier.
   c. Supervisory approval of employee time cards.
   d. Witness the distribution of payroll checks.

**206.** To obtain evidence that no duplicate payments of accounts payable are made, an internal auditor would examine
   a. Purchase orders for proper approval.
   b. Receiving documents to see whether goods were received.
   c. Approved vendor price lists to see whether the company paid the proper amount.
   d. Supporting documentation for cancellation when the check is written to the vendor.

**207.** During the audit of a company's purchasing department, an internal auditor discovered that many purchases were made (at normal prices) from an office supply firm whose owner was the brother of the director of purchasing. There were no policies or controls in place to restrict such purchases, and no fraud appears to have been committed. In this case, the internal auditor should recommend
   a. The development of an approved-vendor file initiated by the buyer and approved by the director of purchasing.
   b. Establishment of a price policy (range) for all goods.
   c. The initiation of a conflict-of-interest policy.
   d. The inspection of all receipts by receiving inspectors.

**208.** Charges and expenses billed by an independent advertising agency are disputed as unauthorized by the marketing department. Which of the following controls would prevent such disputes?
   a. Prompt recording of both commitments and expenditures.
   b. A written agreement containing provisions as to charges and expenses billable.
   c. Separation of duties between sales promotion and advertising.
   d. Monthly reports comparing budget and actual expenditures.

**209.** A means of preventing production delays as a consequence of equipment breakdowns and repairs is to
   a. Schedule production based on capacity utilization.
   b. Budget maintenance department activities based on an analysis of equipment work orders.
   c. Preauthorize maintenance department work orders and overtime pay.
   d. Establish a preventive maintenance program for all production equipment.

**210.** During the audit of the receiving department, an internal auditor examined a physical shipment of goods to verify the accuracy of the completed receiving report. Evidence showed that the number of units in the shipment did not agree with the quantity shown on the receiving report. Which of the following may have led to this error?
   a. Lack of standards for selecting vendors.
   b. Displaying amounts ordered on the receiving department's copy of the purchase order.

c. Failure of receiving personnel to compare the quality of goods received with specifications.
d. Improper authorization of the purchase.

**211.** An auditor observes that controls over the perpetual inventory system are weak. An appropriate audit response would be to
a. Increase the testing of the inventory controls.
b. Perform turnover ratio tests.
c. Recommend that a physical inventory count be scheduled.
d. Apply gross profit analyses by product lines and compare to prior years for reasonableness.

**212.** A utility company with a large investment in repair vehicles would most likely implement which internal control to reduce the risk of vehicle theft or loss?
a. Review insurance coverage for adequacy.
b. Systematically account for all repair work orders.
c. Physically inventory vehicles and reconcile the results with the accounting records.
d. Maintain vehicles in a secured location with release and return subject to approval by a custodian.

**213.** Which of the following audit objectives would be accomplished by tracing a sample of accounts receivable debit entries to customer invoices and related shipping documents?
a. Sales are properly recorded.
b. Sales are billed at the correct prices.
c. Accounts receivable represents valid sales.
d. Customer credit is approved.

**214.** Internal auditing departments are often requested to coordinate their work with that of the external auditors. Which of the following activities would **most** likely be restricted to the external auditor?
a. Evaluating the system of controls over cash collections and similar transactions.
b. Attesting to the fairness of presentation of cash position.
c. Evaluating the adequacy of the organization's overall system of internal controls.
d. Reviewing the system established to ensure compliance with policies and procedures that could have a significant impact on operations.

**215.** An internal auditor is auditing the financial operations of an organization. Which of the following is **not** specified by the IIA *Standards* for inclusion in the scope of the audit?
a. Reviewing the reliability and integrity of financial information.
b. Reviewing systems established to ensure compliance with appropriate policy, plans, procedures, and other types of authority.
c. Appraising economy, efficiency, and effectiveness of the employment of resources.
d. Reviewing the financial decision-making process.

**Information Technology Audit Engagements**

**216.** An internal auditor is conducting an operational audit of the information system department. Which of the following factors would the auditor give the **most** weight to in evaluating the effectiveness of the department?
a. Its objectives and goals are consistent with the overall objectives of its organization.

b. It has a large technical staff.
c. It is given top priority in the budgeting process.
d. It uses leading-edge technology.

**217.** When there is a difference of opinion between the auditor and auditees during new system development audit work, what should the auditor do **first**?
a. Complain to audit management.
b. Discuss it with user management.
c. Convince the auditees.
d. Talk to senior management.

**218.** An information technology (IT) auditor overheard talk about a flaw in system design of a new computer-based application system development project. What should the auditor do **first**?
a. Immediately schedule an audit of the new system.
b. Do nothing since it is hearsay.
c. Discuss the issue with audit management.
d. Talk to the system development project team.

**219.** Which of the following actions impairs the IT auditor's independence during computer system development work?
a. The auditor designs controls.
b. The auditor tests controls.
c. The auditor advises on controls.
d. The auditor designs an integrated test facility.

**220.** Once the IT auditor becomes reasonably certain about a case of fraud, what should the auditor do **next**?
a. Say nothing now since it should be kept secret.
b. Discuss it with the employee suspected of fraud.
c. Report to the law enforcement officials.
d. Report to the company management.

**221.** The **first** step in IT compliance audit testing is to review which of the following?
a. Access security controls.
b. Input controls.
c. Processing controls.
d. Output controls.

**222.** An IT auditor is conducting an application system audit. What source is used to verify the department codes used in the system?
a. Application database files.
b. Application program literal.
c. Systems activity logs.
d. Application parameters.

**223.** During an audit, an IT auditor found no written procedures for an application system. What should the auditor do?
a. Cancel the audit immediately since it is hard to do an audit without documentation.
b. Reschedule the audit when the procedures are written.
c. Report the issue to management.
d. Document the procedures and audit against them.

**224.** A company uses a local area network (LAN) with one client server. The auditor wishes to determine whether LAN users are complying with company policies related to the documentation of applications developed by end users and shared by other users on the LAN. The most appropriate audit procedure would be to

a. Send a questionnaire to end users to determine the extent to which they have developed end-user applications for the LAN.
b. Send a survey to end users to test their knowledge of required application documentation.
c. Take a random sample of end users and examine all applications stored on their computers for compliance with existing policies.
d. Take a random sample of end-user applications stored on the server and examine the applications for compliance with company policies.

**225.** A large data processing center is experiencing processing bottlenecks at peak batch-processing hours. The center is sometimes unable to complete all batch processing by the start of the next business day, creating difficulties in starting online systems in a timely manner. In investigating this problem, the internal auditor should initially focus on controls over

a. Backup/restart procedures.
b. Job scheduling.
c. Console logs.
d. Program documentation.

**Items 226 through 232** are based on the following:

Two major retail companies, both publicly traded and operating in the same geographic area, have recently merged. Both companies are approximately the same size and have audit departments. Company B has invested heavily in information technology and has EDI connections with its major vendors.

The audit committee has asked the internal auditors from both companies to analyze risk areas that should be addressed after the merger. The director of internal auditing of Company B has suggested that the two audit groups have a planning meeting to share audit programs, scope of audit coverage, and copies of audit reports that were delivered to their audit committees. Management has also suggested that the auditors review the compatibility of the companies' two computer systems and control philosophy for individual store operations.

**226.** Which of the following would be the **least** important risk factor when considering the ability to integrate the two companies' computer systems?

a. The number of programmers and systems analysts employed by each company.
b. The extent of EDI connections with vendors.
c. The compatibility of existing operating systems and database structures.
d. The size of company databases and the number of database servers used.

**227.** During the first meeting, a disagreement occurs over the approach taken regarding store compliance. The audit director for Company B questions Company A's extensive use of store compliance testing, stating that the approach is neither responsive to materiality concepts nor an appropriate application of risk assessment. Company A's audit director presents the following reasoning:

I. You have misconstrued materiality. Materiality is not based only on the size of individual stores; it is also based on the control structure that affects the whole organization.

II. Any deviation from a prescribed control procedure is, by definition, material.
III. The only way to ensure that a material amount of the company's control structure is covered is to comprehensively audit all stores.

Which of the statements by the audit director of Company A is(are) valid?
a. I only.
b. I and II only.
c. III only.
d. I, II, and III.

**228.** The audit director for Company B decides to review selected store compliance audit reports issued by the internal audit department of Company A. Upon reviewing the reports, the director comments that most items included in the report are inappropriate because they are very minor and cannot be considered material. The director states that the management of Company B would not tolerate such reports. Which of the following assertions by the audit director of Company A is(are) valid?

I. These are the kinds of reports we have provided since the company has been in operation, and they have served our company well.
II. The reports are consistent with management's control philosophy and are an integral part of the overall control environment.
III. Materiality is in the eyes of the beholder. Any deviation is considered material by my management.

a. I only.
b. II only.
c. III only.
d. II and III.

**229.** In analyzing the differences between the two companies, the audit director of Company A notes that Company A has a formal corporate code of ethics while Company B does not. The code of ethics covers such things as purchase agreements and relationships with vendors as well as a host of other issues to guide individual behavior within the firm. Which of the following statements regarding the existence of the code of ethics in Company A can be logically inferred?

I. Company A exhibits a higher standard of ethical behavior than does Company B.
II. Company A has established objective criteria by which an individual's actions can be evaluated.
III. The absence of a formal corporate code of ethics in Company B would prevent a successful audit of ethical behavior in that company.

a. I and II.
b. II only.
c. III only.
d. II and III.

**230.** Company A's audit director, who is also a CIA, faces an ethical dilemma. For an audit in process, persuasive evidence indicates that a top manager has been involved in insider trading. The extent and type of trading is such that the trading would be considered fraudulent. However, the findings were encountered as a side issue of another audit and are not considered relevant to the compatibility of the computer systems. Regarding this finding, which of the following is the audit director's **most** appropriate action?

a. Discontinue audit work associated with the insider trading and report the preliminary findings to the company's external legal counsel for their investigation. Report the legal counsel findings to management.

b. Discontinue audit work associated with the insider trading. Report the preliminary findings to the chairperson of the audit committee and recommend an investigation.

c. Continue work on the insider trading sufficient to conclusively establish whether fraudulent activity has taken place, then report the findings to the chairperson of the audit committee. Report the matter to government officials if appropriate action is not taken.

d. Discontinue audit work associated with the insider trading since it is not an integral part of the existing audit and the audit committee has established higher priority work for the auditors.

**231.** The two organizations agree to share data on store operations. The data reveal that three stores in company A are characterized by

- Significantly lower gross margins
- Higher-than-average sales volume
- Higher levels of employee bonuses

The three stores are part of a set of six that are managed by a relatively new section manager. In addition, the store managers of the three stores are also relatively new. The **most** likely cause of the observed data is

a. The relative inexperience of the store managers.

b. Problems with employee training and employee ability to meet customer needs.

c. Fraudulent activity whereby goods are taken from the stores, thus resulting in the lower gross margins.

d. Promotional activities that offer large discounts coupled with the payment of commissions to employees who reach targeted sales goals.

**232.** Assume the auditor concludes that the most reasonable explanation of the observed data in the prior question is that inventory fraud is taking place in the three stores. Which of the following audit activities would provide the most persuasive evidence that fraud is taking place?

a. Use an integrated test facility (ITF) to compare individual sales transactions with test transactions submitted through the ITF. Investigate all differences.

b. Interview the three individual store managers to determine if their explanations about the observed differences are the same, and then compare their explanations to that of the section manager.

c. Schedule a surprise inventory audit to include a physical inventory. Investigate areas of inventory shrinkage.

d. Take a sample of individual store prices and compare them with the sales entered on the cash register for the same items.

**233.** A financial institution is overstating revenue by charging too much of each loan payment to interest income and too little to repayment of principal. Which of the following

audit procedures would be **least** effective in detecting this error?

a. Perform an analytical review by comparing interest income this period as a percentage of the loan portfolio with the interest income percentage for the prior period.

b. Use an integrated test facility (ITF) and submit interest payments for various loans in the ITF portfolio to determine if they are recorded correctly.

c. Use test data and submit interest payments for various loans in the test portfolio to determine if they are recorded correctly.

d. Use generalized audit software to take a random sample of loan payments made during the period, calculate the correct posting amounts, and trace the postings that were made to the various accounts.

**234.** Which of the following is **not** a benefit of using information technology in solving audit problems?

a. It helps reduce audit risk.

b. It improves the timeliness of the audit.

c. It increases audit opportunities.

d. It improves the auditor's judgment.

**Items 235 through 240** are based on the following:

An organization has grown rapidly and has just automated its human resource system. The organization has developed a large database that tracks employees, employee benefits, payroll deductions, job classifications, ethnic code, age, insurance, medical protection, and other similar information. Management has asked the internal auditing department to review the new system.

**235.** In order to test whether data currently within the automated system are correct, the auditor should

a. Use test data and determine whether all the data entered are captured correctly in the updated database.

b. Take a sample of data to be entered for a few days and trace the data to the updated database to determine the correctness of the updates.

c. Use generalized audit software to provide a printout of all employees with invalid job descriptions. Investigate the causes of the problems.

d. Use generalized audit software to select a sample of employees from the database and verify the data fields.

**236.** The automated system contains a table of pay rates that is matched to the employee job classifications. The best control to ensure that the table is updated correctly for only valid pay changes would be to

a. Limit access to the data table to management and line supervisors who have the authority to determine pay rates.

b. Require a supervisor in the department who does not have the ability to change the table to compare the changes to a signed management authorization.

c. Ensure that adequate edit and reasonableness checks are built into the automated system.

d. Require that all pay changes be signed by the employee to verify that the change goes to a bona fide employee.

**237.** An employee in the payroll department is contemplating a fraud that would involve the addition of a fictitious employee and the input of fictitious hours worked. The paycheck would then be sent to the payroll employee's home address. The most effective control procedure to prevent this type of fraud would be to require that

a. Someone approves a report of all new employees added outside of the payroll department. Require that reports showing all employees and hours worked be sent to the supervisor's department for review.
b. All new employees and their hours worked be input by the human resources department.
c. Supervisors outside of both human resources and payroll approve all changes to employee records.
d. The payroll department physically delivers paychecks to employees, rather than mailing them to the employees.

**238.** Human resources and payroll are separate departments. Which of the following combinations would provide the **best** segregation of duties?

a. Human resources adds employees, payroll processes hours, and delivers the paychecks to employees.
b. Human resources adds employees, reviews and submits payroll hours to payroll for processing, and delivers paychecks to employees.
c. Human resources adds employees, and payroll processes hours and enters employee bank account numbers. Paychecks are automatically deposited in the employees' bank account.
d. Payroll adds employees and enters employees' bank account numbers but processes hours only as approved by human resources. Paychecks are automatically deposited in the employees' bank accounts.

**239.** The auditor is concerned that retired employees are not receiving the correct benefits. Which of the following auditing procedures would be the **least** effective in addressing this concern?

a. Take a sample of employees added to the retirement list for a specified time period—for example, a day or a week—and determine that they are scheduled for the appropriate benefits.
b. Use an integrated test facility and submit transactions over a period of time to determine if the system is paying the appropriate benefits.
c. Use generalized audit software to take a classical variables sample of retired employees on the database. Verify that all benefit payments are appropriate.
d. Use generalized audit software to take a variables sample stratified on years since retirement and size of benefit payments. Verify that all benefit payments are appropriate.

**240.** The auditor reviews the retirement benefits plan and determines that the pension and medical benefits have been changed several times in the past ten years. The auditor wishes to determine whether there is justification to perform further audit investigation. The most appropriate audit procedure would be to

a. Review the trend of overall retirement expense over the last ten years. If the retirement expense increased, it would indicate the need for further investigation.

b. Use generalized audit software to take a dollar-unit sample of retirement pay and determine whether each retired employee was paid correctly.
c. Review reasonableness of retirement pay and medical expenses on a per-person basis stratified by which plan was in effect when the employee retired.
d. Use generalized audit software to take an attributes sample of retirement pay, and perform detailed testing to determine whether each person chosen was given the proper benefits.

**241.** The internal audit department can be involved with systems development continuously, at the end of specific stages, after implementation, or not at all. An advantage of continuous internal audit involvement compared to the other two types of involvement is that

a. The cost of audit involvement can be minimized.
b. There are clearly defined points at which to issue audit comments.
c. Redesign costs can be minimized.
d. The threat of lack of audit independence can be minimized.

**242.** A decentralized production facility uses a minicomputer to process inventory and production records. The computer system transmits data to the main production facility as a batch process each day. Which of the following would the auditor perform as part of a review of the production facility's general controls?

I. Reviewing the fire suppression capabilities located at the production facility.
II. Reviewing position descriptions for production personnel assigned to computer-related duties.
III. Reviewing error listings of inventory transactions incorrectly entered.
IV. Reviewing record counts of production data transmitted to the central facility.

a. III only.
b. II and IV.
c. I and II only.
d. I, II, and III.

**Items 243 through 248** are based on the following:

A department developed an integrated end user computing (EUC) application involving timekeeping, payroll, and labor cost accounting. The department used its own personnel to design and program the application using a fourth-generation language (4GL). Subsequently, the department hired outside consultants to rewrite certain components. The application was implemented on the departmental local area network (LAN) and connected with the corporate mainframe system to allow the transfer of data between them.

The internal audit department ranked the EUC applications of the organization according to the perceived risk. As a result, the timekeeping/payroll/labor cost accounting application was selected for an IT audit.

**243.** When the labor cost accounting component of the application was first implemented, it did not meet certain business requirements in the department and had to be substantially rewritten. Which one of the following risks associated with EUC application development could have led directly to this result?

a. End-user applications may not receive the independent testing associated with traditional development.

b. There may be insufficient review and analysis of user needs when user and analyst functions are no longer separate.

c. End-user applications may not be adequately documented to facilitate review.

d. Segregation of duties would be inadequate if the same person performed programmer and operator functions.

**244.** Certain payroll transactions were posted to the payroll file but were not uploaded correctly to the general ledger file on the mainframe. The **best** control to detect this type of error would be

a. A standard method for uploading mainframe data files.

b. An appropriate edit and validation of data.

c. A record or log of items rejected during processing.

d. Balancing totals of critical fields.

**245.** Management of the department allowed the outside consultants to test and install new releases of the application software without documenting the changes. Which of the following risks would be **most** closely associated with this practice?

a. The reliability of the information processed may be reduced.

b. An appropriate level of management may not properly authorize initiation of changes.

c. The users may not be aware that changes have been made.

d. The changes may be made to the application without proper testing.

**246.** When planning the controls review of the EUC application, the internal auditor chose to include the general control environment in the scope. Which one of the following statements regarding general controls is the auditor **most** likely to find true?

a. The effectiveness of the general controls is influenced by the application controls.

b. Identifying the person or function responsible for the general controls may be easier here than in a traditional mainframe environment.

c. The need for specific general controls is relatively constant across EUC environments.

d. General controls must be in place before application controls can be relied on.

**247.** A payroll clerk with authorized access to the local area network (LAN) was able to update personnel files directly, independent of the application programs. The **best** control to prevent a clerk from doing this would be to

a. Restrict access to LAN workstations by such means as automatic lock-up after a predefined period of keyboard inactivity.

b. Restrict access to and monitor installation of software products or tools having powerful update capabilities.

c. Use password security to authenticate users as they attempt to log on to the LAN.

d. Establish a security policy for the department that prohibits direct updating of data files.

**248.** The auditor used the reporting capabilities of the 4GL to analyze the data files for unusual activity, such as excessive overtime hours, unusual fluctuations in pay rates, or excessive vacation time. The application controls being verified by this analysis are

a. Edit and validation controls.

b. Rejected and suspense item controls.

c. Controls over update access to the database.

d. Programmed balancing controls.

**Items 249 through 254** are based on the following:

A multinational company has an agreement with a value added network (VAN) that provides the encoding and communications transfer for the company's electronic data interchange (EDI) and electronic funds transfer (EFT) transactions. Before transfer of data to the VAN, the company performs online preprocessing of the transactions. The internal auditor is responsible for assessing preprocessing controls. In addition, the agreement between the company and the VAN states that the internal auditor is allowed to examine and report on the controls in place at the VAN on an annual basis. The contract specifies that access to the VAN can occur on a surprise basis during the second or third quarter of the company's fiscal year. This period was chosen so it would not interfere with processing during the VAN's peak transaction periods. This provision was not reviewed with internal auditing. The annual audit plan approved by the board of directors specifies that a full audit would be done during the current year.

**249.** Which of the following preprocessing controls is **least** likely to provide the auditor with assurance about the validity of transactions?

a. Verification of the requestor.

b. Authentication of information.

c. Exception processing.

d. Decryption of data.

**250.** The auditor wants to obtain assurance that the EFT payments have not been made twice. Computer-assisted audit tools and techniques could be used to perform which of the following procedures?

I. Identification of EFT transactions to the same vendor for the same dollar amount.

II. Extraction of EFT transactions with unauthorized vendor codes.

III. Testing of EFT transactions for reasonableness.

IV. Searching for EFT transactions with duplicate purchase order numbers.

a. I, II, III, and IV.

b. I, III, and IV only.

c. I and III only.

d. I and IV only.

**251.** When the auditor called to arrange the annual control audit during the third quarter, the VAN Provider stated that it could not accommodate the auditor since the peak processing period started earlier than normal this year and all VAN personnel were occupied. This scope limitation, along with its potential effect, must be communicated to which one of the following?

a. The company's board of directors.

b. The board of directors of the VAN Provider.

c. The board of directors of both the company and the VAN provider.

d. This does not need to be reported at the board of director's level.

**252.** Because the VAN did not provide the auditor with access to its system, that portion of the audit program was not completed. Which one of the following should the auditor **not** do?

a. Include the scope limitation in the final report.

b. Rewrite the audit program to eliminate the step.

c. Obtain the approval of the internal audit director.

d. Document the VAN's actions in the workpapers.

**253.** Which one of the following would **not** be included as a reason for the company to use EFT with the EDI system?

a. To take advantage of the time lag associated with negotiable instruments.

b. To allow the company to negotiate discounts with EDI vendors based on prompt payment.

c. To improve its cash management program.

d. To reduce input time and input errors.

**254.** Which one of the following is **least** likely to be recommended by the auditor when an EDI/EFT system is being designed?

a. The identity of the individual approving an electronic document should be stored as a data field.

b. Disaster recovery plans should be established.

c. Data security procedures should be written to prevent changes to data by unauthorized individuals.

d. Remote access to electronic data should be denied.

**255.** An internal auditor was performing an operational audit of the purchasing and accounts payable system. The audit objective was to identify changes to processes that would improve efficiency and effectiveness. Which of the following statements support the auditor's recommendation that electronic data interchange (EDI) should be implemented within a company?

I. There is a small number of transactions.

II. There is a time-sensitive just-in-time purchase environment.

III. There is a large volume of custom purchases.

IV. There are multiple transactions with the same vendor.

a. I only.

b. II and IV only.

c. I and III.

d. II, III, and IV.

**256.** Which one of the following is likely to be a concern in performing an assessment of an EDI purchasing system?

a. Increased turnover of the information technology staff.

b. Increased transaction volume.

c. Increased competition in the market.

d. Decreased competition in the market.

**257.** Which one of the following input controls or edit checks would catch certain types of errors within the payment amount field of a transaction?

a. Record count.

b. Echo check.

c. Check digit.

d. Limit check.

**258.** When assessing application controls, which one of the following input controls or edit checks is **most** likely to be used to detect a data input error in the customer account number field?

a. Limit check.

b. Validity check.

c. Control total.

d. Hash total.

**259.** Management's enthusiasm for computer security seems to vary with changes in the environment, particularly the occurrence of other computer disasters. Which of the following concepts should be addressed when making a comprehensive recommendation regarding the cost-benefit of computer security?

I. Potential loss if security is not implemented.

II. Probability of occurrences.

III. Cost and effectiveness of the implementation and operation of computer security.

a. I only.

b. I and II only.

c. III only.

d. I, II, and III.

**260.** Most large-scale computer systems maintain at least three program libraries: production library (for running programs), source code library (maintains original source coding), and test library (for programs which are being changed). Which of the following statements is correct regarding the implementation of sound controls over computer program libraries?

a. Only programmers should have access to the production library.

b. Users should have access to the test library to determine whether all changes are properly made.

c. Only the program librarian should be allowed to make changes to the production library.

d. The computer operator should have access to both the production library and the source code library to assist in diagnosing computer crashes.

**261.** Most organizations are concerned about the potential compromise of passwords. Which of the following procedures would be the **most** effective in controlling against a perpetrator obtaining someone else's password?

a. Allow only the users to change their passwords, and encourage them to change passwords frequently.

b. Implement a computer program that tests to see that the password is not easily guessed.

c. Implement the use of see-through authentication techniques whereby the user uses a card to generate a password and verifies both the key and the generated password to the system.

d. Limit password authorization to time of day and location.

**262.** An organization uses a database management system (DBMS) as a repository of data. The DBMS in turn supports a number of end-user–developed applications that were created using fourth-generation programming languages. Some of the applications update the database. In evaluating the control procedures over access and use of the database, the auditor would be most concerned that

a. End users have their read-only applications approved by data processing before accessing the database.
b. Concurrency update controls are in place.
c. End-user applications are developed and tested on microcomputers before being ported to the mainframe.
d. A relational database model is adopted so that multiple users can be served at the same time.

**263.** A catalog company has been experiencing an increasing incidence of problems where the wrong products have been shipped to the customer. Most of the customer orders come in over the telephone, and an operator enters the data into the order system immediately. Which of the following control procedures, if properly implemented, would address the problem?

I. Have the computer automatically assign a sequential order number to each customer order.
II. Implement a self-checking digit algorithm for each product number and request entries by product number.
III. Request entries by product number, have the computer program identify the product and price, and require the operator to orally verify the product description with the customer.

    a. II only.
    b. I, II, and III.
    c. II and III.
    d. I and II.

**264.** Responsibility for the control of end-user computing exists at the organizational, departmental, and individual user level. Which of the following should be a direct responsibility of the individual users?
    a. Acquisition of hardware and software.
    b. Taking equipment inventories.
    c. Strategic planning of end-user computing.
    d. Physical security of equipment.

**265.** Which of the following environmental control risks is more likely in a stand-alone microcomputer environment than a mainframe environment?
    a. Copyright violations due to the use of unauthorized copies of purchased software.
    b. Unauthorized access to data.
    c. Lack of data availability due to inadequate data retention policies.
    d. All of the above.

**266.** An auditor reviewed access security over the company's various computer applications. The auditor found that security consisted of access controls programmed into each application. The best recommendation for management in the situation is
    a. Eliminate the built-in access controls.
    b. Consider the use of access control software.
    c. Consider the use of utility software.
    d. Expand the use of the built-in access controls to new applications.

**267.** The best source of evidence to determine if ex-emloyees continue to have access to a company's automated databases is
    a. Discussing the password removal process with the database administrator.

b. Reviewing computer logs of access attempts.
c. Reconciling current payroll lists with database access lists.
d. Reviewing access control software to determine whether the most current version is implemented.

**268.** A controller became aware that a competitor appeared to have access to the company's pricing information. The internal auditor determined that the leak of information was occurring during the electronic transmission of data from branch offices to the head office. Which of the following controls would be **most** effective in preventing the leak of information?
    a. Asynchronous transmission.
    b. Encryption.
    c. Use of fiber optic transmission lines.
    d. Use of passwords.

**269.** In an end-user computing environment, an individual user would be responsible for which one of the following controls?
    a. Data ownership standards.
    b. Backup and recovery.
    c. Technical manuals.
    d. Equipment inventory.

**270.** The auditor's organization has several decades of experience with computing in mainframe environments. Two years ago the organization also implemented end-user computing in several departments. In auditing the end-user computing environment, the auditor is concerned that the end-user environment is less likely to have adequate software and hardware facilities for
    a. Input validation for transactions.
    b. Change control procedures.
    c. Encryption of sensitive data.
    d. Relational database queries.

**271.** A retail company has been using prototyping to accelerate the development of point-of-sale systems. The approach has been so successful that a system that was essentially a prototype was implemented. In response to recommendations from users, changes are being made daily to the online system. A risk associated with this practice is that of
    a. Difficulties in maintaining the system.
    b. Failure to consider alternative approaches.
    c. Increased system development time.
    d. All of the above.

**272.** A retailer of high-priced durable goods operates a catalog-ordering division that accepts customer orders by telephone. The retailer runs frequent price promotions. During these times, the telephone operators enter the promotional prices. The risk of this practice is that
    a. Customers could systematically be charged lower prices.
    b. Frequent price changes could overload the order entry system.
    c. Operators could give competitors notice of the promotional prices.
    d. Operators could collude with outsiders for unauthorized prices.

**273.** The purpose of internal auditing's review of IT data entry operations is to determine if
    a. System development standards exist and have been followed.

b. System developers have the required skills and knowledge for the systems that they develop.

c. Computer operations employ state-of-the-art equipment and procedures.

d. Input/output controls are adequate and effective.

**274.** An internal auditor is planning an operational audit of a computer center. Which of the following items would normally be considered **most** important?

a. Computing required amounts of diskettes, paper, and other supplies.

b. Ascertaining the existence of adequate measures of operational results.

c. Determining the age and condition of the main-frame computer.

d. Conducting a survey of computer vendors to be used in future purchases.

**275.** A company has equipped its staff with personal computers. Several employees also have compatible machines at home and belong to shareware networks and electronic bulletin board systems. They pass along software obtained through these external sources to coworkers at the office. Given this information, an IT auditor should conclude that

a. Management has failed to set quality standards.

b. An exposure exists requiring management attention.

c. A cost-benefit analysis should be done on the use of externally obtained software.

d. Quantitative performance standards are unrealistic.

**276.** Which of the following is **not** a benefit of using information technology in solving audit problems?

a. It helps reduce audit risk.

b. It improves the timeliness of the audit.

c. It increases audit opportunities.

d. It improves the auditor's judgment.

**277.** In a microcomputer environment, significant restrictions on the nature and timing of audit procedures are most often caused by

a. Lack of adequate password protection.

b. Failure to specify backup and recovery procedures.

c. Accessibility of hardware.

d. Limitations on the audit trail.

**278.** Backup and recovery controls are crucial to ensuring the reliability of a teleprocessing network. When reviewing the controls over backup and recovery, which of the following would not be included? Review of

a. Adequacy of user data file backups on the local area network (LAN).

b. Controls over hardware and software failures.

c. Use and adequacy of encryption processes.

d. Adequacy of documents/manuals informing all personnel of their backup and recovery responsibilities.

**279.** Management is investigating the acquisition of an upgraded version of the existing mainframe system to increase its capacity. They have requested that the internal auditor perform an operational audit to determine the efficiency of the existing computer processing resource. What would be the **most** relevant source of information to meet the audit objective?

a. A survey of current user satisfaction.

b. A review of computer job log records, listings of scheduled jobs, and computer downtime.

c. A comparison of mainframe capacity with microcomputer capacity.

d. A detailed analysis of hard disk growth over the last three years.

**280.** At a remote computer center, management installed an automated scheduling system to load data files and execute programs at specific times during the day. The **best** approach for verifying that the scheduling system performs as intended is to

a. Analyze job activity with a queuing model to determine workload characteristics.

b. Simulate the resource usage and compare the results with actual results of operations.

c. Use library management software to track changes to successive versions of application programs.

d. Audit job accounting data for file accesses and job initiation/termination messages.

**281.** Computer output from a large mainframe system should be distributed in accordance with current processing instructions and only after a review of processing results by the

a. Application programmers.

b. Control section.

c. Computer operators.

d. Data processing manager.

**282.** The major purpose of the internal auditor's study and evaluation of the company's IT operations is to

a. Evaluate the competence of IT operating personnel.

b. Ensure the exercise of due professional care.

c. Evaluate the reliability and integrity of financial and operating information.

d. Become familiar with the company's means of identifying, measuring, classifying, and reporting information.

**283.** An unauthorized employee picked up a printout of salary data from the computer center after the last payroll update. The **best** control for ensuring that only authorized employees receive sensitive printouts is logging and

a. Controlled destruction of obsolete printouts.

b. Signed confirmation by recipients.

c. Access control over printout files on disk.

d. Enforced expiration date on sensitive printouts.

**284.** An internal auditor suspected that a master file had been updated twice from the same set of daily transaction data. A technique for determining whether the master file had been updated twice in one day is

a. Job accounting data analysis.

b. Code comparison.

c. Embedded audit data collection.

d. Extended records.

**285.** Inefficient usage of excess computer equipment can be controlled by

a. Contingency planning.

b. System feasibility studies.

c. Capacity planning.

d. Exception reporting.

**Items 286 through 290** are based on the following:

A company uses a local area network (LAN) to connect its four city area sales offices to the headquarter office. Sales information such as credit approval and other customer information, prices, account information, and so on is maintained at headquarters. This office also houses the inventory and shipping functions. Each area office is connected to the headquarters' office computer, and messages/information between the area offices pass through the headquarters' computer. This communication configuration allows for real-time confirmation of shipments as well as billing and account status. The company is concerned about the accuracy and sensitivity of its information and has implemented controls to protect the database used by the area offices. (1) *The data are modeled after a tree structure, with each record type having any number of lower-level dependent records. The relationship is a one-to-many rather than a many-to-many relationship.* When a user enters the system, a series of questions is asked of the user. These (2) *questions include a name and mother's birth date.* The headquarters computer maintains a (3) *matrix of user names and the files/programs the user can access as well as what the user can do to/with the file or program.*

A recent addition to the system controls involves a lockout procedure. This procedure (4) *locks out a particular record to other sales offices while a particular sales office is using the record.* This control ensures that each transaction has the most recent and accurate information available when the sales office is processing the event.

**286.** The local area network (LAN) described above is an example of which of the following LAN topology?
- a. Star.
- b. Hierarchical.
- c. Ring.
- d. Fully interconnected.

**287.** The database system described in (1) above is an example of which type of database model?
- a. Relational.
- b. Hierarchical.
- c. Network.
- d. Distributed.

**288.** The questions described in (2) are primarily intended to provide
- a. Authorization for processing.
- b. Access control to computer hardware.
- c. Authentication of the user.
- d. Data integrity control.

**289.** The matrix described in (3) is primarily intended to provide
- a. Authorization for processing.
- b. Access control to computer hardware.
- c. Authentication of the user.
- d. Data integrity control.

**290.** The control described in (4) is primarily intended to prevent
- a. Duplicate processing of transactions.
- b. LAN server overload.
- c. Transaction processing delay.
- d. Concurrent transaction processing.

**291.** To secure communication networks against wiretapping, the most effective control is
- a. Use of identifiers.
- b. Use of passwords.
- c. Use of logical access methods.
- d. Use of encryption methods.

**292.** In addition to controls over access, processing, program changes, and other functions, a computerized system needs to establish an audit trail of information. Which of the following information would generally **not** be included in an audit trail log designed to summarize unauthorized system access attempts?
- a. A list of authorized users.
- b. The type of event or transaction attempted.
- c. The terminal used to make the attempt.
- d. The data in the program sought.

**293.** You are called upon to audit the security of your firm's online computer system. An internal user-to-data access control program protects the system. You have determined that the data access program is properly installed and is operative. Which of the following statements regarding your knowledge of the data security of the system is **most** accurate?
- a. Restricting specific applications to specific files controls access to data.
- b. Restricting specific terminals to specific applications controls access to data.
- c. Security will be dependent on the controls over the issuance of user IDs and user authentication.
- d. The use of this type of access control software will eliminate any significant control weaknesses.

**294.** In order to ensure the proper addition/deletion of authorizations in an operational audit of data access security, an internal auditor would verify that
- a. Individuals who are not employees have no access privileges.
- b. Revoked access privileges are canceled on a weekly cycle.
- c. Access privileges are activated promptly after they are authorized.
- d. A systems programmer keeps records of all additions/deletions of access changes.

**295.** The audit effort **most** likely to yield relevant evidence in determining the adequacy of an organization's disaster-recovery plan should focus on
- a. The completeness of the plan as to facilities, operations, communications, security, and data processing.
- b. The sufficiency of the list of replacement equipment needed in event of a disaster.
- c. Whether the plan is in the planning or development stage.
- d. The role of the internal auditing department in developing and testing the plan.

**296.** Which of the following would an internal auditor review to evaluate the recovery capabilities of a database management system?
- a. Data journaling procedures.
- b. Edit and validation rules.
- c. Data ownership and accountability policies.
- d. Integrity checking procedures.

**297.** Your firm has recently converted its purchasing cycle from a manual process to an online computer system. Which of the following is a probable result associated with conversion to the new automatic system?
- a. Processing errors are increased.
- b. The nature of the firm's risk exposure is reduced.
- c. Processing time is increased.
- d. Traditional duties are less segregated.

**298.** To determine whether there have been any unauthorized program changes since the last authorized program update, the **best** IT audit technique is for the auditor to conduct a(n)
- a. Code comparison.
- b. Code review.
- c. Test data run.
- d. Analytical review.

**299.** Which of the following is the **most** appropriate activity for an internal auditor to perform during a review of systems development activity?
- a. Serve on the IT steering committee that determines what new systems is to be developed.
- b. Review the methodology used to monitor and control the system development function.
- c. Recommend specific automated procedures to be incorporated into new systems that will provide reasonable assurance that all data submitted to an application is converted to machine-readable form.
- d. Recommend specific operational procedures that will ensure that all data submitted for processing is converted to machine-readable form.

**300.** A hospital is evaluating the purchase of software to integrate a new cost accounting system with its existing financial accounting system. Which of the following describes the **most** effective way for internal audit to be involved in the procurement process?
- a. Evaluate whether performance specifications are consistent with the hospital's needs.
- b. Evaluate whether the application design meets internal development and documentation standards.
- c. Determine whether the prototyped model is validated and reviewed with users before production use begins.
- d. Internal audit has no involvement since the system has already been developed externally.

**301.** In some audits of computer applications, it is appropriate to review the program code to determine whether it satisfies its processing objectives. The code reviewed is the
- a. Object code.
- b. Source code.
- c. Hash code.
- d. Access code.

**302.** Assuming that the internal audit staff possesses the necessary experience and training, which of the following services is appropriate for a staff internal auditor to undertake?
- a. Substitute for the accounts payable supervisor while he is out on sick leave.
- b. Determine the profitability of alternative investment acquisitions and select the best alternative.

- c. As part of an evaluation team review, vendor accounting software internal controls and rank according to exposures.
- d. Participate in an internal audit of the accounting department shortly after transferring from the accounting department.

**303.** The internal auditor can participate in the review of the systems development process at varying intervals including continuous involvement, only at the end of discrete stages, or after implementation of the system. The advantages of continuous internal audit involvement include all of the following **except:**
- a. Improved design and specification of controls.
- b. The opportunity to provide significant suggestions to the design team.
- c. Reduced need for subsequent rework of controls.
- d. Reduced overall internal audit expense when compared to the other intervals.

**304.** An internal auditor is preparing procedures to verify the integrity of data in a database application. The best source of information for the auditor to determine data field definitions is the
- a. Data subschemas.
- b. Data dictionary.
- c. Data definition language.
- d. Data manipulation language.

**305.** An activity appropriately performed by internal auditing is
- a. Designing systems of control.
- b. Drafting procedures for systems of control.
- c. Reviewing systems of control before implementation.
- d. Installing systems of control.

**306.** The internal auditing department was not involved in a major system conversion in which customer records for $100,000 of receivables were lost. Which of the following internal auditing roles would help prevent such losses in the future?
- a. Management of the conversion process.
- b. Performance of a feasibility study.
- c. Involvement in all phases of the system development life cycle.
- d. Use of an integrated test facility.

**307.** The major reason for the internal auditor's involvement in IT system development is for the internal auditor to
- a. Gain familiarity with systems for use in subsequent reviews.
- b. Help assure that systems have adequate control procedures.
- c. Help minimize the cost and development time for new systems.
- d. Propose enhancements for subsequent development and implementation.

**308.** In an audit of a database management system (DBMS), the auditor is concerned about the potential for irregularities in general (integrity) controls. Because of the unique operating characteristics of a DBMS, the irregularity most likely stems from
- a. Unauthorized access to data elements.
- b. Unavailability of data for all applications.

c. Data elements being application owned.
d. Data manipulation by the DBMS.

**309.** By changing the source code, a computer operator of a large mainframe computer added $1,000 to the amount that was paid on a check to a certain vendor. The change was later reversed. The operator then received a kickback from the vendor. Which of the following audit procedures is **most** likely to detect the change to source code?
a. Review of the master copy of source code.
b. Analysis of all program change procedures automatically logged by the computer.
c. Financial ratio analysis of accounts payable.
d. Tests of the existing object code.

**310.** Which of the following techniques is the **most** practical one to detect unauthorized changes to programs?
a. Implement computer program access controls.
b. Comparing production programs with independently controlled copies on a regular basis.
c. Reviewing source code and logic program documentation on a regular basis.
d. Observing activities of computer operators on a surprise basis.

**311.** Employing which of the following can prevent unauthorized alteration of online records?
a. Key verification.
b. Computer sequence checks.
c. Computer matching.
d. Database access controls.

**312.** Passwords for microcomputer software programs are designed to prevent
a. Inaccurate processing of data.
b. Unauthorized access to the computer.
c. Incomplete updating of data files.
d. Unauthorized use of the software.

**313.** A large organization relies on comprehensive user controls over stand-alone microcomputer usage and wishes to gain some assurance as to the control structure over microcomputer-based processing. Which of the following audit strategies is **most** appropriate?
a. Perform tests of user controls.
b. Perform edit tests of data entered into key applications.
c. Perform comprehensive tests of software licensing procedures.
d. Perform substantive tests of executed program logic.

**314.** An internal auditor downloads the invoices, payments, and payables for goods received for the prior month to an audit workstation. The **best** approach for verifying the completeness of the data is for the auditor to use audit software on the workstation to
a. Match invoices to payments; match payments to invoices.
b. Match invoices to payables; match payables to invoices.
c. Match invoices to payments and payables; match payments and payables to invoices.
d. Match invoices to payments; match payments and payables to invoices.

**315.** An internal auditor is reviewing the adequacy of existing policies and procedures concerning end-user computing (EUC) activities. The auditor is testing
a. An application control.
b. An organizational control.
c. An environmental control.
d. A system control.

**316.** The total interruption of processing throughout a distributed IT system is minimized by a control or concept referred to as
a. The system log.
b. Fail-soft protection.
c. Backup and recovery.
d. Data file security.

**317.** An audit procedure for evaluating whether an online order entry system is efficient is to
a. Review copies of weekly and monthly reports that show system availability (uptime) and terminal response times, and compare with service-level objectives.
b. Determine the total number of transactions processed by the system for each of the previous twelve months and note any fluctuations.
c. Compare the cost of processing the orders manually with the cost of the online system.
d. Compare the cost of developing the order entry system with the cost of developing other applications.

**318.** Using test data, an auditor has processed both normal and atypical transactions through a computerized payroll system to test calculation of regular and overtime hours. Sufficient competent evidence of controls exists if
a. No other tests are performed.
b. Test data results are compared to predetermined expectations.
c. Exceptions are mapped to identify the control logic executed.
d. Test result data are tagged to instigate creation of an audit data file.

**319.** Your firm has recently converted its purchasing cycle from a manual to an online computer system. You have been placed in charge of the first postimplementation audit of the new system and have access to a generalized audit software package. One of your objectives is to determine whether all material liabilities for trade accounts payable have been recorded. Which of the following would **most** help you achieve this objective?
a. A listing of all purchase transactions processed after the cutoff date.
b. A listing of all accounts payable ledger accounts with a post office box given as the vendor mailing address.
c. A listing of all duplicates: (1) purchase orders, (2) receiving reports, and (3) vendor invoices.
d. A listing of all vendors with a debit balance in the accounts payable ledgers.

**320.** When computer-matching the employee master file against the payroll transaction file (consisting of time records for each hourly production worker and overtime records for salaried staff), the auditor is essentially testing for the

a. Existence of payments to fictitious employees.
b. Completeness of overtime records.
c. Reasonableness of production worker's pay rates.
d. Reasonableness of staff salaries.

**321.** Erroneous management decisions might be the result of incomplete information. The **best** control to detect a failure to process all valid transactions is
a. Periodic user submission of test data.
b. User review of selected output and transactions rejected by edit checks.
c. Controlled output distribution.
d. Decollation of output.

**322.** Bank tellers might use authorized teller terminals to conceal overdrafts in their personal checking accounts by transferring funds to and from customers' accounts. The **best** control to detect the tellers' unauthorized actions is requiring
a. Supervisor-only authorization for transfers between the bank's customers.
b. Overnight balancing of all accounts by the online teller system.
c. Periodic examination of accounts of employees with access to teller functions.
d. Annual vacations for employees with access to teller functions.

**323.** To ensure the completeness of a file update, the user department retains copies of all unnumbered documents submitted for processing and checks these off individually against a report of transactions processed. This is an example of the use of
a. Established batch totals.
b. One-for-one checking.
c. Computer sequence checks.
d. Computer matching.

**324.** A manufacturing company buys many different types and dimensions of steel for use in production. An internal auditor would most likely use a computer simulation to evaluate the company's steel-purchasing function with respect to
a. Technical specifications adopted for steel purchases.
b. Economy with which the warehousing function is carried out.
c. Effect of alternative purchasing policies on investment in inventory and stock-out costs.
d. Quality of the computer program used to determine economic order quantities.

**325.** Rejection of unauthorized modifications to application systems could be accomplished through the use of
a. Programmed checks.
b. Batch controls.
c. Implementation controls.
d. One-for-one checking.

**326.** The best control for detecting processed data totals that do not agree with input totals is
a. Run-to-run checking.
b. Existence checking.
c. Key verification.
d. Prerecorded inputs.

**327.** Which of the following controls would be **most** efficient in reducing common data input errors?
a. Keystroke verification.
b. A set of well-designed edit checks.
c. Balancing and reconciliation.
d. Batch totals.

**328.** To ensure that a computer file is accurately updated in total for a particular field, the **best** control is
a. Computer matching.
b. Check digit.
c. Transaction log.
d. Run-to-run totals.

**329.** To ensure that a particular data field is properly maintained, manual postings of batch totals for that field to a control account
a. Are of no value in file maintenance.
b. Should be periodically compared to the computer master file.
c. Stand alone as a control.
d. Should be used in combination with hash totals.

**330.** Expert systems consist of
a. Software packages with the ability to make judgment decisions.
b. A panel of outside consultants.
c. Hardware designed to make judgment decisions.
d. Hardware and software used to automate routine tasks.

## Compliance Audit Engagements

**331.** Audits vary in their degree of objectivity. Of the following, which is likely to be the **most** objective?
a. Compliance audit of company's overtime policy.
b. Operational audit of the personnel function hiring and firing procedures.
c. Performance audit of the marketing department.
d. Financial control audit over payroll procedures.

**332.** An auditor is experienced in air-quality issues. While interviewing the manager of a small environmental, safety, and health (ESH) department, the auditor discovers that there is a significant lack of knowledge about legal requirements for controlling air emissions. The auditor should
a. Alter the scope of the audit to focus on activities associated with air emissions.
b. Share the auditor's extensive knowledge with the ESH manager.
c. Take note of the weakness and direct additional questions to help determine the potential effect of the lack of knowledge.
d. Report potential violations in this area to the appropriate regulatory agency.

**333.** Much nonprofit organization fund-raising is done over the telephone. Which of the following control procedures would be **least** effective in gaining assurance that all of the pledges made by telephone are recorded and designated for payment to the organization?
a. Periodic monitoring of phone calls by management personnel.
b. Management reports that compare funds raised this year with funds raised last year on a per-call basis.

c. A confirmation program that randomly selects donations received and confirms the amounts with the donors.

d. Automatic computer recording of all phone calls, coupled with supervisory monitoring of randomly selected phone calls.

**334.** Which of the following control procedures would provide the **greatest** assurance that all donations to a nonprofit organization are immediately deposited to the organization's account?

a. Use a lockbox to receive all donations.

b. Perform periodic internal audits of the organization's cash receipts by tracing deposits to the original posting in the cash receipts records.

c. Require that all donations be made by check.

d. Require issuance of a confirmation receipt to all donors, with the receipt issued by the person who opens and deposits the cash receipts.

**335.** A potential problem facing many nonprofit organizations is public skepticism over the use of funds. For example, there have been instances in which funds were used to support a lavish lifestyle of the organization's president or used to support political causes rather than actual research. Which of the following would be the **least** effective control procedure to address these concerns?

a. Periodic presentation of audited financial statements for review by the public and major donors.

b. Board of directors' review and approval required for all expenditures in excess of a specified dollar amount.

c. Periodic internal audit of expenditures to determine compliance with stated objectives, with the results reported to the audit committee.

d. Periodic payroll audits by the internal auditor to determine compliance with authorized pay rates.

**336.** As part of cash management procedures, the treasurer of a nonprofit organization has decided to invest in a variety of new financial instruments. The audit committee has asked the internal audit department to conduct an audit of the adequacy of controls over the new investing techniques. Which of the following would **not** be required as part of such an audit?

a. Determine if policies exist that describe the risks the treasurer may take and the types of instruments in which the treasurer may make investments.

b. Determine the extent of management oversight over investments in sophisticated instruments.

c. Determine whether the treasurer is getting higher or lower rates of return on investments than are treasurers in comparable organizations.

d. Determine the nature of controls established by the treasurer to monitor the risks in the investments.

**337.** Contributions to a nonprofit organization have been constant for the past three years. The audit committee has become concerned that the president may have embarked on a scheme in which some of the contributions from many sustaining members have been redirected to other organizations. The audit committee suspects that the scheme may involve taking major contributions and depositing them in alternative accounts or soliciting contributions to be made in the name of another organization. Which of the following

audit procedures would be **most** effective in detecting the existence of such a fraud?

a. Use generalized audit software to take a sample of pledged receipts not yet collected and confirm the amounts due with the donors.

b. Take a sample that includes all large donors for the past three years and a statistical sample of others, and request a confirmation of total contributions made to the organization or to affiliated organizations.

c. Take a discovery sample of cash receipts and confirm the amounts of the receipts with the donors. Investigate any differences.

d. Use analytical review procedures to compare contributions generated with those of other comparable institutions over the same period of time. If the amount is significantly less, take a detailed sample of cash receipts and trace to the bank statements.

**Items 338 through 340** are based on the following:

The internal auditors of a financial institution are auditing the institution's investing and lending activities. During the last year, the institution has adopted new policies and procedures for monitoring investments and the loan portfolio. The auditors know that the organization has invested in new types of financial instruments during the year and is heavily involved in the use of financial derivatives to appropriately hedge risks.

**338.** If the auditors were to perform a preliminary review, which of the following procedures should be performed?

a. Review reports of audits performed by regulatory and outside auditors since the last internal audit.

b. Interview management to identify changes made in policies regarding investments or loans.

c. Review minutes of the board of directors' meetings to identify changes in policies affecting investments and loans.

d. All of the above.

**339.** The auditors are evaluating the adequacy of the new policies and procedures in maintaining an appropriate risk profile. Which of the following audit procedures would be **least** relevant to the accomplishment of the audit objective?

a. Meet with operational management to determine its interpretation of those procedures that are not clear.

b. Meet with top management or a board member, if necessary, to clarify policy issues.

c. Test a sample of investments for compliance with the new procedures.

d. Review recent regulatory pronouncements to determine if the new procedures are consistent with regulatory requirements.

**340.** The audit committee has expressed concern that the financial institution has been taking on higher-risk loans in pursuit of short-term profit goals. Which of the following audit procedures would provide the **least** amount of information to address this audit concern?

a. Perform an analytical review of interest income as a percentage of the investment portfolio in comparison with a group of peer financial institutions.

b. Take a random sample of loans made during the period and compare the riskiness of the loans with that of a random sample of loans made two years ago.

c. Perform an analytical review that involves developing a chart to compare interest income plotted over the past ten years.

d. Develop a multiple-regression time-series analysis of income over the past five years, including such factors as interest rate in the economy, size of loan portfolio, and dollar amount of new loans each year.

**341.** During an operational audit, an auditor observes a large number of aboveground storage containers and a large amount of black emissions from a company smokestack. The organization has an environmental safety department. The audit engagement is not designed to consider environmental concerns. The best course of audit action would be to

a. Make a note to consider environmental risk concerns when developing the audit plan for the next year, but do not expand the scope of the existing audit since the budget and risk priorities are already set.

b. Report the observations to the audit committee and seek their advice on whether the audit should be expanded for the environmental audit.

c. Document the observations and report them to the environmental safety department. Determine if their response will be timely, and follow up to determine if they have taken timely action.

d. Inquire of local management as to the use of the storage tanks in order to determine if they are properly classified as an asset. Do not take action on the environmental issues because the auditor is untrained in the area, and such action is the responsibility of an already existing department.

**Items 342 through 345** are based on the following:

A Certified Internal Auditor directs the audit function for a large city and is planning the audit schedule for the next year. The city has a number of different funds, some that are restricted in use by government grants and some that require compliance reports to the government. One of the programs for which the city has received a grant is job retraining and placement. The grant specifies certain conditions a participant in the program must meet in order to be eligible for the funding.

**342.** In some countries, governmental units have established audit standards. For example, in the United States, the General Accounting Office has developed standards for the conduct of governmental audits, particularly those that relate to compliance with government grants. In performing governmental grant compliance audits, the auditor should

a. Be guided only by the governmental standards.

b. Be guided only by the IIA Standards because they are more encompassing.

c. Be guided by the more general standards that have been issued by the public accounting profession.

d. Follow both the IIA *Standards* and any additional governmental standards.

**343.** The auditor randomly selects participants in the job retraining program for the past year to verify that they had

met all the eligibility requirements. This type of audit is best referred to as a(n)

a. Compliance audit.

b. Operational audit.

c. Economy and efficiency audit.

d. Program audit.

**344.** The auditor plans an audit of the job retraining program to verify that the program complies with applicable grant provisions. One of the provisions is that the city adopt a budget for the program and subsequently follow procedures to ensure that the budget is adhered to and that only allowable costs are charged to the program. In performing an audit of compliance with this provision, the auditor should perform all of the following procedures **except:**

a. Determine that the budget was reviewed and approved by supervisory personnel within the city.

b. Determine that the budget was reviewed and approved by supervisory personnel within the granting agency.

c. Select a sample of expenditures to determine that the expenditures are (1) properly classified as to type; (2) appropriate to the program; and (3) designed to meet the program's objectives.

d. Compare actual results with budgeted results and determine the reason for deviations. Determine if appropriate officials have approved such deviations.

**345.** The auditor must determine the applicable laws and regulations. Which of the following procedures would be the **least** effective in learning about the applicable laws and regulations?

a. Make inquiries of the city's chief financial officer, legal counsel, or grant administrators.

b. Review prior year working papers and inquire of officials as to changes.

c. Review applicable grant agreements.

d. Discuss the matter with the audit committee and make inquiries as to the nature of the requirements and the audit committee's objectives for the audit.

**346.** A manufacturing firm uses hazardous materials in production of its products. An audit of these hazardous materials may include

I. Recommending an environmental management system as a part of policies and procedures.

II. Verifying the existence of cradle-to-grave (creation to destruction) tracking records for these materials.

III. Using consultants to avoid self-incrimination of the firm in the event illegalities were detected in an environmental audit.

IV. Evaluating the cost provided for in an environmental liability accrual account.

a. II only.

b. I and II only.

c. I, II, and IV.

d. III and IV.

**347.** Obsolete or scrap materials are charged to a predefined project number. The material is segregated into specified bin locations and eventually transported to a public auction for sale. In order to reduce the risks associated with this process a company would employ which of the following procedures?

I. Require managerial approval for material to be declared scrap or obsolete.

II. Permit employees to purchase obsolete or scrap material prior to auction.

III. Limit obsolete or scrap material sales to a preapproved buyer.

IV. Specify that a fixed fee, rather than a commission, be paid to the auction firm.

    a. II and III.
    b. I only.
    c. II and IV.
    d. I, III, and IV.

**348.** A primary concern of an operational audit of the family welfare department of a governmental unit would be
    a. Determining that proper measures of performances are used.
    b. Generating an adequate return on investment.
    c. Adhering to generally accepted accounting principles (GAAP).
    d. Ensuring that persons with direct client contact have at least a bachelor's degree.

**349.** In a comprehensive audit of a not-for-profit activity, an internal auditor would be primarily concerned with the
    a. Extent of compliance with policies and procedures.
    b. Procedures related to the budgeting process.
    c. Extent of achievement of the organization's mission.
    d. Accuracy of reports on the source and use of funds.

**Items 350 through 355** are based on the following:

The legislative auditing bureau of a country is required to perform compliance auditing of companies that are issued defense contracts on a cost-plus basis. Contracts are clearly written defining acceptable costs, including developmental research cost and appropriate overhead rates.

During the past year, the government has engaged in extensive outsourcing of its activities. The outsourcing included contracts to run cafeterias, provide janitorial services, manage computer operations and systems development, and provide engineering of construction projects. The contracts were modeled after those that had been used for years in the defense industry. The legislative auditors are being called on to expand their audit effort to include compliance audits of these contracts.

Upon initial investigation of these outsourced areas, the auditor found many areas in which the outsourced management has apparently expanded its authority and responsibility. For example, the contractor that manages computer operations has developed a highly sophisticated security program that may represent the most advanced information security in the industry. The auditor reviews the contract and sees reference only to providing appropriate levels of computing security. The auditor suspects that the governmental agency may be incurring developmental costs that the outsourcer may use for competitive advantage in marketing services to other organizations.

**350.** Regarding the audit finding of an advanced computing security system, what is the **most** appropriate course of action by the auditor?
    a. Estimate the amount of cost used to develop the advanced security system and inform the outsourcer that it will be a disallowed cost.

    b. Exclude the finding from the audit report because the contract was vague and the level of security is clearly acceptable.
    c. Estimate the added cost, report it to management, and suggest that management meet with its lawyers and the outsourcer to resolve differences.
    d. Compare the cost with previous costs incurred by governmental operations and inform the outsourcer that the difference will be a disallowed cost.

**351.** The auditor wishes to estimate the additional cost of the added security. Which of the following procedures would be the best first step in providing that evidence? Compare the total costs of computer security under the new contract with the total computer security costs
    a. Previously incurred.
    b. Previously incurred, as a percent of total cost incurred.
    c. Of other governmental entities of similar size.
    d. Of each other entity managed by this outsourcer.

**352.** Assuming that a high degree of security is needed, which of the following potential sources of evidence would also be relevant to the auditor's assessment of whether the governmental unit is being charged for computer security that exceeds the entity's needs?

I. Comparison of the security system with best practices implemented for similar systems.

II. Comparison of the security system with recent publications on state of the art systems.

III. Tests of the functionality of the security system.

    a. II only.
    b. I and II only.
    c. III only.
    d. I, II, and III.

**353.** The auditor is concerned whether all the debits to the computer security expense account are appropriate expenditures. The **most** appropriate audit procedure would be to
    a. Take an attribute sample of computing invoices and determine whether all invoices are properly classified.
    b. Perform an analytical review comparing the amount of expenditures incurred this year with the amounts incurred on a trend line for the past five years.
    c. Take an attribute sample of employee wage expenses incurred by the outsourcing company and trace to the proper account classification.
    d. Take a sample of all debits to the account and investigate by examining source documents to determine the nature and authority of the expenditure.

**354.** Management has asked the auditor to recommend monitoring controls that management could establish to provide timely oversight of the information systems contract. Which of the following would be the **least** effective monitoring control?
    a. Require monthly internal reports summarizing overhead rates used in billings.
    b. Require monthly reports by the outsourcer of total costs billed and services rendered.
    c. Use internal auditors to investigate the appropriateness of costs as part of a yearly audit of the outsourcer.

d. Randomly investigate selected cost accounts throughout the year to determine that all the expenses are properly charged to the governmental unit.

**355.** Assume the auditor investigates and finds that the company providing the computing services is clearly performing research and development activities and charging the governmental entity for those activities because it is experimenting with implementing the security techniques on the governmental entity. Which of the following statements are correct?

I. Fraud must exhibit intentional deception.
II. Determining whether this is a violation of contract terms is a legal function, not an audit function.
III. It would be fraud only if the outsourcer had implemented similar security measures at other entities.

a. I only.
b. II only.
c. I and II only.
d. I, II, and III.

**Items 356 through 360** are based on the following:

A company has two manufacturing facilities. Each facility has two manufacturing processes and a separate packaging process. The processes are similar at both facilities. Raw materials used include aluminum, materials to make plastic, various chemicals, and solvents. Pollution occurs at several operational stages, including raw materials handling and storage, process chemical use, finished goods handling, and disposal. Waste products produced during the manufacturing processes include several that are considered hazardous. The nonhazardous waste is transported to the local landfill. An outside waste vendor is used for the treatment, storage, and disposal of all hazardous waste.

Management is aware of the need for compliance with environmental laws. The company recently developed an environmental policy that includes a statement that each employee is responsible for compliance with environmental laws.

**356.** Management is evaluating the need for an environmental audit program. Which one of the following should **not** be included as an overall program objective?
a. Conduct site assessments at both facilities.
b. Verify company compliance with all environmental laws.
c. Evaluate waste minimization opportunities.
d. Ensure management systems are adequate to minimize future environmental risks.

**357.** If the internal auditing department is assigned the responsibility of conducting an environmental audit, which of the following actions should be performed first?
a. Conduct risk assessments for each site.
b. Review company policies and procedures.
c. Provide the assigned staff with technical training.
d. Review the environmental management system.

**358.** An advantage of conducting environmental audits under the direction of the internal auditing department would be that
a. Independence and authority are already in place.
b. Technical expertise is more readily available.

c. The financial aspects are deemphasized.
d. Internal audit work products are confidential.

**359.** In many countries, the company generating hazardous waste is responsible for the waste from cradle to grave (creation to destruction). A potential risk to the company is the use of an outside vendor to process hazardous waste. Which of the following steps should be performed during a review of the waste vendor?
a. Review the vendor's documentation on hazardous material.
b. Review the financial solvency of the vendor.
c. Review the vendor's emergency response planning.
d. All of the above.

**360.** Management is exploring different ways of reducing or preventing pollution in manufacturing operations. The objective of a pollution prevention audit is to identify opportunities where waste can be minimized and pollution can be eliminated at the source rather than controlled at the end of a process. In what order should the following opportunities to reduce waste be considered?

I. Recycle and reuse.
II. Elimination at the source.
III. Energy conservation.
IV. Recovery as a usable product.
V. Treatment.

a. V, II, IV, I, and III.
b. IV, II, I, III, and V.
c. I, III, IV, II, and V.
d. III, IV, II, V, and I.

**Items 361 and 362** are based on the following:

The auditor of a bank is examining the bank's loan portfolio to determine whether it is in accordance with applicable governmental regulations that

- Limit the amount of loans that can be made to the ten largest customers (as a percent of total bank loans)
- Restrict the amount of loans that can be made in certain industries
- Require additional documentation for all loans over $100,000

The auditor wants to determine whether (1) there are any violations of the applicable regulations, and (2) the system and its control procedures are adequate to prevent violations of the applicable regulations.

**361.** Which of the following audit procedures ought to be included as part of the audit program to address the specific audit concerns identified above?
a. Send confirmations to the ten largest customers to determine the collectibility of the account balances.
b. Select a random sample of all loans over $100,000 and examine supporting documentation to determine if the documentation is in compliance with the applicable regulations.
c. Use audit software to prepare an aging of the loans receivable to determine if a proper allowance for uncollectible accounts has been recorded.
d. All of the above.

**362.** During the audit, the auditor's preliminary evidence indicates that the first concern (loans to the ten largest customers) is not violated. However, upon further investigation of related parties and interlocking organizations, the auditor concludes that although there is not a technical violation, there is some likelihood that the bank may be in violation of the regulation because of loans to a number of related entities that in total exceeds the legal limits. The auditor should

a. Report the findings immediately to management and suggest that legal counsel review the regulations and the audit evidence gathered to date to determine if a violation has taken place.
b. Informally notify management of the finding, but omit any mention of the problem in the formal audit report because the evidence is not persuasive.
c. Report the findings to the regulatory agency and obtain its opinion on whether there is a violation. Include the agency's opinion in the final audit report.
d. Immediately issue an informal report to the audit committee because the findings reflect adversely on management.

**Items 363 through 366** are based on the following:

An international nonprofit organization finances medical research. The majority of its revenue and support comes from fundraising activities, investments, and specific grants from an initial sponsoring corporation. The organization has been in operation over fifteen years and has a small internal audit department. The organization has just finished a major fundraising drive that raised $500 million for the current fiscal period.

The following are selected data from recent financial statements:

|  | Current year | Past year |
|---|---|---|
| Revenue (in millions) | $500 | $425 |
| Investments (average balances) | $210 | $185 |
| Medical research grants made | $418 | $325 |
| Investment income | $16 | $20 |
| Administrative expense | $10 | $8 |

**363.** The auditor wishes to determine if the change in investment income during the current year was due to (1) changes in investment strategy, (2) changes in portfolio mix, or (3) other factors. Which of the following analytical review procedures should the auditor use?

a. Simple linear regression, which compares investment income changes over the past five years to determine the nature of the changes.
b. Ratio analysis, which compares changes in the investment portfolio on a monthly basis.
c. Trend analysis, which compares the changes in investment income as a percentage of total assets and of investment assets over the past five years.
d. Multiple regression analysis, which includes independent variables related to the nature of the investment portfolio and market conditions.

**364.** Auditors must always be alert for the possibility of fraud. Assume the controls over each risk listed below are marginal. Which of the following possible frauds or misuses of organization assets should be considered the area of **greatest** risk?

a. The president is using company travel and entertainment funds for activities that might be considered questionable.

b. Purchases of supplies are made from fictitious vendors.
c. Grants are made to organizations that might be associated with the president or are not for purposes dictated in the organization's charter.
d. The payroll clerk has added ghost employees.

**365.** Assume the auditor finds a number of instances in which travel and entertainment reimbursements going to the president seem excessive and inconsistent with the charter of the organization. Before an audit report is issued, a front-page article appears in a major financial newspaper alleging that the president has been using the organization's funds for personal purposes. The auditor has enough information to confirm the allegations made in the newspaper article. The auditor is called by the newspaper and by a financial magazine in an attempt to confirm the facts. Which of the following would be the **best** response by the auditor?

a. Respond truthfully and fully since the auditor is in a position to confirm the facts that concern the president, not the organization.
b. Direct the inquiry to the audit committee or the board of directors.
c. Provide information off the record so that the article does not state who gave the information.
d. Respond that the investigation is not complete.

**366.** During an examination of grants awarded, the auditor discovered a number of grants made without the approval of the grant authorization committee (which includes outside representatives), as required by the organization's charter. All the grants, however, were approved and documented by the president. The chairperson of the grant authorization committee, who is also a member of the board of directors, proposes that the committee meets and retroactively approves all the grants before the audit report is issued. If the committee meets and approves the grants before the issuance of the audit report, the auditor should

a. Not report the grants in question because they were approved before the issuance of the audit report.
b. Discuss the matter with the chairperson of the grant committee to determine the rationale for not approving the grants earlier. If they are routine grants, then omit discussion in the audit report.
c. Include the items in the report as a breakdown of the organization's controls. Detail the nature of each grant and investigate further for fraud.
d. Report the breakdown in control structure to the audit committee.

**367.** In audit planning, internal auditors should review all relevant information. Which of the following sources of information would **most** likely help identify suspected violations of environmental regulations?

a. Discussions with operating executives.
b. Review of trade publications.
c. Review of correspondence the entity has conducted with governmental agencies.
d. Discussions conducted with the external auditors in coordinating audit efforts.

**368.** During an audit of environmental protection devices at a hazardous materials research center, the auditor has reviewed the architect's alarm device specifications, examined invoices for the devices, and interviewed the plant safety officer responsible for installation. The main concern of these procedures is assurance that

    a.   The alarm system actually works.
    b.   The specified alarm system design is adequate.
    c.   The specified alarm system was purchased and installed.
    d.   The alarm system meets statutory requirements.

**369.** A local government agency received a national government grant that provided funds for assisting families with low incomes. The agency is required to make an investigation of the family's financial condition. The amount of assistance relates to the size of the family, income being received by family members, and the ages and school attendance of family children. The agency's internal auditors plan to perform a compliance audit of the agency's operation in disbursing the grant funds. The **most** appropriate scope of the audit would be to determine

    a.   If the agency is investigating the eligibility of beneficiaries and the propriety of fund disbursement.
    b.   The degree of efficiency the agency is achieving in the disbursement of national funds.
    c.   The accuracy of the disbursement reports furnished to the national government.
    d.   The adequacy of the funds to relieve the family's financial problem.

**370.** The **primary** audit objective for a compliance audit of restricted funds at a government-supported university would be the determination of

    a.   Compliance with accepted accounting principles.
    b.   Adequacy of the institution's budget process.
    c.   Accuracy of financial reports.
    d.   Approval for expenditure of restricted funds.

**371.** In a comprehensive audit of a not-for-profit activity, an internal auditor would be **primarily** concerned with the

    a.   Extent of compliance with policies and procedures.
    b.   Procedures related to the budgeting process.
    c.   Extent of achievement of the organization's mission.
    d.   Accuracy of reports on the source and use of funds.

**372.** In an audit of a nonprofit organization's special fund, the **primary** audit objective would be to determine if the entity

    a.   Complied with existing fund requirements and performed specified activities.
    b.   Managed its resources economically and efficiently.
    c.   Prepared its financial statements in accordance with generally accepted accounting principles.
    d.   Applied the funds in a way that would benefit the greatest number of people.

**373.** Senior management has requested a compliance audit of the company's employee benefits package. Which of the following audit objectives would be considered the **primary** objective by both internal audit and senior management?

    a.   The level of company contributions is adequate to meet the program's demands.
    b.   Individual programs are operating in accordance with corporate policy and government regulations.
    c.   Participation levels support continuation of individual programs.

    d.   Benefit payments, where appropriate, are accurate and timely.

**374.** A compliance audit of the reporting cycle is being planned. The auditors are specifically concerned with the control of sensitive data on quarterly reports that could be used by competitors. The distribution of sensitive financial data should be determined by

    a.   The vice president of finance.
    b.   Approved corporate policy.
    c.   The audit committee.
    d.   The data security officer.

**375.** A consultant's employees will be working on an organization's property using heavy equipment to handle potentially hazardous materials. Although it is believed that the consultant selected is technically competent, which of the following is a control that would **best** ensure that the consultant performs the work in accordance with applicable environmental, safety, and health regulations?

    a.   The contract with the consultant should require that all work be performed in accordance with applicable environmental, safety, and health regulations.
    b.   The consultant should be required to prepare and submit regular reports over the duration of the project demonstrating that employees have been trained, that they are aware of hazards, and that the work area is inspected regularly for practices potentially unsafe or harmful to the environment.
    c.   The organization should provide oversight by calling in regulatory agencies to inspect the work site and review certain records (e.g., injury and illness logs, training records, waste transfer documents), thereby providing assurance about the effectiveness of the consultant's controls.
    d.   The organization should make sure that the consultant has a current copy on site of all applicable environmental, safety, and health regulations and that all employees have read them.

**376.** A company is considering purchasing a commercial property. Because of the location of the property and the known recent history of activities on the property, management has asked the internal audit department, in cooperation with company counsel, to provide a preliminary identification of any environmental liability that may be present. The **strongest** reason supporting management's decision to request such an investigation is

    a.   The potential for future liability may outweigh any advantages achieved by obtaining the property.
    b.   Management will be able to pay a lower price for the property if environmental contamination can be identified.
    c.   The current owner would be required by law to clean up all identified contamination before the sale is closed.
    d.   Regulatory agencies require a purchaser to identify and disclose all actual and potential instances of contamination.

**377.** An internal audit department had been requested to perform an audit to determine whether the organization was in compliance with a particular set of laws and regulations. The audit did not reveal any issues of noncompliance but did reveal that the organization did not have an established system to ensure compliance with the applicable laws and regulations. The auditor's responsibility is to

I. Report that no significant compliance issues were noted.
II. Report that the organization has a significant control deficiency because management has not established a system to ensure compliance.
III. Meet with management to determine what follow-up action will be taken.
IV. Monitor to determine that follow-up action has been taken.

    a.   I only.
    b.   I and II only.
    c.   II and III only.
    d.   I, II, III, and IV.

## Conduct Consulting Engagements

**378.** In planning a system of internal operating controls, the role of the internal auditor is to
    a.   Design the controls.
    b.   Appraise the effectiveness of the controls.
    c.   Establish the policies for controls.
    d.   Create the procedures for the planning process.

**379.** The consultative approach to auditing emphasizes
    a.   Imposition of corrective measures.
    b.   Participation with auditees to improve methods.
    c.   Fraud investigation.
    d.   Implementation of policies and procedures.

**380.** Successful consultative communication in an internal audit is partially based on feedback from auditees about auditors' actions during the audit. This feedback
    a.   Should go only to senior management as a means of reviewing the auditors.
    b.   Should go only to the auditors to help them improve their audit performance.
    c.   Should go to both management and the auditors to ensure business value is being added.
    d.   Will keep auditees on the defensive regarding the auditors.

**381.** As part of the process to improve auditor-auditee relations, it is very important to deal with how internal auditing is perceived. Certain types of attitudes in the work performed will help create these perceptions. From a management perspective, which attitude is likely to be the **most** conducive to a positive perception?
    a.   Objective.
    b.   Investigative.
    c.   Interrogatory.
    d.   Consultative.

**382.** It would be appropriate for internal auditing departments to use consultants with expertise in health care benefits when the internal auditing department is
    a.   Conducting an audit of the organization's estimate of its liability for postretirement benefits that include health care benefits.
    b.   Comparing the cost of the organization's health care program with other programs offered in the industry.
    c.   Training its staff to conduct an audit of health care costs in a major division of the organization.
    d.   All of the above.

## Business Process Review

**383.** A process delivers value through all of the following items **except:**
    a.   Selling.
    b.   Quality.
    c.   Cost reduction.
    d.   Flexibility.

**384.** Which of the following structures yields greater efficiency and production and is achieved by reengineering or process redesign?
    a.   Functional organization.
    b.   Hierarchical organization.
    c.   Horizontal organization.
    d.   Vertical organization.

**385.** An organization should **not** have which of the following business process orientations?
    a.   Functional view.
    b.   Process jobs.
    c.   Process management and measures.
    d.   Process structure.

**386.** Which of the following dimensions of business process orientations is the **most** important one?
    a.   Process view.
    b.   Process jobs.
    c.   Process management and measures.
    d.   Process structure.

**387.** A radical redesign of the entire business cycle is called
    a.   Business process reengineering.
    b.   Benchmarking.
    c.   Best practices.
    d.   Business process improvement.

**388.** Cycle time can be either reduced or speeded up with
    a.   Business process reengineering.
    b.   Benchmarking.
    c.   Best practices.
    d.   Business process improvement.

**389.** "The time between when an order is placed and when it is received by the customer" is known as
    a.   Arrival time.
    b.   Order cycle time.
    c.   Shipping time.
    d.   Order time.

**390.** "The time it takes to deliver a product or service after an order is placed" is called
    a.   Order cycle time.
    b.   Customer response time.
    c.   Order process time.
    d.   Inspection time.

**391.** "The time between when an order is placed and when the order is ready for setup" is called
    a.   Order receipt time.
    b.   Order wait time.
    c.   Order process time.
    d.   Efficiency time.

**392.** "The time between when an order is ready for setup and the setup is complete" is called
    a.   Order receipt time.
    b.   Order wait time.

c. Order process time.

d. Efficiency time.

**393.** Which of the following refers to eliminating unnecessary procedures and activities in a business process?

a. Work standardization.

b. Work simplification.

c. Work customization.

d. Work measurement.

**Items 394 through 396** are based on the following:

A manufacturing company has the following estimates for a specific customer order to produce fifty toy sets:

| | |
|---|---|
| Wait time | 10 hours |
| Inspection time | 1 hour |
| Processing time | 36 hours |
| Move time | 1.5 hours |

**394.** Using these time estimates, what is the value-added time?

a. 36 hours.

b. 37 hours.

c. 38.5 hours.

d. 48.5 hours.

**395.** Using these time estimates, what is the non-value-added time?

a. 2.5 hours.

b. 10.0 hours.

c. 11.0 hours.

d. 12.5 hours.

**396.** Using these time estimates, what is the manufacturing cycle time?

a. 36.00 hours.

b. 46.00 hours.

c. 47.00 hours.

d. 48.50 hours.

**397.** Which of the following actions does **not** help in reducing the cycle time?

a. Changing from parallel flow to linear flow in a process.

b. Using alternate flow paths in a process.

c. Changing the layout of a process.

d. Using technology to improve process flow.

**398.** In reducing cycle time, speed flows from which of the following?

a. Complexity.

b. Simplicity.

c. Homogeneity.

d. Heterogeneity.

**399.** Which of the following is **not** generally associated with reducing cycle time?

a. Expanding work steps.

b. Eliminating work steps.

c. Minimizing work steps.

d. Combining work steps.

**400.** Which of the following is caused by exceeding the capacity limitation of key resources?

a. Fault points.

b. Check points.

c. Critical points.

d. Choke points.

**401.** Which of the following actions does **not** help in reducing the cycle time?

a. Eliminating process waste.

b. Creating continuous work flow.

c. Using self-managed teams.

d. Providing the right resources.

**402.** All of the following are effective ways to shorten the cycle time **except:**

a. Small lot sizes.

b. Synchronized production plans.

c. Just-in-time manufacturing.

d. "Push" production method.

**403.** An internal auditor's involvement in reengineering should include all of the following **except:**

a. Determining whether the process has senior management's support.

b. Recommending areas for consideration.

c. Developing audit plans for the new system.

d. Directing the implementation of the redesigned process.

**404.** Which of the following will allow a manufacturer with limited resources to maximize profits?

a. The Delphi technique.

b. Exponential smoothing.

c. Regression analysis.

d. Linear programming.

**405.** Reengineering is the thorough analysis, fundamental rethinking, and complete redesign of essential business processes. The intended result is a dramatic improvement in service, quality, speed, and cost. An internal auditor's involvement in reengineering should include all of the following **except:**

a. Determining whether the process has senior management's support.

b. Recommending areas for consideration.

c. Developing audit plans for the new system.

d. Directing the implementation of the redesigned process.

**406.** Auditors are operating in organizations in which management is in the process of reengineering operations with strong emphasis on total quality management techniques. In the quest to gain efficiency in processing, many of the traditional control procedures are being deleted from the organization's control structure. As part of this change, management is

a. Placing more emphasis on monitoring control activities.

b. Making different assumptions about human performance and the nature of human motivation from what was done under traditional control techniques.

c. Placing more emphasis on self-correcting control activities and process automation.

d. All of the above.

**407.** An organization has decided to reengineer several major processes. Of the following reasons for employees to resist this change, which is **least** likely?

a. Threat of loss of jobs.

b. Required attendance at training classes.

c. Breakup of existing work groups.

d. Imposition of new processes by top management without prior discussion.

## Benchmarking

**408.** Which of the following involves identifying, studying, and building on the best practices of other organizations?
a. Kaizen.
b. Benchmarking.
c. Plan, Do, Check, and Act cycle.
d. Total quality management.

**409.** Which of the following is true of benchmarking?
a. It is typically accomplished by comparing an organization's performance with the performance of its closest competitors.
b. It can be performed using either qualitative or quantitative comparisons.
c. It is normally limited to manufacturing operations and production processes.
d. It is accomplished by comparing an organization's performance to that of the best-performing organizations.

**410.** An example of an internal nonfinancial benchmark is
a. The labor rate of comparably skilled employees at a major competitor's plant.
b. The average actual cost per pound of a specific product at the company's most efficient plant becomes the benchmark for the company's other plants.
c. The company setting a benchmark of $50,000 for employee training programs at each of the company's plants.
d. The percent of customer orders delivered on time at the company's most efficient plant becomes the benchmark for the company's other plants.

**411.** A company that has many branch stores has decided to benchmark one of its stores for the purpose of analyzing the accuracy and reliability of branch store financial reporting. Which one of the following is the **most** likely measure to be included in a financial benchmark?
a. High turnover of employees.
b. High level of employee participation in setting budgets.
c. High amount of bad debt write-offs.
d. High number of suppliers.

## Information Technology and Systems Development

**412.** Systems development audits include reviews at various points to ensure that development is properly controlled and managed. The reviews should include all of the following **except:**
a. Conducting a technical feasibility study on the available hardware, software, and technical resources.
b. Examining the level of user involvement at each stage of implementation.
c. Verifying the use of controls and quality assurance techniques for program development, conversion, and testing.
d. Determining if system, user, and operations documentation conforms to formal standards.

**413.** A role of internal auditing during evaluation of a new system is to

a. Draft control procedures in cases where the development team omitted them.
b. Determine whether adequate control has been planned and implemented.
c. Document control features for the permanent system documentation file.
d. Rewrite flawed program code affecting control features.

**414.** An outside consultant is developing a system to be used for the management of a city's capital facilities. An appropriate scope of an audit of the consultant's product would be to
a. Review the consultant's contract to determine its propriety.
b. Establish the parameters of the value of the items being managed and controlled.
c. Determine the adequacy of the controls built into the system.
d. Review the handling of idle equipment.

## Performance Measurement

**415.** Which of the following is an example of an efficiency measure?
a. The rate of absenteeism.
b. The goal of becoming a leading manufacturer.
c. The number of insurance claims processed per day.
d. The rate of customer complaints.

**416.** Goal setting is an important component of motivating employees. The goal "We need to do much better than before" would **not** be appropriate because it
a. Does not take into consideration employee needs.
b. Does not specify clear, measurable, and achievable objectives.
c. Does not describe the process by which the goal will be achieved.
d. Is more a strategy than a goal.

**417.** A manager who is concerned with achieving the goals of the organization without much concern for use of resources is
a. Incompetent.
b. Focusing on effectiveness.
c. Focusing on efficiency.
d. Using a goal-setting approach to management.

**418.** Organizational productivity can be defined as the ratio of an organization's total output to its total input, adjusted for inflation, for a specified period of time. For a number of years, Japan's productivity has been held out as an example to emulate. Japan's higher productivity has been mostly attributed to
a. Abundant raw materials and excellent human and financial resources.
b. Better management and the ability to do more with less.
c. Constant refurbishing of the country's infrastructure.
d. A superior educational system that emphasizes creativity.

**419.** Which of the following directives would be **most** useful to a sales department manager in controlling and evaluating the performance of the manager's customer-service group?

a. The customer is always right.
b. Customer complaints should be processed promptly.
c. Employees should maintain a positive attitude when dealing with customers.
d. All customer inquiries should be answered within seven days of receipt.

**420.** In order to meet a deadline, a manager assigned a task to a supervisor. The task, which normally would have been performed by an absent clerk, was completed on schedule and in the same amount of time as if the clerk had done it. This scenario is an example of
a. Sacrificing efficiency for effectiveness.
b. Sacrificing effectiveness for efficiency.
c. A balanced emphasis on effectiveness and efficiency.
d. A situation that is neither efficient nor effective.

**421.** Which of the following can reflect the effectiveness of a firm's personnel department?
a. The ratio of total hiring costs to the total number of hires.
b. The ratio of employees hired at entry level in 2002 and still with the firm in 2004 to total employees hired at entry level in 2002.
c. A comparison over time of the average number of days from the date the approved vacant position requisition is received until the date the new hire starts work.
d. The ratio of the number of job offers accepted to the number of job offers extended.

**422.** Which of the following is **not** related to labor productivity measurement?
a. Work measurement.
b. Time study.
c. Work sampling.
d. Work groups.

**423.** An example of an efficiency measure in a company would be
a. The profit per dollar of sales.
b. The number of contacts a broker makes per day.
c. The percentage of raw materials placed in storage within twenty-four hours of receipt.
d. New insurance policies written by an insurance agent as a percentage of total new and renewed policies.

**424.** Of the following factors that affect efficiency, which is a group-level factor?
a. Values and attitudes.
b. Abilities.
c. Motivation.
d. Leadership.

**425.** Successful organizations are able to balance efficiency and effectiveness. Which of the following scenarios illustrates an organization out of balance by focusing too much on efficiency?
a. The job does not get done and limited resources are wasted.
b. The job gets done but limited resources are wasted.
c. The job does not get done but available resources are not wasted.

d. The job gets done and limited resources are not wasted.

**426.** Productivity is defined as the ratio of outputs of a production process to the inputs that are used. Consider a process that currently produces 2,000 units of output with 500 hours of labor per day. This process can be redesigned to produce 2,520 units of output requiring 600 labor hours per day. The percentage change in productivity from redesigning the process is
a. 5%.
b. 10%.
c. 16%.
d. 22%.

**427.** Traditionally, large manufacturers have believed that economies of scale gained through large production runs of like, or similar, products are the best way to keep production costs down and remain competitive. Select the **most** appropriate response to whether this theory is still valid.
a. Yes, larger economies of scale continue to accrue from ever-larger production runs.
b. Yes, lower per-unit costs for standard products continue to guarantee a competitive advantage.
c. No, economies of scale can no longer be gained from long production runs.
d. No, production flexibility and diversity of products are needed to remain competitive.

## MULTIPLE-CHOICE ANSWERS AND EXPLANATIONS

| | | | | | | | | | | | |
|---|---|---|---|---|---|---|---|---|---|---|---|
| 1. d | | | 63. d | | | 125. d | | | 187. c | | |
| 2. a | | | 64. b | | | 126. c | | | 188. a | | |
| 3. a | | | 65. c | | | 127. c | | | 189. a | | |
| 4. c | | | 66. b | | | 128. a | | | 190. d | | |
| 5. a | | | 67. d | | | 129. a | | | 191. d | | |
| 6. d | | | 68. d | | | 130. d | | | 192. c | | |
| 7. a | | | 69. b | | | 131. c | | | 193. b | | |
| 8. d | | | 70. a | | | 132. a | | | 194. d | | |
| 9. b | | | 71. c | | | 133. a | | | 195. a | | |
| 10. a | | | 72. a | | | 134. a | | | 196. d | | |
| 11. b | | | 73. b | | | 135. b | | | 197. d | | |
| 12. c | | | 74. c | | | 136. d | | | 198. b | | |
| 13. d | | | 75. d | | | 137. d | | | 199. b | | |
| 14. b | | | 76. b | | | 138. c | | | 200. a | | |
| 15. a | | | 77. c | | | 139. c | | | 201. a | | |
| 16. b | | | 78. c | | | 140. d | | | 202. b | | |
| 17. c | | | 79. a | | | 141. a | | | 203. b | | |
| 18. d | | | 80. a | | | 142. c | | | 204. c | | |
| 19. c | | | 81. c | | | 143. a | | | 205. c | | |
| 20. b | | | 82. c | | | 144. d | | | 206. c | | |
| 21. c | | | 83. c | | | 145. b | | | 207. c | | |
| 22. b | | | 84. d | | | 146. b | | | 208. b | | |
| 23. d | | | 85. c | | | 147. c | | | 209. d | | |
| 24. a | | | 86. a | | | 148. c | | | 210. b | | |
| 25. d | | | 87. c | | | 149. c | | | 211. c | | |
| 26. a | | | 88. d | | | 150. b | | | 212. c | | |
| 27. a | | | 89. b | | | 151. b | | | 213. c | | |
| 28. d | | | 90. d | | | 152. c | | | 214. b | | |
| 29. c | | | 91. a | | | 153. b | | | 215. | | |
| 30. d | | | 92. c | | | 154. d | | | 216. a | | |
| 31. b | | | 93. d | | | 155. d | | | 217. c | | |
| 32. a | | | 94. b | | | 156. b | | | 218. c | | |
| 33. c | | | 95. c | | | 157. c | | | 219. a | | |
| 34. c | | | 96. b | | | 158. c | | | 220. d | | |
| 35. d | | | 97. c | | | 159. b | | | 221. a | | |
| 36. d | | | 98. c | | | 160. d | | | 222. a | | |
| 37. b | | | 99. a | | | 161. a | | | 223. d | | |
| 38. a | | | 100. b | | | 162. d | | | 224. d | | |
| 39. d | | | 101. b | | | 163. a | | | 225. b | | |
| 40. c | | | 102. d | | | 164. a | | | 226. a | | |
| 41. d | | | 103. b | | | 165. a | | | 227. a | | |
| 42. b | | | 104. a | | | 166. d | | | 228. b | | |
| 43. c | | | 105. c | | | 167. a | | | 229. b | | |
| 44. d | | | 106. c | | | 168. b | | | 230. b | | |
| 45. d | | | 107. a | | | 169. b | | | 231. d | | |
| 46. a | | | 108. d | | | 170. d | | | 232. c | | |
| 47. a | | | 109. d | | | 171. b | | | 233. a | | |
| 48. a | | | 110. c | | | 172. c | | | 234. d | | |
| 49. a | | | 111. c | | | 173. a | | | 235. d | | |
| 50. a | | | 112. c | | | 174. d | | | 236. b | | |
| 51. d | | | 113. c | | | 175. b | | | 237. a | | |
| 52. d | | | 114. a | | | 176. d | | | 238. c | | |
| 53. b | | | 115. b | | | 177. c | | | 239. a | | |
| 54. c | | | 116. c | | | 178. a | | | 240. c | | |
| 55. c | | | 117. d | | | 179. c | | | 241. c | | |
| 56. a | | | 118. a | | | 180. a | | | 242. c | | |
| 57. b | | | 119. c | | | 181. b | | | 243. b | | |
| 58. a | | | 120. c | | | 182. a | | | 244. d | | |
| 59. a | | | 121. a | | | 183. b | | | 245. c | | |
| 60. b | | | 122. c | | | 184. a | | | 246. d | | |
| 61. b | | | 123. a | | | 185. d | | | 247. b | | |
| 62. d | | | 124. d | | | 186. d | | | 248. a | | |

| | | | | | |
|---|---|---|---|---|---|
| 249. d | | | 311. d | | |
| 250. d | | | 312. d | | |
| 251. a | | | 313. a | | |
| 252. b | | | 314. c | | |
| 253. a | | | 315. b | | |
| 254. d | | | 316. b | | |
| 255. b | | | 317. a | | |
| 256. a | | | 318. b | | |
| 257. c | | | 319. a | | |
| 258. b | | | 320. a | | |
| 259. d | | | 321. b | | |
| 260. c | | | 322. c | | |
| 261. c | | | 323. b | | |
| 262. b | | | 324. c | | |
| 263. c | | | 325. c | | |
| 264. d | | | 326. a | | |
| 265. d | | | 327. b | | |
| 266. b | | | 328. d | | |
| 267. c | | | 329. b | | |
| 268. b | | | 330. a | | |
| 269. b | | | 331. a | | |
| 270. b | | | 332. c | | |
| 271. a | | | 333. c | | |
| 272. d | | | 334. a | | |
| 273. d | | | 335. d | | |
| 274. b | | | 336. c | | |
| 275. b | | | 337. b | | |
| 276. d | | | 338. d | | |
| 277. d | | | 339. c | | |
| 278. c | | | 340. c | | |
| 279. b | | | 341. c | | |
| 280. d | | | 342. d | | |
| 281. b | | | 343. a | | |
| 282. c | | | 344. b | | |
| 283. b | | | 345. d | | |
| 284. a | | | 346. c | | |
| 285. c | | | 347. b | | |
| 286. a | | | 348. a | | |
| 287. b | | | 349. c | | |
| 288. c | | | 350. c | | |
| 289. a | | | 351. a | | |
| 290. d | | | 352. b | | |
| 291. d | | | 353. d | | |
| 292. a | | | 354. c | | |
| 293. c | | | 355. c | | |
| 294. c | | | 356. a | | |
| 295. a | | | 357. c | | |
| 296. a | | | 358. a | | |
| 297. d | | | 359. d | | |
| 298. a | | | 360. b | | |
| 299. b | | | 361. b | | |
| 300. a | | | 362. a | | |
| 301. b | | | 363. d | | |
| 302. c | | | 364. c | | |
| 303. d | | | 365. b | | |
| 304. b | | | 366. d | | |
| 305. c | | | 367. c | | |
| 306. c | | | 368. c | | |
| 307. b | | | 369. a | | |
| 308. a | | | 370. d | | |
| 309. b | | | 371. c | | |
| 310. b | | | 372. a | | |

| | | | | | |
|---|---|---|---|---|---|
| 373. b __ __ | 383. a __ __ | 393. b __ __ | 403. d __ __ | 413. b __ __ | 423. a __ __ |
| 374. b __ __ | 384. c __ __ | 394. a __ __ | 404. d __ __ | 414. c __ __ | 424. d __ __ |
| 375. b __ __ | 385. a __ __ | 395. d __ __ | 405. d __ __ | 415. c __ __ | 425. c __ __ |
| 376. a __ __ | 386. c __ __ | 396. d __ __ | 406. d __ __ | 416. b __ __ | 426. a __ __ |
| 377. d __ __ | 387. a __ __ | 397. a __ __ | 407. b __ __ | 417. b __ __ | 427. d __ __ |
| 378. b __ __ | 388. a __ __ | 398. b __ __ | 408. b __ __ | 418. b __ __ | |
| 379. b __ __ | 389. b __ __ | 399. a __ __ | 409. d __ __ | 419. d __ __ | |
| 380. c __ __ | 390. b __ __ | 400. d __ __ | 410. d __ __ | 420. a __ __ | |
| 381. d __ __ | 391. a __ __ | 401. c __ __ | 411. c __ __ | 421. b __ __ | 1st: __/427 =__% |
| 382. d __ __ | 392. b __ __ | 402. d __ __ | 412. a __ __ | 422. d __ __ | 2nd: __/427 =__% |

## Conduct Assurance Engagements

**1.** **(d)** This is an example of analytical procedures to detect patterns and trends. Choice (a) is incorrect. If the vendor was in collusion with the buyer, either no response or an incorrect response would be elicited. Choice (b) is incorrect. If collusion exists, the purchasing agent can arrange for the invoice. Choice (c) is incorrect. If collusion exists, the purchasing agent can arrange for the purchase order.
Subject Area: Conduct assurance engagements fraud investigation. Source: CIA 591, II-47.

**2.** **(a)** Verifying the beginning balance one month to the ending balance of the prior month is a good quick-change analysis that would catch this diversion. Choice (b) is incorrect. This is not always possible or desired and not necessarily cost justified. Choices (c) and (d) are incorrect. Rumors as to personal finances may be unfounded, and they may be illegal to check out without the employee's knowledge.
Subject Area: Conduct assurance engagements fraud investigation. Source: CIA 591, II-48.

**3.** **(a)** Control is the principal mechanism for the deterrence of fraud. Management, in turn, is primarily responsible for the establishment and maintenance of control. Internal auditors are primarily responsible for the examination and evaluation of the adequacy and effectiveness of actions taken by management in the fulfillment of their obligation. Choice (b) is incorrect. Establishing the system of internal controls for an operating division is a management responsibility. Choice (c) is incorrect. The planning and execution of an operating division's activities are the responsibility of management. Choice (d) is incorrect. Management is primarily responsible for the establishment and maintenance of control.
Subject Area: Conduct assurance engagements fraud investigation. Source: CIA 591, II-50.

**4.** **(c)** Taking an annual physical inventory should lead to the identification of systematic shrinkages in the inventory. The pattern should lead to the pattern of products purchased by the purchasing agent. At that time, a fraud investigation should take place. Choice (a) is incorrect. This would not identify the fraud, since the warehouseman updated the perpetual inventory records before forwarding the receiving report to accounts payable. Choice (b) is incorrect. Taking a sample of purchase orders would not reveal any differences since all the goods were ordered and the perpetrators colluded to make up receiving reports even when the goods were diverted to another location. Choice (d) is incorrect. Sales made would indicate that inventory was on hand. However, potential problems should

have been identified earlier by sales or shipping personnel and would assist the auditor in the investigation.
Subject Area: Conduct assurance engagements fraud investigation. Source: CIA 595, I-68.

**5.** **(a)** Since the parties confessed to the auditor, it should become part of the audit working papers related to the investigation. It is important to have the confession properly recorded, thus it is best that it be reviewed and signed by the perpetrators. Choice (b) is incorrect. The auditor should document the findings because they are an important part of the audit. Choice (c) is incorrect. The confession should be documented. Choice (d) is incorrect. The auditor is not a legal authority. The auditor has no basis on which to inform the perpetrators of their rights. The decision on whether to call in the legal authorities rests with management, not the auditors.
Subject Area: Conduct assurance engagements fraud investigation. Source: CIA 595, I-69.

**6.** **(d)** Based on the knowledge resulting from the audit, the auditor can recommend appropriate further steps. Choice (a) is incorrect. The activity of determining the loss could alert the perpetrator of the fraud, who could destroy or compromise evidence. Choices (b) and (c) are incorrect. This would be done during the fraud investigation phase and may not be done by the internal auditor.
Subject Area: Conduct assurance engagements fraud investigation. Source: CIA 1194, I-10.

**7.** **(a)** The audit director should be informed before pursuing potential fraud. Choice (b) is incorrect. The project engineer has already been asked about the facts and did not resolve the issue. Choice (c) is incorrect. The unexplained payment may be an indicator of fraud. Choice (d) is incorrect. Raising this issue in public may expose the auditor to liability for slander.
Subject Area: Conduct assurance engagements fraud investigation. Source: CIA 1194, I-64.

**8.** **(d)** The audit committee of the board of directors is independent of the management and should be notified of the illegal acts of the senior management members. Choice (a) is incorrect. The auditees at the line level are not in a position to take corrective action. Disclosing sensitive information to this level also creates a situation where rumors can act to the detriment of the company. Choice (b) is incorrect. The internal auditor owes loyalty to the company that employs him or her. This obligation includes maintaining confidentiality of potentially damaging information, which is under investigation. Choice (c) is incorrect. Confronting the implicated officers with the full findings only serves to give them time to hide their misdeeds while other responsibility levels are being notified.

Subject Area: Conduct assurance engagements fraud investigation. Source: CIA 590, I-37.

**9.** **(b)** The report should also summarize findings that serve as the basis for this conclusion, so that management can decide what to do next. Choice (a) is incorrect. Although this is an accurate paraphrase from the "Due Professional Care" *Standard 280*, it is an inappropriate inclusion in a report focusing on an irregularity that has been detected. Choice (c) is incorrect. The questions refer to a preliminary report. If polygraph tests were to be administered, they would come during the investigation, which follows the preliminary report. Choice (d) is incorrect. Design of such tests would take place at the conclusion, rather than the beginning, of the fraud investigation. Also, these tests are internal auditing procedural matters that normally would not be communicated to operating management.

Subject Area: Conduct assurance engagements fraud investigation. Source: CIA 590, I-49.

**10.** **(a)** This is the most appropriate response. The auditors should report all information that represents major breakdowns in control and possible fraud to management on a timely basis so management can take timely corrective and follow-up action. Choice (b) is incorrect. The appropriate reporting chain is through management and the board. They are responsible for taking corrective and follow-up action. Choice (c) is incorrect. All important breakdowns in control should be reported—even if the auditee agrees to correct the problem. Choice (d) is incorrect. This is an important violation of both bank and regulatory rules and should be reported immediately to management for follow-up and corrective action.

Subject Area: Conduct assurance engagements fraud investigation. Source: CIA 597, I-69.

**11.** **(b)** This procedure would assist the auditor in understanding details of the transactions and should be pursued before taking any further action. Choice (a) is incorrect. The auditor should gather some corroborating evidence to the testimonial evidence before bringing the issue to divisional management. Choice (c) is incorrect. This is an important observation related to the operational audit. The auditor should seek a better understanding of the potential problem and potential recommendations before completing the audit. Choice (d) is incorrect. It would be good to take an inventory of the items on hand, but the finding should not be included in an audit report until the auditor has corroborating evidence and an understanding of the nature of the potential problem.

Subject Area: Conduct assurance engagements fraud investigation. Source: CIA 1195, I-61.

**12.** **(c)** Divisional management should be aware of the auditor's findings since management fraud and not personal fraud is involved. It is not clear whether divisional management is an integral part of the scheme to sell the goods, but the important findings should be reviewed with divisional management as the auditee. The IIA *Standards* indicates that findings such as these should be reported to the audit committee and senior management. Choice (a) is incorrect. *Standards* indicate that findings such as these should be reported to the audit committee and senior management. Choice (b) is incorrect. It is not the auditor's re-

sponsibility to report such findings to a regulatory body. The auditor needs to report the findings to the appropriate personnel within the organization. Choice (d) is incorrect because it is a partial answer. The findings should also be reviewed with divisional management.

Subject Area: Conduct assurance engagements fraud investigation. Source: CIA 1195, I-62.

**13.** **(d)** The IIA *Standards* indicate that when financial statements may be materially misstated, the auditor should inform senior management and the board. The audit committee, if one exists, should also be informed. Choices (a), (b), and (c) are incorrect because senior management, the board, and the audit committee come first.

Subject Area: Conduct assurance engagements fraud investigation. Source: CIA 1195, I-63.

**14.** **(b)** This would be the most effective procedure and is consistent with the monitoring concept embodied in the Committee of Sponsoring Organizations (COSO) report on internal accounting controls. Choice (a) is incorrect. The integrated test facility (ITF) is useful in determining the correctness of processing for validly input items. The question with this possible fraud would be the validity of the input items. Choice (c) is incorrect. This would be a very ineffective use of generalized audit software, because an edit control should be built into the application to test for valid policy numbers. Choice (d) is incorrect. Batch controls are designed to ensure that all items submitted are processed; that is, they are not lost or added to. Batch controls serve a control purpose, but the major concern in this situation is the validity of the input. Response (b) would be more effective.

Subject Area: Conduct assurance engagements fraud investigation. Source: CIA 1195, I-64.

**15.** **(a)** This would be the most effective procedure since it would focus on the items that would most likely be fraudulent. Choice (b) is incorrect. This procedure would be less effective than choice (a) because it involves all payments and does not focus on the ones most likely to be improper. Choice (c) is incorrect. This would not be an effective procedure because it focuses on receiving reports. The concern here would be with payments for which no valid support exists. The proper population from which to sample is identified in choice (a). Choice (d) is incorrect. This is not as effective as choice (a) because it (1) focuses only on the last month of the year and (2) does not focus on the items most likely to be fraudulent.

Subject Area: Conduct assurance engagements fraud investigation. Source: CIA 1195, I-65.

**16.** **(b)** Although the substantial difference looks suspicious, the auditor should prepare a more detailed estimate before deciding the most appropriate audit action. Choice (a) is incorrect. The auditor should refine the estimate further before discussing the matter with the treasurer. Even if the auditor has confidence in the first estimate, the suspicion of potential fraud should lead the auditor to do further work, for example, tracing the estimated income developed in step (a) to the cash receipts book before confronting the treasurer. Choice (c) is incorrect. The auditor does not have sufficient evidence to justify the conclusion or this action. Choice (d) is incorrect. This procedure would only provide evidence on cash received for income that was recorded. The analytical procedure indicates a greater concern with income not being recorded.

Subject Area: Conduct assurance engagements fraud investigation. Source: CIA 595, I-42.

**17. (c)** Per the IIA *Standards,* "When an internal auditor suspects wrongdoing, the appropriate authorities within the organization should be informed." Choice (a) is incorrect. Per the IIA *Standards,* "When an internal auditor suspects wrongdoing, the appropriate authorities within the organization should be informed." Law enforcement authorities should be called only after a discussion with and concurrence of management. Choice (b) is incorrect. A confrontation with the cash operations supervisor at this point could not only hinder further investigation, but also lead to slander charges being brought. Choice (d) is incorrect. Per the IIA *Standards,* "When an internal auditor suspects wrongdoing, the appropriate authorities within the organization should be informed." The bonding agency would be notified after discussion with management and, perhaps, legal counsel.

Subject Area: Conduct assurance engagements fraud investigation. Source: CIA 590, II-42.

**18. (d)** Upon the discovery of fraud, the internal auditor should inform executive management. Choice (a) is incorrect. This is a management decision. Choice (b) is incorrect. This is a management responsibility. Choice (c) is incorrect. The auditor's ethical obligations do not include such a responsibility.

Subject Area: Conduct assurance engagements fraud investigation. Source: CIA 596, I-43.

**19. (c)** The *Standards* require notification of authorities and a recommendation of investigation if factors suggest a fraud could be taking place. Choices (a) and (b) are incorrect. Immediate notification of the board is required once additional testing has established that a fraud has taken place. Choice (d) is incorrect. Extended tests to determine extent of fraud are accomplished after the fraud has in fact been determined, not suspected.

Subject Area: Conduct assurance engagements fraud investigation. Source: CIA 594, I-14.

**20. (b)** Fraud investigations are usually team efforts. Choice (a) is incorrect. Fraud investigations are usually team efforts. Choices (c) and (d) are incorrect because internal auditors usually participate in fraud investigations.

Subject Area: Conduct assurance engagements fraud investigation. Source: CIA 591, II-49.

**21. (c)** In carrying out its responsibility for the deterrence of fraud, internal auditing should determine whether such written policy statements exist. Choice (a) is incorrect. On a cost-benefit basis, it is entirely reasonable to have more extensive control policies, practices, and procedures in high-risk areas. Choice (b) is incorrect. Often even the best of internal control systems can be circumvented by collusion. Choice (d) is incorrect. Forgeries, like collusion, can circumvent even the best of internal control systems.

Subject Area: Conduct assurance engagements fraud investigation. Source: CIA 1193, I-49.

**22. (b)** A fraud report is required at the conclusion of the investigation phase. Choice (a) is incorrect. A fraud report is authorized, but not required, at the conclusion of the detection phase. Choice (c) is incorrect. A fraud report is authorized, but not required, at the end of the detection phase. Choice (d) is incorrect. A fraud report is required at the end of the investigation phase.

Subject Area: Conduct assurance engagements fraud investigation. Source: CIA 591, I-50.

**23. (d)** This can be critical in ensuring that the internal auditor avoids providing information to or obtaining misleading information from persons who may be involved. Choice (a) is incorrect. By always giving the impression that additional evidence is in reserve, the internal auditor is more apt to get complete and truthful answers. Choice (b) is incorrect. Fraud investigations usually come up unexpectedly and cannot be scheduled in advance. Also, it is essential that the fraud investigation be conducted by individuals having the appropriate type and level of expertise, even if this means delaying another assignment. Choice (c) is incorrect. Internal auditing should coordinate its activities with the other investigators mentioned.

Subject Area: Conduct assurance engagements fraud investigation. Source: CIA 590, I-50.

**24. (a)** Libel is a written or printed statement of a defamatory nature that causes damage to the person libeled. Reports that are necessary under the circumstances for the performance of the auditor's legitimate duties are considered "privileged communications" and are exempt from libel rules. Choice (b) is incorrect. Slander refers to a spoken, rather than written, defamation. Choice (c) is incorrect. Compounding a felony is, for example, agreeing not to prosecute an employee guilty of fraud if the employee repays the amount stolen. Choice (d) is incorrect. Malicious prosecution is the groundless institution of criminal proceedings.

Subject Area: Conduct assurance engagements fraud investigation. Source: CIA 590, II-48.

**25. (d)** Malicious prosecution is the groundless institution of criminal proceedings. Choice (a) is incorrect. False imprisonment is restraining the free movement of an employee suspected of fraud. Choice (b) is incorrect. Libel is a written or printed statement of a defamatory nature; the words need not be part of a criminal complaint. Choice (c) is incorrect. Slander is a spoken statement of a defamatory nature; the words need not be part of a criminal complaint.

Subject Area: Conduct assurance engagements fraud investigation. Source: CIA 590, II-49.

**26. (a)** Review by legal counsel reduces the possibility of inclusion (and dissemination) of a statement for which the accused employee could sue the organization. If internal auditing wants to invoke client privilege, consideration should be given to addressing the report to legal counsel. Choice (b) is incorrect. The audit committee should receive a final draft of the report only after it has been reviewed and approved by legal counsel. Choice (c) is incorrect. If appropriate, the president may receive a final draft of the report after it has been reviewed and approved by legal counsel. Choice (d) is incorrect. If it is customary to send the outside auditors copies of all internal audit reports, it should be a final draft that has been reviewed and approved by legal counsel.

Subject Area: Conduct assurance engagements fraud investigation. Source: CIA 590, II-50.

**27. (a)** This is true. The internal auditor mainly gathers facts during a fraud investigation. Choice (b) is incorrect. This is considered false imprisonment. Choice (c) is incorrect. This is the role of an investigator. Choice (d) is incorrect. This is considered compounding a felony. The right to punish or forgive a criminal act is reserved to the state.

Subject Area: Conduct assurance engagements fraud investigation. Source: CIA 594, II-14.

**28.** (**d**)   You should avoid creating the impression that you are seeking a confession or a conviction. Choices (a), (b), and (c) are incorrect because each choice is a good interviewing technique to use during a fraud investigation.

Subject Area: Conduct assurance engagements fraud investigation. Source: CIA 594, II-20.

**29.** (**c**)   Such an indication risks compounding a felony. Choices (a), (b), and (d) are incorrect because each choice is an unsound practice.

Subject Area: Conduct assurance engagements fraud investigation. Source: CIA 594, II-50.

**30.** (**d**)   Although the IIA *Standards* state that "the internal auditor should consider . . . the adequacy and effectiveness of internal control," the *Standards* make clear that this consideration must be based on an examination and evaluation, not just an assumption. Choice (a) is incorrect. The *Standards* state the "Due care . . . does not require detailed audits of all transactions." Choice (b) is incorrect. The *Standards* state that "the relative materiality . . . of matters to which audit procedures are applied" is a legitimate consideration. Choice (c) is incorrect. The *Standards* state that "the internal auditor should consider . . . the cost of auditing in relation to potential benefits."

Subject Area: Conduct assurance engagements fraud investigation. Source: CIA 1190, I-49.

**31.** (**b**)   Based on the IIA *Standards*, "The possibility of material irregularities or noncompliance should be considered whenever the internal auditor undertakes an internal auditing assignment." Choice (a) is incorrect. "Due care requires the auditor to conduct examinations and verification to a reasonable extent, but does not require detailed audits of all transactions." Choice (c) is incorrect. "The internal auditor cannot give absolute assurance that noncompliance or irregularities do not exist." Choice (d) is incorrect. "Due care implies reasonable care and competence, not infallibility or extraordinary performance."

Subject Area: Conduct assurance engagements fraud investigation. Source: CIA 590, I-44.

**32.** (**a**)   This is in accord with the IIA *Standards*. Choice (b) is incorrect. Fraud may be perpetrated against the organization. Choice (c) is incorrect. Fraud may be for the benefit of an organization. Choice (d) is incorrect because parts of this statement may or may not be true.

Subject Area: Conduct assurance engagements fraud investigation. Source: CIA 590, I-47.

**33.** (**c**)   The principal means of preventing fraud is internal control; the internal auditor's role is related to evaluating the control. Choice (a) is incorrect. This response relates to the internal auditor's obligation for reporting suspected fraud, not for preventing fraud. Choice (b) is incorrect. Management, not internal auditing, is responsible for establishing these systems. Choice (d) is incorrect. The *Standards* referred to relate to operational efficiency, not to prevention of fraud.

Subject Area: Conduct assurance engagements fraud investigation. Source: CIA 590, II-46.

**34.** (**c**)   The IIA *Standards* require this path for reporting; it is management's decision to make further disclosure. Choices (a), (b), and (d) are incorrect because the *Standards* do not require such reporting.

Subject Area: Conduct assurance engagements fraud investigation. Source: CIA 1193, II-47.

**35.** (**d**)   This is how the responsibility is met according to the IIA *Standards*. Choice (a) is incorrect. This involves detection, not deterrence. Choice (b) is incorrect. Testing for fraud in every audit is not required. Choice (c) is incorrect because this is not the primary means as described in the standards.

Subject Area: Conduct assurance engagements fraud investigation. Source: CIA 593, I-47.

**36.** (**d**)   A written report should be issued at the conclusion of the investigation phase. It should include all findings, conclusions, recommendations, and corrective action taken. This is the list provided by the *Standards*. Choice (a) is incorrect. This is the list of information to include in a final written report at the conclusion of an audit examination that may not include fraud. Since this definition does not include "corrective action," it is incomplete. Choice (b) is incorrect. This is a correct listing of the elements comprising "findings." A fraud report includes more than findings, so this answer is incomplete. Choice (c) is incorrect. The inclusion of background is recommended, but not required for inclusion in a final audit report. There is no mention of it in a fraud report. This list leaves out "conclusions" and "corrective action," so it is incomplete.

Subject Area: Conduct assurance engagements fraud investigation. Source: CIA 593, II-50.

**37.** (**b**)   The director should have periodically checked the status of the case with security. Follow-up is specified by the *Standards*. Choice (a) is incorrect. According to the IIA *Standards,* the director should have ensured that the internal auditing department's responsibilities were met. Choice (c) is incorrect. A security department would generally have more expertise in the investigation of a fraud. Choice (d) is incorrect. The fraud was only suspected when reported to the director. Immediate discharge would have violated the suspect's rights. In addition, the director would not normally have the authority to discharge an employee in an audited area.

Subject Area: Conduct assurance engagements fraud investigation. Source: CIA 593, II-44.

**38.** (**a**)   If the incidence of significant fraud has been established with reasonable certainty, the auditor is responsible for reporting such to senior management or the board. Choice (b) is incorrect. No reporting is required when suspicious acts are reported to the auditor. Choice (c) is incorrect. Irregular transactions under investigation would not require reporting until the investigation phase is completed. Choice (d) is incorrect. Reporting should occur sooner. See choice (a).

Subject Area: Conduct assurance engagements fraud investigation. Source: CIA 1192, II-49.

**39.** (**d**)   Internal auditors are not normally trained in the interrogation of suspected perpetrators and therefore should leave such activity to security or law enforcement specialists. Choice (a) is incorrect. This can be critical to ensuring that internal auditors avoid providing information to or obtaining misleading information from persons who may be involved. Choice (b) is incorrect. This is a responsibility assigned by the *Standards* and will be useful when determining what controls to recommend preventing future occurrences of similar fraud. Choice (c) is incorrect. This is a responsibility assigned by the *Standards* and will tend to ensure a complete and thorough investigation.

Subject Area: Conduct assurance engagements fraud investigation. Source: CIA 1192, II-50.

**40. (c)** The IIA Code of Ethics requires members and CIAs to refrain from undertaking services that cannot be reasonably completed with professional competence. Choice (a) is incorrect. Diligence does not override professional competence or use of good judgment. Choice (b) is incorrect. Loyalty would be better exhibited by consulting professionals in interrogation and knowing your limits of competence. Choice (d) is incorrect. The auditor may violate the suspect's civil rights due to his inexperience, but that is not a certainty.

Subject Area: Conduct assurance engagements fraud investigation. Source: CIA 592, I-47.

**Third Parties and Contract Auditing**

**41. (d)** Test data is the appropriate method to use. Choice (a) is incorrect. The question stub suggests that there are "extensive" transactions. This means that a very large sample must be selected if the plan is to be reasonably effective. Choice (b) is incorrect. The use of a stratification model reduces the standard deviation of the overall sample. This reduces the sample size required to achieve a given level of confidence. Choice (c) is incorrect. Discovery sampling is useful for determining the sample size necessary to have a stated probability that the sample will contain at least one example of the error or irregularity of interest. The procedure is used in cases where errors or irregularities are presumed to exist. There is no mention of such presumption in this case.

Subject Area: Conduct assurance engagements third parties. Source: CIA 1192, II-35.

**42. (b)** Header label is an internal file label that checks for the processing of correct file. It is an example of preventive control. Choice (a) is incorrect. The question is focusing on file updating processing, not data input. File updating comes after data input. Testing for input completeness is an example of a detective control. Choice (c) is incorrect. This is a good control practice, but it is of no use during master file updating. Checking of detail reports is an example of a detective control. Choice (d) is incorrect. This is a good control practice, but it is of no use due to its after-the-fact basis. Exception reports are produced after data files are updated and are an example of a corrective control. A preventive control is needed here.

Subject Area: Conduct assurance engagements third parties. Source: CIA 590, I-25.

**43. (c)** A properly qualified and adequately supervised consultant may be used as needed, according to the IIA *Standards*. Choice (a) is incorrect. It would be inappropriate to delete the audit. Choice (b) is incorrect. This is a direct violation of the *Standards*. Choice (d) is incorrect. Accepting the contractor's representations without adequate testing or disclosure of such would violate the *Standards*.

Subject Area: Conduct assurance engagements—contract auditing. Source: CIA 593, I-6.

**44. (d)** This procedure deals more appropriately with the possible understatement of the account. Further, it is not as effective in dealing with misclassifications as would step b. Choice (a) is incorrect. This would be an effective procedure because it would tell the auditor whether there were computation errors made—even though the underlying expenses were proper. Choice (b) is incorrect. This would provide evidence that all items classified as overhead were appropriately included in the overhead account. The auditor is sampling from the proper population because the concern is with the potential overstatement of the account. Choice (c) is incorrect. This would provide evidence on whether the company submitting the bill properly computed its overhead rate in compliance with the contract terms.

Subject Area: Conduct assurance engagements—contract auditing. Source: CIA 596, I-39.

**45. (d)** All of the responses are correct. The best estimate of the error rate (5%) is the error rate found in the population. The best estimate of the dollar amount of errors is to take the mean-per-unit of items sampled ($53,000/100) times the number of items in the population (1500) giving a result of $795,000. The errors must be occurring on items greater than the average because the average value of items in the population is $8,200 while the average value of an item in error is $53,000/5 errors, or $10,600. Choices (a), (b), and (c) are incorrect since they are part of choice (d).

Subject Area: Conduct assurance engagements—contract auditing. Source: CIA 596, I-40.

**46. (a)** This is a form of testimonial evidence and is insufficient without significant corroborating evidence. Since management has self-interest in certifying it is free from waste and inefficiency, it is the least persuasive evidence. Choice (b) is incorrect. A walk-through provides insight on the efficiency of operations and would be an effective first step in establishing the potential need to investigate for waste and inefficiency. Choice (c) is incorrect. An examination of actual expenditures would indicate whether duplicate expenses have been incurred or whether waste was taking place. Choice (d) is incorrect. Comparison with similar projects, over time or across projects, would provide insight on possible waste and inefficiency.

Subject Area: Conduct assurance engagements—contract auditing. Source: CIA 596, I-41.

**47. (a)** The materiality of the findings should be based on the potential impact to the governmental agency, that is, the potential amount of fines involved since the contract clearly specified the contractor must meet all applicable environmental regulations. Choices (b), (c), and (d) are incorrect. All of the violations are material because they may result in fines. Therefore, all of the environmental regulatory findings should be reported. Regarding choices (c) and (d), the environmental regulator is a reliable source of evidence and has more expertise than the auditor in this area. Therefore, the evidence of the agency should be included in a compliance report.

Subject Area: Conduct assurance engagements—contract auditing. Source: CIA 596, I-42.

**48. (a)** Of the four auditing procedures given, this would be the most important because a cost-plus contract is not self-policed with an incentive for efficiency or economy. Accordingly, without such a provision for system review and cost audits, the company would be at the mercy of the contractor. Choice (b) is incorrect. Seldom will contracts have a strict completion date, especially early on in the construction process. Although the auditor may look at this information, it is not the most crucial. Choice (c) is incorrect. A company should not necessarily select the lowest bid because other factors are considered in selecting a contractor, such as quality of material to be used, reputation of the contractor, and so on. Choice (d) is incorrect. Directly contacting the contractor firm to inquire about its business integrity is not typically an auditing procedure that would be employed.

Subject Area: Conduct assurance engagements—contract auditing. Source: CIA 593, II-15.

**49. (a)** With sound reviews of invoices before payment thereon, including a comparison of items billed with those authorized by the contract, payments of improper billings can be prevented. Choice (b) is incorrect. Adequate record maintenance is essential to good control but does not directly prevent payment of improper billed amounts. Choice (c) is incorrect. Segregation of duties is an essential control, but fails to prevent payment of this overbilling, which originated outside the company. Choice (d) is incorrect. Qualified personnel are needed for control purposes, but they cannot prevent payment of excessive charges unless control procedures related to effective review of invoices before payment are in place.

Subject Area: Conduct assurance engagements—contract auditing. Source: CIA 1191, II-12.

**50. (a)** This involves a risk that the costs charged for the project will be excessive. Choice (b) is incorrect. Income tax provisions related to depreciation charges are not a risk; only those charges that are charged to the contract under the terms of the contract constitute a risk. Choice (c) is incorrect. Budgets inappropriately prepared do not affect contract costs and hence do not constitute a risk. Choice (d) is incorrect. The omission does not involve a risk of contract overcharges or inadequacies in construction; possible delays in payment or underpayments are all that is involved.

Subject Area: Conduct assurance engagements—contract auditing. Source: CIA 1191, I-13.

**51. (d)** Coordination of audit efforts and the efficiency of audit activities should be primary responsibilities of the director of internal auditing. Choice (a) is incorrect. Adopting the full set of quality auditing standards for the internal auditing function would duplicate functions within the organization. Choice (b) is incorrect. The issue is the reporting relationship of internal auditing, not the qualifications of audit staff. Choice (c) is incorrect. Sufficient information in not given to conclude that the internal audit function should be eliminated.

Subject Area: Conduct assurance engagements—quality audits. Source: CIA 595, I-25.

**52. (d)** This is a broad definition of due diligence reviews per the IIA's *Standards*. Choice (a) is incorrect. Although the underwriter may use the reviews, the underwriter does not direct them. Choice (b) is incorrect. The due diligence review is not an operational audit. Choice (c) is incorrect. It is not a review for compliance with company policies.

Subject Area: Conduct assurance engagements—due diligence and due care. Source: CIA 595, I-52.

**53. (b)** The IIA *Standards* include within the definition of due professional care the evaluation of operating standards for acceptability and determining whether they are being met. Choice (a) is incorrect. Communication between the director of internal auditing and the board of directors is part of the Independence standard, not the Due Professional Care standard. Choice (c) is incorrect. The amount of audit time and effort required giving absolute assurance that there are no irregularities would be so great that the audit costs would exceed the benefits. Choice (d) is incorrect. Criteria for filling internal audit positions relate to the Staffing standard; they do not relate directly to the performance of an audit.

Subject Area: Conduct assurance engagements—due diligence and due care. Source: CIA 1190, II-49.

**54. (c)** This would violate the *IIA Standards* because the auditor has not acted on audit evidence, which indicated that the audit should be expanded. Choice (a) is incorrect. This action would be consistent with the *Standards* on due professional care. Choice (b) is incorrect. This action would be consistent with the *Standards* on due professional care. Choice (d) is incorrect. The auditor does not need the auditee's approval to expand the audit test.

Subject Area: Conduct assurance engagements—due diligence and due care. Source: CIA 1195, I-56.

**55. (c)** This is what the IIA *Standards* require in such cases. Choices (a) and (b) are incorrect since the assertions are self-serving. Choice (d) is incorrect. Noting differences in interpretation in the audit report, in and of itself, is not due care. Due care has to do with how the audit is performed and the report written.

Subject Area: Conduct assurance engagements—due diligence and due care. Source: CIA 1193, I-50.

**56. (a)** The exercise of due professional care includes consideration of materiality. Choice (b) is incorrect. The auditor should consider the cost-benefit ratio before beginning an audit. Choice (c) is incorrect. The auditor should evaluate the acceptability of standards as well as whether they are being met. Choice (d) is incorrect. Due care does not require absolute assurance.

Subject Area: Conduct assurance engagements—due diligence and due care. Source: CIA 1191, I-49.

**57. (b)** The *Standards* do not require extensive and detailed audits of all transactions. Choices (a), (c), and (d) are incorrect because the *Standards* specifically identify these items.

Subject Area: Conduct assurance engagements—due diligence and due care. Source: CIA 592, I-50.

**58. (a)** This is what is required by the Code of Ethics of the Institute. Choice (b) is incorrect because there is no specific requirement for this. Choices (c) and (d) are incorrect because each one is too constraining.

Subject Area: Conduct assurance engagements—due diligence and due care. Source: CIA 592, I-49.

**Program and Performance Audit Engagements**

**59. (a)** Program results audits examine effectiveness (outputs) by asking what management or the taxpayer is getting for money spent. Choice (b) is incorrect. Cost savings are sought in audits of economy and efficiency. Choice (c) is incorrect. Historical data are included only in financial and compliance audits. Choice (d) is incorrect. An opinion on the fairness of financial presentation is rendered in a financial audit.

Subject Area: Conduct assurance engagements program and performance audits. Source: CIA 1190, I-17.

**60.** **(b)** A determination that desired results or benefits established by the legislature or other authorizing body are being achieved is a program results audit. Choice (a) is incorrect. An audit of financial statements is a financial audit. Choice (c) is incorrect. Determining if an entity has complied with laws and regulations is a compliance audit. Choice (d) is incorrect. An audit of economy and efficiency is a distinct element of the audit, separate from an audit of program results.

Subject Area: Conduct assurance engagements program and performance audits. Source: CIA 1190, II-17.

**61.** **(b)** This calls for an evaluation of the effectiveness of the agency's achievement of an objective. Choice (a) is incorrect. Evaluating the cost of accomplishing a goal suggests efficiency auditing, a secondary issue in performance auditing. Choice (c) is incorrect. Staffing levels would be a greater issue if the emphasis were on efficiency. Choice (d) is incorrect. Evaluating conformance with policies and procedures is a compliance issue.

Subject Area: Conduct assurance engagements program and performance audits. Source: CIA 1193, II-1.

**Operational Audit Engagements**

**62.** **(d)** Operational auditing is most likely to address a determination of cost savings by focusing on economy and efficiency. Choice (a) is incorrect. Program results auditing addresses accomplishment of program objectives. Choice (b) is incorrect. Financial auditing addresses accuracy of financial records. Choice (c) is incorrect. Compliance auditing addresses compliance with requirements, including legal and regulatory requirements.

Subject Area: Conduct assurance engagements operational audits. Source: CIA 592, II-1.

**63.** **(d)** In an operational audit, all tests are for the purpose of assisting management in its evaluation of effectiveness and efficiency in resource utilization. Choice (a) is incorrect. The comparison will not determine the accuracy of actual costs. Choice (b) is incorrect. The comparison will not measure the effectiveness of the standard costs system. Choice (c) is incorrect. An assessment of the reasonableness of standard costs might be in order, but it cannot be accomplished by simply comparing them to actual costs.

Subject Area: Conduct assurance engagements operational audits. Source: CIA 1191, I-17.

**64.** **(b)** The goal of an operational audit is to assess current performance and make any recommendations for improvement. Choice (a) is incorrect. The auditor would not be concerned with payroll processing during this type of testing and evaluation. Choice (c) is incorrect. Comparison of staffing levels with industry standards will not test the adequacy of internal controls. Choice (d) is incorrect. The auditor would be more concerned with legal requirements during a compliance audit.

Subject Area: Conduct assurance engagements operational audits. Source: CIA 1191, I-10.

**65.** **(c)** Operational and performance auditing deal with the efficiency and effectiveness of systems of controls and operations. Choice (a) is incorrect. A financial audit will focus on assessing the strengths of accounting and financial systems, fairness of financial statements, and the controls that generate financial results and transactions. Choice (b) is incorrect. A compliance audit would test adherence to the control rather than the effectiveness of the control. Choice (d) is incorrect. Program results auditing evaluates the achievement of desired benefits of a program and is normally associated with governmental programs.

Subject Area: Conduct assurance engagements operational audits. Source: CIA 1193, I-2.

**66.** **(b)** Management review of expenditures would provide control over the level of expenditures for small material items. Choice (a) is incorrect. Relocating the bins would limit the efficiency and effectiveness of shop personnel. Choice (c) is incorrect. Locking the bins would limit the efficiency and effectiveness of shop personnel. Choice (d) is incorrect since choice (b) is the correct answer.

Subject Area: Conduct assurance engagements operational audits. Source: CIA 597, I-13.

**67.** **(d)** This would be the least effective because it controls the total amount of expenditures, but does not control where the purchase orders are placed or whether there is receipt of goods for the items purchased. Choice (a) is incorrect. This would be an effective procedure because it would prevent a bogus company being added to authorized vendors. Choice (b) is incorrect. This would be effective because a vendor would not be paid if parts were not used in actual production. Choice (c) is incorrect. This would also be effective because it would ensure that all vendors are authorized.

Subject Area: Conduct assurance engagements operational audits. Source: CIA 597, I-14.

**68.** **(d)** All of the statements are correct. The advantage of the production-based control procedure is that all significant discrepancies between records become known because production will be shut down. Supervisors are then in position to take corrective action. A side benefit is that goods cannot be paid for unless they are used in production. Significant discrepancies with a vendor would, however, have to be investigated. Choices (a), (b), and (c) are incorrect since each one of them is part of the correct answer.

Subject Area: Conduct assurance engagements operational audits. Source: CIA 597, I-15.

**69.** **(b)** This procedure would establish the cause of the problem. Choice (a) is incorrect. Access controls are tangential to the issue. Authorized but incorrect data could also be the problem. Choice (c) is incorrect. This would provide useful information, but it is not as comprehensive as choice (b). Further, choice (b) provides more information on the cause. Choice (d) is incorrect. This tests only one source of the data inaccuracy, that is, the input of production data; other sources of potential error are ignored.

Subject Area: Conduct assurance engagements operational audits. Source: CIA 597, I-16.

**70.** **(a)** This is the most appropriate procedure because: (1) the auditor has already determined that there is a concern; and (2) this procedure results in a direct comparison of current part requirements with purchase orders being generated. Differences can be identified and corrective action taken. Choice (b) is incorrect. This procedure provides evidence that all items entered are processed. Comparison with currently generated purchase orders does not provide evidence on whether the correct parts are being ordered. Choice (c) is incorrect. Generalized audit software is a good method to identify an inventory problem. However, the excess inventory may not be the result of a revised production technique. Choice (a) more directly addresses the audit concern. Choice (d) is incorrect. This procedure provides evidence on the input of data into the system, but does not provide evidence on whether changes in the production process have been implemented.

Subject Area: Conduct assurance engagements operational audits. Source: CIA 597, I-18.

**71.** **(c)** This would be the least effective approach because it only deals with the establishment of vendors—which should be performed independently of the purchasing agent—and does not address the nature of the kickback actions. Choice (a) is incorrect. A specific corporate policy conveys directions to the purchasing agents and is helpful in influencing behavior. Choice (b) is incorrect. Corporate codes of ethics convey directions to the purchasing agents and are helpful in influencing behavior. Choice (d) is incorrect. This is an effective procedure that is increasingly being used by many companies.

Subject Area: Conduct assurance engagements operational audits. Source: CIA 597, I-22.

**72.** **(a)** Verifying is the most often used technique in testing the accuracy of information maintained by a system, whether manual or automated. Choice (b) is incorrect. Test decking of a database will test the program but will not test the accuracy of data in the database. Choice (c) is incorrect. Simulating normal processing would test the program but not the accuracy of data. Choice (d) is incorrect. Tracing would require that additional coding is inserted into the database system programs.

Subject Area: Conduct assurance engagements operational audits. Source: CIA 597, I-61.

**73.** **(b)** This would help the auditor determine that all three pieces of data were appropriately matched before payment. Choices (a) and (c) are incorrect. Each procedure only provides data on whether payments agree with invoices. It does not provide data on whether the invoiced amounts are correct. Choice (d) is incorrect. This provides data only on one day. While it matches items received with those paid, it does not provide data on whether the billings were correct.

Subject Area: Conduct assurance engagements operational audits. Source: CIA 597, I-36.

**74.** **(c)** Balance confirmations usually are done to assess internal accounting procedures. Choice (a) is incorrect. Lot size is directly related to vendor performance. Choice (b) is incorrect. Delivery of only authorized items is directly related to vendor performance. Choice (d) is incorrect. Quality of goods is directly related to vendor performance.

Subject Area: Conduct assurance engagements operational audits. Source: CIA 597, I-38.

**75.** **(d)** Because materials are shipped and used in another business, the analytic comparisons would show an unexplained increase in materials used. Choice (a) is incorrect. Because documents are falsified, all supporting documents would match for each cash disbursement. Choice (b) is incorrect. Vendors would confirm all transactions, because all have been made. Choice (c) is incorrect. Since fraudulent orders are shipped to another location, the receiving dock procedures would appear correct.

Subject Area: Conduct assurance engagements operational audits. Source: CIA 597, I-40.

**76.** **(c)** This represents a change in process that should be brought to the attention of management and documented. Choice (a) is incorrect. The procedures do not represent a deficiency since efficiency has improved without diminishing control. Choice (b) is incorrect. The auditor should not prepare documentation for the auditee. Further, a flowchart is not the best form of documentation. Choice (d) is incorrect. The audit should be completed.

Subject Area: Conduct assurance engagements operational audits. Source: CIA 597, I-41.

**77.** **(a)** A well-designed control system that is set aside at management's discretion can be equivalent to no controls in terms of risk. Choice (b) is incorrect. It is a sufficient control without extenuating circumstances. Choice (c) is incorrect. Assuming both signers review the control is adequate. Choice (d) is incorrect. Absent extenuating circumstances, the purchasing agent would not be in a conflict of interest.

Subject Area: Conduct assurance engagements operational audits. Source: CIA 1196, I-34.

**78.** **(c)** Spreadsheet software is particularly useful for preparing depreciation schedules for fixed assets. Choice (a) is incorrect. Spreadsheet software is not particularly useful for preparing overhead projector slides for an audit presentation. Choice (b) is incorrect. Spreadsheet software is not particularly useful for preparing a narrative report summarizing the results of an audit. Choice (d) is incorrect. Spreadsheet software is not particularly useful for uploading data from a microcomputer to a mainframe.

Subject Area: Conduct assurance engagements operational audits. Source: CIA 597, I-68.

**79.** **(a)** Reconciling the back-order file to shipments daily would identify unfilled orders for appropriate action. Choice (b) is incorrect. Increasing inventory levels might minimize the number of times that out-of-stock conditions occur but will not affect delivery of the items that are out of stock. Choice (c) is incorrect. Implementing electronic data interchange with supply vendors may decrease the time to replenish inventory but will not affect delivery of the items that are out of stock. Choice (d) is incorrect. Reconciling the sum of filled and back orders with the total of all orders placed daily ensures that orders were either filled or back ordered but will not affect delivery of the items that are out of stock.

Subject Area: Conduct assurance engagements operational audits. Source: CIA 597, I-54.

**80.** **(a)** Preventive controls are actions taken prior to the occurrence of transactions with the intent of stopping errors from occurring. Use of an approved vendor list is a control to prevent the use of unacceptable suppliers. Choice (b) is incorrect. A detective control is a control that identifies errors after they have occurred. Choice (c) is incorrect. Corrective controls correct the problems identified by detective controls. Choice (d) is incorrect. Monitoring controls are designed to ensure the quality of the control system's performance over time.

Subject Area: Conduct assurance engagements operational audits. Source: CIA 597, I-59.

**81. (c)** This would be the least effective audit procedure. An ITF tests the correctness of processing, but the fraud that would be occurring here is not because the computer does not process items correctly; it is because items are processed that should not be processed. Choice (a) is incorrect. This would be an effective analytical review procedure because it would help the auditor delineate any unusual deviation from the past year or between the last month of the current year and the first month of the subsequent year. Choice (b) is incorrect. Confirmation with knowledgeable customers would be useful because if the customers respond correctly, they would show a different year-end account balance because of the sales recorded after year-end. Choice (d) is incorrect. This would be an effective procedure because analytical review would show the clear discrepancy in sales between the two months and would present questions the auditor should follow-up as part of the investigation.

Subject Area: Conduct assurance engagements operational audits. Source: CIA 597, I-55.

**82. (c)** The risk of telling the receiving department the quantities ordered is that the receiving department may fail to make an accurate count of the materials received. The receiving department needs to know quantities, but not the receiving clerk counting the materials initially. Choices (a) and (b) are incorrect. Comparing receipts to purchase orders will help detect unauthorized vendors and purchases. Choice (d) is incorrect. Using purchase orders to identify receipts will not require extra time to record purchases. Payment is out of separate department and processing of receipt paperwork is not delayed.

Subject Area: Conduct assurance engagements operational audits. Source: CIA 1196, I-1.

**83. (c)** This is the most effective procedure because it gets at the mechanism that the accountant would have to use to cover up the scheme and not have customers complaining about their account balances. Choice (a) is incorrect. Since the accountant has complete access to the recording mechanism, he or she could pocket the cash and effectively write off the account by debiting the discounts or returns account. The confirmation will not provide evidence on the problem since the customer's account balance will be correctly stated. Choice (b) is incorrect. See response (a) above. Expanding the sample size to 100% of the population with negative confirmations will not make a difference. Choice (d) is incorrect. This procedure would only provide evidence that all items deposited were represented by bona fide credits to cash receipts. The auditor's concern is the other direction—that is, all items where cash is received are recorded and deposited.

Subject Area: Conduct assurance engagements operational audits. Source: CIA 1196, I-2.

**84. (d)** This would be the least persuasive because the stated scenario also assumed that management is turning the goods back around by shipping them out again. If management was not doing this, then taking the physical inventory would lead to a situation where inventory on hand would exceed inventory per the books. Choice (a) is incorrect.

This would be an effective procedure to determine the extent to which previous year's sales had been inflated by poor merchandise sales. Choice (b) is incorrect. This would provide evidence on goods that had been returned but might not yet be accounted for. Choice (c) is incorrect. This would provide valuable evidence that is independent of management.

Subject Area: Conduct assurance engagements operational audits. Source: CIA 1196, I-3.

**85. (c)** The auditor should also attempt to quantify the problem to put it into proper perspective for management. Also, it is possible that the problem is related to communication problems between production and purchasing. Choice (a) is incorrect. This is an appropriate procedure, but so is Statement III. Choices (b) and (d) are incorrect. There is not enough evidence to justify these recommendations. Further, many companies now use more sophisticated materials requirement planning systems. Also, EOQ does not determine level of safety stock.

Subject Area: Conduct assurance engagements operational audits. Source: CIA 1196, I-10.

**86. (a)** An advantage of feedback control is that managers can use the information on past performance to improve future performance. Choice (b) is incorrect. Because the argument is apparently supported in the data, the auditor should consider the sales management data relevant. Choice (c) is incorrect. The sales management data shows that automated controls have, in fact, been successful in meeting the stated objective. Choice (d) is incorrect. The data are not framed to present statistically valid information and are biased to show negative results.

Subject Area: Conduct assurance engagements operational audits. Source: CIA 1194, II-8.

**87. (c)** This procedure would be useful in ensuring that once the order is captured, it is not lost. However, it does not assist in ensuring that the right product is shipped at the right price. Choice (a) is incorrect. Self-checking digits provide effective control to properly identify products for shipment. Choice (b) is incorrect. This is one of the best control procedures because the service representative verified both the product and the price. Choice (d) is incorrect. This procedure provides excellent control over the correct pricing of the products.

Subject Area: Conduct assurance engagements operational audits. Source: CIA 1195, I-33.

**88. (d)** This procedure traces all changes to the specific authorization of the person and would be the most effective procedure. Choice (a) is incorrect. Use of the ITF would provide evidence that the prices invoiced are the same as in the catalog. The data would be limited to the products that were run on the ITF and would not ensure that the marketing manager had approved all the prices in the catalog. Choice (b) is incorrect. The SCARF technique would be effective in identifying unusual transaction for subsequent audit review, but it would not provide any assurance that all changes were authorized. Choice (c) is incorrect. This procedure would tell the auditor whether all authorized price changes were made, but it would not provide assurance that other price changes were not made.

Subject Area: Conduct assurance engagements operational audits. Source: CIA 1195, I-34.

**89.  (b)**   This procedure would work effectively since it takes all items that were initially captured as sales orders and electronically traces them through the processing to determine that they were recorded.  Choice (a) is incorrect.  This procedure would not provide assurance that all items received were shipped.  It only provides evidence on the specific items that were submitted to the ITF.  If the auditor could independently gain assurance that all items were properly captured in the system, then this procedure would help meet the objective.  Choice (c) is incorrect.  Batch control totals provide evidence that the items submitted have been transferred to the sales invoice file.  They do not provide evidence that the specific transactions processed at a number of different terminals were fully captured and processed.  Choice (d) is incorrect.  This is an efficient audit procedure, but only provides evidence that all recorded items are valid.  It does not provide evidence as to whether all items were fully processed.

Subject Area: Conduct assurance engagements operational audits.  Source: CIA 1195, I-35.

**90.  (d)**   The board should develop overall policies that should be implemented and managed by top management.  In rare cases, the board should approve major investments or positions, but it should not get into day-to-day activities of the organization.  Choice (a) is incorrect.  An organization should clearly specify whether derivatives are to be used for investment (speculative) purposes or for hedging.  Choice (b) is incorrect.  The policies should clearly specify the nature, type, and limits on derivative transactions.  This is necessary to limit the potential exposure to the organization.  Choice (c) is incorrect.  Policies should also specify the amount of risk that can be incurred by one trader.

Subject Area: Conduct assurance engagements operational audits.  Source: CIA 1196, I-22 to 24.

**91.  (a)**   This would be the least effective procedure because the problem is not with the amount of individual trades; it is with the nature of the positions taken.  Choice (b) is incorrect.  This procedure would provide evidence on the nature of the hedges and whether the trading is matching the hedges.  Choice (c) is incorrect.  This would provide useful information on transactions used to clear the suspense account.  This is especially true when the credits to the account arose through the recording of speculative gains.  Choice (d) is incorrect.  This would provide evidence on expenditures made to unauthorized brokers—which would have been the case with a false broker.

Subject Area: Conduct assurance engagements operational audits.  Source: CIA 1196, I-23.

**92.  (c)**   The auditor must have the requisite skills and knowledge.  Learning about complex financial instruments "on the job" is not an acceptable substitute for having the skills.  Choice (a) is incorrect.  This is a perfect example of a situation where outsourcing makes sense and should be investigated by the auditor.  Choice (b) is incorrect.  Training staff, if it can be done in a timely fashion, is a reasonable response consistent with the IIA *Standards*.  Choice (d) is incorrect.  Bringing in an outside consultant would be an acceptable alternative as long as the auditors had enough knowledge to understand the consultant's advice and relationship to the audit.

Subject Area: Conduct assurance engagements operational audits.  Source: CIA 1196, I-24.

**93.  (d)**   A payroll account proof would test for completeness but not for validity of cash flow.  Choice (a) is incorrect.  Verification that an employee is actually working is a common procedure to test for nonexistent employees.  Choice (b) is incorrect.  Examining for proper endorsements and comparing to records would possibly detect improper payments.  Choice (c) is incorrect.  Segregation of payroll authorization from hiring and firing would help to eliminate fictitious employees.

Subject Area: Conduct assurance engagements operational audits.  Source: CIA 1196, I-65.

**94.  (b)**   Items 4 and 5 could provide support as to status of vehicles.  Then if it appears that there is a problem, the appropriate authorities within the organization should be consulted.  Choice (a) is incorrect.  Item 1 disqualifies the response.  The superintendent could tip off the investigation and compromise evidence.  Choice (c) is incorrect.  Security personnel should be notified first.  However, Item 1 disqualifies the response.  Choice (d) is incorrect.  Items 2 and 3, although potential indicators, of fraud would not be conclusive evidence.

Subject Area: Conduct assurance engagements operational audits.  Source: CIA 596, I-6.

**95.  (c)**   Economic order quantity does not affect minimum stocking levels.  Choice (a) is incorrect.  Stock-out costs are directly affected by the quantity on hand.  Choice (b) is incorrect.  Seasonal demand directly affects the minimum quantity available.  Choice (d) is incorrect.  Space and obsolescence directly affect stocking levels.

Subject Area: Conduct assurance engagements operational audits.  Source: CIA 596, I-4.

**96.  (b)**   Earnings manipulations generally involve the timing of revenue recognition or the misstatement of inventory.  Choice (a) is incorrect.  Accounts payables manipulation would not affect earnings.  Choice (c) is incorrect.  Such estimates used in interim financial statements are often rough and usually would not materially distort the financial statements.  Choice (d) is incorrect.  Such changes usually must be approved by executive management and generally do not lead to "surprises."

Subject Area: Conduct assurance engagements operational audits.  Source: CIA 596, I-7.

**97.  (c)**   Tables of predefined project numbers and material requirements would allow only acceptable jobs to be recorded.  Choice (a) is incorrect.  Verifying the number of characters does not prevent incorrect charges, only incomplete ones.  Choice (b) is incorrect.  System security does not address data accuracy.  Choice (d) is incorrect.  Internal file labels address processing of data, not the prevention of data errors.

Subject Area: Conduct assurance engagements operational audits.  Source: CIA 596, I-8.

**98.  (c)**   Determining if reports are signed for upon delivery is the only procedure that would provide information on report access.  Choice (a) is incorrect.  Reviewing JCL and report end-of-job indicators would not provide information on report access.  Choice (b) is incorrect.  None of these procedures would provide information on report access.  Choice (d) is incorrect.  Review of end-of-job indicators would not provide information on report access.

Subject Area: Conduct assurance engagements operational audits. Source: CIA 596, I-9.

**99. (a)** This is the only test that selects from the appropriate population (project variances) and verifies that needed approvals and explanations are given. Choices (b) and (c) are incorrect. Recomputing totals does not test the procedure described. Choice (d) is incorrect. Tracing to the monthly report does not ensure that all variances have explanations.
Subject Area: Conduct assurance engagements operational audits. Source: CIA 596, I-10.

**100. (b)** Management review of expenditures would provide control over the level of expenditures for small material items. Choice (a) is incorrect. Relocating the bins would limit the efficiency and effectiveness of shop personnel. Choice (c) is incorrect. Locking the bins would limit efficiency and effectiveness of shop personnel. Choice (d) is incorrect. See choice (b).
Subject Area: Conduct assurance engagements operational audits. Source: CIA 596, I-14.

**101. (b)** Proper valuation of inventory and feedback from control systems are part of an internal control system. Choice (a) is incorrect. Observing inventory transactions would not likely identify material thefts. Choice (c) is incorrect. Comparing standards and reviewing feedback are also part of internal control and auditing. Choice (d) is incorrect. Tracing approved forms to inventory records would not ensure proper authorizations; testing inventory issuance records to authorized material forms would.
Subject Area: Conduct assurance engagements operational audits. Source: CIA 596, I-15.

**102. (d)** Shipping requirements and timing would be recomputed to verify the just-in-time standards utilized for quality control. Choice (a) is incorrect. There are no industry averages for JIT (zero balance). Choice (b) is incorrect. Sales adjustments would meet product quality objectives not stocking standards. Choice (c) is incorrect. Actual stocking levels would meet the objective of meeting just-in-time standards, not establishing them.
Subject Area: Conduct assurance engagements operational audits. Source: CIA 596, I-16.

**103. (b)** Customers take longer to pay (365/4.3 compared to 365/7.3). Choice (a) is incorrect. It should have the opposite effect. Choice (c) is incorrect because it is opposite. Choice (d) is incorrect because it is irrelevant.
Subject Area: Conduct assurance engagements operational audits. Source: CIA 1190, I-24.

**104. (a)** Documentary evidence is the most compelling in evaluating the possibility those fraudulent payments exists. Choice (b) is incorrect. Supervisory personnel may be involved in the fraudulent payments. Choice (c) is incorrect. Testimonial evidence does not test for this specific audit objective. Choice (d) is incorrect. Analytical analysis of payroll costs would be more appropriate evidence for verifying pay/time worked comparisons or proper withholding.
Subject Area: Conduct assurance engagements operational audits. Source: CIA 1190, I-25.

**105. (c)** Items such as broken doors, lack of paint, and leaking and broken machinery can be determined by a tour of the facility. Choice (a) is incorrect. Touring the production facility will not uncover an insurance policy lapse. Choice (b) is incorrect. Application of overhead is an allocation procedure not related to the appearance of the facility. Choice (d) is incorrect. Recorded depreciation is the result of a book entry, and the appearance of the facility is therefore unaffected by depreciation.
Subject Area: Conduct assurance engagements operational audits. Source: CIA 1190, I-14.

**106. (c)** Some unrecorded invoices early in the new fiscal year may relate to incurrences of expenses properly belonging in the previous fiscal year. Choices (a) and (b) are incorrect. The search is for unrecorded expenses, so overstated expenses would likely not be detected by this test. Choice (d) is incorrect. Understated (unrecorded) expenses and payables are being searched for.
Subject Area: Conduct assurance engagements operational audits. Source: CIA 1190, I-15.

**107. (a)** Independent reconciliation of bank accounts in necessary for good internal control. Choice (b) is incorrect. This is not an important internal control consideration. Choice (c) is incorrect. Foreign currency translation rates are not computed, but instead verified. Having two employees in the same department perform the same task will not significantly enhance internal control. Choice (d) is incorrect. This is not an important internal control consideration.
Subject Area: Conduct assurance engagements operational audits. Source: CIA 1190, I-18.

**108. (d)** Reconciliation ensures that data was correct. Choice (a) is incorrect. Reconciliation would not necessarily include review for authorizations. Choice (b) is incorrect. Available material would not be part of the reconciliation. Choice (c) is incorrect. Not all request forms may have been submitted.
Subject Area: Conduct assurance engagements operational audits. Source: CIA 596, I-18.

**109. (d)** Excessive issuance of materials would indicate potential employee fraud. Choice (a) is incorrect. The summary report would not include stocking levels. Choice (b) is incorrect. The summary report deals only with issued items. Choice (c) is incorrect. The summary report does not address valuation.
Subject Area: Conduct assurance engagements operational audits. Source: CIA 596, I-19.

**110. (c)** Items I, II, and III are the only valid quality control steps. Choice (a) is incorrect. Items I and III are valid, but not IV. Choice (b) is incorrect. Item I is also correct. Choice (d) is incorrect. Item IV is not a valid quality control step.
Subject Area: Conduct assurance engagements operational audits. Source: CIA 596, I-20.

**111. (c)** Balance confirmations usually are done to assess internal accounting procedures. Choice (a) is incorrect. Lot size is directly related to vendor performance. Choice (b) is incorrect. Delivery of only authorized items is directly related to vendor performance. Choice (d) is incorrect. Quality of goods is directly related to vendor performance.
Subject Area: Conduct assurance engagements operational audits. Source: CIA 596, I-21.

**112. (c)** Predetermined totals are very important in controlling the processing of transactions. Balancing the transactions back to control totals would detect the error. Choice (a) is incorrect. This is a good control procedure but would not help prevent the **subsequent** error of misposting to the records. Choice (b) is incorrect. Agreeing the monthly statements back to the accounts receivable subsidiary ledger would not detect the initial error of misposting. Choice (d) is incorrect. This is another important control, but would not detect the initial mistake that caused both sets of records to be in error.

Subject Area: Conduct assurance engagements operational audits. Source: CIA 590, I-12.

**113. (c)** Personnel records comprise an independent source of authority for payroll operations such as hiring and termination. Choice (a) is incorrect. Distribution of paychecks is normally a treasury function. Choice (b) is incorrect. Authorization of overtime is an operating department supervisory function. Choice (d) is incorrect. Retention of unclaimed checks is normally a treasury function.
Subject Area: Conduct assurance engagements operational audits. Source: CIA 590, I-9.

**114. (a)** This analysis would indicate any instances where the total purchases exceeded the authorized limits and would indicate that the control procedure was not working properly. Choice (b) is incorrect. The use of test data can tell whether the control procedure is working for the tested purchasing agents for the specific time period examined. Inferences about the working of the control for the whole period cannot be made unless the auditor also gathers assurance that there is no change to the program during that period of time. Choice (c) is incorrect. This is not an appropriate use of parallel simulation. Choice (d) is incorrect. The snapshot approach provides evidence on the correctness of recording of selected transactions, but does not provide evidence on whether the authorized number of purchases is exceeded.

Subject Area: Conduct assurance engagements operational audits. Source: CIA 595, I-30.

**115. (b)** The password control is an absolute necessity, but the other two control procedures are necessary to accomplish the latter part of the objective. Choice (a) is incorrect. Rotating duties is a good control procedure, but it is not relevant to this specific control objective. Choice (c) is incorrect. Passwords accomplish part of the objective, but do not cover the last part of the objectives (authorized vendors and authorized products.) Choice (d) is incorrect. Rotating duties is a good control procedure, but it is not relevant to this specific control objective.

Subject Area: Conduct assurance engagements operational audits. Source: CIA 595, I-31.

**116. (c)** Inspection is a preventive control that prevents inferior or poor-quality goods being accepted. Choice (a) is incorrect. The control procedure is appropriate because one purchase order may generate more than one shipment. It is important that the correct number received is properly recorded, and this reconciliation accomplishes the task. Choice (b) is incorrect. Prenumbered receiving documents are not necessary because they are replaced by a required reference to the purchase order. The latter control is used because the organization is more concerned with accepting incorrect orders than in failing to record an order received. Goods should be inspected in the receiving department for quantity and quality at the time of receipt and receiving in-

formation documented at that time. Choice (d) is incorrect because choices (a) and (b) are incorrect.
Subject Area: Conduct assurance engagements operational audits. Source: CIA 595, I-32.

**117. (d)** The integrated test facility would provide the opportunity for the auditor to test the specific program throughout the year and could identify any breakdowns in the program as it occurs. Choice (a) is incorrect. The generalized audit software would have been a viable alternative had it sampled from the population of paid vendor invoices. Choice (b) is incorrect. The test data approach only tests for one specific point in time. Choice (c) is incorrect. The systems control and audit review file (SCARF) technique would have been a viable alternative had the selection criteria been based on the variance between the vendor invoice and the amount that should have been paid according to the purchase order and receiving document.
Subject Area: Conduct assurance engagements operational audits. Source: CIA 595, I-33.

**118. (a)** As organizations move to EDI and other forms of automated processing, it becomes crucial that a comprehensive data access and security program be implemented. Choice (b) is incorrect. Program changes should always be reviewed and tested by the user and the program librarian, not the programmer, who should only implement the changes. Choice (c) is incorrect. Initiation of changes to the vendor database by the purchasing agent would allow the purchasing agent to establish fictitious vendors. Choice (d) is incorrect. The receiving department needs access to the purchase order information to determine whether a shipment of goods ought to be received.
Subject Area: Conduct assurance engagements operational audits. Source: CIA 595, I-34.

**119. (c)** Hash totals are used to assess input errors, not to limit access. Choice (a) is incorrect. Terminal access restrictions limit access to data input sites. Choice (b) is incorrect. Password requirements help restrict input access. Choice (d) is incorrect. Validity tests on user IDs and product codes assist in determining the authorization of the person doing input.
Subject Area: Conduct assurance engagements operational audits. Source: CIA 596, I-44.

**120. (c)** The manual input and processing in the non-EDI transaction increase the risk of delayed payments and loss of purchase discounts. Choice (a) is incorrect. Open purchase orders have not yet been invoiced or paid. Choice (b) is incorrect. An EDI system is an unlikely to offer cash discounts. In addition, the auditor was involved in the design and testing of the EDI system. Risk assessment by the auditor incorporates knowledge of EDI system procedures. Choice (d) is incorrect since it mixes EDI and non-EDI invoices.
Subject Area: Conduct assurance engagements operational audits. Source: CIA 596, I-45.

**121. (a)** An exception report should be issued so company personnel can examine the discrepancy, determine the cause of the shortage, and take appropriate actions.
Choice (b) is incorrect. Adjusting the inventory for the difference would cause an overstatement. Choice (c) is incorrect. The company should determine the source of the dis-

crepancy. Choice (d) is incorrect. Payment should not be made for items that have not been received.

Subject Area: Conduct assurance engagements operational audits. Source: CIA 596, I-46.

**122. (c)** Sound system development and testing controls mitigate the risks associated with EDI. The internal auditing department's prior involvement affects the reliability of the system. Choice (a) is incorrect. This measure is not representative of the size of the purchases. Choice (b) is incorrect. The case indicates that the amount of purchases is equally divided between EDI and non-EDI purchases. Thus, this is not representative of the degree of risk. Choice (d) is incorrect. If the external auditor had conducted an independent review, this would have mitigated the risk and the internal auditor could take this into consideration. There is no indication why the external auditor did not examine purchase controls. There may have been reliance on the internal auditor's prior work.

Subject Area: Conduct assurance engagements operational audits. Source: CIA 596, I-47.

**123. (a)** The cash receipts/mail clerk is the best person to prepare the turnaround document because he or she has the correct information as to amount remitted. The cash and the turnaround document are segregated, but other control procedures, such as batch reconciliation, would detect any incorrect modification by the clerk. Choice (b) is incorrect. The treasurer could take the cash and cover it up by omitting a turnaround document. Choice (c) is incorrect. The accounts receivable clerk would not know the correct amount. Choice (d) is incorrect. The customer service department should not be handling any recording media.

Subject Area: Conduct assurance engagements operational audits. Source: CIA 595, I-1.

**124. (d)** This would best detect the defalcation because the totals of the debits to cash would not reconcile with the credits to accounts receivable for the batch from which the cash was taken. Choice (a) is incorrect. Analytical procedures can indicate large, unusual fluctuations in an account balance, but would not effectively detect the embezzlement of a single receipt. Choice (b) is incorrect. Customer inquiries reflect a negative image, and some customers would not even bother to report a problem. Choice (c) is incorrect. Periodic confirmation of receivables is a good control, but auditing should not be viewed as a substitute for the implementation of normal processing controls.

Subject Area: Conduct assurance engagements operational audits. Source: CIA 595, I-2.

**125. (d)** This is the most effective procedure because it is comparing interest income with ideal, specified criteria that is designed to measure investing efficiency. Choice (a) is incorrect. Industry averages are too vague and may incorporate too many other variables that would make the comparison meaningless. Choice (b) is incorrect. This would not be an effective comparison because divisions might vary in size and in purchasing requirements. Choice (c) is incorrect. There is no justifiable criterion for the 5% variance.

Subject Area: Conduct assurance engagements operational audits. Source: CIA 595, I-3.

**126. (c)** This is the most effective procedure because it takes into consideration the unique factors affecting each division. Choice (a) is incorrect. While this may work, there may be other costs and disadvantages. There is not enough evidence to justify this conclusion. Choice (b) is incorrect. Delegating the long-term financing to each division would not reduce the amount of borrowing that is taking place or the existence of excess cash by the one division. Choice (d) is incorrect. This might increase the receipt of cash, but would not affect the differences in cash balances between the divisions.

Subject Area: Conduct assurance engagements operational audits. Source: CIA 595, I-4.

**127. (c)** Physical inventories are the most significant control that can be implemented. Choice (a) is incorrect. This step may be added as a control to supplement physical inventories. Choice (b) is incorrect. This may be implemented. However, choice (c) is the best control since it would detect a problem with custody whereas insurance coverage can be used only if a loss is discovered. Choice (d) is incorrect. This may be implemented but is not considered to be a primary control.

Subject Area: Conduct assurance engagements operational audits. Source: CIA 1194, I-26.

**128. (a)** A well-designed control system that is set aside at management's discretion can be equivalent to no controls in terms of risk. Choice (b) is incorrect. It is a sufficient control without extenuating circumstances. Choice (c) is incorrect. Assuming both signers review the control is adequate. Choice (d) is incorrect. Absent extenuating circumstances, the purchasing agent would not be in a conflict of interest.

Subject Area: Conduct assurance engagements operational audits. Source: CIA 1194, I-30.

**129. (a)** This procedure will provide assurance that all shipments are invoiced. Choice (b) is incorrect. This procedure ensures that sales invoices are recorded, not that those shipments are invoiced. Choice (c) is incorrect. This procedure provides no assurance that shipments are invoiced. Choice (d) is incorrect. Customers who are not billed for a delivery may not notify the company.

Subject Area: Conduct assurance engagements operational audits. Source: CIA 1194, I-31.

**130. (d)** Examining bank statement reconciliations, confirming bank balances, verifying cutoff of receipts and disbursements, footing totals, and comparing cash account balances would be appropriate audit procedures to achieve the objective of ensuring that the amount of cash was accurately recorded on the company's financial statements. Choice (a) is incorrect. Audit procedures consisting of reviewing collection procedures, performing an analytical review of accounts receivable, confirming balances of accounts receivable, and verifying the existence of appropriate procedures and facilities would be appropriate for the objective of ensuring that all cash due is received. However, these audit procedures would be inappropriate for ensuring that the amount of cash was accurately recorded on the company's financial statements. Choice (b) is incorrect. Comparing cash receipt lists to the receipts journal and bank deposit slips, reviewing the segregation of duties, observing, and testing cash receipts would be appropriate audit procedures to satisfy the objective of safeguarding cash receipts. However, these audit procedures would be inappropriate for ensuring that the amount of cash was accurately recorded on the company's financial statements. Choice (c) is incorrect.

Reviewing the organizational structure and functional responsibilities; and verifying the existence and describing protection procedures for unused checks, including security measures, would be appropriate audit procedures to achieve the objective of ensuring that appropriate safeguards are in place to protect cash. However, these audit procedures would be inappropriate for ensuring that the amount of cash was accurately recorded on the company's financial statements.

Subject Area. Conduct assurance engagements operational audits. Source: CIA 1194, I-33.

**131. (c)** Since the manager is preparing checks for fake suppliers, there would be no supporting invoice for the payment. Choice (a) is incorrect. This control will not work unless the check signer also determines that the check is made out to a legitimate supplier. Choice (b) is incorrect. Making payment by certified check makes no difference. The problem is that the check is payable to a fake supplier. Choice (d) is incorrect. Accounting for numerical sequence ensures only that all checks are accounted for; it does not verify that the checks were issued to legitimate suppliers.

Subject Area: Conduct assurance engagements operational audits. Source: CIA 1194, I-62.

**132. (a)** Selection of items for cycle count should be done based on the relative value of the item or the relationship of the item to total volume of transactions. Choice (b) is incorrect. An appropriate and effective cycle count process should increase control. Choice (c) is incorrect. The number of adjustments is not indicative of the level of control in this situation. Choice (d) is incorrect. A properly controlled cycle count process could involve stockroom personnel in performing counts.

Subject Area: Conduct assurance engagements operational audits. Source: CIA 1194, I-67.

**133. (a)** Appropriate controls would have provided verification of the serial number by receiving personnel. The auditor should still pursue this issue to identify the customer's basis for citing the original serial numbers sent with the warranty claim to ensure that the related equipment had actually been reported in a sales transaction. Choice (b) is incorrect. Although the circumstances are unusual, the absence of appropriate controls in the receiving area provides a basis for pursuing additional information before alerting authorities within the organization. Choices (c) and (d) are incorrect. The circumstances require obtaining more information about the validity of this transaction.

Subject Area: Conduct assurance engagements operational audits. Source: CIA 1194, I-69.

**134. (a)** Inspection of goods by receiving inspectors is essential to prompt detection and reporting of all materials received that fail to meet specifications. Choice (b) is incorrect. Excessive acquisition is a purchasing function risk and not a receiving department risk. Choice (c) is incorrect. Inappropriate purchasing is involved here, and the risk is associated with noneconomical buying practices and conflicts of interest. Choice (d) is incorrect. This is a significant receiving risk, but returns to vendors are possible since no contract exists. The lack of an order can be detected promptly in either receiving (matching purchase order with the goods received) or in accounting (matching invoice with requisition, receiving report, and purchase order). There is a lesser risk of loss than with undetected substandard materials received.

Subject Area: Conduct assurance engagements operational audits. Source: CIA 590, I-15.

**135. (b)** If personnel records exist for employees for whom a time card exists, the bona fide nature of employment is a reasonable conclusion. Choice (a) is incorrect. Actual pay was not compared to reported hours worked. Choice (c) is incorrect. Pay rate is normally not shown on a time card. Choice (d) is incorrect. Payroll accounting records were not tested; only time cards were reviewed.

Subject Area: Conduct assurance engagements operational audits. Source: CIA 590, I-17.

**136. (d)** This control would provide better control over the number of units of the large-dollar-value items the firm keeps on hand and thereby would assist in the deteriorating working capital situation. Choice (a) is incorrect. This would verify that no inventory records were lost or no new ones added. It would not aid in the inventory acquisition problem. Choice (b) is incorrect. A limit test on the total inventory value would not assist in the inventory acquisition problem; it would only provide information as to when the inventory dollar level reaches a certain point. It would not provide vital information on the makeup of the inventory. Choice (c) is incorrect. Use of authorizing signature would provide control over requisitions but would not provide control over the inventory acquisition process, which is what the firm lacks.

Subject Area: Conduct assurance engagements operational audits. Source: CIA 590, I-26.

**137. (d)** The auditor would trace allowance entries to accounts receivable (which would be credits to accounts receivable) to the supporting credit memos. Appropriate personnel would then examine the credit memos for evidence of approval. Choice (a) is incorrect. The auditor would trace accounts receivable debit entries to sales invoices to determine whether the debits represent valid sales. Choice (b) is incorrect. Tracing accounts receivable credit entries to remittance advices would be a part of determining whether the credits represent actual collections from customers. Choice (c) is incorrect. Tracing accounts receivable entries to shipping documents would be performed to determine whether merchandise was shipped to the customer.

Subject Area: Conduct assurance engagements operational audits. Source: CIA 1190, I-8.

**138. (c)** Inventory is ordered only when supplies reach the predetermined stocking level. This helps prevent ordering unnecessary inventory. Choice (a) is incorrect. Competitive bidding helps ensure inventory is purchased at the lowest possible cost. Choice (b) is incorrect. Approved price lists allow the company to estimate the cost of inventory to be purchased. Choice (d) is incorrect. Negotiated vendor contracts would help ensure the terms of the relationship between the vendor and the company—especially price and quantity.

Subject Area: Conduct assurance engagements operational audits. Source: CIA 1190, I-9.

**139. (c)** This procedure would be the most appropriate means to verify that employees on the payroll are submitting current time cards. Choices (a) and (b) are incorrect. Using this procedure, separated employees who had not been removed from the payroll would continue to receive paychecks. Choice (d) is incorrect. This procedure would detect excessive pay going to current employees but not pay going to separated employees.

Subject Area: Conduct assurance engagements operational audits. Source: CIA 1190, I-10.

**140. (d)** This ideally describes the organizational structure and the functions and responsibilities of each department, which should help eliminate any potential unauthorized changes to payroll. Choice (a) is incorrect. The personnel department should be responsible for maintaining and authorizing all changes to personnel records. Choice (b) is incorrect. The payroll and personnel departments should be independent; neither should supervise the other. Choice (c) is incorrect. The payroll department functions should not include the posting of the payroll entries to the general ledger—this is the responsibility of the accounting department.

Subject Area: Conduct assurance engagements operational audits. Source: CIA 590, II-11.

**141. (a)** Omission of a key control, approval for payment, provides major opportunity for dishonest employees to initiate payments and escape prompt detection. Also, errors are more likely to go undetected for extended periods when this control is absent. Choice (b) is incorrect. Risk is minimal if internal controls are maintained properly, including vacations, supervision, and internal checks. Choice (c) is incorrect. Risk is minimized with proper screening of staff additions. The personnel department should be making background check on all staff additions. Choice (d) is incorrect. Posting does not directly lead to loss of cash; periodic review of accuracy of posting should detect error before significant erroneous payments are made.

Subject Area: Conduct assurance engagements operational audits. Source: CIA 590, II-12.

**142. (c)** Journal entries in the purchase journal can be reviewed to determine if they are supported by properly executed purchase orders. Choices (a), (b), and (d) are incorrect because none of them ensures whether purchases were properly authorized.

Subject Area: Conduct assurance engagements operational audits. Source: CIA 590, II-13.

**143. (a)** Operational audits are directly concerned with cost-benefit relationships as specified in the objective. Choice (b) is incorrect. This is a compliance consideration and not an operational audit objective. Choice (c) is incorrect. Financial statement presentation propriety is important, but is not an operational audit objective. Choice (d) is incorrect. This operational audit objective is not comprehensive and fails to consider such variables as workforce preferences.

Subject Area: Conduct assurance engagements operational audits. Source: CIA 590, II-14.

**144. (d)** A comparison of credit histories would allow for a determination of the consistency of policy application. Choice (a) is incorrect. If a customer was denied credit, there would be no account balance to confirm. Choice (b) is incorrect. If credit was denied, there would be no posting to trace. Choice (c) is incorrect. If credit is denied, there is no receivable and therefore no collection rate.

Subject Area: Conduct assurance engagements operational audits. Source: CIA 1190, II-15.

**145. (b)** Selection of routes and carriers is the chief function of the department, and poor practice may lead to materially excessive shipping costs and/or serious delays. Choice (a) is incorrect. This information is available from other sources, and the confirmation approach is unnecessary. Choice (c) is incorrect. The details of demurrage would not be as significant to the operations of the department as route and carrier selection. Choice (d) is incorrect. This is an internal control matter that, while important, is not central to department objectives.

Subject Area: Conduct assurance engagements operational audits. Source: CIA 1190, II-16.

**146. (b)** The company must protect itself against possible criminal or civil penalties from noncompliance with foreign governmental regulations regarding blocked currencies and multiple exchange rates. Choices (a), (c), and (d) are incorrect since they are unrelated to monetary transfers.

Subject Area: Conduct assurance engagements operational audits. Source: CIA 1190, II-18.

**147. (c)** A physical inventory would almost certainly be requested in an acquisition situation involving significant inventory values. Choice (a) is incorrect. Management certification letters as a means of attesting inventory values were discontinued in the late 1930s with the discovery of major fraud in the McKession & Robbins Company audit. Choice (b) is incorrect. Flowcharting the internal controls would not be an accurate test of inventory value in an acquisition situation. Choice (d) is incorrect. Testimonial evidence is not sufficient in determining the correctness of inventory values.

Subject Area: Conduct assurance engagements operational audits. Source: CIA 1190, II-19.

**148. (c)** Properly approved purchase requisitions vouch for the need for materials, and the issuance of a properly approved purchase order vouches for the authorization of the purchase transaction. Choice (a) is incorrect. Receiving reports are not the correct form of evidence since they are prepared at the end of the material acquisition cycle. Choice (b) is incorrect. Testimonial evidence is not conclusive without supporting documentation. Choice (d) is incorrect. Vendor invoice occurs at the end of the material acquisition cycle and does not vouch for either the need for materials or the authorization of the purchase.

Subject Area: Conduct assurance engagements operational audits. Source: CIA 1190, II-24.

**149. (c)** This would decrease the chance of discovering employees who entered hours they did not work on their time cards. Choice (a) is incorrect. Failing to approve the time cards would not result in duplicate paychecks. Choice (b) is incorrect. This may result if the hourly rates used to calculate pay are not matched to personnel records. Choice (d) is incorrect. This could be prevented by positively identifying paycheck recipients.

Subject Area: Conduct assurance engagements operational audits. Source: CIA 1190, II-8.

**150. (b)** Specifications for materials purchased provide an objective means of determining that the materials meet the minimum quality level required for production. Choice (a) is incorrect. This would not ensure that raw materials are of sufficient quality.  Choice (c) is incorrect.  This would only help ensure that raw materials are used in the proper quantities.  Choice (d) is incorrect.  This would only permit proper determination of spoilage after raw materials have been used in production.

Subject Area: Conduct assurance engagements operational audits.  Source: CIA 1190, II-9.

**151. (b)**  Supervisory review and approval of employees' time records is essential in a properly functioning internal control environment to provide assurance of employee time worked.  Choice (a) is incorrect.  Employees normally have no direct knowledge of the payroll cycle or entries.  Choice (c) is incorrect.  Government authorities will not normally provide such confirmation.  It is the employers' responsibility to ensure accuracy.  Choice (d) is incorrect.  If controls were to be relied on, it would be more appropriate to test to ensure supervisory initials as evidence of control rather than to recalculate.

Subject Area: Conduct assurance engagements operational audits.  Source: CIA 1190, II-29.

**152. (c)**  This procedure will help to ensure that purchases are made only from approved vendors.  Choice (a) is incorrect.  This procedure will control the quantity ordered but will not control the vendor.  Choice (b) is incorrect.  This procedure will help to ensure the maintenance of sufficient quantity on hand but will not control the vendor.  Choice (d) is incorrect.  This procedure will help to identify and evaluate the risks involved in the purchasing function but will not control the vendor.

Subject Area: Conduct assurance engagements operational audits.  Source: CIA 1190, II-10.

**153. (b)**  An operational audit would address the effectiveness, efficiency, and economy of the entire purchasing operation.  This is what the president has requested.  Choice (a) is incorrect.  This type of audit deals almost exclusively with the financial and accounting aspects of operations.  Choice (c) is incorrect.  This type of audit deals almost exclusively with compliance matters.  Choice (d) is incorrect.  Such an audit would deal with financial, compliance, and operational aspects of the whole manufacturing operation.  This goes beyond the president's request.

Subject Area: Conduct assurance engagements operational audits.  Source: CIA 1190, II-11.

**154. (d)**  The allowance for bad debts is determined based on the probability of collecting accounts receivable.  The age of an account is a major determinant of its collectibility.  Choice (a) is incorrect.  Aging accounts receivable would provide no information on sales revenue.  Choice (b) is incorrect.  The balance of the sale returns and allowance account is determined by actual returns and allowance, not by the age of accounts receivable.  Choice (c) is incorrect.  The balance of the accounts receivable account is not affected by the age of accounts receivable.

Subject Area: Conduct assurance engagements operational audits.  Source: CIA 1190, II-13.

**155. (d)**  Most companies large enough to have internal auditing do not physically distribute paychecks on a regular basis.  Moreover, this is generally regarded as an extended procedure most applicable to fraud audits.  Choices (a), (b), and (c) are incorrect because each choice is a routine procedure.

Subject Area: Conduct assurance engagements operational audits.  Source: CIA 594, II-44.

**156. (b)**  Determine if the check was deposited but the posting delayed.  This is an indication of lapping.  Choice (a) is incorrect.  The issue concerns the late deposit, not adjusting the receipt.  Choice (c) is incorrect.  This test deals with late billing, not late posting of receipts.  Choice (d) is incorrect.  This procedure would reconcile bank and book records; the issue is the possible delay in posting the receipt.

Subject Area: Conduct assurance engagements operational audits.  Source: CIA 594, I-31.

**157. (c)**  Comparing daily cash receipt totals to bank deposits would determine if cash was promptly deposited.  Choice (a) is incorrect.  A cash register tape does not ensure that cash is deposited to bank.  Choice (b) is incorrect.  Separating functions will not ensure that cash is deposited to the bank.  Choice (d) is incorrect.  Separate receiving and disbursing functions will not ensure that cash is promptly deposited.

Subject Area: Conduct assurance engagements operational audits.  Source: CIA 1193, I-10.

**158. (c)**  This will allow matching all recorded shipments to related billings.  Choice (a) is incorrect.  Invoices constitute bills; therefore, this is the wrong direction for a test to accomplish this audit objective.  Choice (b) is incorrect.  Accounts receivable is established by billings.  Choice (d) is incorrect.  Cash receipts from customers may be traceable to shipments, but this is the wrong direction for a test to accomplish this audit objective.

Subject Area: Conduct assurance engagements operational audits.  Source: CIA 1193, I-11.

**159. (b)**  is the appropriate control.  The warehouse copy of the purchase order should not list the quantities.  Choice (a) is incorrect.  A receiving function can be effective under normal organizational parameters.  Choice (c) is incorrect.  More than management awareness is needed.  Choice (d) is incorrect.  The receiving clerk must count the goods that are received and note the count on a receiving memo.  The receiving memo is sent to accounting where the quantities and prices are matched and the accounts payable process begins.

Subject Area: Conduct assurance engagements operational audits.  Source: CIA 1193, I-12.

**160. (d)**  The personnel function can only administer programs such as recruiting and job analysis.  It normally will not set staffing levels for individual departments.  Choice (a) is incorrect.  Recruiting does not necessarily address the issue of overstaffing.  Choice (b) is incorrect.  Individual job analyses are performed on positions established by other departments, and their presence or absence would have no impact on overstaffing.  Choice (c) is incorrect.  A centralized personnel function is normal but will not have any impact on the planned audit.

Subject Area: Conduct assurance engagements operational audits.  Source: CIA 1193, I-13.

**161. (a)**  The primary authority for expenditures is the budgetary control established for the project.  Choice (b) is incorrect.  The cost engineer's assurance would not confirm the authorization of these expenditures.  Choice (c) is incorrect.  The primary focus is the validity of the transaction within this construction project.  Choice (d) is incorrect.

There is no basis for reclassifying the transaction within this context.

Subject Area: Conduct assurance engagements operational audits. Source: CIA 1193, I-48.

**162. (d)** The risk of loss in the lack of a receiving report is much larger than the dating of a routine purchase order. Choice (a) is incorrect. The size of the particular exception does not reflect the risk of loss. The lack of a receiving report implicates the whole cash disbursement system. Choice (b) is incorrect. The clerk should not accept verbal assurance. Choice (c) is incorrect. Risk is the probability that an event may adversely affect an organization; it involves more than being related to cost.

Subject Area: Conduct assurance engagements operational audits. Source: CIA 1193, II-3.

**163. (a)** This preventive control provides remedies for uncontrolled access and safeguarding-of-assets considerations. Choice (b) is incorrect. This periodic, detective control would be effective only in compiling the amount of losses; it would not prevent the losses from occurring. Choice (c) is incorrect. This preventive and detective control does not record volume of tools removed from the small tool inventory. Choice (d) is incorrect. This preventive control does not limit access to the small tools inventory.

Subject Area: Conduct assurance engagements operational audits. Source: CIA 1193, II-7.

**164. (a)** Given the three-month manufacturing cycle, setting purchasing lead times uniformly would most likely increase inventory and holding costs. Choice (b) is incorrect. Rotating assignments would not directly affect holding costs. Choice (c) is incorrect. Approval requirements would not increase holding costs. Choice (d) is incorrect. This would address holding costs for finished goods but not for raw materials and subassemblies.

Subject Area: Conduct assurance engagements operational audits. Source: CIA 1193, II-9.

**165. (a)** The amount of cash received for the day as shown in the cash receipts journal should be equal to the amount of the deposit shown in the bank statement. Choice (b) is incorrect. This test would indicate whether cash receipts are being properly posted to customers' accounts, but does not determine when the receipts are being deposited in the bank. Choice (c) is incorrect. This test does not address whether the amounts of the deposits are equal to either amounts of daily cash receipts, or whether the deposits are being made on a timely basis. Choice (d) is incorrect. This test would indicate whether cash receipts are being properly journalized but not whether they are being properly deposited in the bank.

Subject Area: Conduct assurance engagements operational audits. Source: CIA 1193, II-15.

**166. (d)** Comparison of the invoice dates with dates stamped on the remittance advices would indicate whether the discount period had expired. Examination of the cash receipts journal entry would indicate whether the customer had been allowed the discount. Choice (a) is incorrect. A customer who had been allowed to take an improper cash discount is not likely to admit it in a confirmation response. Choice (b) is incorrect. This procedure relates to the timeliness of depositing cash receipts, not to the timeliness of customer payments. Choice (c) is incorrect. None of the documents listed indicates the date that the discount period expired.

Subject Area: Conduct assurance engagements operational audits. Source: CIA 1193, II-16.

**167. (a)** Matching the back-order file to shipments daily would identify unfilled orders for appropriate action. Choice (b) is incorrect. Increasing inventory levels might minimize the number of times that out-of-stock conditions occur but will not affect delivery of the items that are out of stock. Choice (c) is incorrect. Implementing electronic data interchange with supply vendors may decrease the time to replenish inventory but will not affect delivery of the items that are out of stock. Choice (d) is incorrect. Reconciling the sum of filled and back orders with the total of all orders placed daily ensures that orders were either filled or back-ordered but will not affect delivery of the items that are out of stock.

Subject Area: Conduct assurance engagements operational audits. Source: CIA 1193, II-30.

**168. (b)** The weakness affected all inventory purchases during the period. Choice (a) is incorrect. The weakness affected all inventories purchased during the period, not just the inventory still on hand at the end of the year. Choice (c) is incorrect. A weakness over inventory receipts would not be expected to affect other assets. Choice (d) is incorrect. A weakness over inventory receipts would not be expected to affect all operating expenses.

Subject Area: Conduct assurance engagements operational audits. Source: CIA 593, I-10.

**169. (b)** The weakness is most likely to result in unrecorded sales. Selecting bills of lading and tracing to sales invoices will test that goods shipped were billed. Choice (a) is incorrect. Selecting sales invoices from the sales register will not help detect unrecorded sales. Choice (c) is incorrect. Testing the sales register will not help detect unrecorded sales. Choice (d) is incorrect. Testing sales invoices will not help detect unrecorded sales.

Subject Area: Conduct assurance engagements operational audits. Source: CIA 593, I-11.

**170. (d)** After initiation by the personnel department, the functional department should have approval authority. Choices (a) and (b) are incorrect. Each procedure would not prevent or even detect the problem. Choice (c) is incorrect. The personnel department should initiate scheduled pay raises.

Subject Area: Conduct assurance engagements operational audits. Source: CIA 593, I-12.

**171. (b)** The splitting of cost savings encourages the contractor to be efficient and economical. Choice (a) is incorrect. It is unreasonable to expect to eliminate all change orders. Choice (c) is incorrect. The use of an agreed-on price for each unit of work constitutes a unit-price contract, not a cost-plus contract. Choice (d) is incorrect. A checklist approach to the audit of contracts results in sterile reviews.

Subject Area: Conduct assurance engagements operational audits. Source: CIA 593, I-13.

**172. (c)** If the quantities sold are approximately the same as those expected, an auditor could assume that the controls over the sale of scrap are effective. Choice (a) is incorrect. That presupposes that prior periods were correct and that no change quantity produced has occurred. Choice (b) is incorrect. Those persons could speak only of the safeguards in place to handle scrap before its sale. Choice (d) is incorrect. That only verifies the accuracy of perpetual inventory records.

Subject Area: Conduct assurance engagements operational audits. Source: CIA 593, I-18.

**173. (a)** By multiplying the number of trips authorized by the typical charge per trip, the discrepancy can be identified. Choice (b) is incorrect. Multiplying the trips noted on the bills received by the rate specified on the bill will not identify the improper billing related to trips not carried out. Choice (c) is incorrect. Scanning of ledger accounts and bills received is not likely to uncover billings for trips not carried out unless particular bills on ledger entries seriously deviate from expectations. Choice (d) is incorrect. It is unlikely that the internal auditor will be able to observe usage of the messenger service for a long enough period and then trace the usage back to billings. It is impractical on the basis of cost.

Subject Area: Conduct assurance engagements operational audits. Source: CIA 593, I-19.

**174. (d)** The procedures listed will all help to ensure that the allowance for doubtful accounts is accurately stated and therefore that the trade accounts receivable are carried on the balance sheet at their net collectible amounts. Choice (a) is incorrect. To accomplish this objective, the auditor would, at a minimum, select customers' accounts for confirmation, investigate any discrepancies reported, and determine whether any adjustments are necessary. Choice (b) is incorrect. To accomplish this objective, the auditor would, at a minimum, identify liens, security interests, and assets pledged as loan collateral through management inquiries, review of debt agreements, and the confirmation process. Choice (c) is incorrect. To accomplish this objective, the auditor would, at a minimum, have to test procedures to ensure that all goods shipped and all services rendered have been billed and recorded.

Subject Area: Conduct assurance engagements operational audits. Source: CIA 593, II-1.

**175. (b)** Internal control is inadequate because duties are not properly segregated. Choice (a) is incorrect. The system of internal control is not adequate because duties are not properly segregated. Choices (c) and (d) are incorrect. These are not the overall audit opinion; they are facts.

Subject Area: Conduct assurance engagements operational audits. Source: CIA 593, II-40.

**176. (d)** Using cash receipts to cover cash expenditures reduces control effectiveness for both receipts and expenditures. Cash should not be used to meet current expenditures. Instead, short-term financing, such as trade credit, should be used. Choice (a) is incorrect. Exclusive use of interest-bearing accounts maximizes earnings on invested cash. Choice (b) is incorrect. Interbank transfers to consolidate cash would have no effect if all investment accounts were interest bearing. Choice (c) is incorrect. More frequent billings maximize cash availability.

Subject Area: Conduct assurance engagements operational audits. Source: CIA 1192, II-19.

**177. (c)** The departmental supervisors are the most likely to be aware of the goods received by their departments, and segregating ordering authority from payment authority will prevent unauthorized purchases. Choice (a) is incorrect. Purchase orders do not provide evidence that the goods were received. Choice (b) is incorrect. Comparison with lists of authorized vendors does not provide evidence that goods were received. Choice (d) is incorrect. The vice president of finance is unlikely to have knowledge of goods received by the departments.

Subject Area: Conduct assurance engagements operational audits. Source: CIA 593, II-8.

**178. (a)** Management has discretion in deciding whether to capitalize or expense certain fixed asset purchases and repairs. Management may try to increase income by over-capitalizing fixed asset purchases and/or repairs. Subsidiary management has an incentive to overstate income. Auditors should pay special attention to areas where management may overstate revenue or understate expenses. Choice (b) is incorrect. Payroll disbursement procedures have less direct impact on income, require less judgment, and are less susceptible to management override. Choice (c) is incorrect. Bank account reconciliation procedures are low-level work routines that have less direct impact on income and require less judgment. Choice (d) is incorrect. Vendor invoice approval procedures are routine and have no relation to the acquisition of a new business. They are less susceptible to management override.

Subject Area: Conduct assurance engagements operational audits. Source: CIA 593, II-9.

**179. (c)** Use of the master price list assures correct retail price. Choice (a) is incorrect. Timing is not as important as the source of prices. Choice (b) is incorrect. That procedure would not ensure receipt of quantity ordered. Choice (d) is incorrect. Goods may or may not be needed in retail sales.

Subject Area: Conduct assurance engagements operational audits. Source: CIA 593, II-11.

**180. (a)** The types and amounts of insurance should be supported by periodic appraisals. Choice (b) is incorrect. The determination of insurance coverage is not a function of the board of directors. Choice (c) is incorrect. The consumer price index generally does not provide an appropriate adjustment factor for fixed assets. Choice (d) is incorrect. Property tax assessments generally do not correspond to production or real values.

Subject Area: Conduct assurance engagements operational audits. Source: CIA 593, II-12.

**181. (b)** A plan of job classifications is the basic element of compensation analysis and evaluation. Choice (a) is incorrect. Such a vague policy would contribute little if anything to the fair administration of compensation programs. Choice (c) is incorrect. A plan for reviewing individual compensation presupposes a classification plan. Choice (d) is incorrect. Reasonably competitive compensation is predicated on a classification plan.

Subject Area: Conduct assurance engagements operational audits. Source: CIA 1192, I-11.

**182. (a)** Supervisory review at the originating department level is one means of control over the number of items ordered. Choice (b) is incorrect. This procedure could lead to purchases of excess material because it does not consider future plans. Choice (c) is incorrect. This is a control for the risk of accepting unordered goods. Choice (d) is incorrect. This is a control for the risk of receiving an amount other than that ordered.

Subject Area: Conduct assurance engagements operational audits. Source: CIA 1192, I-15.

**183. (b)** A shipment should be rejected if it is not documented by a purchase order in the open file. Choice (a) is incorrect. This would be accomplished by inspecting the goods in a timely manner so they can be released to the appropriate department. Choice (c) is incorrect. The company should require such a count to be made when the goods arrive. Quantities may be left off the receiving department's copy of the purchase order to encourage personnel to make an accurate count. Choice (d) is incorrect. This is accomplished by adequate security over the receiving activities.

Subject Area: Conduct assurance engagements operational audits. Source: CIA 1192, I-19.

**184. (a)** Credit approval should be segregated from sales. Choice (b) is incorrect. Determination of product availability is not a problem and therefore needs no corrective action. Choice (c) is incorrect. Centralized management control does not address the problem of a lack of segregation of duties. Choice (d) is incorrect. Increased profit margins would not address the problem of a lack of segregation of duties.

Subject Area: Conduct assurance engagements operational audits. Source: CIA 1192, I-20.

**185. (d)** Separating the cash receipts and recordkeeping functions prevents an employee from misappropriating cash and altering the records to conceal it. Choice (a) is incorrect. The cash receipts may be physically safeguarded by such measures as a secure cash receiving point. Choice (b) is incorrect. Initial accountability may be fixed by issuing a source document (a receipt) when the cash is received. Choice (c) is incorrect. The cash receipts and disbursements functions should be separated in order to prevent paying cash disbursements directly from cash receipts.

Subject Area: Conduct assurance engagements operational audits. Source: CIA 1192, II-17.

**186. (d)** The written receipt fixes responsibility for the cash to the employee who collected it and issued the receipt. Choice (a) is incorrect. This would be accomplished by counting the cash received and comparing it to the total of the receipts. Choice (b) is incorrect. This would be accomplished by comparing the price charged to an approved price list. Choice (c) is incorrect. This would be ascertained by counting the cash and reconciling the expected total (beginning balance plus receipts).

Subject Area: Conduct assurance engagements operational audits. Source: CIA 1192, II-21.

**187. (c)** This is an audit objective because it states what the audit is to accomplish. Choice (a) is incorrect. Observation is an audit procedure. Choice (b) is incorrect. Analysis is an audit procedure. Choice (d) is incorrect. Recomputation is an audit procedure.

Subject Area: Conduct assurance engagements operational audits. Source: CIA 1192, II-23.

**188. (a)** Periodic rotation of purchasing agent assignments deters long-term relationships that can lead to favoritism, kickbacks, and inappropriate gifts to purchasing agents. Choice (b) is incorrect. Confirmation does not enable internal auditors to detect inappropriate benefits re-

ceived by purchasing agents or deter long-term relationships. Choice (c) is incorrect. Control specified could be helpful in ensuring value received for price paid but does not directly focus on receipt of inappropriate benefits received by purchasing agents. Choice (d) is incorrect. Control does not enable the organization to detect receipt of inappropriate amounts by agent or deter relationships that could lead to such activity.

Subject Area: Conduct assurance engagements operational audits. Source: CIA 1192, II-16.

**189. (a)** Reviewing and canceling the supporting documents would prevent paying a vendor twice for the same purchase. Choice (b) is incorrect. This would prevent the check from being misappropriated. Choice (c) is incorrect. This would ensure that the expenditure is debited to the proper account(s). Choice (d) is incorrect. This would ensure that only authorized purchases are made.

Subject Area: Conduct assurance engagements operational audits. Source: CIA 1192, II-18.

**190. (d)** This is the only control placed in the transaction flow early enough to prevent the addition of bogus employees to the payroll. Choice (a) is incorrect. The clerk could circumvent this control. Choices (b) and (c) are incorrect because these actions are taking place after the fact.

Subject Area: Conduct assurance engagements operational audits. Source: CIA 1192, II-20.

**191. (d)** A vendor invoice would show both the amount and terms of payment for purchase. Choice (a) is incorrect. Receiving reports would indicate the date and quantity received but would not show whether discounts were offered or taken. Choice (b) is incorrect. Purchase orders show only the quantity and expected price of a purchase. Choice (c) is incorrect. Canceled checks would show only the total paid, not whether a discount was offered or taken.

Subject Area: Conduct assurance engagements operational audits. Source: CIA 592, I-40.

**192. (c)** Competitive bids, especially for expensive equipment, are commonly the best way to ensure minimum costs. Choice (a) is incorrect. That procedure would test whether controls are in place to prevent abuse of the system. Choice (b) is incorrect. That procedure would test whether acquisitions were needed. Choice (d) is incorrect. That would only test whether acquisitions were authorized.

Subject Area: Conduct assurance engagements operational audits. Source: CIA 592, I-6.

**193. (b)** Receiving reports should go directly to accounts payable. Choice (a) is incorrect. Good practice ensures accurate communication. Choice (c) is incorrect. It is not a violation if they do not sign checks. Choice (d) is incorrect. It does not pose a threat.

Subject Area: Conduct assurance engagements operational audits. Source: CIA 592, I-19.

**194. (d)** These reports will advise ordering and purchasing personnel of available surplus stock. Choice (a) is incorrect. Purchasing agents would not normally have information on surplus conditions. Choice (b) is incorrect. That would prove the need but not the disposal of the same material. Choice (c) is incorrect. Unless the reorder point system is current, it could result in more surpluses.

Subject Area: Conduct assurance engagements operational audits. Source: CIA 592, I-22.

**195. (a)**   Separating the incompatible functions of access to goods received and authorization for payment is the best preventive control on the clerk's unauthorized actions because the clerk could no longer carry them out alone. Choice (b) is incorrect. Periodically reconciling quantities received with inventory transactions would be likely to detect inventory discrepancies but would not prevent them. Thus this is not a preventive control. Choice (c) is incorrect. Authorizing payment based on vendors' shipping documents would not deter the clerk from these actions because the clerk would authorize full payment anyway. Authorizing payment without comparing goods received with shipping documents might lead to overpayment for goods not received. Choice (d) is incorrect. Requiring passwords for access to the online inventory system would not deter the clerk from these actions because the clerk would be authorized to use the system and hence would have a legitimate password.

   Subject Area: Conduct assurance engagements operational audits.  Source: CIA 592, II-37.

**196. (d)**   If the purchasing agent has to buy from the lowest bidder, it will be much more difficult for the agent to steer business toward a favored vendor. Choice (a) is incorrect. The problem described is not unauthorized purchases; it is improper vendor selection after a purchase has been authorized. Choice (b) is incorrect. Even though the purchasing agent has to purchase important items from two vendors, he or she can continue to buy in high volume from a favored vendor. Choice (c) is incorrect. Decentralization simply puts more buyers in a position to engage in this type of improper activity.

   Subject Area: Conduct assurance engagements operational audits.  Source: CIA 1192, I-46.

**197. (d)**   Testing for paid invoices, which assumes that invoice records are marked paid as checks are produced, would have detected the duplicate check requests and thus prevented the second set of checks from being produced. Choice (a) is incorrect. In a computer agreement of batch totals, the batch totals would have agreed. Thus, the error would not have been prevented. Choice (b) is incorrect. In a manual agreement of a batch register, the batch totals would have agreed. Thus, the error would not have been prevented. Choice (c) is incorrect. In a batch sequence check, only specific ranges are checked for duplicates within the batch. Thus, a batch sequence check would not have prevented this error.

   Subject Area: Conduct assurance engagements operational audits.  Source: CIA 1191, I-30.

**198. (b)**   The purchase order authorizes the purchase. Choice (a) is incorrect. A document produced by the vendor cannot be used to determine if the purchase was authorized. Choice (c) is incorrect. An invoice is a vendor request for payment and is created based on the purchase order and the shipping document—a bill of lading. Choice (d) is incorrect. Policies and procedures are not transaction documents.

   Subject Area: Conduct assurance engagements operational audits.  Source: CIA 1191, I-1.

**199. (b)**   This is an example of inadequate segregation of functions. The treasurer could make unauthorized payments and conceal them. Choice (a) is incorrect. The treasurer should not reconcile the bank statements to accounting records; the controller should. Choice (c) is incorrect. The

stem does not indicate that the treasurer has access to the accounting records. Choice (d) is incorrect. Good control measures would provide the two opportunities to two different persons in positions of responsibility, the treasurer and the controller.

   Subject Area: Conduct assurance engagements operational audits.  Source: CIA 1191, I-12.

**200. (a)**   Irregularities in vendor information indicate potential for invalid liabilities being recorded. Choice (b) is incorrect. Irregularities in vendor information have little bearing on cutoff used. Choice (c) is incorrect. Recorded payables cannot be owned; rather, they can be valid. Choice (d) is incorrect. Valuation is not directly indicated by review of vendor information irregularities.

   Subject Area: Conduct assurance engagements operational audits.  Source: CIA 1191, I-16.

**201. (a)**   Computation of selected sales commissions provides evidence of mathematical accuracy. Choice (b) is incorrect. Calculating commission ratios uses gross sales and does not provide evidence about specific charges. Choice (c) is incorrect. Use of analytical procedures is a test of overall reasonableness. Choice (d) is incorrect. Tests of overall reasonableness are analytical procedures unrelated to specific transactions.

   Subject Area: Conduct assurance engagements operational audits.  Source: CIA 1191, I-18.

**202. (b)**   The payroll clerk should not be authorized such access. Choice (a) is incorrect because the standard form is probably accessible by the payroll clerk. Choice (c) is incorrect because it is too infrequent and is detective rather than preventive. Choice (d) is incorrect because it is a detective rather than a preventive control.

   Subject Area: Conduct assurance engagements operational audits.  Source: CIA 1191, II-11.

**203. (a)**   This is an appropriate objective for an audit of advertising agency billings. Choice (b) is incorrect. An appropriate objective would be to determine if the allowance is appropriate and reflects past collection performance. Choice (c) is incorrect. An appropriate objective would be to determine whether disposals were made in accordance with established policy. Choice (d) is incorrect. A more appropriate objective is to verify the receipt of properly authorized goods and services.

   Subject Area: Conduct assurance engagements operational audits.  Source: CIA 591, I-2.

**204. (c)**   Periodic rotation of buyer assignment will limit the opportunity of any buyer to show favoritism to a particular supplier. Choice (a) is incorrect. Total dollars committed would not detect favoritism shown individual vendors. Choice (b) is incorrect. Detailed product specifications will not prevent buyer favoritism in placing orders. Choice (d) is incorrect. The number of order placed is not relevant to preventing favoritism.

   Subject Area: Conduct assurance engagements operational audits.  Source: CIA 591, I-22.

**205. (c)**   The employee's supervisor would be in the best position to ensure payment of the proper amount. Choice (a) is incorrect. Employees may be properly included on payroll, but the amounts paid may be unauthorized. Choice (b) is incorrect. Undelivered checks provide no evidence regarding the validity of the amounts. Choice (d) is incorrect.

Witnessing a payroll distribution would not ensure that amounts paid are authorized.
  Subject Area: Conduct assurance engagements operational audits. Source: CIA 591, I-23.

**206. (d)** Supporting documentation should be canceled when payment is made to prevent its reuse (which could lead to duplicate payments). Choice (a) is incorrect. This only indicates whether purchases were properly approved. It says nothing about payments. Choice (b) is incorrect. This only indicates whether the goods were received. Choice (c) is incorrect. This would only indicate whether the company paid the proper prices.
  Subject Area: Conduct assurance engagements operational audits. Source: CIA 591, I-27.

**207. (c)** A conflict-of-interest policy should contain directives that restrict business dealings with relatives unless otherwise disclosed to and approved by senior management. Choice (a) is incorrect. An approved-vendor file approved by the director of purchasing would not prevent a situation such as this. Choice (b) is incorrect. Price is not a factor when dealing with conflicts of interest. Choice (d) is incorrect. While this is an appropriate receiving control, it does not pertain to this situation.
  Subject Area: Conduct assurance engagements operational audits. Source: CIA 591, II-20.

**208. (b)** The existence of such a contract would prevent disputes relating to recoverability of charges and expenses. Choice (a) is incorrect. Timely reporting will not resolve the problem. Choice (c) is incorrect. There is no evidence of incompatibility of duty assignment in the problem statement. Choice (d) is incorrect. Monthly report comparisons might detect the problem, but they will not prevent disputes of charges.
  Subject Area: Conduct assurance engagements operational audits. Source: CIA 591, II-21.

**209. (d)** A preventive maintenance program will reduce equipment breakdowns and repairs. Choice (a) is incorrect. Scheduling production based on capacity utilization is nonsense. Choice (b) is incorrect. Budgeting maintenance department activities based on previous work orders will not prevent equipment breakdowns and repairs. Choice (c) is incorrect. Standing authorizations of work orders and overtime will not address the problem posed.
  Subject Area: Conduct assurance engagements operational audits. Source: CIA 591, II-23.

**210. (b)** This may encourage receiving personnel merely to write the same quantity on the receiving report, without counting the shipment. Omitting the quantity on the copy of the purchase order would force receiving personnel to count each shipment. Choice (a) is incorrect. This could lead to selecting a vendor with poor internal control who shipped the wrong quantity. However, the receiving department should have noted the difference in quantity when the shipment was counted. Choice (c) is incorrect. Receiving personnel could inspect the quality of the goods without counting them. Choice (d) is incorrect. This would not lead to the difference in quantity. The number of units in the shipment should still agree with the receiving report.
  Subject Area: Conduct assurance engagements operational audits. Source: CIA 591, II-18.

**211. (c)** Performing a physical inventory would identify any erroneous quantities in the perpetual system that should be corrected to ensure a proper inventory valuation. Choice (a) is incorrect. Since the controls are weak, it would not prove efficient to test those controls. Choice (b) is incorrect. This testing should be performed as an analytical procedure, but it is not the primary audit procedure for weak controls in a perpetual inventory system. Choice (d) is incorrect. Gross profit analyses should also be performed, but would not be the primary procedure.
  Subject Area: Conduct assurance engagements operational audits. Source: CIA 1191, II-22.

**212. (d)** This policy would offer the best means of physical custody to prevent loss or theft. Choice (a) is incorrect. While a good policy, this control addresses the replacement cost if loss or theft occurs; it does not address reducing the risk of loss. Choice (b) is incorrect. It is an internal control designed to ensure control over the work performed; it has no bearing over the risk of loss. Choice (c) is incorrect. It is an excellent procedure that should be performed; however, it is more of an after-the-fact finding than a "prevent" control.
  Subject Area: Conduct assurance engagements operational audits. Source: CIA 592, II-15.

**213. (c)** Debit entries to the accounts are traced to invoices to ascertain whether they represent valid sales. Choice (a) is incorrect. This would be accomplished by tracing a sample of sales invoices to accounts receivable. Choice (b) is incorrect. This would be accomplished by tracing invoice prices to the company's approved price list. Choice (d) is incorrect. This would be accomplished by examining sales documents for evidence of proper approval by credit personnel.
  Subject Area: Conduct assurance engagements operational audits. Source: CIA 591, II-26.

**214. (b)** Attesting to the fairness of financial statements, even interim reports, is the purview of the independent external auditor, since the statements might be relied on by a third party, such as a bank or creditor. Choice (a) is incorrect. Controls over cash collections are part of the work called for by the IIA *Standards*. Choice (c) is incorrect. Evaluating the adequacy of the system of internal controls is a requirement of the *Standards*. Choice (d) is incorrect. Evaluating compliance is a requirement of the *Standards*.
  Subject Area: Conduct assurance engagements—financial audits. Source: CIA 1193, II-2.

**215. (d)** This element of the audit is not included in the IIA *Standards*. Choice (a) is incorrect. Reviewing the reliability and integrity of financial information is the basic element of the audit. Choice (b) is incorrect. The Statement includes compliance, and there are compliance aspects in financial operations. Choice (c) is incorrect. The auditor would review the economy, efficiency, and effectiveness of the financial functions.
  Subject Area: Conduct assurance engagements—financial audits. Source: CIA 1192, II-1.

**Information Technology Audit Engagements**

**216. (a)** Information systems must be aware of where its organization is going in the future in order to adequately support it. Choice (b) is incorrect. Without direction, even the most technical staff is not much use. Choice (c) is incorrect. Information technology is a support function, and money only helps it to be effective if it supports organization goals.  Choice (d) is incorrect.  In many cases the latest leading edge technology is not the most effective solution.

Subject Area: Conduct assurance engagements— information technology audits. CIA 1194, I-41.

**217. (c)**    The job of an auditor is like that of a salesperson: convincing the customer (the auditee) of the auditor's viewpoint.  The auditor should explain the advantages and disadvantages of each party's opinions.  If the first-level auditees are not convinced, then the auditor should escalate the matter to the next level of management in the hierarchy, and so on.

Subject Area: Conduct assurance engagements— information technology audits.  Source: Author.

**218. (c)**    In situations of hearsay, the auditor should handle the matter very carefully so as not to be criticized for using insufficient evidence.  First, the auditor should discuss the issue with audit management to see if they know something about the situation.  The audit management should move the case forward.  The auditor should not dismiss the hearsay matter (choice b.) and should not schedule an audit immediately (choice a.) because the information is unconfirmed.  The auditor should not talk to the system development project team (choice d.) because it is not appropriate at that time.

Subject Area: Conduct assurance engagements— information technology audits.  Source: Author.

**219. (a)**    Independence states that the auditor is to be independent of the auditee in attitude and appearance.  Designing controls is the responsibility of the auditee, and evaluating controls is the responsibility of the auditor.  Auditor lose independence if they designs the controls, but not when they do the other three things mentioned in choices (b), (c), and (d).

Subject Area: Conduct assurance engagements— information technology audits.  Source: Author.

**220. (d)**    In fraud situations, the auditor should proceed with caution.  When certain about a fraud, they should report it to the company management, not to external organizations. (choice c.)  The auditor should not talk to the employee suspected of fraud. (choice b.)  When not certain about fraud, the auditor should talk to the audit management.  The auditor cannot keep it as a secret (choice a.).

Subject Area: Conduct assurance engagements— information technology audits.  Source: Author.

**221. (a)**    In compliance audit testing, the auditor determines whether controls are in place and if they are effective.  Review of access security controls such as input, processing, and output is a part of the review of general controls, which should be done first.  Review of application controls should be performed after the review of general controls (choices b, c, and d).

Subject Area: Conduct assurance engagements— information technology audits.  Source: Author.

**222. (a)**    The application database file contains department name and codes for use in the application programs.  The application parameters contain dates; the log shows what programs are executed; and the program literal indicates the name (ID) of the program used.

Subject Area: Conduct assurance engagements— information technology audits.  Source: Author.

**223. (d)**    The auditor can document the procedures based on interviews and observations of employees' work.  The auditor could show the documentation to auditees for confirmation of his or her understanding prior to auditing against them.  The other three options are not effective in completing the current audit.

Subject Area: Conduct assurance engagements— information technology audits.  Source: Author.

**224. (d)**    This would allow the auditor to examine applications that are shared across users.  Choice (a) is incorrect.  This would provide limited information on end-user–developed applications, but would not provide any information on compliance with company policies.  Choice (b) is incorrect.  This would only provide information on knowledge of the policies, not compliance with the policies.  Choice (c) is incorrect.  This is a good procedure, but it is limited to applications stored on personal computers, not applications that are shared across users and would thus be stored on the server.  This procedure suffers further from the problem of requiring the auditor to look at all applications, not just those shared across users.

Subject Area: Conduct assurance engagements— information technology audits.  Source: CIA 597, I-21.

**225. (b)**    Controls over job scheduling for processing are essential to optimize use of computer resources and would give the best indication of the problem.  Choice (a) is incorrect.  Backup/restart procedures concern abnormally aborted processing of jobs.  Choice (c) is incorrect.  Console logs would only give indications of problems.  Console logs might be used later in the process, but they would not be the initial focus.  Choice (d) is incorrect.  Program documentation is not the correct place to start, but it might help later to determine why a given program was causing a problem.

Subject Area: Conduct assurance engagements— information technology audits.  Source: CIA 597, I-4.

**226. (a)**    This is the least risky area because the number of analysts and programmers may be more of a reflection of operating philosophy (buying new applications versus developing them).  This philosophy is unlikely to affect the probability of the event adversely affecting the operations.  Choice (b) is incorrect.  This is a risk area because (1) one of the companies has little experience with dealing with EDI, and (2) the complexity of computer communications in an EDI environment creates risk for those companies that have not yet established strong communication controls.  Choice (c) is incorrect.  This is a high-risk factor because the two different systems must be made compatible to achieve the economy of objectives and strategic plans of a merged organization.  The conversion from one systems or database structure to another is risky because data or applications may be lost or modified.  Employees will have to be retrained on the surviving system.  There is always increased risk of error when people are not familiar with a computer system.  Choice (d) is incorrect.  This is a heavy risk factor for all the reasons discussed in choice (c) above.

Subject Area: Conduct assurance engagements— information technology audits.  Source: CIA 1196, I-11.

**227. (a)**    Materiality is defined by the potential impact of an item on the organization and is not limited to items that can be assessed only in quantitative terms.  Choice (b) is incorrect.  There may be some control failures of a minor nature that would not be considered material.  Choice (c) is incorrect. Sampling approaches may be used to comprehensively cover the control structure of an organization. Choice (d) is incorrect. Responses II and III are not correct. See Choices (b) and (c) above.

Subject Area: Conduct assurance engagements—information technology audits. Source: CIA 1196, I-12.

**228. (b)** This could be very consistent with management's philosophy and would be considered part of the overall control environment. Detailed internal audit review can be an integral part of an organization's control structure. Choice (a) is incorrect. It is difficult ever to justify an audit approach or reporting style based on tradition. It may indicate the audit director is not in touch with management or that management may not be adopting its control philosophy to substantive changes in the environment. Choice (c) is incorrect. There is a "user" component of materiality, but it would be difficult to consider every situation or deviation as material. Choice (d) is incorrect. See choices (a) and (c).

Subject Area: Conduct assurance engagements—information technology audits. Source: CIA 1196, I-13.

**229. (b)** A formalized corporate code of ethics presents objective criteria by which actions can be evaluated and would thus serve as criteria against which activities could be evaluated. Choice (a) is incorrect. Response I is not correct. The existence of a corporate code of ethics, by itself, does not ensure higher standards of ethical behavior. It must be complemented by follow-up policies and monitoring activities to ensure adherence to the code. Choice (c) is incorrect. The IIA *Standards* that would influence individual actions can occur in other places than the corporate code of ethics. For example, there may be defined policies regarding purchasing activities that may serve the same purpose as a code of ethics. These policies also serve as criteria against which activities may be evaluated. Choice (d) is incorrect. See above responses.

Subject Area: Conduct assurance engagements—information technology audits. Source: CIA 1196, I-15.

**230. (b)** The audit director's preliminary findings should be reported immediately to the audit committee, rather than management, because the audit committee is considered an organization one level above where the alleged fraud is taking place. Choice (a) is incorrect. This response would not be appropriate because the internal auditors are not in a position to engage external legal counsel. Further, the findings should not be reported to management since they might be involved. Choice (c) is incorrect. The IIA *Standards* indicate that the auditors report the suspected fraud to the appropriate levels of the organization to determine whether an investigation is undertaken. The auditors may not be in the best position to determine whether the trading is fraudulent and certainly are not in a position to report the information to government officials. Choice (d) is incorrect. This would not be acceptable because the IIA's Code of Ethics clearly indicates that auditors cannot be associated with any illegal or inappropriate behavior. Ignoring their findings would violate that standard of conduct.

Subject Area: Conduct assurance engagements—information technology audits. Source: CIA 1196, I-16.

**231. (d)** This is the one explanation that could be supported by all the data elements and would thus form a hypothesis for subsequent audit testing. Choice (a) is incorrect. This might be a potential explanation for one store but

is unlikely to occur at all three stores. Choice (b) is incorrect. Although this might be a problem, the data tend to contradict it. Sales are increasing, which would indicate customer satisfaction. Choice (c) is incorrect. There is not enough evidence to indicate that fraud might be present. In order for this hypothesis to hold true, there would have to be significant amounts of inventory shrinkage. This does not explain higher sales and bonuses.

Subject Area: Conduct assurance engagements—information technology audits. Source: CIA 1196, I-17.

**232. (c)** If this type of fraud was occurring, it would result in inventory shrinkage. The surprise inventory count would be an effective audit technique. Choice (a) is incorrect. The ITF only provides evidence on the correctness of computer processing. It would not be relevant to the hypothesized rationale for the operating data. Choice (b) is incorrect. Interviews provide a weak form of evidence and would be better if the auditor first has substantive documentary evidence. Choice (d) is incorrect. The problem is with inventory shrinkage, not whether items are appropriately keyed in or scanned in at the cash register.

Subject Area: Conduct assurance engagements—information technology audits. Source: CIA 1196, I-18.

**233. (a)** This would be the least effective procedure because: (1) it provides only a comparison with the past period, and that past period may have been suffering from the same problem; and (2) it is a global test. Choice (b) is incorrect. Using an ITF would be a very good procedure here because the concern is whether the interest rate calculation is made correctly. Choice (c) is incorrect. Test data would be very effective because they provide a direct test of the interest rate calculation. Choice (d) is incorrect. This would be the most effective procedure because the auditor is taking a detailed sample of actual transactions.

Subject Area: Conduct assurance engagements—information technology audits. Source: CIA 1197, I-48.

**234. (d)** Auditor judgment is a personal characteristic, not a function of the quality of the information. Choice (a) is incorrect. The use of information technology allows more data to be reviewed in greater detail, reducing the possibility of unidentified material errors. Choice (b) is incorrect. Technology can speed the performance of procedures and the reporting of the findings. Choice (c) is incorrect. Information technology can be used to implement a new approach to the audit of an application or function, instead of just automating existing tasks.

Subject Area: Conduct assurance engagements—information technology audits. Source: CIA 1196, I-5.

**235. (d)** This is the only procedure that would address the correctness of data already contained in the database. Choice (a) is incorrect. Test data would provide evidence only about the correctness of processing—at the single point in time it is used—and would not provide information on the correctness of data already in the database. Choice (b) is incorrect. Similar to response (a), this approach would provide information only about the correctness of processing for the data selected. Choice (c) is incorrect. This would provide only partial information on one field of the data. The auditor needs a more comprehensive test, which is included as response (d).

Subject Area: Conduct assurance engagements—information technology audits. Source: CIA 1196, I-35.

**236. (b)** This would be the most appropriate control because it (1) requires supervisory signed approval, (2) limits access to the tables to selected personnel within the payroll department, and (3) provides independent reconciliation of all changes. Choice (a) is incorrect. Access to the database (tables) of employee rates should be severely restricted to authorized personnel within the human resources department or payroll personnel. Proper supervisor personnel should approve the rates but not have access to the tables. Choice (c) is incorrect. Edit checks will not detect invalid changes. Choice (d) is incorrect. The concern is not with bona fide employees. The concern is to gain assurance that all changes to the table are properly authorized and input into the system. Further, one pay rate will apply to more than one employee.

Subject Area: Conduct assurance engagements—information technology audits. Source: CIA 1196, I-36.

**237. (a)** This would be the best control procedure because it appropriately segregates duties and requires review by someone outside of the department. Choice (b) is incorrect. This would be an improper segregation of duties for human resources personnel because they would both input employees' and their own hours. They could commit the same type of fraud. Choice (c) is incorrect. This is a good control, but it would relate only to changes. If someone in payroll input a new employee without supervisory approval and proceeded with the fraud, it would not be detected or prevented by this control. Choice (d) is incorrect. This would not necessarily be effective if the payroll employee withheld the fictitious paycheck for distribution. This would also not be considered a cost-effective technique as companies are moving to automate more of the process.

Subject Area: Conduct assurance engagements—information technology audits. Source: CIA 1196, I-37.

**238. (c)** This is the best response because it takes choice (a) one step further by keeping the completed checks out of the hands of human resources personnel. Choice (a) is incorrect. This is a good procedure because it properly segregates the addition of an employee and the processing of individual paychecks. However, it is not as strong as choice (c), which further segregates the distribution of checks. Choice (b) is incorrect. The human resources department has all the control; it adds employees, submits hours, and distributes the checks. Choice (d) is incorrect. Payroll should not be in a position to add employees because it would then have opportunities to submit fictitious hours for fictitiously created employees.

Subject Area: Conduct assurance engagements—information technology audits. Source: CIA 1196, I-38.

**239. (a)** This is the least effective procedure because it only provides evidence on the transactions that are being processed at this particular point in time. It does not provide evidence that retired employees would actually be paid correctly. The audit concern is with the overall processing, including all data items that were input at the time of conversion from the manual system. Choice (b) is incorrect. The integrated test facility is better than choice (a) because it provides evidence on the correctness of the processing over a greater period of time. Choice (c) is incorrect. Classical variable estimation is the appropriate sampling technique. Choice (d) is incorrect. Selecting data from existing files is appropriate. Stratification can be on attributes other than dollar amounts. The choices appear to be reasonable.

Subject Area: Conduct assurance engagements—information technology audits. Source: CIA 1196, I-39.

**240. (c)** This would be the best procedure because the analytical review is based on a per-person basis consistent with the changes in the pension plans. Choice (a) is incorrect. This would not be the best procedure because it does not take into account the possibility that there may be more retirements in recent years, which could account for increases in benefits paid. Choice (b) is incorrect. The objective is to gather information on the need for further audit work. The best procedure for planning purposes is a well-formulated analytical review. Further, if audit software is to be used, dollar unit or PPS is not the appropriate sampling technique because the auditor is not testing for the possible overstatement of a book value. Choice (d) is incorrect. The objective is to gather information on the need for further audit work. The best procedure for planning purposes is a well-formulated analytical review.

Subject Area: Conduct assurance engagements—information technology audits. Source: CIA 1196, I-40.

**241. (c)** To the extent designs are inadequate, rework will be necessary. The audit involvement approach that minimizes rework costs is continuous involvement. Choice (a) is incorrect. Continuous audit involvement has the highest cost of all the alternatives. Choice (b) is incorrect. If internal audit is involved with systems development at the end of stages, there are clear points at which to issue audit comments. Choice (d) is incorrect. The threat of lack of audit independence is minimized with audit involvement only after implementation.

Subject Area: Conduct assurance engagements—information technology audits. Source: CIA 1196, I-55.

**242. (c)** General controls relate to security and proper segregation of duties. Choice (a) is incorrect. Error listings relate to application controls. Choice (b) is incorrect. Record counts relate to application controls. Choice (d) is incorrect. Error listings relate to application controls.

Subject Area: Conduct assurance engagements—information technology audits. Source: CIA 596, I-11.

**243. (b)** Without formal systems analysts, user-developed applications have no independent review. Also, it may be difficult for users to specify complete requirements. Choice (a) is incorrect. While inadequate testing may fail to detect the missing or erroneous logic, it would not be the underlying cause of the problem. Choice (c) is incorrect. A poorly documented application is more difficult to turn over to another person to operate or change. Choice (d) is incorrect. Lack of segregation of duties is a risk associated with concealment of errors or fraud.

Subject Area: Conduct assurance engagements—information technology audits. Source: CIA 596, I-27.

**244. (d)** Balancing totals should be used to ensure completeness and accuracy of processing. Choice (a) is incorrect. A standard method for uploading data may not include the controls necessary to detect errors in the uploading process. Choice (b) is incorrect. Edit and validation checks are typically designed to identify errors in data entry rather than errors in processing. Choice (c) is incorrect. A record or log of rejected items is a control for monitoring the subsequent correction and processing of the items.

Subject Area: Conduct assurance engagements—information technology audits. Source: CIA 596, I-28.

**245. (c)** There may be confusion over what has changed and the procedures related to the change. Choice (a) is incorrect. The reliability of the information processed may or may not be reduced due to a variety of risks of which this may or may not be one. Choice (b) is incorrect. Departmental management has the responsibility for authorizing all EUC activity and must determine controls accordingly. Choice (d) is incorrect. The consultants may properly test the changes.

Subject Area: Conduct assurance engagements—information technology audits. Source: CIA 596, I-29.

**246. (d)** The relationship between the application controls and the general controls is such that general controls are needed to support the functioning of application controls, and both are needed to ensure complete and accurate information processing. Choice (a) is incorrect. Application controls are dependent on the general controls. Choice (b) is incorrect. In an EUC environment, several individuals in different departments or locations may share responsibility for general controls. Choice (c) is incorrect. The need for specific general controls varies with the complexity and importance of the application.

Subject Area: Conduct assurance engagements—information technology audits. Source: CIA 596, I-30.

**247. (b)** Sophisticated software packages may inadvertently threaten data security by allowing users to bypass existing system level security. Choice (a) is incorrect. Restricting access to LAN workstations is a control to prevent unauthorized persons from gaining access to the network. Choice (c) is incorrect. Password security when logging on may not prevent authorized users of the LAN from accessing unauthorized functions. Choice (d) is incorrect. A security policy may establish responsibility but will not prevent inappropriate update of information.

Subject Area: Conduct assurance engagements—information technology audits. Source: CIA 596, I-31.

**248. (a)** Edit or validation routines should be present in the application to reject or flag these unusual items. Choice (b) is incorrect. Rejected and suspense item controls are relevant only if the data are first subject to edit and validation checks. Choice (c) is incorrect. Controls over update access to the database are general controls rather than application controls. Choice (d) is incorrect. Programmed balancing controls are designed to identify errors in the processing of data rather than in the data itself.

Subject Area: Conduct assurance engagements—information technology audits. Source: CIA 596, I-32.

**249. (d)** Decryption may need to occur after information is received, but encryption is what occurs when information is encoded for transfer. Choice (a) is incorrect. The identity of the requestor should be verified. Choice (b) is incorrect. Information should be authenticated before transfer. Choice (c) is incorrect. Information that is not authenticated is an exception that should be identified for additional processing.

Subject Area: Conduct assurance engagements—information technology audits. Source: CIA 596, I-49.

**250. (d)** These tests can identify duplicate payments. Choice (a) is incorrect. Selection of transactions with unauthorized vendor codes and testing of transactions for reasonableness do not identify duplicate payments. Choices (b) and (c) are incorrect. Testing transaction amounts for reasonableness does not identify duplicate payments.

Subject Area: Conduct assurance engagements—information technology audits. Source: CIA 596, I-50.

**251. (a)** This is a scope limitation. It must be reported to the board of directors unless they were previously communicated to and accepted by the board. Choice (b) is incorrect. Only the board or management should communicate with the board of the VAN. Choice (c) is incorrect. The internal auditor should not communicate directly with the board of the VAN. Choice (d) is incorrect. This must be reported.

Subject Area: Conduct assurance engagements—information technology audits. Source: CIA 596, I-51.

**252. (b)** The original audit program should be annotated but not rewritten. Choice (a) is incorrect. A description of the audit scope limitation should be included in the final report. Choice (c) is incorrect. The approval of the director should be obtained. Choice (d) is incorrect. The VAN's actions should be included in the work papers.

Subject Area: Conduct assurance engagements—information technology audits. Source: CIA 596, I-52.

**253. (a)** Time lag is the amount of time it takes a regular check to arrive at the payee, be deposited, and clear through regular banking channels. All of these processes are eliminated with EFT. Choice (b) is incorrect. EFT can reduce the payment time. Choice (c) is incorrect. EFT allows for control of payments and transfers among accounts. Choice (d) is incorrect. Integration of EDI and EFT eliminates the requirement to manually input transaction data and introduce errors during the process.

Subject Area: Conduct assurance engagements—information technology audits. Source: CIA 596, I-53.

**254. (d)** One of the benefits of an electronic system is that it can provide remote access at any hour of the day across various time zones. However, appropriate controls should prevent unauthorized access. Choice (a) is incorrect. This information is needed to provide an audit trail. Choice (b) is incorrect. Disaster recovery plans are needed to ensure the company can continue to function if the system goes down. Choice (c) is incorrect. Unauthorized individuals should not be provided with the ability to change documents.

Subject Area: Conduct assurance engagements—information technology audits. Source: CIA 596, I-54.

**255. (b)** EDI allows for the rapid ordering of goods that would be beneficial in a just-in-time environment. Choice (a) is incorrect. A large volume of repetitive purchases from the same vendors would suggest that EDI should be considered for implementation. Choice (c) is incorrect. See answer for choice (a). Choice (d) is incorrect. A large volume of custom purchases would be difficult to do on EDI. Also, see answer for choice (a).

Subject Area: Conduct assurance engagements—information technology audits. Source: CIA 596, I-55.

**256. (a)** EDI systems rely on technical personnel for operations. Changes in personnel suggest that increased attention be given to system changes and operating controls and procedures. Choices (b), (c), and (d) are incorrect. Although these items are risk factors for any auditable activity, EDI systems are designed to accommodate fluctuations in volume and competitive activity.

Subject Area: Conduct assurance engagements—information technology audits. Source: CIA 596, I-56.

**257. (d)** A limit test is a test of whether a field amount fits within a predetermined upper and/or lower limit. It can only catch certain errors (i.e., those that exceed the acceptable range). Choice (a) is incorrect. A record count provides the number of documents entered into a process. Choice (b) is incorrect. An echo check is designed to check the reliability of computer hardware. Choice (c) is incorrect. A self-checking number contains digits that are a formula of the other digits. Account numbers with a self-checking digit reduce data input errors.

Subject Area: Conduct assurance engagements—information technology audits. Source: CIA 596, I-57.

**258. (b)** A validity test can compare the value of a customer account number field with a master file containing valid customer accounts. Choice (a) is incorrect. A limit test is a test of whether a field amount fits within a predetermined upper and/or lower limit. It can only catch certain errors (i.e., those that exceed the acceptable range). Choice (c) is incorrect. A control total is the number of transactions in a batch. Choice (d) is incorrect. A hash total is the number obtained from totaling the same field value for each transaction in a batch. The total has no meaning or value other than as a comparison with another hash total.

Subject Area: Conduct assurance engagements—information technology audits. Source: CIA 596, I-58.

**259. (d)** The costs must be considered in terms of the potential benefits of the security. The benefit of implementing security comes through a reduction of exposure, which is measured by items I and II. Choice (a) is incorrect. Potential loss is an important concept and captures information about the amount of dollar damages associated with a security problem or loss of assets. However, it is incomplete by itself. Choice (b) is incorrect. Potential loss times the probability of occurrence is an estimate of the exposure associated with the security problem. It presents a potential benefit amount associated with the implementation of security. However, it is incomplete by itself. Choice (c) is incorrect. In order to perform a cost-benefit analysis, the benefits should be considered. Thus, all three items need to be addressed.

Subject Area: Conduct assurance engagements—information technology audits. Source: CIA 1195, I-31.

**260. (c)** This would appropriately restrict access to the program modules that are running. Choice (a) is incorrect. Good control dictates that programmers cannot make undetected, unrecorded changes to data or programs. Thus, programmers should be restricted from accessing the production library. Choice (b) is incorrect. Programmers should be responsible for making program changes, and users should be responsible for testing the changes. It would be poor control to allow users to have access to the test library. It would decrease accountability. Choice (d) is incorrect. If the operator had access to both program libraries, the operator would be in a position to make unauthorized and undetected changes to the computer programs.

Subject Area: Conduct assurance engagements—information technology audits. Source: CIA 1195, I-32.

**261. (c)** "See-through" authentication techniques, such as the one described, require users to have two of the three important elements to identify themselves to the system: something they possess (the card used to generate the password) and something they know (the key or password to generate the new password). Choice (a) is incorrect. This is the least effective procedure to protect highly sensitive assets since users often pick passwords that are easily guessed—for example, the names of their children. Choice (b) is incorrect. This is an effective approach to maintain hard-to-guess passwords and would be an incremental level of protection above response (a). Choice (d) is incorrect. This provides an incremental level of security over response (a) by limiting access to times and locations where someone unauthorized using the computer terminal would be noted. However, this method is not universal since many systems allow dial-up access from many different locations.

Subject Area: Conduct assurance engagements—information technology audits. Source: CIA 1195, I-36.

**262. (b)** Concurrency controls are important to ensure that all updates to the database are recorded. The controls address the problem of two users attempting to update the database at the same time. Choice (a) is incorrect. End-user computing frees the end user from the need to have each request approved by data processing. This would include end-user applications that use large mainframe databases. Choice (c) is incorrect. Fourth-generation languages have been developed to run efficiently on mainframe computers. The distinction between mainframe and microcomputers is not important here. Choice (d) is incorrect. Relational data models are popular but are not needed to support multiple users or end-user computing.

Subject Area: Conduct assurance engagements—information technology audits. Source: CIA 595, I-26.

**263. (c)** Both the self-checking digit and the oral verification should address the problem of incorrectly identifying the product number. Choice (a) is incorrect. A self-checking digit would address the problem, but so would oral verification. Response (c) is more complete. Choice (b) is incorrect. Assigning a sequential number to the customer's order helps build an audit trail but does not address the product identification issue. Choice (d) is incorrect. The sequential numbering does not address the problem.

Subject Area: Conduct assurance engagements—information technology audits. Source: CIA 595, I-27.

**264. (d)** Users typically have direct responsibility for the physical security of equipment, as they use it directly. Choice (a) is incorrect. Acquisition of hardware and software is typically an organizational and departmental control responsibility. Choice (b) is incorrect. Taking of equipment inventories is typically an organizational and departmental control responsibility. Choice (c) is incorrect. Strategic planning of end-user computing is typically an organizational and departmental control responsibility.

Subject Area: Conduct assurance engagements—information technology audits. Source: CIA 1194, I-37.

**265. (d)** All of the above risks are likely. Choice (a) is incorrect. Copyright violations are a common risk. Choice (b) is incorrect. Unauthorized access is a common risk. Choice (c) is incorrect. Lack of data availability is a common risk.

Subject Area: Conduct assurance engagements—information technology audits. Source: CIA 1194, I-38.

**266. (b)** Access control software provides comprehensive and coordinated security across software types and should be considered as an option. Choice (a) is incorrect. The built-in access controls should not be eliminated until more cost-effective access controls are identified. Choice (c) is incorrect. Utility software is intended primarily for systems development and to assist in operations management of the computer system. Choice (d) is incorrect. Built-in access controls should not be expanded without considering more cost-effective alternatives, such as access control software.

Subject Area: Conduct assurance engagements—information technology audits. Source: CIA 1194, I-27.

**267. (c)** The comparison represents analytical evidence that should identify ex-employees who are accessing the databases but who are not on the current payroll. Choice (a) is incorrect. Although the data base administrator is responsible for security, discussions with the database administrator represent testimonial evidence, which is not conclusive on its own. Choice (b) is incorrect. A log of access attempts will not identify if a person accessing a database is no longer an employee. Choice (d) is incorrect. Review of access control software that is not a specific test designed to identify who has access to the databases.

Subject Area: Conduct assurance engagements—information technology audits. Source: CIA 1194, I-28.

**268. (b)** Encryption is the conversion of data into a code. You may be able be able to access the data by tapping into the transmission line. However, you need an encryption key in order to understand the data being sent. Choice (a) is incorrect. Asynchronous transmission does not prevent theft of data; it speeds up the transmission process. Choice (c) is incorrect. Fiber-optic transmission lines will improve the quality of the transmission but will not prevent theft of data. Choice (d) is incorrect. Use of passwords will control access at the sending location and will limit access to the head office computer. Passwords, however, will not prevent someone from tapping into the transmission line.

Subject Area: Conduct assurance engagements—information technology audits. Source: CIA 1194, I-63.

**269. (b)** Backup and recovery is the responsibility of each individual user in an end-user computing environment. Choice (a) is incorrect. Standards are more properly the responsibility of the organization or department. Choice (c) is incorrect. Most end users do not have the knowledge to read manuals of this nature. Choice (d) is incorrect. The end user has custody of some equipment and therefore should not be responsible for the inventory.

Subject Area: Conduct assurance engagements—information technology audits. Source: CIA 1194, I-42.

**270. (b)** In general, there is no end-user environment equivalent to the mainframe software and procedures (which ensure centralized control) for installing programs and maintaining change histories. Choice (a) is incorrect. Adequate software tools for writing input validation for application programs is available in both environments. Choice (c) is incorrect. Encryption features implemented in hardware or software are available in both the mainframe and the end-user environments. Choice (d) is incorrect. Software for

relational database queries is available for both environments.

Subject Area: Conduct assurance engagements—information technology audits. Source: CIA 1194, I-43.

**271. (a)** Daily changes to the system make it difficult to adequately document. As a result, future changes to the system may be delayed, as system maintainers become familiar with the system the hard way. Choice (b) is incorrect. Instead of failing to consider alternative approaches, using prototyping tends to encourage experimentation to consider alternative approaches. Choice (c) is incorrect. In general, prototyping as a system development approach is associated with faster development. Choice (d) is incorrect since only one answer is correct.

Subject Area: Conduct assurance engagements—information technology audits. Source: CIA 1194, I-44.

**272. (d)** Given the uncontrolled entry of promotional prices, operators could sell goods to outside accomplices at unauthorized prices. Choice (a) is incorrect. It is not likely that customers would be charged a lower price. The charge would probably be higher than the promotional price. Choice (b) is incorrect. The price must be written in every order whether the operator overrides it with a promotional price. Choice (c) is incorrect. Operators could share the special prices with competitors regardless of whether they enter them into the system with each order. Also, the competitor could also get promotional prices from a catalogue.

Subject Area: Conduct assurance engagements—information technology audits. Source: CIA 1194, I-45.

**273. (d)** The purpose of internal auditing's review of IT data entry operations is to determine whether input/output controls are adequate and effective. Choice (a) is incorrect. The purpose of determining whether system development standards exist and have been followed is to assure that systems are developed in a controlled environment. Choice (b) is incorrect. System developers need the skills and knowledge required for the systems they develop, but confirming this is not a function of internal auditing's review of IT operations. Choice (c) is incorrect. Internal auditing is responsible for assessing the effectiveness and efficiency of operations and the adequacy of controls. Employing state-of-the-art equipment and procedures is not necessarily required for effective, efficient systems.

Subject Area: Conduct assurance engagements—information technology audits. Source: CIA 590, II-19.

**274. (b)** A very important aspect of any operational audit is performance measures. Choice (a) is incorrect. This is not a primary concern in an operational audit. Choices (c) and (d) are incorrect since they are relatively unimportant.

Subject Area: Conduct assurance engagements—information technology audits. Source: CIA 1190, II-14.

**275. (b)** There is a definite risk that the company's data or programs could be corrupted by a computer virus that one of the employees contracted through a shareware network or by downloading software from an electronic bulletin board. External, unproven software could also have bugs that may not be evident until it has damaged the integrity of the company's data files. Choice (a) is incorrect. No conclusion can be drawn about the existence of quality standards based on the information given. Choice (c) is incorrect. There is no justification for a cost-benefit analysis on the use of externally obtained software.  Choice (d) is incorrect.  No conclusion can be drawn about quantitative performance standards based on the information given.

Subject Area: Conduct assurance engagements—information technology audits.  Source: CIA 1190, II-6.

**276. (d)**  Auditor judgment is a personal characteristic, not a function of the quality of the information.  Choice (a) is incorrect.  The use of information technology allows more data to be reviewed in greater detail, reducing the possibility of unidentified material errors.  Choice (b) is incorrect.  Technology can speed the performance of procedures and the reporting of the findings.  Choice (c) is incorrect.  Information technology can be used to implement a new approach to the audit of an application or function, instead of just automating existing tasks.

Subject Area: Conduct assurance engagements—information technology audits.  Source: CIA 594, II-3.

**277. (d)**  Limitations on the audit trail (no history files, incomplete printed output, etc.) restrict the nature and timing of audit tests.  Choice (a) is incorrect.  Inadequate password protection does not restrict the nature and timing of audit procedures.  Choice (b) is incorrect.  Failure to specify backup and recovery procedures does not restrict the nature and timing of procedures.  Choice (c) is incorrect.  The fact that microcomputer hardware is accessible does not restrict audit procedures.

Subject Area: Conduct assurance engagements—information technology audits.  Source: CIA 1191, II-34.

**278. (c)**  Encryption is a communication control for security and not related to backup and recovery.  Choice (a) is incorrect.  Data file backups are critical and the auditor would review the adequacy to the backup files.  Choice (b) is incorrect.  The controls over hardware and software failures are included in the review of backup and recovery.  Choice (d) is incorrect.  Documented responsibilities for backup and recovery and personnel knowledge of their responsibilities are very important in the backup and recovery process.  Auditors would review the documentation and knowledge of responsibilities.

Subject Area: Conduct assurance engagements—information technology audits.  Source: CIA 594, I-65.

**279. (b)**  Reviewing job logs, job schedules, and documentation of computer downtime provides an objective record of actual hardware usage.  Choice (a) is incorrect.  User satisfaction surveys are subjective and are not directly related to efficient use of the hardware resources.  Choice (c) is incorrect.  This comparison does not address the audit objective.  Choice (d) is incorrect.  The growth of hard disk use is unrelated to the audit objective.

Subject Area: Conduct assurance engagements—information technology audits.  Source: CIA 1193, II-26.

**280. (d)**  Auditing job accounting data for file accesses and job initiation/termination messages will reveal whether the right data files were loaded/dismounted at the right times and the right programs were initiated/terminated at the right times.  Choice (a) is incorrect.  Analyzing job activity with a queuing model to determine workload characteristics gives information about resource usage but does not verify whether the right data files were loaded/dismounted at the right times and the right programs were initiated/terminated at the right times.  Choice (b) is incorrect.  Simulating the

resource usage and comparing the results with actual results of operating helps management characterize the workload but does not verify whether the right data files were loaded/dismounted at the right times and the right programs were initiated or terminated at the right times.  Choice (c) is incorrect.  Using library management software to track changes to successive versions of application programs permits control of production and test versions but does not verify whether the right data files were loaded/dismounted at the right times and the right programs were initiated or terminated at the right times.

Subject Area: Conduct assurance engagements—information technology audits.  Source: CIA 1193, II-32.

**281. (b)**  The control section should be satisfied that processing was properly completed prior to output distribution.  Choice (a) is incorrect.  Applications programmers are responsible for installing and customizing software and usually perform outside the computer center.  Choice (c) is incorrect.  Review of output is not the responsibility of computer operators.  Choice (d) is incorrect.  The data processing manager performs review of output by the control section and not directly.

Subject Area: Conduct assurance engagements—information technology audits.  Source: CIA 592, I-35.

**282. (c)**  The major purpose of the internal auditor's study and evaluation of a company's IT operations is to evaluate the reliability and integrity of financial and operating information.  Choice (a) is incorrect.  The internal auditor often may evaluate the competence of IT operating personnel during an evaluation of IT operations, but evaluating their competence is not the major purpose of the evaluation.  Choice (b) is incorrect.  One aspect of demonstrating due professional care is by evaluating the means for collecting, manipulating, and reporting financial and operating information, but this is not the major purpose of the auditor's evaluation.  Choice (d) is incorrect.  Becoming familiar with the company's means of identifying, measuring, classifying, and reporting information is necessary to perform the evaluation, but that is not the purpose of the evaluation.

Subject Area: Conduct assurance engagements—information technology audits.  Source: CIA 1191, I-26.

**283. (b)**  Logging identifies sensitive printouts, which would then be released on the signed confirmation by recipients.  This output control would have prevented the unauthorized employee from receiving the printout.  Choice (a) is incorrect.  Controlled destruction of obsolete printouts is an appropriate control, but that would not have prevented the unauthorized employee from receiving the printout.  Choice (c) is incorrect.  Access control over printout files on disk is an appropriate control, but that would not have prevented the unauthorized employee from receiving the printout.  Choice (d) is incorrect.  Enforced expiration date on sensitive printouts is an appropriate control, but that would not have prevented the unauthorized employee from receiving the printout.

Subject Area: Conduct assurance engagements—information technology audits.  Source: CIA 1191, II-30.

**284. (a)**  Job accounting data analysis permits programmatic examination of job initiation/termination, record counts, and processing times.  In this case, the auditor would be looking for duplicate (or near-duplicate) entries for the update run.  Choice (b) is incorrect.  Code comparison is the determination of whether two program files are identical. Choice (c) is incorrect. Embedded audit data collection is the collection of selected transactions by embedded audit routines. Choice (d) is incorrect. Extended records are the collection and combination of information about particular transactions for the purpose of reconstructing the whole work record.

Subject Area: Conduct assurance engagements—information technology audits. Source: CIA 1191, II-27.

**285. (c)** The plan should include goals and objectives, an inventory of current capacity, and a forecast of future needs. Choice (a) is incorrect. Contingency planning refers to the arrangements for alternative processing facilities in the event of equipment failure. Choice (b) is incorrect. The system feasibility study is one of the phases in the systems development life cycle. Choice (d) is incorrect. Exception reports are meant to highlight problems and bring them to the attention of management.

Subject Area: Conduct assurance engagements—information technology audits. Source: CIA 591, I-40.

**286. (a)** "Each computer connected to a central computer with information between area offices passing through the central computer" is the definition of a star topology. Choice (b) is incorrect. The structure is not a tree structure, where all stations receive all transmissions. A tree topology is a variation of bus, which is hierarchical. Choice (c) is incorrect. Each node is connected to a central computer, not to two other nodes, as in the ring topology. Choice (d) is incorrect. No node-to-node connections are present.

Subject Area: Conduct assurance engagements—information technology audits. Source: CIA 594, I-59.

**287. (b)** "Tree structure" and one-to-many relationships describe a hierarchical database system. Choice (a) is incorrect. The data do resemble sequential files and records. Choice (c) is incorrect. Network is a many-to-many relationship. Choice (d) is incorrect. The data are not stored in a remote site, as in a distributed system.

Subject Area: Conduct assurance engagements—information technology audits. Source: CIA 594, I-60.

**288. (c)** The questions and names identify the user. Choice (a) is incorrect. Such names and questions are intended to identify the user entering the system. Choice (b) is incorrect. Access to the computer has already taken place; questions and names do not prevent access to the hardware. Choice (d) is incorrect. Such questions have no effect on the integrity of data.

Subject Area: Conduct assurance engagements—information technology audits. Source: CIA 594, I-61.

**289. (a)** Once the identity of the user is authenticated, the matrix contains the authorized systems to which the user has access. Choice (b) is incorrect. Access to the computer has already taken place. Choice (c) is incorrect. The matrix does not authenticate the user. Choice (d) is incorrect. The matrix does not protect data integrity.

Subject Area: Conduct assurance engagements—information technology audits. Source: CIA 594, I-62.

**290. (d)** This control prevents concurrent processing by allowing only one user to have access to a record at any one point in time. Choice (a) is incorrect. The control prevents processing at the same time by several offices, not processing a transaction over again. Choice (b) is incorrect. The

control does not prevent overload. Choice (c) is incorrect. The control can delay processing while a user is waiting access to a record, not speed it up.

Subject Area: Conduct assurance engagements—information technology audits. Source: CIA 594, I-63.

**291. (d)** Data encryption is used to prevent data theft by wiretapping. Choice (a) is incorrect. Use of identifiers such as passwords protects against unauthorized terminals but not against wiretapping. Choice (b) is incorrect. Passwords are system user identifiers. See choice (a) above. Choice (c) is incorrect. Logical access methods include passwords. See choice (b) above.

Subject Area: Conduct assurance engagements—information technology audits. Source: CIA 591, I-42.

**292. (a)** The list of users and their passwords would not be included in an audit trail log, but in a file within the computer. Choices (b), (c), and (d) are incorrect. The type of event or transaction, the location of the attempted access, and the data sought would all be included in an audit log and are necessary to investigate unauthorized attempted access to the system.

Subject Area: Conduct assurance engagements—information technology audits. Source: CIA 594, I-64.

**293. (c)** This effective administration of user IDs and authentication procedures is the key to enforcing personal accountability, the basis for the user-to-data authorization technique. Choice (a) is incorrect. This is a job-to-data authorization technique. Choice (b) is incorrect. This is terminal-to-data authorization technique. Choice (d) is incorrect. The use of access software alone does not address all access security risks.

Subject Area: Conduct assurance engagements—information technology audits. Source: CIA 1193, II-27.

**294. (c)** Proper addition/deletion of authorizations includes prompt activation of access privileges after they are authorized. Too much delay may tempt users to bypass access control procedures. Choice (a) is incorrect. Individuals external to the organization may need to have access privileges (very limited) in order to participate in interorganization information systems (e.g., electronic data interchange). Choice (b) is incorrect. A weekly cycle may be too long to wait to cancel privileges for employees with changed job responsibilities or for terminated employees. Choice (d) is incorrect. In general, security officers, not systems programmers, are responsible for maintaining records of access changes.

Subject Area: Conduct assurance engagements—information technology audits. Source: CIA 1193, I-28.

**295. (a)** Ascertaining the completeness of the plan as to all key functions, the needed facilities, and the supporting elements in the organization best meet the audit objective of "adequacy." Choice (b) is incorrect. Scope is too limited to provide a good indication of adequacy of the plan. Choice (c) is incorrect. Determining the stage of development of the plan is important but is of little help in determining adequacy of the total plan. Choice (d) is incorrect. The role of internal auditing can be helpful in ensuring the quality of the plan but does not ensure adequacy. If the role has been fulfilled, then this aspect is potentially of great value in assuring adequacy.

Subject Area: Conduct assurance engagements—information technology audits. Source: CIA 590, I-13.

**296. (a)** Adequate journaling procedures require making appropriate copies of any changes to a database to enable recovery from data base failures. Choice (b) is incorrect. Edit and validation are controls over data integrity. Choice (c) is incorrect. It identifies who knows how data are to be used and who is responsible for determining levels of control over access to data. Choice (d) is incorrect. Data integrity procedures test input of data, not recovery of data.

Subject Area: Conduct assurance engagements—information technology audits. Source: CIA 1193, I-35.

**297. (d)** Conversion to automatic data processing usually reduces the existing segregation of duties, because the computer combines many functions that previously could have been performed by separate persons. Such combined functions include (1) authorization, (2) execution, (3) recording, and (4) custody. Choice (a) is incorrect. Conversion to automatic data processing usually reduces processing errors. Choice (b) is incorrect. Conversion to automatic data processing has no effect on the types of risk to which the firm is exposed. Choice (c) is incorrect. Conversion to automatic data processing usually reduces processing time.

Subject Area: Conduct assurance engagements—information technology audits. Source: CIA 1193, I-24.

**298. (a)** Code comparison is the process of comparing two versions of the same program to determine whether the two correspond. It is an efficient technique because it is performed by software. Choice (b) is incorrect. Code review is the process of reading program source code listings to determine whether the code contains potential errors or inefficient statements. Code review can be used as a means of code comparison but is inefficient. Choice (c) is incorrect. Test data runs permit the auditor to verify the processing of preselected transactions. They give no evidence about unexercised portions of the program. Choice (d) is incorrect. Analytical review is the process of creating and evaluating ratios between numbers, often in the context of financial statements.

Subject Area: Conduct assurance engagements—information technology audits. Source: CIA 1193, I-25.

**299. (b)** Reviewing the methodology used by an organization would enable the internal auditor to determine whether he or she could rely on the systems development activity to design and implement appropriate automated controls within applications. Choice (a) is incorrect. Service on a management decision-making committee is an operating responsibility and would impair audit objectivity. Choice (c) is incorrect. Making recommendations for specific automated procedures is an operating responsibility. Choice (d) is incorrect. Making recommendations for specific operational procedures is an operating responsibility.

Subject Area: Conduct assurance engagements—information technology audits. Source: CIA 1193, I-26.

**300. (a)** Internal audit should be involved to ensure the existence of performance specifications consistent with the hospital's needs because incomplete or erroneous specifications may result in the acquisition of unusable software or unenforceable contract terms with the software vendor. Choice (b) is incorrect. Internal audit cannot ensure that the application design meets internal development and documentation standards because an external group with different standards has already developed the system. Choice (c) is incorrect. There is no prototype in procurement of proprietary software. Choice (d) is incorrect. For externally developed systems, the only omitted or abbreviated system development life cycle step is programming of the actual system. All other phases remain, even if they are modified.

Subject Area: Conduct assurance engagements—information technology audits. Source: CIA 1193, III-36.

**301. (b)** Source code is the human-readable version of software that must be compiled into object code before execution by the computer. Choice (a) is incorrect. Object code is the output of a compilation of source code. Choice (c) is incorrect. A hash code is the symbolic address of a record for a fully randomized file. Choice (d) is incorrect. An access code is a sequence of characters that a system recognizes for the purpose of permitting access to some computer resources.

Subject Area: Conduct assurance engagements—information technology audits. Source: CIA 1193, III-28.

**302. (c)** It is appropriate for an internal auditor to provide analysis and counsel to management. Choice (a) is incorrect. It would not be appropriate for an internal auditor to participate in accounting supervision and then perform internal audits. Choice (b) is incorrect. It would not be appropriate for the internal auditor to perform management activities, such as investment decisions, and then perform internal audits. Choice (d) is incorrect. It would never be appropriate for an internal auditor to perform an audit of his or her own work.

Subject Area: Conduct assurance engagements—information technology audits. Source: CIA 593, I-43.

**303. (d)** This is not true—audit involvement on a continuous basis is significantly more expensive in audit resources than any of the other interval choices. Choice (a) is incorrect. Improved design and specifications of controls is a primary objective of auditing systems under development and therefore should be a benefit if the effort is successful. Choice (b) is incorrect. The auditor's continuous involvement in the design gives every opportunity for audit to provide significant input on risks and controls to the design team. Choice (c) is incorrect. Audit involvement on a continuous basis should result in better controls, which will reduce or eliminate the need for a subsequent rework of the systems controls.

Subject Area: Conduct assurance engagements—information technology audits. Source: CIA 593, II-22.

**304. (b)** The data dictionary contains information about data field contents and their definitions. Choice (a) is incorrect. Data subschemas show how fields are related in views for individual applications. Choice (c) is incorrect. The data definition language permits users to define fields and subschemas to the database system. Choice (d) is incorrect. The data manipulation language permits users to manipulate data in the database.

Subject Area: Conduct assurance engagements—information technology audits. Source: CIA 1192, III-34.

**305. (c)** Reviewing systems, even before implementation, is an activity appropriately performed by internal auditing and does not impair objectivity. Choice (a) is incorrect. Designing systems is presumed to impair audit objectivity. Choice (b) is incorrect. Drafting procedures for systems is presumed to impair independence. Choice (d) is incorrect. Installing systems of controls is presumed to impair independence.

Subject Area: Conduct assurance engagements—information technology audits. Source: CIA 592, I-1.

**306. (c)** The auditor should ensure that everything in the system development life cycle is done according to a logical plan. Choice (a) is incorrect. Management of the process by the auditor is overinvolvement and is inappropriate. Choice (b) is incorrect. Performance of a feasibility study alone cannot be relied on to prevent such losses in the future. Choice (d) is incorrect. An integrated test facility processes test data in a live environment. Although useful in testing applications, involvement in all phases of the system development life cycle is more apt to prevent losses.

Subject Area: Conduct assurance engagements—information technology audits. Source: CIA 1191, I-36.

**307. (b)** The major reason for the internal auditor's involvement in IT system development is to help ensure that systems have adequate control procedures. Choice (a) is incorrect. Gaining familiarity with systems in anticipation of subsequent reviews is helpful, but this is not the major reason for the internal auditor's involvement in IT system development. Choice (c) is incorrect. The internal auditor may be asked to monitor the cost and development time of new systems, but this is not the major reason for the internal auditor's involvement in IT system development. Choice (d) is incorrect. Proposing enhancements for subsequent development and implementation is a managerial, not an audit, function.

Subject Area: Conduct assurance engagements—information technology audits. Source: CIA 1191, I-27.

**308. (a)** General or integrity controls concerned with preventing unauthorized access to data have been affected by database technology. Choice (b) is incorrect. By definition, a DBMS makes data available for all applications. Choice (c) is incorrect. By definition, no data elements are application-owned in a DBMS. Choice (d) is incorrect. By definition, the DBMS does, and should, manipulate data.

Subject Area: Conduct assurance engagements—information technology audits. Source: CIA 1191, II-33.

**309. (b)** Program change procedures automatically logged by the computer would identify all instances of changes to the source code. Choice (a) is incorrect. The master copy of source code would have been unaffected. Also, because the change was reversed, the existing copy of source code would not show the alteration. Choice (c) is incorrect. Financial ratio analysis can never be expected to identify one isolated irregularity. Choice (d) is incorrect. The existing object code would be correct and show no alteration.

Subject Area: Conduct assurance engagements—information technology audits. Source: CIA 1191, II-35.

**310. (b)** This is the most practical technique because it is simple, inexpensive, and does not require much computer expertise. Choice (a) is incorrect. This is a preventive control, not a detective control. Choice (c) is incorrect. This is not practical because it is time-consuming and requires a high degree of computer expertise. Choice (d) is incorrect.

Computer operators normally do not possess the expertise to change computer programs.

Subject Area: Conduct assurance engagements—information technology audits. Source: CIA 1191, II-28.

**311. (d)** Users can gain access to databases from terminals only through established recognition and authorization procedures; thus, unauthorized access is prevented. Choice (a) is incorrect. Key verification ensures the accuracy of selected fields by requiring a different individual to rekey them. Choice (b) is incorrect. Sequence checks are used to ensure the completeness of input or update data by checking the use of preassigned document serial number. Choice (c) is incorrect. Computer matching entails checking selected fields on input data with information held in a suspense or master file.

Subject Area: Conduct assurance engagements—information technology audits. Source: CIA 591, I-38.

**312. (d)** Access to the software and/or data is protected by passwords. Choice (a) is incorrect. Passwords deal with access authorization not accuracy of data. Choice (b) is incorrect. Passwords protect access to the software and/or data, not access to the computer. Choice (c) is incorrect. Passwords deal with authorization, not completeness of update.

Subject Area: Conduct assurance engagements—information technology audits. Source: CIA 594, I-32.

**313. (a)** Tests of user controls may be the only logical way to audit microcomputers and are most appropriate when user controls are emphasized. Choice (b) is incorrect. Edit checks are input controls that provide limited assurance only on data input. Choice (c) is incorrect. This provides evidence on only one aspect of control (software licensing). Choice (d) is incorrect. The execution of program logic to change data may not leave an audit trail.

Subject Area: Conduct assurance engagements—information technology audits. Source: CIA 594, I-34.

**314. (c)** Matching invoices to payments and payables ensures that a payment or payable exists for each valid invoice; matching payments and payables to invoices ensures that an invoice exists for each payment or payable. Choice (a) is incorrect. Matching invoices to payments alone does not ensure that a payment or payable exists for each valid invoice; matching payments alone to invoices does not ensure that an invoice exists for each payment or payable. Choice (b) is incorrect. Matching invoices to payables alone does not ensure that a payment or payable exists for each valid invoice; matching payables to invoices alone does not ensure that an invoice exists for each payment or payable. Choice (d) is incorrect. Matching invoices to payments alone does not ensure that a payment or payable exists for each valid invoice.

Subject Area: Conduct assurance engagements—information technology audits. Source: CIA 1193, II-33.

**315. (b)** Policies and procedures are part of the administration of EUC, which is defined at an organizational level. Choice (a) is incorrect. Application controls are specific to the flow of transactions. Choice (c) is incorrect. Environmental controls influence the effective operation of all internal controls. Choice (d) is incorrect. "System controls" is not a specific response.

Subject Area: Conduct assurance engagements—information technology audits. Source: CIA 593 I-22.

**316. (b)** The capability to continue processing at all sites except a nonfunctioning one is called fail-soft protection, and is an advantage of distributed systems. Choice (a) is incorrect. The system log is a file showing details of all activity during processing, which can be used to investigate unusual activity, such as hardware malfunctions, reruns, and abnormal endings. Choice (c) is incorrect. Backup procedures are intended to prevent the recovery process from introducing any erroneous changes into the system after computer failure. Choice (d) is incorrect. Data file security is intended to prevent unauthorized changes to data files.

Subject Area: Conduct assurance engagements—information technology audits. Source: CIA 591, I-39.

**317. (a)** Systems that are frequently unavailable or have slow response times will reduce the efficiency with which transactions can be processed. Choice (b) is incorrect. Examining transaction totals without knowing the associated costs cannot provide the basis for determining efficiency. Choice (c) is incorrect. The cost of processing transactions manually would at best be a guess for a process that is already automated. Choice (d) is incorrect. Examining the cost of developing one application versus another would not provide the basis for establishing the efficiency for an individual system.

Subject Area: Conduct assurance engagements—information technology audits. Source: CIA 1193, I-38.

**318. (b)** To be the best attainable from the test data technique, results must be compared to predetermined expectations. Choice (a) is incorrect. To be competent (best attainable from appropriate audit techniques), results must be compared to predetermined expectations. Choice (c) is incorrect. The identification of program logic that has been executed is not a part of the test data approach and is therefore not required for the test data approach to be competent. Choice (d) is incorrect. Tagging data to instigate the creation of an audit data file is not required for the test data approach and is therefore not required for the test data approach to be competent.

Subject Area: Conduct assurance engagements—information technology audits. Source: CIA 1193, II-18.

**319. (a)** This procedure tests the completeness of accounts payable by the investigation of the potential for the improper timing of the recordation of accounts payable. Choice (b) is incorrect. This procedure is useful in the detection of fraud, but has little efficacy in the determination of the completeness of accounts payable. Choice (c) is incorrect. This procedure helps in the discovery of the potential for duplicate payments, but is not helpful in the search for all legitimate accounts payable. Choice (d) is incorrect. Liability accounts typically have a credit balance. An accounts payable ledger with a debit balance is often the result of the misclassification of a receivable. The result of such an error is the overstatement of accounts payable. The internal auditor is testing for an understatement of accounts payable.

Subject Area: Conduct assurance engagements—information technology audits. Source: CIA 1193, II-24.

**320. (a)** Matching can be expected to identify fictitious employees on the payroll because all legitimate employees

with time records should be on the master file. Choice (b) is incorrect. Since not all salaried staff may work overtime, matching cannot be expected to ensure that all overtime records are entered. Choice (c) is incorrect. Matching of production employee time records is not required to determine reasonableness of pay rates contained in the master file. Choice (d) is incorrect. Matching of overtime records of salaried staff is not required to determine the reasonableness of pay rates contained in the master file.

Subject Area: Conduct assurance engagements—information technology audits. Source: CIA 593, II-26.

**321. (b)** Review of selected output, with selection being made by use of appropriate edit checks, may provide reasonable assurance that only accurate data are processed and reported. Choice (a) is incorrect. Although user submission of test data may detect invalid transactions and failure to process valid transactions, this technique would not be used consistently. Choice (c) is incorrect. Controlled output distribution will not prevent or detect incorrect output. Choice (d) is incorrect. Decollation of output is simply the separation of output copies.

Subject Area: Conduct assurance engagements—information technology audits. Source: CIA 592, I-34.

**322. (c)** Periodic examination of accounts of employees with access to automated teller functions may detect unusual activity to and from employees' accounts. Choice (a) is incorrect. Supervisor-only authorization for transfers between the bank's customer would interfere with normal bank operations, which include transfers between accounts of the bank's customers. Choice (b) is incorrect. Overnight balancing of all accounts by the online teller system ensures that all parts of all transactions are accounted for but does not ensure that all transactions are authorized. Choice (d) is incorrect. Required vacations for employees with access to teller functions might expose the teller's actions to others' scrutiny but would not ensure their detection, especially if the teller remedied any overdrafts before going on vacation.

Subject Area: Conduct assurance engagements—information technology audits. Source: CIA 592, I-36.

**323. (b)** Choice (b) is the correct answer. One-for-one checking is as described. Choice (a) is incorrect. Batch totals require numerical control. Choice (c) is incorrect. Computer sequence checks require that transactions be numbered. Choice (d) is incorrect. Computer matching is performed under program control and not by the user.

Subject Area: Conduct assurance engagements—information technology audits. Source: CIA 592, I-33.

**324. (c)** This is the most appropriate use of computer simulation for testing the purchasing function. Choice (a) is incorrect. Technical specifications are established by the firm and do not involve alternatives. Choice (b) is incorrect. Economy and efficiency measure past production, not future policies. Choice (d) is incorrect. Quality of computer programs is subjective and not easily quantitatively modeled.

Subject Area: Conduct assurance engagements—information technology audits. Source: CIA 592, I-8.

**325. (c)** Implementation controls are designed to ensure that only authorized program procedures are introduced into the system. Choice (a) is incorrect. Programmed checks are used to check the potential accuracy of input data (e.g., a range check). Choice (b) is incorrect. Batch control is used to ensure the completeness and accuracy of input and up-date. Choice (d) is incorrect. One-for-one checking is a technique used to check individual documents for accuracy and completeness of data input or update.

Subject Area: Conduct assurance engagements— information technology audits. Source: CIA 591, I-36.

**326. (a)** During each program run in a series, the computer accumulates the totals of transactions that have been processed and reconciles them with the totals forwarded from the previous program run. Choice (b) is incorrect. Existence checking ensures that individual data codes agree with valid codes held in a file or a program. Choice (c) is incorrect. Key verification ensures the completeness and accuracy of selected fields on individual documents. Choice (d) is incorrect. Prerecorded input (turnaround document) is used to ensure accuracy and completeness of input.

Subject Area: Conduct assurance engagements— information technology audits. Source: CIA 591, I-37.

**327. (b)** A combination of edit checks resulting in exception reports would be the most efficient way of reducing errors. Choice (a) is incorrect. Keystroke verification (a labor-intensive procedure) consists of entering data a second time, with differences detected by a mechanical signal. Choice (c) is incorrect. Balancing and reconciliation make tests of equality and analyze differences. Like choice (a), it is laborious. Choice (d) is incorrect. Batch totals are used to control input via agreement of preestablished totals and are better suited for completeness control.

Subject Area: Conduct assurance engagements— information technology audits. Source: CIA 591, II-34.

**328. (d)** Run-to-run totals are used to ensure completeness of update. Choice (a) is incorrect. Computer matching is used to ensure that data are completely entered. Choice (b) is incorrect. Check digits are used to determine if a number has been keyed incorrectly. Choice (c) is incorrect. A transaction log is used in conjunction with special programs to reperform processing and compare results.

Subject Area: Conduct assurance engagements— information technology audits. Source: CIA 591, II-35.

**329. (b)** To be of benefit, manual postings of batch totals must be agreed to the master file. Choice (a) is incorrect. When agreed, batch totals are useful. Choice (c) is incorrect. Unless agreed or reconciled, batch totals in a control account do not serve as a control. Choice (d) is incorrect. Hash totals are not required or appropriate in this situation.

Subject Area: Conduct assurance engagements— information technology audits. Source: CIA 591, II-36.

**330. (a)** Expert systems consist of software packages with the ability to make judgment decisions—a major purpose of expert systems. Choice (b) is incorrect. Expert systems do not require outside consultants. Inside consultants can be used as well. Choice (c) is incorrect. Hardware does not make judgment decisions, software does. Choice (d) is incorrect. Automation of routine tasks is not the major purpose of expert systems. It is a by-product.

Subject Area: Conduct assurance engagements— information technology audits. Source: CIA 591, II-37.

## Compliance Audit Engagements

**331. (a)** A compliance audit of overtime policy is likely to be the most objective audit because the audit is comparing actual operations against specific management policies and procedures, which are likely to be well defined and documented. Choice (b) is incorrect. An operational audit is more subjective because there is often more than one way to establish operational control. Choice (c) is incorrect. A performance audit is more subjective because criteria to evaluate performance must be agreed upon if not already available. Choice (d) is incorrect. A financial control audit is somewhat subjective because there is often more than one way to establish control. Also, controls must be cost beneficial; thus, a control system may be intentionally less than perfect because of cost restraints.

Subject Area: Conduct assurance engagements— compliance audits. Source: CIA 1194, I-6.

**332. (c)** The auditor should ensure that the fieldwork is designed to identify potential instances of noncompliance and, in the closing conference, should recommend additional training for the ESH manager. Choice (a) is incorrect. Since the auditor is auditing a relatively small operation, it is important to maintain a broad scope and not reduce scope prematurely. Choice (b) is incorrect. While the auditor may be able to contribute to the ESH manager's knowledge of pertinent air-quality matters, it is much more important during this phase of the audit to learn what the manager does. A lecture showing off knowledge will not be as effective as recommendations conveyed within the context of overall performance. Choice (d) is incorrect. It is never appropriate for an auditor to report violations or potential violations to regulatory agencies. Such matters are the responsibility of company counsel.

Subject Area: Conduct assurance engagements— compliance audits. Source: CIA 597, I-24.

**333. (c)** This would be the least effective because it is based only on those people who send in donations. The concern is that callers will send their donations to other locations suggested by the phone solicitors. Choice (a) is incorrect. This is an effective preventive control because phone personnel are aware that all calls could be monitored. Choice (b) is incorrect. This is an overall management control that shows the relative effectiveness of telephone fundraising over time. A substantial decrease in effectiveness should cause management investigation. Choice (d) is incorrect. This would provide assurance similar to that in choice (a). It is a procedure that correctly samples from all phone calls made.

Subject Area: Conduct assurance engagements— compliance audits. Source: CIA 597, I-25.

**334. (a)** Lockboxes ensure that all deposits go directly to the bank and are not handled by organization personnel. Since there is no opportunity for personnel with inappropriate segregation of duties to intervene in the situation, this control procedure best accomplishes the stated objective. Choice (b) is incorrect. Internal audit is an effective control, but this procedure is flawed because it only focuses on deposits that were made. The concern is with cash receipts that were not deposited. Choice (c) is incorrect. This is an effective procedure, but it is not sufficient to keep an individual from taking the check and depositing it to a similarly named organization. Choice (d) is incorrect. The same person is handling both the cash receipts and the confirmations. The person could send out confirmations even if the cash receipts were diverted for other purposes.

Subject Area: Conduct assurance engagements—compliance audits. Source: CIA 597, I-26.

**335. (d)** This is the least effective control because it only addresses whether payroll is made at the correct rates. Many of the problems discussed in the question could relate to inappropriate payments other than payroll. Choice (a) is incorrect. This is an effective control because it provides accountability to the public at large. It provides detail on the amount of expenditures for administrative purposes. Donors and sponsors can utilize this information to determine whether the appropriate amounts are used for designated purposes. Choice (b) is incorrect. Board of directors' approvals in a nonprofit organization provide an effective control against unauthorized administrative actions. Choice (c) is incorrect. This audit procedure provides direct assurance that expenditures are used for designated purposes.

Subject Area: Conduct assurance engagements—compliance audits. Source: CIA 597, I-27.

**336. (c)** Although this might be informational, there is no need to develop a comparison of investment returns with other organizations. Indeed, recent financial investment scandals show that such comparisons can be highly misleading because high returns were due to taking on a high level of risk. Also, this is not a test of the adequacy of the controls. Choice (a) is incorrect. Part of the audit is to determine compliance with company policies. Since new financial instruments are very risky, the first step of such an audit should be to determine the nature of policies established for the investments. Choice (b) is incorrect. Oversight by a management committee is an important control. Therefore, the auditor should determine the nature of the oversight set up to monitor and authorize such investments. Choice (d) is incorrect. A fundamental control concept over cash is that someone establishes a mechanism to monitor the risks.

Subject Area: Conduct assurance engagements—compliance audits. Source: CIA 597, I-28.

**337. (b)** This would be the best procedure because it covers all large donors who gave in prior years and confirms all pledged and paid contributions to this organization or to any other organization that may have been represented as an affiliate organization. Discrepancies would provide an area for the auditor to investigate. Choice (a) is incorrect. This would provide some evidence, but it is not as thorough as choice (b). This response only shows the amounts that are listed as unpaid and would not account for any contributions previously paid or shifted to another organization. Choice (c) is incorrect. This procedure only deals with cash receipts that have been recorded by the organization and would not provide any insight on receipts that were not recorded or were diverted elsewhere. Choice (d) is incorrect. Analytical review of the nature described would be of limited use. The follow-up audit procedure only provides evidence that those receipts that were recorded were also deposited and does not directly relate to the potential fraud described.

Subject Area: Conduct assurance engagements—compliance audits. Source: CIA 597, I-29.

**338. (d)** All of the procedures should be performed. See the IIA *Standards,* which describes a preliminary review. Choices (a), (b), and (c) are incorrect. All of the procedures should be performed. The IIA *Standards* describes a preliminary review.

Subject Area: Conduct assurance engagements—compliance audits. Source: CIA 597, I-42.

**339. (c)** This would be least relevant, since compliance with procedures is not relevant to evaluating the adequacy of the procedures themselves. Choice (a) is incorrect. It is often necessary to obtain a clear understanding of criteria to be used in evaluating activities before the audit begins. This would be an appropriate step. Choice (b) is incorrect. If there were questions on the interpretation of the broad policies, it would be useful to seek clarification from top management or a board member. Choice (d) is incorrect. It would be useful to determine whether the criteria used by the organization are consistent with regulatory activities.

Subject Area: Conduct assurance engagements—compliance audits. Source: CIA 597, I-43.

**340. (c)** This would be the least useful procedure because it is a time series of interest income only, without considering other important economic factors, such as size of the portfolio, changes in interest rate in the economy, and so on. Choice (a) is incorrect. This would be a good procedure because it would provide a valid comparison of the riskiness of the existing loan portfolio with that of other peer institutions. A higher interest rate would be indicative of greater risk in the loan portfolio. Choice (b) is incorrect. This would be an effective procedure because it is comparing a generalizable sample of loans made during two discrete periods of time and would thus provide information on whether the current issuance of loans has higher risk than that incurred two years ago. Choice (d) is incorrect. This would be a highly effective procedure because it develops a model that would be effective in explaining changes in the interest income as a result of relevant factors and could show how much of the change might be due to a change in the riskiness of the loans.

Subject Area: Conduct assurance engagements—compliance audits. Source: CIA 597, I-44.

**341. (c)** The auditor cannot ignore information gathered during the course of an audit. Since environmental concerns present large risks to most organizations, the auditor should determine that the environmental safety department is aware of the concerns and is actively monitoring the potential exposure to the organization. Follow-up is necessary. Choice (a) is incorrect. The auditor should follow up to determine whether there are concerns that should be immediately addressed by the organization. Choice (b) is incorrect. The auditor should first gather more information before going to the audit committee. The auditor should proceed with discussions with the environmental safety department. Choice (d) is incorrect. See explanation given for the choice (c).

Subject Area: Conduct assurance engagements—compliance audits. Source: CIA 1196, I-54.

**342. (d)** Members and CIA's are required to follow the IIA *Standards.* Additional governmental audit standards should also be followed on these governmental grant audits. Choice (a) is incorrect. Although there are minimal differences in the *Standards,* the auditor ought to be guided by the most applicable set of standards. Choice (b) is incorrect. Although there are minimal differences in the *Standards*, the auditor ought to be guided by the most applicable set of standards. Choice (c) is incorrect. The applicable IIA and governmental standards should guide the internal auditor.

Subject Area: Conduct assurance engagements—compliance audits. Source: CIA 1196, I-6.

**343. (a)** The auditor is determining that the participants have complied with the eligibility requirements. Choice (b) is incorrect. An operational audit would focus on the overall operations of the job-retraining program. Choice (c) is incorrect. An economy and efficiency program would address the cost of the program and compare it with the objectives achieved. Choice (d) is incorrect. A program audit is broader in context and will address the achievement of the overall program objectives.

Subject Area: Conduct assurance engagements—compliance audits. Source: CIA 1196, I-7.

**344. (b)** The overall regulation provides that the city establish a budget in a manner consistent with the objectives of the program. The requirements do not require that the agency approve the budget; it only requires that the entity develop a reporting mechanism to provide assurance that it is in compliance with the objectives of the grant and the applicable laws and regulations. Choice (a) is incorrect. This would be an appropriate procedure and relates to the objectives established in the regulation. Choice (c) is incorrect. This would be an appropriate procedure since expenditures could be deliberately charged to the wrong account to bypass budgeting control. Choice (d) is incorrect. This would be an appropriate procedure and relates to the objectives established in the regulation.

Subject Area: Conduct assurance engagements—compliance audits. Source: CIA 1194, I-8.

**345. (d)** This would not be relevant or the best attainable. First, the audit committee would not be responsible for understanding all the underlying laws and regulations. Second, determining the audit committee's objective for the audit does not help the auditor understand the applicable laws and regulations. Choice (a) is incorrect. These individuals should be familiar with the applicable laws and regulations. Choice (b) is incorrect. This common procedure allows the auditor to benefit from the research of prior auditors. Choice (c) is incorrect. The grant or loan agreements will often reference the applicable laws and regulations to be followed.

Subject Area: Conduct assurance engagements—compliance audits. Source: CIA 1194, I-9

**346. (c)** Policies, tracking and estimates of potential liability relate to control of hazardous material inventories. Choice (a) is incorrect. Cradle-to-grave activities would be necessary to assure proper disposal. Items I and IV are also appropriate procedures. Choice (b) is incorrect. Cradle-to-grave activities would be necessary to assure proper disposal. Item IV is also an appropriate procedure. Choice (d) is incorrect. See choice (c).

Subject Area: Conduct assurance engagements—compliance audits. Source: CIA 596, I-12.

**347. (b)** Obsolete or scrap sales should be approved prior to declaration. Choice (a) is incorrect. Strong internal control would preclude employees from purchasing obsolete

inventory prior to auction. Choices (c) and (d) are incorrect because neither III nor IV reduces risk.

Subject Area: Conduct assurance engagements—compliance audits. Source: CIA 596, I-13.

**348. (a)** This is a very important factor. Choice (b) is incorrect. A family welfare department of a governmental unit does not generate a profit. Choice (c) is incorrect. GAAP applies to for-profit enterprises. Choice (d) is incorrect. This is not primary concern.

Subject Area: Conduct assurance engagements—compliance audits. Source: CIA 1190, I-16.

**349. (c)** Not-for-profit organizations are funded to accomplish a specific goal or mission. Choice (a) is incorrect. Compliance, although rightfully included in a comprehensive audit, is not the primary issue in an audit of not-for-profit entities. Choice (b) is incorrect. Budget procedures, although rightfully included in a comprehensive audit, are not the primary issue in an audit of not-for-profit entities. Choice (d) is incorrect. Accuracy of financial reports, although rightfully included in a comprehensive audit, is not the primary issue in an audit of not-for-profit entities.

Subject Area: Conduct assurance engagements—compliance audits. Source: CIA 590, II-1.

**350. (c)** This is the most appropriate response. It includes an identification of the significance of the item, the cause (vague contract), potential impact, and potential cure. Choice (a) is incorrect. The auditor does not have the authority to make the decision that this is a "disallowed cost." The contract is vague and differences should be reported to management for reconciliation. Choice (b) is incorrect. It would be inappropriate to exclude the finding. It is an issue that should be resolved by management. Choice (d) is incorrect. The contract does not specify that cost savings are in integral part of the contract.

Subject Area: Conduct assurance engagements—compliance audits. Source: CIA 596, I-33.

**351. (a)** This would be the best answer because it gives some an estimate of incremental costs incurred. Although the data are not conclusive, they do present a starting point for further analysis—for example, was the previous level of security adequate, and so on. Choice (b) is incorrect. This is not the best because it is not an apples-to-apples comparison. Total computing costs may have increased under this new contract. The auditor wants to first focus on the difference associated with the identified expenditure. Choice (c) is incorrect. Although potentially useful, there are too many variables that may affect this comparison—for example, the level of security desired at the other entities. Choice (d) is incorrect. Although potentially useful, it does not take into account items that could vary at the other entities.

Subject Area: Conduct assurance engagements—compliance audits. Source: CIA 596, I-34.

**352. (b)** This would be the best approach because it compares the system being developed with cutting edge or state-of-the art systems and provides the auditor with a basis to address the outsourcer's claim that the system is the minimum necessary for the organization. Choice (a) is incorrect. This would be a piece of evidence. However, response I provides similar evidence. Choice (c) is incorrect. Testing the functionality of the system provides information on whether the system works, not whether the system is sufficient or more than sufficient for the entity. Choice (d) is incorrect. Response III would not help to compare with other systems.

Subject Area: Conduct assurance engagements—compliance audits. Source: CIA 596, I-35.

**353. (d)** This would be the most appropriate response because it samples from the population of interest, that is, debits to the expense account. Choice (a) is incorrect. The sample would be too broad to be efficient. The auditor is specifically interested in the debits to the computing security account and should sample from a population that consists of those debits. Choice (b) is incorrect. Analytical review provides evidence on whether the total expense is reasonable. It does not provide evidence on the whether specific debits to the account balance are correct. Choice (c) is incorrect. This would provide some evidence on the wage part of the costs, but would not provide evidence on other aspects of costs incurred.

Subject Area: Conduct assurance engagements—compliance audits. Source: CIA 596, I-36.

**354. (c)** The audit activity described here is one of compliance auditing, not monitoring. The control procedure is not timely because it occurs only once a year and does not provide timely feedback for monitoring operations. Choices (a) and (b) are incorrect. A monitoring control is one that provides timely information to management as to whether an activity may be out of control. The reporting mechanism described here meets that objective. Choice (d) is incorrect. By randomly selecting transactions throughout the year, management has established a test by which to monitor the validity of expenses.

Subject Area: Conduct assurance engagements—compliance audits. Source: CIA 596, I-37.

**355. (c)** Per the IIA *Standards*, fraud is an intentional act. Whenever contracts are involved, the use of an expert (in this case a lawyer) would be necessary to determine if the activity is in violation of the contract. If it is not in violation, then it could not be considered an intentional deception. Choice (a) is incorrect. This statement is correct, but so is statement II. Choice (b) is incorrect. This statement is correct, but so is statement I. Choice (d) is incorrect. An intentional deception would not require that the company had actually implemented the security techniques at other companies.

Subject Area: Conduct assurance engagements—compliance audits. Source: CIA 596, I-38.

**356. (a)** This is a step that would be performed during a specific audit, such as a compliance or transaction audit. Choice (b) is incorrect. This would be a potential program objective. Choices (c) and (d) are incorrect. Each would be a potential program objective.

Subject Area: Conduct assurance engagements—compliance audits. Source: CIA 596, I-22.

**357. (c)** If the internal auditing department is tasked with environmental audits, the first action that should be accomplished is training auditors with the technical expertise needed to identify and recommend corrective actions for environmental issues. Choices (a), (b), and (d) are incorrect because technical training is a prerequisite.

Subject Area: Conduct assurance engagements—compliance audits. Source: CIA 596, I-23.

**358. (a)** The internal auditing department normally has a broad charter and realm of responsibility and can readily assimilate the new auditing function. Choice (b) is incorrect. Environment audits are highly complex and require technical expertise. This would be an advantage for an environmental auditing group directed by a technically oriented department. Internal auditing groups normally do not have the technical expertise necessary to assume primary responsibility. Choices (c) and (d) are incorrect. See choice (a).

Subject Area: Conduct assurance engagements—compliance audits. Source: CIA 596, I-24.

**359. (d)** All of the above actions should be accomplished. Choice (a) is incorrect. The storage facility should have documentation on all hazardous waste on site, method of treatment, and method of disposal. Choice (b) is incorrect. The costs of remediation can be extensive; the waste vendor should have adequate financial resources to operate long term. Choice (c) is incorrect. A waste vendor should have a written plan and equipment available to respond to all emergencies.

Subject Area: Conduct assurance engagements—compliance audits. Source: CIA 596, I-25.

**360. (b)** The prioritization of the steps should be (1) recovery as a usable product; (2) elimination at the source; (3) recycle and reuse; (4) energy conservation; and (5) treatment. Therefore, by definition, choices (a), (c), and (d) are incorrect.

Subject Area: Conduct assurance engagements—compliance audits. Source: CIA 596, I-26.

**361. (b)** This audit procedure directly addresses the third regulation. Choice (a) is incorrect. There is no need to confirm accounts receivable to address the specific regulations noted in the scenario. Choice (c) is incorrect. There is no requirement to age loans receivable and determine the proper allowance to address the three regulations noted in the scenario. Choice (d) is incorrect because responses (a) and (c) are not required.

Subject Area: Conduct assurance engagements—compliance audits. Source: CIA 595, I-23.

**362. (a)** Since it is unclear as to whether a violation has taken place, the auditor should inform management and seek the opinion of legal counsel. Choice (b) is incorrect. The auditor should not issue a formal report until the status of the violation is decided. Thus, it would not be appropriate to omit mention of the finding. Choice (c) is incorrect. It is not an audit function to report to the regulatory agency unless law specifically requires it. The auditor should seek an opinion on the legality of the loans from legal counsel, not the regulatory agency. Choice (d) is incorrect. The auditor should inform management and seek an opinion from legal counsel. The audit report will go to the audit committee during the normal course of processing. The auditor should go to the audit committee immediately only if there is evidence that the audit investigation is being impeded.

Subject Area: Conduct assurance engagements—compliance audits. Source: CIA 595, I-24.

**363. (d)** This would be the best approach because it allows the auditor to capture information on the potential causes of the change in investment income. Choice (a) is incorrect. Simple linear regression would be useful but not as insightful as multiple regression analysis could be (for example, partition stocks into high volatility and low volatility, as measured by market beta). Thus, choice (d) is superior. Choice (b) is incorrect. Ratio analysis provides some insight, but it is designed only to provide data on the relative composition of interest-bearing instruments versus stock investments. More information can be gathered through multiple regression. Choice (c) is incorrect. Trend analysis only verifies that a change has taken place and shows the broad nature of the change. It does not provide insight on the causes of the change in investment income.

Subject Area: Conduct assurance engagements—compliance audits. Source: CIA 597, I-31.

**364. (c)** This would be the area of greatest risk because the dollars expended are very large and inadequate controls could lead to grants used for fraudulent purposes. Choice (a) is incorrect. This is an area that is often misused, but it does not have the dollar amounts associated with it that inappropriate grants would have, since total administrative costs are only $10 million. Choice (b) is incorrect. This is a risk area, but the dollar amounts would be much more moderate than those in response (c). Choice (d) is incorrect. Total administrative costs are only $10 million in the current year.

Subject Area: Conduct assurance engagements—compliance audits. Source: CIA 597, I-32.

**365. (b)** The board of directors and audit committee are responsible for the oversight function and are the appropriate authorities to respond to press inquiries. Choice (a) is incorrect. See the response for (b). Choice (c) is incorrect. The proper response should come from the oversight function in the organization. Choice (d) is incorrect. Even if the investigation was not complete, the auditors should give the response in (b).

Subject Area: Conduct assurance engagements—compliance audits. Source: CIA 597, I-33.

**366. (d)** Auditors are required to report the results of their audit work. The results indicate a breakdown in an important control procedure that should be brought to the attention of senior oversight officials. Choice (a) is incorrect. The control breakdown should be reported. Choice (b) is incorrect. The control breakdown should be reported. Even though the grants were approved retroactively, there was a breakdown in the control procedures that should be brought to the attention of the audit committee. Choice (c) is incorrect. There is a need to provide detail on the nature of each grant only if the auditor has reason to believe that fraud may have been suspected. Also, the IIA *Standards* provide that the auditor should inform management if wrongdoing is suspected. Management decides whether to pursue investigation.

Subject Area: Conduct assurance engagements—compliance audits. Source: CIA 597, I-33.

**367. (c)** This is the best answer since such correspondence may very well deal with potential violations. Choice (a) is incorrect. It is not the best answer, as the source may be biased. Choice (b) is incorrect because the source is not specific enough. Choice (d) is incorrect. It is not the best answer because external auditors do not have ready access to needed information.

Subject Area: Conduct assurance engagements—compliance audits. Source: CIA 591, II-12.

**368. (c)** Procedures described will determine if the specified system was purchased and installed. Choice (a) is incorrect. Actual testing of the alarms is the only procedure to determine if the system actually works. Choice (b) is incorrect. Appropriate tests were not performed to determine adequacy of system design. Choice (d) is incorrect. Appropriate tests were not performed to determine if the system meets statutory requirements.

Subject Area: Conduct assurance engagements—compliance audits. Source: CIA 1192, I-26.

**369. (a)** Compliance with national government regulations is the essence of the administration of the grant. This, along with the disbursement of proper funds, is the area of greatest risk. Choice (b) is incorrect. This aspect is important as an administrative item. However, inefficiency would not result in financial disallowance to the agency. Choice (c) is incorrect. As a part of a financial audit, auditors would audit this aspect. Choice (d) is incorrect. This is not relevant except as a special study.

Subject Area: Conduct assurance engagements—compliance audits. Source: CIA 1192, I-1.

**370. (d)** The approval of restricted-fund expenditures indicates effectiveness of fund management and is the primary objective of a compliance audit. Choice (a) is incorrect. Although proper accounting is important, effectiveness of fund management is indicated primarily by the reasonableness of expenditures. Choice (b) is incorrect. Although budgeting is important, effectiveness of fund management is indicated primarily by the reasonableness of expenditures. Choice (c) is incorrect. Although accuracy is important, effectiveness of fund management is indicated primarily by the reasonableness of expenditures.

Subject Area: Conduct assurance engagements—compliance audits. Source: CIA 1192, II-24.

**371. (c)** Not-for-profit organizations are funded to accomplish a specific goal or mission. Choice (a) is incorrect. Compliance, although rightfully included in a comprehensive audit, is not the primary issue in an audit of not-for-profit entities. Choice (b) is incorrect. Budget procedures, although rightfully included in a comprehensive audit, are not the primary issue in an audit of not-for-profit entities. Choice (d) is incorrect. Accuracy of financial reports, although rightfully included in a comprehensive audit, is not the primary issue in an audit of not-for-profit entities.

Subject Area: Conduct assurance engagements—compliance audits. Source: CIA 1192, II-14.

**372. (a)** A fund is defined as an accounting entity for the purpose of carrying on specific activities in accordance with special instructions. Choice (b) is incorrect. The special purpose of the fund outweighs issues of economy and efficiency. Choice (c) is incorrect. Most nonprofit entities use a modified accrual accounting system that is not GAAP. Choice (d) is incorrect. Only the activities specified by fund restrictions are meant to be carried out.

Subject Area: Conduct assurance engagements—compliance audits. Source: CIA 593, I-17.

**373. (b)** This objective takes overwhelming precedence over all others since it tests the most basic aspect of the programs. Choice (a) is incorrect. While this objective has merit, it would be addressed annually by the external auditors. Choice (c) is incorrect. While this objective has merit, it is in terms of long-range planning.  Choice (d) is incorrect.  Since benefit payments are most often the responsibility of a third-person provider, this objective would serve to help decide on future contracts.

Subject Area: Conduct assurance engagements—compliance audits.  Source: CIA 1193, II-13.

**374. (b)**  A corporate policy should be developed to address distribution of sensitive data.  Choice (a) is incorrect.  The VP Finance would not determine the distribution of sensitive data.  Choice (c) is incorrect.  The audit committee would not determine distribution of sensitive data.  Choice (d) is incorrect.  The data security officer may distribute sensitive data but only in accordance with corporate policy.

Subject Area: Conduct assurance engagements—compliance audits.  Source: CIA 1193, II-10.

**375. (b)**  If the consultant is tracking and reporting actions taken pertaining to maintaining a safe work environment and preventing damage to the environment, there is an important element of accountability added to the project by management's assessment of performance.  That is, the performance standard established in the contract or by regulation provides a strong control.  Choice (a) is incorrect.  While it is necessary to establish the consultant's responsibility, the contract alone does not ensure that the work will be performed in accordance with applicable environmental, safety, and health regulations.  Choice (c) is incorrect.  It is rarely advisable to invite a regulatory agency to inspect one's activities, nor would one wish to rely on the results of an inspection over which one had no control.  Choice (d) is incorrect.  While it is necessary to know what the regulations require, a written document alone does not ensure that appropriate action will be taken.

Subject Area: Conduct assurance engagements—compliance audits.  Source: CIA 1196, I-21.

**376. (a)**  In many countries, a current landowner may be held responsible for contamination whether that landowner caused the contamination.  Choice (b) is incorrect.  The presence of contamination would likely affect the value of a property, but it is not likely to be management's primary reason for wanting knowledge of it.  Choice (c) is incorrect.  The current owner may agree within the terms of the sale to clean up all contamination before the sale is closed, but remediation is not necessarily required before a property can be sold.  Choice (d) is incorrect.  The potential purchaser is not required to disclose what liability is identified during such an investigation, but would likely decide not to purchase the property.

Subject Area: Conduct assurance engagements—compliance audits.  Source: CIA 1196, I-25.

**377. (d)**  This description fully describes the auditor's responsibility for reporting on significant deficiencies in controls, the findings of the current audit, and providing follow-up work to determine if sufficient actions have been taken.

Subject Area: Conduct assurance engagements—compliance audits.  Source: CIA 1196, I-60.

## Conduct Consulting Engagements

**378. (b)**  This is the proper role of the internal auditor, and to report the results to management.  Choices (a), (c),

and (d) are incorrect because they are the role of management.

Subject Area: conduct consulting engagements—internal audits.  Source: CIA 1190, I-11.

**379. (b)**  Since auditors alone cannot implement audit recommendations, auditee participation and involvement makes it better.  Choice (a) is incorrect.  Imposition implies an adversarial relationship.  Choice (c) is incorrect.  Fraud Investigation is a unique requirement of auditing.  Choice (d) is incorrect.  Due to the requirement for independence, auditors should never implement policies and procedures.

Subject Area: conduct consulting engagements—internal audits.  Source: CIA 595, III-2.

**380. (c)**  Both management and auditors should be involved in improving the image of internal audit in the organization.  Choice (a) is incorrect.  The auditors also need to know the feedback so they can improve relations with auditees for the next audit.  Choice (b) is incorrect.  Management should also know if communication is poor because of some auditor behavior.  Choice (d) is incorrect.  Involving the auditees should reduce conflict and defensiveness and make the audit more participative.

Subject Area: conduct consulting engagements—internal audits.  Source: CIA 1196, I-22.

**381. (d)**  A consultative attitude leads to two-way communication.  Choice (a) is incorrect.  An objective attitude is desirable, but by itself it will not lead to a more positive relationship.  Choice (b) is incorrect.  An investigative attitude is not likely to enhance the relationship.  Choice (c) is incorrect.  An interrogatory attitude is not likely to enhance the relationship.

Subject Area: conduct consulting engagements—internal audits.  Source: CIA 1195, III-7.

**382. (d)**  All of the above items are appropriate uses of consultants.  Choice (a) is incorrect.  This would be an appropriate use of such experts according to the IIA *Standards*.  However, choice (b) and (c) also describe appropriate uses of consultants.  Choice (b) is incorrect.  This is an example of an operational audit and would be an appropriate use of such experts according to the IIA *Standards*.  However, choices (a) and (c) also describe appropriate uses of consultants.  Choice (c) is incorrect.  This would be an appropriate example of training.  However, choices (a) and (b) also describe appropriate uses of consultants.

Subject Area: conduct consulting engagements—internal audits.  Source: CIA 1195, I-18.

## Business Process Review

**383. (a)**  Selling is not the only one that can deliver value.  Others, such as production, supply chain, and logistics, can deliver value equally.  The other three items are essential in delivering value.

Subject Area: conduct consulting engagements—business process review.  Source: CBM, Volume 2.

**384. (c)**  The horizontal organization is described as eliminating both hierarchy and functional boundaries and is operated with multidisciplinary teams.  Few layers of management are practiced between the top and the bottom of the hierarchy.  There are many layers of management in the vertical organization.

Subject Area: conduct consulting engagements—business process review. Source: CBM, Volume 2.

**385. (a)** A process view, not the functional view, of the business is required. All the other three items are required for a proper business process orientation.

Subject Area: conduct consulting engagements—business process review. Source: CBM, Volume 2.

**386. (c)** Process-oriented measures are, by definition, cross-functional, which contributes to a common cause. It might also be said that what gets measured and rewarded gets done.

Subject Area: conduct consulting engagements—business process review. Source: CBM, Volume 2.

**387. (a)** Business process reengineering requires a radical rethinking and redesigning of a process.

Subject Area: conduct consulting engagements—business process review. Source: CBM, Volume 2.

**388. (a)** Business process reengineering can be used to reduce the cycle time or speed it up.

Subject Area: conduct consulting engagements—business process review. Source: CBM, Volume 2.

**389. (b)** The time between when an order is placed and when the customer receives it is known as order cycle time.

Subject Area: conduct consulting engagements—business process review. Source: CBM, Volume 2.

**390. (b)** The time it takes to deliver a product or service after an order is placed is called customer response time.

Subject Area: conduct consulting engagements—business process review. Source: CBM, Volume 2.

**391. (a)** The time between when an order is placed and when the order is ready for setup is called order receipt time.

Subject Area: conduct consulting engagements—business process review. Source: CBM, Volume 2.

**392. (b)** The time between when an order is ready for setup and when the setup is complete is called order wait time.

Subject Area: conduct consulting engagements—business process review. Source: CBM, Volume 2.

**393. (b)** "Work simplification" refers to eliminating unnecessary procedures and activities in a business process. Work measurement uses industrial engineering techniques to estimate labor time and material standards.

Subject Area: conduct consulting engagements—business process review. Source: CBM, Volume 2.

**394. (a)** Processing time (36 hours) is the only task that adds value to a specific customer.

Subject Area: conduct consulting engagements—business process review. Source: CBM, Volume 2.

**395. (d)** Wait time (10 hours), inspection time (1 hour), and move time (1.5 hours) are examples of non–value-added time (12.5 hours) from a customer's viewpoint.

Subject Area: conduct consulting engagements—business process review. Source: CBM, Volume 2.

**396. (d)** The manufacturing cycle time (48.5 hours) is the combination of value-added time (36 hours) and non-value-added time (12.5 hours).

Subject Area: conduct consulting engagements—business process review. Source: CBM, Volume 2.

**397. (a)** Cycle time can be reduced by (1) reducing process complexity through work or process simplification, (2) changing from linear process flow to parallel flow, (3) using alternate process flow paths, (4) changing the sequence or layout of a process, (5) using technology to improve process flow, and (6) letting customer or suppliers share some of the process work.

Subject Area: conduct consulting engagements—business process review. Source: CBM, Volume 2.

**398. (b)** Speed flows from simplicity of tasks, activities, and operations. On the other hand, complexity reduces speed.

Subject Area: conduct consulting engagements—business process review. Source: CBM, Volume 2.

**399. (a)** The goal of reducing the cycle time is to eliminate, minimize, combine, or improve the work steps or time. Expanding the work steps usually increases the cycle time.

Subject Area: conduct consulting engagements—business process review. Source: CBM, Volume 2.

**400. (d)** Exceeding the capacity limitation of key resources causes choke points in a process. Here capacity is defined as the potential output over a time period. Choke points cause major delays in the cycle time.

Subject Area: conduct consulting engagements—business process review. Source: CBM, Volume 2.

**401. (c)** Cross-functional teams, not self-managed teams, focus on completing a specific work activity to reduce the cycle time. Cross-functional work teams are multidisciplined and are an attempt to organize employees around work itself. Self-managed teams are high-performance teams that assume traditional managerial duties, such as planning and staffing. Managers should act as facilitators, although they can be at times a barrier to self-managed teams. Members in self-managed teams come from one department whereas members in cross-functional teams come from multiple department or functions.

Subject Area: conduct consulting engagements—business process review. Source: CBM, Volume 2.

**402. (d)** When products are made in large lot sizes, the cycle times must be long because it is necessary to complete a large quantity in each step of the process. Synchronized production plans use just-in-time (JIT) manufacturing to organize the shop floor so that each work cell produces components, subassemblies, and final assemblies in the right quantities and at the right time. The use of Kanban cards can help to synchronize production through the "pull" production methods. In the "push" production methods, products are made before they are needed whereas in the "pull" method, products are not made until they are needed.

Subject Area: conduct consulting engagements—business process review. Source: CBM, Volume 2.

**403. (d)** Internal auditors should not become directly involved in the implementation of the redesigned process. This would impair their independence and objectivity. Choices (a), (b), and (c) are incorrect because internal auditors should perform these functions.

Subject Area: conduct consulting engagements—business process review. Source: CIA Model Exam 1998, III-8.

**404. (d)** Linear programming is a mathematical technique for maximizing or minimizing a given objective subject to certain constraints. It is the correct technique to optimize the problem of limited resources. Choice (a) is incorrect because the Delphi technique is a qualitative forecasting method that obtains forecasts through group consensus. Choice (b) is incorrect because exponential smoothing is a forecasting technique that uses past time series values to arrive at forecasted values. Choice (c) is incorrect because regression analysis is a statistical technique used to develop forecasts based on the relationship between two or more variables.

Subject Area: conduct consulting engagements—business process review. Source: CIA Model Exam 1998, III-35.

**405. (d)** Internal auditors should not become directly involved in the implementation of the redesign process. This would impair their independence and objectivity. Choices (a), (b), and (c) are incorrect because internal auditors should perform these functions.

Subject Area: conduct consulting engagements—business process review. Source: CIA 597, III-32.

**406. (d)** See responses given for choices (a), (b), and (c). Choice (a) is incorrect because all of the statements are reflective of the differences in approaches to controls in reengineered organizations. Reengineering places more emphasis on monitoring controls to let management know when an operation may be out of control and signals the need for corrective action. Choice (b) is incorrect because most of the reengineering and total quality management techniques assume that humans will be motivated to actively work in improving the process when they are involved from the beginning. Choice (c) is incorrect because there is an increasing emphasis on self-correcting and automated controls.

Subject Area: conduct consulting engagements—business process review. Source: CIA 1195, I-68.

**407. (b)** Employee training programs facilitate doing jobs in a new or different way. Choice (a) is incorrect because real or imagined loss of job(s) is a common reason for employees to resist any change. Choice (c) is incorrect because members of work groups often exert peer pressure on one another to resist change, especially if social relationships are changed. Choice (d) is incorrect because lack of communication and discussion of the need for switching to new processes threatens the status quo.

Subject Area: conduct consulting engagements—business process review. Source: CIA 596, III-18.

### Benchmarking

**408. (b)** Benchmarking is identifying, studying, and building on the best practices of other organizations. Benchmarking establishes standards that provide feed-forward control by warning people when they deviate from standards. Kaizen is continuous improvement. Plan, do, check and act (PDCA) is called Shewhart cycle in quality and later was modified by Deming to plan, do, study, and act (PDSA) cycle.

Subject Area: conduct consulting engagements—benchmarking. Source: CBM, Volume 2.

**409. (d)** Benchmarking is accomplished by comparing an organization's performance to that of the best-performing organizations. Choice (a) is incorrect because benchmarking involves a comparison against industry leaders or "world-class" operations. Benchmarking either uses industry-wide figures (to protect the confidentiality of information provided by participating organizations) or figures from cooperating organizations. Choice (b) is incorrect because benchmarking requires measurements, which involve quantitative comparisons. Choice (c) is incorrect because benchmarking can be applied to all the functional areas in a company. In fact, because manufacturing often tends to be industry-specific whereas things like processing an order or paying an invoice are not, there is a greater opportunity to improve by learning from global leaders.

Subject Area: conduct consulting engagements—benchmarking. Source: CIA Model Exam 2002, III-15.

**410. (d)** This is an example of an internal nonfinancial benchmark. Choice (a) is incorrect because this is an example of an external financial benchmark. Choices (b) and (c) are incorrect because each is an example of an internal financial benchmark.

Subject Area: conduct consulting engagements—benchmarking. Source: CIA 595, III-22.

**411. (c)** A high level of bad debt write-offs could indicate fraud and the compromising of the accuracy and reliability of financial reports. Choice (a) is incorrect because high turnover of employees may indicate a morale problem but not necessarily a problem with the accuracy and reliability of financial reports. Choice (b) is incorrect because a high level of employee participation in budget setting is an example of decentralization and would not necessarily impact the accuracy and reliability of financial reports. Choice (d) is incorrect because a high number of suppliers would not necessarily indicate a problem with the accuracy and reliability of financial reports.

Subject Area: conduct consulting engagements—benchmarking. Source: CIA 596, II-1.

### Information Technology and Systems Development

**412. (a)** A feasibility study should be conducted in the systems analysis stage. Choice (b) is incorrect. The involvement of users in the development process at various points is important. Choice (c) is incorrect. This ensures the quality in the development process at various points. Choice (d) is incorrect. Without good documentation, an information system may be difficult, if not impossible, to operate, maintain, or use.

Subject Area: conduct consulting engagements—information technology and systems development. Source: CIA 597, I-67.

**413. (b)** An internal audit role during evaluation of a new system is to recommend the level of control needed and review procedures before they are implemented. Choice (a) is incorrect. Drafting control procedures in any case is presumed to impair the internal auditor's objectivity. Drafting control procedures is a development, not an audit activity. Choice (c) is incorrect. Documenting control features for the permanent system documentation file is a development, not an audit activity, and is presumed to impair the internal auditor's objectivity. Choice (d) is incorrect. Rewriting flawed program code affecting control features is a development, not an audit activity, and is presumed to impair the internal auditor's objectivity.

Subject Area: conduct consulting engagements—information technology and systems development. Source: CIA 591, III-41.

**414. (c)** This is a normal area of internal audit expertise. Choice (a) is incorrect. This aspect is related to a procurement action. Choice (b) is incorrect. This is a top management financial decision. Choice (d) is incorrect. This is a management policy. Some equipment may be retained for emergency use.

Subject Area: conduct consulting engagements—information technology and systems development. Source: CIA 1191, II-9.

## Performance Measurement

**415. (c)** Efficiency is the ratio of effective output to the input required to achieve it. Insurance claims processed per day measures the output (claims processed) to the input (a day's work). Choice (a) is incorrect. There is not any comparison of input to output. Choice (b) is incorrect. This is an example of effectiveness, not efficiency. Choice (d) is incorrect. There is not any comparison of input to output.

Subject Area: conduct consulting engagements—performance measurement. Source: CIA 597, III-22.

**416. (b)** A good goal should be clear, measurable, and achievable. Choice (a) is incorrect. Employee needs are not an essential component of goal setting. Choice (c) is incorrect. The process of goal implementation is not one of the components of the goal itself. A goal may be appropriate and still poorly implemented. Choice (d) is incorrect. Strategies are general statements of the direction of a department or an organization. The statement is not a strategy.

Subject Area: conduct consulting engagements—performance measurement. Source: CIA 597, III-26.

**417. (b)** The question is aimed at distinguishing between the concepts of effectiveness and efficiency as measures of organizational performance. Focus on goals is the key to effectiveness. Choice (a) is incorrect. Although sole focus on either effectiveness or efficiency could lead to mismanagement, it does not necessarily mean that the manager is incompetent. Choice (c) is incorrect. Focusing on efficiency means being concerned with proper use of resources. Choice (d) is incorrect. The second part of the question—lack of concern for resources—makes it not applicable to goal setting concepts.

Subject Area: conduct consulting engagements—performance measurement. Source: CIA 1196, III-19.

**418. (b)** Most of the credit for Japanese success has been given to their management systems and their ability to be efficient with the limited resources that the country has. Although the reindustrialization after World War II has been cited as a potential cause for the success of Japan, it is by no means the strongest factor. Choice (a) is incorrect. Japan has limited materials, although it has a large population and, as a result of its success, gained access to tremendous financial resources. Choice (c) is incorrect. Japanese people are efficient. Choice (d) is incorrect. The Japanese educational system has been found to be high quality; however, its emphasis is not on creativity, and education has not been found to be the major factor in the country's success.

Subject Area: conduct consulting engagements—performance measurement. Source: CIA 1196, III-20.

**419. (d)** Performance has been measured against the standard seven days to see if objective is being met. Choice (a) is incorrect. No standard has been set in which to measure employee perfection. Choice (b) is incorrect. An inadequate measure has been specified to the employee. Choice (c) is incorrect. No measure of positive attitude has been specified for the employee.

Subject Area: conduct consulting engagements—performance measurement. Source: CIA 596, III-13.

**420. (a)** Since the task was completed on schedule and in the allotted time, it would be considered to be an effective use of resources. However, using a supervisor to complete a task that could have been done by a clerk would not be considered an efficient use of resources (assuming supervisors are more expensive resources than clerks are). Choice (b) is incorrect. As explained in choice (a), this would not be an efficient use of resources. Choice (c) is incorrect. A balanced emphasis on effectiveness and efficiency means the job gets done and a minimum amount of resources were used. Choice (d) is incorrect. The task was performed effectively but not efficiently.

Subject Area: conduct consulting engagements—performance measurement. Source: CIA 593, III-2.

**421. (b)** Effectiveness measures the degree to which a predetermined objective is met. Choices (a), (c), and (d) are incorrect because each measures efficiency (inputs used to achieve a given level of output).

Subject Area: conduct consulting engagements—performance measurement. Source: CIA 594, III-63.

**422. (d)** Work groups are a collection of people working together; they are not a labor productivity measurement. Choice (a) is incorrect. Work measurement is used to estimate the amount of worker time required to generate one unit of work. Choice (b) is incorrect. In a time study, analysts use stopwatches to time operations being performed by workers. Choice (c) is incorrect. Work sampling is a work measurement technique that randomly samples the work of one or more workers at periodic intervals to determine the proportion of the total operation that is accounted for in one particular activity.

Subject Area: conduct consulting engagements—performance measurement. Source: CIA 594, III-67.

**423. (a)** It is an efficiency measure of cost control by stating the profit as a percentage of sales. Choice (b) is incorrect. The number of contacts a broker makes per day would be a measure of effectiveness. Choice (c) is incorrect. The percentage of raw materials placed in storage without damage would be a measure of effectiveness. Choice (d) is incorrect. The percentage of new insurance policies written by an insurance agent would be a measure of effectiveness.

Subject Area: conduct consulting engagements—performance measurement. Source: CIA 596, III-27.

**424. (d)** It is a group-level factor that impacts efficiency. Choices (a), (b), and (c) are incorrect because each one is an individual-level factor that impacts efficiency.

Subject Area: conduct consulting engagements—performance measurement. Source: CIA 596, III-28.

**425. (c)** This scenario illustrates an organization out of balance by focusing too much on efficiency. Choice (a) is incorrect. This scenario illustrates an organization out of balance by having no focus on either effectiveness or efficiency. Choice (b) is incorrect. This scenario illustrates an organization out of balance by focusing too much on effectiveness. Choice (d) is incorrect. This scenario illustrates an organization perfectly balancing efficiency and effectiveness.

Subject Area: conduct consulting engagements—performance measurement. Source: CIA 1195, III-30.

**426. (a)** Productivity = output/input
Productivity before redesign = 2,000 units/500 hours = 4.0 units per hour
Productivity after redesign = 2,520 units/600 hours = 4.2 units per hour
Percentage change in productivity = (4.2 – 4.0)/4.0 = (0.2)/4.0 = 0.05 × 100 = 5%
Therefore, by definition, choices (b), (c), and (d) are incorrect.

Subject Area: conduct consulting engagements—performance measurement. Source: CIA 1195, III-84.

**427. (d)** Global competition and more rapidly changing consumer tastes are lessening the need for long production runs and are increasing the need for diversity of products and flexibility of production. Choice (a) is incorrect. Economies of scale cannot continue to be achieved if the products are not salable. Choice (b) is incorrect. If the item being produced is not the item that is desired, low cost is not an issue. Choice (c) is incorrect. Economies of scale can still be achieved from long production runs if the goods are salable.

Subject Area: conduct consulting engagements—performance measurement. Source: CIA 595, III-29.

# 3 MONITOR ENGAGEMENT OUTCOMES (5–15%)

## THEORY

### 3.1 Audit Monitoring and Follow-up

Audit monitoring and follow-up can be sophisticated or simple depending on a number of factors, including the size and complexity of the audit organization. Regardless of the type chosen, each audit should include: a firm basis for monitoring and follow-up actions, active status monitoring, and a determination of the results of actions taken on recommendations.

---

**Audit Follow-up**

---

The director of internal auditing should ensure follow-up of prior audit findings and recommendations to determine if corrective action was taken and is achieving the desired results.

---

Auditee responses to the audit report are reviewed to assess their adequacy and timeliness and appropriateness of proposed corrective actions. Auditee responses and their corrective actions are monitored to ensure their timely completion. Effective follow-up is essential to get the full benefits of audit work. If monitoring and follow-up disclose that action on major recommendations is not progressing, additional steps should be promptly considered. Follow-up should be elevated to progressively higher levels of management of the organization to obtain prompt action. Continued attention is required until expected results are achieved. At this point, audit recommendations are closed.

Reasons for closing audit recommendations include only one of these: the recommendation was effectively implemented, an alternative action was taken that achieved the intended results, circumstances have so changed that the recommendation is no longer valid, or the recommendation was not implemented despite the use of all feasible strategies. When a recommendation is closed for the last reason, a judgment is made on whether the objectives are significant enough to be pursued at a later date in another assignment.

### 3.2 IIA's *Performance Standards*

#### (a) Monitoring Progress

**2500—Monitoring Progress**—The chief audit executive should establish and maintain a system to monitor the disposition of results communicated to management.

> **2500.A1**—The chief audit executive should establish a follow-up process to monitor and ensure that management actions have been effectively implemented or that senior management has accepted the risk of not taking action.
>
> **2500.C1**—The internal audit activity should monitor the disposition of results of consulting engagements to the extent agreed on with the client.

**IIA's Practice Advisory 2500-1: Monitoring Progress**

*Nature of This Practice Advisory*

Internal auditors should consider these suggestions when monitoring progress on results communicated to management. This guidance is not intended to represent all the considerations that may be necessary, but simply a recommended set of items that should be addressed. *Compliance with Practice Advisories is optional.*

1.  The chief audit executive (CAE) should establish procedures to include

    *   A time frame within which management's response to the engagement observations and recommendations is required
    *   An evaluation of management's response
    *   A verification of the response (if appropriate)
    *   A follow-up engagement (if appropriate)
    *   A communications procedure that escalates unsatisfactory responses/actions, including the assumption of risk, to the appropriate levels of management

2.  Certain reported observations and recommendations may be so significant as to require immediate action by management. These conditions should be monitored by the internal audit activity until corrected because of the effect they may have on the organization.

3.  Techniques used to effectively monitor progress include

    *   Addressing engagement observations and recommendations to the appropriate levels of management responsible for taking corrective action
    *   Receiving and evaluating management responses to engagement observations and recommendations during the engagement or within a reasonable time period after the engagement results are communicated. Responses are more useful if they include sufficient information for the CAE to evaluate the adequacy and timeliness of corrective action.
    *   Receiving periodic updates from management in order to evaluate the status of management's efforts to correct previously communicated conditions
    *   Receiving and evaluating information from other organizational units assigned responsibility for procedures of a follow-up or corrective nature
    *   Reporting to senior management or the board on the status of responses to engagement observations and recommendations

## IIA's Practice Advisory 2500.A1-1: Follow-up Process

### Nature of This Practice Advisory

Internal auditors should consider these suggestions when establishing follow-up processes. This guidance is not intended to represent all the considerations that may be necessary during such an evaluation, but simply a recommended set of items that should be addressed. *Compliance with Practice Advisories is optional.*

1.  Internal auditors should determine that corrective action was taken and is achieving the desired results, or that senior management or the board has assumed the risk of not taking corrective action on reported observations.

2.  Follow-up by internal auditors is defined as a process by which they determine the adequacy, effectiveness, and timeliness of actions taken by management on reported engagement observations and recommendations, including those made by external auditors and others.

3.  Responsibility for follow-up should be defined in the internal audit activity's written charter. The nature, timing, and extent of follow-up should be determined by the CAE. Factors that should be considered in determining appropriate follow-up procedures are

    *   The significance of the reported observation or recommendation
    *   The degree of effort and cost needed to correct the reported condition
    *   The impact that may result should the corrective action fail
    *   The complexity of the corrective action
    *   The time period involved

4.  There may also be instances where the CAE judges that management's oral or written response shows that action already taken is sufficient when weighed against the relative importance of the engagement observation or recommendation. On such occasions, follow-up may be performed as part of the next engagement.

5.  Internal auditors should ascertain those actions taken on engagement observations and recommendations remedy the underlying conditions.

6.  The CAE is responsible for scheduling follow-up activities as part of developing engagement work schedules. Scheduling of follow-up should be based on the risk and exposure involved, as

well as on the degree of difficulty and the significance of timing in implementing corrective action.

(b) **Resolution of Management's Acceptance of Risks**

**2600—Resolution of Management's Acceptance of Risks**—When the chief audit executive believes that senior management has accepted a level of residual risk that **may be** unacceptable to the organization, the CAE should discuss the matter with senior management. If the decision regarding residual risk is not resolved, the CAE and senior management should report the matter to the board for resolution.

**IIA's Practice Advisory 2600-1: Management's Acceptance of Risks**

*Nature of This Practice Advisory*

Internal auditors should consider these suggestions involving management's acceptance of risks. This guidance is not intended to represent all the considerations that may be necessary, but simply a recommended set of items that should be addressed. *Compliance with this Practice Advisory is optional.*

1. Management is responsible for deciding the appropriate action to be taken in response to reported engagement observations and recommendations. The CAE is responsible for assessing such management action for the timely resolution of the matters reported as engagement observations and recommendations. In deciding the extent of follow-up, internal auditors should consider procedures of a follow-up nature performed by others in the organization.
2. As stated in Section 2060 of the *International Standards for the Professional Practice of Internal Auditing (Standards)*, paragraph 3 of Practice Advisory 2060-1, senior management may decide to assume the risk of not correcting the reported condition because of cost or other considerations. The board should be informed of senior management's decision on all significant engagement observations and recommendations.

**MULTIPLE-CHOICE QUESTIONS (1-52)**

**Items 1 and 2** are based on the following:

An internal audit team recently completed an audit of the company's compliance with its lease-versus-purchase policy concerning company automobiles. The audit report noted that the basis for several decisions to lease rather than purchase automobiles had not been documented and was not auditable. The report contained a recommendation that operating management ensure that such lease agreements not be executed without proper documentation of the basis for the decision to lease rather than buy. The internal auditors are about to perform follow-up work on this audit report.

1. The primary purpose for performing a follow-up review is to
   a. Ensure timely consideration of the internal auditors' recommendations.
   b. Ascertain that appropriate action was taken on reported findings.
   c. Allow the internal auditors to evaluate the effectiveness of their recommendations.
   d. Document what management is doing in response to the audit report and close the audit file in a timely manner.

2. Assume that senior management has decided to accept the risk involved in failure to document the basis for lease-versus-purchase decisions involving company automobiles. In such a case, what would be the auditors' reporting obligation?
   a. The auditors have no further reporting responsibility.
   b. Management's decision and the auditors' concern should be reported to the company's board of directors.
   c. The auditors should issue a follow-up report to management clearly stating the rationale for the recommendation that the basis for lease-versus-purchase decisions be properly documented.
   d. The auditors should inform the external auditor and any responsible regulatory agency that no action has been taken on the finding in question.

3. Auditors realize that at times corrective action is not taken even when agreed to by the appropriate parties. This should lead an internal auditor to
   a. Decide the extent of necessary follow-up work.
   b. Allow management to decide when to follow-up, since it is management's ultimate responsibility.
   c. Decide to conduct follow-up work only if management requests the auditor's assistance.
   d. Write a follow-up audit report with all findings and their significance to the operations.

4. Follow-up activity may be required to ensure that corrective action has taken place for certain findings. The internal audit department's responsibility to perform follow-up activities as required should be defined in the
   a. Internal auditing department's written charter.
   b. Mission statement of the audit committee.
   c. Engagement memo issued prior to each audit assignment.
   d. Purpose statement within applicable audit reports.

5. Given the acceptance of the cost savings audits and the scarcity of internal audit resources, the audit manager also decided that follow-up action was not needed. The manager reasoned that cost savings should be sufficient to motivate the auditee to implement the auditor's recommendations. Therefore, follow-up was not scheduled as a regular part of the audit plan. Does the audit manager's decision violate the IIA *Standards*?
   a. No. The *Standards* do not specify whether follow-up is needed.
   b. Yes. The *Standards* require the auditors to determine whether the auditee has appropriately implemented all of the auditor's recommendations.
   c. Yes. Scarcity of resources is not a sufficient reason to omit follow-up action.
   d. No. When there is evidence of sufficient motivation by the auditee, there is no need for follow-up action.

6. Reporting to senior management and the board is an important part of the auditor's obligation. Which of the following items is **not required to be reported** to senior management and/or the board?
   a. Subsequent to the completion of an audit, but prior to the issuance of an audit report, the audit senior in charge of the audit was offered a permanent position in the auditee's department.
   b. An annual report summary of the department's audit work schedule and financial budget.
   c. Significant interim changes to the approved audit work schedule and financial budget.
   d. An audit plan was approved by senior management and the board. Subsequent to the approval, senior management informed the audit director not to perform an audit of a division because the division's activities were very sensitive.

7. During an audit of purchasing, internal auditors found several violations of company policy concerning competitive bidding. The same condition that had been reported in an audit report last year, and corrective action had not been taken. Which of the following **best** describes the appropriate action concerning this repeat finding?
   a. The audit report should note that this same condition had been reported in the prior audit.
   b. During the exit interview, management should be made aware that a finding from the prior report had not been corrected.
   c. The director of internal auditing should determine whether management or the board has assumed the risk of not taking corrective action.
   d. The director of internal auditing should determine whether this condition should be reported to the independent auditor and any regulatory agency.

8. Which of the following audit committee activities would be of the greatest benefit to the internal auditing department?
   a. Review and approval of audit programs.
   b. Assurance that the external auditor will rely on the work of the internal auditing department whenever possible.
   c. Review and endorsement of all internal audit reports prior to their release.
   d. Support for appropriate follow-up of recommendations made by the internal auditing department.

9.  An internal auditor reported a suspected fraud to the director of internal auditing. The director turned the entire case over to the security department. Security failed to investigate or report the case to management. The perpetrator continued to defraud the organization until being accidentally discovered by a line manager two years later. Select the most appropriate action for the audit director.

a.  The director's actions were correct.
b.  The director should have periodically checked the status of the case with security.
c.  The director should have conducted the investigation.
d.  The director should have discharged the perpetrator.

10. If an internal auditor finds that no corrective action has been taken on a prior audit finding that is still valid, the IIA *Standards* states that the internal auditor should

a.  Restate the prior finding along with the findings of the current audit.
b.  Determine whether management or the board has assumed the risk of not taking corrective action.
c.  Seek the board's approval to initiate corrective action.
d.  Schedule a future audit of the specific area involved.

11. Internal auditing is responsible for reporting fraud to senior management or the board when

a.  The incidence of fraud of a material amount has been established to a reasonable certainty.
b.  Suspicious activities have been reported to internal auditing.
c.  Irregular transactions have been identified and are under investigation.
d.  The review of all suspected fraud-related transactions is complete.

12. Why should organizations require auditees to promptly reply and outline the corrective action that has been implemented on reported deficiencies?

a.  To close the open audit issues as soon as possible.
b.  To effect savings as early as possible.
c.  To indicate concurrence with the audit findings.
d.  To ensure that the auditor performance is evaluated.

13. Following a negative performance evaluation by a supervisor, a staff auditor went to the audit director to seek a change in the evaluation. The director was familiar with the auditor's performance and agreed with the evaluation. The director agreed to meet and discuss the situation. Which of the following is the best course of action for the director to take?

a.  Have the supervisor participate in the meeting, so that there is no misunderstanding about the facts.
b.  Have a human resources administrator present to ensure that improper statements are not made.
c.  Meet privately with the employee. Tell the employee of the director's agreement with the performance evaluation and express interest in any additional facts the employee may wish to present.
d.  Meet privately with the employee. Encourage discussion by asking for the employee's side of the issue and disclaiming any agreement with the supervisor.

14. The requirements for staffing level, education and training, and audit research should be included in

a.  The internal auditing department's charter.
b.  The internal auditing department's policies and procedures manual.
c.  The annual plan for the internal auditing department.
d.  Job descriptions for the various staff positions.

15. Which of the following activities is **not** included in determining the audit schedule?

a.  Developing audit programs.
b.  Assessing risk factors.
c.  Planning workload requirements.
d.  Identifying auditable locations.

16. The internal audit director of a multinational company must form an audit team to examine a newly acquired subsidiary in another country. Consideration should be given to which of the following factors?

I.   Local customs.
II.  Language skills of the auditor.
III. Experience of the auditor.
IV.  Monetary exchange rate.

a.  I, II, III.
b.  II, III, IV.
c.  I and III.
d.  I and II.

17. A quality assurance program of an internal audit department provides reasonable assurance that audit work conforms to applicable standards. Which of the following activities are designed to provide feedback on the effectiveness of an audit department?

I.   Proper supervision.
II.  Proper training.
III. Internal reviews.
IV.  External reviews.

a.  I, II, and III.
b.  II, III, and IV.
c.  I, III, and IV.
d.  I, II, III, and IV.

18. If the internal audit staff does **not** have the skills to perform a particular task, a specialist could be brought in from

I.   The organization's external audit firm.
II.  An outside consulting firm.
III. The department currently being audited.
IV.  A college or university.

a.  I and II.
b.  II and IV.
c.  I, II, and III.
d.  I, II, and IV.

19. The **best** rationale for rotating internal auditors so those different individuals are assigned to consecutive audits of a given auditee is to

a.  Prevent burnout on the part of the internal auditor, which may lead to excessive turnover in the internal audit department.
b.  Promote rapid professional development on the part of internal auditors by exposing them to the full range of organizational activities.

c.   Increase the diligence exercised by internal auditors who know that the quality of their work will be apparent to the next set of internal auditors.

d.   Avoid the development of bias toward a given auditee.

**20.** Which of the following activities does **not** constitute audit supervision?

a.   Preparing a preliminary audit program.

b.   Providing appropriate instructions to the auditors.

c.   Reviewing audit workpapers.

d.   Seeing that audit objectives are achieved.

**21.** The audit team leader is **least** likely to have a primary role in

a.   Allocating budget audit hours among assigned staff.

b.   Updating the permanent files.

c.   Reviewing the working papers.

d.   Preparing the critique sheet for the audit.

**22.** In which of the following duties would the audit director **least** likely have a primary role?

a.   Determine the need for expanded testing.

b.   Review the summary findings sheet.

c.   Select or approve team members.

d.   Organize and draft the audit report.

**23.** An element of authority that should be included in the charter of the internal auditing department is

a.   Identification of the operational departments which the audit department must audit.

b.   Identification of the types of disclosures which should be made to the audit committee.

c.   Access to records, personnel, and physical properties relevant to the performance of audits.

d.   Access to the external auditor's working papers.

**24.** Having been given the task of developing a performance appraisal system for evaluating the audit performance of a large internal auditing staff, you should

a.   Provide for an explanation of the appraisal criteria methods at the time the appraisal results are discussed with the internal auditor.

b.   Provide general information concerning the frequency of evaluations and the way evaluations will be performed without specifying their timing and uses.

c.   Provide primarily for the evaluation of criteria such as diligence, initiative, and tact.

d.   Provide primarily for the evaluation of specific accomplishments directly related to the performance of the audit program.

**25.** The key factor to the success of an audit organization's human resources program is

a.   An informal program for developing and counseling staff.

b.   A compensation plan based on years of experience.

c.   A well developed set of selection criteria.

d.   A program for recognizing the special interests of individual staff members.

**26.** Which of the following would be the **best** source of an internal audit director's information for planning staffing requirements?

a.   Discussions of audit needs with executive management and the audit committee.

b.   Review of audit staff education and training records.

c.   Review audit staff size and composition of similar sized companies in the same industry.

d.   Interviews with existing audit staff.

**27.** Which of the following is **most essential** for guiding the audit staff in maintaining daily compliance with the department's standards of performance?

a.   Quality control reviews.

b.   Position descriptions.

c.   Performance appraisals.

d.   Policies and procedures.

**28.** You have been selected to develop an internal auditing department for your company. Your approach would most likely be to hire

a.   Internal auditors each of whom possesses all the skills required to handle all audit assignments.

b.   Inexperienced personnel and train them the way the company wants them trained.

c.   Degreed accountants since most audit work is accounting related.

d.   Internal auditors who collectively have the knowledge and skills needed to complete all internal audit assignments.

**29.** The director of a newly formed internal auditing department is in the process of drafting a formal written charter for the department. Which one of the following items, related to the operational effectiveness of the internal audit department, should be included in the charter?

a.   The frequency of the audits to be performed.

b.   The manner by which audit findings will be reported.

c.   The procedures which the internal auditors will employ in investigating and reporting fraud.

d.   The internal auditors' unlimited access to those records, personnel, and physical properties that are relevant to the performance of the audits.

**30.** A director of internal auditing has reviewed credentials, checked references, and interviewed a candidate for a staff position. The director concludes that the candidate has a thorough understanding of internal auditing techniques, accounting, and management. However, the director notes that the candidate has limited knowledge of economics and computer science. Which of the following actions would be **most** appropriate?

a.   Reject the candidate because of the lack of knowledge required by the IIA *Standards*.

b.   Offer the candidate a position despite the lack of knowledge in certain essential areas.

c.   Encourage the candidate to obtain additional training in economics and computer science and then reapply.

d.   Offer the candidate a position if other staff members possess sufficient knowledge in economics and computer science.

**31.** Which audit-planning tool is general in nature and is used to ensure adequate audit coverage over time?

a.   The long-range schedule.

b.   The audit program.

c.   The department budget.

d.   The department charter.

**32.** A professional engineer applied for a position in the internal auditing department of a high-technology firm. The engineer became interested in the position after observing several internal auditors while they were auditing the engineering department. The director of internal auditing
   a. Should not hire the engineer because of the lack of knowledge of internal auditing standards.
   b. May hire the engineer in spite of the lack of knowledge of internal auditing standards.
   c. Should not hire the engineer because of the lack of knowledge of accounting and taxes.
   d. May hire the engineer because of the knowledge of internal auditing gained in the previous position.

**Items 33 through 35** are based on the following:

Upon being appointed, a new director of internal auditing found an inexperienced audit staff that was over budget on most audits. A detailed review of audit working papers revealed no evidence of progressive reviews by audit supervisors. Additionally, there was no evidence that a quality assurance program existed.

**33.** As a means of controlling projects and avoiding time-budget overruns, decisions to revise time budgets for an audit should normally be made
   a. Immediately after the preliminary survey.
   b. When a significant deficiency has been substantiated.
   c. When inexperienced audit staff is assigned to an audit.
   d. Immediately after expanding tests to establish reliability of findings.

**34.** Determining that audit objectives have been met is part of the overall supervision of an audit assignment and is the ultimate responsibility of the
   a. Staff internal auditor.
   b. Audit committee.
   c. Internal auditing supervisor.
   d. Director of internal auditing.

**35.** To properly evaluate the operations of an internal auditing department, a quality assurance program should include
   a. Periodic supervision of internal audit work on a sample basis.
   b. Internal reviews, by other than the internal audit staff, to appraise the quality of department operations.
   c. External reviews at least once every three years by qualified persons who are independent of the organization.
   d. Periodic rotation of audit managers.

**36.** The internal auditing department of a large corporation has established its operating plan and budget for the coming year. The operating plan is restricted to the following categories: a prioritized listing of all audits, staffing, a detailed expense budget, and the commencement date of each audit. Which of the following **best** describes the major deficiency of this operating plan?
   a. Requests by management for special projects are not considered.
   b. Opportunities to achieve operating benefits are ignored.
   c. Measurability criteria and targeted dates of completion are not provided.

   d. Knowledge, skills, and disciplines required to perform work are ignored.

**37.** The capabilities of individual staff members are key features in the effectiveness of an internal auditing department. Select the primary consideration used when staffing an internal auditing department.
   a. Background checks.
   b. Job descriptions.
   c. Continuing education.
   d. Organizational orientation.

**38.** Internal audit staff members should be afforded an appropriate means through which they can discuss problems and receive updates regarding departmental policies. The most appropriate forum for this objective is
   a. The department's informal communication lines.
   b. Intradepartment memoranda.
   c. Staff meetings.
   d. Employee evaluation conferences.

**39.** The peer review process can be performed internally or externally. A distinguishing feature of the external review is its objective to
   a. Identify tasks that can be performed better.
   b. Determine if audit activities meet professional standards.
   c. Set forth the recommendations for improvement.
   d. Provide an independent evaluation.

**40.** Exit conferences serve to ensure the accuracy of the information used by an internal auditor. A secondary purpose of an exit conference is to
   a. Get immediate action on a recommendation.
   b. Improve relations with auditees.
   c. Agree to the appropriate distribution of the final report.
   d. Brief senior management on the results of the audit.

**41.** The advantage attributed to the establishment of internal auditing field offices for work at remote locations is best described as
   a. The possibility of increased objectivity of personnel assigned to a field office.
   b. A reduction of travel time and related travel expense.
   c. The increased ease of maintaining uniform company-wide standards.
   d. More contact with senior audit personnel leading to an increase in control.

**42.** The director of internal auditing is preparing the work schedule for the next budget year and has limited audit resources. In deciding whether to schedule the purchasing or the personnel department for an audit, which of the following would be the **least** important factor?
   a. There have been major changes in operations in one of the departments.
   b. The audit staff has recently added an individual with expertise in one of the areas.
   c. There are more opportunities to achieve operating benefits in one of the departments than in the other.
   d. The potential for loss is significantly greater in one department than the other.

**43.** According to the IIA *Standards*, an internal auditing department's activity reports should
    a.   List the material findings of major audits.
    b.   List unresolved findings.
    c.   Report the weekly activities of the individual auditors.
    d.   Compare audits completed with audits planned.

**44.** The best means for the internal auditing department to determine whether its goal of implementing broader audit coverage of functional activities has been met is through
    a.   Accumulation of audit findings by auditable area.
    b.   Comparison of the audit plan to actual audit activity.
    c.   Surveys of management satisfaction with the internal auditing function.
    d.   Implementation of a quality assurance program.

**45.** Why should organizations require auditees to promptly reply and outline the corrective action that has been implemented on reported deficiencies?
    a.   To remove items from the "pending" list as soon as possible.
    b.   To institute compliance as early as possible.
    c.   To indicate concurrence with the audit findings.
    d.   To ensure that the audit schedule is kept up-to-date.

**46.** Which of the following factors serves as a direct input to the internal auditing department's financial budget?
    a.   Audit work schedules.
    b.   Activity reports.
    c.   Past effectiveness of the internal auditing department in identifying cost savings.
    d.   Auditing department's charter.

**47.** While attending a social function, an internal auditor described to a group of friends the elements of a sensitive audit on which he was working. The internal auditing director's best avenue for proceeding is to
    a.   Fire the auditor to set an example for other auditors.
    b.   Remove the auditor from all audits in that area, or in other sensitive areas.
    c.   Reprimand the auditor for "talking shop" at a social function.
    d.   Explain that the act is an ethical violation of the profession and that further such action could result in dismissal or other serious effects.

**48.** The internal auditing department for a large corporation recently concluded an audit of sales department travel expenses. Which of the following groups should receive a copy of the audit report?
    a.   Sales director and vice president for marketing.
    b.   Chairman of the board, chief operating officer, and vice president for marketing.
    c.   Chairman of the board, controller, and sales director.
    d.   Chief financial officer, sales director, and chief executive officer.

**49.** External review of an internal auditing department is **not** likely to evaluate
    a.   Adherence to the internal auditing department's charter.
    b.   Compliance with the IIA *Standards*.

    c.   Detailed cost-benefit analysis of the internal auditing department.
    d.   Audit planning documents, particularly those submitted to senior management and the audit committee.

**50.** An internal auditing manager has a small team of employees, but each individual is self-motivated and could be termed a "high achiever." The audit manager has been given a particularly difficult assignment. Even for a high achiever, the probability that this job can be completed by one individual by the required deadline is low. Select the best course for the audit manager.
    a.   Assign one individual since high achievers thrive on high risks.
    b.   Assign two staff members to moderate the risk of failure.
    c.   Assign the entire staff to ensure the risk of failure is low.
    d.   Ask company management to cancel the job.

**51.** Recent criticism of an internal auditing department suggested that audit coverage was not providing adequate feedback to senior management on the processes used in the organization's key lines of business. The problem was further defined as lack of feedback on the recent implementation of automated support systems. Which two functions does the director of internal auditing need to improve?
    a.   Staffing and communicating.
    b.   Staffing and decision making.
    c.   Planning and organizing.
    d.   Planning and communicating.

**52.** In some cultures and organizations, managers insist that the internal auditing function is not needed to provide a critical assessment of the organization's operations. A management attitude such as this will most probably have an adverse affect on the internal auditing department's
    a.   Operating budget variance.
    b.   Charter.
    c.   Performance appraisals.
    d.   Policies and procedures.

MULTIPLE-CHOICE ANSWERS AND EXPLANATIONS

| | | | | | | | | | |
|---|---|---|---|---|---|---|---|---|---|
| 1. b __ __ | 12. b __ __ | 23. c __ __ | 34. d __ __ | 45. b __ __ |
| 2. a __ __ | 13. c __ __ | 24. d __ __ | 35. c __ __ | 46. a __ __ |
| 3. a __ __ | 14. c __ __ | 25. c __ __ | 36. c __ __ | 47. d __ __ |
| 4. a __ __ | 15. a __ __ | 26. a __ __ | 37. b __ __ | 48. a __ __ |
| 5. c __ __ | 16. a __ __ | 27. d __ __ | 38. c __ __ | 49. c __ __ |
| 6. a __ __ | 17. c __ __ | 28. d __ __ | 39. d __ __ | 50. b __ __ |
| 7. c __ __ | 18. d __ __ | 29. d __ __ | 40. b __ __ | 51. d __ __ |
| 8. d __ __ | 19. d __ __ | 30. d __ __ | 41. b __ __ | 52. b __ __ |
| 9. b __ __ | 20. a __ __ | 31. a __ __ | 42. b __ __ | |
| 10. b __ __ | 21. b __ __ | 32. b __ __ | 43. d __ __ | 1st: __/52 = __% |
| 11. a __ __ | 22. d __ __ | 33. a __ __ | 44. b __ __ | 2nd: __/52 = __% |

**1.** **(b)** This is what the IIA *Standards* require. Choice (a) is incorrect because it is not the best answer. It implies that the auditor's recommendations, not the findings, are the most important elements of the report. Choice (c) is incorrect because it is not the best choice. This implies that the auditor's recommendations, not findings, are primary. Choice (d) is incorrect because this implies that processes in the internal auditing activity are primary.

Subject Area: Internal audit—monitor engagement outcomes. Source: CIA 596, I-1.

**2.** **(a)** When senior management has assumed such risk, reporting to the board is required only for significant findings. There is no indication that the failure to document several decisions is significant enough to report to the board. Choice (b) is incorrect because of explanation given in choice (a). Choice (c) is incorrect because senior management has already indicated that it understands and has accepted the related risk. Choice (d) is incorrect because reporting to anyone outside the organization is not required or appropriate.

Subject Area: Internal audit—monitor engagement outcomes. Source: CIA 596, I-2.

**3.** **(a)** The IIA *Standards* state that the director of internal auditing should determine the nature, timing, and extent of follow-up. Choices (b) and (c) are incorrect because the IIA *Standards* state that follow-up work is not management's responsibility. Choice (d) is incorrect because the auditor has to provide an opinion as to the decision made with regard to lack of action.

Subject Area: Internal audit—monitor engagement outcomes. Source: CIA 596, I-3.

**4.** **(a)** Responsibility for follow-up should be defined in the internal auditing department's written charter. Choice (b) is incorrect. Follow-up is not specified in the content of the audit committee's mission statement. Choice (c) is incorrect. This memo may contain a statement about responsibility for follow-up, but such a statement should be based on the wording and authority of the departmental charter. Choice (d) is incorrect. Follow-up authority and responsibility may be cited in applicable audit reports, but the definition should be first contained in the departmental charter.

Subject Area: Internal audit—monitor engagement outcomes. Source: CIA 596, I-60.

**5.** **(c)** The IIA *Standards* require follow-up action. Lack of resources is not a sufficient reason. Choice (a) is incorrect. Follow-up is required. Choice (b) is incorrect. Follow-up is to see that actions are taken, not just that the auditor's recom-

mendations have been implemented. Choice (d) is incorrect. Follow-up is required.

Subject Area: Internal audit—monitor engagement outcomes. Source: CIA 595, I-40.

**6.** **(a)** This would not have to be communicated. The audit work was done. The director of internal auditing would have to determine that there was no impairment of the independence of the senior's work. If there was none, the report could be issued without reporting the personnel change. Choices (b) and (c) are incorrect. Both are a standard part of the required reporting to senior management and the board. Choice (d) is incorrect. Both senior management and the board had approved the audit plan. The change dictated by senior management should be reported to the board.

Subject Area: Internal audit—monitor engagement outcomes. Source: CIA 595, I-58.

**7.** **(c)** This action meets the requirements of the IIA *Standards*. Choices (a) and (b) are incorrect because these actions are insufficient. Choice (d) is incorrect because this action would be inappropriate.

Subject Area: Internal audit—monitor engagement outcomes. Source: CIA 590, I-42.

**8.** **(d)** The audit committee can lend considerable weight to the recommendations of internal auditing. Choice (a) is incorrect. Review and approval of audit programs is the responsibility of internal audit supervision. Choice (b) is incorrect. External audit's reliance on the work of internal auditing is the subject of an AICPA pronouncement. Choice (c) is incorrect. Review and approval of internal audit reports is the responsibility of the director of internal auditing or designee.

Subject Area: Internal audit—monitor engagement outcomes. Source: CIA 590, II-5.

**9.** **(b)** The director should have periodically checked the status of the case with security. Follow-up is specified by the IIA *Standards*. Choice (a) is incorrect. According to the *Standards*, the director should have ensured that the internal auditing department's responsibilities were met. Choice (c) is incorrect. A security department would generally have more expertise in the investigation of a fraud. Choice (d) is incorrect. The fraud was only suspected when reported to the director. Immediate discharge would have violated the suspect's rights. In addition, the director would not normally have the authority to discharge an employee in an audited area.

Subject Area: Internal audit—monitor engagement outcomes. Source: CIA 593, II-44.

**10.** **(b)** As per the IIA *Standards*, and therefore, by definition, choices (a), (c), and (d) will be incorrect.

Subject Area: Internal audit—monitor engagement outcomes. Source: CIA 1192, I-47.

**11.** **(a)** If the incidence of significant fraud has been established with reasonable certainty, the auditor is responsible for reporting such to senior management or the board. Choice (b) is incorrect. No reporting is required when suspicious acts are reported to the auditor. Choice (c) is incorrect. Irregular transactions under investigation would not require reporting until the investigation phase is completed. Choice (d) is incorrect. Reporting should occur sooner. See choice (a).

Subject Area: Internal audit—monitor engagement outcomes. Source: CIA 1192, II-49.

**12.** **(b)** The objective of the audit is to effect savings resulting from the auditee's corrective action as early as possible so that the organization will benefit from the action taken. Choice (a) is incorrect. This is a mechanical aspect of the audit reporting process. Choice (c) is incorrect. The auditee may not concur with the audit finding all the time. Choice (d) is incorrect. This is an administrative function of the audit department.

Subject Area: Internal audit—monitor engagement outcomes. Source: CIA 1191, I-44 (modified).

**13.** **(c)** Private conversation signals to the employee that the director is interested in what he or she has to say and will not be measuring his or her words against those of another. However, the director must establish a position and show support for the supervisor. There may be more than one valid viewpoint, but that does not necessarily mean that the employee's is valid. Choice (a) is incorrect. The supervisor, as author of a critical performance review, will only add to the element of management intimidation. Choice (b) is incorrect. Again, the presence of a third party would inhibit the director's listening effectiveness. Unless the director thinks the auditor's concerns are so serious that the human resources department must be informed, it is preferable to meet with the employee privately. Choice (d) is incorrect. It is never appropriate to mislead an employee in order to obtain information or to determine the employee's view on a matter.

Subject Area: Internal audit—monitor engagement outcomes. Source: CIA 597, I-21.

**14.** **(c)** The annual plan should be comprised of both an audit schedule and a budget and, as such, should include all of these issues. Choice (a) is incorrect. The charter outlines the purpose, authority, and responsibilities of the department, not the details related to staffing and such. Choice (b) is incorrect. The policies and procedures manual spells out how audits should be conducted. It does not cover areas such as staffing levels. Choice (d) is incorrect. Job descriptions do not reflect staffing level requirements.

Subject Area: Internal audit—monitor engagement outcomes. Source: CIA 590, II-8.

**15.** **(a)** The development of audit programs occurs during the planning phase of an individual audit. It is not included within the scope of developing the audit schedule. Choices (b), (c), and (d) are incorrect because each choice is considered to determine the audit schedule.

Subject Area: Internal audit—monitor engagement outcomes. Source: CIA 594, III-3.

**16.** **(a)** In addition to language skills, local customs must be considered. For example, gender and ethnic compatibility may be important in some Middle Eastern countries because religious restrictions and incompatibilities are relevant. As always, experience levels are relevant in making audit assignments. Choice (b) is incorrect. The monetary exchange rate would not be a factor in determining the needed traits of the team members. Choice (c) is incorrect. It includes appropriate factors, but does not identify all the acceptable choices. Choice (d) is incorrect. It includes an incomplete answer. See choice (c).

Subject Area: Internal audit—monitor engagement outcomes. Source: CIA 594, III-4.

**17.** **(c)** The purpose of a quality assurance program is to evaluate the operations of the internal audit department. The IIA *Standards* note that a program should include supervision, internal reviews, and external reviews. Choices (a), (b), and (d) are incorrect. Proper training is an important component of maintaining a current staff, but does not provide feedback.

Subject Area: Internal audit—monitor engagement outcomes. Source: CIA 594, III-5.

**18.** **(d)** The key point is independence and objectivity. A specialist from the department currently being audited would not be independent due to a natural bias toward that department. Choices (a) and (b) are incorrect. They include acceptable consultants, but do not identify all the acceptable choices. Choice (c) is incorrect. A specialist from the same department is unacceptable since the person would not be independent or objective.

Subject Area: Internal audit—monitor engagement outcomes. Source: CIA 594, III-7.

**19.** **(d)** This is the primary reason. The alternatives may be desirable, but they are not the basis for the rotation preference. Choice (a) is incorrect. It is a secondary reason. For example, auditor burnout can be reduced with less travel. Choice (b) is incorrect. It is a secondary reason. Professional development can be obtained in other ways, such as attending conferences, seminars, and taking the CIA exam. Choice (c) is incorrect. It is a secondary reason. This approach establishes a precedent or standard for others to follow.

Subject Area: Internal audit—monitor engagement outcomes. Source: CIA 594, III-91.

**20.** **(a)** This choice is a planning task. Choices (b), (c), and (d) are incorrect because each choice is a supervisory task.

Subject Area: Internal audit—monitor engagement outcomes. Source: CIA 594, III-92.

**21.** **(b)** This is a task most likely performed by the audit staff. Choice (a), (c), and (d) are incorrect because each choice is a common team leader task.

Subject Area: Internal audit—monitor engagement outcomes. Source: CIA 594, III-93.

**22.** **(d)** This is a task most likely performed by the team leader. Choices (a), (b), and (c) are incorrect because each choice is a common audit director task.

Subject Area: Internal audit—monitor engagement outcomes. Source: CIA 594, III-94.

**23.** **(c)** The auditor must have access to all audit evidence in order to fulfill obligations and responsibilities. Choice (a) is incorrect. The internal audit department should not specifically identify what activities will be audited. Choice (b) is incorrect. The auditor is obligated to make all needed disclosures to the audit committee. Choice (d) is incorrect. Access to the external auditor's working papers cannot be guaranteed in the charter.

Subject Area: Internal audit—monitor engagement outcomes. Source: CIA 1193, I-3.

**24.** **(d)** The appraisal of audit performance should deal primarily with specific accomplishments related to audits. This provides a more objective appraisal than focusing on traits, which are largely subjective. Choice (a) is incorrect. The personnel whose performance is being appraised should be made aware of the criteria and methods at the time they begin the employment, not at the time of the performance review. Choice (b) is incorrect. The frequency and use of the evaluation are important criteria that should be clearly communicated. Choice (c) is incorrect. The criteria named are traits, not accomplishments. Although traits are important, a performance evaluation system for evaluating audit performance should primarily focus on specific accomplishments not traits.

Subject Area: Internal audit—monitor engagement outcomes. Source: CIA 591, I-9.

**25.** **(c)** Selection of individuals with the attributes and education needed for internal auditing is essential if the staff is to develop properly. A well-developed set of selection criteria is important in any organization, whether it is audit or nonaudit function. Choice (a) is incorrect. The success of any training program will be heavily dependent on the attributes of those being trained. Choice (b) is incorrect. While compensation is an important factor in attracting and retaining staff, it is probably not the most important in staff development. Choice (d) is incorrect because such a program should be fair and equitable to all staff members.

Subject Area: Internal audit—monitor engagement outcomes. Source: CIA 591, I-10.

**26.** **(a)** This is a good source of information concerning staff size or skill requirements. Choice (b) is incorrect. It is not the best choice since there is not obvious link with scheduled work. Choice (c) is incorrect. That would not account for the unique needs of a particular organization. Choice (d) is incorrect. It is not the best choice since there is not obvious link with scheduled work.

Subject Area: Internal audit—monitor engagement outcomes. Source: CIA 591, I-11.

**27.** **(d)** Comprehensive policies and procedures provided by the director of internal audit guide the audit staff on a daily basis to ensure compliance with department's standards of performance. Choice (a) is incorrect. Quality control reviews would evaluate compliance and not serve as a daily guide to the audit staff. Choice (b) is incorrect. Position descriptions provide the purpose description and responsibilities of individual positions but are not effective in the day-to-day management of the function. Choice (c) is incorrect. Performance evaluations are a periodic function and will not be effective on a day-to-day basis.

Subject Area: Internal audit—monitor engagement outcomes. Source: CIA 591, I-12.

**28.** **(d)** Having a collective mix of knowledge and skills is an integral part of the IIA *Standards*. No internal audit department can have a credible program without this mix.

Choice (a) is incorrect. The scope of internal auditing is so broad that it is not possible for one individual to have the requisite expertise in all areas. Choice (b) is incorrect. It is desirable to have various skill levels to match auditors appropriately with varying assignment complexities. It is also necessary to have experienced auditors available to train and supervise less experienced staff members. Choice (c) is incorrect. Many skills are needed in internal auditing. Computer skills are widely needed in companies that perform information technology audits. Many industries find it necessary to have the skills of engineers and other disciplines available on a regular basis.

Subject Area: Internal audit—monitor engagement outcomes. Source: CIA 591, II-8.

**29.** **(d)** The IIA *Standards* state that the charter should include the internal auditors' access to those records, personnel and physical properties that are relevant to their work. Having limitations on such access would impact the operational effectiveness of the internal audit department because the internal auditor would not be able to conduct the audit in the proper approach that he designed it. Choice (a) is incorrect. The *Standards* state that "the charter should (a) establish the department's position within the organization; (b) authorize access to records, personnel, and physical properties relevant to the performance of audits; and (c) define the scope of internal auditing activities." Accordingly, not only is the frequency of audits not included in the charter, but also such information is not related to the operational effectiveness of the internal audit department. Choice (b) is incorrect. The manner of reporting audit findings (how it is reported, to whom it will be reported, etc.) is not included in the charter and is not related to operational effectiveness of the internal audit department. Choice (c) is incorrect. The procedures to be employed by internal auditors in investigating and reporting fraud are not included in the charter.

Subject Area: Internal audit—monitor engagement outcomes. Source: CIA 1193, II-4.

**30.** **(d)** This is the most realistic way to address the department's staffing needs. Choice (a) is incorrect. The IIA *Standards* state the general subjects that staff should possess knowledge of, but clearly states that every auditor need not possess knowledge of all of them. Choice (b) is incorrect. The department's needs may be for additional expertise in economics or computer science. Choice (c) is incorrect. This may be good advice, but it does not adequately address the department's present needs.

Subject Area: Internal audit—monitor engagement outcomes. Source: CIA 1193, II-5.

**31.** **(a)** The long-range program gives evidence of coverage of key functions at planned intervals. Choice (b) is incorrect. The audit program is limited in scope to a particular project. Choice (c) is incorrect. The department budget may be used to justify head count, but it is not used to ensure adequate audit coverage over time. Choice (d) is incorrect. The department charter is not an audit-planning tool.

Subject Area: Internal audit—monitor engagement outcomes. Source: CIA 592, I-4.

**32.** **(b)** Internal auditing standards are required to be known by the department collectively. Individual internal auditing staff members may, however, bring special skills to the department instead of specific knowledge of internal auditing standards. Choice (a) is incorrect. Each new employee of an internal auditing department is not required to have knowledge of internal auditing standards. It is required that the department collectively has this knowledge. Choice (c) is incorrect. Each individual internal auditor is not required to have knowledge of accounting or taxes. Choice (d) is incorrect. What knowledge that was acquired by observing is irrelevant to the skills necessary for internal auditing.

Subject Area: Internal audit—monitor engagement outcomes. Source: CIA 592, I-5.

**33.    (a)**    Time budgets should be appraised for revision after the preliminary survey and preparation of the audit program. Choice (b) is incorrect. When a deficiency has been substantiated, no further audit work is required. Choice (c) is incorrect. The assignment of inexperienced staff should have no effect on the time budget. Choice (d) is incorrect. Expanded tests should have no effect on the time budget; the budget would have already been expanded as necessary.

Subject Area: Internal audit—monitor engagement outcomes. Source: CIA 592, I-15.

**34.    (d)**    The director of internal auditing is responsible for supervision, including determining that audit objectives are being met. Choices (a), (b), and (c) are incorrect because according to the IIA *Standards*, the director of internal auditing is responsible for supervision.

Subject Area: Internal audit—monitor engagement outcomes. Source: CIA 592, I-16.

**35.    (c)**    External reviews should be conducted at least once every three years. Choice (a) is incorrect. Supervision should be carried out continually, not just on a periodic test basis. Choice (b) is incorrect. Internal reviews should be conducted by internal auditors and should focus on specific audit projects. Choice (d) is incorrect. Periodic rotation of audit managers is not required.

Subject Area: Internal audit—monitor engagement outcomes. Source: CIA 592, I-17.

**36.    (c)**    This is a requirement of the IIA *Standards*. Choices (a) and (b) are incorrect because prioritizing audits would consider these factors. Choice (d) is incorrect. Staffing for each audit would include this consideration.

Subject Area: Internal audit—monitor engagement outcomes. Source: CIA 592, II-20.

**37.    (b)**    Properly formulated job descriptions provide a basis for the identifying job qualifications (including training and experience). Choice (a) is incorrect. Background checks help ensure that statements made by prospective employees are accurate. However, they are not the primary requisite. Choice (c) is incorrect. Continuing education occurs after the proper people are hired. Choice (d) is incorrect. A thorough orientation helps the new employee become productive more rapidly. However, it will not overcome hiring the wrong person.

Subject Area: Internal audit—monitor engagement outcomes. Source: CIA 1192, II-8.

**38.    (c)**    Formal staff meetings provide the best opportunity for ensuring that issues are addressed timely and efficiently. Choice (a) is incorrect. Informal communication is not the most appropriate forum. Choice (b) is incorrect. Memoranda are generally impersonal and do not afford a good opportunity for maximum exchange of ideas. Choice (d) is incorrect. The employee evaluation conference is not a timely place to discuss problems and receive updates.

Subject Area: Internal audit—monitor engagement outcomes. Source: CIA 1192, II-9.

**39.    (d)**    External review process will provide independent evaluation for management and the audit committee. Choice (a) is incorrect. The internal peer review process will identify things that can be done better. Choice (b) is incorrect. The internal review process will assess if audit activities meet professional standards. Choice (c) is incorrect. The internal review process will set forth recommendations for improvement.

Subject Area: Internal audit—monitor engagement outcomes. Source: CIA 1192, II-10.

**40.    (b)**    The exit conference can be used to allow operating management to air their views and to present any operational objections to specific recommendations. Choice (a) is incorrect. An interim report would have been used to accomplish this. Choice (c) is incorrect. The distribution of reports is not a secondary purpose of an exit conference. Choice (d) is incorrect. Senior management should be given a greatly condensed view of the results of an audit.

Subject Area: Internal audit—monitor engagement outcomes. Source: CIA 1192, II-14.

**41.    (b)**    It is an advantage of the field office. Choice (a) is incorrect. Objectivity of field office personnel decreases. Choice (c) is incorrect. It is a disadvantage; it decreases the ease of maintaining standards. Choice (d) is incorrect. Senior audit personnel are expected to be at corporate level.

Subject Area: Internal audit—monitor engagement outcomes. Source: CIA 1192, II-2.

**42.    (b)**    Audit needs, not auditor skill availability, should drive audit schedules. Choices (a), (c) and (d) are incorrect because each one is an important factor according to the IIA *Standards*.

Subject Area: Internal audit—monitor engagement outcomes. Source: CIA 592, II-11.

**43.    (d)**    This information is a status report to be provided to the audit oversight authority. Choices (a), (b), and (c) are incorrect because each one of them is not an activity report as defined by the IIA *Standards*.

Subject Area: Internal audit—monitor engagement outcomes. Source: CIA 592, II-7.

**44.    (b)**    Comparison of the plan to actual activity will reveal if the planned breadth was achieved. Choice (a) is incorrect. The number of audit findings is not an indicator of audit breadth or quality. Choice (c) is incorrect. Management satisfaction does not directly relate to the expressed goal (broader audit coverage). Choice (d) is incorrect. Implementation of a quality assurance program has no bearing on the stated goal.

Subject Area: Internal audit—monitor engagement outcomes. Source: CIA 1191, I-5.

**45.    (b)**    The objective of the audit is to institute compliance with the auditee's corrective action as early as possible so that the organization will benefit from the action taken. Choice (a) is incorrect. This is an immaterial aspect of the audit reporting process. Choice (c) is incorrect. The auditee may not concur with the audit finding at all times. Choice (d) is incorrect. This is an administrative function of the audit department.

Subject Area: Internal audit—monitor engagement outcomes. Source: CIA 1191, I-44 (modified).

**46. (a)** As specified in the IIA *Standards*, audit work schedules determine both staffing plans and financial budgets. Choice (b) is incorrect. Activity reports compare actual performance with goals and schedules and compare actual expenditures with financial budgets. Choice (c) is incorrect. While past performance is an indicator of the value of internal auditing, it will not impact the funds committed to current operations. Choice (d) is incorrect. The charter for an internal auditing department defines the purpose, authority, and responsibility of the department.

Subject Area: Internal audit—monitor engagement outcomes. Source: CIA 1191, I-7.

**47. (d)** This is an instructive solution and explains the defect in the actions of the internal auditor. Choice (a) is incorrect. There was no intent to do wrong. The sanction is probably too severe. Also, the staff may lose a good auditor. Choice (b) is incorrect. The single occurrence described does not warrant this action. Choice (c) is incorrect. This is partly correct but it has no instructive value.

Subject Area: Internal audit—monitor engagement outcomes. Source: CIA 1191, II-49.

**48. (a)** Audit reports should be distributed to those members of the organization who are able to ensure that audit results are given due consideration. In this case, the sales director and vice president of marketing would be sufficient. Choice (b) is incorrect. The distribution should include only that shown in choice (a). The chairman of the board and chief operating officer need not be involved unless significant problems were revealed. Choice (c) is incorrect. The distribution should include only that shown in choice (a). The chairman of the board and controller need not be involved unless significant problems were revealed. Choice (d) is incorrect. The distribution should include only that shown in choice (a). Chief financial officer and chief executive officer involvement would not be needed.

Subject Area: Internal audit—monitor engagement outcomes. Source: CIA 1191, II-40.

**49. (c)** The cost benefit of internal auditing is neither easily quantifiable nor the subject of an external review. Choices (a), (b), and (c) are incorrect. Each is included in the evaluation of the performance of an internal auditing department per the IIA *Standards*.

Subject Area: Internal audit—monitor engagement outcomes. Source: CIA 1191, II-3.

**50. (b)** High achievers thrive when the job provides for personal responsibility, feedback, and moderate risks. Choices (a), (c), and (d) are incorrect because high achievers prefer moderate risks. They perform best with moderate risks.

Subject Area: Internal audit—monitor engagement outcomes. Source: CIA 595, III-25.

**51. (d)** The problem of lack of feedback indicates the director has problems in planning and allocating audit resources and communicating this need to the audit staff. Choice (a) is incorrect. There is no indication that there are staffing problems (i.e., insufficient audit personnel) or that audit personnel lack necessary skills to provide feedback on automated support systems. Choice (b) is incorrect. There is no indication that staffing or decision making is a problem.

Choice (c) is incorrect. There is no indication that organizing is a problem.

Subject Area: Internal audit—monitor engagement outcomes. Source: CIA 595, III-33.

**52. (b)** In this type of situation, management is highly averse to analysis or possible criticism of their actions and will not grant the internal auditors an adequate charter. Choice (a) is incorrect. An operating budget variance report is a control device used to monitor actual performance versus budget. Management foot-dragging could cause unfavorable variances, but favorable variances could also occur if many audits were cut short due to scope impairments. Choice (c) is incorrect. An unbiased evaluation of audit staff would not be affected by lack of cooperation on the part of nonaudit management. Choice (d) is incorrect. Policies and procedures of the internal audit function are developed by the internal audit department and should not be affected by nonaudit management.

Subject Area: Internal audit—monitor engagement outcomes. Source: CIA 1194, III-14.

# 4 FRAUD KNOWLEDGE ELEMENTS (5–15%)

## THEORY

### 4.1 Discovery Sampling

An auditor could use attribute sampling to estimate the percentage of checks that have problem endorsements. Attribute sampling can be used to determine the deviation rate. Variable sampling could help an auditor determine if a subunit manager of a large company had overstated an asset to increase net income and his bonus.

Discovery sampling, a special kind of attribute sampling, is very useful to fraud examiners when trying to determine whether critical errors exist. Discovery sampling allows examiners to conclude with a certain percentage confidence level whether any problem endorsements or similar critical errors exist in a population. Discovery sampling is attribute sampling with a zero expected error rate. More is said about discovery sampling in Chapter 5.

> **Uses of Discovery Sampling**
>
> Attribute sampling is more useful in fraud examination than variable sampling. Discovery sampling, an extension of attribute sampling, is primarily an investigative technique.

### 4.2 Interrogation Techniques

(a) **Investigative Process.** The investigative process for a fraud incident can be divided into three phases.

- **Phase 1: Initiating the investigation.** This phase includes securing the crime scene, collecting evidence, developing incident hypothesis, and investigating alternative explanations.
- **Phase 2: Analyzing the incident.** This phase covers analysis of the evidence collected in the first phase along with alternative explanations to determine whether a crime has occurred.
- **Phase 3: Analyzing the evidence.** This phase involves preparing to present the incident with findings and recommendations to management or law enforcement authorities.

The *order* of investigation is

1.  Gather facts
2.  Interview witnesses
3.  Develop incident hypothesis
4.  Test the hypothesis
5.  Report to management and others

(b) **Team Composition.** Investigating a fraud or computer-related crime requires a team approach with many participants, where the talent and skills of each participant are required. Each participant has a specific task to complete, consistent with his or her skills and experience. These participants (specialists) can include representatives from corporate investigations, law enforcement officials, system auditors, corporate counsel, consultants, information technology (IT) security management, and functional user management. The objectives of the system auditor and the IT security management are similar during a computer crime investigation. The duties of the manager of the crime team are clear while the duties of team participants may not be clear due to overlapping functions and responsibilities.

(c) **Target.** A victim organization should practice a "delay" technique when its computer system is attacked. If a system perpetrator can be delayed longer while attacking, investigative authorities can trace the perpetrator's origins and location.

It is important for the investigative team to know what the intruder is targeting for an attack. Although there are many targets, Peter Stephenson describes these targets as part of denial-of-service attacks.

- **Hard disks.** An attacker can fill up the hard disk to overload it in order to make it inoperable.
- **Bandwidth.** An attacker can fill up the bandwidth so that the network becomes useless.
- **Caches.** An attacker can block the cache or bypass it for further use.
- **Swap space.** An attacker can fill up the swap space so that it cannot be used.
- **Random access memory (RAM).** An attacker can allocate a large amount of RAM. Some system resources, such as mail servers, will become sensitive to too much RAM because they do not need much RAM to begin with. Users can notice that RAM is missing in a personal computer (PC) during a system BIOS boot-up.
- **Kernel tables.** Attackers try to overflow the kernel tables, causing serious problems on the system. Systems with write-through caches and small write buffers are sensitive to this type of attack.[1]

(d) **Objects/Subjects.** An investigation revolves around two things: objects and subjects. Examples of **objects** include computers, networks, switches, processes, data, and programs. **Subjects** include employees (former and current) and outsiders (hackers, crackers, virus writers, cloners, and phrackers).

(e) **Forensics**

(i) **Software forensics.** The term **forensics** means using computer hardware and software to gather and analyze the evidence. Use of sophisticated **software forensics** may identify authorship of various code modules. By routinely analyzing modules on protected systems, substitution of valid software by intruders can be detected. This esoteric approach theoretically offers protection against attacks that would not be detected by network perimeter defenses, such as those that use covert channels, or attacks by internal users where those users are knowledgeable and sophisticated enough to circumvent normal host security. The possible benefit of this method must be balanced against the normally low probability of such an attack and the complexity of the defense as well as its limits in detecting software modification, such as introducing Trojan horse programs.

Examples of forensic tools include virus detection software, audit software, password cracking programs, disk imaging software, auditing tools, operating system file utility programs, file zip and unzip utility programs, cable testers, line monitors, alcohol cleaning kits, and antistatic sealing tapes.

In a computer crime—for that matter in any crime—successful prosecution depends heavily on presenting good evidence to the court. Computer forensics is used to provide that good evidence. Computer forensics is the art of retrieving computer data in such a way that will make it admissible in court. Computer forensics can be used to convict a computer criminal.

[1] Peter Stephenson, *Investigating Computer-Related Crime* (Boca Raton, FL: CRC Press, Florida, 2000).

**Safeguards to Protect Evidence**

- Regular backups
- Off-site storage of backups
- Transaction logging
- Data storage on a tape/CD-ROM
- Chain-of-custody rules

The victim organization should be able to know who used a computer system and why, trace the criminal's activity through transaction logs, and protect the evidence. From a court's viewpoint, the evidence needs to be (1) understandable to a judge and jury; (2) credible; and (3) defensible. This requires the security manager to think like a lawyer, police officer, and criminal.

(ii) **Guidelines to a successful computer forensics.** This list provides guidelines to a successful computer forensics.

- If one suspects that a computer system has been used in a crime, he should cut off its links to the network immediately.
- When evidence is found, it should be left untouched. This requires freezing or taking a snapshot of the computer records and data.
- Don't create a "reasonable doubt" situation to a judge or jury.
- Prove when each transaction has occurred with time and date stamp.
- Protect the evidential matter (e.g., programs, data, and hardware) in such a way that it will not be modified, tainted, or fabricated. This is very important to the court.
- Store that evidential matter (e.g., data and programs) in an immutable form (e.g., tape or CD-ROM) so that it is inexpensive, defensible in a court, and easy to handle, present, and protect.

(iii) **Use of hash algorithms in computer forensics.** The US (NIST) National Institute of Standards and Technology has developed a national software reference library (NSRL) that includes known program executable files, library files, word processors, network browsers, accounting packages, compressed files used to install applications, operating system files, and so on. On a specific computer, these files can make up from 25 to 95% of the total number of files. Reviewing these files for evidence can take hundreds of staff hours. In most cases, these files do not contain evidence. Without some automated process, an investigator must review each file manually to determine whether it can be used in the evidence.

The idea is to collect as many different examples, versions, and updates of software as possible in order to generate file signatures for as many known files as possible. Each file within a package is "fingerprinted" by passing the file through a program that computes a hash code. The code is computed in such as a way that if one bit in the file is changed, a completely different hash code is produced. The primary hash value used here is the secure hash algorithm (SHA-1). Several other standard hash values also are computed for each file. These include message digest 4 (MD4), message digest 5 (MD5), and a 32-bit cyclic redundancy checksum (CRC32).

When a computer hard disk, CD, or other storage medium becomes part of an investigation, the files stored on it can be "fingerprinted" using SHA-1, MD4, MD5, or CRC32. These fingerprints can be compared to the known file fingerprints in the NSRL's reference data set (RDS) database. Those files that have matching hash values can be discarded from the investigation without further examination; those that do not match the RDS database should be examined further. Expected files may be missing if they do not show up in the known file list. This may indicate that files were deleted to cover up illegal activity and may prompt the investigator to pursue other means of investigating the file system.

The major benefit of this approach is savings in investigator's time because he or she does not have to review all the files on a computer involved in a computer crime. Only the files that changed the hash value need to be looked at.

(f) **Search and Seizure.** Ownership, occupancy, and possession are three influencing factors in a crime warrant search. A search warrant or court order is necessary to use the "trap and trace" technique, which involves the telephone company finding the intruder. Traps can be placed on in-circuit emulators, network protocol analyzers, and hardware analyzers.

   If computer equipment involved in a computer crime is not covered by a search warrant, the investigator should leave it alone until a warrant can be obtained. A court order is also required to access the evidence and to conduct surveillance techniques. To get a court-ordered search, one has to show that there is probable cause to believe that the suspect is committing an offense and that normal procedures have failed or are unlikely to work or are dangerous to health and life. An independent judge must issue the court order, not a police officer, security investigator, law enforcement agent, or prosecutor.

(g) **Interrogation.** During evidence collection activities, the investigative team interviews and interrogates many individuals. The interviewing and interrogation processes are quite different in terms of objectives, techniques, and timing. The goal of the interview is obtaining information about the incident. Here the intent is finding the answers to the five Ws: *who, what, when, where,* and *why.* This requires talking to as many witnesses as possible. The goal of interrogation, however, is to establish enough evidence to consider the subject a suspect.

## INTERVIEWING VERSUS INTERROGATION

- When gathering evidence, use the interview process: individuals become witnesses.
- When an interviewee becomes a suspect, use the interrogation process: witnesses become suspects.

   Interrogation should be left to experienced investigators since they need to balance between the accused's privacy rights and their own job duties. Investigators must be soft-spoken with clear communications skills and must have incontrovertible facts. Making a false accusation that results in embarrassment or damage to the suspect can cost the organization significantly if the wrongly accused decides to take legal action against the organization.

### 4.3 Forensic Auditing

   Auditing for fraud is called forensic auditing. The purpose of forensic examination (auditing) is to establish whether a fraud has occurred. One of the major purposes of financial auditing is to attest the financial statements of an organization. Unlike financial auditing, forensic auditing has no generally accepted auditing standards. In fact, most self-proclaimed forensic auditors are certified public accountants or internal auditors specializing in fraud detection.

   According to Joseph Wells[2], forensic auditing can be divided into four phases: (1) problem recognition and planning, (2) evidence collection, (3) evidence evaluation, and (4) communication of results (see Exhibit 4.1).

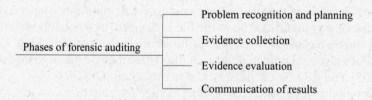

Phases of forensic auditing
- Problem recognition and planning
- Evidence collection
- Evidence evaluation
- Communication of results

**Exhibit 4.1:  Phases of forensic auditing**

(a) **Phase 1: Problem Recognition and Planning.** In the problem recognition and planning phase, the pertinent facts and circumstances regarding fraud are gathered. Here fraud examiners learn as much about the potential fraud as possible, without actually gathering evidence. There must be some indication of fraud for an examiner to become involved. The suspected fraud may have become known because of an anonymous tip, a fraud symptom such as a questionable document, suspicion on the part of an employee, or an unusual event or relationship.

   The important point is that there must be a legitimate reason to believe that fraud exists. Background checks into the suspects, the environment, and other conditions are conducted. Possible explanations for

[2]  *Joseph Wells,* **Fraud Examination: Investigative and Audit Procedures** *(New York: Quorum Books, 1992).*

the potential problem are explored. The problem could be a mistake or unintentional error rather than a fraud. At this stage, no one is convicted or incriminated. Indeed, evidence has not yet been gathered.

(b) **Phase 2: Evidence Collection.** The purpose of the evidence collection phase is twofold: to determine whether (1) the initial evidence of suspected fraud is misleading, and (2) if further action is recommended to gather sufficient, competent, and relevant evidence to resolve the fraud.

Several rules must be remembered in the evidence-gathering stage. To be effective in detecting fraud, the auditor or the examiner must attempt to identify the three elements of fraud—act, concealment, and conversion—and work on the easiest element first. Most frauds can be resolved by concentrating on the most obvious solutions and the weakest point in the fraud. If someone has an opportunity to commit fraud and/or appears suspicious, he or she probably is the perpetrator.

Another method of obtaining evidence is to search for fraud opportunities by using vulnerability charts and internal control critical combination charts. Fraud cannot occur unless there is an opportunity. The greater or more accessible the opportunity, the more often it is likely to be exploited. Vulnerability charts and critical combinations of controls help examiners arrange risks in the order of their probabilities.

---

**Timely Resolution of a Fraud**

In determining when the examination will take place, it should always be remembered that delaying an investigation can lead to destroyed or lost evidence. Early resolution of a fraud case protects both the victim and the perpetrator.

---

These charts involve correlating stolen assets with potential thieves, possible methods of fraud, effectiveness of controls around the fraud, possible concealment courses, and possibilities of conversion. These charts are objective ways of focusing on the most likely fraud perpetrators. Document examination is another technique to uncover concealment efforts.

Sometimes the gathering of evidence involves using employee searches. This detection technique involves examining employees' desks, lockers, lunchboxes, and other personal effects. When searching, it is important not to violate personal rights. If a search is conducted in an improper way, it can lead to allegations of invasion of privacy, false imprisonment, defamation of character, assault, and/or battery against the examiner. Evidence can be declared inadmissible if obtained illegally.

A seldom-used but powerful method of obtaining evidence is invigilation. Invigilation is the close supervision of suspects during an examination period. It involves imposing such strict temporary controls that during the period of supervision, fraud is almost impossible to commit. Invigilation requires top-management support, as it is expensive and time-consuming. It should be applicable only in high-risk areas. Invigilation has been successfully used to catch fraud committed by suppliers, night watchmen, and warehouse employees.

(c) **Phases 3 and 4: Evidence Evaluation and Communication of Results.** After evidence for fraud is properly evaluated, the auditor or the examiner needs to communicate the results of the work to the interested parties. The written report is the only evidence of the work performed and is the best vehicle to communicate results of the examination work. Fraud cases are frequently won or lost on the strength of the report.

## 4.4 Types of Fraud

(a) **Overview of fraud.** What is fraud? Here is the legal definition of fraud by most statutes: Fraud is a generic term and embraces all the multifarious means that human ingenuity can devise, which are resorted to by one individual, to get an advantage over another by false representations. It includes all surprise, trick, cunning, and unfair ways by which another is cheated. Fraud is a term of law, applied to certain facts as a conclusion from them, but is not in itself a fact. It has been defined as any cunning deception or artifice used to cheat or deceive another.

**Cheat and defraud** means every kind of trick and deception, from false representation and intimidation to suppression and concealment of any fact and information by which a party is induced to part with property for less than its value or to give more than it is worth for the property of another. The terms **fraud** and **bad faith** are synonymous when applied to the conduct of public offenders.

(b) **Types of Fraud.** There are many varieties of frauds, limited only by the ingenuity of the perpetrators. Fraud can be classified in a number of ways from a discovery point of view. The reason for this classification is that different approaches and procedures are required to discover each type of fraud and to control each type's occurrence.

Howard Davia and his coauthors present four types of fraud: (1) theft of assets, (2) fraud by frequency, (3) fraud by conspiracy, and (4) varieties of fraud (see Exhibit 4.2).[3]

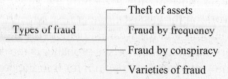

**Exhibit 4.2:  Types of fraud**

(i) **Theft of assets.** Theft of assets is classified into three categories.

1. Theft of assets that appears openly on the books as distinct accounting entries (fraud open on the books are the least difficult to discover)
2. Theft of assets that appears on the books, but is hidden as a part of other larger otherwise legitimate accounting entries (fraud hidden on the books)
3. Theft of assets is not on the books and could never be detected by an examination of "booked" accounting transactions (fraud off the books, most difficult to discover)

**Fraud open on the books** includes criminal acts that involve discrete entries in the accounting records. Here the term "discrete entry" means that the fraud involves the entire transaction; if that transaction is selected by an auditor for examination, this type of fraud offers the best chance for discovery (e.g., a fraudulent duplicate payment that stands by it).

**Fraud hidden on the books** involves acts of fraud that are included in accounting entries that appear on the books, but are not discrete entries. That is, the amount of the fraud is always buried in a larger, legitimate accounting entry, never appearing as a discrete amount (e.g., kickbacks).

In **fraud off the books,** the amount of the fraud is neither a discrete accounting entry nor a hidden part of an accounting entry. It is the loss of a valuable asset for the victim. Examples include diverting vending machine sales money and conversion of payment on accounts receivable that have been written off.

(ii) **Fraud by frequency.** Another way of classifying fraud is by its frequency of occurrence: nonrepeating or repeating. In nonrepeating fraud, a fraudulent act, even though repeated many times, is singular in nature in that it must be triggered by the perpetrator each time (e.g., a weekly payroll check requires a time card every week in order to generate the fraudulent paycheck).

In repeating fraud, a defrauding act may occur many times; however, it needs to be initiated only once. It then keeps running until it is stopped. It could possibly recur in perpetuity (e.g., a salaried payroll check that does not require input each time in order to generate the paycheck. It continues until a stop order is issued).

| Three Elements of Fraud |
| --- |
| 1. An intent to defraud |
| 2. The commission of a fraudulent act |
| 3. The accomplishment of the fraud |

For the auditor, the significance of whether a fraud is nonrepeating or repeating lies in where to look for the evidence. For example, the auditor would have to review a computer application program to obtain evidence of a repeating fraud involving skimming of a few cents off every bank customer's account service charge.

(iii) **Fraud involving conspiracy.** Fraud can be classified as that involving conspiracy, that which does not involve conspiracy, and that involving partial (pseudo-) conspiracy. Here the word "conspiracy"

---

[3] *Management Accountant's Guide to Fraud Discovery and Control*, Howard R. Davia, Patrick C. Coggins, John C. Wideman, and Joseph T. Kastantin, John Wiley & Sons, New York, 1992.

is synonymous with "collusion." It has been proven that most frauds involve conspiracy, either bona fide or pseudo. In the bona fide conspiracy, all parties involved are fully aware of the fraudulent intent; in the pseudoconspiracy, one or more of the parties to the fraud is innocent of fraudulent intent.

(iv) **Varieties of fraud.** The varieties of fraud can be grouped in two categories: (1) "specialized" fraud, which is unique to people working in certain kinds of business operations, and (2) the "garden varieties" of fraud, which all people are likely to encounter in general business operations.

Examples of specialized fraud include: embezzlement of assets entrusted by depositors to financial institutions such as banks, savings and loans, credit unions, pension funds (called "custodial" fraud), and false insurance claims for life, health, auto, and property coverage.

Examples of garden varieties of fraud include kickbacks, defective pricing, unbalanced contracts or purchase orders, reopening completed contracts, duplicate payments, double payments, shell payments, and defective delivery. These eight types of fraud are the more common frauds occurring today.

According to Jack Bologna, corporate fraud can be generated internally (perpetrated by directors, officers, employees, or agents of a corporation for or against it or against others) and externally (perpetrated by others—suppliers, vendors, customers, hackers) against the corporation.[4] Bologna includes management fraud as a part of corporate fraud as the intentional overstatements of corporate or division profits. It is inspired, perpetrated, or induced by managers who seek to benefit in terms of promotions, job stability, larger bonuses, and status symbols.

## 4.5 Risk Factors, Red Flags, and Symptoms of Fraud

(a) **Risk Factors in Fraud.** The internal auditors should be aware of risk factors related to general fraud as well as computer fraud.

---

**RISK FACTORS RELATED TO GENERAL FRAUD (RED FLAGS OF CORPORATE FRAUD)**

- Infighting among top management.
- Low morale and motivation among employees.
- Understaffed accounting departments.
- High level of complaints against the organization from customers, suppliers, or regulatory authorities.
- Inconsistent and surprising cash flow deficiencies.
- Sales or income are decreasing while accounts payable and receivable are rising.
- The company's line of credit is used to its limit for long periods of time.
- There is a significant excess inventory.
- There is an increasing number of year-end adjusting journal entries.

*SOURCE: Association of Certified Fraud Examiners, "The White Paper," Vol. 7, No. 5 (October/November 1993). Original source: KPMG Canada, "The Fraud Prevention Primer."*

---

The degree of fraud can be linked to the environment of an organization, as described below.

- **High Fraud Environment.** Low management integrity, poor control environment, loose accountability, and high pressure for results.
- **Low Fraud Environment.** A culture of honesty, management openness, and employee assistance programs, and total quality management.

The user-friendliness of computer systems and the increase in user computer literacy combined with a lack of or inadequate system controls could have significant effect on computer crime and fraud. The rewards of computer crime can be greater than other crimes, and there is less chance of being discovered and convicted. Embarrassment, expense, and time are the reasons given for not prosecuting computer criminals. This is compounded by the fact that it is difficult to prove malicious intent. A computer is used as a tool but is also the means to perpetrate fraud. The motivations for, or causes of, computer abuse or fraud include

---

[4] *Jack Bologna, **Handbook on Corporate Fraud** (Stoneham, MA: Butterworth-Heinemann, 1993).*

- Situational pressures
- Opportunities
- Personal or financial gain
- Revenge

Situational pressures can include when an honest employee becomes addicted to alcohol or drugs, or incurs large debts because of gambling. Opportunities are provided by weak policies and procedures and/or a poor system of controls or lack of audit trails. Given the opportunity, employees will find a "shortcut" around certain controls. Some employees will steal given any opportunity. System users can reveal system vulnerabilities due to their close working knowledge with the system—both manual and automated. Other causes include personal or financial gain and revenge against employers and co-workers.

Creating a team environment can help employees feel that they are a part of the decision-making process and be content with the job condition. This in turn motivates employees to behave in a normal manner and be less tempted to commit computer crime and fraud.

## CONTROL/AUDIT RISKS: COMPUTER FRAUD AND CRIME

- Good internal controls do not deter some employees who will always steal. However, good internal controls do detect the fraud at an early date and, therefore, lessen the loss. Internal controls are there for honest employees.
- Most computer crimes and frauds are committed internally, by employees of the organization.
- More and more frauds are being committed by individuals outside the organization, such as consultants, contractors, and hackers.
- People will take advantage of any weakness in the computer system and company policies and procedures as well as their employment position.
- Application program development and maintenance work are equal targets for computer crime and fraud activities.
- Additions, deletions, and changes to computer data files are a major source for committing computer crime and fraud.
- Employees may sell computer-based client/customer lists, vendor names and addresses, bid information, or other sensitive and confidential information to competitors and others for money, to take revenge, or for other reasons.
- Employees may walk out the door with the organization's data and programs through diskettes and tapes.
- Third-shift service bureau employees may conduct computer work for their own clients without the knowledge of the service bureau management.
- For each irregularity or fraud discovered, there might be hundreds of dead ends.
- The reliability of applications software is one of the weakest links in the security and fraud chain.
- Programmers, systems analysts, tape librarians, database analysts and administrators, and functional users all are capable of committing computer crime and fraud.
- Passwords and other identification codes can be cracked with a "brute-force" approach.
- Spool area print files can be the targets of fraud where files can be copied before they are printed

(b) **Red Flags for Fraud. Red flags** do not signal that a fraud has occurred, but rather that the opportunity for a fraud exists. Some examples of red flags are
- Concealed assets
- Missing or destroyed records and documents
- Split purchases
- Excessive "voids" or "refunds"
- Rapid turnover of financial managers and executives

According to Belden Menkus, all types of frauds, including computer frauds, are characterized by certain contributing factors related to the values and motivations of the fraud perpetrator and the management of the defrauded organization.[5] Understanding how computer fraud can occur will not eliminate the menace; however, auditors have no alternative but to ferret out weaknesses and develop counterstrategies. The *eight factors* are

1. **Inadequate design of the information system.** Inadequate design deals with the flaws and errors in the system. The system's performance does not rest on a reliable foundation and its results are not predictable in any reasonable or consistent fashion. This provides opportunity for fraud.

2. **Aggregation of the information system's transaction processing steps so that a review of what is taking place becomes impossible.** The "separation of duties' within the system may be reduced or eliminated as a result of this information system design technique called "chaining." Verification of the operation becomes difficult if not impossible.

3. **Insufficient discrimination as to the legitimacy of the transactions processed by the information system.** Data editing and validation routines at data entry and update activities may not be available or too primitive to be of any use.

4. **Error toleration by the information system—either in data content or processing results.** Users may establish some arbitrary upper limit on individual errors that would disguise fraudulent activity as apparent error. This means that the fraud perpetrator who does not become either greedy or careless becomes almost impossible for the auditor to detect, except by accident.

5. **Detachment of the information system's ongoing operation from the physical or functional reality that it is supposed to reflect.** For example, an inventory database does not reflect the actual items. In this situation, it is possible for a set of numbers to look right, but for them to be essentially worthless.

6. **Unrestrained, unmediated remote access to an information system that is subject to possible compromise or manipulation.** Sometimes it is difficult to isolate the actual identity or even the location of the individual perpetrating the fraud.

7. **Restricted ability to collect sufficient knowledge about the fraud itself—especially its scope and the extent of the loss that has occurred.** The fraud perpetrator may not leave sufficient evidence of his or her actions or the evidence may have been destroyed. This can occur when the system permits files to be modified without leaving any trace of what was added, changed, or deleted.

8. **Limits in the investigative tools for analyzing the knowledge that auditors may gain about the fraud.** The volume, volatility, and complexity of the data that must be considered in detecting and investigating computer frauds may exceed the auditor's ability to deal constructively and in a timely manner.

## BUSINESS RISKS: FRAUD

- Employee hiring efforts could be ineffective since computer criminals usually have the same characteristics that organizations are seeking for possible employment.
- Employees will not take seriously a code of conduct if it is not consistently enforced.
- Not prosecuting employees caught in committing a computer crime could send a wrong signal to other employees that illegal acts are considered acceptable.
- If organizations quietly suspend without prosecuting employees who committed computer crime and fraud, the problem is never solved and the suspended employee will find another job where he or she is more than likely to resume such behavior.
- If the employee's rights are violated either by improper search or lack of evidence when suspected of computer crime, the organization may be legally liable for damages.
- Computer crime will never be completely eliminated because the elements of controls are themselves subject to human error and manipulation.

---

[5] *Belden Menjus, "Eight Factors Contributing to Computer Fraud," Internal Auditor (October 1990).*

(c) **Symptoms of Fraud**

(i) **Symptoms of management fraud.** Management fraud tends to involve a number of people with conspiracy in mind. It occurs because senior managers, due to their position of power, circumvent internal controls. According to Bologna, the major symptoms of management fraud are the intentional understatement of losses and liabilities and overstatement of assets or profits. For example

- Profits can be manipulated by overstating revenues or understating costs.
- Revenues can be overstated by recording fictitious sales, recording unfinalized sales, recording consignments as sales, or recording shipments to storage facilities as sales.
- Costs can be manipulated by deferring them to the next accounting period or understating them in the current period. This is accomplished by such ploys as overstating ending inventories of raw materials, work-in-process, and finished goods, or understating purchases of raw materials.

In almost every case of management fraud, signs (**red flags**) of the fraud exist for some time before the fraud itself is detected or disclosed by a third party. These signs include

- Knowledge that the company is having financial difficulties, such as frequent cash flow shortages, declining sales and profits, and loss of market share.
- Signs of management incompetence, such as poor planning, organization, communication, and controls; poor motivation and delegation; management indecision and confusion about corporate mission, goals, and strategies; management ignorance of conditions in the industry and in the general economy.
- Autocratic management, low trust of employees, poor promotion opportunities, high turnover of employees, poorly defined business ethics.
- Some of accounting-related transaction-based **red flags** include
  - Cash flow is diminishing.
  - Sales and income are diminishing.
  - Payables and receivables are increasing.
  - Unusual or second endorsements on checks.
  - Inventory and cost of sales are increasing.
  - Income and expense items are continually reclassified.
  - Suspense items are not reconciled at all or reconciled in an untimely manner.
  - Suspense items are written off without explanation.
  - Accounts receivable write-offs are increasing.
  - Journal entries are adjusted heavily at year-end.
  - Old outstanding checks.
  - Heavy customer complaints.

---

**Accounting Fraud by High-Level Managers**

- Early booking of sales
- Expense deferrals
- Inventory overstatement
- Expense account padding

---

In planning and performing inventory procedures, auditors should be aware that reported methods of fraudulently misstating inventory have involved: nonexistent items recorded as inventory; goods that have been sold (and recorded as sales) included in inventory; goods shipped between two sites and recorded as inventory at both locations; scrap materials substituted for genuine inventory for the physical inventory observation; false invoices or journal entries; inflated inventory costs; inventory that has been excluded from the physical count because management states it has been sold when, under the terms of the bill-and-hold arrangement, title has not yet passed to the customer; and inadequate reserves for slow-moving and obsolete inventory.[6]

---

[6] *Audit of Inventories, Auditing Procedure Study* (New York: American Institute of Certified Public Accountants, 1993).

**IIA *PROFESSIONAL STANDARDS***

According to the IIA's *Standards* "Due Professional Care," fraud encompasses an array of irregularities and illegal acts characterized by intentional deception. It can be perpetrated for the benefit of or to the detriment of the organization and by persons outside as well as inside the organization. Management fraud is perpetrated by anyone in an organization with responsibilities for setting and/or achieving objectives. Generally, fraud is perpetrated for the direct or indirect benefit of an employee, outside individual, or another firm.

---

(ii) **Symptoms of employee fraud.** Embezzlement and corruption are two major types of employee fraud. The crime of embezzlement consists of the fraudulent misappropriation of the property of an employer by an employee to whom the possession of that property has been entrusted. Here is the difference between embezzlement and larceny: Embezzlement occurs when the embezzler gains initial possession of property lawfully but subsequently misappropriates it. Larceny is committed when property is taken without the owner's consent.

*Common embezzlement techniques include these schemes.*

- Cash disbursement embezzlement involves the creation of fake documents or false expense entries using phony invoices, time cards, and receipts.
- Cash receipts fraud involving the lapping of cash or accounts receivable. Here the embezzler "borrows" from today's receipts and replaces them with tomorrow's receipts. Other examples are skimming, where the proceeds of cash sales are intercepted before any entry is made of their receipts, and granting fake credits for discounts, refunds, rebates, returns, and allowances, possibly through collusion with a customer.
- Theft of property involving assets such as tools, supplies, equipment, finished goods, raw materials, and intellectual property, such as software, data, and proprietary information.

**Accounting Fraud by Lower-Level Employees**

- Check kiting
- Lapping of receivables
- Phony vendor invoices
- Phony benefit payment claims
- Expense account padding

Corruption is another common type of employee fraud. Vendors, suppliers, service providers, or contractors often corrupt the employees of an organization on both a small-scale level (e.g., gifts and free tickets of nominal value) and a large-scale level (e.g., commissions, payoffs, free trips, free airline tickets and hotel accommodations).

**KEY CONCEPTS TO REMEMBER: SYMPTOMS OF EMPLOYEE FRAUD**

- Adjusting journal entries that lack management authorization and supporting details
- Expenditures that lack supporting documents
- False and improper entries in books of accounts
- Destruction, counterfeiting, and forgery of documents that support payments
- Short shipments received
- Overpricing of goods purchased
- Double-billing
- Substitution of inferior goods

(iii) **Professional skepticism in fraud.** The planning and performance of an audit are to be carried out by an auditor with an attitude of professional skepticism. This means "the auditor neither assumes that management is dishonest nor assumes unquestioned honesty." An objective evaluation of the situation and management integrity are important considerations for the auditor. *The auditor needs to balance between excessive audit costs due to suspicion and time constraints.*

The auditor should use professional skepticism in establishing the audit scope and in gathering audit evidence. The auditor needs to be aware of the inherent limitations of the auditing process, which include flaws in the audit procedures, auditor errors, risks created by management override of controls, collusion, forgeries, and unrecorded transactions.

The audit engagement needs to be planned so as to provide reasonable assurance of determining material errors or irregularities. *Errors are unintentional mistakes. Irregularities are intentional distortions, misrepresentations, and fraud.*

The auditor's understanding of the internal control structure influences the degree of professional skepticism applied in the course of the audit. The auditor gains an understanding of the internal control structure through previous experiences in the auditable area and by reviewing evidence obtained through preliminary audit survey work, which includes inquiry, inspection, and observation. *The more comfortable the auditor is with the internal control structure, the less skeptical he or she would be.*

---

**KEY CONCEPTS TO REMEMBER: SEQUENCE OF AUDIT ACTIVITIES RELATED TO PROFESSIONAL SKEPTICISM**

- Reviewing internal control structure
- Performing audit planning work
- Determining the audit scope
- Collecting audit evidence
- Reviewing accounting estimates
- Issuing an audit opinion

---

It is good to remain skeptical throughout the course of an audit even if the preliminary survey results indicate no existence of irregularities. If internal auditors discover errors and irregularities during the audit, they are required to inform the audit committee by quantifying their effects after obtaining sufficient evidence of their existence. In essence, it is good for internal auditors to maintain a posture of professional skepticism at all times.

(iv) **Management representations versus risk.** The auditor needs to assess the risk of management misrepresentations and to consider the effects of such risks in establishing an overall audit strategy and the scope of the audit. Examples of situations (red flags) that could lead to risk of management representations include

- Frequent disputes about aggressive application of generally accepted accounting principles.
- Excessive emphasis on meeting targets upon which management compensation program is based.
- Responses to audit inquiries are evasive.
- Employees lack necessary knowledge and experience, yet develop various estimates including accounting.
- Supervisors of employees generating estimates appear careless or inexperienced in reviewing and approving the estimates.
- A history of unreliable or unreasonable estimates has developed.
- Crisis conditions exist constantly in operating and accounting areas of the organization.
- Frequent and excessive back orders, shortages of materials and products, delays, or lack of documentation of major transactions arise.
- Access to computer-based application systems initiating or controlling the movement of assets is not restricted.
- High levels of transaction processing errors are observed.
- Unusual delays occur in providing operating results and accounting reports.

**Value of Auditee Representations**

Auditee representations are not good substitutes for effective auditing procedures.

(v) **Review of accounting estimates.** Many assumptions go into accounting estimates. The internal auditor should understand this assumptions and should evaluate to determine whether the assumptions are subjective and are susceptible to misstatements and bias.

The auditor should show professional skepticism during the review and evaluation of the reasonableness of accounting estimates. These estimates contain both subjective and objective factors. Professional skepticism is important with respect to subjective factors where personal bias could be significant.

*Examples of accounting estimates include:* uncollectible receivables; allowance for loan losses; revenues to be earned on contracts; subscription income; losses on sales contracts; professional membership or union dues income; valuation of financial securities; trading versus investment security classifications; compensation in stock option plans and deferred plans; probability of loss; obsolete inventory; net realizable value of inventories; losses in purchase commitments; property and causality insurance accruals; loss reserves; warranty claims; taxes on real estate and personal property.

In addition to review, the auditor should test management's process of developing accounting estimates or develop an independent estimation. The auditor can compare prior estimates with subsequent results to assess the reliability of the process used to develop estimates. The auditor should also review whether the accounting estimates are consistent with the operational plans and programs of the entity.

## 4.6 Acts and Profiles of Fraud Perpetrators

(a) **Acts of Fraudulent Behavior.** A list of fraudulent behavior acts about which an internal auditor must be concerned follows:

- Significant changes in the behavior of the defrauder (e.g., easygoing attitude, irregular work habits, and expensive social life)
- Knowledge that the defrauder is undergoing an emotional trauma at home or in the work place
- Knowledge that the defrauder is betting heavily
- Knowledge that the defrauder is drinking heavily
- Knowledge that the defrauder is heavily in debt
- Audit findings of errors or irregularities that are considered immaterial when discovered
- Works quietly, works hard, works long hours, often works alone
- Appearance of living beyond means
- Expensive car or clothes

(b) **Profiles of Fraud Perpetrators**

(i) **Traits of managers.** According to Joseph Wells, personality traits of managers associated with frauds include wheeler-dealers, a management that is feared, impulsive, too number-oriented, and insensitive to people (especially to employees).[7] Obviously, the contrast is a management that is friendly, calm, generous with time, self-confident, and goal oriented.

Many frauds occur where an autocratic management arbitrarily sets budgets for lower-level managers to meet. When these budgets are unattainable, the managers have a choice to either cheat or fail. When their jobs, reputations, and careers are at stake, cheating is sometimes easier than failing.

(ii) **Traits of employees.** These traits are suggested as an indication of fraudulent behavior.

- Managers and executives seem to be the major sources of ethical attitudes within organization. That is, there is pressure from superiors to commit unethical behavior. Superiors pressure subordinates to support incorrect viewpoints, sign false documents, overlook superiors' wrong-

---

[7] *Wells, Ibid.*

doing, and do business with superiors' friends. The chief executive officer sets the ethical tone of his organization.

- Be wary of employees who never take vacations, live beyond their means, or suffer from mood swings.
- Males arrested for embezzlement outnumber females by about two to one.
- The age demographics of embezzlers show that about one-third of both males and females are 22 to 29 years of age; they constitute the largest groupings of all.

(iii) **White-collar crime**. White-collar crime is a breach of trust, confidence, or fiduciary duty. Someone relies on and trusts another, to his or her economic detriment. White-collar crime is classified as that directed against consumers and that directed against employers. It is caused by greed and by weak internal control mechanisms. Jack Bologna defines white-collar crime as occupational, corporate, economic, or financial.[8]

The common characteristics of each of the so-called white-collar crimes are intentional deception (fraud theft, embezzlement, and corruption), destruction of property (industrial sabotage), gross negligence (product liability), and failure to comply with government regulations on environmental pollution, unfair pricing practices, untrue advertising, unsafe and unhealthy products, stock fraud, tax fraud, and so on. *High-level employee crimes are perceived to be based on economic greed, while low-level employee crimes are perceived as based on economic need.*

In his book *White Collar Crime,* Edwin Sutherland gave examples of violations by larger American corporations.[9] These involved restraints of trade; misrepresentation in advertising; patent, trademark, and copyright infringements; unfair labor practices; illegal rebates; and other types of violations. He found that many of the corporations were serious repeaters.

Irwin Ross, writing for *Fortune* magazine, compiled statistics on fraud committed by the largest industrial and nonindustrial corporations.[10] Included were five kinds of offenses, all of which were committed for the benefit of the organization rather than for personal profit: bribe-taking or bribe-giving by high-level corporate officials (including kickbacks and illegal rebates), criminal fraud, illegal campaign contributions, tax evasion, and criminal antitrust violations.

### PROFILE OF A CORPORATE FRAUDSTER

- Extravagant purchases or lavish lifestyle
- Unexplained mood swings or compulsive behavior (e.g., workaholics, alcohol, or drug abusers, overeaters, gamblers)
- Unable to deal with pressure
- Able to rationalize their thefts
- Able to exploit internal control weaknesses to cover up their fraud
- Reluctance to take vacations or is away from the office
- Chronic job frustration, low morale
- Unusually close ties to vendors or a sudden switch in a long-term vendor
- Suggestions of heavy personal debt

*SOURCE: Association of Certified Fraud Examiners, "The White Paper Journal" 7, no. 5 (October/November 1993).  Original source was from "The Fraud Prevention Primer," KPMG Canada.*

(iv) **Profiles of organizational crime.** Research by Edwin Sutherland, Marshall B. Clinard, and Peter Yeager found these profiles for organizations committing crime: the oil, pharmaceutical, and motor vehicle industries were the most likely to violate the law; firms that were relatively more prosperous tended more often to pollute illegally; larger corporations in general commit no more violations per unit size than do smaller corporations.[11] In some cases, larger corporations had more infractions

---

[8]   *Bologna, Ibid.*
[9]   *Quoted in Gary S. Green, **Occupational Crime** (Chicago: Nelson-Hall, 1990). Originally from Edwin O. Sutherland, **White Collar Crime** (New York: CBS, 1961).*
[10]  *Quoted in ibid.. Originally from Irwin Ross, "How Lawless Are Big Companies?" Fortune, December 1, 1980.*
[11]  *Quoted in ibid., based on research studies conducted by Sutherland, Clinard, and Yeager in 1949, 1980, and 1983.*

generally, but smaller corporations had more violations per unit size. More diversified firms will violate more often. (This is because they are exposed to a greater number of regulations. More diversified firms seem more likely to violate labor and manufacturing laws than those less diversified.) Firms with more market power had slightly fewer violations per unit size than less dominant firms, which suggests that market power may diminish pressures to violate the law. Firms and industries with greater labor concentration tend to have more official censures for labor violations.

## 4.7 Integrating Analytical Relationships to Detect Fraud

(a) **Major Impetus.** The major impetus for the need to integrate analytical relationships in detecting fraud was the recommendation of the Treadway Commission that analytical procedures should be used more extensively to identify areas with a high risk of fraudulent financial reporting.

The results of a research study sponsored by the Institute of Management Accountants (IMA) entitled *The Role of Analytical Procedures in Detecting Management Fraud* indicated that analytical procedures can be an effective supplement to an overall program to detect and prevent fraud.[12] However, the IMA study also says that a question remains unresolved as to exactly what types of errors (unintentional mistakes) or irregularities (fraudulent financial reporting or defalcation) are detected effectively through the use of analytical procedures.

The participants in the IMA study included internal auditors, controllers, and external auditors, and the findings showed that analytical procedures are not being used effectively to detect management fraud due to: differing views concerning the participants' responsibility to use the procedures and lack of specific guidance and training in fraud detection methods. When fraud is detected, it is usually through other audit procedures, although commonly it is revealed by informal disclosures rather than detected.

### TREADWAY COMMISSION: RECOMMENDATION ABOUT ANALYTICAL REVIEW PROCEDURES

**Recommendation for the Independent Public Accountant**. The Auditing Standards Board should establish standards which require independent public accountants to perform analytical review procedures in all audit engagements and which provide improved guidance on the appropriate use of these procedures.

The public accounting profession widely recognizes the usefulness of analytical review procedures, and auditors perform such procedures in many audits today. Analytical review procedures can encompass a broad range of audit steps. Usually involving comparisons of relationships among data, they range from relatively simple comparisons of ratios and trends to sophisticated statistical modeling techniques. Regardless of specific form, they focus on the overall reasonableness of a reported amount in relation to the surrounding circumstances.

The potential of analytical review procedures for detecting fraudulent financial reporting has not been fully realized. Unusual year-end transactions, deliberate manipulation of estimates or reserves, and misstatements of revenues and assets often introduce aberrations in otherwise predictable amounts, ratios, or trends that will stand out to a skeptical auditor. The Commission observed a number of cases where performing analytical review procedures would have increased the likelihood of the auditor's detecting fraudulent financial reporting.

Existing auditing standards allow, but do not require, analytical review procedures. The Commission recommends that auditing standards be revised to require the use of analytical review procedures on all audit engagements. The revised standards should require auditors to use analytical review procedures throughout the audit including at the planning phase.

SOURCE: *Report of the National Commission on Fraudulent Financial Reporting (October 1987):* 52.

Further, the Commission recommends that the public accounting profession provide greater guidance on the application of analytical review procedures. Executive-level auditors should be required to participate in selecting the analytical review procedures to be performed and evaluating the results. Meaningful audit evidence from these procedures depends on the seasoned judgment of executive-level

---

[12] Edward Blocher, "The Role of Analytical Procedures in Detecting Management Fraud" (Montvale, NJ: IMA 1993, 73 pp).

professionals, who should have a greater understanding than the nonexecutives of the company's industry as well as the environmental, institutional, and individual factors that increase the risk of fraudulent financial reporting.

The Treadway Commission defined fraudulent financial reporting as intentional or reckless conduct, whether by act or omission, that results in materially misleading financial statements. Fraudulent financial reporting can involve many factors and take many forms. It may entail gross and deliberate distortion of corporate records, such as inventory count tags, or falsified transactions, such as fictitious sales or orders. It may entail the misapplication of accounting principles. Company employees at any level may be involved, from top to middle management to lower-level personnel. If the conduct is intentional, or so reckless that it is the legal equivalent of intentional conduct, and results in fraudulent financial statements, it comes within the commission's operating definition of the term "fraudulent financial reporting."

Fraudulent financial reporting differs from other causes of materially misleading financial statements such as unintentional errors. The commission also distinguished fraudulent financial reporting from other corporate improprieties, such as employee embezzlements, violation of environmental or product safety regulations, and tax fraud, which do not necessarily cause the financial statements to be materially inaccurate.

(b) **Types of Analytical Procedures.** The IMA research study investigated the use and effectiveness of analytical procedures in the possible link between different types of analytical procedures and the detection of management fraud.[13] The three principal types of analytical procedures are trend analysis, ratio analysis, and modeling techniques (see Exhibit 4.3).

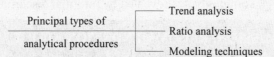

**Exhibit 4.3: Principal types of analytical procedures**

**Trend analysis** examines the trend of the account balances as a basis for determining whether the current period data potentially are misstated, that is, whether they depart significantly from the trend of the prior data. Trend analysis techniques vary from the simplest two-period comparisons to statistically based time-series models. Trend analysis is the most commonly employed analytical procedure.

**Ratio analysis** refers to procedures that involve the simultaneous analysis of two or more financial statement accounts. The value in using ratios is that often the relationship between the two (or more) accounts in the ratio is relatively stable over time, so that a variation in a ratio is a direct and clear signal of an underlying unusual condition: It can be a fraud, a simple error, or simply an unusual combination of environmental events. Ratio analysis is potentially a far more useful method for detecting error and fraud than trend analysis because ratio analysis uses the assumed stable relationship between accounts, while trend analysis looks at the behavior of only a single account. The behavior of a ratio is expected to be stable, while a single account balance can change for a number of reasons related to normal operating factors that do not reflect error or fraud.

A third type of analytical procedure, based on **modeling techniques,** can be more effective than either ratio analysis or trend analysis. The modeling approach is distinguished by the attempt to identify meaningful, stable relationships between financial and operating data.

A common type of modeling approach is the reasonableness test. This procedure involves the use of selected operating data, associated financial data, and external data to predict an account balance.

Reasonableness tests of the expense accounts are common. Two examples are: (1) the auditor or analyst estimates a value for utilities expense based on average temperature and hours of operation, and (2) payroll expense is estimated from operating data on the number of employees, the average pay rates, and the number of days of applicable operations.

The reasonableness test can be particularly effective because it links the financial data directly to relevant operating data. When, as is often the case, variations in operations are the principal cause for variations in the related accounts (especially the expense accounts), reasonableness tests provide a relatively precise means of detecting errors and frauds affecting these accounts; when a fraud is committed,

---

[13] *Ibid.*

*4: CONDUCT ENGAGEMENTS*        441

it is likely that the reported financial and operating facts will not agree. That is, the perpetrator will find it difficult to disguise both the financial data and the related operating data.

For example, a reasonableness test of payroll expense can be an effective means of detecting fraud, if there are "phony" employees or excess time is charged, because personnel records also must be manipulated fraudulently in the same pattern to prevent detection. Because these methods effectively model the relationships between the financial data and the operating transactions that are the basis for the recorded financial data, reasonableness tests are potentially the most effective of the analytical procedures.

(i) **Use of analytical procedures in practice.** Analytical procedures are a substantive audit procedure and oriented to detecting rather than preventing management fraud. The participants in the research study have a different perspective about their role in management fraud as indicated below.

## IMA RESEARCH FINDINGS

- Internal auditors saw their role as preventing fraud or investigating a fraud that had already been revealed. They tended not to use analytical procedures.
- External auditors saw their role as detecting fraud within the context of developing an opinion on the financial statements. They tended to use analytical procedures extensively.
- Controllers saw their role similar to internal auditors in both preventing and detecting fraud. They were found to be the best-trained and most extensive users of analytical procedures.

According to the IMA research study, internal auditors should take a more proactive role in the detection of management fraud.[14] The current guidance in IIA's *Standards* provides necessary guidance in this area. The key point is that internal auditors should take greater responsibility in the detection of management fraud.

(ii) **Implications for internal auditors.** A pervasive finding in the IMA research study is that there are significant differences among the three participant groups. *Internal auditors took a prevention-oriented and control-based approach to fraud. External auditors and controllers tended to take a detection-oriented and analytical approach to fraud. The respective approaches were found to be effective.*

In view of the Treadway Commission's recommendation for greater use of analytical procedures by external auditors, the IMA research study findings suggest

- Controllers, internal auditors, and others might employ analytical procedures more effectively as well.
- The analytical procedures now being done by the controllers to explain changes in account balances need to be redirected in part to looking for potential management fraud.
- As directed in the IIA's *Standards,* the control-based approach of the internal auditors needs to be augmented by analytical procedures to improve the overall effectiveness of the auditors in detecting fraud

(iii) **More examples of analytical procedures.** Joseph Wells[15] recommends financial statement analysis (ratio analysis, trend analysis, net worth method), statistical sampling, and flowcharting techniques to detect fraud (see Exhibit 4.4). Each of these techniques is explained below.

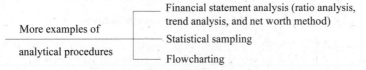

**Exhibit 4.4: Examples of analytical procedures**

[14] *Ibid.*
[15] *Wells, Ibid.*

(iv) **Financial statement analysis.** If financial statements are prepared with integrity, changes in account balances from one period to another should have logical explanations. Manipulating financial statements to hide missing assets or other problems sometimes hides frauds. Using ratios and trend analysis, fraud examiners or auditors can identify unusual relationships suggesting errors or irregularities. The discussion of financial statement analysis includes two elements: (1) analysis of the balance sheet and income statement using ratios and trends, and (2) analysis of changes in cash balances from period to period using a statement of cash flows.

(A) *Analyzing the balance sheet and income statement.* The balance sheet and income statement can be analyzed three ways to reveal fraud and other types of errors. First, financial statement data from the current period can be compared with results from prior periods to look for unusual relationships. Second, financial statement data can be compared with similar information from other companies, or with industry statistics to look for unusual relationships. Because comparisons between similar companies are so valuable, industry-wide financial statements are distributed widely by several publishing companies.

Third, financial statements data can be associated with nonfinancial data to see if the numbers on the statements make sense. When searching for fraud, examiners should be inquisitive and challenge things that appear out of order or out of sequence. There should always be analytical relationships between representation in financial statements and physical goods or movements of assets.

---

**KEY CONCEPTS TO REMEMBER: PLAUSIBLE RELATIONSHIPS**

- If sales are increasing, examiners would see buildup of inventory.
- If sales are increasing, examiners would see accounts receivable increasing.
- If sales are increasing, examiners would see the cost of outbound freight increasing.
- If purchases are increasing, examiners would see the cost of inbound freight increasing.
- If inventory is increasing, examiners would see increases in the costs of warehousing, storage, and handling activities.
- If manufacturing volume is increasing, examiners would expect the per-unit cost of labor and material to be decreasing.
- If manufacturing volume is going up, examiners would see increases in the dollar amount of scrap sales and discounts on purchases.
- If profits are increasing, examiners would see increases in cash flows from operations.

---

Examining financial statement data to see if they make sense with respect to nonfinancial statement data is one of the best ways to detect fraud. Examiners who ask themselves if reported amounts are too small, too large, too early, too late, too often, and too rare or who look for things that are reported at odd times, by odd people, and using odd procedures are much more likely to detect fraud than those who view the financial statement without sufficient professional skepticism.

Three techniques can be helpful in comparing financial statement data from period to period: (1) ratio analysis, (2) vertical analysis, and (3) horizontal analysis (see Exhibit 4.5).

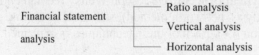

Financial statement analysis
— Ratio analysis
— Vertical analysis
— Horizontal analysis

**Exhibit 4.5: Financial statement analysis**

**Ratio analysis** involves computing key ratios to compare significant financial statement relationships from period to period. The most helpful ratios in detecting whether financial statements are reasonable include current ratio, quick ratio, and cash ratio.

### Scope of Internal Fraud

Much of internal fraud involves the theft of cash or inventory or the manipulation of receivables—major components of current assets.

These ratios only suggest potential problem areas. By themselves, they do not incriminate anyone or prove conclusively that fraud exists. When the current ratio, quick ratio, or cash ratios suggest a potential problem in either receivables or inventory, five additional ratios can be useful. These five ratios include: accounts receivable turnover, days to collect receivables, inventory turnover, days to sell inventory, and days to convert inventory to cash.

The examiner's responsibility is to use these ratios to identify significant, unexplained fluctuations and then determine if those fluctuations have logical explanations. If they do not, someone may be overstating or understating current assets or liabilities to conceal dishonest acts. Unexplained changes in the ratios can signal problems.

**Vertical analysis** is a technique for analyzing the relationships between line items on an income statement or balance sheet by expressing components as percentages. In vertical analysis of an income statement, net sales are assigned 100%. For a balance sheet, total assets are assigned 100%. All other items on the statements are then expressed as a percentage of these two numbers.

**Horizontal analysis** is a technique for analyzing the percentage change in individual income statements or balance sheet items from one year to the next. Horizontal analysis supplements ratio and vertical analysis and allows an examiner to determine whether any particular item has changed in an unusual way in relation to the change in net sales or total assets from one period to the next.

(B) *Statement of cash flows.* The statement of cash flows identifies sources and uses of cash during a period. The statement is extremely useful for identifying how an entity is funding its operation—whether from investments, earnings, or borrowing; and what it is doing with its money—whether it is being distributed to the principals, used to make additional investments, or used in operations.

*Because cash is the asset most often misappropriated, the statement of cash flows is useful for identifying potential fraudulent acts.*

The statement of cash flows can be very helpful when detecting fraud, especially for small businesses. In one fraud case, an accountant was stealing money instead of paying payroll taxes and other bills. The statement of cash flows highlighted the significant increase in payables. In another fraud case, cash receipts were stolen over a period of six years. The statement of cash flows showed significant increases in receivables. The discrepancies went unnoticed.

### "RED FLAGS" TO WATCH IN THE STATEMENT OF CASH FLOWS

- When sales are increasing, accounts receivable is decreasing.
- Inventory could be overstated to make net income look better.
- Cash could be stolen when accounts payable balance is increasing and delayed payment is occurring.
- Accounts payable balance increases when raw material inventory purchases are decreased.

The examiner or the auditor should convert the traditional net income from operations reported in the income statement to obtain the net amount of cash from operation. This conversion helps in understanding the relationships of various components of cash flows.

---

## FORMULA FOR DETERMINING NET AMOUNT OF CASH FROM OPERATIONS

|  | Net income from operations |
|---|---|
| plus | Depreciation |
| minus | Increase in accounts receivable |
| plus | Decrease in inventory |
| plus | Increase in accounts payable |
| equals | NET AMOUNT OF CASH FROM OPERATIONS |

---

(v) **Flowcharting techniques.** Flowcharting techniques are useful in detecting fraud. The flowcharting method, despite its indirect approach, can prove money-laundering activities. Enterprises used to launder funds will generally have common ownership or other connections, usually under the control of the targets. Therefore, corporate and other business filings and records showing the principals in the suspect business should be obtained and patterns of ownership noted. Financial and bank records can then be subpoenaed to trace the flow of funds between the enterprises. Other charting techniques that were explained earlier include link network diagrams, time-flow diagrams, and matrices to show the relationships between persons, organizations, and events.

(c) **Proving Illicit Financial Transactions.** This section describes various audit and examination techniques to identify and track the secret movement of funds in fraud, corruption, and money-laundering schemes. Joseph Wells[16] collected many examples, of which a few are briefly presented here. In all these cases, the illegal objectives may differ, but the means are the same, and the means are relatively limited in number.

- Company funds can be used to purchase expensive personal items as a form of embezzlement as well as for corrupt gifts.
- Money can be siphoned from a company account by cash or check for the benefit of the owners as well as to bribe another.
- Hidden interests can be taken in related transactions to earn fraudulent profits or can be given as a means of a payoff.

*Typical schemes and devices that are utilized to conceal embezzlement, corrupt payments, and other illicit transfers fall into two categories: "on-book" and "off-book" schemes.*

(i) **On-book and off-book schemes. On-book schemes** occur after the point of receipt of funds. Here illicit funds are drawn from the regular bank accounts and recorded on books, disguised as a legitimate trade payable, salary payment, or other business expense. Such payments are often made by regular business check, often payable to a sham business, through an intermediary. The payer may also cash the check, with the currency given to the recipient or used to create a slush fund for illegal purposes. Direct cash withdrawals are difficult to explain and deduce, if in significant amounts. Relatively small amounts of cash are often generated by fictitious charges to travel, entertainment, or miscellaneous accounts.

**Off-book schemes** refer to those schemes in which the funds used for illegal payments or transfers are not drawn from regular, known bank accounts. The payments do not appear anywhere on the books and records. In relatively small amounts, such payments may come directly from other ventures. In larger schemes, the funds are usually generated by unrecorded sales or by failing to record legitimate rebates from suppliers. Off-book schemes are often employed by businesses with significant cash sales (e.g., restaurants, bars, and retail shops).

The net worth method or comparative net worth analysis is used to prove illicit income circumstantially by showing that the suspect's assets or expenditures for a given period exceed that which can be accounted for from admitted sources of income. The technique is most useful when the recipient is taking currency or other payments that cannot be traced directly, and when the amount of illicit income generally exceeds the recipient's legitimate income. Net worth evidence is also useful to corroborate testimony of hidden illicit payments.

---

[16] *Ibid.*

(ii) **Net worth computation methods.** According to Joseph Wells[17], there are two basic methods of net worth computation: the asset method and the expenditures method (sources and application of funds method) (see Exhibit 4.6).

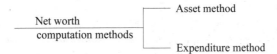

**Exhibit 4.6: Net worth computation methods**

The **asset method** should be used when the suspect has invested illegal funds to accumulate wealth and acquire assets, causing net worth (value of assets over liabilities) to increase year to year. The **expenditure method** is best used when the suspect spends his ill-gotten gains on lavish living, travel, and entertainment, which would not be reflected in an increase in net worth.

## ASSET METHOD FORMULA

|  | ASSETS |
|---|---|
| minus | liabilities |
| equals | NET WORTH |
| minus | prior year's net worth |
| equals | NET WORTH INCREASE |
| plus | living expenses |
| equals | INCOME (or EXPENDITURES) |
| minus | funds from known sources |
| equals | FUNDS FROM UNKNOWN SOURCES |

These steps should be undertaken for the asset method.

1. All assets should be valued at cost, not fair market value. Subsequent appreciation or depreciation of assets is ignored.
2. The amount of funds available to the suspect from legitimate sources should be estimated or computed generously. Any doubts should be resolved in favor of the suspect.
3. Attempt to interview the suspect, in order to identify all alleged sources of funds and to negate defenses that he or she may raise later.

## EXPENDITURES METHOD FORMULA

|  | EXPENDITURES (APPLICATION OF FUNDS) |
|---|---|
| minus | known sources of funds |
| equals | FUNDS FROM UNKNOWN SOURCES |

These steps should be undertaken for the expenditure method.

1. Establish the suspect's known expenditures for the relevant year. Expenditures include the use or application of funds for any purpose, including deposits to bank accounts, purchase of major assets, travel and entertainment expenses, and payment of loan and credit card debts.
2. Identify all sources of funds available to the suspect, including loans and gifts, as well as cash on hand from previous years.
3. The difference between the amount of the suspect's expenditures and known income is the amount attributed to unknown sources.

---

[17] *Ibid.*

(iii) **Money laundering.** An examiner tracing illicit funds may find an apparently legitimate source at the end of the trail: a prosperous cash retail business, a profitable real estate transaction, or offshore "loans" or investments. This is the realm of money laundering. Although money laundering is now itself a crime (as a result of the Money Laundering Act of 1986), it is usually detected as a result of the investigation of the underlying offenses. Effective investigation measures have included visual and electronic surveillance, sting and undercover operations.

Laundering schemes conducted through a front business are best proven through the cooperation of an insider, such as the business's accountant or tax preparer, or by infiltrating an agent.

Indirect methods of proving laundering activity include these techniques.

1. **Ratio analysis and sampling techniques.** Overreporting revenues of a front business to launder funds may result in an imbalance of the normal ratio of costs to sales: cost will appear unduly low compared to reported revenues (this is why the ideal laundering operation would have relatively low fixed costs against sales). Surveillance of the suspect enterprise may provide additional evidence that revenues are being underreported, by showing low customer traffic. Surveillance may also permit sampling procedures wherein a count of the number of customers or sales during a given period is used to extrapolate total sales.

2. **Flowcharting technique.** A laundering operation may also be revealed by the flowcharting technique, which was presented earlier.

(iv) **Federal sentencing guidelines for organizational defendants.** New federal sentencing guidelines for organizational defendants became effective in November of 1991. These guidelines provide judges with a compacted formula for sentencing business organizations for various **white-collar crimes**. Included are federal securities, employment and contract laws, as well as the crimes of mail and wire fraud, kickbacks and bribery, and money laundering.

These guidelines represent a unique carrot-and-stick approach calling for business organizations found guilty of crimes to face sanctions reaching potentially hundreds of millions of dollars (the "stick"). Organizations may be given offsetting credits against these penalties if they can demonstrate that: they exercised **due diligence** prior to the offense, the wrongdoing was investigated, and they cooperated with government investigators (the "carrot").

An organization is well advised to be able to demonstrate, prior to the accusation of any offense, that it exercised due diligence in seeking to prevent and detect criminal conduct by its agents. Due diligence requires that the organization has taken, at a minimum, these seven steps.

1. Established compliance policies that define standards and procedures
2. Assigned specific high-level responsibility to ensure compliance with these standards and procedures
3. Used due care in not delegating substantial discretionary authority to individuals who could engage in illegal activities
4. Communicated standards and procedures to all employees (by requiring participation in training programs and disseminating publications)
5. Taken reasonable steps to achieve compliance with standards (by utilizing monitoring and auditing systems including a system for employees to report violations without fear of reprisal)
6. Consistently enforced standards through appropriate disciplinary mechanisms
7. Taken all reasonable steps to prevent future similar offenses

**Internal auditors** should play an active role in educating management about the importance of the federal sentencing guidelines and assist in the development of new or expanded programs to address their requirements.

## 4.8 Use of Computers in Analyzing Data for Fraud and Crime

(a) **Collection and Preservation of Computer Evidence**

(i) **Guidelines for the care and handling of computer evidence.** Investigation of computer-related crimes more often than not involves highly technical matters, making it imperative during a search that appropriate steps are taken to ensure both the proper handling and preservation of evidence. There are seven recognized considerations involved in the care and handling of evidence.

1. Discovery and recognition
2. Protection
3. Recording
4. Collection
5. Identification
6. Preservation
7. Transportation

(A) ***Discovery and recognition.*** The investigator's capability to discover and to recognize the potential source of evidence is vital. When a computer is involved, the evidence is probably not apparent or visible. Nevertheless, the investigator must recognize that computer storage devices are nothing more than electronic or magnetic file cabinets and should be searched if it would normally be reasonable to search a file cabinet.

(B) ***Protection.*** The physical condition of evidence collected and seized is a major concern. Care should be taken to protect the area where evidence is located. Documents should be handled so as not to destroy latent prints or identifying characteristics. Computer-related evidence is sensitive to heat and humidity and should not be stored in the back seat or trunk of a car without special precautions.

(C) ***Recording.*** The alleged crime scene should be properly recorded. The use of a video camera to videotape computer equipment, workstations, and so on, and related written documentation at the crime scene is highly encouraged. Examiners should remember to photograph the rear side of the computer (particularly the cable connections).

(D) ***Collection.*** Collecting computer-related evidence is somewhat different from collecting other forms of evidence. When collecting evidence, examiners should take these precautions:

- When collecting evidence, go after original books, records, magnetic storage media, or printouts where possible.
- Be aware of degaussing equipment. A degausser is an electronic appliance that creates a strong magnetic field used to effectively erase a magnetic tape or disk. When collecting this type of evidence, ensure that any degaussing equipment is secured or rendered inoperative.
- Documents and paper should be handled with cloth gloves, placed in an evidence container, and sealed.
- It is vital to seize all storage media, even ones that purportedly have been erased. Technical personnel may still be able to capture data thought to have been erased or determine that erasures never occurred. (Disk-operating system "delete" commands do not actually erase disk sectors but merely make them available to magnetically write new information over existing information).

## Care and Handling of Computer Evidence

Considerations involved in the care and handling of computer evidence include discovery and recognition, protection, recording, collection, identification, preservation, and transportation.

(E) ***Identification.*** It is usually more difficult to identify computer evidence than other forms of evidence; special knowledge of the thing being marked is required. A list of things to look for during the gathering of computer evidence follows:

- Information on the evidence tag should include the hardware identification and operating system used to produce the tapes, disks, printouts, and so on.
- Do not write on a magnetic disk surface.
- Diskettes should be marked only with a felt-tip pen or a label that has been filled out, then attached.
- Printouts should be marked with permanent marking pens.
- Reel-to-reel magnetic tapes can be marked on the nonshiny side, within the first 10 to 15 feet (leader part).

(F) *Preservation.* Computer evidence can be very volatile. For example, turning the computer's power off prematurely can lose evidence. A list of things to preserve computer evidence follows:

- Remove evidence as soon as possible to prevent tampering. Tapes and disks can be erased or damaged quickly and easily.
- Write-protect magnetic media as soon as possible to prevent deliberate or inadvertent alteration of evidence.
- Store magnetic media in a proper temperature (40 to 90°F) and humidity (20 to 80%) in a dust-free environment. Tobacco smoke is also damaging. Avoid placing near strong magnetic fields (e.g., telephones, radio transmitters, photocopiers, or degaussers).

(G) *Transportation.* Particular care should be taken in the handling of computer evidence while in transit. A list of things to do during transportation of computer evidence follows:

- Transport magnetic media at the proper temperature and humidity.
- Write-protect all magnetic media and label disks and diskettes.
- Label the wires connecting various devices at both ends to aid in system reassembly at a later time.
- Photograph the labeled equipment and wires before disconnecting.
- Disassemble, tag, and inventory the equipment.
- Carefully pack seized devices in suitable containers for transport.
- Transport magnetic media in dust-free, climate-controlled environments. Temperature extremes may render magnetically stored evidence unreadable, and various types of contamination can damage electronic equipment.
- Do not take magnetic media through metal detectors, conveyor belts, or X-ray machines. This equipment generates strong magnetic fields that could destroy computer evidence.

(ii) **Guidelines for the preservation and submission of computer evidence.** These guidelines are applicable to preservation and submission of computer evidence, specifically to hardware, magnetic media, and documentation.

I. **Hardware**

A. PC/central processing output (CPU)

1. Determine if the system has an internal hard drive. If possible, secure hard drive read/write heads with the appropriate software command. Do not remove the internal hard drive from the computer.
2. Secure read/write heads in the floppy disk drives with a blank floppy diskette.
3. Label cables and ports.
4. Initial and date PC as required by the department's chain-of-custody procedures.
5. Wrap in plastic, and box for shipment to the laboratory.

B. Monitor and keyboard

1. Label cables.
2. Initial and date the monitor and keyboard as required by the department's chain-of-custody procedures.
3. Wrap in plastic, and box for shipment to the laboratory.

C. External/removable hard drives, external floppy diskette drives, external tape drives, and printers/plotters

1. Secure the hard drive read/write heads, if possible. Some are secured by software commands, and others are secured automatically.
2. Remove floppy diskettes from drive(s). Secure the read/write heads with a blank floppy diskette, if possible.
3. Note and record the switch setting for the external tape drive. Remove the tape cartridge from the drive.
4. Note and record the switch settings for printers and plotters. Remove the ribbon, and initial and date the ribbon canister.
5. Initial and date each item as required by the department's chain-of-custody procedures.
6. Wrap each item in plastic, and box for shipment to the laboratory.

    D. Modems/acoustic couplers, and cables

      1. Disconnect the modem or acoustic coupler from telephone.
      2. Label both ends of each cable, describing connection to PC, printer, and so on.
      3. Label all ports.
      4. Initial and date each item as required by the department's chain-of-custody procedures.
      5. Wrap each item in plastic, and box for shipment to the laboratory.

**II. Magnetic Media**

    A. Floppy diskettes and cartridge tapes

      1. Keep them away from magnetic fields.
      2. Initial and date using felt-tip pen as required by the department's chain-of-custody procedures.
      3. Place them in appropriate evidence container. Do not use plastic envelopes because of the risk of static electric discharge.
      4. Label the outside of shipment container "DO NOT X-RAY " to warn that evidence should be kept away from magnetic fields, and ship to the laboratory.

**III. Documentation**

    A. Manuals/handwritten notes, printouts/listings

      1. Handle with gloves to preserve for latent fingerprint examination.
      2. Initial and date all loose sheets, note pads, manuals, and other paper documents as required by the department's chain-of-custody procedures.
      3. Place in appropriate evidence container.
      4. Ship to the laboratory.

(iii) **Guidelines for the examination of computer evidence.** Guidelines for examination of computer evidence, specifically for receipt of evidence, examination of evidence, and reporting results follow:

**I. Receipt of evidence**

    A. Log evidence into appropriate evidence control system and assign to an examiner.

      1. Record date and time received by some unique numbering system.
      2. Identify the examiner.
      3. Prepare documentation for chain-of-custody from evidence control to the examiner.

    B. Transfer evidence to the examiner.

      1. Determine if other expert analyses, such as accounting and latent fingerprint examination, is necessary.
      2. Prepare chain-of-custody documentation for other experts as necessary for complete examination.
      3. Determine that all pieces of equipment listed as having been submitted are actually present.
      4. Mark and initial each piece of evidence as required by the laboratory system and prepare working papers for notes.

**II. Examination of evidence**

    A. Determine if the submitted system is operational.

      1. Review submitting communication to determine if the system was operational at the time of seizure.
      2. Take logical steps to render the system operational.

    B. Floppy diskettes and hard disk systems

      1. Write-protect all diskettes.
      2. Write-protect the hard disk using appropriate software.
      3. Identify the computer to be used for examination.
      4. Convert the operating system if necessary.
      5. Create directory/subdirectory listings.

6. Check for hidden and deleted files using appropriate commercial or custom software.
7. Display and print files.

   III.  **Reporting results**

     A. Prepare reports, documenting what was done and the results.
     B. Send printouts and report to the contributor or subject matter expert for additional analysis.
     C. Repack the computer and all disks.
     D. Return the evidence to contributor.

(iv) **Using a computer as an investigative tool.** Computers can be used to collect and compile large amounts of data and provide statistics, reports, and graphs to assist the investigator in analysis and decision making. In deciding whether to employ computer resources to assist in an investigation, these requirement analysis factors should be carefully considered.

- Is automation necessary or appropriate?
- What output is desired?
- What software or hardware is available?
- What data elements are required based on output requirements?
- Who will do the data entry, how many records will have to be entered, how long will it take to enter all of the data, and what are the data characteristics (alpha, numeric, field size)?
- If there are calculated fields in the report, can the software create those fields?
- Who needs the report (agent or prosecutor)?
- Will the software or the hardware handle the number of records required?
- What is the security classification of the data to be entered?
- How much time is there for program development, and will an existing investigative tool suffice?
- Will the design of input/output screen layouts, report formats, sequence-of-data presentation, design of menus to drive the system, and design of a backup system is available?
- Will the development of a user's guide be available and training of prospective system users be provided?

(b) **Chain of Computer Evidence.** This section addresses various aspects of properly maintaining computer-related evidence. These procedures are important in avoiding problems of proof caused by improper care and handling of such evidence.

- Maintaining evidence in the form of computer storage media presents problems that differ from handling other types of evidence. Because they are subject to erasure and easily damaged, magnetic or electronic storage devices must be carefully guarded and kept under controlled temperature and humidity to avoid deterioration.
- In investigating and prosecuting a case involving such evidence, one of the early steps a prosecutor should take is to retain an appropriate computer expert or technical assistance. This can be critical in avoiding problems resulting from inept maintenance procedures or inadvertent loss of key information.
- Sometimes the contents of dozens or even hundreds of computer tapes or disks must be copied to allow the business to continue operating while the case is being prosecuted. This must be done under the close supervision of an expert who cannot only ensure that it is done right but can also determine the least costly procedure.
- Initials of the seizing agent and the date should be scratched on each storage media container, and a **chain-of-custody** sheet or log should be made for every container. The log should show, at a minimum, the date, place, and specific location of the seizure and the name of the agent making the seizure.

The agents investigating the case are likely to have considerable expertise in maintaining computer evidence, gained from training and experience. Their advice and assistance can be invaluable to the prosecutor in minimizing problems of proof inherent in computer-related crimes.

(c) **Computer Fraud and Crime Examples**

(i) **Military and intelligence attacks.** *Espionage can take three forms such as industrial espionage, economic espionage, and foreign government espionage.* **Industrial espionage** is the act of gathering proprietary data from private companies or the government for the purpose of aiding another company. Industrial espionage can be perpetrated either by companies seeking to improve their competitive advantage or by governments seeking to aid their domestic industries. The three most damaging types of industrial espionage include pricing data, manufacturing process information, and product development/specification information (trade secrets).

Foreign industrial espionage carried out by a government is often referred to as **economic espionage**. Information related to technology, information on commodities, interest rates, and contract data are the targets of economic espionage. In addition to possible economic espionage, **foreign intelligence services** may target unclassified systems to further their intelligence acts. Some unclassified information that may be of interest includes: travel plans of senior officials; civil defense and emergency preparedness; satellite data; personnel and payroll data; and law enforcement, investigative, and security files. **Countermeasures** against intelligence attacks include implementing user awareness, education, and training programs.

**Wiretapping** (electronic eavesdropping) is listening in on another's communication during transmission of messages and information. It also occurs when data flowing over cables is intercepted. **Countermeasures** include: locking up the cable closet, using traffic padding technique to confuse the eavesdropper, and implementing voice encryption techniques with (SSL) Security Socket Layer protocol.

**Data leakage** is removal of data from a computer system by covert means. It might be possible to examine computer operating system usage journals to determine if and when data files may have been accessed. Data leakage attacks might be conducted through the use of Trojan horse, logic bomb, or scavenging methods. **Countermeasures** include encryption, access controls, and cryptographic techniques.

(ii) **Business attacks. Employee sabotage** is the most common business attack. The number of incidents of employee sabotage is much *smaller* than instances of employee theft, but the cost of such incidents can be quite high. Common examples of computer-related employee sabotage include: destroying hardware or facilities, planting logic bombs that destroy programs or data, "crashing" computer systems, and entering data incorrectly, deleting data, or changing data (data diddling).

**Data diddling** involves changing data before or during input to computers or during output from a computer system. The changing can be done by anybody associated with or having access to the process of creating, recording, transporting, encoding, examining, checking, converting, and transforming data that ultimately enter a computer. Examples include: forging or counterfeiting documents; exchanging valid computer magnetic media with prepared replacements; source document entry violations; and neutralizing, bypassing, or avoiding manual controls. *Manipulating input is the most common method of perpetrating fraud using a computer. Data diddling attacks can be prevented with access controls, program change controls, and integrity checking software.*

**Superzapping,** an example of a business attack, it involves unauthorized use of a computer utility program to modify, destroy, copy, disclose, insert, use, or deny use of data stored in a computer system or computer media. This powerful utility program bypasses operating system security controls and even the access control security software controls. By definition, superzapping is not a computer crime by itself. *A reliable way to detect superzapping work is by comparing current data files with previous data files.*

Simply **writing computer virus programs** is not a criminal activity. However, using, releasing, and spreading a virus with bad intentions of destroying computer resources are the basis for criminal activity.

(iii) **Financial attacks. The salami technique** of financial attacks involves theft of small amounts of assets (primarily money) from a number of sources. For example, the perpetrator steals a few cents from each customer account on a large number of bank accounts, theft that is unnoticed by most customers. However, the account totals will be kept in balance with double-entry recordkeeping system. The salami technique can also be affected by "round-down" fractions of money, which can be moved into the perpetrator's bank account.

Collecting customers' credit card information through Web sites and unauthorized access to **wire transfer fund** accounts in a financial institution are other examples of financial attacks. Transfer of money between two parties without a financial institution's involvement is another example of a financial attack.

**Toll fraud** through telephone cloning is another example of a financial attack; this type of fraud costs telephone companies significant amounts of money.

(iv) **Terrorist attacks.** Terrorists can hold data hostage, or they can demand ransom money for data and programs stolen.

(v) **Grudge attacks.** Employees who were fired may have a grudge against the organization where they have worked. The general public may have a grudge against an organization where they do not like what the organization is doing or has done.

(vi) **"Fun" attacks.** People can target organizations for fun and challenge to get publicity and to satisfy their intellectual curiosity. Their goal is not to make money.

## RELATED CONCEPTS IN COMPUTER CRIME

- A person must have a motive, the opportunity, and the means to commit a crime.
- Computer crime is possible when controls are predictable and avoidable (bypassable).
- System predictability is a key to a successful computer crime; that is, users and attackers know how the system reacts to a given condition.
- Computer crime can be minimized with dynamic controls and variable features.
- White-collar crimes tend to be situation-oriented, meaning that a change in a person's lifestyle and job situations can make the person commit crime.
- Unknown misbehavior of unknown perpetrators is the major reason for the inability to calculate the risk resulting from computer crime.

**MULTIPLE-CHOICE QUESTIONS (1-101)**

**1.** When an auditor's sampling objective is to obtain a measurable assurance that a sample will contain at least one occurrence of a specific critical exception existing in a population, the sampling approach to use is
   a. Random.
   b. Discovery.
   c. Probability proportional to size.
   d. Variables.

**2.** Management is legally required to prepare a shipping document for all movement of hazardous materials. The document must be filed with bills of lading. Management expects 100% compliance with the procedure. Which of the following sampling approaches would be **most** appropriate?
   a. Attributes sampling.
   b. Discovery sampling.
   c. Targeted sampling.
   d. Variables sampling.

**3.** The appropriate sampling plan to use to identify at least one irregularity, assuming some number of such irregularities exist in a population, and then to discontinue sampling when one irregularity is observed is
   a. Stop-and-go sampling.
   b. Discovery sampling.
   c. Variables sampling.
   d. Attributes sampling.

**4.** After partially completing an internal control review of the accounts payable department, the auditor suspects that some type of fraud has occurred. To ascertain whether the fraud is present, the **best** sampling approach would be to use
   a. Simple random sampling to select a sample of vouchers processed by the department during the past year.
   b. Probability-proportional-to-size sampling to select a sample of vouchers processed by the department during the past year.
   c. Discovery sampling to select a sample of vouchers processed by the department during the past year.
   d. Judgmental sampling to select a sample of vouchers processed by clerks identified by the department manager as acting suspiciously.

**5.** Because of control weaknesses, it is possible that the individual managers of 122 restaurants could have placed fictitious employees on the payroll. Each restaurant employs between 25 and 30 people. To efficiently determine whether this fraud exists at less than a 1% level, the auditor should use
   a. Attributes sampling.
   b. Judgment sampling.
   c. Directed sampling.
   d. Discovery sampling.

**6.** In the audit of a health insurance claims processing department, a sample is taken to test for the presence of fictitious payees, although none is suspected. The most appropriate sampling plan would be
   a. Attributes sampling.
   b. Discovery sampling.
   c. Variables sampling.
   d. Stop-and-go sampling.

**7.** An auditor applying a discovery sampling plan with a 5% risk of overreliance may conclude that there is
   a. A 95% probability that the actual rate of occurrence in the population is less than the critical rate if only one exception is found.
   b. A 95% probability that the actual rate of occurrence in the population is less than the critical rate if no exceptions are found.
   c. A 95% probability that the actual rate of occurrence in the population is less than the critical rate if the occurrence rate in the sample is less than the critical rate.
   d. Greater than a 95% probability that the actual rate of occurrence in the population is less than the critical rate if no exceptions are found.

**8.** An internal auditor suspects fraud. Which of the following sample plans should be used if the purpose is to select a sample with a given probability of containing at least one example of the irregularity?
   a. Attributes.
   b. Discovery.
   c. Stop and go.
   d. Probability proportional to size.

**9.** What is a data diddling technique?
   a. Changing data before input to a computer system.
   b. Changing data during input to a computer system.
   c. Changing data during output from a computer system.
   d. Choices a, b, and c.

**10.** What is a salami technique?
   a. Taking small amounts of assets.
   b. Using "rounding-down" concept.
   c. Stealing small amounts of money from bank accounts.
   d. Choices a, b, and c.

**11.** Data diddling can be prevented by all of the following **except:**
   a. Access controls.
   b. Program change controls.
   c. Rapid correction of data.
   d. Integrity checking.

**12.** A reliable way to detect superzapping work is by
   a. Comparing current data files with previous data files.
   b. Examining computer usage logs.
   c. Noting discrepancies by those who receive reports.
   d. Reviewing undocumented transactions.

**13.** With respect to computer security and fraud, a legal liability exists to an organization under which of the following conditions?
   a. When estimated security costs are greater than estimated losses.
   b. When estimated security costs are equal to estimated losses.
   c. When estimated security costs are less than estimated losses.
   d. When actual security costs are equal to actual losses.

**14.** Are an investigator's handwritten notes considered valid evidence in court of law?

   a. No.
   b. Maybe.
   c. Yes.
   d. Depends.

**15.** A security investigator or law enforcement officer should observe which of the following during a computer crime investigation?
   a. Chain of events.
   b. Chain of custody.
   c. Chain of computers.
   d. Chain of logs.

**16.** Which of the following security techniques allow time for response by investigative authorities?
   a. Deter.
   b. Detect.
   c. Delay.
   d. Deny.

**17.** Most of the evidence submitted in a computer crime case is
   a. Legal evidence.
   b. Documentary evidence.
   c. Secondary evidence.
   d. Admissible evidence.

**18.** When computers and peripheral equipment are seized in relation to a computer crime, it is an example of
   a. Duplicate evidence.
   b. Physical evidence.
   c. Best evidence.
   d. Collateral evidence.

**19.** From a computer security viewpoint, courts expect what amount of care from organizations?
   a. Super care.
   b. Due care.
   c. Extraordinary care.
   d. Great care.

**20.** Which of the following is **not** a criminal activity in **most** jurisdictions?
   a. Writing a computer virus program.
   b. Using a computer virus program.
   c. Releasing a computer virus program.
   d. Spreading a computer virus program.

**21.** Once evidence is seized, a law enforcement officer should follow which of the following?
   a. The chain of command.
   b. The chain of control.
   c. The chain of custody.
   d. The chain of communications.

**22.** The concept of admissibility of evidence does **not** include which of the following?
   a. Relevance.
   b. Competence.
   c. Materiality.
   d. Sufficiency.

**23.** The chain of custody does **not** ask which of the following questions?
   a. Who damaged the evidence?
   b. Who collected the evidence?
   c. Who stored the evidence?
   d. Who controlled the evidence?

**24.** When large volumes of writing are presented in court, which type of evidence is inapplicable?
   a. Best evidence.
   b. Flowchart evidence.
   c. Magnetic tapes evidence.
   d. Demonstrative evidence.

**25.** Evidence is needed to do which of the following?
   a. Charge a case.
   b. Classify a case.
   c. Make a case.
   d. Prove a case.

**26.** What determines whether a computer crime has been committed?
   a. When the crime is reported.
   b. When a computer expert has completed his or her work.
   c. When the allegation has been substantiated.
   d. When the investigation is completed.

**27.** The correct sequence of preliminary investigation is

  I. Consult with a computer expert.
  II. Prepare an investigative plan.
  III. Consult with a prosecutor.
  IV. Substantiate the allegation.

   a. IV, I, II, and III.
   b. III, I, II, and IV.
   c. IV, II, III, and I.
   d. I, IV, II, and III.

**28.** The objective of which of the following team members is similar to that of the information systems security officer involved in a computer crime investigation?
   a. An investigator.
   b. A district attorney.
   c. A computer expert.
   d. An internal systems auditor.

**29.** A search warrant is required
   a. Before the allegation has been substantiated.
   b. After establishing the probable cause(s).
   c. Before identifying the number of investigators needed.
   d. After seizing the computer and related equipment.

**30.** In a computer-related crime investigation, computer evidence is
   a. Volatile and invisible.
   b. Apparent and magnetic
   c. Electronic and inadmissible.
   d. Difficult and erasable.

**31.** In a computer-related crime investigation, maintenance of evidence is important for which of the following reasons?
   a. To record the crime.
   b. To collect the evidence.
   c. To protect the evidence.
   d. To avoid problems of proof.

**32.** If a computer or peripheral equipment involved in a computer crime is **not** covered by a search warrant, what should the investigator do?
   a. Seize it before someone takes it away.
   b. Leave it alone until a warrant can be obtained.

c. Analyze the equipment or its contents, and record it.
d. Store it in a locked cabinet in a secure warehouse.

**33.** All of the following are proper ways to handle the computer equipment and magnetic media items involved in a computer crime investigation **except:**
  a. Seal, store, and tag the items.
  b. Seal and store items in a cardboard box.
  c. Seal and store items in a paper bag.
  d. Seal and store items in a plastic bag.

**34.** Indicate the **most** objective and relevant evidence in a computer environment involving fraud.
  a. Physical examination.
  b. Physical observation.
  c. Inquiries of people.
  d. Computer logs.

**35.** Which of the following is needed to produce technical evidence in computer-related crimes?
  a. Audit methodology.
  b. System methodology.
  c. Forensic methodology.
  d. Criminal methodology.

**36.** The final stage of reporting results of computer evidence life cycle is
  a. Return.
  b. Receive.
  c. Examine.
  d. Report.

**37.** Which of the following investigative tools is **most** effective when large volumes of evidence need to be analyzed?
  a. Interviews.
  b. Questionnaires.
  c. Forensic analysis.
  d. Computer.

**38.** Which of the following methods is acceptable to handle computer equipment seized in a computer crime investigation?
  a. Exposing the magnetic media to radio waves.
  b. Laying the magnetic media on top of electronic equipment.
  c. Subjecting the magnetic media to forensic testing.
  d. Leaving the magnetic media in the trunk of a vehicle containing a radio unit.

**39.** Computer fraud is discouraged by
  a. Being willing to prosecute.
  b. Ostracizing whistle-blowers.
  c. Overlooking inefficiencies in the judicial system.
  d. Accepting the lack of integrity in the system.

**40.** Identify the computer-related crime and fraud method that involves obtaining information that may be left in or around a computer system after the execution of a job.
  a. Data diddling.
  b. Salami technique.
  c. Scavenging.
  d. Piggybacking.

**41.** Computer fraud is increased when
  a. Employees are not trained.
  b. Documentation is not available.
  c. Audit trails are not available.
  d. Employee performance appraisals are not given.

**42.** Internal auditors would be **more likely** to detect fraud if they developed/strengthened their ability to
  a. Recognize and question changes which occur in organizations.
  b. Interrogate fraud perpetrators to discover why the fraud was committed.
  c. Develop internal controls to prevent the occurrence of fraud.
  d. Document computerized operating system programs.

**43.** According to the IIA *Standards*, which of the following **best** describes the two general categories or types of fraud that concern most internal auditors?
  a. Improper payments (i.e., bribes and kickbacks) and tax fraud.
  b. Fraud designed to benefit the organization and fraud perpetrated to the detriment of the organization.
  c. Acceptance of bribes or kickbacks and improper related-party transactions.
  d. Acceptance of kickbacks or embezzlement and misappropriation of assets.

**44.** A company hired a highly qualified accounts payable manager who had been terminated from another company for alleged wrongdoing. Six months later the manager diverted $12,000 by sending duplicate payments of invoices to a relative. A control that might have prevented this situation would be to
  a. Adequately check prior employment backgrounds for all new employees.
  b. Not hire individuals who appear overqualified for a job.
  c. Verify educational background for all new employees.
  d. Check to see if close relatives work for vendors.

**45.** Red flags are conditions that indicate a higher likelihood of fraud. Which of the following would **not** be considered a red flag?
  a. Management has delegated the authority to make purchases under a certain dollar limit to subordinates.
  b. An individual has held the same cash-handling job for an extended period without any rotation of duties.
  c. An individual handling marketable securities is responsible for making the purchases, recording the purchases, and reporting any discrepancies and gains/losses to senior management.
  d. The assignment of responsibility and accountability in the accounts receivable department is not clear.

**46.** Internal auditors and management have become increasingly concerned about computer fraud. Which of the following control procedures would be **least** important in preventing computer fraud?
  a. Program change control that requires a distinction between production programs and test programs.
  b. Testing of new applications by users during the systems development process.

c.  Segregation of duties between the applications programmer and the program librarian function.

d.  Segregation of duties between the programmer and systems analyst.

**47.** During a regularly scheduled IT audit of a major division, the IT auditor discovers a complicated programming algorithm that adds costs to a cost-plus program billing the government. The amount added accounted for 95% of the net income for the division for the most recent year. Upon further investigation, the IT auditor finds that only the marketing manager, the divisional manager, and the programmer know of the algorithm.

The company has a separate section to investigate fraud. The auditor communicates with management and the special investigation section, and the investigation is turned over to that group. However, after a month, it becomes apparent that senior management has instructed the group to "not make waves" and to drop the investigation. The internal audit department should

a.  Immediately report the circumstances and the IT auditor's findings to the audit committee.

b.  Immediately report the circumstances and the IT auditor's findings to the appropriate governmental regulatory agency because the auditor cannot knowingly be a party to an illegal act.

c.  Take no further action. The nature of the fraud has been reported to the proper authorities within the company and the auditor has no power to pursue the investigation further.

d.  Report the findings to the external auditor because the external auditor should be aware of any material misstatement of account balances.

**48.** Which of the following statements correctly characterize(s) the "red flags" literature that has recently developed in the auditing profession?

I.  Red flags are items or actions that have been associated with fraudulent conduct.

II. The auditor should document all red flags that may have been noted on an audit engagement.

III. Many red flags are "subjective" in nature and might not come to the auditor's attention during the course of an audit that is properly planned and conducted in accordance with the *Standards*.

a.  I and II.
b.  I and III.
c.  II and III.
d.  III only.

**49.** An employee of an insurance company processed a fraudulent policy loan application for an amount less than the established level requiring supervisory review. The employee then obtained the check and cashed it by forging the endorsement. To prevent the loan's appearance on a subsequent policyholder statement, the loan amount was transferred to a "suspense" account. Which of the following should expose this situation at the earliest date?

a.  A computer report identifying unusual entries to the suspense account.

b.  The use of prenumbered checks which are periodically accounted for.

c.  An annual internal audit.

d.  Regular reconciliation of the "suspense" account performed by an independent employee.

**50.** The primary purpose of operating a fraud hot line within a company is to

a.  Reduce total costs of operating the company.

b.  Measure how well organizational units are achieving the organization's goals.

c.  Establish channels of communication for people to report suspected improprieties.

d.  Concentrate on areas that deserve attention and to place less attention on areas operating as expected.

**51.** A programmer accumulating round-off errors into one account that is later accessed by the programmer is a type of computer fraud. The best way to prevent this type of fraud is to

a.  Build in judgment with reasonableness tests.

b.  Independently test programs during development and limit access to the programs.

c.  Segregate duties of systems development and programming.

d.  Use control totals and check the results of the computer.

**52.** Which of the following statements is(are) correct regarding the deterrence of fraud?

I.  The primary means of deterring fraud is through an effective control system initiated by top management.

II. Internal auditors are responsible for assisting in the deterrence of fraud by examining and evaluating the adequacy of the control system.

III. Internal auditors should determine whether communication channels provide management with adequate and reliable information regarding the effectiveness of the control system and the occurrence of unusual transactions.

a.  I only.
b.  I and II only.
c.  II only.
d.  I, II, and III.

**53.** A significant employee fraud took place shortly after an internal audit. The Internal auditor may **not** have properly fulfilled the responsibility for the deterrence of fraud by failing to note and report that

a.  Policies, practices, and procedures to monitor activities and safeguard assets were less extensive in low-risk areas than in high-risk areas.

b.  A system of control that depended on separation of duties could be circumvented by collusion among three employees.

c.  There were no written policies describing prohibited activities and the action required whenever violations are discovered.

d.  Divisional employees had not been properly trained to distinguish between bona fide signatures and cleverly forged ones on authorization forms.

**54.** Fraudulent use of corporate credit cards would be minimized by which of the following internal control procedures?

a.  Establishing a corporate policy on the issuance of credit cards to authorized employees.

b. Reviewing the validity of credit card need at executive and operating levels on a periodic basis.

c. Reconciling the monthly statement from the credit card company with the submitted copies of the cardholders' charge slips.

d. Subjecting credit card charges to the same expense controls as those used on regular company expense forms.

**Items 55 through 57** are based on the following:

A fraud was perpetrated in a moderate-sized company when the accounting clerk was delegated too much responsibility. During the year, the company switched suppliers of a service to a new vendor. The accounting clerk continued to submit fraudulent invoices from the "old supplier." Because contracting for services and approval of supplier invoices had been delegated to the clerk, it was possible for her to continue billings from the old supplier and deposit the subsequent checks, which she was responsible to mail, into a new account she opened in the name of the old supplier. The clerk was considered an excellent employee and eventually was improperly given the added responsibility of preparing the department budgets. This added responsibility allowed her to actually budget for the amount of the fraudulent payments.

**55.** Analytical tests can be useful in detecting frauds. Which of the following analytical procedures would **most** likely have signaled the existence of the fraud?

a. Current production with prior period production.

b. Current and prior period service expenses.

c. Budget to actual service expense.

d. Company cost of goods sold to industry cost of goods sold.

**56.** Which of the following controls would be **least** likely to prevent or detect the fraud described above?

a. Require authorization of payments by someone other than the clerk negotiating the contract.

b. Comparison by person signing checks of invoices to an independent verification of services received.

c. Budget preparation by someone other than person signing contract and approving payment.

d. Mailing of check by someone other than persons responsible for check signing or invoice approval.

**57.** Which of the following audit procedures would **most** likely lead to the detection of the fraud?

a. Take a sample of paid invoices and verify receipt of services by departments involved.

b. Trace a sample of checks disbursed to approved invoices for services.

c. Perform bank statement reconciliation and account for all outstanding checks.

d. Trace a sample of receiving documents to invoices and to checks disbursed.

**58.** A production manager for a moderate-sized manufacturing company began ordering excessive raw materials and had them delivered to a wholesale company he runs as a side business. He falsified receiving documents and approved the invoices for payment. Which of the following audit procedures would **most** likely detect this fraud?

a. Take a sample of cash disbursements; compare purchase orders, receiving reports, invoices, and check copies.

b. Take a sample and confirm the amount purchased, purchase price, and date of shipment with the vendors.

c. Observe the receiving dock and count material received; compare your counts to receiving reports completed by receiving personnel.

d. Prepare analytical tests, comparing production, material purchased, and raw material inventory levels and investigates differences.

**Items 59 through 61** are based on the following:

A purchasing agent acquired items for personal use with company funds. The company allowed designated employees to purchase as much as $250 per day in merchandise under open-ended contracts. Supervisory approval of the purchases was required, but that information was not communicated to the vendor. Instead of reviewing and authorizing each purchase order, supervisors routinely signed the authorization sheet at the end of the month without reviewing any of the supporting documentation. Since purchases of this nature were not subject to normal company receiving policies, the dishonest employee picked up the supplies at the vendor's warehouse. All purchases were for items routinely ordered by the company. During the past year, the employee amassed enough merchandise to start a printing and photography business.

**59.** Which of the following internal controls would have been most effective in preventing this fraud?

a. Allowing purchases only from a list of preapproved vendors.

b. Requiring the use of prenumbered purchase orders for all purchases of merchandise.

c. Canceling supporting documents, such as purchase orders and receiving reports, at the time invoices are paid.

d. Establishing separation of duties between the ordering and receiving of merchandise.

**60.** Which of the following audit procedures performed by the internal auditor would be most effective in leading to the discovery of this fraud?

a. Tracing selected canceled checks to the cash payments journal and to the related vendors' invoices.

b. Performing a trend analysis of printing supplies expenses for a two-year period.

c. Tracing prices and quantities on selected vendors' invoices to the related purchase orders.

d. Recomputing the clerical accuracy of selected vendors' invoices, including discounts and sales taxes.

**61.** Once the internal auditor becomes reasonably certain that this defalcation is taking place, what should the auditor do next?

a. Immediately report the matter to the appropriate law enforcement official, since a potential felony is involved.

b. Say nothing now, but include a description of the suspected defalcation in the audit.

c. Immediately report the matter to the appropriate level of management.

d. Immediately discuss the matter with the employee suspected of the defalcation in order to confirm the audit findings.

**Items 62 and 63** are based on the following:

Management discovers that a supervisor at one of their restaurant locations removes excess cash and resets sales totals throughout the day on the point-of-sale (POS) system. At closing the supervisor deposits cash equal to the recorded sales on the POS system and keeps the rest.

The supervisor forwards the close-of-day POS reports from the POS system along with a copy of the bank deposit slip to the company's revenue accounting department. The revenue accounting department records the sales and the cash for the location in the general ledger and verifies the deposit slip to the bank statement. Any differences between sales and deposits are recorded in an over/short account and, if necessary, followed up with the location supervisor. The customer food order checks are serially numbered, and it is the supervisor's responsibility to see that they are accounted for at the end of each day. Customer checks and the transaction journal tapes from the POS system are kept by the supervisor for one week at the location and then destroyed.

**62.** Which of the following control procedures allowed the fraud to occur?
   a.  The accounting of customer food checks by the supervisor.
   b.  The deposit of cash receipts by the supervisor.
   c.  The matching of the bank deposit slips to the bank statement by revenue accounting.
   d.  The forwarding of the close-of-day POS reports to revenue accounting.

**63.** Which of the following audit procedures would have detected the fraud?
   a.  Flowcharting the controls over the verification of bank deposit.
   b.  Comparing a sample of the close of day POS reports to copies of the bank deposit slips.
   c.  On a test basis, verifying that the serial-numbered customer food checks are accounted for.
   d.  For selected days, reconciling the total of customer food checks to daily bank deposits.

**64.** The IIA *Standards* require internal auditors to have knowledge about factors (red flags) that have proven to be associated with management fraud. Which of the following factors have generally **not** been associated with management fraud?
   a.  Generous performance-based reward systems.
   b.  A domineering management.
   c.  Regular comparison of actual results to budgets.
   d.  A management preoccupation with increased financial performance.

**65.** A personnel department is responsible for processing placement agency fees for new hires. A recruiter established some bogus placement agencies and, when interviewing walk-in applicants, the recruiter would list one of the bogus agencies as referring the candidate. A possible means of detection or deterrence is to
   a.  Process all personnel agency invoices via a purchase order through the purchasing department.
   b.  Verify new vendors to firms listed in a professional association catalog and/or verify the vendor name and address through the telephone book.
   c.  Monitor the closeness of the relationships of recruiters with specific vendors.

   d.  Require all employees to sign an annual conflict of interest statement.

**66.** Experience has shown that certain conditions in an organization are symptoms of possible management fraud. Which of the following conditions would **not** be considered an indicator of possible fraud?
   a.  Managers regularly assume subordinates' duties.
   b.  Managers dealing in matters outside their profit center's scope.
   c.  Mangers not complying with corporate directives and procedures.
   d.  Managers subject to formal performance reviews on a regular basis.

**67.** Which of the following is an indicator of possible financial reporting fraud being perpetrated by management of a manufacturer?
   a.  A trend analysis discloses (1) sales increases of 50% and (2) cost of goods sold increases of 25%.
   b.  A ratio analysis discloses (1) sales of $50 million and (2) cost of goods sold of $25 million.
   c.  A cross-sectional analysis of common size statements discloses: (1) the firm's ratio of cost of goods sold to sales is 0.4 and (2) the industry average ratio of cost of goods sold to sales is 0.5.
   d.  A cross-sectional analysis of common size statements discloses: (1) the firm's ratio of cost of goods sold to sales is 0.5 and (2) the industry average ratio of cost of goods sold to sales is 0.4.

**68.** Which of the following might be considered a red flag indicating possible fraud in a large manufacturing company with several subsidiaries?
   a.  The existence of a financial subsidiary.
   b.  A consistent record of above average return on investment for all subsidiaries.
   c.  Complex sales transactions and transfers of funds between affiliated companies.
   d.  Use of separate bank accounts for payrolls by each subsidiary.

**69.** A subsidiary president terminated a controller and hired a replacement without the required corporate approvals. Sales, cash flow, and profit statistics were then manipulated by the new controller and president via accelerated depreciation and sale of capital assets to obtain larger performance bonuses for the controller and the subsidiary president. An approach that might detect this fraudulent activity would be
   a.  Analysis of overall management control for segregation of duties.
   b.  Required exit interviews for all terminated employees.
   c.  Periodic changes of outside public accountants.
   d.  Regular analytical review of operating divisions.

**Items 70 through 73** are based on the following:

Bank management suspects that a bank loan officer frequently made loans to fictitious companies, disbursed loan proceeds to personally established accounts, and then let the loans go into default. Some pertinent facts about the loan officer include

   •  A high standard of living, explained as the result of sound investments and not taking vacations

- An expensive personal car obtained through business contacts
- Gasoline and repair bills submitted for an assigned company car that is higher than company average (mileage logs were submitted on a quarterly basis)
- Marked annoyance with questions from auditors

**70.** In this situation, typical indicators of the suspected fraud would include all of the following **except:**
   a. Not taking an annual vacation.
   b. Becoming easily annoyed with auditor inquiries about questionable loans.
   c. Explaining a high standard of living as the result of investments.
   d. Submitting gasoline and repair bills that are higher than company average.

**71.** The most appropriate trend analysis to indicate this potential fraud is
   a. Loan default rates by loan officer.
   b. Accumulation of unpaid vacation days.
   c. Automobile operating expenses by loan officer.
   d. Total dollar volume of loans by loan officer.

**72.** The extent of loans made to fictitious borrowers by the loan officer could **best** be determined by
   a. Reviewing a representative sample of the loan officer's transactions for compliance with bank policies and procedures.
   b. Reviewing a representative sample of loan files for properly completed documents, such as loan agreements, credit approvals, and approval of secured collateral.
   c. Comparing current loan approval balances with those of prior years.
   d. Requesting positive confirmations for all outstanding loans made by the loan officer.

**73.** The above fraud would **least** likely be discovered by
   a. Analyses of the number of loans made by each loan officer.
   b. Analysis of total dollar volume of loans by loan officer.
   c. External or internal audits of loan files.
   d. Reconciliation of total loans outstanding to the general ledger balance.

**74.** Which of the following policies is most likely to result in an environment conducive to the occurrence of fraud?
   a. Budget preparation input by the employees who are responsible for meeting the budget.
   b. Unreasonable sales and production goals.
   c. The division's hiring process frequently results in the rejection of adequately trained applicants.
   d. The application of some accounting controls on a sample basis.

**75.** Internal auditors must exercise due care if they are to meet their responsibilities for fraud detection. Thus, the existence of certain conditions should raise red flags and arouse auditors' professional skepticism concerning possible fraud. Which of the following is **most likely** to be considered an indication of possible fraud?
   a. A new management team installed as the result of a takeover.
   b. Rapid turnover of financial executives.

   c. Rapid expansion into new markets.
   d. An Internal Revenue Service audit of tax returns.

**76.** In order for internal auditors to be able to recognize potential fraud, they must be aware of the basic characteristics of fraud. Which of the following is **not** a characteristic of fraud?
   a. Intentional deception.
   b. Taking unfair or dishonest advantage.
   c. Perpetration for the benefit or detriment of the organization.
   d. Negligence on the part of executive management.

**77.** Auditors have been advised to look at red flags to determine whether management is involved in a fraud. Which of the following does **not** represent a difficulty in using the red flags as fraud indicators?
   a. Many common red flags are also associated with situations where no fraud exists.
   b. Some red flags are difficult to quantify or to evaluate.
   c. Red flag information is not gathered as a normal part of an audit engagement.
   d. The red flags literature is not well enough established to have a positive impact on auditing.

**Items 78 through 80** are based on the following:

Management of a nonprofit organization has been monitoring spending and is concerned because payments to some vendors appear to be unusually high. Most purchases are made through the purchasing function, which is organized around three buyers, each with defined purchasing areas. The purchasing agents place the purchase orders and receive copies of receiving reports to ensure goods are received. They review the reports and compare them with the purchase orders before sending the items to accounts payable with their approval for payment. All vendor invoices are sent directly to accounts payable even though receiving reports first go through the purchasing agents. The organization has a policy of requiring three bids on all purchases that exceed $10,000.

**78.** Which of the following, if observed, would **not** indicate the need to search for other indicators of fraud?
   a. The standard of living of one of the purchasing agents has increased.
   b. The internal control structure has significant weaknesses.
   c. Management, at the purchasing agents' request, has adopted a policy of paying vendors on a more timely basis to avoid incurring penalty charges.
   d. The cost of goods procured seems to be excessive in comparison with previous years.

**79.** Which of the following statements regarding the internal auditor's responsibility for detecting fraud in the environment described in the scenario above is **not** correct? The auditor should
   a. Detect fraud if red flags are present in the environment.
   b. Have sufficient knowledge to correctly identify indicators that fraud may have been committed.
   c. Identify control weaknesses that could allow fraud to occur.
   d. Evaluate the indicators of fraud sufficiently to determine if a fraud investigation should take place.

**80.** Management has requested that the auditor investigate the possibility of kickbacks going to a purchasing agent. Which of the following procedures would be **least** effective in addressing management's concern?
a. Confirm all contract terms with vendors.
b. Analyze, by purchasing agent, all increases in cost of procured goods from specific vendors.
c. Take a statistical sample of goods purchased and compare purchase prices for goods with those of other sources of similar goods, such as other companies or catalogs.
d. Observe any changes in the lifestyles or individual consumption habits of the purchasing agents involved.

**Items 81 through 83** are based on the following:

An auditor is investigating the performance of a division with an unusually large increase in sales, gross margin, and profit.

**81.** Which of the following indicators is **least** likely to indicate the possibility of sales-related fraud in the division?
a. A significant portion of divisional management compensation is based on reported divisional profits.
b. There is an unusually large amount of sales returns recorded after year-end.
c. The auditor has taken a random sample of sales invoices, but cannot locate a shipping document for a number of the sales transactions selected for November and December.
d. One of the division's major competitors went out of business during the year.

**82.** If the auditor continued to suspect fraudulent recording of transactions to increase reported profits, which of the following audit procedures would be **least effective**?
a. Take a physical inventory.
b. Develop a schedule of inventory by month and investigate unusual fluctuations by reference to the perpetual inventory records.
c. Prepare a schedule of sales fluctuations and gross margin by month. Investigate unusually high months of sales and gross margin by examining support for sales.
d. Perform year-end sales and purchase cutoff tests.

**83.** Without prejudice to answers on the previous question, assume that the analysis shows unusually high sales and gross margin during the months of November and December and the auditor wishes to investigate further. Which of the following audit procedures would be **most effective** in analyzing whether fraudulent sales may have been recorded?
a. Take a sample of shipping documents and trace to related sales invoice, noting that all items were properly billed.
b. Confirm accounts receivable with large customers.
c. Perform an analytical review comparing sales and gross margin with the previous 10 months and the first month of the following year.
d. Use regression analysis techniques for the first 10 months to estimate the sales and cost of goods sold for the last 2 months.

**Items 84 through 87** are based on the following:

The internal auditing department has been assigned to perform an audit of a division. Based on background review, the auditor knows the following about management policies:

- Company policy is to rapidly promote divisional managers who show significant success. Thus, successful managers rarely stay at a division for more than three years.
- A significant portion of division management's compensation comes in the form of bonuses based on the division's profitability.

The division was identified by senior management as a turnaround opportunity. The division is growing, but is not scheduled for a full audit by the external auditors this year. The division has been growing about 7% per year for the past three years and uses a standard cost system.

During the preliminary review, the auditor notes the following changes in financial data compared to the prior year:

- Sales have increased by 10%.
- Cost of goods sold has increased by 2%.
- Inventory has increased by 15%.
- Divisional net income has increased by 8%.

**84.** Which of the following items might alert the auditor to the possibility of fraud in the division?
a. The division is not scheduled for an external audit this year.
b. Sales have increased by 10%.
c. A significant portion of management's compensation is directly tied to reported net income of the division.
d. All of the above.

**85.** It is November and the audit manager is finalizing plans for a year-end audit of the division. Based on the above data, the audit procedure with highest priority would be to
a. Select sales transactions and trace shipping documents to entries into cost of goods sold to determine if all shipments were recorded.
b. Schedule a complete count of inventory at year-end and have the auditor observe and test the year-end inventory.
c. Schedule a complete investigation of the standard cost system by preparing cost buildups of a sample of products.
d. Schedule a year-end sales cutoff test.

**86.** If the auditor decides there are significant problems with the standard cost system, the next audit step to perform would be to
a. Interview divisional management to determine why the standard cost system has not been updated on a timely basis.
b. Select a random sample of products and review the standard cost buildup by tracing purchases to the standard cost record.
c. Use generalized audit software to prepare a listing of gross margin by product by comparing standard cost with sales price. Select all high-gross-margin items for further investigation.

d. Schedule all variances and determine their source and their disposition, that is, whether they are allocated to inventory or cost of goods sold.

**87.** Assume the auditor found that there was a plan to overstate inventory and therefore increase reported profits for the division. If reported correctly, the division would not have shown an increase in net income. The auditor has substantial evidence that the divisional manager was aware of and approved the plan to overstate inventory. There is also some evidence that the manager may have been responsible for the implementation of the plan. The appropriate audit action would be to

a. Continue to conduct interviews with subordinates until a clear-cut case is made. Then report the case to the audit committee.

b. Inform management and the audit committee of the findings and discuss proper follow-up action and/or further investigation with them.

c. Inform the divisional manager of the audit suspicions and obtain the manager's explanation of the findings before pursuing the matter further.

d. Document the case thoroughly and report the suspicions to the external auditor for further review and external reporting.

**88.** The following are facts about a subsidiary:

I. The subsidiary company has been in business for several years and enjoyed good profit margins although the general economy was in a recession, which affected competitors.

II. The working capital ratio had declined from a healthy 3:1 to 0.9:1.

III. Turnover for the last several years has included three controllers, two supervisors of accounts receivable, four payables supervisors, and numerous staff in other financial positions.

IV. Corporate purchasing policy requires three bids. However, the supervisor of purchasing at the subsidiary has instituted a policy of sole-source procurement to reduce the number of suppliers.

When conducting a financial audit of the subsidiary, the internal auditor would

a. Be unlikely to detect I, II, or III.

b. Ignore II since the economy had a downturn during this period.

c. Consider III to be normal turnover, but be concerned about II and IV as warning signals of fraud.

d. Consider I, II, III, and IV as warning signals of fraud.

**89.** When comparing perpetrators who have embezzled company funds to perpetrators of financial statement fraud (falsified financial statements), those who have falsified financial statements would be **less likely** to

a. Have experienced an autocratic management style.

b. Be living beyond their obvious means of support.

c. Rationalize the fraudulent behavior.

d. Use company expectations as justification for the act.

**Items 90 through 96** are based on the following:

Randy and John had known each other for many years. They had become best friends in college, where they both majored in accounting. After graduation, Randy took over the family business from his father. His family had been in the grocery business for several generations. When John had difficulty finding a job, Randy offered him a job in the family store. John proved to be a very capable employee. As John demonstrated his abilities, Randy began delegating more and more responsibility to him. After a period of time, John was doing all of the general accounting and authorization functions for checks, cash, inventories, documents, records, and bank statement reconciliations. (I) *John was trusted completely and handled all financial functions.* No one checked his work.

Randy decided to expand the business and opened several new stores. (II) *Randy was always handling the most urgent problem . . . crisis management is what his college professors had termed it.* John assisted with the problems when his other duties allowed him time. Although successful at work, John had (III) *difficulties with personal financial problems.*

At first, the amounts stolen by John were small. John did not even worry about making the accounts balance. But he became greedy. "How easy it is to take the money," he said. He felt that he was a critical member of the business team, (IV) *and that he contributed much more to the success of the company than was represented by his salary.* It would take two or three people to replace me, he often thought to himself. As the amounts became larger and larger, (V) *he made the books balance.* Because of these activities, John was able to purchase an expensive car and take his family on several trips each year. (VI) *He also joined an expensive country club.* Things were changing at home, however. (VII) *John's family observed that he was often argumentative and at other times very depressed.*

The fraud continued for six years. Each year the business performed more and more poorly. In the last year the stores lost over $200,000. Randy's bank required an audit. John confessed when he thought the auditors had discovered his embezzlements. When discussing frauds, the pressures, opportunities, and rationalizations that cause/allow a perpetrator to commit the fraud are often identified. Symptoms of fraud are also studied.

Identify the numbered and italicized factors (from the case) as being one of the symptoms, pressures, opportunities, or rationalizations given.

**90.** Number I, "John was trusted completely . . . " is an example of a(n)

a. Document symptom.

b. Situational pressure.

c. Opportunity to commit.

d. Physical symptom.

**91.** Number II, "Randy was always handling the most urgent . . . " is an example of a(n)

a. Opportunity to commit.

b. Analytical symptom.

c. Situational pressure.

d. Rationalization.

**92.** Number III; "Difficulties with personal financial problems" is an example of a(n)

a. Behavioral symptom.

b. Situational pressure.

c. Rationalization.

d. Opportunity to commit.

**93.** Number IV, "and that he contributed much more . . . " is an example of a
   a.   Rationalization.
   b.   Behavioral symptom.
   c.   Situational pressure.
   d.   Physical symptom.

**94.** Number V, "he made the books balance," is an example of a(n)
   a.   Physical symptom.
   b.   Analytical symptom.
   c.   Lifestyle symptom.
   d.   Document symptom.

**95.** Number VI, "He also joined an expensive country club," is an example of a
   a.   Rationalization.
   b.   Lifestyle symptom.
   c.   Behavioral symptom.
   d.   Physical symptom.

**96.** Number VII, "John's family observed that he was often argumentative . . . " is an example of a
   a.   Rationalization.
   b.   Lifestyle symptom.
   c.   Behavioral symptom.
   d.   Physical symptom.

**97.** An internal auditor would be concerned about the possibility of fraud if
   a.   Cash receipts, net of the amounts used to pay petty cash-type expenditures, are deposited in the bank daily.
   b.   The same employee who maintains the perpetual inventory records performs the monthly bank statement reconciliation.
   c.   The same person maintains the accounts receivable subsidiary ledger and accounts payable subsidiary ledger.
   d.   One person, acting alone, has sole access to the petty cash fund (except for a provision for occasional surprise counts by a supervisor or auditor).

**Items 98 and 99** are based on the following:

   When following up on a $200,000 increase in maintenance supplies during the past year, a purchasing agent explained to the auditor that the main reason for the increase was painting services and supplies. The auditor found a blanket purchase order without the normal bid or quote documentation. The blanket purchase order had been signed by the general manager and named the general manager's father as the sole contractor for painting services on company projects. The auditor also found a number of large invoices authorized for payment by the general manager that showed the general manager's father as the person who signed for receipt of the material at the supplier.

**98.** Which is not a symptom of fraud as described in this situation?
   a.   Purchased material is not received by authorized company personnel.
   b.   Routine controls are suspended for certain transactions.
   c.   Purchased material is not delivered to a central location on company premises.
   d.   The use of blanket purchase orders.

**99.** The common indicator of fraud recognized by the auditor in this scenario is
   a.   Analytical procedures revealed an extraordinary increase in account balances.
   b.   Paint and supplies are being purchased for a contractor.
   c.   The purchasing agent is selecting the contractor on the basis of a blanket purchase order.
   d.   Invoices are being authorized for payment by the general manager.

**Items 100 and 101** are based on the following:

   Jane Jackson had been the regional sales manager for a company over ten years. During this time she had become a very close friend with Frank Hansen, an internal audit manager. In addition to being neighbors, Jane and Frank had many of the same interests and belonged to the same tennis club. They trusted each other. Frank had helped Jane solve some sales problems, and Jane had given Frank some information that led to significant audit findings during the past three audits.

   Below are selected analytical data from the company that have led staff auditors to believe that there has been a financial statement fraud. The perpetrator appears to have falsified sales information for the past two years. Frank is concerned because he recently completed an audit in the area and accepted Jane's explanation for differences in the analytical data. Frank is now certain that Jane is involved in the fraud.

**100.** Which combination of the following analytical data provides the strongest indication of the possibility of the fraud?

|  | Current year | Last year | -2 year | -3 year | -4 year |
|---|---|---|---|---|---|
| Percent increase in sales | 10% | 8% | 6% | 4% | 5% |
| Inventory turnover | 5 | 4 | 5 | 3.5 | 4 |
| Gross margin percentage | 54 | 49 | 42 | 39 | 40 |
| Percent change in sales returns | 8% | 6% | 3% | 2.5% | 3% |

   a.   Percent increase in sales **and** inventory turnover.
   b.   Gross margin percentage **and** change in sales returns.
   c.   Inventory turnover **and** change in sales returns.
   d.   Percent increase in sales **and** gross margin percentage.

**101.** The current dilemma in which Frank finds himself was **least** likely caused by
   a.   Not rotating audit assignments every year.
   b.   Accepting an audit assignment in an area where he was a close personal friend of management.
   c.   Failure to select the appropriate analytical procedures.
   d.   Accepting the response of management without additional audit testing.

## MULTIPLE-CHOICE ANSWERS AND EXPLANATIONS

| | | | | | | | | | | | |
|---|---|---|---|---|---|---|---|---|---|---|---|
| 1. b | __ __ | 20. a | __ __ | 39. a | __ __ | 58. d | __ __ | 77. d | __ __ | 96. c | __ __ |
| 2. b | __ __ | 21. c | __ __ | 40. c | __ __ | 59. d | __ __ | 78. c | __ __ | 97. a | __ __ |
| 3. b | __ __ | 22. d | __ __ | 41. c | __ __ | 60. b | __ __ | 79. a | __ __ | 98. d | __ __ |
| 4. c | __ __ | 23. a | __ __ | 42. a | __ __ | 61. c | __ __ | 80. a | __ __ | 99. a | __ __ |
| 5. d | __ __ | 24. a | __ __ | 43. b | __ __ | 62. a | __ __ | 81. d | __ __ | 100. b | __ __ |
| 6. b | __ __ | 25. d | __ __ | 44. a | __ __ | 63. d | __ __ | 82. b | __ __ | 101. c | __ __ |
| 7. b | __ __ | 26. c | __ __ | 45. a | __ __ | 64. c | __ __ | 83. b | __ __ | | |
| 8. b | __ __ | 27. a | __ __ | 46. d | __ __ | 65. b | __ __ | 84. c | __ __ | | |
| 9. d | __ __ | 28. d | __ __ | 47. a | __ __ | 66. d | __ __ | 85. b | __ __ | | |
| 10. d | __ __ | 29. b | __ __ | 48. b | __ __ | 67. a | __ __ | 86. d | __ __ | | |
| 11. c | __ __ | 30. a | __ __ | 49. a | __ __ | 68. c | __ __ | 87. b | __ __ | | |
| 11. a | __ __ | 31. d | __ __ | 50. c | __ __ | 69. d | __ __ | 88. d | __ __ | | |
| 13. c | __ __ | 32. b | __ __ | 51. b | __ __ | 70. d | __ __ | 89. b | __ __ | | |
| 14. c | __ __ | 33. d | __ __ | 52. d | __ __ | 71. a | __ __ | 90. c | __ __ | | |
| 15. b | __ __ | 34. d | __ __ | 53. c | __ __ | 72. b | __ __ | 91. a | __ __ | | |
| 16. c | __ __ | 35. c | __ __ | 54. d | __ __ | 73. d | __ __ | 92. b | __ __ | | |
| 17. b | __ __ | 36. a | __ __ | 55. b | __ __ | 74. b | __ __ | 93. a | __ __ | | |
| 18. b | __ __ | 37. d | __ __ | 56. d | __ __ | 75. b | __ __ | 94. d | __ __ | 1st: __/101 = __% |
| 19. b | __ __ | 38. c | __ __ | 57. a | __ __ | 76. d | __ __ | 95. b | __ __ | 2nd: __/101 = __% |

**1.** **(b)** Discovery sampling is structured to measure the probability of at least one exception occurring in a sample if there are a minimum number of errors in the population. Choice (a) is incorrect. Random sampling deals only with the technique used to choose the sample. Choice (c) is incorrect. Probability-proportional-to-size (PPS) sampling deals with the technique used to select items but does not apply when attempting to discover critical occurrences. Choice (d) is incorrect. Variables sampling need not include at least one exception of a critical occurrence.

Subject Area: Fraud knowledge elements—discovery sampling. Source: CIA 597, II-46.

**2.** **(b)** Discovery sampling is best because this application deals with an attribute that is expected to be quite rare. Choice (a) is incorrect. Attributes sampling is too broad. Choice (c) is incorrect. Targeted sampling is a nonsense term. Choice (d) is incorrect. Variables sampling deals with monetary amounts.

Subject Area: Fraud knowledge elements—discovery sampling. Source: CIA 1195, II-48.

**3.** **(b)** Choice (b) involves identifying characteristics that could include "discovering" single instances of suspected special characteristics (irregularities). Choice (a) is incorrect. It involves discontinuing the sampling when a target error rate is achieved. Choice (c) is incorrect. It involves reducing sample size by separating the population into groups of items with similar values. Choice (d) is incorrect. It involves identifying characteristics of the sample and projecting those to the population.

Subject Area: Fraud knowledge elements—discovery sampling. Source: CIA 596, II-50.

**4.** **(c)** The purpose here is to determine whether any fraud has taken place, rather than to estimate its overall frequency. Discovery sampling is a method designed specifically to do this. Choice (a) is incorrect. This approach would be appropriate if the extent of fraud were to be estimated. Choice (b) is incorrect. This approach would be appropriate if the monetary value of fraud were to be estimated. Choice (d) is incorrect. It would be difficult to determine what an adequate

sample would be in this case, but a more important issue is restricting the population considered to the vouchers processed by workers that the department manager considers suspicious. This presents a significant potential for biasing the sample because of the potential conflict of interest of the department manager.

Subject Area: Fraud knowledge elements—discovery sampling. Source: CIA 1195, II-28.

**5.** **(d)** Discovery sampling is most often interested in the occurrence of fraud. It efficiently defines a sampling effort that will have a specified probability of containing at least one occurrence of the attribute within the population, given that it is expected to occur at a certain rate. Choice (a) is incorrect. Attribute sampling could work, but it would not be as efficient as discovery sampling. Choice (b) is incorrect. Judgment sampling cannot provide the needed statistical assurance. Choice (c) is incorrect. Directed sampling focuses on certain transactions or locations that are likely to contain errors. Its use is not indicated.

Subject Area: Fraud knowledge elements—discovery sampling. Source: CIA 1193, II-39.

**6.** **(b)** Discovery sampling is appropriate when a near-zero error rate is expected and the characteristic under scrutiny is critical. Choice (a) is incorrect. Attributes sampling implies a fixed sample size and a need to project a sample occurrence rate. Choice (c) is incorrect. Sampling for attributes not a variable. Choice (d) is incorrect. It is not in accord with the audit objective.

Subject Area: Fraud knowledge elements—discovery sampling. Source: CIA 593, I-34.

**7.** **(b)** If no exceptions are found, the correct conclusion is that the occurrence rate is less than the critical rate at a given probability level. Choice (a) is incorrect. There is a 95% probability that the actual rate of occurrence is equal to or greater than the critical rate if one exception is found. Choice (c) is incorrect. There is a 95% probability that the actual rate is equal to or exceeds the critical rate if any exceptions are found. Choice (d) is incorrect. The probability does not increase because no exceptions were found.

Subject Area: Fraud knowledge elements—discovery sampling. Source: CIA 1191, I-37.

**8.   (b)**   Discovery sampling is used when the internal auditor suspects a rare but material error or fraud. The plan seeks to select a sample just large enough to include one example of the error or irregularity a specified percentage of the time. Choice (a) is incorrect. Attribute sampling is for normal compliance testing. It is not used when very, very few errors are expected. Choice (c) is incorrect. Stop-and-go is a form of attribute sampling. Choice (d) is incorrect. Probability-proportional-to-size (monetary-unit) sampling is used for substantive testing. It allows the verification of values whose range lies between positive and negative infinity.

Subject Area: Fraud knowledge elements—discovery sampling. Source: CIA 592, II-41.

**9.   (d)**   Data diddling involves changing data before or during input to computers or during output from a computer system.

Subject Area: Fraud knowledge elements—use of computers in analyzing data. Source: Author.

**10.   (d)**   A salami technique is a theft of small amounts of assets and money from a number of sources (e.g., bank accounts, inventory accounts, and accounts payable and receivable accounts). It is also using the "rounding-down" concept, where a fraction of money is taken from bank accounts.

Subject Area: Fraud knowledge elements—use of computers in analyzing data. Source: Author.

**11.   (c)**   Data diddling can be prevented by limiting access to data and programs and limiting the methods used to perform modification to such data and programs. Integrity checking also helps in prevention. Rapid detection is needed—the sooner the better—because correcting data diddling is expensive.

Subject Area: Fraud knowledge elements—use of computers in analyzing data. Source: Author.

**12.   (a)**   Superzapping leaves no evidence of file changes, and the only reliable way to detect this activity is by comparing current data files with previous generations of the same file. Computer usage logs (choice b.) may not capture superzapping activity. Users may not detect changes in their reports (choice c.). It is very difficult to find, let alone review, the undocumented transactions (choice d.). Even if these transactions are found, there is no assurance that the task is complete.

Subject Area: Fraud knowledge elements—use of computers in analyzing data. Source: Author.

**13.   (c)**   Courts do not expect organizations to spend more money than losses resulting from a security flaw, threat, risk, or vulnerability. Implementing countermeasures and safeguards to protect information system assets cost money. Losses can result from risks, that is, exploitation of vulnerabilities. When estimated costs are less than estimated losses, then a legal liability exists. Courts can argue that the organization's management should have installed safeguards but did not and that management did not exercise due care and due diligence. Choice (a) poses no legal liability because costs are greater than losses. Choice (b) requires judgment and qualitative considerations because costs are equal to losses. Choice (d) is not applicable because actual costs and losses are not known at the time of implementing safeguards.

Subject Area: Fraud knowledge elements—use of computers in analyzing data. Source: Author.

**14.   (c)**   An investigator's handwritten notes are considered valid evidence as long as the affected parties can read and understood the notes. Handwritten notes are no different from typed or printed versions.

Subject Area: Fraud knowledge elements—interrogation techniques. Source: Author.

**15.   (b)**   Chain of custody is required when evidence is collected and handled so that there is no dispute about it.

Subject Area: Fraud knowledge elements—evidence. Source: Author.

**16.   (c)**   If a system perpetrator can be delayed longer while attacking a computer system, investigative authorities can trace his or her origins and location. Choices (a), (b), and (d) would not allow such a trap.

Subject Area: Fraud knowledge elements—interrogation techniques. Source: Author.

**17.   (b)**   Documentary evidence is created information, such as letters, contracts, accounting records, invoices, and management information reports on performance and production. Legal evidence is a broad term, and is not be useful here. Secondary evidence is any evidence offered to prove the writing other than the writing itself and is a part of the best evidence rule. The best evidence is original. Admissible evidence is evidence that is revealed to the jury or other trier of fact with express or implied permission to use it in deciding disputed issues of fact.

Subject Area: Fraud knowledge elements—evidence. Source: Author.

**18.   (b)**   Direct inspection or observation of people, property, or events obtains physical evidence. Duplicate evidence is a document that is produced by some mechanical process that makes it more reliable evidence of the contents of the original than other forms of secondary evidence (e.g., a photocopy of the original). Modern statutes make duplicates easily substitutable for an original. Duplicate evidence is a part of the best evidence rule. Best evidence is evidence that is the most natural and reliable. The best evidence is primary. Collateral evidence is evidence relevant only to some evidential fact and that is not by itself relevant to a consequential fact.

Subject Area: Fraud knowledge elements—evidence. Source: Author.

**19.   (b)**   Courts will find computer owners responsible for their insecure systems. Courts will not find liability every time a computer is hijacked. Rather, courts will expect organizations to become reasonably prudent computer owners taking due care (reasonable care) to ensure adequate security. The term "due care" means having the right policies and procedures, access controls, firewalls, and other reasonable security measures in place. Computer owners need not take super care, great care, or extraordinary care.

Subject Area: Fraud knowledge elements—evidence. Source: Author.

**20.   (a)**   It is the intentions of the developer of a computer virus program that matter the most in deciding what is a criminal activity. Simply writing a virus program is not a criminal activity. However, using, releasing, and spreading a virus with bad intentions of destroying computer resources are the basis for criminal activity.

Subject Area: Fraud knowledge elements—evidence. Source: Author.

**21.** **(c)** The chain of custody or the chain of evidence is a method of authenticating an object by the testimony of witnesses who can trace possession of the object from hand to hand and from the beginning to the end. The term "chain of command" choice (a) refers to relationships between a superior and a subordinate in a workplace setting. Both the chain of control, choice (b), and communications, choice (d), are distracters.

Subject Area: Fraud knowledge elements—evidence.
Source: Author.

**22.** **(d)** Laying a proper foundation for evidence is "the practice or requirement of introducing evidence of things necessary to make further evidence relevant, material, or competent." Sufficiency is not part of the concept of admissibility of evidence. Relevant evidence is evidence that had some logical tendency to prove or disprove a disputed consequential fact. Competent evidence (i.e., admissible evidence) is evidence that satisfied all the rules of evidence except those dealing with relevance. Materiality is the notion that evidence must be relevant to a fact that is in dispute between the parties.

Subject Area: Fraud knowledge elements—evidence.
Source: Author.

**23.** **(a)** The chain of custody deals with who collected, stored, and controlled the evidence and does not ask who damaged the evidence. It looks at the positive side of the evidence. If the evidence is damaged, there is nothing to show in the court.

Subject Area: Fraud knowledge elements—evidence.
Source: Author.

**24.** **(a)** Best evidence is primary evidence, which is the most natural evidence. Best evidence gives the most satisfactory proof of the fact under investigation. It is confined to documents, records, and papers. A recommendation for cases with a large volume of evidence is to assemble a single exhibit book containing all documents, send copies to the defense and to the judge, and introduce it as a single exhibit in court. This saves time in court. Also, prepare a record of exhibits, the counts each is connected with, and the names of the witnesses who are to testify as to each item. Both flowchart evidence and magnetic tape evidence are proper. Demonstrative evidence or visual aids can be real things (i.e., a gun of the same type used in a homicide) or representation of real things (i.e., a photograph or map).

Subject Area: Fraud knowledge elements—evidence.
Source: Author.

**25.** **(d)** Proper elements of proof and correct types of evidence are needed to prove a case.

Subject Area: Fraud knowledge elements—evidence.
Source: Author.

**26.** **(c)** A computer crime is committed when the allegation is substantiated with proper evidence that is relevant, competent, and material.

Subject Area: Fraud knowledge elements—evidence.
Source: Author.

**27.** **(a)** Step 1 is substantiating the allegation. Step 2 is consulting with a computer expert, as appropriate. Step 3 is preparing an investigation plan that sets forth the scope of the investigation and serves as a guide in determining how much technical assistance will be needed. Step 4 is consulting with a prosecutor, depending on the nature of the allegation and scope of the investigation. Items to discuss with the prosecutor may include the elements of proof, evidence required, and parameters of a prospective search.

Subject Area: Fraud knowledge elements—investigation.
Source: Author.

**28.** **(d)** A team approach is desirable when a computer-related crime case is a complex one. Each person has a definite and different role and brings varied capabilities to the team approach. Both the internal system auditor's and the security officer's objectives are the same since they work for the same organization. The objectives are to understand system vulnerabilities, to strengthen security controls, and to support the investigation. A district attorney's role is to prove the case while the objective of the investigator is to gather facts.

Subject Area: Fraud knowledge elements—investigation.
Source: Author.

**29.** **(b)** Once the allegation has been substantiated, the prosecutor should be contacted to determine if there is probable cause for a search. Because of the technical orientation of a computer-related crime investigation, presenting a proper technical perspective in establishing probable cause becomes crucial to securing a search warrant.

Subject Area: Fraud knowledge elements—investigation.
Source: Author.

**30.** **(a)** Discovery and recognition is one of the seven considerations involved in the care and handling of evidence. It is the investigator's capability to discover and to recognize the potential source of evidence. When a computer is involved, the evidence is probably not apparent or visible. Nevertheless, the investigator must recognize that computer storage devices are nothing more than electronic or magnetic file cabinets and should be searched if it would normally be reasonable to search an ordinary file cabinet. The evidence is highly volatile, that is, subject to change.

Subject Area: Fraud knowledge elements—investigation.
Source: Author.

**31.** **(d)** It is proper to maintain computer-related evidence. Special procedures are needed to avoid problems of proof caused by improper care and handling of such evidence.

Subject Area: Fraud knowledge elements—investigation.
Source: Author.

**32.** **(b)** If a computer or peripheral equipment involved in a computer crime is not covered by a search warrant, leave it alone until a warrant can be obtained. The point is that a warrant is required for anything to be collected by the investigator.

Subject Area: Fraud knowledge elements—investigation.
Source: Author.

**33.** **(d)** After all equipment and magnetic media have been labeled and inventoried, seal and store each item in a paper bag or cardboard box to keep out dust. An additional label should be attached to the bag identifying its contents and noting any identifying numbers, such as the number of the evidence tag. Do not use plastic bags or sandwich bags to store any piece of computer equipment and/or magnetic storage media, since plastic material can cause both static electricity and condensation, which can damage electronically stored data and sensitive electronic components.

Subject Area: Fraud knowledge elements—investigation.
Source: Author.

**34.** **(d)** Relevant evidence is essential for a successful computer fraud examination. For example, data usage and access control security logs will identify (1) who has accessed the computer, (2) what information was accessed, (3) where the computer was accessed, and (4) how long the access lasted. These logs can be manually or computer maintained; the latter method is more timely and reliable than the former method. Physical examination—choice (a)—and physical observation—choice (b)—may not be possible in a computer environment due to automated records. Inquiries of people choice (c)—may not give in-depth answers due to their lack of specific knowledge about how a computer system works.

Subject Area: Fraud knowledge elements—evidence. Source: Author.

**35.** **(c)** A forensic methodology is a process for the analysis of electronically stored data. The process must be completely documented to ensure that the integrity of the evidence is not questioned in court. The forensic methodology deals with technical evidence. The audit methodology deals with reviewing business transactions and systems and reaching an opinion by an auditor. The phrases system methodology and criminal methodology are too vague; they have many meanings.

Subject Area: Fraud knowledge elements—forensic auditing. Source: Author.

**36.** **(a)** The first stage is preparing a report documenting what was done and the results obtained. The second stage is sending printouts and reports to the contributor or subject matter expert for additional analysis. The third stage is repacking the computer and all magnetic disks. The final stage is returning the evidence to the contributor.

Subject Area: Fraud knowledge elements—evidence. Source: Author.

**37.** **(d)** Computers can be used to collect and compile large amounts of data and provide statistics, reports, and graphs to assist the investigator in analysis and decision making. Forensic analysis is the art of retrieving computer data in such a way that will make it admissible in court.

Subject Area: Fraud knowledge elements—evidence. Source: Author.

**38.** **(c)** Forensic analysis is the art of retrieving computer data in such a way that will make it admissible in court. Exposing magnetic media to magnetic fields, such as radio waves, may alter or destroy data. Do not carry magnetic media in the trunk of a vehicle containing a radio unit, and do not lay magnetic media on top of any electronic equipment.

Subject Area: Fraud knowledge elements—forensic auditing. Source: Author.

**39.** **(a)** Situational pressures (e.g., gambling, drugs), opportunities to commit fraud (e.g., weak system of controls), and personal characteristics (e.g., lack of integrity, honesty) are major causes of fraud, whether computer-related or not. There is nothing new about the act of committing fraud. There is no new way to commit fraud because someone has already tried it somewhere. Choices (b), (c), and (d) encourage computer fraud whereas choice (a) discourages it. Willingness to prosecute sends a strong message to the potential perpetrators.

Subject Area: Fraud knowledge elements—computer-related crime and fraud. Source: Author.

**40.** **(c)** Scavenging fits the description. Choice (a) is incorrect. Data diddling involves changing data before or during input to computers or during output from a computer system. Choice (b) is incorrect. The salami technique is a theft of small amounts of assets (primarily money) from a number of sources. Choice (d) is incorrect. Piggybacking can be done physically and electronically. Both involve gaining access to a controlled area without authorization.

Subject Area: Fraud knowledge elements—computer-related crime and fraud. Source: Author.

**41.** **(c)** Audit trails indicate what actions are taken by the system. The fact that the system has adequate and clear audit trails will deter fraud perpetrators because they fear getting caught. There is no direct correlation between computer fraud and the other three things indicated in the three choices.

Subject Area: Fraud knowledge elements—computer-related crime and fraud. Source: Author.

**42.** **(a)** The recognition and questioning of change is critical to the detection of fraud. Choice (b) is incorrect. Interrogation of fraud perpetrators occurs after detection. Choice (c) is incorrect. The controls mentioned are preventive, not detective. Choice (d) is incorrect. Documentation of operating systems is not within the scope of internal auditing, and would do little to enhance fraud detection skills.

Subject Area: Fraud knowledge elements—types of fraud and red flags. Source: CIA 594, I-13.

**43.** **(b)** These are the two overall categories or types of fraud given in the IIA *Standards*. Choice (a) is incorrect. These are examples of kinds of fraud within the two general categories or types given in the *Standards*. Choice (c) is incorrect. These are examples of kinds of fraud within the two general categories or types given in the *Standards*. Choice (d) is incorrect. These are examples of kinds of fraud within the two general categories or types given in the *Standards*.

Subject Area: Fraud knowledge elements—types of fraud and red flags. Source: CIA 1191, I-50.

**44.** **(a)** This practice might give some leads to previous shortcomings. Choice (b) is incorrect. Individuals in their declining years may be forced to accept jobs below their full capabilities. Choice (c) is incorrect. This does not include checking prior employment. Choice (d) is incorrect. This is not an adequate control in this scenario.

Subject Area: Fraud knowledge elements—types of fraud and red flags. Source: CIA 591, I-48.

**45.** **(a)** This is an acceptable control procedure aimed at limiting risk while promoting efficiency. It is not, by itself, considered a red flag. Choice (b) is incorrect. Lack of rotation of duties or cross-training for sensitive jobs is one of the red-flag list factors. Choice (c) is incorrect. This would be an example of an inappropriate segregation of duties, which is an identified red flag. Choice (d) is incorrect. This is an identified red flag.

Subject Area: Fraud knowledge elements—types of fraud and red flags. Source: CIA 597, I-53.

**46.** **(d)** This would be the least important control procedure. The analyst is responsible for communicating the nature of the design to the programmer. There is no control reason not to combine these functions. Choice (a) is incorrect. This is one of the elements of good program change control. Choice (b) is incorrect. Testing of new applications by users is one of the most important controls to help prevent computer fraud. Choice (c) is incorrect. An adequate control structure over program changes is one of the most important control procedures in a computerized environment.

Subject Area: Fraud knowledge elements—types of fraud and red flags. Source: CIA 595, I-48.

**47. (a)** The auditor cannot knowingly be a party to any illegal act. If the auditor does not do anything, he or she might be perceived as a party. The auditor should report the problem directly to the audit committee and await its decision as to further action to be taken. Choice (b) is incorrect. Although the action recommended is necessary to ultimately disassociate the auditor from the fraud, alternatives within the organization should be pursued first. That alternative is represented in response (a). Choice (c) is incorrect. Doing nothing is not acceptable. The auditor could be perceived as a party to the fraud if no action is taken. Choice (d) is incorrect. The auditor is not required to report the finding to the external auditor, but should be free to communicate the problem if the external auditor makes an inquiry.

Subject Area: Fraud knowledge elements—types of fraud and red flags. Source: CIA 595, I-59.

**48. (b)** Red flags are associated with fraudulent conduct. However, many red flags are personal in nature and would not necessarily come to the attention of the auditor. These would include items such as excessive living style by a manager, excessive gambling, and so on. Choice (a) is incorrect. The auditor is to be alert to red flags and should investigate any situations that might include potential fraud. But the auditor is not required to document all personal red flags, for example, excessive gambling debts or excessive living style. The requirement to document these red flags is pertinent only when the auditor continues a fraud investigation or the item is pertinent to a particular audit finding. Choice (c) is incorrect because Item II is not required. Choice (d) is incorrect because item I is also a correct statement.

Subject Area: Fraud knowledge elements—types of fraud and red flags. Source: CIA 595, I-67.

**49. (a)** A programmed computer output notification identifying unusual entries would identify the write off of the payee's account to suspense as an unusual item immediately when it occurs. Choice (b) is incorrect because this is a good control procedure. Choice (c) is incorrect. The annual internal audit may detect the fraud, but it is unlikely to do so because of the small amount involved. In any case the timing of the internal audit may delay discovery. Choice (d) is incorrect. Regular reconciliation of the suspense account would occur at a date later than the computer output notification.

Subject Area: Fraud knowledge elements—types of fraud and red flags. Source: CIA 1194, I-65.

**50. (c)** Fraud hotlines may identify areas where existing internal controls need to be modified or enhanced. Choice (a) is incorrect. Performance measures focus on reducing the total costs of the company as a whole. Choice (b) is incorrect. Responsibility accounting is concerned with measuring how well organizational members are achieving the organization's goals. Choice (d) is incorrect. Management by exception concentrates on areas that deserve attention and places less attention on areas operating as expected.

Subject Area: Fraud knowledge elements—types of fraud and red flags. Source: CIA 595, III-21.

**51. (b)** The accumulation of round-off errors into one person's account is a procedure written into the program. In-

dependent testing of a program will lead to discovery of this programmed fraud. If access to programs was not limited, it would be possible for a programmer to change a program without approval. Choice (a) is incorrect. Reasonableness tests will not overcome this error, since in this particular type of fraud all the amounts will balance. Choice (c) is incorrect. Segregation of duties between systems development and programming would not generally prevent this type of error, since programmers possess the skills required to construct the program. Unless the controls outlined in choice (b) are present, the fraud would go undetected. Choice (d) is incorrect. Since the particular fraud results in a balanced entry, control totals would not detect the fraud.

Subject Area: Fraud knowledge elements—types of fraud and red flags. Source: CIA 1194, I-59.

**52. (d)** All three items are correct statements according to the IIA Standards.

Subject Area: Fraud knowledge elements—types of fraud and red flags. Source: CIA 597, I-58.

**53. (c)** In carrying out its responsibility for the deterrence of fraud, internal auditing should determine whether such written policy statements exist. Choice (a) is incorrect. On a cost/benefit basis, it is entirely reasonable to have more extensive control policies, practices, and procedures in high-risk areas. Choice (b) is incorrect. Even the best of internal control systems can often be circumvented by collusion. Choice (d) is incorrect. Forgeries, like collusion, can circumvent even the best of internal control systems.

Subject Area: Fraud knowledge elements—types of fraud and red flags. Source: CIA 590, II-47.

**54. (d)** Subjecting credit card expenses to the same controls used in processing similar expense reports. In this way, per diems and authorization limits would be reviewed. Choice (a) is incorrect. Establishing a corporate policy on the issuance of credit cards does nothing to prevent fraudulent usage by those authorized to use company cards. Choice (b) is incorrect. This procedure helps ensure the validity of issuance rather than usage within prescribed limitations. Choice (c) is incorrect. Reconciling the monthly statement with the cardholders' charge slips would determine that the amount of the separate charge items and the vendor codes were in agreement. However, amounts charged may exceed authorized limits and amounts incurred may not be business related. The same expense controls should be applied to charge transactions as those applied to currency.

Subject Area: Fraud knowledge elements—types of fraud and red flags. Source: CIA 1191, II-45.

**55. (b)** Period-to-period analysis of expenses would have shown a sudden increase in material costs. Choice (a) is incorrect. Comparison of production totals would not provide information concerning suppliers or the amount of materials used. Choice (c) is incorrect. At the time the fraud was uncovered, the amount taken was included in the organization's budget. Choice (d) is incorrect. The service may not have been part of cost of goods sold, but if so, comparison to industry averages is not as likely to reveal the extra cost as is comparison of company data period to period.

Subject Area: Fraud knowledge elements—types of fraud and red flags. Source: CIA 594, I-2.

**56. (d)** Once invoices have been approved and checks are prepared and signed, the mailing of the check by an independent person provides no means of preventing improper payments. Choice (a) is incorrect. Separating contracting for service and approval of invoices would have prevented the fraud. Choice (b) is incorrect. An independent verification of services received, reviewed by the check signor, would have prevented payment for services not received. Choice (c) is incorrect. Independent budget preparation would have allowed an actual to budget comparison to detect the payments.

Subject Area: Fraud knowledge elements—types of fraud and red flags. Source: CIA 594, I-3.

**57.   (a)**   Confirming with the using department the receipt of services that have been paid for would uncover the fraud. Choice (b) is incorrect. The clerk approved the fraudulent invoices, and an "approved" invoice would therefore support each check. Choice (c) is incorrect. Bank statement reconciliations do not test the validity of the cash payments. Choice (d) is incorrect. The test begins with valid receiving reports; the fraudulent payments would not be detected.

Subject Area: Fraud knowledge elements—types of fraud and red flags. Source: CIA 594, I-4.

**58.   (d)**   Because materials are shipped and used in another business, the analytic comparisons would show an unexplained increase in materials used. Choice (a) is incorrect. Because documents are falsified, all supporting documents would match for each cash disbursement. Choice (b) is incorrect. Vendors would confirm all transactions, because all have been made. Choice (c) is incorrect. Fraudulent orders are shipped to another location; the receiving dock procedures would appear correct.

Subject Area: Fraud knowledge elements—types of fraud and red flags. Source: CIA 594, I-10.

**59.   (d)**   If the supplies in question had been sent to the company and a receiving report had been signed by an employee other than the one ordering them, the fraud could not have occurred. Choice (a) is incorrect. There is nothing suggesting inappropriate actions by the vendor or collusion between the vendor and the dishonest employee. Choice (b) is incorrect. Purchase orders are being issued by the dishonest employee, who has the authority to do so. They may be prenumbered—that would not prevent him from engaging in this fraud. Choice (c) is incorrect. This control is to prevent the same document from being used to support two identical payments; that is not the case here.

Subject Area: Fraud knowledge elements—types of fraud and red flags. Source: CIA 593, I-48.

**60.   (b)**   Analytical procedures would identify an excess use of supplies. Choice (a) is incorrect. There is a legitimate vendor's invoice for each cash payment related to this fraud. Choice (c) is incorrect. There is nothing in this scenario that would cause the invoice prices or quantities to be different from those on the purchase order prepared by the dishonest employee. Choice (d) is incorrect. Recomputations prove accuracy of invoices, but do not detect fraud.

Subject Area: Fraud knowledge elements—types of fraud and red flags. Source: CIA 593, I-49.

**61.   (c)**   The IIA *Standards* state: "When an internal auditor suspects wrongdoing, the appropriate authorities within the organization should be informed." Choice (a) is incorrect. The *Standards* state that "internal auditors are not responsible for notifying outside authorities of suspected wrongdoing." Choice (b) is incorrect. A delay in reporting the suspected

defalcation will allow it to continue and/or give the suspected dishonest employee time to destroy or conceal important evidence. Choice (d) is incorrect. Once the dishonest employee knows that he or she is suspected, the person has an opportunity to destroy or to conceal important evidence or to flee to avoid apprehension.

Subject Area: Fraud knowledge elements—types of fraud and red flags. Source: CIA 593, I-50.

**62.   (a)**   An inappropriate segregation of duties was created when responsibility for accounting for customer food checks and the depositing of receipts was given to the supervisor. Choice (b) is incorrect. The depositing of receipts by the supervisor by itself is not the problem; it is the access to cash and ability to reset POS totals throughout the day that allowed the fraud. Choice (c) is incorrect. This is an independent verification of the deposits made by the supervisor. Choice (d) is incorrect. This is a step in the process of independently verifying sales.

Subject Area: Fraud knowledge elements—types of fraud and red flags. Source: CIA 1193, II-37.

**63.   (d)**   Using the total of the customer food checks as a confirmation of sales would have detected the shortage in the bank deposit. Choice (a) is incorrect. The fraud involved receipts, not deposits. Choice (b) is incorrect. The fraud involved altering the amounts on the close-of-day POS reports by resetting the POS system totals to zero. Choice (c) is incorrect. The accounting for individual customer food checks would not have detected the fraud because it did not involve manipulation of these devices.

Subject Area: Fraud knowledge elements—types of fraud and red flags. Source: CIA 1193, II-38.

**64.   (c)**   Regular actual to budget comparisons encourage performance and detect problems before they become too large. Choice (a) is incorrect. Generous reward systems can lead managers to falsify records so that rewards can be achieved. Choice (b) is incorrect. Domineering management cause managers to falsify records so as to meet the demands of upper management. Choice (d) is incorrect. Preoccupation with increased financial performance can cause management to falsify records to show increased performance.

Subject Area: Fraud knowledge elements—types of fraud and red flags. Source: CIA 594, I-11.

**65.   (b)**   This type of checking would prove that the agency is a genuine one. Choice (a) is incorrect. Invoices being processed through purchasing will not add any additional controls. Purchasing would have to make an independent source selection of the vendor. Choice (c) is incorrect. This is not practical for all employees. The degree of closeness in itself is not a conflict nor might it be subject to scrutiny. Choice (d) is incorrect. If a person was unethical, he or she probably would not disclose any illegal activity that the person is processing through the company.

Subject Area: Fraud knowledge elements—types of fraud and red flags. Source: CIA 591, II-46.

**66.   (d)**   This would be internal control strength. Choices (a), (b), and (c) are incorrect because each one of them is a symptom of possible fraud.

Subject Area: Fraud knowledge elements—types of fraud and red flags. Source: CIA 591, II-44.

**67.   (a)**   A 50% increase in sales supported by a 25% increase in cost of goods sold is either fortuitous or fraudulent.

Increases in sales are usually accompanied by close to proportional increases in cost of goods sold. Examples of situation in which increases in sales can be disproportionately larger than increases in cost of goods sold include: (1) operations within the realm of economies of scale (increasing returns to scale) and (2) the introduction of a highly accepted fashion item. Cases where disproportionately large sales increases indicate fraudulent conduct include: (1) collusion by the host firm's sales personnel and the buying firm's purchasing personnel and (2) collusion by members of two departments within the host firm, such as sales and transportation. Since the internal auditor would not know whether the disproportionately large increase in sales is legitimate, the auditor should view this as an indicator of possible fraud. Choice (b) is incorrect. Sales of $50 million and cost of goods sold of $25 million yield a gross profit margin (GPM) of 50%. Manufacturers can expect a range of 40 to 60% on this ratio. Choice (c) is incorrect. These data indicate an industry GPM of 0.5 and host firm GPM of 0.4. The greater GPM realized by the host firm may result from any number of reasonable causes. These include: (1) greater efficiencies exercised by the host firm, (2) greater sales effort (or a more highly accepted product), and (3) measurement errors. Choice (d) is incorrect. These data indicate an industry GPM of 0.4 and a host firm GPM of 0.5. The lower GPM realized by the host firm may result from such causes as: (1) host firm inefficiencies, (2) less acceptance of host firm product or less sales effort, and (3) measurement errors.

Subject Area: Fraud knowledge elements—types of fraud and red flags. Source: CIA 1192, II-48.

**68.** **(c)** Experience shows that such transfers are often used in fraud schemes. This is the only red flag among the options. Choice (a) is incorrect. Mere existence does not indicate fraud. Choice (b) is incorrect. A consistent record of above-average return on investment can be an indication of good management. Choice (d) is incorrect. Use of separate bank accounts is normal and convenient.

Subject Area: Fraud knowledge elements—types of fraud and red flags. Source: CIA 591, I-47.

**69.** **(d)** Analytical review of the divisions would reveal trends that might indicate fraud. Choice (a) is incorrect. Analysis of segregation of duties will not detect fraudulent activity; it only shows areas where opportunity exists. Choice (b) is incorrect. Exit interviews are not as effective at the officer level, since most individuals will not want to compromise severance arrangements. Choice (c) is incorrect. Changing outside auditor's coverage of divisions will not mandate better due diligence reviews.

Subject Area: Fraud knowledge elements—types of fraud and red flags. Source: CIA 591, I-49.

**70.** **(d)** Choice (d) is not correlated to making fraudulent loans. Choice (a) is incorrect. Not taking an annual vacation is a fraud indicator. Choice (b) is incorrect. Becoming easily annoyed with auditor questions is a fraud indicator. Choice (c) is incorrect. Explaining a high standard of living is a fraud indicator.

Subject Area: Fraud knowledge elements—types of fraud and red flags. Source: CIA 593, II-46.

**71.** **(a)** Trend analysis would detect an increase in the default rate due to bogus loans. Choice (b) is incorrect. Trend analysis would not detect annual vacation not taken. Choice (c) is incorrect. Although trend analysis could detect higher-

than-average expenses for operation of the company car, it has no relationship to suspected fraudulent loans. Choice (d) is incorrect. Total dollar value of loans made would not correlate to fraudulent loans.

Subject Area: Fraud knowledge elements—types of fraud and red flags. Source: CIA 593, II-47.

**72.** **(b)** Secured collateral would be difficult to obtain. Choice (a) is incorrect. A compliance audit would not show which loans were made to fictitious borrowers. Choice (c) is incorrect because the loan officer's level of activity might be higher or lower without regard to fraudulent activity. Choice (d) is incorrect because the perpetrator could easily make positive account confirmations.

Subject Area: Fraud knowledge elements—types of fraud and red flags. Source: CIA 593, II-48.

**73.** **(d)** Reconciling outstanding loans to the general ledger would be least likely discover this fraud. Choices (a), (b), and (c) are incorrect because each of these procedures has some possibility of detecting fraud.

Subject Area: Fraud knowledge elements—types of fraud and red flags. Source: CIA 593, II-49.

**74.** **(b)** A prod to achieve an unrealistically high sales or production quota can become a prod to falsify the records so that it appears the quota has been met. Choice (a) is incorrect. Participatory budgeting can reduce antagonism to budgets and reduce the likelihood of inappropriate means of meeting the budget. Choice (c) is incorrect. First, hiring policies should be based on factors other than adequate training—such as the applicants' personal integrity. Second, in many labor markets the large number of applicants may make cause rejection of qualified ones to be unavoidable. Choice (d) is incorrect. Under the "reasonable assurance" concept, the cost of controls should not exceed their benefits. It is quite possible that, in some areas, the additional cost of applying controls to all relevant transactions, rather than just a sample of them, may be greater than the resultant savings.

Subject Area: Fraud knowledge elements—types of fraud and red flags. Source: CIA 593, II-45.

**75.** **(b)** This is considered a red flag that indicates possible fraud. Choices (a), (c), and (d) are incorrect. These are not unusual and, in and of themselves, are not an indication of possible fraud.

Subject Area: Fraud knowledge elements—types of fraud and red flags. Source: CIA 590, I-48.

**76.** **(d)** Negligence is not fraud because it does not involve willful wrongdoing. Choices (a), (b), and (c) are incorrect because these are characteristics of fraud.

Subject Area: Fraud knowledge elements—types of fraud and red flags. Source: CIA 590, II-45.

**77.** **(d)** This is not a difficulty. The red flags literature is well established. Although red flags will be refined in the future as research is done, this does not preclude their effective use. Choice (a) is incorrect. This is a difficulty in using red flags. Red flags are developed through correlation analysis, not necessarily causation analysis. Choice (b) is incorrect. Many red flags, such as management's attitude, are difficult to quantify. Choice (c) is incorrect. When performing an audit, internal auditors should be alert to the possibility of intentional wrongdoing, errors, omissions, inefficiency, waste, ineffectiveness, and conflicts of interest.

Subject Area: Fraud knowledge elements—types of fraud and red flags. Source: CIA 1195, I-50.

**78. (c)** This, by itself, would not be considered a red flag. It represents a valid business reason for more timely payment. Choice (a) is incorrect. This is generally considered a red flag, which is most indicative of possible fraud. Choice (b) is incorrect. Significant deficiencies are one of the major factors associated with fraud. Choice (d) is incorrect. An unexpected, and unusual, increase in costs could be considered a red flag.

Subject Area: Fraud knowledge elements—types of fraud and red flags. Source: CIA 1196, I-61.

**79. (a)** The presence of red flags does not make the auditor responsible for detecting fraud. Choices (b), (c), and (d) are incorrect because each one is a responsibility identified in the IIA *Standards*.

Subject Area: Fraud knowledge elements—types of fraud and red flags. Source: CIA 1196, I-62.

**80. (a)** This would be the least useful procedure because the contract terms are already known. The confirmation would have to be expanded to inquire as to whether pressure was brought to bear by the purchasing agent to generate kickbacks—and that approach would be successful only if the kickbacks were initiated by the purchasing agent rather than the vendor. Choice (b) is incorrect. This would be the best procedure to gather more insight as to what products and which purchasing agent might be involved. It would be an important first step. Choice (c) is incorrect. This would provide information on excess purchase prices. Choice (d) is incorrect. Most (although not all) frauds are accompanied by changes in lifestyles of those committing the fraud. Although not the best procedure, it provides more information than choice (a).

Subject Area: Fraud knowledge elements—types of fraud and red flags. Source: CIA 1196, I-63.

**81. (d)** A decrease in the number of competitors during the year could be a potential explanation for the increase in sales and profits. Choice (a) is incorrect. Significant management compensation tied to reported profits has been identified as a red flag for potential fraud investigation. Choice (b) is incorrect. An unusually large amount of sales returns after year-end could indicate that a large amount of nonvalid (without substance) sales were recorded near the end of the year. Choice (c) is incorrect. The lack of receiving documents would be a good indicator that nonvalid sales were recorded during November and December.

Subject Area: Fraud knowledge elements—types of fraud and red flags. Source: CIA 1195, I-58.

**82. (b)** This would be the least effective procedure. The auditor would have more information by conducting a year-end physical inventory. Choice (a) is incorrect. This would be an effective procedure because one way to overstate the gross margin would be to overstate inventory. Choice (c) is incorrect. Sales and gross margin fluctuation analysis identifying unusual months would be a useful procedure to indicate the possibility of fraudulent transactions. Choice (d) is incorrect. Performing year-end cutoff tests would be effective in identifying transactions recorded in the wrong period.

Subject Area: Fraud knowledge elements—types of fraud and red flags. Source: CIA 1195, I-59.

**83. (b)** If fictitious sales were recorded, the most likely corresponding debit would be to accounts receivable. Thus, confirming accounts receivable would be an effective procedure, assuming that the customers are willing to respond to confirmations. The alternative best procedure would be to select recorded sales and trace them back to the underlying documents. However, that procedure was not given as an alternative. Choice (a) is incorrect. Selecting a sample of shipping documents only provides evidence that all shipments were billed. The concern here is that sales have been recorded for shipments not made. A more appropriate procedure would be to select recorded sales and trace back to the underlying documents. Choice (c) is incorrect. Analytical review procedures have already been performed and indicate the possibility of a misstatement. The auditor now needs to perform detailed tests to determine the existence of misstatements. Choice (d) is incorrect. Regression analysis would potentially indicate the existence of misstatements. That has already been accomplished by the analytical review techniques.

Subject Area: Fraud knowledge elements—types of fraud and red flags. Source: CIA 1195, I-60.

**84. (c)** This is one of the most common red flags identified in the IIA Standards. Choice (a) is incorrect. This factor has not been identified as a significant red flag. In addition, the division is audited by the internal audit department. Choice (b) is incorrect. Sales have normally been increasing by about 7% at this division. Thus, an increase of 10%, by itself, is not unexpected and would not raise a red flag. Choice (d) is incorrect because neither choice (b) nor (c) is a red flag.

Subject Area: Fraud knowledge elements—types of fraud and red flags. Source: CIA 595, I-44.

**85. (b)** The data would seem to indicate that inventory is overstated and cost of goods sold is understated. Inventory might be overstated because of either quantity or cost differences. Since we are nearing year-end, the most appropriate procedure would be to begin with a physical observation of inventory and expand to price tests after establishing the existence of inventory. Choices (a) and (c) are incorrect. Each would be an appropriate procedure, but the major problem appears to be existence of inventory, and the auditor should start there. Choice (d) is incorrect. The problem is occurring during normal operations. Because of the red flags, the auditor should schedule a cutoff test, but the existing red flags point primarily to a problem with inventory overstatement.

Subject Area: Fraud knowledge elements—types of fraud and red flags. Source: CIA 595, I-45.

**86. (d)** If there is a problem with standard costs, it will show up in variances. Since this is an analytical procedure, it is not costly and provides the best direction for further detailed testing. Choice (a) is incorrect. It would be inappropriate to interview management to determine why the standard costs have not been updated when the auditor does not yet have evidence that the standard costs are misstated. Choice (b) is incorrect. This would follow choice (a), and would need to test more than the correct recording of purchases. It would also need to test for proper allocation of labor and overhead costs. Choice (c) is incorrect. This procedure may have merit, but there is no indication that higher-gross-margin products are the ones with standard cost problems. Again, it would be a supplemental procedure after choice (a) is performed.

Subject Area: Fraud knowledge elements—types of fraud and red flags. Source: CIA 595, I-46.

**87. (b)** This is the correct response according to the IIA *Standards*. Choice (a) is incorrect. The auditor has sufficient evidence to bring the matter to the attention of management and leave it to them to decide the method of further investigation. Choice (c) is incorrect. There is no need to inform divisional management of suspicions. It would be appropriate to interview divisional management, but primarily as a fact-finding chore. Choice (d) is incorrect. The auditor's responsibility is for reporting inside the organization. There is no need to report the item to the external auditor.

Subject Area: Fraud knowledge elements—types of fraud and red flags. Source: CIA 595, I-47.

**88. (d)** Insufficient working capital may indicate such problems as overexpansion, decreases in revenues, transfer of funds to other companies, insufficient credit, and excessive expenditures. The auditor should be on the lookout for diversion of funds to personal use through such methods as unrecorded sales and falsified expenditures. Rapid turnover in financial positions may signify existing problems that the individuals feel uncomfortable with but do not want to disclose. Accountability for funds and other resources should be determined upon termination of employment. Use of sole-source procurement is not a practice that encourages competition to assure that the organization is obtaining the required materials or equipment at the best price. Sole-source procurement, if not adequately justified, indicates potential favoritism or kickbacks. Choice (a) is incorrect. The items described can be detected through usual audit procedures in a financial audit. Choice (b) is incorrect. Although the economy had a downturn, the change in working capital is unusual in light of the continuing strong profit margins and should be investigated. Choice (c) is incorrect. Items II, III, and IV are all warning signals.

Subject Area: Fraud knowledge elements—types of fraud and red flags. Source: CIA 1194, I-66.

**89. (b)** Living beyond one's means has been linked to employee (embezzlement) fraud, not to financial statement fraud. Choice (a) is incorrect. Autocratic management styles have been linked to management (financial statement) fraud. Choice (c) is incorrect. Rationalization is common to all fraud. Choice (d) is incorrect. High expectations are often given as a motivating factor by those who have committed financial statement fraud.

Subject Area: Fraud knowledge elements—types of fraud and red flags. Source: CIA 594, I-12.

**90. (c)** Complete trust is an opportunity to commit a fraud. Therefore, by definition, choices (a), (b), and (d) are incorrect.

Subject Area: Fraud knowledge elements—types of fraud and red flags. Source: CIA 594, I-48.

**91. (a)** "Crisis management" provides an opportunity to commit a fraud. Therefore, by definition, choices (b), (c), and (d) are incorrect.

Subject Area: Fraud knowledge elements—types of fraud and red flags. Source: CIA 594, I-49.

**92. (b)** Personal financial problem is a situational pressure to commit a fraud. Therefore, by definition, choices (a), (c), and (d) are incorrect.

Subject Area: Fraud knowledge elements—types of fraud and red flags. Source: CIA 594, I-50.

**93. (a)** Contributing more than paid is a rationalization. Therefore, by definition, choices (b), (c), and (d) are incorrect.

Subject Area: Fraud knowledge elements—types of fraud and red flags. Source: CIA 594, I-51.

**94. (d)** To make the "books balance" is an example of a document symptom. Therefore, by definition, choices (a), (b), and (c) are incorrect.

Subject Area: Fraud knowledge elements—types of fraud and red flags. Source: CIA 594, I-52.

**95. (b)** "Joining an expensive country club" is an example of a lifestyle symptom. Therefore, by definition, choices (a), (c), and (d) are incorrect.

Subject Area: Fraud knowledge elements—types of fraud and red flags. Source: CIA 594, I-53.

**96. (c)** Being "argumentative" is an example of a behavioral symptom. Therefore, by definition, choices (a), (b), and (d) are incorrect.

Subject Area: Fraud knowledge elements—types of fraud and red flags. Source: CIA 594, I-54.

**97. (a)** Paying petty cash–type expenditures from cash receipts facilitates the unauthorized removal of cash before deposit. All cash receipts should be deposited intact daily. Petty cash–type expenditures should be handled through an imprest fund. Choice (b) is incorrect. The monthly bank reconciliation should not be performed by a person who makes deposits or writes checks, but there is no problem with the inventory clerk doing it. Choice (c) is incorrect. There is no direct relationship between the transactions posted to the accounts receivable and accounts payable subsidiary ledgers; having the same person maintain both does not create a control weakness. Choice (d) is incorrect. In order to pinpoint responsibility for petty cash, it is desirable that only one person has access to the fund.

Subject Area: Fraud knowledge elements—types of fraud and red flags. Source: CIA 593, I-46.

**98. (d)** The use of blanket purchase orders is an acceptable business practice. Choice (a) is incorrect. The receipt of goods or services by noncompany personnel is a symptom of fraud. Choice (b) is incorrect. The scenario refers to normal and appropriate procedures that are suspended for these transactions. Choice (c) is incorrect. The receipt of goods or services off-site is a symptom of fraud.

Subject Area: Fraud knowledge elements—types of fraud and red flags. Source: CIA 1193, II-49.

**99. (a)** The indicators include an extraordinary change in account balances as discovered during analytical review procedures. Choice (b) is incorrect. The provision of paint is not an issue. Choice (c) is incorrect. The purchasing agent is fulfilling this responsibility in accordance with the authority of a purchasing agent's position. Choice (d) is incorrect. The painting contractor is bound by company procedures in this manner.

Subject Area: Fraud knowledge elements—types of fraud and red flags. Source: CIA 1193, II-50.

**100. (b)** One would expect rapid increases in gross margin percentage if sales were fictitious; the large increase in returns is also symptomatic of falsified sales. Choice (a) is incorrect. The increase in percent change in sales is not unreasonable, and given the constant increase, one might expect increases in inventory that could keep turnover constant. Choice (c) is incorrect. See choice (a) for turnover. The turnover and return figures, when taken together, are not indications of sales overstatements. Choice (d) is incorrect. If the increase in sales was due to a market sales price increase, one might expect these results.

Subject Area: Fraud knowledge elements—types of fraud and red flags. Source: CIA 594, I-19.

**101. (c)** From the information given, it appears Frank found the analytic data, but accepted management's explanation of the findings. Choices (a) and (b) are incorrect because failure to rotate assignments and close personal friendships seem to have contributed to Frank's decision to accept management's explanation for the analytic findings. Choice (d) is incorrect because Frank should not accept management's response on its face value.

Subject Area: Fraud knowledge elements—types of fraud and red flags. Source: CIA 594, I-20.

# 5 ENGAGEMENT TOOLS (15–25%)

## THEORY

### 5.1 Sampling

(a) **Sampling Theory and Nonstatistical Sampling.** The primary reason for an auditor to use statistical sampling is to allow the auditor to quantify, and therefore control, the risk of making an incorrect decision based on sample evidence. It is not true that statistical sampling prevents auditors from using professional judgment in conducting reviews. Statistical sampling is merely a tool to help them make wise decisions. Auditors still decide what type of review to make, how and when to use sampling, and how to interpret the results. In applying statistical sampling techniques to audit testing, auditors must make six decisions that involve professional judgment.

1. **Auditors must define the problem.** They must decide what to measure, what type of information will provide sufficient facts for the formation of an opinion, and what testing procedures to use.

2. **They must specify the level of confidence.** This is precision, or the probability that an estimate made from the sample will fall within a stated interval of the true value for the population as a whole. Auditors may think of it as the percentage of times that a correct decision (within the specified precision limits) will result from using an estimate based on a sample.

3. **Auditors must define the population for size and other characteristics.** They decide what type of items will be included and excluded, and specify the time period to be covered.

4. **They must determine the areas applicable to sampling.** The auditors' assessment of the internal control system for an area may determine whether statistical sampling is appropriate. A strong internal control system may reduce testing to the minimum necessary for verification and may, therefore, call for a different sampling plan or no statistical sampling at all. Prior experience, as well as information from prior audits, plays a role here. Prior audits may suggest that certain kinds of records are more prone to error and need higher verification rates than other kinds of records. Thus, auditors may have to stratify the population between records likely to have a high error rate and those likely to have a low error rate.

5. **Auditors must decide the maximum error rate that they will consider acceptable, and they must define an error.** Or, if auditors are attempting to estimate the value of some balance sheet amount, they must determine the required precision of the estimate in terms of the materiality of the amount being examined and the overall objective.

6. **They must draw conclusions about the population from the sampling results.** In arriving at these conclusions, auditors must judge the significance of the errors they have discovered.

    Because statistical sampling provides more and better information, it permits greater use of professional judgment and enables auditors to more effectively analyze the results of tests. And by reducing the workload, statistical sampling allows more time to use professional judgment.

Basically there are two approaches to audit sampling: (1) statistical and (2) nonstatistical. The choice is based on costs and benefits. Sampling risk—the risk that the sample is not a representative of the population—is present in both approaches. Exhibit 5.1 summarizes similarities and differences between statistical and nonstatistical sampling approaches.

| *Statistical sampling approaches* | *Nonstatistical sampling approaches* |
|---|---|
| • Require auditor's judgment | • Require auditor's judgment |
| • Basic audit procedures are the same | • Basic audit procedures are the same |
| • Permitted as a professional standard | • Permitted as a professional standard |
| • Use the laws of probabilities to measure sampling risk associated with the sampling procedures | • Cannot measure the sampling risk |
| • Sample selection methods use statistics | • Sample selection methods may use statistics, but evaluation of the sample results could be nonstatistical |
| • Additional costs involved due to technical training required | • Fewer costs due to minimal training requirements |
| • Sampling risk can be explicitly measured and controlled | • Sampling risk cannot be explicitly measured or controlled |
| • Require computer software and hardware for efficient use | • Do not require computer facilities |
| • Provide objective conclusions based on sample results | • Provide subjective conclusions that are subjected to challenge |
| • Compatible with limited number of sample selection methods | • Compatible with a wider variety of sample selection methods |
| • Sample is larger and is based on mathematics | • Sample is smaller and is based on judgment |

**Exhibit 5.1: Statistical and nonstatistical approaches**

---

**KEY CONCEPTS TO REMEMBER: WHAT MAKES A GOOD SAMPLE?**

- A good sample should have four characteristics: representative, corrective, protective, and preventive.
- "Representative" means that the sample estimates the true population characteristic as accurately as possible.

> - "Corrective" means that the sample will locate as many error items as possible, so that they can be corrected.
> - "Protective" means that the person who does the sampling attempts to include the maximum number of high-value items in the sample. This approach is common when auditors isolate the high-value items from the rest of the population, gather data on all these items, and gather data from a sample of the remaining items.
> - "Preventive" means that the sampling method gives auditees no idea which items will be selected during the audit.

### (i) Sampling plan and operations

(A) *Sampling plan.* When designing a sampling plan, auditors should keep in mind the desirability of obtaining a sample that is as representative, corrective, protective, and preventive as possible. To do so, they should stratify the population on the basis of dollar value and the likelihood that the items contain errors, use some random method to select the sample from each stratum, and weight the results from each stratum to compute overall estimates for the population. It is not possible, however, to optimize all four characteristics in a single sample. Instead, a balance must be struck, depending on which characteristic is most important in view of the audit objective. Also, in certain types of audits, one or more of the characteristics may not require consideration at all.

## Sample Size Factors

If all other factors in a sampling plan are held constant: (1) changing the measure of tolerable error to a smaller value would cause the sample size to be larger, or (2) changing the audit risk from 5% to 3% would cause the sample size to be larger.

One of the auditor's objectives is to answer questions about a universe of people or things. This universe is called the population. This objective can be achieved by looking at a sample of things, if the sample is representative of the population. A representative sample has approximately the same distribution of characteristics as the population from which it was drawn.

(B) *Sampling operations.* There are three components in the sampling operations: (1) sample design, (2) sample selection procedures, and (3) estimation procedures. The term "sample design" refers to the plans made for the overall way in which a sample will be related to a population. Selection procedures are the methods used to select units of samples from a population. Estimation procedures are the ways of estimating the characteristics of a population from information acquired about a sample.

Interrelationships exist among these three components.

1. The sample design will affect the estimation procedures to be used, and it may also affect the selection procedures. Conversely, the sample design is often affected by the estimation procedures to be used.
2. Selection procedures can have a major effect on how precision is estimated.
3. The types of estimates to be developed can have a bearing on the selection procedures to be used.

Auditors usually form conclusions through testing, or "sampling," a portion of a collection of items (a population). The method by which they choose a sample and the degree to which the sample is representative of every item in the population determine whether they can form valid conclusions.

(C) *Sample size.* The determination of an appropriate sample size is part of sample design. Before selecting the sample size, the auditor should decide on the sampling method to be used, the estimation procedure, the sample precision required, and the confidence level desired.

### KEY CONCEPTS TO REMEMBER: SAMPLE SIZE

- A decision to decrease the precision interval (i.e., high precision) would result in an increase in the required sample size.
- A decision to increase the precision interval from 4% to 5% (i.e., less precision) would result in a decrease in the required sample size.
- Sample size varies directly with changes in confidence level, inversely with changes in precision.
- Sample size increases with the use of higher confidence levels.
- Sample size will decrease when the auditor increases the amount of tolerable error.
- Stop-and-go sampling plan will minimize the sample size whenever a low rate of non-compliance is expected.
- When relatively few items of high-dollar value constitute a large proportion of an account balance, stratified sampling technique and complete testing of the high-dollar-value items will generally result in a reduction in sample size.
- In an attribute sampling application, holding other factors constant, sample size will increase as the planned precision becomes smaller.
- In variables sampling application, sample size will increase when the confidence level is changed from 90% to 95%.

(D) **Precision.** Specifying the precision needed for sample estimates is an important part of sample design. The desired precision is the amount of sampling error that can be tolerated but that will still permits the results to be useful. This is sometimes called tolerable error or the bound on error.

In terms of a stated confidence level, precision is the range into which an estimate of a population characteristic is expected to fall. Factors in the choice of a desired precision include the tolerable level of sampling error, the size of an account balance error considered material, and the objectives of the audit test being conducted. Audit resources available for execution of the sampling plan are not a factor.

*An application of precision follows.* Based on a random sample, it is estimated that 4%, plus or minus 2%, of a firm's invoices contain errors. The plus or minus 2% is known as the estimate's precision.

## PRECISION VS. SAMPLING RISK

- Precision is under the auditor's full control because he or she specifies it.
- Sampling risk is not under the auditor's full control.
- Precision applies to both attributes sampling and variables sampling.
- Sampling risk is present in both attribute sampling and variables sampling work.

### KEY CONCEPTS TO REMEMBER: PRECISION

- The application of the finite correction factor to the precision interval will cause the precision interval to become smaller.
- When a confidence level is changed from 95.5% to 99.7%, and no change in sample standard deviation takes place, the sample size would be larger, but achieved precision would not change.
- When planning an attribute sampling application, the difference between the expected error rate and the maximum tolerable error rate is the planned precision.
- In an attribute sampling application, holding other factors constant, sample size will increase as the planned precision becomes smaller.

(E) **Precision and confidence.** Because precision is a way of expressing the amount of error that can be tolerated, it is related to the accounting concept of materiality. Materiality, or importance, is a relative concept rather than absolute. For example, a $100,000 overstatement of the assets for a company whose total assets are only $200,000 would be material while it would be immaterial for a company with total assets of a multibillion dollars.

In addition to specifying the precision of the estimate, auditors must specify the degree of confidence that they want placed in the estimate. This is referred to as confidence level, expressed as a percentage. Confidence level is the complement of the chance that our estimate and its precision will not contain the true but unknown population value. The confidence level should be determined by the importance of the sample results to the overall objectives of the audit.

Two examples will illustrate the relationship between confidence level and risk.

1. A confidence level of 90% means that there are 90 chances out of 100 that the sample results will not vary from the true characteristics of the population by more than specified amount.
2. The complement of the risk that an internal auditor will erroneously conclude adequate compliance with a specific management policy is the confidence level.

## PRECISION VS. ACCURACY

- "Precision" refers to the maximum amount, stated at a certain confidence level, that we can expect the estimate from a single sample to deviate from the results obtained by applying the same measuring procedures to all the items in the population.
- "Accuracy" refers to the difference between the value of the population from which the sample is selected and the true characteristic that we intend to measure.

---

(F) **Types of risks.** Basically, there are two types of risks: (1) sampling and (2) nonsampling risks. **Sampling risk** is the risk that the conclusions reached based on a sample will differ from those conclusions that would be reached by examining the entire population. Usually, the smaller the sample size, the greater will be the sampling risk.

**Nonsampling risk** arises even if the entire population is tested and is due to errors in auditor judgment, such as use of inappropriate audit procedures and not recognizing errors during sampling. This risk can be controlled with better audit planning and supervision.

The American Institute of Certified Public Accountants (AICPA) in its Statement on Auditing Standards (SAS) 39 describes the two aspects of sampling risk in performing substantive testing.

1. The **risk of incorrect rejection** is the risk that the sample supports the conclusion that the recorded account balance is materially misstated when it is not materially misstated. *This is known as Alpha Risk, Type I error.*
2. The **risk of incorrect acceptance** is the risk that the sample supports the conclusion that the recorded account balance is not materially misstated when it is materially misstated. *This is known as Beta Risk, Type II error.*

According to SAS 39, the auditor is also concerned with two aspects of sampling *risk in performing compliance tests* of internal accounting control.

1. The **risk of overreliance** on internal accounting control is the risk that the sample supports the auditor's planned degree of reliance on the control when the true compliance rate does not justify such reliance.
2. The **risk of underreliance** on internal accounting control is the risk that the sample does not support the auditor's planned degree of reliance on the control when the true compliance rate supports such reliance.

The risk of incorrect rejection and the risk of underreliance on internal accounting control relate to the efficiency of the audit. For example, if the auditor's evaluation of an audit sample leads him or her to the initial erroneous conclusion that a balance is materially misstated when it is not, the application of additional audit procedures and consideration of other audit evidence would ordinarily lead the auditor to the correct conclusion.

Similarly, if the auditor's evaluation of a sample leads him or her to unnecessarily reduce the planned degree of reliance on internal accounting control, the auditor would ordinarily increase the scope of substantive tests to compensate for the perceived inability to rely on internal accounting control to the extent originally planned. Although the audit may be less efficient in these circumstances, the audit is, nevertheless, effective.

*The risk of incorrect acceptance and the risk of overreliance on internal accounting control relate to the effectiveness of an audit in detecting an existing material misstatement.*

---

**KEY CONCEPTS TO REMEMBER: SAMPLING RISK**

- Sampling risk is choosing a sample that has proportionately more errors than the population.
- The term "sampling risk" refers to the possibility that even though a sample is properly chosen, it may not be representative of the population.
- Each time an auditor draws a conclusion based on evidence drawn from a sample, a sampling risk is introduced that draws an erroneous conclusion from sample data.

---

(ii) **Statistical sampling and judgmental sampling.** The use of any statistical sample requires a high degree of professional judgment to determine the confidence level and the reliability desired, and thus what sample criteria to use. It takes judgment to evaluate the effectiveness of internal control procedures in order to test the accuracy and reliability of records, as well as to recognize any errors in the items examined.

In using a statistical sample, the auditor must use caution in that any exceptions or irregularities noted in performing any auditing procedure must be investigated by appropriate means: This may include a subsequent increase in the sample size. If there are no exceptions, the sample size should not be arbitrarily increased. Statistical sampling helps ensure that audit tests are adequate but not excessive and demonstrates objectivity.

When the choice is made to use statistical sampling, the first step is to devise a sampling plan. A statistical sampling plan includes five major steps.

---

**KEY CONCEPTS TO REMEMBER: STEPS INVOLVED IN A STATISTICAL SAMPLING PLAN**

1. Define the audit objectives.
2. Define the population as clearly as possible, noting any distributional or systematic patterns. This step will establish the population size.
3. Determine the appropriate sampling method and sample selection technique that best fits the characteristics of the population.
4. Determine the precision and reliability desired.
5. Calculate the sample size.

---

One common error is the assumption that statistical sampling techniques are limited to customer confirmation programs. Auditors should look at all records and transactions that should be reviewed but, due to volume, must be sampled. Statistical sampling may apply to documentation tests, signature verifications, expenses, and so forth.

The auditor must be careful with statistical sampling. There are many different sampling techniques, and not all of them are appropriate in a given circumstance. Correct application of the wrong method is an error that is fairly common and should be avoided.

The auditor must not let the mere application of a statistical method lead to a false sense of security. Statistical samples are subject to some degree of error. Absolutely no inferences can be made from a statistical sample except that of the likelihood of the sample being representative of the population from which it is drawn. Statistical sampling is no substitute for judgment. The auditor must decide the sampling method most appropriate, the confidence level and precision that are appropriate, and even the correct definition of "population." An error in any of these judgments can lead to incorrect conclusions in spite of the elegance of the mathematics.

Although using statistical methods will almost always be preferable to samples selected judgmentally, judgmental sample selection may be appropriate in some circumstances. However, auditors should always justify their use of judgmental sample selection in the working papers.

Sampling, whether statistical or nonstatistical (judgmental), is **not** appropriate when: examination of 100% of an account balance is required; inquiry and observation techniques are used to collect audit evidence; and analytical procedures are used to evaluate the appropriateness of values reported by the auditee. Analytical procedures examine the entire population, instead of examining only part as in sampling. Accounts with low risk of material errors are included in the sample and examination of few items is done without evaluating the characteristics of the population.

Auditors should document the conclusions drawn from the samples, whether statistically or judgmentally selected. When the population size and audit objectives are sufficient to warrant statistical samples, the samples will provide certain mathematical confidence levels to support the conclusions.

Exceptions must be classified as either critical or noncritical. Critical errors are those that cannot be tolerated (e.g., errors caused by deliberate falsification of transactions or account balances). Any critical errors must be analyzed and the underlying causes determined. The scope of the work also must be increased.

Noncritical errors are those exceptions that have a lesser impact (e.g., clerical or typing errors). If numerous clerical errors exist, the department should be required to resolve the problems and sufficient follow-up audit procedures should be pursued.

(b) **Statistical Sampling**

(i) **Sample selection methods**. **Selection** procedures involve the method of actually picking the sampling units—called drawing the sample (see Exhibit 5.2). All types of statistical sampling use random selection procedures. Several selection procedures may be used for a single sample design.

**Overview Diagram for Sample Selection Methods**

Statistical sample selection methods
- Random sampling
  - Using computer programs
  - Using number tables
- Systematic sampling
- Cluster sampling

Nonstatistical sample selection methods
- Haphazard selection
- Block selection
- Judgment selection

Statistical and nonstatistical selection method → Stratified sampling

**Exhibit 5.2: Overview diagram for sample selection methods**

(A) *Statistical sample selection methods: random sampling.* Statistical sample selection methods include simple random sampling, systematic sampling, cluster sampling, and stratified sampling. Simple, or unrestricted, random sampling is the simplest method of drawing a statistical sample, and this design is basic to others. The assumptions underlying the use of simple random sampling are that the population is homogeneous and is in one location, or it can be sampled from a single list of sampling units if it is in several locations, and that there is only moderate variation among the values of the items in the population.

**Random Sampling**

The only factor involved in random selection is chance. Subjective considerations, whether conscious or otherwise, are completely avoided.

No attempt is made to segregate any portion of the population into separate groups before the sample is selected. Thus, each individual item in the population has an equal probability of being included in the sample. *Random sampling uses a concept called sampling without replacement, which means that once an item has been selected, it is removed from the population and is not subject to reselection.*

Computer programs can be used. Programmed random number generators are available for use with most large or small computers. These generators are designed to produce a selection of random numbers that will be suitable for, or can be adapted to, most numbering systems. Obviously, the time required for random number selection is reduced with the use of computers.

Alternatively, random number tables can be used to select the random digits. The beginning and ending numbers of the items in the population are determined. Then numbers falling between the beginning and ending numbers equal to the specified sample size are selected from a table of random digits. The sampling units having numbers that correspond to the selected random numbers constitute the sample.

### Examples of random number tables

If we want to select a sample of 200 items from a population of 8,894 items numbered from 265 through 9,158, we start at some random point in the table. Going either down the table columns or across the rows, we select the first 200 four-digit numbers that fall between 0265 and 9,158, inclusive. Note that we must look at four-digit numbers because the largest number in the population has four digits. The quantity of digits in the numbers that are read must always equal the quantity of digits in the largest number of the population. Numbers that duplicate a number that has already been drawn are discarded, and the quantity of additional random numbers that will achieve the required sample size is selected. When preliminary results indicate that the sample is larger than needed, the auditor may want to decrease the sample size.

Applications of random sampling method follow. In order to project the frequency of shipments to wrong addresses, an auditor chose a random sample from the busiest month of each of the four quarters of the most recent year. The auditor violated this concept of statistical sampling: failing to give each item in the population an equal chance of selection. Simple random sampling is the most appropriate method for drawing a sample of checks when the accounts payable checks are consecutively numbered.

(B)  *Statistical sample selection methods: systematic sampling.* Systematic sampling or systematic selection with a random start is simple and useful in many audit situations, and easier to use than random sampling. The sample is selected from the population on the basis of a fixed, or uniform, interval between sampling units, after a random starting point has been determined. *The uniform interval is obtained by dividing a given sample size into the population size and dropping any decimals in the result. The random start is selected from a table of random digits and is the first combination of digits that is between one and the uniform sampling interval, inclusive.*

Systematic sampling with monetary units (e.g., dollars) is a special case of probability proportional to size (PPS).

### Example of Systematic Sampling

We want to draw a sample of 200 items from a file containing 10,100 items. Dividing the sample size into the population size gives a quotient of 50.5 (i.e., 10,100/200). Rounding downward to the nearest whole number gives a sampling interval of 50. From a table of random digits, the first number between 1 and 50 is selected to obtain the starting point. Suppose the random starting number between 1 and 50 is 36. We start with item number 36 and pull every 50th item thereafter; the 36th item, 86th item, 136th item, and so on will constitute the sample.

Systematic sampling may be used when the sampling units are not numbered or when it would be too cumbersome to attempt to match the sampling units against random numbers. Specifically, systematic sampling should be used when: the sampling units are long lists or pages of lists (e.g., checks, accounts, inventory items, dollars), the sampling units are filed on index cards that are not serially numbered, or, if they are numbered, they are not in numerical sequence; the sampling units are numbered in blocks of numbers, and some blocks are not used; and the sampling units are not suitably numbered and are intermingled with other items that are not to be included in the sample.

## Ways to Reduce Bias in Systematic Sampling

Systematic sampling can produce a nonrepresentative sample if the population contains a systematic bias. This bias can be minimized or reduced by (1) making sure that the population is in random order and (2) using multiple random starts.

Some cautions are in order while using the systematic selection procedure. Make sure that the sample is drawn from the entire population. If the sample is to be drawn from a list of items, the list must be complete; if the sample is to be drawn from a file, all the folders must be in the file. Once the sample has been selected, it is not permissible to substitute other items for sample items that are missing or for sample items that may not have adequate supporting material to permit the audit work. Every effort should be made to locate the missing items or supporting material. If they cannot be located, this fact should be noted and reported as one of the sample results.

Before using systematic sampling, the auditor should determine whether there is a direct relationship between the arrangement of the population and the characteristic being measured. If the sampling units are arranged in ascending or descending order of magnitude, a systematic sample will yield a smaller estimate of the sampling error than a random number sample.

(C) ***Statistical sample selection methods: cluster sampling.*** Cluster sampling is the selection of groups of sampling units (or clusters) rather than the selection of individual sampling units directly. Examples of clusters are folders in filing cabinet drawers, baskets of produce, counties in a state, and the persons in a household. Cluster sampling should be used when a built-in pattern is not expected in the population or data.

Three types of cluster sampling exist: one stage, two stage, and three stage—depending on the size and complexity of population (see Exhibit 5.3).

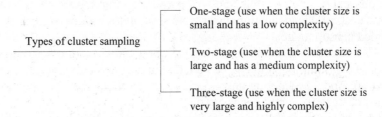

**Exhibit 5.3: Types of cluster sampling**

- **One-stage sampling:** Use one-stage sampling when all the sampling units within the sampled cluster can be examined in one step.
- **Two-stage sampling:** Use two-stage sampling when a selection of random sample of units within the selected cluster is required.
- **Three-stage sampling:** Use three-stage sampling when an extension of the two-stage is required. First, take a sample of clusters (primary sampling units), and then take a sample of units from within the cluster (secondary sampling units). Finally, take a sample of the elements (the unit, object, thing or person on which the measurement is taken) from each of the selected secondary sampling units.

**Examples of cluster sampling method**

1. A survey of suburban households is conducted to obtain data on television viewing habits. A statistical sample of suburban areas is first selected. Within the chosen areas, statistical samples of whole blocks are selected, and within the selected blocks, random samples of households are selected.
2. A car rental agency has branches located throughout the world that are essentially small-scale representations of the entire population. Cluster sampling method is good to determine the average net revenue per vehicle in inventory.

(D) ***Nonstatistical sample selection methods.*** Haphazard selection, block selection, and judgment selection are examples of nonstatistical sample selection methods. All these methods require the auditor's subjective knowledge, which is not necessarily bad.

Judgment sampling is discretionary; that is, the auditor bases the selection of a sample on knowledge or judgment about the characteristics of the population. Haphazard selection, or catch-as-catch-can samples—for example, selecting a few items "at random"—are usually included in the category of judgment sampling. Block selection includes selecting a block of documents, whether prenumbered or not (e.g., invoices, purchase orders, or all invoices for a particular month). For example, selecting 100% of most recent express-mail shipping transactions does not allow a statistical generalization about all express-mail transactions.

Judgment samples have valid uses. When one does not need to generalize to a population or a statistical sample is not necessary, a small judgment sample would be cost effective. However, judgment samples lack three characteristics of statistical samples: (1) random selection of the units to be examined, (2) mathematical determination of the sample size, and (3) mathematical measurement of the risk of being wrong because a sample was used.

(E) *Statistical and nonstatistical selection method—stratified sampling.* The term "stratified sampling" refers to the situation in which the population is divided into two or more parts (strata) and a simple random sample is selected for each part (stratum). An estimate is determined separately for each stratum, and these are combined to form an estimate for the entire population. A stratum is a subpopulation from the total population.

The terms "high income," "middle income," and "low income" indicate three strata of a population of people classified by the income they received. Tax returns might be divided into strata based on the asset size of the company submitting the return.

A stratified sample can be used to: obtain equal precision with a smaller sample or tighter precision with the same size sample; obtain separate estimates for the groups in the individual strata, if such estimates would be useful for comparison purposes; and give special emphasis to certain groups within the population, such as invoices of high-dollar values or those with a great error potential.

Sometimes stratification is necessary because the population is divided up among several locations and it is not possible to develop a single sampling frame. Stratification may be desirable if the costs of data collection differ from stratum to stratum (e.g., personal interviews versus mailed questionnaires).

When defining strata and setting their boundaries, auditors should keep certain rules in mind: Each sampling unit can be included in one, and only one, stratum. The strata must not overlap. And the sampling units in each stratum should be as much alike as possible in relation to the characteristic being measured.

Each stratum is treated as if it were a separate population from which items are selected independently, that is, the sample selected in one stratum must not depend on, or be related to, the sample selected in another stratum. One of the acceptable random selection procedures is used to draw the sample in each stratum.

The total sample may be allocated to each stratum in proportion or in disproportion to the number of sampling units in that stratum. With proportional allocation, the sampling fraction (i.e., sample size divided by the population size) is the same in each stratum. With disproportional allocation, sampling fractions differ in two or more strata. Disproportional allocation may be based on professional judgment or on mathematical formulas, in order to minimize the overall precision or the overall cost of data collection.

One of the objectives is to achieve a reduced sample size by reducing variation within each subpopulation. A major advantage of the systematic sampling is that it can be used in both statistical and nonstatistical sampling plans, as shown below.

- For a statistical plan, variation is measured in terms of standard deviation.
- For a nonstatistical plan, variation is measured in qualitative terms, such as small, moderate, or large.

---

**KEY CONCEPTS TO REMEMBER: STRATIFIED SAMPLING**

- Stratification generally reduces the cost of a sample for a given precision.
- Depending on the arrangement of the items in the subpopulations and numbering systems employed, it might be advisable to use random number sampling in some of the strata and systematic selection with a random start in others.
- "Number of items" would be least likely used as criteria to classify inventory items into strata to evaluate a large, heterogeneous inventory. "Dollar values" would most likely be used.
- A population that is physically separated into two or more distinct groups based on the sample variation being less than that for the entire population is called a stratified sample.
- Stratified sampling is the most appropriate method to use when 40% of the checks were issued to a single vendor who offered unusually large cash discounts.

---

## DEFINITIONS OF KEY TERMS: SAMPLING

- **Attribute.** A characteristic that describes a person, thing, or event. An inherent quality that an item either has or does not have.
- **Attribute sampling.** The measurement or evaluation of selected sampling units in terms of whether they have the attribute of interest, and the computation of some statistical measure (statistic) from these measurements to estimate the proportion of the population that has the attribute.
- **Bias.** The existence of a factor that causes an estimate made on the basis of a sample to differ systematically from the population parameter being estimated. Bias may originate from poor sample design, deficiencies in carrying out the sampling process, or an inherent characteristic of the measuring or estimating technique used.
- **Cluster sample.** A simple random sample in which each sampling unit is a collection of elements.
- **Coefficient of variation.** The ratio produced by dividing the standard deviation by the mean value. It provides an indication of the consistency of the data.
- **Confidence coefficient.** A measure (usually expressed as a percentage) of the degree of assurance that the estimate obtained from a sample differs from the population parameter being estimated by less than the measure of precision (sampling error).
- **Confidence interval.** An estimate of a population parameter that consists of a range of values bounded by statistics called upper and lower confidence limits.
- **Confidence level.** A number, stated as a percentage, that expresses the degree of certainty associated with an interval estimate of a population parameter. It is the probability that an estimate based on a random sample falls within a specified range.
- **Confidence limits.** Two statistics that form the upper and lower bounds of a confidence interval.
- **Degrees of freedom.** A random sample of size $n$ is said to have $n$-1 degrees of freedom for estimating the population variance, in the sense that there are $n$-1 independent deviations from the sample mean on which to base such an estimate.
- **Deviation.** The difference between the particular number and the average of the set of number under consideration.
- **Dispersion.** The extent to which the elements of a sample or the elements of a population are not all alike in the measured characteristic, are spread out, or vary from one another. Items that measure dispersion include: range, deviation, mean absolute deviation, variance, standard deviation, and coefficient of variation.
- **Finite population correction (FPC) factor**. A multiplier that makes adjustments for the sampling efficiency gained when sampling is without replacement and when the sample size is large (greater than 5 or 10%) with respect to the population size. This multiplier reduces the sampling error for a given sample size or reduces the required sample size for a specified measure of precision (in this case, desired sampling error).
- **Interval estimate.** General term for an estimate of a population parameter that is a range of numerical values. The estimation of a parameter in terms of an interval, called an "interval estimate,"

for which one can assert with a given probability (or degree of confidence) that it contains the actual value of the parameter.

- **Interval variable.** A quantitative variable the attributes of which are ordered and for which the numerical differences between adjacent attributes are interpreted as equal.
- **Judgment sample.** Unlike a probability sample, a sample in whose selection personal judgment plays a significant part. Though judgment samples are sometimes required by practical consideration, and may lead to satisfactory results, they do not lend themselves to analysis by standard statistical methods.
- **Mean.** A measure of central tendency; a statistic used primarily with interval-ratio variables following symmetrical distributions. The sum of all the values in a set of observations divided by the number of observations. Also known as "average" or "arithmetic mean," it indicates the typical value for a set of observations. If five students make the grades 15, 75, 80, 95, and 100, the mean is 73.
- **Mean absolute deviation (MAD).** A measure of the difference between the individual items in a population and the mean value. MAD is the average of the total unsigned differences.
- **Median.** A measure of central tendency; a statistic used primarily with ordinal variables and asymmetrically distributed interval-ratio variables. The middle measurement when the items are arranged in order of size or, if there is no middle one, then the average of the two middle ones. If five students make the grades 15, 75, 80, 95, and 100, the median is 80.
- **Mode.** A measure of central tendency; a statistic used primarily with nominal variables. The most frequent value of a set of numbers. If more students (of a given group) make 75 than any other one grade, then 75 is the mode.
- **Nominal variable.** A quantitative variable the attributes of which have no inherent order.
- **Ordinal variable.** A quantitative variable the attributes of which are ordered but for which the numerical difference between adjacent attributes is not necessarily interpreted as equal.
- **Outlier.** An extremely large or small observation; applies to ordinal, interval, and ratio variables.
- **Parameter.** A number that describes a population. A measure such as mean, median, standard deviation, or proportion that is calculated or defined by using every item in the population.
- **Point estimate.** An estimate of a population parameter that is a single numerical value.
- **Population.** A set of persons, things, or events about which there are questions. All the numbers of a group to be studied as defined by the auditor; the total collection of individuals or items from which a sample is selected. Population is also called a universe.
- **Precision.** See *sampling error*.
- **Random number sampling.** A sampling method in which combinations of random digits, within the range of the number of items in a population, are selected by using one of the random number generation methods until a given sample size is obtained. For example, if a sample of 60 items is required from a population numbered 1 through 2,000, then 60 random numbers between 1 and 2,000 are selected.
- **Random selection.** A selection method that uses an acceptable method of generating random numbers in a standard manner. The method minimizes the influence of nonchance factors in selecting the sample items.
- **Range.** The distance (or difference) between the highest and lowest values. This is a quick measure of the dispersion (spread) of the distribution. It is a statistic used primarily with interval-ratio variables.
- **Ratio estimate.** An estimate of a population parameter that is obtained by multiplying the known population total for another variable by a ratio of appropriate sample values of the two variables.
- **Ratio variable.** A quantitative variable the attributes of which are ordered, spaced equally, and with a true zero point.
- **Sample.** A portion of a population that is examined or tested in order to obtain information or draw conclusions about the entire population.
- **Sampling distribution.** The distribution of a statistic.
- **Sampling error or precision.** Each estimate generated from a probability sample has a measurable precision, or sampling error, that may be expressed as a plus or minus figure. A sampling error indicates how closely we can reproduce from a sample the results that we would obtain if we were to take a complete count of the population using the same measurement methods.

By adding the sampling error to and subtracting from the estimate, we can develop upper and lower bounds for each estimate. This range is called a "confidence interval." Sampling errors and confidence intervals are stated at a certain confidence level. For example, a confidence interval at the 95% confidence level means that in 95 of 100 instances, the sampling procedure we used would produce a confidence interval containing the population value we are estimating.

- **Sampling frame.** A means of access to a population, usually a list of the sampling units contained in the population. The list may be printed on paper, a magnetic tape/disk file, or a physical file of such things as payroll records or accounts receivable.
- **Simple random sample.** A probability sample in which each member of the population has an equal chance of being drawn to the sample.
- **Spread.** General term for the extent of variation among cases.
- **Standard deviation.** A measure of spread; a statistic used with interval-ratio variables. A numerical measurement of the dispersion, or scatter, of a group of values about their mean. Also called root mean square deviation.
- **Standard deviation.** A numerical measure of the spread of a group of values about their mean. It is a measure of the average squared deviation from the mean. It is the square root of the variance. We take the square root to account for the fact that we squared the differences in computing the variance. It is the measure of variability of a statistical sample that serves as an estimate of the population variability. This is the most common and useful of the dispersion measures.
- **Standard error of the mean.** The standard deviation of the sampling distribution of a sample statistic. It is a measure of the variability within a sample.
- **Statistic.** A number computed from data on one or more variables.
- **Statistical estimate.** A numerical value assigned to a population parameter on the basis of evidence from a sample.
- **Strata.** Two or more mutually exclusive subdivisions of a population defined in such a way that each sampling unit can belong to only one subdivision or stratum.
- **Stratified random sample.** If the population to be sampled is first subclassified into several sub-populations called "strata," the sample may be drawn by taking random samples from each stratum. The samples need not be proportional to the strata sizes.
- **Symmetric measure of association.** A measure of association that does not make a distinction between independent and dependent variables.
- **Systematic selection with a random start.** A sampling method in which a given sample size is divided into the population size in order to obtain a sampling interval. A random starting point between 1 and the sampling interval is obtained. This item is selected first; then every item whose number or location is equal to the previously selected item plus the sampling interval is selected, until the population is used up.
- **Tolerable error.** The specified precision or the maximum sampling error that will still permit the results to be useful. It is also called "bound on error."
- **Variable sampling.** Sampling in which the selected sampling units are measured or evaluated (in terms of dollars, pounds, days, etc.), and some statistical measure (statistic) is computed from these measurements to estimate the population parameter or measure.
- **Variance.** Sometimes called the average squared deviation. It is computed by taking the difference between individual value and the mean, squaring it, then adding all the squared differences and dividing by the number of items.

---

(iii) **Basic estimation procedures.** Two basic estimation procedures are available: attribute sampling, which is sampling for attributes, and variable sampling, which is sampling for variables. Attributes estimation is used for estimating discrete (e.g., yes or no) characteristics of a population while variables estimation is used for estimating the value of a population (see Exhibit 5.4).

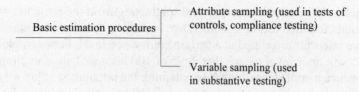

Exhibit 5.4:  Basic estimation procedures

When **sampling for attributes,** we want to determine how frequently items having a certain characteristic occur in a population. The characteristic(s) that we are interested in is called the attribute of the item. Either the item has the characteristic or it does not, although a third, unknown value can be ascribed.

Some examples of attributes for which we might sample are: travel orders without proper approval, health insurance claims that were paid without supporting documentation, error rates on travel reimbursement claims exceeding the level set by management, determining whether the credit department is requiring a credit check for credit sales when needed, and determining error rates in cash disbursements.

**Sampling for variables** is used when we are estimating something that can be quantified or measured in dollars, pounds, feet, and so on. This measurement is known as a variable. The measure of variability most useful in variable sampling is the standard deviation. A confidence level of 95% for a variables sampling application can be interpreted as a 95% probability that results of repeated samples will not vary from population characteristics by more than a specified amount.

Some examples of variables are: the dollar error in an accounts-receivable balance, a person's weight, the value of a population of accounts receivable outstanding, reviewing the accuracy of total charges to employee fringe benefit accounts, estimating the number of units in a certain class of inventory without counting each one, and estimating the average account balance of a bank depositor's based on a sample.

We can use a single sample to develop estimates for both variables and attributes. For example, in examining purchase orders, we can take one sample to estimate both the rate of occurrence and the dollar amount of unadjusted purchases. However, *in general, the sample sizes required for estimating variables are larger than those required for estimating attributes.* Therefore, when we calculate the sample size, we should base it on the precision we want to obtain for the variables estimate, not the attributes estimate.

## ATTRITUBUTE SAMPLING VS. VARIABLE SAMPLING

- Attribute sampling is sampling for error rates (percent). Attributes are counted.
- Variable sampling is sampling for amounts (dollars). Variables are measured.
- Attribute sampling is applied in compliance testing (tests of controls).
- Variable sampling is applied in substantive testing.
- Attribute sampling is mostly used by internal auditors.
- Variable sampling is mostly used by external auditors.

(A) *Attribute sampling.* Sometimes we want to estimate the proportion, percentage, or total number of items in a population that possess some characteristic (attribute) or that fall into some defined classification. When sampling for errors, the auditor is looking for one of only two possible conditions: the presence or absence of an error. The attributes sampling method is used to sort the erroneous accounts from the good accounts.

The sample selection methods can be fixed or sequential. Under a fixed approach, the auditor selects a single sample of a calculated size in one step. Multiple steps are used in a sequential sampling plan where each step is dependent on the audit results of the previous step.

One example of application of attribute sampling is the percentages of the purchase requisitions that were not approved. Assume that the auditors are reviewing a supply store's efficiency of operations in a manufacturing plant. For this audit, they want to estimate the number of requisitions the store was unable to fill during the past fiscal year because requisitioned items were out of stock and the rate at which the store was unable to fill them. The population consists of all 12,000 requisitions received by the store that year.

We use $N$ to represent the size of the population and $n$ to represent the sample size. In the example, the sample consists of a simple random sample of 100 requisitions. Therefore, $N$ equals 12,000 and $n$ equals 100.

The characteristic of interest is, of course, a requisition that was not filled because the item was out of stock. We will let $a$ represent the number of items in the sample that have the characteristic of interest. In this case, assume $a$ equals 36. We calculate the estimated rate of occurrences, $p$, as

$$p = a/n = 36/100 = 0.36 = 36\%$$

Given an estimated rate of occurrence of 36% for unfilled requisitions in our population of 12,000, after multiplying the population size times the rate of occurrence, we estimate that the number of unfilled requisitions is 4,320 (i.e., $12,000 \times 0.36 = 4,320$).

(B) *Calculating the sampling error for attribute sampling.* To calculate the sampling error of the estimated rate of occurrence ($E_p$) and of the estimated number of occurrences ($E_i$), we use the formulas below. Let $q$ equal $1 - p$.

$$E_p = t\sqrt{\frac{pq}{n}}$$

where $t$ is t-value from the tables, $p$ is estimated rate of occurrences, $q$ is complement of $p$, that is, $(1 - p)$, and $n$ is sample size.

At the 90% confidence level and with a $t$ value of 1.645, the sampling error is calculated as:

$$E_p = 1.645\sqrt{\frac{(0.36)(0.64)}{100}}$$

$$E_p = (1.645)(0.048) = 0.07896$$

$$E_i = E_p \times 12,000 = 0.07896 \times 12,000 = 948$$

Based on the results obtained above, we can say that the number of unfilled requisitions is within 948 of the 4,320 at the 90% confidence level; that is, the number of unfilled requisitions falls between 3,372 (i.e., $4,320 - 948$) and 5,268 (i.e., $4,320 + 948$) at the 90% confidence level, or the best estimate of the number of unfilled requisitions is 4,320 within a sampling error of 948 as stated at the 90% confidence level.

If a large number of samples were taken from the same universe, 68% of them would be within 1 sampling error of the percentage, about 90% would be within 1.645 sampling errors, about 95% would be within 1.96 (or 2) sampling errors, and 99% would be within 2.58 (or 3) sampling errors.

(C) *Calculating sampling size for attribute sampling.* The formula for calculating the sample size for an attribute sampling method is:

$$n = \frac{t^2 pq}{E^2}$$

Suppose we wanted to reduce the sampling error of the percentage of unfilled requisitions to 4 percentage points at the 95% confidence level. Since tolerable error ($E$) equals 0.04, we have

$$n = \frac{(2)^2(0.36)(0.64)}{(0.04)^2} = 576$$

Thus, we would have to sample 476 requisitions in addition to the 100 already sampled. With attribute sampling, if the sample size is more than 5% of the universe, we should use the finite population correction (FPC) factor. *FPC is used to reduce the sampling error and to reduce the sample size.* If the FPC is used to compute the sample size, it should be used to compute the sampling error. Otherwise, the computed sampling error will be greater than the specified tolerable error.

(D) *Special cases of attribute sampling.* Sequential sampling (stop-and-go sampling, discovery sampling, and acceptance sampling) plans are special cases of attribute sampling. In this section, focus is on the stop-and-go sampling; the other two topics are discussed elsewhere.

The stop-and-go sampling method is designed to accept a small number of errors or low rate of noncompliance with statistical conclusions. The sample items include a number of blocks, and each block is tested in order. The inclusion of each block is conditional on the results of the previous block. Once a given block has been completed, the auditor stops and applies these decision rules.

- **Rule 1:** If the number of deviations noted is less than the number of blocks tested, then the desired conclusion has been reached. The sampling is stopped.
- **Rule 2:** If the number of deviations noted is equal to or greater than the number of blocks tested, then the desired conclusion has not been reached. The sampling is either continued or stopped.

The main advantage of stop-and-go sampling is that it may reduce the size of the sample that needs to be taken from a population, thus reducing sampling costs. Stop-and-go sampling differs from fixed-sample size attribute sampling in that total expected sample size will always be smaller.

(E) *Variable sampling.* Variables are things that can be quantified, or measured in dollars, pounds, and the like. When sampling for variables, we usually want to estimate the total value for the universe of interest; for example, the total amount of assessed taxes that were not collected.

Assume that our objective is to estimate the dollar amount of small purchases made by a company during a specific fiscal year, and there were 100 such purchases.

*Calculating the sampling error for variable sampling.* To compute the sampling error, or precision, of the estimated total, we first compute the standard deviation of the purchases amounts. The standard deviation is a numerical measure of the dispersion of a group of values about their mean. It is a measure of the average squared deviation from the mean.

The sampling error is calculated by multiplying the standard deviation by a $t$ value corresponding to the stipulated level of confidence and dividing by the square root of the sample size. The formula is:

$$E_y = \frac{ts}{\sqrt{n}}$$

Suppose that we have previously decided that the confidence level for the precision of our estimate should be 95%. The $t$ factor for 95% is 1.96 or 2. Using this value and $48.71 for $s$, and assuming a simple random sample size of 30, we obtain

$$E_y = \frac{(1.96)(48.71)}{\sqrt{30}} = 17.43$$

Thus, the sampling error of the mean is $17.43. To get the sampling error of the total, we simply multiply the sampling error of the mean by the number of items in the universe. Thus, the sampling error of the total is $(100) \times (17.43) = \$1,743$.

Using the 95% confidence level, we state that if all small purchase orders were reviewed, the chances are 19 in 20 that the results of a review would differ from the estimate obtained from the sample by less than the sampling error. The best estimate, the point that is likely to be closest to the true population total, is $18,230. This is obtained by multiplying the arithmetic mean of the sample purchases, 182.3, by the number of small purchases, 100.

*Calculating the sample size for variable sampling.* Whether we sample for variables or sample for attributes, one advantage of statistical sampling is that it permits us to determine objectively the sample size required to achieve a given degree of precision at a specified confidence level. To make this computation, we need to estimate the standard deviation of the universe, not the sample.

In computing the sample size, we must consider three factors: (1) confidence level, (2) precision, and (3) standard deviation. The auditor specifies two factors—confidence level and precision. The third factor, the standard deviation, is based on the characteristics of the universe.

Suppose we want to reduce the sampling error of the total small purchases in the example given above from $1,743 to $1,400 at the 95% confidence level. The first step is to convert the precision that is wanted (or tolerable error) of the total to the tolerable error of the mean (E). The computation is E = desired precision of estimated total divided by $N$. In our example, it is E =

1,400/100 = 14. Thus, the tolerable error of the mean is $14. Once we have the tolerable error of the mean, we compute the required sample size by using the formula

$$n = \frac{t^2 s^2}{E^2} = \frac{(1.96)^2 (48.71)^2}{(14)^2} = 46.48 = 46$$

This means that 16 purchase orders, in addition to the first sample of 30, would have to be sampled in order to achieve the required precision. Note that we have used the standard deviation obtained from our first sample as an estimate of the true universe standard deviation. If the true standard deviation was known, we would not be sampling.

Occasionally, it is incorrectly stated that a larger universe requires a larger sample or that the sample must always be a certain percentage of the universe. This is not true. As noted in the formula for calculating sample size, the size of the universe does not enter into the calculations.

(iv) **Advanced estimation procedures.** Ratio estimation, difference estimation, and mean-per-unit estimation procedures are different approaches to variables sampling. Selection of an approach depends on the data being audited. Ratio estimation and difference estimation procedures are advanced estimation sampling procedures that yield more efficient (or precise) estimates and give more information than basic estimation procedures, such as attribute sampling and variables sampling (see Exhibit 5.5).

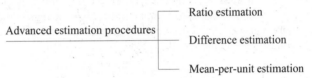

**Exhibit 5.5: Advanced estimation procedures**

(A) *Ratio estimation procedure.* Sometimes, in a sampling application, the summary statistic we want to estimate is a ratio between two variables, both of which can vary from sampling unit to sampling unit: for example, the ratio of Medicare reimbursements for prescription drugs to total reimbursements.

---
**Ratio Estimation and Sampling Error**

Ratio estimation yields a smaller sampling error because the positive correlation between the auxiliary and primary variables reduces the sampling error.

---

In other applications, we may want to estimate the total value of an unknown variable that is related to another variable for which we already know the universe total value. For example, we may want to estimate the total meals cost claimed on a department's travel vouchers for a year, when we already know the total amount of travel reimbursement (the population total) for the year and the number of vouchers paid (the population size). We record two variables for each sample travel voucher: the auxiliary (independent) variable describes the amount paid, and the primary (dependent) variable describes the amount of meals claimed. The summary statistic is the ratio in which the total of the primary variables (the meal costs) is the numerator and the total of the auxiliary variables (the amount paid) is the denominator.

We should also use ratio estimation when we suspect that there is a positive correlation between the two variables, even if we are interested not in the ratio, but only in the estimated total of the primary variable. If the correlation is positive and if it is strong enough, the estimate that can be obtained will be more precise than the estimate that can be obtained with simple expansion estimation.

---
**SIMPLE ESTIMATION VS. ADVANCED ESTIMATION**

- In simple expansion estimation, we calculate a sample mean or proportion and multiply it by the population size to obtain the estimated total or the estimated number of occurrences in the population.

• In advanced estimation, we take account of other information that we can obtain from the samples and the population.

---

The ratio estimate has a slight mathematical bias that can usually be ignored if the sample size is large, say 50 or more. The bias results from the assumption that the line representing the ratio is a straight line passing through the origin. This almost never happens in practice.

Ratio estimation can be used with more complex sample designs, such as stratified samples and single-stage and multistage cluster samples.

Note that with ratio estimation, we obtain two estimated results, ratio and total. For many purposes, the ratio is more meaningful than the total, because it permits us to make useful statements about meeting the audit objective.

### Examples of ratio estimation procedures

1.  A department made 10,000 small purchases totaling $5,100,000 over one year. The auditors, suspecting that purchases could have been made at a lower cost, decided to estimate the savings that would have resulted if suppliers offering lower costs had been used. The confidence level is set at 95%, and a preliminary random sample of 50 cases is taken. The sum of the savings in the sample is $3,600, and the sum of the purchase costs is $24,800.

    The first step is to compute the ratio of savings to the department purchase costs ($R$) by dividing the sum of the savings in the sample ($3,600) by the sum of the department purchase costs in the sample ($24,800).

    $$R = \$3,600/\$24,800 = 0.14516$$

    The ratio of 0.14516 tells us that 14.5 cents of every dollar could have been saved had purchases cost less.

    The next step is to estimate the total savings ($Y$) by multiplying the total purchase costs ($X$) of $5,100,000 by 0.14516, the ratio of savings to costs.

    $$\text{Total savings} = \$5,100,000 \times 0.14516 = \$740,316$$

2.  An auditor discovered that discounts for prompt payment were frequently not being taken. About 30% of the suppliers' invoices offered discounts ranging from 2% to 5% of the invoice amount. To estimate the amount lost from not taking these discounts during the past year, the most efficient and effective sampling technique would be ratio estimation.

(B) *Difference estimation.* Difference estimation is used when we want to obtain a "corrected" estimate of a previously stated "book" value. For example, suppose we wanted to estimate the "correct" total value of an inventory when we know the value per book and can take a sample from the inventory items and correct the items examined in the sample, if necessary. It is also an attempt to increase precision by obtaining two measurements on a single sampling unit. However, difference estimation will increase precision only if the differences between the primary and auxiliary variables are very small. To use difference estimation, we must know the population total for the auxiliary variable.

### Example of difference estimation procedures

Using the same example as used for the ratio estimation, assume that the auditors decided to audit the accuracy of the payments that were made. To save work, they decided to use the same sample of 50 purchases. We need to obtain or calculate three items: (1) the purchase costs, (2) the audited amounts that should have been paid, and (3) the differences between the first two items.

The first step is to calculate the mean difference as the sum of all differences (+ $1,048) divided by the sample size, which is equal to + $1,048/50 = + 20.96.

The next step is to obtain the estimated total difference as multiplying the mean difference by the population of 10,000. This is equal to 10,000 × 20.96 = + 209,600.

The next step is to add or subtract the estimated total difference to the population total of $5,100,000. Since the estimated total difference is positive, we should be adding to the population total. This gives $5,100,000 + 209,600 = $5,309,600.

Thus, using the difference method, we can estimate the correct amount that should have been paid at $5,309,600. The actual payments were more than this amount by $5,309,600 − $5,100,000 = $209,600.

## RATIO ESTIMATION VS. DIFFERENCE ESTIMATION

- One big advantage of ratio and difference estimation procedures is that they adjust the sample results to known population data when we compute totals.
- If the sample mean for the auxiliary variable turns out to be lower than the population mean, the sample results are adjusted upward.
- If the sample means for the auxiliary variable turns out to be higher than the population mean, the sample results are adjusted downward.
- When the calculations must be done manually, difference estimation has one advantage over ratio estimation: the formulas for computing estimates and sampling errors are simple. Also, because of the simplicity of the formulas, difference estimation can be easily adapted to stratified sampling.

---

(C) *Mean-per-unit estimation procedures.* Mean-per-unit is a sampling plan that can be used to estimate unknown values, such as that of an inventory where book values either do not exist or are unreliable. An important measure for such estimates is the standard error of the mean. Sample size affects the size of the standard error.

In general, the mean-per-unit method is used when the book value of a population is unknown, the population can be stratified, and the variability of the book value is low. This procedure can be performed with a nonstatistical population. Mean-per-unit method, discovery sampling, and attributes sampling methods are based on normal-curve mathematics while dollar-unit-sampling method is not. A major characteristic of normal-curve mathematics is that the sampling distribution of the sample means approaches the normal distribution as the sample size becomes larger and larger.

### Example of mean-per-unit estimation procedures

Mean-per-unit method is appropriate when an auditor for the state highway and safety department needs to estimate the average highway weight of tractor-trailer trucks using the state's highway system.

(v) **Discovery sampling procedures.** Discovery sampling is a type of sampling procedure that has a specified probability of including at least one item that occurs very rarely in the population. It is used when there is a possibility of finding such things as fraud and avoidance of internal controls. In discovery sampling, the auditors can specify the probability of including in the sample at least one item with a particular characteristic, if the characteristic occurs at a specified rate in the population. If the sample does not turn up an item with this characteristic, the auditors can make a probability statement that the characteristic's rate of occurrence is less than that specified.

Discovery sampling can be regarded as a special case of attribute sampling. However, in its usual applications, it does not yield an estimated rate of occurrence, and usually it is used only if the particular characteristic's rate of occurrence is thought to be very small—that is, close to zero. For example, discovery sampling is usually used in financial audits to guard against an intolerable rate of fraud.

(A) *Procedures.* The auditor must specify two things: the rate of error, fraud, or abuse that would be intolerable and the probability of finding at least one occurrence in the sample. The sample sizes can be found from the tables (consisting of sample size versus total errors in population size) or calculated using the logarithms.

Then the auditors select a simple random sample of items and examine each item until they find one with an error or until they have examined the entire sample and found no errors. If they find an error, they know that the error rate is at least as great as the specified intolerable rate and can extend the review perhaps to the entire population. If they find no deficiencies, they can conclude that the rate of occurrence of deficiencies is less than that specified as intolerable.

(B) *Advantages.* An advantage of discovery sampling is that the probability of finding at least one error will increase if the rate of occurrence of deficiencies is greater than the intolerable rate specified by the auditors. Thus, the likelihood of more quickly finding the one error in the sample is increased, and the average sample size that actually has to be examined is smaller.

**Example of discovery sampling procedures**

An auditor samples cash disbursement records for significant errors of $5 or more. Upon finding one such error, these records are scheduled for a complete review. This conclusion is based on a discovery sample.

---

**KEY CONCEPTS TO REMEMBER: DISCOVERY SAMPLING**

- Discovery sampling is good to detect fictitious employees on the payroll.
- It is generally inappropriate if the objective is to perform a substantive test.
- It controls the risks of an erroneous decision due to observation of at least one sample occurrence.
- It is suitable to test for the presence of fictitious payees for health insurance claims, although none are suspected.
- One minus the confidence level can be interpreted to mean the probability of being incorrect in placing reliance on the results of the sample.
- A 5% risk of overreliance would conclude that there is a 95% probability that the actual rate of occurrence in the population is less than the critical rate if no exceptions are found.
- An auditor might use discovery sampling to compute the upper precision limit of an infrequently occurring error.
- When fraud is suspected, a discovery sampling plan should be used if the purpose is to select a sample with a given probability of containing at least one example of the irregularity.
- The primary difference between discovery and acceptance sampling is that a discovery-sampling plan is primarily an investigative technique, while an acceptance sampling is a quality control tool.

---

(vi) **Monetary unit sampling procedures.** Monetary unit sampling is an efficient method used to determine how many items need to be examined and the reliability of the conclusions drawn from sampling results. The monetary unit sampling procedure is used for substantive audit testing and is based on the assumption that the variable to be measured is highly correlated with some data already known about the cluster, such as the dollar value of transactions. If the assumption is correct, this selection method will yield a smaller sampling error than other methods would.

(A) *Sampling unit.* The sampling unit is each dollar in the population. This means that if an accounts receivable account has a balance of $100,000, there would be 100,000 sampling units in the population. Audit procedures will be performed on the customer account that contains the dollar that was selected. The customer account is called a logical unit because it will be subjected to the audit work. The auditor must define the population, sampling unit, and logical unit before determining the sample size.

Here sampling with replacement is used, which means that when the random numbers are selected, duplicates are not eliminated. Sampling with replacement is a characteristic of the monetary unit sampling procedure. The monetary unit sampling procedure is also called the probability-proportional-to-size (PPS) and dollar-unit sampling. The major use of PPS is in two-stage cluster sampling where the cluster sizes vary greatly.

**Example of monetary unit sampling procedures**

Suppose we want to estimate the dollar value of the insurance claims that were paid by claims-paying offices. It is reasonable to assume that the dollar value of claims that were paid is approximately proportional to the number of claims that were paid. Assume that the maximum number of offices that can be audited is 20.

First, we set up a range of cumulative numbers of claims for each office. Next, we select 20 random numbers between one and the total number of claims paid—say between 1 and 30,447. Then we enter each random number on the line for the office whose range of paid claims includes the random number. This identifies the sample office. Sampling with replacement does not allow some offices to be identified in the sample more than once.

Each office's probability of selection is proportional to the number of paid claims. Yet each office, from the smallest to the largest, has an opportunity of being selected.

(B) *Selection with probability proportional to size (PPS).* When auditors apply random selection procedures to cluster sampling, the clusters can be selected with PPS or with a related variable that can be used as a measure of size. The cluster sampling method is based on the assumption that the variable to be measured is highly correlated with some data already known about the cluster, such as dollar volume of transactions. If the assumption is correct, the PPS method will yield a smaller sampling error than other methods would.

If clusters were chosen with equal probability, the variation in cluster sizes would increase the computed variation between clusters and thus the overall precision of the estimate. Using two-stage cluster sampling and PPS sampling to select the primary units, the auditor can calculate subsampling rates within the primary units in a way such that the second-stage sample sizes within each primary unit are equal and, at the same time, the sample is self-weighing. Therefore, the sample can be treated as if it were a simple random sample of cluster, which greatly simplifies the calculations.

---

**KEY CONCEPTS TO REMEMBER: MONETARY UNIT SAMPLING AND PPS**

- Monetary unit sampling is not efficient if the audit objective is oriented to understatements. It is good to (1) test for overstatement of accounts payable or receivable book balances and (2) estimate overstatement of error of an account balance in the balance sheet category.
- The monetary unit sampling method automatically provides stratification when using systematic selection.
- An inherent limitation of the PPS sampling method is that error rates must be small and the errors must be overstatements. PPS is good for detecting material overstatements.
- The use of PPS sampling method would be inefficient if each account is of equal importance.
- If no errors are expected, a smaller sample size is suggested.
- If errors are expected, a moderate to larger sample size is suggested.

---

## 5.2 Statistical Analyses

A system should be put in place to allow the organization to determine systematically the degree to which products and services please customers and to focus on internal process improvement. Data should be collected on features of customer satisfaction such as responsiveness, reliability, accuracy, and ease of access. The measurement systems should also focus on internal processes, especially on processes that generate variation in quality and cycle time. *Cycle time* is the time required from conception to completion of an idea or a process. When customer data indicate a problem, or when the organization wants to raise the level of customer satisfaction, the organization should focus on improving the processes that deliver the product or service.

In order to ensure that processes are continuously improved, data should be collected and analyzed on a continuing basis, with particular attention to variation in processes. The causes of variation are examined to determine whether they result from special circumstances (special causes) or from recurring (common) causes. Different strategies should be adopted to correct each occurrence. The immediate objectives of the analysis and measurement effort are to reduce rework, waste, and cycle time and to improve cost-effectiveness and accuracy. The ultimate objectives are to ensure that the organization understands the extent to which customer satisfaction is being realized and where there are deficiencies and why, and to isolate causes that can be attacked systematically.

(a) **Variation.** It is true in manufacturing that no two products are ever made exactly alike. Similarly, no two individuals provide the same service in exactly the same way. The term "variation" means deviation from specifications, standards, or targets. The variation concept is a law of nature: no two items are the same. Variation can result in poor quality to the customer and cost to the producer. Variation must be measured and reduced for proper functioning of a process. The ability to measure variation is a requirement before it can be controlled or stabilized. When the variation is reduced, quality is improved and costs are reduced. Both input and process variation must be reduced in order to reduce the overall variation in a product. These relationships can be shown in the next equation.

Reduced input variation + Reduced process variation = Reduced product variation

Variation is present in every process as a result of a combination of four variables: (1) operator variation (due to physical and emotional conditions), (2) equipment variation (due to wear and tear), (3) materials variation (due to thickness, moisture content, and old and new materials), and (4) environmental variation (due to changes in temperature, light, and humidity). Variation is either expected or unexpected.

Variation affects the proper functioning of a process; this process output deviates from the established target (**off-target**). From a statistics point of view, the term "off-target" relates to a process average. **Common causes** affect the standard deviation of a process, and are caused by factors internal to a process. These causes, which are present in all processes, are called *chance* (random) *causes*. Chance causes are small in magnitude and are difficult to identify. Examples of common random causes include worker availability, number and complexity of orders, job schedules, equipment testing, work center schedules, changes in raw materials, truck schedules, and worker performance.

**Special causes** affect the standard deviation of a process and are factors external to a process. Special causes, also known as *assignable causes,* are large in magnitude and are not so difficult to identify. They may or may not be present in a process. Examples of special (assignable) causes include equipment breakdowns, operator changes, new raw materials, new products, new competition, and new customers.

**Structural causes** affect the standard deviation of a process; they are factors both internal and external to a process. They may or may not be present in a process; they are a blend of common and special causes. Examples of structural causes include sudden sales/production volume increase due to a new product or a new customer, seasonal sales, and sudden increase in profits.

(b) **Control Charts.** A control chart is a statistical tool that distinguishes between natural (common) and unnatural (special) variations. The control chart method is used to measure variations in quality. The control chart is a picture of the process over time. It shows whether a process is in a stable state and is used to improve the process quality.

Natural variation is the result of random causes. Management intervention is required to achieve quality improvement or quality system. It has been stated that 80% to 85% of quality problems are due to management or the quality system and that 15% to 20% of problems are due to operators or workers. Supervisors, operators, and technicians can correct the unnatural variation. Control charts can be drawn for variables and attributes.

The control chart method for **variables** is a means of visualizing the variations that occur in the central tendency and dispersion of a set of observations. It measures the quality of a particular characteristic, such as length, time, or temperature.

A variable chart is an excellent technique for achieving quality improvement. True process capability can be achieved only after substantial quality improvement has been made. Once true process capability is obtained, effective specifications can be determined. Here is the sequence of events taking place with the control chart.

Variable chart ⟶ Quality improvement ⟶ Process capability ⟶ Specifications

The attribute chart refers to those quality characteristics that conform to specifications (specs) or do not conform to specifications. It is used where measurements are not possible, such as for color, missing parts, scratches, or damage.

(c) **Stable and Unstable Process.** When only chance causes of variation are present in a process, the process is considered to be in a state of statistical control (i.e., the process is stable and predictable). When a process is in control (stable), there occurs a natural pattern of variation, and only chance causes of variation are present. Small variations in operator performance, equipment performance, materials, and environmental characteristics are expected and are considered to be part of a stable process. Further improvements in the process can be achieved only by changing the input factors, that is, operator, equipment, materials, and environment. These changes require action by management through quality improvement ideas.

When an assignable cause of variation is present in a process, it is considered to be out of statistical control (i.e., the process is unstable and unpredictable). When an observed measurement falls outside its control limits, the process is said to be out of control (unstable). This means that an assignable cause of variation is present. The unnatural, unstable variation makes it impossible to predict future variation. The assignable causes must be found and corrected before a natural, stable process can continue.

(d) **Attribute and Variable Control Charts**

(i) **Attribute control charts.** Two types of attribute control charts exist: (1) the chart for nonconforming units and (2) the chart for nonconformities. A nonconforming unit is a product or service containing at least one nonconformity. A nonconformity is a departure of quality characteristic from its intended level that is not meeting a specification requirement.

The nonconforming unit is based on the binomial distribution. It is shown as proportion chart (p chart) that is expressed as a fraction or a percent of nonconforming units in a sample. Another chart is number proportion chart (np chart) to represent the number of nonconforming units. The fraction nonconforming, $p$, is usually quite small, say 5% or less. Values greater than 5% require drastic measures other than a control chart. The p chart can be used to measure the quantity produced by a work center, by a department, by a production shift, or by an entire plant. It is also used to report the performance of an operator.

### Example: Calculation for p chart

Formula is $p = np/n$, where $p$ is proportion of nonconformities in a sample, $np$ is number of nonconforming units in the sample, and $n$ is the number of units in the sample.

During the second shift of production, 400 inspections are made of shipments and 4 nonconforming shipments are found. The second shift produced 10,000 units. What is the fraction of shipments nonconforming?

$$p = np/n = 4/400 = 0.01 = 1\%$$

Since 1% is less than 5% target, shipments conform to specifications or standards. Here, 10,000 production is not relevant.

The nonconformity is based on the Poisson distribution. It has two charts: (1) the c chart, which shows the count of nonconformities in an inspected unit, and (2) the u chart, which shows the count of nonconformities per unit. The u chart is similar to the c chart except in scale and size. The scale for a u chart is continuous, but the scale for a c chart is discrete. This makes the u chart more flexible. The subgroup size is one for the c chart, and it varies for the u chart.

The most common types of attribute control charts are

- The p chart is used to control the fraction of units with some characteristic such as the fraction defective. It is based on binomially distributed counts.
- The np chart is used to control the number of units with some characteristic, such as the number of defectives per batch. It is based on binomially distributed count.
- The c chart is used to control the number of events, such as defects in some fixed area of opportunity, (e.g. single unit.) It is an example of an area of opportunity chart and based on Poisson distribution.
- The u chart is used to control the number of events, such as defects in a changeable area of opportunity, (e.g., square yards). It is an example of an area of opportunity chart and is based on Poisson distribution.
- The individual chart is used to control the count when the assumptions for the other attribute charts cannot be met. It is used when attribute data are neither binomial nor Poisson in nature.

(ii) **Variable control charts.** To improve the process continuously, variable control charts can be used to overcome the limitations of the attribute control charts. Continuous process improvement is the highest level of quality consciousness. Control charts based on variable data reduce unit-to-unit variation, even within specification limits. Variable data consist of measurements such as weight, length, width, height, time, temperature. Variable data contain more information than attribute data. Variable control charts can decrease the difference between customer needs and process performance.

Two types of variable control charts exist: the X bar chart, which is used to record the variation in the average value of samples (process average) and the R chart, which measures the range or the dispersion (process spread, standard deviation, or variability).

The most common types of variable control charts are

- The X bar chart is used to control the process average.
- The R chart is used to control the process range.
- The s chart is used to control the process standard deviation.
- The median chart is used as a simple alternative to the combination of an X bar and an R chart.
- The individual chart is used to control subgroups of size one drawn from a process; it frequently is used when sampling is expensive or only one observation is available per subgroup (e.g., production per month).

## 5.3 Data-Gathering Tools and Techniques

Auditors use several data-gathering tools and techniques to obtain background information on the auditee's operations, collect audit evidence, and pertinent data for the audit purpose. These techniques include questionnaires, anecdotal records, unobtrusive measures, checklists, interviews, focus group, and observation (see Exhibit 5.6).

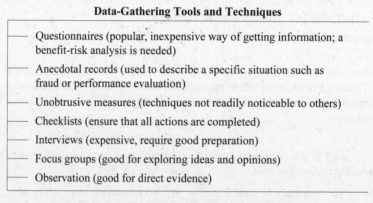

**Data-Gathering Tools and Techniques**

— Questionnaires (popular, inexpensive way of getting information; a benefit-risk analysis is needed)

— Anecdotal records (used to describe a specific situation such as fraud or performance evaluation)

— Unobtrusive measures (techniques not readily noticeable to others)

— Checklists (ensure that all actions are completed)

— Interviews (expensive, require good preparation)

— Focus groups (good for exploring ideas and opinions)

— Observation (good for direct evidence)

**Exhibit 5.6: Data-gathering tools and techniques**

### (a) Interviewing

(i) **Types of interviews.** Interviews are of two types: structured and unstructured (i.e., less structured). A **structured interview** is one in which auditors ask the same questions of numerous individuals or individuals representing numerous organizations in a precise manner, offering each interviewee the same set of possible responses.[1] In contrast, an **unstructured interview** contains many open-ended questions, which are not asked in a structured, precise manner. With unstructured interviews, different auditors interpret questions and often offer different explanations when respondents ask for clarification. The structured interview technique is good to apply in an organization with multiple locations, units, or divisions. The less-structured and less-guided type of unstructured interview may be more useful to one-of-a-kind interview.

## STRUCTURED VS. UNSTRUCTURED INTERVIEWS

- Structured interviews are good for repetitive types of interviews.
- Unstructured interviews are good for one-of-a-kind interviews.

The telephone interview and, even more, the face-to-face interview enable the interviewer to establish rapport with respondents. Individuals who would not answer certain questions on their own can be persuaded to provide truthful answers in a telephone or face-to-face interview.

In comparison to the telephone interview, the face-to-face interview gives the interviewer the opportunity to observe as well as listen. More complex questions can be asked in a face-to-face interview than in a telephone interview. More questions can be asked in a face-to-face interview since the time can last up to an hour (optimum time) while 30 minutes is the usual limit for telephone interviews. In comparison with mail questionnaires, face-to-face and telephone interviews are much faster methods of gathering data.

---

[1] *Using Structured Interviewing Techniques* (Washington, DC: U.S. General Accounting Office 1991).

A good preparation for an interview requires several dimensions, such as making sure that interview questions are appropriate, that is, relevant to the audit, directed to the proper persons, and easily answered.

- **Relevance** requires that interview questions should have a good probability of yielding data needed for the final audit report. Auditors should not go on "fishing expeditions" and try to include all sorts of variables that can create an unnecessary burden on the interviewee and distract attention from the central purpose of the interview.
- **Selection of respondents.** Consideration should be given to auditees who can be expected to answer given questions. A question may be relevant to a given audit, but the choice of persons to answer it may be inappropriate.
- **Ease of response.** Interviews are meant to obtain data that may otherwise not be documented or, if documented, may need some interpretation. Questions should be constructed that are relatively easy to answer and do not cause undue burden to the interviewee (auditee).

If needed, ask sensitive questions in a mail questionnaire where confidentiality or anonymity can be granted. Also avoid questions that could cause unnecessary confrontation, causing the interviewer and interviewee to take sides and do battle.

Also avoid questions that have no answers, and avoid questions that, if you attempt to ask them, produce unusable results. These are not to be confused with questions for which the legitimate answer might be "no basis to judge" or "no opinion."

(ii) **Organizing interview questions.** The order in which the questions are presented in an interview is important. Early questions, which set the tone for the data collection procedure and can influence responses to later questions, also help the auditor get to know the interviewee and to establish the rapport essential to a successful interview. Remember that the questions should hold the interviewee's attention; thus, the auditor must begin to introduce some "interesting" questions.

The questions should be presented in a logical manner, keeping the flow of questions in chronological or reverse order, as appropriate. It is good to avoid haphazardly jumping from one topic to another. Also avoid introducing bias in the ordering of questions.

(iii) **Interview design.** There are ways to compose good interview questions and to forestall problems with comprehension or bias. The appropriateness and level of language used in the interview, the effects of qualifying language, and the importance of clarity are all important to consider. The auditor needs to be familiar with the various kinds of bias that can creep into the wording of interview questions and their effect on the validity of the audit results (see Exhibit 5.7).

**Considerations in Designing
Interview Questions**

— Appropriateness of the language
— Level of language
— Speaking down to an interviewee
— Use of qualifying language
— Clarity of language

**Exhibit 5.7: Considerations in designing interview questions**

(A) *Appropriateness of the language*. Whether interviewing language is appropriate or inappropriate may relate to what is said, how it is said, or when it is said. What is said in the interview is basically dictated by the writer's structured data collection instrument. How it is said concerns the speech and mannerisms of the interviewer who controls the "presentation" and whose delivery of questions may alter their intended meaning. When it is said refers to the context of the interview in which each question is placed. If the interviewee expresses concern or sensitivity to a given question, changing the language of a subsequent question might defuse the concern.

(B) *Level of language*. When composing interview questions, consider the level of the language used. Seek to communicate at the level the interviewee understands and to create a verbal setting that is conducive to serious data gathering yet one in which the interviewee is comfortable. One problem often encountered is maintaining a level of language that is neither above nor below the interviewee's level of understanding. Speaking over the interviewee's head includes the use of complex, rare, and foreign words and expressions; words of many syllables; abbreviations; acronyms; and certain jargon. Such language, while it may seem appropriate to the interviewer or audit team, may not be understood by the interviewee. Thus, to speak over the interviewee's head hinders communication. Interviewees who are embarrassed at their lack of understanding may either not answer or guess at the meaning, which can lead to incorrect answers. Or interviewees may get the impression that the auditor really does not care about the answer and lose interest in the interview.

(C) *Speaking down to an interviewee.* This is just as bad. Oversimplifying the language in the data collection instrument can make the interviewees feel you regard them as ignorant. This approach is demeaning. The auditor has contacted these individuals because they have important information to impart. To treat a person condescendingly—or to let it appear that one does—negates that importance. Likewise, care should be taken in using slang, folksy expressions, and certain jargon. While such language may help the auditor develop rapport with the interviewee, the exactness of the communication may be lessened. To avoid error in either direction, **pretest** both the final wording of the data collection instrument and the interview questions.

(D) *Use of qualifying language.* After composing an interview question, the auditor may find it requires an adjective or qualifying phrase or a time specified to make the item complete or to give the interviewee sufficient or complete information. For example, "How many employees do you have?" might become "How many full-time-equivalent employees do you have?" If the auditor did not include the necessary qualifiers in the data collection instrument, another auditor may qualify it in a different way. This could make the resulting data difficult to summarize and analyze. Also interviewees, not realizing that qualifying language is absent, may answer the question as they interpret it. Thus, different interviewees would be responding to different questions, based on their own interpretations.

(E) *Clarity of language.* The style in which a question is couched can affect the clarity of communication. A question that contains too many ideas or concepts may be too complex for the interviewee to understand, especially if it is presented orally, which makes it difficult for the interviewee to review parts of the question. The auditor should limit one thought to one sentence and give the interviewee the proper framework.

Likewise, a sentence may contain clutter—words that do not clarify the message. Questions should be worded concisely. Here are a few suggestions to reduce sentence clutter.

- Delete "that" wherever possible—for example, "Others suggest [that] training can be improved."
- Use plain language. For example, for "aforementioned," use "previous" or "previously mentioned."
- Avoid the passive voice. Substitute pronouns ("I," "we," or "they") and active verbs; instead of "It is necessary to obtain," use "We need."

A double-barreled question is a classic example of an unclear question. In this case, it is good to state the question separately if it contains too many parts. In phrasing a question, avoid the double negative, which is difficult to answer. For example, "Indicate which of the organizational goals listed below are not considered unattainable within the 2-year period" should be reworded to read "Indicate which of the organizational goals listed below are considered attainable within the 2-year period."

Avoid such words as "all," "none," "everything," "never," and others that represent extreme values. There are cases when the use of "all" or "none" is appropriate, but they are few. Where "yes" or "no" answers are expected, the results can be misleading. For example, if one employee is not covered in a question such as "Are all of your employees covered by medical insurance," a "yes" answer is impossible. This is because some employees may not have been covered. A better question would be "About what percent of your employees are covered by medical insurance?" Where possible, define key words and comments used in questions. For example, when speaking of "employees," define and clarify the term. Are we talking about part-time, full-time, permanent, temporary, volunteer, white-collar, blue-collar employees?

(iv) **Biased questions in interviews.** A question is biased when it causes interviewees to answer in a way that does not reflect their true positions on an issue. An interviewee may or may not be aware of the bias. Problems result when the interviewees are

- Unaware of the bias and influenced to respond in the way that is directed by the wording
- Aware of the bias and either deliberately answer in a way that does not reflect their opinions
- Refuse to answer because the question is biased

Bias can appear in the stem (or statement) portion of the question or in the response-alternative portion. Bias may also result when a question carries an implied answer, choices of answer are unequal, "loaded" words are used, or a scaled question is unbalanced.

(v) **Conducting interviews.** Each participant in the interview—interviewer (auditor) and interviewee (auditee)—has a role to perform and a set of behaviors that assist in the performance. Because the role and behaviors of each one influence the conduct of the interview, they affect the other participant. To oversimplify, the role of the auditor is to ask the questions; that of the auditee is to respond with answers. Actually, the auditor must perform these major tasks.

- Develop rapport with the auditee and show interest.
- Give the auditee a reason to participate.
- Elicit responsiveness from the auditee.
- Ask questions in a prescribed order and manner.
- Ensure understanding.
- Ensure nonbias.
- Obtain sufficient answers.
- Show sensitivity to the auditee's burden.

(A) *Developing rapport and showing interest.* Auditors should seek to establish a balance relationship between the auditee and themselves as empathetic, friendly individuals who are not too different from the auditee but who are also independent, unbiased, and honest collectors of data. The auditors' appearance, verbal mannerisms, body language, and voice will determine the rapport, starting with the contact that sets up the interview.

The auditors should make their verbal and voice cues calm and unflustered. They should speak so the auditee need not strain to hear and understand. Changes in voice inflection, sighs, or other noises give clues to the auditors' feelings or moods, as do facial expressions and body language. These nonverbal communications can be imprecise. The auditors should control these so that the auditee does not pick up impatience, disapproval, or other negative feelings. Ideally, the auditors should not experience such feelings during the interview, since they are supposed to be impartial, unbiased, and tolerant observers. Likewise, the auditors should control expressions of positive feelings or agreement with what the auditee is saying.

It is important that the auditors be aware of characteristic nonlinguistic cues, such as change in voice, facial expressions, or gestures, since as much as half of the communication that takes place during the interview is conveyed by these modes of expression. Failure to understand those cues may result in miscommunication.

The auditors' appearance is still another variable that influence rapport and, therefore, the tone of the interview. Auditors should dress to fit both the interview and the interviewee. This means wearing warehouse-type clothing (e.g., casual) to meet the auditee during physical inventory taken in a warehouse or manufacturing plant and wearing office-type clothing (e.g., suit and tie) to meet an auditee manager in the office. The auditors' appearance indicates to the auditee (1) the auditors understand the nature of his circumstances, and (2) that the auditors are not totally different from the auditee.

(B) *Giving the auditee a reason to participate.* Some auditees understand the nature of audits in general and the role of the auditor in the organization, while the others do not. Auditees who are not aware of the importance of the audit work and how they can help may not give sincere and well-thought-out answers. Therefore, an auditor's explanations to the auditee are important to the validity of the resulting data.

(C) *Helping the auditee to be responsive.* Some auditees may have never before been interviewed during an audit. The auditor needs to make the auditee comfortable and capable as a respondent. This can be done by reinforcing the auditee with such verbal cues as "I see," "Let me get that down," "I want to make sure that I have that right," "I see, that is helpful to know," "It is useful to get your ideas on this."

(D) ***Asking questions in a prescribed order and manner.*** Questions should be ordered so as to lead the auditee through various topics, correctly position sensitive questions, and hold the auditee's interest. These suggestions may help.

- Ask the questions exactly as they are worded in the questionnaire.
- Ask the questions in the order in which they are presented in the questionnaire.
- Ask every question specified in the questionnaire.
- Read each question slowly (i.e., two words per second).
- Repeat questions that are misunderstood or misinterpreted.
- Do not let the auditee stray from the questions in the interview.
- Keep nonverbal cues as neutral as possible.

*Remember that for telephone interviews, the lack of visual contact decreases the ability to make the auditee understand.*

(E) ***Ensuring understanding.*** At times, an auditee will not understand a question, as indicated by telling the auditor so, by not answering, or by providing an answer that seems inconsistent or wrong. When this happens, the auditor should use an appropriate probing technique such as

- Repeat the question.
- Give an expectant pause.
- Repeat the respondent's reply.
- Make neutral questions or comments, such as "Anything else?" "How do you mean?" "What do you mean?"

The auditor should use these probing questions with care so as not bias the auditee. At this time, rephrasing the question or adding new questions should be avoided as much as possible to minimize confusion.

(F) ***Ensuring nonbias.*** A bias can be introduced in many ways, such as in the way a question is written, in the selection of auditees, in the way the auditor poses the contents of the query, in the introduction of an auditor's own ideas into a probe, in the auditor adding certain verbal emphasis, or using certain body language. All these can destroy the neutrality that should characterize the auditor's presentation.

(G) ***Obtaining sufficient answers.*** Auditors must learn to judge when an answer is sufficient before going to the next question. If the answer is incomplete or vague, auditors should ensure that the question is understood or draw more out of the auditee to complete the answer. Auditors can check the accuracy of the answers given by asking for supporting documentation from the auditee.

(H) ***Showing sensitivity to auditee's burden.*** Before conducting an interview, give the auditee a general statement of how long it is expected to take. Then the auditor is under obligation to adhere to this time limitation. Besides the length of time taken, the interview can be burdensome because of the amount of work the auditee needs to go through to produce the information requested.

(b) **Questionnaires**

(i) **Purpose of questionnaires.** Three phases occur in questionnaires: (1) data design, (2) data collection, and (3) data analysis. A questionnaire is a data collection instrument, and auditors employ it: to ask auditees for figures, statistics, amounts, and other facts; to describe conditions and procedures that affect the work, organizations, and systems with which they are involved; for their judgments and views about processes, performance, adequacy, efficiency, and effectiveness; to report past events and to make forecasts; to describe their attitudes and opinions; and to describe their behavior and the behavior of others.[2]

Questionnaires are popular because they can be a relatively inexpensive way of getting auditees to provide information. However, because questionnaires rely on people to provide answers, a benefit-risk consideration is associated with their use. People with the ability to observe, select, ac-

---

[2] ***Developing and Using Questionnaires*** *(Washington, DC: U.S. General Accounting Office, 1993).*

quire, process, evaluate, interpret, sort, retrieve, and report can be a valuable and versatile source of information under the right circumstances. However, the human mind is a very complex and vulnerable observation instrument. *If we do not ask the right people the right questions in the right way, we will not get high-quality answers.*

## WHAT KINDS OF QUESTIONS SHOULD BE ASKED?

Three kinds of audit questions should be asked: descriptive, normative, and causal (impact). As the name implies, the answers to **descriptive questions** provide descriptive information about specific conditions or events, and focus on "what is." An example is the number of people who received certain types of medical benefits in a given year.

The answers to **normative questions** compare an observed outcome to an expected level of performance, and focus on "what should be." An example is the comparison between airline safety violations and the standard that has been set for safety.

The answers to **impact (cause-and-effect) questions** help reveal whether observed conditions or events can be attributed to business operations. An example is determining the effect of changing a policy or a procedure.

Auditor should use these three kinds of questions in questionnaires since they are all relevant to most common audit situations. The best way to achieve the right balance is to see if each question can be labeled as one of the three kinds of questions. If a question does not belong to either of these types of questions, the auditors need to decide whether to drop the question or use it as a general background, information-gathering information.

---

*Questions must be clear, interesting, and easy to understand and answer. The answers to the questionnaires become input to audit report writing.*

(ii) **When to use questionnaires.** The decision to use a questionnaire should be made only after carefully considering the comparative advantages and disadvantages of the various ways of administering a questionnaire over other data collection techniques.

Data can be collected in a variety of ways, such as field observations, reviews of records or published reports, interviews, mail questionnaires, and face-to-face or telephone questionnaires. The selection of one technique over another involves trade-offs between staff requirements, costs, time constraints, and, most important, the depth and type of information needed.

Questionnaires are frequently used with sample survey strategies to answer descriptive and normative audit questions. They are often less central in studies answering cause-and-effect questions since good answers require an in-depth qualitative and quantitative analysis. Questionnaires can be used in all types of audits—operational, financial, and compliance—to confirm or expand the audit scope.

Questionnaires can be useful when the auditor needs a cost-effective way to collect a large amount of standardized information, when the information to be collected varies in complexity, when a large number of auditees are needed, when different populations are involved, and when auditees in those populations are in widely separated locations.

---

### Constraints in Using Questionnaires

- Time, cost, and staff expertise are examples of primary constraints while location and facilities are a secondary constraint in using and administering questionnaires. For example, if location and facilities are a constraint, use of a mail questionnaire or telephone interviews are advised compared to face-to-face interviews.
- If money is tight and the subject matter can be phrased intelligibly for the respondent population, use the mail.
- If time is tight and staff time is not, use the face-to-face or telephone interview methods.

Furthermore, questionnaires are usually more versatile than other methods. They can be used to collect more types of information from a wider variety of sources than other methods because they use people, who can report facts, figures, amounts, statistics, dates, attitudes, opinions, experiences, events, assessments, and judgments during a single contact.

Questionnaires are difficult to use if the respondent population cannot be readily identified or if the information being sought is not widely distributed among the population of those who hold the knowledge. Furthermore, questionnaires should not be used if the respondents are likely to be unable or unwilling to answer or to provide accurate and unbiased answers or if the questions are inappropriate or compromising.

In general, questionnaires should not be used to gather information that taxes the limitations of the respondent. Sometimes people are not knowledgeable as accurate reporters of certain kinds of information. They remember recent events much better than long-past events. They remember salient and routine events and meaningful facts, but do not remember details, dates, and incidental events very well.

Structured questionnaires are also not particularly well suited for broad, global, or exploratory questions. Because respondents have many different forms of reference, levels of knowledge, and question interpretations, the structured methodology limits the auditor's ability to vary the focus, scope, depth, and direction of the line of inquiry. Such flexibility is necessary to accommodate variances in the respondents' perceptions and understanding that result from such questions.

Mail questionnaires are usually more cost-effective but require longer time periods than personal or telephone interviews. While mail questionnaires usually have higher development costs than telephone or face-to-face interviews, this is generally offset by the relatively inexpensive data collection costs. Extra care must be taken with the mail questionnaires because, unlike the other choices, there is no interviewer (auditor) to help the respondent (auditee). Also, mail is a slow means of transmission, and mail questionnaires take two or three follow-ups.

If the contact people are likely to conceal the identity of the intended respondent, and this is likely to make a difference, or if the auditor is not sure that the intended respondent will get the questionnaire, then personal contact is better than telephone and telephone is better than mail.

---

**KEY CONCEPTS TO REMEMBER: QUESTIONNAIRES VS. INTERVIEWS**

- Auditors should review the conditions and requirements of the data collection methods before deciding to use questionnaires and again before deciding the methods for administering the questionnaire.
- Mail questionnaires are a versatile, low-cost method of collecting detailed data. They are particularly adaptable to survey methods when the population is big, difficult to contact, likely to be inconvenienced, concerned about privacy, and widely dispersed. But mail questionnaires usually have a long turnaround time. The auditors must be willing to invest the time required to carefully design and test these questions. And the respondents must be willing and able to provide unbiased answers.
- Interview methods, while much more expensive and more prone to bias, help ensure against respondent error, have less turnaround time if sufficient staff is provided, and can be used to provide some auditor verifications during the interviews.

---

(iii) **Formatting the questions.** Before preparing the questionnaire, the auditors need to choose the format for each question, which is a design issue. Basically, two types of formats exist: open-ended and closed-ended questions (see Exhibit 5.8).

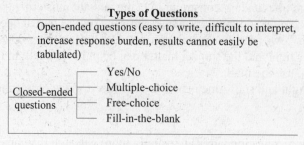

**Types of Questions**

Open-ended questions (easy to write, difficult to interpret, increase response burden, results cannot easily be tabulated)

Closed-ended questions
— Yes/No
— Multiple-choice
— Free-choice
— Fill-in-the-blank

**Exhibit 5.8:  Types of questions**

(iv) **Open-ended questions.** Open-ended questions are easy to write and require very little knowledge of the subject or operation. These types of questions provide very unstandardized, often incomplete, and ambiguous answers, and it is very difficult to use such answers in a quantitative analysis. Respondents will write some salient factors that they happen to think of, but will leave out some important factors because at that moment they did not think of them.

## Care in Developing Questionnaires

Good questionnaires can be seriously compromised if they are not presented in a format that is easy to read and understand by respondents.

Open-ended questions do not help respondents consider a range of factors; rather, they depend on the respondents' unaided recall. There is no way of knowing what is important but not recalled, and because not all respondents consider the same set of factors, it may be extremely difficult or impossible to aggregate the responses. *Open-ended questions are easy for the auditors and difficult for the auditees.*

Also, the auditors may not know how to interpret the answers due to their descriptive nature. Another problem is that open-ended questions cannot easily be tabulated. Rather, a complicated process called "content analysis" must be used, in which someone reads and rereads a substantial number of the written responses, identifies the major categories of themes, and develops rules for assigning responses to these categories.

Still another problem is that open-ended questions substantially increase response burden. They usually take several minutes to answer, rather than a few seconds. Because respondents must compose and organize their thoughts and then try to express them in concise language, they are much less likely to answer.

However, open-ended questions do sometimes have advantages. Their use may be unavoidable when, for example, we are uncertain about criteria or we are engaged in exploratory work. If we ask enough people an open-ended question, we can develop a list of alternatives for closed-ended questions, but not the other way around. We can also use open-ended questions to make sure our list of structured alternatives did not omit an important item or qualification. We can also ask open-ended questions to obtain responses that might further clarify the meaning of answers to closed-ended questions or to gather respondent examples that can be used to illustrate points. In other words, *answers to open-ended questions can become an input to the closed-ended questions.*

(v) **Closed-ended questions. Yes/no questions** are very popular. Although they have some advantages, they have many problems and few uses. Yes/no questions are ideal for dichotomous variables, such as black and white, because they measure whether the condition or trait is present or absent. They are therefore very good for filters in the line of questioning and can be used to move respondents to the questions that apply to them.

<u>*Yes/No Filter Question*</u>
Did you get training?  (Check one)
☐Yes (continue)
☐No (go to question 5)

Consider the question: "Were the terms of the contracts clear?" Most auditees would have trouble with this question because it involves several different considerations: (1) Some contracts may have been clear and others may not have been; (2) some contracts may have been neither clear nor unclear or of marginal clarity; (3) parts of some contracts may have been clear and others not clear.

## When to Use Yes/no Questions

Yes/no questions are good in dealing with measures that are absolute. They are not good for measures that span a range of values and conditions.

Because so little information is obtained from each yes/no question, several rounds of questions individually have to be administered to get the information needed. "Did you have a plan?" "Was the plan in writing?" "Was it a formal plan?" "Was it approved?" This method of inquiry is usually so boring as to discourage respondents.

Sometimes question writers try to compress their line of inquiry and cause serious item-construction flaws. They ask for two things at once—a double-barreled question. For instance, a yes/no answer to "Did you get mission and site support training?" is imprecise. How do respondents answer if they got mission but not site support training? A related question-writing mistake is mixing yes/no and multiple choice.

Yes/no questions are prone to bias and misinterpretation for two reasons: (1) Many people like to say "yes." Some have the opposite bias and like to say "no." (2) Questions such as "Do you submit reports?" have what is called an "inferred bias" toward the "yes" response. The most common way to counter this bias is to add the negative alternative—for example, "Do you submit reports or not?" However, if this is done, the use of yes/no choices in the answer must be qualified or avoided. Without this precaution, a simple "yes" answer may be read as applying to both parts of the question, "Yes, I submit" and "Yes, I do not submit." A simple "no" might also be read as "No, I do not submit"—a double negative. To prevent confusion, qualify the answer choices to avoid yes/no answers.

<u>*Balanced and Unambiguous Yes/No Question*</u>
Do you submit reports? (Check one)
☐Yes, I submit reports
☐No, I do not submit reports

**(A)** **"Implied-no" choices.** The implied-no choice format, a variation of yes/no format, is used because it is easy to read and quick to answer. A failure to check an item implies "no." When auditors want to emphasize the "no" alternative, they can expand the implied-no format to include one column for "yes" answer and one for "no." If "no" is not included as an alternative, nos will be overreported, because the auditors will not be able to differentiate real nos from omissions and nonresponses.

**(B)** **Single-item choices.** In single-item choices, which is another variation of the yes/no format, respondents choose not "yes" or "no" but one of two or more alternatives. This is because "yes" and "no" are not one of the choices given. Since yes/no and single-item choices are similar, they have the same types of problems, but the difficulties are less pronounced in some respects and accentuated in others.

If used carefully, the single-item choice can be efficient. It often serves to filter people out or to skip them through parts of the questionnaire. It is not likely to be overused and cause excessive cycles of repetition. Furthermore, the question writer is not likely to compress the question into a double-barreled item. The single-item-choice format is also not subject to bias from yea-sayers or naysayers. And eliminating the negative alternative reduces misinterpretation.

But there are problems. In the single-item choice format, the writer is more apt to bias one of the choices by understating or overstating it. Some writers may not properly emphasize the second alternative; others, aware of this tendency, overcompensate.

**(C)** **Expanded yes/no questions.** One way around the yes/no constraints is to use an expanded yes/no format. The expanded yes/no format gives a measure of intensity; avoids some of the biases common to yes/no, implied-no, and single-item choice questions; and resolves the problem of quibbling.

<u>*Expanded Yes/No Format*</u>
☐Yes
☐Probably yes
☐Probably no
☐No

The expanded alternatives can have qualifiers other then "probably yes" and "probably no." Qualifiers can be changed to meet the situation—"generally yes" and "generally no" or "for the most part yes" and "for the most part no."

**(D)** **Multiple-choice questions.** The most efficient format—and the most difficult to design—is the multiple-choice question. The respondent is exposed to a range of choices and must pick one or more. Usually four or five choices are included, the "other—specify" being the final choice.

Multiple-choice questions are difficult to write because the writer must provide a comprehensive range of nonoverlapping choices. They must be a logical and reasonable grouping of the types of experience the respondents are likely to have encountered.

(E) **Free-choice questions.** Yes/no, implied-no, single-item, and expanded formats are forced choices in that respondents must answer one way or the other. Forced-choice items generally simplify measurement and analysis because they divide the population clearly into those who do and those who do not or those who have and those who have not. Unfortunately, putting the population into just two categories may also oversimplify the picture and yield error, bias, and unreliable answers. To avoid this problem and to reduce the respondent's burden, a middle category can be added.

*Expanded Yes/No Format*
*with Middle Category*
☐ Yes
☐ Probably yes
☐ Uncertain
☐ Probably no
☐ No

Even though the proportion of yeses to nos will not change, the auditor will have a better measure of the yes/no polarization, because the middle category absorbs those who are uncertain. *A good rule of thumb is that if we are not certain that nearly everyone can make a clear choice, we include a middle category.*

Usually the question writer will also put in an "escape choice" to filter out those for whom the question is not relevant. Examples are "not applicable," "no basis to judge," "have not considered the issue," and "can't recall."

*Expanded Yes/No Format with*
*Escape Choice*
☐ Yes
☐ Probably yes
☐ Uncertain
☐ Probably no
☐ No
☐ Have not considered the issue

(F) **Fill-in-the-blank questions.** Each questionnaire usually has some fill-in-the-blank questions. They are not open-ended because the blanks are accompanied by parenthetical directions that specify the units in which the respondent is to answer.

*Fill-in-the-Blank Questions*
What is your manufacturing plant? _____ (in square feet)
What is your department budget? _____ (in dollars)

Fill-in-the-blank questions should be reserved for very specific requests. The instructions should be explicit and should specify the answer units. Sometimes several fill-in-the blank questions are asked at once in a row, column, or matrix format.

(vi) **Quality of questionnaires.** The quality of questionnaires can be checked by several methods, some of which are carried out during the design phase and others during the data collection or analysis phase. During the design phase, the questionnaire should be pretested (or pilot tested) on selected persons or departments that represent the range of conditions likely to influence the auditor's results. The questionnaires should also be sent out for review by experts who are familiar with both the issue area and the respondent group. In addition to expert reviews, peer reviews can be done by an auditor who worked on the auditable area before or a new auditor who never worked before in that area.

## Quality Assurance of Questionnaires

The quality of questionnaires can be checked by four methods

1. Pretesting
2. Expert review
3. Peer review
4. Validation and verification techniques

The first three methods belong to the data design phase, while the fourth method is used in the data collection and data analysis phases.

Pretesting and expert review are some of the best ways to ensure that the instrument actually communicates what it was intended to communicate, that it is standardized and will be uniformly interpreted by the target population, and that it will be free of design flaws that could lead to inaccurate answers.

Validating, verifying, or corroborating responses, conducting reliability studies, and analyzing nonresponses are important parts of quality assurance effort. These tasks are conducted during data collection and analysis phases.

(vii) **Pretesting.** By testing the questionnaire before it is distributed, auditors can assess whether they are asking the right group of auditees the right questions in the right way and whether the respondents are willing and able to give the auditors the information they need. Pretests are conducted with a small set of respondents from the population that will eventually be considered for the full-scale study. Troublesome questions discovered in the pretest can be dropped.

Mail questionnaires are pretested by means of personal interviews. During the interviews, a wealth of information can be obtained by observing respondents as they complete the form and by debriefing them about the question-answering experience. The purpose of debriefing is not only to identify items that are difficult or misunderstood but also to get at the cause of these problems.

(viii) **Expert review.** Expert review seeks outside comments on the questionnaire approach. The purpose of this expert review is twofold: (1) We want to determine whether the questions and the manner in which we ask them are adequate for addressing the larger questions posed by the audit; and (2) we want to find out whether the target population for the survey has the knowledge to answer the questions. People who provide expert reviews do not act as pretest interviewees; they do not answer the questions but provide a critique. Some sources of expert reviews include audit managers from the same or other business units or divisions, auditee managers, and business school professors.

(ix) **Data validation, verification, corroboration, and reliability of questionnaires. Validation** is an effort to ensure that the questionnaire is actually measuring the variables it was designed to measure. The concept of "construct validation" requires the demonstration of relationship between the measurement and the construct being measured in a setting as controlled as possible. Construct validity is tested with a number of people under controlled conditions. A very practical method of assessing validity is to use "content validity." In this approach, auditors might ask experts to make sure that the measure includes the content they want to measure. Validity can be tested by looking at the relationships between factors that should be positively correlated or negatively correlated. For example, measures of the quality of training ought to correlate positively with productivity. If they do, we have some confidence in the validity of the measures. The measure of a participative management style ought to correlate inversely with a measure of an authoritative management style. If it does, confidence in the validity of the measure is strengthened.

## Criteria for Questionnaires

- The term "validation" refers to the purpose of measure (shows that the observation measures what it is supposed to measure).
- The term "verification" refers to the accuracy of data.
- The term "corroboration" refers to validation in some cases.
- The term "reliability" refers to the consistency of measures.

Validation is important because if the questions are not valid measures of the constructs we are studying, even answers verified as accurate will not provide us with the quality data needed for our findings, conclusions, and recommendations.

**Verification** is a way of checking or testing questionnaire answers with records or direct observation to reduce the risk of using data that are inaccurate. The accuracy of data is tested by comparing the data against an accurate source, by putting in controls that reduce observation errors, or by repeating the measurement process. The extent of verification should be based on the type of data, its use as evidence to address the assignment's objectives, the relative risk of it being erroneous, and an alternative available to verify data, including time and resource constraints.

The most convincing method of verification is to compare on a test basis the respondent's answers with evidence developed from an on-site inspection that involves direct observation or a review of documents and records. Such verifications are ideally conducted on a statistical sample of the respondent population. Practically, a judgment sample considered typical of the population is often used.

## VERIFICATION VS. VALIDATION

- Verification is different from validation.
- Verification is ideally conducted by testing a sample, which is time-consuming and expensive.
- Validation does not require sampling approaches.

**Corroboration** (referred to as validation in some circumstances) of questionnaire results against similar information from another, independent source can also provide supporting evidence to increase confidence in the relative accuracy of questionnaire data.

The **reliability** of questionnaire results tests whether a question always gets the same results when repeated under similar conditions. *Answers can be highly reliable without being either verified or valid.* A reliable measure is one that, used repeatedly in order to make observations, produces consistent results. Testing reliability is difficult and expensive, because the auditors have to either replicate the data collection or return to those who were questioned before. People do not like to be retested.

## VERIFICATION VS. RELIABILITY

- It is important to note that the procedures for testing the reliability of answers are different from those for verifying answers.
- When information is verified, auditors usually go to a different source for the same information or use a different technique on the same source, such as observations or in-depth interviews.
- To test reliability, auditors have to administer the same test to the same source.

Why do auditors have to validate, verify, corroborate, and make reliability checks during data collection or analysis phases? Nonstandardized questionnaires require this kind of checking. We are either measuring things that have not been measured before or measuring previously measured things under different circumstances. Standardized questionnaires have already been tested during their design and development phase.

(x) **Analysis of questionnaire nonresponses.** Nonresponses to questionnaires, whether an individual item or a section is not completed, must be analyzed because high or disproportionate nonresponse rates can threaten the credibility and generalizability of the findings. The real problem is not so much the decreased sample size but whether those who chose not to answer had disproportionately different views from those who did. This would threaten the representativeness of the sample and the ability to generalize from the sample to the population. Inductive generalizations cannot be made under these circumstances. Therefore, reasons for nonresponses should be investigated.

(xi) **Quality instructions for questionnaires.** A questionnaire should be easy to read, attractive, and interesting. Good graphics and layout can catch the respondent's attention, counteract negative impressions, cut the respondent's time in half, and reduce completion errors.

The first part of the questionnaire should present the introduction and instructions. The instructions should: state the purpose of the survey; explain who the data collector is, the basis of its authority, and why it is conducting the survey; tell how and why the respondents were selected; explain why their answers are important; tell how to complete the form; provide mail-back instructions; list the person to call if help is needed to complete the form; provide assurances of confidentiality and anonymity when appropriate; tell how long it will typically take to complete the form; explain how the data will be used; explain who will have access to the information; disclose data uses that may affect the respondents; and present the response efforts as a favor and thank the respondents for their cooperation. The instructions should be concise, courteous, and businesslike.

(xii) **Use of rating scales for questionnaires.** Questions are subject to ranking and rating. Ranking questions are used to make very difficult distinction between things that are of nearly equal value. The question forces the respondent to value one alternative over another no matter how close they are. The value that is assigned is a relative value. Rating questions are used when the alternatives are likely to vary somewhat in value and when auditors want to know how valuable the alternative is rather than if it is a little more or less valuable than the next alternative. The next list discusses ranking and rating.

- **Ranking.** In ranking, the respondents are asked to tell which alternative has the highest value, which has the second highest, and so on. They rank the choices with respect to one another, but their answers tell little about the intrinsic value of their choices. Ranking starts to get hard for people when there are more than seven categories. Respondents begin to lose track of where they are with respect to the first, last, and middle positions. When this happens, they make mistakes. Ranking questions have to be written very carefully. The slightest lapse in clarity in the question or the instruction given will cause some people to rank in the reverse order or to assign two alternatives the same rank or to forget to rank every alternative. Nonetheless, sometimes ranking must be used—when an order of issues or items is important.

- **Rating.** Rating questions are perhaps the most useful format because we usually want to know the actual or absolute value of the trait we are measuring. Ratings are assigned solely on the basis of the score's absolute position within a range of possible values. For example, a rating scale might be assigned these categories: of little importance, somewhat important, moderately important, and so on. In writing rating questions, we should try to categorize the scales in equal intervals and anchor the scale positions whenever possible. Aside from the scaling, rating questions are easier to write properly and cause less error than ranking questions. Ratings usually provide an adequate level of quantification for most purposes, and rating formats are simpler than ranking formats.

*Example of a Rating Question*

Based on what we discussed, how would you classify the risk involved in your accounts receivable operations?  (Check one)

☐Maximum risk
☐Moderate risk
☐Minimum risk
☐No risk

Other question formats include the Gutman format and intensity scale format, where the latter includes the Likert scale, and amount and frequency intensity scales. In questions written in the *Gutman format*, the alternatives increase in comprehensiveness; that is, the higher-valued alternatives include the lower-valued alternatives. The intensity scale format is usually used to measure the strength of an attitude or an opinion.

Another frequently used intensity scale format is the *Likert or agree-or-disagree scale*. The Likert scale is easy to construct. However, if the writer is not careful, the simplicity and adaptability of the Likert scale format are often paid for by greater error and threats to validity.

Consider an example of the Likert scale: "My supervisor never lets me participate in decisions (agree or disagree)." First, there is bias. The Likert scale presents only one side of an argument, and some people have a natural tendency to agree with the status quo or the argument presented.

This bias can be countered by presenting the converse statement also: "My supervisor lets me participate in decisions (agree or disagree)."

Another problem is that the extent of the respondent's agreement or disagreement with a statement may not correspond directly to the strength of the respondent's attitude about the Likert statement posed in the question. The respondent may consider the statement either true or false and respond as if the question were in an either/or format rather than a graduated scale measuring the intensity of a belief.

The Likert question uses the statement as a reference point or anchor. Hence, what is measured may be not the strength of the respondent's attitude over the complete range of intensities but, rather, the range of intensities bounded or referenced by the position of the anchoring statement at one end of the range and unbounded at the other end of the range. The indirect approach in the Likert scale may produce misleading results for a variety of reasons. It is usually better to use a direct approach that measures the strength of the respondent's actual attitude over a complete range of intensities. For example, it is better to reformulate the item from "My supervisor never lets me participate in decisions" to "To what extent, if at all, do you participate?"

However, one situation in which the Likert scale is very useful is when the extent of an agreement or disagreement is closely and indirectly related to the statement. For instance, the respondent may be asked about the extent to which he or she agrees or disagrees with a policy.

<u>*Example of a Likert Scale Question*</u>
How do you feel about policy A?  (Check one)
☐Strongly agree
☐Agree more than disagree
☐Undecided
☐Disagree more than agree
☐Strongly disagree

Many audit questions ask the respondent to "quantify" either amounts or frequencies. These questions are relatively simple. They use certain derivative words to characterize the amount, frequency, or number of items being measured. For example, traits like "help," "hindrance," "effect," "increase," or "decrease," can be quantified by adding "little," "some," "moderate," "great," or "very great." Certain adjectives like "some" and "great" have a stable and relatively precise level of quantification. Quantities can also be implied by the sequence of numbered alternatives ordered with respect to increasing or decreasing intensity.

<u>*Example of Amount Intensity Scale*</u>
☐Little or no hindrance
☐Some hindrance
☐Moderate hindrance
☐Great hindrance
☐Very great hindrance

Frequencies or occurrences of events are treated the same way. Question writers know that words like "sometimes" and "great many" or "very often" mean about one-fourth of the amount or 25% of the time and three-fourths or 75% of the time, respectively, to most people. Similarly, words like "about half" and "moderate" anchor the midpoints. As with amount intensity scales, it is important to use both numbered, ordered scalar presentations and words to quantify the scale intervals.

<u>*Example of Frequency Intensity Scale*</u>
☐Seldom if ever
☐Sometimes
☐Often
☐Very often
☐Always or almost always

In many amount and frequency measures, where ambiguities are likely to occur, it is also important to use proportional anchors, such as fractions and percents, or verbal descriptive anchors, such as once a day or once a month, in addition to the adjective and scale number anchors.

*Example of Frequency Intensity Scale with Proportional Anchors*
☐Seldom if ever (0 to 10% of the time)
☐Sometimes (about ¼ of the time)
☐Often (about ½ of the time)
☐Very often (about ¾ of the time)
☐Always or almost always (90 to 100% of the time)

(xiii) **Application of rating scales.** Rating scales can be applied in many instances. For example, rating scales can be used as a method of employee performance evaluation. In the graphic rating scale method, a set of performance factors, such as quantity and quality of work, depth of knowledge, co-operation, and initiative, can be used to rate each factor on an incremental scale of 1 (poor) to 5 (excellent). Advantages of rating scales are that they are less time-consuming to develop and administer and allow for quantitative analysis and comparisons. The disadvantage is a lack of depth of information on the performance factors when compared to anecdotal records (discussed below).

Behavioral anchored rating scales combine major elements from the anecdotal records and graphic rating scale approaches. Examples of behavioral descriptions that are used to rate include plans, anticipates, executes, and solves problems. The appraiser rates the employee based on actual behavior on the job rather than general descriptions or traits.

(xiv) **Methods for gathering feedback.** Auditors face some degree of nonrespondent problem whether they are conducting personal interviews or mailing questionnaires. The reason is that auditees may not be available, may be unable to locate, or did not answer the questions completely or sufficiently. In some cases auditors may want to obtain feedback on the quality and relevancy of interview or the questionnaire. The higher the nonrespondent problem, the lower the feedback.

The best approach to gather feedback would be to conduct a short phone survey of auditees, using some of the critical questions on the data collection instrument or second-mail the questionnaire.

Some other common methods for gathering feedback would include sending standardized letters for comments, requesting customized written responses, receiving voice mail answers, and receiving electronic mail answers. A stratified sample can be selected to determine the number of auditees to request for feedback.

---

**KEY CONCEPTS TO REMEMBER: QUESTIONNAIRES**

- The primary purpose of an internal control questionnaire (ICQ) is to make preliminary appraisals of controls to be tested.
- The primary advantage of using an ICQ is that it reduces the risk of overlooking important aspects of the system.
- The major disadvantage of using an ICQ is that questionnaires may be routinely completed without auditors really understanding overall operations of internal control systems.
- ICQ provides indirect audit evidence that might need corroboration. The "verification" technique is most appropriate for testing the quality of the preaudit of payment vouchers described in an ICQ.
- The most appropriate use of questionnaires is to help review internal control.
- The ICQ does not highlight the interaction of departments; it is a static data collection instrument.

---

(c) **Checklists.** Auditors are familiar with using checklists for various purposes. They are memory aids to ensure that all required steps or actions are completed. Checklists can be used in any phase of the audit: planning, survey, fieldwork, report writing. Checklists are especially useful during working paper review to ensure that all components of the quality assurance program are addressed properly.

Supervisors can use checklists to document their review comments when they look at the auditor's working papers. The supervisor can later use the review comment sheet (also called point sheet) for follow-up to ensure that all points that were raised are cleared by the auditor who worked on the audit. There is no limit to the number of applications of the checklists, and it really depends on the creativity of the auditor. Audit quality can be enhanced with the use of checklists since they provide a discipline and framework to work with by all parties involved in an audit. For example, checklists can be used during a peer review of working papers to mark compliance with the requirements.

**(d) Focus Groups**

(i) **Purpose of focus groups.** The primary purpose of focus groups is to collect qualitative data, with quantitative data being the secondary purpose. Focus groups do represent an important tool for discovery and exploration of ideas and opinions. They are a choice between individual interviews or focus group interviews. Focus groups, which consist of 6 to 12 people, produce a rich body of data expressed in the respondents' own words and context.

Surveys ask for responses expressed on point rating scale or other constrained response categories. Surveys produce more artificial responses than focus groups due to absence of interaction among respondents. The data provided by focus groups is idiosyncratic and difficult to summarize. In surveys, the response categories may or may not be those with which the respondents are comfortable, although they may still be selecting answers.

## SURVEYS VS. FOCUS GROUPS

- Surveys produce artificial responses due to lack of interaction among respondents.
- Focus groups do not produce artificial responses due to interaction among respondents.

(ii) **The process.** The process begins with a statement of the problem. The group has focus and a clearly identifiable agenda. Then a sampling frame is identified. A moderator needs to be located to design the questions used in the group interview. The moderator leads the group through the questions and seeks to facilitate discussion among all the group members. The moderator should be perceived as nonevaluative and nonthreatening. Analysis and interpretation of data and report writing concludes the process.

(iii) **Uses and misuses.** Focus group interviews should be considered when these circumstances are present.

- Insights are needed in exploratory or preliminary studies, with limited scope or limited resources. The goal might be to gain reactions to areas needing improvement.
- There is a communication or understanding gap between groups or categories of people. Focus groups bring people together.
- The moderator desires ideas to emerge from the group. Focus groups possess the capacity to become more than the sum of their participants, to exhibit a synergy that individuals alone cannot achieve.

Focus group interviews should **not** be considered when these circumstances are present.

- The environment is emotionally charged, issues are polarized, trust had deteriorated, and the participants are in a confrontational mode.
- The moderator has lost control over critical aspects of the study. The moderator should maintain control over the participants' selection, question development, and analysis protocol.
- Statistical projections or estimations are needed. Focus groups do not involve sufficient number of participants, nor does the sampling strategy lend itself to statistical projections. The types of generalizations that arise from focus group results tend to be more general than specific, more tentative, and more descriptive.

(iv) **Advantages and disadvantages of focus groups.** Some major **advantages** resulting from the focus groups include

- Focus groups provide data from a group of individuals much more quickly and at less cost than would be the case if each individual were interviewed separately. They also can be assembled on much shorter notice than would be required for a more systematic and larger survey.
- The focus group interview process is objective and rigorous as it rests on an extensive body of empirical theory and research, as well practice.
- Focus groups allow the moderator to interact directly with respondents. This provides opportunities for the clarification of responses, for follow-up questions, and for the probing of

responses. Respondents can qualify responses or give contingent answers to questions. In addition, it is possible for the moderator to observe nonverbal responses such as gestures, smiles, frowns, and so forth.

- The open response format provides an opportunity to obtain large and rich amounts of data in the respondents' own words. It allows respondents to react to and build on the responses of other group members.

Some major **disadvantages** resulting from the focus groups include

- The results obtained in a focus group may be biased by a very dominant or highly opinionated member of the group. More reserved group members may be hesitant to talk.
- The open-ended nature of responses obtained in focus groups often makes summarization and interpretation of results difficult.
- The moderator may bias results by knowingly or unknowingly providing cues about what types of responses and answers are desirable.
- Each focus group really represents a single observation although it is a group of people. Group consensus is given here. Therefore, there should be more than one focus group conducted on a specific topic.

(v) **Audit application of focus groups.** Focus groups can be used in the survey phase of an audit when little is known about the area to be audited. For example, they can be used to obtain general background information about an area; to diagnose the potential for problems with a new policy, program, product, or service; to generate impressions of policies, products, programs, or services; and to interpret previously obtained quantitative data through mail surveys.

## 5.4 Analytical Review Techniques

(a) **Ratio Estimation.** Four types of measures are used to analyze a company's financial statements and its financial position: (1) common-size analysis, (2) trend analysis, (3) comparative ratios, and (4) single ratios (see Exhibit 5.9).

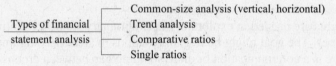

Types of financial statement analysis
— Common-size analysis (vertical, horizontal)
— Trend analysis
— Comparative ratios
— Single ratios

**Exhibit 5.9: Types of financial statement analysis**

**Common-size analysis** expresses items in percentages, which can be compared with similar items of other firms or with those of the same firm over time. For example, common-size balance sheet line items (both assets and liabilities) are expressed as a percentage of total assets (e.g., receivables as *x* percent of total assets). Similarly, common-size income statement line items are expressed as a percentage of total sales (e.g., cost of goods sold as *x* percent of total sales).

Variations of common-size analysis include vertical analysis and horizontal analysis. **Vertical analysis** expresses all items on a financial statement as a percentage of some base figure, such as total assets or total sales. Comparing these relationships between competing organizations helps to isolate strengths and areas of concern.

In **horizontal analysis,** the financial statements for two years are shown together with additional columns showing dollar differences and percentage changes. Thus, the direction, absolute amount, and relative amount of change in account balances can be calculated. Trends that are difficult to isolate by examining the financial statements of individual years or comparisons with competitors can be identified.

**Trend analysis** shows trends in ratios, which gives insight whether the financial situation of a firm is improving, declining, or stable. It shows a graph of ratios over time, which can be compared with a firm's own performance as well as that of its industry.

**Comparative ratios** show key financial ratios, such as current ratio and net sales to inventory, by industry, such as beverages and bakery products. These ratios represent average financial ratios for all firms within an industry category. Many organizations supply ratio data, and each one designs ratios for its own purpose, such as small firms or large firms. Also, the focus of these ratios is different, such as creditor's viewpoint or investor's viewpoint. Another characteristic of the ratio data-supplying organization is that each has its own definitions of the ratios and their components. Due to these differences, examiners must be cautious when interpreting these ratios.

Another type of comparative analysis is comparing the financial statements for the current year with those of the most recent year. By comparing summaries of financial statements for the last five to ten years, one can identify trends in operations, capital structure, and the composition of assets. This comparative analysis provides insight into the normal or expected account balance or ratio, information about the direction of changes in ratios and account balances, and insight into the variability or fluctuation in an organization's assets or operations.

## TREND ANALYSIS VS. COMPARATIVE RATIO ANALYSIS

- In trend analysis, trends are shown over time between the firm and its industry.
- In comparative ratio analysis, a single point (one-to-one) comparison is shown between the firm and its industry.
- In both analyses, the industry's ratio is an average ratio, while the firm's ratio is not.

Next, our focus will shift to **single ratios or simple ratios.** Certain accounts or items in an organization's financial statements have logical relationships with each other. If the dollar amounts of these related accounts or items are expressed in fraction form, then they are called **ratios**. These ratios are grouped into five categories: (1) liquidity ratios, (2) asset management ratios, (3) debt management ratios, (4) profitability ratios, and (5) market value ratios. Exhibit 5.10 presents individual ratios for each ratio category.

| *Ratio category* | *Individual ratios* |
|---|---|
| Liquidity (1) | Current, quick, or acid test |
| Asset management (2) | Inventory turnover, days sales outstanding, fixed assets turnover, total assets turnover |
| Debt management (3) | Debt to total assets, time-interest-earned, fixed charge coverage, cash flow coverage |
| Profitability (4) = (1) + (2) + (3) | Profit margin on sales, basic earning power, return on total assets, return on common equity, earnings per share, payout |
| Market value (5) = (1) + (2) + (3) + (4) | Price/earnings, book value per share, market/book |

**Exhibit 5.10: Ratio categories with examples**

(b) **Variance Analysis.** Budgets and standards are used to plan an operation and measure its progress. **Variance** is the difference between budget or standard and actual. For example, if actual spending is greater than the budget, it results in a negative variance. If actual spending is less than the budget, it results in a positive variance. Managers need to analyze both positive and negative variances for reasonableness because people play psychological games with budgets, such as inflating the budget for personal gain.

(c) **Other Reasonableness Tests.** The reasonableness test procedure involves the use of selected operating data, associated financial data, and external data to predict an account balance. Reasonableness tests can be used to determine whether input data, updated data, calculated data, or output data are reasonable. Ascending or descending checks for numeric and alphabetic data can be performed. Tolerance tests measuring dollar or percentage deviation can be designed.

Reasonableness tests of the expense accounts are common. Two examples are: (1) the auditor or analyst estimates a value for utilities expense based on average temperature and hours of operation, and (2) payroll expense is estimated from operating data on the number of employees, the average pay rates, and the number of days of applicable operations.

The reasonableness test can be particularly effective because it links the financial data directly to relevant operating data. When variations in operations are the principal cause for variations in the related accounts (especially the expense accounts), reasonableness tests provide a relatively precise means of detecting errors and frauds affecting these accounts. That is, when a fraud is committed, it is likely that the reported financial and operating facts will not agree. The perpetrator will find it difficult to disguise both the financial data and the related operating data.

For example, a reasonableness test of payroll expense can be an effective means of detecting fraud, if there are "phony" employees or excess time is charged, because personnel records also must be manipulated fraudulently in the same pattern to prevent detection. Because these methods effectively model the relationships between the financial data and the operating transactions that are the basis for the recorded financial data, reasonableness tests are potentially the most effective of the analytical procedures.

Examples of generic reasonableness tests include

- Airline passenger departure flight time is not reasonable with arrival flight time for the same day.
- Customer order quantity is not reasonable with historical order.
- Prices on purchase orders are not reasonable with the prices on purchase invoices or purchase requisitions.
- Stock-status dollar values are not reasonable with general-ledger amounts.
- Shipment values are not reasonable with billed amounts.

### 5.5 Observations, Unobtrusive Measures, and Anecdotal Records

(a) **Observations.** Observation is a direct notice of things, events, and people's actions. It is the ability to see what is happening in an individual and/or within a group, and to respond appropriately. Watching body language in addition to words and actions is an additional benefit of observation. In other words, body language says more than the words and actions of people.

Observation is considered a reliable audit procedure, but one that is limited in usefulness. It is not sufficient to satisfy any audit assertion other than existence. Observation provides information on how transactions are handled at one particular point in time, not how they are processed throughout the period under study. It provides a snapshot of operations. The reason why observation is limited is that individuals can react differently when being observed.

(b) **Unobtrusive Measures.** An **unobtrusive measure** is the one that is not readily noticeable to others. An auditor can use an unobtrusive measure, for example, to check to see if all hourly employees in a manufacturing plant are clocking in when they report to their workstation, as opposed to someone else representing them. An auditor would stay in an area in an unobtrusive manner where employees clock in to determine their natural motions and actions. Compliance with procedure is the auditor's major objective here.

Another application is to determine whether security guards at a retail store are checking all bags and personal belongings of all employees when they leave the store building. An auditor would observe this in an unobtrusive manner so that the security guard would not notice the auditor. It is a test of control compliance with the store policy that all employee bags are checked every day at quitting time.

(c) **Anecdotal Records.** Anecdotal records constitute a description or narrative of a specific situation or condition. For example, during the employee performance evaluation process, the appraiser writes down anecdotes that describe what the employee did that was especially effective or ineffective. The appraiser can be the immediate supervisor, peers, self-evaluation by the employee, or immediate subordinate(s).

Another example of use of anecdotal records is allowing a fraud suspect to make a narrative response concerning the incident after the interviewer has established rapport and sold the suspect on the need to cooperate in the interview.

### 5.6 Problem Solving and Decision Making

(a) **Problem-Solving Tools**

(i) **What is a problem?** In this section, we first discuss the theory behind problem solving followed by its application to internal auditing. A problem exists when there is a gap between "what is" and "what should be." Individuals recognize a problem when they feel frustrated, frightened, angry, or anxious about a situation. Organizations recognize problems when outputs and productivity are low; when quality of products and services is poor; when people are not cooperating, sharing information, or communicating; or when there is a dysfunctional degree of conflict among people in various departments. When the gap between "what is" and "what should be" causes anxiety and inefficiency, something needs to be done to solve the problem.

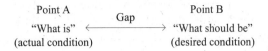

A problem is the gap between where one is and where one wants to be. The process of closing the gap between the actual situation and the desired situation is problem solving. Problems do not solve themselves—people solve problems. In a way, audit reports are problem-solving tools. The deficiency findings contained in the audit report describe and compare the actual condition (what is) with the desired condition (what should be), thus creating a gap. The auditor's recommendations are aimed at closing this gap. Audit work is then a type of problem solving. According to the IIA *Standard* 430, *Communicating Results*, audit findings are the result of comparing "what should be" with "what is" and analyzing the impact. This is shown below.

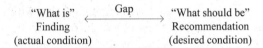

If internal auditing reports are problem-solving tools, then internal auditors are problem solvers since the audit work is done by the auditor, who then prepares the report. The management principle behind the problem solving is "Theory Y" in that both managers and auditors will take responsibility for and are interested in solving organizational problems. *Effective written and oral communication skills are prerequisites to effective problem-solving skills.*

(ii) **Problem-solving process.** Problem solving is a systematic process of bringing the actual situation or condition closer to the desired condition. Although there are many ways to handle problems, Robert Kreitner defines managerial problem solving as a four-step sequence: (1) identifying the problem, (2) generating alternative solutions, (3) selecting a solution, and (4) implementing and evaluating the solution.[3] These four steps are depicted in Exhibit 5.11 with a possible recycling from steps 3 and 4 to steps 1 and 2.

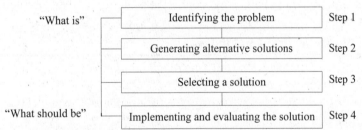

**Exhibit 5.11:  Steps in the problem-solving process**

(A) **Step 1: Identifying the problem.** The scope of this step includes awareness of a problem, problem diagnosis and identification, and criteria for solution. Identifying the problem is a major, crucial work. It can consist of initial awareness that something is not right. The problem-solving cycle begins with some felt need. If there is no felt need, the cycle is unnecessary. Some examples of problem indications include

- A production manager finds a gap between actual weekly production and the desired level.
- A plant department manager finds a gap between actual attendance levels and desired attendance levels.
- A marketing manager finds a gap between the actual market share for a product and the desired market share.
- A financial manager finds a gap between the actual earnings for a quarter and the desired earnings.
- An audit manager finds a gap between the actual report issuance time and the desired report issuance time.

---

[3]  Robert Kreitner,  **Management**, 9th ed. (Boston: Houghton Mifflin Company,  2004).

The adage "A fully developed problem is half-solved" is truly applicable here. Problem identification is a two-dimensional process. The first dimension deals with the degree or condition of the problem, and the second one addresses the structure of the problem. Each dimension is discussed briefly.

*Degree or condition of the problem.* It is necessary to understand the degree or intensity of a problem in order to plan the appropriate timing and strategies for its solutions. There are three issues involved here: stable, dynamic, and critical.

A **stable issue** is one in which there is a little or no controversy. The decision maker requires little input and can usually solve the problem in a task-oriented fashion. A **dynamic issue** is one around which there is a good deal of controversy and the decision maker turns to a group for input. Leadership is process-oriented. A **critical issue** is immersed in controversy and requires resolution by senior management. Leadership is most effective in resolving critical issues when it is task- as well as process- oriented.

*Structure of the problem.* Structure has to do with the routineness of the decision required. Questions to ask include: How much is known or understood about the problem? Is this a new problem? Do mechanisms exist within the organization to deal with this problem?

Two types of problems exist: structured and unstructured problems. Structured problems have only one unknown and have routine programs available to respond; unstructured problems have at least two unknowns and no routine programs available. As an organization faces the same unstructured problem repeatedly, it will gradually develop mechanisms to respond to the problem, which then becomes structured.

After being aware of the problem, it is good to obtain valid information about the problem in order to identifying what it is. Problem identification is a description of the present conditions, the symptoms, and the underlying causes. The outcome should be a written statement identifying the root problem.

Defining the criteria for solution addresses what the desired condition should be. This condition should be measurable and specific. True agreement on the criteria that a solution must meet is important to help avoid conflict at a later time in the problem-solving cycle.

---

**Stumbling Blocks for Problem Finders**

- *Defining the problem according to a possible solution* means ruling out alternative solutions in the way one states a problem
- *Focusing on narrow, low-priority areas* means ignoring organization goals and objectives
- *Diagnosing problems in terms of their symptoms* means inability to differentiate between short-run and long-run handling of symptoms. Treating symptoms rather than underlying causes is acceptable in the short run, but is not acceptable in the long run since symptoms tend to reappear. The real cause(s) of the problem should be discovered. Causes are variables, whether they are controllable or uncontrollable. The problem can be solved or the gap can disappear by focusing on adding or removing these variables.

---

(B)   ***Step 2: Generating alternative solutions.*** During this step, the problem solver needs to identify the possible methods and means to get from "what is" to "what should be." The information collection effort includes researching new ideas and methods and resources for achieving the goals. Generating alternative solutions is time-consuming and demanding mental work.

People have a tendency to settle for the first answer or alternative without really developing several answers or alternatives from which to choose. Developing several alternatives requires a combination of careful and thorough analysis, intuition, creativity, and a sense of humor. Several techniques using individual and group creativity are available to develop alternatives. These include brainstorming, synectics, and others, which are discussed later in the section.

(C)   ***Step 3: Selecting a solution.*** In this step, the various alternatives are evaluated against the established criteria for the solutions. In this way, the solution that best fits the criteria can be selected. Each alternative must be compared to others. Since "best" is a relative term, the alternative solutions must be evaluated to provide a reasonable balance of effectiveness and efficiency, considering the constraints and intangibles, if any.

If during this step the problem solver cannot establish a satisfactory solution, it may be necessary to return to Step 1 in order to redefine the problem or to repeat Step 2 in order to generate more realistic alternatives and solution criteria.

As part of the decision-making process, alternative solutions should be screened for the most appealing balance of effectiveness and efficiency in view of relevant constraints and intangibles. Russell Ackoff, a specialist in managerial problem solving, contends that three things can be done about problems: They can be resolved, solved, or dissolved (see Exhibit 5.12).

**Exhibit 5.12: How are problems handled?**

**Resolving the problem** includes selecting a course of action that is good enough to meet the minimum constraints. Here the problem solver satisfices rather than optimizes. Optimizing or maximizing is selecting the best possible solution. When a problem is resolved by selecting a course of action that meets the minimum constraints, a manager is said to be satisficing. The manager uses a minimal amount of information to make a quick, good enough, and not the best, decision. Satisficing has been criticized as a shortsighted and passive technique emphasizing survival instead of growth. Idealizing involves dreaming that no problem would exist or changing the current situation so that the problem no longer exists.

## SATSIFICE VS. OPTIMIZE VS. IDEALIZE

- Satisfice is settling for a solution that is good enough.
- Optimize is systematically searching for a solution with the best combination of resources and benefits.
- Idealize is changing the nature of a problem's situation.

**Solving the problem** is when one selects the best possible solution with the best combination of benefits. A **problem is dissolved** when the situation in which it occurs is changed so that the problem no longer exists. Problem dissolvers are said to idealize because they actually change the nature of the system in which a problem resides.

## RESOLVING VS. SOLVING VS. DISSOLVING

- Resolving the problem requires a qualitative, subjective approach.
- Solving the problem requires scientific observations and quantitative measurements.
- Dissolving the problem requires a combination of quantitative and qualitative tools.

(D) ***Step 4: Implementing and evaluating the solution.*** Once a solution has been chosen, implementation must be planned in detail. This step includes deciding who will do what and when. It requires implementation plans, checkpoints, schedules, and resources. The implementation of the action plan should have moved the situation from "what is" to "what should be."

## PROBLEM-SOLVING STRATEGY CHECKLIST

- Look for a pattern.
- Account for all possibilities.
- Act it out.
- Make a model or diagram.

- Work backward.
- Reason hypothetically.
- Restate the problem or change the problem representation (taking the point of view of an observer).
- Identify given, wanted, needed information.

---

At this point, both product and process evaluation are important. The outcomes must be measured against the desired criteria to determine if the goal has been reached and the problem solved. If people are still uncomfortable with the way things are, it may be necessary to start again at Step 1.

(iii) **Impediments to problem solving.** Business problems are solved either by individuals or by groups. The most neglected area of problem solving is human resources, the people who participate in the problem-solving group. The group leader can encourage new ideas and creativity in group members by following these guidelines.

- Practice effective listening because people think much more rapidly than they speak. Effective listening is the best way to gather information. Try not to be distracted.
- Practice "stroking," a concept borrowed from transactional analysis. A stroke is a unit of recognition. Provide recognition to people and ideas. Positive stroking makes people more important and secure and invites more ideas and creativity.
- Discourage "discounting" (i.e., not paying attention), another concept borrowed from transactional analysis. When discounting is high, group members will feel reluctant to respond to questions and will be constantly ready to attack or retreat. This is not a healthy climate for successful problem solving, and it encourages dysfunctional behavior and uncooperative attitudes among the members of the group.
- Keep the group members informed about progress and what is expected of them.

Reasons frequently cited by psychology researchers for people making mistakes in solving problems include lack of understanding of concepts, reasoning errors, failure to note details, and insufficient computation skills.[4] Researchers have identified common traits that good problem solvers possess.

- Good estimation and analysis skills
- Ability to perceive similarities and differences
- Reflective and creative thinking
- Ability to visualize relationships
- Strong understanding of concepts and terms
- Ability to disregard irrelevant data
- Capability to switch methods easily, but not impulsively
- Ability to generalize on the basis of a few examples
- Ability to interpret quantitative data
- Strong self-esteem

A problem-solving attitude, an inquiring and questioning mind, can be developed. It does not occur by accepting from others truths and conclusions that the learner ought to establish by him- or herself. The attitude is produced by continued experience in solving real problems, one consequence of which is that the learner comes to expect new problems and to look for them. Auditors have the same agenda in mind. The ability to discriminate among possible alternatives is a valuable life skill. One should not think of problem-solving skills as a single, uniform capability. *Problems of different kinds may require substantially different problem-solving skills.*

Problem-solving expertise consists of skill in identifying obstacles that can be easily circumvented and of ingenuity in dealing with particular obstacles. The identification of problem obstacles is generally given too little priority because we are "solution-oriented." We spend too little time in exploring the problem situation.

---

[4] *Problem Solving–Volume 2 (Columbus, OH: Ohio Department of Education, State Board of Education, 1980).*

## IDEA GETTING VS. IDEA EVALUATION

- Reaching a final solution depends on both idea getting (generating alternatives) and idea evaluation (choosing the best alternative). Sometimes we do not achieve a satisfactory solution because we put too little effort into considering alternatives or we make a poor selection from those alternatives evaluated. Frequently the obstacle to successful problem solving is the tendency to evaluate and select an alternative before better ideas have been generated.
- Unless idea getting is stressed and idea evaluation temporarily suppressed, the presence of available alternatives can impede the possible consideration of other, more viable alternatives.

(iv) **Problem solving and creativity.** The reorganization of experience into new configurations is called "creativity." The best argument in favor of creativity is that environmental changes make creativity essential for long-term survival. Stagnation can lead to organizational failure or demise. Creativity is not easy to get or to manage, as it requires hiring intelligent people and motivating them to deliver to the fullest extent of their skills.

A creative act is one that is original, valuable, and suggests that the person performing the act has unusual mental abilities.[5] A creative act is a problem-solving act; in particular it is the solution of an ill-defined problem. Four cognitive processes especially important for creativity include: (1) problem finding, (2) idea generation, (3) planning, and (4) preparation.

The discovery of a new problem not suggested by anyone else is important in any field. Three procedures that can help us to find problems are bug listing, searching for counterexamples, and searching for alternative interpretations.

Sometimes, when we are trying to solve an ill-defined problem, we are blocked by difficulty in generating ideas for solution. Brainstorming and discovering analogies may help us out of this difficulty. Planning is important in creative activities, as it is in any form of problem solving. Good writing and good art depend on good planning.

Internal auditors need to use creative skills during audit planning and the preliminary survey and during development of the audit program. Identification of audit objectives is important in the audit planning phase. Development of a good approach to conduct the preliminary survey requires creativity. Deciding what audit procedures need to be performed requires creativity during audit program development. Both new audits and repeat audits benefit from applying creative skills.

(v) **Reasons why individuals solve problems differently.** Problem-solving skills are different with different people. Five factors have a major play in a person's problem-solving capabilities: (1) value system, (2) information filtration, (3) interpretation, (4) internal representation, and (5) external representation (see Exhibit 5.13).

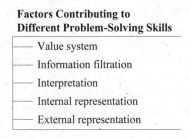

**Factors Contributing to Different Problem-Solving Skills**

- Value system
- Information filtration
- Interpretation
- Internal representation
- External representation

**Exhibit 5.13: Factors contributing to different problem-solving skills**

(A) *Value system.* Individuals make decisions and solve problems differently due to the different value system each one of us has. If two people make different choices in the same situation, it does not mean that one of them is wrong; it may just be that they have different values. This means that we cannot tell how good people's decision-making processes are by the choices they make. However, training in formal decision-making methods and problem-solving skills would

---

[5] John R. Hayes, *The Complete Problem Solver*, 2nd ed. (Mahwah, NJ: Lawrence Erlbaum Associates, 1989).

help. No matter what people's values are, if they use good decision-making methods, they should tend to agree with themselves when they make the same decision again.

(B) *Information filtration.* Some people can filter relevant information from the irrelevant. It is a skill that can be acquired through reasoning and practice. Problem solving would be simpler for people who can think simply and clearly in their minds. Also, a multiple-level organization structure is most likely to produce information filtration. Information is subject to distortion or filtration as it moves through many channels of communication. The greater the level of communication, the greater the information filtration.

Even when two people represent the same problem, they may not represent it in the same way. A person who is very good at filtering out irrelevant details may produce a very sparse representation. Another person who is not good at filtering out irrelevant details may produce a complex and ornate representation.

(C) *Interpretation.* Forming a representation is a very active process in which a person adds and subtracts information and interprets information in the original situation. Pictures can be used during the process of interpretation.

(D) *Internal representation.* Internal representation deals with analogies and schemas in our minds. When we encounter a problem, we recognize that we have seen a similar problem before. This is called "analogy." An example would be a car stalling and a similar audit situation. A problem schema is a package of information about the properties of a particular problem type. Problem schemas are an important part of the knowledge we use to solve problems.

### Internal Representation of a Problem

Examples of internal representation of a problem include imaging, inferencing, decision making, and retrieving of knowledge from memory in an effort to understand the problem.

Our skill in problem solving depends in a very important way on our store of problem schemas. Each problem schema we know gives us a very valuable advantage in solving a whole class of problems—an advantage that may consist in knowing what to pay attention to, or how to represent the problem, or how to search for a solution, or all three. *Clearly, the more schemas we know, the better prepared we are as problem solvers.*

Different people may create different internal representations of the same problem. There are more differences between representations, though, than just the amount of detail they contain. One person may represent a problem in visual imagery, another in sentences, and a third in auditory images. If two people represent a problem in visual images, they may not use the same images. For example, people frequently use both auditory and visual imagery in solving arithmetic problems. While doing problems in their heads, people use visual images of the digits of the answer and of marks indicating borrowing or cancellation.

(E) *External representation.* In many cases, an external representation is very helpful for solving problems. Drawing a sketch, jotting down lists, writing out equations, and making diagrams can help us to remember information and to notice new relations in the problem. Some relations in problems are easier to discover when diagrams are used. For example, a matrix representation is useful in solving control identification problems (e.g., matching controls to control objectives).

External representations are very helpful in solving complex problems, but they are not useful without an internal representation of the problem. An internal representation is essential for intelligent problem solving since it is the medium in which people think—the same way the words are the medium for speech. Sometimes an internal representation is sufficient for solving simple problems. However, external representation alone is not useful. Both representations are needed for most cases.

(vi) **Prospective and retrospective methods.** Often management asks auditors to deal with forward-looking, future-oriented problems or questions. Collectively they are referred to as prospective methods to distinguish them from approaches designed to answer questions about what is happening now or what has happened in the past—that is, retrospective methods. An auditor's problem-solving skill set should address both of these methods. Conducting a repeat audit of accounts payable is an example of a retrospective method. Performing a due diligence review is an example of a prospective method of problem solving.

---

**Examples of Types of Prospective Methods**

Four types of methods exist: actual, empirical, logical, and judgmental.

1. Actual types include experimental test and demonstration programs.
2. Empirical types include simulation and forecasting.
3. Logical types include front-end analysis, risk assessment, systems analysis, scenario building, and anticipatory analysis.
4. Judgmental types include Delphi technique and expert opinion.

---

Basically, two types of forward-looking questions exist: anticipate the future or improve the future. In both situations, auditors would be critiquing others' analyses or would do their own analyses. Future needs, costs, and consequences are analyzed when anticipating the future issues. Courses of action that have the best potential for success are analyzed to improve the future. These types of questions are most appropriate in acquisition and divestiture audits.

The type of questions being addressed dictates the need for a systematic method of analysis. Where the questions are controversial, far-reaching, sensitive, and more systematic methods may be called for. Simple questions need simple methods. Some advantages of using systematic methods include: the full range of existing information can be brought to bear on the question, and high-quality standards of evidence and analysis can be used in documenting the basis for answers about the future. Exhibit 5.14 compares retrospective methods with prospective methods.

| *Retrospective methods* | *Prospective methods* |
|---|---|
| • Require less judgment due to the lower level of uncertainty involved | • Require more judgment due to higher degree of uncertainty involved |
| • Decreased need for alternatives and options | • Increased need for alternatives and options |
| • Source of questions: existing criteria, issues, and policies | • Sources of questions: ideas and assumptions about problems, probable causes, possible solutions |
| • Primary sources of information: documents, administrative data, interviews, observations, survey | • Primary sources of information: prior research, theory, pilot tests, experimental tests of proposed approaches, expert opinion |
| • Primary types of analysis: qualitative and quantitative approaches to empirical data, information syntheses in relation to criteria and issues | • Primary types of analysis: simulations, forecasting, and information syntheses in relation to conceptual and operational assumptions of proposed solutions; Delphi techniques; analyses of likely effects |

**Exhibit 5.14: Comparison of retrospective methods with prospective methods of problem solving**

(vii) **Tools and techniques for problem solving.** Many tools and techniques are available for the problem solver to solve problems. They include brainstorming, synectics, nominal group technique, force-field approach, systems analysis, and others (see Exhibit 5.15).[6] Differences exist among the problem-solving methods, and all of them do not work equally well in different situations. In any given situation, one or two methods might have a greater probability of leading to the desired outcomes.

---

[6] *Francis L. Ulschak, Leslie Nathanson, and Peter G. Gillan, **Small Group Problem Solving** (Reading, MA: Addison-Wesley, 1981).*

**Tools and Techniques for Problem Solving**

— Brainstorming (the more ideas, the better; encourages uninhibited flow of ideas)

— Synectics (a highly structured approach; uses excursions, fantasies, and analogies)

— Nominal group technique (no real group exists, uses a very structured approach

— Force-field analysis (identifies inhibiting and facilitating forces)

— Systems analysis (breaks down a large problem into many smaller problems)

**Exhibit 5.15: Tools and techniques for problem solving**

(viii) **Brainstorming.** The purpose of the brainstorming technique is to generate a great number of ideas; that is, its purpose is idea generation. The key is to let the members of the group feel free to express whatever ideas come to mind without fear of judgment or criticism. Uninhibited flow of ideas is permitted; negative thinking is not permitted. Recording all ideas and deferring judgment until the later phases of the analysis is the hallmark of brainstorming. See Exhibit 5.16 for advantages and disadvantages of brainstorming technique.

| *Advantages* | *Disadvantages* |
|---|---|
| • Rapid generation of ideas | • Process focuses on idea generation, not on specific solutions |
| • Identification of many factors of a particular topic | • Process does not work well where problems are not open-ended |
| • Expression of a cross-section of views from various disciplines | |

**Exhibit 5.16: Advantages and disadvantages of brainstorming technique**

The brainstorming technique is most effective when the presence of an expert is not necessary, the high level of creativity is seen as a bonus rather than an irritant, and a large quantity of ideas is needed.

## Misconceptions about Brainstorming

There are two misconceptions about brainstorming: (1) there is a total lack of control and direction in a brainstorming session, and (2) brainstorming does not involve judgment or evaluation of ideas; all ideas are seen as equally effective and productive.

There *are four rules for effective brainstorming sessions.*

1. **Postpone evaluation of ideas.** Postpone evaluation of ideas of others as well as one's own. This rule is the most critical, because the best way to reduce effective idea generation is to make premature evaluations and\or judgments.
2. **"Free-wheeling" is welcome and invited.** "Free-wheeling" means that any idea is permitted, no matter how outlandish or fanciful. One person's flight of fantasy may be the trigger for another's generation of a very workable idea.
3. **Many ideas are wanted.** The greater the number of ideas, the greater the possibility that quality ideas will emerge.
4. **Encourage hitchhiking.** Hitchhiking is the art of combining and improving on ideas; in other words, building on another's suggestion. Frequently, a group will develop a cue for members to use when they want to hitchhike; for example; snapping a finger. Hitchhiking is a by-product of brainstorming.

(ix) **Synectics.** Synectics is a technique for creating an environment that encourages creative approaches to problem solving. It is a highly structured approach for an individual who needs a group to help solve a problem. *It involves the use of nontraditional activities, such as excursions and fantasies, and analogies.* Synectics is good for idea generation and team building. See Exhibit 5.17 for advantages and disadvantages of synectics technique.

| Advantages | Disadvantages |
|---|---|
| • The method works exceptionally well when people feel in a rut or blocked with a problem | • Participants many have difficulty with the excursion; some may be reluctant to fantasize |
| • The process is fun—there is a lot of energy flowing | • The process works best with small groups consisting of six to eight members |
| • It generates a great number of new perspectives on the problem | • The process works better for individual problems than for group problems |
| • In addition to structure, there is plenty of room for flexibility | • Although the process sounds easy, much preparation is required |
| • Participants feel very involved in the process | |

**Exhibit 5.17: Advantages and disadvantages of synectics technique**

*Excursions and fantasies* are a deliberate move to get participants away from consciously thinking about the problem. Synectics utilizes the excursion for employing the subconscious mind to work on the problem and find clues to possible solutions. Excursions are productive with regard to developing possible solutions, and they also serve to energize the group members.

*Analogies* are an important source of ideas when searching for problem solutions. A checklist is prepared for each type of analogy, including personal, direct, symbolic, fantasy, and attribute. The user works through the checklist and tries to find analogies of each type. Personal analogy is where the problem solver puts him- or herself directly into the problem situation. Direct analogy involves searching for a setting where the same function is accomplished.

Symbolic analogy is associated with symbols, notations, figures, and pictures. Fantasy analogy includes magic and science fiction. In an attribute analogy system, the checklist would list attributes of an object—its name, form, function, color, and material. After listing the attributes, analogies are attached to each one by screening for useful insights. Analogies and symbols are also called free association, where unconventional thinking is encouraged.

(x) **Nominal group technique.** The nominal group technique (NGT) is an idea-generating, consensus-building tool. *No real group exists—in name only.* A strength of this process is that it permits a problem to become focused in a short period of time. It uses a very structured approach and is an excellent technique to use when the group members are drawn from various levels of the organizational hierarchy or when they are in conflict with one another. The technique gives everyone an opportunity to express ideas without being interrupted by others in the group. See Exhibit 5.18 for advantages and disadvantages of NGT.

| Advantages | Disadvantages |
|---|---|
| • The technique can be used with groups of varying backgrounds, cultures, education, or work roles who share a common problem or goal. | • The technique calls for a trained leader or group facilitator. |
| • NGT can be used in groups where participants do not have previous training in group process or communication skills. | • It can deal with only one question at a time. |
| • The highly structured process is a quick method of bringing people together to approach a common task. | • NGT is inappropriate to use in a group where interacting problem-solving and team-building skills are to be developed. |
| • NGT promotes the generation of many ideas surrounding an issue. | |
| • NGT allows for a maximum and equal participation of all group members, encouraging input from many areas of expertise. | |
| • The process is easy to run. | |

**Exhibit 5.18: Advantages and disadvantages of nominal group technique**

Generally social psychology researchers have found that individuals working in groups generate more ideas than when they work alone. Furthermore, nominal groups—groups "in name only," where people are brought together but not allowed to communicate—have been found to be more effective for idea generation than interacting groups, where people meet to discuss, brainstorm, and exchange information. Such interacting groups tend to inhibit creative thinking. However, for purposes such as attitude change, team building, and consensus generation, interacting groups have been found superior.

## BRAINSTORMING VS. SYNECTICS VS. NOMINAL GROUP TECHNIQUE

- If the goal is idea generation, use brainstorming or synectics since they facilitate more diverse or creative thinking.
- If the goal is for a group of relative strangers to meet in order to reach a group consensus concerning common issues, use nominal group technique since it is a structured process of consensus building.

---

The unique NGT process combines a silent time for idea generation with the social reinforcement of an interacting group setting. This structured process forces equality of participation among members in generating and sharing information about the issue. The NGT group may consist of five to eight participants.

(xi) **Force-field analysis.** Force-field analysis involves the identification of a problem, the factors or forces contributing to making it a problem, and steps for generating solutions. Two main sets of forces are identified: (1) inhibiting forces—those that resist the resolution of the problem; and (2) facilitating forces—those that push the problem toward resolution. Once the forces acting on a problem are identified, actions can be taken to decrease the major resisting forces, increase the major facilitating forces, or both. This process, then, is basically an analysis of the forces acting to keep the problem a problem. See Exhibit 5.19 for advantages and disadvantages of force-field analysis.

| *Advantages* | *Disadvantages* |
|---|---|
| • The outcome of the process is a detailed action plan with evaluation criteria built in. | • The group may get lost in arguments about what the problem really is, what forces are the most important, which action steps to begin with, and so on. |
| • It is an excellent process for a group to use in dealing with group problems. | |
| • It is an effective tool to define problems, analyze problems, and develop solutions into workable action plans. | • Problems that are not easily and clearly defined many be difficult for this process. |
| • Group size is not a critical factor, and it can be used as a team-building process. | • The team leader needs to be a good listener and should be able to help the team weight and rank alternatives. |

**Exhibit 5.19:  Advantages and disadvantages of force-field analysis**

Force-field analysis calls for the definition of present conditions and desired conditions. Once a clear image of these conditions is established, effective intervention strategies can be devised to move from the present to the desired condition. As a problem-solving process, force-field analysis involves identifying and analyzing problems, developing strategies for change, and clarifying specific steps to be taken to confront the problem. It is an excellent analytical tool. The outcome will be a detailed action plan outlining when, to whom, and how the problem will be addressed. The force-field approach is useful for viewing a problem that involves the entire group, and it may be combined with other problem-solving methods in order to establish a long-term plan of action.

(xii) **Systems analysis.** Systems analysis breaks down a large problem into many smaller problems. It is an excellent technique if the desired outcome of the problem-solving session is a detailed understanding of a problem. The technique offers a structure for analyzing a problem and various alternative solutions. However, it does not structure the roles of the participants. The major strength of this process is that it offers a method of reviewing the total context of a problem. The phrase "systems analysis" does not mean analysis of computer-based information systems. The scope is broader than that—manual, automated, or both. See Exhibit 5.20 for advantages and disadvantages of systems analysis.

| *Advantages* | *Disadvantages* |
|---|---|
| • The problem is fully analyzed, touching on important questions and areas of concern. | • There may be a tendency for the group to get bogged down in the process. |
| • Several alternatives are developed, leaving abundant options for choice. | |
| • It can be combined with other problem-solving methods. | |

**Exhibit 5.20:  Advantages and disadvantages of systems analysis**

This method requires the problem solver to look beyond the unit of the problem to the environment for various possible solutions. It focuses on three attributes: (1) open systems, (2) multiple reasons and causes, and (3) the entire picture.

The first attribute of systems theory assumes that a system is open; it interacts with its environment and can be represented by three models: hierarchical, input-output, and entities model. In the hierarchical model, systems are seen within a structure of subsystems. This framework may be useful in identifying the context in which the group finds itself. An input-output model may be useful in identifying the inputs that are needed and how they are to be transformed toward the desired outputs. The entities model may be used to form tentative hypotheses about how the group members may interact.

The second attribute of systems theory looks at multiple reasons or causes for things; it keeps the problem solver from having tunnel vision concerning the nature of the problem. The systems approach moves away from linear causation, which assumes that the effects of a situation are based on single causes. Realizing that problems often have more than one cause helps to attack the problem from several fronts.

The third attribute of the system model examines the entire picture rather than only one part or element. Remember the classic elephant story—different views of the elephant by six blind men.

(xiii) **More problem-solving tools and techniques.** Additional problem-solving tools include

- **Imagineering.** Imagineering involves the visualization of a complex process, procedure, or operation with all waste eliminated. The imagineer assumes the role of dreamer, realist, and critic. The steps in imagineering consist of taking an action, comparing the results with the person's imagined perfect situation, and making mental correction for the next time. This approach will eventually improve the situation and bring it to the desired level. Imagineering is similar to value-analysis.

- **Value analysis.** Value analysis is a systematic study of a business process or product with a view to improving the process or product and reducing cost. Creative skills are required while doing value analysis. Its goal is to ensure that the right activities are performed in the right way the first time. Industrial engineering techniques, such as work measurement and simplification methods, can be used to achieve the goals.

  A group approach that encourages free discussion and exchange of ideas is required to conduct value analysis in order to determine how the functions of particular parts, materials, or services can be performed as well or better at a lower cost. Techniques such as brainstorming, hitchhiking, and leapfrogging are used during value analysis.

- **Leapfrogging.** Leapfrogging is taking a big step forward in thinking up idealistic solutions to a problem. For example, leapfrogging can be applied to value-analyzing comparable products to identify their best features and design. These ideas are then combined into a hybrid product that, in turn, can bring new superior products to enter a new market.

- **Blasting, creating, and refining.** Blasting, creating, and refining are used when a completely new way of thinking or speculation is required or when answering a question such as "What else will do the job? Blasting is good when the group members are free to speculate and come up with totally new ideas that were never heard of or thought about before. Creativity comes into full play.

- **Attribute listing.** Attribute listing emphasizes the detailed observation of each particular characteristic or quality of an item or situation. Attempts are then made to profitably change the characteristic or to relate it to a different item.

- **Edisonian.** Edisonian, named after Thomas Edison, involves trial-and-error experimentation. This method requires a tedious and persistent search for the solution.

- **Investigative questions.** The scope includes asking six investigative (journalism) questions: who, what, when, where, why, and how—to understand the root causes of issues and problems better.

- **Cause and effect diagrams.** Cause and effect (C&E) diagrams (also called Ishikawa or fishbone diagrams) can be used to identify possible causes for a problem. The problem solver looks for the root causes by asking the "why" five or six times to move from broad (possible) causes to specific (root) causes. The idea is that by repeating the same question "why," the true source of a problem is discovered. This process will help identify the real problem. Then the problem solver chooses the most likely cause for further review. Brainstorming can be used in developing the C&E diagrams.

C&E diagrams can be used to explain audit findings to an auditee and to validate the causes by the auditee. This brings the auditee involvement and buy-in into the audit findings and recommendations. A graph can be drawn showing the relationship between a cause (independent variable on *x*-axis) and effect (dependent variable on *y*-axis). Scatter diagrams can be used to show the root causes of a problem while the C&E diagrams can be used to show possible causes.

- **Pareto charts.** Pareto charts can be drawn to separate the "vital few" from the "trivial many." They are based on the 80/20 rule, that is, 20% of items contribute to 80% of problems.
- **Psychodramatic approaches.** These approaches involve role-playing and role-reversal behavior. In psychodrama, the attempt is made to bring into focus all elements of an individual's problem; in sociodrama, the emphasis is on shared problems of group members.
- **Checklists.** Checklists focus one's attention on a logical list of diverse categories to which the problem could conceivably relate.
- **General semantics.** These include approaches that help the individual to discover multiple meanings or relationships in words and expressions.
- **Morphological analysis.** This is a system involving the methodical interrelating of all elements of a problem in order to discover new approaches to a solution.
- **Panel consensus technique.** This technique is a way to process a large number of ideas, circumventing organizational restraints to idea creation, using extensive participation and emphasizing methods for selecting good ideas.
- **Delphi technique.** This technique is a method used to avoid groupthink. Group members do not meet face-to-face to make decisions. Rather, each group member independently and anonymously writes down suggestions and submits comments, which are then centrally compiled. The compiled results are then distributed to the group members who, independently and anonymously, write additional comments. These comments are again centrally compiled and the process repeated until consensus is obtained. The Delphi technique is a group decision-making method.
- **Work measurement.** This industrial engineering program applies some of the general principles of creative problem solving to the simplification of operations or procedures.
- **Storyboards.** Storyboarding is a group problem-solving technique to create a picture of relevant information. A storyboard can be created for each group that is making decisions. A positive outcome of storyboarding is that it takes less time than interviewing, and many employees can get involved in problem solving, not just the managers.
- **Humor.** In addition to being a powerful tool to relieve tension and hostility, humor is a problem-solving tool. When correctly executed, it opens the mind to seeking creative solutions to the problem. Humor can be in the form of detached jokes, quips, games, puns, and anecdotes. Humor gives perspective and solves problems. Stepping back and viewing a problem with a certain level of detachment restores perspective. A sense of humor sends messages of self-confidence, security, and control of the situation. However, humor should not be sarcastic or scornful.
- **Operations research.** Operations research is a management science discipline attempting to find optimal solutions to business problems using mathematical techniques, such as simulation, linear programming, statistics, and computers.
- **Intuitive approach.** The intuitive approach is based on hunches (gut feelings). It does not use a scientific approach and uses subjective estimates or probabilities, which are difficult to replicate.
- **T-Analysis.** T-analysis is a tabular presentation of strengths on one side and weaknesses on the other side of the letter "T." The goal is to address the weaknesses (problems).
- **Closure.** Closure is a perceptual process that allows a person to solve a complex problem with incomplete information. It is the last step in problem solving.
- **TRIZ.** TRIZ is a theory of solving inventive problems. It supports the idea that unsolved problems are the result of contradicting goals (constraints) and nonproductive thinking. It

suggests to breakout of nonproductive thinking mold by reframing the contradicting and competing goals in such a way that the contradictions disappear.

(xiv) **Considerations of problem solving: traits and behaviors.** All auditors should be familiar with certain traits and behaviors during problem solving. While certain problem-solving behaviors, such as conjecturing, predicting, and drawing conclusions, can be learned and taught, the other behaviors and problem-solving traits, such as self-reliance, risk taking, creative thinking, and interacting, are examples of affective-related behaviors that are fostered through individual encouragement.[7]

An auditor needs to focus on these traits and behaviors.

- *Traits*

  - **Curious.** Eager to investigate, to learn new approaches and techniques, to understand how a problem is solved.
  - **Keen.** Interested in problems, quick to respond to individual challenges.
  - **Interactive.** Participates freely with others, seeking and sharing ideas.
  - **Creative.** Responds to problem situations in new or unusual ways; not confined in problem approaches or ways of thinking.
  - **Receptive.** Willing to listen to and consider ideas of others.
  - **Intuitive.** Able to act on hunches or educated guesses.
  - **Retentive.** Draws on and applies previously acquired information in new situations.
  - **Self-confident.** Believes that skills and abilities are adequate to meet the challenge of new problems.
  - **Relishes challenges.** Desires and enjoys pitting abilities against problems.
  - **Critical.** Evaluates ideas and explanations carefully; looks for exceptions to generalizations.
  - **Organized.** Approaches the problems systematically, investigates problem ideas in an orderly, sequential manner; keeps a record of successful and unsuccessful attempts.
  - **Tolerant.** Listens to ideas and problem approaches that are not personal choices; willing to bide time in making and seeing suggestions acted on; respects problem-solving efforts and achievement of others.
  - **Resourceful.** Able to overcome obstacles in more than one way.
  - **Flexible.** Capable of changing or expanding thinking to incorporate new or different ideas from others.
  - **Self-directed.** Motivated from within to pursue and continue with challenges.
  - **Introspective.** Considers own thinking processes in problem solving; reflects on how new knowledge or discoveries integrate with previous information or thinking.
  - **Risk-taker.** Unafraid to be wrong in ideas or to be unsuccessful in efforts to solve a problem; willing to present ideas about a problem to others for evaluation.

- *Behaviors*

  - **Questions.** Expands on problem-solving discussion by asking about other cases, how the situation varies by changing givens; pursues matters that need clarification in own or others' thinking.
  - **Notes details.** Considers all information that may affect the outcome of a problem; alert to recognizing relationships among variable quantities.
  - **Discriminates.** Perceives similarities and differences among objects or relationships that are important to the problem; distinguishes relevant information from irrelevant problem material.
  - **Recognizes patterns.** Detects similarities that characterize a set of information; able to predict missing elements.
  - **Anticipates.** Examines alternatives using cause and effect reasoning without carrying action to conclusion; capable of meeting problems before they arise.
  - **Predicts.** Foresees or foretells the outcomes of or results to a problem based on previous background, experience, or reasoning.

---

[7] *Problem Solving—Volume 2.*

- **Generalizes.** Extends the results of a particular problem or set of data to a larger and more general situation.
- **Visualizes.** Forms mental images of problem variables to perceive interrelationships among them.
- **Infers.** Examines problem information carefully to derive hypotheses and draw conclusions.
- **Speculates.** Reflects on and reasons about problem components, interrelationships, and implications; forms educated conjectures from available evidence.
- **Concentrates.** Summons all of his or her skills and resources to attack a problem; overcomes extraneous influences and distractions.
- **Synthesizes.** Integrates individually acquired skills and information into a larger understanding of the processes and components of problem solving.
- **Draws conclusions.** Able to bring thinking to a decision to direct problem-solving actions; able to summarize the results of problems or implications.
- **Deliberates.** Recognizes the appropriate times to consider carefully the information of a problem before acting, the implications of a result before generalizing, the alternatives before choosing.
- **Perseveres.** Persists with a problem despite lack of success, discouragement, or opposition to his or her ideas; reluctant to "give up" on a problem.
- **Makes refined judgments.** Able to adjust thinking or statements based on additional information; able to improve the work of others by noting subtleties, distinctions, exceptions, or special cases.
- **Uses divergent thinking.** Able to perceive more than one implication or consequence to a problem action; able to consider unique or unusual approaches or outcomes to a problem; able to expand thinking throughout a problem rather than narrowing it.

(xv) **Problem solving and the internal auditor:  applications.** Auditors solve problems when they engage in an audit. An example of a problem-solving skill required of internal auditors is that of determining which audit procedures are most appropriate for a given situation. Because internal auditing involves examining evidence and reaching conclusions based on that evidence, auditors must understand and be adept in the use of inductive reasoning. In addition, internal auditors must be able to evaluate a specific situation and deduce, for example, what evidence should be gathered to reach a valid conclusion. Several audit situations are presented to apply problem-solving skills.

- **Audit Situation No. 1.** An internal auditor wishes to determine whether the accounts payable ledgers accurately reflect the obligations of the firm to vendors. Goods are shipped FOB to the buyer's plant. The auditor needs to select the type of documents that provide the best evidence and are useful. Given the documents such as vendors' packing slips, purchase orders, receiving reports, vendors' invoices, and purchase requisitions, the auditor would select purchase orders, receiving reports, and vendors' invoices.
- **Audit Situation No. 2.** During a preliminary survey of the accounts receivable function, an internal auditor discovered a potentially major control deficiency while preparing a flowchart. Since this is a major control problem, the auditor should take an immediate action by reporting it to the level of management responsible for corrective action and highlighting the control weakness to ensure that audit work steps to test it are included in the audit program.
- **Audit Situation No. 3.** An internal auditor observed that only 1 of the company's 10 divisions had a large number of material sales transactions close to the end of the fiscal year. In terms of risk analysis, this would most likely lead the auditor to conclude that there is a relatively higher risk of overstatement of revenues for this division than for other divisions.
- **Audit Situation No. 4.** During an audit for the state tax department, one of the audit objectives is to determine if reporting taxpayers are correctly disclosing their sales taxes. The audit procedure that would most effectively achieve that objective is to conduct field examinations of selected taxpayers.
- **Audit Situation No. 5.** Due to a widespread failure of department managers to meet their budgets, senior management has requested an internal audit of the budget process. The primary objective of such an audit would be to determine if budget-setting policies and procedures are adequate and are in use. The audit objective would not be whether individual vari-

ances are accurately reported or whether first-line managers are given an opportunity to provide inputs into their budgets.

- **Audit Situation No. 6.** One of the objectives of a computerized inventory system audit is to determine if merchandise levels are replenished on a timely basis. An appropriate audit procedure for this objective would involve detailed testing of the update program that creates new purchase orders. It would not involve an edit program that lists all quantities sold or batch totals for shipments or an update program that creates new part numbers.
- **Audit Situation No. 7.** To determine the sufficiency of evidence regarding interpretation of a contract, an auditor uses the best obtainable evidence, subjective judgments, objective evaluations, and logical relationships between evidence and issues.
- **Audit Situation No. 8.** While planning an audit, an internal auditor establishes audit objectives to describe what is to be accomplished. A key issue to consider in developing audit objectives is the auditee's objectives and control structure. It is not the qualifications of the audit staff selected for the engagement, recommendations of the auditee's employees, or the recipients of the audit report.
- **Audit Situation No. 9.** When receiving, reports are forwarded to the purchasing department where they are matched to purchase orders and then sent to accounts payable. This is a problem situation that should cause the auditor to question the adequacy of internal controls in a purchasing function. The problem is solved when the accounts payable department receives all receiving reports directly, matches them to purchase orders, and prepares payments.
- **Audit Situation No. 10.** In an audit of an automated inventory control system, the audit approach that would provide the best evidence that purchase orders are authorized is testing to ensure that only authorized persons are able to change parameters in the computer program that generates purchase orders. It is not tracing purchase orders to the computer listing, comparing receiving reports with purchase order details, or reviewing system documentation to determine proper functioning of the program.
- **Audit Situation No. 11.** A company manufacturing special-order products is experiencing excessive rates of rejection of finished products. An audit procedure to identify the source of the problem is evaluating communication from the sales department to the production department. It is not evaluating communication from the production department to the sales department, analyzing customer demand for the product, or testing whether supply of the product is sufficient to meet customer demand.
- **Audit Situation No. 12.** An internal auditor is planning an operational audit of the traffic department. The audit objective that best describes the focus of the audit would be to verify that the selection of carriers and routes provides the most economical and timely shipments of supplies and finished goods. It would not be to determine the market potential for the company's products, determine that the proper goods and services are obtained at the right price, or ensure that distributors give extra attention to sales of the company's products.
- **Audit Situation No. 13.** An audit of the purchasing function disclosed that orders were placed for materials that at that time were being disposed of as surplus. The best solution to this problem would be a recommendation to develop and distribute periodic reports of surplus stocks. It is not having all purchase requisitions approved by the responsible purchasing agent, scheduling purchases based on past orders placed, or employing a historical reorder point system.
- **Audit Situation No. 14.** An internal auditor is evaluating the propriety of a payment to a consultant. The most appropriate evidence for the auditor to obtain and review would be documentary evidence in the form of a contract. It would not be oral evidence in the form of opinions of operating management, analytical evidence in the form of comparisons with prior years' expenditures on consultants, or physical evidence in the form of the consultant's report.
- **Audit Situation No. 15.** An internal auditor is evaluating the reasonableness of account balances. The most relevant form of evidence to obtain to achieve this audit objective would be an analytical evidence, not documentary, physical, or testimonial evidence.
- **Audit Situation No. 16.** A large public charity raises funds for medical research from the general public by using a wide variety of solicitation techniques. In an audit of donations, the auditor would select these audit procedures: written confirmation of a sample of direct mail

pledges, reconciliation of depository bank accounts, and reconciliation of raffle tickets sold to amounts deposited in the bank. The auditor would not select "Surprise observation of door-to-door solicitation teams" since it is not an effective audit procedure.

- **Audit Situation No. 17.** A large hospital is faced with quality problems in housekeeping services. The most reliable source of information for an auditor to evaluate the quality of such services would be to interview with a sample of medical personnel since they can give first-hand information about quality problems. The following sources would not provide reliable information since they would not be objective: scrutiny of survey forms returned by medical personnel directly to the administrator of the hospital (medical personnel may be inhibited from saying the truth to the administrator); a review of records maintained by the medical records department of the hospital; and a personal interview with the dean of the school of medicine that is affiliated with the hospital (the dean would not be close to the action).

- **Audit Situation No. 18.** One payroll audit objective is to determine whether employees received pay in amounts recorded in the payroll journal. The auditor needs to select an audit procedure that would achieve the audit objective. Comparing the canceled payroll checks to the payroll journal would be the best audit procedure since the endorsement on the back of the check is an indication of the right employee receiving the amount. These audit procedures would not be meaningful to use: reconciling the payroll bank account, requesting that a company official distribute all paychecks, or determining whether a proper segregation of duties exists between recording payroll and reconciling the payroll bank account.

- **Audit Situation No. 19.** The auditor is evaluating the adequacy of a company's insurance coverage. The auditor developed a detailed schedule of current insurance policies in force. The most likely source of information for the working paper would be the files containing insurance policies with various carriers. These sources would not be appropriate: original journal entries found in the cash disbursements journal and supported by canceled check; management's charter prescribing the insurance staff objectives, authority, and responsibilities; or the current fiscal year's budget for prepaid insurance together with the beginning balance sheet amount.

- **Audit Situation No. 20.** In examining whether an auditee is conforming to the company's affirmative action policy, the internal auditor has found that: 5% of the employees are from minority groups, and no one from a minority group has been hired this year. The most appropriate conclusion the auditor should draw is that insufficient evidence exists of compliance with the affirmative action policy. The reason for insufficient evidence is that target percent of minority hiring is not known and how many total employees were hired this year is not known.

- **Audit Situation No. 21.** During an early phase of an extensive audit of a manufacturing company's inventory management system, an auditor discovered that there had been recurring stock-outs for some high-demand items and that this had led to expensive expediting and work stoppages. Further investigation revealed that the purchasing department had regularly ordered these items based on purchase orders produced automatically by the computerized inventory system. The quantity ordered had been based on an economic order quantity (EOQ) model included in the computerized inventory system. The auditor determined that the EOQ model was properly designed and that the problem had resulted from failure to update data in the model concerning the time required for delivery. The auditor is now faced with selecting an appropriate action to resolve the problem at hand. Some examples are

  - The auditor would most likely conclude that these facts indicate an important problem that should be included in the audit report.
  - If the auditor decided that the situation warranted management's immediate attention and the entire audit would not be completed for several weeks, communication with management would probably take the form of a written interim report to operating management. An oral report would not be proper since statistics and facts may be presented that require a written document.
  - The importance of the problem outlined would probably cause the auditing department to follow up on action taken by management as a result of an audit communication. Follow-up should be conducted by scheduling a review of this area in the near future.

- **Audit Situation No. 22.** A company has computerized sales and cash receipts journals. The computer programs for these journals have been properly debugged (i.e., tested). The auditor discovered that the total of the accounts receivable subsidiary accounts differs materially from the accounts receivable control account. A reason for this problem could be that credit memoranda are being improperly recorded. These would not be good reasons for causing the problem: lapping of receivables, receivables not being properly aged, and statements being intercepted prior to mailing.
- **Audit Situation No. 23.** An auditor performing a payroll audit wants to be assured that persons for whom paychecks are produced actually exist and are employees of the organization. The most appropriate evidence to achieve these objectives would be visual or physical evidence obtained by observing the distribution of paychecks. This evidence is more direct and firsthand. This evidence would not be appropriate: documentary evidence in the form of time cards signed by supervisors, documentary evidence in the form of personnel and payroll records, or oral evidence obtained by discussions with supervisors and payroll clerks. Fraud could be present in these three procedures.
- **Audit Situation No. 24.** An auditor is testing for the misclassification of capital acquisitions as expenditures. The most efficient testing procedures would be to scan the repair and maintenance records and investigate large-dollar-value entries. There is a tendency to misclassify high-dollar-value items instead of low-dollar-value items to obtain big impact. These testing procedures would not be efficient: taking a physical tour of plant facilities before starting an audit, reviewing company capital-acquisition policies with purchasing personnel, or tracing capital additions back to source documents.
- **Audit Situation No. 25.** A machinist claims that his poor-quality output is due to a contracted maintenance service employee's failure to perform required service on his equipment. The most convincing evidence for the auditor to determine whether the service was performed is whether the shop supervisor initialed the serviceperson's work order for the work in question. These items would not provide convincing evidence: a label attached to the equipment has checkmarks showing the maintenance work was performed on the scheduled dates, the maintenance service's invoice listing the equipment in question was paid, or the plant engineer approval of the listed services as adequate for the equipment.
- **Audit Situation No. 26.** An auditor's objective is to verify ownership of selected vehicles. The best source of evidence would be vehicle titles and current license certificates since they are official documents. These items would not provide best source of evidence because they cannot be relied on: property records containing vehicle identification numbers, properly approved purchase orders, or invoices from dealers.
- **Audit Situation No. 27.** An auditor who wishes to substantiate the gross balance of the account "Trade Notes Receivable" is considering the advisability of performing these four procedures.

    1. Age the receivables.
    2. Confirm the notes with the makers.
    3. Inspect the notes.
    4. Trace a sample of postings from the sales journal to the notes receivable ledger.

    The auditor needs to select appropriate audit procedures to meet his objective. The auditor would select procedures 2 and 3 to accomplish the objective.
- **Audit Situation No. 28.** The audit objective is to determine that nonrecurring purchases, initiated by various user organizations, have been properly authorized. All purchases are made through the purchasing department. The auditor would select purchase requisitions for tracing purchases since they provide a starting point for purchases. Other documents, such as purchase orders, invoices, and receiving reports, would not help in achieving the audit objective since they come after purchase requisitions.
- **Audit Situation No. 29.** A large university has relatively poor internal accounting control—a problem. The university's auditor seeks assurance that all tuition revenue has been recorded. The auditor could best obtain the desired assurance by comparing business office revenue records with registrar's office records of students enrolled since they provide a direct link. These audit procedures would not solve the problem: confirming a sample of tuition payments

with the students, observing tuition payment procedures on a surprise basis, or preparing year-end bank reconciliation.

- **Audit Situation No. 30.** A company invests material amounts of idle cash in marketable securities. The auditor has reason to believe that suboptimal use (a problem) is being made of the idle cash. The audit procedure that would provide the most reliable evidence is computation of the rate of return earned on investments and comparison with alternative investments.

    Analytical evidence is being sought here in order to obtain a feel for the reasonableness of investments and returns. These audit procedures would not provide reliable evidence: review of the minutes of the company's investment committee; confirmation of security transactions, and income received, with the company's independent stockbrokers; or comparison of actual with budgeted investment income earned. These three procedures do not provide solid evidence.

- **Audit Situation No. 31.** An audit discloses payments for unauthorized purchases. The auditor needs to recommend specific control procedures that require management's closer attention. The auditor would recommend approval of purchase requisitions and purchase orders since this is a preventive control procedure. The auditor would not recommend these control procedures: verification of agreement of voucher with invoice, comparison of invoice with receiving report, or comparison of voucher with supporting invoices by check signers. These three procedures are detective control procedures and do not help in controlling unauthorized purchases.

(b) **Decision-Making Tools.** In this section, we will first discuss the theory behind decision making, followed by its application to internal auditing. Decision making is a process of choosing among alternative courses of action. The correct sequence of the decision-making process is shown in Exhibit 5.21.

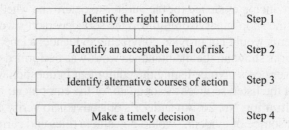

| | |
|---|---|
| Identify the right information | Step 1 |
| Identify an acceptable level of risk | Step 2 |
| Identify alternative courses of action | Step 3 |
| Make a timely decision | Step 4 |

**Exhibit 5.21: Steps in the decision-making process**

Note the difference between problem-solving and decision-making steps. Identify an acceptable level of risk (step 2) does not enter into the problem-solving process. Risk is unique to decision making and is an integral part of it. Decision-making reduces or increases the risk, depending on the quality of the decision making and the level of uncertainty.

The process of management is fundamentally a process of decision making. The functions of management (planning, organizing, directing, and controlling) all involve the process of initiating, selecting, and evaluating courses of action. Therefore, decision making at the center of the functions comprises the management process. The manager makes decisions in establishing objectives: planning decisions, organizing decisions, motivating decisions, and control decisions.

Professor Igor Ansoff classifies the organizational decisions into three categories: strategic decisions, administrative decisions, and operating decisions (see Exhibit 5.22).[8]

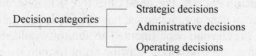

Decision categories — Strategic decisions
                    — Administrative decisions
                    — Operating decisions

**Exhibit 5.22: Decision categories**

**Strategic decisions** are primarily concerned with the external rather than the internal problems of the firm. Examples include product mix and markets to sell.

---

[8] Igor H. Ansoff, *Corporate Strategy* (New York: McGraw-Hill, 1965).

**Administrative decisions** are concerned with structuring the firm's resources to create maximum performance potential.

Administrative decisions are further divided into organizational structure and resource acquisition and development. Organizational structure involves structuring of authority and responsibility relationships, work flows, information flows, distribution channels, and location of facilities. Resource acquisition and development involves the development of raw material sources, personnel training, personnel development, financing, acquisition of facilities, and equipment.

**Operating decisions** are primarily concerned with maximizing the profitability of current operations. They include pricing, establishing market strategy, setting production schedules and inventory levels, and deciding on the relative expenditures in support of research and development, marketing, and operations.

Basically, a decision must be made when the organization faces a problem, when it is dissatisfied with existing conditions, or when it is given a choice. There is no unified agreed-on structure for decision theory because each decision maker has a different value system. A significant amount of work is performed by staff and line people in discovering problems, defining the problems, and preparing the alternatives for decisions. The actual decision is only the conclusion of a decision-making process. The intelligence phase in the decision-making process includes finding the problem.

The three-step sequence of setting objectives is

1. Broad objectives are established at the senior managerial levels
2. Strategies and department goals are developed from the broad objectives. The department goals provide a framework for decision making at lower managerial levels.
3. The manager needs to balance multiple objectives, conflicting objectives, and the hierarchy of objectives.

As the name indicates, the term "multiple objectives" mean that the manager is focusing on two or more objectives at the same time. Examples include market growth, diversification, profit/sales maximization, employee attitudes, social responsibility, and employee development. Quantification is difficult to obtain on the latter three objectives.

*Conflicting objectives* arise when two objectives are at odds with each other. For example, social responsibility, such as pollution control projects, may adversely affect profit margins.

*Hierarchy of objectives* means that objectives of organizational units must be consistent with the objectives of higher organizational units. This means there are objectives within objectives. If the cascade of organizational objectives is not consistent, suboptimization results. It occurs where a departmental level maximizes its own objectives, but, in doing so, it subverts the overall objectives of the organization. Examples include dichotomies where the sales manager prefers large inventories, the production manager prefers large production runs, the warehouse manager prefers minimum inventory, the purchasing agent prefers large lot purchases, and the financing manager prefers low inventories, low production runs, and so on.

(i) **Many facets of decision making.** Managers and leaders make decisions. The type of decision made depends on the level of that manager in the organization hierarchy. To accommodate this diversity, many facets of decision making exist, as depicted in Exhibit 5.23.

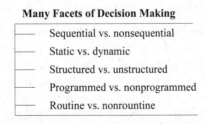

**Many Facets of Decision Making**

— Sequential vs. nonsequential
— Static vs. dynamic
— Structured vs. unstructured
— Programmed vs. nonprogrammed
— Routine vs. nonrountine

**Exhibit 5.23: Many facets of decision making**

(A) *Sequential/nonsequential decision making.* Sequential decision making is the process of successively solving interrelated subproblems comprising a large complex problem. It uses the principle of divide and conquer. Decision C cannot be made until decisions A and B are made. Most of senior managements' decisions are nonsequential in nature for strategic issues; lower-level management mostly makes sequential decisions.

### Decision Rules

Decision rules are behind the programmed decisions procedures. Decision rules require that there is a standard approach to resolve recurring problems and that the problems need to be solved only once.

There are no decision rules behind nonprogrammed decision making. Every situation is different, unique, and complex, requiring innovative and creative problem-solving approaches.

(B) *Static/dynamic decision making.* Static decisions are onetime events leading to one-shot decisions. Dynamic decision making emphasizes that management's decisions are not usually a one-time event, but are successive over a time frame. Future management decisions are influenced to some degree by past decisions.

(C) *Structured/unstructured decision making.* Structured decisions have formal rules, while unstructured decisions have no rules. Examples of structured decisions include production scheduling, inventory reordering, and materials requirements planning. These models have a rigid structure to the decision processes and are programmed to perform routinely without much human involvement. Examples of unstructured decision models include decision support systems and executive support systems. All decision models are rational within their own limits and boundaries. Structured decisions can mean programmed decision making; unstructured decisions can mean nonprogrammed decision making.

(D) *Programmed/nonprogrammed decision making.* Programmed decisions are those that are repetitive and routine, requiring definite procedures. Examples of programmed decisions are employee hiring decisions, billing decisions, supply order decisions, consumer loan decisions, and pricing decisions. In contrast, nonprogrammed decisions are unstructured and novel; there are no set patterns for handling them. Higher levels of management are associated with the unstructured, nonprogrammed decisions.

Nonprogrammed decisions are complex, important situations, often under new and unfamiliar circumstances. Nonprogrammed decisions are made much less frequently than are programmed decisions. Examples of nonprogrammed decisions include building a new manufacturing plant or warehouse, and merger and acquisition decisions. There is no cut-and-dried method for handling nonprogrammed decisions because the problem has not arisen before, or because its precise nature and structure are not clear, or because it is so important that it deserves a custom-tailored approach. See Exhibit 5.24 for a hierarchy of management decision making.

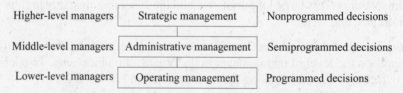

**Exhibit 5.24: Hierarchy of management decision making**

Senior-level managers make nonprogrammed (nonroutine) decisions for strategic management purposes. Programmed (routine) decision address lower-level and highly repetitive tasks, as they are fully programmed. Clerks and computers are involved in routine programmed decisions, such as production scheduling and machine loading. Programmed decisions serve the needs of operating management. However, there is an overlap with semiprogrammed decisions in the sense that such decisions are made by both higher-level managers and middle-level managers.

The Institute of Management Accountant's research study identified nine models to describe nonroutine decision making environments and labeled them as semiprogrammed decisions.[9] These nine decision models include

[9]   *World-Class Accounting for World-Class Manufacturing* (Montvale, NJ: Institute of Management Accountants, 1990).

1. New product decision
2. Distribution channels decision
3. Acquisition decision
4. Divestment (product abandonment) decision
5. Capital expenditure decision
6. Make or buy decision
7. Lease or buy decision
8. Pricing decision
9. Manpower planning decision

(F) ***Routine/nonroutine decision making.*** Routine decisions involve structured and programmed tasks. Nonroutine decisions involve unstructured and nonprogrammed tasks. Higher levels of management deal with nonroutine decision making while lower-level management handles routine decisions. Exhibit 5.25 depicts who makes what decisions.

| Type of decision | Lower-level management | Higher-level management |
|---|---|---|
| Sequential decisions | x | |
| Nonsequential decisions | | x |
| Structured decisions | x | |
| Unstructured decisions | | x |
| Programmed decisions | x | |
| Nonprogrammed decisions | | x |
| Routine decisions | x | |
| Nonroutine decisions | | x |

**Exhibit 5.25: Who makes what decisions?**

(ii) **Decision-making models.** Models are predetermined procedures that specify the step-by-step actions to be taken in a particular situation. Two types of decision models exist: normative and empirical models. Normative models prescribe the decision-making process—what should be. These models do not describe actual management practice in decision making. Instead, they describe how a decision procedure should be followed.

Empirical decision models do not describe how a decision maker should go about making a decision. Instead, they describe the actual decision processes followed by a decision maker—what is. A decision process is any interrelated set of activities leading to a "decision"—a commitment of resources. Reconciliation is needed between the normative and descriptive results in order to develop theories and hypotheses about how managers make use of information. *When there is no set of procedures for a decision process, then by definition there is no "model" for it. Examples include crisis handling and leadership.*

Normative models are programmed decisions. They help lower-level operating management to implement programs such as production scheduling or inventory control. Empirical models are nonprogrammed decisions. They help middle to senior management in making strategic decisions such as pricing and new product introduction.

## NORMATIVE MODELS VS. EMPIRICAL MODELS

- Normative models are prescriptive in nature, address "what and how should be," and are programmed.
- Empirical models are descriptive in nature, address "what is," and are nonprogrammed.

(iii) **Types of data used in decision making.** Decision making is a process that incorporates the estimating and predicting of the outcome of future events. When specific events are known with certainty, the decision maker does not use probabilities in the evaluation of alternatives. When specific events are uncertain, the decision maker uses probabilities in the evaluation of alternatives. The decision maker often uses the most likely outcome stated in deterministic format rather than incorporating all outcomes in a probabilistic (stochastic) format.

*A decision maker uses two types of data: deterministic data and probabilistic data.* Deterministic data are known and not subject to any error or distribution of error. They are based on historical data; their environment is stable and predictable. Decision results will be certain with a single unique payoff. There is only a single outcome for each possible action.

Probabilistic data is used by the decision maker to evaluate decisions under situations of risk and uncertainty. An estimation of distribution of possible outcomes can be made, not an assured or a predictable outcome. The environment is characterized as unstable and unpredictable since each event is assigned a probability of occurrence. Probabilistic data allows for better risk evaluation since sensitivity analysis can be performed on each action to measure the material impact of the various events.

An estimated payoff table or decision tree can be developed for analysis. A drawback of using probabilistic data is the availability and integrity of data to determine multiple courses of action.

## DETERMINISTIC DATA VS. PROBABILISTIC DATA

- Deterministic data are known, and the environment is stable and predictable.
- Probabilistic data are not known, and the environment is unstable and unpredictable.

---

(iv) **Types of decisions.** Decision making is a frequent and important human activity and is especially a managerial activity. Decisions are not all of one kind. The procedure for making one decision, such as buying a home, is entirely different from making another decision, such as taking a CIA examination.

Decision making is related to risk levels. With respect to risk, individuals act differently, and can be grouped into three categories: risk takers, risk neutral, and risk averters. When contrasted with a risk-taking entrepreneur, a professional manager (or an auditor) is likely to be more cautious as a risk taker (i.e., either risk neutral or risk averter). Another factor is that risks are related to returns. The higher the risk, the greater the return, and vice versa. Also, controls are related to risks. The higher the risk, the greater the need for controls, and vice versa. Controls reduce or eliminate risks and exposures.

Four general types of decisions exist that require different decision procedures: (1) decisions under certainty, (2) decisions under risk, (3) decisions under uncertainty, and (4) decisions under conflict or competition (see Exhibit 5.26).

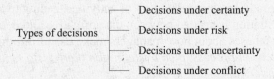

**Exhibit 5.26: Types of decisions**

(A) *Decision making under certainty.* A decision maker is operating in an environment where all of the facts surrounding a decision are known exactly, and each alternative is associated with only one possible outcome. The environment is known as certainty.

Five different methods exist that are useful for making decisions under certainty. The first four methods are optimization methods—that is, they attempt to identify the very best alternative available. The fifth method, satisficing, simply looks for the first satisfactory alternative (see Exhibit 5.27).

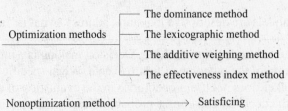

**Exhibit 5.27: Optimization methods**

The **dominance method** is the simplest of the decision procedures. To use it in making decisions, it is necessary to find the dominance relations among the alternatives. One alternative dominates another if both of the following are satisfied:

1. It is at least as good as the other on all properties, and
2. It is better on at least one property.

Any alternative that is dominated by another is dropped from consideration since it will never be judged the best alternative by any reasonable decision procedure. Any alternative that dominates all the others is chosen as best.

**Decision-Making Choices**

- If two people make different choices in the same situation, it does not mean that one of them is wrong; it may just be that they have different values. Therefore, the correct choice in any decision-making situation depends on the decision maker's individual value system.
- Generating alternatives, examining their properties, and choosing among the alternatives are all activities that may add considerable cost to the decision-making process.

The advantage of this method is that people can agree about which alternatives are dominant. It is easy to apply, and its results are reliable. The disadvantages of this method are that it is not a powerful decision-making method because it usually does not eliminate very many of the alternatives. Examples of applications of decision making under certainty are linear programming, transportation problems, inventory models, and break-even analysis.

The **lexicographic method** is so named because of its resemblance to the procedure for ordering words in the dictionary. In this method, look first at the most important property. If two alternatives have the same value on this property, then one decides on the basis of the second most important property, and so on. It is necessary to specify the order of importance of the properties of the alternatives.

To make a decision by this method, consider the most important property first. If one alternative is better than the other alternatives on the most important property, then that alternative is the one chosen. If two or more alternatives are tied on the most important property, then drop the other alternatives from consideration and consider the next most important property in order to break ties. If any ties remain unbroken, then consider the third property, and so on. Changing the order of importance of the properties in the lexicographic method does not always change the alternative chosen as best.

The lexicographic method is most appropriate when one of the properties outweighs all of the others in importance. The method's major strengths under these circumstances are that it is quick and easy to apply. This method is least appropriate when the properties are roughly equal in importance. Under these circumstances, the method may lead us to choose an alternative that has a slight advantage in the most important property, even though that advantage is outweighed by big disadvantages in other properties. This happens because the lexicographic method typically ignores all but the most important property.

The **additive weighing method** takes all of the properties into account but does not give them equal weight. The more important properties receive heavy weights and the less important ones lighter weights. To use this method, numbers both for weights of the properties and for the values of the properties reflecting values to the decision maker must be available.

To make a decision by the additive weighing method, multiply numerical values of the properties by the weights of the properties for each alternative. Then choose the alternative with the largest sum as "best." This method takes all of the properties into account in making the decision, but does not take the interactions of the properties into account. Therefore, this method can lead to inappropriate decisions by ignoring these interactions, just as the lexicographic method can lead to inappropriate decisions by ignoring the less important properties. The major drawback of this method is that it is time consuming and difficult to obtain the numbers for the weights and values of the properties.

## Decision Methods

Decision methods such as lexicography and additive weighing are useful because they allow people to substitute reliable objective procedures for unreliable subjective ones.

The **effectiveness index method** takes into account the interactions that the additive weighing method ignores. This method is used when the interactions are especially strong or because errors in decisions are very costly, or both. This method requires an extensive analysis of the situation under consideration, and designing and implementing such a method is very expensive and time consuming.

**Satisficing** is a nonoptimizing approach to decision making under certainty. The satisficing method requires the decision maker to identify the worst value he or she is willing to accept for each of the attributes. The decision maker then considers all of the alternatives in order, rejecting any alternatives that fall below the minimal values of the attributes and accepting the first alternative that meets all of the minimal values.

The satisficing method is particularly useful when we have to choose among a very large number of alternatives and it is not essential to find the best. This method is less costly since it does not examine all of the alternatives and may not yield a decision at all if the decision-making standards are very high.

---

### KEY CONCEPTS TO REMEMBER: DECISION MAKING UNDER CERTAINTY

- All optimizing methods are designed to find the best available alternative and are suitable for idealized situations. They examine all alternatives available.
- The nonoptimizing method is not designed to identify the best alternative. Rather, it is designed to find the first satisfactory alternative that is more suitable to real-world situations. Only some alternatives are examined.

---

(B) *Decision making under risk.* When a decision maker is faced with a decision and the probabilities of various outcomes are known, the situation is said to be decision making under risk (see Exhibit 5.28). Gambling decisions are typical of decisions under risk. An essential feature of decisions under risk is that we can calculate a probability for the effect of the chance event. Tossing a fair coin, rotating roulette, and rolling a die are examples of decisions under risk. Examples of decision making under risk can be found in queuing theory, statistical quality control, acceptance sampling, program evaluation and review techniques (PERT), and so on. Decision trees are used to assist the decision maker under conditions of risk.

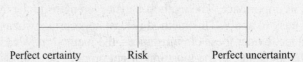

Exhibit 5.28: **Perfect certainty vs. risk vs. perfect uncertainty**

Risk is a condition faced by managers when they have to make a decision based on incomplete but reliable information. Uncertain conditions exist when little or no reliable information is available. Certainty conditions exist when complete, reliable information is available.

One widely recommended technique for making risky decisions is to choose the action that has the greatest expected value. The expected value of an action is the average payoff value we can expect if we repeat the action many times.

**Example of Expected Value**

Game 1. Win $2.00 whether the coin comes up heads or tails when a fair coin is tossed.
Game 2. Win $10.00 if the coin comes up heads and lose $5.00 if it comes up tails.

Expected value = average payoff = probability of a head (*PH*) × payoff for heads (*VH*) + probability of a tail (*PT*) × payoff for tails (*VT*)

$$EV = PH \times VH + PT \times VT$$

here *PH* and *PT* have equal chances, that is, 1/2

$$EV \text{ (for game 2)} = 1/2 \,(10.00) + 1/2 \,(-5.00) = 5.00 - 2.50 = 2.50$$

$$EV \text{ (for game 1)} = 1/2 \,(2.00) + 1/2 \,(2.00) = 1.00 + 1.00 = 2.00$$

Since the expected value of game 2 is greater than the expected value of game 1, we should choose game 2 in order to maximize our expected value. Whether we choose to play game 1 or 2 depends on whether we are risk averse or not. Game 1 is a no-lose game while game 2 is not.

(C) *Decision making under uncertainty.* Like decisions under risk, decisions under uncertainty involve a chance factor. The unique feature of decisions under uncertainty is that we cannot calculate a probability for the effect of the chance event. This is a situation in which a decision must be made on the basis of little or no reliable factual information. When considering pricing of competitors, actions of regulatory agencies, and strikes of suppliers, the decision maker is addressing the problem of uncertainty.

Multiple outcomes are possible. The first task is to establish subjective probabilities of occurrence for the multiple outcomes. Under conditions of uncertainty, the rational, economic decision maker will use "expected monetary value" as the decision criteria. The expected monetary value of an act is the sum of the conditional profit (loss) of each event times the probability of each event occurring.

Four strategies for making decisions under uncertainty include: (1) the mini-max strategy, (2) the maxi-max strategy, (3) the Hurwicz strategy, and (4) and the mini-max regret strategy (see Exhibit 5.29).

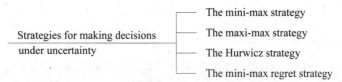

**Exhibit 5.29: Strategies for making decisions under uncertainty**

The **mini-max strategy** is a very conservative, pessimistic strategy that assumes that whatever action we choose, nature is against us and will cause the worst possible outcome. The values of the worst outcomes are the row minima. This strategy calls for choosing the action that gives us the best (largest) of these minima. That is, it chooses the action whose worst possible outcomes is not as bad as the worst possible outcomes of the other actions.

The best examples of applications for uncertainty are in problems of the military, war, and various types of athletic competition, product development, product pricing, collective bargaining, arbitration, foreign policy decisions, contract bidding, and oligopolistic and monopolistic market conditions.

The mini-max strategy has the nice property that it guarantees an outcome that is no worse than the minimum value for the action. The outcome may be better than the minimum, but it will certainly be no worse. However, this strategy, which focuses on preventing disaster, has the unfortunate property that it may eliminate the best outcomes from consideration.

The **maxi-max strategy** is an optimistic strategy that assumes that nature will cooperate with us to provide the best possible outcome for the action we choose—the row maxima. This strategy chooses the action that yields the best of the possible outcomes. However, it does not defend the decision maker against the possibility of containing the worst possible outcome, as does the mini-max strategy. Decision makers who are attracted to large gains would most likely use the maxi-max decision rule.

## Approaches to Decision Problems

Whatever strategy we decide to use in approaching decision problems, it is wise to make a habit of determining if any of the alternatives is dominating, and could therefore be eliminated.

The **Hurwicz strategy** is a compromise between the very pessimistic mini-max strategy and the very optimistic maxi-max strategy. A value between 0 and 1 is chosen for the coefficient of optimism, A, keeping in mind that low values of A are an indication of pessimism and high values of A are an indication of optimism. The goal is to find both the row minima and the row maxima and choose the activity that yields the maximum of the computed quantities. When A is zero, the Hurwicz is the same as the mini-max strategy; when A is 1, the Hurwicz strategy is the same as the maxi-max strategy.

## MINI-MAX STRATEGY VS. MAXI-MAX STRATEGY

- The mini-max strategy is a pessimistic strategy and finds the *row minima*. It gives a conservative feel when playing a game against nature but not when playing against a human opponent. This is because we know our opponents.
- The maxi-max strategy is an optimistic strategy and finds the *row maxima*.

The **mini-max regret strategy** is good for situations where the expected values concept fails. Why does the expected value technique fail? Expected values are averages of values. They are appropriate when we are trying to balance values that are close together, for example, the chance of losing $2.00 versus the chance of winning $4.00. Averages are much less appropriate when we balance values that are very different, such as the cost of a modest insurance premium versus the risk of being impoverished by a serious car accident.

The mini-max regret decision criteria choose the strategy that minimizes the maximum opportunity cost. To measure regret, take the difference between the value of the outcome actually obtained and the maximum value that could have been obtained if a different alternative had been chosen.

## DECISIONS UNDER RISK VS. DECISIONS UNDER UNCERTAINTY

- Probabilities can be computed for decisions under risk.
- Probabilities cannot be computed for decisions under uncertainty.

(D) *Decision making under conflict.* Decision making under conflict is referred to as game theory. The mini-max strategy is used for analyzing decisions under conflict or competition. There are two types of games under conflict: zero-sum game and nonzero-sum game.

**Game theory** is used when the states of nature of the decision maker are the strategies of the opponent. When one opponent gains at the loss of the other, it is called **zero-sum games** involving a complete conflict of interest. Games with less than complete conflict of interest are termed **nonzero-sum games**. In nonzero-sum games, the gains of one competitor are not completely at the expense of the other competitors.

The majority of business competitive actions involve nonzero-sum games. Nonzero-sum games require that the payoffs be given for each player since the payoff of one player can no longer be deducted from the payoff of the other, as in zero-sum games. **Prisoner's dilemma** is a type of business game situation where one firm is concerned about the actions of its rivals. The outcome of the prisoner's dilemma game cannot be predicted conclusively. An example of payoff table is shown in Exhibit 5.30.

**States of Nature**

|   | 1 | 2 | 3 | 4 | Expected profit |
|---|---|---|---|---|---|
| A |   |   |   |   |   |
| B |   |   |   |   |   |
| C |   |   |   |   |   |

**Exhibit 5.30: Payoff table**

States of nature are uncontrollable future events that can affect the outcomes of a decision. The best examples of applications of zero-sum games are in problems of the military, war, and various types of athletic competition. The best examples of applications of nonzero-sum games are in product development, product pricing, collective bargaining, arbitration, foreign policy decisions, contract bidding, and oligopolistic and monopolistic market conditions.

The simplest type of gain is the two-person zero-sum game. The players, X and Y, are equal in intelligence and ability. The term "zero sum" is used because the sum of gains exactly equals the sum of losses. The sum of player X's gains (or losses) and player Y's losses (or gains) is zero. Such a game, in which the sum of gains and losses added up over all players is zero, is called a zero-sum game.

### Example of Utility for Alternatives

Assume a linear utility for money and a risk-neutral decision maker. From the payoff table below one can conclude that the utility for alternative A is

|  | *State of Nature* | | |
|---|---|---|---|
|  | *S1* | *S2* | *Expected Profit* |
| Alternative A | 100 | 200 | $160 |
| Alternative B | 140 | 40 | $ 80 |

a. $300.
b. High.
c. Exactly twice that of B.
d. Approximately twice that of B.

The correct answer is (c). The utility function for money would be linear, and the decision maker's behavior would be consistent with the maximization of expected profit. A risk neutral decision maker will select the alternative with the highest profit, that is, alternative A, which is exactly twice that of B (160/80 = 2). Choice (a) is incorrect. Utility is measured in "utils, not in dollars." It does not compare the two alternatives. Choice (b) is incorrect. This requires a judgment about the utility function of the decision maker, which is unknown. Choice (d) is incorrect. The linearity assumption leads to exact statements, not approximations.

(v) **Pure strategy and mixed strategy.** A pure strategy exists if there is one strategy for player X and one strategy for player Y that will be played each time. The payoff, which is obtained when each player pays the pure strategy, is called a **saddle point**. The saddle point represents an equilibrium condition that is optimum for both competitors.

The **Wald criterion,** which is a variant of decision making under uncertainty, is a useful technique to determine if a pure strategy exists. A saddle point can be recognized because it is both the smallest numerical value in its row and largest numerical value in its column. Not all two-person zero-sum games have a saddle point. When a saddle point is present, complex calculations to determine optimum strategies and game values are unnecessary.

When a pure strategy does not exist, a fundamental theorem of game theory states that the optimum can be found by using a mixed strategy. In a mixed strategy, each competitor randomly selects the strategy to employ according to a previously determined probability of usage for each strategy. Using a mixed strategy involves making a selection each time period by tossing a coin, selecting a number from a table of random numbers, or by using some probabilistic process.

There is a simple test to determine whether a pure or mixed strategy is best. If the maximum of the row minima (the maxi-min) equals the minimum of the column maxima (the mini-max), then a pure strategy is best. Otherwise, use the mixed strategy.

---

### KEY CONCEPTS TO REMEMBER: WHICH DECISION CRITERIA IS WHAT?

Mini-max criteria $\longrightarrow$ Minimizing the maximum losses

Maxi-max criteria $\longrightarrow$ Maximizing the maximum profits

Maxi-min criteria $\longrightarrow$ Maximizing the minimum profits

Mini-min criteria $\longrightarrow$ Minimizing the minimum losses or maximum profits (not worth pursuing)

Mini-max regret criteria $\longrightarrow$ Minimizing the maximum opportunity cost

---

(vi) **Decision making vs. problem solving.** Decision making and problem solving are not the same—they have two different time dimensions. *The basic difference is that decision making is future-oriented and problem solving is past-oriented. Decision making deals with risk, while problem solving does not.*

Decision making is the probability of success. Examples of decision-making situations include investing in a new product line, buying new equipment, and selecting an employee for a key position. Examples of problem-solving situations include handling a tardy employee, correcting a poor-quality production, and working with a slow-paying customer.

Exhibit 5.31 presents an overview of differences between decision making and problem solving.

| *Decision making* | *Problem solving* |
|---|---|
| • Decision making is concerned with future consequences; it changes the environment and the situation. | • Problem solving is concerned with looking back; this is the way it should be and it no longer is. |
| • A decision is made to create a change and therefore generates a new set of circumstances. | • A problem is solved now so that decision making is not needed later. This is because the problem-solving approach has restored the process where it should be. |
| • Decision making focuses on making things happen in the future. | • Problem solving can be greatly overdone because it creates a fear of change. |
| • A decision has a risk and an uncertainty, but it also creates an opportunity. | • A change should be seen as an opportunity to go forward, not to go back to the past. |

SOURCE: Drucker, Peter F. *The Frontiers of Management.* (New York: Harper & Row; 1986.)

**Exhibit 5.31: Differences between decision making and problem solving**

(vii) **Tools and techniques for decision making.** The following list provides additional tools and techniques for making decisions.

- **Differential analysis.** Differential analysis is a technique to compare differences in revenues or costs of two or more alternatives.
- **Decision table.** A decision table is a tool that documents rules used to select one or more actions based on one or more conditions. These conditions and their corresponding actions can be presented either in a matrix or tabular form.
- **Flowcharts.** Flowcharts help a decision maker in analyzing a large, complex problem. Flowcharts and decision trees both show flow or sequencing. Unlike the flowchart, a decision tree shows outcome probabilities.
- **Discriminant analysis.** Discriminant analysis is a qualitative, subjective tool to differentiate between effective and ineffective procedures or actions.
- **Management science.** Operations research or management science provides management an approach that focuses on decision making and reliance on formal mathematical models.
- **Decision trees.** A decision tree is a graphical representation of possible decisions, events, or states of nature resulting from each decision with its associated probabilities, and the outcomes of the events or states of nature. The decision problem displays the sequential nature of the decision-making situation. The decision tree has nodes, branches, and circles to represent junction boxes, connectors between the nodes, and states-of-nature nodes, respectively.

Examples of application of decision trees include

- A company has two new products ready for market but cannot afford to introduce them simultaneously. Management plans to initially market one product, then use some of the revenue to either (1) expand the introduction of the original product or (2) introduce the second product. Odds of profitability and first-year profits for each course of action can be predicted with reasonable accuracy.
- A company has the option of either buying or manufacturing a component. It is possible to develop the probabilities of three levels of demand (low, medium, and high). The number of payoffs for this problem would be six (i.e., three levels of demand for each outcome of buy or manufacture, 3+3 = 6).
- A group of training specialists has to choose among three different sites for a proposed seminar. The sites are priced according to size (small, medium, or large). Public acceptance of the seminar is expected to be either high or low. The number of state-of-nature branches for a decision tree of this problem would be six, computed as three branches for high and three branches for low.

- **Payoff table.** A payoff table is a tabular representation of the payoffs for a decision problem. It shows losses and gains for each outcome of the decision alternatives.
- **Cost-benefit analysis.** Cost-benefit analysis is a decision procedure in which we compare the expected costs and benefits of alternative actions. We choose the action for which the expected value of the benefits minus the expected value of the costs is greatest. The expected value is the desirability of alternative multiplied by the probability of success. The likelihood of an occurrence that is derived mathematically from reliable historical data is called objective probabilities. However, subjective probabilities do not have mathematical reliability since they are derived from intuition and "gut feel" of the decision maker.
- **Success-failure analysis.** Success-failure analysis is a qualitative approach to brainstorm conditions for both success and failure. A T-column can be used with headings "What will guarantee success" and "What will guarantee failure."
- **Devil's advocate techniques.** In the devil's advocate technique, the decision maker is focusing on failures and identifies ways an action or an alternative can be less than successful.
- **Reality check.** The reality check decision is tested in the pseudo–real-world conditions. A T-column is used with headings "Our expectations" and "Our concerns" to facilitate the analysis.
- **Risk-analysis.** Risk analysis is the analysis of possible risks to be encountered and the means to handle them that can be performed. A T-column can be used with headings "Anticipated Risks" and "Actions to overcome risks."
- **Activity analysis.** All current activities can be labeled as either value-added or non-value-added using a T-account diagram. The goal is to eliminate or reduce non-value-added activities since they are adding little or no value to the process at hand. Decisions affecting costs incurred for non–value-added activities can then be challenged or revisited by performing a detailed analysis of all tasks and activities with the purpose of eliminating or reducing them. A T-column can be used with headings "Value-added activities" and "Non-value-added activities" to facilitate the activity analysis.

(viii) **Decision making and the internal auditor: applications.** In order for auditors to reach decisions, they must understand how the various pieces of information are combined. For example, the issues of materiality, conflicting evidence, and determining whether sufficient evidence has been gathered all influence the auditor's decision-making process.

The internal auditor will be making decisions under various circumstances. When the auditor must make an important decision in a hurry and that decision is based on incomplete information, the decision-making process would be called "satisficing," not maximizing, minimizing, or rationalizing. "Satisficing" is a nonoptimization decision-making method. The auditor presents several audit situations that require a decision.

- **Audit Situation No. 1.** The director of internal auditing of a manufacturing company is updating the long-range audit schedule. Several possible audit assignments can fill a given time spot. Information on potential dollar exposure and key internal controls has been gathered.

The director has four choices to choose from, based on perceived audit risks, and needs to select the assignment of greatest merit. The four choices are

1. Precious metals inventory—book value, $1,000,000; separately stored, but access not restricted.
2. Branch office petty cash—ledger amount, $50,000; 10 branch offices, equal amounts; replenishment of accounts requires three separate approvals
3. Sales force travel expenses—budget, $1,000,000; 50 salespeople; all expenditures over $25 must be receipted.
4. Expendable tools inventory—book value, $500,000; issued by tool crib attendant upon receipt of authorization form.

The audit director will select the choice 1 because of its relatively high risk. Precious metals include gold and silver, which are subject to theft or loss. Also, the access is not restricted. Choice 2 is not a high-risk situation because replenishment of petty cash requires three separate approvals and the total dollar amount is less than choice 1. Choice 3 is not a high-risk situation since all expenditures over $25 must be receipted. Choice 4 is not a high-risk situation because tool crib attendant upon receipt of authorization form issues expendable tools. Key internal controls are adequate in situations described by choices 2, 3, and 4. Controls are inadequate in choice 1.

- **Audit Situation No. 2.** An internal auditor is planning an audit of the personnel department of her company. She needs to make a decision about audit objectives. The appropriate audit objective would be to determine if reference checks of prospective employees are being performed. It would not determine whether: hourly employees are being paid only for hours actually worked as indicated by time cards or similar reports; an equitable training program exists that provides all employees with approximately the same amount of training each year; or recruitment is being delegated to the various departments that have personnel needs.

- **Audit Situation No. 3.** During an audit of the human resources department, an internal auditor plans to evaluate controls over the termination process. If audit work steps are to be prioritized, the auditor should do this audit step first: Evaluate procedures used to communicate termination actions to the payroll department. The auditor should not first examine employee turnover rates for the most recent years, reasons for termination as shown in exit interviews, or costs associated with replacing terminated employees.

- **Audit Situation No. 4.** An internal auditing team has identified findings that should significantly improve a division's operating efficiency. Out of appreciation of this fact, and because it is the Christmas season, the division manager presents the in-charge auditor with a gift that has a value of approximately $100. The auditor needs to make a decision between his personal ethics and the IIA's Code of Ethics. The correct decision is that he should not accept the gift without the knowledge and consent of the director of internal auditing and that he should not accept it, regardless of other circumstances, because its value is significant.

- **Audit Situation No. 5.** An internal auditor is involved in a fraud investigation. She needs to make a decision about the most appropriate audit activity that she should undertake. The correct approach is to design procedures to follow in attempting to identify the perpetrators and causes of the fraud. She should not supervise the activities of security personnel and other investigators, serve as liaison with law enforcement personnel and the press, or conduct public interrogations of suspected perpetrators.

- **Audit Situation No. 6.** An internal auditor is examining accounts receivable balances. He needs to make a decision to obtain the most competent type of evidence. He should receive positive confirmations directly from the customers. The least competent evidence would be when he interviews the personnel who records accounts receivable, verifies that postings to the receivable account from journals have been made, and assures himself that no response has been received for a request for a negative confirmation.

- **Audit Situation No. 7.** An internal auditor is preparing working papers in connection with plant maintenance costs audit. She needs to differentiate between necessary and unnecessary features of preparing a working paper. It is unnecessary to prepare a schedule of total acquisition cost of property, plant, and equipment for the preceding month. It is necessary to prepare a schedule showing total repair expense for the month preceding the audit.

- **Audit Situation No. 8.** An audit objective is to verify that the correct goods or services are received on time, at the right price, and in the right quantity. Based on this objective, an internal auditor needs to decide whether to audit the receiving department, the purchasing department, the manufacturing department, or the payroll department. The correct decision is to audit the purchasing department because it is the objective of the purchasing department to procure goods or services with all those attributes present (i.e., price, delivery, quantity, and quality).
- **Audit Situation No. 9.** A company makes a practice of investing excess short-term cash in marketable securities. An internal auditor is faced with a decision to select a reliable audit test of the valuation of those securities. The correct approach is to compare cost data with current market quotations. The following audit tests would not provide reliable tests for the valuation of those securities: confirmation of securities held by the broker, recalculation of investment carrying value using the equity method, or calculation of premium or discount amortization.
- **Audit Situation No. 10.** An internal auditor is planning to obtain evidence to support the legal ownership of real property. The best audit procedure he could choose would be an examination of closing document, deeds, and ownership documents registered and on file at the county courthouse. The following audit procedures would not provide the best audit evidence: examination of corporate minutes and board resolutions with regard to approvals to acquire real property discussion with corporate legal counsel concerning the acquisition of a specific piece of property, and confirmation with the title company that handled the escrow account and disbursement of proceeds on the closing of the property.
- **Audit Situation No. 11.** An internal auditor is performing an audit of the receiving department to determine if only authorized purchases are being accepted. She needs to make a decision about the type of documents that should be examined. The correct approach is to examine a "blind" (no quantities shown) copy of the purchase order received directly from the purchasing department. She should not examine: a bill of lading that has been accepted directly by the receiving department, an invoice that has been sent by the supplier directly to accounts payable, or a note documenting a telephone conversation with a purchasing agent.
- **Audit Situation No. 12.** A preliminary survey of the purchasing function indicates that: department managers initiate purchase requests that must be approved by the plant superintendent; purchase orders are typed by the purchasing department using prenumbered and controlled forms; buyers regularly update the official vendor listing as new sources of supply become known; rush orders can be placed with a vendor by telephone but must be followed by a written purchase order before delivery can be accepted; and vendor invoice payment requests must be accompanied by a purchase order and receiving report.

  An internal auditor is faced with a situation to decide what is relevant and what is irrelevant information with respect to controls, and he needs to identify one possible fault of this system. A risk exists that purchases could be made from a vendor controlled by a buyer at prices higher than normal.
- **Audit Situation No. 13.** An internal auditor is verifying a company's ownership of equipment. She needs to decide a course of action that would provide her the best evidence of ownership. She should choose to verify a canceled check written to acquire the equipment. Actions that would not provide the best evidence of ownership include: reviewing the current year's depreciation expense journal entry, conducting an interview with the equipment custodian verifying company ownership, or checking the presence of the equipment on the company's balance sheet.
- **Audit Situation No. 14.** The auditor is reviewing insurance coverage. His objective is to determine whether specified insurance coverage is being obtained economically. He needs to decide which audit procedure would be most appropriate to accomplish his objective. He would determine whether competitive bids were obtained from qualified insurance agents. He would not: inspect the insurance policies currently in force to determine compliance with company policies and the propriety of premiums; compare current-year insurance costs with those of the preceding two years on a total and on a risk-by-risk basis; or interview the head of the insurance department to ascertain procedures employed in identifying risks, purchasing insurance, and obtaining dividends.

- **Audit Situation No. 15.** Bank teller supervisors might manipulate accounts using their privileged computer access codes. They could withdraw money for their own use and move money among accounts when depositors complain to the bank about errors. The auditor needs to decide which procedures would most likely detect this potential problem. She would review transactions on privileged access codes since they are high-risk codes. She would not: review transactions for employees' accounts, verify proof records for teller access codes, or test the accuracy of account posting programs. These three procedures are good procedures for a normal audit, but not for the problem situation described above.

- **Audit Situation No. 16.** During an audit of a construction contract, it was discovered that the contractor was being paid for each ton of dirt removed. The contract called for payment made on cubic yards removed. There is a problem of mismatching the units of measure (i.e., ton versus cubic yards). The auditor needs to decide which documents need to be reviewed to correct this error. He would compare invoices to purchase orders or contracts since they indicate what should be the correct unit of measure. The auditor would not: compare invoices to receiving reports, compare actual cots to budgeted costs, or check the mathematical accuracy of invoice amounts. These three steps would not provide the official proof of the correct unit of measure since they are after-the-fact documents. A contract is the first and official document from which purchase orders are written.

- **Audit Situation No. 17.** An auditor is reviewing payments, and her objective is to ascertain the existence of improper payments. The auditor needs to decide which documents to review to satisfy her audit objective. She would decide to review payment-voucher supporting documents for receiving reports, invoices, purchase orders and approval-to-pay initials. The idea is that these documents would reveal any improper payments since they are the ones required for proper payment. The auditor would not: ask the treasurer's office personnel about the existence of duplicate payments, observe payment procedures in the treasurer's office for conformance to policies and procedures manual specifications, or compare total payments by type this year with those of prior years. These three procedures do not provide sufficient evidence to reach a valid conclusion.

- **Audit Situation No. 18.** Senior management has asked the internal auditing staff to conduct an audit of manufacturing safety facilities using an audit program originally designed by government auditors for use in Occupational Safety and Health Act investigations. The auditor can justify using this standardized program because one responsibility of the internal auditor is to review systems to ensure compliance with laws. Audit objectives not pertinent to this request would include the means of safeguarding assets, the reliability and integrity of financial and operating information, and activities in coordination with others.

- **Audit Situation No. 19.** A car rental agency has branch offices throughout the world. Each branch is organized into three separate departments: maintenance, operations, and accounting. The auditor needs to decide the objectives for an operational audit. The information that would be most useful for the auditor is the objectives of each department. An operational audit would be more meaningful when the audit objectives include the objectives of the area to be audited. The following information would not be useful: the most recent financial data for each department, activity reports showing rental information for the different branches, and a complete listing of the perpetual inventory for the branch to be audited.

- **Audit Situation No. 20.** An auditor wishes to test the efficiency of a company's use of labor resources. He needs to decide an audit objective that would lead him to a test of the efficiency of labor resources. The audit objective would be to determine that employees are assigned to work situations equivalent to their training and skill level. The following audit objectives would not be relevant for the auditor's decision making: to determine that all employees are paid in accordance with union wages (may be useful in a payroll audit), to determine that the quality of performance by labor meets company standards, or to determine that only authorized employees are paid (may be useful in a payroll audit).

- **Audit Situation No. 21.** An auditor needs to decide an audit procedure that best meets the objectives of determining that all sales are recorded. The appropriate audit procedure would be to test company controls that are designed to capture initial sales transactions as they occur. The following audit procedures would not achieve the desired objective: tracing sales invoices to subsidiary accounts receivable records, comparing current recorded sales totals with prior period, or vouching recorded sales from sales invoices to shipping documents.

- **Audit Situation No. 22.** An auditor noted that the accounts receivable department is separate from other accounting activities. Credit is approved by a separate credit department. Control accounts and subsidiary ledgers are balanced monthly. Similarly, accounts are aged monthly. The accounts receivable manager writes off delinquent accounts after one year, or sooner if a bankruptcy or other unusual circumstances are involved. Credit memoranda are prenumbered and must correlate with receiving reports. The auditor needs to decide which of the following areas could be viewed as an internal control weakness: write-offs of delinquent accounts, credit approvals, monthly aging of receivables, or handling of credit memos. Write-offs of delinquent accounts are a control weakness because the manager is not trying other avenues of collecting receivables prior to writing them off. The problem is that the manager is writing off delinquent accounts too soon.

- **Audit Situation No. 23.** Management wishes to include in their internal controls over factory payroll a procedure to ensure that employees are paid only for work actually performed. The auditor needs to decide an internal control action that would be most appropriate to achieve management's objective. She would compare piecework records with inventory additions from production since this provides her an objective basis for calculating the payroll. The following control actions would not achieve the objective: have foremen distribute paychecks to employees in their sections, use time cards, or keep unused paychecks in a vault. These three actions do not measure the work performed.

- **Audit Situation No. 24.** While performing an audit of cash, an auditor begins to suspect check kiting. The auditor needs to decide the best type of evidence that he can get concerning whether kiting is taking place. He would accomplish this by preparing a schedule of interbank transfers. Kiting is a term used for a scheme in which a depositor with accounts in two or more banks takes advantage of the time required for checks to clear in order to obtain unauthorized credit. Therefore, a schedule of interbank transfers would detect check kiting. The following evidence would not be useful: documentary evidence obtained by vouching entries in the cash account to supporting documents, documentary evidence obtained by vouching credits on the latest bank statements to supporting documents, or oral evidence obtained by discussion with controller personnel.

- **Audit Situation No. 25.** An auditor wishes to estimate inventory shrinkage by weighing a sample of inventory items. From past experience, he knows that few specific items are subject to unusually large amounts of shrinkage. The auditor wants to decide the best course of action using statistical sampling. He should stratify the inventory population so those items subject to unusually large amounts of shrinkage are reviewed separately. The following courses of action would not be useful: eliminating any of the items known to be subject to unusually large amounts of shrinkage, increasing the sample size to lessen the effect of the items subject to unusually large amount of shrinkage, or continuing to draw new samples until a sample is drawn that includes none of the items known to be subject to large amounts of shrinkage.

- **Audit Situation No. 26.** An auditor is planning an audit program for her company's purchasing department. The auditor discovered four situations related to purchasing activities.

  1. User departments, instead of purchasing, are selecting suppliers and ordering goods.
  2. Make-or-buy committee does not have a written set of procedures.
  3. Quantitative and qualitative yardsticks on purchasing activities are absent.
  4. Rotation of buyer assignments is not accomplished.

  The audit objective is to determine if goods and services are obtained at the best price. The auditor needs to make a decision how best to allocate audit resources to the four purchasing activities. A risk ranking approach would be useful here. She would review activity 1 first, activity 4 next, activity 3 next, and activity 2 last, because activity 1 is a high risk and activity 2 is a low risk.

- **Audit Situation No. 27.** In an audit of a purchasing and payables system, the auditor has determined that invoices are sometimes paid twice, goods are paid for that were never received, materials have been shipped to an assistant buyer's home, and invoices for goods returned to vendors are sometimes paid—few problems! The auditor's objective is to obtain sufficient evidence for each one of these problems.

- A random sample found 10 paid vouchers without an accompanying original invoice. All 10 had been paid twice. This form of evidence would be both competent and sufficient in determining that invoices are paid twice.
- A receiving report signed by the assistant buyer would be the strongest indicator that company-paid materials have been shipped to an assistant buyer's home.
- An examination and accounting of shipping documents prepared for all returns would provide sufficient evidence to support a conclusion that invoices are sometimes paid even though goods are returned to vendors.

- **Audit Situation No. 28.** An auditor wishes to test the effectiveness of data processing access controls. He needs to decide the audit procedure that would assist him in satisfying the audit objective. He would review access logs since they capture all accesses whether successful or not. He would not: study various access control software costs (may be appropriate in a software acquisition audit); analyze object code controlling access; or process test data simulating exception conditions. These three procedures do not achieve the audit objective at hand.

- **Audit Situation No. 29.** An auditor is verifying the existence of newly acquired fixed assets recorded in the accounting records. She needs to decide the best evidence to help achieve this objective. She would conduct a physical examination of a sample of newly recorded fixed assets to provide direct, firsthand evidence. The following items do not provide direct evidence: documentary support obtained by vouching entries to subsidiary records and invoices, oral evidence obtained by discussion with operating management, or documentary support obtained by reviewing titles and tax returns.

- **Audit Situation No. 30.** An auditor must make a decision about a test to determine whether purchase orders are being processed on a timely basis. The appropriate test would be to compare dates of selected purchase orders with those of purchase requisitions. Elapsed times can be measured with this test. The following tests would not be appropriate: determining the dates of unpaid accounts payable invoices, selecting a block of used purchase order numbers and account for all numbers in the block, or discussing processing procedures with operating personnel and observing actual processing of purchases. These three tests do not measure the elapsed time.

- **Audit Situation No. 31.** An auditor might use several different procedures to test for the proper accounting for retirement of plant and equipment. She needs to make a decision about a test that would be the most effective in providing evidence of retiring fixed assets. She would do analysis of debits to the accumulated depreciation account since this entry is done to retire fixed assets. The following tests would not be effective in achieving the stated objective: analysis of debits to the fixed-asset account (which is used to add new fixed assets); determination of whether fully depreciated assets still in use are included in the asset accounts; or examination of the cash account for unusual entries (assets may be retired without receiving any cash).

- **Audit Situation No. 32.** An auditor is evaluating the reasonableness of advertising expense. He needs to select the audit procedure providing the best evidence to achieve his objective. Analytical evidence developed by comparing the ratio of advertising expenses to sales with historical data for the company and industry would provide the auditor with the best evidence to meet his objectives. The following procedures would not provide the best evidence: oral evidence obtained through discussions with company marketing executives and representatives of the advertising agency retained; documentary evidence obtained by vouching charges to the account and by retracing charges from source documents to the account; or arithmetical evidence developed by recomputing charges submitted by the advertising agency and paid by the company.

- **Audit Situation No. 33.** The internal auditor in a consumer-products company plans to review marketing activities. She needs to decide actions that would contribute the most to determining whether the product-planning-and-development group has executed its responsibilities effectively. She would evaluate the acceptance of the company's products in the market by comparison with those of competitors. She would not: evaluate the organizational status of the group and its organizational structure; evaluate the coordination between the group and other interested parties such as sales, finance, market research, and production; or evaluate the qualifications of personnel working in the group in relation to their specific assignments.

- **Audit Situation No. 34.** A logical substantive test for accrued interest receivable would be to recalculate interest earned and compare it to the amounts received. The following tests would not be logical: comparing the interest income with published interest-investment records; verifying the interest income by a calculation based on the face amount of notes and the nominal interest rate; or verifying the cost, carrying value, and market value of notes receivable. These three tests do not recalculate interest earned for checking its accuracy and do not compare to the amounts received, which is the focus of the substantive test.

- **Audit Situation No. 35.** An auditor is in the process of verifying the correct sales date for an item sold FOB shipping point. He needs to select the source document that would help him achieve his objective. He should select the carrier's bill of lading, not the customer's payment document, purchase order, or sales invoice. The bill of lading will indicate the correct shipping date at which the risk and ownership were transferred to the buyer. The other documents may or may not show the shipping date, let alone its accuracy.

- **Audit Situation No. 36.** While auditing a new computer system, the auditor discovered the design team had not complied with the company's system-development standards. What should the auditor do? She should expand test procedures as warranted by the deficiencies noted. She should not: instruct the design team to remedy the development deficiencies before reauditing the system, report the deficiencies to the external auditors, or terminate the audit.

- **Audit Situation No. 37.** A plant maintenance shop is experiencing excessive overtime. An auditor is planning to establish an appropriate objective for the audit. The objective should be to determine whether minimizing overtime requires a combination of preventive and corrective controls. The following would not be appropriate: developing work schedules based on the availability of skilled labor force; writing work order instructions in clear, understandable language; or delivering appropriate quantities of materials to work sites to meet work schedules.

- **Audit Situation No. 38.** A Certified Internal Auditor was found to be violating the IIA Code of Ethics. He should be anticipating the following action by the IIA board of directors. He should expect to forfeit the Certified Internal Auditor designation. He should not expect the following to happen: be discharged by his employer, pay a fine in the appropriate court, or receive an official reprimand.

## 5.7 Risk and Control Self-Assessment

The IIA's "Perspective on Control Self-Assessment" (CSA) identifies three primary approaches to CSA: (1) facilitated team meeting (also known as workshops), (2) questionnaires (also known as surveys), and (3) management-produced analysis (also known as self-certification). Various tools and usage ideas are suggested, including

- Use facilitated workshops with anonymous voting to assess risk as one of the factors in developing the annual audit plans. This helps manage the risks involved in preparing the plan.
- Use workshops for major business processes that cross the departmental boundaries.
- Send a questionnaire to management asking them to assess standard list of control objectives within their department, and select audits to perform based on the responses.
- Use a facilitated interview process at the start of traditional audits to gather data and set the scope of the audit.
- Alternate CSA consulting and traditional auditing, that is, conduct a traditional audit one year and hold a self-assessment workshop the next year.
- Use CSA as a "preventive" auditing tool. It is a consulting engagement outside the annual opinion on controls issued.
- A department that is totally separate from internal auditing uses CSA workshops to help employees understand their objectives, risks, and controls.
- Send an annual questionnaire to management that is used to support an annual opinion on controls required by outside regulators.

- Use the "wall writing" approach, where the participants respond to two questions: "What things help you achieve your organization's objectives?" and "What things hinder you in achieving your organization's objectives?"
- Use self-assessment workshop to evaluate the overall control environment of the organization.
- Use questionnaires followed by one-on-one interviews with senior management to identify organization-wide risks.

To conduct the CSA consulting engagement, internal auditors need to be proficient in interpersonal skills, including observation, listening, and questioning skills. The auditor's role should be changed to a facilitator, not as a police officer, in collecting data and information that assists in the effective management of risks.

## 5.8 Computerized Audit Tools and Techniques

(a) **Auditing around the Computer versus Auditing with the Computer.** There are two approaches to testing computer-based data. They are characterized as auditing around the computer or auditing with the computer. The appropriate approach or combination of approaches is dependent on the nature of the related system (see Exhibit 5.32).

|  | *Auditing around the Computer* | *Auditing with the Computer* |
|---|---|---|
| Time involved to do the audit | High | Low |
| Cost involved to do the audit | Low/Medium | Medium/High |
| Audit effectiveness | Low/Medium | High |
| Technical knowledge required of auditor | Low | High |

Exhibit 5.32: Auditing around the computer and auditing with the computer

(i) **Auditing around the computer.** Auditing around the computer assumes that techniques and procedures the computer uses to process data need not be considered as long as there is a visible audit trail and/or the result can be manually verified. This approach bypasses the computer in either of two ways.

In the first way, computer output is compared to or confirmed by an independent source. This approach confirms computer-processed data with third parties or compares data with physical counts, inspections, records, files, and reports from other sources. Physical counts and inspections can verify quantity, type, and condition of tangible assets.

Auditors can also conduct common-sense examinations of printed data output to reveal potential reliability problems. These inspections can establish data reliability when a low to very low level of data testing is required. When a moderate to high level of testing is required, these tests should be supplemented by more extensive procedures. The following questions are examples of common-sense data tests: Are amounts too small? Are amounts too large? Are data fields complete? Are calculations correct?

Although confirmations and comparisons directly test the accuracy of computer output and effectively disclose fictitious data, they may not detect incomplete data input. When data completeness is in doubt, confirmations or comparisons should be supplemented by tracing a sample of source records to computer output.

The second way to bypass the computer in confirming data reliability is to select source transactions, manually duplicate the computer processes, and compare the results with computer output. Examples include salary payments, specific benefit payments, and loan balances and delinquent amounts.

Although this approach can test the completeness of computer output as well as the accuracy of computer processing, it does not disclose fictitious data (i.e., data that have been entered into the computer but are not supported by source records). If fictitious data are an issue, tracing data from the computer to source records should be considered.

The usefulness of auditing around the computer diminishes as the number and complexity of computer decisions increases. It may be impractical when sophisticated data processing activities are involved. *A principal disadvantage of auditing around the computer is that the integrity of the audit trail through the computer is not tested.*

(ii) **Auditing with the computer.** Auditing with the computer means that computer-programmed tests are used, in part, to measure data reliability.

After determining the completeness and accuracy of computer input by manually tracing data to and/or from a sample of source records, this approach uses auditor-developed computer-programmed tests to examine data reasonableness and identify defects that would make data unreliable.

An advantage of auditing with the computer is that it can be used regardless of the computer system's complexity or the number of decisions the computer makes. Auditing with the computer is also fast and accurate, permitting a much larger scope of testing than would be practical with other methods.

The first step in developing computer-programmed tests is to identify what computer information is to be used as evidence and what data elements were used to produce it. Auditors should test all data elements that affect the assignment objective(s).

When an audit-significant data element is derived (i.e., calculated by the computer based on two or more data elements), auditors should also test the source data elements. For example, the element "net pay" might be planned for use as evidence to meet an assignment's objective(s). Review of the system's data dictionary shows that a computer program uses three other data elements to calculate net pay—"hourly rate," "hours worked," and "deductions." Errors in any of these data elements would make "net pay" incorrect. Therefore, auditors should determine the accuracy of each data element.

After identifying the relevant data elements, the data dictionary can be examined to define the attributes of each and identify rules which each should meet. If a data element fails these requirements, the computer may exclude it or process it in a way that does not ensure an accurate result. Computer programs frequently have default logic that may cause a missing or defective data element to be erroneously processed due to incorrect assumptions.

Understanding a data element also makes it possible for audit staff to develop reasonableness assumptions that can be programmed as common-sense tests. Data attributes should also consider expected relationships among data elements. Although developed independently, a data element may have a reasonable relationship to another data element. For example, some kinds of medical procedures are age- or gender-related. Determining and testing relationships can reveal errors by disclosing irrational or unlikely relationships, such as a hysterectomy on a male patient.

When auditors have learned about each of the data elements that affects the information relied on, tests are developed to detect errors. Tests are of two types: (1) those that disclose failures of data elements to meet established requirements (called unconditional data tests) and (2) those that disclose illogical relationships (called conditional data tests).

After data tests are developed, the computer is programmed to apply them. The programmed data tests must be validated and tested to ensure that errors revealed during the data testing are the result of incorrect data and not the result of invalid test programs. *Data tests can be developed without knowledge of the technical design of the database, its structure, and layout. This knowledge, however, is needed to program the tests.*

Whether a microcomputer or a mainframe computer should be used to process data test depends on factors such as the size of the database, the number and complexity of data tests, required processing speed, computer accessibility, and team expertise. The key point is to ensure that test requirements are properly matched to the application and to the operating environment (micro- versus mainframe computer).

(b) **Embedded Audit Modules.** Embedded audit data collection modules use one or more specially designed data collection modules embedded in the computer application system to select and record data for subsequent analysis and evaluation. The data collection modules are inserted in the application system or program at points determined by the auditor to be appropriate. The auditor also determines the criteria for selection and recording. Other automated or manual methods may be used to analyze the collected data. This technique is intended to highlight unusual transactions and subject them to audit review and testing. Another name given to this technique is system control audit review file (SCARF).

Unlike other audit methods, this technique uses "in-line" code; that is, the computer application program performs the audit data collection function at the same time it processes the data for normal production purposes. This has two important consequences for the auditor: (1) in-line code ensures the availability of a comprehensive or very specialized sample of data as desired by the auditor, since strategically placed modules have access to every data element being processed; (2) retrofitting this technique to an existing system is more costly than implementing the audit module during system development. Therefore, it is preferable for auditors to specify requirements in this regard while the application system is being designed. Ideally, data collection control points should be inserted in the application program processing logic where errors, irregularities, or security breaches are most likely to occur.

(c) **Data Extraction Techniques.** Many data extraction tools and techniques are available, such as fourth-generation programming languages, audit hooks, and extended records, and others.

    (i) **Fourth-generation programming languages.** Relatively speaking, the fourth-generation programming languages (4GLs) are easy to learn and easy to use. 4GLs have online real-time, interactive, query characteristics with a quick turnaround time. 4GLs are command driven and user-friendly software and use nonprocedural statements, unlike the third-generation programming languages (e.g., COBOL) and the traditional audit software packages. Some 4GLs contain both procedural and nonprocedural statements.

        With the use of 4GLs, the auditor can make inquiries against online data files. 4GLs can merge different data records and data files. Many 4GLs perform most of the functions that a traditional audit software package does, but 4GLs do not come with some functions, such as accounts receivable aging and confirmations and statistical sampling, that are common to traditional audit software packages. If these functions are needed, the auditor has to insert them in the 4GLs by developing them as special subroutines written in COBOL, FORTRAN, or PL/1 programming languages.

        An advantage of 4GLs is their free-format report requests. Auditors' productivity may be enhanced with the use of a 4GL package. Any viable 4GL package is recommended for use as a supplement to the traditional audit software package but not as a substitute for it.

    (ii) **Audit hooks.** Audit hooks are similar to "red flags" to auditors. They are computer programs used in high-risk systems and are triggered by a condition or event designed by the auditor in conjunction with the information systems (IS) staff and the user. The objective is to act before an error, abnormality, or irregularity gets out of hand. Audit hooks are inserted in application programs to function as red flags. For example, bank internal auditors can use the audit hook in a program that processes dormant customer accounts to observe the activity in the account and, if need be, initiate timely action to correct or eliminate any irregularities that are identified. The difference between the audit hooks technique and the SCARF technique is that an audit hook is used more discretely for sensitive applications.

    (iii) **Extended records.** The extended record technique collects, by means of a special program(s), all the significant data that have affected the processing of an individual transaction. This includes the accumulation of the results of processing into a single record covering the time period that the transaction required to complete processing. The extended record includes data from all the computer application systems that contributed to the processing of a transaction. Such extended records are compiled into files that provide a conveniently accessible source of transaction data. Auditors can extract the transactions that have such extended records using generalized audit software or utility programs, and prepare reports for audit review and analysis.

        With this technique, the auditor no longer needs to review several computer data files to determine how a specific transaction was processed. With extended records, data are consolidated from different accounting periods and from systems interfacing with the application system being reviewed so that a complete transaction audit trail is physically included in one computer record. This facilitates tests of compliance to organization policies and procedures.

(d) **Generalized Audit Software.** Generalized audit software (e.g., ACL and IDEA) should be used to achieve cost-effective audits of computer-based systems where similar audit tasks are required to meet a variety of objectives. Generalized audit software can: provide totals of unusual items; check for duplications, missing information, or range of values; verify calculation totals and analyses produced; examine the existence and consistency of data maintained in files; perform concurrent auditing of data files; and select and generate audit confirmations.

    The audit software is most effective in verifying the clerical accuracy of an account balance. It is least effective in evaluating the logic of a specific computer program, evaluating the adequacy of internal controls embedded in a computer program, or confirming the existence of internal controls in manual operational procedures.

A limitation to using the audit software is that it can only be used on hardware with compatible operating systems. The audit software does not require significant programming knowledge to be used effectively. It does not require lengthy detailed instructions in order to accomplish specific tasks. It does not require significant modification of the program to be of use. The audit software cannot specify which data elements will be tested and the criteria to be used. The auditor specifies the criteria.

Generalized audit software is the most widely used technique for auditing computer application systems. This technique permits the auditor to independently analyze a computer-application system data file.

Most generalized audit software packages, because of their widespread use and long history, are reliable, highly flexible, and extensively and accurately documented. They are used to test the functions of data editing and validation routines in computer programs.

Generalized audit software packages can foot, cross-foot, balance, stratify, select a statistical sample, select transactions, total, compare, and perform calculations on diverse data elements contained within various data files.

These extensive capabilities are available to the auditor to substantively test computer application programs. Generally, this audit method is used to test the integrity of computer records in a data file or files and not to test the application program logic. However, some insights into the logic may surface through the use of generalized audit software.

Generalized audit software packages are available for batch and online systems. However, in a database environment, generalized audit software may not be usable directly because of complex data storage and access structures. In this case, there are two approaches to this problem.

1. Copy the required portion of the database onto a sequential file that can be accessed with the generalized audit software.
2. Develop a computer interface program that uses the database management system software to access the database.

Many audit software packages that are currently available examine data in microcomputer files independently and interactively. Required data files can be downloaded from the host to a microcomputer based on some selection criteria. Downloading is a process for selecting and retrieving data from another computer system in a way that makes it usable on a microcomputer. This requires that a compatible communication link be established between the microcomputer and the mainframe computer. This method is used when data exist in automated form already. The data may be available on the computer system or on another electronic medium, such as magnetic tape.

Downloading is frequently used when selecting data from very large data files stored on a mainframe or on tape used on the mainframe. To establish the link between the micro- and mainframe computer, the auditor must determine the appropriate communication protocol and have access rights on the mainframe computer. Standard software for downloading data can be used to select the desired data elements for use. Once the data have been downloaded into the microcomputer, they may have to be reformated for use with available microcomputer software.

Another method of entering data into a particular microcomputer is to communicate it from another microcomputer. Two compatible microcomputers can exchange data by using diskettes or by using existing phone lines and a communications program. Communication links among microcomputers permit data entered into a microcomputer in the field to be transferred to a headquarters system. A local area network (LAN) permits data to be transferred to designated recipients on the network or to be stored in common storage files with relative ease.

In some cases, the audit software can be developed on the microcomputer and then uploaded to the host computer for program execution. After the program is executed, the results can either stay on the host or be downloaded to a microcomputer.

Some microcomputer-based packages include interactive procedures for performing a full range of audit tests, such as analyzing data fields, sampling transactions and records, validating data, testing and converting dates, and producing statistical summaries. Reports required by the auditor can be produced in the graph, normal, or hard copy manner.

An example of application of microcomputer audit software in a payroll audit follows.

- Compare current period amounts with previous period amounts for employee gross and net payroll wages. Identify employees with unusual pay amounts after performing reasonableness tests.
- Select all transactions in specified activity codes and in excess of predetermined amounts. Trace them to proper authorization in personnel files in order to determine if payroll changes are authorized.

Advantages of generalized audit software are

- It is most widely used to analyze and extract data from computer files.
- It allows the auditor to examine more data on computer records in more detail as compared to manual records.
- It can be used to automate working paper preparation.
- It enables auditors to control their own programming and testing work.
- It minimizes the audit staff time allocated to audit testing.
- It minimizes the cost of adapting audit program routines to frequent changes in the application program being used due to parameter-driven approach used in the audit software.

Disadvantages of generalized audit software are

- It is least likely to be used for inquiry of online data files.
- It cannot flowchart an application program logic.
- It cannot perform a physical count of inventory or cash.
- It cannot perform continuous monitoring and analysis of transactions.
- It can require IS technical knowledge.

(i) **Terminal audit software.** Terminal audit software accesses, extracts, manipulates, and displays data from online databases using remote terminal inquiry commands. This technique provides the same basic functional capability as the more widely used batch-oriented generalized audit software. It has the advantages of a quicker turnaround and interactive investigation. It provides direct access to data files for periodic audit examination without extensive setup procedures or separate processing. It is, however, useful only in situations where online databases have been established and are already in use.

(ii) **Special-purpose or customized audit software.** These computer programs are specially developed to extract and report data from a specific application system's data files. A focused approach in meeting audit needs is the major advantage.

Disadvantages associated with the use of these audit programs are their limited applicability, inflexibility, development cost and time, and high level of computer programming expertise required.

Another problem encountered in using these programs is the maintenance needed to keep pace with changing audit requirements and changing application system functions. On occasion, utility programs can be used for audit purposes.

(e) **Spreadsheet Analysis.** Auditors perform spreadsheet analysis very extensively with the use of microcomputer-based software packages such as Spreadsheet Auditor and Spreadsheet Analyst. These software packages are designed to serve as an aid in creating error-free spreadsheets. The software prints out a description of ranges; a map indicating which cells contain formulas, labels, numbers, or macros; and a formula report. A critical point is the accuracy of formulas used in spreadsheet cells and their applicability to business rules.

A list of suggested controls for spreadsheet work follows:

- Spreadsheets should be mapped out clearly to show how the spreadsheet should look. A record of changes should be maintained for important data.
- Proper analysis should be conducted to ensure that the data required for analysis are included and entered in a format amenable to the analytic techniques planned.
- A specific area within the spreadsheet should be designated for data entry to minimize data entry errors. All data should be entered in that area and verified before the data are used.
- A specific area should be denoted in the spreadsheet for parameters of the data entry.
- Sampling and validation criteria should be established for each individual spreadsheet based on principles and judgment.
- Critical data should undergo more vigorous verification methods.

- Adequate quality assurance measures should be implemented during the data entry and analysis stage. This will help eliminate errors and facilitate supervisory review and referencing. Some guidelines include

  - Minimize data entry errors by using the pointer method to specify a cell or range rather than typing in cell addresses, and copying formulas and then editing. Take the time to verify the formula before copying it.
  - Use range names, as they are a good way to identify cells. To facilitate the supervisor's and referencer's review, prepare a list of all named ranges and their locations in the spreadsheet.
  - Protect formulas and key data by using the range protect command.
  - Test the spreadsheet's features, including its formulas and macros, with a small part of the database to ensure that the spreadsheet works as planned. Using a partial database rather than a complete spreadsheet saves time and makes it easier to identify errors in logic.
  - Correct mistakes as soon as they are identified.
  - Format cells using two decimals.
  - Write out macros by spelling what each macro command means.

- To ensure the accuracy of data entry, the following precautions should be taken prior to printing the spreadsheet:

  - Use foots and cross foots. By adding an extra row and column of formulas that bracket the totals, the accuracy of the preliminary results can be checked.
  - Use hash totals. To verify that all records are included in the spreadsheet, various hash totals can be used. This total can be arrived at by adding up the data elements to be used in the subsequent analysis.
  - Use automatic recalculations feature. Each spreadsheet should be set on automatic recalculation for a final recalculation before the information is used in the report and the spreadsheet is given to a referencer or supervisor to be used as support for a statement of fact.
  - Protect your spreadsheet. After verification, when no further changes are anticipated to the spreadsheet, the entire spreadsheet should be protected using the global protect feature.
  - Print out spreadsheet formulas. Printing the formulas facilitates spreadsheet review for accuracy.
  - Include reasonableness checks into formula or particular cells; for example, tax rate should not exceed a certain percentage.

- Some spreadsheets may require more extensive documentation than is practical to place within the spreadsheet itself. In such instances, external documentation should be used for detailed explanation of the spreadsheet. The external documentation should be placed in word processing software or other means. The internal documentation would still contain the elements listed below, with keys to the external documentation.

  - Job title and code, title of the spreadsheet, workpaper index
  - Purpose of the spreadsheet, reviewer and date, description of the spreadsheet, source of data entered
  - Documenting the cell addresses for each component of the spreadsheet showing data entry, formula explanations, macro explanations and purpose, range names and their cell addresses

- Maintain backup copies of spreadsheet data whenever changes are made. Backup copies should be kept in a location that is secure and different from the location where originals are kept.
- Spreadsheet applications should be reviewed and tested, both manually and by using audit software. Typical functions that can be provided by spreadsheet-audit software include

  - Documenting the contents of macros used within the spreadsheet as a basis for verifying the logic
  - Providing a global view of the contents of the spreadsheet application to scan reports for particular patterns or configurations
  - Verifying for circular references
  - Displaying the contents of a cell

- Adequate training should be provided to potential users of the spreadsheet software.

(f) **Automated WorkPapers.** Automated workpaper software helps auditors to increase efficiency and productivity because it relieves the boredom of writing out by hand. The software automatically references to audit work program sections and related audit objectives. Any corrections or changes can be done with ease and without losing the continuity.

Other documentation aids can also help the internal auditor during the fieldwork. One of the ways that an auditor can make sure that the intentions of program/system changes have indeed been achieved is through the use of automated documentation aids. If used properly, these documentation aids can provide flowcharts, tables, or graphs of the program or the system that can be compared at two different points in time, that is, before and after the program change. Any differences indicate changes to the program logic, data file contents, and Job Control Language procedures. The auditor then locates and analyzes the supporting documentation prepared to authorize and implement the changes.

Program or system flowcharts, tables, or graphs generated by the automated documentation aids provide a correct picture of what is in the computer programs and data files as opposed to relying on incorrect, obsolete, or incomplete documentation maintained on paper. Some of the features of automated documentation aids are

- Automated flowchart software packages, which read the source code for a computer program and convert it into an easy-to-read flowchart
- Computer data file translation software packages, which read the data file descriptions in the computer program and convert them into a convenient and readable format (tabular and graphic)
- Job Control Language software packages, which depict the job control flow as a graph or table showing the sequence of jobs or steps executed and indicating their procedure names and numbers.

(g) **Source Code Comparison.** The best audit tool and technique that an auditor in charge of reviewing program changes can find is a source code compare utility program. Why review and compare source code? It is the media through which program changes, whether authorized or unauthorized, can be made. Source code explains the functions, features, and capabilities of a computerized application system. Programmers write a source code in a programming language, such as COBOL. Hence it is most vulnerable to program changes. After the source code is developed, it is placed in a production source code library, which is often protected from unauthorized modifications by the use of program library management software packages.

Simply stated, a source code compare utility program takes two versions of a source code, compares each line of code, and indicates differences and whether the line of code is added, changed, or deleted. This output can be used in a structured walk-through or for management and auditor reviews. The auditor then locates and analyzes the supporting documentation (system, program, computer operations, and user) prepared to authorize and implement the program changes. Lack of supporting documentation is a weakness in controls, which is an indication of potential risk and exposure. The auditor needs to inform management to strengthen internal controls over software maintenance activities.

(h) **Object Code Comparison.** As indicated in the previous section, programmers write source code in a programming language such as COBOL. Later the source code is translated into machine-readable language, object code, for proper execution of the program. Compiler software supplied by vendors performs the translation of source code into object code. Load/executable code, which comes after the object code is link-edited, is then placed in a production library and used for the processing of live data for an application system.

The source code compare utility software package, described in the previous section, by itself may not be sufficient to ensure that programs are changed properly and effectively. An additional approach is needed to ensure that the object code being executed in production mode is in agreement with the authorized source code.

The auditor can use object code compare utility software packages for comparison of two versions of a program's object code to report any differences. This is accomplished through four steps.

1. Identify the current version of production source code.
2. Recompile the current version of production source code to obtain the corresponding object code (say Item 1).
3. Inspect the production job control language for correct program name and production library where the object code to be compared (say Item 2) is placed.
4. Compare Item 1 and Item 2 of object code with the use of an object code compare utility software package.

Any differences indicate that the object code in the production library that is used for program processing is not generated from the corresponding source code. This requires analysis and corrective action by the information technology (IT) staff and the auditor. Combined with the source code compare, an object code compare tool is an effective method of detecting, identifying, and controlling program/system changes.

(i) **File Comparison Utility Program.** File compare is performed by a utility program supplied by a software vendor (e.g., IBM's IEBCOMPR). The purpose of the tool is to identify differences in data field names and values in two files of data at a static point in time. For example, in a manufacturing environment, "on-hand inventory balance" data field appearing in two different files can be compared with the use of file compare utility program to determine if the values are the same. If not, it indicates an abnormal situation. This may require analysis and correction if the two values are supposed to be the same.

Another example is to compare file control totals in accounts receivable or payable subsidiary ledger files to file control totals maintained in the general ledger file. Accounting logic requires that these two file control totals be the same. If not, it indicates an abnormal situation. Also, this tool can be used to compare JCL file contents at two points in time to detect any changes. The auditor needs to be imaginative to use this powerful tool either in the software maintenance or development activities.

(j) **Test Data Method.** The test data method verifies computer-processing accuracy of application programs by executing these programs using manually prepared sets of test cases, test data, and expected results of processing. Actual processing results are compared with the expected results. If the two results are identical, then the auditor may infer that the program logic is consistent with the documentation.

This method provides auditors with a procedure for review, testing, and evaluation of computer program logic. However, because of continual program changes, it is very difficult and time-consuming to prepare and maintain test data manually. In addition, the test data method is not an appropriate technique for verification of the accuracy and completeness of production data or master files.

Automated test data generators are available to create large volumes of test data in complex data formats with relatively little effort. They can be used as input to the application program to be tested. This technique, combined with an automated code optimizer program, provides statistics on the number of times a program statement line code was executed and highlights the program sections that were not used during computer processing. Automated code optimizer programs can be used to evaluate test data prepared either manually or by an automated test data generator program. Test data method can be used to test both batch and online programs.

(k) **Base Case System Evaluation.** Base case system evaluation (BCSE) is a technique that applies a standardized body of data (input, parameters, and output) to the testing of computer application programs. User staff, with auditor participation, establishes this body of data (the base case) as the criterion for correct functioning of the computer application system. This testing process is widely used as a technique for validation of production systems.

Some organizations are using the base case approach as a means to: test computer programs during their development; demonstrate the successful operation of the system prior to its implementation; and verify its continuing and accurate processing during its production life. As a result, this approach requires and represents a total commitment by data processing and user department management to the principles and disciplines of BCSE.

(l) **Integrated Test Facility.** Integrated test facility (ITF) is a technique to review application program logic and functions to provide the auditor with evidence on operating procedures (computer and/or manual) and error handling conditions. The auditor's test data for a fictitious entity (i.e., a branch, department, division, or subsidiary) are used to compare ITF processing results to precalculated and expected test results. Here the auditor's test data are processed with normal production data. The auditor, however, must ensure that the ITF results for the fictitious entity are removed from the regular production data files either at the end of testing process or later, in order to eliminate its impact on the organization's financial and operating transactions and records. ITF can be used in batch and online application systems.

(m) **Parallel Simulation.** Parallel simulation is the use of one or more special computer programs to process "live" data files and simulate normal computer application processing. As opposed to the test data method and the integrated test facility, which process test data through "live" programs, the parallel simulation method processes "live" data through test programs. Generalized audit software can be used to create a test model or simulation of relatively simple application systems or a portion of more complex application systems.

Parallel simulation programs include only the application logic, calculations, and controls that are relevant to specific audit objectives. As a result, simulation programs are usually much less complex than their application program counterparts. Often large segments of major applications that consist of several computer programs can be simulated for audit purposes with a single parallel simulation program. Parallel simulation permits the auditors to independently verify complex and critical application program controls and procedures. Parallel simulation is also used to test computer programs and complex processing logic, such as interest calculations, during system development projects.

(n) **Snapshot.** Both auditors and IT staff periodically encounter difficulty in reconstructing the computer decision-making process. The cause is a failure to keep together all the data elements involved in that process. Snapshot is a technique that, in effect, takes a picture of the parts of computer memory that contain the data elements involved in a computerized decision-making process at the time the decision is made.

Input transactions are tagged and written to an audit log file with date, time, and indication of the point in the program at which the snapshot occurred. The results of the snapshot are printed in a report for review and analysis.

The snapshot audit technique offers the capability of listing all the data that were involved in a specific decision-making process. The technique requires the necessary logic to be preprogrammed in the system. A mechanism, usually a special code in the transaction record, is added for triggering, logging, and printing of the data in question for analysis.

The snapshot audit technique may help auditors answer questions as to why computer application systems produce questionable results. It provides information to explain why the computer made a particular decision.

Used in conjunction with other audit techniques (e.g., integrated test facility or tracing), this technique aids in the determination of what results would occur if a certain type of input entered the application system. The snapshot technique can also be an invaluable aid to systems and programming staff in debugging the application system because it can provide "pictures" of the computer memory. Ideally, the snapshot technique should be designed as part of the original application system development process. The auditor participates in the system development process by defining requirements and reviewing system design specifications and system test results.

(o) **Tracing.** A traditional audit technique in a manual environment is to follow the path of a transaction during processing. For example, an auditor picks up a customer order as it is received into an organization and follows the flow from department to department. The auditor inquires of the employee involved what actions were taken at that particular step in the processing cycle.

Since the auditor understands the policies and procedures of the organization, he or she can judge whether they are being adequately followed. By the time the auditor has walked through the processing cycle, he or she has an appreciation of how work flows through the organization.

In an IS environment, it is not possible to follow the path of a transaction through its processing cycle solely by following the paperwork flow, since the computer accomplishes many of the functions performed by employees and no hard copy documents are produced. A new type of audit evidence (electronic) is introduced.

Tracing is an audit technique that provides the auditor with the ability to perform an electronic walk-through of a computer application system. The audit objective of tracing is to verify compliance with policies and procedures by substantiating, by examining the path a transaction followed through a program, how that transaction was processed. Tracing can be used to detect omissions.

Tracing shows what instructions have been executed in a computer program and in which sequence they have been executed. Since the instructions in a computer program represent the steps in processing, the processes that have been executed can be determined from the results of the tracing audit technique. Once an auditor knows what instructions in a program have been executed, he or she can perform an analysis to determine if the processing conformed to the organization's policies and procedures.

(p) **Mapping.** Mapping is a technique used to assess the extent of system testing and to identify specific program logic that has not been tested. Mapping is performed by software measurement tools that analyze a computer program during execution and indicate which program statements have been executed. The software measurement tool can also determine the amount of central processing unit (CPU) time consumed by each program segment.

The original intent of the mapping concept was to help computer programmers ensure the quality of their programs. Auditors can use the same software measurement tools, however, to look for unexecuted program statements. This analysis can provide auditors with insight into the efficiency of program operation and can reveal unauthorized program segments or statements included, if any exist.

(q) **Control Flowcharting.** In a complex business environment, it is difficult to thoroughly understand the total system of control of an organization within its total business and operational context. A graphic technique, or flowchart, for simplifying the identification and interrelationships of controls can be a great help in evaluating the adequacy of those controls and in assessing the impact of system changes on the overall control profile.

Flowcharts facilitate the explanation of controls to a system analyst, auditor, or people unfamiliar with specific functions of the system. They also aid in ascertaining that controls are operating as originally intended or planned.

The control flowcharting technique provides the documentation necessary to explain the system of control. Often an organization's information about controls is fragmented. This fragmentation makes obtaining a clear picture of the controls operating within the organization difficult. The availability of an overall picture of controls, using several levels of flowcharts, facilitates understanding.

(r) **Control Reprocessing.** Control reprocessing is a technique to identify lost or incomplete records during an update cycle. An update cycle of importance is reprocessed to compare against the original update to determine whether the results are the same between the two updates—original and reprocessed. If the results are not the same, analysis is conducted to identify the sources causing the difference.

---

### WHICH COMPUTER-ASSISTED AUDIT TECHNIQUE (CAAT) METHOD USES WHAT?

- The test data method uses test data with production programs.
- The parallel simulation method uses production data with test programs.
- The integrated test facility method uses test data with production programs.
- The embedded audit data collection, generalized audit software, snapshot, audit hooks, tracing, mapping, extended records, and transaction selection methods all use production data with production programs.

---

(s) **Conventional and Concurrent Audit Techniques.** In a conventional audit using a computer-assisted audit technique on an after-the-fact-basis, auditors evaluate the controls at periodic intervals. Using concurrent audit techniques, controls are evaluated on a continuing basis. Audit evidence is collected in a timely manner.

Exhibit 5.33 presents a comparison between conventional and concurrent audit techniques.

| *Conventional audit techniques* | *Concurrent audit techniques* |
| --- | --- |
| • Examples: generalized audit software, test data method, transaction selection, extended records, tracing, mapping, utility programs. | • Examples: ITF, SCARF, simulation, snapshots, audit hooks. |
| • Most appropriate for computerized batch, simple, and normal application systems. | • Most appropriate for computerized online, complex, and sensitive application systems. |
| • Require less data processing technical knowledge on the part of the auditor. | • Require more data processing technical knowledge on the part of the auditor. |
| • Mostly use test data instead of production data | • Mostly use production data instead of test data. |
| • Not part of user production application systems. | • Part of production application systems. |
| • Auditor has more control over test data. | • Auditor has less control over test data. |
| • Auditor initiates CAAT program execution to test plans and schedules. | • Application system initiates CAAT program execution according to specified event, transaction, date, time, and other criteria. |

**Exhibit 5.33: Conventional and concurrent audit techniques**

## 5.9 Process Mapping Including Flowcharting

(a) **Process Mapping.** Robert Damelio identified three tools to map a process, activity, or function to understand it and to improve it.[10] These tools include relationship maps, cross-functional process maps, and flowcharts.

Relationship maps show the customer-supplier relationships or linkages that exist between parts of an organization. These maps show the big-picture view that portrays how the major functions of the business interact with each other. They can also be used to show any individual function.

Cross-functional process maps show how an organization's major work processes cut across several functions. These maps show the sequence of steps that make up the work process, as well as the inputs and outputs associated with each process step.

Flowcharts are good to illustrate work processes since they help define, document, and analyze processes at the detailed level, especially about the individual performing the work or to develop the work procedures step by step. The next section presents flowcharts in a detailed manner.

Process maps can be used in a variety of ways, such as (1) to orient new employees, (2) to organize work, (3) to clarify employee roles and contributions, (4) to identify improvement opportunities, (5) to reduce cycle time, and (6) to measure performance. For example, cross-functional process maps and flowcharts can be used to reduce costs, reduce defects, conduct benchmarks, and reengineer a process. Similarly, relationship maps, cross-functional process maps, and flowcharts can be used to design performance measurement system and to measure customer satisfaction.

(b) **Flowcharting.** The three most widely used audit tools include flowcharts, questionnaires, and interviews. These tools will be discussed more heavily than other tools such as anecdotes (narratives), unobtrusive measures, and checklists.

Flowcharts are most valuable in providing a summary outline and overall description of the process of transactions in a system. The objective of a flowchart is to present a clear and concise picture and description of a system or operation, whether manual or automated. This description provides a basis for an understanding of information flow and for subsequent audit work required in testing and evaluating internal controls. Usually flowcharts are supplemented by other forms of documentation, such as narratives, policies and procedures, internal control questionnaires (ICQs), or interviews (see Exhibit 5.34 for benefits of flowcharts).

**Benefits of Flowcharts**

— Can visualize things better—provides visual thoughts
— Can clearly see missing pieces easily
— Is easy to understand a complex system or procedure
— Can see the "big" picture of a system or operation
— Is easy to present to others—communication tool
— Can see the interfaces within and between systems
— Can locate control points
— Can identify information paths and flows
— Can trace document movement from source to destination

**Exhibit 5.34: Benefits of flowcharts**

Since systems are complex, it is advised to prepare flowcharts in two stages: summary level and detail level. The summary-level flowchart gives a quick synopsis of the entire system, while the detail-level flowchart is used for internal control testing and evaluation. Care should be taken to ensure that these two types of flowcharts do not contradict or duplicate each other in terms of flow of information. For example, a summary flowchart for a revenue cycle can have several detailed flowcharts, such as sales, credit, billing, and accounting receivable functions, and should not contain any unrelated functions.

When a large system is divided into several subsystems, it is important to make sure that interaction between subsystems is kept to a minimum to eliminate overlaps, errors, and confusing flow of documents. Good advice to a flowchart preparer is to keep the interfaces between documents simpler for a clear understanding.

---

[10] Robert Damelio, **The Basics of Process Mapping** (Portland, OR: Productivity, Inc., 1996).

Every flowchart should have at least three key elements: (1) departments involved or activities undertaken; (2) symbols to denote documents, nature of work done (posted, filed), and the sequence of documents related to the activities; and (3) information flow lines that show how documents and records are processed.

Flowcharts are of two types: horizontal flowcharts and vertical flowcharts. A flowchart is horizontal when it shows the document movement from source to final destination and from filing to destruction among departments. The information flow is from left to right. A flowchart is vertical when it shows the movement of documents from source to final destination and from filing to destruction within a department or operation. The information flow is from top to bottom. The horizontal flowchart is used to document the procedures followed by several interacting departments; the vertical flowchart does not show such interaction. The horizontal flowchart is more commonly used than the vertical one.

## QUESTIONNAIRE VS. FLOWCHART

- The questionnaire is a data collection instrument—a means of gathering information about documents processed, forms used, procedures followed, record contents, program logic, and data editing details. However, questionnaires are not useful for document analysis and control evaluation purposes.
- Flowcharts overcome this weakness.

For example, flowcharts developed to describe a computer system can show programmed decisions, master file updates, and computer-generated transactions, in addition to manually generated transactions.

### Uses of Flowcharts

Flowcharts make it a lot simpler to see what should be happening. For example, in a computer operation, when something goes wrong, such as figures are not balancing or a job failed in the middle of processing, the flowchart is the first thing that should be checked to see where the job was or what correction needs to be made. A flowchart is a problem-solving tool since it can be used to compare "what is" and "what should be."

For effective control evaluation, auditors need to make sure that the flowchart, whether prepared by the auditors or developed by the auditee, is in fact representative of the actual system in operation. If not, the auditors' conclusions will be questionable. Verification is the process of ensuring that the system described in the flowchart and the actual system is the same. The verification of the transaction or the document flow can be achieved by tracing several different types of transactions or documents taken at random and walking through the entire system. This verification procedure provides a reasonably accurate description of the system and is not intended to provide any reliable information as to whether the systems are operating effectively. These procedures provide a partial answer in obtaining observation-type evidence.

For example, the verification procedure can be used to test a small sample of transaction posting from each book of original entry to the general ledger or to trace issuance of credit memos for goods returned by customers, price adjustments, or invoice errors.

(i) **Other uses of flowcharts.** Flowcharts are used in business functions other than auditing. Flowcharts are increasingly the focus now due to total quality management (TQM) programs. Flowcharting is the most effective way to describe how a process works now, how to fix it when it does not work, and how it is going to be improved in the future. To improve a process, repetitive tasks or activities need to be looked at for streamlining, to improve consistency and quality, and to reduce confusion.

Another use of flowcharting is to improve and facilitate training. People learn more quickly with a flowchart because they can see and understand the process as a whole—a picture is worth 1,000 words.

---

**KEY CONCEPTS TO REMEMBER: FLOWCHARTS**

- Flowcharts would most likely be used in the evaluation of controls in a complex system, not in a simple but well-documented system.
- An auditor develops a flowchart primarily to analyze a system and identify internal controls, to determine whether there is inefficiency and lack of controls.
- Flowcharts would be most appropriate during the preliminary stage of an area that has not previously been audited. Flowcharts help auditors in evaluating the internal control system.
- As a means of internal control evaluation, flowcharts allow users to follow information flow more easily than do questionnaires and descriptive narratives.

---

(ii) **Interpreting charts and graphs.** The basic purpose of a chart or graph is to give a visual comparison between two or more things. For example, changes in budget from one year to the next may be represented in a graph. One significant reason for visualizing a comparison is to reinforce its comprehension.

Charts and graphs are used to dramatize a statement, a fact, a point of view, or an idea. Visual aids assist in the quick comprehension of both simple and complex data, statistics, or problems.

A chart should explain itself in silence; it should be completely understood without the assistance of a caption. The caption must act only as reinforcement to its comprehension.

Various charts, such as tabular charts, column charts, bar charts, pie charts, line charts, and layer charts, are discussed briefly (see Exhibit 5.35).

**Types of Charts**

- Tabular (used to represent items of interest)
- Column (used for comparison of things)
- Gantt (bar) (used for milestone scheduling)
- Pie (used to represent 100% of total)
- Line (used for comparison of things)
- Layer (used for accumulation of individual facts)

**Exhibit 5.35: Types of charts**

The **tabular chart** is used to represent items of interest. It requires a fair amount of study in order to grasp the full meaning of the figures. This is because it takes longer to digest the meaning of an itemization of compiled figures than if the same figures are presented graphically. The **column chart** is most commonly used for demonstrating a comparison between two or more things. The column chart is vertical.

The **Gantt chart** is a bar chart and is essentially a column chart on its side, and is used for the same purpose. The bar chart is horizontal. It is a tool that allows a manager to evaluate whether existing resources can handle work demand or whether activities should be postponed. The Gantt chart is used for milestone scheduling where each milestone has start and completion dates. A milestone represents a major activity or task to be accomplished (e.g., design phase in a computer system development project).

A Gantt chart is a graphical illustration of a scheduling technique. The structure of the chart shows output plotted against units of time. It does not include cost information. It highlights activities over the life of a project and contrasts actual times with projected times using a horizontal (bar) chart. It gives a quick picture of a project's progress in terms of actual time lines and projected time lines.

The **pie chart** is used to represent a 100% total of two or more items. The **line chart** is exceptionally impressive when comparing several things but could present a visual problem if the comparisons are too many or too close in relation to one another. Advantages are that it is simple to draw. Disadvantages are that if the lines are close to each other, it is difficult to distinguish some of the plotted points.

The **layer chart** is linear in appearance but has a different representation. It depicts the accumulation of individual facts stacked one over the other to create the overall total. This chart is more complex than the others, since it illustrates much more. In addition to showing the comparison of layers that add up to the total, this type of chart also shows how each group of layers relates to subsequent groups. The layer chart requires more work to prepare than the other charts. There is more arithmetic involved, and it requires a good deal of concentration to draw the chart.

## MULTIPLE-CHOICE QUESTIONS (1-296)

## Sampling and Statistical Analysis

**1.** For which of the following sample results is sampling risk the **smallest**?

| | Sample size | Tolerable error rate | Sample error rate |
|---|---|---|---|
| a. | 40 | 5% | 2% |
| b. | 60 | 5% | 1% |
| c. | 80 | 4% | 3% |
| d. | 100 | 1% | 1% |

**2.** If an auditor is sampling to test compliance with a particular company policy, which of the following factors should **not** affect the allowable level of sampling risk?
- a. The experience and knowledge of the auditor.
- b. The adverse consequences of noncompliance.
- c. The acceptable level of risk of making an incorrect audit conclusion.
- d. The cost of performing auditing procedures on sample selections.

**3.** Which of the following techniques could be used to estimate the standard deviation for a sampling plan?
- a. Difference estimation.
- b. Pilot sample.
- c. Regression.
- d. Discovery sampling.

**4.** Identification of an appropriate population to sample is dependent on audit objectives. A population of entries in an asset repairs expense file would be an appropriate population if the audit objective were to determine whether
- a. Expenditures for fixed assets have been improperly expensed.
- b. Noncapital repair expenditures have been properly charged to expense.
- c. Noncapital repair expenditures have been recorded in the proper period.
- d. Expenditures for fixed assets have been recorded in the proper period.

**5.** To test compliance with a policy regarding sales returns recorded during the most recent year, an auditor systematically selected 5% of the actual returns recorded in March and April. Returns during these two busiest months of the year represented about 25% of total annual returns. Error projections from this sample have limited usefulness because
- a. The small size of the sample relative to the population makes sampling risk unacceptable.
- b. The failure to stratify the population according to sales volume results in bias.
- c. The systematic selection of returns during the two months is not sufficiently random.
- d. The error rates during the two busiest months may not be representative of the whole year.

**6.** Using random numbers to select a sample
- a. Is required for a variables sampling plan.
- b. Is likely to result in an unbiased sample.
- c. Results in a representative sample.
- d. Allows auditors to use smaller samples.

**7.** An auditor tested a population by examining sixty items selected judgmentally and found one error. The main limitation of the auditor's sample is the inability to

- a. Quantify sampling risk.
- b. Quantify the acceptable error rate.
- c. Project the population's error rate.
- d. Determine whether the sample is random.

**8.** The degree to which the auditor is justified in believing that the estimate based on a random sample will fall within a specified range is called
- a. Sampling risk.
- b. Nonsampling risk.
- c. Confidence level.
- d. Precision.

**9.** An auditor is designing a sampling plan to test the accuracy of daily production reports over the past three years. All of the reports contain the same information except that Friday reports also contain weekly totals and are prepared by managers rather than by supervisors. Production normally peaks near the end of a month. If the auditor wants to select two reports per month using an interval-sampling plan, which of the following techniques **reduces** the likelihood of bias in the sample?
- a. Estimating the error rate in the population.
- b. Using multiple random starts.
- c. Increasing the confidence level.
- d. Increasing the precision.

**10.** In a sampling application, the group of items about which the auditor wants to estimate some characteristic is called the
- a. Population.
- b. Attribute of interest.
- c. Sample.
- d. Sampling unit.

**11.** In a sampling application, the standard deviation represents a measure of the
- a. Expected error rate.
- b. Level of confidence desired.
- c. Degree of data variability.
- d. Extent of precision achieved.

**12.** An auditor selected a random sample of 100 items from a population of 2,000 items. The total dollars in the sample were $10,000, and the standard deviation was $10. If the achieved precision based on this sample was plus or minus $4,000, the **minimum** acceptable value of the population would be
- a. $204,000
- b. $196,000
- c. $199,000
- d. $199,800

**13.** An auditor prepared a working paper that consisted of a list of employee names and identification numbers as well as the following statement: By matching random numbers with employee identification numbers, forty employee personnel files were selected to verify that they contain all documents required by company policy 501. No exceptions were noted.

The auditor did not place any tick marks on this working paper. Which one of the following changes would improve the auditor's working paper the most?
- a. Use of tick marks to show that each file was examined.
- b. Removal of the employee names to protect their confidentiality.
- c. Justification for the sample size.

d.   Listing of the actual documents examined for each employee.

**14.** The standard deviation of a sample will usually decrease with
a.   A decrease in sample size.
b.   The use of stratification.
c.   An increase in desired precision.
d.   An increase in confidence level.

**15.** Statistical sampling would be appropriate to estimate the value of an auto dealer's 3,000 line-item inventory because statistical sampling is
a.   Reliable and objective.
b.   Thorough and complete.
c.   Thorough and accurate.
d.   Complete and precise.

**16.** An important difference between a statistical sample and a judgmental sample is that with a statistical sample
a.   No judgment is required, everything is by formula.
b.   A smaller sample size can be used.
c.   More accurate results are obtained.
d.   Population estimates with measurable reliability can be made.

**17.** Sample size
a.   Increases with the use of higher confidence levels.
b.   Decreases with the use of higher confidence levels.
c.   Remains unchanged with changes in confidence levels.
d.   Increases with the use of lower confidence levels.

**18.** Using the following results from a variables sample, compute the standard error of the mean.

| | |
|---|---|
| Population size | = 10,000 |
| Sample size | = 144 |
| Sample standard deviation | = $24.00 |
| Confidence level | = 90% (Z=1.65) |
| Mean | = $84.00 |

a.   $60.00
b.   $ 7.00
c.   $ 2.30
d.   $ 2.00

**19.** During an internal control inspection, an auditor is evaluating the contents of a large warehouse that contains records from both the retail and the wholesale divisions of the client company. Upon inspecting the contents of one particular randomly selected box, the auditor discovers that the contents do not match the computer-generated label taped to the outside of the box. On average, errors of this kind have occurred in 6% of retail boxes and 2% of wholesale boxes. Unfortunately, some water has leaked onto the label and smeared the part that indicated the division of origin. The auditor does know that two-thirds of the boxes in this warehouse come from the wholesale division and one-third from the retail division. Which of the following can be concluded?
a.   The box is more likely to have come from the retail division than from the wholesale division.
b.   The box is more likely to have come from the wholesale division than from the retail division.
c.   The proportion of retail boxes in the warehouse is probably much larger than the auditor thought.
d.   The proportion of wholesale boxes in the warehouse is probably much larger than the auditor thought.

**20.** Which one of the following statements about sampling is **true**?
a.   A larger sample is always more representative of the underlying population than a smaller sample.
b.   For very large populations, the absolute size of a sample has more impact on the precision of its results than does its size relative to its population.
c.   For a given sample size, a simple random sample always produces the most representative sample.
d.   The limitations of an incomplete sample frame can almost always be overcome by careful sampling techniques.

**21.** Which one of the following is **not** an important consideration in determining the appropriate sample size?
a.   Whether the sample is designed to estimate a mean or a proportion.
b.   The amount of variability in the population under study.
c.   The sensitivity of the decision using this sample to errors of estimation.
d.   The cost per sample observation.

**22.** An auditor is considering a sample size of fifty to estimate the average amount per invoice in a large trucking company. How would the precision of the sample results be affected if the sample size were increased to 200?
a.   The larger sample would be about two times as precise as the smaller sample.
b.   The larger sample would be about four times as precise as the smaller sample.
c.   Although precision would not be increased that much, a possible downward bias in the estimate of the average per invoice would be corrected.
d.   Since both sample sizes are larger than 30, the increase would not have that much of an effect on precision.

**23.** A 90% confidence interval for the mean of a population based on the information in a sample always implies that there is a 90% chance that the
a.   Estimate is equal to the true population mean.
b.   True population mean is no larger than the largest end point of the interval.
c.   Standard deviation will not be any greater than 10% of the population mean.
d.   True population mean lies within the specified confidence interval.

**24.** The auditor is concerned that a computer program is not properly computing the amount of freight to be added to shipments of merchandise ordered through the catalog. Management considers the occurrence of any freight costing errors to be critical. The auditor is considering sampling techniques to examine the freight charges on invoices to customers or considering the use of computer audit tools. Which of the following sampling or audit approaches would provide the greatest assurance as to the correctness of the freight charge computations at the current time?
a.   Use discovery sampling selecting transactions from invoices, which should have freight charges added to them.
b.   Use either test data or parallel simulation to test the computer application.

    c.    Use difference estimation by selecting transactions from invoices, which should have freight charges added to them.

    d.    Use generalized audit software to select a monetary unit sample of invoices that have been billed to customers.

**25.** If all other factors specified in an attributes-sampling plan remain constant, decreasing the confidence level from 95% to 90% would cause the required sample size to

    a.    Increase.

    b.    Decrease.

    c.    Change by 5%.

    d.    Remain the same.

**26.** In sampling applications, the standard deviation represents a measure of the

    a.    Expected error rate.

    b.    Level of confidence desired.

    c.    Degree of data variability.

    d.    Extent of precision achieved.

**27.** In preparing a sampling plan for an inventory-pricing test, which of the following describes an advantage of statistical sampling over nonstatistical sampling?

    a.    Requires nonquantitative expression of sample results.

    b.    Provides a quantitative measure of sampling risk.

    c.    Minimizes nonsampling risk.

    d.    Reduces the level of tolerable error.

**28.** An internal auditor wishes to determine whether the finished goods perpetual inventory records are being properly updated for completed production. To accomplish this, the auditor traces inventory quantity and cost records from production reports to perpetual inventory records, using an appropriate sample size based on a 95% confidence level, estimated error rate of 4%, and desired precision of 2%. If the error rate in the sample is, as expected, 4%, and 2,000 production reports were posted to perpetual inventory records during the year, the auditor can be 95% sure that the number incorrectly posted was

    a.    At least 100.

    b.    At least 80.

    c.    Between 60 and 140.

    d.    Between 40 and 120.

**29.** A company with 14,344 customers determines that the mean and median accounts receivable balances for the year are $15,412 and $10,382, respectively. From this information, the auditor can conclude that the distribution of the accounts receivable balances is continuous and

    a.    Negatively skewed.

    b.    Positively skewed.

    c.    Symmetrically skewed.

    d.    Evenly distributed between the mean and median.

**30.** The following data relate to a variables-sampling application:

$x = \$78.50$, $s = \$13.00$, $s_x = \$1.00$, confidence level = 90% ($Z = 1.65$).

The achieved precision is equal to

    a.    $ 1.65

    b.    $21.45

    c.    $70.65

    d.    $80.15

**31.** The measure of variability most useful in variables-sampling is the

    a.    Median.

    b.    Range.

    c.    Standard deviation.

    d.    Mean.

**32.** The primary reason for an auditor to use statistical sampling is to

    a.    Obtain a smaller sample than would be required by nonstatistical sampling techniques.

    b.    Obtain a sample more representative of the population than would be obtained by nonstatistical sampling techniques.

    c.    Allow the auditor to quantify, and therefore control, the risk of making an incorrect decision based on sample evidence.

    d.    Meet requirements of the IIA *Standards*.

**33.** During the audit of inventories, an internal auditor specified a precision of 5% instead of the 4% contained in the preliminary audit program. What would be the impact of the change in precision?

    a.    A decrease in population standard deviation.

    b.    An increase in population standard deviation.

    c.    A decrease in required sample size.

    d.    An increase in required sample size.

**34.** Based on a random sample, it is estimated that 4%, plus or minus 2%, of a firm's invoices contain errors. The plus or minus 2% is known as the estimate's

    a.    Precision.

    b.    Accuracy.

    c.    Confidence level.

    d.    Standard error.

**35.** The measure of variability of a statistical sample that serves as an estimate of the population variability is the

    a.    Basic precision.

    b.    Range.

    c.    Standard deviation.

    d.    Interval.

**36.** Internal auditors employ confidence levels in the context of audit sampling. In a given sample plan, the confidence level

    a.    Is a decision variable that the internal auditor specifies after considering the economic consequences of drawing the wrong conclusion as a result of sampling error.

    b.    Is a characteristic of the audit population and is not under the direct control of the internal auditor.

    c.    Is essentially a measure of the accuracy of the sample results obtained after the sample has been selected and tested.

    d.    Is not normally specified before the sample size is determined. Rather it is computed once the sample has been selected and tested.

**37.** Internal auditors employ the concept of precision in audit sampling contexts. In this context, precision is

    a.    A characteristic of the population at hand and is not under the direct control of the auditor.

    b.    A measure of the accuracy with which one has generated sample estimates. Desired precision must be established before the sample is obtained and evaluated.

c. Evaluated independently of reliability in a given sample.

d. Important for evaluating variables samples, but not attributes samples.

**38.** In audit sampling applications there are risks of Type I and Type II errors. These risks

a. Result directly from the chance that the sample obtained by the internal auditor is unrepresentative of the population.

b. Can be decreased by using more reliable, albeit more expensive, audit procedures.

c. Have a magnitude that is based only on the economic consequences of incorrect sample-based conclusions.

d. Refer respectively to the risks that (1) internal controls will fail and (2) the resultant error will go undetected.

**39.** The size of a given audit sample is jointly a result of characteristics of the population of interest and decisions made by the internal auditor. Everything else being equal, sample size will

a. Increase if the internal auditor decides to accept more risk of incorrectly concluding that controls are effective when they are in fact ineffective.

b. Double if the internal auditor finds that the variance of the population is twice as large as was indicated in the pilot sample.

c. Decrease if the internal auditor increases the amount of tolerable error.

d. Increase as the risk of sampling error increases.

**40.** The auditor notes an unexpectedly weak correlation between lower interest rates and large mortgages closed and seeks an explanation for the rejection of most large mortgages. The auditor should

a. Take a judgment sample directed toward applications for large mortgages.

b. Take a random sample of all mortgages closed.

c. Develop a regression model to explain the relationship.

d. Use linear programming to analyze allocation of funds.

**41.** Assuming no change in sample standard deviation, how would sample size and achieved precision be affected by a change in confidence level from 95.5% to 99.7%?

a. Sample size would be smaller, but achieved precision would be larger.

b. Sample size would be larger, but achieved precision would not change.

c. Sample size would be smaller, but achieved precision would not change.

d. Sample size would be larger, but achieved precision would be smaller.

**42.** In testing payroll transactions, an auditor discovers that 4 out of a statistical sample of 100 selected time cards were not signed by the appropriate supervisor. To evaluate the materiality or significance of this control deficiency, the auditor should

a. Compare the tolerable error rate with the expected error rate.

b. Compute an upper precision limit and compare with the tolerable error.

c. Evaluate the dollar amount of the 4 time cards in relation to the financial statements.

d. Report the errors and let management assess the significance because they are in the best position to know.

**43.** Each time an internal auditor draws a conclusion based on evidence drawn from a sample, an additional risk—sampling risk—is introduced. An example of sampling risk is

a. Projecting the results of sampling beyond the population tested.

b. Using an improper audit procedure with a sample.

c. Incorrectly applying an audit procedure to sample data.

d. Drawing an erroneous conclusion from sample data.

**44.** A confidence level of 90% means that

a. The expected error rate is equal to 10%.

b. The point estimate obtained is within 10% of the true population value.

c. There are 90 chances out of 100 that the sample results will not vary from the true characteristics of the population by more than a specified amount.

d. A larger sample size is required than if the desired confidence level were equal to 95%.

**45.** Internal auditing is conducting an operational audit of the organization's mailroom activities to determine whether the use of express mail service is limited to cases of necessity. To test cost-effectiveness, the auditor selects the 100 most recent express-mail transactions for review. A major limitation of such a sampling technique is that it

a. Does not allow a statistical generalization about all express-mail transactions.

b. Results in a sample size that is too small to project to the population.

c. Does not evaluate existing controls in this area.

d. Does not describe the population from which it was drawn.

**46.** The supervisor of claims-processing department for a health insurance firm selects all claims processed in the past two days by a particular employee for audit. From this sample, the supervisor can develop

a. An overall representative view of employee work for the year.

b. A quantification of sampling error.

c. Conclusions about the correctness of processing for the department.

d. Understanding of the details contained in the processing task.

**47.** To audit invoices paid over the past year, an auditor selects the two busiest months, which account for 60% of invoices. Following a random start, every tenth invoice is chosen yielding a sample of 116 invoices. This sample may not be valid because it is not a

a. Representative sample.

b. Random sample.

c. Large enough sample.

d. None of the above—sample is valid.

**48.** A sample of 100 items was taken from a population of 5,000 items. The mean value was $200 and the standard deviation was $30. The computed confidence interval for a 95% confidence level (Z=1.96) is

a. $970,600 to $1,029,400.

b.   $706,000 to $1,294,000.
c.   $996,733 to $1,003,267.
d.   $997,060 to $1,002,940.

**49.**  The probability that an estimate based on a random sample falls within a specified range is known as the
a.   Error rate.
b.   Lower precision limit.
c.   Confidence level.
d.   Standard error of the mean.

**50.**  The range into which an estimate of a population characteristic is expected to fall at a stated confidence level is known as the
a.   Precision.
b.   Measure of central tendency.
c.   Standard deviation.
d.   Sampling field.

**51.**  One measure of the variability within a sample is the
a.   Median.
b.   Standard error of the mean.
c.   Upper precision limit.
d.   Mean.

**52.**  An internal auditor suspects that the invoices from a small number of vendors contain serious errors and therefore limits the sample to only those vendors. A major disadvantage of selecting such a directed sample of items to examine is the
a.   Difficulty in obtaining sample items.
b.   Inability to quantify the sampling error related to the total population of vendor invoices.
c.   Absence of a normal distribution.
d.   Tendency to sample a greater number of units.

**53.**  An electronics manufacturer is planning to purchase a large quantity of computer chips, which are available at a bargain price. However, before doing so, it would like to know whether these chips are of sufficient quality. To determine the number of chips to be tested in order to estimate the quality of these computer chips, the manufacturer should use
a.   Linear programming.
b.   Regression analysis.
c.   Queuing theory.
d.   Statistical sampling.

**54.**  The fundamental difference between judgmental sampling and statistical sampling techniques is that
a.   A nonrandom sample will be more representative of the population than a sample chosen by statistical sampling.
b.   Statistical sampling results in smaller sample sizes than judgmental sampling.
c.   Judgmental sampling does not permit sampling risk to be measured.
d.   Statistical sampling results in more accurate point estimates of the parameters than judgmental sampling.

**55.**  An auditor wishes to obtain substantive evidence concerning a division's accounts receivable balances. The receivables are of four types.

| Type | Number of accounts | Balance per book |
|---|---|---|
| Retail | 3,800 | $1,500,000 |
| Commercial | 875 | 6,700,000 |
| Government agencies | 34 | 900,000 |
| Miscellaneous receivables | 900 | 375,000 |

In which of the following instances would the auditor be precluded from using statistical inferences?
a.   The auditor randomly selects 100 commercial accounts for confirmations.
b.   The auditor sends confirmations to 30 of the miscellaneous receivables customers.  From a serial number of a dollar bill, the auditor takes the first two digits falling between 1 and 30 to determine the starting point and selects every 30th account to send confirmations.
c.   In examining the retail accounts, the auditor decides to confirm all accounts with a balance in excess of $2,000. This results in the selection of 87 accounts. The auditor, using simple random sampling, selects additional 23 accounts with balances less than $2,000 for confirmation.
d.   For the accounts with governmental agencies, the auditor decides not to send confirmations but to trace the accounts to subsequent cash collections. The auditor then selects the five largest accounts and from each selected account takes the first purchase transaction at least 60 days old to trace to subsequent collections.

**56.**  Sampling risk refers to the possibility that
a.   The auditor may use a less than optimal statistical method for the circumstances, for example, difference estimation instead of ratio estimation.
b.   The auditor may fail to recognize an error that is included in the sample.
c.   Even though a sample is properly chosen, it may not be representative of the population.
d.   The confidence level and/or precision established by the auditor are not appropriate.

**57.**  An advantage of statistical over nonstatistical sampling is that statistical sampling
a.   Enables auditors to objectively measure the reliability of their sample results.
b.   Permits use of a smaller sample size than would be necessary with nonstatistical sampling.
c.   Is compatible with a wider variety of sample selection methods than is nonstatistical sampling.
d.   Allows auditors to inject their subjective judgment in determining sample size and selection process in order to audit items of greatest value and highest risk.

**58.**  An auditor is checking the accuracy of a computer-printed inventory listing to determine whether the total dollar value of inventory is significantly overstated. Because there is no time or resources to check all items in the warehouse, a sample of inventory items must be used. If the sample size were fixed, which one of the following would be the **most accurate** sampling approach in this case?
a.   Select those items that are most easily inspected.
b.   Employ simple random sampling.
c.   Sample so that the probability of a given inventory item being selected is proportional to the number of units sold for that item.
d.   Sample so that the probability of a given inventory item being selected is proportional to its book value.

**59.**  A distinguishing characteristic of random number sample selection is that each

a. Item is selected from a stratum having minimum variability.
b. Item's chance for selection is proportional to its dollar value.
c. Item in the population has an equal chance of being selected.
d. Stratum in the population has an equal number of items selected.

**60.** Which one of the following statements is true regarding two random samples drawn in the same way from the same population, one of size 30 and one of size 300?
a. The two samples would have the same expected value.
b. The larger sample is more likely to produce a large sample mean.
c. The smaller sample will have a smaller 95% confidence interval for the mean.
d. The smaller sample will, on the average, produce a lower estimate of the variance of the population.

**61.** An auditor is conducting a survey of perceptions and beliefs of employees concerning an organization health care plan. The **best** approach to selecting a sample would be to
a. Focus on people who are likely to respond so that a larger sample can be obtained.
b. Focus on managers and supervisors because they can also reflect the opinions of the people in their departments.
c. Use stratified sampling where the strata are defined by marital and family status, age, and salaried/ hourly status.
d. Use monetary unit sampling according to employee salaries.

**62.** An internal auditor uses a number of techniques to select samples. A frequently, and appropriately, used technique is random selection. In which of the following situations would random selection be **least** justified? The auditor needs to
a. Test sales transactions to determine that they were properly authorized and are supported by shipping documents.
b. Confirm accounts receivable and has already selected the 10 largest accounts for confirmation. The remaining accounts are not numbered. The auditor only has a computer listing of the accounts in alphabetical order approximately 250 pages long with 50 account balances on every page.
c. Obtain evidence on the proper sales cutoff by sampling items from the monthly sales journal to determine if the items were recorded in the correct time period.
d. Test the perpetual inventory records to ensure that the sample covers the largest dollar value items in the account.

**63.** Systematic selection can be expected to produce a representative when
a. Random number tables are used to determine the items included in the sample.
b. The population is arranged randomly with respect to the audit objective.
c. The sample is determined using multiple random starts and includes more items than required.
d. Judgmental sampling is used by the auditor to offset any sampling bias.

**64.** An internal auditor used regression analysis to evaluate the relationship between utility costs and machine hours. The following information was developed using a computer software program:

| | |
|---|---|
| Intercept | 2,050 |
| Regression coefficient | .825 |
| Correlation coefficient | .800 |
| Standard error of the estimate | 200 |
| Number of observations | 36 |

What is the expected utility cost if the company's 10 machines will be used 2,400 hours next month?
a. $4,050
b. $4,030
c. $3,970
d. $3,930

**65.** An internal auditor wants to select a statistically representative sample from a population of 475 inventory control sheets. Each sheet lists the description, physical count, bar code, and unit cost for 50 inventory items. The auditor uses a random number table to construct the sample; the first two columns are listed below. The randomly chosen starting point is 14326; the sample's first item is found on page 143, line 26. (The route used by the auditor is down Column A to the top of Column B.)

| Column A | Column B |
|---|---|
| 75233 | 06852 |
| 14326 | 42904 |
| 76562 | 64854 |
| 28123 | 04978 |
| 64227 | 33150 |
| 80938 | 04301 |
| 22539 | 41240 |
| 29452 | 69521 |

Where is the fifth item in the sample located?
a. Page 809, line 38.
b. Page 429, line 04.
c. Page 331, line 50.
d. Page 068, line 52.

**66.** The most appropriate methodology for drawing a sample from 3,000 time cards to check for signatures would be
a. Interval sampling.
b. Cluster sampling.
c. Stratified sampling.
d. Variables sampling.

**67.** A car rental agency has branches located throughout the world that are essentially small-scale representations of the entire population. What is the appropriate sampling method for determining the average net revenue per vehicle in inventory?
a. Stratified sampling.
b. Cluster sampling.
c. Attributes sampling.
d. Systematic sampling.

**68.** In obtaining a sample for the purpose of reaching a conclusion about the population from which it is drawn, the internal auditor
a. Can statistically quantify the sample results only if the sample was selected in such a way that each population item has an equal or known probability of selection.
b. Should use judgmental sampling and concentrate on high-risk items.

c.   Cannot use random sampling procedures unless the items to be sampled are available in machine-readable form.

d.   Will usually use random sampling with replacement.

**69.**  An auditor wishes to sample 200 sales receipts from a population of 5,000 receipts issued during the last year. The receipts have preprinted serial numbers and are arranged in chronological (and thus serial number) order. The auditor randomly chooses a receipt from the first 25 receipts and then selects every 25th receipt thereafter. The sampling procedure described here is called

a.   Systematic random sampling.
b.   Dollar-unit sampling.
c.   Judgmental interval sampling.
d.   Variables sampling

**70.**  In a regional survey of suburban households to obtain data on television viewing habits, a statistical sample of suburban areas is first selected. Within the chosen areas, statistical samples of whole blocks are selected, and within the selected blocks, random samples of households are selected. This type of sample selection can best be described as

a.   Attributes sampling.
b.   Stratified sampling.
c.   Cluster sampling.
d.   Interval sampling.

**71.**  An internal auditor with an international shipping company needs to sample shipping records over the past six months. To do so, the auditor draws a random sample for ships operating in the Mediterranean and a separate sample for those operating in the North Atlantic. This method of sampling is called

a.   Cluster sampling.
b.   Haphazard.
c.   Interval sampling.
d.   Stratified sampling.

**72.**  A sample from a population of over 10,000 bills of lading is needed to estimate an error rate. Since a sample size of 250 will satisfy precision and confidence level needs, a sampling interval of 40 is chosen. For ease of implementation, the auditor randomly selects a number between 1 and 40, and then selects each succeeding 40th item. Which of the following is true?

a.   The sample lacks randomness and will not be correct.
b.   Interval sampling is not an acceptable statistical method.
c.   If the population lacks bias, the sample is statistically valid.
d.   Interval sampling eliminates the use of auditor judgment.

**73.**  An inventory listing consisting of approximately 2,050 unnumbered items is arranged by category, with 10 items in each category. Within each category, the most expensive (per unit) items are listed first. An auditor wishes to use an interval-sampling plan to select a representative sample of at least 100 items from this population. The best technique is to

a.   Select a random number from 1 to 20 as the starting point and then select every 20th item, moving through the entire population.

b.   Select a random number from 1 to 15 as the starting point and then select every 15th item until he has 100 items.

c.   Select 7 random digits from 1 to 135 as the starting points and then select every 135th item per pass, moving through the entire population 7 times.

d.   Select the 50 largest items (i.e., extensions with the highest dollar amounts); then, excluding the 50 largest items already selected, select a random number from 1 to 37 as the starting point and select every 37th item, moving through the entire population.

**Items 74 and 75** are based on the following:

You are to audit the timeliness of the payment of vendor invoices based on a representative sample of checks written. The sample population consists of a total of 967 consecutively numbered checks that have been issued for accounts payable.

**74.**  The most appropriate method for drawing a sample of checks is

a.   Cluster sampling.
b.   Interval sampling.
c.   Simple random sampling.
d.   Stratified sampling.

**75.**  If you know that 40% of the checks were issued to a single vendor who offered unusually large cash discounts, the most appropriate method of sampling would be

a.   Cluster sampling.
b.   Interval sampling.
c.   Simple random sampling.
d.   Stratified sampling.

**76.**  An auditor using statistical sampling wishes to select a sample from an aged trial balance of 750 accounts receivable. There are no account numbers; the accounts are listed in alphabetical order by customer name. Account balances range from $50 to $10,000. Which of the following selection schemes is most likely to produce a random sample of 75 items? (In choices a. and b., you are to assume that the digit "3" was appropriately chosen from a random number table.)

a.   Select all accounts in which the fourth digit to the left of the decimal point in the account balance (i.e. the thousands digit) is a "3."

b.   Select the 3rd account, then the 13th, 23rd, and so on, on through the 743rd.

c.   Select the 75 accounts with the largest total balances.

d.   Select the 50 accounts with the largest total balances plus the 25 accounts (other than those included in the first 50) with the largest past due balances.

**77.**  To use stratified variables sampling to evaluate a large, heterogeneous inventory, an appropriate criterion for classifying inventory items into strata is

a.   Dollar values.
b.   Number of items.
c.   Turnover volume.
d.   Storage locations.

**78.**  Which of the following would **not** be appropriate if the auditor expects a built-in pattern in the population?

a.   Dollar-unit sampling.
b.   Systematic sampling with multiple random starts.
c.   Cluster sampling.

d.   Stratifying the population in anticipation of the pattern.

**79.**   An auditor designed an attribute sample to test the effectiveness of a control procedure. The auditor designed the sample to achieve an upper precision limit of 4% at a confidence level of 95% with a 1% expected error rate. Based on those factors, the auditor selected 156 items and found three errors. The auditor can conclude that there is

a.   At least a 95% chance that the error rate in the population exceeds 4%.
b.   At least a 95% chance that the error rate in the population is less than 4%.
c.   Less than a 95% chance that the error rate in the population is less than 4%.
d.   More than a 95% chance that the error rate in the population exceeds 1%.

**80.**   Which of the following must be known to evaluate the results of an attributes sample?

a.   Estimated dollar value of the population.
b.   Standard deviation of the sample values.
c.   Actual size of the sample selected.
d.   Finite population correction factor.

**81.**   In evaluating an attribute sample, the range within which the estimate of the population characteristic is expected to fall is called the

a.   Confidence level.
b.   Precision.
c.   Upper error limit.
d.   Expected error rate.

**82.**   An auditor wishes to determine if the error rate on travel reimbursement claims is within the 5% tolerance level set by management. What sampling plan should the auditor use?

a.   Variable sampling.
b.   Attributes sampling.
c.   Judgmental sampling.
d.   Dollar-unit sampling.

**83.**   A bank internal auditor wishes to determine if loans that were not funded were rejected using criteria consistent with that contained in bank policies. A lending officer initially processes all loan requests. Those that the officer deems appropriate to be funded are forwarded to the lending committee for its approval. The **most** efficient audit procedure to address this objective would be to

a.   Select an attribute sample of loans not funded and review the loan applications and the reasons for rejecting them.
b.   Select an attribute sample of loans that were funded, review the loan applications, and determine if the funded loans complied with bank policies.
c.   Take a sample of all loan applications, review the applications, and trace them to either a funded or rejected loan to determine if all actions taken were consistent with bank policies.
d.   Take a sample of loans presented to the lending committee for approval and determine if committee actions taken were consistent with bank policies.

**84.**   An auditor has taken an attribute sample of a bank's existing loan portfolio. Out of a sample of sixty loans, the auditor finds

• Four that were not properly collateralized,

• Five that are not in compliance with bank policies (other than lack of collateralization), and
• Four that were part of a related-party group, but were set up as separate loan entities.

Of the sixty loans selected in the sample, these errors were noted on a total of ten loans. Several loans had multiple problems. Which of the following conclusions can the auditor reach from these findings?

I.   There is sufficient evidence that fraudulent activity is taking place by one or more of the bank's lending officers.
II.   The financial statements will be misstated as a result of these actions.
III.   There are significant noncompliance audit findings that should be reported.

a.   I and II.
b.   I and III.
c.   II and III.
d.   III only.

**85.**   In selecting a sample of items for attributes testing, an auditor must consider the confidence level factor, the desired precision, and the

a.   Recorded dollar value of the population.
b.   Sampling interval.
c.   Expected occurrence rate.
d.   Standard deviation in the population.

**86.**   An auditor is planning to use attributes sampling to test the effectiveness of a specific internal control related to approvals for cash disbursements. In attributes sampling, decreasing the estimated occurrence rate from 5% to 4% while keeping all other sample size planning factors exactly the same would result in a revised sample size which would be

a.   Larger.
b.   Smaller.
c.   Unchanged.
d.   Indeterminate.

**87.**   If all other sample size planning factors were exactly the same in attributes sampling, changing the confidence level from 95% to 90% and changing the desired precision from 2% to 5% would result in a revised sample size which would be

a.   Larger.
b.   Smaller.
c.   Unchanged.
d.   Indeterminate.

**88.**   Which of the following must be known to evaluate the results of an attribute sample?

a.   Estimated dollar value of the population.
b.   Standard deviation of the sample values.
c.   Actual size of the sample selected.
d.   Finite population correction factor.

**89.**   An auditor has to make a number of decisions when using attribute sampling. The term "efficiency" is used to describe anything that affects sample size. The term "effectiveness" is used to describe the likelihood that the statistical sample result will be a more accurate estimate of the true population error rate. Assume an auditor expects a control procedure failure rate of 0.5%. The auditor is making a decision on whether to use a 90% or a 95% confidence level and whether to set the tolerable control failure rate at 3% or 4%.

Which of the following statements regarding efficiency and effectiveness of an attribute sample is **true**?
- a. Decreasing the confidence level to 90% and decreasing the tolerable control failure rate to 3% will result in both increased efficiency and effectiveness.
- b. Decreasing the tolerable failure rate from 4% to 3% will increase audit efficiency.
- c. Increasing the confidence level to 95% and decreasing the tolerable control failure rate to 3% will increase audit effectiveness.
- d. Increasing the confidence level to 95% will increase audit efficiency.

**Items 90 through 92** are based on the following:

An auditor is testing on a company's large, normally distributed accounts receivable file. The objectives of the audit are to test end-of-period dollar balances and accounts receivable posting exception (error) rates.

**90.** The expected population exception rate is 3% for the accounts receivable posting processes. If the auditor has established a 5% tolerable rate, the auditor would use which sampling plan for testing the actual exception rate?
- a. Difference or mean per unit estimation.
- b. Discovery.
- c. Stratified.
- d. Attribute.

**91.** To test the accounts receivable file to compute an estimated dollar total, the auditor could use any one of the following sampling techniques except:
- a. Difference or ratio estimation.
- b. Unstratified mean-per-unit estimation.
- c. Probability proportional to size.
- d. Attribute.

**92.** The accounts receivable file contains a large number of small dollar balances and a small number of large dollar balances and the auditor expects to find numerous errors in the account balances. The most appropriate sampling technique to estimate the dollar amount of errors would be
- a. Difference or ratio estimation.
- b. Unstratified mean-per-unit.
- c. Probability proportional to size.
- d. Attribute.

**93.** An internal auditor planning an attribute sample from a large number of invoices must estimate the tolerable error. Which factor below is the most important for the auditor to consider?
- a. Audit objective.
- b. Population size.
- c. Desired confidence level.
- d. Population variance.

**94.** To use stratified sampling to evaluate a large, heterogeneous inventory, which of the following would **least** likely be used as criteria to classify inventory items into strata?
- a. Dollar values.
- b. Number of items.
- c. Turnover volume.
- d. Storage locations.

**95.** Using company policies to establish when approval is needed, an auditor has sampled accounts receivable balances exceeding $1,000 to determine whether the credit department is requiring a credit check for credit sales when appropriate. This is an example of
- a. Dollar-unit sampling.
- b. Mean-per-unit sampling.
- c. Attributes sampling.
- d. Variables sampling.

**96.** An audit of accounts payable was made to determine if the error rate was within the stated policy of 0.5%. One hundred of the 10,000 accounts payable transactions were randomly selected using a 95% confidence level. No errors were found. With 95% certainty, one can conclude that the sample results
- a. Indicate another sample is needed.
- b. Prove there are no errors in accounts payable.
- c. Indicate the null hypothesis is false.
- d. Fail to prove the error rate is above 0.5%.

**97.** What is the chief advantage of stop-or-go sampling?
- a. The error rate in the population can be projected to within certain precision limits.
- b. It may reduce the size of the sample that needs to be taken from a population, thus reducing sampling costs.
- c. It allows sampling analysis to be performed on populations that are not homogeneous.
- d. It allows the sampler to increase the confidence limits of his analysis without sacrificing precision.

**98.** A statistical sampling technique which will minimize sample size whenever a low rate of noncompliance is expected is called
- a. Ratio-estimation sampling.
- b. Difference-estimation sampling.
- c. Stratified mean-per-unit sampling.
- d. Stop-or-go sampling.

**99.** In order to estimate the value of 2,500 accounts receivable outstanding, the best sampling method would be
- a. Variables estimation.
- b. Stop-and-go sampling.
- c. Cluster sampling.
- d. Attributes estimation.

**100.** In selecting a sample of items for variables testing, an auditor must consider the desired precision, the standard deviation, and the
- a. Recorded dollar value of the population.
- b. Acceptable risk level.
- c. Expected occurrence rate.
- d. Sampling interval.

**101.** In a variable-sampling application, if the achieved dollar precision range of the statistical sample at a given confidence level is greater than the desired dollar precision range, this is an indication that the
- a. Occurrence rate was smaller than expected.
- b. Occurrence rate was greater than expected.
- c. Standard deviation was less than expected.
- d. Standard deviation was greater than expected.

**102.** In a variables-sampling application, which of the following factors will vary directly with a change in confidence level from 90 to 95%?
- a. Standard error of the mean.
- b. Nonsampling error.

c. Achieved precision.

d. Point estimate of the arithmetic mean.

**103.** In determining the sample size for variables sampling, the internal auditor requires some knowledge of the variability of the population. In obtaining this preliminary information the internal auditor

a. Can seldom rely on the results of prior years' sample results since they pertain only to the prior years' populations.

b. Frequently takes a convenience pilot sample of 30 to 50 items and use this to estimate the variability of the population.

c. Frequently takes a random pilot sample of 30 to 50 items, applies audit tests to these items, and uses the variability in these items to estimate the variability in the population of audit values. The pilot sample is then discarded and the real sample is taken from the remaining population.

d. Will frequently take a random pilot sample of 30 to 50 items, compute the range in this sample, and use this range as an estimate of the population variability for purposes of computing sample size.

**104.** An internal auditor wishes to estimate the number of units in a certain class of inventory without counting each one. Which of the following sample plans would be appropriate?

a. Attributes.

b. Discovery.

c. Stop-or-go.

d. Variables.

**105.** Ratio estimation sampling would be **inappropriate** to use to project the dollar error in a population if

a. The recorded book values and audited values are approximately proportional.

b. A number of observed differences exist between book values and audited values.

c. Observed differences between book values and audited values are proportional to book values.

d. Subsidiary ledger book balances for some inventory items are unknown.

**106.** The auditor wishes to sample the perpetual inventory records to develop an estimate of the dollar amount of misstatement, if any, in the account balance. The account balance is made up of a large number of small value items and a small number of large value items. The auditor has decided to audit all items over $50,000 plus a random selection of others. This audit decision is made because the auditor expects to find a large amount of errors in the perpetual inventory records, but is not sure that it will be enough to justify taking a complete physical inventory. The auditor expects the errors to vary directly with the value recorded in the perpetual records. The most efficient sampling procedure to accomplish the auditor's objectives would be

a. Dollar-unit sampling.

b. Ratio estimation.

c. Attribute sampling.

d. Stratified mean-per-unit sampling.

**107.** Difference estimation sampling would be appropriate to use to project the dollar error in a population if

a. Subsidiary ledger book balances for some individual inventory items are unknown.

b. Virtually no differences between the individual book values and the audited values exist.

c. A number of nonproportional differences between book values and audited values exist.

d. Observed differences between book values and audited values are proportional to book values.

**108.** An internal auditor is interested in the processing accuracy of a sales invoice preparation system. The monetary amount of individual invoices is highly variable. The internal auditor has sound reasons for believing that the error rate in invoice processing is between 3% and 10% but has no idea of the monetary magnitude of the errors. In evaluating which specific approach to variables sampling to employ, the internal auditor should be aware that

a. Since the error magnitude is uncertain, a stratified mean per unit estimator will perform poorly in this case.

b. With error rates in this range, there is little advantage to stratifying the population.

c. Either a difference estimator or a ratio estimator will be more efficient than an unstratified mean per unit estimator in this case.

d. Neither a difference or ratio estimator is practical in this case unless an audit value and a book value exist for each item in the population.

**109.** An auditor randomly selects 100 items of finished goods perpetual inventory, physically counts them, and computes an "audited value" for each (calculated as quantity times unit cost per production reports). The internal auditor then compares the audited value with the "book value" (inventory cost per perpetual inventory records) and uses difference estimation to estimate the correct total for the finished goods inventory. Results of the 100-item sample are as follows:

| | |
|---|---|
| Total audited value | $605,000 |
| Total book value (of these 100 items) | $630,000 |
| Number of items incorrectly stated (out of 100) | 17 |

The total book value of the entire finished goods inventory (1,100 items) is $6,988,000. On the basis of difference estimation, the auditor's best guess (point estimate) as to the correct total is

a. $6,655,000

b. $6,713,000

c. $6,963,000

d. $7,263,000

**Items 110 through 113** are based on the following:

Using mean-per-unit sampling to estimate the value of inventory, an auditor had the following results:

| | |
|---|---|
| Projected inventory value | $3,000,000 |
| Confidence level | 95% |
| Confidence interval | $2,800,000 to $3,200,000 |
| Standard error | $100,000 |
| (Standard error = standard deviation/ square root of sample size) | |
| Z value (approximately) | 2.0 |
| Precision | $200,000 |

The recorded value of inventory was $3,075,000.

**110.** Which of the following is a logical conclusion from the sample?

a. There is a 95% chance that the misstatement of inventory is less than $100,000.

b.   There is a 5% chance that $200,000 or more mis-
     states the inventory amount.
c.   Inventory is materially misstated.
d.   There is a 2.5% chance that the inventory amount is
     greater than $3,200,000.

**111.**  Which of the following changes would result in a narrower confidence interval?
a.   An increase in the confidence level from 95 to 99%.
b.   A decrease in the confidence level from 95 to 90%.
c.   A decrease in the allowable risk of incorrect accep-
     tance.
d.   An increase in the precision.

**112.**  The standard error of $100,000 reflects
a.   The projected population error based on errors in the
     sample.
b.   The average rate of error in the sample.
c.   The degree of variation in the dollar amount of sam-
     ple items.
d.   The error in the population that the auditor can ac-
     cept.

**113.**  If the auditor had used nonstatistical sampling instead of
statistical sampling, which of the following would be true?
a.   The confidence level could not be quantified.
b.   The precision would be larger.
c.   The projected value of inventory would be less reli-
     able.
d.   The risk of incorrect acceptance would be higher.

**114.**  The auditor is performing a test to determine whether
the gas and electric appliance company should move its service center from one location to another. The service center
houses the service trucks that are used to drive to the customers' locations to service their appliances. The auditor wants to
determine the reduction in average miles driven as a result of
moving to the other location. Which of the following statistical sampling methods would be most appropriate for this test?
a.   Attribute sampling.
b.   Discovery sampling.
c.   Probability proportional to size (dollar-unit) sam-
     pling.
d.   Mean-per-unit sampling.

**115.**  An auditor is designing stratified, mean-per-unit variables sampling plan. To which one of the following strata
should the auditor allocate the largest proportion of the overall
sample size?

|    | Number of items | Expected mean | Expected standard deviation | Total dollar value |
|----|-----------------|---------------|-----------------------------|--------------------|
| a. | 2,000           | $100          | $9                          | $200,000           |
| b. | 2,250           | $200          | $4                          | $450,000           |
| c. | 3,000           | $80           | $2                          | $240,000           |
| d. | 3,100           | $150          | $1                          | $465,000           |

**Items 116 through 118** are based on the following:

An internal auditor has obtained the following data by
selecting a random sample from an inventory population.

|            | Number of items | Audited value | Book value   |
|------------|-----------------|---------------|--------------|
| Sample     | 200             | $220,000      | $ 200,000    |
| Population | 5,000           |               | $5,200,000   |

**116.**  The estimate of the population dollar value using mean-
per-unit sampling would be
a.   $5,000,000
b.   $5,420,000
c.   $5,500,000
d.   $5,720,000

**117.**  The estimate of the population dollar value using difference estimation sampling would be
a.   $4,700,000
b.   $5,500,000
c.   $5,680,000
d.   $5,700,000

**118.**  The estimate of the population dollar value using ratio
estimation would be
a.   $4,727,273
b.   $5,500,000
c.   $5,700,000
d.   $5,720,000

**119.**  The internal auditor for an insurance company is conducting an audit of claims processing and wants to assess the
average length of time that it takes to process automobile
claims to determine whether processing is being completed
within standards set by company policy.
    The auditor plans to take a sample of claims made during
the year and perform the needed analysis. The most appropriate sampling method would be
a.   Mean-per-unit variables sampling.
b.   Probability proportion to size.
c.   Attribute sampling.
d.   Discovery sampling.

**120.**  What effect does an increase in the standard deviation
have on the required sample size of mean-per-unit estimation
and probability pro-portion to size sampling? Assume no
change in any of the other characteristics of the population
and no change in desired precision and confidence.

|    | Mean-per-unit             | Probability proportional to size (PPS) |
|----|---------------------------|----------------------------------------|
| a. | Increase in sample size   | Increase in sample size                |
| b. | No change in sample size  | Decrease in sample size                |
| c. | Increase in sample size   | No change in sample size               |
| d. | Decrease in sample size   | No change in sample size               |

**121.**  By statistically projecting the population value based on
the average value of sampled subsidiary accounts, the auditor
has estimated the value of the total equipment account to be
$2,800,000. This is an example of
a.   Dollar-unit sampling.
b.   Mean-per-unit sampling.
c.   Attributes sampling.
d.   Statistical difference estimation.

**122.**  An audit of a wholesale company's inventory was conducted to estimate its value. The inventory contained 20,000
items with a book value of $1 million. The audit plan was to
estimate inventory value with a precision of plus or minus 2%
at a 90% confidence level. The sample results were

Sample Size: 300
Sample Mean per unit: $52
Sample Standard Deviation per unit: $10.80
Sample Precision per unit: $1.03

Based on the sample results, the estimated inventory value is between
- a. $784,000 and $1,216,000.
- b. $844,000 and $1,256,000.
- c. $1,019,400 and $1,060,600.
- d. $979,400 and $1,020,600.

**123.** An auditor is using the mean-per-unit method of variables sampling to estimate the correct total value of a group of inventory items. Based on the sample, the auditor estimates, with a precision of plus or minus 4% and confidence of 90%, that the correct total is $800,000. This means that
- a. There is a 4% chance that the actual correct total is less than $720,000 or more than $880,000.
- b. There is a 10% chance that the actual correct total is less than $768,000 or more than $832,000.
- c. The probability that the inventory is not significantly overstated is between 6% and 14%.
- d. The inventory is not likely to be overstated by more than 4.4% ($35,200) or understated by more than 3.6% ($28,800).

**124.** What effect does an increase in the standard deviation have on the required sample size of mean-per-unit estimation and dollar-unit sampling? Assume no change in any of the other characteristics of the population and no change in desired precision and confidence.

| | Mean-per-unit estimation | Dollar-unit sampling |
|---|---|---|
| a. | Decrease in sample size | No change in sample size |
| b. | No change in sample size | Decrease in sample size |
| c. | Increase in sample size | No change in sample size |
| d. | No change in sample size | Increase in sample size |

**125.** An auditor applied dollar-unit sampling to select a sample of costs charged by a contractor. The sample design and results were as follows:

| | |
|---|---|
| Contract costs charged | $10,000,000 |
| Number of invoices in population | 2,000 |
| Tolerable error | 1% |
| Confidence level | 95% |
| Reliability factor | 3.0 |
| Sampling interval | $33,333 |
| Sample size | 300 |
| Expected error | None |
| Detected error | None |

Which of the following is **true** about this sample?
- a. The probability of selecting any particular invoice is 15% (300/2000).
- b. There is a 1% chance that the contract invoices contain significant errors.
- c. The sampling risk is acceptable if errors do not exceed $33,333.
- d. There is a 95% chance that the costs are not overstated more than $100,000 (1% of $10,000,000).

**126.** In which of the following situations would monetary-unit sampling be **more** effective and efficient than ratio estimation?
- a. The population contains a large number of differences between the recorded amount and the actual amount.
- b. The population is expected to contain few differences between the recorded amount and the actual amount.

- c. The population has a high degree of variability in dollar amount.
- d. The population has a low degree of variability in dollar amount.

**127.** An auditor is using dollar-unit sampling with a fixed interval to test an account with a balance of $750,000. Sample size is 50. The auditor started the selection process with a random start of 04719. Which of the following items would be the **third** sample item selected?

| | Invoice amount | Cumulative amount |
|---|---|---|
| a. | $ 7,985 | $31,374 |
| b. | $ 4,108 | $35,482 |
| c. | $12,305 | $47,787 |
| d. | $ 456 | $48,243 |

**128.** Monetary-unit sampling is most useful when the internal auditor
- a. Is testing the accounts payable balance.
- b. Cannot cumulatively arrange the population items.
- c. Expects to find several material errors in the sample.
- d. Is concerned with overstatements.

**129.** The book value of a 3,000th item inventory is $3,000,000. An auditor specifies a maximum tolerable error of $60,000 and a 95% confidence level (reliability factor = 3.0). Assuming that no individual item in the population exceeds the monetary value of the interval, the expected sample size for monetary-unit sampling would be
- a. Less than 70.
- b. From 70 to 140.
- c. From 140 to 160.
- d. Greater than 160.

**130.** An auditor is planning to use monetary-unit sampling for testing the dollar value of a large accounts receivable population. The advantages of using monetary-unit sampling include all of the following **except:**
- a. It is an efficient model for establishing that a low error rate population is not materially misstated.
- b. It does not require the normal distribution approximation required by variable sampling.
- c. It can be applied to a group of accounts, since the sampling units are homogenous.
- d. It results in a smaller sample size than that required when using classical sampling, as errors increase.

**131.** Which of the following factors would most likely preclude the auditor from using monetary unit sampling?
- a. The auditor expects to find a limited number of understatements of individual account balances.
- b. The auditor expects to find that a large percentage of items sampled have misstatements.
- c. Individual accounts are not assigned a number, but are listed only alphabetically.
- d. The auditor expects to find more errors in the larger dollar value items than in the smaller dollar value items.

**132.** Many firms are beginning to use the statistical processing control techniques as part of their total quality management approach. Which of the following would **not** constitute a part of statistical processing control techniques?
- a. Acceptance sampling.
- b. Dollar-unit sampling.

c. Quality control charts.
d. Continuous monitoring and feedback.

**133.** Dollar-unit sampling is not efficient if
a. Computerized account balances are being audited.
b. Statistical inferences are to be made.
c. The audit objective is oriented to understatements.
d. The account contains a large number of transactions.

**134.** An internal auditor is considering the use of dollar-unit (probability-proportional-to-size, PPS) sampling. This technique is likely to be especially beneficial if
a. The auditor is interested in testing the proper valuation of accounts payable.
b. The auditor believes that the items to be tested are just as likely to be overstated as understated.
c. The auditor is interested in testing the accuracy and valuation of accounts receivable.
d. The error rate in the population is believed to be quite large.

**135.** A sampling plan is needed to test for overstatement of a $3 million accounts payable book balance. The auditor determines that a $100,000 error is material and a 95% confidence level is appropriate. Based on these determinations, the sample of size 90 is needed. The sampling plan **most** likely used is
a. Stop and go.
b. Cluster sampling.
c. Dollar-unit sampling.
d. Attributes sampling.

**136.** An internal auditor is preparing to sample accounts receivable for overstatement. A statistical sampling method that automatically provides stratification when using systematic selection is
a. Attributes sampling.
b. Ratio-estimation sampling.
c. Dollar-unit sampling.
d. Mean-per-unit sampling.

**137.** An auditor wishes to select a dollar-unit sample of 100 sales invoices that are included in receivables. Total receivables consist of 1,600 invoices, beginning with invoices number 1781, ranging in value from $25 to $3,000 and totaling $700,000. A partial list is

| Invoice No. | Amount | Cumulative amount |
|---|---|---|
| 1781 | $ 75 | $ 75 |
| 1790 | 1,400 | 1,475 |
| 1795 | 1,500 | 2,975 |
| . | . | . |
| . | . | . |
| . | . | . |
| 1804 | 1,470 | 8,450 |
| 1805 | 30 | 8,480 |

Assuming the 4-digit random number 1461 is selected as a starting point, the first two invoice numbers to be included in the sample are
a. 1790 and 1795.
b. 1790 and 1805.
c. 1795 and 1804.
d. 1795 and 1805.

**Data-Gathering Tools and Techniques**

Items 138 through 144 are based on the following:

Management of a property and casualty insurance company is concerned about the efficiency and effectiveness of the claims processing activities. It has two major concerns: (1) some claims are being paid that should not be paid or are being paid in amounts in excess of the policy; and (2) many claimants are not being paid on a timely basis. In preparing for an audit of the area, the internal auditor decides to perform a preliminary survey to gather more information about the nature of processing and potential problems.

**138.** Which of the following procedures would be the **least** effective in gathering information about the nature of the processing and potential problems?
a. Interview supervisors in the claims department to find out more about the procedures used and the rationale for the procedures, and obtain their observations about the nature and efficiency of processing.
b. Send an electronic mail message to all clerical personnel detailing the alleged problems and request them to respond.
c. Interview selected clerical employees in the claims department to find out more about the procedures used and the rationale for the procedures, and obtain their observations about the nature and efficiency of processing.
d. Distribute a questionnaire to gain a greater understanding of the responsibilities for claims processing and the control procedures utilized.

**139.** The auditor used a questionnaire during interviews to gather information about the nature of claims processing. Unfortunately, the questionnaire did not cover a number of pieces of information offered by the person being interviewed. Consequently, the auditor did not document the potential problems for further audit investigation. The primary deficiency with the above process is that
a. The auditor failed to consider the importance of the information offered.
b. The use of a questionnaire in a situation where a structured interview should have been used.
c. Questionnaires do not allow for opportunities to document other information.
d. All of the above.

**140.** A clerical employee approaches the auditor and indicates that she has important information about a collusion within her department to process fraudulent claims and split the proceeds among the members of a small group. She is willing to discuss the matter with the auditor, but wishes to remain anonymous. The auditor should
a. Request that the conversation be videotaped so that it will be available as evidence should fraud be found.
b. Reply that the matter must be reported to appropriate organizational officials for subsequent follow-up.
c. Document the information and use it to plan the audit. Change the nature of the audit from one of economy and efficiency to one of fraud.
d. Obtain the information and develop procedures that could corroborate the information.

**141.** The auditor conducted an interview with the supervisor. The auditor noted that the supervisor became uncomfortable and nervous and changed the subject whenever the auditor raised questions about certain types of claims. The supervisor's answers were consistent with company policies and procedures. When documenting the interview, the auditor should

- a. Document the supervisor's answers, noting the nature of the nonverbal communications.
- b. Not document the nonverbal communication because it is subjective and is not corroborated.
- c. Conclude that the nonverbal communication is persuasive and that sufficient evidence exists to charge fraud against the group.
- d. Ignore the specific answers given in the interview, because they are self-serving.

**142.** After informing management, the auditor is directed to go ahead with a fraud investigation. The auditor has identified the parties most likely to have been involved in the fraud, if indeed one is taking place. The auditor sends each potential participant a personal electronic mail message indicating the nature of the investigation and urges the individual to come forward and explain the nature of the fraud. The auditor states that this is strictly an audit investigation and legal authorities are not involved. A major problem with this particular communication is

- a. The medium. A paper-based document, such as a letter, should have been used instead of electronic mail message.
- b. The medium. Personal interviews should have been used instead of electronic mail.
- c. The nature of the communication. The auditor should have sent a questionnaire to each employee, rather than seeking an open-ended response.
- d. The nature of the message. The auditor should have detailed the specific allegations against each employee and allowed them the opportunity to respond. The message, as written, is too general.

**143.** After pursuing the investigation, two clerical employees corroborate the allegations and indicate that it was a plan developed by the supervisor and that they were put under pressure to go along with the scheme. The auditor decides to question the supervisor, who becomes very hostile in responding to the auditor's questions. The auditor should

- a. Indicate that if the supervisor will not cooperate, the auditor will turn the matter over to legal authorities for further investigation.
- b. Indicate this is not a fraud audit and that the purpose is to identify the nature of incorrectly processed transactions and the reason for the problems encountered. Emphasize that the supervisor's cooperation will be documented in the workpapers.
- c. Respond in a like manner and indicate the evidence the auditor has already obtained. Put pressure on the supervisor to confess to the fraud and to name others involved in the scheme.
- d. Describe the purpose of the interview and the nature of the evidence sought. Encourage the supervisor to continue the interview.

**144.** The supervisor has a change of heart and indicates the amount of fraud was less than $85,000 out of $85 million in claims processed, a clearly immaterial amount in the supervisor's opinion. The supervisor makes an offer to: (1) name all employees involved; (2) describe the circumvention of controls that allowed the fraud to take place; and (3) implement the necessary controls *if* the auditor would agree to describe

the situation as a control procedure breakdown and not report it to management as a fraud. The amounts represent less than 0.1 percent of the claims processed. Otherwise, the supervisor will not cooperate in the investigation, will order the others involved not to cooperate, and will engage legal counsel.

The auditor is already well over time budget and is intrigued by the opportunity to negotiate an end to the investigation and improve the control procedures. Which of the following would represent an appropriate response to the supervisor?

- I. Indicate the situation is open to negotiation, but that more details on the nature of the fraud would be needed and the supervisor would have to sign an agreement as to the compromise reached.
- II. Indicate that the auditor has no authority to negotiate.
- III. Indicate that if the supervisor wishes to negotiate, the matter must be first reported as a fraud and the negotiations would have to take place with management.

- a. I only.
- b. II only.
- c. III only.
- d. II and III only.

**Items 145 through 149** are based on the following:

An audit team has been assigned to review "the customer satisfaction measurement system" that the industrial products division implemented two years ago. This system consists of the division's customer service office conducting an annual mail survey. A survey is sent to 100 purchasing departments randomly selected from all customers who made purchases in the prior 12 months. The survey is three pages long and its 30 questions use a mixture of response modes (e.g., some questions are open-ended, some multiple choice, and others use a response scale). The customer service office mails the survey in September and tabulates the results for questionnaires returned by October 15. Only one mailing is sent. If the customer does not return the questionnaire, no follow-up is conducted. When the survey was last conducted, 45 of the questionnaires were not returned.

**145.** Nonresponse bias is often a concern in conducting mail surveys. The main reason that nonresponse bias can cause difficulties in a sample such as the one taken by the customer service office is that

- a. The sample means and standard errors are harder to compute.
- b. Those who did not respond may be systematically different from those who did.
- c. The questionnaire is too short.
- d. Confidence intervals are narrower.

**146.** One of the steps of the audit program is to review the quality of the questionnaire's design. Which of the following is a common error made in designing multiple-choice questions in a survey questionnaire?

- a. Unipolar rather than bipolar labels are used for the response categories.
- b. The alternative response categories for the questions are not mutually exclusive.
- c. Likert scaling is used instead of semantic differential scaling.
- d. The question itself uses terms that are very familiar to the respondent.

**147.** Which of the following is **not** an advantage of face-to-face interviews over mail surveys?
    a.   The response rate is typically higher.
    b.   Interviewers can increase a respondent's comprehension of questions.
    c.   Survey designers can use a wider variety of types of questions.
    d.   They are less expensive since mailing costs are avoided.

**148.** Many questionnaires are made up of a series of different questions that use the same response categories (e.g., strongly agree, agree, neither, disagree, strongly disagree). Some designs will have different groups of respondents answer alternative versions of the questionnaire that present the questions in different orders and reverse the orientation of the endpoints of the scale (e.g., agree on the right and disagree on the left or vice versa). The purpose of such questionnaire variations is to
    a.   Eliminate intentional misrepresentations.
    b.   Reduce the effects of pattern response tendencies.
    c.   Test whether respondents are reading the questionnaire.
    d.   Make it possible to get information about more than one population parameter using the same questions.

**149.** Several of the audit team members are concerned about the low response rate, the poor quality of the questionnaire design, and the potentially biased wording of some of the questions. They suggest that the customer service office might want to supplement the survey with some unobtrusive data collection, such as observing customer interactions in the office or collecting audiotapes of phone conversations with customers. Which of the following is **not** a potential advantage of unobtrusive data collection compared to surveys or interviews?
    a.   Interactions with customers can be observed as they occur in their natural setting.
    b.   It is easier to make precise measurements of the variables under study.
    c.   Unexpected or unusual events are more likely to be observed.
    d.   People are less likely to alter their behavior because they are being studied.

**150.** An audit team developed a preliminary questionnaire with the following response choices

  I. Probably not a problem.
 II. Possibly a problem.
III. Probably a problem.

The questionnaire illustrates the use of
    a.   Trend analysis.
    b.   Ratio analysis.
    c.   Unobtrusive measures or observations.
    d.   Rating scales.

**151.** An audit of the quality control department is being planned. Which of the following would **least** likely be used in the preparation of a preliminary survey questionnaire?
    a.   An analysis of quality control documents.
    b.   The permanent audit file.
    c.   The prior audit report.
    d.   Management's charter for the quality control department.

**152.** In advance of a preliminary survey, an audit director sends a memorandum and questionnaire to the supervisors of the department to be audited. What is the most likely result of that procedure?
    a.   It creates apprehension about the audit.
    b.   It involves the auditee's supervisory personnel in the audit.
    c.   It is an uneconomical approach to obtaining information.
    d.   It is only useful for audits of distant locations.

**Items 153 through 154** are based on the following:

Management answered "yes" to every question when filling out an internal control questionnaire and stated that all listed requirements and control activities were part of its procedures. An internal auditor retrieved this questionnaire from management during the preliminary survey visit but did not review the responses with management while on site.

**153.** The auditor's supervisor should be critical of the above procedure based on the fact that
    a.   Audit information must be corroborated in some way.
    b.   Internal control questionnaires cannot be relied on.
    c.   The auditors were not present while the questionnaire was being filled out.
    d.   The questionnaire was not designed to address accounting operations and controls.

**154.** The auditor's supervisor is writing the performance assessment for the auditor on this preliminary survey assignment. The supervisor cites the need to review management's responses on the control questionnaire. The auditor should have interviewed management for additional information because the interview technique
    a.   Provides the opportunity to insert questions to probe promising areas.
    b.   Is the most efficient way to upgrade the information to the level of objective evidence.
    c.   Is the least costly audit technique when a large amount of information is involved.
    d.   Is the only audit procedure that does not require confirmation and walk-through of the information that is obtained.

**155.** An auditor is considering developing a questionnaire to research employee attitude toward control procedures. Which of the following represents criteria that should **not** be considered in designing the questionnaire?
    a.   Questions must be worded to ensure a valid interpretation by the respondents.
    b.   Questions must be reliably worded so that they measure what was intended to be measured.
    c.   The questionnaire should be short to increase the response rate.
    d.   Questions should be worded such that a "no" answer indicates a problem.

**156.** Which of the following statements describes an internal control questionnaire? It
    a.   Provides detailed evidence regarding the substance of the control system.
    b.   Takes less of the auditee's time to complete than other control evaluation devices.
    c.   Requires that the auditor be in attendance to properly administer it.

d. Provides indirect audit evidence that might need corroboration.

**157.** Which of the following **best** describes the major disadvantage of using a questionnaire rather than a flowchart to evaluate internal controls?

a. Questionnaires usually take more time to complete and are more cumbersome.

b. Responses do not efficiently flag potential internal control weaknesses.

c. It is difficult for auditors to develop or obtain questionnaires that are appropriate for most internal control systems.

d. Auditors may complete questionnaires without really understanding overall operations of internal control systems.

**158.** Which of the following is the primary advantage of using an internal control questionnaire?

a. It provides a clear picture of the interrelationships that exist between the various controls.

b. It reduces the risk of overlooking important aspects of the system.

c. It forces an auditor to acquire a full understanding of the system.

d. The negative responses indicate the only areas needing further audit work.

**159.** An audit manager is conducting the annual meeting with manufacturing division management to discuss proposed audit plans and activities for the next year. After some discussion about the past year's audit activity at twelve plants in the division, the divisional vice president agrees that all significant recommendations made by the audit staff refer to key controls and related operating activities that are correctly described for local management within the volume of standard operating procedures for the division. The vice president proposes to transcribe key control activities from the division's extensive written procedures to a self-audit standard operating procedure (SOP) questionnaire. What significance should the audit manager attach to such SOP questionnaires in relation to the proposed audit schedule for the next year?

a. The SOP questionnaires should improve control adequacy, but the auditors need to verify that controls are working as documented in the SOP.

b. Adding this control should eliminate significant audit recommendations in the coming year, so the scope of audit activities can be reduced accordingly.

c. Audit activity can be reduced if the vice president agrees to require internal auditing department approval on all divisional standard operating procedures.

d. SOP questionnaires must be mailed and controlled by the internal auditing department to be considered in relation to the proposed audit schedule.

**160.** Checklists used to assess audit risk have been criticized for all of the following reasons **except:**

a. Providing a false sense of security that all relevant factors are addressed.

b. Inappropriately implying equal weight to each item on the checklist.

c. Decreasing the uniformity of data acquisition.

d. Being incapable of translating the experience or sound reasoning intended to be captured by each item on the checklist.

**161.** When an internal auditor is interviewing to gain information, the auditor will not be able to remember everything that was said in the interview. The most effective way to record interview information for later use is to

a. Write notes quickly, trying to write down everything in detail, as it is said; then highlight important points after the meeting.

b. Tape-record the interview to capture everything that everyone says; then type everything said into a computer for documentation.

c. Hire a professional secretary to take notes, allowing complete concentration on the interview; then delete unimportant points after the meeting.

d. Organize notes around topics on the interview plan and note responses in the appropriate area, reviewing the notes after the meeting to make additions.

**162.** As part of the test of the effectiveness of a disaster recovery plan, the auditor plans to interview five employees from each of five different departments (25 employees in all). After the first few interviews, what would be the best way for the auditor to remain attentive during the remaining interviews?

a. Make up completely different questions to stay interested.

b. Ask the questions in a slightly different format and in a different sequence.

c. Have the rest of the employees write down their responses.

d. Interview the remaining employees in groups of four or five.

**163.** When conducting interviews during the early stages of an internal audit, it is more effective to

a. Ask for specific answers that can be quantified.

b. Ask people about their jobs.

c. Ask surprise questions about daily procedures.

d. Take advantage of the fact that fear is an important part of the audit.

**164.** The current audit of disbursement activities shows a significant number of errors made during the accounts payable vouchering process that have resulted in lost discounts and an extraordinary number of adjustments and credit memos. To date the causes have not been fully identified for all types of errors noted. The most appropriate course of action for the auditor to take related to these problems is to

a. Interview accounts payable clerks and those involved in processing these transactions.

b. Expand sample sizes for attributes already tested in transactions entered by accounts payable and purchasing.

c. Concentrate on audit program requirements for cash disbursements testing to discover any related information from those tests.

d. Describe the transaction-related problems identified to date in a special report to management without expressing a cause or an auditor's conclusion about the situation.

**165.** Interviewing techniques are used frequently by internal auditors. When considering the potential use of interviewing techniques to gather audit evidence, auditors should be aware those interviews

a. Are more objective than questionnaires in gathering data.

b. Provide a systematic format to ensure audit coverage.
c. Should be corroborated by gathering objective data.
d. Are best suited to reaching audit conclusions.

## Analytical Review Techniques

**166.** Management has requested an audit of promotional expenses. The sales department has been giving away expensive items in conjunction with new product sales to stimulate demand. The promotion seems successful, but management believes the cost may be too high. Which of the following audit procedures would be the **least** useful to determine the effectiveness of the promotion?
a. A comparison of product sales during the promotion period with sales during a similar nonpromotion period.
b. A comparison of the unit cost of the products sold before and during the promotion period.
c. An analysis of marginal revenue and marginal cost for the promotion period, compared to the period before the promotion.
d. A review of the sales department's reasons for believing that the promotion has been successful.

**167.** An internal auditor plans to use an analytical review to verify the correctness of various operating expenses in a division. The use of an analytical review as a verification technique would **not** be a preferred approach if
a. The auditor notes strong indicators of a specific fraud involving this account.
b. The company has relatively stable operations that have not changed much over the past year.
c. The auditor would like to identify large, unusual, or nonrecurring transactions during the year.
d. The operating expenses vary in relation to other operating expenses, but not in relation to revenue.

**168.** During an audit, the internal auditor should consider the following factor(s) in determining the extent to which analytical procedures should be used:
a. Adequacy of the system of internal control.
b. Significance of the area being examined.
c. Precision with which the results of analytical audit procedures can be predicted.
d. All of the above.

**169.** A restaurant food chain has over 680 restaurants. All food orders for each restaurant are required to be input into an electronic device that records all orders by food servers and transmits the order to the kitchen for preparation. All food servers are responsible for collecting cash for all their orders and must turn in cash at the end of their shift equal to the sales value of food ordered for their ID number. The manager then reconciles the cash received for the day with the computerized record of food orders generated. All differences are investigated immediately by the restaurant.

Corporate headquarters has established monitoring controls to determine when an individual restaurant might not be recording all its revenue and transmitting the applicable cash to the corporate headquarters. Which one of the following would be the **best** example of a monitoring control?
a. The restaurant manager reconciles the cash received with the food orders recorded on the computer.

b. All food orders must be entered on the computer, and there is segregation of duties between the food servers and the cooks.
c. Management prepares a detailed analysis of gross margin per store and investigates any store that shows a significantly lower gross margin.
d. Cash is transmitted to corporate headquarters on a daily basis.

**Items 170 and 171** are based on the following:

The auditor of a construction company that builds foundations for bridges and large buildings performed a review of the expense accounts for equipment (augers) used to drill holes in rocks to set the foundation for the buildings. During the review, the auditor noted that the expenses related to some of the auger accounts had increased dramatically during the year. The auditor spoke to the construction manager, who explained that the augers last two to three years and are expensed when purchased. Thus, the auditor should see a decrease in the expense accounts for these augers in the next year, but would expect an increase in the expenses of other augers. The auditor also found out that the construction manager is responsible for the inventorying and receiving of the augers and is a part owner of a company that supplies augers to the company. To improve the quality of equipment, the president of the company approved the supplier.

**170.** Which of the following procedures would be the **least appropriate** audit procedure to address these analytical findings?
a. Note the explanation in the working papers for investigation during the next audit and perform no further work at this time.
b. Develop a comparative analysis of auger expense over the past few years to determine if the relationship held in previous years.
c. Take a sample of debits to the auger expense account and trace to independent shipping documents and to invoices for the augers.
d. Arrange to take an inventory of augers to determine if the augers purchased this year were on hand and would be available for use in the next two years.

**171.** Assume the auditor did not find a satisfactory explanation for the results of the analytical procedures performed and has conducted the appropriate follow-up procedures. The audit of the area is otherwise complete. Which of the following would be the **most** appropriate action to take?
a. Note the actions and follow-up next year. Defer the reporting to management until a satisfactory explanation can be obtained.
b. Expand audit procedures by observing the receipt of all augers during a reasonable period of time and trace the receipts to the appropriate accounts. Determine causes of any discrepancies.
c. Report the findings, as they are, to management and recommend an investigation for possible irregularities.
d. Report the findings to the construction manager and insist that appropriate internal controls, such as independent receiving reports, be implemented. Follow up to see if the controls are properly implemented.

**172.** An auditor performs an analytical review by comparing the gross margins of various divisional operations with those of other divisions and with the individual division's performance in previous years. The auditor notes a significant increase in the gross margin at one division. The auditor does some preliminary investigation and also notes that there were no changes in products, production methods, or divisional management during the year. Based on the above information, the **most** likely cause of the increase in gross margin would be

    a.   An increase in the number of competitors selling similar products.

    b.   A decrease in the number of suppliers of the material used in manufacturing the product.

    c.   An overstatement of year-end inventory.

    d.   An understatement of year-end accounts receivable.

**173.** During an operational audit, an auditor compares the inventory turnover rate of a subsidiary with established industry standards in order to

    a.   Evaluate the accuracy of the subsidiary's internal financial reports.

    b.   Test the subsidiary's controls designed to safeguard assets.

    c.   Determine if the subsidiary is complying with corporate procedures regarding inventory levels.

    d.   Assess the performance of the subsidiary and indicate where additional audit work may be needed.

**Items 174 and 175** are based on the following:

During an audit of a smaller division, the auditor notes the following regarding the purchasing function:

- There are three purchasing agents. Agent 1 is responsible for ordering all large component parts, Agent 2 is responsible for electric motors, and Agent 3 is responsible for smaller parts, such as fasteners.
- There are separate accounts payable and receiving departments.
- In order to hold vendors more responsible, all invoices are sent to the purchasing agent placing the order. The purchasing agent matches the vendor invoice, receiving slip, and purchase order. If all match, the purchasing agent sends the documents forward to the accounts payable department. The purchasing agent investigates differences.
- Only the accounts payable department has the ability to authorize an item for payment.
- All recorded receipts are immediately recorded into a perpetual inventory record by the department to which the goods are transferred after receipt.

The auditor interviewed both management and the purchasing agents. Both groups were very satisfied with the current system because it helped maintain vendor accountability and provided sufficient segregation of duties since only the accounts payable department can authorize an item for payment.

**174.** Which of the following audit procedures would be **most effective** in determining whether material fraud was taking place?

    a.   Take a random sample of cash disbursements and trace to approved purchase orders and receiving slips.

    b.   Reconcile the perpetual inventory to the general ledger and investigate any differences.

    c.   Take a random sample of purchase orders. Trace each purchase order to a receiving slip, vendor invoice, and approval by the accounts payable department.

    d.   Perform an analytical review of inventory by product line to determine whether a particular product line has increased. Inquire of the purchasing agent as to the reason for the inventory increase.

**175.** The auditor is responsible for evaluating the control structure to determine if the structure would allow for undetected fraud. Based on the above scenario, the most likely undetected fraud, if any, would be

    a.   The purchasing agents could be purchasing the majority of products from a favorite vendor since rotation among purchasing agents is not mandatory.

    b.   The purchasing agents could be sending fake purchase orders to a dummy vendor, inserting a receiving slip, and having payments made to the dummy vendor.

    c.   The receiving department could be diverting receipts to different locations and failing to create receiving reports.

    d.   The production department could be deflating the price of products purchased and thereby increasing the reported gross margin of sales.

**176.** Which of the following control procedures, if properly implemented, would **best** decrease the likelihood of fraud in the environment described above?

    a.   Require periodic rotation of purchases among different vendors.

    b.   Require rotation of duties among the three purchasing agents.

    c.   Require receiving reports be sent directly to accounts payable.

    d.   Require that the receiving department make the updates to the perpetual inventory record.

**177.** Analytical procedures

    a.   Are considered direct evidence of the assertion being evaluated.

    b.   Are compelling evidence when they involve recomputation.

    c.   May provide the best available evidence for the completeness assertion.

    d.   Are not sufficient by themselves for management assertions, but should be used for fraud.

**178.** A company makes a practice of investing excess short-term cash in marketable equity securities. A reliable test of the valuation of those securities would be a

    a.   Comparison of cost data with current market quotations.

    b.   Confirmation of securities held by the broker.

    c.   Recalculation of investment carrying value using the equity method.

    d.   Calculation of premium or discount amortization.

**179.** Analytical procedures in which current financial statements are compared with budgets or previous statements are primarily intended to determine

    a.   Adequacy of financial statement disclosure.

    b.   Existence of specific errors or omissions.

    c.   Overall reasonableness of statement contents.

    d.   Use of an erroneous cutoff date.

## Problem Solving

**180.** During an internal audit, the auditor experienced difficulty obtaining required information from a specific employee. When this situation continued for one week, the auditor requested a private meeting with the employee for the purpose of identifying the problem and resolving the difficulty through open discussion. Which conflict management technique was the auditor applying?

  a.  Problem solving.
  b.  Expansion of resources.
  c.  Authoritative command.
  d.  Altering the human variable.

**Items 181 and 182** are based on the following:

An audit supervisor is preparing the annual evaluation of a senior auditor's overall performance. For each of the following criteria, select the one statement the supervisor could make that addresses the criterion and is appropriate for an evaluation.

**181.** Problem-solving skills.

  a.  You need to further analyze alternatives before selecting a solution.
  b.  Your ability to communicate ideas clearly is exemplary.
  c.  You could expedite your problem solving by focusing on logic instead of reasoning activities.
  d.  You are able to reduce conflict with ease and without putting individuals on the defensive.

**182.** Human resources management.

  a.  Your ability to effectively socialize within the organization has had a positive impact on the department.
  b.  You have successfully handled numerous issues that have challenged your decision-making abilities.
  c.  You have developed quite a strong reputation outside the department thereby increasing your credibility.
  d.  Your motivational skills in the field increased morale within this department.

**183.** An organization's executive committee, meeting to solve an important problem, spent 30 minutes analyzing data and debating the cause of the problem. Finally, members agreed and could move on to the next step. Possible steps in the creative problem-solving process are listed below. Which step should the committee perform next?

  a.  Select a solution.
  b.  Generate alternative solutions.
  c.  Identify the problem.
  d.  Consider the reaction of competitors to various courses of action.

**184.** The president of an organization believes employees should be rewarded for innovative ideas and has established a formal method for employees to submit their ideas for consideration by top management. All employees who submit ideas are praised, and those whose ideas increase profits receive cash bonuses. Why do programs like this often result in greater innovation?

  a.  Innovation is intrinsically rewarding because it results in personal satisfaction and the pleasure derived from a job.

  b.  The employees have been classically conditioned to be innovative.
  c.  Employees who do not contribute innovative ideas are essentially punished because they do not receive praise and bonuses.
  d.  Positive reinforcements, such as praise and cash bonuses, increase the probability that employees will submit innovative ideas.

**185.** An operational audit of your organization's budget process has revealed that department heads frequently circumvent budget controls by actions such as padding their budgets and concealing opportunities to cut costs. One of the audit recommendations involves forming a group comprised of department heads to find a solution for this problem. Which one of the following methods is likely to generate a high level of commitment to the solution among members of the group?

  a.  The brainstorming technique in which group members orally identify as many alternatives as possible without criticism from other members.
  b.  A mandate from top management.
  c.  The Delphi technique in which a series of questionnaires is used to arrive at a consensus.
  d.  An open discussion of the problem and potential solutions until a consensus is reached.

**186.** The auditor has recognized that a problem exists because the organizational unit has been too narrow in its definition of goals. The goals of the unit focus on profits, but the overall organizational goals are much broader. The auditor also recognizes that the auditee will resist any recommendations about adopting broader goals. The best course of action would be to

  a.  Avoid conflict and present only those goals that are consistent with the auditee's views since all others will be ignored.
  b.  Identify the broader organizational goals and present a set of recommendations that attempts to meet both the organizational and auditee goals.
  c.  Subtly mix the suggested solution with the problem definition so that the auditee will identify the solution apparently independently of the auditor.
  d.  Only report the conditions found and leave the rest of the analysis to the auditees.

**187.** Which of the following problem-solving tools is an idea-generating and consensus-building technique?

  a.  Brainstorming.
  b.  Synectics.
  c.  Systems analysis.
  d.  Nominal group technique.

**188.** A company has recently introduced total quality management (TQM). The director of internal auditing is faced with determining a new and innovative approach to auditing in this new environment. The director should

  a.  Seek isolation from all distractions in order to think the problem through.
  b.  Bring the audit team together for a brainstorming session.
  c.  Rely on the audit supervisor to develop a new approach.
  d.  Use a disciplined problem-solving approach.

**Items 189 through 191** are based on the following:

A company has four manufacturing plants spread throughout the country. Major decisions regarding production, product pricing, and strategic directions are controlled and coordinated through central headquarters. Two manufacturing plants (C and D) serve as suppliers to the other two plants (A and B) that produce the company's two major lines of industrial products. Since there are many interdependencies between the plants, a great deal of production, sales, and intracompany product transfers are controlled through central headquarters.

Each plant is responsible for its own computer systems and for making purchases to support production. Sales orders come from sales representatives located throughout the country and can be transmitted directly to the production plant for processing or can be transmitted through central headquarters to the production plant for shipping and billing. All sales prices are determined at central headquarters.

**189.** During the preliminary survey in conjunction with an upcoming audit of plant B, the auditor discovers that the plant has experienced production problems with costs far in excess of what management had planned and with finished goods inventory levels that are clearly excessive. Which of the following management control procedures would have **best** brought the problems to management's attention earlier?

    a. Standard costing procedures are implemented at each plant with a summary of variances reported to central headquarters on a weekly basis.

    b. Perpetual inventory control procedures are implemented at each plant. A report is prepared detailing any inventory items with levels in excess of two weeks' production. The report goes to plant management and central headquarters.

    c. Production plans based on management forecasts are sent to the plants on a monthly basis. A weekly report compares actual production with forecasted production and weekly costs with budgeted costs.

    d. A weekly report is prepared which compares actual sales with forecasted sales and budgeted gross margin with actual gross margins. Inventory costs going into cost of goods sold should be computed on a last in, first out basis to be the most up-to-date.

**190.** All sales prices are determined centrally and are electronically sent to the plant to update their sales price table (file). All sales transactions should be based on the prices in the computerized table. Any pricing deviations must be approved by the plant-marketing manager and by a manager in the marketing department at central headquarters for updating the tables. The internal auditor wishes to know how this processing is functioning. The **most** appropriate audit procedure and audit tools to use would be to

    a. Document the flow of sales price information from headquarters to the plant, how the table is accessed and updated, and the use of the table in the billing program.

    b. Develop a flowchart of the sales order process to determine how orders are taken and priced.

    c. Use a questionnaire to identify who approves the shipment of goods and how the goods are priced.

    d. Obtain a copy of the existing program flowchart from the plant to determine how price data are accessed.

**191.** The auditor wishes to develop a flowchart of (1) the process of receiving sales order information at headquarters; (2) the transmission of the data to the plants to generate the shipment; and (3) the plants processing of the information for shipment. The auditor should

    a. Start with management's decisions to set sales prices. Gather internal documentation on the approval process for changing sales prices. Complement documentation with a copy of the program flowchart. Prepare an overview flowchart that links these details.

    b. Start with a shipment of goods and trace the transaction back through the origination of the sales order as received from the sales representative.

    c. Start with the receipt of a sales order from a sales representative and walk-through both the manual and computerized processing at headquarters and the plant until the goods are shipped and billed.

    d. Obtain a copy of the plant's systems flowchart for the sales process, interview relevant personnel to determine if any changes have been made, then develop an overview flowchart that will highlight the basic process.

**192.** A manager recently transferred from a manufacturing company to a service-oriented affiliate. When the manager unexpectedly announced a set of production standards, two employees quit on the spot, three others transferred out within a week, and the remaining employees were openly hostile. Select the best method for resolving this dysfunctional conflict situation.

    a. Conflict triggering.

    b. Forcing.

    c. Smoothing.

    d. Problem solving.

**193.** A chief executive officer (CEO) believes that a major competitor may be planning a new campaign. The CEO sends a questionnaire to key personnel asking for original thinking concerning what the new campaign may be. The CEO selects the best possibilities then sends another questionnaire asking for the most likely option. The process employed by the CEO is called the

    a. Least squares technique.

    b. Delphi technique.

    c. Maximum likelihood technique.

    d. Optimizing of expected payoffs.

**Items 194 through 201** are based on the following:

Listed below are situations and techniques for generating creative alternatives in solving problems. For each question, identify the technique most appropriate for each situation. (Answers are only used once.)

**194.** A company wishes to determine what advertising mix among radio, television, and newspapers offers the optimal desired result in increased sales and improved public image.

    a. Synectics.

    b. Value analysis.

    c. Brainstorming.

    d. Forced relationship.

**195.** A company cannot identify why production has been decreasing at a particular plant. All efforts to isolate the cause with conventional accounting and administrative systems have failed. As a final effort before closing the plant, you need to

gain the cooperation of selected employees from all levels. A small group will be formed to identify and solve this significant problem. All group-member suggestions will be evaluated equally, regardless of their position.
    a.   Brainstorming.
    b.   Synectics.
    c.   Blast then refine.
    d.   Operations research.

**196.** Costs of a specific department must be cut by 40% and quality must improve or it cannot compete in the marketplace. This drastic charge was recently given to your department. You do not have time for more traditional techniques. You must come up with something quickly. Conventional cost-cutting techniques have been attempted but to no avail. You decide to employ a radical new production arrangement.
    a.   Blast then refine.
    b.   Edisonian.
    c.   Morphological matix analysis.
    d.   Operations research.

**197.** All attempts to solve a problem based on affirmative action program goals have failed. A very structured group to view the problem from management and various minority group perspectives has been created. All group members will be required to study the complaints and slogans of the various minority groups in order to produce a new program.
    a.   Synectics.
    b.   Forced relationship.
    c.   Brainstorming.
    d.   Attribute listing.

**198.** A company is about to introduce a new service and wishes to develop a new slogan and logo to be utilized in advertising and on company publications. You have been chosen to participate in this process and to look at past slogans, logos, and suggestions given by the advertising agency. You are not limited to the suggested ideas and have been encouraged to suggest original ideas of your own.
    a.   Brainstorming.
    b.   Value analysis.
    c.   Free association.
    d.   Attribute listing.

**199.** A company has a computer that it no longer needs because of a discontinued operation. Currently there are several computer projects that may be able to utilize the machine, but some modification will be necessary if such new application is to be successful.
    a.   Attribute listing.
    b.   Operations research.
    ç.   Morphological matrix analysis.
    d.   Synectics.

**200.** A company has experienced numerous complaints because a passenger door has not opened smoothly. All attempts to repair the door have failed. The item is no longer under warranty and the manufacturer has informed the company that a very expensive new door must be purchased and installed to solve the problem. You have been asked to supervise an attempt by your engineering department to come up with less expensive alternative solutions.
    a.   Free association.
    b.   Operations research.
    c.   Blast then refine.
    d.   Edisonian.

**201.** A company is concerned that spare parts inventories are too large. It has attempted to keep critical parts for its fleet in stock so that equipment will have minimal downtime. Management wants to know what the optimal spare parts inventory should be if downtime is estimated to cost $150 per day. Carrying cost and order cost have not been measured. You have been asked to make a formal recommendation on spare parts stocking levels.
    a.   Operations research.
    b.   Value analysis.
    c.   Attribute listing.
    d.   Brainstorming.

**202.** Management activities can be classified in three levels: strategic planning, management control, and operational control. Information requirements vary with the level of management activity. Which of the following **best** describes the information requirements for strategic planning?
    a.   Frequent use, external, aggregate information.
    b.   Future-oriented, outdated, detailed information.
    c.   Highly current, accurate, largely internal information.
    d.   Wide scope, aggregate, future-oriented information.

**Risk and Control Self-Assessment**

**203.** The control self-assessment (CSA) is a
    a.   Directive auditing tool.
    b.   Preventive auditing tool.
    c.   Detective auditing tool.
    d.   Corrective auditing tool.

**204.** The control self-assessment (CSA) is a
    a.   Compliance audit engagement.
    b.   Consulting engagement.
    c.   Financial audit engagement.
    d.   Operational audit engagement.

**205.** The most popular approach to control self-assessment (CSA) is the
    a.   Workshop approach.
    b.   Questionnaire approach.
    c.   Survey approach.
    d.   "Wall-writing" approach.

**206.** When the culture of an organization is supportive of candid employee responses in a control self-assessment workshop, which of the following is favored by most organizations?
    a.   Audit-facilitated workshops.
    b.   Client-facilitated workshops.
    c.   Questionnaire approach.
    d.   Management-produced analyses.

**207.** When the culture of an organization is **not** supportive of candid employee responses in a control self-assessment workshop, which of the following can be suggested to organizations?
    a.   Audit-facilitated workshops.
    b.   Client-facilitated workshops.
    c.   Questionnaire approach.
    d.   Meeting approach.

**208.** Which of the following is used when an organization wants to investigate a control breakdown?
    a.   Management-produced analyses.
    b.   Surveys.

c.  Questionnaires.
d.  Workshops.

**209.** Which of the following control self-assessment (CSA) approaches or formats are used about 70% of the time?

I. Workshops.
II. Surveys.
III. Questionnaires.
IV. Interviews.

a.  I or II.
b.  II or III.
c.  I or IV.
d.  III or IV.

**210.** The work flow in the control self-assessment (CSA) workshops "objectives-risks-controls-residual risks-assessment" is referred to as
a.  Objective-based approach.
b.  Risk-based approach.
c.  Control-based approach.
d.  Process-based approach.

**211.** Which of the following components of the enterprise risk management (ERM) framework addresses processes and people in an organization?
a.  Strategic risks.
b.  Operational risks.
c.  Financial risks.
d.  Hazard risks.

**212.** Which of the following is **not** the goal of enterprise risk management (ERM) initiatives?
a.  Integrating risks.
b.  Creating shareholder value.
c.  Protecting shareholder value.
d.  Enhancing shareholder value.

**213.** The scope of enterprise risk management (ERM) encompasses which of the following?

I. Creating opportunities.
II. De-risking opportunities.
III. Analyzing strengths.
IV. Focusing on weaknesses.

a.  I and II.
b.  I and III.
c.  III and IV.
d.  I, III, and IV.

**214.** The enterprise risk management (ERM) focuses on which of the following?
a.  Value-added potential.
b.  Risk management process.
c.  Asset management principles.
d.  Management accountability.

**215.** The role and focus of the internal audit function in enterprise risk management (ERM) with the objective of improving corporate governance includes which of the following?

I. Follow-up on ERM scorecards.
II. Internal controls for ERM.
III. The IIA's *Standards* on ERM.
IV. Follow-up on ERM metrics.

a.  I and II.
b.  II and III.

c.  I and IV.
d.  III and IV.

**216.** Which of the following attributes of the internal audit department can hinder the implementation of enterprise risk management (ERM) in the auditor's organization?

I. Control-based audit approach.
II. Use of traditional auditing tools.
III. Consultant role.
IV. Facilitation skills.

a.  I and II.
b.  II and III.
c.  I and IV.
d.  III and IV.

**217.** According to the control self-assessment (CSA) approach, which of the following address soft controls?
a.  Control self-assessment techniques.
b.  Dual controls.
c.  Authorization techniques.
d.  Traditional audit techniques.

**218.** The role of an internal auditor in introducing a control self-assessment (CSA) program into the organization is that of a(n)
a.  Enabler.
b.  Reviewer.
c.  Evaluator.
d.  Enforcer.

**219.** In the implementation of control self-assessment (CSA), which of the following examines a given business process in depth?
a.  Horizontal sessions.
b.  Diagonal sessions.
c.  Vertical sessions.
d.  Individual sessions.

**220.** The **major** purpose of control self-assessment (CSA) is
a.  Control.
b.  Improvement.
c.  Documentation.
d.  Auditing.

**221.** Control self-assessment (CSA) is a process that involves employees in assessing the adequacy of controls and identifying opportunities for improvement within an organization. Which of the following are reasons to involve employees in this process?

I. Employees become more motivated to do their jobs right.
II. Employees are objective about their jobs.
III. Employees can provide an independent assessment of internal controls.
IV. Managers want feedback from their employees.

a.  I and II.
b.  III and IV.
c.  I and IV.
d.  II and IV.

**Computerized Audit Tools and Techniques**

**222.** An auditor becomes concerned that fraud in the form of payments to bogus companies may exist. Buyers, who are responsible for all purchases for specific product lines, are able to approve expenditures up to $50,000 without any other approval. Which of the following audit procedures would be **most** effective in addressing the auditor's concerns?

a. Use generalized audit software to list all purchases over $50,000 to determine whether they were properly approved.
b. Develop a "snapshot" technique to trace all transactions by suspected buyers.
c. Use generalized audit software to take a random sample of all expenditures under $50,000 to determine whether they were properly approved.
d. Use generalized audit software to list all major vendors by product line; select a sample of paid invoices to new vendors and examine evidence which shows that services or goods were received.

**223.** An auditor wishes to determine the extent to which invalid data could be contained in a human resources computer system. Examples would be an invalid job classification, age in excess of retirement age, or an invalid ethnic classification. The **best** approach to determine the extent of the potential problem would be to

a. Submit test data to test the effectiveness of edit controls over the input of data.
b. Review and test access controls to ensure that access is limited to authorized individuals.
c. Use generalized audit software to develop a detailed report of all data outside specified parameters.
d. Use generalized audit software to select a sample of employees. Use the sample to determine the validity of data items and project the result to the population as a whole.

**224.** A bank internal auditor wishes to determine whether all loans are backed by sufficient collateral, properly aged as to current payments, and properly categorized as current or noncurrent. The **best** audit procedure to accomplish this objective would be to

a. Use generalized audit software to read the total loan file, age the file by last payment due, and take a statistical sample stratified by the current and aged population. Examine each loan selected for proper collateralization and aging.
b. Take a block sample of all loans in excess of a specified dollar limit and determine if they are current and properly categorized. For each loan approved, verify aging and categorization.
c. Take a discovery sample of all loan applications to determine whether each application contains a statement of collateral.
d. Take a sample of payments made on the loan portfolio and trace them to loans to see that the payments are properly applied. For each loan identified, examine the loan application to determine that the loan has proper collateralization.

**Items 225 and 226** are based on the following:

A retail company uses electronic data interchange (EDI) to order all of its merchandise. The goods are received at a central warehouse, where they are electronically scanned into the computer to determine that a purchase order had been issued and to record the goods. The goods are price-marked at the warehouse and shipped to individual stores within twenty-four to forty-eight hours. Inventory and accounts payable is updated when the goods are received. The company receives

an invoice electronically from the vendor. A computer program matches the invoice with the applicable purchase order and receiving information. If the items match, the invoice is scheduled for payment and a report is made to the treasurer. If the invoice does not match the other items within predefined ranges, a report is generated and sent to accounts payable for further investigation. All the applicable documents are electronically marked, cross-referenced, and retained in open files.

**225.** The auditor wants to determine whether the computer program is appropriately matching the purchase receipts and vendor invoices throughout the year. Which one of the following computerized audit techniques would be **most** efficient and effective in accomplishing this objective?

a. Use the test data method during the last quarter.
b. Use an integrated test facility throughout the year.
c. Use "parallel simulation" technique and apply on a monthly basis.
d. Use the SCARF (systems control audit review file) on a daily basis.

**226.** The auditor wants to determine the extent to which items are not matched at year-end and investigate the potential cause of the nonmatching items. Which one of the following audit procedures would be **most** effective in determining the items to investigate?

a. Submit test data to identify attributes of nonmatching items. Follow up by investigating the attributes identified.
b. Use generalized audit software to read the purchase order file for the year. Select a statistical sample of purchase orders and trace to applicable receiving and vendor invoice files.
c. Use SCARF to identify unusual items. Take an attribute sample and trace to the underlying paper documents.
d. Use generalized audit software to read the electronically marked unmatched items.

**227.** Governmental auditors have been increasingly called on to perform audits to determine whether individuals are getting extra social welfare payments. One common type of welfare fraud is individuals receiving more than one social welfare payment. This is often accomplished by filing multiple claims under multiple names, but using the same address. Which of the following computer audit tools and techniques would be **most** helpful in identifying the existence of this type of fraud?

a. Tagging and tracing.
b. Generalized audit software.
c. Integrated test facility.
d. Spreadsheet analysis.

**Items 228 and 229** are based on the following:

The auditor determines that a major user application is implemented on a spreadsheet. The spreadsheet takes input regarding projected freight deliveries from the mainframe computer and develops an optimal freight-dispatching plan. When first used two years ago, the spreadsheet helped reduce costs dramatically. However, freight costs have been increasing, and no one, other than the developer, has reviewed the spreadsheet. The freight-dispatching algorithm is complicated, but the auditor has researched the area and understands the algorithm and its correct computation.

**228.** The auditor wishes to gain assurance on whether the spreadsheet has properly implemented the freight-dispatching algorithm. Which of the following audit procedures would accomplish the task?

I. Develop an independent spreadsheet and run test data through it and through the user's spreadsheet. Compare the results.

II. Use a product to print out the logic of the user spreadsheet. Examine the logic to determine if it has been correctly incorporated into the spreadsheet.

III. Develop a set of test data and manually calculate the expected results. Run the test data through the user application.

    a.   II only.
    b.   I and III.
    c.   I, II, and III.
    d.   I only.

**229.** Assume the audit testing performed in the previous question indicates that the spreadsheet has correctly implemented the freight-dispatching algorithm. Which of the following conclusions is(are) justified from the audit evidence?

I. The spreadsheet must be obtaining incorrect data when it is downloaded from the mainframe.

II. Although the algorithm is correctly implemented, it is not the most efficient algorithm.

III. The increased freight costs must be due to some other cause than the spreadsheet calculation.

    a.   III only.
    b.   I, II, and III.
    c.   I and II.
    d.   II only.

**230.** The auditor wishes to test controls over computer program changes. The specific objective to be addressed in the following audit step is that only authorized changes have been made to computer programs (i.e., there are no unauthorized program changes). The organization uses an automated program library system, and the auditor obtains copies of the table of contents of the program library system at various periods of time. The table of contents indicates the date a change was last made to the program, the version number of the program, and the length of the program. Which of the following audit procedures would **best** address the stated objective?

    a.   Use generalized audit software to randomly select a sample of current applications. Trace those selected to program change authorization forms.

    b.   Take a sample of all program change requests. Trace the requests to proper authorization and to changes in the program library.

    c.   Use generalized audit software to compare the table of contents of the program library currently with an auditor copy made previously. Compare and identify differences. Select a sample of the differences for further investigation.

    d.   Obtain a list of programming projects implemented by the data processing manager during the last six months. Take a sample from the list and trace to program change authorization forms.

**231.** Auditors have learned that increased computerization has created more opportunities for computer fraud, but has also led to the development of computer audit techniques to detect frauds. A type of fraud that has occurred in the banking industry is a programming fraud where the programmer designs a program to calculate daily interest on savings accounts to four decimal points. The programmer then truncates the last two digits and adds it to his or her account balance. Which of the following computer audit techniques would be most effective in detecting this type of fraud?

    a.   Parallel simulation.
    b.   Generalized audit software that selects account balances for confirmation with the depositor.
    c.   Snapshot.
    d.   SCARF (systems control and audit review file).

**Items 232 and 233** are based on the following:

While performing analytical procedures related to an audit of a social services agency of a government entity, the auditor noted that there was an unusually large increase in payments to individual recipients who are under the direction of a particular social worker in the agency.

**232.** Which of the following audit procedures would be the **best** procedure to investigate this observation?

    a.   Use generalized audit software to sort payments to recipients by social worker. Then sort the payments by common addresses and names.

    b.   Implement an integrated test facility and monitor transactions throughout the year to identify unusual items.

    c.   Implement the snapshot approach and tag transactions that are related to the social worker identified with the unusually large increases.

    d.   Use generalized audit software to take a random sample of recipients and investigate by sending confirmations to each recipient to determine if they had received proper payments.

**233.** The auditor is considering making a recommendation on appropriate controls to address a potential problem of fictitious recipients. The auditor has identified the following control procedures as potential items to include in the recommendation.

I. Require that all additions to the recipient file be independently investigated and approved by a supervisor of the social workers.

II. Require the use of self-checking digits on the account numbers of all recipients so that any duplicates will be immediately noted by the system.

III. Incorporate a code into the computer program to search for duplicate names and addresses. Develop an exception report that will go the section supervisor whenever duplicates are noted.

IV. Require social workers to be rotated among recipients.

Which of the following control combinations would effectively address the auditor's concerns and improve control over valid recipients?

    a.   I, II, III, and IV.
    b.   I, II, and III.
    c.   I and IV.
    d.   I, III, and IV.

**234.** Many public utility companies operate complex customer service systems (CSS) to manage their customer service function. CSS operate in an online, real-time environment, which allows customer service data to be directly entered online from customer telephone calls. Which of the following

IT auditing techniques provides the auditor with the capability to continuously monitor customer service data that are collected from telephone calls in CSS?

- a. Generalized audit software.
- b. Control flowcharting.
- c. Embedded audit data collection.
- d. Integrated test facility (ITF).

**235.** Which of the following information systems auditing techniques processes real transaction data (or a copy of the real data) through auditor-developed test programs?

- a. Integrated test facility.
- b. Tracing.
- c. Parallel simulation.
- d. Mapping.

**236.** To determine if there have been any unauthorized program changes since the last authorized program update, the best IT audit technique is for the auditor to conduct a(n)

- a. Code comparison.
- b. Code review.
- c. Test date run.
- d. Analytical review.

**237.** In auditing an online perpetual inventory system, an auditor selected certain file-updating transactions for detailed testing. The audit technique that will provide a computer trail of all relevant processing steps applied to a specific transaction is described as

- a. Simulation.
- b. Snapshot.
- c. Code comparison.
- d. Tagging and tracing.

**238.** Which of the following statements is **not** true concerning the tasks that generalized audit software is able to perform?

- a. Provide totals of unusual items.
- b. Check for duplications, missing information, or ranges of values.
- c. Specify which data elements will be tested and the criteria to be used.
- d. Verify calculation totals and analyses produced.

**239.** Generalized audit software can be used to

- a. Examine the existence and consistency of data maintained on files.
- b. Perform concurrent auditing of data files.
- c. Verify processing logic of operating systems software.
- d. Access complex data structures without using host language extensions.

**240.** A primary reason auditors are reluctant to use integrated test facility (ITF) is that it requires them to

- a. Reserve specific master file records and process them at regular intervals.
- b. Collect transaction and master file records in a separate file.
- c. Notify user personnel so they can make manual adjustments to output.
- d. Identify and reverse the fictitious entries to avoid contamination of the master file.

**241.** Embedded audit modules

- a. Identify unexecuted computer code.
- b. Aid in debugging application systems.
- c. Analyze the efficiency of programming.
- d. Enable continuous monitoring of transaction processing.

**242.** An internal auditing department implemented an integrated test facility (ITF) to test its payroll processing. The auditing department identified the key controls, processing steps built into the computer program, and developed test data to test them. The department submitted test transactions throughout the year. Assuming the auditors did not find any differences in their test results, the auditors can conclude

- a. The system is properly capturing the hours worked by employees during the year and the hours have been properly submitted to payroll and processed correctly.
- b. All employees were correctly paid during the year and their pay was correctly computed.
- c. The computer application and its control procedures were processing payroll transactions correctly during the past year.
- d. All of the above.

**243.** The greatest impact information technology has had on the audit process is

- a. Its use to track personnel performance and development of audit staff.
- b. Its use in the audit reporting process, such as automated working paper packages.
- c. Its use to conduct audits utilizing various computer-assisted techniques.
- d. Its use as a strategic tool to develop the audit plan.

**244.** Generalized audit software is designed to allow auditors to

- a. Monitor the execution of application programs.
- b. Process test data against master files that contain real and fictitious entities.
- c. Select sample data from files and check computations.
- d. Insert special audit routines into regular application programs.

**245.** An internal auditor was assigned to confirm whether operating personnel had corrected several errors in transaction files that were discovered during a recent audit. Which of the following automated tools is the auditor **most** likely to use?

- a. Online inquiry.
- b. Parallel simulation.
- c. Mapping.
- d. Tracing.

**246.** An audit test to substantiate that a company is complying with software copyright requirements is to

- a. Review the corporate policy on copyrights.
- b. Compare the software on a sample of microcomputers with the purchase documentation.
- c. Inventory all the software that is being run on microcomputers.
- d. Review the minutes of the MIS steering committee or similar body.

**247.** A principal disadvantage of auditing around rather than through the computer is

- a. The time involved in testing controls for simulation programs is extensive.
- b. The costs involved in testing controls over computer processing are high.

c.  The integrity of the audit trail through the computer is not tested.

d.  The technical expertise to compensate for auditing around the computer is extensive.

**Items 248 and 249** are based on the following:

**248.** An accounting clerk developed a scheme to input fraudulent invoices for nonexistent vendors. All the payments were sent to the same address. The auditor suspects a possible fraud. The **most** effective computer audit technique to investigate the fraud would be to

a.  Use test-data for multiple vendors and investigate unexpected results.

b.  Perform a complete audit of computer program changes.

c.  Use generalized audit software to compare addresses across multiple files and print out duplicates for investigation.

d.  Test application controls through an integrated test facility and investigate unexpected results.

**249.** In the audit example described in the previous question, the auditor would test all of the vendor information rather than a sample of the vendor transactions because

a.  Although nonsampling error is reduced, sampling error is larger when computers are used to draw the sample.

b.  The audit procedures used to compare vendor information require the reading of all records.

c.  Audit standards prohibit the use of sampling if fraud is expected.

d.  The only effective procedures require auditing through the computer.

**250.** To achieve cost-effective audits of computer-based systems where similar audit tasks are required to meet a variety of objectives, the auditor should use

a.  Comparison programs.

b.  Custom audit software.

c.  Query functions and report writers.

d.  Generalized audit software.

**251.** Which of the following is an appropriate audit procedure that may be used to test the adequacy of application controls over computer-based accounts payable?

a.  Observing the computer library and operations area to obtain evidence to support an opinion about the security of accounts payable data files.

b.  Manually comparing vendor invoice numbers with those listed on computer-generated lists of accounts payable to assess the effectiveness of computer-based sequence checks.

c.  Testing purchase transactions using a test-data approach.

d.  Using a computer-generated questionnaire to obtain reliable information about the accuracy and completeness of input and update of accounts payable data from the organization's computer management personnel.

**252.** The internal auditing department has begun an audit of an automated payroll system. Audit staff members have been trained in the use of an audit software package and have a working knowledge of the database employed for this system but do not have programming experience. In the system being audited, employees report their hours on time sheets, which

are keyed each week by an assigned individual in each department.

The transaction file of payroll hours is maintained by the system as a primary source of payroll input. After the department manager reviews the gross hours, the information is released to the online payroll system. The payroll is then processed and pay stubs are printed and distributed to the employees. All payments are through direct deposit. In order to preserve the confidentiality of the payroll information of employees, detailed reports that reconcile payroll expenses charged to the department are not generated. Management wants to know whether the payroll program is reliable. Given the skill level of the assigned staff, which of the following methods will **most likely** be applied to test the accuracy of the payroll calculation?

a.  Parallel simulation.

b.  Integrated test facility.

c.  Tagging and tracing.

d.  Mapping and program analysis.

**253.** To identify lost or incomplete sales accounting record updates using the computer, the **most appropriate** approach is

a.  Test data.

b.  Parallel simulation.

c.  Controlled reprocessing.

d.  Integrated test facility.

**254.** You have been assigned to review the propriety of the duplicate payments edit control in the accounts payable system of a public agency. The agency purchases spare parts from approximately 2,000 vendors. In addition, the agency is building a heavy rail system and makes payments to contractors and subcontractors for this $2 billion project. You have been told that vendors have recently reported several duplicate payments.

Management believes that some unreported duplicate payments may exist for which the agency should seek refund. The director of management information systems (MIS) stated that the duplicate payments were isolated instances that would eventually have been discovered by controls outside of the computer system. All payments are matched against a 60-day payment history file. Whenever there is a match on amount, invoice number, and vendor number, duplicate payments warning is sent to the accounts payable clerk. Only the manager of accounts payable is capable of overriding this edit. Which of the following is the **best** computer-assisted audit technique or tool to use in this situation?

a.  Statistical sampling.

b.  Source code desk checking.

c.  Integrated test facility.

d.  Generalized audit software.

**255.** When concerned with the validity of certain recurring transactions, which of the following computer-assisted audit techniques would allow the auditor to select predefined transactions for audit during normal processing?

a.  Extended records.

b.  Tracing.

c.  Mapping.

d.  Embedded audit data collection.

**256.** To test that all inventory shipments are billed to customers, an auditor would compare computer-generated

a.  Receivables ledger updates with detailed sales invoices.

b.   Shipping records with detailed sales invoices.

c.   Shipping records with original customer orders.

d.   Shipping records with customer credit limits.

**257.** Which of the following **best** describes the operation of an integrated test facility (ITF)?

a.   Establishing a dummy entity against which test data are processed and stored.

b.   Developing a simulation program to compare actual data and test data.

c.   Using specially coded inputs to trace test data through the transaction trail.

d.   Translating business transactions into a format that the operating system processes.

**258.** An internal auditor identifies a situation where there is doubt whether all overhead is completely allocated to cost centers by the computer program. The best procedure to test the completeness of the allocation by the program is

a.   Use of control flowcharting.

b.   Inquiry of the systems programmers.

c.   Use of extended records and mapping.

d.   The test-data approach.

**259.** Modern computer technology makes it possible to perform "paperless audits." For example, in an audit of computer-processed customer accounts receivable balances, an auditor might utilize a microcomputer to directly access the accounts receivable files and copy selected customer records into the microcomputer for audit analysis. Which of the following is an advantage of this type of "paperless audit" of accounts receivable balances?

a.   It reduces the amount of substantive testing required.

b.   It allows immediate processing of audit data on a spreadsheet working paper.

c.   It increases the amount of technical skill required of the auditor.

d.   It allows direct confirmation of customer account balances.

**260.** To ensure that goods received are the same as those shown on the purchase invoice, a computerized system should

a.   Match selected fields of the purchase invoice to goods received.

b.   Maintain control totals of inventory value.

c.   Calculate batch totals for each input.

d.   Use check digits in account numbers.

**261.** Which of the following is a disadvantage of using an integrated test facility (ITF) when auditing a computer application?

a.   The ITF may be useful in verifying the correctness of account balances, but not in determining the presence of processing controls.

b.   The test transactions could enter the live data environment.

c.   The ITF technique cannot be used with simulated master file records, during application testing.

d.   The test data must be processed by IT staff with substantial technical skills.

**262.** Which of the following is one purpose of an embedded audit module?

a.   Enable continuous monitoring of transaction processing.

b.   Identify program code that may have been inserted for unauthorized purposes.

c.   Verify the correctness of account balances on a master file.

d.   Review the contents of a specific portion of computer memory.

## Process Mapping Including Flowcharting

**263.** Which of the following is true of a horizontal flowchart as compared to a vertical flowchart?

a.   It provides more room for written descriptions that parallel the symbols.

b.   It brings into sharper focus the assignment of duties and independent checks on performance.

c.   It is usually longer.

d.   It does not provide as broad a picture at a glance.

**264.** Of the following, which is the **most efficient** source for an auditor to use to evaluate a company's overall control system?

a.   Control flowcharts.

b.   Copies of standard operating procedures.

c.   A narrative describing departmental history, activities, and forms usage.

d.   Copies of industry operating standards.

**265.** Which of the following tools would **best** give a graphical representation of a sequence of activities and decisions?

a.   Flowchart.

b.   Control chart.

c.   Histogram.

d.   Run chart.

**266.** Of the techniques available to an auditor, which is the **most** valuable in providing a summary outline and overall description of the process of transactions in an information system?

a.   Flowcharts.

b.   Transaction retrievals.

c.   Test decks.

d.   Software code comparisons.

**267.** An auditor reviews and adapts a systems flowchart to understand the flow of information in the processing of cash receipts. Which of the following statements is **true** regarding the use of such flowcharts? The flowcharts

a.   Show specific control procedures used, such as edit tests that are implemented and batch control reconciliations.

b.   Are good guides to potential segregation of duties.

c.   Are generally kept up to date for systems changes.

d.   Show only computer processing, not manual processing.

**268.** In documenting the procedures used by several interacting departments, the internal auditor will **most** likely use

a.   A horizontal (or systems) flowchart.

b.   A vertical flowchart.

c.   A Gantt chart.

d.   An internal control questionnaire.

**269.** Which method of evaluating internal controls during the preliminary review provides the auditor with the **best** visual grasp of a system and a means for analyzing complex operations?

a.   A flowcharting approach.

b.   A questionnaire approach.

c. A matrix approach.

d. A detailed narrative approach.

## Risk and Control Self-Assessment 2

**270.** From enterprise risk management (ERM) viewpoint, control processes are implemented in which of the following?

a. Risk assessment.

b. Risk mitigation.

c. Risk financing.

d. Risk monitoring

**271.** From enterprise risk management (ERM) viewpoint, the scope of traditional risk management includes which of the following?

a. Insurance.

b. Earnings growth.

c. Revenue growth.

d. Corporate governance.

**272.** In implementing enterprise risk management (ERM), most organizations are following a(n)

a. Layered approach.

b. Total risk approach.

c. Early wins approach.

d. Pilot project approach.

**273.** From enterprise risk management (ERM) viewpoint, all of the following can oversee risk management activities except

a. Chief financial officer.

b. Chief executive officer.

c. Chief audit executive.

d. Chief risk officer.

**274.** Organizations do not view enterprise risk management (ERM) as a(n)

a. Analytical tool.

b. Risk mapping tool.

c. Optimization software tool.

d. Performance management system tool.

**275.** Which of the following is the primary driver for enterprise risk management (ERM) activity?

a. Corporate governance guidelines.

b. Desire for a unifying framework.

c. Competitive pressure.

d. Desire for earnings stability.

**276.** According to the IIA survey regarding enterprise risk management (ERM), which of the following is ranked as the highest business issue today?

a. Earnings consistency.

b. Expense control.

c. Earnings growth.

d. Revenue growth.

**277.** Enterprise resource management (ERM) is seen as providing immediate value in which of the following areas?

I. Capital management.

II. Earnings consistency.

III. Contingency planning.

IV. Expense control.

a. I only.

b. II only.

c. I and III.

d. II and IV.

**278.** Which of the following is the major barrier to implementing enterprise risk management (ERM) program?

a. Unclear benefits.

b. Lack of tools.

c. Organizational turf battles.

d. Organizational culture.

**279.** Comprehensive risk assessment does **not** exist in which of the following functions?

a. Human resources.

b. Finance.

c. Operations.

d. Internal audit.

**280.** Risk management has evolved from which of the following?

a. Operations research.

b. Decision theory.

c. Insurance management.

d. Management science.

**281.** Risk management is concerned primarily with

a. Dynamic risks.

b. Pure risks.

c. Speculative risks.

d. Fundamental risks.

**282.** A business firm with an inventory of obsolete stock that is overinsured might represent which of the following?

a. A moral hazard.

b. A morale hazard.

c. A physical hazard.

d. A legal hazard.

**283.** Which of the following techniques for dealing with risk may represent a special variation of other techniques?

a. Risk financing.

b. Risk retention.

c. Risk sharing.

d. Risk transfer.

**284.** Risk avoidance should be used in those instances in which

a. The severity of loss is high.

b. The exposure has catastrophic potential and the risk cannot be reduced or transferred.

c. The frequency of loss is high.

d. The frequency or severity cannot be determined.

**285.** The term "enterprise risk management" (ERM) refers to which of the following?

a. Risks related to financial derivatives and futures.

b. Market risk, financial risk, and operational risks.

c. Pure, financial, operational, strategic, and speculative risks.

d. Dynamic risks, static risks, and pure risks.

**286.** The two broad approaches to dealing with risk management are

a. Risk retention and risk transfer.

b. Risk avoidance and risk transfer.

c. Risk avoidance and risk reduction.

d. Risk control and risk financing.

**287.** Which of the following steps in the risk management process is **most likely** to be overlooked?

a. Evaluation of risks.

b. Determination of objectives.

    c.    Identification of risks.
    d.    Selection of risk treatments.

**288.** The ultimate goal of risk management is to
    a.    Minimize insurance expenditures.
    b.    Minimize uninsured losses.
    c.    Minimize the adverse effects of losses and uncertainty connected with pure risks.
    d.    Eliminate financial and operational losses.

**289.** Risk retention is most appropriate for situations in which there is a
    a.    Low frequency and a high severity.
    b.    High frequency and a high severity.
    c.    Low frequency and a low severity.
    d.    High frequency and a low severity.

**290.** Insurance is most appropriate for situations in which there is a
    a.    Low frequency and a high severity.
    b.    High frequency and a high severity.
    c.    Low frequency and a low severity.
    d.    High frequency and a low severity.

**291.** Regarding enterprise resource management (ERM) framework, the cost of financing risk is a(n)
    a.    Marginal cost.
    b.    Opportunity cost.
    c.    Average cost.
    d.    Interest cost.

**292.** From an enterprise risk management (ERM) viewpoint, the term "hazard" refers to
    a.    The same thing as risk.
    b.    The same thing as exposure.
    c.    A condition that increases the chance of loss.
    d.    Uncertainty regarding loss.

**293.** When creating new businesses, organizations must consider
    a.    Delinking opportunities.
    b.    Desizing opportunities.
    c.    Derisking opportunities.
    d.    Desourcing opportunities.

**294.** Which of the following enterprise risk management (ERM) frameworks address market risk?
    a.    Strategic risks.
    b.    Operational risks.
    c.    Financial risks.
    d.    Hazard risks.

**295.** Regarding enterprise risk management (ERM), which of the following are more difficult to identify and assess?
   I. Hazard risks.
   II. Financial risks.
  III. Strategic risks.
  IV. Operational risks.

    a.    I only.
    b.    II only.
    c.    I and II.
    d.    III and IV.

**296.** Enterprise risk management (ERM) should encompass which of the following?
   I. Hazards.
   II. Opportunities.
  III. Strengths.
  IV. Weaknesses.

    a.    I only.
    b.    II only.
    c.    I and II.
    d.    III and IV.

## MULTIPLE-CHOICE ANSWERS AND EXPLANATIONS

| | | | | | | | | | | | | | | |
|---|---|---|---|---|---|---|---|---|---|---|---|---|---|---|
| 1. b | __ __ | 51. b | __ __ | 101. d | __ __ | 151. a | __ __ | 201. a | __ __ | 251. c | __ __ |
| 2. a | __ __ | 52. b | __ __ | 102. c | __ __ | 152. b | __ __ | 202. d | __ __ | 252. a | __ __ |
| 3. b | __ __ | 53. d | __ __ | 103. b | __ __ | 153. a | __ __ | 203. b | __ __ | 253. c | __ __ |
| 4. a | __ __ | 54. c | __ __ | 104. d | __ __ | 154. a | __ __ | 204. b | __ __ | 254. d | __ __ |
| 5. d | __ __ | 55. d | __ __ | 105. d | __ __ | 155. d | __ __ | 205. a | __ __ | 255. d | __ __ |
| 6. b | __ __ | 56. c | __ __ | 106. b | __ __ | 156. d | __ __ | 206. a | __ __ | 256. b | __ __ |
| 7. a | __ __ | 57. a | __ __ | 107. c | __ __ | 157. d | __ __ | 207. c | __ __ | 257. a | __ __ |
| 8. c | __ __ | 58. d | __ __ | 108. c | __ __ | 158. b | __ __ | 208. a | __ __ | 258. d | __ __ |
| 9. b | __ __ | 59. c | __ __ | 109. b | __ __ | 159. a | __ __ | 209. c | __ __ | 259. b | __ __ |
| 10. a | __ __ | 60. a | __ __ | 110. d | __ __ | 160. c | __ __ | 210. b | __ __ | 260. a | __ __ |
| 11. c | __ __ | 61. c | __ __ | 111. b | __ __ | 161. d | __ __ | 211. b | __ __ | 261. b | __ __ |
| 11. b | __ __ | 62. c | __ __ | 112. c | __ __ | 162. b | __ __ | 212. a | __ __ | 262. a | __ __ |
| 13. c | __ __ | 63. b | __ __ | 113. a | __ __ | 163. b | __ __ | 213. a | __ __ | 263. b | __ __ |
| 14. b | __ __ | 64. b | __ __ | 114. d | __ __ | 164. a | __ __ | 214. a | __ __ | 264. a | __ __ |
| 15. a | __ __ | 65. c | __ __ | 115. a | __ __ | 165. c | __ __ | 215. c | __ __ | 265. a | __ __ |
| 16. d | __ __ | 66. a | __ __ | 116. c | __ __ | 166. b | __ __ | 216. a | __ __ | 266. a | __ __ |
| 17. a | __ __ | 67. b | __ __ | 117. d | __ __ | 167. a | __ __ | 217. a | __ __ | 267. b | __ __ |
| 18. d | __ __ | 68. a | __ __ | 118. d | __ __ | 168. d | __ __ | 218. a | __ __ | 268. a | __ __ |
| 19. b | __ __ | 69. a | __ __ | 119. a | __ __ | 169. c | __ __ | 219. c | __ __ | 269. a | __ __ |
| 20. b | __ __ | 70. c | __ __ | 120. c | __ __ | 170. a | __ __ | 220. b | __ __ | 270. b | __ __ |
| 21. a | __ __ | 71. d | __ __ | 121. b | __ __ | 171. c | __ __ | 221. c | __ __ | 271. a | __ __ |
| 22. a | __ __ | 72. c | __ __ | 122. c | __ __ | 172. c | __ __ | 222. d | __ __ | 272. c | __ __ |
| 23. d | __ __ | 73. c | __ __ | 123. b | __ __ | 173. d | __ __ | 223. c | __ __ | 273. b | __ __ |
| 24. b | __ __ | 74. c | __ __ | 124. c | __ __ | 174. b | __ __ | 224. a | __ __ | 274. d | __ __ |
| 25. b | __ __ | 75. d | __ __ | 125. d | __ __ | 175. b | __ __ | 225. b | __ __ | 275. b | __ __ |
| 26. c | __ __ | 76. b | __ __ | 126. b | __ __ | 176. c | __ __ | 226. d | __ __ | 276. c | __ __ |
| 27. b | __ __ | 77. a | __ __ | 127. b | __ __ | 177. c | __ __ | 227. b | __ __ | 277. c | __ __ |
| 28. d | __ __ | 78. c | __ __ | 128. d | __ __ | 178. a | __ __ | 228. c | __ __ | 278. d | __ __ |
| 29. b | __ __ | 79. c | __ __ | 129. c | __ __ | 179. c | __ __ | 229. a | __ __ | 279. a | __ __ |
| 30. a | __ __ | 80. c | __ __ | 130. d | __ __ | 180. a | __ __ | 230. c | __ __ | 280. c | __ __ |
| 31. c | __ __ | 81. b | __ __ | 131. b | __ __ | 181. a | __ __ | 231. a | __ __ | 281. b | __ __ |
| 32. c | __ __ | 82. b | __ __ | 132. b | __ __ | 182. d | __ __ | 232. a | __ __ | 282. a | __ __ |
| 33. c | __ __ | 83. a | __ __ | 133. c | __ __ | 183. b | __ __ | 233. d | __ __ | 283. c | __ __ |
| 34. a | __ __ | 84. d | __ __ | 134. c | __ __ | 184. d | __ __ | 234. c | __ __ | 284. b | __ __ |
| 35. c | __ __ | 85. c | __ __ | 135. c | __ __ | 185. d | __ __ | 235. c | __ __ | 285. c | __ __ |
| 36. a | __ __ | 86. b | __ __ | 136. c | __ __ | 186. b | __ __ | 236. a | __ __ | 286. d | __ __ |
| 37. b | __ __ | 87. b | __ __ | 137. b | __ __ | 187. d | __ __ | 237. d | __ __ | 287. b | __ __ |
| 38. a | __ __ | 88. c | __ __ | 138. b | __ __ | 188. b | __ __ | 238. c | __ __ | 288. c | __ __ |
| 39. c | __ __ | 89. c | __ __ | 139. a | __ __ | 189. c | __ __ | 239. a | __ __ | 289. c | __ __ |
| 40. a | __ __ | 90. d | __ __ | 140. d | __ __ | 190. a | __ __ | 240. d | __ __ | 290. a | __ __ |
| 41. b | __ __ | 91. d | __ __ | 141. a | __ __ | 191. c | __ __ | 241. d | __ __ | 291. b | __ __ |
| 42. b | __ __ | 92. a | __ __ | 142. b | __ __ | 192. d | __ __ | 242. c | __ __ | 292. c | __ __ |
| 43. d | __ __ | 93. a | __ __ | 143. d | __ __ | 193. b | __ __ | 243. c | __ __ | 293. c | __ __ |
| 44. c | __ __ | 94. b | __ __ | 144. d | __ __ | 194. b | __ __ | 244. c | __ __ | 294. c | __ __ |
| 45. a | __ __ | 95. c | __ __ | 145. b | __ __ | 195. a | __ __ | 245. a | __ __ | 295. d | __ __ |
| 46. d | __ __ | 96. d | __ __ | 146. b | __ __ | 196. a | __ __ | 246. b | __ __ | 296. c | __ __ |
| 47. a | __ __ | 97. b | __ __ | 147. d | __ __ | 197. a | __ __ | 247. c | __ __ | | |
| 48. a | __ __ | 98. d | __ __ | 148. b | __ __ | 198. c | __ __ | 248. c | __ __ | | |
| 49. c | __ __ | 99. a | __ __ | 149. b | __ __ | 199. a | __ __ | 249. b | __ __ | 1st: __/296 = __% |
| 50. a | __ __ | 100. b | __ __ | 150. d | __ __ | 200. d | __ __ | 250. d | __ __ | 2nd: __/296 = __% |

### Sampling and Statistical Analysis

**1. (b)** Compared to the other responses, the percentage of error in the sample is small relative to the tolerable error rate. Choice (a) is incorrect. Sampling risk would be higher for the sample because the sample size is smaller and because the 2% error rate is larger than the 1% in choice (b), while the tolerable error rate is the same. Choice (c) is incorrect. Sampling risk would be higher than in choice (b) because the sample error rate is very large compared to the tolerable error rate. Although the sample size is larger than that in choice (b), the increase in the sample size is not large enough to compensate for the size of the sample error rate relative to the tolerable error rate. Choice (d) is incorrect. Although this is the largest sample, the sampling risk is extremely high because the sample error rate equals the tolerable error rate.

Subject Area: Engagement tools—sampling. Source: CIA 597, II-31.

**2.** **(a)** The allowable level of sampling risk is the risk an auditor is willing to take that a conclusion based on the sample may be incorrect. The auditor's experience and knowledge should have no bearing on that decision; however, the auditor's experience and knowledge may affect his or her decision to use statistical or nonstatistical sampling and may be a factor in assessing nonsampling risks. Choice (b) is incorrect. As adverse consequences of noncompliance increase, the allowable level of sampling risk tends to decrease. Choice (c) is incorrect. The acceptable level of risk of making an incorrect audit conclusion is directly related to the allowable level of sampling risk. Choice (d) is incorrect. The cost of performing auditing procedures on sample selections is one of the factors an auditor should consider when assessing the allowable level of sampling risk. The cost of performing the auditing procedures is weighed against the benefit of minimizing the chance of making an incorrect audit decision.

Subject Area: Engagement tools—sampling. Source: CIA 597, II-35.

**3.** **(b)** Auditors use a pilot sample to estimate the standard deviation in a population. This enables auditors to estimate the confidence interval that would be achieved by the sample and therefore helps them decide how large of a sample to select. Choice (a) is incorrect. Difference estimation is a type of variables sampling plan. It is not a technique for estimating standard deviation. Choice (c) is incorrect. Auditors use regression to project balances of accounts or other populations. Choice (d) is incorrect. Discovery sampling is a type of sampling plan, not a technique for estimating standard deviation.

Subject Area: Engagement tools—sampling. Source: CIA 597, II-39.

**4.** **(a)** Sampling of this transaction file would be appropriate to ascertain if the cost of fixed assets is improperly expensed. Choice (b) is incorrect. Ascertaining that all noncapital expenditures have been expensed would require testing of expense accounts and selected asset accounts in addition to the repair expense account. Choice (c) is incorrect. Ascertaining that noncapital repair expenditures have been recorded in the proper time period would require sampling from more than one time period. Choice (d) is incorrect. Ascertaining that capital fixed assets expenditures were recorded in the proper time period would involve sampling from the fixed assets file.

Subject Area: Engagement tools—sampling. Source: CIA 597, II-49.

**5.** **(d)** The auditor has selected items from only two months. That sampling plan may enable the auditor to make conclusions about the overall error rates during those two months, but not about error rates during the whole year. Choice (a) is incorrect. Although sampling risk is related to sample size, it is not related to sample size relative to the population size. In addition, this problem does not contain sufficient information to evaluate the acceptability of sampling risk. Choice (b) is incorrect. The objective of stratifying a population is to decrease the sampling risk, not to reduce bias. This problem does not give enough information to decide whether stratification might have enabled the auditor to use a smaller sample. Choice (c) is incorrect. Systematic selection with a random start is unbiased if the population is randomly organized.

Subject Area: Engagement tools—sampling. Source: CIA 1196, II-39.

**6.** **(b)** This is why auditors often use random numbers to select sample items. In a random sample, each sampling unit and each combination of sampling units has an equal probability of selection and is therefore likely to be unbiased. Choice (a) is incorrect. Although random-number sampling may be used for variables sampling plan, it is not required. Systematic selection is also acceptable unless the population is not randomly organized. Choice (c) is incorrect. The use of random numbers does not always result in a representative sample. Statistics allow auditors to estimate the probability that a random sample is not representative. Choice (d) is incorrect. The use of random numbers does not affect sample size.

Subject Area: Engagement tools—sampling. Source: CIA 1196, II-40.

**7.** **(a)** The limitation of all nonstatistical sampling techniques is the auditor's inability to quantify sampling risk. Based on past experience and intuition, the auditor may believe that sampling risk is acceptable, but the auditor is not able to quantify the risk level without using statistical sampling. Choice (b) is incorrect. The auditor could quantify the acceptable error rate independently of the sample design. Choice (c) is incorrect. The auditor can project an error rate of 1/60, or .0167. The problem is that the auditor cannot quantify the risk that the rate in the sample is significantly different from the rate in the population. Choice (d) is incorrect. A mathematician may be able to determine whether the auditor's selections are random, although it is unlikely that they are. If the sample is representative, it does not matter whether it is random or not.

Subject Area: Engagement tools—sampling. Source: CIA 1196, II-42.

**8.** **(c)** This is the definition of confidence level. Choice (a) is incorrect. Sampling risk is the complement of the confidence level. Choice (b) is incorrect. Nonsampling risk is the risk of improperly auditing the sampled items and cannot be quantified. Choice (d) is incorrect. Precision is the specified range, not the degree of justification.

Subject Area: Engagement tools—sampling. Source: CIA 1196, II-44.

**9.** **(b)** Using multiple random starts would increase the likelihood that the population includes a representative number of reports for each day of the week and for each day of the month. Choice (a) is incorrect. Estimating the error rate has no effect on bias. Bias is related to the selection method. Choice (c) is incorrect. Increasing the confidence level has no effect on bias. Choice (d) is incorrect. Increasing the precision has no effect on bias.

Subject Area: Engagement tools—sampling. Source: CIA 1196, II-46.

**10.** **(a)** This is the definition of the population. Choice (b) is incorrect. The attribute is the characteristic the auditor wants to estimate about the population. Choice (c) is incorrect. The sample is a subset of the population used to estimate the characteristic. Choice (d) is incorrect. Sampling unit refers to the item that is actually selected for examination and is a subset of the population.

Subject Area: Engagement tools—sampling. Source: CIA 1196, II-49.

**11.** **(c)** Standard deviation is a measure of data (item) variability. Choice (a) is incorrect. Expected error rate is associated with attribute sampling and is not involved with the standard deviation. Choice (b) is incorrect. Confidence level is determined by auditor judgment. Choice (d) is incorrect. Achieved precision in variables sampling is computed using the standard deviation.

Subject Area: Engagement tools—sampling. Source: CIA 1196, II-50.

**12.   (b)**   $10,000/100 = $100 and $100 (2000) = $200,000 and $200,000 – $4000 = $196,000. Choice (a) is incorrect. Precision of $4,000 should be subtracted, not added to the estimate of the population. Choice (c) is incorrect. This calculation uses standard deviation for determining the precision factor, but the precision has been given as $4,000. The amount is determined as follows: $10 × 100 = $1,000 and $200,000 – 1,000 = $199,000. Choice (d) is incorrect. This calculation uses standard deviation for determining the precision factor, but the precision has been given as $4,000. The amount is determined as: ($10/100) 2,000 = $200 and 200,000 – 200 = $199,800.

Subject Area: Engagement tools—sampling. Source: CIA 596, II-40.

**13.   (c)**   The working paper should specify the sampling risk and the confidence level or precision achieved by the sample or the method of determining size. Choice (a) is incorrect. It is not necessary to use tick marks in this case because the same procedures were applied to all sample selections and no exceptions were detected. Choice (b) is incorrect. The audit work papers are themselves kept confidential so it is not necessary to remove employee names. Choice (d) is incorrect. In this case, reference to the company policy is equivalent to listing the documents that were examined.

Subject Area: Engagement tools—sampling. Source: CIA 1195, II-7.

**14.   (b)**   Because high-value items can be sampled 100%, a large segment of variability can be eliminated. Choice (a) is incorrect. A larger sample might more closely approximate the population standard deviation, but that could be either higher or lower depending on the point of reference. A smaller sample might go either way without the increased reliability. Choices (c) and (d) are incorrect. To the extent that sample size is affected, the results might be the same as in the choice (a) above.

Subject Area: Engagement tools—sampling. Source: CIA 590, I-32.

**15.   (a)**   This fits the definition. Choices (b) and (c) are incorrect because each is neither. Choice (d) is incorrect because it is precise but not complete.

Subject Area: Engagement tools—sampling. Source: CIA 1190, I-39.

**16.   (d)**   It is the only way to measure reliability. Choice (a) is incorrect because judgment is needed for sample size. Choice (b) is incorrect because this may need a large sample. Choice (c) is incorrect because there is no way to determine this.

Subject Area: Engagement tools—sampling. Source: CIA 1190, I-40.

**17.   (a)**   In its simplest form, the sample-size formula shows that sample size is equal to [(Confidence level factor squared × Estimated standard deviation squared)/(Precision squared)], thus any increase in confidence level would be accompanied by an increase in sample size. By definition, choices (b), (c), and (d) are incorrect.

Subject Area: Engagement tools—sampling. Source: CIA 590, II-27.

**18.   (d)**   The standard error of the mean is equal to the sample standard deviation divided by the square root of sample size. ($24.00/12 = $2.00). By definition, choices (a), (b), and (c) are incorrect.

Subject Area: Engagement tools—sampling. Source: CIA 590, II-28.

**19.   (b)**   Errors are three times as likely in retail boxes as in wholesale boxes, but wholesale boxes are twice as frequent in the warehouse. Thus, the evidence points slightly more toward the retail division. Alternatively, by the Bayes theorem, we have:  P (Retail/Error) = 0.06 × 1/3)/0.06 × 1/3 + 0.02 × 2/3) = 0.60. Choice (a) is incorrect. See response (b). Choice (c) is incorrect. The contents of any one box are insufficient grounds to conclude anything about the whole warehouse. Choice (d) is incorrect. See response (c).

Subject Area: Engagement tools—sampling. Source: CIA 1195, II-41.

**20.   (b)**   When the size of the population is very large, the effect on precision of the finite population correction factor is very limited. Choice (a) is incorrect. A large sample selected in a biased way leads to less representatives than a smaller but more carefully selected sample. Choice (c) is incorrect. The advantage of most variations on simple random sampling is that for a given sample size, they produce a more representative sample. Choice (d) is incorrect. Things that are not in the sampling frame cannot be put there by an appropriate sampling technique.

Subject Area: Engagement tools—sampling. Source: CIA 1195, II-42.

**21.   (a)**   Sample size considerations are the same for both of these parameters. Choice (b) is incorrect. The greater the variability, the greater the required sample size. Choice (c) is incorrect. The more sensitive the decision is to estimation errors, the greater the appropriate sample size. Choice (d) is incorrect. The greater the cost per observation, the smaller the appropriate sample size.

Subject Area: Engagement tools—sampling. Source: CIA 1195, II-43.

**22.   (a)**   The precision of sample results is proportional to the square root of the sample size. Choice (b) is incorrect. The precision of sample results does not increase at the same rate as sample size. Choice (c) is incorrect. The expected value of the sample mean is the same regardless of sample size, and thus no "downward bias" is present. Choice (d) is incorrect. See explanation given for the choice (a).

Subject Area: Engagement tools—sampling. Source: CIA 1195, II-44.

**23.   (d)**   This is the definition of a confidence interval. Choice (a) is incorrect. A confidence interval concerns only whether the population parameter is contained inside the interval and says nothing directly about the exact value of the parameter. Choice (b) is incorrect. This could be true if the confidence interval were one-sided (i.e., all probability bunched below the mean), but it is not true for the more common two-sided confidence intervals, for which the correct chance of exceeding the top of the interval in a 90% confidence interval would be 5%. Choice (c) is incorrect. The confidence interval is based on the standard deviation, but it has no bearing on the size of the standard deviation.

Subject Area: Engagement tools—sampling. Source: CIA 1195, II-46.

**24.   (b)**   The major concern is whether the computer program is properly calculating the freight charges. Test data or parallel simulation would allow a comprehensive test of the computer program at this one point in time and would provide more evidence than sampling procedures. Choice (a) is incorrect. Discovery sampling would not be as comprehensive or as efficient as either of the computer audit techniques in choice (b). Choice (c) is incorrect. Difference estimation is used to estimate the dollar amount of error in a population, not to discover whether such errors take place. The auditor is more interested in finding whether errors take place. Choice (d) is incorrect. A computer audit tool is used, but the basic technique is a monetary unit sample, which is designed to test the hypothesis of material errors in the account balance. The task cited is to determine whether such errors are occurring.

Subject Area: Engagement tools—sampling. Source: CIA 595, II-43.

**25.   (b)**   Lower confidence level allows smaller sample size. Choices (a) and (d) are incorrect. Lower confidence level allows smaller sample size. Choice (c) is incorrect. The percentage change is not a corresponding percent—only a decrease.

Subject Area: Engagement tools—sampling. Source: CIA 1194, II-36.

**26.   (c)**   Standard deviation is a measure of data (items) variability. Choice (a) is incorrect. Expected error rate is associated with attribute sampling and is not involved with the standard deviation. Choice (b) is incorrect. Confidence level is determined by auditor judgment. Choice (d) is incorrect. Achieved precision in variables sampling is computed using the standard deviation.

Subject Area: Engagement tools—sampling. Source: CIA 1194, II-38.

**27.   (b)**   Statistical sampling provides quantifiable risk and results. Choice (a) is incorrect. Statistical sampling provides quantified results. Choice (c) is incorrect. Nonsampling risk exists in statistical and nonstatistical sampling. Choice (d) is incorrect. Tolerable error is related to materiality and auditor judgment.

Subject Area: Engagement tools—sampling. Source: CIA 1194, II-39.

**28.   (d)**   There is a 95% probability that the number of errors is between 2% (4% − 2%) and 6% (4% + 2%) of the population of 2,000 items. Choice (a) is incorrect. This response (5% × 2,000 items) confuses the confidence level with the estimated error rate. Choice (b) is incorrect. Although 80 (4% × 2,000) is the best guess as to the number of errors, the actual number of errors will be fewer than 80 approximately as often as it exceeds 80 (indicated by the stated precision of 2%). Choice (c) is incorrect. This response (5%± 2% × 2,000 items) also confuses the confidence level with the estimated error rate.

Subject Area: Engagement tools—sampling. Source: CIA 1194, II-44.

**29.   (b)**   This answer is correct because the mean is greater than the median and the distribution is continuous. Choice (a) is incorrect because the mean is greater than the median and

the distribution is continuous. Choice (c) is incorrect. This answer would be correct for a continuous distribution when the mean, median, and mode are equal. Choice (d) is incorrect. Distributions spread evenly between two values are uniform distributions.

Subject Area: Engagement tools—sampling. Source: CIA 1194, II-49.

**30.   (a)**   Achieved precision (A) = $s_x t$;  A = $1.00 (1.65) = $1.65. Therefore, by definition, choices (b), (c), and (d) are incorrect.

Subject Area: Engagement tools—sampling. Source: CIA 590, I-27.

**31.   (c)**   Use of the standard deviation enables an auditor to extend the results of a sample to the population. Choice (a) is incorrect. The median is a measure of central tendency. Choice (b) is incorrect. Although the range is a measure of variability, its use is considerably limited when compared to the standard deviation. Choice (d) is incorrect. The mean is a measure of central tendency.

Subject Area: Engagement tools—sampling. Source: CIA 590, I-28.

**32.   (c)**   The primary difference between statistical and nonstatistical sampling is that statistical sampling allows sampling risk to be measured and thus controlled. Choice (a) is incorrect. Statistical sampling will not necessarily prescribe a smaller sample size than nonstatistical sampling techniques. It will, however, aid the auditor in designing an efficient sample. Choice (b) is incorrect. Statistical sampling does not guarantee that the sample obtained will be more representative than a sample selected by nonstatistical sampling techniques, only that the sampling risk can be quantified. Choice (d) is incorrect. The IIA *Standards* do not require statistical sampling. Both statistical and nonstatistical samples can provide sufficient evidential matter. The auditor chooses between them after considering their relative cost and effectiveness in the circumstances.

Subject Area: Engagement tools—sampling. Source: CIA 590, I-29.

**33.   (c)**   Sample size is equal to (Standard deviation squared × Confidence-level factor squared) / Desired precision squared. Choice (a) is incorrect. Population standard deviation is a factor of the variability of data only. Choice (b) is incorrect. Population standard deviation is a factor of the variability of data only. Choice (d) is incorrect because choice (c) is the correct answer. It was just reversed.

Subject Area: Engagement tools—sampling. Source: CIA 590, II-31.

**34.   (a)**   Precision refers to the maximum amount, stated at a certain confidence level, that we can expect the estimate from a single sample to deviate from the results obtained by applying the same measuring procedures to all the items in the population. Choice (b) is incorrect because it is not used in connection with sampling. Choice (c) is incorrect because it is a probability. Choice (d) is incorrect because it is too general.

Subject Area: Engagement tools—sampling. Source: CIA 1190, II-39.

**35.   (c)**   The standard deviation is the measure of variability of a statistical sample that serves as an estimate of the population variability. Choice (a) is incorrect. The variance is the square of the standard deviation, which is the measure of variability of a statistical sample that serves as an estimate of the population variability. Choice (b) is incorrect. The range is the difference between the largest and smallest values of a sample or population. Choice (d) is incorrect. The interval is a set of numbers or observations that consists of all the numbers or observations between and including the end points.

Subject Area: Engagement tools—sampling. Source: CIA 1190, II-41.

**36. (a)** Confidence level is the probability that an estimate based on a random sample falls within a specified range. Choice (b) is incorrect because confidence is a decision variable, not a population characteristic. Choice (c) is incorrect because precision, not confidence level, is a measure of accuracy. Choice (d) is incorrect because planned confidence must be specified before sample size can be computed.

Subject Area: Engagement tools—sampling. Source: CIA 594, II-31.

**37. (b)** Precision is the range into which an estimate of a population characteristic is expected to fall. Choice (a) is incorrect because precision is under the auditor's control. Choice (c) is incorrect because precision and reliability are dependent on one another. Choice (d) is incorrect because precision applies to attribute samples as well.

Subject Area: Engagement tools—sampling. Source: CIA 594, II-32.

**38. (a)** Sampling risk results from the possibility that the sample might not be representative in this population. Choice (b) is incorrect because these errors refer to sampling risk, which is independent of the quality of audit procedures. Choice (c) is incorrect because these risks do not inherently depend on economic consequences. Choice (d) is incorrect because it deals with aspects of audit risk, a different concept.

Subject Area: Engagement tools—sampling. Source: CIA 594, II-33.

**39. (c)** If tolerable error is increased, sample size will decrease. Choice (a) is incorrect. This decision will cause sample size to decrease. Choice (b) is incorrect. This will cause the sample size to more that double. Choice (d) is incorrect. This would cause sample size to decrease.

Subject Area: Engagement tools—sampling. Source: CIA 594, II-34.

**40. (a)** A directed nonstatistical (judgment) sample is desirable when reasons exist for focusing audit attention on specific transactions, as in this case for large mortgage applications. Choice (b) is incorrect. A random sample is inefficient in this case, and the population (mortgages closed) is inappropriate. Choice (c) is incorrect. A regression analysis would not explain the cause of the weak correlation. Choice (d) is incorrect. Linear programming to allocate the funds is irrelevant to the issue at hand.

Subject Area: Engagement tools—sampling. Source: CIA 1193, I-39.

**41. (b)** If all other factors remain constant, the sample size will increase to the size required to keep achieved precision constant. Choices (a) and (c) are incorrect. Sample size would be larger and achieved precision would not change. Choice (d) is incorrect because precision would not change. It is good to remember that sample size varies directly with changes in confidence level and inversely with changes in precision.

Subject Area: Engagement tools—sampling. Source: CIA 593, I-32.

**42. (b)** An upper precision limit can be calculated based on the size of the sample and the observed error rate. This should be compared with the maximum tolerable error. Choice (a) is incorrect. Both the expected error rate and the tolerable error rate are known before sampling. Choice (c) is incorrect. Any monetary errors discovered in the sample must first be extrapolated to the population before their materiality can be assessed. Choice (d) is incorrect. It is the responsibility of the auditor to determine the significance of detected errors.

Subject Area: Engagement tools—sampling. Source: CIA 593, II-10.

**43. (d)** Sampling error is the likelihood that sampled items do not reflect the population for which conclusions are made. Choice (a) is incorrect. Drawing a conclusion beyond the population tested is an example of a nonsampling error. Choice (b) is incorrect. Using an improper audit procedure is an example of nonsampling error. Choice (c) is incorrect. Incorrectly applying an audit procedure is another example of a nonsampling error.

Subject Area: Engagement tools—sampling. Source: CIA 593, II-30.

**44. (c)** A confidence level of 90% does mean that 90 times out of 100, the sample results will not vary from the true characteristics of the whole population by more than a specified amount. Ten times out of 100 they will. Choice (a) is incorrect. A confidence level of 90% does not necessarily mean that the expected error rate will be 10%. If it is, it is only by chance. Choice (b) is incorrect. A confidence level of 90% does not mean that any point estimate obtained is within 10% of the value of the true population value. Choice (d) is incorrect. A smaller sample size is required if the desired confidence level was equal to 95%.

Subject Area: Engagement tools—sampling. Source: CIA 593, II-31.

**45. (a)** Along with the inability to quantify sampling error, this is a major limitation of a judgmental sample. Choice (b) is incorrect because the sample size is not the reason for not being able to project; 100 might be enough. Choice (c) is incorrect because the auditor is testing for cost effectiveness. Choice (d) is incorrect because 100 might be enough.

Subject Area: Engagement tools—sampling. Source: CIA 593, II-32.

**46. (d)** Since the sample is highly limited due to selection of all claims processed in the past two days, the intention of the supervisor is to gain an understanding of the details of the work performed by a particular employee. Conclusions cannot be generalized. Choice (a) is incorrect. It is not representative of the employees' work for the whole year. Choice (b) is incorrect. This is a judgment sample. Choice (c) is incorrect. Conclusions for the whole department cannot be drawn.

Subject Area: Engagement tools—sampling. Source: CIA 1192, I-39.

**47. (a)** The two busiest months may not be representative of the entire year. Choice (b) is incorrect. The sample is random. Choice (c) is incorrect. There is insufficient information to judge size. Choice (d) is incorrect since choice (a) is the correct answer.

Subject Area: Engagement tools—sampling. Source: CIA 1192, II-36.

**48.** **(a)** The computed precision is $1.96 \times 30 \times 5,000/10 =$ 29,400. This amount added to the population of $5,000 \times$ mean of $200 equals $1,000,000 plus $29,400 and minus $29,400. Choice (b) is incorrect. If the square root of the sample is incorrectly omitted, the computed precision is $1.96 \times 30 \times 5,000 = 294,000$. Choice (c) is incorrect. If the standard deviation and the square root of the sample size are incorrectly reversed, the computed precision is $1.96 \times 10 \times 5,000/30 = 3,267$. Choice (d) is incorrect. If the sample size is incorrectly used (not the square root), the computed precision is $1.96 \times 30 \times 5000/100 = 2,940$.

Subject Area: Engagement tools—sampling. Source: CIA 592, I-42.

**49.** **(c)** The confidence level is the estimated probability that a value falls within the precision limits. Choice (a) is incorrect. The error rate is the proportion of incorrect items in a population. Choice (b) is incorrect. The lower limit is the bound below which a population value is not expected to fall at a specified confidence level. Choice (d) is incorrect. The standard error of the mean is a value equal to the standard deviation divided by the square root of sample size.

Subject Area: Engagement tools—sampling. Source: CIA 592, I-37.

**50.** **(a)** The precision is the range in which a population parameter is expected to fall, at a specified confidence level. Choice (b) is incorrect. The average or mean is an example of central tendency. Choice (c) is incorrect. Standard deviation is a measure of the variability of the data around the mean. Choice (d) is incorrect. The field is the population.

Subject Area: Engagement tools—sampling. Source: CIA 592, II-38.

**51.** **(b)** The standard error is a measure of the sample's variability. It is computed by dividing sample standard deviation by the square root of sample size. Choice (a) is incorrect. The median, a form of the average, is the central item in an array. Choice (c) is incorrect. The upper limit is the bound above which a population parameter is not expected to fall, at a specified confidence level. Choice (d) is incorrect. The mean, a form of the average, is the sum of the population values, divided by the number of units in the population.

Subject Area: Engagement tools—sampling. Source: CIA 592, II-39.

**52.** **(b)** Sampling error cannot be quantified if judgmental sampling is used. This makes the auditor's conclusions difficult to defend. Choice (a) is incorrect. The stem of this question describes judgmental sampling. Judgmental sampling is often used to make sample selection easier. Choice (c) is incorrect. Judgmental sampling does not rely on any statistical concepts, including assumptions about the distribution of the population. Choice (d) is incorrect. An auditor who uses judgmental sampling often samples fewer units than a statistical plan would have specified.

Subject Area: Engagement tools—sampling. Source: CIA 592, II-40.

**53.** **(d)** Statistical sampling is a procedure for estimating the value of a population parameter of interest by examining only a few observations from the population. Choice (a) is incorrect. Linear programming is a mathematical technique for maximizing or minimizing a given objective subject to certain constraints. Choice (b) is incorrect. Regression analysis is a statistical procedure for estimating the relation between

variables. Choice (c) is incorrect. Queuing theory is used to minimize the cost of waiting in line plus the cost of servicing waiting lines when items arrive randomly at a service point and are serviced sequentially.

Subject Area: Engagement tools—sampling. Source: CIA 592, III-65.

**54.** **(c)** The basic difference between judgmental and statistical sampling is that the sampling risk cannot be quantified in judgmental sampling because the behavior of the sample draw cannot be predicted in terms of the laws of the theory of probability. Choice (a) is incorrect. Representativeness of population is the goal of all sampling. Judgmental and random (statistical) selection both attempt to achieve it. There is no general rule that judgmental will be better than statistical in obtaining it. Choice (b) is incorrect. Statistical sampling may or may not result in a smaller sample size than judgmental sampling. Choice (d) is incorrect. Judgmental sampling does not necessarily give less accurate point estimates.

Subject Area: Engagement tools—sampling. Source: CIA 1191, II-36.

**55.** **(d)** The transactions chosen are judgmental. The selection or the transactions does not meet the criteria of probability sampling since all are not available for selection. Choice (a) is incorrect. Although the sample size is arbitrarily chosen, sampling risk can still be quantified since the sample items are selected according to the criteria of probability sampling. Choice (b) is incorrect. Here systematic selection with a random starting point is used. In practice, this is assumed to meet the criteria of probability sampling. Choice (c) is incorrect. Stratification is used here. The upper stratum is examined 100% and those in the lower stratum are randomly selected. Thus, the criteria of probability sampling are met.

Subject Area: Engagement tools—sampling. Source: CIA 1191, II-37.

**56.** **(c)** This response gives the correct definition of "sampling risk." It can be measured, and increasing sample size can reduce it. Choice (a) is incorrect. This choice may result in an inefficient or unnecessarily large sample, but it is not called "sampling risk." Choice (b) is incorrect. Failure to recognize an error included in a sample is referred to as "nonsampling risk." Choice (d) is incorrect. Confidence level and precision are a matter of auditor judgment; faulty judgment is not called "sampling risk."

Subject Area: Engagement tools—sampling. Source: CIA 591, II-38.

**57.** **(a)** Statistical sampling enables auditors to compute the reliability (confidence) and precision of their sample results. Choice (b) is incorrect. While statistical sampling may sometimes result in a smaller sample than nonstatistical sampling, it may at other times require a larger sample. Choice (c) is incorrect. Statistical sampling requires use of a random sample. Nonstatistical sampling permits the use of nonrandom selection techniques, such as high-value and high-risk items. Choice (d) is incorrect. Statistical sampling results in an objective computation of sample size and, as stated above, requires a random rather than subjective selection technique.

Subject Area: Engagement tools—sampling. Source: CIA 591, II-39.

**58.** **(d)** Since the total dollar value is under study, the probability-in-proportion-to-size (book value) approach is most efficient here. Choice (a) is incorrect. How easy it is to inspect an item has nothing necessarily to do with its value. Choice (b) is incorrect. The approach described in the choice (d) is more appropriate than simple random sampling. Choice (c) is incorrect. Although this approach is better than simple random sampling, items with high sales volumes may have low prices, and thus this method is not as good as that described in the choice (d).

Subject Area: Engagement tools—sampling. Source: CIA 1195, II-19.

**59. (c)** Equal opportunity for selection is a feature of random selection. Choice (a) is incorrect. Stratifying the population is not required for random selection. Choice (b) is incorrect. Dollar values are not used in random selection. Choice (d) is incorrect. Stratifying the population is not required for random selection.

Subject Area: Engagement tools—sampling. Source: CIA 596, II-48.

**60. (a)** The expected value of a random sample of any size is equal to the population mean. Choice (b) is incorrect. The smaller sample is less reliable and is therefore more likely to produce unusually large (or small) sample means. Choice (c) is incorrect. The smaller sample is less reliable and therefore will have a wider 95% confidence interval. Choice (d) is incorrect. The variance is also a population parameter, and the expected value of the sample variance does not change with sample size.

Subject Area: Engagement tools—sampling. Source: CIA 1195, II-47.

**61. (c)** Because different employees probably have different situations, needs, and experiences, stratified sampling would best ensure that a representative sample would result. Choice (a) is incorrect. This convenience sample is likely to emphasize people with lots of time on their hands at the expense of key employees who are too busy with company work to respond. Choice (b) is incorrect. Managers and supervisors often do not have the same needs and perceptions as their subordinates and also often misperceive their views. Choice (d) is incorrect. This approach would produce a disproportionate number of highly paid employees who may not have the same needs as lower-paid employees.

Subject Area: Engagement tools—sampling. Source: CIA 1195, II-49.

**62. (c)** This is the least justified situation to use random selection because the auditor is concerned that the monthly sales journal has been held open to record the next month sales. The auditor should select transactions from the latter part of the month and examine supporting evidence to determine if they were recorded in the proper time period. Choice (a) is incorrect. This is an ideal place to use random selection because it could provide evidence on the quality of processing throughout the year. Choice (b) is incorrect. This would be a very appropriate situation in which to use random selection. Individual account balances could be selected using dollar-unit (PPS) sampling or could be randomly selected by randomly selecting a page number and then selecting an account item (1–50) within each page. Choice (d) is incorrect. This is an ideal place to apply dollar-unit sampling to gain confidence about potential dollar misstatement of account balances.

Subject Area: Engagement tools—sampling. Source: CIA 595, II-38.

**63. (b)** Samples selected using a systematic sampling procedure and a random start will behave as if they were a random sample when the population is randomly ordered with respective to the audit objective. Sampling bias due to the systematic procedure will be small because the population items do not have a pattern with respect to the audit objective. Choice (a) is incorrect. This is the description of a random selection procedure where each item in the population has an equal chance of being included in the sample. Choice (c) is incorrect. The number of items in a sample is not relevant to the procedures used to select the specific items comprising the sample. The use of multiple random starts might increase the chance that a sample will behave randomly but only if the population is arranged randomly. Choice (d) is incorrect. Judgmental sampling will not increase the randomness of a sample but will introduce sampling bias into the sample. In fact, the use of any judgment by an internal auditor in determining which items are included in a sample increases the sampling bias.

Subject Area: Engagement tools—sampling. Source: CIA 1194, II-50.

**64. (b)** $2,050 + .825(2,400)$. Choice (a) is incorrect. $2,050 + 10(200)$ [incorrectly uses the standard error of the estimate]. Choice (c) is incorrect. [$2,050 + .825(2,400)] – 100$ [incorrectly uses the standard error of the estimate]. Choice (d) is incorrect. $2,050 + .800(2,400)$ [incorrectly uses the correlation coefficient instead of the regression coefficient].

Subject Area: Engagement tools—sampling. Source: CIA 1194, II-47.

**65. (c)** This is the fifth usable number. Choice (a) is incorrect. This answer is the fifth random number but not the fifth usable number. For example, the random number following the starting point (14326) is 76562, which represents page 765, line 62. However, there are only 475 sheets and only 50 lines per sheet. Choice (b) is incorrect. This is the fourth usable number. Choice (d) is incorrect. This is the fifth usable **page** number, but the line limitation is exceeded.

Subject Area: Engagement tools—sampling. Source: CIA 1194, II-48.

**66. (a)** This fits the definition. Choice (b) is incorrect. There are no clusters. Choice (c) is incorrect. There are no strata. Choice (d) is incorrect. It does not allow reliable estimates.

Subject Area: Engagement tools—sampling. Source: CIA 1190, I-41.

**67. (b)** In this case savings would occur because the auditor would not have to travel to all sight to draw a representative sample. Choice (a) is incorrect. Stratified sampling is used to give special emphasis to certain categories in the population. Skewed or unusual values are not indicated in this case. Choice (c) is incorrect. Attribute sampling is not appropriate for estimating a variable such as dollar amount. Choice (d) is incorrect. Systematic (judgmental) sampling is not appropriate for projecting sample results to a population.

Subject Area: Engagement tools—sampling. Source: CIA 590, II-30.

**68. (a)** The only way to statistically evaluate a sample is if each item has an equal or known probability of selection. Choice (b) is incorrect. Judgment sampling is an unsatisfactory alternative for reaching conclusions about a population.

Choice (c) is incorrect. Random sampling does not require machine-readable data. Choice (d) is incorrect. Sampling without replacement is normal.

Subject Area: Engagement tools—sampling. Source: CIA 594, II-36.

**69.** **(a)** With systematic random sampling, every *n*th element is selected from the sample, with the starting point among the first *n* elements determined at random. Choice (b) is incorrect. With dollar-unit sampling, the probability of an item being chosen is directly proportionate to its dollar value. Choice (c) is incorrect. Judgmental interval sampling is a "nonsense" term, since interval sampling is a statistical, not judgmental, sampling approach. Choice (d) is incorrect. Variables sampling is a sampling methodology, not a sample selection method.

Subject Area: Engagement tools—sampling. Source: CIA 593, I-35.

**70.** **(c)** Cluster sampling samples groups of items rather than individual items and is most appropriate when each aggregate sampling group is representative of the entire population. Choice (a) is incorrect. Attributes sampling describes a sampling model, not a selection technique. Choice (b) is incorrect. Stratified sampling separates the population into several strata with the elements in each stratum possessing some common attribute. The sample is then chosen using a statistical sampling approach. Choice (d) is incorrect. Interval sampling selects every *n*th item for sampling with a randomized starting point.

Subject Area: Engagement tools—sampling. Source: CIA 593, II-34.

**71.** **(d)** Two strata are being used—Mediterranean and North Atlantic. Choice (a) is incorrect. Not enough information is given, such as (1) sampling units are not defined and (2) stages are not defined. Choice (b) is incorrect since it is not a sampling term. Choice (c) is incorrect. Interval sampling involves taking every *n*th item from a total population.

Subject Area: Engagement tools—sampling. Source: CIA 1192, II-37.

**72.** **(c)** If the population contains no systematic bias, interval sampling with a random start is valid. Choice (a) is incorrect. The sample has a random start. Choice (b) is incorrect. Interval sampling, with a random start, is statistically valid. Choice (d) is incorrect. Auditor judgment is required when using statistical methods.

Subject Area: Engagement tools—sampling. Source: CIA 1192, I-38.

**73.** **(c)** The 7 different starting points, plus the fact that the sampling interval (135) is not an exact multiple of the population pattern interval (10), should result in a representative sample. Choice (a) is incorrect. Due to the pattern of this population, this technique could result in a sample consisting almost entirely of high-value items (starting numbers = 1, 2, 11, or 12) or low-value items (starting numbers = 8, 9, 18, or 19). Choice (b) is incorrect. The sample will be complete after he has moved through three-quarters of the population, so items in the last one-quarter/4 of the population will have zero chance of being selected. Choice (d) is incorrect. This is a stratified sample. While it may be a desirable sampling procedure for some purposes, it might not constitute a representative sample, since the interval, 25, would result in every other

item being a multiple of 10. Thus, 40 of the items could be from an extreme value.

Subject Area: Engagement tools—sampling. Source: CIA 1192, II-39.

**74.** **(c)** It is easy to do since checks are numbered consecutively. Choice (a) is incorrect. It may be misleading. Choice (b) is incorrect. It is not as good as answer choice (c). There may be a pattern in the way the checks were written. Choice (d) is incorrect. There is no reason to stratify.

Subject Area: Engagement tools—sampling. Source: CIA 592, II-42.

**75.** **(d)** Two strata could be used, the single vendor and all others. Choice (a) is incorrect because there is no basis for this. Choice (b) and (c) are incorrect because they would not subdivide the population.

Subject Area: Engagement tools—sampling. Source: CIA 592, II-43.

**76.** **(b)** Since there appears to be no pattern in the sequencing of this population, use of interval sampling with a random start gives each account an equal chance of being selected and should provide an unbiased sample. Choice (a) is incorrect. This would provide only accounts with balances in the $3,000 to $3,999 range, and thus would not be representative of the population. Choice (c) is incorrect. While this scheme will provide the maximum dollar coverage, it is not random because large accounts have a greater chance of being selected than small accounts. Choice (d) is incorrect. This scheme may lead to the selection of accounts most likely to be in error or to invoice collection problems. However, it is not random because all accounts do not have an equal chance of being selected.

Subject Area: Engagement tools—sampling. Source: CIA 591, I-44.

**77.** **(a)** In variables sampling, the objective is to estimate the dollar value of the inventory. Strata based on dollar values are the usual population characteristic. Choice (b) is incorrect. Dollar values are the usual characteristic to create strata in variables sampling, not number of items. Choice (c) is incorrect. Turnover volume could be a characteristic of interest in attribute sampling but not in variables sampling. Choice (d) is incorrect. Storage location is not a relevant characteristic when creating strata for variables sampling.

Subject Area: Engagement tools—sampling. Source: CIA 1191, I-39.

**78.** **(c)** Cluster sampling is a selection method resulting in contiguous sampling units and does not overcome patterns. Choice (a) is incorrect. Dollar-unit sampling includes a random start and a selection based on dollar value sampling increments. Choice (b) is incorrect. Multiple random starts overcome the existence of a pattern by using a number of different starting points. Choice (d) is incorrect. Stratified sampling is dividing the population into two or more strata using the variability of values; recognizing a pattern in advance permits appropriate sampling techniques.

Subject Area: Engagement tools—sampling. Source: CIA 1191, II-38.

**79.** **(c)** The auditor knows this because the error rate in the sample was more than 1%. If the error rate was equal to 1%, the auditor would know that the probability was 95% that the error rate in the population was no higher than 4%. Choice (a) is incorrect. The error rate may exceed 4%, but the probability that it does it less than 95%. Choice (b) is incorrect. The error rate may be less than 4%, but that probability is less than 95%. Choice (d) is incorrect. The error rate may be higher than 1%, but that probability is less than 95%.

Subject Area: Engagement tools—sampling. Source: CIA 1196, II-45.

**80.** **(c)** Sample size is used to evaluate the actual occurrence rate. Choice (a) is incorrect. Dollar values are irrelevant to attributes sampling. Choice (b) is incorrect. Standard deviation is irrelevant to attributes sampling. Choice (d) is incorrect. The finite population correction factor is used to adjust an initial computed sample size.

Subject Area: Engagement tools—sampling. Source: CIA 597, II-50.

**81.** **(b)** This is the definition of precision. Choice (a) is incorrect. Confidence level is a measure of how reliable the auditor wants the sample results to be. Choice (c) is incorrect. Precision is the range between the lower and upper error limits. Choice (d) is incorrect. The expected error rate is a measure of how frequently the auditor expects the characteristic of interest to exist in the population prior to selecting and evaluating the sample.

Subject Area: Engagement tools—sampling. Source: CIA 1196, II-47.

**82.** **(b)** Attribute sampling is used to estimate how many, such as the rate of erroneous claims. Choice (a) is incorrect. Variable sampling is used to estimate how much, such as total dollar amount or total weight. Choice (c) is incorrect. Judgmental sampling is not appropriate if inferences are to be made about a population. Choice (d) is incorrect. Dollar-unit sampling, like variable sampling, is used to estimate how much an account balance is in error.

Subject Area: Engagement tools—sampling. Source: CIA 590, II-29.

**83.** **(a)** This would be the most appropriate audit procedure because the audit objective only asks for a determination that rejected loans have been rejected for proper reasons. It is not concerned with approval of loans that should not have been made. Choice (b) is incorrect. This only provides information on loans that were funded. The concern is with loans that may have been inappropriately rejected. Choice (c) is incorrect. This is an excellent procedure to determine whether all the loans (both funded and unfunded) are being handled consistent with the stated policies and procedures. However, the audit objective only dealt with loans that were not funded; therefore, this procedure would cause the auditors to review more loans and would not be as efficient as the procedure noted in choice (a). Choice (d) is incorrect. This uses a sample of loans that were presented to the lending committee. It does not include loans that would have already been rejected by an individual lending officer.

Subject Area: Engagement tools—sampling. Source: CIA 597, II-47.

**84.** **(d)** These are significant audit findings (item III). Item I is incorrect. Although these findings are significant audit findings, there is not sufficient evidence to conclude fraudulent activity on the part of the bank's lending officers. There must be intent to deceive for some personal gain to infer fraud. Item II is incorrect. The financial statements will not necessarily be incorrect as long as the bank can determine

that the loans receivable are properly classified as to term and are carried at their net realizable value.

Subject Area: Engagement tools—sampling. Source: CIA 597, II-49.

**85.** **(c)** The expected occurrence rate is one necessary factor in selecting samples for attributes sampling. Choice (a) is incorrect. The dollar value of the population relates to a variable often involved in sample selection when testing for variables. Choice (b) is incorrect. The sampling interval is used in monetary-unit sampling to select items based on monetary-unit value distributions. Choice (d) is incorrect. The standard deviation is not a variable having relevance when selecting samples for attributes sampling.

Subject Area: Engagement tools—sampling. Source: CIA 597, II-47.

**86.** **(b)** A smaller estimated occurrence rate results in a smaller sample size when all other factors are the same. Therefore, choices (a), (c), and (d) are incorrect.

Subject Area: Engagement tools—sampling. Source: CIA 596, II-46.

**87.** **(b)** A lower confidence level and a less rigorous precision allow a smaller sample with other factors constant. Therefore, choices (a), (c), and (d) are incorrect.

Subject Area: Engagement tools—sampling. Source: CIA 596, II-47.

**88.** **(c)** Sample size is used to evaluate the actual occurrence rate. Choice (a) is incorrect. Dollar values are irrelevant to attribute sampling. Choice (b) is incorrect. Standard deviation is irrelevant to attribute sampling. Choice (d) is incorrect. The finite population correction factor is used to adjust an initial computed sample size.

Subject Area: Engagement tools—sampling. Source: CIA 1194, II-35.

**89.** **(c)** Increasing the confidence level and decreasing the tolerable failure rate will result in a much larger sample size and will give the auditor a more precise estimate of the population parameters. Choice (a) is incorrect. Decreasing the confidence level results in a decrease in effectiveness, while decreasing the tolerable failure rate results in a decrease in efficiency. Choice (b) is incorrect. Decreasing the tolerable failure rate will result in a larger sample size, resulting in a decrease in efficiency as defined in the problem. Choice (d) is incorrect. Increasing the confidence level results in a larger sample size, which decreases audit efficiency.

Subject Area: Engagement tools—sampling. Source: CIA 595, II-44.

**90.** **(d)** Attribute sampling is used to reach conclusions about exception occurrence rates in populations. Choice (a) is incorrect. Difference or mean estimation is used when sampling for dollar values. Choice (b) is incorrect. Discovery is only used when exception rates are expected to be very low. Choice (c) is incorrect. Stratified sampling arranges populations for more efficient sampling.

Subject Area: Engagement tools—sampling. Source: CIA 1194, II-40.

**91.** **(d)** Attribute sampling does not involve dollar-balance estimation. Choice (a) is incorrect. Difference or ratio estimation can be used to estimate population dollar values. Choice (b) is incorrect. Mean-per-unit estimation can be used to estimate population dollar values. Choice (c) is incorrect.

Probability-proportional-to-size (PPS) can be used for estimating population dollar values.

Subject Area: Engagement tools—sampling. Source: CIA 1194, II-41.

**92.** **(a)** Difference or ratio estimation is used when estimating dollar amounts of errors for normally distributed populations. Choice (b) is incorrect. Mean-per-unit estimation is used to project a total dollar value for a population, but would be inappropriate since there are a large number of small balance account errors. Choice (c) is incorrect. Probability-proportional-to-size (PPS) is used for estimating dollar values of errors when the expected error frequency is low. Choice (d) is incorrect. Attribute sampling does not involve dollar-balance estimation.

Subject Area: Engagement tools—sampling. Source: CIA 1194, II-42.

**93.** **(a)** Tolerable error is the specified precision or the maximum sampling error that will still permit the results to be useful. Since the precision is under the control of the auditor, the audit objective is the most important factor to be considered. Choice (b) is incorrect. Knowing the population is large is sufficient. Choice (c) is incorrect. This factor is independent of precision. Choice (d) is incorrect. It is a consideration but not the most important one.

Subject Area: Engagement tools—sampling. Source: CIA 1193, I-40.

**94.** **(b)** The number of items is not generally associated with the risk of misstatement. Choice (a) is incorrect. The extent of risk of misstatement is associated with the dollar values of inventory items. Choice (c) is incorrect. Turnover volume could be associated with the risk of misstatement of the items. Choice (d) is incorrect. Storage location may be associated with the risk of misstatement of the items.

Subject Area: Engagement tools—sampling. Source: CIA 593, I-31.

**95.** **(c)** Attributes sampling typically involve tests of the effectiveness of controls. Choice (a) is incorrect. Dollar-unit sampling is used to estimate dollar amounts. Choice (b) is incorrect. Mean-per-unit sampling is used to estimate dollar amounts. Choice (d) is incorrect. Variables sampling describes methods used to estimate dollar amounts. Choice (d) is incorrect. The report should be made to management and coordinated with the external auditor.

Subject Area: Engagement tools—sampling. Source: CIA 1192, II-40.

**96.** **(d)** This is the definition of 95% confidence level. Choice (a) is incorrect. The sample is adequate. Choice (b) is incorrect. No sample could prove this. Choice (c) is incorrect. Null hypothesis is Error Rate <= 0.5%

Subject Area: Engagement tools—sampling. Source: CIA 1191, II-39.

**97.** **(b)** Stop-or-go sampling helps prevent oversampling for attributes by permitting the sampler to halt an audit test at the earliest possible moment. Choice (a) is incorrect. Only upper precision limits and statements are made. Choice (c) is incorrect. The populations must be homogeneous in all attribute-sampling plans. Choice (d) is incorrect. An increase in the confidence limits will result in a loss of precision (assuming contact sample size).

Subject Area: Engagement tools—sampling. Source: CIA 1191, I-38.

**98.** **(d)** The stop-or-go sampling technique will yield a smaller sample size if the error rate is low. It is also the only technique listed that is applicable to estimates of rate of compliance (attributes sampling). Choice (a) is incorrect. Rate of noncompliance is not applicable to ratio-estimation sampling (a variables-sampling technique). Choice (b) is incorrect. Difference-estimation sampling is used when we want to obtain a "corrected" estimate of a previously stated "book" value (a variables-sampling technique). Choice (c) is incorrect. Stratified mean-per-unit sampling is used in substantive testing (a variables-sampling technique).

Subject Area: Engagement tools—sampling. Source: CIA 593, II-33.

**99.** **(a)** Variables sampling method is good for estimating the dollar value. Choices (b) and (c) are incorrect. Each is is an inappropriate plan for drawing samples. Choice (d) is incorrect. It is for estimating discrete characteristics, not values.

Subject Area: Engagement tools—sampling. Source: CIA 1190, II-40.

**100.** **(b)** Risk level is a necessary criterion to include in the sample selection process for variables. Choice (a) is incorrect. The recorded dollar value is not needed for variables testing. Choice (c) is incorrect. The expected occurrence rate is not a criterion in sample selection for variables. Choice (d) is incorrect. The sampling (skip) interval is the monetary-unit interval when selecting samples using monetary-unit sampling.

Subject Area: Engagement tools—sampling. Source: CIA 597, II-48.

**101.** **(d)** Standard deviation (variability) directly affects the computed precision. Choices (a) and (b) are incorrect. Occurrence rate is irrelevant for computing achieved precision. Choice (c) is incorrect. A lower actual variability would result in achieved precision being lower than desired precision.

Subject Area: Engagement tools—sampling. Source: CIA 1194, II-37.

**102.** **(c)** Achieved precision (sampling error) is equal to the confidence level factor times the standard error of the mean. Choice (a) is incorrect. The standard error of the mean is dependent on only the standard deviation and sample size. Choice (b) is incorrect. Nonsampling error is not variable according to sampling criteria; it is the result of such as misclassifications. Choice (d) is incorrect. The point estimate of the sample mean does not include a confidence interval.

Subject Area: Engagement tools—sampling. Source: CIA 590, I-31.

**103.** **(b)** Pilot samples are often used to estimate variability. Choice (a) is incorrect. This is a common practice. Choice (c) is incorrect. It would be inefficient to disregard the audit evidence found in the pilot sample. Choice (d) is incorrect. The sample range is not the correct measure of variability for this purpose.

Subject Area: Engagement tools—sampling. Source: CIA 594, II-30.

**104.** **(d)** Variables sampling is used for substantive testing. It allows the verification of values whose range lies between positive and negative infinity. Choice (a) is incorrect. Attribute sampling is for compliance testing. It calls for yes-or-no, right-or-wrong answers. The range of values is limited to 0 through 1. Choice (b) is incorrect. Discovery sampling is used when the internal auditor suspects a gross error or fraud. The plan seeks to select a sample just large enough to include one example of the error or irregularity a specified percentage of the time. Choice (c) is incorrect. Stop-or-go sampling is an attribute-sampling plan.

Subject Area: Engagement tools—sampling. Source: CIA 592, I-41.

**105. (d)** Individual item amounts must be known to use ratio estimation. Choice (a) is incorrect. Proportional relationships tend to support the use of ratio estimation. Choice (b) is incorrect. A minimum number of differences must be present to validly use ratio estimation. Choice (c) is incorrect. Ratio estimation is supported by proportional differences.

Subject Area: Engagement tools—sampling. Source: CIA 596, II-43.

**106. (b)** Ratio estimation is the most efficient sampling methodology because the auditor expects a large number of errors and expects the errors to vary directly with size of the account balance on the perpetual record. Choice (a) is incorrect. Dollar-unit sampling becomes less accurate when a large number of errors are expected. Choice (c) is incorrect. Attribute sampling is not used to estimate a dollar amount. Choice (d) is incorrect. Stratified mean-per-unit sampling could be used, but it is not as efficient as ratio estimation when a large number of errors are expected in the account balance.

Subject Area: Engagement tools—sampling. Source: CIA 595, II-39.

**107. (c)** There must be a sufficient number of nonproportional errors to generate a reliable sample estimate. Choice (a) is incorrect. Individual item amounts must be known to use difference estimation. Choice (b) is incorrect. There must be sufficient errors in the population to generate a reliable sample estimate. Choice (d) is incorrect. Ratio estimation is supported by proportional differences.

Subject Area: Engagement tools—sampling. Source: CIA 596, II-42.

**108. (c)** Ratio or difference estimates would be more efficient in this situation. Choice (a) is incorrect because the stratified mean per unit would work here. The error magnitude is unimportant. Choice (b) is incorrect because the advantage of stratification is not dependent on error rates. Choice (d) is incorrect because these estimators do not require an audit value for every item in the population. If such values were available, there would be no need to sample at all.

Subject Area: Engagement tools—sampling. Source: CIA 594, II-29.

**109. (b)** The average overstatement error in the sample is $250 per item ($630,000 – $605,000 / 100 items). Thus the projected overstatement is $275,000 (1,100 items × $250), and the estimated total is $6,988,000 minus $275,000. Choice (a) is incorrect. This answer (1,100 items × the average audited value of $6,050 per item) is based on mean-per-unit estimation, not difference estimation. Choice (c) is incorrect. This response was obtained by subtracting the $25,000 total sample overstatement from the book value. As explained above, it is the *projected* overstatement that must be subtracted. Choice (d) is incorrect. This is the book value plus the projected overstatement. Since the difference is an overstatement, it must be subtracted from, not added to, the book value.

Subject Area: Engagement tools—sampling. Source: CIA 1194, II-45.

**110. (d)** This is a valid statement about the confidence interval. There is also a 2.5% chance that inventory is less than $2,800,000. There is a 95% chance that the true inventory value falls between $2,800,000 and $3,200,000. Choice (a) is incorrect. This conclusion is not supported by the facts given. There is, however, a 95% chance that the true value of inventory is more than $2,800,000 and less than $3,200,000. Choice (b) is incorrect. This conclusion is also not supported by the facts given in the problem. Instead, there is a 5% chance that the true value of inventory is more than $3,200,000 or less $2,800,000. Choice (c) is incorrect. It is not possible to conclude from the information given that inventory is materially misstated.

Subject Area: Engagement tools—sampling. Source: CIA 597, II-40.

**111. (b)** The confidence interval = mean ± $Z$ value × standard error. Decreasing the confidence level would decrease the $Z$ value and that would result in a smaller confidence interval. Choice (a) is incorrect. Increasing the confidence level would result in a wider confidence interval. Choice (c) is incorrect. Decreasing the allowable risk of incorrect acceptance would increase the confidence level, which would result in a wider confidence interval. Choice (d) is incorrect. Increasing the precision would make the confidence interval wider.

Subject Area: Engagement tools—sampling. Source: CIA 597, II-41.

**112. (c)** The standard error is a function of the standard deviation, which is a measurement of the average variation from the mean of the sample. The standard error is used to compute precision and the confidence interval. The larger the standard error, the wider the interval. Choice (a) is incorrect. The standard error is not a projection of error in the population. Choice (b) is incorrect. The standard error is not a measurement of the errors in the sample. Choice (d) is incorrect. The amount of error that the auditor would be willing to accept (the tolerable error) is the auditor's decision; it is not the result of a statistical calculation. The amount of tolerable error has no effect on the standard error.

Subject Area: Engagement tools—sampling. Source: CIA 597, II-42.

**113. (a)** Statistical sampling enables an auditor to quantify the confidence level or the sampling risk. Nonstatistical sampling does not. Choice (b) is incorrect. Unless the auditor uses statistical sampling, the auditor would not be able to quantify precision. Choice (c) is incorrect. The value of inventory could not be projected when nonstatistical sampling is used. Choice (d) is incorrect. The risk of incorrect acceptance could not be quantified when nonstatistical sampling is used.

Subject Area: Engagement tools—sampling. Source: CIA 597, II-43.

**114. (d)** This is the only statistical sampling method designed to estimate a variable for which there are not available individual book values making up the value of a population. Choice (a) is incorrect. Attribute sampling will not produce a quantitative value. Choice (b) is incorrect. Discovery sampling is used to uncover an attribute that exists in the population with a low rate of occurrence, not to estimate a variable. Choice (c) is incorrect. Individual book values adding up to a total book value is required for this method to be used.

Subject Area: Engagement tools—sampling. Source: CIA 1196, II-48.

**115. (a)** This stratum has the largest expected standard deviation. Allocating more selections to strata with larger standard deviations decreases the standard error of the mean, which results in a smaller confidence interval. The objective of stratifying a sample is to reduce variation in order to be able to use a smaller sample than would be required without stratification. Choice (b) is incorrect. Although this stratum has the largest mean, it has a smaller standard deviation than stratum defined in the choice (a). Choice (c) is incorrect. Although this stratum has the largest number of items, is has the smallest standard deviation. Choice (d) is incorrect. The total dollar value is directly related to the mean and number of items in a stratum. As explained above, neither of these factors is a normal consideration in allocating sample size to strata.

Subject Area: Engagement tools—sampling. Source: CIA 1196, II-41.

**116. (c)** Mean-per-unit = $220,000/200 = $1100 and $1100 (5000) = $5,500,000. Choice (a) is incorrect. This calculation uses the means of the book value of the sample rather than the mean of the audit sample: $200,000/200 = $1,000; 1,000 × 5,000 = $5,000,000. Choice (b) is incorrect. This calculation added the audit value of the sample to the book value of the population: $220,000 + 5,200,000 = $5,420,000. Choice (d) is incorrect. Ratio estimation = $220,000/$200,000 = 1.1 and 1.1 ($5,200,000) = $5,720,000.

Subject Area: Engagement tools—sampling. Source: CIA 596, II-37.

**117. (d)** Difference estimation = $220,000 – $200,000 = $20,000 and $20,000/200 = $100 and $100 (5000) = $500,000 and $500,000 + $5,200,000 = $5,700,000. Choice (a) is incorrect. Estimated difference of $500,000 per choice (d) should be added to $5,200,000, not deducted from $5,200,000. Choice (b) is incorrect. Mean-per-unit = $220,000/200 = $1100 and $1100 (5000) = $5,500,000. Choice (c) is incorrect. This is an incorrect calculation using the difference in units between the population and sample and then adding this incorrect amount to the book value as follows: [(220,000 – 200,000)/200] × (5,000 – 200) = 480,000 and $5,200,000 + 480,000 = $5,680,000.

Subject Area: Engagement tools—sampling. Source: CIA 596, II-38.

**118. (d)** Ratio estimation = $220,000/$200,000 = 1.1 and 1.1 ($5,200,000) = $5,720,000. Choice (a) is incorrect. This calculation reverses the correct ratio estimation as: Ratio estimation = $200,000/$220,000 = .90909091 and .90909091 ($5,200,000) = $4,727,273. Choice (b) is incorrect. Mean-per-unit = $220,000/200 = $1100 and $1100 (5000) = $5,500,000. Choice (c) is incorrect. Difference estimation = $220,000 – $200,000 = $20,000 and $20,000/200 = $100 and $100 (5000) = $500,000 and $500,000 + $5,200,000 = $5,700,000.

Subject Area: Engagement tools—sampling. Source: CIA 596, II-39.

**119. (a)** Mean-per-unit variables sampling is the most appropriate sampling procedure because it allows the auditor to calculate a mean of the processing time and build confidence levels around the mean. The normal sampling distribution will allow the auditor to also estimate the percentage of claims that are not processed within the time limit contained in the company's policy. Choice (b) is incorrect. Probability proportion to size is not appropriate in this situation. Choice (c) is incorrect. Attribute sampling would not lead to an esti-

mate of the average length of time to process the claims. It could, however, be used to estimate the probability that a claim is not processed within the company's defined standard. Choice (d) is incorrect. Discovery sampling is used to determine if an isolated event is occurring in the population. It would be used here only if exceeding the policy for claims processing was expected to be extremely rare and extremely important.

Subject Area: Engagement tools—sampling. Source: CIA 595, II-42.

**120. (c)** An increase in the standard deviation represents an increase in the variability of the population and therefore the sample size would increase when using mean-per-unit estimation. A change in the standard deviation has no effect on the required sample size when probability proportional to size sampling is used, since the sampling units are homogeneous. Choice (a) is incorrect. See explanations for choice (c). Choice (b) is incorrect. A change in the standard deviation has no effect on the required sample size when dollar-unit sampling is used, since the sampling units are homogeneous—the individual dollars. Choice (d) is incorrect. An increase in the standard deviation represents an increase in the variability of the population and therefore requires increasing, not decreasing, the sample size.

Subject Area: Engagement tools—sampling. Source: CIA 1194, II-43.

**121. (b)** Mean-per-unit sampling uses subsidiary account balances or records as a basis for projecting total account balances. Choice (a) is incorrect. Dollar-unit sampling uses individual dollars instead of account balances as the sampling units. Choice (c) is incorrect. Attributes sampling estimates the presence of a qualitative characteristic, such as internal control errors. Choice (d) is incorrect. Difference estimation uses differences between audit and book values to project population values.

Subject Area: Engagement tools—sampling. Source: CIA 1192, II-38.

**122. (c)** 20,000 (52 ± 1.03) = $1,040,000 ± 20,600 or $1,019,400 to $1,060,600. Based on the data given: Precision of sample result = 1.03/52 = 1.98%. This is within the plan goal of ± 2%. Choice (a) is incorrect. It uses book plus or minus value mean and standard deviation rather than sample mean and precision to compute the confidence interval. Choice (b) is incorrect. It uses standard deviation instead of precision to compute confidence interval. Choice (d) is incorrect. It is centered on book value mean.

Subject Area: Engagement tools—sampling. Source: CIA 1191, I-40.

**123. (b)** A 90% confidence level implies that 10% of the time the true population total will be outside the computed range. Precision of plus or minus 4% gives the boundaries of the computed range: 4% × $800,000 = $32,000. $800,000 ± $32,000 provides a range of $768,000 to $832,000. Choice (a) is incorrect. The computation underlying this response transposes the correct definitions of "precision" and "confidence." Choice (c) is incorrect. This response improperly uses precision to modify confidence and fails to specify a dollar amount for the range within which the correct total is apt to lie. Choice (d) is incorrect. This response improperly uses confidence to modify precision, and the phrase "not likely" is ambiguous.

Subject Area: Engagement tools—sampling. Source: CIA 591, I-43.

**124. (c)** In mean-per-unit estimation, an increase in the standard deviation increases the sample size since it is used to estimate unknown values, such as inventory. In dollar-unit sampling, an increase in the standard deviation has no effect on the sample size since it yields a smaller sampling error. Choice (a) is incorrect. An increase in the standard deviation represents an increase in the variability of the population and therefore requires increasing, not decreasing, the sample size. Choice (b) is incorrect. A change in the standard deviation has no effect on the required sample size when dollar-unit sampling is used, since the sampling units are homogeneous—the individual dollars. Choice (d) is incorrect. See explanations for choices (a) and (b).

Subject Area: Engagement tools—sampling. Source: CIA 591, II-40.

**125. (d)** No errors were detected in the sample. Therefore, the desired confidence level and precision were achieved. Choice (a) is incorrect. The probability of selecting any particular invoice is proportional to the dollar amount of the invoice. Choice (b) is incorrect. The chance is 5% that errors are more than 1% of $10,000,000. Choice (c) is incorrect. The acceptable level of sampling risk is 5%, which is 100% less 95%. Sampling risk is the complement of the confidence level.

Subject Area: Engagement tools—sampling. Source: CIA 597, II-44.

**126. (b)** Monetary-unit sampling is especially efficient and effective when there are a small number of differences. Ratio estimation, however, requires a large number of differences to be effective. Choice (a) is incorrect. Monetary-unit sampling is generally inefficient and less effective than variables sampling when there are a larger number of differences. The ratio approach, however, tends to be especially efficient in such circumstances. Choice (c) is incorrect. A high degree of variability in the dollar amount within the population makes both of these methods efficient relative to alternative statistical methods. A high degree of variability in the dollar amount of the population generally has no effect on the effectiveness of these two methods relative to each other. Choice (d) is incorrect. A low degree of variability among the items in the population reduces the relative efficiency of both of these methods compared to alternative statistical sampling methods. A low degree of variability does not affect the effectiveness of these methods.

Subject Area: Engagement tools—sampling. Source: CIA 597, II-45.

**127. (b)** The cumulative amount is the first amount greater than $34,719, which would be the threshold for the third selection (i.e., $4719 + 15,000 + $15,000). The selection interval is $750,000/50 = $15,000. It contains dollars 31,375 through 35,482, thus it contains 34,719. Choice (a) is incorrect. The cumulative amount is less than $34,719. Choice (c) is incorrect. This item would not be selected because it does not contain the 34,719th dollar. Choice (d) is incorrect. This item would not be selected because it does not contain the 34,719th dollar.

Subject Area: Engagement tools—sampling. Source: CIA 1196, II-9.

**128. (d)** Overstated items have a greater chance of being included in the sample. Additionally, samples under this procedure include more of the "higher-dollar" accounts because of the way the sample is conducted. Errors in these accounts are more likely to result in material misstatements and are thus more critical to the internal auditor. Choice (a) is incorrect. Monetary-unit sampling is "generally not appropriate for testing understatement of liabilities since the more a balance is understated, the less its chance of being included in the sample." Choice (b) is incorrect. This is one of the requirements for using monetary-unit sampling. Choice (c) is incorrect. Again, one of the assumptions for using monetary-unit sampling is the error rate in the population should be small (e.g., less than 10%). The internal auditor should not use this procedure if material errors are expected.

Subject Area: Engagement tools—sampling. Source: CIA 596, II-41.

**129. (c)** (3) ($3,000,000/$60,000) = 150, which represents the correct sample size. Choices (a), (b), and (d) are incorrect.

Subject Area: Engagement tools—sampling. Source: CIA 596, II-44.

**130. (d)** Monetary unit sampling would result in a larger sample size, and this is not an advantage. Choice (a) is incorrect. Monetary unit sampling is being an efficient model; this is an advantage. Choice (b) is incorrect. Monetary unit sampling does not assume normally distributed populations; this is an advantage. Choice (c) is incorrect. Monetary unit sampling uses dollar units as the homogenous units; this is an advantage.

Subject Area: Engagement tools—sampling. Source: CIA 596, II-45.

**131. (b)** Monetary unit sampling is not as effective in calculating an upper error estimate when a very large number of errors are expected. Choice (a) is incorrect. Monetary unit sampling can effectively handle a small number of understatement errors. Choice (c) is incorrect. Account numbers do not have to be assigned to use monetary unit sampling. Choice (d) is incorrect. This would not preclude the use of monetary unit sampling because: (1) most large-dollar-value items are selected and a census of that data is performed; and (2) the probability of any item being selected is proportional to its size. Thus, monetary unit sampling works especially well in the situation described here.

Subject Area: Engagement tools—sampling. Source: CIA 595, II-45.

**132. (b)** Dollar unit is a sampling technique that has been uniquely applied to auditing. It is not used in statistical processing control. Choice (a) is incorrect. Acceptance sampling is a standard statistical process control technique. Choice (c) is incorrect. Quality control charts are an integral part of total quality management approaches. Choice (d) is incorrect. Continuous monitoring and frequent feedbacks are two of the important elements of statistical quality control.

Subject Area: Engagement tools—sampling. Source: CIA 595, II-48.

**133. (c)** Dollar unit sampling, because it samples each individual dollar, automatically stratifies. If the audit objective is to identify understatements, dollar-unit sampling is not appropriate because the larger the understatement, the least likely it is to be identified. Choice (a) is incorrect. The issue of manual or computerized accounts would not have any impact on sampling efficiency. Choice (b) is incorrect. Dollar-unit sampling is an accepted method of estimating the dollar error of an account balance. Choice (d) is incorrect. The number of transactions is not the issue, the number of dollars is.

Subject Area: Engagement tools—sampling. Source: CIA 590, I-30.

**134. (c)** Dollar-unit sampling is often used for these purposes. Choices (a) and (b) are incorrect because each technique is ineffective at detecting understatements, which are of significant concern for accounts payable. Choice (d) is incorrect. Dollar-unit sampling performs relatively poorly with very large error rates.

Subject Area: Engagement tools—sampling. Source: CIA 594, II-35.

**135. (c)** Dollar-unit sampling is the only quantitative method listed. Choice (a) is incorrect. A quantitative materiality amount cannot apply to stop or go, a form of attributes sampling. Choice (b) is incorrect. It requires a definition of a cluster. Choice (d) is incorrect. This question involves a variable and, like choice (a), cannot apply to attributes sampling.

Subject Area: Engagement tools—sampling. Source: CIA 1193, II-40.

**136. (c)** It stratifies, in that each dollar is a sampling unit and the larger the account balance, the greater the chance of selection. Choices (a), (b), and (d) are incorrect. They do not automatically stratify.

Subject Area: Engagement tools—sampling. Source: CIA 593, I-33.

**137. (b)** Invoice number 1790 includes cumulative amount $1,461, and invoice number 1805 includes cumulative amount $8,461. Choice (a) is incorrect. The sampling interval is $7,000 (population total of $700,000 / sample size of 100). Thus the first two dollars to be selected are cumulative amounts $1,461 (the starting point) and $8,461 ($1,461 + $7,000). Invoice number 1795 is obtained by adding 1461 to the initial selection and does not reflect the $7,000 interval. Choice (c) is incorrect. Invoice number 1795 includes cumulative amounts $1,476 through $2,975, and thus does not include the starting point of $1,461; and, as explained in choice (a) above, invoice number 1804 does not include the second cumulative amount of $8,461. Choice (d) is incorrect. See explanation given for the choice (c) above.

Subject Area: Engagement tools—sampling. Source: CIA 1192, I-41.

### Data-Gathering Tools and Techniques

**138. (b)** This is the least effective communication and information-gathering technique of the four responses because it is impersonal and it alleges inefficiencies before there is evidence that the problems are due to inefficiencies in the processing. The impersonal method may have been applicable if the auditor wished open responses, but not enough guidance is given here to lead to that kind of response. Choice (a) is incorrect. This would be a good method to learn more about the nature of processing and to solicit input from employees as to the potential cause of the situation being investigated. Choice (c) is incorrect. This would supplement the supervisor's perceptions with those from individuals intimately involved with the processing of transactions. This would be an effective communication technique. Choice (d) is incorrect. This is not as good of a procedure as choices (b) and (c), but

would represent an efficient method of gathering preliminary information that would be useful in structuring the interviews.

Subject Area: Engagement tools—data-gathering tools. Source: CIA 595, II-21.

**139. (a)** The major problem is that the auditor was too oriented to the questionnaire and failed to appropriately consider the other information that was offered. Questionnaires may be limited, but the auditor needs to be flexible enough to gather other information when it is offered. Choice (b) is incorrect. This is not an inappropriate use of a questionnaire. The problem was the auditor did not listen well enough to expand the information-gathering process. Choice (c) is incorrect. Questionnaires are limited, but the problem is with its application, not necessarily the nature of the questionnaires. Choice (d) is incorrect. Choices (b) and (c) are not appropriate conclusions.

Subject Area: Engagement tools—data-gathering tools. Source: CIA 595, II-22.

**140. (d)** The auditor should attempt to corroborate the oral information before changing the nature of the audit or reporting it to company officials. Choice (a) is incorrect. The employee has requested anonymity. No formal investigation has yet begun. The auditor should not require that the interview be videotaped at this time. Choice (b) is incorrect. The information is strictly "hearsay" evidence at this point in time. The auditor should gather enough information to determine if there is other evidence available that might corroborate the assertion and provide a basis for further investigation. Choice (c) is incorrect. The auditor should determine if there are available sources to corroborate the assertion made by the employee before changing the nature of the investigation. The auditor will focus on the possibility of fraud, but should not completely change the direction of the investigation without corroborating evidence.

Subject Area: Engagement tools—data-gathering tools. Source: CIA 595, II-23.

**141. (a)** Auditors frequently encounter and act on nonverbal communication. If the nonverbal communication affects the auditor's perception of the information gathered, it should be documented so that it can be considered as the audit proceeds. Choice (b) is incorrect. If the nonverbal communication affects the auditor's perception of the information gathered, it should be documented so that it can be considered as the audit proceeds. Choice (c) is incorrect. Nonverbal communication is not sufficient to reach a conclusion that fraud has taken place. However, along with the allegations made by the employee, it may be sufficient to perform a fraud investigation. Choice (d) is incorrect. The answers given should be documented, but the process of only documenting the verbal responses, especially in a situation like this where nonverbal actions may indicate untruthfulness, would result in incomplete documentation of the auditee's response.

Subject Area: Engagement tools—data-gathering tools. Source: CIA 595, II-24.

**142. (b)** The nature of the communication is highly sensitive and personal. A more personal form of communication, such as the direct interview, should have been used to elicit the response from the auditees. Choice (a) is incorrect. The major problem is with the impersonal form of the communication, not whether it was delivered electronically or on paper. Choice (c) is incorrect. There is a need for personal communication. Questionnaires are used to gain an understanding about the nature of processing. The auditor has already obtained most of this information and is interested in more specific facts as to how a fraud may have taken place and who was involved in the fraud if one had taken place. Choice (d) is incorrect. The auditor is not in position to detail the allegations against each specific employee. The auditor wants to gain more information about the nature of the fraud, if it exists. It would not be proper to detail allegations to each individual employee at this point.

Subject Area: Engagement tools—data-gathering tools. Source: CIA 595, II-25.

**143.** **(d)** The auditor should not react adversely to the hostile actions by the supervisor, but should carefully explain the situation and provide an opportunity for the supervisor to calm down and continue the interview. Choice (a) is incorrect. The auditor's responsibility is to refer the matter to management and the audit committee. It is up to them to decide whether to turn the investigation over to legal authorities. Choice (b) is incorrect. This would be incorrect communication because the auditor has explicitly embarked on a fraud audit. Choice (c) is incorrect. This is a fraud audit, not a fraud interrogation. The auditor should not respond with hostility or threaten the supervisor to get a confession. The auditor should be prepared to turn the investigation over to proper authorities if the supervisor will not cooperate, but should not act as a fraud interrogator.

Subject Area: Engagement tools—data-gathering tools. Source: CIA 595, II-26.

**144.** **(d)** If the supervisor wants to negotiate, the negotiation should be performed with management and the assigned fraud investigation team. Choice (a) is incorrect. This would be an inappropriate response for the auditor. Choice (b) is incorrect. This is a correct communication, but response III is also an appropriate communication. Choice (c) is incorrect. This is a correct communication, but response II is also an appropriate communication.

Subject Area: Engagement tools—data-gathering tools. Source: CIA 595, II-27.

**145.** **(b)** This can result because people may choose not to respond for reasons related to the purpose of the questionnaire. Choice (a) is incorrect. Formulas are equally easy to compute with bad as with good data. Choice (c) is incorrect. Longer questionnaires actually increase nonresponse bias. Choice (d) is incorrect. Nonresponse decreases sample size, so, if anything, confidence intervals would be wider rather than narrower.

Subject Area: Engagement tools—data-gathering tools. Source: CIA 1195, II-9.

**146.** **(b)** Overlapping categories frequently cause respondent difficulty. Choices (a) and (c) are incorrect. Both of these are valid scaling choices for multiple-choice questions. Choice (d) is incorrect. This is a desirable feature of a question.

Subject Area: Engagement tools—data-gathering tools. Source: CIA 1195, II-10.

**147.** **(d)** One of the principal advantages of mail surveys is their cost efficiency because mailing costs are less than interview labor costs. Choice (a) is incorrect. Mail surveys often have notoriously low response rates. Choice (b) is incorrect. The interviewer's flexibility to interpret responses and rephrase questions increases response quality. Choice (c) is

incorrect. Audio-visual aids, complex sequences, and other varieties of questions are made possible by the interactive nature of interviews.

Subject Area: Engagement tools—data-gathering tools. Source: CIA 1195, II-11.

**148.** **(b)** There are many known effects of the sequence and format of questions. One method for dealing with these is to use questionnaire variations that cause these biases to average out across the sample. Choices (a), (c), and (d) are incorrect due to explanation given for the choice (b).

Subject Area: Engagement tools—data-gathering tools. Source: CIA 1195, II-12.

**149.** **(b)** Lack of experimental control and measurement precision is the chief weaknesses of unobtrusive measures. Choice (a) is incorrect. Observing the phenomenon in its natural setting is a principal advantage of unobtrusive measures. Choice (c) is incorrect. Unobtrusive measures are useful for exploratory investigations for this reason. Choice (d) is incorrect. Since people are going about their normal business, they are less likely to do what they think the researcher wants, censor their comments, and so on.

Subject Area: Engagement tools—data-gathering tools. Source: CIA 1195, II-13.

**150.** **(d)** The auditors are using a numerical rating for the organization audited (source: Sawyer's Internal Auditing IIA). Choice (a) is incorrect. Trend analysis is a specialized form of analytical review procedure, used primarily to analyze the changes in account balances over time. Choice (b) is incorrect. Ratio analysis is a subset of trend analysis used in analytical review. It is unrelated to the subject. Choice (c) is incorrect. "Observing means seeing, noticing, not passing over. It implies a careful, knowledgeable look at people and things. It means a visual examination with a purpose, a mental comparison with standards, an evaluative sighting." Use of rating scales requires the participant to actively participate, it is not unobtrusive.

Subject Area: Engagement tools—data-gathering tools. Source: CIA 596, II-9.

**151.** **(a)** Such analysis is a part of fieldwork, which comes after the preliminary survey. Choice (b) is incorrect. This file probably contains information, such as questions used in prior audits and problems detected in prior years, that will help in the development of appropriate questions to ask this year. Choice (c) is incorrect. The report will identify prior findings and recommendations that should be followed up on this year. Choice (d) is incorrect. Knowing what the department is supposed to do will help the auditor develop knowledgeable questions.

Subject Area: Engagement tools—data-gathering tools. Source: CIA 597, II-13.

**152.** **(b)** This helps involve the supervisors of the auditee's department and encourages a more collegial approach to the audit. Choice (a) is incorrect. Greater knowledge of the upcoming audit is more likely to remove some of the apprehension about it. Choice (c) is incorrect. It will normally be more economical since the legwork will be done by those most competent to do it rapidly. Choice (d) is incorrect. Even though it is very useful for audits of distant locations, it can also be advantageous in other circumstances.

Subject Area: Engagement tools—data-gathering tools. Source: CIA 597, II-6.

**153. (a)** Self-audit questionnaires provide indirect evidence, which must be confirmed. Choice (b) is incorrect. The ability to adapt general-purpose internal control questionnaires (ICQs) to different organizational units, personnel, and functional units is one of the strengths of these audit tools. Choice (c) is incorrect. ICQs can be designed so that the auditee can answer the questions without the auditor being present. Choice (d) is incorrect. An ICQ does not need to address accounting information to ensure integrity.

Subject Area: Engagement tools—data-gathering tools. Source: CIA 596, II-11.

**154. (a)** During face-to-face contact, a skilled interviewer can react to potential problems and expand questioning of more relevant subjects. Choice (b) is incorrect. Interviews do not produce objective evidence unless the information corroborates facts already in evidence. Choice (c) is incorrect. Interviews tend to be more costly in relation to the amount of information that must be included because of the preparation and discussion time involved. Choice (d) is incorrect. Critical information obtained during an interview must be followed up and confirmed.

Subject Area: Engagement tools—data-gathering tools. Source: CIA 596, II-12.

**155. (d)** Questions can be multiple choice, fill-in-the-blank, essay, Likert scales, and so on. Choices (a) and (b) are incorrect. Validity and reliability of each question is extremely important. Choice (c) is incorrect. When questionnaires are too long, people tend not to fill them out.

Subject Area: Engagement tools—data-gathering tools. Source: CIA 594, II-13.

**156. (d)** The evidence provided is indirect and therefore could require corroboration in some way. Choice (a) is incorrect. "Yes" and "no" answers may be very general and not specific as to degree. Choice (b) is incorrect. They are tiring for auditees to complete due to their length. Choice (c) is incorrect. The structured questionnaire asks for specific "yes" or "no" answers plus brief explanations.

Subject Area: Engagement tools—data-gathering tools. Source: CIA 592, II-13.

**157. (d)** This is the major disadvantage of using questionnaires. Developing or reviewing flowcharts is an extremely effective way to gain an overall understanding of the system and pinpoint control points and the lack of controls. Choice (a) is incorrect. The opposite is true. Choice (b) is incorrect. This is an advantage of questionnaires. Choice (c) is incorrect. Such are readily obtained or developed.

Subject Area: Engagement tools—data-gathering tools. Source: CIA 1191, II-23.

**158. (b)** It can be prepared in advance and functions very much like a checklist. Choices (a) and (c) are incorrect because they are advantages of flowcharts. Choice (c) is incorrect because it is an advantage of a flowchart. Choice (d) is incorrect because positive responses must also be tested to determine compliance.

Subject Area: Engagement tools—data-gathering tools. Source: CIA 1191, II-14.

**159. (a)** A specific advantage of a SOP questionnaire is that it may be used by local management to periodically ensure that employee practices remain current with relevant, valid, and up-to-date standard operating procedures; this improves the overall level of control and the control environ-

ment when follow-up is included to ensure performance. Choice (b) is incorrect. These SOP questionnaires have no impact on inherent risk, and there is no evidence that such a control would be effective; there is no basis in fact for reducing the proposed scope. Choice (c) is incorrect. Standard operating procedures, as described, are providing directive controls, which appear to be adequate; adding internal auditing department approval does not impact the effectiveness of these controls. Choice (d) is incorrect. Control of SOP questionnaires by the internal auditing department would not affect the level of evidence obtained in this manner; information obtained via questionnaires must be verified to be considered objective.

Subject Area: Engagement tools—data-gathering tools. Source: CIA 1195, II-29.

**160. (c)** Checklists increase the uniformity of data acquisition. Choices (a), (b), and (d) are incorrect because each choice is a criticism of checklists.

Subject Area: Engagement tools—data-gathering tools. Source: CIA 594, II-16.

**161. (d)** Organizing note taking ahead of time helps you have time during the interview to listen and evaluate the responses and the reactions of your respondent. Choice (a) is incorrect. Extensive note taking may interfere with your communication with your respondent, since you cannot maintain eye contact or notice nonverbal as well when you are occupied with your own notes. Choice (b) is incorrect. Tape recording might be used for controversial material, but generally will not elicit positive feelings from your respondent. For most organizational purposes, you will not need exact quotes, the major benefit of a recording. Choice (c) is incorrect. Aside from cost, this option would not work because of confidentiality and negative reaction from your respondent. This interview is *your* job, not someone else's.

Subject Area: Engagement tools—data-gathering tools. Source: CIA 596, II-10.

**162. (b)** Changing the wording of the questions and the sequence in which they are asked may eliminate some of the tedium associated with a series of interviews and may also allow the auditor to refine the technique during the process. Choice (a) is incorrect. The results of the auditor's test depend on comparing responses to the same questions. Choice (c) is incorrect. Written responses to questions are often very different from verbal responses, and the interviewer does not have the option of immediately pursuing a particular answer. Choice (d) is incorrect. Employees are less likely to be forthcoming in a group, particularly when their responses may be critical of management.

Subject Area: Engagement tools—data-gathering tools. Source: CIA 597, II-9.

**163. (b)** Individuals feel more important when they are asked people questions rather than control questions. This will improve the important interpersonal part of building the audit relationship. Choice (a) is incorrect. Later fieldwork will cover information that can be quantified. Building rapport is more important in the early interviews. Choice (c) is incorrect. Unless fraud is suspected or the audit deals with cash or negotiable securities, it is more effective to defuse the anxiety of anticipating the audit by providing information ahead of time explaining the audit process and how to prepare for it. Choice (d) is incorrect. Auditee fear may be a natural part of anticipating the audit, but the auditor should keep it from being an important continuing part of the audit by using good interpersonal skills to build a positive participative relationship with auditees.

Subject Area: Engagement tools—data-gathering tools. Source: CIA 1196, II-24.

**164. (a)** The three methods of gathering feedback include observing, analyzing, and questioning; questioning the personnel and others affected within the organization represents the remaining method. Choice (b) is incorrect. Expanding sample sizes will generate more factual information about error rates in these attributes, but it will not provide feedback. Choice (c) is incorrect. The cash disbursements testing will show results of transaction processing after the vouchering process has been performed and corrections have been posted to the system; this information will not provide additional feedback. Choice (d) is incorrect. The auditor is looking to gather feedback.

Subject Area: Engagement tools—data-gathering tools. Source: CIA 1196, II-13.

**165. (c)** Evidence obtained by interviews should be corroborated. Choice (a) is incorrect. Interviews are not more objective than questionnaires. Choice (b) is incorrect. Interviews do not provide a systematic format. Choice (d) is incorrect. Evidence from interviews is not conclusive.

Subject Area: Engagement tools—data-gathering tools. Source: CIA 594, II-15.

**Analytical Review Techniques**

**166. (b)** There is no indication that cost of the products sold has changed. The challenge is to address the effectiveness of the promotion. Choice (a) is incorrect. This comparison would help highlight the effectiveness of the promotion in increasing sales. Choice (c) is incorrect. This is the key analysis, as it would show the extent of additional revenue versus cost. Choice (d) is incorrect. This would be helpful because the sales department may have useful information on new customers and repeat purchases.

Subject Area: Engagement tools—analytical review techniques. Source: CIA 597, I-37.

**167. (a)** If the auditor already suspects fraud, a more directed audit approach would be appropriate. Choice (b) is incorrect. Relatively stable operating data are a good scenario for using analytical review. Choice (c) is incorrect. Analytical review would be useful in identifying whether large, nonrecurring, or unusual transactions occurred. Choice (d) is incorrect. Analytical review only needs to have accounts related to other accounts or other independent data. It does not require that they be related to revenue.

Subject Area: Engagement tools—analytical review techniques. Source: CIA 597, I-63.

**168. (d)** All of the above factors would be considered in determining the extent of analytical audit procedures to be used. Choice (a) is incorrect. Adequacy of the system of internal control would be used to determine the extent of analytical audit procedures to be completed. Choice (b) is incorrect. The significance of the area being examined would be a factor in determining the extent of the analytical audit procedures to be used. Choice (c) is incorrect. The precision of the prediction of the internal audit results would be a factor in determining the extent of analytical audit procedures to be used.

Subject Area: Engagement tools—analytical review techniques. Source: CIA 1194, I-5.

**169. (c)** Monitoring is a process that assesses the quality of the internal control structure's performance over time. It involves appropriate personnel assessing the design and operation of controls on a timely basis and taking necessary actions. Monitoring can be done through *ongoing activities* or *separate evaluations*. Ongoing monitoring procedures are built into the normal recurring activities of an entity and include regular management and supervisory activities. Choice (a) is incorrect. This is an example of a reconciliation control applied at the store level. Monitoring refers to an overall control, which will tell management whether its other controls are operating effectively. Choice (b) is incorrect. These are operational and segregation controls. Choice (d) is incorrect. This is a daily operational control.

Subject Area: Engagement tools—analytical review techniques. Source: CIA 1195, I-16.

**170. (a)** This is the least appropriate audit procedure because it just defers the investigation to the following year. If a fraud was being conducted, it would not be appropriate to defer investigative action to the following year. Choice (b) is incorrect. This would be an effective procedure to establish the "face validity" of the manager's explanation. If the relationship is valid, it should also hold for the previous years. Choice (c) is incorrect. This would be an appropriate attempt to establish some independent evidence as to whether the goods were received, because the construction manager has a conflict of interest. The auditor should look for the existence of receiving reports signed by someone other than the construction manager and should verify that the individuals signing the reports exist. Choice (d) is incorrect. This would be a good procedure to determine if the augers exist since they are supposed to be used over a two- to three-year period.

Subject Area: Engagement tools—analytical review techniques. Source: CIA 1195, I-25.

**171. (c)** The IIA *Standards* states: "Results, or relationships from applying analytical auditing procedures that are not sufficiently explained should be communicated to the appropriate levels of management." Choice (a) is incorrect. This would only delay the reporting of an important finding. Choice (b) is incorrect. The results should be reported to management. The suggested audit procedure is incomplete and would not likely answer the question on the causes of the problem. Choice (d) is incorrect. The results should be reported to other levels of management because the auditor has already noted that the construction manager has a conflict of interest. Further, the auditor cannot insist that controls be implemented; the auditor can only recommend.

Subject Area: Engagement tools—analytical review techniques. Source: CIA 1195, I-26.

**172. (c)** An overstatement of year-end inventory would result in an increase in the gross margin. Choice (a) is incorrect. An increase in the number of competitors would result in price competition and a likely decrease in gross margin. Choice (b) is incorrect. A decrease in the number of suppliers would cause less price competition on the incoming side and, all else being equal, would result in a decreased gross margin. Choice (d) is incorrect. A decrease in accounts receivable would be very unlikely to signal an increase in the gross margin.

Subject Area: Engagement tools—analytical review techniques. Source: CIA 1195, I-27.

**173. (d)**    Such an analytical procedure will provide an indication of the efficiency and effectiveness of the subsidiary's management of the inventory. Choice (a) is incorrect. Comparison with industry standards will not test the accuracy of internal reporting. Choice (b) is incorrect. Comparison with industry standards will not test the controls designed to safeguard the inventory. Choice (c) is incorrect. Comparison with industry standards will not test compliance.

Subject Area: Engagement tools—analytical review techniques. Source: CIA 590, I-2.

**174. (b)**    A fraud would result in an overstatement of inventory in the ledger, but the perpetual inventory would reflect actual purchases. Choice (a) is incorrect. This would not be an effective procedure because, by definition, all cash disbursements would be accompanied by approved documents. Choice (c) is incorrect. This procedure would only verify that purchase orders were processed. It would not indicate the existence of fictitious purchase orders. Choice (d) is incorrect. This procedure would provide limited evidence on the possibility of fraud, but would not be as complete as choice (a).

Subject Area: Engagement tools—analytical review techniques. Source: CIA 595, I-61.

**175. (b)**    This type of fraud would not be detected by the control system since the purchasing agent could insert the fictitious receiving slip. Choice (a) is incorrect. There may be good reason to purchase most goods from a particular vendor. Nothing in the scenario suggests fraudulent activities. Choice (c) is incorrect. This possible fraud would be detected because no receiving report would be available to support the vendor's invoice. Choice (d) is incorrect. This response is unrelated to the purchasing environment described above.

Subject Area: Engagement tools—analytical review techniques. Source: CIA 595, I-62.

**176. (c)**    This change in procedures would make it difficult for the purchasing agent to insert a fictitious receiving report. An even better procedure would be to have both the receiving reports and vendor invoices be sent to accounts payable. Choice (a) is incorrect. This might partially deal with the problem, but the purchasing agent could just develop new dummy vendors. Further, this would be a trend away from establishing long-term relationships with key vendors as part of many TQM programs. Choice (b) is incorrect. Rotation of duties would not affect the type of fraud that could take place in this environment. The purchasing agent could just develop another dummy vendor for the new product line. Choice (d) is incorrect. This would just create an additional opportunity for fraud by the receiving department.

Subject Area: Engagement tools—analytical review techniques. Source: CIA 595, I-63.

**177. (c)**    Analytical relationships provide evidence that related transactions have been recorded. Choice (a) is incorrect. Although relevant, analytical evidence is not direct. Choice (b) is incorrect. It is not a recomputation or compelling. Choice (d) is incorrect. For assertions and accounts of low materiality, analytical evidence is often considered sufficient.

Subject Area: Engagement tools—analytical review techniques. Source: CIA 594, I-28.

**178. (a)**    This procedure would provide most competent evidence about value of the marketable equity securities. Choice (b) is incorrect. This procedure would not provide evidence about value. Choice (c) is incorrect. Marketable equity investments held for the short term are not subject to the equity method of accounting. Choice (d) is incorrect. There is no amortization of premium or discount on equity investments only on bonds and other debtor investments held for long-term purposes.

Subject Area: Engagement tools—analytical review techniques. Source: CIA 1192, I-4.

**179. (c)**    A determination of overall reasonableness can be made based on analytical procedures. Choice (a) is incorrect. Analytical procedures do not generally provide evidence regarding the adequacy of disclosure. Choice (b) is incorrect. Analytical procedures do not disclose specific errors or omissions. Choice (d) is incorrect. Analytical procedures will not disclose specific errors of cutoff.

Subject Area: Engagement tools—analytical review techniques. Source: CIA 1191, II-16.

**Problem Solving**

**180. (a)**    Problem solving involves face-to-face meetings. Choice (b) is incorrect. Expansion or resources requires more resources. Choice (c) is incorrect. The auditor does not use formal authority. Choice (d) is incorrect. The organizational structure has not changed.

Subject Area: Engagement tools—problem solving. Source: CIA 1196, II-33.

**181. (a)**    These skills are part of the problem-solving process. Choice (b) is incorrect because this is an interpersonal skill. Choice (c) is incorrect because both logic and reasoning skills are critical components of problem solving. Choice (d) is incorrect because this skill falls into the interpersonal category.

Subject Area: Engagement tools—problem solving. Source: CIA 597, II-36.

**182. (d)**    This is a primary activity in human resource management. Choice (a) is incorrect because this is an activity found in networking. Choice (b) is incorrect because decision making is an activity associated with traditional management. Choice (c) is incorrect because this activity is found in networking.

Subject Area: Engagement tools—problem solving. Source: CIA 597, II-37.

**183. (b)**    This is the second step in the process and the one the group should take up next. Choice (a) is incorrect. This is the third step and cannot be taken prior to identifying alternatives. Choice (c) is incorrect. Identifying the problem includes three parts: what is the actual situation, what is the desired situation, and, finally, identifying the cause of the problem. The stem describes completion of this step. Choice (d) is incorrect. This would be part of evaluating alternative solutions.

Subject Area: Engagement tools—problem solving. Source: CIA 596, II-2.

**184. (d)**    Although innovation is intrinsically rewarding to many people, employees of many companies do not believe innovation will be rewarded so they do not try to innovate or they keep their ideas to themselves. Programs like the one described in this problem offer extrinsic rewards. Choice (a) is incorrect due to explanation given for the choice (d). Choice (b) is incorrect because classical conditioning applies to reflexive behavior. The desired employee behavior in this problem—innovation—is voluntary. Choice (c) is incorrect because programs like the one described in this problem do not punish anyone. They merely reward innovators and encourage all employees to participate voluntarily.

Subject Area: Engagement tools—problem solving. Source: CIA 1195, II-35.

**185. (d)** Open discussion in which the members reach consensus is the most effective technique for obtaining commitment to the solution. Choice (a) is incorrect. Brainstorming is a good technique for generating a large number of ideas because it helps group members overcome the pressure to conform while the group is identifying options. It has no predictable effect, however, on the group's commitment to the solution. Choice (b) is incorrect. Top management mandates are unlikely to result in a high level of commitment, and they make group formation pointless. Choice (c) is incorrect. The Delphi technique is effective for generating a large number of ideas and for arriving at a consensus. It is not designed, however, for obtaining a high level of group commitment to the solution.

Subject Area: Engagement tools—problem solving. Source: CIA 1195, II-3.

**186. (b)** The auditor is responsible to the organization, not just the auditee, and should therefore report the problem to the auditee. Choice (a) is incorrect. Organizations cannot avoid conflict. It is now becoming accepted that some levels of conflict are necessary in order for organizations to grow and adapt to a changing environment. Choice (c) is incorrect. Mixing solutions with problem identification is a frequent problem cited in the managerial literature, but is not an effective means of dealing with the problem identified. Choice (d) is incorrect. This would be a violation of the *Standards,* which specify reporting criteria.

Subject Area: Engagement tools—problem solving. Source: CIA 595, II-36.

**187. (d)** The nominal group technique is an idea-generating and consensus-building problem solving tool. This technique gives everyone an opportunity to express ideas without being interrupted by others in the group. Choice (a) is incorrect because brainstorming is a technique to generate a great number of ideas. Choice (b) is incorrect because synectics involves the use of nontraditional activities such as excursions, fantasies, and analogies. Choice (c) is incorrect because systems analysis breaks down a large problem into many smaller problems.

Subject Area: Engagement tools—problem solving. Source: Author.

**188. (b)** Group decisions tend to be more creative than individual decisions. Choice (a) is incorrect. Group decisions tend to be more creative than individual decisions because they bring many points of view to bear on the problem. Choice (c) is incorrect. The supervisor is still an individual. Choice (d) is incorrect. The best way to enhance creativity is to involve other people.

Subject Area: Engagement tools—problem solving. Source: CIA 596, II-35.

**189. (c)** This is a type of management control that, if implemented correctly, should have brought the problem to management's attention much sooner. Since there is a great deal of central coordination needed, it is important that management establish a reporting and control system to compare actual performance with budgeted performance. Choice (a) is

incorrect. A good standard cost system would assist management in identifying the causes of the cost overruns, but a report on variances, by itself, would not totally address the cost overruns or the excess production problems. Choice (b) is incorrect. Perpetual inventory records would be useful but not sufficient to address the cost overrun and the excessive inventory level. There is no rationale given for the criteria to be used in developing the management report. The choice of two weeks of production in inventory may be low, or it may be excessive. It appears to be an arbitrary judgment that should be better justified. Choice (d) is incorrect. The problem is with production levels and production costs. Data on sales and gross margin do not provide timely input into the nature of the problem.

Subject Area: Engagement tools—problem solving. Source: CIA 595, II-9.

**190. (a)** This is the most complete answer. There are three potential problems: (1) the correct transfer of the data to the plants; (2) the ability to access and/or change the price data that are used by the computer program to develop sales invoices; and (3) the use of the tables in the billing program. This procedure develops information on all aspects of the process. Choice (b) is incorrect. This procedure provides information on the sales order process, but only limited information on how individual invoices are priced. It does not gather as much information as choice (a). Choice (c) is incorrect. This is a limited procedure. Choice (d) is incorrect. This procedure would provide information about how the computer program is supposed to work, but may not be up-to-date and does not provide information on how the data are entered into the price tables.

Subject Area: Engagement tools—problem solving. Source: CIA 595, II-10.

**191. (c)** This provides the most complete description of the total process. Additionally, starting with the initiation of the transaction and tracing it through to the completion of the transaction allows the auditor to "walk through" and define both the processing and the relevant control procedures. Choice (a) is incorrect. This is a good procedure to understand the process of making changes to the sales price data, but does not cover the processing of sales orders. Choice (b) is incorrect. Starting with the completed transaction does not provide as complete an understanding the full process. It will not identify flows where documents or data were "peeled off" and processed separately. Choice (d) is incorrect. This is a good procedure, but focuses only on the part of the processing that takes place at the plant level.

Subject Area: Engagement tools—problem solving. Source: CIA 595, II-11.

**192. (d)** Problem solving is the only method that can remove the source of the conflict. However, it does require time. Choice (a) is incorrect. A conflict trigger is a means of stimulating conflict. Choice (b) is incorrect. This method may submerge the conflict for a period of time, but it will not resolve the hurt feelings and mistrust. Choice (c) is incorrect. This is a stopgap measure and, like forcing, will not get to the root of the problem.

Subject Area: Engagement tools—problem solving. Source: CIA 1190, III-10.

**193. (b)** The Delphi approach seeks to obtain group consensus on a relatively narrow set of alternatives through a series of iterations such as those described in the stem. Choice

(a) is incorrect. The least squares method refers to regression analysis and involves specified variables. Choice (c) is incorrect. The maximum likelihood technique is a complex alternative to least squares. Choice (d) is incorrect. Optimizing expected payoffs is used in decision-making alternatives, which relies on historical information.

Subject Area: Engagement tools—problem solving. Source: CIA 592, III-74.

**194. (b)** Value analysis is primarily designed to optimize performance at a minimum cost. Choice (a) is incorrect. Synectics is a highly structured approach to problem solving. It uses excursions, fantasies, and analogies. Choice (c) is incorrect. The purpose of brainstorming is to generate a great number of ideas. Choice (d) is incorrect. Forced relationship involves the identification of a problem, the factors or forces contributing to making it a problem, and steps for generating solutions.

Subject Area: Engagement tools—problem solving. Source: CIA 592, III-86.

**195. (a)** Brainstorming is a group approach to breaking down broadly based problems into essential elements. Choice (b) is incorrect. Synectics is a highly structured approach to problem solving. It uses excursions, fantasies, and analogies. Choice (c) is incorrect. Blasting, creating, and refining are used when a completely new way of thinking or speculation is required or when answering a question such as "What else will do the job"? Choice (d) is incorrect. Operations research is a management science discipline attempting to find optimal solutions to business problems.

Subject Area: Engagement tools—problem solving. Source: CIA 592, III-87.

**196. (a)** Blast then refine is the technique being utilized. The old ways were completely disregarded and an entirely new approach was devised to meet the objectives of cost cutting and improved quality. Choice (b) is incorrect. Edisonian technique involves trial-and-error experimentation toward reaching a solution. Choice (c) is incorrect. Morphological matrix analysis is a system involving the methodical interrelating of all elements of a problem in order to discover new approaches to a solution. Choice (d) is incorrect. Operations research is a management science discipline attempting to find optimal solutions to business problems.

Subject Area: Engagement tools—problem solving. Source: CIA 592, III-88.

**197. (a)** Synectics is a highly structured group approach utilizing various analogies and metaphors to assist in viewing problems from widely divergent viewpoints. Choice (b) is incorrect. Forced relationship involves the identification of a problem, the factors or forces contributing to making it a problem, and steps for generating solutions. Choice (c) is incorrect. The purpose of brainstorming is to generate a great number of ideas. Choice (d) is incorrect. Attribute listing emphasizes the detailed observation of each particular characteristic or quality of an item or situation.

Subject Area: Engagement tools—problem solving. Source: CIA 592, III-89.

**198. (c)** Free association is the approach to idea stimulation whereby other symbols and ideas are to be freely associated with a problem. Choice (a) is incorrect. The purpose of brainstorming is to generate a great number of ideas. Choice (b) is incorrect. Value analysis is primarily designed to opti-

mize performance at a minimum cost. Choice (d) is incorrect. Attribute listing emphasizes the detailed observation of each particular characteristic or quality of an item or situation.

Subject Area: Engagement tools—problem solving. Source: CIA 592, III-90.

**199. (a)** Attribute listing is applied primarily to improve tangible objects by listing the parts and essential features of the object and systematically analyzing modifications to improve the object. Choice (b) is incorrect. Operations research is a management science discipline attempting to find optimal solutions to business problems. Choice (c) is incorrect. Morphological matrix analysis is a system involving the methodical interrelating of all elements of a problem in order to discover new approaches to a solution. Choice (d) is incorrect. Synectics is a highly structured approach to problem solving. It uses excursions, fantasies, and analogies.

Subject Area: Engagement tools—problem solving. Source: CIA 592, III-91.

**200. (d)** The Edisonian approach has been chosen here. Edisonian technique involves trial-and-error experimentation toward reaching a solution. Choice (a) is incorrect. Free association is the approach to idea stimulation whereby other symbols and ideas are to be freely associated with a problem. Choice (b) is incorrect. Operations research is a management science discipline attempting to find optimal solutions to business problems. Choice (c) is incorrect. Blasting, creating, and refining are used when a completely new way of thinking or speculation is required or when answering a question such as "What else will do the job?"

Subject Area: Engagement tools—problem solving. Source: CIA 592, III-92.

**201. (a)** Operations research attempts to find optimal solutions utilizing classical concepts such as statistics, simulation, and logical thinking to develop and test hypothesis. This application closely fits the problem and charge given. Choice (b) is incorrect. Value analysis is primarily designed to optimize performance at a minimum cost. Choice (c) is incorrect. Attribute listing emphasizes the detailed observation of each particular characteristic or quality of an item or situation. Choice (d) is incorrect. The purpose of brainstorming is to generate a great number of ideas.

Subject Area: Engagement tools—problem solving. Source: CIA 592, III-93.

**202. (d)** The focus of a strategic planning is on broad issues dealing with a time horizon of five to ten years and looking at a macro level. Choice (a) is incorrect. It is not a frequent use. Choice (b) is incorrect. It is not detailed or necessarily outdated. Choice (c) is incorrect. None applies.

Subject Area: Engagement tools—problem solving. Source: CIA 592, III-25.

**Risk and Control Self-Assessment**

**203. (b)** The CSA is a preventive auditing tool in that it identifies issues and problems earlier before they get bigger.

Subject Area: Engagement tools—risk and control self-assessment. Source: Author.

**204. (b)** The CSA is not a traditional audit engagement applied to financial, operational, and compliance areas. It is a consulting engagement in identifying problems and solving them for the benefit of the organization.

Subject Area: Engagement tools—risk and control self-assessment. Source: Author.

**205. (a)** The workshop is the most popular approach to CSA in assessing risks and evaluating controls for a given objective or process. In the "wall-writing" approach, meeting participants respond to questions posed by the facilitator of the workshop (meeting). The questionnaire approach and the survey approach are the same.

Subject Area: Engagement tools—risk and control self-assessment. Source: Author.

**206. (a)** A CSA approach using facilitated workshops (meetings) with the internal auditors as facilitators is favored by most organizations. This approach is especially good when the culture of the organization is supportive of candid participant responses in the workshops. Self-certification is an output of management-produced analyses.

Subject Area: Engagement tools—risk and control self-assessment. Source: Author.

**207. (c)** When an organization's culture does not support a participative approach like facilitated workshops, questionnaires and management-produced analyses of controls can be used. The meeting approach is the facilitated workshop approach, whether it is an audit or client facilitated.

Subject Area: Engagement tools—risk and control self-assessment. Source: Author.

**208. (a)** Management-produced analysis is a special type of self-assessment and used in self-certification of internal controls, annual representation letter required by external auditors, during a new computer system development project, during business combinations, or during an investigation into the reasons why a particular control breakdown or fraud occurred.

Subject Area: Engagement tools—risk and control self-assessment. Source: Author.

**209. (c)** Workshops or interviews are used in about 70% of CSA efforts; surveys or questionnaires are used about 30% of the time.

Subject Area: Engagement tools—risk and control self-assessment. Source: Author.

**210. (b)** The risk-based approach examines risks first in achieving an objective, looks at controls next, and finally identifies any significant residual risks. The risk-based workshop takes the participants through the entire sequence of objectives-risks-controls. The work flow in the objective-based approach is objectives-controls-residual risks-assessment. The work flow in the control-based approach is objectives-risks-controls-assessment. The work flow in the process-based approach is overall objectives-activity-level objectives-risks-controls-assessment.

Subject Area: Engagement tools—risk and control self-assessment. Source: Author.

**211. (b)** The operational risk is related to the organization's internal systems, products, services, processes, technology, and people. The strategic risks include risks related to strategy, political, economic, regulatory, and global market conditions. It also includes reputation risks, leadership risks, brand management risks, and customer risks. The financial risk includes risks from volatility in foreign currencies, interest rates, and commodities. It also includes credit risk, liquidity risk, and market risk. The hazard risk includes risks that

are insurable, such as natural disasters, various insurable liabilities, impairment of physical assets and property, and terrorism. The ERM includes both upside and downside risks.

Subject Area: Engagement tools—risk and control self-assessment. Source: Author.

**212. (a)** The ERM approach is more than just integrating risks, where risks are a part of uncertainty. The goal of an ERM initiative is to create, protect, and enhance shareholder value by managing the uncertainties that could influence in achieving the organization's objectives.

Subject Area: Engagement tools—risk and control self-assessment. Source: Author.

**213. (a)** According to the IIA Research Foundation, ERM defines risk as any event or action that could adversely influence an organization's ability to achieve its objectives. ERM encompasses the more traditional view of potential hazards (threats) as well as opportunities. Management must consider derisking the opportunities when creating and evaluating new opportunities. Risks and opportunities move together, and the key is to determine if the potential of a given opportunity exceed the risks. Items III and IV are part of the strength, weaknesses, opportunity, and threat (SWOT) analysis used in strategic management. When companies fail to manage risks, opportunities are missed, and shareholder value can be lost, which creates great pressure on management to improve corporate governance.

Subject Area: Engagement tools—risk and control self-assessment. Source: Author.

**214. (a)** According to the IIA Research Foundation, the chief audit executives (CAEs) of the study companies understand the value-added potential of ERM, which made them very effective ERM champions. ERM adds value because it is both inward-looking and forward-thinking. The other three choices are part of the value-added potential.

Subject Area: Engagement tools—risk and control self-assessment. Source: Author.

**215. (c)** Traditionally, the internal audit's role has been to provide reliable, overall assessment of risks and internal control effectiveness. In light of ERM implementation in improving corporate governance, internal auditors now (1) take a more business-oriented approach to audit company's operations, (2) change their audit approach to focus on business risk, (3) perform more effective follow-up on open ERM scorecards and metrics to increase management accountability, and (4) review formal action plans developed by management as part of the ERM implementation. Scorecards, metrics, and formal action plans are key part of the ERM infrastructure.

Subject Area: Engagement tools—risk and control self-assessment. Source: Author.

**216. (a)** In order to meet the ERM implementation challenge, the internal auditor should (1) use a risk-based audit approach (not a control-based approach), (2) be a consultant to the ERM implementation team (not as a policeman), (3) focus on future events (not past events), and (4) acquire competent skills to become an ERM facilitator (not use traditional accounting and auditing tools and skills).

Subject Area: Engagement tools—risk and control self-assessment. Source: Author.

**217. (a)** Control self-assessment (CSA) is a management technique where an organization's members identify and analyze controls and risks within business processes for continuous improvement. CSA techniques address soft controls while traditional audit techniques focus on hard controls. Soft controls are informal while hard controls are formal. Soft controls are more difficult to assess than hard controls. An example of a hard control is: Is there a code of ethics in place? An example of a soft control is: Are the employees willing to follow it?

Subject Area: Engagement tools—risk and control self-assessment. Source: Author.

**218.  (a)**    The internal auditor is am enabler (facilitator) in introducing the control self-assessment program into his or her organization. The roles mentioned in the other choices reflect the various roles in traditional audits.

Subject Area: Engagement tools—risk and control self-assessment. Source: Author.

**219.  (c)**    The implementation of the CSA program is categorized as either "vertical" or "horizontal." Vertical sessions are process-specific sessions that examine a given business process in depth. Horizontal sessions are organization-wide (or division-wide) sessions that cut across departmental responsibilities to identify and control risks that have a broader effect. Diagonal and individual sessions are distracters.

Subject Area: Engagement tools—risk and control self-assessment. Source: Author.

**220.  (b)**    Most people react badly to the concept of being controlled and audited. The chore of documentation is not exciting to many either. Improvement resulting from a self-assessment exercise where interested parties in the organization are involved from the beginning in the evaluation process will lead to effective results and outcomes.

Subject Area: Engagement tools—risk and control self-assessment. Source: Author.

**221.  (c)**    Items I and IV are the reasons for involving employees in the process. Item II is incorrect. Employees in general are not felt to be objective about their jobs and/or performance. Item III is incorrect. Although employees can be involved in assessing internal controls, these would not be considered independent assessments.

Subject Area: Engagement tools—risk and control self-assessment. Source: CIA 597, III-35.

## Computerized Audit Tools and Techniques

**222.  (d)**    This is the most comprehensive procedure because it identifies major vendors, concentrates on new vendors, and searches for underlying support that goods or services were provided by the vendor. Choice (a) is incorrect. This would provide evidence only on purchases above $50,000, which must be approved by someone other than the buyer. Choice (b) is incorrect. This would only provide information on whether the transactions that were authorized by the buyer were properly processed. It does not provide evidence on whether the transaction should have been processed. Choice (c) is incorrect. This would provide information on whether transactions under $50,000 contained the buyer's authorization. That is not the question here; the question is whether there is support for the expenditure. Further, this procedure is limited because it is not directed to the specific indicators that a fraud might exist.

Subject Area: Engagement tools—computerized audit tools and techniques. Source: CIA 597, I-11.

**223.  (c)**    This is both the most effective and the most efficient procedure as it provides a comprehensive analysis of the extent that obviously incorrect data is included in the database. Choice (a) is incorrect. Test data would provide evidence on whether the edit controls are currently working. The concern, however, is that data may have entered the system earlier and may be corrupted. Choice (b) is incorrect. Access controls are important, but they do not address the auditor's major concern, which is to determine the extent of the potential problem as a precursor for planning the extent to which additional audit work is necessary. Choice (d) is incorrect. This is a valid procedure, but given the auditor's more limited objective, choice (c) provides more comprehensive and efficient evidence.

Subject Area: Engagement tools—computerized audit tools and techniques. Source: CIA 597, I-35.

**224.  (a)**    This is the best procedure because it takes a sample from the total loan file and tests to determine that the loan is properly categorized as well as properly collateralized. Choice (b) is incorrect. This sample only deals with large-dollar items and does not test for proper collateralization. Choice (c) is incorrect. This is an inefficient audit procedure because it samples from loan applications, not loans approved. Choice (d) is incorrect. This would be an ineffective procedure because it is based only on loans in which payments are currently being made—it does not include loans that should have been categorized differently because payments are not being made.

Subject Area: Engagement tools—computerized audit tools and techniques. Source: CIA 597, I-46.

**225.  (b)**    The integrated test facility would allow the auditor to submit data periodically during the year to determine how well the program worked throughout the year. Choice (a) is incorrect. The test data method is limited to a point in time in which the testing is accomplished. Using it only during the last quarter of the year would not be effective unless there was also a test of program changes. Choice (c) is incorrect. Parallel simulation would not be an efficient technique because it would cause the auditor to develop a massive parallel system. Choice (d) is incorrect. The SCARF method is used to identify outliers (transactions with unusual characteristics or transactions that are processed when they do not pass normal edit controls). It simply writes these transactions out to a file for further audit investigation. It would not be a good technique for addressing the audit objective.

Subject Area: Engagement tools—computerized audit tools and techniques. Source: CIA 1195, I-29.

**226.  (d)**    This would be the best method because it would sample from a population that has been explicitly identified as nonmatching. It allows the auditor to analyze the potential problems before investigating further. Choice (a) is incorrect. The test data method would only tell us whether the computer program is working correctly at one point in time. It would not identify all the problems encountered during the year. Choice (b) is incorrect. Generalized audit software is a good tool, but it would not be used efficiently here since it is reading the purchase order file only. Many of the items selected may have been appropriately matched and some may not have been filled. Choice (d) is more efficient. Choice (c) is incorrect. SCARF would not be an effective audit tool because the auditor wishes to identify nonmatched items. Choice (d) is a more encompassing solution.

Subject Area: Engagement tools—computerized audit tools and techniques. Source: CIA 1195, I-30.

**227. (b)** Generalized audit software could be used to develop a list of multiple recipients at one address. The list could then be investigated further to determine the possibility of fraud. Choice (a) is incorrect. Tagging and tracing is most effective to determine that items properly submitted are processed correctly. Choice (c) is incorrect. The ITF is most effective to determine that items properly submitted are processed correctly. Choice (d) is incorrect. This would not be the most effective technique.

Subject Area: Engagement tools—computerized audit tools and techniques. Source: CIA 1195, I-57.

**228. (c)** All three audit approaches would work. If we were to rank order the effectiveness, it would be I, III, then II. However, if properly implemented, procedure II would work. Choices (a), (b), and (d) are incorrect because all three of the procedures would work.

Subject Area: Engagement tools—computerized audit tools and techniques. Source: CIA 595, I-28.

**229. (a)** The only justifiable conclusion that can be reached based on the audit tests is that something other than the calculation is causing the increase in freight costs. Choice (b) is incorrect. Although hypotheses I and II may be potential explanations, they would need to be tested. They represent hypotheses, not conclusions. Choice (c) is incorrect. Although hypotheses I and II may be potential explanations, they would need to be tested. They represent hypotheses, not conclusions. Choice (d) is Incorrect because the auditor has researched the potential algorithms and did not conclude that the one implemented is not sufficient. There is not enough evidence to justify this conclusion.

Subject Area: Engagement tools—computerized audit tools and techniques. Source: CIA 595, I-29.

**230. (c)** This would be the best procedure. Since the auditor is looking for unauthorized changes, the auditor must first identify all changes that have taken place. The auditor then investigates the changes to see if they had been authorized. Choice (a) is incorrect. This would be an inefficient procedure. Many programs will not have changes made to them during the applicable time period. Thus, there will not be program change request forms for many items selected. Choice (b) is incorrect. Sampling from authorized changes will tell the auditor only that authorized changes had been made. The auditor is searching for unauthorized changes. Choice (d) is incorrect. Similar to response (b), the population only identifies those projects that have been authorized. The auditor is concerned with unauthorized changes.

Subject Area: Engagement tools—computerized audit tools and techniques. Source: CIA 595, I-35.

**231. (a)** This method would work best because the amounts credited to each account would be compared to that calculated by the auditor's parallel program. Choice (b) is incorrect. It is doubtful that confirmation of an account balance would detect errors less than 1 cent made on a daily basis. Choice (c) is incorrect. Snapshot is a technique for tracing the processing of transactions through a system. It would not be applicable here. Choice (d) is incorrect. SCARF is an audit technique that captures unusual transactions (or transactions in excess of edit checks) that have been submitted for process-

ing. The auditor can later evaluate the items. It is not applicable here.

Subject Area: Engagement tools—computerized audit tools and techniques. Source: CIA 595, I-64.

**232. (a)** This would be the best procedure because it would be an efficient manner to determine if there were any easily seen fraudulent pattern associated with the payments under the control of the social worker. Choice (b) is incorrect. The integrated test facility is designed to test the correctness of processing, not whether only valid recipients are receiving payment. Choice (c) is incorrect. This is a future-oriented approach and would not provide much information about the possibility of fraudulent items currently contained in the file. Like the ITF, snapshot concentrates on the processing of data, not the addition of new recipients to the files. Choice (d) is incorrect. Sending confirmations to the recipients listed on the file would not be the first approach that is being used for two reasons: (1) response (a) better establishes whether there is a defined pattern of potential fraud; (2) if the recipients are indeed fraudulent, the social worker will receive the confirmation (all sent to a common address) and will be able to respond positively.

Subject Area: Engagement tools—computerized audit tools and techniques. Source: CIA 595, I-65.

**233. (d)** All three of these responses would be effective in dealing with the audit and control concern identified by the auditor: Item I segregates duties, Item III incorporates an important computer check, and Item IV rotates duties so that a new worker will find that some recipients are not valid. Choice (a) is incorrect. Item II would not add to the control. Choice (b) is incorrect. The self-checking digit would not improve the control procedure. Each recipient set up in the system would have a unique self-checking digit. The concern is over the process of setting up valid recipients. Choice (c) is incorrect. Item III would also contribute.

Subject Area: Engagement tools—computerized audit tools and techniques. Source: CIA 595, I-66.

**234. (c)** Embedded audit data collection provides the auditor with the capability to continuously monitor the operation of an application. Choice (a) is incorrect because generalized audit software can be used for data collection, but operates independently—and thus not continuously—from an application. Choice (b) is incorrect because control flowcharting is developed to document and/or review the controls in an application system. Choice (d) is incorrect because ITF is used to test programs, not to collect data.

Subject Area: Engagement tools—computerized audit tools and techniques. Source: CIA 1194, I-36.

**235. (c)** Parallel simulation processes real transaction data through auditor-developed test programs. Choice (a) is incorrect. The integrated test facility involves the use of test data and also the creation of fictitious entities (e.g., vendors and employees) on master files. Choice (b) is incorrect. Tracing provides a detailed listing of the sequence of program statement execution. Choice (d) is incorrect. Mapping is a procedure for reporting code usage within a program.

Subject Area: Engagement tools—computerized audit tools and techniques. Source: CIA 1194, I-40.

**236. (a)** Code comparison is the process of comparing two versions of the same program to determine whether the two correspond. It is an efficient technique because it is performed by software. Choice (b) is incorrect. Code review is the process of reading program source code listings to determine whether the code contains potential errors or inefficient statements. Code review can be used as a means of code comparison but is inefficient. Choice (c) is incorrect. Test data runs permit the auditor to verify the processing of preselected transactions. It gives no evidence about unexercised portions of the program. Choice (d) is incorrect. Analytical review is the process of creating and evaluating ratios between numbers, often in the context of financial statements.

Subject Area: Engagement tools—computerized audit tools and techniques. Source: CIA 590, I-19.

**237. (d)** Tagging is an audit technique to obtain a computer trail of processing steps relevant to a given transaction. Choice (a) is incorrect. Simulation permits comparisons of live data processing but does not produce a trail of processing steps. Choice (b) is incorrect. Snapshot is a technique for taking a picture of computer memory to aid in verifying a decision process. Choice (c) is incorrect. Code comparison verifies that program changes and maintenance are correctly followed.

Subject Area: Engagement tools—computerized audit tools and techniques. Source: CIA 1190, I-37.

**238. (c)** This is a manual function that must be performed by the auditor. Choices (a), (b), and (d) are incorrect because these are examples of functions that generalized audit software is able to perform.

Subject Area: Engagement tools—computerized audit tools and techniques. Source: CIA 590, I-24.

**239. (a)** The software compares two files for data consistency. Choice (b) is incorrect. Generalized audit software only permits ex-post (after the fact) auditing. Choice (c) is incorrect. Generalized audit software cannot verify operating system logic. Choice (d) is incorrect. Using a host language extension, an auditor can gain direct access to the database.

Subject Area: Engagement tools—computerized audit tools and techniques. Source: CIA 1190, II-36.

**240. (d)** This is the major reason for not using ITF. Choice (a) is incorrect. Reserving specific master file records and processing them at regular intervals pertains to base case system evaluation instead of ITF. Choice (b) is incorrect. Collecting transaction and master file records in a separate file is a feature of embedded audit data collection, not ITF. Choice (c) is incorrect. Making manual adjustments to output does not reverse the fictitious entries in the master file.

Subject Area: Engagement tools—computerized audit tools and techniques. Source: CIA 1190, III-26.

**241. (d)** They can be continuously monitored or specifically activated. Choice (a) is incorrect because it is a characteristic of snapshot. Choice (b) is incorrect because it is a characteristic of tracing. Choice (c) is incorrect because it is a characteristic of mapping.

Subject Area: Engagement tools—computerized audit tools and techniques. Source: CIA 596, III-74.

**242. (c)** The auditor's inference can only be to the operation of computerized controls and the correctness of computer processing during the year because the integrated test facility tests only tests the computerized portion of the application, not that all data have been entered correctly. Choice (a) is incorrect. The ITF only provides audit evidence on the correctness of processing of data that has been submitted to the

computer application. Thus, it does not provide evidence that all hours worked have been entered into the system for processing. Choice (b) is incorrect. The auditor cannot conclude that all employees were paid correctly and that their pay was correctly recorded because to do so the auditor would need evidence that all employees were correctly classified as to pay rate and that all their time was correctly submitted to the computer program. Choice (d) is incorrect. Response (b) and (c) are not correct.

Subject Area: Engagement tools—computerized audit tools and techniques. Source: CIA 595, II-8.

**243. (c)** Computer-assisted techniques have had the greatest impact on the audit process. They have changed the audit scope and test procedures, and so on. Choice (a) is incorrect. This task can be performed manually without the use of information technology. Choice (b) is incorrect. While it has changed audit documentation, it has not impacted the audit scope or test procedures. Choice (d) is incorrect. Whether using information technology or not, the audit risk is the same.

Subject Area: Engagement tools—computerized audit tools and techniques. Source: CIA 594, II-4.

**244. (c)** This is a function of generalized audit software. Choice (a) is incorrect. This is a function of mapping. Choice (b) is incorrect. This is a function of an integrated test facility. Choice (d) is incorrect. This is a function of an embedded audit routine.

Subject Area: Engagement tools—computerized audit tools and techniques. Source: CIA 594, III-10.

**245. (a)** Online inquiry is an interactive procedure that allows an auditor or other authorized personnel to select and view individual records or transactions. Choice (b) is incorrect. Parallel simulation processes real data through audit programs so simulated output and regular output can be compared. Choice (c) is incorrect. Mapping monitors the execution of a program. Choice (d) is incorrect. Tracing provides an audit trail of the instructions that are executed when a program is run.

Subject Area: Engagement tools—computerized audit tools and techniques. Source: CIA 594, III-11.

**246. (b)** Comparing a sample of software being run on personal computers with purchase documentation will establish a basis for determining compliance. Choice (a) is incorrect. Reviewing the policy will not determine compliance with copyright limitations. Choice (c) is incorrect. An inventory of software alone cannot determine compliance without comparing it to supporting purchase documentation. Choice (d) is incorrect. Reviewing the minutes may determine the intent to comply with copyright laws but cannot establish compliance.

Subject Area: Engagement tools—computerized audit tools and techniques. Source: CIA 1193, I-36.

**247. (c)** Auditing around the computer does not involve testing the transaction (audit) trail. Choice (a) is incorrect. Simulation programs involve computer applications and require auditing through the computer. Choice (b) is incorrect. High costs are not involved with testing controls when auditing around the computer. Choice (d) is incorrect. A high level of technical expertise is a disadvantage of auditing through the computer—not around the computer.

Subject Area: Engagement tools—computerized audit tools and techniques. Source: CIA 1191, II-32.

**248.** **(c)** This software could check the mailing addresses of vendors and detect common address, or other commonalities of the billings. Choice (a) is incorrect. Test data would check the processing of information, not the validity of the input information. Choice (b) is incorrect. The fraud did not involve a program change. Choice (d) is incorrect. This test is not designed to test for the processing of invalid information.

Subject Area: Engagement tools—computerized audit tools and techniques. Source: CIA 594, I-35.

**249.** **(b)** The audit procedure to be applied in this case requires a matching of all records to identify vendor addresses that are the same. Choice (a) is incorrect. Sampling error is not larger when computers are used to draw the sample. Choice (c) is incorrect. Standards do not prohibit the use of sampling. Choice (d) is incorrect. This is not an example of "auditing through the computer." The test uses audit software to extract and compare data.

Subject Area: Engagement tools—computerized audit tools and techniques. Source: CIA 594, I-36.

**250.** **(d)** Generalized audit software allows many different audits to be done where similar audit tasks are required. It is cost effective. Choice (a) is incorrect. Comparison programs compare source versions of operational programs with authorized copies and identify only changes or deviations in logic. Choice (b) is incorrect. Custom audit software is written for a specific audit and cannot be used on different systems. Choice (c) is incorrect. It requires the auditor to learn rules of each environment—usually limited to retrieval.

Subject Area: Engagement tools—computerized audit tools and techniques. Source: CIA 593, I-26.

**251.** **(c)** The use of test data is a useful audit procedure to test application controls. Choice (a) is incorrect. Data file security is a general control concern. The question deals with application controls. Choice (b) is incorrect. Computer-based sequence checks are applications controls. It is appropriate for an internal auditor to seek to determine whether the checks are working. However, this question involves the document numbers on vendor invoices. Since the vendors generate these document numbers, the purchasing firm has no access to a sequencing of such invoices. Choice (d) is incorrect. It is never acceptable for an internal auditor to rely on the representations of an auditee.

Subject Area: Engagement tools—computerized audit tools and techniques. Source: CIA 593, II-21.

**252.** **(a)** Use of audit software to perform parallel simulation is an acceptable audit application. Choice (b) is incorrect. Use of an integrated facility usually requires advanced planning before a system is implemented. Installing an integrated test facility after the fact can be quite costly and time consuming. Choice (c) is incorrect. Tagging and tracing is more difficult to employ than parallel simulation. Choice (d) is incorrect. Mapping and program analysis requires a strong programming background, something not available on this audit team.

Subject Area: Engagement tools—computerized audit tools and techniques. Source: CIA 1192, I-36.

**253.** **(c)** Controlled reprocessing allows update inputs to be inexpensively reprocessed and compared to original update results. Choice (a) is incorrect. Test data checks specific controls, but would not allow identification of lost or incomplete updates. Choice (b) is incorrect. Parallel simulation is quite expensive and is inappropriate for a one-time identification of lost or incomplete updates. Choice (d) is incorrect. An integrated test facility tests the system on a continuous basis, but may contaminate actual transaction data.

Subject Area: Engagement tools—computerized audit tools and techniques. Source: CIA 1192, I-25.

**254.** **(d)** Generalized audit software can be utilized to review 100% of the file for duplicate payments using any matching requirements and thus help identify potential duplicate payments claims. Choice (a) is incorrect. Statistical sampling is most useful in estimating the size of a population (variables sampling) or the degree of error (attribute sampling). Specific identification of duplicate payments is the problem here. Choice (b) is incorrect. While desk checking the source code might detect a program error, it is not the solution to the problem at hand. Choice (c) is incorrect. An integrated test facility is useful for passing test data through a production system, but it does not address the duplicate payments problem.

Subject Area: Engagement tools—computerized audit tools and techniques. Source: CIA 592, II-30.

**255.** **(d)** Embedded audit data collection requires screening routines be inserted within production runs and thus allows identification and selection of transactions meeting predefined criteria. Choice (a) is incorrect. Extended records combine elements from different files into a single record. Choice (b) is incorrect. Tracing is used to identify the execution and sequence of computer instructions. Choice (c) is incorrect. Mapping is used to determine if any unexecuted code exists.

Subject Area: Engagement tools—computerized audit tools and techniques. Source: CIA 1191, I-35.

**256.** **(b)** Comparing shipping records with sales invoices would disclose any shipments that were not billed. Choice (a) is incorrect. Comparing entries in the receivable ledger with sales invoices only demonstrates that the prepared invoices were posted. Choice (c) is incorrect. Comparing shipping records with original customer orders only demonstrates that shipments were made to customers—not those customers were billed. Choice (d) is incorrect. Comparing shipping records with credit limits demonstrates only that credit limits might not have been exceeded.

Subject Area: Engagement tools—computerized audit tools and techniques. Source: CIA 1191, I-33.

**257.** **(a)** An integrated test facility uses a fictitious or dummy entity against which data are processed and stored. Choice (b) is incorrect. Simulation programs are techniques using separate programs to process actual data and then compare results. Choice (c) is incorrect. Snapshot is a technique using specially coded inputs to trace the transaction trail. Choice (d) is incorrect. Data conversion is the process of translating transactions into a form compatible with an operating system.

Subject Area: Engagement tools—computerized audit tools and techniques. Source: CIA 1191, II-31.

**258.** **(d)** The test data approach inputs data into the application and allows output to be compared to predetermined results, thus identifying the degree of completeness of the allocation. Choice (a) is incorrect. Control flowcharting is generally at the systems level rather than the program level. Choice (b) is incorrect. Inquiry of the systems programmer would be of little help in relation to specific program logic problems. Choice (c) is incorrect. Extended records are used to capture an audit trail through a system.

Subject Area: Engagement tools—computerized audit tools and techniques. Source: CIA 1191, II-17.

**259. (b)** A major advantage of this type of auditing is the ability to immediately process data using microcomputer software without first having to manually enter the data into the microcomputer. Choice (a) is incorrect. Audit technology has no direct effect on the amount of substantive testing required. Choice (c) is incorrect. While this is true, it is not an advantage. Choice (d) is incorrect. Processing computer files does not in itself provide confirmation of customer account balances.

Subject Area: Engagement tools—computerized audit tools and techniques. Source: CIA 1191, III-23.

**260. (a)** Computer matching of fields such as goods received number, product code, supplier code, and quantity assures agreement between goods received and goods invoiced. Choice (b) is incorrect. Control totals do not identify specific item-by-item differences. Choice (c) is incorrect. Batch totals only provide a total value for a field and do not allow for detail matching. Choice (d) is incorrect. Check digits only provide for validation of predefined account numbers.

Subject Area: Engagement tools—computerized audit tools and techniques. Source: CIA 591, I-41.

**261. (b)** An acknowledged risk of using the ITF is the contamination of live master files. Choice (a) is incorrect. The ITF is utilized to test programs in operation, including the presence of processing controls. Choice (c) is incorrect. The ITF technique can be used for both system development and application testing. Choice (d) is incorrect. Minimal technical skill is required to process test data when using an ITF.

Subject Area: Engagement tools—computerized audit tools and techniques. Source: CIA 597, III-66.

**262. (a)** An embedded audit module enables continuous monitoring and analysis transaction processing, including the functioning of processing controls. Choice (b) is incorrect. Mapping is a technique for determining whether a computer program contains any unexecuted code that should be examined. Choice (c) is incorrect. Retrieval and analysis programs such as generalized audit software offer the features and flexibility suitable for verifying the correctness of information on a computer file. Choice (d) is incorrect. The snapshot method is a technique utilized to capture and print all data pertinent to the analysis of a specific moment in the processing cycle.

Subject Area: Engagement tools—computerized audit tools and techniques. Source: CIA 597, III-56.

## Process Mapping Including Flowcharting

**263. (b)** By emphasizing the flow of processing between departments and/or people, it more clearly shows any inappropriate separation of duties and lack of independent checks on performance. Choice (a) is incorrect. A vertical flowchart is usually designed to provide for written descriptions. Choice (c) is incorrect. It is usually shorter because space for written descriptions is not provided. Choice (d) is incorrect. More of the flow of processing can be depicted on one page than in a vertical flowchart with written descriptions.

Subject Area: Engagement tools—process mapping including flowcharting. Source: CIA 597, II-15.

**264. (a)** Control flowcharting provides an efficient and comprehensive method of describing relatively complex activities, especially those involving several departments. Choice (b) is incorrect. Copies of procedures and related forms do not provide an efficient method of reviewing the processing activities. Choice (c) is incorrect. A narrative review covering the history and forms' usage of the department is not as efficient or comprehensive as flowcharting for communicating relevant information about controls. Choice (d) is incorrect. Industry standards do not provide a picture of existing practice for subsequent audit activity.

Subject Area: Engagement tools—process mapping including flowcharting. Source: CIA 596 II-13.

**265. (a)** The definition of a flowchart is that it is a graphical representation of a sequence of activities and decisions. Choice (b) is incorrect. A control chart is used to monitor actual versus desired quality measurements during repetition operation. Choice (c) is incorrect. A histogram is a bar chart showing conformance to a standard bell curve. Choice (d) is incorrect. A run chart tracks the frequency or amount of a given variable over time.

Subject Area: Engagement tools—process mapping including flowcharting. Source: CIA 596, III-58.

**266. (a)** A flowchart is most valuable in providing a summary outline and description of transaction flows. Choice (b) is incorrect. Transaction retrievals are used to select items for testing and review. Choice (c) is incorrect. Test decks are used to verify processing accuracy. Choice (d) is incorrect. Software code comparisons are used to validate that programs in production correspond to an authorized copy of the software.

Subject Area: Engagement tools—process mapping including flowcharting. Source: CIA 1193, III-19.

**267. (b)** Systems flowcharts show segregation of duties and the transfer of data between different segments in the organization. Choice (a) is incorrect. The systems flowchart shows the overall flow, but would not identify the specific edit tests implemented. Those would be found in a programming flowchart. Choice (c) is incorrect. The flowcharts are generally not kept up-to-date for changes. Therefore, the auditor will have to interview key personnel to determine changes in processing since the flowchart was developed. Choice (d) is incorrect. A systems flowchart should show both the manual processing and the computer processing.

Subject Area: Engagement tools—process mapping including flowcharting. Source: CIA 595, I-5.

**268. (a)** It highlights the interaction between departments. Choices (b) and (d) are incorrect because they do not highlight the interaction of departments. Choice (c) is incorrect because it is not a procedure-oriented documenting tool.

Subject Area: Engagement tools—process mapping including flowcharting. Source: CIA 594, II-43.

**269. (a)** A flowchart provides a visual grasp of the system and a means of analysis that cannot be achieved by other methods. Choice (b) is incorrect. A questionnaire approach provides only an agenda for evaluation. Choice (c) is incorrect. A matrix approach does not provide the visual grasp of the system that a flowchart does. Choice (d) is incorrect. A detailed narrative does not provide the means of evaluating complex operations that a flowchart does.

Subject Area: Engagement tools—process mapping including flowcharting. Source: CIA 592, I-18.

## Risk and Control Self-Assessment 2

**270. (b)** Controls are implemented in the risk mitigation phase in order to reduce the effects of risks. Risk assessment includes identification, analysis, measurement, and prioritization of risks— choice (a). Risk financing deals with internal funding and external transfer of risk—choice (c). Risk monitoring addresses internal and external reporting and feedback into risk assessment—choice (d).

Subject Area: Engagement tools—risk and control self-assessment. Source: Author.

**271. (a)** Traditionally, risk management has been focused more narrowly in terms of scope of risks, types of risk management strategies, and the impact and nature of risk. The strategies have concentrated on insurance solutions primarily. Now the focus of ERM is broad, covering areas such as earnings growth, revenue growth, and corporate governance.

Subject Area: Engagement tools—risk and control self-assessment. Source: Author.

**272. (c)** Most organizations are seeking early wins that will help build momentum and promote further development toward their ideal ERM process. Some organizations are using a layered approach of risk, one at a time, into their risk assessment and risk mitigation processes—choice (a). Some organizations are embracing all sources of risk at the outset, but are tackling the processes one at a time, with most starting with risk assessment—choice (b). Other organizations taking on all risk sources and all processes, but on a small, manageable subset of their operations as a pilot project—choice (d).

Subject Area: Engagement tools—risk and control self-assessment. Source: Author.

**273. (b)** According to the IIA survey respondents, 30% felt that chief audit executive is responsible for overseeing enterprise risk management or compliance activities. The chief financial officer was second with 24% and the chief risk officer was third with 21%. Chief executive officer was not involved in this activity.

Subject Area: Engagement tools—risk and control self-assessment. Source: Author.

**274. (d)** The IIA survey indicated that some organizations see ERM as an analytical tool rather than as a performance management system. Other tools of importance include risk mapping or optimization software.

Subject Area: Engagement tools—risk and control self-assessment. Source: Author.

**275. (b)** More than half of the IIA survey respondents cited the desire for a unifying framework is the primary driver for ERM, and 38% cited corporate governance guidelines as another important driver.

Subject Area: Engagement tools—risk and control self-assessment. Source: Author.

**276. (c)** Earnings growth received the highest rating. Similarly, revenue growth was the second highest ranked business issue. Expense control or reduction was ranked as the third most important issue today; however, few years from now earnings consistency will be viewed to be the third most important issue.

Subject Area: Engagement tools—risk and control self-assessment. Source: Author.

**277. (c)** The IIA survey respondents indicated that capital management and contingency plans provide significant and immediate value. They also believed that ERM could assist with earnings consistency and expense control.

Subject Area: Engagement tools—risk and control self-assessment. Source: Author.

**278. (d)** The IIA survey respondents indicated that organizational culture is the top barrier followed by unclear benefits to senior management, lack of formalized process, organizational turf battles, and lack of tools.

Subject Area: Engagement tools—risk and control self-assessment. Source: Author.

**279. (a)** The IIA survey respondents reported that most internal auditing, finance, and operations functions have a formal, comprehensive risk assessment process in place. In contrast, only 21% of respondents reported that risk assessment activity related to the human resource function.

Subject Area: Engagement tools—risk and control self-assessment. Source: Author.

**280. (c)** Risk management has evolved from insurance management. The strategic factor in the transition from insurance management to risk management was the evolution of decision theory, operations research, and management science disciplines. Choices (a), (b), and (d) use a scientific approach to decision making. Decision theory provides a basis for judging the goodness or badness of decisions before the outcome is known. Decision theory has its roots in operations research and management science.

Subject Area: Engagement tools—risk and control self-assessment. Source: Author.

**281. (b)** Pure risks are those in which there is a chance of loss or no loss only. Pure risks are of several types, including personal risks, property risks, liability risks, and performance risks. Examples include personal risks (death, sickness, or disability), property risks (damage to or destruction of property, and the loss of use of property that has been damaged), liability risks (liability suits arising out of automobiles), performance risks (risks resulting from human failure of a contractor to complete a project, default of a debtor). Risk management deals with both insurable and uninsurable risks. Although the major focus of most risk managers is on insurable risks, the more appropriate realm of risk management is pure risk. The risk manager cannot ignore those pure risks that are not insurable (e.g., shoplifting losses in a retail store that are rarely insurable). Dynamic risks (choice a.) are those that arise from changes in the economy (e.g., unemployment, high interest rates, and high inflation rates). Speculative risks (choice c.) involve the chance of loss or gain (e.g., hedging, options, and derivatives). Fundamental risks (choice d.) are those that are impersonal in origin and consequences—they are generally beyond the control of the individual. They are group risks, caused for the most part by economic, social, and political phenomena, although they may also result from physical occurrences.

Subject Area: Engagement tools—risk and control self-assessment. Source: Author.

**282. (a)** A hazard is a condition that increases the probability of loss from a peril. Examples include faulty wiring and improper storage of flammables. Moral hazard is a dishonest tendency, and examples include businesses that are losing money, obsolete inventory that is overinsured, and false claims to defraud an insurer. Morale hazard (choice b.) is reflected in a careless attitude that may accompany the existence of insurance, or the inflated losses that occur simply because the loss is insured. Physical hazards (choice c.) include conditions such as faulty housekeeping, defective wiring, storage of flammables, and road conditions. Legal hazards (choice d.) include statutes, court decisions, and the legal environment that can influence the probability of loss.

Subject Area: Engagement tools—risk and control self-assessment. Source: Author.

**283.  (c)**    Risk sharing is viewed as a special case of risk transfer, in which the risk is transferred from the individual to the group. It may also be a form of risk retention, depending on the success of the risk-sharing arrangement. Both risk retention and risk transfer and part of risk financing.

Subject Area: Engagement tools—risk and control self-assessment. Source: Author.

**284.  (b)**    Risk situations that have high severity and high frequency should be either avoided or reduced. Reduction is appropriate when it is possible to reduce either the severity or the frequency to a manageable level. Otherwise, the risk should be avoided or transferred.

Subject Area: Engagement tools—risk and control self-assessment. Source: Author.

**285.  (c)**    ERM is a broad concept that includes many areas, such as pure risks, financial risks, operational risks, strategic risks, and speculative risks. Pure risks are those in which there is a chance of loss or no loss only (e.g., default of a debtor, disability). Financial risks include credit risk and interest rate risk. Operational risks include risks related to systems, processes, technology, and people. Strategic risks include reputation risk and leadership risk. Speculative risks involve the chance of loss or gain (e.g., hedging, options, and derivatives).

Subject Area: Engagement tools—risk and control self-assessment. Source: Author.

**286.  (d)**    Risk management is broken down into two major categories: risk control ad risk financing. Risk control focuses on minimizing the risk of loss to which the organization is exposed. Risk financing concentrates on arranging the availability of funds to meet the losses that do occur. Risk control includes risk avoidance and risk reduction (choice c.). Risk financing includes risk retention and risk transfer (choice a.). Choice (b) is meaningless in that it combines parts of the two categories.

Subject Area: Engagement tools—risk and control self-assessment. Source: Author.

**287.  (b)**    Despite its importance, determining the objectives of the program is the first step in the risk management process that is most likely to be overlooked. Consequently, the risk management efforts of many firms are fragmented and inconsistent. The risk management process properly handles the other choices.

Subject Area: Engagement tools—risk and control self-assessment. Source: Author.

**288.  (c)**    Risk management is concerned with pure risk. Minimizing the adverse effects of losses and uncertainty connected with pure risks is necessary. Risk management is a process that involves managing the pure risks.

Subject Area: Engagement tools—risk and control self-assessment. Source: Author.

**289.  (c)**    Risk retention is most appropriate for situations in which there is a low probability of occurrence (frequency) with a low potential severity. Severity dictates whether a risk should be retained. If the potential severity is more than the organization can afford, retention is not recommended. Frequency determines whether the risk is economically insurable. The higher the probabilities of loss, the higher the expected value of loss and the higher the cost of transfer.

Subject Area: Engagement tools—risk and control self-assessment. Source: Author.

**290.  (a)**    Insurance is most appropriate for situations in which there is a low frequency and a high severity. The high severity implies a catastrophic impact if the loss should occur, and a low probability (frequency) implies a low expected value and a low cost of transfer.

Subject Area: Engagement tools—risk and control self-assessment. Source: Author.

**291.  (b)**    Financing involves paying for the losses out of current income or existing assets, by earmarking funds or by the purchase of insurance. The cost of financing losses is the amount of funds that is paid for the losses that occur. The cost of risk for retained risks is the opportunity cost on the funds that must be earmarked and that cannot be used for other purposes.

Subject Area: Engagement tools—risk and control self-assessment. Source: Author.

**292.  (c)**    A hazard is a condition that increases the probability (chance) of loss from a peril. Perils are causes of loss, and examples include fire and flood. Uncertainty can exist where there is no risk. Risk or exposure is the possibility of loss.

Subject Area: Engagement tools—risk and control self-assessment. Source: Author.

**293.  (c)**    As organizations think about the future and actually create the future of their business, they must consider derisking opportunities. In capitalizing on opportunities, the goal is to be a market leader but yet reduce risk.

Subject Area: Engagement tools—risk and control self-assessment. Source: Author.

**294.  (c)**    Financial risk includes risks from volatility in foreign currencies, interest rates, and commodities. It also includes credit risk, liquidity risk, and market risk.

Subject Area: Engagement tools—risk and control self-assessment. Source: Author.

**295.  (d)**    ERM integrates the management of all risks, including the more traditional hazard and financial risks, with operational and strategic risks. The latter two risks are new and are more difficult to identify, assess, and evaluate.

Subject Area: Engagement tools—risk and control self-assessment. Source: Author.

**296.  (c)**    It is important to emphasize that the uncertainties could have a potential upside or downside so that ERM encompasses the more traditional view of potential hazards as well as opportunities. Hazard risks include both insurable and uninsurable risks.

Subject Area: Engagement tools—risk and control self-assessment. Source: Author.

Internal control questionnaires (ICQs), 221, 512
Internal controls, 334–336
Internal control training, 352
Internal fraud, 443
Internal sources, 5
International business divisions, 338
Interrogations:
  in fraud investigations, 81–82
  interviewing vs., 84–85, 428
  role of interrogator in, 83–84
  silence in, 84
  techniques for, 425–428
Interval estimate, 484
Interval variable, 484
Interviews/interviewing, 496–501
  biased questions in, 499
  conducting, 499–501
  design of, 498–499
  in fraud investigations, 81–82
  interrogation vs., 84–85, 428
  memorandum of, 92–93
  organizing questions for, 497
  questionnaires vs., 503
  role of interviewer in, 83–84
  silence in, 84
  types of, 497
Intuitive approach, 530
Inventory control:
  ABC method of, 128
  examples of computer-assisted audit techniques, 155–156
  forecasting guidelines, 155
  formulas in, 155
  production/conversion cycle, 151–156
Investigative process for fraud, 425–426
Investigative questions, 529
Investment management, 190–194
Invoicing, 112
Irregularities, 331
IS, *see* Information systems
ITF (integrated test facility), 562
IT/IS auditing, *see* Information technology/systems auditing

**J**

JIT (just-in-time) systems, 129
Job scheduling audits, 297–299
Job setup procedures, 298
Joint ventures, 20–21
Journal entry preparation, 203
Judgmental sampling, *see* Nonstatistical sampling
Judgment sample, 484
Judgment selection, 482
Just-in-time (JIT) systems:
  for purchasing, 129
  for receiving, 133

**K**

Kernel tables, 426
Key performance indicators (KPIs), 108
Knowledge, 4
KPIs (key performance indicators), 108

**L**

LANs, *see* Local area networks
Language:
  appropriateness of, 498
  clarity of, 498–499
  level of, 498
  oversimplifying, 498

qualifying, use of, 498
Layer charts, 567
Leapfrogging, 528
Legal considerations:
  in communicating results, 28–29
  in fraud investigations, 85–87
  in granting access to engagement records, 25–26
Legal department, 338
Lexicographic method, 540–541
Liability accrual audits, 337
Libel, 86
Licensing, software, 307–308
Likert scale, 510
Line charts, 567
Link network diagrams, 91–92
Local area networks (LANs), 252–255
Location of information, 224
Logs:
  error, 221
  system, 306
  system console, 301–302
  transaction, 221
Logical access security controls, 222
Logical security, 107
Lot size variance, 178
Low fraud environment, 432

**M**

MAD (mean absolute deviation), 484
Magnetic media (as evidence), 450
Mail questionnaires, 502–503
Maintainability, 234
Maintenance:
  plant, 169–172, 284
  preventive, 303–304
  software, 240–242
Malicious prosecution, 86
Management decision making, 537–538
Management fraud, 434–435, 438
Management issues, e-commerce and, 330–331
Management-produced analysis (self-certification), 99, 553
Management representations, risk vs., 436–437
Management responses, 15–16
Management science, 546
Manual development, 238
Manually-prepared audit working papers, 9–10
Manual reconciliations, 222
Mapping, 563
Marketing administration, 120–122
Marketing function, 338
Master catalog changes, 230
Materials requirements planning (MRP) systems, 129
Materiality, 477
Material Safety Data Sheets (MSDS), 347
Matrix technique, 92
Maxi-max strategy, 543, 546
Maxi-min strategy, 546
MD4 (message digest 4), 427
MD5 (message digest 5), 427
Mean, 484
Mean absolute deviation (MAD), 484
Mean-per-unit estimation procedures, 491
Median, 484
Median chart, 496
Message digest 4 (MD4), 427
Message digest 5 (MD5), 427

Methodology:
  of audit reporting, 12–13
  statement of, 12
Microfiche and microfilm controls, 296
Military attacks, 452
Mini-max regret strategy, 543, 546
Mini-max strategy, 542–544, 546
Mini-min strategy, 546
Mirroring technique, 85
Misunderstandings, 2
Mixed decision-making strategy, 545
Models, decision-making, 538–539
Modeling techniques, 441, 484
Monetary unit sampling procedures, 492–493
Money laundering, 447
Monitoring:
  aggressive, 17
  of consulting audits, 362
  of progress, 411–412
Monitoring Progress (standard), 362, 411–413
Morphological analysis, 529
Movement of documents, 224
MRP (materials requirements planning) systems, 129
MSDS (Material Safety Data Sheets), 347
Multiple-choice questions, 505
Multiple objectives, 536

**N**

National Institute of Standards and Technology (NIST), 427
National software reference library (NSRL), 427
Natural disaster preparedness, 275–276
Nature of Work (standard), 324–331, 342–345
Net change, 155
Net work, computation of, 446
Network changes, 256–257
Network configuration management, 250–251
Network management systems, 248–252
Network security, 251
Network services, 104
Network terminal expansion system, 252
New hire testing (for drugs), 349
NIST (National Institute of Standards and Technology), 427
Nominal group technique, 526–527
Nominal variable, 484
Nonbias, ensuring, 501
Noncompliance, 28, 331
Nonconformity, 495
Nonprogrammed decision making, 537–538
Nonresponses, analysis of, 508–509
Nonroutine decision making, 538
Nonsampling risk, 477
Nonsequential decision making, 537
Nonstatistical sampling, 474, 478–479
  haphazard/block/judgment selection in, 482
  stratified, 482–483
Nonverbal behavior, 82–83
Nonzero-sum games, 544
Normative decision models, 538–539
Normative questions, 501
Noteworthy accomplishments, 16
np chart, *see* Number proportion chart